COLLINS
POCKET
GERMAN
DICTIONARY

GERMAN ▶ ENGLISH ENGLISH ▶ GERMAN

HarperCollins*Publishers*

third edition/dritte Auflage 1998

HarperCollins Publishers
P.O. Box, Glasgow G4 0NB, Great Britain
ISBN 0 00 470771-0

Veronika Calderwood-Schnorr • Ute Nicol • Peter Terrell
Bob Grossmith • Helga Holtkamp • Horst Kopleck • John Whitlam

editorial staff/Manuskriptbearbeitung
Joyce Littlejohn • Elspeth Anderson
Christine Bahr • John Podbielski

series editor/Gesamtleitung
Lorna Sinclair Knight

Typeset by Morton Word Processing Ltd, Scarborough

*Printed and bound in Great Britain by Caledonian International
Book Manufacturing Ltd, Glasgow, G64*

INTRODUCTION

We are delighted you have decided to buy the Collins Pocket German Dictionary and hope you will enjoy and benefit from using it at home, at school, on holiday or at work.

The innovative use of colour guides you quickly and efficiently to the word you want, and the comprehensive wordlist provides a wealth of modern and idiomatic phrases not normally found in a dictionary this size.

In addition, the supplement provides you with guidance on using the dictionary, along with entertaining ways of improving your dictionary skills.

We hope that you will enjoy using it and that it will significantly enhance your language studies.

ZUM GEBRAUCH IHRES COLLINS
TASCHENWÖRTERBUCHS

Das Wörterbuch enthält eine Fülle von Informationen, die mit Hilfe von unterschiedlichen Schriften und Schriftgrößen, Symbolen, Abkürzungen und Klammern vermittelt werden. Die dabei verwendeten Regeln und Symbole werden in den folgenden Abschnitten erklärt.

Stichwörter

Die Wörter, die Sie im Wörterbuch nachschlagen — „Stichwörter" — sind alphabetisch geordnet. Sie sind **rot** gedruckt, damit man sie schnell erkennt. Die beiden Stichwörter oben auf jeder Seite geben das erste und letzte Wort an, das auf der betreffenden Seite behandelt wird.

Informationen zur Verwendung oder zur Form bestimmter Stichwörter stehen in Klammern hinter der Lautschrift. Sie erscheinen meist in abgekürzter Form und sind kursiv gedruckt (z.B. (*fam*), (*COMM*)).

Wo es angebracht ist, werden mit dem Stichwort verwandte Wörter im selben Artikel behandelt (z.B. **accept, acceptance**). Sie sind wie das Stichwort fett, aber etwas kleiner gedruckt.

Häufig verwendete Ausdrücke, in denen das Stichwort vorkommt (z.B. **to be cold**), sind in einer anderen Schrift halbfett gedruckt.

Lautschrift

Die Lautschrift für jedes Stichwort (zur Angabe seiner Aussprache), steht in eckigen Klammern direkt hinter dem Stichwort (z.B. **Quark** [kvark]; **knead** [ni:d]). Die Symbole der Lautschrift sind auf Seite xii erklärt.

Übersetzungen

Die Übersetzungen des Stichworts sind normal gedruckt. Wenn es mehr als eine Bedeutung oder Verwendung des Stichworts gibt, sind diese durch ein Semikolon voneinander getrennt. Vor den Übersetzungen stehen oft andere, kursiv gedruckte Wörter in Klammern. Sie geben an, in welchem Zusammenhang das Stichwort erscheinen könnte (z.B. **rough** (*voice*) oder (*weather*)), oder sie sind Synonyme (z.B. **rough** (*violent*)).

Schlüsselwörter

Besonders behandelt werden bestimmte deutsche und englische Wörter, die man als „Schlüsselwörter" der jeweiligen Sprache betrachten kann. Diese Wörter kommen beispielsweise sehr häufig vor oder werden unterschiedlich verwendet (z.B. **sein, auch; get, that**). Mit Hilfe von Rauten und Ziffern können Sie die verschiedenen Wortarten und Verwendungen unterscheiden. Weitere nützliche Hinweise finden Sie kursiv und in Klammern in der jeweiligen Sprache des Benutzers.

Grammatische Informationen

Wortarten stehen in abgekürzter Form kursiv gedruckt hinter der Aussprache des Stichworts (z.B. *vt, adv, conj*).

Die unregelmäßigen Formen englischer Substantive und Verben stehen in Klammern vor der Wortart (z.B. **man** (*pl* **men**) *n*, **give** (*pt* **gave**, *pp* **given**) *vt*).

Die deutsche Rechtschreibreform

Stichwörter und übersetzungen, die von der Rechtschreibreform betroffen sind, werden im Wörterbuch mit △ gekennzeichnet. Weitere Informationen zu den neuen Screibweisen finden Sie ab Seite 615.

USING YOUR COLLINS POCKET DICTIONARY

A wealth of information is presented in the dictionary, using various typefaces, sizes of type, symbols, abbreviations and brackets. The conventions and symbols used are explained in the following sections.

Headwords

The words you look up in a dictionary — "headwords" — are listed alphabetically. They are printed in **red type** for rapid identification. The two headwords appearing at the top of each page indicate the first and last word dealt with on the page in question.

Information about the usage or form of certain headwords is given in brackets after the phonetic spelling. This usually appears in abbreviated form and in italics (e.g. (*umg*), (*COMM*)).

Where appropriate, words related to headwords are grouped in the same entry (**Glück, glücken**) in a slightly smaller bold type than the headword.

Common expressions in which the headword appears are shown in a different bold roman type (e.g. **Glück haben**).

Phonetic spellings

The phonetic spelling of each headword (indicating its pronunciation) is given in square brackets immediately after the headword (e.g. **Quark** [kvark]). A list of these symbols is given on page xii.

Meanings

Headword translations are given in ordinary type and, where more than one meaning or usage exists, these are separated by a semi-colon. You will often find other words in italics in brackets before the translations. These offer suggested contexts in which the headword might appear (e.g. **eng** (*Kleidung*) or (*Freundschaft*)) or provide synonyms (e.g. **eng** (*fig: Horizont*)).

"Key" words

Special status is given to certain German and English words which are considered as "key" words in each language. They may, for example, occur very frequently or have several types of usage (e.g. **sein, auch; get, that**). A combination of lozenges and numbers helps you to distinguish different parts of speech and different meanings. Further helpful information is provided in brackets and in italics in the relevant language for the user.

Grammatical information

Parts of speech are given in abbreviated form in italics after the phonetic spellings of headwords (e.g. *vt, av, kong*).

Genders of German nouns are indicated as follows: *m* for a masculine and *f* for a feminine and *nt* for a neuter noun. The genitive and plural forms of regular nouns are shown on the table on page xi. Nouns which do not follow these rules have the genitive and plural in brackets immediately preceding the gender (e.g. **Spaß**, (**-es**, **ˬe**), *m*).

Adjectives are normally shown in their basic form (e.g. **groß** *adj*), but where they are only used attributively (i.e. before a noun) feminine and neuter endings follow in brackets (**hohe** (**r, s**) *adj attrib*).

German spelling changes

German headwords and translations affected by the spelling reforms are marked in the text by △. Further information is given on page 615.

ABKÜRZUNGEN

ABBREVIATIONS

Abkürzung	**abk, abbr**	abbreviation
Akkusativ	**acc**	accusative
Adjektiv	**adj**	adjective
Adverb	**adv**	adverb
Landwirtschaft	**AGR**	agriculture
Akkusativ	**akk**	accusative
Anatomie	**ANAT**	anatomy
Architektur	**ARCHIT**	architecture
Astrologie	**ASTROL**	astrology
Astronomie	**ASTRON**	astronomy
attributiv	**attrib**	attributive
Kraftfahrzeuge	**AUT**	automobiles
Hilfsverb	**aux**	auxiliary
Luftfahrt	**AVIAT**	aviation
besonders	**bes**	especially
Biologie	**BIOL**	biology
Botanik	**BOT**	botany
britisch	**BRIT**	British
Chemie	**CHEM**	chemistry
Film	**CINE**	cinema
Handel	**COMM**	commerce
Komparativ	**compar**	comparative
Computer	**COMPUT**	computing
Konjunktion	**conj**	conjunction
Kochen und Backen	**COOK**	cooking
zusammengesetztes Wort	**cpd**	compound
Dativ	**dat**	dative
bestimmter Artikel	**def art**	definite article
Diminutiv	**dimin**	diminutive
kirchlich	**ECCL**	ecclesiastical
Eisenbahn	**EISENB**	railways
Elektrizität	**ELEK, ELEC**	electricity
besonders	**esp**	especially
und so weiter	**etc**	et cetera
etwas	**etw**	something
Euphemismus, Hüllwort	**euph**	euphemism
Interjektion, Ausruf	**excl**	exclamation
Femininum	**f**	feminine
übertragen	**fig**	figurative
Finanzwesen	**FIN**	finance
nicht getrennt gebraucht	**fus**	(phrasal verb) inseparable
Genitiv	**gen**	genitive
Geographie	**GEOG**	geography
Geologie	**GEOL**	geology
Grammatik	**GRAM**	grammar

Geschichte	HIST	history
unpersönlich	impers	impersonal
unbestimmter Artikel	indef art	indefinite article
umgangssprächlich (! vulgär)	inf(!)	informal (! particularly offensive)
Infinitiv, Grundform	infin	infinitive
nicht getrennt gebraucht	insep	inseparable
unveränderlich	inv	invariable
unregelmäßig	irreg	irregular
jemand	jd	somebody
jemandem	jdm	(to) somebody
jemanden	jdn	somebody
jemandes	jds	somebody's
Rechtswesen	JUR	law
Kochen und Backen	KOCH	cooking
Komparativ	kompar	comparative
Konjunktion	konj	conjunction
Sprachwissenschaft	LING	linguistics
Literatur	LITER	of literature
Maskulinum	m	masculine
Mathematik	MATH	mathematics
Medizin	MED	medicine
Meteorologie	MET	meteorology
militärisch	MIL	military
Bergbau	MIN	mining
Musik	MUS	music
Substantiv, Hauptwort	n	noun
nautisch, Seefahrt	NAUT	nautical, naval
Nominativ	nom	nominative
Neutrum	nt	neuter
Zahlwort	num	numeral
Objekt	obj	object
oder	od	or
sich	o.s.	oneself
Parlament	PARL	parliament
abschätzig	pej	pejorative
Photographie	PHOT	photography
Physik	PHYS	physics
Plural	pl	plural
Politik	POL	politics
Präfix, Vorsilbe	pp	prefix
Präposition	präp, prep	preposition
Typographie	PRINT	printing
Pronomen, Fürwort	pron	pronoun
Psychologie	PSYCH	psychology
1. Vergangenheit, Imperfekt	pt	past tense
Radio	RAD	radio
Eisenbahn	RAIL	railways
Religion	REL	religion

jemand(-en, -em)	sb	someone, somebody
Schulwesen	SCH	school
Naturwissenschaft	SCI	science
Singular, Einzahl	sg	singular
etwas	sth	something
Konjunktiv	sub	subjunctive
Subjekt	subj	(grammatical) subject
Superlativ	superl	superlative
Technik	TECH	technology
Nachrichtentechnik	TEL	telecommunications
Theater	THEAT	theatre
Fernsehen	TV	television
Typographie	TYP	printing
umgangssprachlich (! vulgär)	umg(!)	informal (! particularly offensive)
Hochschulwesen	UNIV	university
unpersönlich	unpers	impersonal
unregelmäßig	unreg	irregular
(nord)amerikanisch	US	(North) America
gewöhnlich	usu	usually
Verb	vb	verb
intransitives Verb	vi	intransitive verb
reflexives Verb	vr	reflexive verb
transitives Verb	vt	transitive verb
Zoologie	ZOOL	zoology
zusammengesetztes Wort	zW	compound
zwischen zwei Sprechern	—	change of speaker
ungefähre Entsprechung	≃	cultural equivalent
eingetragenes Warenzeichen	®	registered trademark

Warenzeichen

Wörter, die unseres Wissens eingetragene Warenzeichen darstellen, sind als solche gekennzeichnet. Es ist jedoch zu beachten, daß weder das Vorhandensein noch das Fehlen derartiger Kennzeichnungen die Rechstlage hinsichtlich eingetragener Warenzeichen berührt.

Note on trademarks

Words which we have reason to believe constitute trademarks have been designated as such. However, neither the presence nor the absence of such designation should be regarded as affecting the legal status of any trademark.

REGULAR GERMAN NOUN ENDINGS

nom		gen	pl
-ant	*m*	-anten	-anten
-anz	*f*	-anz	-anzen
-ar	*m*	-ar(e)s	-are
-chen	*nt*	-chens	-chen
-e	*f*	-	-n
-ei	*f*	-ei	-eien
-elle	*f*	-elle	-ellen
-ent	*m*	-enten	-enten
-enz	*f*	-enz	-enzen
-ette	*f*	-ette	-etten
-eur	*m*	-eurs	-eure
-euse	*f*	-euse	-eusen
-heit	*f*	-heit	-heiten
-ie	*f*	-ie	-ien
-ik	*f*	-ik	-iken
-in	*f*	-in	-innen
-ine	*f*	-ine	-inen
-ion	*f*	-ion	-ionen
-ist	*m*	-isten	-isten
-ium	*nt*	-iums	-ien
-ius	*m*	-ius	-iusse
-ive	*f*	-ive	-iven
-keit	*f*	-keit	-keiten
-lein	*nt*	-leins	-lein
-ling	*m*	-lings	-linge
-ment	*nt*	-ments	-mente
-mus	*m*	-mus	-men
-schaft	*f*	-schaft	-schaften
-tät	*f*	-tät	-täten
-tor	*m*	-tors	-toren
-ung	*f*	-ung	-ungen
-ur	*f*	-ur	-uren

PHONETIC SYMBOLS / LAUTSCHRIFT

[ː] length mark/Längezeichen ['] stress mark/Betonung
['] glottal stop/Knacklaut

all vowel sounds are approximate only
alle Vokallaute sind nur ungefähre Entsprechungen

lie	[aɪ]	weit	day	[eɪ]		
now	[aʊ]	Haut	girl	[ɜː]		
above	[ə]	bitte	board	[ɔː]		
green	[iː]	viel	root	[uː]	Hut	
pity	[ɪ]	Bischof	come	[ʌ]	Butler	
rot	[ɒ,ɔ]	Post	salon	[ʒ]	Champignon	
full	[ʊ]	Pult	avant	[ɑ̃]	Ensemble	
			(garde)			
bet	[b]	Ball	fair	[ɛə]	mehr	
dim	[d]	dann	beer	[ɪə]	Bier	
face	[f]	Faß	toy	[ɔɪ]	Heu	
go	[g]	Gast	pure	[ʊə]		
hit	[h]	Herr	wine	[w]		
you	[j]	ja	thin	[θ]		
cat	[k]	kalt	this	[əʊ]		
lick	[l]	Last				
must	[m]	Mast	Hast	[a]	mash	
nut	[n]	Nuß	Ensemble	[ã]	avant	
bang	[ŋ]	lang			(garde)	
pepper	[p]	Pakt	Metall	[e]	meths	
sit	[s]	rasse	häßlich	[ɛ]		
shame	[ʃ]	Schal	Cousin	[ɛ̃]		
tell	[t]	Tal	vital	[i]		
vine	[v]	was	Moral	[o]		
loch	[x]	Bach	Champignon	[õ]	salon	
zero	[z]	Hase	ökonomisch	[ø]		
leisure	[ʒ]	Genie	gönnen	[œ]		
			Heu	[ɔY]	toy	
bat	[æ]		kulant	[u]		
farm	[ɑː]	Bahn	physisch	[y]		
set	[e]	Kette	Müll	[ʏ]		
			ich	[ç]		

[ʳ] r can be pronounced before a vowel; Bindungs-R

NUMMER

NUMBERS

ein(s)	1	one	
zwei	2	two	
drei	3	three	
vier	4	four	
fünf	5	five	
sechs	6	six	
sieben	7	seven	
acht	8	eight	
neun	9	nine	
zehn	10	ten	
elf	11	eleven	
zwölf	12	twelve	
dreizehn	13	thirteen	
vierzehn	14	fourteen	
fünfzehn	15	fifteen	
sechzehn	16	sixteen	
siebzehn	17	seventeen	
achtzehn	18	eighteen	
neunzehn	19	nineteen	
zwanzig	20	twenty	
einundzwanzig	21	twenty-one	
zweiundzwanzig	22	twenty-two	
dreißig	30	thirty	
vierzig	40	forty	
fünfzig	50	fifty	
sechzig	60	sixty	
siebzig	70	seventy	
achtzig	80	eighty	
neunzig	90	ninety	
hundert	100	a hundred	
hunderteins	101	a hundred and one	
zweihundert	200	two hundred	
zweihunderteins	201	two hundred and one	
dreihundert	300	three hundred	
dreihunderteins	301	three hundred and one	
tausend	1000	a thousand	
tausend(und)eins	1001	a thousand and one	
fünftausend	5000	five thousand	
eine Million	1000000	a million	

erste(r,s)	1.	first	1st
zweite(r,s)	2.	second	2nd
dritte(r,s)	3.	third	3rd
vierte(r,s)	4.	fourth	4th

fünfte(r,s)	5.	fifth	5th
sechste(r,s)	6.	sixth	6th
siebte(r,s)	7.	seventh	7th
achte(r,s)	8.	eighth	8th
neunte(r,s)	9.	ninth	9th
zehnte(r,s)	10.	tenth	10th
elfte(r,s)	11.	eleventh	11th
zwölfte(r,s)	12.	twelfth	12th
dreizehnte(r,s)	13.	thirteenth	13th
vierzehnte(r,s)	14.	fourteenth	14th
fünfzehnte(r,s)	15.	fifteenth	15th
sechzehnte(r,s)	16.	sixteenth	16th
siebzehnte(r,s)	17.	seventeenth	17th
achtzehnte(r,s)	18.	eighteenth	18th
neunzehnte(r,s)	19.	nineteenth	19th
zwanzigste(r,s)	20.	twentieth	20th
einundzwanzigste(r,s)	21.	twenty-first	21st
dreißigste(r,s)	30.	thirtieth	30th
hundertste(r,s)	100.	hundredth	100th
hunderterste(r,s)	101.	hundred-and-first	101st
tausendste(r,s)	1000.	thousandth	1000th

Brüche usw.

Fractions etc.

ein Halb	$\frac{1}{2}$	a half	
ein Drittel	$\frac{1}{3}$	a third	
ein Viertel	$\frac{1}{4}$	a quarter	
ein Fünftel	$\frac{1}{5}$	a fifth	
null Komma fünf	0,5	(nought) point five	0.5
drei Komma vier	3,4	three point four	3.4
sechs Komma acht neun	6,89	six point eight nine	6.89
zehn Prozent	10%	ten per cent	
hundert Prozent	100%	a hundred per cent	

Beispiele

Examples

er wohnt in Nummer 10	he lives at number 10
es steht in Kapitel 7	it's in chapter 7
auf Seite 7	on page 7
er wohnt im 7. Stock	he lives on the 7th floor
er wurde 7.	he came in 7th
im Maßstab eins zu zwanzigtausend	scale one to twenty thousand

UHRZEIT

THE TIME

wieviel Uhr ist es?, wie spät ist es?

what time is it?

es ist ...

it's ...

Mitternacht, zwölf Uhr nachts
ein Uhr (morgens *or* früh)
fünf nach eins, ein Uhr fünf
zehn nach eins, ein Uhr zehn
Viertel nach eins, ein Uhr fünfzehn
fünf vor halb zwei, ein Uhr
  fünfundzwanzig
halb zwei, ein Uhr dreißig
fünf nach halb zwei, ein Uhr
  fünfunddreißig
zwanzig vor zwei, ein Uhr vierzig
Viertel vor zwei, ein Uhr
  fünfundvierzig
zehn vor zwei, ein Uhr fünfzig
zwölf Uhr (mittags), Mittag
halb eins (mittags *or* nachmittags),
  zwölf Uhr dreißig
zwei Uhr (nachmittags)

halb acht (abends)

midnight, twelve p.m.
one o'clock (in the morning), one (a.m.)
five past one
ten past one
a quarter past one, one fifteen
twenty-five past one, one twenty-five

half past one, one thirty
twenty-five to two, one thirty-five

twenty to two, one forty
a quarter to two, one forty-five

ten to two, one fifty
twelve o'clock, midday, noon
half past twelve, twelve thirty (p.m.)

two o'clock (in the afternoon), two
  (p.m.)
half past seven (in the evening), seven
  thirty (p.m.)

um wieviel Uhr?

at what time?

um Mitternacht
um sieben Uhr

at midnight
at seven o'clock

in zwanzig Minuten
vor fünfzehn Minuten

in twenty minutes
fifteen minutes ago

WÖRTERBUCH
DEUTSCH-ENGLISCH

GERMAN-ENGLISH
DICTIONARY

DEUTSCH – ENGLISCH
GERMAN – ENGLISH

A, a

Aal [aːl] (-(e)s, -e) m eel

Aas [aːs] (-es, -e od **Äser**) nt carrion

SCHLÜSSELWORT
---

ab [ap] *präp +dat* from; **Kinder ab 12 Jahren**
children from the age of 12; **ab morgen**
from tomorrow; **ab sofort** as of now
♦ *adv* 1 off; **links ab** to the left; **der Knopf
ist ab** the button has come off; **ab nach
Hause!** off you go home
2 (*zeitlich*): **von da ab** from then on; **von
heute ab** from today, as of today
3 (*auf Fahrplänen*): **München ab 12.20**
leaving Munich 12.20
4: **ab und zu** od **an** now and then od again

Abänderung [ˈap|ɛndərʊŋ] f alteration

Abbau [ˈapbaʊ] (-(e)s) m (+gen) dismantling;
(*Verminderung*) reduction (in); (*Verfall*)
decline (in); (MIN) mining; quarrying;
(CHEM) decomposition; **a~en** vt to
dismantle; (MIN) to mine; to quarry;
(*verringern*) to reduce; (CHEM) to break
down

abbeißen [ˈapbaɪsən] (*unreg*) vt to bite off

abbekommen [ˈapbəkɔmən] (*unreg*) vt
(*Deckel, Schraube, Band*) to loosen; **etwas ~**
(*beschädigt werden*) to get damaged;
(: *Person*) to get injured

abbestellen [ˈapbəʃtɛlən] vt to cancel

abbezahlen [ˈapbətsaːlən] vt to pay off

abbiegen [ˈapbiːɡən] (*unreg*) vi to turn off;
(*Straße*) to bend ♦ vt (*verhindern*)
to ward off

abbilden [ˈapbɪldən] vt to portray;
Abbildung f illustration

abblenden [ˈapblɛndən] vt, vi (AUT) to dip
(BRIT), to dim (US)

Abblendlicht [ˈapblɛntlɪçt] nt dipped (BRIT)
od dimmed (US) headlights pl

abbrechen [ˈapbrɛçən] (*unreg*) vt, vi to
break off; (*Gebäude*) to pull down; (*Zelt*) to
take down; (*aufhören*) to stop; (COMPUT) to
abort

abbrennen [ˈapbrɛnən] (*unreg*) vt to burn
off; (*Feuerwerk*) to let off ♦ vi (aux sein) to
burn down

abbringen [ˈapbrɪŋən] (*unreg*) vt: **jdn von
etw ~** to dissuade sb from sth; **jdn vom
Weg ~** to divert sb

abbröckeln [ˈapbrœkəln] vt, vi to crumble
off od away

Abbruch [ˈapbrʊx] m (von Verhandlungen
etc) breaking off; (von Haus) demolition;
jdm/etw ~ tun to harm sb/sth; **a~reif** adj
only fit for demolition

abbrühen [ˈapbryːən] vt to scald;
abgebrüht (*umg*) hard-boiled

abbuchen [ˈapbuːxən] vt to debit

abdanken [ˈapdaŋkən] vi to resign; (*König*)
to abdicate; **Abdankung** f resignation;
abdication

abdecken [ˈapdɛkən] vt (Loch) to cover;
(*Tisch*) to clear; (*Plane*) to uncover

abdichten [ˈapdɪçtən] vt to seal; (NAUT) to
caulk

abdrehen [ˈapdreːən] vt (Gas) to turn off;
(*Licht*) to switch off; (*Film*) to shoot ♦ vi
(*Schiff*) to change course

Abdruck [ˈapdrʊk] m (Nachdrucken)
reprinting; (*Gedrucktes*) reprint; (Gips~,
Wachs~) impression; (Finger~) print; **a~en**
vt to print, to publish

abdrücken [ˈapdrʏkən] vt (Waffe) to fire;
(*Person*) to hug, to squeeze

Abend [ˈaːbənt] (-s, -e) m evening; **guten ~**
good evening; **zu ~ essen** to have dinner
od supper; **a~** △ adv: **heute a~** this
evening; **~brot** nt supper; **~essen** nt
supper; **~garderobe** f evening dress;

△ *For information on spelling reform see page 615*

~kasse f box office; **~kleid** nt evening dress; **~kurs** m evening classes pl; **~land** nt (Europa) West; **a~lich** adj evening; **~mahl** nt Holy Communion; **~rot** nt sunset; **a~s** adv in the evening

Abenteuer ['a:bəntɔʏər] (-s, -) nt adventure; **a~lich** adj adventurous; **~urlaub** m adventure holiday

Abenteurer (-s, -) m adventurer; **~in** f adventuress

aber ['a:bər] konj but; (jedoch) however ♦ adv: **tausend und ~ tausend** thousands upon thousands; **das ist ~ schön** that's really nice; **nun ist ~ Schluß!** now that's enough!; **vielen Dank – ~ bitte!** thanks a lot – you're welcome; **A~glaube** m superstition; **~gläubisch** adj superstitious

aberkennen ['apˈɛrkɛnən] (unreg) vt (JUR): **jdm etw ~** to deprive sb of sth, to take sth (away) from sb

abermals ['a:bəma:ls] adv once again

Abf. abk (= Abfahrt) dep.

abfahren ['apfa:rən] (unreg) vi to leave, to depart ♦ vt to take od cart away; (Strecke) to drive; (Reifen) to wear; (Fahrkarte) to use

Abfahrt ['apfa:rt] f departure; (SKI) descent; (Piste) run; **~szeit** f departure time

Abfall ['apfal] m waste; (von Speisen etc) rubbish (BRIT), garbage (US); (Neigung) slope; (Verschlechterung) decline; **~eimer** m rubbish bin (BRIT), garbage can (US); **a~en** (unreg) vi (auch fig) to fall or drop off; (sich neigen) to fall od drop away

abfällig ['apfɛlɪç] adj disparaging, deprecatory

abfangen ['apfaŋən] (unreg) vt to intercept; (Person) to catch; (unter Kontrolle bringen) to check

abfärben ['apfɛrbən] vi to lose its colour; (Wäsche) to run; (fig) to rub off

abfassen ['apfasən] vt to write, to draft

abfertigen ['apfɛrtɪgən] vt to prepare for dispatch, to process; (an der Grenze) to clear; (Kundschaft) to attend to

Abfertigungsschalter m (Flughafen) check-in desk

abfeuern ['apfɔʏərn] vt to fire

abfinden ['apfɪndən] (unreg) vt to pay off ♦ vr to come to terms; **sich mit jdm ~/ nicht abfinden** to put up with/not get on with sb

Abfindung f (von Gläubigern) payment; (Geld) sum in settlement

abflauen ['apflauən] vi (Wind, Erregung) to die away, to subside; (Nachfrage, Geschäft) to fall od drop off

abfliegen ['apfli:gən] (unreg) vi (Flugzeug) to take off; (Passagier auch) to fly ♦ vt (Gebiet) to fly over

abfließen ['apfli:sən] (unreg) vi to drain away

Abflug ['apflu:k] m departure; (Start) take-off; **~halle** f departure lounge; **~zeit** f departure time

Abfluß △ ['apflʊs] m draining away; (Öffnung) outlet; **~rohr** △ nt drain pipe; (von sanitären Anlagen auch) waste pipe

abfragen ['apfra:gən] vt (bes SCH) to test orally (on)

Abfuhr ['apfu:r] (-, -en) f removal; (fig) snub, rebuff

abführen ['apfy:rən] vt to lead away; (Gelder, Steuern) to pay ♦ vi (MED) to have a laxative effect

Abführmittel ['apfy:rmɪtəl] nt laxative, purgative

abfüllen ['apfʏlən] vt to draw off; (in Flaschen) to bottle

Abgabe ['apga:bə] f handing in; (von Ball) pass; (Steuer) tax; (eines Amtes) giving up; (einer Erklärung) giving

Abgang ['apgaŋ] m (von Schule) leaving; (THEAT) exit; (Abfahrt) departure; (der Post, von Waren) dispatch

Abgas ['apga:s] nt waste gas; (AUT) exhaust

abgeben ['apge:bən] (unreg) vt (Gegenstand) to hand od give in; (Ball) to pass; (Wärme) to give off; (Amt) to hand over; (Schuß) to fire; (Erklärung, Urteil) to give; (darstellen, sein) to make ♦ vr: **sich mit jdm/etw ~** to associate with sb/bother with sth; **jdm etw ~** (überlassen) to let sb have sth

abgebrüht ['apgəbry:t] (umg) adj (skrupellos) hard-boiled

△ *Informationen zur Rechtschreibreform Seite 615*

abgehen ['apgeːən] (*unreg*) *vi* to go away, to leave; (*THEAT*) to exit; (*Knopf etc*) to come off; (*Straße*) to branch off ♦ *vt* (*Strecke*) to go *od* walk along; **etw geht jdm ab** (*fehlt*) sb lacks sth

abgelegen ['apgəleːgən] *adj* remote

abgemacht ['apgəmaxt] *adj* fixed; **~!** done!

abgeneigt ['apgənaikt] *adj* disinclined

abgenutzt ['apgənʊtst] *adj* worn

Abgeordnete(r) ['apgəʔɔrdnətə(r)] *f(m)* member of parliament; elected representative

abgeschlossen ['apgəʃlɔsən] *adj attrib* (*Wohnung*) self-contained

abgeschmackt ['apgəʃmakt] *adj* tasteless

abgesehen ['apgəzeːən] *adj*: **es auf jdn/ etw ~ haben** to be after sb/sth; **~ von ...** apart from ...

abgespannt ['apgəʃpant] *adj* tired out

abgestanden ['apgəʃtandən] *adj* stale; (*Bier auch*) flat

abgestorben ['apgəʃtɔrbən] *adj* numb; (*BIOL, MED*) dead

abgetragen ['apgətraːgən] *adj* shabby, worn out

abgewinnen ['apgəvɪnən] (*unreg*) *vt*: **einer Sache etw/Geschmack ~** to get sth/ pleasure from sth

abgewöhnen ['apgəvøːnən] *vt*: **jdm/sich etw ~** to cure sb of sth/give sth up

abgrenzen ['apgrɛntsən] *vt* (*auch fig*) to mark off; to fence off

Abgrund ['apgrʊnt] *m* (*auch fig*) abyss

abhacken ['aphakən] *vt* to chop off

abhaken ['aphaːkən] *vt* (*auf Papier*) to tick off

abhalten ['aphaltən] (*unreg*) *vt* (*Versammlung*) to hold; **jdn von etw ~** (*fernhalten*) to keep sb away from sth; (*hindern*) to keep sb from sth

abhanden [ap'handən] *adj*: **~ kommen** to get lost

Abhandlung ['aphandlʊŋ] *f* treatise, discourse

Abhang ['aphaŋ] *m* slope

abhängen ['aphɛŋən] *vt* (*Bild*) to take down; (*Anhänger*) to uncouple; (*Verfolger*) to shake off ♦ *vi* (*unreg: Fleisch*) to hang; **von jdm/etw ~** to depend on sb/sth

abhängig ['aphɛŋɪç] *adj*: **~ (von)** dependent (on); **A~keit** *f*: **A~keit (von)** dependence (on)

abhärten ['aphɛrtən] *vt, vr* to toughen (o.s.) up; **sich gegen etw ~** to inure o.s. to sth

abhauen ['aphaʊən] (*unreg*) *vt* to cut off; (*Baum*) to cut down ♦ *vi* (*umg*) to clear off *od* out

abheben ['apheːbən] (*unreg*) *vt* to lift (up); (*Karten*) to cut; (*Geld*) to withdraw, to take out ♦ *vi* (*Flugzeug*) to take off; (*Rakete*) to lift off ♦ *vr* to stand out

abheften ['aphɛftən] *vt* (*Rechnungen etc*) to file away

abhetzen ['aphɛtsən] *vr* to wear *od* tire o.s. out

Abhilfe ['aphɪlfə] *f* remedy; **~ schaffen** to put things right

abholen ['aphoːlən] *vt* (*Gegenstand*) to fetch, to collect; (*Person*) to call for; (*am Bahnhof etc*) to pick up, to meet

abholzen ['aphɔltsən] *vt* (*Wald*) to clear

abhorchen ['aphɔrçən] *vt* (*MED*) to listen to a patient's chest

abhören ['aphøːrən] *vt* (*Vokabeln*) to test; (*Telefongespräch*) to tap; (*Tonband etc*) to listen to

Abhörgerät *nt* bug

Abitur [abi'tuːr] (*-s, -e*) *nt* German school-leaving examination; **~i'ent(in)** *m(f)* candidate for school-leaving certificate

---

ABITUR

The Abitur is the German school-leaving examination taken in four subjects by pupils at a Gymnasium at the age of 18 or 19. It is necessary for entry to university.

Abk. *abk* (= *Abkürzung*) abbr.

abkapseln ['apkapsəln] *vr* to shut *od* cut o.s. off

abkaufen ['apkaʊfən] *vt*: **jdm etw ~** (*auch fig*) to buy sth from sb

abkehren ['apkeːrən] *vt* (*Blick*) to avert, to

⚠ *For information on spelling reform see page 615*

turn away ♦ *vr* to turn away

abklingen ['apklɪŋən] (*unreg*) *vi* to die away; (*Radio*) to fade out

abknöpfen ['apknœpfən] *vt* to unbutton; **jdm etw ~** (*umg*) to get sth off sb

abkochen ['apkɔxən] *vt* to boil

abkommen ['apkɔmən] (*unreg*) *vi* to get away; **von der Straße/von einem Plan ~** to leave the road/give up a plan; **A~** **(-s, -)** *nt* agreement

abkömmlich ['apkœmlɪç] *adj* available, free

abkratzen ['apkratsən] *vt* to scrape off ♦ *vi* (*umg*) to kick the bucket

abkühlen ['apky:lən] *vt* to cool down ♦ *vr* (*Mensch*) to cool down *od* off; (*Wetter*) to get cool; (*Zuneigung*) to cool

abkürzen ['apkʏrtsən] *vt* to shorten; (*Wort auch*) to abbreviate; **den Weg ~** to take a short cut

Abkürzung *f* (*Wort*) abbreviation; (*Weg*) short cut

abladen ['apla:dən] (*unreg*) *vt* to unload

Ablage ['apla:gə] *f* (*für Akten*) tray; (*für Kleider*) cloakroom

ablassen ['aplasən] (*unreg*) *vt* (*Wasser, Dampf*) to let off; (*vom Preis*) to knock off ♦ *vi*: **von etw ~** to give sth up, to abandon sth

Ablauf ['aplauf] *m* (*Abfluß*) drain; (*von Ereignissen*) course; (*einer Frist, Zeit*) expiry (*BRIT*), expiration (*US*); **a~en** (*unreg*) *vi* (*abfließen*) to drain away; (*Ereignisse*) to happen; (*Frist, Zeit, Paß*) to expire ♦ *vt* (*Sohlen*) to wear (down *od* out)

ablegen ['aple:gən] *vt* to put *od* lay down; (*Kleider*) to take off; (*Gewohnheit*) to get rid of; (*Prüfung*) to take, to sit; (*Zeugnis*) to give

Ableger (**-s, -**) *m* layer; (*fig*) branch, offshoot

ablehnen ['aple:nən] *vt* to reject; (*Einladung*) to decline, to refuse ♦ *vi* to decline, to refuse

ablehnend *adj* (*Haltung, Antwort*) negative; (*Geste*) disapproving; **ein ~er Bescheid** a rejection

Ablehnung *f* rejection; refusal

ableiten ['aplaɪtən] *vt* (*Wasser*) to divert; (*deduzieren*) to deduce; (*Wort*) to derive; **Ableitung** *f* diversion; deduction; derivation; (*Wort*) derivative

ablenken ['aplɛŋkən] *vt* to turn away, to deflect; (*zerstreuen*) to distract ♦ *vi* to change the subject; **Ablenkung** *f* distraction

ablesen ['aple:zən] (*unreg*) *vt* to read out; (*Meßgeräte*) to read

ablichten ['aplɪçtən] *vt* to photocopy

abliefern ['apli:fərn] *vt* to deliver; **etw bei jdm ~** to hand sth over to sb

Ablieferung *f* delivery

ablösen ['aplø:zən] *vt* (*abtrennen*) to take off, to remove; (*in Amt*) to take over from; (*Wache*) to relieve

Ablösung *f* removal; relieving

abmachen ['apmaxən] *vt* to take off; (*vereinbaren*) to agree; **Abmachung** *f* agreement

abmagern ['apma:gərn] *vi* to get thinner

Abmagerungskur *f* diet; **eine ~ machen** to go on a diet

abmarschieren ['apmarʃi:rən] *vi* to march off

abmelden ['apmɛldən] *vt* (*Zeitungen*) to cancel; (*Auto*) to take off the road ♦ *vr* to give notice of one's departure; (*im Hotel*) to check out; **jdn bei der Polizei ~** to register sb's departure with the police

abmessen ['apmɛsən] (*unreg*) *vt* to measure; **Abmessung** *f* measurement

abmontieren ['apmɔnti:rən] *vt* to take off

abmühen ['apmy:ən] *vr* to wear o.s. out

Abnahme ['apna:mə] *f* (*+gen*) removal; (*COMM*) buying; (*Verringerung*) decrease (in)

abnehmen ['apne:mən] (*unreg*) *vt* to take off, to remove; (*Führerschein*) to take away; (*Prüfung*) to hold; (*Maschen*) to decrease ♦ *vi* to decrease; (*schlanker werden*) to lose weight; **(jdm) etw ~** (*Geld*) to get sth (out of sb); (*kaufen, umg: glauben*) to buy sth (from sb); **jdm Arbeit ~** to take work off sb's shoulders

Abnehmer (**-s, -**) *m* purchaser, customer

Abneigung ['apnaɪgʊŋ] *f* aversion, dislike

abnorm [ap'nɔrm] *adj* abnormal

⚠ *Informationen zur Rechtschreibreform Seite 615*

abnutzen ['apnʊtsən] *vt* to wear out;
  Abnutzung *f* wear (and tear)
Abo ['abo] (*umg*) *nt abk* = **Abonnement**
Abonnement [abɔn(ə)'mãː] (**-s, -s**) *nt*
  subscription; **Abonnent(in)** *m(f)*
  subscriber; **abonnieren** *vt* to subscribe to
Abordnung ['apˌɔrdnʊŋ] *f* delegation
abpacken ['appakən] *vt* to pack
abpassen ['appasən] *vt* (*Person, Gelegenheit*)
  to wait for
Abpfiff ['appfɪf] *m* final whistle
abplagen ['appla:gən] *vr* to wear o.s. out
abprallen ['appralən] *vi* to bounce off; to
  ricochet
abraten ['apra:tən] (*unreg*) *vi*: **jdm von etw**
  ~ to advise *od* warn sb against sth
abräumen ['apˌrɔymən] *vt* to clear up *od*
  away
abreagieren ['apreagi:rən] *vt*: **seinen Zorn**
  (an jdm / etw) ~ to work one's anger off
  (on sb/sth) ♦ *vr* to calm down
abrechnen ['apreçnən] *vt* to deduct, to
  take off ♦ *vi* to settle up; (*fig*) to get even
Abrechnung *f* settlement; (*Rechnung*) bill
Abrede ['apre:də] *f*: **etw in ~ stellen** to
  deny *od* dispute sth
Abreise ['apraɪzə] *f* departure; **a~n** *vi* to
  leave, to set off
abreißen ['apraɪsən] (*unreg*) *vt* (*Haus*) to tear
  down; (*Blatt*) to tear off
abrichten ['apˌrɪçtən] *vt* to train
abriegeln ['apˌri:gəln] *vt* (*Straße, Gebiet*) to
  seal off
Abruf ['apru:f] *m*: **auf ~** on call; **a~en**
  (*unreg*) *vt* (*Mensch*) to call away; (*COMM:
  Ware*) to request delivery of
abrunden ['apˌrʊndən] *vt* to round off
abrupt [a'brʊpt] *adj* abrupt
abrüsten ['apˌrʏstən] *vi* to disarm;
  Abrüstung *f* disarmament
abrutschen ['apˌrʊtʃən] *vi* to slip; (*AVIAT*) to
  sideslip
Abs. *abk* (= *Absender*) sender, from
Absage ['apza:gə] *f* refusal; **a~n** *vt* to
  cancel, to call off; (*Einladung*) to turn down
  ♦ *vi* to cry off; (*ablehnen*) to decline
absahnen ['apza:nən] *vt* to skim ♦ *vi* (*fig*) to

rake in
Absatz ['apzats] *m* (*COMM*) sales *pl*;
  (*Bodensatz*) deposit; (*neuer Abschnitt*)
  paragraph; (*Treppen~*) landing; (*Schuh~*)
  heel; **~gebiet** *nt* (*COMM*) market
abschaffen ['apʃafən] *vt* to abolish, to do
  away with; **Abschaffung** *f* abolition
abschalten ['apʃaltən] *vt, vi* (*auch umg*) to
  switch off
abschätzen ['apʃɛtsən] *vt* to estimate;
  (*Lage*) to assess; (*Person*) to size up
abschätzig ['apʃɛtsɪç] *adj* disparaging,
  derogatory
Abschaum ['apʃaʊm] (**-(e)s**) *m* scum
Abscheu ['apʃɔy] (**-(e)s**) *m* loathing,
  repugnance; **a~erregend** *adj* repulsive,
  loathsome; **a~lich** [ap'ʃɔylɪç] *adj*
  abominable
abschicken ['apʃɪkən] *vt* to send off
abschieben ['apʃi:bən] (*unreg*) *vt* to push
  away; (*Person*) to pack off; (: *POL*) to deport
Abschied ['apʃi:t] (**-(e)s, -e**) *m* parting;
  (*von Armee*) discharge; **(von jdm) ~**
  nehmen to say goodbye (to sb), to take
  one's leave (of sb); **seinen ~ nehmen** (*MIL*)
  to apply for discharge; **~sbrief** *m* farewell
  letter; **~sfeier** *f* farewell party
abschießen ['apʃi:sən] (*unreg*) *vt* (*Flugzeug*)
  to shoot down; (*Geschoß*) to fire
abschirmen ['apʃɪrmən] *vt* to screen
abschlagen ['apʃla:gən] (*unreg*) *vt*
  (*abhacken, COMM*) to knock off; (*ablehnen*)
  to refuse; (*MIL*) to repel
abschlägig ['apʃlɛ:gɪç] *adj* negative
Abschlagszahlung *f* interim payment
Abschlepp- ['apʃlɛp] *zW*: **~dienst** *m* (*AUT*)
  breakdown service (*BRIT*), towing company
  (*US*); **a~en** *vt* to (take in) tow; **~seil** *nt*
  towrope
abschließen ['apʃli:sən] (*unreg*) *vt* (*Tür*) to
  lock; (*beenden*) to conclude, to finish;
  (*Vertrag, Handel*) to conclude ♦ *vr* (*sich
  isolieren*) to cut o.s. off; **~d** *adj* concluding
Abschluß ⚠ ['apʃlʊs] *m* (*Beendigung*) close,
  conclusion; (*COMM: Bilanz*) balancing; (*von
  Vertrag, Handel*) conclusion; **zum ~** in
  conclusion; **~feier** ⚠ *f* (*SCH*) end of term

⚠ *For information on spelling reform see page 615*

party; **~prüfung** △ *f* final exam
abschneiden ['apʃnaɪdən] (*unreg*) *vt* to cut off ♦ *vi* to do, to come off
Abschnitt ['apʃnɪt] *m* section; (*MIL*) sector; (*Kontroll~*) counterfoil; (*MATH*) segment; (*Zeit~*) period
abschrauben ['apʃraubən] *vt* to unscrew
abschrecken ['apʃrɛkən] *vt* to deter, to put off; (*mit kaltem Wasser*) to plunge in cold water; **~d** *adj* deterrent; **~des Beispiel** warning
abschreiben ['apʃraɪbən] (*unreg*) *vt* to copy; (*verloren geben*) to write off; (*COMM*) to deduct
Abschrift ['apʃrɪft] *f* copy
Abschuß △ ['apʃʊs] *m* (*eines Geschützes*) firing; (*Herunterschießen*) shooting down; (*Tötung*) shooting
abschüssig ['apʃʏsɪç] *adj* steep
abschwächen ['apʃvɛçən] *vt* to lessen; (*Behauptung, Kritik*) to tone down ♦ *vr* to lessen
abschweifen ['apʃvaɪfən] *vi* to digress
abschwellen ['apʃvɛlən] (*unreg*) *vi* (*Geschwulst*) to go down; (*Lärm*) to die down
abschwören ['apʃvøːrən] *vi* ((+*dat*)) to renounce
absehbar ['apzeːbaːr] *adj* foreseeable; **in ~er Zeit** in the foreseeable future; **das Ende ist ~** the end is in sight
absehen ['apzeːən] (*unreg*) *vt* (*Ende, Folgen*) to foresee ♦ *vi*: **von etw ~** to refrain from sth; (*nicht berücksichtigen*) to leave sth out of consideration
abseilen ['apzaɪlən] *vr* (*Bergsteiger*) to abseil (down)
abseits ['apzaɪts] *adv* out of the way ♦ *präp* +*gen* away from; **A~** *nt* (*SPORT*) offside
absenden ['apzɛndən] (*unreg*) *vt* to send off, to dispatch
Absender (**-s, -**) *m* sender
absetzen ['apzɛtsən] *vt* (*niederstellen, aussteigen lassen*) to put down; (*abnehmen*) to take off; (*COMM: verkaufen*) to sell; (*FIN: abziehen*) to deduct; (*entlassen*) to dismiss; (*König*) to depose; (*streichen*) to drop; (*hervorheben*) to pick out ♦ *vr* (*sich entfernen*) to clear off; (*sich ablagern*) to be deposited
Absetzung *f* (*FIN: Abzug*) deduction; (*Entlassung*) dismissal; (*von König*) deposing
absichern ['apzɪçərn] *vt* to make safe; (*schützen*) to safeguard ♦ *vr* to protect o.s.
Absicht ['apzɪçt] *f* intention; **mit ~** on purpose; **a~lich** *adj* intentional, deliberate
absinken ['apzɪŋkən] (*unreg*) *vi* to sink; (*Temperatur, Geschwindigkeit*) to decrease
absitzen ['apzɪtsən] (*unreg*) *vi* to dismount ♦ *vt* (*Strafe*) to serve
absolut [apzoˈluːt] *adj* absolute; **A~ismus** *m* absolutism
absolvieren [apzɔlˈviːrən] *vt* (*SCH*) to complete
absonder- ['apzɔndər] *zW*: **~lich** *adj* odd, strange; **~n** *vt* to separate; (*ausscheiden*) to give off, to secrete ♦ *vr* to cut o.s. off; **A~ung** *f* separation; (*MED*) secretion
abspalten ['apʃpaltən] *vt* to split off
abspannen ['apʃpanən] *vt* (*Pferde*) to unhitch; (*Wagen*) to uncouple
abspeisen ['apʃpaɪzən] *vt* (*fig*) to fob off
abspenstig ['apʃpɛnstɪç] *adj*: (**jdm**) ~ **machen** to lure away (from sb)
absperren ['apʃpɛrən] *vt* to block *od* close off; (*Tür*) to lock; **Absperrung** *f* (*Vorgang*) blocking *od* closing off; (*Sperre*) barricade
abspielen ['apʃpiːlən] *vt* (*Platte, Tonband*) to play; (*SPORT: Ball*) to pass ♦ *vr* to happen
Absprache ['apʃpraːxə] *f* arrangement
absprechen ['apʃprɛçən] *vt* (*vereinbaren*) to arrange; **jdm etw ~** to deny sb sth
abspringen ['apʃprɪŋən] (*unreg*) *vi* to jump down/off; (*Farbe, Lack*) to flake off; (*AVIAT*) to bale out; (*sich distanzieren*) to back out
Absprung ['apʃprʊŋ] *m* jump
abspülen ['apʃpyːlən] *vt* to rinse; (*Geschirr*) to wash up
abstammen ['apʃtamən] *vi* to be descended; (*Wort*) to be derived; **Abstammung** *f* descent; derivation
Abstand ['apʃtant] *m* distance; (*zeitlich*) interval; **davon ~ nehmen, etw zu tun** to refrain from doing sth; **mit ~ der beste** by

far the best
abstatten ['apʃtatən] vt (Dank) to give; (Besuch) to pay
abstauben ['apʃtaubən] vt, vi to dust; (umg: stehlen) to pinch; (: schnorren) to scrounge
Abstecher ['apʃteçər] (-s, -) m detour
abstehen ['apʃteːən] (unreg) vi (Ohren, Haare) to stick out; (entfernt sein) to stand away
absteigen ['apʃtaigən] (unreg) vi (vom Rad etc) to get off, to dismount; **(in die zweite Liga) ~** to be relegated (to the second division)
abstellen ['apʃtɛlən] vt (niederstellen) to put down; (entfernt stellen) to pull out; (hinstellen: Auto) to park; (ausschalten) to turn od switch off; (Mißstand, Unsitte) to stop
Abstellraum m storage room
abstempeln ['apʃtɛmpəln] vt to stamp
absterben ['apʃtɛrbən] (unreg) vi to die; (Körperteil) to go numb
Abstieg ['apʃtiːk] (-(e)s, -e) m descent; (SPORT) relegation; (fig) decline
abstimmen ['apʃtɪmən] vi to vote ♦ vt: ~ **(auf** +akk) (Instrument) to tune (to); (Interessen) to match (with); (Termine, Ziele) to fit in (with) ♦ vr to agree
Abstimmung f vote
Abstinenz [apstiˈnɛnts] f abstinence; teetotalism; ~**ler(in)** (-s, -) m(f) teetotaller
abstoßen ['apʃtoːsən] (unreg) vt to push off od away; (verkaufen) to unload; (anekeln) to repel, to repulse; ~**d** adj repulsive
abstrakt [apˈstrakt] adj abstract ♦ adv abstractly, in the abstract
abstreiten ['apʃtraitən] (unreg) vt to deny
Abstrich ['apʃtriç] m (Abzug) cut; (MED) smear; ~**e machen** to lower one's sights
abstufen ['apʃtuːfən] vt (Hang) to terrace; (Farben) to shade; (Gehälter) to grade
Absturz ['apʃturts] m fall; (AVIAT) crash
abstürzen ['apʃtyrtsən] vi to fall; (AVIAT) to crash
absuchen ['apzuːxən] vt to scour, to search
absurd [apˈzʊrt] adj absurd
Abszeß ⚠ [apsˈtsɛs] (-sses, -sse) m ·

abscess
Abt [apt] (-(e)s, ̈e) m abbot
Abt. abk (= Abteilung) dept.
abtasten ['aptastən] vt to feel, to probe
abtauen ['aptauən] vt, vi to thaw
Abtei [apˈtai] (-, -en) f abbey
Abteil [apˈtail] (-(e)s, -e) nt compartment; '**abteilen** vt to divide up; (abtrennen) to divide off; ~**ung** f (in Firma, Kaufhaus) department; (in Krankenhaus) section; (MIL) unit
abtippen ['aptɪpən] vt (Text) to type up
abtransportieren ['aptranspɔrtiːrən] vt to take away, to remove
abtreiben ['aptraibən] (unreg) vt (Boot, Flugzeug) to drive off course; (Kind) to abort ♦ vi to be driven off course; to abort
Abtreibung f abortion
abtrennen ['aptrɛnən] vt (lostrennen) to detach; (entfernen) to take off; (abteilen) to separate off
abtreten ['aptreːtən] (unreg) vt to wear out; (überlassen) to hand over, to cede ♦ vi to go off; (zurücktreten) to step down
Abtritt ['aptrɪt] m resignation
abtrocknen ['aptrɔknən] vt, vi to dry
abtun ['aptuːn] (unreg) vt (fig) to dismiss
abwägen ['apvɛːgən] (unreg) vt to weigh up
abwälzen ['apvɛltsən] vt (Schuld, Verantwortung): ~ **(auf** +akk) to shift (onto)
abwandeln ['apvandəln] vt to adapt
abwandern ['apvandərn] vi to move away; (FIN) to be transferred
abwarten ['apvartən] vt to wait for ♦ vi to wait
abwärts ['apvɛrts] adv down
Abwasch ['apvaʃ] (-(e)s) m washing-up; a~**en** (unreg) vt (Schmutz) to wash off; (Geschirr) to wash (up)
Abwasser ['apvasər] (-s, -wässer) nt sewage
abwechseln ['apvɛksəln] vi, vr to alternate; (Personen) to take turns; ~**d** adj alternate; **Abwechslung** f change; **abwechslungsreich** adj varied
abwegig ['apveːgɪç] adj wrong
Abwehr ['apveːr] (-) f defence; (Schutz)

⚠ For information on spelling reform see page 615

protection; (~*dienst*) counterintelligence (service); **a~en** *vt* to ward off; (*Ball*) to stop
abweichen ['apvaiçən] (*unreg*) *vi* to deviate; (*Meinung*) to differ
abweisen ['apvaizən] (*unreg*) *vt* to turn away; (*Antrag*) to turn down; **~d** *adj* (*Haltung*) cold
abwenden ['apvɛndən] (*unreg*) *vt* to avert ♦ *vr* to turn away
abwerfen ['apvɛrfən] (*unreg*) *vt* to throw off; (*Profit*) to yield; (*aus Flugzeug*) to drop; (*Spielkarte*) to discard
abwerten ['apvɛrtən] *vt* (*FIN*) to devalue
abwertend *adj* (*Worte, Sinn*) pejorative
Abwertung *f* (*von Währung*) devaluation
abwesend ['apveːzənt] *adj* absent
Abwesenheit ['apveːzənhait] *f* absence
abwickeln ['apvikəln] *vt* to unwind; (*Geschäft*) to wind up
abwimmeln ['apviməln] (*umg*) *vt* (*Menschen*) to get shot of
abwischen ['apviʃən] *vt* to wipe off *od* away; (*putzen*) to wipe
Abwurf ['apvurf] *m* throwing off; (*von Bomben etc*) dropping; (*von Reiter, SPORT*) throw
abwürgen ['apvyrgən] (*umg*) *vt* to scotch; (*Motor*) to stall
abzahlen ['aptsaːlən] *vt* to pay off
abzählen ['aptsɛːlən] *vt, vi* to count (up)
Abzahlung *f* repayment; **auf ~ kaufen** to buy on hire purchase
abzapfen ['aptsapfən] *vt* to draw off; **jdm Blut ~** to take blood from sb
abzäunen ['aptsɔynən] *vt* to fence off
Abzeichen ['aptsaiçən] *nt* badge; (*Orden*) decoration
abzeichnen ['aptsaiçnən] *vt* to draw, to copy; (*Dokument*) to initial ♦ *vr* to stand out; (*fig: bevorstehen*) to loom
abziehen ['aptsiːən] (*unreg*) *vt* to take off; (*Tier*) to skin; (*Bett*) to strip; (*Truppen*) to withdraw; (*subtrahieren*) to take away, to subtract; (*kopieren*) to run off ♦ *vi* to go away; (*Truppen*) to withdraw
abzielen ['aptsiːlən] *vi*: **~ auf** +*akk* to be aimed at

Abzug ['aptsuːk] *m* departure; (*von Truppen*) withdrawal; (*Kopie*) copy; (*Subtraktion*) subtraction; (*Betrag*) deduction; (*Rauch~*) flue; (*von Waffen*) trigger
abzüglich ['aptsyːkliç] *präp* +*gen* less
abzweigen ['aptsvaigən] *vi* to branch off ♦ *vt* to set aside
Abzweigung *f* junction
ach [ax] *excl* oh; **~ ja!** (oh) yes; **~ so!** I see; **mit A~ und Krach** by the skin of one's teeth
Achse ['aksə] *f* axis; (*AUT*) axle
Achsel ['aksəl] (**-, -n**) *f* shoulder; **~höhle** *f* armpit
acht [axt] *num* eight; **~ Tage** a week; **A~**[1] (**-, -en**) *f* eight; (*beim Eislaufen etc*) figure eight
Acht[2] (**-, -en**) *f*: **sich in a~ nehmen (vor** +*dat*) to be careful (of), to watch out (for); **etw außer a~ lassen** to disregard sth; **a~bar** *adj* worthy
acht- *zW*: **~e(r, s)** *adj* eighth; **A~el** *num* eighth; **~en** *vt* to respect ♦ *vi*: **~en (auf** +*akk*) to pay attention (to); **~en, daß ...** to be careful that ...
ächten ['ɛçtən] *vt* to outlaw, to ban
Achterbahn ['axtɐr-] *f* roller coaster
acht- *zW*: **~fach** *adj* eightfold; **~geben** △ (*unreg*) *vi*: **~geben (auf** +*akk*) to pay attention (to); **~hundert** *num* eight hundred; **~los** *adj* careless; **~mal** *adv* eight times; **~sam** *adj* attentive
Achtung ['axtʊŋ] *f* attention; (*Ehrfurcht*) respect ♦ *excl* look out!; (*MIL*) attention!; **alle ~!** good for you/him *etc*
achtzehn *num* eighteen
achtzig *num* eighty
ächzen ['ɛçtsən] *vi* to groan
Acker ['akɐr] (**-s, ¨**) *m* field; **a~n** *vt, vi* to plough; (*umg*) to slog away
ADAC [aːdeːˈaˈtseː] *abk* (= *Allgemeiner Deutscher Automobil-Club*) ≈ AA, RAC
Adapter [aˈdaptɐr] (**-s, -**) *m* adapter
addieren [aˈdiːrən] *vt* to add (up); **Addition** [aditsiˈoːn] *f* addition
Adel ['aːdəl] (**-s**) *m* nobility; **a~ig** *adj* noble; **a~n** *vt* to raise to the peerage

⚠ *Informationen zur Rechtschreibreform Seite 615*

Ader ['aːdər] (-, -n) f vein

Adjektiv ['atjektiːf] (-s, -e) nt adjective

Adler ['aːdlər] (-s, -) m eagle

adlig adj noble

Adopt- zW: **a~ieren** [adɔp'tiːrən] vt to adopt; **~ion** [adɔptsi'oːn] f adoption; **~iveltern** pl adoptive parents; **~ivkind** nt adopted child

Adreßbuch ⚠ nt directory; (privat) address book

Adress- zW: **~e** [a'drɛsə] f address; **a~ieren** [adrɛ'siːrən] vt: **a~ieren (an** +akk) to address (to)

Adria ['aːdria] (-) f Adriatic

Advent [at'vɛnt] (-(e)s, -e) m Advent; **~skalender** m Advent calendar; **~skranz** m Advent wreath

Adverb [at'vɛrp] nt adverb

Aerobic [ae'roːbik] nt aerobics sg

Affäre [a'fɛːrə] f affair

Affe ['afə] (-n, -n) m monkey

Affekt [a'fɛkt] (-(e)s, -e) m: **im ~ handeln** to act in the heat of the moment; **a~iert** [afɛk'tiːrt] adj affected

Affen- zW: **a~artig** adj like a monkey; **mit a~artiger Geschwindigkeit** like a flash; **~hitze** (umg) f incredible heat

affig ['afɪç] adj affected

Afrika ['aːfrika] (-s) nt Africa; **~ner(in)** [-'kaːnər(ɪn)] (-s, -) m(f) African; **a~nisch** [-'kaːnɪʃ] adj African

AG [aː'geː] abk (= Aktiengesellschaft) ≈ plc (BRIT), ≈ Inc. (US)

Agent [a'gɛnt] m agent; **~ur** f agency

Aggregat [agre'gaːt] (-(e)s, -e) nt aggregate; (TECH) unit

Aggress- zW: **~ion** [agrɛsi'oːn] f aggression; **a~iv** [agrɛ'siːf] adj aggressive; **~ivität** [agrɛsiviˈtɛːt] f aggressiveness

Agrarpolitik [a'graːr-] f agricultural policy

Ägypten [ɛ'gʏptən] (-s) nt Egypt; **ägyptisch** adj Egyptian

aha [a'haː] excl aha!

ähneln ['ɛːnəln] vi +dat to be like, to resemble ♦ vr to be alike od similar

ahnen ['aːnən] vt to suspect; (Tod, Gefahr) to have a presentiment of

ähnlich ['ɛːnlɪç] adj (+dat) similar (to); **Ä~keit** f similarity

Ahnung ['aːnʊŋ] f idea, suspicion; presentiment; **a~slos** adj unsuspecting

Ahorn ['aːhɔrn] (-s, -e) m maple

Ähre ['ɛːrə] f ear

Aids [eːdz] nt AIDS sg

Airbag ['ɛːəbɛk] (-s, -s) m airbag

Akademie [akade'miː] f academy; **Aka'demiker(in)** (-s, -) m(f) university graduate; **akademisch** adj academic

akklimatisieren [aklimati'ziːrən] vr to become acclimatized

Akkord [a'kɔrt] (-(e)s, -e) m (MUS) chord; **im ~ arbeiten** to do piecework

Akkordeon [a'kɔrdeɔn] (-s, -s) nt accordion

Akku ['aku] (-s, -s) m rechargeable battery

Akkusativ ['akuzatiːf] (-s, -e) m accusative

Akne ['aknə] f acne

Akrobat(in) [akro'baːt(ɪn)] (-en, -en) m(f) acrobat

Akt [akt] (-(e)s, -e) m act; (KUNST) nude

Akte ['aktə] f file

Akten- zW: **~koffer** m attaché case; **a~kundig** adj on the files; **~schrank** m filing cabinet; **~tasche** f briefcase

Aktie ['aktsiə] f share

Aktien- zW: **~gesellschaft** f public limited company; **~index** (-(es), -e od -indices) m share index; **~kurs** m share price

Aktion [aktsi'oːn] f campaign; (Polizei~, Such~) action

Aktionär [aktsio'nɛːr] (-s, -e) m shareholder

aktiv [ak'tiːf] adj active; (MIL) regular; **~ieren** [-'viːrən] vt to activate; **A~i'tät** f activity

Aktualität [aktuali'tɛːt] f topicality; (einer Mode) up-to-dateness

aktuell [aktu'ɛl] adj topical; up-to-date

Akupunktur [akupʊŋk'tuːr] f acupuncture

Akustik [a'kʊstɪk] f acoustics pl

akut [a'kuːt] adj acute

Akzent [ak'tsɛnt] m accent; (Betonung) stress

akzeptabel [aktsɛp'taːbl] adj acceptable

akzeptieren [aktsɛp'tiːrən] vt to accept

Alarm [a'larm] (-(e)s, -e) m alarm; **a~bereit** adj standing by; **~bereitschaft** f stand-by; **a~ieren** [-'miːrən] vt to alarm

⚠ For information on spelling reform see page 615

Albanien [al'ba:niən] **(-s)** *nt* Albania
albanisch *adj* Albanian
albern ['albərn] *adj* silly
Album ['albʊm] **(-s, Alben)** *nt* album
Alge ['algə] *f* algae
Algebra ['algebra] **(-)** *f* algebra
Algerier(in) [al'ge:riər] **(-s, -)** *m(f)* Algerian
algerisch *adj* Algerian
alias ['a:lias] *adv* alias
Alibi ['a:libi] **(-s, -s)** *nt* alibi
Alimente [ali'mɛntə] *pl* alimony *sg*
Alkohol ['alkoho:l] **(-s, -e)** *m* alcohol; **a~frei** *adj* non-alcoholic; **~iker(in)** [alko'ho:likar(ɪn)] **(-s, -)** *m(f)* alcoholic; **a~isch** *adj* alcoholic; **~verbot** *nt* ban on alcohol
All [al] **(-s)** *nt* universe
all|abendlich *adj* every evening
'**allbekannt** *adj* universally known

alle(r, s) ['alə(r,s)] *adj* **1** (*sämtliche*) all; **wir alle** all of us; **alle Kinder waren da** all the children were there; **alle Kinder mögen ...** all children like ...; **alle beide** both of us/them; **sie kamen alle** they all came; **alles Gute** all the best; **alles in allem** all in all
2 (*mit Zeit- oder Maßangaben*) every; **alle vier Jahre** every four years; **alle fünf Meter** every five metres
♦ *pron* everything; **alles was er sagt** everything he says, all that he says
♦ *adv* (*zu Ende, aufgebraucht*) finished; **die Milch ist alle** the milk's all gone, there's no milk left; **etw alle machen** to finish sth up

Allee [a'le:] *f* avenue
allein [a'laɪn] *adv* alone; (*ohne Hilfe*) on one's own, by oneself ♦ *konj* but, only; **nicht ~** (*nicht nur*) not only; **A~erziehende(r)** △ *f(m)* single parent; **A~gang** *m*: **im A~gang** on one's own; **~stehend** △ *adj* single
allemal ['alə'ma:l] *adv* (*jedesmal*) always; (*ohne weiteres*) with no bother; **ein für ~** once and for all
allenfalls ['alən'fals] *adv* at all events;

(*höchstens*) at most
aller- ['alər] *zW*: **~beste(r, s)** *adj* very best; **~dings** *adv* (*zwar*) admittedly; (*gewiß*) certainly
Allergie [aler'gi:] *f* allergy; **al|lergisch** *adj* allergic
aller- *zW*: **~hand** (*umg*) *adj inv* all sorts of; **das ist doch ~hand!** that's a bit much; **~hand!** (*lobend*) good show!; **A~heiligen** *nt* All Saints' Day; **~höchstens** *adv* at the very most; **~lei** *adj inv* all sorts of; **~letzte(r, s)** *adj* very last; **A~seelen** **(-s)** *nt* All Souls' Day; **~seits** *adv* on all sides; **prost ~seits!** cheers everyone!

i **Allerheiligen** (*All Saints' Day*) *is celebrated on November 1st and is a public holiday in some parts of Germany and in Austria. Allerseelen (All Souls' Day) is celebrated on November 2nd in the Roman Catholic Church. It is customary to visit cemeteries and place lighted candles on the graves of relatives and friends.*

Allerwelts- *in zW* (*Durchschnitts-*) common; (*nichtssagend*) commonplace
alles *pron* everything; **~ in allem** all in all; **~ Gute!** all the best!
Alleskleber **(-s, -)** *m* multi-purpose glue
allgemein ['algəmaɪn] *adj* general; **im ~en** in general; **~gültig** △ *adj* generally accepted; **A~wissen** *nt* general knowledge
Alliierte(r) [ali'i:rtə(r)] *m* ally
all- *zW*: **~jährlich** *adj* annual; **~mächtig** *adj* almighty; **~mählich** *adj* gradual; **A~tag** *m* everyday life; **~täglich** *adj*, *adv* daily; (*gewöhnlich*) commonplace; **~tags** *adv* on weekdays; **~'wissend** *adj* omniscient; **~zu** *adv* all too; **~zuoft** △ *adv* all too often; **~zuviel** △ *adv* too much
Allzweck- ['altsvɛk-] *in zW* multi-purpose
Alm [alm] **(-, -en)** *f* alpine pasture
Almosen ['almo:zən] **(-s, -)** *nt* alms *pl*
Alpen ['alpən] *pl* Alps; **~vorland** *nt* foothills *pl* of the Alps

Alphabet [alfa'be:t] (-(e)s, -e) *nt* alphabet; **a~isch** *adj* alphabetical

Alptraum ⚠ ['alptraʊm] *m* nightmare

SCHLÜSSELWORT
---

als [als] *konj* **1** (*zeitlich*) when; (*gleichzeitig*) as; **damals, als ...** (in the days) when ...; **gerade, als ...** just as ...
2 (*in der Eigenschaft*) than; **als Antwort** as an answer; **als Kind** as a child
3 (*bei Vergleichen*) than; **ich kam später als er** I came later than he (did) *od* later than him; **lieber ... als ...** rather ... than ...; **nichts als Ärger** nothing but trouble
4: als ob/wenn as if

also ['alzo:] *konj* so; (*folglich*) therefore; **~ gut** *od* **schön!** okay then; **~, so was!** well really!; **na ~!** there you are then!

Alsterwasser ['alstər-] *nt* shandy (BRIT), beer and lemonade

Alt [alt] (-s, -e) *m* (MUS) alto

alt *adj* old; **alles beim ~en lassen** to leave everything as it was

Altar [al'ta:r] (-(e)s, -äre) *m* altar

Alt- *zW*: **~bau** *m* old building; **a~bekannt** *adj* long-known; **~bier** *nt* top-fermented German dark beer; **~eisen** *nt* scrap iron

Alten(wohn)heim *nt* old people's home

Alter ['altər] (-s, -) *nt* age; (*hohes*) old age; **im ~ von** at the age of; **a~n** *vi* to grow old, to age

Alternativ- [alterna'ti:f] *in zW* alternative; **~e** *f* alternative

Alters- *zW*: **~grenze** *f* age limit; **~heim** *nt* old people's home; **~rente** *f* old age pension; **a~schwach** *adj* (*Mensch*) frail; **~versorgung** *f* old age pension

Altertum ['altərtu:m] *nt* antiquity

alt- *zW*: **A~glas** *nt* glass for recycling; **A~glascontainer** *m* bottle bank; **~klug** *adj* precocious; **~modisch** *adj* old-fashioned; **A~papier** *nt* waste paper; **A~stadt** *f* old town

Alufolie ['a:lufo:liə] *f* aluminium foil

Aluminium [alu'mi:niʊm] (-s) *nt* aluminium, aluminum (US)

Alzheimerkrankheit ['altshaɪmər-'kraŋkhaɪt] *f* Alzheimer's (disease)

am [am] = **an dem**; **~ Schlafen** (umg) sleeping; **~ 15. März** on March 15th; **~ besten/schönsten** best/most beautiful

Amateur [ama'tø:r] *m* amateur

Amboß ⚠ ['ambɔs] (-sses, -sse) *m* anvil

ambulant [ambu'lant] *adj* outpatient; **Ambulanz** *f* outpatients *sg*

Ameise ['a:maɪzə] *f* ant

Ameisenhaufen *m* ant hill

Amerika [a'me:rika] (-s) *nt* America; **~ner(in)** [-'ka:nər(ɪn)] (-s, -) *m(f)* American; **a~nisch** [-'ka:nɪʃ] *adj* American

Amnestie [amnɛs'ti:] *f* amnesty

Ampel ['ampəl] (-, -n) *f* traffic lights *pl*

amputieren [ampu'ti:rən] *vt* to amputate

Amsel ['amzəl] (-, -n) *f* blackbird

Amt [amt] (-(e)s, -̈er) *nt* office; (*Pflicht*) duty; (TEL) exchange; **a~ieren** [am'ti:rən] *vi* to hold office; **a~lich** *adj* official

Amts- *zW*: **~richter** *m* district judge; **~stunden** *pl* office hours; **~zeichen** *nt* dialling tone; **~zeit** *f* period of office

amüsant [amy'zant] *adj* amusing

amüsieren [amy'zi:rən] *vt* to amuse ♦ *vr* to enjoy o.s.

Amüsierviertel *nt* nightclub district

SCHLÜSSELWORT
---

an [an] *präp +dat* **1** (*räumlich: wo?*) at; (*auf, bei*) on; (*nahe bei*) near; **an diesem Ort** at this place; **an der Wand** on the wall; **zu nahe an etw** too near to sth; **unten am Fluß** down by the river; **Köln liegt am Rhein** Cologne is on the Rhine
2 (*zeitlich: wann?*) on; **an diesem Tag** on this day; **an Ostern** at Easter
3: arm an Fett low in fat; **an etw sterben** to die of sth; **an (und für) sich** actually
♦ *präp +akk* **1** (*räumlich: wohin?*) to; **er ging ans Fenster** he went (over) to the window; **etw an die Wand hängen/schreiben** to hang/write sth on the wall
2 (*zeitlich: woran?*): **an etw denken** to think of sth
3 (*gerichtet an*) to; **ein Gruß/eine Frage**

⚠ *For information on spelling reform see page 615*

an dich greetings/a question to you
♦ *adv* **1** (*ungefähr*) about; **an die hundert** about a hundred
2 (*auf Fahrplänen*): **Frankfurt an 18.30** arriving Frankfurt 18.30
3 (*ab*): **von dort/heute an** from there/today onwards
4 (*angeschaltet, angezogen*) on; **das Licht ist an** the light is on; **ohne etwas an** with nothing on; *siehe auch* **am**

analog [ana'lo:k] *adj* analogous; **A~ie** [-'gi:] *f* analogy

Analphabet(in) [an|alfa'be:t(ɪn)] (**-en, -en**) *m(f)* illiterate (person)

Analyse [ana'ly:zə] *f* analysis

analysieren [analy'zi:rən] *vt* to analyse

Ananas ['ananas] (**-, -** *od* **-se**) *f* pineapple

Anarchie [anar'çi:] *f* anarchy

Anatomie [anato'mi:] *f* anatomy

anbahnen ['anba:nən] *vt, vr* to open up

Anbau ['anbau] *m* (*AGR*) cultivation; (*Gebäude*) extension; **a~en** *vt* (*AGR*) to cultivate; (*Gebäudeteil*) to build on

anbehalten ['anbəhaltən] (*unreg*) *vt* to keep on

anbei [an'baɪ] *adv* enclosed

anbeißen ['anbaɪsən] (*unreg*) *vt* to bite into ♦ *vi* to bite; (*fig*) to swallow the bait; **zum A~** (*umg*) good enough to eat

anbelangen ['anbəlaŋən] *vt* to concern; **was mich anbelangt** as far as I am concerned

anbeten ['anbe:tən] *vt* to worship

Anbetracht ['anbətraxt] *m*: **in ~** +*gen* in view of

anbieten ['anbi:tən] (*unreg*) *vt* to offer ♦ *vr* to volunteer

anbinden ['anbɪndən] (*unreg*) *vt* to tie up; **kurz angebunden** (*fig*) curt

Anblick ['anblɪk] *m* sight; **a~en** *vt* to look at

anbraten ['anbra:tən] *vt* to brown

anbrechen ['anbrɛçən] (*unreg*) *vt* to start; (*Vorräte*) to break into ♦ *vi* to start; (*Tag*) to break; (*Nacht*) to fall

anbrennen ['anbrɛnən] (*unreg*) *vi* to catch

fire; (*KOCH*) to burn

anbringen ['anbrɪŋən] (*unreg*) *vt* to bring; (*Ware*) to sell; (*festmachen*) to fasten

Anbruch ['anbrʊx] *m* beginning; **~ des Tages/der Nacht** dawn/nightfall

anbrüllen ['anbrʏlən] *vt* to roar at

Andacht ['andaxt] (**-, -en**) *f* devotion; (*Gottesdienst*) prayers *pl*; **andächtig** *adj* ['andɛçtɪç] devout

andauern ['andauərn] *vi* to last, to go on; **~d** *adj* continual

Anden ['andən] *pl* Andes

Andenken ['andɛŋkən] (**-s, -**) *nt* memory; souvenir

andere(r, s) ['andərə(r, z)] *adj* other; (*verschieden*) different; **ein ~s Mal** another time; **kein ~r** nobody else; **von etw ~m sprechen** to talk about something else; **~rseits** *adv* on the other hand

andermal *adv*: **ein ~** some other time

ändern ['ɛndərn] *vt* to alter, to change ♦ *vr* to change

andernfalls ['andərnfals] *adv* otherwise

anders ['andərs] *adv*: **~ (als)** differently (from); **wer ~?** who else?; **jd/irgendwo ~** sb/somewhere else; **~ aussehen/klingen** to look/sound different; **~artig** *adj* different; **~herum** *adv* the other way round; **~wo** *adv* somewhere else; **~woher** *adv* from somewhere else

anderthalb ['andərt'halp] *adj* one and a half

Änderung ['ɛndərʊŋ] *f* alteration, change

Änderungsschneiderei *f* tailor (who does alterations)

anderweitig ['andər'vaɪtɪç] *adj* other ♦ *adv* otherwise; (*anderswo*) elsewhere

andeuten ['andɔɪtən] *vt* to indicate; (*Wink geben*) to hint at; **Andeutung** *f* indication; hint

Andrang ['andraŋ] *m* crush

andrehen ['andre:ən] *vt* to turn *od* switch on; **jdm etw ~** (*umg*) to unload sth onto sb

androhen ['andro:ən] *vt*: **jdm etw ~** to threaten sb with sth

aneignen ['an|aɪgnən] *vt*: **sich** *dat* **etw ~** to

⚠ *Informationen zur Rechtschreibreform Seite 615*

acquire sth; *(widerrechtlich)* to appropriate sth

aneinander [anaɪ'nandər] *adv* at/on/to *etc* one another *od* each other; **~geraten** △ *(unreg) vi* to clash

Anekdote [anɛk'do:tə] *f* anecdote

anekeln ['anˌe:kəln] *vt* to disgust

anerkannt ['anˌɛrkant] *adj* recognized, acknowledged

anerkennen ['anˌɛrkɛnən] *(unreg) vt* to recognize, to acknowledge; *(würdigen)* to appreciate; **~d** *adj* appreciative

Anerkennung *f* recognition, acknowledgement; appreciation

anfachen ['anfaxən] *vt* to fan into flame; *(fig)* to kindle

anfahren ['anfa:rən] *(unreg) vt* to deliver; *(fahren gegen)* to hit; *(Hafen)* to put into; *(fig)* to bawl out ♦ *vi* to drive up; *(losfahren)* to drive off

Anfahrt ['anfa:rt] *f (Anfahrtsweg, Anfahrtszeit)* journey

Anfall ['anfal] *m (MED)* attack; **a~en** *(unreg) vt* to attack; *(fig)* to overcome ♦ *vi (Arbeit)* to come up; *(Produkt)* to be obtained

anfällig ['anfɛlɪç] *adj* delicate; **~ für etw** prone to sth

Anfang ['anfaŋ] (**-(e)s, -fänge**) *m* beginning, start; **von ~ an** right from the beginning; **zu ~** at the beginning; **~ Mai** at the beginning of May; **a~en** *(unreg) vt, vi* to begin, to start; *(machen)* to do

Anfänger(in) ['anfɛŋər(ɪn)] (**-s, -**) *m(f)* beginner

anfänglich ['anfɛŋlɪç] *adj* initial

anfangs *adv* at first; **A~buchstabe** *m* initial *od* first letter; **A~gehalt** *nt* starting salary

anfassen ['anfasən] *vt* to handle; *(berühren)* to touch ♦ *vi* to lend a hand ♦ *vr* to feel

anfechten ['anfɛçtən] *(unreg) vt* to dispute

anfertigen ['anfɛrtɪgən] *vt* to make

anfeuern ['anfɔʏɐn] *vt (fig)* to spur on

anflehen ['anfle:ən] *vt* to implore

anfliegen ['anfli:gən] *(unreg) vt* to fly to

Anflug ['anflu:k] *m (AVIAT)* approach; *(Spur)* trace

anfordern ['anfɔrdərn] *vt* to demand; *(COMM)* to requisition

Anforderung *f (+gen)* demand (for)

Anfrage ['anfra:gə] *f* inquiry; **a~n** *vi* to inquire

anfreunden ['anfrɔʏndən] *vr* to make friends

anfügen ['anfy:gən] *vt* to add; *(beifügen)* to enclose

anfühlen ['anfy:lən] *vt, vr* to feel

anführen ['anfy:rən] *vt* to lead; *(zitieren)* to quote; *(umg: betrügen)* to lead up the garden path

Anführer *m* leader

Anführungszeichen *pl* quotation marks, inverted commas

Angabe ['anga:bə] *f* statement; *(TECH)* specification; *(umg: Prahlerei)* boasting; *(SPORT)* service

angeben ['anɡe:bən] *(unreg) vt* to give; *(anzeigen)* to inform on; *(bestimmen)* to set ♦ *vi (umg)* to boast; *(SPORT)* to serve

Angeber (**-s, -**) *(umg) m* show-off; **Angebe|rei** *(umg) f* showing off

angeblich ['anɡe:plɪç] *adj* alleged

angeboren ['anɡəbo:rən] *adj* inborn, innate

Angebot ['anɡəbo:t] *nt* offer; **~ (an +dat)** *(COMM)* supply (of)

angebracht ['anɡəbraxt] *adj* appropriate, in order

angegriffen ['anɡəɡrɪfən] *adj* exhausted

angeheitert ['anɡəhaɪtərt] *adj* tipsy

angehen ['anɡe:ən] *(unreg) vt* to concern; *(angreifen)* to attack; *(bitten)* **jdn ~ (um)** to approach sb (for) ♦ *vi (Feuer)* to light; *(umg: beginnen)* to begin; **~d** *adj* prospective

angehören ['anɡəhø:rən] *vi (+ dat)* to belong to; *(Partei)* to be a member of

Angehörige(r) *f(m)* relative

Angeklagte(r) ['anɡəkla:ktə(r)] *f(m)* accused

Angel ['aŋəl] (**-, -n**) *f* fishing rod; *(Tür~)* hinge

Angelegenheit ['anɡələ:ɡənhaɪt] *f* affair, matter

Angel- *zW:* **~haken** *m* fish hook; **a~n** *vt* to catch ♦ *vi* to fish; **~n** (**-s**) *nt* angling,

---

⚠ *For information on spelling reform see page 615*

fishing; **~rute** f fishing rod; **~schein** m fishing permit

angemessen ['angəmɛsən] adj appropriate, suitable

angenehm ['angəneːm] adj pleasant; **~!** (bei Vorstellung) pleased to meet you

angeregt [angəreːkt] adj animated, lively

angesehen ['angəzeːən] adj respected

angesichts ['angəzɪçts] präp +gen in view of, considering

angespannt ['angəʃpant] adj (Aufmerksamkeit) close; (Arbeit) hard

Angestellte(r) ['angəʃtɛltə(r)] f(m) employee

angestrengt ['angəʃtrɛŋt] adv as hard as one can

angetan ['angətaːn] adj: **von jdm/etw ~ sein** to be impressed by sb/sth; **es jdm ~ haben** to appeal to sb

angetrunken ['angətrʊŋkən] adj tipsy

angewiesen ['angəviːzən] adj: **auf jdn/etw ~ sein** to be dependent on sb/sth

angewöhnen ['angəvøːnən] vt: **jdm/sich etw ~** to get sb/become accustomed to sth

Angewohnheit ['angəvoːnhait] f habit

angleichen ['anglaiçən] (unreg) vt, vr to adjust

Angler ['anlər] (-s, -) m angler

angreifen ['angraifən] (unreg) vt to attack; (beschädigen) to damage

Angreifer (-s, -) m attacker

Angriff ['angrɪf] m attack; **etw in ~ nehmen** to make a start on sth

Angst (-, ¨e) f fear; **jdm ist a~** sb is afraid od scared; **~ haben** (vor +dat) to be afraid od scared (of); **~ haben um jdn/etw** to be worried about sb/sth; **jdm a~ machen** to scare sb; **~hase** (umg) m chicken, scaredy-cat

ängst- ['ɛŋst] zW: **~igen** vt to frighten ♦ vr: **sich ~igen (vor +dat od um)** to worry (o.s.) (about); **~lich** adj nervous; (besorgt) worried; **Ä~lichkeit** f nervousness

anhaben ['anhaːbən] (unreg) vt to have on; **er kann mir nichts ~** he can't hurt me

anhalt- ['anhalt] zW: **~en** (unreg) vt to stop

♦ vi to stop; (andauern) to persist; **(jdm) etw ~en** to hold sth up (against sb); **jdn zur Arbeit/Höflichkeit ~en** to make sb work/be polite; **~end** adj persistent; **A~er(in)** (-s, -) m(f) hitch-hiker; **per A~er fahren** to hitch-hike; **A~spunkt** m clue

anhand [an'hant] präp +gen with

Anhang ['anhaŋ] m appendix; (Leute) family; supporters pl

anhäng- ['anhɛŋ] zW: **~en** (unreg) vt to hang up; (Wagen) to couple up; (Zusatz) to add (on); **A~er** (-s, -) m supporter; (AUT) trailer; (am Koffer) tag; (Schmuck) pendant; **A~erschaft** f supporters pl; **~lich** adj devoted; **A~lichkeit** f devotion; **A~sel** (-s, -) nt appendage

Anhäufung ['anhɔyfʊŋ] f accumulation

anheben ['anheːbən] (unreg) vt to lift up; (Preise) to raise

anheizen ['anhaitsən] vt (Stimmung) to lift; (Moral) to boost

Anhieb ['anhiːb] m: **auf ~** at the very first go; (kurz entschlossen) on the spur of the moment

Anhöhe ['anhøːə] f hill

anhören ['anhøːrən] vt to listen to; (anmerken) to hear ♦ vr to sound

animieren [ani'miːrən] vt to encourage, to urge on

Anis [a'niːs] (-es, -e) m aniseed

Ank. abk (= Ankunft) arr.

Ankauf ['ankauf] m (von Wertpapieren, Devisen, Waren) purchase; **a~en** vt to purchase, to buy

Anker ['aŋkər] (-s, -) m anchor; **vor ~ gehen** to drop anchor

Anklage ['anklaːgə] f accusation; (JUR) charge; **~bank** f dock; **a~n** vt to accuse; **jdn (eines Verbrechens) a~n** (JUR) to charge sb (with a crime)

Ankläger ['anklɛːgər] m accuser

Anklang ['anklaŋ] m: **bei jdm ~ finden** to meet with sb's approval

Ankleidekabine f changing cubicle

ankleiden ['anklaidən] vt, vr to dress

anklopfen ['anklɔpfən] vi to knock

anknüpfen ['anknʏpfən] vt to fasten od tie

on; (fig) to start ♦ vi (anschließen): ~ **an** +akk to refer to

ankommen ['ankɔmən] (unreg) vi to arrive; (näherkommen) to approach; (Anklang finden): **bei jdm (gut)** ~ to go down well with sb; **es kommt darauf an** it depends; (wichtig sein) that (is what) matters; **es darauf** ~ **lassen** to let things take their course; **gegen jdn/etw** ~ to cope with sb/sth; **bei jdm schlecht** ~ to go down badly with sb

ankreuzen ['ankrɔytsən] vt to mark with a cross; (hervorheben) to highlight

ankündigen ['ankʏndɪgən] vt to announce; **Ankündigung** f announcement

Ankunft ['ankʊnft] (-, -künfte) f arrival; **~szeit** f time of arrival

ankurbeln ['ankʊrbəln] vt (fig) to boost

Anlage ['anla:gə] f disposition; (Begabung) talent; (Park) gardens pl; (Beilage) enclosure; (TECH) plant; (FIN) investment; (Entwurf) layout

Anlaß ⚠ ['anlas] (-sses, -lässe) m: ~ **(zu)** cause (for); (Ereignis) occasion; **aus** ~ +gen on the occasion of; ~ **zu etw geben** to give rise to sth; **etw zum** ~ **nehmen** to take the opportunity of sth

anlassen (unreg) vt to leave on; (Motor) to start ♦ vr (umg) to start off

Anlasser (-s, -) m (AUT) starter

anläßlich ⚠ ['anlɛslɪç] präp +gen on the occasion of

Anlauf ['anlaʊf] m run-up; **a~en** (unreg) vi to begin; (neuer Film) to show; (SPORT) to run up; (Fenster) to mist up; (Metall) to tarnish ♦ vt to call at; **rot a~en** to blush; **angelaufen kommen** to come running up

anlegen ['anle:gən] vt to put; (anziehen) to put on; (gestalten) to lay out; (Geld) to invest ♦ vr to dock; **etw an etw** akk ~ to put sth against od on sth; **ein Gewehr** ~ **(auf** +akk) to aim a weapon (at); **es auf etw** akk ~ to be out for sth/to do sth; **sich mit jdm** ~ (umg) to quarrel with sb

Anlegestelle f landing place

anlehnen ['anle:nən] vt to lean; (Tür) to leave ajar; **(sich) an etw** akk ~ to lean on/

against sth

Anleihe ['anlaɪə] f (FIN) loan

anleiten ['anlaɪtən] vt to instruct; **Anleitung** f instructions pl

anliegen ['anli:gən] (unreg) vi (Kleidung) to cling; **A~** (-s, -) nt matter; (Wunsch) wish; **~d** adj adjacent; (beigefügt) enclosed

Anlieger (-s, -) m resident; „~ **frei"** "residents only"

anmachen ['anmaxən] vt to attach; (Elektrisches) to put on; (Zigarette) to light; (Salat) to dress

anmaßen ['anma:sən] vt: **sich** dat **etw** ~ (Recht) to lay claim to sth; **~d** adj arrogant

Anmaßung f presumption

anmelden ['anmɛldən] vt to announce ♦ vr (sich ankündigen) to make an appointment; (polizeilich, für Kurs etc) to register

Anmeldung f announcement; appointment; registration

anmerken ['anmɛrkən] vt to observe; (anstreichen) to mark; **sich** dat **nichts** ~ **lassen** to not give anything away

Anmerkung f note

anmieten ['anmi:tən] vt to rent; (auch Auto) to hire

Anmut ['anmu:t] (-) f grace; **a~en** vt to give a feeling; **a~ig** adj charming

annähen ['annɛ:ən] vt to sew on

annähern ['annɛ:ərn] vr to get closer; **~d** adj approximate

Annäherung f approach

Annäherungsversuch m advances pl

Annahme ['anna:mə] f acceptance; (Vermutung) assumption

annehm- ['anne:m] zW: **~bar** adj acceptable; **~en** (unreg) vt to accept; (Namen) to take; (Kind) to adopt; (vermuten) to suppose, to assume ♦ vr (+gen) to take care (of); **A~lichkeit** f comfort

Annonce [a'nõ:sə] f advertisement

annoncieren [anõ'si:rən] vt, vi to advertise

annullieren [anʊ'li:rən] vt to annul

anonym [ano'ny:m] adj anonymous

Anorak ['anorak] (-s, -s) m anorak

anordnen ['anʔɔrdnən] vt to arrange; (befehlen) to order

⚠ For information on spelling reform see page 615

Anordnung f arrangement; order

anorganisch ['an|ɔrga:nɪʃ] *adj* inorganic

anpacken ['anpakən] *vt* to grasp; (*fig*) to tackle; **mit ~** to lend a hand

anpassen ['anpasən] *vt*: **(jdm) ~** to fit (on sb); (*fig*) to adapt ♦ *vr* to adapt

anpassungsfähig *adj* adaptable

Anpfiff ['anpfɪf] *m* (*SPORT*) (starting) whistle; kick-off; (*umg*) rocket

anprallen ['anpralən] *vi*: **~ (gegen** *od* **an** +*akk***)** to collide (with)

anprangern ['anpraŋərn] *vt* to denounce

anpreisen ['anpraɪzən] (*unreg*) *vt* to extol

Anprobe ['anpro:bə] *f* trying on

anprobieren ['anprobi:rən] *vt* to try on

anrechnen ['anrɛçnən] *vt* to charge; (*fig*) to count; **jdm etw hoch ~** to value sb's sth greatly

Anrecht ['anrɛçt] *nt*: **~ (auf** +*akk***)** right (to)

Anrede ['anre:də] *f* form of address; **a~n** *vt* to address; (*belästigen*) to accost

anregen ['anre:gən] *vt* to stimulate; **angeregte Unterhaltung** lively discussion; **~d** *adj* stimulating

Anregung *f* stimulation; (*Vorschlag*) suggestion

anreichern ['anraɪçərn] *vt* to enrich

Anreise ['anraɪzə] *f* journey; **a~n** *vi* to arrive

Anreiz ['anraɪts] *m* incentive

Anrichte ['anrɪçtə] *f* sideboard; **a~n** *vt* to serve up; **Unheil a~n** to make mischief

anrüchig ['anrʏçɪç] *adj* dubious

anrücken ['anrʏkən] *vi* to approach; (*MIL*) to advance

Anruf ['anru:f] *m* call; **~beantworter** [-bə|antvɔrtər] **(-s, -)** *m* answering machine; **a~en** (*unreg*) *vt* to call out to; (*bitten*) to call on; (*TEL*) to ring up, to phone, to call

ans [ans] = **an das**

Ansage ['anza:gə] *f* announcement; **a~n** *vt* to announce ♦ *vr* to say one will come; **~r(in) (-s, -)** *m(f)* announcer

ansammeln ['anzaməln] *vt* (*Reichtümer*) to amass ♦ *vr* (*Menschen*) to gather, to assemble; (*Wasser*) to collect;
Ansammlung *f* collection; (*Leute*) crowd

ansässig ['anzɛsɪç] *adj* resident

Ansatz ['anzats] *m* start; (*Haar~*) hairline; (*Hals~*) base; (*Verlängerungsstück*) extension; (*Veranschlagung*) estimate; **~punkt** *m* starting point

anschaffen ['anʃafən] *vt* to buy, to purchase; **Anschaffung** *f* purchase

anschalten ['anʃaltən] *vt* to switch on

anschau- ['anʃaʊ] *zW*: **~en** *vt* to look at; **~lich** *adj* illustrative; **A~ung** *f* (*Meinung*) view; **aus eigener A~ung** from one's own experience

Anschein ['anʃaɪn] *m* appearance; **allem ~ nach** to all appearances; **den ~ haben** to seem, to appear; **a~end** *adj* apparent

anschieben ['anʃi:bən] *vt* to push

Anschlag ['anʃla:k] *m* notice; (*Attentat*) attack; (*COMM*) estimate; (*auf Klavier*) touch; (*Schreibmaschine*) character; **a~en** ['anʃla:gən] (*unreg*) *vt* to put up; (*beschädigen*) to chip; (*Akkord*) to strike; (*Kosten*) to estimate ♦ *vi* to hit; (*wirken*) to have an effect; (*Glocke*) to ring; **an etw** *akk* **a~en** to hit against sth

anschließen ['anʃli:sən] (*unreg*) *vt* to connect up; (*Sender*) to link up ♦ *vi*: **an etw** *akk* **~** to adjoin sth; (*zeitlich*) to follow sth ♦ *vr*: **sich jdm/etw ~** to join sb/sth; (*beipflichten*) to agree with sb/sth; **sich an etw** *akk* **~** to adjoin sth; **~d** *adj* adjacent; (*zeitlich*) subsequent ♦ *adv* afterwards

Anschluß △ ['anʃlʊs] *m* (*ELEK*, *EISENB*) connection; (*von Wasser etc*) supply; **im ~ an** +*akk* following; **~ finden** to make friends; **~flug** △ *m* connecting flight

anschmiegsam ['anʃmi:ksa:m] *adj* affectionate

anschnallen ['anʃnalən] *vt* to buckle on ♦ *vr* to fasten one's seat belt

anschneiden ['anʃnaɪdən] (*unreg*) *vt* to cut into; (*Thema*) to introduce

anschreiben ['anʃraɪbən] (*unreg*) *vt* to write (up); (*COMM*) to charge up; (*benachrichtigen*) to write to

anschreien ['anʃraɪən] (*unreg*) *vt* to shout at

Anschrift ['anʃrɪft] *f* address

Anschuldigung ['anʃʊldɪgʊŋ] *f* accusation

anschwellen ['anʃvɛlən] (*unreg*) *vi* to swell (up)

anschwindeln ['anʃvɪndəln] *vt* to lie to

ansehen ['anzeːən] (*unreg*) *vt* to look at; **jdm etw ~** to see sth (from sb's face); **jdn/etw als etw ~** to look on sb/sth as sth; **~ für** to consider; **A~** (**-s**) *nt* respect; (*Ruf*) reputation

ansehnlich ['anzeːnlɪç] *adj* fine-looking; (*beträchtlich*) considerable

ansetzen ['anzɛtsən] *vt* (*festlegen*) to fix; (*entwickeln*) to develop; (*Fett*) to put on; (*Blätter*) to grow; (*zubereiten*) to prepare ♦ *vi* (*anfangen*) to start, to begin; (*Entwicklung*) to set in; (*dick werden*) to put on weight ♦ *vr* (*Rost etc*) to start to develop; **~ an** +*akk* (*anfügen*) to fix on to; (*anlegen, an Mund etc*) to put to

Ansicht ['anzɪçt] *f* (*Anblick*) sight; (*Meinung*) view, opinion; **zur ~** on approval; **meiner ~ nach** in my opinion; **~skarte** *f* picture postcard; **~ssache** *f* matter of opinion

ansonsten [an'zɔnstən] *adv* otherwise

anspannen ['anʃpanən] *vt* to harness; (*Muskel*) to strain; **Anspannung** *f* strain

anspielen ['anʃpiːlən] *vi* (*SPORT*) to start play; **auf etw** *akk* **~** to refer *od* allude to sth

Anspielung *f*: **~ (auf** +*akk*) reference (to), allusion (to)

Anspitzer ['anʃpɪtsər] (**-s, -**) *m* pencil sharpener

Ansporn ['anʃpɔrn] (**-(e)s**) *m* incentive

Ansprache ['anʃpraːxə] *f* address

ansprechen ['anʃprɛçən] (*unreg*) *vt* to speak to; (*bitten, gefallen*) to appeal to ♦ *vi*: **(auf etw** *akk***) ~** to react (to sth); **jdn auf etw** *akk* **(hin) ~** to ask sb about sth; **~d** *adj* attractive

anspringen ['anʃprɪŋən] (*unreg*) *vi* (*AUT*) to start ♦ *vt* to jump at

Anspruch ['anʃprʊx] *m* (*Recht*): **~ (auf** +*akk*) claim (to); **hohe Ansprüche stellen/haben** to demand/expect a lot; **jdn/etw in ~ nehmen** to occupy sb/take up sth; **a~slos** *adj* undemanding; **a~svoll** *adj* demanding

anstacheln ['anʃtaxəln] *vt* to spur on

Anstalt ['anʃtalt] (**-, -en**) *f* institution; **~en machen, etw zu tun** to prepare to do sth

Anstand ['anʃtant] *m* decency

anständig ['anʃtɛndɪç] *adj* decent; (*umg*) proper; (*groß*) considerable

anstandslos *adv* without any ado

anstarren ['anʃtarən] *vt* to stare at

anstatt [an'ʃtat] *präp* +*gen* instead of ♦ *konj*: **~ etw zu tun** instead of doing sth

Ansteck- ['anʃtɛk] *zW*: **a~en** *vt* to pin on; (*MED*) to infect; (*Pfeife*) to light; (*Haus*) to set fire to ♦ *vr*: **ich habe mich bei ihm angesteckt** I caught it from him ♦ *vi* (*fig*) to be infectious; **a~end** *adj* infectious; **~ung** *f* infection

anstehen ['anʃteːən] (*unreg*) *vi* to queue (up) (*BRIT*), to line up (*US*)

ansteigen ['anʃtaɪgən] *vt* (*Straße*) to climb; (*Gelände, Temperatur, Preise*) to rise

anstelle [an'ʃtɛlə] *präp* +*gen* in place of; **~n** ['an-] *vt* (*einschalten*) to turn on; (*Arbeit geben*) to employ; (*machen*) to do ♦ *vr* to queue (up) (*BRIT*), to line up (*US*); (*umg*) to act

Anstellung *f* employment; (*Posten*) post, position

Anstieg ['anʃtiːk] (**-(e)s, -e**) *m* (+*gen*) climb; (*fig: von Preisen etc*) increase (in)

anstiften ['anʃtɪftən] *vt* (*Unglück*) to cause; **jdn zu etw ~** to put sb up to sth

anstimmen ['anʃtɪmən] *vt* (*Lied*) to strike up with; (*Geschrei*) to set up

Anstoß ['anʃtoːs] *m* impetus; (*Ärgernis*) offence; (*SPORT*) kick-off; **der erste ~** the initiative; **~ nehmen an** +*dat* to take offence at; **a~en** (*unreg*) *vt* to push; (*mit Fuß*) to kick ♦ *vi* to knock, to bump; (*mit der Zunge*) to lisp; (*mit Gläsern*): **a~en (auf** +*akk*) to drink (to), to drink a toast (to)

anstößig ['anʃtøːsɪç] *adj* offensive, indecent

anstreichen ['anʃtraɪçən] (*unreg*) *vt* to paint

anstrengen ['anʃtrɛŋən] *vt* to strain; (*JUR*) to bring ♦ *vr* to make an effort; **~d** *adj* tiring

Anstrengung *f* effort

Anstrich ['anʃtrɪç] *m* coat of paint

⚠ *For information on spelling reform see page 615*

Ansturm ['anʃtʊrm] *m* rush; (*MIL*) attack

Antarktis [ant'ʔarktɪs] (-) *f* Antarctic

antasten ['antastən] *vt* to touch; (*Recht*) to infringe upon; (*Ehre*) to question

Anteil ['antaɪl] (-**s**, -**e**) *m* share; (*Mitgefühl*) sympathy; ~ **nehmen** (**an** +*dat*) to share (in); (*sich interessieren*) to take an interest (in); ~**nahme** (-) *f* sympathy

Antenne [an'tɛnə] *f* aerial

Anti- ['anti] *in zW* anti; ~**alko'holiker** *m* teetotaller; **a~autori'tär** *adj* anti-authoritarian; ~**babypille** *f* contraceptive pill; ~**biotikum** [antibi'o:tikʊm] (-**s**, -**ka**) *nt* antibiotic

antik [an'ti:k] *adj* antique; **A~e** *f* (*Zeitalter*) ancient world

Antiquariat [antikvari'a:t] (-(**e**)**s**, -**e**) *nt* secondhand bookshop

Antiquitäten [antikvi'tɛ:tən] *pl* antiques; ~**händler** *m* antique dealer

Antrag ['antra:k] (-(**e**)**s**, -**träge**) *m* proposal, (*PARL*) motion; (*Gesuch*) application; ~**steller(in)** (-**s**, -) *m(f)* claimant; (*für Kredit*) applicant

antreffen ['antrɛfən] (*unreg*) *vt* to meet

antreiben ['antraɪbən] (*unreg*) *vt* to drive on; (*Motor*) to drive

antreten ['antre:tən] (*unreg*) *vt* (*Amt*) to take up; (*Erbschaft*) to come into; (*Beweis*) to offer; (*Reise*) to start, to begin ♦ *vi* (*MIL*) to fall in; (*SPORT*) to line up; **gegen jdn** ~ to play/fight (against) sb

Antrieb ['antri:p] *m* (*auch fig*) drive; **aus eigenem** ~ of one's own accord

antrinken ['antrɪŋkən] (*unreg*) *vt* (*Flasche, Glas*) to start to drink from; **sich** *dat* **Mut/ einen Rausch** ~ to give o.s. Dutch courage/get drunk; **angetrunken sein** to be tipsy

Antritt ['antrɪt] *m* beginning, commencement; (*eines Amts*) taking up

antun ['antu:n] (*unreg*) *vt*: **jdm etw** ~ to do sth to sb; **sich** *dat* **Zwang** ~ to force o.s.; **sich** *dat* **etwas** ~ to (try to) take one's own life

Antwort ['antvɔrt] (-, -**en**) *f* answer, reply; **a~en** *vi* to answer, to reply

anvertrauen ['anfertrauən] *vt*: **jdm etw** ~ to entrust sb with sth; **sich jdm** ~ to confide in sb

anwachsen ['anvaksən] (*unreg*) *vi* to grow; (*Pflanze*) to take root

Anwalt ['anvalt] (-(**e**)**s**, -**wälte**) *m* solicitor; lawyer; (*fig*) champion

Anwältin ['anvɛltɪn] *f siehe* **Anwalt**

Anwärter ['anvɛrtər] *m* candidate

anweisen ['anvaɪzən] (*unreg*) *vt* to instruct; (*zuteilen*) to assign

Anweisung *f* instruction; (*COMM*) remittance; (*Post-, Zahlungs~*) money order

anwend- ['anvɛnd] *zW*: ~**bar** [anvɛnt-] *adj* practicable, applicable; ~**en** (*unreg*) *vt* to use, to employ; (*Gesetz, Regel*) to apply; **A~ung** *f* use; application

anwesend ['anve:zənt] *adj* present; **die A~en** those present

Anwesenheit *f* presence

anwidern ['anvi:dərn] *vt* to disgust

Anwohner(in) ['anvo:nər(ɪn)] (-**s**, -) *m(f)* neighbour

Anzahl ['antsa:l] *f*: ~ (**an** +*dat*) number (of); **a~en** *vt* to pay on account; ~**ung** *f* deposit, payment on account

Anzeichen ['antsaɪçən] *nt* sign, indication

Anzeige ['antsaɪɡə] *f* (*Zeitungs~*) announcement; (*Werbung*) advertisement; (*bei Polizei*) report; ~ **erstatten gegen jdn** to report sb (to the police); **a~n** *vt* (*zu erkennen geben*) to show; (*bekanntgeben*) to announce; (*bei Polizei*) to report

anziehen ['antsi:ən] (*unreg*) *vt* to attract; (*Kleidung*) to put on; (*Mensch*) to dress; (*Seil*) to pull tight; (*Schraube*) to tighten; (*Knie*) to draw up ♦ *vr* to get dressed; ~**d** *adj* attractive

Anziehung *f* (*Reiz*) attraction; ~**skraft** *f* power of attraction; (*PHYS*) force of gravitation

Anzug ['antsu:k] *m* suit; (*Herankommen*): **im** ~ **sein** to be approaching

anzüglich ['antsy:klɪç] *adj* personal; (*anstößig*) offensive; **A~keit** *f* offensiveness; (*Bemerkung*) personal remark

anzünden ['antsʏndən] *vt* to light

⚠ *Informationen zur Rechtschreibreform Seite 615*

anzweifeln ['antsvaɪfəln] *vt* to doubt

apathisch [a'pa:tɪʃ] *adj* apathetic

Apfel ['apfəl] (**-s**, **̈**) *m* apple; **~saft** *m* apple juice; **~sine** [-'zi:nə] *f* orange; **~wein** *m* cider

Apostel [a'pɔstəl] (**-s**, **-**) *m* apostle

Apotheke [apo'te:kə] *f* chemist's (shop), drugstore (*US*); **a~npflichtig** [-pflɪçtɪç] *adj* available only at a chemist's shop (*BRIT*) or pharmacy; **~r(in)** (**-s**, **-**) *m(f)* chemist, druggist (*US*)

APOTHEKE

i The **Apotheke** is a pharmacy selling medicines available only on prescription and toiletries. The pharmacist is qualified to give advice on medicines and treatments.

Apparat [apa'ra:t] (**-(e)s**, **-e**) *m* piece of apparatus; camera; telephone; (*RAD, TV*) set; **am ~!** speaking!; **~ur** [-'tu:r] *f* apparatus

Appartement [apart(ə)'mã:] (**-s**, **-s**) *nt* flat

appellieren [ape'li:rən] *vi*: **~ (an** +*akk*) to appeal (to)

Appetit [ape'ti:t] (**-(e)s**, **-e**) *m* appetite; **guten ~!** enjoy your meal; **a~lich** *adj* appetizing; **~losigkeit** *f* lack of appetite

Applaus [ap'laus] (**-es**, **-e**) *m* applause

Aprikose [apri'ko:zə] *f* apricot

April [a'prɪl] (**-(s)**, **-e**) *m* April

Aquarell [akva'rɛl] (**-s**, **-e**) *nt* watercolour

Äquator [ɛ'kva:tɔr] (**-s**) *m* equator

Arab- ['arab] *zW*: **~er(in)** (**-s**, **-**) *m(f)* Arab; **~ien** [a'ra:biən] (**-s**) *nt* Arabia; **a~isch** [a'ra:bɪʃ] *adj* Arabian

Arbeit ['arbaɪt] (**-**, **-en**) *f* work *no art*; (*Stelle*) job; (*Erzeugnis*) piece of work; (*wissenschaftliche*) dissertation; (*Klassen~*) test; **das war eine ~** that was a hard job; **a~en** *vi* to work ♦ *vt* to work, to make; **~er(in)** (**-s**, **-**) *m(f)* worker; (*ungelernt*) labourer; **~erschaft** *f* workers *pl*, labour force; **~geber** (**-s**, **-**) *m* employer; **~nehmer** (**-s**, **-**) *m* employee

Arbeits- *in zW* labour; **a~am** *adj* industrious; **~amt** *nt* employment exchange; **~erlaubnis** *f* work permit;

a~fähig *adj* fit for work, able-bodied; **~gang** *m* operation; **~kräfte** *pl* (*Mitarbeiter*) workforce; **a~los** *adj* unemployed, out-of-work; **~lose(r)** *f(m)* unemployed person; **~losigkeit** *f* unemployment; **~markt** *m* job market; **~platz** *m* job; place of work; **a~scheu** *adj* workshy; **~tag** *m* work(ing) day; **a~unfähig** *adj* unfit for work; **~zeit** *f* working hours *pl*; **~zimmer** *nt* study

Archäologe [arçeo'lo:gə] (**-n**, **-n**) *m* archaeologist

Architekt(in) [arçi'tɛkt(ɪn)] (**-en**, **-en**) *m(f)* architect; **~ur** [-'tu:r] *f* architecture

Archiv [ar'çi:f] (**-s**, **-e**) *nt* archive

arg [ark] *adj* bad, awful ♦ *adv* awfully, very

Argentinien [argɛn'ti:niən] (**-s**) *nt* Argentina, the Argentine

argentinisch *adj* Argentinian

Ärger ['ɛrgər] (**-s**) *m* (*Wut*) anger; (*Unannehmlichkeit*) trouble; **ä~lich** *adj* (*zornig*) angry; (*lästig*) annoying, aggravating; **ä~n** *vt* to annoy ♦ *vr* to get annoyed

arg- *zW*: **~listig** *adj* cunning, insidious; **~los** *adj* guileless, innocent

Argument [argu'mɛnt] *nt* argument

argwöhnisch *adj* suspicious

Arie ['a:riə] *f* aria

Aristokrat [aristo'kra:t] (**-en**, **-en**) *m* aristocrat; **~ie** [-'ti:] *f* aristocracy

Arktis ['arktɪs] (**-**) *f* Arctic

Arm [arm] (**-(e)s**, **-e**) *m* arm; (*Fluß~*) branch

arm *adj* poor

Armatur [arma'tu:r] *f* (*ELEK*) armature; **~enbrett** *nt* instrument panel; (*AUT*) dashboard

Armband *nt* bracelet; **~uhr** *f* (wrist) watch

Arme(r) *f(m)* poor man (woman); **die ~n** the poor

Armee [ar'me:] *f* army

Ärmel ['ɛrməl] (**-s**, **-**) *m* sleeve; **etw aus dem ~ schütteln** (*fig*) to produce sth just like that; **~kanal** *m* English Channel

ärmlich ['ɛrmlɪç] *adj* poor

armselig *adj* wretched, miserable

Armut ['armu:t] (**-**) *f* poverty

⚠ *For information on spelling reform see page 615*

Aroma [a'ro:ma] (**-s, Aromen**) *nt* aroma; **~therapie** *f* aromatherapy; **a~tisch** [aro'ma:tɪʃ] *adj* aromatic

arrangieren [arã:'ʒi:rən] *vt* to arrange ♦ *vr* to come to an arrangement

Arrest [a'rɛst] (**-(e)s, -e**) *m* detention

arrogant [aro'gant] *adj* arrogant

Arroganz [aro'gants] *f* arrogance

Arsch [arʃ] (**-es, ¨e**) (*umg!*) *m* arse (*BRIT!*), ass (*US!*)

Art [a:rt] (**-, -en**) *f* (*Weise*) way; (*Sorte*) kind, sort; (*BIOL*) species; **eine ~ (von) Frucht** a kind of fruit; **Häuser aller ~** houses of all kinds; **es ist nicht seine ~, das zu tun** it's not like him to do that; **ich mache das auf meine ~** I do that my (own) way

Arterie [ar'te:riə] *f* artery; **~nverkalkung** *f* arteriosclerosis

artig ['a:rtɪç] *adj* good, well-behaved

Artikel [ar'ti:kəl] (**-s, -**) *m* article

Artillerie [artɪlə'ri:] *f* artillery

Artischocke [arti'ʃɔkə] *f* artichoke

Artist(in) [ar'tɪst(ɪn)] (**-en, -en**) *m(f)* (circus/variety) artiste *od* performer

Arznei [a:rts'naɪ] *f* medicine; **~mittel** *nt* medicine, medicament

Arzt [a:rtst] (**-es, ¨e**) *m* doctor; **~helferin** *f* (doctor's) receptionist

Ärztin ['ɛ:rtstɪn] *f* doctor

ärztlich ['ɛ:rtstlɪç] *adj* medical

As ⚠ [as] (**-ses, -se**) *nt* ace

Asche ['aʃə] *f* (**-, -n**) ash, cinder

Aschen- *zW:* **~bahn** *f* cinder track; **~becher** *m* ashtray

Aschermittwoch *m* Ash Wednesday

Äser ['ɛ:zər] *pl von* **Aas**

Asiat(in) [azi'a:t(ɪn)] (**-en, -en**) *m(f)* Asian; **a~isch** [-'a:tɪʃ] *adj* Asian

Asien ['a:ziən] (**-s**) *nt* Asia

asozial ['azotsia:l] *adj* antisocial; (*Familien*) asocial

Aspekt [as'pɛkt] (**-(e)s, -e**) *m* aspect

Asphalt [as'falt] (**-(e)s, -e**) *m* asphalt; **a~ieren** *vt* to asphalt

aß *etc* [a:s] *vb siehe* **essen**

Asse ['asə] *pl von* **As**

Assistent(in) [asɪs'tɛnt(ɪn)] *m(f)* assistant

Assoziation [asotsiatsi'o:n] *f* association

Ast [ast] (**-(e)s, ¨e**) *m* bough, branch

ästhetisch [ɛs'te:tɪʃ] *adj* aesthetic

Asthma ['astma] (**-s**) *nt* asthma; **~tiker(in)** (**-s, -**) *m(f)* asthmatic

Astro- [astro] *zW:* **~'loge** (**-n, -n**) *m* astrologer; **~lo'gie** *f* astrology; **~'naut** (**-en, -en**) *m* astronaut; **~'nom** (**-en, -en**) *m* astronomer; **~no'mie** *f* astronomy

Asyl [a'zy:l] (**-s, -e**) *nt* asylum; (*Heim*) home; (*Obdachlosen~*) shelter; **~ant(in)** [azy'lant(ɪn)] (**-en, -en**) *m(f)* asylum-seeker

Atelier [atəli'e:] (**-s, -s**) *nt* studio

Atem ['a:təm] (**-s**) *m* breath; **den ~ anhalten** to hold one's breath; **außer ~** out of breath; **a~beraubend** *adj* breathtaking; **a~los** *adj* breathless; **~not** *f* difficulty in breathing; **~pause** *f* breather

Atheismus [ate'ɪsmʊs] *m* atheism

Atheist *m* atheist; **a~isch** *adj* atheistic

Athen [a'te:n] (**-s**) *nt* Athens

Äthiopien [ɛti'o:piən] (**-s**) *nt* Ethiopia

Athlet [at'le:t] (**-en, -en**) *m* athlete

Atlantik [at'lantɪk] (**-s**) *m* Atlantic (Ocean)

Atlas ['atlas] (**-** *od* **-ses, -se** *od* **Atlanten**) *m* atlas

atmen ['a:tmən] *vt, vi* to breathe

Atmosphäre [atmo'sfɛ:rə] *f* atmosphere; **atmosphärisch** *adj* atmospheric

Atmung ['a:tmʊŋ] *f* respiration

Atom [a'to:m] (**-s, -e**) *nt* atom; **a~'ar** *adj* atomic; **~bombe** *f* atom bomb; **~energie** *f* atomic *od* nuclear energy; **~kern** *m* atomic nucleus; **~kraftwerk** *nt* nuclear power station; **~krieg** *m* nuclear *od* atomic war; **~müll** *m* atomic waste; **~strom** *m* (electricity generated by) nuclear power; **~versuch** *m* atomic test; **~waffen** *pl* atomic weapons; **a~waffenfrei** *adj* nuclear-free; **~zeitalter** *nt* atomic age

Attentat [atɛn'ta:t] (**-(e)s, -e**) *nt*: **~ (auf +akk)** (attempted) assassination (of)

Attentäter [atɛn'tɛ:tər] *m* (would-be) assassin

Attest [a'tɛst] (**-(e)s, -e**) *nt* certificate

Attraktion [atraktsi'o:n] *f* (*Tourismus, Zirkus*) attraction

⚠ *Informationen zur Rechtschreibreform Seite 615*

attraktiv [atrak'tiːf] *adj* attractive
Attrappe [a'trapə] *f* dummy
Attribut [atri'buːt] **(-(e)s, -e)** *nt* (GRAM) attribute
ätzen ['ɛtsən] *vi* to be caustic; **~d** *adj* (Säure) corrosive; (fig: Spott) cutting
au [aʊ] *excl* ouch!; **~ ja!** oh yes!
Aubergine [obɛr'ʒiːnə] *f* aubergine, eggplant

SCHLÜSSELWORT
---

auch [aʊx] *adv* 1 (ebenfalls) also, too, as well; **das ist auch schön** that's nice too *od* as well; **er kommt - ich auch** he's coming - so am I, me too; **auch nicht** not ... either; **ich auch nicht** nor I, me neither; **oder auch** or; **auch das noch!** not that as well! 2 (selbst, sogar) even; **auch wenn das Wetter schlecht ist** even if the weather is bad; **ohne auch nur zu fragen** without even asking
3 (wirklich) really; **du siehst müde aus - bin ich auch** you look tired - (so) I am; **so sieht es auch aus** it looks like it too
4 (auch immer): **wer auch** whoever; **was auch** whatever; **wie dem auch sei** be that as it may; **wie sehr er sich auch bemühte** however much he tried

---
SCHLÜSSELWORT
---

auf [aʊf] *präp +dat* (wo?) on; **auf dem Tisch** on the table; **auf der Reise** on the way; **auf der Post/dem Fest** at the post office/party; **auf der Straße** on the road; **auf dem Land/der ganzen Welt** in the country/the whole world
♦ *präp +akk* 1 (wohin?) on(to); **auf den Tisch** on(to) the table; **auf die Post gehen** go to the post office; **auf das Land** into the country; **etw auf einen Zettel schreiben** to write sth on a piece of paper
2: **auf deutsch** in German; **auf meine Lebenszeit** for my/his lifetime; **bis auf ihn** except for him; **auf einmal** at once; **auf seinen Vorschlag (hin)** at his suggestion
♦ *adv* 1 (offen) open; **das Fenster ist auf** the window is open
2 (hinauf) up; **auf und ab** up and down; **auf und davon** up and away; **auf!** (los!) come on!
3 (aufgestanden) up; **ist er schon auf?** is he up yet?
♦ *konj*: **auf daß** (so) that

---

aufatmen ['aʊflaːtmən] *vi* to heave a sigh of relief
aufbahren ['aʊfbaːrən] *vt* to lay out
Aufbau ['aʊfbaʊ] *m* (Bauen) building, construction; (Struktur) structure; (aufgebautes Teil) superstructure; **a~en** *vt* to erect, to build (up); (Existenz) to make; (gestalten) to construct; **a~en (auf +dat)** (gründen) to found *od* base (on)
aufbauschen ['aʊfbaʊʃən] *vt* to puff out; (fig) to exaggerate
aufbekommen ['aʊfbəkɔmən] (unreg) *vt* (öffnen) to get open; (Hausaufgaben) to be given
aufbessern ['aʊfbɛsərn] *vt* (Gehalt) to increase
aufbewahren ['aʊfbəvaːrən] *vt* to keep; (Gepäck) to put in the left-luggage office (BRIT) *od* baggage check (US)
Aufbewahrung *f* (safe)keeping; (Gepäck~) left-luggage office (BRIT), baggage check (US)
aufbieten ['aʊfbiːtən] (unreg) *vt* (Kraft) to summon (up); (Armee, Polizei) to mobilize
aufblasen ['aʊfblaːzən] (unreg) *vt* to blow up, to inflate ♦ *vr* (umg) to become bigheaded
aufbleiben ['aʊfblaɪbən] (unreg) *vi* (Laden) to remain open; (Person) to stay up
aufblenden ['aʊfblɛndən] *vt* (Scheinwerfer) to switch on full beam ♦ *vi* (Fahrer) to have the lights on full beam; (AUT: Scheinwerfer) to be on full beam
aufblicken ['aʊfblɪkən] *vi* to look up; **~ zu** to look up at; (fig) to look up to
aufblühen ['aʊfblyːən] *vi* to blossom, to flourish
aufbrauchen ['aʊfbraʊxən] *vt* to use up
aufbrausen ['aʊfbraʊzən] *vi* (fig) to flare

⚠ *For information on spelling reform see page 615*

up; **~d** adj hot-tempered
aufbrechen ['aʊfbrɛçən] (*unreg*) vt to break
od prise (*BRIT*) open ♦ vi to burst open;
(*gehen*) to start, to set off
aufbringen ['aʊfbrɪŋən] (*unreg*) vt (*öffnen*)
to open; (*in Mode*) to bring into fashion;
(*beschaffen*) to procure; (*FIN*) to raise;
(*ärgern*) to irritate; **Verständnis für etw ~**
to be able to understand sth
Aufbruch ['aʊfbrʊx] m departure
aufbrühen ['aʊfbryːən] vt (*Tee*) to make
aufbürden ['aʊfbʏrdən] vt: **jdm etw ~** to
burden sb with sth
aufdecken ['aʊfdɛkən] vt to uncover
aufdrängen ['aʊfdrɛŋən] vt: **jdm etw ~** to
force sth on sb ♦ vr (*Mensch*): **sich jdm ~**
to intrude on sb
aufdrehen ['aʊfdreːən] vt (*Wasserhahn etc*)
to turn on; (*Ventil*) to open up
aufdringlich ['aʊfdrɪŋlɪç] adj pushy
aufeinander [aʊfaɪˈnandər] adv on top of
each other; (*schießen*) at each other;
(*vertrauen*) each other; **~folgen** ⚠ vi to
follow one another; **~folgend** ⚠ adj
consecutive; **~prallen** ⚠ vi to hit one
another
Aufenthalt ['aʊfɛnthalt] m stay;
(*Verzögerung*) delay; (*EISENB*: *Halten*) stop;
(*Ort*) haunt
Aufenthaltserlaubnis f residence permit
auferlegen ['aʊfɛrleːgən] vt: **(jdm) ~** to
impose (upon sb)
Auferstehung ['aʊfɛrʃteːʊŋ] f resurrection
aufessen ['aʊfɛsən] (*unreg*) vt to eat up
auffahr- ['aʊffaːr] zW: **~en** (*unreg*) vi
(*herankommen*) to draw up; (*hochfahren*) to
jump up; (*wütend werden*) to flare up; (*in
den Himmel*) to ascend ♦ vt (*Kanonen,
Geschütz*) to bring up; **~en auf** +akk (*Auto*)
to run od crash into; **~end** adj hot-
tempered; **A~t** f (*Hausauffahrt*) drive;
(*Autobahnauffahrt*) slip road (*BRIT*), (*freeway*)
entrance (*US*); **A~unfall** m pile-up
auffallen ['aʊffalən] (*unreg*) vi to be
noticeable; **jdm ~** to strike sb
auffällig ['aʊffɛlɪç] adj conspicuous, striking
auffangen ['aʊffaŋən] (*unreg*) vt to catch;

(*Funkspruch*) to intercept; (*Preise*) to peg
auffassen ['aʊffasən] vt to understand, to
comprehend; (*auslegen*) to see, to view
Auffassung f (*Meinung*) opinion;
(*Auslegung*) view, concept; (*auch*: **~sgabe**)
grasp
auffindbar ['aʊffɪntbaːr] adj to be found
auffordern ['aʊffɔrdərn] vt (*befehlen*) to call
upon, to order; (*bitten*) to ask
Aufforderung f (*Befehl*) order; (*Einladung*)
invitation
auffrischen ['aʊffrɪʃən] vt to freshen up;
(*Kenntnisse*) to brush up; (*Erinnerungen*) to
reawaken ♦ vi (*Wind*) to freshen
aufführen ['aʊffyːrən] vt (*THEAT*) to perform;
(*in einem Verzeichnis*) to list, to specify ♦ vr
(*sich benehmen*) to behave
Aufführung f (*THEAT*) performance; (*Liste*)
specification
Aufgabe ['aʊfgaːbə] f task; (*SCH*) exercise;
(*Haus~*) homework; (*Verzicht*) giving up;
(*von Gepäck*) registration; (*von Post*) posting;
(*von Inserat*) insertion
Aufgang ['aʊfgaŋ] m ascent; (*Sonnen~*) rise;
(*Treppe*) staircase
aufgeben ['aʊfgeːbən] (*unreg*) vt (*verzichten*)
to give up; (*Paket*) to send, to post;
(*Gepäck*) to register; (*Bestellung*) to give;
(*Inserat*) to insert; (*Rätsel, Problem*) to set
♦ vi to give up
Aufgebot ['aʊfgəboːt] nt supply; (*Ehe~*)
banns pl
aufgedunsen ['aʊfgədʊnzən] adj swollen,
puffed up
aufgehen ['aʊfgeːən] (*unreg*) vi (*Sonne, Teig*)
to rise; (*sich öffnen*) to open; (*klarwerden*) to
become clear; (*MATH*) to come out exactly;
~ (in +dat) (*sich widmen*) to be absorbed
(in); **in Rauch/Flammen ~** to go up in
smoke/flames
aufgelegt ['aʊfgəleːkt] adj: **gut/schlecht ~
sein** to be in a good/bad mood; **zu etw ~
sein** to be in the mood for sth
aufgeregt ['aʊfgəreːkt] adj excited
aufgeschlossen ['aʊfgəʃlɔsən] adj open,
open-minded
aufgeweckt ['aʊfgəvɛkt] adj bright,

⚠ *Informationen zur Rechtschreibreform Seite 615*

intelligent

aufgießen ['aʊfgiːsən] (*unreg*) *vt* (*Wasser*) to pour over; (*Tee*) to infuse

aufgreifen ['aʊfgraɪfən] (*unreg*) *vt* (*Thema*) to take up; (*Verdächtige*) to pick up, to seize

aufgrund [aʊf'grʊnt] *präp +gen* on the basis of; (*wegen*) because of

aufhaben ['aʊfhaːbən] (*unreg*) *vt* to have on; (*Arbeit*) to have to do

aufhalsen ['aʊfhalzən] (*umg*) *vt*: **jdm etw ~** to saddle *od* lumber sb with sth

aufhalten ['aʊfhaltən] (*unreg*) *vt* (*Person*) to detain; (*Entwicklung*) to check; (*Tür, Hand*) to hold open; (*Augen*) to keep open ♦ *vr* (*wohnen*) to live; (*bleiben*) to stay; **sich mit etw ~** to waste time over sth

aufhängen ['aʊfhɛŋən] (*unreg*) *vt* (*Wäsche*) to hang up; (*Menschen*) to hang ♦ *vr* to hang o.s.

Aufhänger (**-s, -**) *m* (*am Mantel*) loop; (*fig*) peg

aufheben ['aʊfheːbən] (*unreg*) *vt* (*hochheben*) to raise, to lift; (*Sitzung*) to wind up; (*Urteil*) to annul; (*Gesetz*) to repeal, to abolish; (*aufbewahren*) to keep ♦ *vr* to cancel itself out; **bei jdm gut aufgehoben sein** to be well looked after at sb's; **viel A~(s) machen (von)** to make a fuss (about)

aufheitern ['aʊfhaɪtərn] *vt, vr* (*Himmel, Miene*) to brighten; (*Mensch*) to cheer up

aufhellen ['aʊfhɛlən] *vt, vr* to clear up; (*Farbe, Haare*) to lighten

aufhetzen ['aʊfhɛtsən] *vt* to stir up

aufholen ['aʊfhoːlən] *vt* to make up ♦ *vi* to catch up

aufhorchen ['aʊfhɔrçən] *vi* to prick up one's ears

aufhören ['aʊfhøːrən] *vi* to stop; **~, etw zu tun** to stop doing sth

aufklappen ['aʊfklapən] *vt* to open

aufklären ['aʊfklɛːrən] *vt* (*Geheimnis etc*) to clear up; (*Person*) to enlighten; (*sexuell*) to tell the facts of life to; (*MIL*) to reconnoitre ♦ *vr* to clear up

Aufklärung *f* (*von Geheimnis*) clearing up; (*Unterrichtung, Zeitalter*) enlightenment;

(*sexuell*) sex education; (*MIL, AVIAT*) reconnaissance

aufkleben ['aʊfkleːbən] *vt* to stick on; **Aufkleber** (**-s, -**) *m* sticker

aufknöpfen ['aʊfknœpfən] *vt* to unbutton

aufkommen ['aʊfkɔmən] (*unreg*) *vi* (*Wind*) to come up; (*Zweifel, Gefühl*) to arise; (*Mode*) to start; **für jdn/etw ~** to be liable *od* responsible for sb/sth

aufladen ['aʊflaːdən] (*unreg*) *vt* to load

Auflage ['aʊflaːgə] *f* edition; (*Zeitung*) circulation; (*Bedingung*) condition

auflassen ['aʊflasən] (*unreg*) *vt* (*offen*) to leave open; (*aufgesetzt*) to leave on

auflauern ['aʊflaʊərn] *vi*: **jdm ~** to lie in wait for sb

Auflauf ['aʊflaʊf] *m* (*KOCH*) pudding; (*Menschen~*) crowd

aufleben ['aʊfleːbən] *vi* (*Mensch, Gespräch*) to liven up; (*Interesse*) to revive

auflegen ['aʊfleːgən] *vt* to put on; (*Telefon*) to hang up; (*TYP*) to print

auflehnen ['aʊfleːnən] *vt* to lean on ♦ *vr* to rebel

Auflehnung *f* rebellion

auflesen ['aʊfleːzən] (*unreg*) *vt* to pick up

aufleuchten ['aʊflɔʏçtən] *vi* to light up

auflisten ['aʊflɪstən] *vt* to list

auflockern ['aʊflɔkərn] *vt* to loosen; (*fig: Eintönigkeit etc*) to liven up

auflösen ['aʊfløːzən] *vt* to dissolve; (*Haare etc*) to loosen; (*Mißverständnis*) to sort out ♦ *vr* to dissolve; to come undone; to be resolved; (**in Tränen**) **aufgelöst sein** to be in tears

Auflösung *f* dissolving; (*fig*) solution

aufmachen ['aʊfmaxən] *vt* to open; (*Kleidung*) to undo; (*zurechtmachen*) to do up ♦ *vr* to set out

Aufmachung *f* (*Kleidung*) outfit, get-up; (*Gestaltung*) format

aufmerksam ['aʊfmɛrkzaːm] *adj* attentive; **jdn auf etw** *akk* **~ machen** to point sth out to sb; **A~keit** *f* attention, attentiveness

aufmuntern ['aʊfmʊntərn] *vt* (*ermutigen*) to encourage; (*erheitern*) to cheer up

Aufnahme ['aʊfnaːmə] *f* reception; (*Beginn*)

⚠ *For information on spelling reform see page 615*

beginning; (*in Verein etc*) admission; (*in Liste etc*) inclusion; (*Notieren*) taking down; (*PHOT*) shot; (*auf Tonband etc*) recording; **a~fähig** *adj* receptive; **~prüfung** *f* entrance test

aufnehmen ['aʊfneːmən] (*unreg*) *vt* to receive; (*hochheben*) to pick up; (*beginnen*) to take up; (*in Verein etc*) to admit; (*in Liste etc*) to include; (*fassen*) to hold; (*notieren*) to take down; (*fotografieren*) to photograph; (*auf Tonband, Platte*) to record; (*FIN: leihen*) to take out; **es mit jdm ~ können** to be able to compete with sb

aufopfern ['aʊfɔpfərn] *vt, vr* to sacrifice; **~d** *adj* selfless

aufpassen ['aʊfpasən] *vi* (*aufmerksam sein*) to pay attention; **auf jdn/etw ~** to look after sb/etw; **aufgepaßt!** look out!

Aufprall ['aʊfpral] (**-s, -e**) *m* impact; **a~en** *vi* to hit, to strike

Aufpreis ['aʊfpraɪs] *m* extra charge

aufpumpen ['aʊfpʊmpən] *vt* to pump up

aufräumen ['aʊfrɔʏmən] *vt, vi* (*Dinge*) to clear away; (*Zimmer*) to tidy up

aufrecht ['aʊfrɛçt] *adj* (*auch fig*) upright; **~erhalten** (*unreg*) *vt* to maintain

aufreg- ['aʊfreːg] *zW*: **~en** *vt* to excite ♦ *vr* to get excited; **~end** *adj* exciting; **A~ung** *f* excitement

aufreibend ['aʊfraɪbənt] *adj* strenuous

aufreißen ['aʊfraɪsən] (*unreg*) *vt* (*Umschlag*) to tear open; (*Augen*) to open wide; (*Tür*) to throw open; (*Straße*) to take up

aufreizen ['aʊfraɪtsən] *vt* to incite, to stir up; **~d** *adj* exciting, stimulating

aufrichten ['aʊfrɪçtən] *vt* to put up, to erect; (*moralisch*) to console ♦ *vr* to rise; (*moralisch*): **sich ~ (an** +*dat*) to take heart (from)

aufrichtig ['aʊfrɪçtɪç] *adj* sincere, honest; **A~keit** *f* sincerity

aufrücken ['aʊfrʏkən] *vi* to move up; (*beruflich*) to be promoted

Aufruf ['aʊfruːf] *m* summons; (*zur Hilfe*) call; (*des Namens*) calling out; **a~en** (*unreg*) *vt* (*Namen*) to call out; (*auffordern*): **jdn a~en (zu)** to call upon sb (for)

Aufruhr ['aʊfruːr] (**-(e)s, -e**) *m* uprising, revolt

aufrührerisch ['aʊfryːrərɪʃ] *adj* rebellious

aufrunden ['aʊfrʊndən] *vt* (*Summe*) to round up

Aufrüstung ['aʊfrʏstʊŋ] *f* rearmament

aufrütteln ['aʊfrʏtəln] *vt* (*auch fig*) to shake up

aufs [aʊfs] = **auf das**

aufsagen ['aʊfzaːgən] *vt* (*Gedicht*) to recite

aufsässig ['aʊfzɛsɪç] *adj* rebellious

Aufsatz ['aʊfzats] *m* (*Geschriebenes*) essay; (*auf Schrank etc*) top

aufsaugen ['aʊfzaʊgən] (*unreg*) *vt* to soak up

aufschauen ['aʊfʃaʊən] *vi* to look up

aufscheuchen ['aʊfʃɔʏçən] *vt* to scare *od* frighten away

aufschieben ['aʊfʃiːbən] (*unreg*) *vt* to push open; (*verzögern*) to put off, to postpone

Aufschlag ['aʊfʃlaːk] *m* (*Ärmel~*) cuff; (*Jacken~*) lapel; (*Hosen~*) turn-up; (*Aufprall*) impact; (*Preis~*) surcharge; (*Tennis*) service; **a~en** [-gən] (*unreg*) *vt* (*öffnen*) to open; (*verwunden*) to cut; (*hochschlagen*) to turn up; (*aufbauen: Zelt, Lager*) to pitch, to erect; (*Wohnsitz*) to take up ♦ *vi* (*aufprallen*) to hit; (*teurer werden*) to go up; (*Tennis*) to serve

aufschließen ['aʊfʃliːsən] (*unreg*) *vt* to open up, to unlock ♦ *vi* (*aufrücken*) to close up

aufschlußreich ⚠ *adj* informative, illuminating

aufschnappen ['aʊfʃnapən] *vt* (*umg*) to pick up ♦ *vi* to fly open

aufschneiden ['aʊfʃnaɪdən] (*unreg*) *vt* (*Brot*) to cut up; (*MED*) to lance ♦ *vi* to brag

Aufschneider (**-s, -**) *m* boaster, braggart

Aufschnitt ['aʊfʃnɪt] *m* (slices of) cold meat

aufschrauben ['aʊfʃraʊbən] *vt* (*festschrauben*) to screw on; (*lösen*) to unscrew

aufschrecken ['aʊfʃrɛkən] *vt* to startle ♦ *vi* (*unreg*) to start up

aufschreiben ['aʊfʃraɪbən] (*unreg*) *vt* to write down

aufschreien ['aʊfʃraɪən] (*unreg*) *vi* to cry

out

Aufschrift ['aʊfʃrɪft] f (*Inschrift*) inscription; (*auf Etikett*) label

Aufschub ['aʊfʃuːp] (**-(e)s, -schübe**) m delay, postponement

Aufschwung ['aʊfʃvʊŋ] m (*Elan*) boost; (*wirtschaftlich*) upturn, boom; (*SPORT*) circle

aufsehen ['aʊfzeːən] (*unreg*) vi to look up; ~ **zu** to look up at; (*fig*) to look up to; **A~** (**-s**) nt sensation, stir; **~erregend** ⚠ adj sensational

Aufseher(in) (**-s, -**) m(f) guard; (*im Betrieb*) supervisor; (*Museums~*) attendant; (*Park~*) keeper

aufsein ⚠ ['aʊfzaɪn] (*unreg*) (*umg*) vi (*Tür, Geschäft etc*) to be open; (*Mensch*) to be up

aufsetzen ['aʊfzɛtsən] vt to put on; (*Dokument*) to draw up ♦ vr to sit up(right) ♦ vi (*Flugzeug*) to touch down

Aufsicht ['aʊfzɪçt] f supervision; **die ~ haben** to be in charge

Aufsichtsrat m (supervisory) board

aufsitzen ['aʊfzɪtsən] (*unreg*) vi (*aufrecht hinsitzen*) to sit up; (*aufs Pferd, Motorrad*) to mount, to get on; (*Schiff*) to run aground; **jdm ~** (*umg*) to be taken in by sb

aufsparen ['aʊfʃpaːrən] vt to save (up)

aufsperren ['aʊfʃpɛrən] vt to unlock; (*Mund*) to open wide

aufspielen ['aʊfʃpiːlən] vr to show off

aufspießen ['aʊfʃpiːsən] vt to spear

aufspringen ['aʊfʃprɪŋən] (*unreg*) vi (*hochspringen*) to jump up; (*sich öffnen*) to spring open; (*Hände, Lippen*) to become chapped; **auf etw** akk ~ to jump onto sth

aufspüren ['aʊfʃpyːrən] vt to track down, to trace

aufstacheln ['aʊfʃtaxəln] vt to incite

Aufstand ['aʊfʃtant] m insurrection, rebellion; **aufständisch** ['aʊfʃtɛndɪʃ] adj rebellious, mutinous

aufstehen ['aʊfʃteːən] (*unreg*) vi to get up; (*Tür*) to be open

aufsteigen ['aʊfʃtaɪɡən] (*unreg*) vi (*hochsteigen*) to climb; (*Rauch*) to rise; **auf etw** akk ~ to get onto sth

aufstellen ['aʊfʃtɛlən] vt (*aufrecht stellen*) to

put up; (*aufreihen*) to line up; (*nominieren*) to nominate; (*formulieren: Programm etc*) to draw up; (*leisten: Rekord*) to set up

Aufstellung f (*SPORT*) line-up; (*Liste*) list

Aufstieg ['aʊfʃtiːk] (**-(e)s, -e**) m (*auf Berg*) ascent; (*Fortschritt*) rise; (*beruflich, SPORT*) promotion

aufstocken ['aʊfʃtɔkən] vt (*Kapital*) to increase

aufstoßen ['aʊfʃtoːsən] (*unreg*) vt to push open ♦ vi to belch

aufstützen ['aʊfʃtʏtsən] vt (*Körperteil*) to prop, to lean; (*Person*) to prop up ♦ vr: **sich auf etw** akk ~ to lean on sth

aufsuchen ['aʊfzuːxən] vt (*besuchen*) to visit; (*konsultieren*) to consult

Auftakt ['aʊftakt] m (*MUS*) upbeat; (*fig*) prelude

auftanken ['aʊftaŋkən] vi to get petrol (*BRIT*) od gas (*US*) ♦ vt to refuel

auftauchen ['aʊftaʊxən] vi to appear; (*aus Wasser etc*) to emerge; (*U-Boot*) to surface; (*Zweifel*) to arise

auftauen ['aʊftaʊən] vt to thaw ♦ vi to thaw; (*fig*) to relax

aufteilen ['aʊftaɪlən] vt to divide up; (*Raum*) to partition; **Aufteilung** f division; partition

Auftrag ['aʊftraːk] (**-(e)s, -träge**) m order; (*Anweisung*) commission; (*Aufgabe*) mission; **im ~ von** on behalf of; **a~en** [-ɡən] (*unreg*) vt (*Essen*) to serve; (*Farbe*) to put on; (*Kleidung*) to wear out; **jdm etw a~en** to tell sb sth; **dick a~en** (*fig*) to exaggerate; **~geber** (**-s, -**) m (*COMM*) purchaser, customer

auftreiben ['aʊftraɪbən] (*unreg*) vt (*umg: beschaffen*) to raise

auftreten ['aʊftreːtən] (*unreg*) vt to kick open ♦ vi to appear; (*mit Füßen*) to tread; (*sich verhalten*) to behave; **A~** (**-s**) nt (*Vorkommen*) appearance; (*Benehmen*) behaviour

Auftrieb ['aʊftriːp] m (*PHYS*) buoyancy, lift; (*fig*) impetus

Auftritt ['aʊftrɪt] m (*des Schauspielers*) entrance; (*Szene: auch fig*) scene

⚠ *For information on spelling reform see page 615*

aufwachen ['aʊfvaxən] *vi* to wake up

aufwachsen ['aʊfvaksən] (*unreg*) *vi* to grow up

Aufwand ['aʊfvant] **(-(e)s)** *m* expenditure; (*Kosten auch*) expense; (*Luxus*) show

aufwärmen ['aʊfvɛrmən] *vt* to warm up; (*alte Geschichten*) to rake up

aufwärts ['aʊfvɛrts] *adv* upwards; **A~entwicklung** *f* upward trend

Aufwasch ['aʊfvaʃ] *m* washing-up

aufwecken ['aʊfvɛkən] *vt* to wake up, to waken up

aufweisen ['aʊfvaɪzən] (*unreg*) *vt* to show

aufwenden ['aʊfvɛndən] (*unreg*) *vt* to expend; (*Geld*) to spend; (*Sorgfalt*) to devote

aufwendig △ *adj* costly

aufwerfen ['aʊfvɛrfən] (*unreg*) *vt* (*Fenster etc*) to throw open; (*Probleme*) to throw up, to raise

aufwerten ['aʊfvɛrtən] *vt* (*FIN*) to revalue; (*fig*) to raise in value

aufwickeln ['aʊfvɪkəln] *vt* (*aufrollen*) to roll up; (*umg: Haar*) to put in curlers

aufwiegen ['aʊfviːgən] (*unreg*) *vt* to make up for

Aufwind ['aʊfvɪnt] *m* up-current

aufwirbeln ['aʊfvɪrbəln] *vt* to whirl up; **Staub ~** (*fig*) to create a stir

aufwischen ['aʊfvɪʃən] *vt* to wipe up

aufzählen ['aʊftsɛːlən] *vt* to list

aufzeichnen ['aʊftsaɪçnən] *vt* to sketch; (*schriftlich*) to jot down; (*auf Band*) to record

Aufzeichnung *f* (*schriftlich*) note; (*Tonband~*) recording; (*Film~*) record

aufzeigen ['aʊftsaɪgən] *vt* to show, to demonstrate

aufziehen ['aʊftsiːən] (*unreg*) *vt* (*hochziehen*) to raise, to draw up; (*öffnen*) to pull open; (*Uhr*) to wind; (*umg: necken*) to tease; (*großziehen: Kinder*) to raise, to bring up; (*Tiere*) to rear

Aufzug ['aʊftsuːk] *m* (*Fahrstuhl*) lift, elevator; (*Aufmarsch*) procession, parade; (*Kleidung*) get-up; (*THEAT*) act

aufzwingen ['aʊftsvɪŋən] (*unreg*) *vt*: **jdm etw ~** to force sth upon sb

Augapfel ['aʊk|apfəl] *m* eyeball; (*fig*) apple of one's eye

Auge ['aʊgə] **(-s, -n)** *nt* eye; (*Fett~*) globule of fat; **unter vier ~n** in private

Augen- *zW*: **~blick** *m* moment; **im ~blick** at the moment; **a~blicklich** *adj* (*sofort*) instantaneous; (*gegenwärtig*) present; **~braue** *f* eyebrow; **~optiker(in)** *m(f)* optician; **~weide** *f* sight for sore eyes; **~zeuge** *m* eye witness

August [aʊ'gʊst] **(-(e)s od -, -e)** *m* August

Auktion [aʊktsi'oːn] *f* auction

Aula ['aʊla] **(-, Aulen od -s)** *f* assembly hall

SCHLÜSSELWORT
---

aus [aʊs] *präp +dat* **1** (*räumlich*) out of; (*von ... her*) from; **er ist aus Berlin** he's from Berlin; **aus dem Fenster** out of the window

2 (*gemacht/hergestellt aus*) made of; **ein Herz aus Stein** a heart of stone

3 (*auf Ursache deutend*) out of; **aus Mitleid** out of sympathy; **aus Erfahrung** from experience; **aus Spaß** for fun

4: **aus ihr wird nie etwas** she'll never get anywhere

♦ *adv* **1** (*zu Ende*) finished, over; **aus und vorbei** over and done with

2 (*ausgeschaltet, ausgezogen*) out; (*Aufschrift an Geräten*) off; **Licht aus!** lights out!

3 (*in Verbindung mit von*): **von Rom aus** from Rome; **vom Fenster aus** out of the window; **von sich aus** (*selbständig*) of one's own accord; **von ihm aus** as far as he's concerned

ausarbeiten ['aʊs|arbaɪtən] *vt* to work out

ausarten ['aʊs|artən] *vi* to degenerate

ausatmen ['aʊs|aːtmən] *vi* to breathe out

ausbaden ['aʊsbaːdən] (*umg*) *vt*: **etw ~ müssen** to carry the can for sth

Ausbau ['aʊsbaʊ] *m* extension, expansion; removal; **a~en** *vt* to extend, to expand; (*herausnehmen*) to take out, to remove; **a~fähig** *adj* (*fig*) worth developing

ausbessern ['aʊsbɛsərn] *vt* to mend, to repair

ausbeulen ['ausbɔʏlən] *vt* to beat out

Ausbeute ['ausbɔʏtə] *f* yield; (*Fische*) catch; **a~n** *vt* to exploit; (*MIN*) to work

ausbild- ['ausbɪld] *zW:* **~en** *vt* to educate; (*Lehrling, Soldat*) to instruct, to train; (*Fähigkeiten*) to develop; (*Geschmack*) to cultivate; **A~er** (**-s, -**) *m* instructor; **A~ung** *f* education; training, instruction; development; cultivation

ausbleiben ['ausblaɪbən] (*unreg*) *vi* (*Personen*) to stay away, not to come; (*Ereignisse*) to fail to happen, not to happen

Ausblick ['ausblɪk] *m* (*auch fig*) prospect, outlook, view

ausbrechen ['ausbrɛçən] (*unreg*) *vi* to break out ♦ *vt* to break off; **in Tränen/Gelächter ~** to burst into tears/out laughing

ausbreiten ['ausbraɪtən] *vt* to spread (out); (*Arme*) to stretch out ♦ *vr* to spread; **sich über ein Thema ~** to expand *od* enlarge on a topic

ausbrennen ['ausbrɛnən] (*unreg*) *vt* to scorch; (*Wunde*) to cauterize ♦ *vi* to burn out

Ausbruch ['ausbrʊx] *m* outbreak; (*von Vulkan*) eruption; (*Gefühls~*) outburst; (*von Gefangenen*) escape

ausbrüten ['ausbryːtən] *vt* (*auch fig*) to hatch

Ausdauer ['ausdauər] *f* perseverance, stamina; **a~nd** *adj* persevering

ausdehnen ['ausdeːnən] *vt, vr* (*räumlich*) to expand; (*zeitlich, auch Gummi*) to stretch; (*Nebel, fig: Macht*) to extend

ausdenken ['ausdɛŋkən] (*unreg*) *vt:* **sich** *dat* **etw ~** to think sth up

Ausdruck ['ausdrʊk] *m* expression, phrase; (*Kundgabe, Gesichts~*) expression; (*COMPUT*) print-out, hard copy; **a~en** *vt* (*COMPUT*) to print out

ausdrücken ['ausdrʏkən] *vt* (*auch vr: formulieren, zeigen*) to express; (*Zigarette*) to put out; (*Zitrone*) to squeeze

ausdrücklich *adj* express, explicit

ausdrucks- *zW:* **~los** *adj* expressionless, blank; **~voll** *adj* expressive; **A~weise** *f* mode of expression

auseinander [aus|ar'nandər] *adv* (*getrennt*) apart; **~ schreiben** to write as separate words; **~bringen** △ (*unreg*) *vt* to separate; **~fallen** △ (*unreg*) *vi* to fall apart; **~gehen** △ (*unreg*) *vi* (*Menschen*) to separate; (*Meinungen*) to differ; (*Gegenstand*) to fall apart; **~halten** △ (*unreg*) *vt* to tell apart; **~nehmen** △ (*unreg*) *vt* to take to pieces, to dismantle; **~setzen** △ *vt* (*erklären*) to set forth, to explain ♦ *vr* (*sich verständigen*) to come to terms, to settle; (*sich befassen*) to concern o.s.; **A~setzung** *f* argument

ausfahren ['ausfaːrən] (*unreg*) *vt* (*spazierenfahren: im Auto*) to take for a drive; (*: im Kinderwagen*) to take for a walk; (*liefern*) to deliver

Ausfahrt ['ausfaːrt] *f* (*des Zuges etc*) leaving, departure; (*Autobahn~*) exit; (*Garagen~ etc*) exit, way out; (*Spazierfahrt*) drive, excursion

Ausfall ['ausfal] *m* loss; (*Nichtstattfinden*) cancellation; (*MIL*) sortie; (*radioaktiv*) fall-out; **a~en** (*unreg*) *vi* (*Zähne, Haare*) to fall *od* come out; (*nicht stattfinden*) to be cancelled; (*wegbleiben*) to be omitted; (*Person*) to drop out; (*Lohn*) to be stopped; (*nicht funktionieren*) to break down; (*Resultat haben*) to turn out; **~straße** *f* arterial road

ausfertigen ['ausfɛrtɪgən] *vt* (*förmlich: Urkunde, Paß*) to draw up; (*Rechnung*) to make out

Ausfertigung ['ausfɛrtɪgʊŋ] *f* drawing up; making out; (*Exemplar*) copy

ausfindig ['ausfɪndɪç] *adj:* **~ machen** to discover

ausfließen ['ausfliːsən] (*unreg*) *vt* (*herausfließen*): **~ (aus)** to flow out (of); (*auslaufen: Öl etc*): **~ (aus)** to leak (out of)

Ausflucht ['ausflʊxt] (**-, -flüchte**) *f* excuse

Ausflug ['ausfluːk] *m* excursion, outing; **Ausflügler** ['ausflyːklər] (**-s, -**) *m* tripper

Ausflugslokal *nt* tourist café

Ausfluß △ ['ausflʊs] *m* outlet; (*MED*) discharge

ausfragen ['ausfraːgən] *vt* to interrogate, to question

ausfressen ['ausfrɛsən] (*unreg*) *vt* to eat up; (*aushöhlen*) to corrode; (*umg: anstellen*) to

△ *For information on spelling reform see page 615*

be up to

Ausfuhr ['ausfuːr] (-, -en) f export, exportation ♦ *in zW* export

ausführ- ['ausfyːr] *zW:* **~en** vt (verwirklichen) to carry out; (*Person*) to take out; (*Hund*) to take for a walk; (*COMM*) to export; (*erklären*) to give details of; **~lich** adj detailed ♦ adv in detail; **A~lichkeit** f detail; **A~ung** f execution, performance; (*Durchführung*) completion; (*Herstellungsart*) version; (*Erklärung*) explanation

ausfüllen ['ausfʏlən] vt to fill up; (*Fragebogen etc*) to fill in; (*Beruf*) to be fulfilling for

Ausgabe ['ausgaːbə] f (*Geld*) expenditure, outlay; (*Aushändigung*) giving out; (*Gepäck~*) left-luggage office; (*Buch*) edition; (*Nummer*) issue; (*COMPUT*) output

Ausgang ['ausgaŋ] m way out, exit; (*Ende*) end; (*Ausgangspunkt*) starting point; (*Ergebnis*) result; (*Ausgehtag*) free time, time off; **kein ~** no exit

Ausgangs- *zW:* **~punkt** m starting point; **~sperre** f curfew

ausgeben ['ausgeːbən] (*unreg*) vt (*Geld*) to spend; (*austeilen*) to issue, to distribute ♦ vr: **sich für etw/jdn ~** to pass o.s. off as sth/sb

ausgebucht ['ausgəbuːxt] adj (*Vorstellung, Flug, Maschine*) fully booked

ausgedient ['ausgədiːnt] adj (*Soldat*) discharged; (*verbraucht*) no longer in use; **~ haben** to have done good service

ausgefallen ['ausgəfalən] adj (*ungewöhnlich*) exceptional

ausgeglichen ['ausgəglɪçən] adj (well-)balanced; **A~heit** f balance; (*von Mensch*) even-temperedness

ausgehen ['ausgeːən] (*unreg*) vi to go out; (*zu Ende gehen*) to come to an end; (*Benzin*) to run out; (*Haare, Zähne*) to fall od come out; (*Feuer, Ofen, Licht*) to go out; (*Strom*) to go off; (*Resultat haben*) to turn out; **mir ging das Benzin aus** I ran out of petrol (*BRIT*) od gas (*US*); **von etw ~** (*wegführen*) to lead away from sth; (*herrühren*) to come from sth; (*zugrunde legen*) to proceed from

sth; **wir können davon ~, daß ...** we can take as our starting point that ...; **leer ~** to get nothing

ausgelassen ['ausgəlasən] adj boisterous, high-spirited

ausgelastet ['ausgəlastət] adj fully occupied

ausgelernt ['ausgəlɛrnt] adj trained, qualified

ausgemacht ['ausgəmaxt] adj settled; (*umg: Dummkopf etc*) out-and-out, downright; **es war eine ~e Sache, daß ...** it was a foregone conclusion that ...

ausgenommen ['ausgənɔmən] *präp +gen* except ♦ *konj* except; **Anwesende sind ~** present company excepted

ausgeprägt ['ausgəprɛːkt] adj distinct

ausgerechnet ['ausgəreçnət] adv just, precisely; **~ du/heute** you of all people/ today of all days

ausgeschlossen ['ausgəʃlɔsən] adj (*unmöglich*) impossible, out of the question

ausgeschnitten ['ausgəʃnɪtən] adj (*Kleid*) low-necked

ausgesprochen ['ausgəʃprɔxən] adj (*Faulheit, Lüge etc*) out-and-out; (*unverkennbar*) marked ♦ adv decidedly

ausgezeichnet ['ausgətsaɪçnət] adj excellent

ausgiebig ['ausgiːbɪç] adj (*Gebrauch*) thorough, good; (*Essen*) generous, lavish; **~ schlafen** to have a good sleep

ausgießen ['ausgiːsən] vt to pour out; (*Behälter*) to empty

Ausgleich ['ausglaɪç] (-(e)s, -e) m balance; (*Vermittlung*) reconciliation; (*SPORT*) equalization; **zum ~ einer Sache** *gen* in order to offset sth; **a~en** (*unreg*) vt to balance (out); to reconcile; (*Höhe*) to even up ♦ vi (*SPORT*) to equalize

ausgraben ['ausgraːbən] (*unreg*) vt to dig up; (*Leichen*) to exhume; (*fig*) to unearth

Ausgrabung f excavation; (*Ausgraben auch*) digging up

Ausguß ⚠ ['ausgʊs] m (*Spüle*) sink; (*Abfluß*) outlet; (*Tülle*) spout

aushalten ['aushaltən] (*unreg*) vt to bear, to stand; (*Geliebte*) to keep ♦ vi to hold out;

das ist nicht zum A~ that is unbearable
aushandeln ['aʊshandəln] vt to negotiate
aushändigen ['aʊshɛndɪgən] vt: **jdm etw ~** to hand sth over to sb
Aushang ['aʊshaŋ] m notice
aushängen ['aʊshɛŋən] (unreg) vt (Meldung) to put up; (Fenster) to take off its hinges ♦ vi to be displayed
ausharren ['aʊsharən] vi to hold out
ausheben ['aʊshe:bən] (unreg) vt (Erde) to lift out; (Grube) to hollow out; (Tür) to take off its hinges; (Diebesnest) to clear out; (MIL) to enlist
aushecken ['aʊshɛkən] (umg) vt to cook up
aushelfen ['aʊshɛlfən] (unreg) vi: **jdm ~** to help sb out
Aushilfe ['aʊshɪlfə] f help, assistance; (Person) (temporary) worker
Aushilfs- zW: **~kraft** f temporary worker; **a~weise** adv temporarily, as a stopgap
ausholen ['aʊsho:lən] vi to swing one's arm back; (zur Ohrfeige) to raise one's hand; (beim Gehen) to take long strides
aushorchen ['aʊshɔrçən] vt to sound out, to pump
auskennen ['aʊskɛnən] (unreg) vr to know a lot; (an einem Ort) to know one's way about; (in Fragen etc) to be knowledgeable
Ausklang ['aʊsklaŋ] m end
auskleiden ['aʊsklaɪdən] vr to undress ♦ vt (Wand) to line
ausklingen ['aʊsklɪŋən] (unreg) vi (Ton, Lied) to die away; (Fest) to peter out
ausklopfen ['aʊsklɔpfən] vt (Teppich) to beat; (Pfeife) to knock out
auskochen ['aʊskɔxən] vt to boil; (MED) to sterilize; **ausgekocht** (fig) out-and-out
Auskommen (-s) nt: **sein ~ haben** to have a regular income
auskommen (unreg) vi: **mit jdm ~** to get on with sb; **mit etw ~** to get by with sth
auskosten ['aʊskɔstən] vt to enjoy to the full
auskundschaften ['aʊskʊntʃaftən] vt to spy out; (Gebiet) to reconnoitre
Auskunft ['aʊskʊnft] (-, -künfte) f information; (nähere) details pl, particulars

pl; (Stelle) information office; (TEL) directory inquiries sg
auslachen ['aʊslaxən] vt to laugh at, to mock
ausladen ['aʊsla:dən] (unreg) vt to unload; (umg: Gäste) to cancel an invitation to
Auslage ['aʊsla:gə] f shop window (display); **~n** pl (Ausgabe) outlay sg
Ausland ['aʊslant] nt foreign countries pl; **im ~** abroad; **ins ~** abroad
Ausländer(in) ['aʊslɛndər(ɪn)] (-s, -) m(f) foreigner
ausländisch adj foreign
Auslands- zW: **~gespräch** nt international call; **~reise** f trip abroad; **~schutzbrief** m international travel cover
auslassen ['aʊslasən] (unreg) vt to leave out; (Wort etc auch) to omit; (Fett) to melt; (Kleidungsstück) to let out ♦ vr: **sich über etw** akk **~** to speak one's mind about sth; **seine Wut** etc **an jdm ~** to vent one's rage etc on sb
Auslassung f omission
Auslauf ['aʊslaʊf] m (für Tiere) run; (Ausfluß) outflow, outlet; **a~en** (unreg) vi to run out; (Behälter) to leak; (NAUT) to put out (to sea); (langsam aufhören) to run down
Ausläufer ['aʊslɔyfər] m (von Gebirge) spur; (Pflanze) runner; (MET: von Hoch) ridge; (: von Tief) trough
ausleeren ['aʊsle:rən] vt to empty
auslegen ['aʊsle:gən] vt (Waren) to lay out; (Köder) to put down; (Geld) to lend; (bedecken) to cover; (Text etc) to interpret
Auslegung f interpretation
ausleiern ['aʊslaɪərn] vi (Gummi) to wear out
Ausleihe ['aʊslaɪə] f issuing; (Stelle) issue desk; **a~n** (unreg) vt (verleihen) to lend; **sich** dat **etw a~n** to borrow sth
Auslese ['aʊsle:zə] f selection; (Elite) elite; (Wein) choice wine; **a~n** (unreg) vt to select; (umg: zu Ende lesen) to finish
ausliefern ['aʊsli:fərn] vt to deliver (up), to hand over; (COMM) to deliver; **jdm/etw ausgeliefert sein** to be at the mercy of sb/sth

⚠ For information on spelling reform see page 615

auslöschen ['auslœʃən] *vt* to extinguish; (*fig*) to wipe out, to obliterate

auslosen ['auslo:zən] *vt* to draw lots for

auslösen ['auslø:zən] *vt* (*Explosion, Schuß*) to set off; (*hervorrufen*) to cause, to produce; (*Gefangene*) to ransom; (*Pfand*) to redeem

ausmachen ['ausmaxən] *vt* (*Licht, Radio*) to turn off; (*Feuer*) to put out; (*entdecken*) to make out; (*vereinbaren*) to agree; (*beilegen*) to settle; (*Anteil darstellen, betragen*) to represent; (*bedeuten*) to matter; **macht es Ihnen etwas aus, wenn ...?** would you mind if ...?

ausmalen ['ausma:lən] *vt* to paint; (*fig*) to describe; **sich** *dat* **etw ~** to imagine sth

Ausmaß ['ausma:s] *nt* dimension; (*fig auch*) scale

ausmessen ['ausmɛsən] (*unreg*) *vt* to measure

Ausnahme ['ausna:mə] *f* exception; **~fall** *m* exceptional case; **~zustand** *m* state of emergency

ausnahms- *zW:* **~los** *adv* without exception; **~weise** *adv* by way of exception, for once

ausnehmen ['ausne:mən] (*unreg*) *vt* to take out, to remove; (*Tier*) to gut; (*Nest*) to rob; (*umg: Geld abnehmen*) to clean out; (*ausschließen*) to make an exception of ♦ *vr* to look, to appear; **~d** *adj* exceptional

ausnützen ['ausnytsən] *vt* (*Zeit, Gelegenheit*) to use, to turn to good account; (*Einfluß*) to use; (*Mensch, Gutmütigkeit*) to exploit

auspacken ['auspakən] *vt* to unpack

auspfeifen ['auspfaifən] (*unreg*) *vt* to hiss/boo at

ausplaudern ['ausplaudərn] *vt* (*Geheimnis*) to blab

ausprobieren ['ausprobi:rən] *vt* to try (out)

Auspuff ['auspuf] (**-(e)s, -e**) *m* (*TECH*) exhaust; **~rohr** *nt* exhaust (pipe)

ausradieren ['ausradi:rən] *vt* to erase, to rub off; (*fig*) to annihilate

ausrangieren ['ausrãʒi:rən] (*umg*) *vt* to chuck out

ausrauben ['ausraubən] *vt* to rob

ausräumen ['ausrɔymən] *vt* (*Dinge*) to clear

away; (*Schrank, Zimmer*) to empty; (*Bedenken*) to dispel

ausrechnen ['ausrɛçnən] *vt* to calculate, to reckon

Ausrede ['ausre:də] *f* excuse; **a~n** *vi* to have one's say ♦ *vt*: **jdm etw a~n** to talk sb out of sth

ausreichen ['ausraiçən] *vi* to suffice, to be enough; **~d** *adj* sufficient, adequate; (*SCH*) adequate

Ausreise ['ausraizə] *f* departure; **bei der ~** when leaving the country; **~erlaubnis** *f* exit visa; **a~n** *vi* to leave the country

ausreißen ['ausraisən] (*unreg*) *vt* to tear *od* pull out ♦ *vi* (*Riß bekommen*) to tear; (*umg*) to make off, to scram

ausrenken ['ausrɛŋkən] *vt* to dislocate

ausrichten ['ausrɪçtən] *vt* (*Botschaft*) to deliver; (*Gruß*) to pass on; (*Hochzeit etc*) to arrange; (*in gerade Linie bringen*) to get in a straight line; (*angleichen*) to bring into line; (*TYP*) to justify; **ich werde es ihm ~** I'll tell him; **etwas/nichts bei jdm ~** to get somewhere/nowhere with sb

ausrotten ['ausrɔtən] *vt* to stamp out, to exterminate

Ausruf ['ausru:f] *m* (*Schrei*) cry, exclamation; (*Bekanntmachung*) proclamation; **a~en** (*unreg*) *vt* to cry out, to exclaim; to call out; **~ezeichen** *nt* exclamation mark

ausruhen ['ausru:ən] *vt, vr* to rest

ausrüsten ['ausrystən] *vt* to equip, to fit out

Ausrüstung *f* equipment

ausrutschen ['ausrutʃən] *vi* to slip

Aussage ['ausza:gə] *f* (*JUR*) statement; **a~n** *vt* to say, to state ♦ *vi* (*JUR*) to give evidence

ausschalten ['ausʃaltən] *vt* to switch off; (*fig*) to eliminate

Ausschank ['ausʃaŋk] (**-(e)s, -schänke**) *m* dispensing, giving out; (*COMM*) selling; (*Theke*) bar

Ausschau ['ausʃau] *f*: **~ halten (nach)** to look out for, to watch (for); **a~en** *vi*: **a~en (nach)** to look out (for), to be on the look-out (for)

ausscheiden ['ausʃaidən] (*unreg*) *vt* to take

out; (*MED*) to secrete ♦ *vi*: ~ **(aus)** to leave; (*SPORT*) to be eliminated (from) *od* knocked out (of)

Ausscheidung *f* separation; secretion; elimination; (*aus Amt*) retirement

ausschenken ['aʊsʃɛŋkən] *vt* (*Alkohol, Kaffee*) to pour out; (*COMM*) to sell

ausschildern ['aʊsʃɪldərn] *vt* to signpost

ausschimpfen ['aʊsʃɪmpfən] *vt* to scold, to tell off

ausschlafen ['aʊsʃlaːfən] (*unreg*) *vi, vr* to have a good sleep ♦ *vt* to sleep off; **ich bin nicht ausgeschlafen** I didn't have *od* get enough sleep

Ausschlag ['aʊsʃlaːk] *m* (*MED*) rash; (*Pendel~*) swing; (*Nadel~*) deflection; **den ~ geben** (*fig*) to tip the balance; **a~en** [-gən] (*unreg*) *vt* to knock out; (*auskleiden*) to deck out; (*verweigern*) to decline ♦ *vi* (*Pferd*) to kick out; (*BOT*) to sprout; **a~gebend** *adj* decisive

ausschließen ['aʊsʃliːsən] (*unreg*) *vt* to shut *od* lock out; (*fig*) to exclude

ausschließlich *adj* exclusive ♦ *adv* exclusively ♦ *präp* +*gen* exclusive of, excluding

Ausschluß ⚠ ['aʊsʃlʊs] *m* exclusion

ausschmücken ['aʊsʃmʏkən] *vt* to decorate; (*fig*) to embellish

ausschneiden ['aʊsʃnaɪdən] (*unreg*) *vt* to cut out; (*Büsche*) to trim

Ausschnitt ['aʊsʃnɪt] *m* (*Teil*) section; (*von Kleid*) neckline; (*Zeitungs~*) cutting; (*aus Film etc*) excerpt

ausschreiben ['aʊsʃraɪbən] (*unreg*) *vt* (*ganz schreiben*) to write out (in full); (*ausstellen*) to write (out); (*Stelle, Wettbewerb etc*) to announce, to advertise

Ausschreitung ['aʊsʃraɪtʊŋ] *f* (*usu pl*) riot

Ausschuß ⚠ ['aʊsʃʊs] *m* committee, board; (*Abfall*) waste, scraps *pl*; (*COMM: auch: ~ware*) reject

ausschütten ['aʊsʃʏtən] *vt* to pour out; (*Eimer*) to empty; (*Geld*) to pay ♦ *vr* to shake (with laughter)

ausschweifend ['aʊsʃvaɪfənt] *adj* (*Leben*) dissipated, debauched; (*Phantasie*) extravagant

aussehen ['aʊszeːən] (*unreg*) *vi* to look; **es sieht nach Regen aus** it looks like rain; **es sieht schlecht aus** things look bad; **A~ (-s)** *nt* appearance

aussein ⚠ ['aʊszaɪn] (*unreg*) (*umg*) *vi* (*zu Ende sein*) to be over; (*nicht zu Hause sein*) to be out; (*nicht brennen*) to be out; (*abgeschaltet sein: Radio, Herd*) to be off

außen ['aʊsən] *adv* outside; (*nach ~*) outwards; ~ **ist es rot** it's red (on the) outside

Außen- *zW*: ~**dienst** *m*: **im ~dienst sein** to work outside the office; ~**handel** *m* foreign trade; ~**minister** *m* foreign minister; ~**ministerium** *nt* foreign office; ~**politik** *f* foreign policy; **a~politisch** *adj* (*Entwicklung, Lage*) foreign; ~**seite** *f* outside; ~**seiter (-s, -)** *m* outsider; ~**stände** *pl* outstanding debts; ~**stehende(r)** *f(m)* outsider; ~**welt** *f* outside world

außer ['aʊsər] *präp* +*dat* (*räumlich*) out of; (*abgesehen von*) except ♦ *konj* (*ausgenommen*) except; ~ **Gefahr** out of danger; ~ **Zweifel** beyond any doubt; ~ **Betrieb** out of order; ~ **Dienst** retired; ~ **Landes** abroad; ~ **sich** *dat* **sein** to be beside o.s.; ~ **sich** *akk* **geraten** to go wild; ~ **wenn** unless; ~ **daß** except; ~**dem** *konj* besides, in addition

äußere(r, s) ['ɔysərə(r,s)] *adj* outer, external

außergewöhnlich *adj* unusual

außerhalb *präp* +*gen* outside ♦ *adv* outside

äußerlich *adj* external

äußern *vt* to utter, to express; (*zeigen*) to show ♦ *vr* to give one's opinion; (*Krankheit etc*) to show itself

außerordentlich *adj* extraordinary

außerplanmäßig *adj* unscheduled

äußerst ['ɔysərst] *adv* extremely, most; ~**e(r, s)** *adj* utmost; (*räumlich*) farthest; (*Termin*) last possible; (*Preis*) highest

Äußerung *f* remark, comment

aussetzen ['aʊszɛtsən] *vt* (*Kind, Tier*) to abandon; (*Boote*) to lower; (*Belohnung*) to offer; (*Urteil, Verfahren*) to postpone ♦ *vi*

⚠ *For information on spelling reform see page 615*

(*aufhören*) to stop; (*Pause machen*) to have a break; **jdm/etw ausgesetzt sein** to be exposed to sb/sth; **an jdm/etw etwas ~** to find fault with sb/sth

Aussicht ['aʊszɪçt] *f* view; (*in Zukunft*) prospect; **etw in ~ haben** to have sth in view

Aussichts- *zW:* **a~los** *adj* hopeless; **~punkt** *m* viewpoint; **a~reich** *adj* promising; **~turm** *m* observation tower

aussöhnen ['aʊszø:nən] *vt* to reconcile ♦ *vr* to reconcile o.s., to become reconciled

aussondern ['aʊszɔndərn] *vt* to separate, to select

aussortieren ['aʊszɔrti:rən] *vt* to sort out

ausspannen ['aʊsʃpanən] *vt* to spread *od* stretch out; (*Pferd*) to unharness; (*umg: Mädchen*): **(jdm) jdn ~** to steal sb (from sb) ♦ *vi* to relax

aussperren ['aʊsʃpɛrən] *vt* to lock out

ausspielen ['aʊsʃpi:lən] *vt* (*Karte*) to lead; (*Geldprämie*) to offer as a prize ♦ *vi* (*KARTEN*) to lead; **jdn gegen jdn ~** to play sb off against sb; **ausgespielt haben** to be finished

Aussprache ['aʊsʃpra:xə] *f* pronunciation; (*Unterredung*) (frank) discussion

aussprechen ['aʊsʃprɛçən] *vt* to pronounce; (*äußern*) to say, to express ♦ *vr* (*sich äußern*): **sich ~ (über** +*akk*) to speak (about); (*sich anvertrauen*) to unburden o.s. (about *od* on); (*diskutieren*) to discuss ♦ *vi* (*zu Ende sprechen*) to finish speaking

Ausspruch ['aʊsʃprʊx] *m* saying, remark

ausspülen ['aʊsʃpy:lən] *vt* to wash out; (*Mund*) to rinse

Ausstand ['aʊsʃtant] *m* strike; **in den ~ treten** to go on strike

ausstatten ['aʊsʃtatən] *vt* (*Zimmer etc*) to furnish; (*Person*) to equip, to kit out

Ausstattung *f* (*Ausstatten*) provision; (*Kleidung*) outfit; (*Aufmachung*) make-up; (*Einrichtung*) furnishing

ausstechen ['aʊsʃtɛçən] (*unreg*) *vt* (*Augen, Rasen, Graben*) to dig out; (*Kekse*) to cut out; (*übertreffen*) to outshine

ausstehen ['aʊsʃte:ən] (*unreg*) *vt* to stand,

to endure ♦ *vi* (*noch nicht dasein*) to be outstanding

aussteigen ['aʊsʃtaɪgən] (*unreg*) *vi* to get out, to alight

ausstellen ['aʊsʃtɛlən] *vt* to exhibit, to display, to show; (*umg: ausschalten*) to switch off; (*Rechnung etc*) to make out; (*Paß, Zeugnis*) to issue

Ausstellung *f* exhibition; (*FIN*) drawing up; (*einer Rechnung*) making out; (*eines Passes etc*) issuing

aussterben ['aʊsʃtɛrbən] (*unreg*) *vi* to die out

Aussteuer ['aʊsʃtɔʏər] *f* dowry

Ausstieg ['aʊsʃti:k] (**-(e)s, -e**) *m* exit

ausstopfen ['aʊsʃtɔpfən] *vt* to stuff

ausstoßen ['aʊsʃto:sən] (*unreg*) *vt* (*Luft, Rauch*) to give off, to emit; (*aus Verein etc*) to expel, to exclude; (*Auge*) to poke out

ausstrahlen ['aʊsʃtra:lən] *vt, vi* to radiate; (*RAD*) to broadcast

Ausstrahlung *f* radiation; (*fig*) charisma

ausstrecken ['aʊsʃtrɛkən] *vt, vr* to stretch out

ausstreichen ['aʊsʃtraɪçən] (*unreg*) *vt* to cross out; (*glätten*) to smooth (out)

ausströmen ['aʊsʃtrø:mən] *vi* (*Gas*) to pour out, to escape ♦ *vt* to give off; (*fig*) to radiate

aussuchen ['aʊszu:xən] *vt* to select, to pick out

Austausch ['aʊstaʊʃ] *m* exchange; **a~bar** *adj* exchangeable; **a~en** *vt* to exchange, to swap

austeilen ['aʊstaɪlən] *vt* to distribute, to give out

Auster ['aʊstər] (**-, -n**) *f* oyster

austoben ['aʊsto:bən] *vr* (*Kind*) to run wild; (*Erwachsene*) to sow one's wild oats

austragen ['aʊstra:gən] (*unreg*) *vt* (*Post*) to deliver; (*Streit etc*) to decide; (*Wettkämpfe*) to hold

Australien [aʊs'tra:liən] (**-s**) *nt* Australia; **Australier(in)** (**-s, -**) *m(f)* Australian; **australisch** *adj* Australian

austreiben ['aʊstraɪbən] (*unreg*) *vt* to drive out, to expel; (*Geister*) to exorcize

austreten ['aʊstreːtən] (unreg) vi (zur Toilette) to be excused ♦ vt (Feuer) to tread out, to trample; (Schuhe) to wear out; (Treppe) to wear down; **aus etw ~** to leave sth

austrinken ['aʊstrɪŋkən] (unreg) vt (Glas) to drain; (Getränk) to drink up ♦ vi to finish one's drink, to drink up

Austritt ['aʊstrɪt] m emission; (aus Verein, Partei etc) retirement, withdrawal

austrocknen ['aʊstrɔknən] vt, vi to dry up

ausüben ['aʊsyːbən] vt (Beruf) to practise, to carry out; (Funktion) to perform; (Einfluß) to exert; **einen Reiz auf jdn ~** to hold an attraction for sb; **eine Wirkung auf jdn ~** to have an effect on sb

Ausverkauf ['aʊsfɛrkaʊf] m sale; **a~en** vt to sell out; (Geschäft) to sell up; **a~t** adj (Karten, Artikel) sold out; (THEAT: Haus) full

Auswahl ['aʊsvaːl] f: **eine ~ (an +dat)** a selection (of), a choice (of)

auswählen ['aʊsvɛːlən] vt to select, to choose

Auswander- ['aʊsvandər] zW: **~er** m emigrant; **a~n** vi to emigrate; **~ung** f emigration

auswärtig ['aʊsvɛrtɪç] adj (nicht am/vom Ort) out-of-town; (ausländisch) foreign

auswärts ['aʊsvɛrts] adv outside; (nach außen) outwards; **~ essen** to eat out

Auswärtsspiel ['aʊsvɛrtsʃpiːl] nt away game

auswechseln ['aʊsvɛksəln] vt to change, to substitute

Ausweg ['aʊsveːk] m way out; **a~los** adj hopeless

ausweichen ['aʊsvaɪçən] (unreg) vi: **jdm/etw ~** to move aside od make way for sb/sth; (fig) to side-step sb/sth; **~d** adj evasive

ausweinen ['aʊsvaɪnən] vr to have a (good) cry

Ausweis ['aʊsvaɪs] (-es, -e) m identity card; passport; (Mitglieds~, Bibliotheks~ etc) card; **a~en** [-zən] (unreg) vt to expel, to banish ♦ vr to prove one's identity; **~kontrolle** f identity check; **~papiere** pl identity papers; **~ung** f expulsion

ausweiten ['aʊsvaɪtən] vt to stretch

auswendig ['aʊsvɛndɪç] adv by heart

auswerten ['aʊsveːrtən] vt to evaluate; **Auswertung** f evaluation, analysis; (Nutzung) utilization

auswirken ['aʊsvɪrkən] vr to have an effect; **Auswirkung** f effect

auswischen ['aʊsvɪʃən] vt to wipe out; **jdm eins ~** (umg) to put one over on sb

Auswuchs ['aʊsvuːks] m (out)growth; (fig) product

auszahlen ['aʊstsaːlən] vt (Lohn, Summe) to pay out; (Arbeiter) to pay off; (Miterbe) to buy out ♦ vr (sich lohnen) to pay

auszählen ['aʊstsɛːlən] vt (Stimmen) to count

auszeichnen ['aʊstsaɪçnən] vt to honour; (MIL) to decorate; (COMM) to price ♦ vr to distinguish o.s.

Auszeichnung f distinction; (COMM) pricing; (Ehrung) awarding of decoration; (Ehre) honour; (Orden) decoration; **mit ~** with distinction

ausziehen ['aʊstsiːən] (unreg) vt (Kleidung) to take off; (Haare, Zähne, Tisch etc) to pull out; (nachmalen) to trace ♦ vr to undress ♦ vi (aufbrechen) to leave; (aus Wohnung) to move out

Auszubildende(r) ['aʊstsʊbɪldəndə(r)] f(m) trainee

Auszug ['aʊstsuːk] m (aus Wohnung) removal; (aus Buch etc) extract; (Konto~) statement; (Ausmarsch) departure

Auto ['aʊto] (-s, -s) nt (motor)car; **~ fahren** to drive; **~atlas** m road atlas; **~bahn** f motorway; **~bahndreieck** nt motorway junction; **~bahngebühr** f toll; **~bahnkreuz** nt motorway intersection; **~bus** m bus; **~fähre** f car ferry; **~fahrer(in)** m(f) motorist, driver; **~fahrt** f drive

autogen [aʊto'geːn] adj autogenous

Auto- [aʊto] zW: **~'gramm** nt autograph; **~'mat** (-en, -en) m machine; **~matik** [aʊto'maːtɪk] f (AUT) automatic; **a~'matisch** adj automatic; **a~nom** [-'noːm] adj autonomous

⚠ For information on spelling reform see page 615

AUTOBAHN

i An Autobahn *is a motorway. In former West Germany there is a widespread motorway network but in the former* **DDR** *the motorways are somewhat less extensive. There is no overall speed limit but a limit of 130 km/hour is recommended and there are lower mandatory limits on certain stretches of road. As yet there are no tolls payable on German Autobahnen. However, a yearly toll is payable in Switzerland and tolls have been introduced in Austria.*

Autor(in) ['autoːr(ɪn)] **(-s, -en)** *m(f)* author
Auto- *zW:* **~radio** *nt* car radio; **~reifen** *m* car tyre; **~reisezug** *m* motorail train; **~rennen** *nt* motor racing
autoritär [autoriˈtɛːr] *adj* authoritarian
Autorität *f* authority
Auto- *zW:* **~telefon** *nt* car phone; **~unfall** *m* car *od* motor accident; **~vermietung** *m* car hire *(BRIT) od* rental *(US)*; **~waschanlage** *f* car wash
Axt [akst] **(-, ¨e)** *f* axe

B, b

Baby ['beːbi] **(-s, -s)** *nt* baby; **~nahrung** *f* baby food; **~sitter (-s, -)** *m* baby-sitter
Bach [bax] **(-(e)s, ¨e)** *m* stream, brook
Backbord (-(e)s, -e) *nt (NAUT)* port
Backe ['bakə] *f* cheek
backen ['bakən] *(unreg) vt, vi* to bake
Backenzahn *m* molar
Bäcker ['bɛkər(ɪn)] **(-s, -)** *m* baker; **~ei** *f* bakery; *(Bäckereiladen)* baker's (shop)
Back- *zW:* **~form** *f* baking tin; **~obst** *nt* dried fruit; **~ofen** *m* oven; **~pflaume** *f* prune; **~pulver** *nt* baking powder; **~stein** *m* brick
Bad [baːt] **(-(e)s, ¨er)** *nt* bath; *(Schwimmen)* bathe; *(Ort)* spa
Bade- ['baːdə] *zW:* **~anstalt** *f* (swimming) baths *pl;* **~anzug** *m* bathing suit; **~hose** *f* bathing *od* swimming trunks *pl;* **~kappe** *f*

bathing cap; **~mantel** *m* bath(ing) robe; **~meister** *m* baths attendant; **b~n** *vi* to bathe, to have a bath ♦ *vt* to bath; **~ort** *m* spa; **~tuch** *nt* bath towel; **~wanne** *f* bath (tub); **~zimmer** *nt* bathroom
Bagatelle [bagaˈtɛlə] *f* trifle
Bagger ['bagər] **(-s, -)** *m* excavator; *(NAUT)* dredger; **b~n** *vt, vi* to excavate; to dredge
Bahn [baːn] **(-, -en)** *f* railway, railroad *(US)*; *(Weg)* road, way; *(Spur)* lane; *(Renn~)* track; *(ASTRON)* orbit; *(Stoff~)* length; **b~brechend** *adj* pioneering; **~Card** ['baːŋkaːrd] **(-, -s)** Ⓡ *f* ≈ railcard; **~damm** *m* railway embankment; **b~en** *vt:* **sich/ jdm einen Weg b~en** to clear a way/a way for sb; **~fahrt** *f* railway journey; **~fracht** *f* rail freight; **~hof** **(-, -¨e)** *m* station; **auf dem ~hof** at the station; **~hofshalle** *f* station concourse; **~linie** *f* (railway) line; **~steig** *m* platform; **~übergang** *m* level crossing, grade crossing *(US)*
Bahre ['baːrə] *f* stretcher
Bakterien [bakˈteːriən] *pl* bacteria *pl*
Balance [baˈlãːsə] *f* balance, equilibrium
balan'cieren *vt, vi* to balance
bald [balt] *adv (zeitlich)* soon; *(beinahe)* almost; **~ig** ['baldɪç] *adj* early, speedy
Baldrian ['baldriaːn] **(-s, -e)** *m* valerian
Balkan ['balkaːn] **(-s)** *m:* **der ~** the Balkans *pl*
Balken ['balkən] **(-s, -)** *m* beam; *(Trag~)* girder; *(Stütz~)* prop
Balkon [balˈkõː] **(-s, -s** *od* **-e)** *m* balcony; *(THEAT)* (dress) circle
Ball [bal] **(-(e)s, ¨e)** *m* ball; *(Tanz)* dance, ball
Ballast ['balast] **(-(e)s, -e)** *m* ballast; *(fig)* weight, burden
Ballen ['balən] **(-s, -)** *m* bale; *(ANAT)* ball; **b~** *vt (formen)* to make into a ball; *(Faust)* to clench ♦ *vr (Wolken etc)* to build up; *(Menschen)* to gather
Ballett [baˈlɛt] **(-(e)s, -e)** *nt* ballet
Ballkleid *nt* evening dress
Ballon [baˈlõː] **(-s, -s** *od* **-e)** *m* balloon
Ballspiel *nt* ball game
Ballungsgebiet ['baluŋsgəbiːt] *nt*

⚠ *Informationen zur Rechtschreibreform Seite 615*

conurbation

Baltikum ['baltikʊm] (**-s**) *nt*: **das ~** the Baltic States

Banane [ba'naːnə] *f* banana

Band¹ [bant] (**-(e)s**, **ëe**) *m* (*Buch~*) volume

Band² (**-(e)s**, **ër**) *nt* (*Stoff~*) ribbon, tape; (*Fließ~*) production line; (*Ton~*) tape; (*ANAT*) ligament; **etw auf ~ aufnehmen** to tape sth; **am laufenden ~** (*umg*) non-stop

Band³ (**-(e)s**, **-e**) *nt* (*Freundschafts~ etc*) bond

Band⁴ [bɛnt] (**-**, **-s**) *f* band, group

band *etc vb* **siehe** **binden**

Bandage [ban'daːʒə] *f* bandage

banda'gieren *vt* to bandage

Bande ['bandə] *f* band; (*Straßen~*) gang

bändigen ['bɛndɪgən] *vt* (*Tier*) to tame; (*Trieb, Leidenschaft*) to control, to restrain

Bandit [ban'diːt] (**-en**, **-en**) *m* bandit

Band- *zW*: **~nudel** *f* (*KOCH: gew pl*) ribbon noodles *pl*; **~scheibe** *f* (*ANAT*) disc; **~wurm** *m* tapeworm

bange ['baŋə] *adj* scared; (*besorgt*) anxious; **jdm wird es ~** sb is becoming scared; **jdm ~ machen** to scare sb; **~n** *vi*: **um jdn/etw ~n** to be anxious *od* worried about sb/sth

Bank¹ [baŋk] (**-**, **ëe**) *f* (*Sitz~*) bench; (*Sand~ etc*) (sand)bank, (sand)bar

Bank² [baŋk] (**-**, **-en**) *f* (*Geld~*) bank; **~anweisung** *f* banker's order; **~einzug** *m* direct debit

Bankett [baŋ'ket] (**-(e)s**, **-e**) *nt* (*Essen*) banquet; (*Straßenrand*) verge (*BRIT*), shoulder (*US*)

Bankier [baŋki'eː] (**-s**, **-s**) *m* banker

Bank- *zW*: **~konto** *nt* bank account; **~leitzahl** *f* bank sort code number; **~note** *f* banknote; **~raub** *m* bank robbery

Bankrott [baŋ'krɔt] (**-(e)s**, **-e**) *m* bankruptcy; **~ machen** to go bankrupt; **b~** *adj* bankrupt

Bankverbindung *f* banking arrangements *pl*; **geben Sie bitte Ihre ~ an** please give your account details

Bann [ban] (**-(e)s**, **-e**) *m* (*HIST*) ban; (*Kirchen~*) excommunication; (*fig: Zauber*) spell; **b~en** *vt* (*Geister*) to exorcize; (*Gefahr*)

to avert; (*bezaubern*) to enchant; (*HIST*) to banish

Banner (**-s**, **-**) *nt* banner, flag

Bar (**-**, **-s**) *f* bar

bar [baːr] *adj* (*+gen*) (*unbedeckt*) bare; (*frei von*) lacking (in); (*offenkundig*) utter, sheer; **~(e)s Geld** cash; **etw (in) ~ bezahlen** to pay sth (in) cash; **etw für ~e Münze nehmen** (*fig*) to take sth at its face value

Bär [bɛːr] (**-en**, **-en**) *m* bear

Baracke [ba'rakə] *f* hut

barbarisch [bar'baːrɪʃ] *adj* barbaric, barbarous

Bar- *zW*: **b~fuß** *adj* barefoot; **~geld** *nt* cash, ready money; **b~geldlos** *adj* non-cash

Barkauf *m* cash purchase

Barkeeper ['baːrkiːpər] (**-s**, **-**) *m* barman, bartender

barmherzig [barm'hertsɪç] *adj* merciful, compassionate

Baron [ba'roːn] (**-s**, **-e**) *m* baron; **~in** *f* baroness

Barren ['barən] (**-s**, **-**) *m* parallel bars *pl*; (*Gold~*) ingot

Barriere [bari'eːrə] *f* barrier

Barrikade [bari'kaːdə] *f* barricade

Barsch [barʃ] (**-(e)s**, **-e**) *m* perch

barsch [barʃ] *adj* brusque, gruff

Bar- *zW*: **~schaft** *f* ready money; **~scheck** *m* open *od* uncrossed cheque (*BRIT*), open check (*US*)

Bart [baːrt] (**-(e)s**, **ëe**) *m* beard; (*Schlüssel~*) bit; **bärtig** ['bɛːrtɪç] *adj* bearded

Barzahlung *f* cash payment

Base ['baːzə] *f* (*CHEM*) base; (*Kusine*) cousin

Basel ['baːzəl] *nt* Basle

Basen *pl von* **Base**; **Basis**

basieren [ba'ziːrən] *vt* to base ♦ *vi* to be based

Basis ['baːzɪs] (**-**, **Basen**) *f* basis

Baß △ [bas] (**Basses**, **Bässe**) *m* bass

Bassin [ba'sɛ̃ː] (**-s**, **-s**) *nt* pool

basteln ['bastəln] *vt* to make ♦ *vi* to do handicrafts

bat *etc* [baːt] *vb* **siehe** **bitten**

Bataillon [batal'joːn] (**-s**, **-e**) *nt* battalion

⚠ *For information on spelling reform see page 615*

Batik 36 *DEUTSCH-ENGLISCH*

Batik ['baːtɪk] f (*Verfahren*) batik
Batterie [batə'riː] f battery
Bau [bau] (-(e)s) m (*Bauen*) building, construction; (*Auf~*) structure; (*Körper~*) frame; (*~stelle*) building site; (*pl Baue: Tier~*) hole, burrow; (: *MIN*) working(s); (*pl Bauten: Gebäude*) building; **sich im ~ befinden** to be under construction; **~arbeiten** pl building od construction work sg; **~arbeiter** m building worker
Bauch [baux] (-(e)s, Bäuche) m belly; (*ANAT auch*) stomach, abdomen; **~fell** nt peritoneum; **b~ig** adj bulbous; **~nabel** m navel; **~redner** m ventriloquist; **~schmerzen** pl stomachache; **~weh** nt stomachache
Baudenkmal nt historical monument
bauen ['bauən] vt, vi to build; (*TECH*) to construct; **auf jdn/etw ~** to depend od count upon sb/sth
Bauer¹ ['bauər] (-n od -s, -n) m farmer; (*Schach*) pawn
Bauer² ['bauər] (-s, -) nt od m (bird)cage
Bäuerin ['bɔyərɪn] f farmer; (*Frau des Bauers*) farmer's wife
bäuerlich adj rustic
Bauern- zW: **~haus** nt farmhouse; **~hof** m farm(yard)
Bau- zW: **b~fällig** adj dilapidated; **~gelände** f building site; **~genehmigung** f building permit; **~gerüst** nt scaffolding; **~herr** m purchaser; **~kasten** m box of bricks; **~land** nt building land; **b~lich** adj structural
Baum [baum] (-(e)s, Bäume) m tree
baumeln ['bauməln] vi to dangle
bäumen ['bɔymən] vr to rear (up)
Baum- zW: **~schule** f nursery; **~stamm** m tree trunk; **~stumpf** m tree stump; **~wolle** f cotton
Bau- zW: **~plan** m architect's plan; **~platz** m building site
bauspar- zW: **~en** vi to save with a building society; **B~kasse** f building society; **B~vertrag** m building society savings agreement
Bau- zW: **~stein** m building stone,

freestone; **~stelle** f building site; **~teil** nt prefabricated part (of building); **~ten** pl von **Bau**; **~unternehmer** m building contractor; **~weise** f (method of) construction; **~werk** nt building; **~zaun** m hoarding
Bayern ['baiərn] nt Bavaria
bayrisch ['bairɪʃ] adj Bavarian
Bazillus [ba'tsɪlʊs] (-, Bazillen) m bacillus
beabsichtigen [bə'apzɪçtɪgən] vt to intend
beacht- [bə'axt] zW: **~en** vt to take note of; (*Vorschrift*) to obey; (*Vorfahrt*) to observe; **~lich** adj considerable; **B~ung** f notice, attention, observation
Beamte(r) [bə'amtə(r)] (-n, -n) m official; (*Staats~*) civil servant; (*Bank~ etc*) employee
Beamtin f siehe **Beamte(r)**
beängstigend [bə'ɛŋstɪgənt] adj alarming
beanspruchen [bə'anʃprʊxən] vt to claim; (*Zeit, Platz*) to take up, to occupy; **jdn ~** to take up sb's time
beanstanden [bə'anʃtandən] vt to complain about, to object to
beantragen [bə'antraːgən] vt to apply for, to ask for
beantworten [bə'antvortən] vt to answer; **Beantwortung** f ((+gen)) reply (to)
bearbeiten [bə'arbaitən] vt to work; (*Material*) to process; (*Thema*) to deal with; (*Land*) to cultivate; (*CHEM*) to treat; (*Buch*) to revise; (*umg: beeinflussen wollen*) to work on
Bearbeitung f processing; cultivation; treatment; revision
Bearbeitungsgebühr f handling charge
Beatmung [bə'aːtmʊŋ] f respiration
beaufsichtigen [bə'aufzɪçtɪgən] vt to supervise; **Beaufsichtigung** f supervision
beauftragen [bə'auftraːgən] vt to instruct; **jdn mit etw ~** to entrust sb with sth
Beauftragte(r) f(m) (*dekl wie adj*) representative
bebauen [bə'bauən] vt to build on; (*AGR*) to cultivate
beben ['beːbən] vi to tremble, to shake; **B~** (-s, -) nt earthquake
Becher ['bɛçər] (-s, -) m mug; (*ohne Henkel*)

⚠ *Informationen zur Rechtschreibreform Seite 615*

tumbler

Becken ['bɛkən] (**-s, -**) nt basin; (MUS) cymbal; (ANAT) pelvis

bedacht [bə'daxt] adj thoughtful, careful; **auf etw** akk **~ sein** to be concerned about sth

bedächtig [bə'dɛçtɪç] adj (umsichtig) thoughtful, reflective; (langsam) slow, deliberate

bedanken [bə'daŋkən] vr: **sich (bei jdm) ~** to say thank you (to sb)

Bedarf [bə'darf] (**-(e)s**) m need, requirement; (COMM) demand; **je nach ~** according to demand; **bei ~** if necessary; **~ an etw** dat **haben** to be in need of sth

Bedarfs- zW: **~fall** m case of need; **~haltestelle** f request stop

bedauerlich [bə'dauərlɪç] adj regrettable

bedauern [bə'dauərn] vt to be sorry for; (bemitleiden) to pity; **B~** (**-s**) nt regret; **~swert** adj (Zustände) regrettable; (Mensch) pitiable, unfortunate

bedecken [bə'dɛkən] vt to cover

bedeckt adj covered; (Himmel) overcast

bedenken [bə'dɛŋkən] (unreg) vt to think over, to consider

Bedenken (**-s, -**) nt (Überlegen) consideration; (Zweifel) doubt; (Skrupel) scruple

bedenklich adj doubtful; (bedrohlich) dangerous, risky

Bedenkzeit f time to think

bedeuten [bə'dɔytən] vt to mean; to signify; (wichtig sein) to be of importance; **~d** adj important; (beträchtlich) considerable

bedeutsam adj (wichtig) significant

Bedeutung f meaning; significance; (Wichtigkeit) importance; **b~slos** adj insignificant, unimportant; **b~svoll** adj momentous, significant

bedienen [bə'di:nən] vt to serve; (Maschine) to work, to operate ♦ vr (beim Essen) to help o.s.; **sich jds/einer Sache ~** to make use of sb/sth

Bedienung f service; (Kellnerin) waitress; (Verkäuferin) shop assistant; (Zuschlag)

service (charge)

Bedienungsanleitung f operating instructions pl

bedingen [bə'dɪŋən] vt (verursachen) to cause

bedingt adj (Richtigkeit, Tauglichkeit) limited; (Zusage, Annahme) conditional

Bedingung f condition; (Voraussetzung) stipulation; **b~slos** adj unconditional

bedrängen [bə'drɛŋən] vt to pester, to harass

bedrohen [bə'dro:ən] vt to threaten; **Bedrohung** f threat, menace

bedrücken [bə'drʏkən] vt to oppress, to trouble

bedürf- [bə'dʏrf] zW: **~en** (unreg) vi +gen to need, to require; **B~nis** (**-ses, -se**) nt need; **~tig** adj in need, poor, needy

beeilen [bə'ʔaɪlən] vr to hurry

beeindrucken [bə'ʔaɪndrʊkən] vt to impress, to make an impression on

beeinflussen [bə'ʔaɪnflʊsən] vt to influence

beeinträchtigen [bə'ʔaɪntrɛçtɪgən] vt to affect adversely; (Freiheit) to infringe upon

beend(ig)en [bə'ʔɛnd(ɪg)ən] vt to end, to finish, to terminate

beengen [bə'ʔɛŋən] vt to cramp; (fig) to hamper, to oppress

beerben [bə'ʔɛrbən] vt: **jdn ~** to inherit from sb

beerdigen [bə'ʔe:rdɪgən] vt to bury; **Beerdigung** f funeral, burial

Beere ['be:rə] f berry; (Trauben~) grape

Beet [be:t] (**-(e)s, -e**) nt bed

befähigen [bə'fɛ:ɪgən] vt to enable

befähigt adj (begabt) talented; **~ (für)** (fähig) capable (of)

Befähigung f capability; (Begabung) talent, aptitude

befahrbar [bə'fa:rba:r] adj passable; (NAUT) navigable

befahren [bə'fa:rən] (unreg) vt to use, to drive over; (NAUT) to navigate ♦ adj used

befallen [bə'falən] (unreg) vt to come over

befangen [bə'faŋən] adj (schüchtern) shy, self-conscious; (voreingenommen) biased

befassen [bə'fasən] vr to concern o.s.

⚠ *For information on spelling reform see page 615*

Befehl [bə'fe:l] (-(e)s, -e) m command, order; **b~en** (unreg) vt to order ♦ vi to give orders; **jdm etw b~en** to order sb to do sth; **~sverweigerung** f insubordination

befestigen [bə'fɛstɪɡən] vt to fasten; (stärken) to strengthen; (MIL) to fortify; **~ an** +dat to fasten to

Befestigung f fastening; strengthening; (MIL) fortification

befeuchten [bə'fɔʏçtən] vt to damp(en), to moisten

befinden [bə'fɪndən] (unreg) vr to be; (sich fühlen) to feel ♦ vt: **jdn/etw für od als etw ~** to deem sb/sth to be sth ♦ vi: **~ (über** +akk) to decide (on), to adjudicate (on); **B~** (-s) nt health, condition; (Meinung) view, opinion

befolgen [bə'fɔlɡən] vt to comply with, to follow

befördern [bə'fœrdərn] vt (senden) to transport, to send; (beruflich) to promote; **Beförderung** f transport; promotion

befragen [bə'fra:ɡən] vt to question

befreien [bə'fraɪən] vt to set free; (erlassen) to exempt; **Befreiung** f liberation, release; (Erlassen) exemption

befreunden [bə'frɔʏndən] vr to make friends; (mit Idee etc) to acquaint o.s.

befreundet adj friendly

befriedigen [bə'fri:dɪɡən] vt to satisfy; **~d** adj satisfactory

Befriedigung f satisfaction, gratification

befristet [bə'frɪstət] adj limited

befruchten [bə'frʊxtən] vt to fertilize; (fig) to stimulate

Befruchtung f: **künstliche ~** artificial insemination

Befugnis [bə'fu:knɪs] (-, -se) f authorization, powers pl

befugt adj authorized, entitled

Befund [bə'fʊnt] (-(e)s, -e) m findings pl; (MED) diagnosis

befürchten [bə'fʏrçtən] vt to fear; **Befürchtung** f fear, apprehension

befürworten [bə'fy:rvɔrtən] vt to support, to speak in favour of; **Befürworter (-s, -)** m supporter, advocate

begabt [bə'ɡa:pt] adj gifted

Begabung [bə'ɡa:bʊŋ] f talent, gift

begann [bə'ɡan] vb siehe **beginnen**

begeben [bə'ɡe:bən] (unreg) vr (gehen) to betake o.s.; (geschehen) to occur; **sich ~ nach** od **zu** to proceed to(wards); **B~heit** f occurrence

begegnen [bə'ɡe:ɡnən] vi: **jdm ~** to meet sb; (behandeln) to treat sb; **einer Sache** dat **~** to meet with sth

Begegnung f meeting

begehen [bə'ɡe:ən] (unreg) vt (Straftat) to commit; (abschreiten) to cover; (Straße etc) to use, to negotiate; (Feier) to celebrate

begehren [bə'ɡe:rən] vt to desire

begehrt adj in demand; (Junggeselle) eligible

begeistern [bə'ɡaɪstərn] vt to fill with enthusiasm, to inspire ♦ vr: **sich für etw ~** to get enthusiastic about sth

begeistert adj enthusiastic

Begierde [bə'ɡi:rdə] f desire, passion

begierig [bə'ɡi:rɪç] adj eager, keen

begießen [bə'ɡi:sən] (unreg) vt to water; (mit Alkohol) to drink to

Beginn [bə'ɡɪn] (-(e)s) m beginning; **zu ~** at the beginning; **b~en** (unreg) vt, vi to start, to begin

beglaubigen [bə'ɡlaʊbɪɡən] vt to countersign; **Beglaubigung** f countersignature

begleichen [bə'ɡlaɪçən] (unreg) vt to settle, to pay

Begleit- [bə'ɡlaɪt] zW: **b~en** vt to accompany; (MIL) to escort; **~er (-s, -)** m companion; (Freund) escort; (MUS) accompanist; **~schreiben** nt covering letter; **~umstände** pl concomitant circumstances; **~ung** f company; (MIL) escort; (MUS) accompaniment

beglücken [bə'ɡlʏkən] vt to make happy, to delight

beglückwünschen [bə'ɡlʏkvʏnʃən] vt: **~ (zu)** to congratulate (on)

begnadigen [bə'ɡna:dɪɡən] vt to pardon; **Begnadigung** f pardon, amnesty

begnügen [bə'ɡny:ɡən] vr to be satisfied, to

⚠ *Informationen zur Rechtschreibreform Seite 615*

content o.s.

begonnen *etc* [bəˈgɔnən] *vb siehe* **beginnen**

begraben [bəˈgraːbən] (*unreg*) *vt* to bury;
Begräbnis (-ses, -se) *nt* burial, funeral

begreifen [bəˈgraɪfən] (*unreg*) *vt* to
understand, to comprehend

begreiflich [bəˈgraɪflɪç] *adj* understandable

begrenzen [bəˈgrɛntsən] *vt* (*beschränken*) to
limit

Begrenztheit [bəˈgrɛntsthaɪt] *f* limitation,
restriction; (*fig*) narrowness

Begriff [bəˈgrɪf] (-(e)s, -e) *m* concept, idea;
im ~ sein, etw zu tun to be about to do
sth; **schwer von ~** (*umg*) slow, dense

begriffsstutzig *adj* slow, dense

begründ- [bəˈgrʏnd] *zW*: **~en** *vt* (*Gründe
geben*) to justify; **~et** *adj* well-founded,
justified; **B~ung** *f* justification, reason

begrüßen [bəˈgryːsən] *vt* to greet, to
welcome; **Begrüßung** *f* greeting, welcome

begünstigen [bəˈgʏnstɪgən] *vt* (*Person*) to
favour; (*Sache*) to further, to promote

begutachten [bəˈguːtˌʔaxtən] *vt* to assess

begütert [bəˈgyːtərt] *adj* wealthy, well-to-do

behaart [bəˈhaːrt] *adj* hairy

behagen [bəˈhaːgən] *vi*: **das behagt ihm
nicht** he does not like it

behaglich [bəˈhaːklɪç] *adj* comfortable,
cosy; **B~keit** *f* comfort, cosiness

behalten [bəˈhaltən] (*unreg*) *vt* to keep, to
retain; (*im Gedächtnis*) to remember

Behälter [bəˈhɛltər] (-s, -) *m* container,
receptacle

behandeln [bəˈhandəln] *vt* to treat;
(*Thema*) to deal with; (*Maschine*) to handle

Behandlung *f* treatment; (*von Maschine*)
handling

beharren [bəˈharən] *vi*: **auf etw** *dat* **~** to
stick *od* keep to sth

beharrlich [bəˈharlɪç] *adj* (*ausdauernd*)
steadfast, unwavering; (*hartnäckig*)
tenacious, dogged; **B~keit** *f* steadfastness;
tenacity

behaupten [bəˈhauptən] *vt* to claim, to
assert, to maintain; (*sein Recht*) to defend
♦ *vr* to assert o.s.

Behauptung *f* claim, assertion

beheben [bəˈheːbən] (*unreg*) *vt* to remove

behelfen [bəˈhɛlfən] (*unreg*) *vr*: **sich mit
etw ~** to make do with sth

behelfsmäßig *adj* improvised, makeshift;
(*vorübergehend*) temporary

behelligen [bəˈhɛligən] *vt* to trouble, to
bother

beherbergen [bəˈhɛrbɛrgən] *vt* to put up,
to house

beherrsch- [bəˈhɛrʃ] *zW*: **~en** *vt* (*Volk*) to
rule, to govern; (*Situation*) to control;
(*Sprache, Gefühle*) to master ♦ *vr* to control
o.s.; **~t** *adj* controlled; **B~ung** *f* rule;
control; mastery

beherzigen [bəˈhɛrtsigən] *vt* to take to
heart

beherzt *adj* courageous, brave

behilflich [bəˈhɪlflɪç] *adj* helpful; **jdm ~ sein
(bei)** to help sb (with)

behindern [bəˈhɪndərn] *vt* to hinder, to
impede

Behinderte(r) *f(m)* disabled person

Behinderung *f* hindrance; (*Körper~*)
handicap

Behörde [bəˈhøːrdə] *f* (*auch pl*) authorities *pl*

behördlich [bəˈhøːrtlɪç] *adj* official

behüten [bəˈhyːtən] *vt* to guard; **jdn vor
etw** *dat* **~** to preserve sb from sth

behutsam [bəˈhuːtzaːm] *adj* cautious,
careful; **B~keit** *f* caution, carefulness

SCHLÜSSELWORT

bei [baɪ] *präp +dat* **1** (*nahe bei*) near; (*zum
Aufenthalt*) at, with; (*unter, zwischen*)
among; **bei München** near Munich; **bei
uns** at our place; **beim Friseur** at the
hairdresser's; **bei seinen Eltern wohnen** to
live with one's parents; **bei einer Firma
arbeiten** to work for a firm; **etw bei sich
haben** to have sth on one; **jdn bei sich
haben** to have sb with one; **bei Goethe** in
Goethe; **beim Militär** in the army

2 (*zeitlich*) at, on; (*während*) during;
(*Zustand, Umstand*) in; **bei Nacht** at night;
bei Nebel in fog; **bei Regen** if it rains; **bei
solcher Hitze** in such heat; **bei meiner
Ankuft** on my arrival; **bei der Arbeit** when

⚠ *For information on spelling reform see page 615*

I'm etc working; **beim Fahren** while driving

beibehalten ['baɪbəhaltən] (*unreg*) *vt* to keep, to retain

beibringen ['baɪbrɪŋən] (*unreg*) *vt* (*Beweis, Zeugen*) to bring forward; (*Gründe*) to adduce; **jdm etw ~** (*lehren*) to teach sb sth; (*zu verstehen geben*) to make sb understand sth; (*zufügen*) to inflict sth on sb

Beichte ['baɪçtə] *f* confession; **b~n** *vt* to confess ♦ *vi* to go to confession

beide(s) ['baɪdə(s)] *pron, adj* both; **meine ~n Brüder** my two brothers, both my brothers; **die ersten ~n** the first two; **wir ~** we two; **einer von ~n** one of the two; **alles ~s** both (of them)

beider- ['baɪdər] *zW*: **~lei** *adj inv* of both; **~seitig** *adj* mutual, reciprocal; **~seits** *adv* mutually ♦ *präp +gen* on both sides of

beieinander [baɪaɪˈnandər] *adv* together

Beifahrer ['baɪfaːrər] *m* passenger

Beifall ['baɪfal] **(-(e)s)** *m* applause; (*Zustimmung*) approval

beifügen ['baɪfyːgən] *vt* to enclose

beige ['beːʒ] *adj* beige, fawn

beigeben ['baɪgeːbən] (*unreg*) *vt* (*zufügen*) to add; (*mitgeben*) to give ♦ *vi* (*nachgeben*) to give in

Beihilfe ['baɪhɪlfə] *f* aid, assistance; (*Studien~*) grant; (*JUR*) aiding and abetting

beikommen ['baɪkɔmən] (*unreg*) *vi +dat* to get at; (*einem Problem*) to deal with

Beil [baɪl] **(-(e)s, -e)** *nt* axe, hatchet

Beilage ['baɪlaːgə] *f* (*Buch~ etc*) supplement; (*KOCH*) vegetables and potatoes *pl*

beiläufig ['baɪlɔyfɪç] *adj* casual, incidental ♦ *adv* casually, by the way

beilegen ['baɪleːgən] *vt* (*hinzufügen*) to enclose, to add; (*beimessen*) to attribute, to ascribe; (*Streit*) to settle

Beileid ['baɪlaɪt] *nt* condolence, sympathy; **herzliches ~** deepest sympathy

beiliegend ['baɪliːgənt] *adj* (*COMM*) enclosed

beim [baɪm] = **bei dem**

beimessen ['baɪmɛsən] (*unreg*) *vt* (*+dat*) to

attribute (to), to ascribe (to)

Bein [baɪn] **(-(e)s, -e)** *nt* leg

beinah(e) ['baɪnaː(ə)] *adv* almost, nearly

Beinbruch *m* fracture of the leg

beinhalten [bəˈʔɪnhaltən] *vt* to contain

Beipackzettel ['baɪpaktsetəl] *m* instruction leaflet

beipflichten ['baɪpflɪçtən] *vi*: **jdm/etw ~** to agree with sb/sth

beisammen [baɪˈzamən] *adv* together; **B~sein (-s)** *nt* get-together

Beischlaf ['baɪʃlaːf] *m* sexual intercourse

Beisein ['baɪzaɪn] **(-s)** *nt* presence

beiseite [baɪˈzaɪtə] *adv* to one side, aside; (*stehen*) on one side, aside; **etw ~ legen** (*sparen*) to put sth by

beisetzen ['baɪzɛtsən] *vt* to bury; **Beisetzung** *f* funeral

Beisitzer ['baɪzɪtsər] **(-s, -)** *m* (*bei Prüfung*) assessor

Beispiel ['baɪʃpiːl] **(-(e)s, -e)** *nt* example; **sich** *+dat* **an jdm ein ~ nehmen** to take sb as an example; **zum ~** for example; **b~haft** *adj* exemplary; **b~los** *adj* unprecedented; **b~sweise** *adv* for instance *od* example

beißen ['baɪsən] (*unreg*) *vt, vi* to bite; (*stechen: Rauch, Säure*) to burn ♦ *vr* (*Farben*) to clash; **~d** *adj* biting, caustic; (*fig auch*) sarcastic

Beistand ['baɪʃtant] **(-(e)s, ̈e)** *m* support, help; (*JUR*) adviser

beistehen ['baɪʃteːən] (*unreg*) *vi*: **jdm ~** to stand by sb

beisteuern ['baɪʃtɔyərn] *vt* to contribute

Beitrag ['baɪtraːk] **(-(e)s, ̈e)** *m* contribution; (*Zahlung*) fee, subscription; (*Versicherungs~*) premium; **b~en** ['baɪtraːgən] (*unreg*) *vt, vi*: **b~en (zu)** to contribute (to); (*mithelfen*) to help (with)

beitreten ['baɪtreːtən] (*unreg*) *vi +dat* to join

Beitritt ['baɪtrɪt] *m* joining, membership

Beiwagen ['baɪvaːgən] *m* (*Motorrad~*) sidecar

beizeiten [baɪˈtsaɪtən] *adv* in time

bejahen [bəˈjaːən] *vt* (*Frage*) to say yes to, to answer in the affirmative; (*gutheißen*) to

⚠ *Informationen zur Rechtschreibreform Seite 615*

agree with

bekämpfen [bə'kɛmpfən] *vt* (*Gegner*) to fight; (*Seuche*) to combat ♦ *vr* to fight; **Bekämpfung** *f* fight, struggle

bekannt [bə'kant] *adj* (well-)known; (*nicht fremd*) familiar; **mit jdm ~ sein** to know sb; **jdn mit jdm ~ machen** to introduce sb to sb; **das ist mir ~** I know that; **es/sie kommt mir ~ vor** it/she seems familiar; **B~e(r)** *f(m)* acquaintance; friend; **B~enkreis** *m* circle of friends; **~geben** △ (*unreg*) *vt* to announce publicly; **~lich** *adv* as is well known, as you know; **~machen** △ *vt* to announce; **B~machung** *f* publication; announcement; **B~schaft** *f* acquaintance

bekehren [bə'ke:rən] *vt* to convert ♦ *vr* to be *od* become converted

bekennen [bə'kɛnən] (*unreg*) *vt* to confess; (*Glauben*) to profess; **Farbe ~** (*umg*) to show where one stands

Bekenntnis [bə'kɛntnɪs] (**-ses, -se**) *nt* admission, confession; (*Religion*) confession, denomination

beklagen [bə'kla:gən] *vt* to deplore, to lament ♦ *vr* to complain

bekleiden [bə'klaɪdən] *vt* to clothe; (*Amt*) to occupy, to fill

Bekleidung *f* clothing

beklemmen [bə'klɛmən] *vt* to oppress

beklommen [bə'klɔmən] *adj* anxious, uneasy

bekommen [bə'kɔmən] (*unreg*) *vt* to get, to receive; (*Kind*) to have; (*Zug*) to catch, to get ♦ *vi*: **jdm ~** to agree with sb

bekömmlich [bə'kœmlɪç] *adj* easily digestible

bekräftigen [bə'krɛftɪgən] *vt* to confirm, to corroborate

bekreuzigen [bə'krɔʏtsɪgən] *vr* to cross o.s.

bekunden [bə'kʊndən] *vt* (*sagen*) to state; (*zeigen*) to show

belächeln [bə'lɛçəln] *vt* to laugh at

beladen [bə'la:dən] (*unreg*) *vt* to load

Belag [bə'la:k] (**-(e)s, ⸚e**) *m* covering, coating; (*Brot~*) spread; (*Zahn~*) tartar; (*auf Zunge*) fur; (*Brems~*) lining

belagern [bə'la:gərn] *vt* to besiege; **Belagerung** *f* siege

Belang [bə'laŋ] (**-(e)s**) *m* importance; **~e** *pl* (*Interessen*) interests, concerns; **b~los** *adj* trivial, unimportant

belassen [bə'lasən] (*unreg*) *vt* (*in Zustand, Glauben*) to leave; (*in Stellung*) to retain

belasten [bə'lastən] *vt* to burden; (*fig: bedrücken*) to trouble, to worry; (*COMM: Konto*) to debit; (*JUR*) to incriminate ♦ *vr* to weigh o.s. down; (*JUR*) to incriminate o.s.; **~d** *adj* (*JUR*) incriminating

belästigen [bə'lɛstɪgən] *vt* to annoy, to pester; **Belästigung** *f* annoyance, pestering

Belastung [bə'lastʊŋ] *f* load; (*fig: Sorge etc*) weight; (*COMM*) charge, debit(ing); (*JUR*) incriminatory evidence

belaufen [bə'laʊfən] (*unreg*) *vr*: **sich ~ auf** +*akk* to amount to

beleben [bə'le:bən] *vt* (*anregen*) to liven up; (*Konjunktur, jds Hoffnungen*) to stimulate ♦ *vr* (*Augen*) to light up; (*Stadt*) to come to life

belebt [bə'le:pt] *adj* (*Straße*) busy

Beleg [bə'le:k] (**-(e)s, -e**) *m* (*COMM*) receipt; (*Beweis*) documentary evidence, proof; (*Beispiel*) example; **b~en** *vt* to cover; (*Kuchen, Brot*) to spread; (*Platz*) to reserve, to book; (*Kurs, Vorlesung*) to register for; (*beweisen*) to verify, to prove; (*MIL: mit Bomben*) to bomb; **~schaft** *f* personnel, staff; **b~t** *adj*: **b~tes Brot** open sandwich

belehren [bə'le:rən] *vt* to instruct, to teach; **Belehrung** *f* instruction

beleibt [bə'laɪpt] *adj* stout, corpulent

beleidigen [bə'laɪdɪgən] *vt* to insult, to offend; **Beleidigung** *f* insult; (*JUR*) slander, libel

beleuchten [bə'lɔʏçtən] *vt* to light, to illuminate; (*fig*) to throw light on

Beleuchtung *f* lighting, illumination

Belgien ['bɛlgiən] *nt* Belgium; **Belgier(in)** *m(f)* Belgian; **belgisch** *adj* Belgian

belichten [bə'lɪçtən] *vt* to expose

Belichtung *f* exposure; **~smesser** *m* exposure meter

Belieben [bə'li:bən] *nt*: **(ganz) nach ~**

△ *For information on spelling reform see page 615*

(just) as you wish

beliebig [bə'li:bɪç] *adj* any you like ♦ *adv* as you like; **ein ~es Thema** any subject you like *od* want; **~ viel/viele** as much/many as you like

beliebt [bə'li:pt] *adj* popular; **sich bei jdm ~ machen** to make o.s. popular with sb; **B~heit** *f* popularity

beliefern [bə'li:fərn] *vt* to supply

bellen ['bɛlən] *vi* to bark

belohnen [bə'lo:nən] *vt* to reward; **Belohnung** *f* reward

Belüftung [bə'lʏftʊŋ] *f* ventilation

belügen [bə'ly:gən] *(unreg) vt* to lie to, to deceive

belustigen [bə'lʊstɪgən] *vt* to amuse; **Belustigung** *f* amusement

bemalen [bə'ma:lən] *vt* to paint

bemängeln [bə'mɛŋəln] *vt* to criticize

bemerk- [bə'mɛrk] *zW:* **~bar** *adj* perceptible, noticeable; **sich ~bar machen** (*Person*) to make *od* get o.s. noticed; (*Unruhe*) to become noticeable; **~en** *vt* (*wahrnehmen*) to notice, to observe; (*sagen*) to say, to mention; **~enswert** *adj* remarkable, noteworthy; **B~ung** *f* remark; (*schriftlich auch*) note

bemitleiden [bə'mɪtlaɪdən] *vt* to pity

bemühen [bə'my:ən] *vr* to take trouble *od* pains; **Bemühung** *f* trouble, pains *pl*, effort

benachbart [bə'naxba:rt] *adj* neighbouring

benachrichtigen [bə'na:xrɪçtɪgən] *vt* to inform; **Benachrichtigung** *f* notification, information

benachteiligen [bə'na:xtaɪlɪgən] *vt* to put at a disadvantage; to victimize

benehmen [bə'ne:mən] *(unreg) vr* to behave; **B~** *(-s) nt* behaviour

beneiden [bə'naɪdən] *vt* to envy; **~swert** *adj* enviable

benennen [bə'nɛnən] *(unreg) vt* to name

Bengel ['bɛŋəl] *(-s, -) m* (little) rascal *od* rogue

benommen [bə'nɔmən] *adj* dazed

benoten [bə'no:tən] *vt* to mark

benötigen [bə'nø:tɪgən] *vt* to need

benutzen [bə'nʊtsən] *vt* to use

Benutzer *(-s, -) m* user

Benutzung *f* utilization, use

Benzin [bɛnt'si:n] *(-s, -e) nt* (*AUT*) petrol (*BRIT*), gas(oline) (*US*); **~kanister** *m* petrol (*BRIT*) *od* gas can; **~tank** *m* petrol tank (*BRIT*), gas tank (*US*); **~uhr** *f* petrol (*BRIT*) *od* gas gauge

beobachten [bə'o:baxtən] *vt* to observe; **Beobachter** *(-s, -) m* observer; (*eines Unfalls*) witness; (*PRESSE, TV*) correspondent; **Beobachtung** *f* observation

bepacken [bə'pakən] *vt* to load, to pack

bequem [bə'kve:m] *adj* comfortable; (*Ausrede*) convenient; (*Person*) lazy, indolent; **~en** *vr:* **sich ~en(, etw zu tun)** to condescend (to do sth); **B~lichkeit** [-'lɪçkaɪt] *f* convenience, comfort; (*Faulheit*) laziness, indolence

beraten [bə'ra:tən] *(unreg) vt* to advise; (*besprechen*) to discuss, to debate ♦ *vr* to consult; **gut/schlecht ~ sein** to be well/ill advised; **sich ~ lassen** to get advice

Berater *(-s, -) m* adviser

Beratung *f* advice; (*Besprechung*) consultation; **~sstelle** *f* advice centre

berauben [bə'raʊbən] *vt* to rob

berechenbar [bə'rɛçənba:r] *adj* calculable

berechnen [bə'rɛçnən] *vt* to calculate; (*COMM: anrechnen*) to charge; **~d** *adj* (*Mensch*) calculating, scheming

Berechnung *f* calculation; (*COMM*) charge

berechtigen [bə'rɛçtɪgən] *vt* to entitle; to authorize; (*fig*) to justify

berechtigt [bə'rɛçtɪçt] *adj* justifiable, justified

Berechtigung *f* authorization; (*fig*) justification

bereden [bə're:dən] *vt* (*besprechen*) to discuss; (*überreden*) to persuade ♦ *vr* to discuss

Bereich [bə'raɪç] *(-(e)s, -e) m* (*Bezirk*) area; (*PHYS*) range; (*Ressort, Gebiet*) sphere

bereichern [bə'raɪçərn] *vt* to enrich ♦ *vr* to get rich

bereinigen [bə'raɪnɪgən] *vt* to settle

bereisen [bə'raɪzən] *vt* (*Land*) to travel

⚠ *Informationen zur Rechtschreibreform Seite 615*

through

bereit [bə'raɪt] adj ready, prepared; **zu etw ~ sein** to be ready for sth; **sich ~ erklären** to declare o.s. willing; **~en** vt to prepare, to make ready; (*Kummer, Freude*) to cause; **~halten** (*unreg*) vt to keep in readiness; **~legen** vt to lay out; **~machen** vt, vr to prepare, to get ready; **~s** adv already; **B~schaft** f readiness; (*Polizei*) alert; **B~schaftsdienst** m emergency service; **~stehen** (*unreg*) vi (*Person*) to be prepared; (*Ding*) to be ready; **~stellen** vt (*Kisten, Pakete etc*) to put ready; (*Geld etc*) to make available; (*Truppen, Maschinen*) to put at the ready; **~willig** adj willing, ready; **B~willigkeit** f willingness, readiness

bereuen [bə'rɔʏən] vt to regret

Berg [bɛrk] (-(e)s, -e) m mountain; hill; **b~ab** adv downhill; **~arbeiter** m miner; **b~auf** adv uphill; **~bahn** f mountain railway; **~bau** m mining

bergen ['bɛrgən] (*unreg*) vt (*retten*) to rescue; (*Ladung*) to salvage; (*enthalten*) to contain

Berg- zW: **~führer** m mountain guide; **~gipfel** m peak, summit; **b~ig** ['bɛrgɪç] adj mountainous; hilly; **~kette** f mountain range; **~mann** (pl **~leute**) m miner; **~rettungsdienst** m mountain rescue team; **~rutsch** m landslide; **~steigen** nt mountaineering; **~steiger(in)** (-s, -) m(f) mountaineer, climber; **~tour** f mountain climb

Bergung ['bɛrgʊŋ] f (*von Menschen*) rescue; (*von Material*) recovery; (*NAUT*) salvage

Berg- zW: **~wacht** f mountain rescue service; **~wanderung** f hike in the mountains; **~werk** nt mine

Bericht [bə'rɪçt] (-(e)s, -e) m report, account; **b~en** vt, vi to report; **~erstatter** (-s, -) m reporter; (newspaper) correspondent

berichtigen [bə'rɪçtɪgən] vt to correct; **Berichtigung** f correction

Bernstein ['bɛrnʃtaɪn] m amber

bersten ['bɛrstən] (*unreg*) vi to burst, to split

berüchtigt [bə'rʏçtɪçt] adj notorious, infamous

berücksichtigen [bə'rʏkzɪçtɪgən] vt to consider, to bear in mind; **Berücksichtigung** f consideration

Beruf [bə'ru:f] (-(e)s, -e) m occupation, profession; (*Gewerbe*) trade; **b~en** (*unreg*) vt: **b~en zu** to appoint to ♦ vr: **sich auf jdn/etw b~en** to refer od appeal to sb/sth ♦ adj competent, qualified; **b~lich** adj professional

Berufs- zW: **~ausbildung** f job training; **~berater** m careers adviser; **~beratung** f vocational guidance; **~geheimnis** nt professional secret; **~leben** nt professional life; **~schule** f vocational od trade school; **~sportler** [-ʃpɔrtlər] m professional (sportsman); **b~tätig** adj employed; **b~unfähig** adj unfit for work; **~verkehr** m rush-hour traffic

Berufung f vocation, calling; (*Ernennung*) appointment; (*JUR*) appeal; **~ einlegen** to appeal

beruhen [bə'ru:ən] vi: **auf etw** dat **~** to be based on sth; **etw auf sich ~ lassen** to leave sth at that

beruhigen [bə'ru:ɪgən] vt to calm, to pacify, to soothe ♦ vr (*Mensch*) to calm (o.s.) down; (*Situation*) to calm down

Beruhigung f soothing; (*der Nerven*) calming; **zu jds ~** (in order) to reassure sb; **~smittel** nt sedative

berühmt [bə'ry:mt] adj famous; **B~heit** f (*Ruf*) fame; (*Mensch*) celebrity

berühren [bə'ry:rən] vt to touch; (*gefühlsmäßig bewegen*) to affect; (*flüchtig erwähnen*) to mention, to touch on ♦ vr to meet, to touch

Berührung f contact

besagen [bə'za:gən] vt to mean

besänftigen [bə'zɛnftɪgən] vt to soothe, to calm

Besatz [bə'zats] (-es, ̈-e) m trimming, edging

Besatzung f garrison; (*NAUT, AVIAT*) crew

Besatzungsmacht f occupying power

beschädigen [bə'ʃɛːdɪgən] vt to damage; **Beschädigung** f damage; (*Stelle*) damaged spot

⚠ *For information on spelling reform see page 615*

beschaffen [bəˈʃafən] *vt* to get, to acquire ♦ *adj*: **das ist so ~, daß** that is such that; **B~heit** *f* (*von Mensch*) constitution, nature
Beschaffung *f* acquisition
beschäftigen [bəˈʃɛftɪgən] *vt* to occupy; (*beruflich*) to employ ♦ *vr* to occupy *od* concern o.s.
beschäftigt *adj* busy, occupied
Beschäftigung *f* (*Beruf*) employment; (*Tätigkeit*) occupation; (*Befassen*) concern
beschämen [bəˈʃɛːmən] *vt* to put to shame; **~d** *adj* shameful; (*Hilfsbereitschaft*) shaming
beschämt *adj* ashamed
Bescheid [bəˈʃaɪt] (**-(e)s, -e**) *m* information; (*Weisung*) directions *pl*; **~ wissen (über** +*akk*) to be well-informed (about); **ich weiß ~** I know; **jdm ~ geben** *od* **sagen** to let sb know
bescheiden [bəˈʃaɪdən] (*unreg*) *vr* to content o.s. ♦ *adj* modest; **B~heit** *f* modesty
bescheinen [bəˈʃaɪnən] (*unreg*) *vt* to shine on
bescheinigen [bəˈʃaɪnɪgən] *vt* to certify; (*bestätigen*) to acknowledge
Bescheinigung *f* certificate; (*Quittung*) receipt
beschenken [bəˈʃɛŋkən] *vt*: **jdn mit etw ~** to give sb sth as a present
bescheren [bəˈʃeːrən] *vt*: **jdm etw ~** to give sb sth as a Christmas present; **jdn ~** to give Christmas presents to sb
Bescherung *f* giving of Christmas presents; (*umg*) mess
beschildern [bəˈʃɪldərn] *vt* to put signs/a sign on
beschimpfen [bəˈʃɪmpfən] *vt* to abuse; **Beschimpfung** *f* abuse, insult
Beschlag [bəˈʃlaːk] (**-(e)s, ¨e**) *m* (*Metallband*) fitting; (*auf Fenster*) condensation; (*auf Metall*) tarnish; finish; (*Hufeisen*) horseshoe; **jdn/etw in ~ nehmen** *od* **mit ~ belegen** to monopolize sb/sth; **b~en** [bəˈʃlaːgən] (*unreg*) *vt* to cover; (*Pferd*) to shoe ♦ *vi, vr* (*Fenster etc*) to mist over; **b~en sein (in** *od* **auf** +*dat*) to be well

versed (in); **b~nahmen** *vt* to seize, to confiscate; to requisition; **~nahmung** *f* confiscation, sequestration
beschleunigen [bəˈʃlɔʏnɪgən] *vt* to accelerate, to speed up ♦ *vi* (*AUT*) to accelerate; **Beschleunigung** *f* acceleration
beschließen [bəˈʃliːsən] (*unreg*) *vt* to decide on; (*beenden*) to end, to close
Beschluß △ [bəˈʃlʊs] (**-sses, ¨sse**) *m* decision, conclusion; (*Ende*) conclusion, end
beschmutzen [bəˈʃmʊtsən] *vt* to dirty, to soil
beschönigen [bəˈʃøːnɪgən] *vt* to gloss over
beschränken [bəˈʃrɛŋkən] *vt, vr*: **(sich) ~ (auf** +*akk*) to limit *od* restrict (o.s.) (to)
beschränk- *zW*: **~t** *adj* confined, restricted; (*Mensch*) limited, narrow-minded; **B~ung** *f* limitation
beschreiben [bəˈʃraɪbən] (*unreg*) *vt* to describe; (*Papier*) to write on
Beschreibung *f* description
beschriften [bəˈʃrɪftən] *vt* to mark, to label; **Beschriftung** *f* lettering
beschuldigen [bəˈʃʊldɪgən] *vt* to accuse; **Beschuldigung** *f* accusation
Beschuß △ [bəˈʃʊs] *m*: **jdn/etw unter ~ nehmen** (*MIL*) to open fire on sb/sth
beschützen [bəˈʃʏtsən] *vt*: **~ (vor** +*dat*) to protect (from); **Beschützer** (**-s, -**) *m* protector
Beschwerde [bəˈʃveːrdə] *f* complaint; (*Mühe*) hardship; **~n** *pl* (*Leiden*) trouble
beschweren [bəˈʃveːrən] *vt* to weight down; (*fig*) to burden ♦ *vr* to complain
beschwerlich *adj* tiring, exhausting
beschwichtigen [bəˈʃvɪçtɪgən] *vt* to soothe, to pacify
beschwindeln [bəˈʃvɪndəln] *vt* (*betrügen*) to cheat; (*belügen*) to fib to
beschwingt [bəˈʃvɪŋt] *adj* in high spirits
beschwipst [bəˈʃvɪpst] (*umg*) *adj* tipsy
beschwören [bəˈʃvøːrən] (*unreg*) *vt* (*Aussage*) to swear to; (*anflehen*) to implore; (*Geister*) to conjure up
beseitigen [bəˈzaɪtɪgən] *vt* to remove; **Beseitigung** *f* removal
Besen [ˈbeːzən] (**-s, -**) *m* broom; **~stiel** *m*

broomstick

besessen [bəˈzɛsən] *adj* possessed

besetz- [bəˈzɛts] *zW:* **~en** *vt* (*Haus, Land*) to occupy; (*Platz*) to take, to fill; (*Posten*) to fill; (*Rolle*) to cast; (*mit Edelsteinen*) to set; **~t** *adj* full; (*TEL*) engaged, busy; (*Platz*) taken; (*WC*) engaged; **B~tzeichen** *nt* engaged tone; **B~ung** *f* occupation; filling; (*von Rolle*) casting; (*die Schauspieler*) cast

besichtigen [bəˈzɪçtɪgən] *vt* to visit, to have a look at; **Besichtigung** *f* visit

besiegen [bəˈziːgən] *vt* to defeat, to overcome

besinn- [bəˈzɪn] *zW:* **~en** (*unreg*) *vr* (*nachdenken*) to think, to reflect; (*erinnern*) to remember; **sich anders ~en** to change one's mind; **B~ung** *f* consciousness; **zur B~ung kommen** to recover consciousness; (*fig*) to come to one's senses; **~ungslos** *adj* unconscious

Besitz [bəˈzɪts] (*-es*) *m* possession; (*Eigentum*) property; **b~en** (*unreg*) *vt* to possess, to own; (*Eigenschaft*) to have; **~er(in)** (*-s, -*) *m(f)* owner, proprietor; **~ergreifung** *f* occupation, seizure

besoffen [bəˈzɔfən] (*umg*) *adj* drunk, stoned

besohlen [bəˈzoːlən] *vt* to sole

Besoldung [bəˈzɔldʊŋ] *f* salary, pay

besondere(r, s) [bəˈzɔndərə(r, s)] *adj* special; (*eigen*) particular; (*gesondert*) separate; (*eigentümlich*) peculiar

Besonderheit [bəˈzɔndərhaɪt] *f* peculiarity

besonders [bəˈzɔndərs] *adv* especially, particularly; (*getrennt*) separately

besonnen [bəˈzɔnən] *adj* sensible, level-headed

besorg- [bəˈzɔrg] *zW:* **~en** *vt* (*beschaffen*) to acquire; (*kaufen auch*) to purchase; (*erledigen: Geschäfte*) to deal with; (*sich kümmern um*) to take care of; **B~nis** (*-, -se*) *f* anxiety, concern; **~t** [bəˈzɔrçt] *adj* anxious, worried; **B~ung** *f* acquisition; (*Kauf*) purchase

bespielen [bəˈʃpiːlən] *vt* to record

bespitzeln [bəˈʃpɪtsəln] *vt* to spy on

besprechen [bəˈʃprɛçən] (*unreg*) *vt* to discuss; (*Tonband etc*) to record, to speak onto; (*Buch*) to review ♦ *vr* to discuss, to consult; **Besprechung** *f* meeting, discussion; (*von Buch*) review

besser [ˈbɛsər] *adj* better; **~gehen** △ (*unreg*) *vi unpers:* **es geht ihm ~** he is feeling better; **~n** *vt* to make better, to improve ♦ *vr* to improve; (*Menschen*) to reform; **B~ung** *f* improvement; **gute B~ung!** get well soon!; **B~wisser** (*-s, -*) *m* know-all

Bestand [bəˈʃtant] (*-(e)s, ̈e*) *m* (*Fortbestehen*) duration, stability; (*Kassen~*) amount, balance; (*Vorrat*) stock; **~ haben, von ~ sein** to last long, to endure

beständig [bəˈʃtɛndɪç] *adj* (*ausdauernd: auch fig*) constant; (*Wetter*) settled; (*Stoffe*) resistant; (*Klagen etc*) continual

Bestandsaufnahme [bəˈʃtantsaʊfnaːmə] *f* stocktaking

Bestandteil *m* part, component; (*Zutat*) ingredient

bestärken [bəˈʃtɛrkən] *vt:* **jdn in etw** *dat* **~** to strengthen *od* confirm sb in sth

bestätigen [bəˈʃteːtɪgən] *vt* to confirm; (*anerkennen, COMM*) to acknowledge; **Bestätigung** *f* confirmation; acknowledgement

bestatten [bəˈʃtatən] *vt* to bury

Bestattung *f* funeral

Bestattungsinstitut *nt* funeral director's

bestaunen [bəˈʃtaʊnən] *vt* to marvel at, gaze at in wonder

beste(r, s) [ˈbɛstə(r, s)] *adj* best; **so ist es am ~n** it's best that way; **am ~n gehst du gleich** you'd better go at once; **jdn zum ~n haben** to pull sb's leg; **einen Witz etc zum ~n geben** to tell a joke *etc*; **aufs ~** in the best possible way; **zu jds B~n** for the benefit of sb

bestechen [bəˈʃtɛçən] (*unreg*) *vt* to bribe; **bestechlich** *adj* corruptible; **Bestechung** *f* bribery, corruption

Besteck [bəˈʃtɛk] (*-(e)s, -e*) *nt* knife, fork and spoon, cutlery; (*MED*) set of instruments

bestehen [bəˈʃteːən] (*unreg*) *vi* to be; to exist; (*andauern*) to last ♦ *vt* (*Kampf, Probe, Prüfung*) to pass; **~ auf** +*dat* to insist on; **~**

⚠ *For information on spelling reform see page 615*

aus to consist of

bestehlen [bəˈʃteːlən] (*unreg*) *vt*: **jdn (um etw) ~** to rob sb (of sth)

besteigen [bəˈʃtaɪɡən] (*unreg*) *vt* to climb, to ascend; (*Pferd*) to mount; (*Thron*) to ascend

Bestell- [bəˈʃtɛl] *zW*: **~buch** *nt* order book; **b~en** *vt* to order; (*kommen lassen*) to arrange for see; (*nominieren*) to name; (*Acker*) to cultivate; (*Grüße, Auftrag*) to pass on; **~formular** *nt* order form; **~nummer** *f* order code; **~ung** *f* (COMM) order; (*Bestellen*) ordering

bestenfalls [ˈbɛstənˈfals] *adv* at best

bestens [ˈbɛstəns] *adv* very well

besteuern [bəˈʃtɔɪərn] *vt* (*jdn, Waren*) to tax

Bestie [ˈbɛstiə] *f* (*auch fig*) beast

bestimm- [bəˈʃtɪm] *zW*: **~en** *vt* (*Regeln*) to lay down; (*Tag, Ort*) to fix; (*beherrschen*) to characterize; (*vorsehen*) to mean; (*ernennen*) to appoint; (*definieren*) to define; (*veranlassen*) to induce; **~t** *adj* (*entschlossen*) firm; (*gewiß*) certain, definite; (*Artikel*) definite ♦ *adv* (*gewiß*) definitely, for sure; **suchen Sie etwas B~tes?** are you looking for something in particular?; **B~theit** *f* firmness; certainty; **B~ung** *f* (*Verordnung*) regulation; (*Festsetzen*) determining; (*Verwendungszweck*) purpose; (*Schicksal*) fate; (*Definition*) definition; **B~ungsland** *nt* (country of) destination; **B~ungsort** *m* (place of) destination

Bestleistung *f* best performance

bestmöglich *adj* best possible

bestrafen [bəˈʃtraːfən] *vt* to punish; **Bestrafung** *f* punishment

bestrahlen [bəˈʃtraːlən] *vt* to shine on; (MED) to treat with X-rays

Bestrahlung *f* (MED) X-ray treatment, radiotherapy

Bestreben [bəˈʃtreːbən] (**-s**) *nt* endeavour, effort

bestreiten [bəˈʃtraɪtən] (*unreg*) *vt* (*abstreiten*) to dispute; (*finanzieren*) to pay for, to finance

bestreuen [bəˈʃtrɔɪən] *vt* to sprinkle, to dust; (*Straße*) to grit

bestürmen [bəˈʃtʏrmən] *vt* (*mit Fragen, Bitten etc*) to overwhelm, to swamp

bestürzend [bəˈʃtʏrtsənd] *adj* (*Nachrichten*) disturbing

bestürzt [bəˈʃtʏrtst] *adj* dismayed

Bestürzung *f* consternation

Besuch [bəˈzuːx] (**-(e)s, -e**) *m* visit; (*Person*) visitor; **einen ~ machen bei jdm** to pay sb a visit *od* call; **~ haben** to have visitors; **bei jdm auf** *od* **zu ~ sein** to be visiting sb; **b~en** *vt* to visit; (SCH *etc*) to attend; **gut b~t** well-attended; **~er(in)** (**-s, -**) *m(f)* visitor, guest; **~szeit** *f* visiting hours *pl*

betätigen [bəˈtɛːtɪɡən] *vt* (*bedienen*) to work, to operate ♦ *vr* to involve o.s.; **sich als etw ~** to work as sth

Betätigung *f* activity; (*beruflich*) occupation; (TECH) operation

betäuben [bəˈtɔɪbən] *vt* to stun; (*fig: Gewissen*) to still; (MED) to anaesthetize

Betäubung *f* (*Narkose*): **örtliche ~** local anaesthetic

Betäubungsmittel *nt* anaesthetic

Bete [ˈbeːtə] *f*: **rote ~** beetroot (BRIT), beet (US)

beteilig- [bəˈtaɪlɪɡ] *zW*: **~en** *vr*: **sich ~en (an** +*dat*) to take part (in), to participate (in), to share (in); (*an Geschäft: finanziell*) to have a share (in) ♦ *vt*: **jdn ~en (an** +*dat*) to give sb a share *od* interest (in); **B~te(r)** *f(m)* (*Mitwirkender*) partner; (*finanziell*) shareholder; **B~ung** *f* participation; (*Anteil*) share, interest; (*Besucherzahl*) attendance

beten [ˈbeːtən] *vt, vi* to pray

beteuern [bəˈtɔɪərn] *vt* to assert; (*Unschuld*) to protest

Beton [beˈtõː] (**-s, -s**) *m* concrete

betonen [bəˈtoːnən] *vt* to stress

betonieren [betoˈniːrən] *vt* to concrete

Betonung *f* stress, emphasis

betr. *abk* (= *betrifft*) re

Betracht [bəˈtraxt] *m*: **in ~ kommen** to be considered *od* relevant; **etw in ~ ziehen** to take sth into consideration; **außer ~ bleiben** not to be considered; **b~en** *vt* to look at; (*fig*) to look at, to consider; **~er(in)** (**-s, -**) *m(f)* observer

⚠ *Informationen zur Rechtschreibreform Seite 615*

beträchtlich [bəˈtrɛçtlɪç] *adj* considerable

Betrachtung *f* (*Ansehen*) examination; (*Erwägung*) consideration

Betrag [bəˈtraːk] **(-(e)s, ̈-e)** *m* amount; **b~en** (*unreg*) *vt* to amount to ♦ *vr* to behave; **~en (-s)** *nt* behaviour

Betreff *m*: **~ Ihr Schreiben vom ...** re your letter of ...

betreffen [bəˈtrɛfən] (*unreg*) *vt* to concern, to affect; **was mich betrifft** as for me; **~d** *adj* relevant, in question

betreffs [bəˈtrɛfs] *präp +gen* concerning, regarding; (*COMM*) re

betreiben [bəˈtraɪbən] (*unreg*) *vt* (*ausüben*) to practise; (*Politik*) to follow; (*Studien*) to pursue; (*vorantreiben*) to push ahead; (*TECH: antreiben*) to drive

betreten [bəˈtreːtən] (*unreg*) *vt* to enter; (*Bühne etc*) to step onto ♦ *adj* embarrassed; **B~ verboten** keep off/out

Betreuer(in) [bəˈtrɔyər(ɪn)] **(-s, -)** *m(f)* (*einer Person*) minder; (*eines Gebäudes, Arbeitsgebietes*) caretaker; (*SPORT*) coach

Betreuung *f* care

Betrieb [bəˈtriːp] **(-(e)s, -e)** *m* (*Firma*) firm, concern; (*Anlage*) plant; (*Tätigkeit*) operation; (*Treiben*) traffic; **außer ~ sein** to be out of order; **in ~ sein** to be in operation

Betriebs- *zW*: **~ausflug** *m* works outing; **b~bereit** *adj* operational; **b~fähig** *adj* in working order; **~ferien** *pl* company holidays (*BRIT*), company vacation *sg* (*US*); **~klima** *nt* (working) atmosphere; **~kosten** *pl* running costs; **~rat** *m* workers' council; **b~sicher** *adj* safe (to operate); **~störung** *f* breakdown; **~system** *nt* (*COMPUT*) operating system; **~unfall** *m* industrial accident; **~wirtschaft** *f* economics

betrinken [bəˈtrɪŋkən] (*unreg*) *vr* to get drunk

betroffen [bəˈtrɔfən] *adj* (*bestürzt*) full of consternation; **von etw ~ werden** *od* **sein** to be affected by sth

betrüben [bəˈtryːbən] *vt* to grieve

betrübt [bəˈtryːpt] *adj* sorrowful, grieved

Betrug [bəˈtruːk] **(-(e)s)** *m* deception; (*JUR*) fraud

betrügen [bəˈtryːgən] (*unreg*) *vt* to cheat; (*JUR*) to defraud; (*Ehepartner*) to be unfaithful to ♦ *vr* to deceive o.s.

Betrüger (-s, -) *m* cheat, deceiver; **b~isch** *adj* deceitful; (*JUR*) fraudulent

betrunken [bəˈtrʊŋkən] *adj* drunk

Bett [bɛt] **(-(e)s, -en)** *nt* bed; **ins** *od* **zu ~ gehen** to go to bed; **~bezug** *m* duvet cover; **~decke** *f* blanket; (*Daunenbett*) quilt; (*Überwurf*) bedspread

Bettel- [ˈbɛtəl] *zW*: **b~arm** *adj* very poor, destitute; **~ei** [bɛtəˈlaɪ] *f* begging; **b~n** *vi* to beg

bettlägerig [ˈbɛtlɛːgərɪç] *adj* bedridden

Bettlaken *nt* sheet

Bettler(in) [ˈbɛtlər(ɪn)] **(-s, -)** *m(f)* beggar

Bett- *zW*: **~(t)uch** *nt* ⚠ sheet; **~vorleger** *m* bedside rug; **~wäsche** *f* bed linen; **~zeug** *nt* bed linen *pl*

beugen [ˈbɔygən] *vt* to bend; (*GRAM*) to inflect ♦ *vr* (*sich fügen*) to bow

Beule [ˈbɔylə] *f* bump, swelling

beunruhigen [bəˈʔʊnruːɪgən] *vt* to disturb, to alarm ♦ *vr* to become worried

Beunruhigung *f* worry, alarm

beurlauben [bəˈʔuːrlaʊbən] *vt* to give leave *od* a holiday to (*BRIT*), to grant vacation time to (*US*)

beurteilen [bəˈʔʊrtaɪlən] *vt* to judge; (*Buch etc*) to review

Beurteilung *f* judgement; review; (*Note*) mark

Beute [ˈbɔytə] **(-)** *f* booty, loot

Beutel (-s, -) *m* bag; (*Geld~*) purse; (*Tabak~*) pouch

Bevölkerung [bəˈfœlkərʊŋ] *f* population

bevollmächtigen [bəˈfɔlmɛçtɪgən] *vt* to authorize

Bevollmächtigte(r) *f(m)* authorized agent

bevor [bəˈfoːr] *konj* before; **~munden** *vt insep* to treat like a child; **~stehen** (*unreg*) *vi*: **(jdm) ~stehen** to be in store (for sb); **~stehend** *adj* imminent, approaching; **~zugen** *vt insep* to prefer

bewachen [bəˈvaxən] *vt* to watch, to guard

⚠ *For information on spelling reform see page 615*

Bewachung f (*Bewachen*) guarding; (*Leute*) guard, watch

bewaffnen [bə'vafnən] vt to arm

Bewaffnung f (*Vorgang*) arming; (*Ausrüstung*) armament, arms pl

bewahren [bə'va:rən] vt to keep; **jdn vor jdm/etw ~** to save sb from sb/sth

bewähren [bə'vɛ:rən] vr to prove o.s.; (*Maschine*) to prove its worth

bewahrheiten [bə'va:rhaɪtən] vr to come true

bewährt adj reliable

Bewährung f (*JUR*) probation

bewältigen [bə'vɛltɪgən] vt to overcome; (*Arbeit*) to finish; (*Portion*) to manage

bewandert [bə'vandərt] adj expert, knowledgeable

bewässern [bə'vɛsərn] vt to irrigate

Bewässerung f irrigation

bewegen [bə've:gən] vt, vr to move; **jdn zu etw ~** to induce sb to do sth; **~d** adj touching, moving

Beweg- [bə've:k] zW: **~grund** m motive; **b~lich** adj movable, mobile; (*flink*) quick; **b~t** adj (*Leben*) eventful; (*Meer*) rough; (*ergriffen*) touched

Bewegung f movement, motion; (*innere*) emotion; (*körperlich*) exercise; **~sfreiheit** f freedom of movement; (*fig*) freedom of action; **b~slos** adj motionless

Beweis [bə'vaɪs] (**-es, -e**) m proof; (*Zeichen*) sign; **b~en** [-zən] (*unreg*) vt to prove; (*zeigen*) to show; **~mittel** nt evidence

Bewerb- [bə'vɛrb] zW: **b~en** (*unreg*) vr to apply (for); **~er(in)** (**-s, -**) m(f) applicant; **~ung** f application

bewerkstelligen [bə'vɛrkʃtɛlɪgən] vt to manage, to accomplish

bewerten [bə've:rtən] vt to assess

bewilligen [bə'vɪlɪgən] vt to grant, to allow

Bewilligung f granting

bewirken [bə'vɪrkən] vt to cause, to bring about

bewirten [bə'vɪrtən] vt to feed, to entertain (to a meal)

bewirtschaften [bə'vɪrtʃaftən] vt to manage

Bewirtung f hospitality

bewog etc [bə'vo:k] vb siehe **bewegen**

bewohn- [bə'vo:n] zW: **~bar** adj habitable; **~en** vt to inhabit, to live in; **B~er(in)** (**-s, -**) m(f) inhabitant; (*von Haus*) resident

bewölkt [bə'vœlkt] adj cloudy, overcast

Bewölkung f clouds pl

Bewunder- [bə'vʊndər] zW: **~er** (**-s, -**) m admirer; **b~n** vt to admire; **b~nswert** adj admirable, wonderful; **~ung** f admiration

bewußt ⚠ [bə'vʊst] adj conscious; (*absichtlich*) deliberate; **sich** dat **einer Sache** gen **~ sein** to be aware of sth; **~los** ⚠ adj unconscious; **B~losigkeit** ⚠ f unconsciousness; **B~sein** ⚠ nt consciousness; **bei B~sein** conscious

bezahlen [bə'tsa:lən] vt to pay for

Bezahlung f payment

bezaubern [bə'tsaubərn] vt to enchant, to charm

bezeichnen [bə'tsaɪçnən] vt (*kennzeichnen*) to mark; (*nennen*) to call; (*beschreiben*) to describe; (*zeigen*) to show, to indicate; **~d** adj: **~d (für)** characteristic (of), typical (of)

Bezeichnung f (*Zeichen*) mark, sign; (*Beschreibung*) description

bezeugen [bə'tsɔygən] vt to testify to

Bezichtigung [bə'tsɪçtɪgʊŋ] f accusation

beziehen [bə'tsi:ən] (*unreg*) vt (*mit Überzug*) to cover; (*Bett*) to make; (*Haus, Position*) to move into; (*Standpunkt*) to take up; (*erhalten*) to receive; (*Zeitung*) to subscribe to, to take ♦ vr (*Himmel*) to cloud over; **etw auf jdn/etw ~** to relate sth to sb/sth; **sich ~ auf** +akk to refer to

Beziehung f (*Verbindung*) connection; (*Zusammenhang*) relation; (*Verhältnis*) relationship; (*Hinsicht*) respect; **~en haben** (*vorteilhaft*) to have connections od contacts; **b~sweise** adv or; (*genauer gesagt auch*) that is, or rather

Bezirk [bə'tsɪrk] (**-(e)s, -e**) m district

Bezug [bə'tsu:k] (**-(e)s, ̈-e**) m (*Hülle*) covering; (*COMM*) ordering; (*Gehalt*) income, salary; (*Beziehung*): **~ (zu)** relation(ship) (to); **in b~ auf** +akk with reference to; **~ nehmen auf** +akk to refer to

bezüglich [bə'tsy:klɪç] *präp +gen* concerning, referring to ♦ *adj* (*GRAM*) relative; **auf etw** *akk* ~ relating to sth

bezwecken [bə'tsvɛkən] *vt* to aim at

bezweifeln [bə'tsvaɪfəln] *vt* to doubt, to query

BH *m abk von* **Büstenhalter**

Bhf. *abk* (= *Bahnhof*) station

Bibel ['bi:bəl] (-, -n) *f* Bible

Biber ['bi:bər] (-s, -) *m* beaver

Biblio- [bi:blio] *zW:* ~**graphie** △ [-gra'fi:] *f* bibliography; ~**thek** [-'te:k] (-, -en) *f* library; ~**thekar(in)** [-te'ka:r(ɪn)] (-s, -e) *m(f)* librarian

biblisch ['bi:blɪʃ] *adj* biblical

bieder ['bi:dər] *adj* upright, worthy; (*Kleid etc*) plain

bieg- ['bi:g] *zW:* ~**en** (*unreg*) *vt, vr* to bend ♦ *vi* to turn; ~**sam** ['bi:k-] *adj* flexible; **B~ung** *f* bend, curve

Biene ['bi:nə] *f* bee

Bienenhonig *m* honey

Bienenwachs *nt* beeswax

Bier [bi:r] (-(e)s, -e) *nt* beer; ~**deckel** *m* beer mat; ~**garten** *m* beer garden; ~**krug** *m* beer mug; ~**zelt** *nt* beer tent

Biest [bi:st] (-s, -er) (*umg: pej*) *nt* (*Tier*) beast, creature; (*Mensch*) beast

bieten ['bi:tən] (*unreg*) *vt* to offer; (*bei Versteigerung*) to bid ♦ *vr* (*Gelegenheit*): **sich jdm** ~ to present itself to sb; **sich** *dat* **etw** ~ **lassen** to put up with sth

Bikini [bi'ki:ni] (-s, -s) *m* bikini

Bilanz [bi'lants] *f* balance; (*fig*) outcome; ~ **ziehen** (**aus**) to take stock (of)

Bild [bɪlt] (-(e)s, -er) *nt* (*auch fig*) picture; photo; (*Spiegel~*) reflection; ~**bericht** *m* photographic report

bilden ['bɪldən] *vt* to form; (*erziehen*) to educate; (*ausmachen*) to constitute ♦ *vr* to arise; (*erziehen*) to educate o.s.

Bilderbuch *nt* picture book

Bilderrahmen *m* picture frame

Bild- *zW:* ~**fläche** *f* screen; (*fig*) scene; ~**hauer** (-s, -) *m* sculptor; **b~hübsch** *adj* lovely, pretty as a picture; **b~lich** *adj*

figurative; pictorial; ~**schirm** *m* television screen; (*COMPUT*) monitor; **b~schön** *adj* lovely

Bildung [-dʊŋ] *f* formation; (*Wissen, Benehmen*) education

Billard ['bɪljart] (-s, -e) *nt* billiards *sg*; ~**kugel** *f* billiard ball

billig ['bɪlɪç] *adj* cheap; (*gerecht*) fair, reasonable; ~**en** ['bɪlɪgən] *vt* to approve of

Binde ['bɪndə] *f* bandage; (*Arm~*) band; (*MED*) sanitary towel; ~**gewebe** *nt* connective tissue; ~**glied** *nt* connecting link; ~**hautentzündung** *f* conjunctivitis; **b~n** (*unreg*) *vt* to bind, to tie; ~**strich** *m* hyphen

Bindfaden ['bɪnt-] *m* string

Bindung *f* bond, tie; (*Ski~*) binding

binnen ['bɪnən] *präp* (+*dat od gen*) within; **B~hafen** *m* river port; **B~handel** *m* internal trade

Bio- [bio-] *in zW* bio-; ~**chemie** *f* biochemistry; ~**graphie** △ [-gra'fi:] *f* biography; ~**laden** *m* wholefood shop; ~**loge** [-'lo:gə] (-n, -n) *m* biologist; ~**logie** [-lo'gi:] *f* biology; **b~logisch** [-'lo:gɪʃ] *adj* biological; ~**top** *m od nt* biotope

---

BIOLADEN

i A **Bioladen** is a shop specializing in environmentally-friendly products such as phosphate-free washing powders, recycled paper and organically-grown vegetables.

Birke ['bɪrkə] *f* birch

Birne ['bɪrnə] *f* pear; (*ELEK*) (light) bulb

SCHLÜSSELWORT

bis [bɪs] *präp +akk, adv* **1** (*zeitlich*) till, until; (*bis spätestens*) by; **Sie haben bis Dienstag Zeit** you have until *od* till Tuesday; **bis Dienstag muß es fertig sein** it must be ready for Tuesday; **bis auf weiteres** until further notice; **bis in die Nacht** into the night; **bis bald/gleich** see you later/soon **2** (*räumlich*) up to; **ich fahre bis Köln** I'm going to *od* I'm going as far as Cologne; **bis an unser Grundstück** (right *od* up) to

△ *For information on spelling reform see page 615*

our plot; **bis hierher** this far
3 (*bei Zahlen*) up to; **bis zu** up to
4: **bis auf etw** *akk* (*außer*) except sth; (*einschließlich*) including sth
♦ *konj* 1 (*mit Zahlen*) to; **10 bis 20** 10 to 20
2 (*zeitlich*) till, until; **bis es dunkel wird** till *od* until it gets dark; **von ... bis ...** from ... to ...

Bischof ['bɪʃɔf] (**-s, -̈e**) *m* bishop; **bischöflich** *adj* episcopal
bisher [bɪs'he:r] *adv* till now, hitherto; **~ig** *adj* till now
Biskuit [bɪs'kvi:t] (**-(e)s, -s** *od* **-e**) *m od nt* (fatless) sponge
Biß △ [bɪs] (**-sses, -sse**) *m* bite
biß △ *etc vb siehe* **beißen**
bißchen △ ['bɪsçən] *adj, adv* bit
Bissen ['bɪsən] (**-s, -**) *m* bite, morsel
bissig ['bɪsɪç] *adj* (*Hund*) snappy; (*Bemerkung*) cutting, biting
bist [bɪst] *vb siehe* **sein**
bisweilen [bɪs'vaɪlən] *adv* at times, occasionally
Bitte ['bɪtə] *f* request; **b~** *excl* please; (*wie bitte?*) (I beg your) pardon? ♦ *interj* (*als Antwort auf Dank*) you're welcome; **darf ich? - aber b~!** may I? - please do; **b~ schön!** it was a pleasure; **b~n** (*unreg*) *vt, vi*: **b~n (um)** to ask (for); **b~nd** *adj* pleading, imploring
bitter ['bɪtər] *adj* bitter; **~böse** *adj* very angry; **B~keit** *f* bitterness; **~lich** *adj* bitter
Blähungen ['blɛːʊŋən] *pl* (*MED*) wind *sg*
blamabel [bla'maːbəl] *adj* disgraceful
Blamage [bla'maːʒə] *f* disgrace
blamieren [bla'miːrən] *vr* to make a fool of o.s., to disgrace o.s. ♦ *vt* to let down, to disgrace
blank [blaŋk] *adj* bright; (*unbedeckt*) bare; (*sauber*) clean, polished; (*umg: ohne Geld*) broke; (*offensichtlich*) blatant
blanko ['blaŋko] *adv* blank; **B~scheck** *m* blank cheque
Blase ['blaːzə] *f* bubble; (*MED*) blister; (*ANAT*) bladder; **~balg** (**-(e)s, -bälge**) *m* bellows *pl*; **b~n** (*unreg*) *vt, vi* to blow;

~nentzündung *f* cystitis
Blas- ['blaːs] *zW*: **~instrument** *nt* wind instrument; **~kapelle** *f* brass band
blaß △ [blas] *adj* pale
Blässe ['blɛsə] (**-**) *f* paleness, pallor
Blatt [blat] (**-(e)s, -̈er**) *nt* leaf; (*von Papier*) sheet; (*Zeitung*) newspaper; (*KARTEN*) hand
blättern ['blɛtərn] *vi*: **in etw** *dat* **~** to leaf through sth
Blätterteig *m* flaky *od* puff pastry
blau [blau] *adj* blue; (*umg*) drunk, stoned; (*KOCH*) boiled; (*Auge*) black; **~er Fleck** bruise; **Fahrt ins B~e** mystery tour; **~äugig** *adj* blue-eyed
Blech [blɛç] (**-(e)s, -e**) *nt* tin, sheet metal; (*Back~*) baking tray; **~büchse** *f* tin, can; **~dose** *f* tin, can; **b~en** (*umg*) *vt, vi* to fork out; **~schaden** *m* (*AUT*) damage to bodywork
Blei [blaɪ] (**-(e)s, -e**) *nt* lead
Bleibe ['blaɪbə] *f* roof over one's head; **b~n** (*unreg*) *vi* to stay, to remain; **b~nd** *adj* (*Erinnerung*) lasting; (*Schaden*) permanent; **b~nlassen** △ (*unreg*) *vt* to leave (alone)
bleich [blaɪç] *adj* faded, pale; **~en** *vt* to bleach
Blei- *zW*: **b~ern** *adj* leaden; **b~frei** *adj* (*Benzin*) lead-free; **~stift** *m* pencil
Blende ['blɛndə] *f* (*PHOT*) aperture; **b~n** *vt* to blind, to dazzle; (*fig*) to hoodwink; **b~nd** (*umg*) *adj* grand; **b~nd aussehen** to look smashing
Blick [blɪk] (**-(e)s, -e**) *m* (*kurz*) glance, glimpse; (*Anschauen*) look; (*Aussicht*) view; **b~en** *vi* to look; **sich b~en lassen** to put in an appearance; **~fang** *m* eye-catcher
blieb *etc* [bliːp] *vb siehe* **bleiben**
blind [blɪnt] *adj* blind; (*Glas etc*) dull; **~er Passagier** stowaway; **B~darm** *m* appendix; **B~darmentzündung** *f* appendicitis; **B~enschrift** ['blɪndən-] *f* Braille; **B~heit** *f* blindness; **~lings** *adv* blindly
blink- ['blɪŋk] *zW*: **~en** *vi* to twinkle, to sparkle; (*Licht*) to flash, to signal; (*AUT*) to indicate ♦ *vt* to flash, to signal; **B~er** (**-s, -**) *m* (*AUT*) indicator; **B~licht** *nt* (*AUT*)

△ *Informationen zur Rechtschreibreform Seite 615*

indicator; (*an Bahnübergängen usw*) flashing light

blinzeln ['blɪntsəln] *vi* to blink, to wink

Blitz [blɪts] **(-es, -e)** *m* (flash of) lightning; **~ableiter** *m* lightning conductor; **b~en** *vi* (*aufleuchten*) to flash, to sparkle; **es b~t** (*MET*) there's a flash of lightning; **~licht** *nt* flashlight; **b~schnell** *adj* lightning ♦ *adv* (as) quick as a flash

Block [blɔk] **(-(e)s, -e)** *m* block; (*von Papier*) pad; **~ade** [blɔ'ka:də] *f* blockade; **~flöte** *f* recorder; **b~frei** *adj* (*POL*) unaligned; **~haus** *nt* log cabin; **b~ieren** [blɔ'ki:rən] *vt* to block ♦ *vi* (*Räder*) to jam; **~schrift** *f* block letters *pl*

blöd [blø:t] *adj* silly, stupid; **~eln** ['blø:dəln] (*umg*) *vi* to fool about (*fam*), to fool around; **B~sinn** *m* nonsense; **~sinnig** *adj* silly, idiotic

blond [blɔnt] *adj* blond, fair-haired

SCHLÜSSELWORT

---

bloß [blo:s] *adj* **1** (*unbedeckt*) bare; (*nackt*) naked; **mit der bloßen Hand** with one's bare hand; **mit bloßem Auge** with the naked eye

2 (*alleinig, nur*) mere; **der bloße Gedanke** the very thought; **bloßer Neid** sheer envy ♦ *adv* only, merely; **laß das bloß!** just don't do that!; **wie ist das bloß passiert?** how on earth did that happen?

Blöße ['blø:sə] *f* bareness; nakedness; (*fig*) weakness

bloßstellen *vt* to show up

blühen ['bly:ən] *vi* to bloom (*lit*), to be in bloom; (*fig*) to flourish; **~d** *adj* (*Pflanze*) blooming; (*Aussehen*) blooming, radiant; (*Handel*) thriving, booming

Blume ['blu:mə] *f* flower; (*von Wein*) bouquet

Blumen- *zW*: **~kohl** *m* cauliflower; **~topf** *m* flowerpot; **~zwiebel** *f* bulb

Bluse ['blu:zə] *f* blouse

Blut [blu:t] **(-(e)s)** *nt* blood; **b~arm** *adj* anaemic; (*fig*) penniless; **b~befleckt** *adj* bloodstained; **~bild** *nt* blood count;

~druck *m* blood pressure

Blüte ['bly:tə] *f* blossom; (*fig*) prime

Blut- *zW*: **b~en** *vi* to bleed; **~er** *m* (*MED*) haemophiliac; **~erguß** ⚠ *m* haemorrhage; (*auf Haut*) bruise

Blütezeit *f* flowering period; (*fig*) prime

Blut- *zW*: **~gruppe** *f* blood group; **b~ig** *adj* bloody; **b~jung** *adj* very young; **~probe** *f* blood test; **~spender** *m* blood donor; **~transfusion** *f* (*MED*) blood transfusion; **~ung** *f* bleeding, haemorrhage; **~vergiftung** *f* blood poisoning; **~wurst** *f* black pudding

Bö [bø:] **(-, -en)** *f* squall

Bock [bɔk] **(-(e)s, -e)** *m* buck, ram; (*Gestell*) trestle, support; (*SPORT*) buck; **~wurst** *f* type of pork sausage

Boden ['bo:dən] **(-s, -)** *m* ground; (*Fuß~*) floor; (*Meeres~, Faß~*) bottom; (*Speicher*) attic; **b~los** *adj* bottomless; (*umg*) incredible; **~nebel** *m* ground mist; **~personal** *nt* (*AVIAT*) ground staff; **~schätze** *pl* mineral resources; **~see** *m*: **der ~see** Lake Constance; **~turnen** *nt* floor exercises *pl*

Böe ['bø:ə] *f* squall

Bogen ['bo:gən] **(-s, -)** *m* (*Biegung*) curve; (*ARCHIT*) arch; (*Waffe, MUS*) bow; (*Papier*) sheet

Bohne ['bo:nə] *f* bean

bohnern *vt* to wax, to polish

Bohnerwachs *nt* floor polish

Bohr- ['bo:r] *zW*: **b~en** *vt* to bore; **~er** **(-s, -)** *m* drill; **~insel** *f* oil rig; **~maschine** *f* drill; **~turm** *m* derrick

Boiler ['bɔylər] **(-s, -)** *m* (hot-water) tank

Boje ['bo:jə] *f* buoy

Bolzen ['bɔltsən] **(-s, -)** *m* bolt

bombardieren [bɔmbar'di:rən] *vt* to bombard; (*aus der Luft*) to bomb

Bombe ['bɔmbə] *f* bomb

Bombenangriff *m* bombing raid

Bombenerfolg (*umg*) *m* smash hit

Bon [bɔŋ] **(-s, -s)** *m* voucher, chit

Bonbon [bõ'bõː] **(-s, -s)** *m od nt* sweet

Boot [bo:t] **(-(e)s, -e)** *nt* boat

Bord [bɔrt] **(-(e)s, -e)** *m* (*AVIAT, NAUT*) board

⚠ *For information on spelling reform see page 615*

♦ *nt* (*Brett*) shelf; **an ~** on board

Bordell [bɔrˈdɛl] (**-s, -e**) *nt* brothel

Bordstein *m* kerb(stone)

borgen [ˈbɔrgən] *vt* to borrow; **jdm etw ~** to lend sb sth

borniert [bɔrˈniːrt] *adj* narrow-minded

Börse [ˈbœːrzə] *f* stock exchange; (*Geld~*) purse; **~nmakler** *m* stockbroker

Borte [ˈbɔrtə] *f* edging; (*Band*) trimming

bös [bøːs] *adj* = **böse**

bösartig [ˈbøːz-] *adj* malicious

Böschung [ˈbœʃʊŋ] *f* slope; (*Ufer~ etc*) embankment

böse [ˈbøːzə] *adj* bad, evil; (*zornig*) angry

boshaft [ˈboːshaft] *adj* malicious, spiteful

Bosheit *f* malice, spite

Bosnien [ˈbɔsniən] (**-s**) *nt* Bosnia; **~ und Herzegowina** [-hɛrtsəˈgoːvina] *nt* Bosnia (and) Herzegovina

böswillig [ˈbøːsvɪlɪç] *adj* malicious

bot *etc* [boːt] *vb siehe* **bieten**

Botanik [boˈtaːnɪk] *f* botany; **botanisch** *adj* botanical

Bot- [boːt] *zW:* **~e** (**-n, -n**) *m* messenger; **~schaft** *f* message, news; (*POL*) embassy; **~schafter** (**-s, -**) *m* ambassador

Bottich [ˈbɔtɪç] (**-(e)s, -e**) *m* vat, tub

Bouillon [buˈljõ:] (**-, -s**) *f* consommé

Bowle [ˈboːlə] *f* punch

Box- [ˈbɔks] *zW:* **b~en** *vi* to box; **~er** (**-s, -**) *m* boxer; **~kampf** *m* boxing match

boykottieren [bɔykɔˈtiːrən] *vt* to boycott

brach *etc* [braːx] *vb siehe* **brechen**

brachte *etc* [ˈbraxtə] *vb siehe* **bringen**

Branche [ˈbrãːʃə] *f* line of business

Branchenverzeichnis *nt* yellow pages *pl*

Brand [brant] (**-(e)s, ¨e**) *m* fire; (*MED*) gangrene; **b~en** [ˈbrandən] *vi* to surge; (*Meer*) to break; **b~marken** *vt* to brand; (*fig*) to stigmatize; **~salbe** *f* ointment for burns; **~stifter** [-ʃtɪftər] *m* arsonist, fire raiser; **~stiftung** *f* arson; **~ung** *f* surf

Branntwein [ˈbrantvaɪn] *m* brandy

Brasilien [braˈziːliən] *nt* Brazil

Brat- [ˈbraːt] *zW:* **~apfel** *m* baked apple; **b~en** (*unreg*) *vt* to roast; to fry; **~en** (**-s, -**) *m* roast, joint; **~hähnchen** *nt* roast

chicken; **~huhn** *nt* roast chicken; **~kartoffeln** *pl* fried *od* roast potatoes; **~pfanne** *f* frying pan

Bratsche [ˈbraːtʃə] *f* viola

Bratspieß *m* spit

Bratwurst *f* grilled/fried sausage

Brauch [braʊx] (**-(e)s, Bräuche**) *m* custom; **b~bar** *adj* usable, serviceable; (*Person*) capable; **b~en** *vt* (*bedürfen*) to need; (*müssen*) to have to; (*umg: verwenden*) to use

Braue [ˈbraʊə] *f* brow

brauen [ˈbraʊən] *vt* to brew

Braue'rei [braʊəˈtiːraɪ] *f* brewery

braun [braʊn] *adj* brown; (*von Sonne auch*) tanned

Bräune [ˈbrɔynə] (**-**) *f* brownness; (*Sonnen~*) tan; **b~n** *vt* to make brown; (*Sonne*) to tan

braungebrannt ⚠ *adj* tanned

Brause [ˈbraʊzə] *f* shower bath; (*von Gießkanne*) rose; (*Getränk*) lemonade; **b~n** *vi* to roar; (*auch vr: duschen*) to take a shower

Braut [braʊt] (**-, Bräute**) *f* bride; (*Verlobte*) fiancée

Bräutigam [ˈbrɔytɪgam] (**-s, -e**) *m* bridegroom; fiancé

Brautpaar *nt* bride and (bride)groom, bridal pair

brav [braːf] *adj* (*artig*) good; (*ehrenhaft*) worthy, honest

bravo [ˈbraːvo] *excl* well done

BRD [beːˈɛrˈdeː] (**-**) *f abk* = **Bundesrepublik Deutschland**

BRD

ⓘ The **BRD** (*Bundesrepublik Deutschland*) is the official name for the Federal Republic of Germany. It comprises 16 *Länder* (*see* **Land**). It was formerly the name given to West Germany as opposed to East Germany (the **DDR**). The two Germanies were reunited on 3rd October 1990.

Brech- [ˈbrɛç] *zW:* **~eisen** *nt* crowbar; **b~en** (*unreg*) *vt, vi* to break; (*Licht*) to refract; (*fig: Mensch*) to crush; (*speien*) to vomit; **~reiz** m nausea, retching

Brei [braɪ] (-(e)s, -e) m (*Masse*) pulp; (*KOCH*) gruel; (*Hafer~*) porridge

breit [braɪt] adj wide, broad; **B~e** f width; (*bes bei Maßangaben*) breadth; (*GEOG*) latitude; **~en** vt: **etw über etw** akk **~en** to spread sth over sth; **B~engrad** m degree of latitude; **~machen** △ vr to spread o.s. out; **~treten** (*unreg*) (*umg*) vt to go on about

Brems- ['brɛms] zW: **~belag** m brake lining; **~e** [-zə] f brake; (*ZOOL*) horsefly; **b~en** [-zən] vi to brake; (*Auto*) to brake; (*fig*) to slow down; **~flüssigkeit** f brake fluid; **~licht** nt brake light; **~pedal** nt brake pedal; **~spur** f skid mark(s pl); **~weg** m braking distance

Brenn- ['brɛn] zW: **b~bar** adj inflammable; **b~en** (*unreg*) vi to burn, to be on fire; (*Licht, Kerze etc*) to burn ♦ vt (*Holz etc*) to burn; (*Ziegel, Ton*) to burn; (*Kaffee*) to roast; **darauf b~en, etw zu tun** to be dying to do sth; **~(n)essel** △ f stinging nettle; **~punkt** m (*PHYS*) focal point; (*Mittelpunkt*) focus; **~stoff** m fuel

brenzlig ['brɛntslɪç] adj (*fig*) precarious

Bretagne [brə'tanjə] f: **die ~** Brittany

Brett [brɛt] (-(e)s, -er) nt board, plank; (*Bord*) shelf; (*Spiel~*) board; **~er** pl (*SKI*) skis; (*THEAT*) boards; **Schwarze(s) ~** notice board; **~erzaun** m wooden fence; **~spiel** nt board game

Brezel ['breːtsəl] (-, -n) f pretzel

brichst etc [brɪçst] vb siehe **brechen**

Brief [briːf] (-(e)s, -e) m letter; **~freund** m penfriend; **~kasten** m letterbox; **b~lich** adj, adv by letter; **~marke** f (postage) stamp; **~papier** nt notepaper; **~tasche** f wallet; **~träger** m postman; **~umschlag** m envelope; **~waage** f letter scales; **~wechsel** m correspondence

briet etc [briːt] vb siehe **braten**

Brikett [bri'kɛt] (-s, -s) nt briquette

brillant [brɪl'jant] adj (*fig*) brilliant; **B~** (-en, -en) m brilliant, diamond

Brille ['brɪlə] f spectacles pl; (*Schutz~*) goggles pl; (*Toiletten~*) (toilet) seat;

~ngestell nt (spectacle) frames

bringen ['brɪŋən] (*unreg*) vt to bring; (*mitnehmen, begleiten*) to take; (*einbringen: Profit*) to bring in; (*veröffentlichen*) to publish; (*THEAT, CINE*) to show; (*RAD, TV*) to broadcast; (*in einen Zustand versetzen*) to get; (*umg: tun können*) to manage; **jdn dazu ~, etw zu tun** to make sb do sth; **jdn nach Hause ~** to take sb home; **jdn um etw ~** to make sb lose sth; **jdn auf eine Idee ~** to give sb an idea

Brise ['briːzə] f breeze

Brit- ['briːt] zW: **~e** m Briton; **~in** f Briton; **b~isch** adj British

bröckelig ['brœkəlɪç] adj crumbly

Brocken ['brɔkən] (-s, -) m piece, bit; (*Fels~*) lump of rock

brodeln ['broːdəln] vi to bubble

Brokkoli ['brɔkoli] pl (*BOT*) broccoli

Brombeere ['brɔmbeːrə] f blackberry, bramble (*BRIT*)

Bronchien ['brɔnçiən] pl bronchia(l tubes) pl

Bronchitis [brɔn'çiːtɪs] (-) f bronchitis

Bronze ['brõːsə] f bronze

Brosche ['brɔʃə] f brooch

Broschüre [brɔ'ʃyːrə] f pamphlet

Brot [broːt] (-(e)s, -e) nt bread; (*Laib*) loaf

Brötchen ['brøːtçən] nt roll

Bruch [brʊx] (-(e)s, -e) m breakage; (*zerbrochene Stelle*) break; (*fig*) split, breach; (*MED: Eingeweide~*) rupture, hernia; (*Bein~ etc*) fracture; (*MATH*) fraction

brüchig ['brʏçɪç] adj brittle, fragile; (*Haus*) dilapidated

Bruch- zW: **~landung** f crash landing; **~strich** m (*MATH*) line; **~stück** nt fragment; **~teil** m fraction; **~zahl** [brʊxtsaːl] f (*MATH*) fraction

Brücke ['brʏkə] f bridge; (*Teppich*) rug

Bruder ['bruːdər] (-s, ") m brother; **brüderlich** adj brotherly

Brühe ['bryːə] f broth, stock; (*pej*) muck

brüllen ['brʏlən] vi to bellow, to roar

brummen ['brʊmən] vi (*Bär, Mensch etc*) to growl; (*Insekt*) to buzz; (*Motoren*) to roar; (*murren*) to grumble

△ *For information on spelling reform see page 615*

brünett [brymɛt] *adj* brunette, dark-haired

Brunnen ['brʊnən] (**-s, -**) *m* fountain; (*tief*) well; (*natürlich*) spring

Brust [brʊst] (**-, "e**) *f* breast; (*Männer~*) chest

brüsten ['brʏstən] *vr* to boast

Brust- *zW:* **~kasten** *m* chest; **~schwimmen** *nt* breast-stroke

Brüstung ['brʏstʊŋ] *f* parapet

Brut [bru:t] (**-, -en**) *f* brood; (*Brüten*) hatching

brutal [bru'ta:l] *adj* brutal; **B~i'tät** *f* brutality

brüten ['bry:tən] *vi* (*auch fig*) to brood

Brutkasten *m* incubator

brutto ['brʊto] *adv* gross; **B~einkommen** *nt* gross salary; **B~gehalt** *nt* gross salary; **B~gewicht** *nt* gross weight; **B~lohn** *m* gross wages *pl*; **B~sozialprodukt** *nt* gross national product

BSE *f abk* (= *Bovine Spongiforme Enzephalopathie*) BSE

Bube ['bu:bə] (**-n, -n**) *m* (*Schurke*) rogue; (*KARTEN*) jack

Buch [bu:x] (**-(e)s, "er**) *nt* book; (*COMM*) account book; **~binder** *m* bookbinder; **~drucker** *m* printer

Buche *f* beech tree

buchen *vt* to book; (*Betrag*) to enter

Bücher- ['by:çər] *zW:* **~brett** *nt* bookshelf; **~ei** [-'rai] *f* library; **~regal** *nt* bookshelves *pl*, bookcase; **~schrank** *m* bookcase

Buch- *zW:* **~führung** *f* book-keeping, accounting; **~halter(in)** (**-s, -**) *m(f)* book-keeper; **~handel** *m* book trade; **~händler(in)** *m(f)* bookseller; **~handlung** *f* bookshop

Büchse ['bʏksə] *f* tin, can; (*Holz~*) box; (*Gewehr*) rifle; **~nfleisch** *nt* tinned meat; **~nmilch** *f* (*KOCH*) evaporated milk, tinned milk; **~nöffner** *m* tin od can opener

Buch- *zW:* **~stabe** (**-ns, -n**) *m* letter (of the alphabet); **b~stabieren** [bu:xʃta'bi:rən] *vt* to spell; **b~stäblich** ['bu:xʃtɛ:plɪç] *adj* literal

Bucht ['bʊxt] (**-, -en**) *f* bay

Buchung ['bu:xʊŋ] *f* booking; (*COMM*) entry

Buckel ['bʊkəl] (**-s, -**) *m* hump

bücken ['bʏkən] *vr* to bend

Bude ['bu:də] *f* booth, stall; (*umg*) digs *pl* (*BRIT*)

Büfett [by'fɛt] (**-s, -s**) *nt* (*Anrichte*) sideboard; (*Geschirrschrank*) dresser; **kaltes ~** cold buffet

Büffel ['bʏfəl] (**-s, -**) *m* buffalo

Bug [bu:k] (**-(e)s, -e**) *m* (*NAUT*) bow; (*AVIAT*) nose

Bügel ['by:gəl] (**-s, -**) *m* (*Kleider~*) hanger; (*Steig~*) stirrup; (*Brillen~*) arm; **~brett** *nt* ironing board; **~eisen** *nt* iron; **~falte** *f* crease; **b~frei** *adj* crease-resistant, noniron; **b~n** *vt, vi* to iron

Bühne ['by:nə] *f* stage; **~nbild** *nt* set, scenery

Buhruf ['bu:ru:f] *m* boo

buk *etc* [bu:k] *vb siehe* **backen**

Bulgarien [bʊl'ga:riən] *nt* Bulgaria

Bull- ['bʊl] *zW:* **~auge** *nt* (*NAUT*) porthole; **~dogge** *f* bulldog; **~dozer** (**-s, -**) *m* bulldozer; **~e** (**-n, -n**) *m* bull

Bumerang ['bu:məraŋ] (**-s, -e**) *m* boomerang

Bummel ['bʊməl] (**-s, -**) *m* stroll; (*Schaufenster~*) window-shopping; **~ant** [-'lant] *m* slowcoach; **~ei** [-'lai] *f* wandering; dawdling; skiving; **b~n** *vi* to wander, to stroll; (*trödeln*) to dawdle; (*faulenzen*) to skive, to loaf around; **~streik** ['bʊməlʃtraik] *m* go-slow

Bund¹ [bʊnt] (**-(e)s, "e**) *m* (*Freundschafts~ etc*) union; (*Organisation*) union; (*POL*) confederacy; (*Hosen~, Rock~*) waistband

Bund² (**-(e)s, -e**) *nt* bunch; (*Stroh~*) bundle

Bündel ['bʏndəl] (**-s, -**) *nt* bundle, bale; **b~n** *vt* to bundle

Bundes- ['bʊndəs] *in zW* Federal; **~bürger** *m* German citizen; **~hauptstadt** *f* Federal capital; **~kanzler** *m* Federal Chancellor; **~land** *nt* Land; **~liga** *f* football league; **~präsident** *m* Federal President; **~rat** *m* upper house of German Parliament; **~regierung** *f* Federal government; **~republik** *f* Federal Republic (of Germany); **~staat** *m* Federal state; **~straße** *f* Federal road; **~tag** *m* German

Parliament; **~wehr** f German Armed Forces pl; **b~weit** adj nationwide

---
BUNDESPRÄSIDENT

i The **Bundespräsident** is the head of state of the Federal Republic of Germany. He is elected every 5 years - no-one can be elected more than twice - by the members of the **Bundesversammlung**, a body formed especially for this purpose. His role is to represent Germany at home and abroad. In Switzerland the **Bundespräsident** is the head of the government, known as the **Bundesrat**. The **Bundesrat** is the Upper House of the German Parliament whose 68 members are nominated by the parliaments of the **Länder**. Its most important function is to approve federal laws concerned with the jurisdiction of the **Länder**, it can raise objections to other laws, but can be outvoted by the **Bundestag**. In Austria the **Länder** are also represented in the **Bundesrat**.

BUNDESTAG

i The **Bundestag** is the Lower House of the German Parliament and is elected by the people by proportional representation. There are 672 MPs, half of them elected directly from the first vote (**Erststimme**), and half from the regional list of parliamentary candidates resulting from the second vote (**Zweitstimme**). The **Bundestag** exercises parliamentary control over the government.

Bündnis ['byntnɪs] **(-ses, -se)** nt alliance
Bunker ['bʊŋkar] **(-s, -)** m bunker
bunt [bʊnt] adj coloured; (*gemischt*) mixed; **jdm wird es zu ~** it's getting too much for sb; **B~stift** m coloured pencil, crayon
Burg [bʊrk] **(-, -en)** f castle, fort
Bürge ['byrgə] **(-n, -n)** m guarantor; **b~n** vi: **b~n für** to vouch for
Bürger(in) ['byrgər(ɪn)] **(-s, -)** m(f) citizen;

member of the middle class; **~krieg** m civil war; **b~lich** adj (*Rechte*) civil; (*Klasse*) middle-class; (*pej*) bourgeois; **~meister** m mayor; **~recht** nt civil rights pl; **~schaft** f (*Vertretung*) City Parliament; **~steig** m pavement
Bürgschaft f surety; **~ leisten** to give security
Büro [by'ro:] **(-s, -s)** nt office; **~angestellte(r)** f(m) office worker; **~klammer** f paper clip; **~kra'tie** f bureaucracy; **b~'kratisch** adj bureaucratic; **~schluß** m office closing time
Bursche ['bʊrʃə] **(-n, -n)** m lad, fellow; (*Diener*) servant
Bürste ['byrstə] f brush; **b~n** vt to brush
Bus [bʊs] **(-ses, -se)** m bus; **~bahnhof** m bus/coach (*BRIT*) station
Busch [bʊʃ] **(-(e)s, "e)** m bush, shrub
Büschel ['byʃəl] **(-s, -)** nt tuft
buschig adj bushy
Busen ['bu:zən] **(-s, -)** m bosom; (*Meer~*) inlet, bay
Bushaltestelle f bus stop
Buße ['bu:sə] f atonement, penance; (*Geld*) fine
büßen ['by:sən] vi to do penance, to atone ♦ vt to do penance for, to atone for
Bußgeld ['bu:sgɛlt] nt fine; **~bescheid** m notice of payment due (*for traffic offence etc*)
Büste ['bystə] f bust; **~nhalter** m bra
Butter ['bʊtar] **(-)** f butter; **~blume** f buttercup; **~brot** nt (piece of) bread and butter; (*umg*) sandwich; **~brotpapier** nt greaseproof paper; **~dose** f butter dish; **~milch** f buttermilk; **b~weich** ['bʊtərvaɪç] adj soft as butter; (*fig, umg*) soft
b.w. abk (= *bitte wenden*) p.t.o.
bzgl. abk (= *bezüglich*) re
bzw. abk = **beziehungsweise**

⚠ *For information on spelling reform see page 615*

C, c

ca. [ka] *abk* (= *circa*) approx.

Café [ka'fe:] **(-s, -s)** *nt* café

Cafeteria [kafete'ri:a] **(-, -s)** *f* cafeteria

Camcorder **(-s, -)** *m* camcorder

Camp- ['kɛmp] *zW*: **c~en** *vi* to camp; **~er** **(-s, -)** *m* camper; **~ing** **(-s)** *nt* camping; **~ingführer** *m* camping guide (book); **~ingkocher** *m* camping stove; **~ingplatz** *m* camp(ing) site

CD-Spieler *m* CD (player)

Cello ['tʃɛlo] **(-s, -s** *od* **Celli)** *nt* cello

Celsius ['tsɛlziʊs] **(-)** *nt* centigrade

Champagner [ʃam'panjər] **(-s, -)** *m* champagne

Champignon ['ʃampɪnjõ] **(-s, -s)** *m* button mushroom

Chance ['ʃã:s(ə)] *f* chance, opportunity

Chaos ['ka:ɔs] **(-, -)** *nt* chaos; **chaotisch** [ka'o:tɪʃ] *adj* chaotic

Charakter [ka'raktər, *pl* karak'te:rə] **(-s, -e)** *m* character; **c~fest** *adj* of firm character, strong; **c~i'sieren** *vt* to characterize; **c~istisch** [karakte'rɪstɪʃ] *adj*: **c~istisch (für)** characteristic (of), typical (of); **c~los** *adj* unprincipled; **~losigkeit** *f* lack of principle; **~schwäche** *f* weakness of character; **~stärke** *f* strength of character; **~zug** *m* characteristic, trait

charmant [ʃar'mant] *adj* charming

Charme [ʃarm] **(-s)** *m* charm

Charterflug ['tʃartərflu:k] *m* charter flight

Chauffeur [ʃɔ'fø:r] *m* chauffeur

Chauvinist [ʃovi'nɪst] *m* chauvinist, jingoist

Chef [ʃɛf] **(-s, -s)** *m* head; (*umg*) boss; **~arzt** *m* senior consultant; **~in** (*umg*) *f* boss

Chemie [çe'mi:] **(-)** *f* chemistry; **~faser** *f* man-made fibre

Chemikalie [çemi'ka:liə] *f* chemical

Chemiker ['çe:mikər] **(-s, -)** *m* (industrial) chemist

chemisch ['çe:mɪʃ] *adj* chemical; **~e Reinigung** dry cleaning

Chicorée △ [ʃiko're:] **(-s)** *m od f* chicory

Chiffre ['ʃɪfrə] *f* (*Geheimzeichen*) cipher; (*in Zeitung*) box number

Chile ['tʃi:le] *nt* Chile

Chin- ['çi:n] *zW*: **~a** *nt* China; **~akohl** *m* Chinese leaves; **~ese** *m* Chinese; **~esin** *f* Chinese; **c~esisch** *adj* Chinese

Chip [tʃɪp] **(-s, -s)** *m* (*Kartoffelchips*) crisp (*BRIT*), chip (*US*); (*COMPUT*) chip; **~karte** *f* smart card

Chirurg [çi'rʊrg] **(-en, -en)** *m* surgeon; **~ie** [-'gi:] *f* surgery; **c~isch** *adj* surgical

Chlor [klo:r] **(-s)** *nt* chlorine; **~oform** **(-s)** *nt* chloroform

cholerisch [ko'le:rɪʃ] *adj* choleric

Chor [ko:r] **(-(e)s, ̈e)** *m* choir; (*Musikstück, THEAT*) chorus; **~al** [ko'ra:l] **(-s, -äle)** *m* chorale

Choreograph △ [koreo'gra:f] **(-en, -en)** *m* choreographer

Christ [krɪst] **(-en, -en)** *m* Christian; **~baum** *m* Christmas tree; **~entum** *nt* Christianity; **~in** *f* Christian; **~kind** *nt* ≈ Father Christmas; (*Jesus*) baby Jesus; **c~lich** *adj* Christian; **~us** **(-)** *m* Christ

Chrom [kro:m] **(-s)** *nt* (*CHEM*) chromium; chrome

Chron- ['kro:n] *zW*: **~ik** *f* chronicle; **c~isch** *adj* chronic; **c~ologisch** [-o'lo:gɪʃ] *adj* chronological

circa ['tsɪrka] *adv* about, approximately

Clown [klaʊn] **(-s, -s)** *m* clown

Cocktail ['kɔkte:l] **(-s, -s)** *m* cocktail

Cola ['ko:la] **(-, -s)** *f* Coke ®

Computer [kɔm'pju:tər] **(-s, -)** *m* computer; **~spiel** *nt* computer game

Cord [kɔrt] **(-s)** *m* cord, corduroy

Couch [kaʊtʃ] **(-, -es** *od* **-en)** *f* couch

Coupon [ku'põ] **(-s, -s)** *m* coupon

Cousin [ku'zɛ̃] **(-s, -s)** *m* cousin; **~e** [ku'zi:nə] *f* cousine

Creme [krɛ:m] **(-, -s)** *f* cream; (*Schuh~*) polish; (*Zahn~*) paste; (*KOCH*) mousse; **c~farben** *adj* cream(-coloured)

cremig ['kre:mɪç] *adj* creamy

Curry ['kari] **(-s)** *m od nt* curry powder; **~pulver** *nt* curry powder; **~wurst** *f* curried sausage

△ *Informationen zur Rechtschreibreform Seite 615*

D, d

da [da:] *adv* **1** (*örtlich*) there; (*hier*) here; **da draußen** out there; **da bin ich** here I am; **da, wo** where; **ist noch Milch da?** is there any milk left?
2 (*zeitlich*) then; (*folglich*) so
3: da haben wir Glück gehabt we were lucky there; **da kann man nichts machen** nothing can be done about it
♦ *konj* (*weil*) as, since

dabehalten (*unreg*) *vt* to keep
dabei [da'baɪ] *adv* (*räumlich*) close to it; (*noch dazu*) besides; (*zusammen mit*) with them; (*zeitlich*) during this; (*obwohl doch*) but, however; **was ist schon ~?** what of it?; **es ist doch nichts ~, wenn ...** it doesn't matter if ...; **bleiben wir ~** let's leave it at that; **es bleibt ~** that's settled; **das Dumme/Schwierige ~** the stupid/difficult part of it; **er war gerade ~, zu gehen** he was just leaving; **~sein** ⚠ (*unreg*) *vi* (*anwesend*) to be present; (*beteiligt*) to be involved; **~stehen** (*unreg*) *vi* to stand around

Dach [dax] (**-(e)s, "er**) *nt* roof; **~boden** *m* attic, loft; **~decker** (**-s, -**) *m* slater, tiler; **~fenster** *nt* skylight; **~gepäckträger** *m* roof rack; **~luke** *f* skylight; **~pappe** *f* roofing felt; **~rinne** *f* gutter

Dachs [daks] (**-es, -e**) *m* badger
dachte *etc* ['daxtə] *vb siehe* **denken**
Dackel ['dakəl] (**-s, -**) *m* dachshund
dadurch [da'dʊrç] *adv* (*räumlich*) through it; (*durch diesen Umstand*) thereby, in that way; (*deshalb*) because of that, for that reason ♦ *konj*: **~, daß** because

dafür [da'fy:r] *adv* for it; (*anstatt*) instead; **er kann nichts ~** he can't help it; **er ist bekannt ~** he is well-known for that; **was bekomme ich ~?** what will I get for

it?
dafürkönnen ⚠ (*unreg*) *vt*: **er kann nichts dafür** he can't help it
dagegen [da'ge:gən] *adv* against it; (*im Vergleich damit*) in comparison with it; (*bei Tausch*) for it/them ♦ *konj* however; **ich habe nichts ~** I don't mind; **ich war ~** I was against it; **~ kann man nichts tun** one can't do anything about it; **~halten** (*unreg*) *vt* (*vergleichen*) to compare with it; (*entgegnen*) to object to it; **~sprechen** (*unreg*) *vi*: **es spricht nichts ~** there's no reason why not

daheim [da'haɪm] *adv* at home; **D~** (**-s**) *nt* home
daher [da'he:r] *adv* (*räumlich*) from there; (*Ursache*) from that ♦ *konj* (*deshalb*) that's why

dahin [da'hɪn] *adv* (*räumlich*) there; (*zeitlich*) then; (*vergangen*) gone; **~'gegen** *konj* on the other hand; **~gehend** *adv* on this matter; **~gestellt** *adv*: **~gestellt bleiben** to remain to be seen; **~gestellt sein lassen** to leave open *od* undecided

dahinten [da'hɪntən] *adv* over there
dahinter [da'hɪntər] *adv* behind it; **~kommen** ⚠ (*unreg*) *vi* to get to the bottom of it

dalli ['dali] (*umg*) *adv* chop chop
damalig ['da:ma:lɪç] *adj* of that time, then
damals ['da:ma:ls] *adv* at that time, then
Dame ['da:mə] *f* lady; (*SCHACH, KARTEN*) queen; (*Spiel*) draughts *sg*; **~nbinde** *f* sanitary towel *od* napkin (*US*); **d~nhaft** *adj* ladylike; **~ntoilette** *f* ladies' toilet *od* restroom (*US*); **~nwahl** *f* ladies' excuse-me

damit [da'mɪt] *adv* with it; (*begründend*) by that ♦ *konj* in order that, in order to; **was meint er ~?** what does he mean by that?; **genug ~!** that's enough!

dämlich ['dɛ:mlɪç] (*umg*) *adj* silly, stupid
Damm [dam] (**-(e)s, "e**) *m* dyke; (*Stau~*) dam; (*Hafen~*) mole; (*Bahn~, Straßen~*) embankment
dämmen ['dɛmən] *vt* (*Wasser*) to dam up; (*Schmerzen*) to keep back
dämmer- *zW*: **~ig** *adj* dim, faint; **~n** *vi*

⚠ *For information on spelling reform see page 615*

(*Tag*) to dawn; (*Abend*) to fall; **D~ung** *f* twilight; (*Morgendämmerung*) dawn; (*Abenddämmerung*) dusk

Dampf [dampf] **(-(e)s, ⁻e)** *m* steam; (*Dunst*) vapour; **d~en** *vi* to steam

dämpfen [ˈdɛmpfən] *vt* (*KOCH*) to steam; (*bügeln*) to iron with a damp cloth; (*fig*) to dampen, to subdue

Dampf- *zW:* **~schiff** *nt* steamship; **~walze** *f* steamroller

danach [daˈnaːx] *adv* after that; (*zeitlich*) after that, afterwards; (*gemäß*) accordingly; according to which; according to that; **er sieht ~ aus** he looks it

Däne [ˈdɛːnə] **(-n, -n)** *m* Dane

daneben [daˈneːbən] *adv* beside it; (*im Vergleich*) in comparison; **~benehmen** (*unreg*) *vr* to misbehave; **~gehen** (*unreg*) *vi* to miss; (*Plan*) to fail

Dänemark [ˈdɛːnəmark] *nt* Denmark; **Dänin** *f* Dane; **dänisch** *adj* Danish

Dank [daŋk] **(-(e)s)** *m* thanks *pl*; **vielen** *od* **schönen ~** many thanks; **jdm ~ sagen** to thank sb; **d~** *präp* (*+dat od gen*) grateful to; **d~bar** *adj* grateful; (*Aufgabe*) rewarding; **~barkeit** *f* gratitude; **d~e** *excl* thank you, thanks; **d~en** *vi +dat* to thank; **d~enswert** *adj* (*Arbeit*) worthwhile; rewarding; (*Bemühung*) kind; **d~sagen** *vi* to express one's thanks

dann [dan] *adv* then; **~ und wann** now and then

daran [daˈran] *adv* on it; (*stoßen*) against it; **es liegt ~, daß ...** the cause of it is that ...; **gut/schlecht ~ sein** to be well-/badly off; **das Beste/Dümmste ~** the best/stupidest thing about it; **ich war nahe ~, zu ...** I was on the point of ...; **er ist ~ gestorben** he died from it *od* of it; **~gehen** (*unreg*) *vi* to start; **~setzen** *vt* to stake

darauf [daˈrauf] *adv* (*räumlich*) on it; (*zielgerichtet*) towards it; (*danach*) afterwards; **es kommt ganz ~ an, ob ...** it depends whether ...; **die Tage ~** the days following *od* thereafter; **am Tag ~** the next day; **~folgend** ⚠ *adj* (*Tag, Jahr*) next, following; **~legen** *vt* to lay *od* put on top

daraus [daˈraus] *adv* from it; **was ist ~ geworden?** what became of it?; **~ geht hervor, daß ...** this means that ...

Darbietung [ˈdaːrbiːtʊŋ] *f* performance

darf *etc* [darf] *vb siehe* **dürfen**

darin [daˈrɪn] *adv* in (there), in it

darlegen [ˈdaːrleːgən] *vt* to explain, to expound, to set forth; **Darlegung** *f* explanation

Darleh(e)n **(-s, -)** *nt* loan

Darm [darm] **(-(e)s, ⁻e)** *m* intestine; (*Wurst~*) skin; **~grippe** *f* (*MED*) gastric influenza *od* flu

darstell- [ˈdaːrʃtɛl] *zW:* **~en** *vt* (*abbilden, bedeuten*) to represent; (*THEAT*) to act; (*beschreiben*) to describe ♦ *vr* to appear to be; **D~er(in)** **(-s, -)** *m(f)* actor (actress); **D~ung** *f* portrayal, depiction

darüber [daˈryːbər] *adv* (*räumlich*) over it, above it; (*fahren*) over it; (*mehr*) more; (*währenddessen*) meanwhile; (*sprechen, streiten*) about it; **~ geht nichts** there's nothing like it

darum [daˈrʊm] *adv* (*räumlich*) round it ♦ *konj* that's why; **er bittet ~** he is pleading for it; **es geht ~, daß ...** the thing is that ...; **er würde viel ~ geben, wenn ...** he would give a lot to ...; **ich tue es ~, weil ...** I am doing it because ...

darunter [daˈrʊntər] *adv* (*räumlich*) under it; (*dazwischen*) among them; (*weniger*) less; **ein Stockwerk ~** one floor below (it); **was verstehen Sie ~?** what do you understand by that?

das [das] *def art* the ♦ *pron* that

Dasein [ˈdaːzain] **(-s)** *nt* (*Leben*) life; (*Anwesenheit*) presence; (*Bestehen*) existence

dasein ⚠ (*unreg*) *vi* to be there

daß ⚠ [das] *konj* that

dasselbe [dasˈzɛlbə] *art, pron* the same

dastehen [ˈdaːʃteːən] (*unreg*) *vi* to stand there

Datei [daˈtai] *f* file

Daten- [ˈdaːtən] *zW:* **~bank** *f* data base; **~schutz** *m* data protection; **~verarbeitung** *f* data processing

datieren [daˈtiːrən] *vt* to date

Dativ ['da:ti:f] (**-s, -e**) *m* dative (case)

Dattel ['datl] (**-, -n**) *f* date

Datum ['da:tʊm] (**-s, Daten**) *nt* date; **Daten** *pl* (*Angaben*) data *pl*

Dauer ['dauər] (**-, -n**) *f* duration; (*gewisse Zeitspanne*) length; (*Bestand, Fortbestehen*) permanence; **es war nur von kurzer ~** it didn't last long; **auf die ~** in the long run; (*auf längere Zeit*) indefinitely; **~auftrag** *m* standing order; **d~haft** *adj* lasting, durable; **~karte** *f* season ticket; **~lauf** *m* jog(ging); **d~n** *vi* to last; **es hat sehr lang gedauert, bis er ...** it took him a long time to ...; **d~nd** *adj* constant; **~parkplatz** *m* long-stay car park; **~welle** *f* perm, permanent wave; **~wurst** *f* German salami; **~zustand** *m* permanent condition

Daumen ['daumən] (**-s, -**) *m* thumb

Daune ['daunə] *f* down; **~ndecke** *f* down duvet, down quilt

davon [da'fɔn] *adv* of it; (*räumlich*) away; (*weg von*) from it; (*Grund*) because of it; **das kommt ~!** that's what you get; **~ abgesehen** apart from that; **~ sprechen/ wissen** to talk/know of *od* about it; **was habe ich ~?** what's the point?; **~kommen** (*unreg*) *vi* to escape; **~laufen** (*unreg*) *vi* to run away

davor [da'fo:r] *adv* (*räumlich*) in front of it; (*zeitlich*) before (that); **~ warnen** to warn about it

dazu [da'tsu:] *adv* (*legen, stellen*) by it; (*essen, singen*) with it; **und ~ noch** and in addition; **ein Beispiel/seine Gedanken ~** one example for/his thoughts on this; **wie komme ich denn ~?** why should I?; **~ fähig sein** to be capable of it; **sich ~ äußern** to say something on it; **~gehören** *vi* to belong to it; **~kommen** (*unreg*) *vi* (*Ereignisse*) to happen too; (*an einen Ort*) to come along

dazwischen [da'tsvɪʃən] *adv* in between; (*räumlich auch*) between (them); (*zusammen mit*) among them; **~kommen** (*unreg*) *vi* (*hineingeraten*) to get caught in it; **es ist etwas ~gekommen** something cropped up; **~reden** *vi* (*unterbrechen*) to interrupt;

(*sich einmischen*) to interfere; **~treten** (*unreg*) *vi* to intervene

Debatte [de'batə] *f* debate

Deck [dɛk] (**-(e)s, -s** *od* **-e**) *nt* deck; **an ~ gehen** to go on deck

Decke *f* cover; (*Bett~*) blanket; (*Tisch~*) tablecloth; (*Zimmer~*) ceiling; **unter einer ~ stecken** to be hand in glove; **~l** (**-s, -**) *m* lid; **d~n** *vt* to cover ♦ *vr* to coincide

Deckung *f* (*Schützen*) covering; (*Schutz*) cover; (*SPORT*) defence; (*Übereinstimmen*) agreement

Defekt [de'fɛkt] (**-(e)s, -e**) *m* fault, defect; **d~** *adj* faulty

defensiv [defɛn'si:f] *adj* defensive

definieren [defi'ni:rən] *vt* to define; **Definition** [definitsi'o:n] *f* definition

Defizit ['de:fitsɪt] (**-s, -e**) *nt* deficit

deftig ['dɛftɪç] *adj* (*Essen*) large; (*Witz*) coarse

Degen ['de:gən] (**-s, -**) *m* sword

degenerieren [degene'ri:rən] *vi* to degenerate

dehnbar ['de:nba:r] *adj* elastic; (*fig: Begriff*) loose

dehnen *vt, vr* to stretch

Deich [daɪç] (**-(e)s, -e**) *m* dyke, dike

deichseln (*umg*) *vt* (*fig*) to wangle

dein(e) [daɪn(ə)] *adj* (*Dein in Briefen*) your; **~e(r, s)** *pron* yours; **~er** (*gen von* **du**) *pron* of you; **~erseits** *adv* on your part; **~esgleichen** *pron* people like you; **~etwegen** *adv* (*für dich*) for your sake; (*wegen dir*) on your account; **~etwillen**

adv: **um ~etwillen = deinetwegen; ~ige**
pron: **der/die/das ~ige** yours

Deklination [deklinatsi'o:n] *f* declension

deklinieren [dekli'ni:rən] *vt* to decline

Dekolleté △ [dekɔl'te:] **(-s, -s)** *nt* low neckline

Deko- [deko] *zW*: **~rateur** [-ra'tø:r] *m* window dresser; **~ration** [-ratsi'o:n] *f* decoration; (*in Laden*) window dressing; **d~rativ** [-ra'ti:f] *adj* decorative; **d~rieren** [-'ri:rən] *vt* to decorate; (*Schaufenster*) to dress

Delegation [delegatsi'o:n] *f* delegation

delegieren [dele'gi:rən] *vt*: **~ an** +*akk* (*Aufgaben*) to delegate to

delikat [deli'ka:t] *adj* (*zart, heikel*) delicate; (*köstlich*) delicious

Delikatesse [delika'tɛsə] *f* delicacy; **~n** *pl* (*Feinkost*) delicatessen food; **~ngeschäft** *nt* delicatessen

Delikt [de'lıkt] **(-(e)s, -e)** *nt* (*JUR*) offence

Delle ['dɛlə] (*umg*) *f* dent

Delphin △ [dɛl'fi:n] **(-s, -e)** *m* dolphin

dem [de:m] *art dat von* **der**

Demagoge [dema'go:gə] **(-n, -n)** *m* demagogue

dementieren [demɛn'ti:rən] *vt* to deny

dem- *zW*: **~gemäß** *adv* accordingly; **~nach** *adv* accordingly; **~nächst** *adv* shortly

Demokrat [demo'kra:t] **(-en, -en)** *m* democrat; **~ie** [-'ti:] *f* democracy; **d~isch** *adj* democratic; **d~isieren** [-i'zi:rən] *vt* to democratize

demolieren [demo'li:rən] *vt* to demolish

Demon- [demɔn] *zW*: **~strant(in)** [-'strant(ın)] *m(f)* demonstrator; **~stration** [stratsi'o:n] *f* demonstration; **d~strativ** [-stra'ti:f] *adj* demonstrative; (*Protest*) pointed; **d~strieren** [-'stri:rən] *vt, vi* to demonstrate

Demoskopie [demosko'pi:] *f* public opinion research

Demut ['de:mu:t] **(-)** *f* humility

demütig ['de:my:tıç] *adj* humble; **~en** ['de:my:tıgən] *vt* to humiliate; **D~ung** *f* humiliation

demzufolge ['de:mtsu'fɔlgə] *adv* accordingly

den [de(:)n] *art akk von* **der**

denen ['de:nən] *pron dat pl von* **der; die; das**

Denk- ['dɛŋk] *zW*: **d~bar** *adj* conceivable; **~en (-s)** *nt* thinking; **d~en** (*unreg*) *vt, vi* to think; **d~faul** *adj* lazy; **~fehler** *m* logical error; **~mal (-s, ̈-er)** *nt* monument; **~malschutz** *m* protection of historical monuments; **unter ~malschutz stehen** to be classified as a historical monument; **d~würdig** *adj* memorable; **~zettel** *m*: **jdm einen ~zettel verpassen** to teach sb a lesson

denn [dɛn] *konj* for ♦ *adv* then; (*nach Komparativ*) than; **warum ~?** why?

dennoch ['dɛnnɔx] *konj* nevertheless

Denunziant [denuntsi'ant(ın)] *m* informer

Deodorant [de|odo'rant] **(-s, -s** *od* **-e)** *nt* deodorant

Deponie [depo'ni:] *f* dump

deponieren [depo'ni:rən] *vt* (*COMM*) to deposit

Depot [de'po:] **(-s, -s)** *nt* warehouse; (*Bus~, EISENB*) depot; (*Bank~*) strongroom, safe (*US*)

Depression [deprɛsi'o:n] *f* depression; **depres'siv** *adj* depressive

deprimieren [depri'mi:rən] *vt* to depress

SCHLÜSSELWORT

---

der [de(:)r] (*f* **die**, *nt* **das**, *gen* **des, der, des**, *dat* **dem, der, dem**, *akk* **den, die, das**, *pl* **die**) *def art* the; **der Rhein** the Rhine; **der Klaus** (*umg*) Klaus; **die Frau** (*im allgemeinen*) women; **der Tod/das Leben** death/life; **der Fuß des Berges** the foot of the hill; **gib es der Frau** give it to the woman; **er hat sich die Hand verletzt** he has hurt his hand

♦ *relativ pron* (*bei Menschen*) who, that; (*bei Tieren, Sachen*) which, that; **der Mann, den ich gesehen habe** the man who *od* whom *od* that I saw

♦ *demonstrativ pron* he/she/it; (*jener, dieser*) that; (*pl*) those; **der/die war es** it was him/her; **der mit der Brille** the one with

---

glasses; **ich will den (da)** I want that one

derart ['de:r|a:rt] *adv* so; *(solcher Art)* such; **~ig** *adj* such, this sort of

derb [dɛrp] *adj* sturdy; *(Kost)* solid; *(grob)* coarse

der- *zW:* **'der'gleichen** *pron* such; **'derjenige** *pron* he; she; it; the one (who); that (which); **'der'maßen** *adv* to such an extent, so; **~'selbe** *art, pron* the same; **'der'weil(en)** *adv* in the meantime; **'der'zeitig** *adj* present, current; *(damalig)* then

des [dɛs] *art gen von* **der**

desertieren [dezɛr'ti:rən] *vi* to desert

desgleichen ['dɛs'glaɪçən] *adv* likewise, also

deshalb ['dɛs'halp] *adv* therefore, that's why

Desinfektion [dɛzɪnfɛktsi'o:n] *f* disinfection; **~smittel** *nt* disinfectant

desinfizieren [dɛzɪnfi'tsi:rən] *vt* to disinfect

dessen ['dɛsən] *pron gen von* **der**; **das**; **~'ungeachtet** ⚠ *adv* nevertheless, regardless

Dessert [dɛ'sɛ:r] **(-s, -s)** *nt* dessert

destillieren [dɛstɪ'li:rən] *vt* to distil

desto ['dɛsto] *adv* all the, so much the; **~ besser** all the better

deswegen ['dɛs've:gən] *konj* therefore, hence

Detail [de'taɪ] **(-s, -s)** *nt* detail

Detektiv [detɛk'ti:f] **(-s, -e)** *m* detective

deut- ['dɔyt] *zW:* **~en** *vt* to interpret, to explain ♦ *vi:* **~en (auf** +*akk*) to point (to *od* at); **~lich** *adj* clear; *(Unterschied)* distinct; **D~lichkeit** *f* clarity; distinctness

Deutsch [dɔytʃ] *nt* German

deutsch *adj* German; **auf ~** in German; **D~e Demokratische Republik** German Democratic Republic, East Germany; **~es Beefsteak** ≈ hamburger; **D~e** *f* German; **D~er** *m* German; **ich bin D~er** I am German; **D~land** *nt* Germany

Devise [de'vi:zə] *f* motto, device; **~n** *pl* (*FIN*) foreign currency, foreign exchange

Dezember [de'tsɛmbər] **(-s, -)** *m* December

dezent [de'tsɛnt] *adj* discreet

dezimal [detsi'ma:l] *adj* decimal; **D~system** *nt* decimal system

d.h. *abk* (= *das heißt*) i.e.

Dia ['di:a] **(-s, -s)** *nt* (*PHOT*) slide, transparency

Diabetes [dia'be:tes] **(-, -)** *m* (*MED*) diabetes

Diagnose [dia'gno:zə] *f* diagnosis

diagonal [diago'na:l] *adj* diagonal

Dialekt [dia'lɛkt] **(-(e)s, -e)** *m* dialect; **d~isch** *adj* dialectal; *(Logik)* dialectical

Dialog [dia'lo:k] **(-(e)s, -e)** *m* dialogue

Diamant [dia'mant] *m* diamond

Diaprojektor ['di:aprojɛktɔr] *m* slide projector

Diät [di'ɛ:t] **(-, -en)** *f* diet

dich [dɪç] *(akk von du) pron* you; yourself

dicht [dɪçt] *adj* dense; *(Nebel)* thick; *(Gewebe)* close; *(undurchlässig)* (water)tight; *(fig)* concise ♦ *adv:* **~ an/bei** close to; **~bevölkert** ⚠ *adj* densely *od* heavily populated; **D~e** *f* density; thickness; closeness; (water)tightness; *(fig)* conciseness

dichten *vt* *(dicht machen)* to make watertight, to seal; *(NAUT)* to caulk; *(LITER)* to compose, to write ♦ *vi* to compose, to write

Dichter(in) **(-s, -)** *m(f)* poet; *(Autor)* writer; **d~isch** *adj* poetical

dichthalten *(unreg) (umg) vi* to keep one's mouth shut

Dichtung *f* (*TECH*) washer; (*AUT*) gasket; *(Gedichte)* poetry; *(Prosa)* (piece of) writing

dick [dɪk] *adj* thick; *(fett)* fat; **durch ~ und dünn** through thick and thin; **D~darm** *m* (*ANAT*) colon; **D~e** *f* thickness; fatness; **~flüssig** *adj* viscous; **D~icht** **(-s, -e)** *nt* thicket; **D~kopf** *m* mule; **D~milch** *f* soured milk

die [di:] *def art siehe* **der**

Dieb(in) [di:p, 'di:bɪn] **(-(e)s, -e)** *m(f)* thief; **d~isch** *adj* thieving; *(umg)* immense; **~stahl** **(-(e)s, ¨e)** *m* theft; **~stahlversicherung** *f* insurance against theft

Diele ['di:lə] *f* *(Brett)* board; *(Flur)* hall, lobby

dienen ['di:nən] *vi:* **(jdm) ~** to serve (sb)

⚠ *For information on spelling reform see page 615*

Diener (**-s, -**) m servant; **~in** f (maid)servant; **~schaft** f servants pl

Dienst [di:nst] (**-(e)s, -e**) m service; **außer ~** retired; **~ haben** to be on duty

Dienstag ['di:nsta:k] m Tuesday; **d~s** adv on Tuesdays

Dienst- zW: **~bote** m servant; **~geheimnis** nt official secret; **~gespräch** nt business call; **d~habend** ⚠ adj (Arzt) on duty; **~leistung** f service; **d~lich** adj official; **~mädchen** nt (house)maid; **~reise** f business trip; **~stelle** f office; **~vorschrift** f official regulations pl; **~weg** m official channels pl; **~zeit** f working hours pl; (MIL) period of service

dies [di:s] pron (demonstrativ: sg) this; (: pl) these; **~bezüglich** adj (Frage) on this matter; **~e(r, s)** ['di:zə(r, s)] pron this (one)

Diesel ['di:zəl] m (Kraftstoff) diesel

dieselbe [di:'zɛlbə] pron, art the same

Dieselmotor m diesel engine

diesig ['di:zɪç] adj drizzly

dies- zW: **~jährig** adj this year's; **~mal** adv this time; **~seits** präp +gen on this side; **D~seits** (**-**) nt this life

Dietrich ['di:trɪç] (**-s, -e**) m picklock

diffamieren [dıfa'mi:rən] (pej) vt to defame

Differenz [dıfə'rɛnts] (**-, -en**) f (Unterschied) difference; **~en** pl (Meinungsverschiedenheit) difference (of opinion); **d~ieren** vt to make distinctions in; **d~iert** adj (Mensch etc) complex

digital [digi'ta:l] adj digital

Dikt- [dıkt] zW: **~aphon** [-a'fo:n] ⚠ nt dictaphone; **~at** [-'ta:t] (**-(e)s, -e**) nt dictation; **~ator** [-'ta:tɔr] m dictator; **d~atorisch** [-a'to:rıʃ] adj dictatorial; **~atur** [-a'tu:r] f dictatorship; **d~ieren** [-'ti:rən] vt to dictate

Dilemma [di'lɛma] (**-s, -s** od **-ta**) nt dilemma

Dilettant [dile'tant] m dilettante, amateur; **d~isch** adj amateurish, dilettante

Dimension [dimɛnzi'o:n] f dimension

DIN f abk (= Deutsche Industrie-Norm) German Industrial Standard

Ding [dıŋ] (**-(e)s, -e**) nt thing, object;

⚠ Informationen zur Rechtschreibreform Seite 615

d~lich adj real, concrete; **~s(bums)** ['dıŋks(bʊms)] (**-**) (umg) nt thingummybob

Diplom [di'plo:m] (**-(e)s, -e**) nt diploma, certificate; **~at** [-'ma:t] (**-en, -en**) m diplomat; **~atie** [-a'ti:] f diplomacy; **d~atisch** [-'ma:tıʃ] adj diplomatic; **~ingenieur** m qualified engineer

dir [di:r] (dat von du) pron (to) you

direkt [di'rɛkt] adj direct; **D~flug** m direct flight; **D~or** m director; (SCH) principal, headmaster; **D~übertragung** f live broadcast

Dirigent [diri'gɛnt(ın)] m conductor

dirigieren [diri'gi:rən] vt to direct; (MUS) to conduct

Diskette [dıs'kɛtə] f diskette, floppy disk

Diskont [dıs'kɔnt] (**-s, -e**) m discount; **~satz** m rate of discount

Diskothek [dısko'te:k] (**-, -en**) f disco(theque)

diskret [dıs'kre:t] adj discreet; **D~ion** f discretion

diskriminieren [dıskrimi'ni:rən] vt to discriminate against

Diskussion [dıskusi'o:n] f discussion; debate; **zur ~ stehen** to be under discussion

diskutieren [dısku'ti:rən] vt, vi to discuss; to debate

Distanz [dıs'tants] f distance; **distan'zieren** vr: **sich von jdm/etw d~ieren** to distance o.s. from sb/sth

Distel ['dıstəl] (**-, -n**) f thistle

Disziplin [dıstsi'pli:n] f discipline

Dividende [divi'dɛndə] f dividend

dividieren [divi'di:rən] vt: (**durch etw**) **~** to divide (by sth)

DM [de:'|ɛm] abk (= Deutsche Mark) German Mark

D-Mark ['de:mark] f D Mark, German Mark

SCHLÜSSELWORT

doch [dɔx] adv **1** (dennoch) after all; (sowieso) anyway; **er kam doch noch** he came after all; **du weißt es ja doch besser** you know better than I do anyway; **und doch ...** and yet ...

2 (*als bejahende Antwort*) yes I do/it does *etc*; **das ist nicht wahr - doch!** that's not true - yes it is!

3 (*auffordernd*): **komm doch** do come; **laß ihn doch** just leave him; **nicht doch!** oh no!

4: sie ist doch noch so jung but she's still so young; **Sie wissen doch, wie das ist** you know how it is(, don't you?); **wenn doch** if only

♦ *konj* (*aber*) but; (*trotzdem*) all the same; **und doch hat er es getan** but still he did it

Docht [dɔxt] **(-(e)s, -e)** *m* wick
Dock [dɔk] **(-s, -s** *od* **-e)** *nt* dock
Dogge ['dɔgə] *f* bulldog
Dogma ['dɔgma] **(-s, -men)** *nt* dogma; **d~tisch** *adj* dogmatic
Doktor ['dɔktɔr, *pl* -'toːrən] **(-s, -en)** *m* doctor
Dokument [doku'mɛnt] *nt* document
Dokumentar- [dokumɛn'taːr] *zW:* **~bericht** *m* documentary; **~film** *m* documentary (film); **d~isch** *adj* documentary
Dolch [dɔlç] **(-(e)s, -e)** *m* dagger
dolmetschen ['dɔlmɛtʃən] *vt, vi* to interpret; **Dolmetscher(in) (-s, -)** *m(f)* interpreter
Dom [doːm] **(-(e)s, -e)** *m* cathedral
dominieren [domi'niːrən] *vt* to dominate
♦ *vi* to predominate
Donau ['doːnaʊ] *f* Danube
Donner ['dɔnər] **(-s, -)** *m* thunder; **d~n** *vi unpers* to thunder
Donnerstag ['dɔnərstaːk] *m* Thursday
doof [doːf] (*umg*) *adj* daft, stupid
Doppel ['dɔpəl] **(-s, -)** *nt* duplicate; (*SPORT*) doubles; **~bett** *nt* double bed; **d~deutig** *adj* ambiguous; **~fenster** *nt* double glazing; **~gänger (-s, -)** *m* double; **~punkt** *m* colon; **~stecker** *m* two-way adaptor; **d~t** *adj* double; **in d~ter Ausführung** in duplicate; **~verdiener** *m* person with two incomes; (*pl: Paar*) two-income family; **~zentner** *m* 100 kilograms;

~zimmer *nt* double room.
Dorf [dɔrf] **(-(e)s, ¨er)** *nt* village; **~bewohner** *m* villager
Dorn [dɔrn] **(-(e)s, -en)** *m* (*BOT*) thorn; **d~ig** *adj* thorny
Dörrobst ['dœroːpst] *nt* dried fruit
Dorsch [dɔrʃ] **(-(e)s, -e)** *m* cod
dort [dɔrt] *adv* there; **~ drüben** over there; **~her** *adv* from there; **~hin** *adv* (to) there; **~ig** *adj* of that place; in that town
Dose ['doːzə] *f* box; (*Blech~*) tin, can
Dosen *pl von* **Dose; Dosis**
Dosenöffner *m* tin *od* can opener
Dosis ['doːzɪs] **(-, Dosen)** *f* dose
Dotter ['dɔtər] **(-s, -)** *m* (egg) yolk
Drache ['draxə] **(-n, -n)** *m* (*Tier*) dragon
Drachen (-s, -) *m* kite; **~fliegen (-s)** *nt* hang-gliding
Draht [draːt] **(-(e)s, ¨e)** *m* wire; **auf ~ sein** to be on the ball; **d~ig** *adj* (*Mann*) wiry; **~seil** *nt* cable; **~seilbahn** *f* cable railway, funicular
Drama ['draːma] **(-s, Dramen)** *nt* drama, play; **~tiker (-s, -)** *m* dramatist; **d~tisch** [-'maːtɪʃ] *adj* dramatic
dran [dran] (*umg*) *adv:* **jetzt bin ich ~!** it's my turn now; *siehe* **daran**
Drang [draŋ] **(-(e)s, ¨e)** *m* (*Trieb*): **~ (nach)** impulse (for), urge (for), desire (for); (*Druck*) pressure
drängeln ['drɛŋəln] *vt, vi* to push, to jostle
drängen ['drɛŋən] *vt* (*schieben*) to push, to press; (*antreiben*) to urge ♦ *vi* (*eilig sein*) to be urgent; (*Zeit*) to press; **auf etw** *akk* **~** to press for sth
drastisch ['drastɪʃ] *adj* drastic
drauf [draʊf] (*umg*) *adv* = **darauf**; **D~gänger (-s, -)** *m* daredevil
draußen ['draʊsən] *adv* outside, out-of-doors
Dreck [drɛk] **(-(e)s)** *m* mud, dirt; **d~ig** *adj* dirty, filthy
Dreh- ['dreː] *zW:* **~arbeiten** *pl* (*CINE*) shooting *sg*; **~bank** *f* lathe; **~buch** *nt* (*CINE*) script; **d~en** *vt* to turn, to rotate; (*Zigaretten*) to roll; (*Film*) to shoot ♦ *vi* to turn, to rotate ♦ *vr* to turn; (*handeln von*):

⚠ *For information on spelling reform see page 615*

es d~t sich um ... it's about ...; **~orgel** f barrel organ; **~tür** f revolving door; **~ung** f (Rotation) rotation; (Umdrehung, Wendung) turn; **~zahl** f rate of revolutions; **~zahlmesser** m rev(olution) counter

drei [draɪ] num three; **D~eck** nt triangle; **~eckig** adj triangular; **~einhalb** num three and a half; **~erlei** adj inv of three kinds; **~fach** adj triple, treble ♦ adv three times; **~hundert** num three hundred; **D~königsfest** nt Epiphany; **~mal** adv three times; **~malig** adj three times

dreinreden ['draɪnreːdən] vi: **jdm ~** (dazwischenreden) to interrupt sb; (sich einmischen) to interfere with sb

Dreirad nt tricycle

dreißig ['draɪsɪç] num thirty

dreist [draɪst] adj bold, audacious

Dreistigkei f boldness, audacity

drei- zW: **~viertel** △ num three-quarters; **D~viertelstunde** f three-quarters of an hour; **~zehn** num thirteen

dreschen ['drɛʃən] (unreg) vt (Getreide) to thresh; (umg: verprügeln) to beat up

dressieren [drɛˈsiːrən] vt to train

drillen ['drɪlən] vt (bohren) to drill, to bore; (MIL) to drill; (fig) to train

Drilling m triplet

drin [drɪn] (umg) adv = **darin**

dringen ['drɪŋən] (unreg) vi (Wasser, Licht, Kälte): **~ (durch/in** +akk) to penetrate (through/into); **auf etw** akk **~** to insist on sth

dringend ['drɪŋənt] adj urgent

Dringlichkeit f urgency

drinnen ['drɪnən] adv inside, indoors

dritte(r, s) [drɪtə(r, s)] adj third; **~ Welt** Third World; **D~s Reich** Third Reich; **D~l** (-s, -) nt third; **~ns** adv thirdly

DRK [deːˈʔɛrˈkaː] nt abk (= Deutsches Rotes Kreuz) German Red Cross

droben ['droːbən] adv above, up there

Droge ['droːgə] f drug

drogen zW: **~abhängig** adj addicted to drugs; **D~händler** m drug pedlar, pusher

Drogerie [drogəˈriː] f chemist's shop

DROGERIE

ⓘ The **Drogerie** as opposed to the **Apotheke** sells medicines not requiring a prescription. It tends to be cheaper and also sells cosmetics, perfume and toiletries.

Drogist [droˈgɪst] m pharmacist, chemist

drohen ['droːən] vi: **(jdm) ~** to threaten (sb)

dröhnen ['drøːnən] vi (Motor) to roar; (Stimme, Musik) to ring, to resound

Drohung ['droːʊŋ] f threat

drollig ['drɔlɪç] adj droll

Drossel ['drɔsəl] (-, -n) f thrush

drüben ['dryːbən] adv over there, on the other side

drüber ['dryːbər] (umg) adv = **darüber**

Druck [drʊk] (-(e)s, -e) m (PHYS: Zwang) pressure; (TYP: Vorgang) printing; (: Produkt) print; (fig: Belastung) burden, weight; **~buchstabe** m block letter

drücken ['drʏkən] vt (Knopf, Hand) to press; (zu eng sein) to pinch; (fig: Preise) to keep down; (: belasten) to oppress, to weigh down ♦ vi to press; to pinch ♦ vr: **sich vor etw** dat **~** to get out of (doing) sth; **~d** adj oppressive

Drucker (-s, -) m printer

Drücker (-s, -) m button; (Tür~) handle; (Gewehr~) trigger

Druck- zW: **~e'rei** f printing works, press; **~erschwärze** f printer's ink; **~fehler** m misprint; **~knopf** m press stud, snap fastener; **~sache** f printed matter; **~schrift** f block od printed letters pl

drum [drʊm] (umg) adv = **darum**

drunten ['drʊntən] adv below, down there

Drüse ['dryːzə] f gland

Dschungel ['dʒʊŋəl] (-s, -) m jungle

du [duː] (nom) pron (Du in Briefen) you; **D~sagen** = **duzen**

Dübel ['dyːbəl] (-s, -) m Rawlplug ®

ducken ['dʊkən] vt (Kopf, Person) to duck; (fig) to take down a peg or two ♦ vr to duck

Duckmäuser ['dʊkmɔʏzər] (-s, -) *m* yes man

Dudelsack ['du:dəlzak] *m* bagpipes *pl*

Duell [du'ɛl] (-s, -e) *nt* duel

Duft [dʊft] (-(e)s, "e) *m* scent, odour; **d~en** *vi* to smell, to be fragrant; **d~ig** *adj* (*Stoff, Kleid*) delicate, diaphanous

dulden ['dʊldən] *vt* to suffer; (*zulassen*) to tolerate ♦ *vi* to suffer

dumm [dʊm] *adj* stupid; (*ärgerlich*) annoying; **der D~e sein** to be the loser; **~erweise** *adv* stupidly; **D~heit** *f* stupidity; (*Tat*) blunder, stupid mistake; **D~kopf** *m* blockhead

dumpf [dʊmpf] *adj* (*Ton*) hollow, dull; (*Luft*) musty; (*Erinnerung, Schmerz*) vague

Düne ['dy:nə] *f* dune

düngen ['dyŋən] *vt* to manure

Dünger (-s, -) *m* dung, manure; (*künstlich*) fertilizer

dunkel ['dʊŋkəl] *adj* dark; (*Stimme*) deep; (*Ahnung*) vague; (*rätselhaft*) obscure; (*verdächtig*) dubious, shady; **im ~n tappen** (*fig*) to grope in the dark

Dunkel- *zW*: **~heit** *f* darkness; (*fig*) obscurity; **~kammer** *f* (*PHOT*) darkroom; **d~n** *vi unpers* to grow dark; **~ziffer** *f* estimated number of unreported cases

dünn [dyn] *adj* thin; **~flüssig** *adj* watery, thin

Dunst [dʊnst] (-es, "e) *m* vapour; (*Wetter*) haze

dünsten ['dynstən] *vt* to steam

dunstig ['dʊnstɪç] *adj* vaporous; (*Wetter*) hazy, misty

Duplikat [dupli'ka:t] (-(e)s, -e) *nt* duplicate

Dur [du:r] (-, -) *nt* (*MUS*) major

SCHLÜSSELWORT

durch [dʊrç] *präp +akk* **1** (*hindurch*) through; **durch den Urwald** through the jungle; **durch die ganze Welt reisen** to travel all over the world

2 (*mittels*) through, by (means of); (*aufgrund*) due to, owing to; **Tod durch Herzschlag/den Strang** death from a heart attack/by hanging; **durch die Post**

by post; **durch seine Bemühungen** through his efforts

♦ *adv* **1** (*hindurch*) through; **die ganze Nacht durch** all through the night; **den Sommer durch** during the summer; **8 Uhr durch** past 8 o'clock; **durch und durch** completely

2 (*durchgebraten etc*): **(gut) durch** well-done

---

durch- *zW*: **~arbeiten** *vt, vi* to work through ♦ *vr* to work one's way through; **~'aus** *adv* completely; (*unbedingt*) definitely; **~aus nicht** absolutely not

Durchblick ['dʊrçblɪk] *m* view; (*fig*) comprehension; **d~en** *vi* to look through; (*umg: verstehen*): **(bei etw) d~en** to understand (sth); **etw d~en lassen** (*fig*) to hint at sth

durchbrechen ['dʊrçbrɛçən] (*unreg*) *vt, vi* to break

durch'brechen ['dʊrçbrɛçən] (*unreg*) *vt insep* (*Schranken*) to break through; (*Schallmauer*) to break; (*Gewohnheit*) to break free from

durchbrennen ['dʊrçbrɛnən] (*unreg*) *vi* (*Draht, Sicherung*) to burn through; (*umg*) to run away

durchbringen (*unreg*) *vt* (*Kranken*) to pull through; (*umg: Familie*) to support; (*durchsetzen: Antrag, Kandidat*) to get through; (*vergeuden: Geld*) to get through, to squander

Durchbruch ['dʊrçbrʊx] *m* (*Öffnung*) opening; (*MIL*) breach; (*von Gefühlen etc*) eruption; (*der Zähne*) cutting; (*fig*) breakthrough; **zum ~ kommen** to break through

durch- *zW*: **~dacht** [-'daxt] *adj* well thought-out; **~'denken** (*unreg*) *vt* to think out; **~drehen** *vt* (*Fleisch*) to mince ♦ *vi* (*umg*) to crack up

durcheinander [dʊrçai'nandər] *adv* in a mess, in confusion; (*umg: verwirrt*) confused; **D~** (-s) *nt* (*Verwirrung*) confusion; (*Unordnung*) mess; **~bringen** ⚠ (*unreg*) *vt* to mess up; (*verwirren*) to confuse; **~reden** ⚠ *vi* to talk at the same

⚠ *For information on spelling reform see page 615*

time
durch- *zW:* **~fahren** (*unreg*) *vi* (*durch Tunnel usw*) to drive through; (*ohne Unterbrechung*) to drive straight through; (*ohne anzuhalten*): **der Zug fährt bis Hamburg ~** the train runs direct to Hamburg; (*ohne Umsteigen*): **können wir ~fahren?** can we go direct?, can we go non-stop?; **D~fahrt** *f* transit; (*Verkehr*) thoroughfare; **D~fall** *m* (*MED*) diarrhoea; **~fallen** (*unreg*) *vi* to fall through; (*in Prüfung*) to fail; **~finden** (*unreg*) *vr* to find one's way through; **~fragen** *vr* to find one's way by asking

durchführ- ['dʊrçfyːr] *zW:* **~bar** *adj* feasible, practicable; **~en** *vt* to carry out; **D~ung** *f* execution, performance

Durchgang ['dʊrçgaŋ] *m* passage(way); (*bei Produktion, Versuch*) run; (*SPORT*) round; (*bei Wahl*) ballot; **„~ verboten"** "no thoroughfare"

Durchgangsverkehr *m* through traffic

durchgefroren ['dʊrçgəfroːrən] *adj* (*Mensch*) frozen stiff

durchgehen ['dʊrçgeːən] (*unreg*) *vt* (*behandeln*) to go over ♦ *vi* to go through; (*ausreißen: Pferd*) to break loose; (*Mensch*) to run away; **mein Temperament ging mit mir durch** my temper got the better of me; **jdm etw ~ lassen** to let sb get away with sth; **~d** *adj* (*Zug*) through; (*Öffnungszeiten*) continuous

durch- *zW:* **~greifen** (*unreg*) *vi* to take strong action; **~halten** (*unreg*) *vi* to last out ♦ *vt* to keep up; **~kommen** (*unreg*) *vi* to get through; (*überleben*) to pull through; **~'kreuzen** *vt insep* to thwart, to frustrate; **~lassen** (*unreg*) *vt* (*Person*) to let through; (*Wasser*) to let in; **~lesen** (*unreg*) *vt* to read through; **~'leuchten** *vt insep* to X-ray; **~machen** *vt* to go through; **die Nacht ~machen** to make a night of it

Durchmesser (**-s, -**) *m* diameter

durch- *zW:* **~'nässen** *vt insep* to soak (through); **~nehmen** (*unreg*) *vt* to go over; **~numerieren** ⚠ *vt* to number consecutively; **~queren** [dʊrç'kveːrən] *vt insep* to cross; **D~reise** *f* transit; **auf der**

D~reise passing through; (*Güter*) in transit; **~ringen** (*unreg*) *vr* to reach a decision after a long struggle

durchs [dʊrçs] = **durch das**

Durchsage ['dʊrçzaːgə] *f* intercom *od* radio announcement

durchschauen ['dʊrçʃauən] *vi* to look *od* see through; (*Person, Lüge*) to see through

durchscheinen ['dʊrçʃaɪnən] (*unreg*) *vi* to shine through; **~d** *adj* translucent

Durchschlag ['dʊrçʃlaːk] *m* (*Doppel*) carbon copy; (*Sieb*) strainer; **d~en** [-gən] (*unreg*) *vt* (*entzweischlagen*) to split (in two); (*sieben*) to sieve ♦ *vi* (*zum Vorschein kommen*) to emerge, to come out ♦ *vr* to get by

durchschlagend *adj* resounding

durchschneiden ['dʊrçʃnaɪdən] (*unreg*) *vt* to cut through

Durchschnitt ['dʊrçʃnɪt] *m* (*Mittelwert*) average; **über/unter dem ~** above/below average; **im ~** on average; **d~lich** *adj* average ♦ *adv* on average

Durchschnittswert *m* average

durch- *zW:* **D~schrift** *f* copy; **~sehen** (*unreg*) *vt* to look through; **~setzen** *vt* to enforce ♦ *vr* (*Erfolg haben*) to succeed; (*sich behaupten*) to get one's way; **seinen Kopf ~setzen** to get one's way; **~'setzen** *vt insep* to mix

Durchsicht ['dʊrçzɪçt] *f* looking through, checking; **d~ig** *adj* transparent

durch- *zW:* '**durchsprechen** (*unreg*) *vt* to talk over; '**durchstehen** (*unreg*) *vt* to live through; **~stellen** *vt* (*an Telefon*) to put through; **~stöbern** (*auch untr*) *vt* (*Kisten*) to rummage through, to rifle through; (*Haus, Wohnung*) to ransack; '**durchstreichen** (*unreg*) *vt* to cross out; **~'suchen** *vt insep* to search; **D~'suchung** *f* search; **~'wachsen** *adj* (*Speck*) streaky; (*fig: mittelmäßig*) so-so; **D~wahl** *f* (*TEL*) direct dialling; **~weg** *adv* throughout, completely; **~ziehen** (*unreg*) *vt* (*Faden*) to draw through ♦ *vi* to pass through; **D~zug** *m* (*Luft*) draught; (*von Truppen, Vögeln*) passage

⚠ *Informationen zur Rechtschreibreform Seite 615*

SCHLÜSSELWORT

dürfen ['dʏrfən] (*unreg*) *vi* **1** (*Erlaubnis haben*) to be allowed to; **ich darf das** I'm allowed to (do that); **darf ich?** may I?; **darf ich ins Kino?** can *od* may I go to the cinema?; **es darf geraucht werden** you may smoke

2 (*in Verneinungen*): **er darf das nicht** he's not allowed to (do that); **das darf nicht geschehen** that must not happen; **da darf sie sich nicht wundern** that shouldn't surprise her

3 (*in Höflichkeitsformeln*): **darf ich Sie bitten, das zu tun?** may *od* could I ask you to do that?; **was darf es sein?** what can I do for you?

4 (*können*): **das dürfen Sie mir glauben** you can believe me

5 (*Möglichkeit*): **das dürfte genug sein** that should be enough; **es dürfte Ihnen bekannt sein, daß ...** as you will probably know ...

---

dürftig ['dʏrftıç] *adj* (*ärmlich*) needy, poor; (*unzulänglich*) inadequate

dürr [dʏr] *adj* dried-up; (*Land*) arid; (*mager*) skinny, gaunt

Dürre *f* aridity; (*Zeit*) drought; (*Magerkeit*) skinniness

Durst [dʊrst] (**-(e)s**) *m* thirst; **~ haben** to be thirsty

durstig *adj* thirsty

Dusche ['dʊʃə] *f* shower; **d~en** *vi, vr* to have a shower

Düse ['dy:zə] *f* nozzle; (*Flugzeug~*) jet

Düsen- *zW*: **~antrieb** *m* jet propulsion; **~flugzeug** *nt* jet (plane); **~jäger** *m* jet fighter

Dussel ['dʊsəl] (**-s, -**) *m* (*umg*) twit

düster ['dy:stər] *adj* dark; (*Gedanken, Zukunft*) gloomy

Dutzend ['dʊtsənt] (**-s, -e**) *nt* dozen; **d~(e)mal** *adv* a dozen times

duzen ['du:tsən] *vt*: **(jdn) ~** to use the familiar form of address "du" (to *od* with sb)

DUZEN

i There are two different forms of address in Germany: du and Sie. **Duzen** means addressing someone as 'du' - used with children, family and close friends - and siezen means addressing someone as 'Sie' - used for all grown-ups and older teenagers. Students almost always use 'du' to each other.

Dynamik [dy'na:mık] *f* (*PHYS*) dynamics *sg*; (*fig: Schwung*) momentum; (*von Mensch*) dynamism; **dynamisch** *adj* (*auch fig*) dynamic

Dynamit [dyna'mi:t] (**-s**) *nt* dynamite

Dynamo [dy'na:mo] (**-s, -s**) *m* dynamo

DZ *nt abk* = **Doppelzimmer**

D-Zug ['de:tsu:k] *m* through train

E, e

Ebbe ['ɛbə] *f* low tide

eben ['e:bən] *adj* level, flat; (*glatt*) smooth ♦ *adv* just; (*bestätigend*) exactly; **~ deswegen** just because of that; **~bürtig** *adj*: **jdm ~bürtig sein** to be sb's equal; **E~e** *f* plain; (*fig*) level; **~falls** *adv* likewise; **~so** *adv* just as

Eber ['e:bər] (**-s, -**) *m* boar

ebnen ['e:bnən] *vt* to level

Echo ['ɛço] (**-s, -s**) *nt* echo

echt [ɛçt] *adj* genuine; (*typisch*) typical; **E~heit** *f* genuineness

Eck- ['ɛk] *zW*: **~ball** *m* corner (kick); **~e** *f* corner; (*MATH*) angle; **e~ig** *adj* angular; **~zahn** *m* eye tooth

ECU [e'ky:] (**-, -s**) *m* (*FIN*) ECU

edel ['e:dəl] *adj* noble; **E~metall** *nt* rare metal; **E~stahl** *m* high-grade steel; **E~stein** *m* precious stone

EDV [e:de:'fau] (**-**) *f abk* (= *elektronische Datenverarbeitung*) electronic data processing

Efeu ['e:fɔy] (**-s**) *m* ivy

Effekt [ɛ'fɛkt] (**-s, -e**) *m* effect

⚠ *For information on spelling reform see page 615*

Effekten [ɛˈfɛktən] *pl* stocks

effektiv [ɛfɛkˈtiːf] *adj* effective, actual

EG [ˈeːˈɡeː] *f abk* (= *Europäische Gemeinschaft*) EC

egal [eˈɡaːl] *adj* all the same

Ego- [eːɡo] *zW:* **~ismus** [-ˈɪsmʊs] *m* selfishness, egoism; **~ist** [-ˈɪst] *m* egoist; **e~istisch** *adj* selfish, egoistic

Ehe [ˈeːə] *f* marriage

ehe *konj* before

Ehe- *zW:* **~beratung** *f* marriage guidance (counselling); **~bruch** *m* adultery; **~frau** *f* married woman; wife; **~leute** *pl* married people; **e~lich** *adj* matrimonial; (*Kind*) legitimate

ehemalig *adj* former

ehemals *adv* formerly

Ehe- *zW:* **~mann** *m* married man; husband; **~paar** *nt* married couple

eher [ˈeːər] *adv* (*früher*) sooner; (*lieber*) rather, sooner; (*mehr*) more

Ehe- *zW:* **~ring** *m* wedding ring; **~schließung** *f* marriage ceremony

eheste(r, s) [ˈeːəstə(r, s)] *adj* (*früheste*) first, earliest; **am ~n** (*liebsten*) soonest; (*meist*) most; (*wahrscheinlichst*) most probably

Ehr- [ˈeːr] *zW:* **e~bar** *adj* honourable, respectable; **~e** *f* honour; **e~en** *vt* to honour

Ehren- [ˈeːrən] *zW:* **e~amtlich** *adj* honorary; **~gast** *m* guest of honour; **e~haft** *adj* honourable; **~platz** *m* place of honour *od* (*US*) honor; **~runde** *f* lap of honour; **~sache** *f* point of honour; **e~voll** *adj* honourable; **~wort** *nt* word of honour

Ehr- *zW:* **~furcht** *f* awe, deep respect; **e~fürchtig** *adj* reverent; **~gefühl** *nt* sense of honour; **~geiz** *m* ambition; **e~geizig** *adj* ambitious; **e~lich** *adj* honest; **~lichkeit** *f* honesty; **e~los** *adj* dishonourable; **~ung** *f* honour(ing); **e~würdig** *adj* venerable

Ei [aɪ] (**-(e)s, -er**) *nt* egg

Eich- *zW:* **~e** [ˈaɪçə] *f* oak (tree); **~el** (**-, -n**) *f* acorn; **~hörnchen** *nt* squirrel

Eichmaß *nt* standard

Eid [aɪt] (**-(e)s, -e**) *m* oath

Eidechse [ˈaɪdɛksə] *f* lizard

eidesstattlich *adj:* **~e Erklärung** affidavit

Eidgenosse *m* Swiss

Eier- *zW:* **~becher** *m* eggcup; **~kuchen** *m* omelette; pancake; **~likör** *m* advocaat; **~schale** *f* eggshell; **~stock** *m* ovary; **~uhr** *f* egg timer

Eifer [ˈaɪfər] (**-s**) *m* zeal, enthusiasm; **~sucht** *f* jealousy; **e~süchtig** *adj:* **e~süchtig (auf +***akk***)** jealous (of)

eifrig [ˈaɪfrɪç] *adj* zealous, enthusiastic

Eigelb [ˈaɪɡɛlp] (**-(e)s, -**) *nt* egg yolk

eigen [ˈaɪɡən] *adj* own; (*~artig*) peculiar; **mit der/dem Ihm ~en ...** with that ... peculiar to him; **sich ***dat*** etw zu ~ machen** to make sth one's own; **E~art** *f* peculiarity; characteristic; **~artig** *adj* peculiar; **E~bedarf** *m:* **zum E~bedarf** for (one's own) personal use/domestic requirements; **der Vermieter machte E~bedarf geltend** the landlord showed he needed the house/flat for himself; **~händig** *adj* with one's own hand; **E~heim** *nt* owner-occupied house; **E~heit** *f* peculiarity; **~mächtig** *adj* high-handed; **E~name** *m* proper name; **~s** *adv* expressly, on purpose; **E~schaft** *f* quality, property, attribute; **E~sinn** *m* obstinacy; **~sinnig** *adj* obstinate; **~tlich** *adj* actual, real ♦ *adv* actually, really; **E~tor** *nt* own goal; **E~tum** *nt* property; **E~tümer(in)** (**-s, -**) *m(f)* owner, proprietor; **~tümlich** *adj* peculiar; **E~tümlichkeit** *f* peculiarity; **E~tumswohnung** *f* freehold flat

eignen [ˈaɪɡnən] *vr* to be suited; **Eignung** *f* suitability

Eil- [aɪl] *zW:* **~bote** *m* courier; **~brief** *m* express letter; **~e** *f* haste; **es hat keine ~e** there's no hurry; **e~en** *vi* (*Mensch*) to hurry; (*dringend sein*) to be urgent; **e~ends** *adv* hastily; **~gut** *nt* express goods *pl*, fast freight (*US*); **e~ig** *adj* hasty, hurried; (*dringlich*) urgent; **es e~ig haben** to be in a hurry; **~zug** *m* semi-fast train, limited stop train

Eimer [ˈaɪmər] (**-s, -**) *m* bucket, pail

ein [aɪn] *adv:* **nicht ~ noch aus wissen** not to know what to do

---

⚠ *Informationen zur Rechtschreibreform Seite 615*

ein(e) ['aɪn(ə)] *num* one ♦ *indef art* a, an

einander [aɪ'nandər] *pron* one another, each other

einarbeiten ['aɪnʔarbaɪtən] *vt* to train ♦ *vr*: **sich in etw** *akk* **~** to familiarize o.s. with sth

einatmen ['aɪnʔaːtmən] *vt, vi* to inhale, to breathe in

Einbahnstraße ['aɪnbaːnʃtraːsə] *f* one-way street

Einband ['aɪnbant] *m* binding, cover

einbauen ['aɪnbaʊən] *vt* to build in; (*Motor*) to install, to fit

Einbaumöbel *pl* built-in furniture *sg*

einbegriffen ['aɪnbəgrɪfən] *adj* included

einberufen ['aɪnbəruːfən] (*unreg*) *vt* to convene; (*MIL*) to call up

Einbettzimmer *nt* single room

einbeziehen ['aɪnbətsiːən] (*unreg*) *vt* to include

einbiegen ['aɪnbiːgən] (*unreg*) *vi* to turn

einbilden ['aɪnbɪldən] *vt*: **sich** *dat* **etw ~** to imagine sth

Einbildung *f* imagination; (*Dünkel*) conceit; **~skraft** *f* imagination

Einblick ['aɪnblɪk] *m* insight

einbrechen ['aɪnbrɛçən] (*unreg*) *vi* (*in Haus*) to break in; (*Nacht*) to fall; (*Winter*) to set in; (*durchbrechen*) to break; **~ in** *+akk* (*MIL*) to invade

Einbrecher (-s, -) *m* burglar

einbringen ['aɪnbrɪŋən] (*unreg*) *vt* to bring in; (*Geld, Vorteil*) to yield; (*mitbringen*) to contribute

Einbruch ['aɪnbrʊx] *m* (*Haus~*) break-in, burglary; (*Eindringen*) invasion; (*des Winters*) onset; (*Durchbrechen*) break; (*MET*) approach; (*MIL*) penetration; **(bei/vor) ~ der Nacht** at/before nightfall; **e~sicher** *adj* burglar-proof

einbürgern ['aɪnbʏrgərn] *vt* to naturalize ♦ *vr* to become adopted

einbüßen ['aɪnbyːsən] *vt* to lose, to forfeit

einchecken ['aɪntʃɛkən] *vt, vi* to check in

eincremen ['aɪnkreːmən] *vt* to put cream on

eindecken ['aɪndɛkən] *vr*: **sich (mit etw) ~**
to lay in stocks (of sth); to stock up (with sth)

eindeutig ['aɪndɔʏtɪç] *adj* unequivocal

eindringen ['aɪndrɪŋən] (*unreg*) *vi*: **~ (in** *+akk*) to force one's way in(to); (*in Haus*) to break in(to); (*in Land*) to invade; (*Gas, Wasser*) to penetrate; **(auf jdn) ~** (*mit Bitten*) to pester (sb)

eindringlich *adj* forcible, urgent

Eindringling *m* intruder

Eindruck ['aɪndrʊk] *m* impression

eindrücken ['aɪndrʏkən] *vt* to press in

eindrucksvoll *adj* impressive

eine(r, s) *pron* one; (*jemand*) someone

eineiig ['aɪnʔaɪɪç] *adj* (*Zwillinge*) identical

eineinhalb ['aɪnʔaɪn'halp] *num* one and a half

einengen ['aɪnʔɛŋən] *vt* to confine, to restrict

einer- ['aɪnər] *zW*: **'E~'lei (-s)** *nt* sameness; **'~'lei** *adj* (*gleichartig*) the same kind of; **es ist mir ~lei** it is all the same to me; **~seits** *adv* on the one hand

einfach ['aɪnfax] *adj* simple; (*nicht mehrfach*) single ♦ *adv* simply; **E~heit** *f* simplicity

einfädeln ['aɪnfɛːdəln] *vt* (*Nadel, Faden*) to thread; (*fig*) to contrive

einfahren ['aɪnfaːrən] (*unreg*) *vt* to bring in; (*Barriere*) to knock down; (*Auto*) to run in ♦ *vi* to drive in; (*Zug*) to pull in; (*MIN*) to go down

Einfahrt *f* (*Vorgang*) driving in; pulling in; (*MIN*) descent; (*Ort*) entrance

Einfall ['aɪnfal] *m* (*Idee*) idea, notion; (*Licht~*) incidence; (*MIL*) raid; **e~en** (*unreg*) *vi* (*Licht*) to fall; (*MIL*) to raid; (*einstürzen*) to fall in, to collapse; (*einstimmen*): **(in etw** *akk*) **e~en** to join in (with sth); **etw fällt jdm ein** sth occurs to sb; **das fällt mir gar nicht ein** I wouldn't dream of it; **sich** *dat* **etwas e~en lassen** to have a good idea

einfältig ['aɪnfɛltɪç] *adj* simple(-minded)

Einfamilienhaus [aɪnfa'miːliənhaʊs] *nt* detached house

einfarbig ['aɪnfarbɪç] *adj* all one colour; (*Stoff etc*) self-coloured

einfetten ['aɪnfɛtən] *vt* to grease

⚠ *For information on spelling reform see page 615*

einfließen ['aɪnfliːsən] (*unreg*) *vi* to flow in

einflößen ['aɪnfløːsən] *vt*: **jdm etw ~** to give sb sth; (*fig*) to instil sth in sb

Einfluß △ ['aɪnfluːs] *m* influence; **~bereich** △ *m* sphere of influence

einförmig ['aɪnfœrmɪç] *adj* uniform; **E~keit** *f* uniformity

einfrieren ['aɪnfriːrən] (*unreg*) *vi* to freeze (up) ♦ *vt* to freeze

einfügen ['aɪnfyːgən] *vt* to fit in; (*zusätzlich*) to add

Einfuhr ['aɪnfuːr] (-) *f* import; **~beschränkung** *f* import restrictions *pl*; **~bestimmungen** *pl* import regulations

einführen ['aɪnfyːrən] *vt* to bring in; (*Mensch, Sitten*) to introduce; (*Ware*) to import

Einführung *f* introduction

Eingabe ['aɪngaːbə] *f* petition; (*COMPUT*) input

Eingang ['aɪngaŋ] *m* entrance; (*COMM: Ankunft*) arrival; (*Erhalt*) receipt

eingeben ['aɪngeːbən] (*unreg*) *vt* (*Arznei*) to give; (*Daten etc*) to enter

eingebildet ['aɪngəbɪldət] *adj* imaginary; (*eitel*) conceited

Eingeborene(r) ['aɪngəboːrənə(r)] *f(m)* native

Eingebung *f* inspiration

eingefleischt ['aɪngəflaɪʃt] *adj* (*Gewohnheit, Vorurteile*) deep-rooted

eingehen ['aɪngeːən] (*unreg*) *vi* (*Aufnahme finden*) to come in; (*Sendung, Geld*) to be received; (*Tier, Pflanze*) to die; (*Firma*) to fold; (*schrumpfen*) to shrink ♦ *vt* to enter into; (*Wette*) to make; **auf etw** *akk* **~** to go into sth; **auf jdn ~** to respond to sb; **jdm ~** (*verständlich sein*) to be comprehensible to sb; **~d** *adj* exhaustive, thorough

Eingemachte(s) ['aɪngəmaːxtə(s)] *nt* preserves *pl*

eingenommen ['aɪngənɔmən] *adj*: **~ (von)** fond (of), partial (to); **~ (gegen)** prejudiced (against)

eingeschrieben ['aɪngəʃriːbən] *adj* registered

eingespielt ['aɪngəʃpiːlt] *adj*: **aufeinander**

~ sein to be in tune with each other

Eingeständnis ['aɪngəʃtɛntnɪs] (**-ses, -se**) *nt* admission, confession

eingestehen ['aɪngəʃteːən] (*unreg*) *vt* to confess

eingestellt ['aɪngəʃtɛlt] *adj*: **auf etw ~ sein** to be prepared for sth

eingetragen ['aɪngətraːgən] *adj* (*COMM*) registered

Eingeweide ['aɪngəvaɪdə] (**-s, -**) *nt* innards *pl*, intestines *pl*

Eingeweihte(r) ['aɪngəvaɪtə(r)] *f(m)* initiate

eingewöhnen ['aɪngəvøːnən] *vr*: **sich ~ in** +*akk* to settle (down) in

eingleisig ['aɪnglaɪzɪç] *adj* single-track

eingreifen ['aɪngraɪfən] (*unreg*) *vi* to intervene, to interfere; (*Zahnrad*) to mesh

Eingriff ['aɪngrɪf] *m* intervention, interference; (*Operation*) operation

einhaken ['aɪnhaːkən] *vt* to hook in ♦ *vr*: **sich bei jdm ~** to link arms with sb ♦ *vi* (*sich einmischen*) to intervene

Einhalt ['aɪnhalt] *m*: **~ gebieten** +*dat* to put a stop to; **e~en** (*unreg*) *vt* (*Regel*) to keep ♦ *vi* to stop

einhändigen ['aɪnhɛndɪgən] *vt* to hand in

einhängen ['aɪnhɛŋən] *vt* to hang; (*Telefon*) to hang up ♦ *vi* (*TEL*) to hang up; **sich bei jdm ~** to link arms with sb

einheimisch ['aɪnhaɪmɪʃ] *adj* native; **E~e(r)** *f(m)* local

Einheit ['aɪnhaɪt] *f* unity; (*Maß, MIL*) unit; **e~lich** *adj* uniform; **~spreis** *m* standard price

einholen ['aɪnhoːlən] *vt* (*Tau*) to haul in; (*Fahne, Segel*) to lower; (*Vorsprung aufholen*) to catch up with; (*Verspätung*) to make up; (*Rat, Erlaubnis*) to ask ♦ *vi* (*einkaufen*) to shop

einhüllen ['aɪnhylən] *vt* to wrap up

einhundert ['aɪn'hʊndərt] *num* one hundred, a hundred

einig ['aɪnɪç] *adj* (*vereint*) united; **sich** *dat* **~ sein** to be in agreement; **~ werden** to agree

einige(r, s) ['aɪnɪgə(r, s)] *adj, pron* some ♦ *pl* some; (*mehrere*) several; **~mal** △ *adv* a few times

einigen vt to unite ♦ vr: **sich ~ (auf** +akk**)** to agree (on)

einigermaßen adv somewhat; (leidlich) reasonably

einig- zW: **~gehen** ⚠ (unreg) vi to agree; **E~keit** f unity; (Übereinstimmung) agreement; **E~ung** f agreement; (Vereinigung) unification

einkalkulieren ['aɪnkalkuliːrən] vt to take into account, to allow for

Einkauf ['aɪnkaʊf] m purchase; **e~en** vt to buy ♦ vi to shop; **e~en gehen** to go shopping

Einkaufs- zW: **~bummel** m shopping spree; **~korb** m shopping basket; **~wagen** m shopping trolley; **~zentrum** nt shopping centre

einklammern ['aɪnklamərn] vt to put in brackets, to bracket

Einklang ['aɪnklaŋ] m harmony

einklemmen ['aɪnklɛmən] vt to jam

einkochen ['aɪnkɔxən] vt to boil down; (Obst) to preserve, to bottle

Einkommen ['aɪnkɔmən] **(-s, -)** nt income; **~(s)steuer** f income tax

Einkünfte ['aɪnkʏnftə] pl income sg, revenue sg

einladen ['aɪnlaːdən] (unreg) vt (Person) to invite; (Gegenstände) to load; **jdn ins Kino ~** to take sb to the cinema

Einladung f invitation

Einlage ['aɪnlaːgə] f (Programm~) interlude; (Spar~) deposit; (Schuh~) insole; (Fußstütze) support; (Zahn~) temporary filling; (KOCH) noodles pl, vegetables pl etc in soup

einlagern ['aɪnlaːgərn] vt to store

Einlaß ⚠ ['aɪnlas] **(-sses, -lässe)** m (Zutritt) admission

einlassen ['aɪnlasən] (unreg) vt to let in; (einsetzen) to set in ♦ vr: **sich mit jdm/auf etw** akk **~** to get involved with sb/sth

Einlauf ['aɪnlaʊf] m arrival; (von Pferden) finish; (MED) enema; **e~en** (unreg) vi to arrive, to come in; (in Hafen) to enter; (SPORT) to finish; (Wasser) to run in; (Stoff) to shrink ♦ vt (Schuhe) to break in ♦ vr

(SPORT) to warm up; (Motor, Maschine) to run in; **jdm das Haus e~en** to invade sb's house

einleben ['aɪnleːbən] vr to settle down

einlegen ['aɪnleːgən] vt (einfügen: Blatt, Sohle) to insert; (KOCH) to pickle; (Pause) to have; (Protest) to make; (Veto) to use; (Berufung) to lodge; (AUT: Gang) to engage

einleiten ['aɪnlaɪtən] vt to introduce, to start; (Geburt) to induce; **Einleitung** f introduction; induction

einleuchten ['aɪnlɔʏçtən] vi: **(jdm) ~** to be clear od evident (to sb); **~d** adj clear

einliefern ['aɪnliːfərn] vt: **~ (in** +akk**)** to take (into)

Einlieferungsschein m certificate of posting

Einliegerwohnung ['aɪnliːgərvoːnʊŋ] f self-contained flat; (für Eltern, Großeltern) granny flat

einlösen ['aɪnløːzən] vt (Scheck) to cash; (Schuldschein, Pfand) to redeem; (Versprechen) to keep

einmachen ['aɪnmaxən] vt to preserve

einmal ['aɪnmaːl] adv once; (erstens) first; (zukünftig) sometime; **nehmen wir ~ an** just let's suppose; **noch ~** once more; **nicht ~** not even; **auf ~** all at once; **es war ~** once upon a time there was/were; **E~eins** nt multiplication tables pl; **~ig** adj unique; (nur einmal erforderlich) single; (prima) fantastic

Einmarsch ['aɪnmarʃ] m entry; (MIL) invasion; **e~ieren** vi to march in

einmischen ['aɪnmɪʃən] vr: **sich ~ (in** +akk**)** to interfere (with)

einmütig ['aɪnmyːtɪç] adj unanimous

Einnahme ['aɪnnaːmə] f (von Medizin) taking; (MIL) capture, taking; **~n** pl (Geld) takings, revenue sg; **~quelle** f source of income

einnehmen ['aɪnneːmən] (unreg) vt to take; (Stellung, Raum) to take up; **~ für/gegen** to persuade in favour of/against; **~d** adj charming

einordnen ['aɪnʔɔrdnən] vt to arrange, to fit in ♦ vr to adapt; (AUT) to get into lane

⚠ For information on spelling reform see page 615

einpacken ['aɪnpakən] *vt* to pack (up)

einparken ['aɪnparkən] *vt* to park

einpendeln ['aɪnpɛndəln] *vr* to even out

einpflanzen ['aɪnpflantsən] *vt* to plant; (*MED*) to implant

einplanen ['aɪnpla:nən] *vt* to plan for

einprägen ['aɪnprɛ:gən] *vt* to impress, to imprint; (*beibringen*): **(jdm) ~** to impress (on sb); **sich** *dat* **etw ~** to memorize sth

einrahmen ['aɪnra:mən] *vt* to frame

einräumen ['aɪnrɔʏmən] *vt* (*ordnend*) to put away; (*überlassen: Platz*) to give up; (*zugestehen*) to admit, to concede

einreden ['aɪnre:dən] *vt*: **jdm/sich etw ~** to talk sb/o.s. into believing sth

einreiben ['aɪnraɪbən] (*unreg*) *vt* to rub in

einreichen ['aɪnraɪçən] *vt* to hand in; (*Antrag*) to submit

Einreise ['aɪnraɪzə] *f* entry; **~bestimmungen** *pl* entry regulations; **~erlaubnis** *f* entry permit; **~genehmigung** *f* entry permit; **e~n** *vi*: **(in ein Land) e~n** to enter (a country)

einrichten ['aɪnrɪçtən] *vt* (*Haus*) to furnish; (*schaffen*) to establish, to set up; (*arrangieren*) to arrange; (*möglich machen*) to manage ♦ *vr* (*in Haus*) to furnish one's house; **sich ~ (auf** +*akk*) (*sich vorbereiten*) to prepare o.s. (for); (*sich anpassen*) to adapt (to)

Einrichtung *f* (*Wohnungs~*) furnishings *pl*; (*öffentliche Anstalt*) organization; (*Dienste*) service

einrosten ['aɪnrɔstən] *vi* to get rusty

einrücken ['aɪnrʏkən] *vi* (*MIL: in Land*) to move in

Eins [aɪns] (**-, -en**) *f* one; **e~** *num* one; **es ist mir alles e~** it's all one to me

einsam ['aɪnza:m] *adj* lonely, solitary; **E~keit** *f* loneliness, solitude

einsammeln ['aɪnzaməln] *vt* to collect

Einsatz ['aɪnzats] *m* (*Teil*) inset; (*an Kleid*) insertion; (*Verwendung*) use, employment; (*Spiel~*) stake; (*Risiko*) risk; (*MIL*) operation; (*MUS*) entry; **im ~** in action; **e~bereit** *adj* ready for action

einschalten ['aɪnʃaltən] *vt* (*einfügen*) to insert; (*Pause*) to make; (*ELEK*) to switch on; (*Anwalt*) to bring in ♦ *vr* (*dazwischentreten*) to intervene

einschärfen ['aɪnʃɛrfən] *vt*: **jdm etw ~** to impress sth (up)on sb

einschätzen ['aɪnʃɛtsən] *vt* to estimate, to assess ♦ *vr* to rate o.s.

einschenken ['aɪnʃɛnkən] *vt* to pour out

einschicken ['aɪnʃɪkən] *vt* to send in

einschl. *abk* (= *einschließlich*) incl.

einschlafen ['aɪnʃla:fən] (*unreg*) *vi* to fall asleep, to go to sleep

einschläfernd ['aɪnʃlɛ:fərnt] *adj* (*MED*) soporific; (*langweilig*) boring; (*Stimme*) lulling

Einschlag ['aɪnʃla:k] *m* impact; (*fig: Beimischung*) touch, hint; **e~en** [-gən] (*unreg*) *vt* to knock in; (*Fenster*) to smash, to break; (*Zähne, Schädel*) to smash in; (*AUT: Räder*) to turn; (*kürzer machen*) to take up; (*Ware*) to pack, to wrap up; (*Weg, Richtung*) to take ♦ *vi* to hit; (*sich einigen*) to agree; (*Anklang finden*) to work, to succeed; **in etw** *akk*/**auf jdn e~en** to hit sth/sb

einschlägig ['aɪnʃlɛ:gɪç] *adj* relevant

einschließen ['aɪnʃli:sən] (*unreg*) *vt* (*Kind*) to lock in; (*Häftling*) to lock up; (*Gegenstand*) to lock away; (*Bergleute*) to cut off; (*umgeben*) to surround; (*MIL*) to encircle; (*fig*) to include, to comprise ♦ *vr* to lock o.s. in

einschließlich *adv* inclusive ♦ *präp* +*gen* inclusive of, including

einschmeicheln ['aɪnʃmaɪçəln] *vr*: **sich ~ (bei)** to ingratiate o.s. (with)

einschnappen ['aɪnʃnapən] *vi* (*Tür*) to click to; (*fig*) to be touchy; **eingeschnappt sein** to be in a huff

einschneidend ['aɪnʃnaɪdənt] *adj* drastic

Einschnitt ['aɪnʃnɪt] *m* cutting; (*MED*) incision; (*Ereignis*) decisive point

einschränken ['aɪnʃrɛŋkən] *vt* to limit, to restrict; (*Kosten*) to cut down, to reduce ♦ *vr* to cut down (on expenditure); **Einschränkung** *f* restriction, limitation; reduction; (*von Behauptung*) qualification

Einschreib- ['aɪnʃraɪb] *zW*: **~(e)brief** *m*

recorded delivery letter; **e~en** (*unreg*) *vt* to write in; (*Post*) to send recorded delivery ♦ *vr* to register; (*UNIV*) to enrol; **~en** *nt* recorded delivery letter

einschreiten ['aɪnʃraɪtən] (*unreg*) *vi* to step in, to intervene; **~ gegen** to take action against

einschüchtern ['aɪnʃʏçtərn] *vt* to intimidate

einschulen ['aɪnʃuːlən] *vt*: **eingeschult werden** (*Kind*) to start school

einsehen ['aɪnzeːən] (*unreg*) *vt* (*hineinsehen in*) to realize; (*Akten*) to have a look at; (*verstehen*) to see; **E~** (**-s**) *nt* understanding; **ein E~ haben** to show understanding

einseitig ['aɪnzaɪtɪç] *adj* one-sided

Einsend- ['aɪnzɛnd] *zW*: **e~en** (*unreg*) *vt* to send in; **~er** (**-s, -**) *m* sender, contributor; **~ung** *f* sending in

einsetzen ['aɪnzɛtsən] *vt* to put (in); (*in Amt*) to appoint, to install; (*Geld*) to stake; (*verwenden*) to use; (*MIL*) to employ ♦ *vi* (*beginnen*) to set in; (*MUS*) to enter, to come in ♦ *vr* to work hard; **sich für jdn/ etw ~** to support sb/sth

Einsicht ['aɪnzɪçt] *f* insight; (*in Akten*) look, inspection; **zu der ~ kommen, daß ...** to come to the conclusion that ...; **e~ig** *adj* (*Mensch*) judicious; **e~slos** *adj* unreasonable; **e~svoll** *adj* understanding

einsilbig ['aɪnzɪlbɪç] *adj* (*auch fig*) monosyllabic; (*Mensch*) uncommunicative

einspannen ['aɪnʃpanən] *vt* (*Papier*) to insert; (*Pferde*) to harness; (*umg*: *Person*) to rope in

Einsparung ['aɪnʃpaːrʊŋ] *f* economy, saving

einsperren ['aɪnʃpɛrən] *vt* to lock up

einspielen ['aɪnʃpiːlən] *vr* (*SPORT*) to warm up ♦ *vt* (*Film*: *Geld*) to bring in; (*Instrument*) to play in; **sich aufeinander ~** to become attuned to each other; **gut eingespielt** running smoothly

einsprachig ['aɪnʃpraːxɪç] *adj* monolingual

einspringen ['aɪnʃprɪŋən] (*unreg*) *vi* (*aushelfen*) to help out, to step into the breach

Einspruch ['aɪnʃprʊx] *m* protest, objection; **~srecht** *nt* veto

einspurig ['aɪnʃpuːrɪç] *adj* (*EISENB*) single-track; (*AUT*) single-lane

einst [aɪnst] *adv* once; (*zukünftig*) one day, some day

einstecken ['aɪnʃtɛkən] *vt* to stick in, to insert; (*Brief*) to post; (*ELEK*: *Stecker*) to plug in; (*Geld*) to pocket; (*mitnehmen*) to take; (*überlegen sein*) to put in the shade; (*hinnehmen*) to swallow

einstehen ['aɪnʃteːən] (*unreg*) *vi*: **für jdn/ etw ~** to guarantee sb/sth; (*verantworten*): **für etw ~** to answer for sth

einsteigen ['aɪnʃtaɪgən] (*unreg*) *vi* to get in od on; (*in Schiff*) to go on board; (*sich beteiligen*) to come in; (*hineinklettern*) to climb in

einstellen ['aɪnʃtɛlən] *vt* (*aufhören*) to stop; (*Geräte*) to adjust; (*Kamera etc*) to focus; (*Sender, Radio*) to tune in; (*unterstellen*) to put; (*in Firma*) to employ, to take on ♦ *vi* (*Firma*) to take on staff/workers ♦ *vr* (*anfangen*) to set in; (*kommen*) to arrive; **sich auf jdn ~** to adapt to sb; **sich auf etw** *akk* **~** to prepare o.s. for sth

Einstellung *f* (*Aufhören*) suspension, cessation; adjustment; focusing; (*von Arbeiter etc*) appointment; (*Haltung*) attitude

Einstieg ['aɪnʃtiːk] (**-(e)s, -e**) *m* entry; (*fig*) approach

einstig ['aɪnstɪç] *adj* former

einstimmig ['aɪnʃtɪmɪç] *adj* unanimous; (*MUS*) for one voice

einstmals *adv* once, formerly

einstöckig ['aɪnʃtœkɪç] *adj* two-storeyed

Einsturz ['aɪnʃtʊrts] *m* collapse

einstürzen ['aɪnʃtʏrtsən] *vi* to fall in, to collapse

einst- *zW*: **~weilen** *adv* meanwhile; (*vorläufig*) temporarily, for the time being; **~weilig** *adj* temporary

eintägig ['aɪntɛːgɪç] *adj* one-day

eintauschen ['aɪntauʃən] *vt*: **~ (gegen** *od* **für)** to exchange (for)

eintausend ['aɪn'tauzənt] *num* one thousand

⚠ *For information on spelling reform see page 615*

einteilen ['aɪntaɪlən] vt (in Teile) to divide (up); (Menschen) to assign

einteilig adj one-piece

eintönig ['aɪntøːnɪç] adj monotonous

Eintopf ['aɪntɔpf] m stew

Eintracht ['aɪntraxt] (-) f concord, harmony; **einträchtig** ['aɪntrɛçtɪç] adj harmonious

Eintrag ['aɪntraːk] (-(e)s, -̈e) m entry; **amtlicher ~** entry in the register; **e~en** [-gən] (unreg) vt (in Buch) to enter; (Profit) to yield ♦ vr to put one's name down

einträglich ['aɪntrɛːklɪç] adj profitable

eintreffen ['aɪntrɛfən] (unreg) vi to happen; (ankommen) to arrive

eintreten ['aɪntreːtən] (unreg) vi to occur; (sich einsetzen) to intercede ♦ vt (Tür) to kick open; **~ in** +akk to enter; (in Club, Partei) to join

Eintritt ['aɪntrɪt] m (Betreten) entrance; (Anfang) commencement; (in Club etc) joining

Eintritts- zW: **~geld** nt admission charge; **~karte** f (admission) ticket; **~preis** m admission charge

einüben ['aɪnˈyːbən] vt to practise

Einvernehmen ['aɪnfɛrneːmən] (-s, -) nt agreement, harmony

einverstanden ['aɪnfɛrʃtandən] excl agreed, okay ♦ adj: **~ sein** to agree, to be agreed

Einverständnis ['aɪnfɛrʃtɛntnɪs] nt understanding; (gleiche Meinung) agreement

Einwand ['aɪnvant] (-(e)s, -̈e) m objection

Einwand- zW: **~erer** m immigrant; **e~ern** vi to immigrate; **~erung** f immigration

einwandfrei adj perfect ♦ adv absolutely

Einweg- ['aɪnveːg-] zW: **~flasche** f no-deposit bottle; **~spritze** f disposable syringe

einweichen ['aɪnvaɪçən] vt to soak

einweihen ['aɪnvaɪən] vt (Kirche) to consecrate; (Brücke) to open; (Gebäude) to inaugurate; **~ (in** +akk) (Person) to initiate (in); **Einweihung** f consecration; opening; inauguration; initiation

einweisen ['aɪnvaɪzən] (unreg) vt (in Amt) to install; (in Arbeit) to introduce; (in Anstalt) to send

einwenden ['aɪnvɛndən] (unreg) vt: **etwas ~ gegen** to object to, to oppose

einwerfen ['aɪnvɛrfən] (unreg) vt to throw in; (Brief) to post; (Geld) to put in, to insert; (Fenster) to smash; (äußern) to interpose

einwickeln ['aɪnvɪkəln] vt to wrap up; (fig: umg) to outsmart

einwilligen ['aɪnvɪlɪgən] vi: **~ (in** +akk) to consent (to), to agree (to); **Einwilligung** f consent

einwirken ['aɪnvɪrkən] vi: **auf jdn/etw ~** to influence sb/sth

Einwohner ['aɪnvoːnər] (-s, -) m inhabitant; **~'meldeamt** nt registration office; **~schaft** f population, inhabitants pl

Einwurf ['aɪnvʊrf] m (Öffnung) slot; (von Münze) insertion; (von Brief) posting; (Einwand) objection; (SPORT) throw-in

Einzahl ['aɪntsaːl] f singular; **e~en** vt to pay in; **~ung** f paying in; **~ungsschein** m paying-in slip, deposit slip (US)

einzäunen ['aɪntsɔynən] vt to fence in

Einzel ['aɪntsəl] (-s, -) nt (TENNIS) singles; **~fahrschein** m one-way ticket; **~fall** m single instance, individual case; **~handel** m retail trade; **~handelspreis** m retail price; **~heit** f particular, detail; **~kind** nt only child; **e~n** adj single; (vereinzelt) the odd ♦ adv singly; **e~n angeben** to specify; **der/die e~ne** the individual; **das e~ne** the particular; **ins e~ne gehen** to go into detail(s); **~teil** nt component (part); **~zimmer** nt single room; **~zimmerzuschlag** m single room supplement

einziehen ['aɪntsiːən] (unreg) vt to draw in, to take in; (Kopf) to duck; (Fühler, Antenne, Fahrgestell) to retract; (Steuern, Erkundigungen) to collect; (MIL) to draft, to call up; (aus dem Verkehr ziehen) to withdraw; (konfiszieren) to confiscate ♦ vi to move in; (Friede, Ruhe) to come; (Flüssigkeit) to penetrate

einzig ['aɪntsɪç] adj only; (ohnegleichen) unique; **das ~e** the only thing; **der/die ~e** the only one; **~artig** adj unique

Einzug ['aɪntsuːk] m entry, moving in

⚠ *Informationen zur Rechtschreibreform Seite 615*

Eis [ais] **(-es, -)** nt ice; (Speiseeis) ice cream; **~bahn** f ice od skating rink; **~bär** m polar bear; **~becher** m sundae; **~bein** nt pig's trotters pl; **~berg** m iceberg; **~café** nt ice-cream parlour (BRIT) od parlor (US); **~decke** f sheet of ice; **~diele** f ice-cream parlour

Eisen ['aizən] **(-s, -)** nt iron

Eisenbahn f railway, railroad (US); **~er (-s, -)** m railwayman, railway employee, railroader (US); **~schaffner** m railway guard; **~wagen** m railway carriage

Eisenerz nt iron ore

eisern ['aizərn] adj iron; (Gesundheit) robust; (Energie) unrelenting; (Reserve) emergency

Eis- zW: **e~frei** adj clear of ice; **~hockey** nt ice hockey; **e~ig** ['aizɪç] adj icy; **e~kalt** adj icy cold; **~kunstlauf** m figure skating; **~laufen** nt ice skating; **~pickel** m ice axe; **~schrank** m fridge, icebox (US); **~würfel** m ice cube; **~zapfen** m icicle; **~zeit** f ice age

eitel ['aitəl] adj vain; **E~keit** f vanity

Eiter ['aitər] **(-s)** m pus; **e~ig** adj suppurating; **e~n** vi to suppurate

Eiweiß **(-es, -e)** nt white of an egg; (CHEM) protein

Ekel¹ ['e:kəl] **(-s, -)** nt (umg: Mensch) nauseating person

Ekel² ['e:kəl] **(-s)** m nausea, disgust; **e~erregend** ⚠ adj nauseating, disgusting; **e~haft** adj nauseating, disgusting; **e~ig** adj nauseating, disgusting; **e~n** vt to disgust ♦ vr: **sich e~n (vor** +dat) to loathe, to be disgusted (at); **es e~t jdn** od **jdm** sb is disgusted; **eklig** adj nauseating, disgusting

Ekstase [ɛk'staːzə] f ecstasy

Ekzem [ɛk'tseːm] **(-s, -e)** nt (MED) eczema

Elan [e'lãː] **(-s)** m elan

elastisch [e'lastɪʃ] adj elastic

Elastizität [elastitsiˈtɛːt] f elasticity

Elch [ɛlç] **(-(e)s, -e)** m elk

Elefant [ele'fant] m elephant

elegant [ele'gant] adj elegant

Eleganz [ele'gants] f elegance

Elek- [e'lɛk] zW: **~triker** [-trikər] **(-s, -)** m electrician; **e~trisch** [-trɪʃ] adj electric;

e~trisieren [-tri'ziːrən] vt (auch fig) to electrify; (Mensch) to give an electric shock to ♦ vr to get an electric shock; **~trizität** [tritsi'tɛːt] f electricity; **~trizitätswerk** nt power station; (Gesellschaft) electric power company

Elektro- [e'lɛktro] zW: **~de** [-'troːdə] f electrode; **~gerät** nt electrical appliance; **~herd** m electric cooker; **~n (-s, -en)** nt electron; **~nenrechner** [elɛk'troːnən-] m computer; **~nik** f electronics sg; **e~nisch** adj electronic; **~rasierer** m electric razor; **~technik** f electrical engineering

Element [ele'mɛnt] **(-s, -e)** nt element; (ELEK) cell, battery; **e~ar** [-'taːr] adj elementary; (naturhaft) elemental

Elend ['eːlɛnt] **(-(e)s)** nt misery; **e~** adj miserable; **~sviertel** nt slum

elf [ɛlf] num eleven; **E~ (-, -en)** f (SPORT) eleven

Elfe f elf

Elfenbein nt ivory

Elfmeter m (SPORT) penalty (kick)

Elite [e'liːtə] f elite

Ell- zW: **~bogen** m elbow; **~e** f ell; (Maß) yard; **~enbogen** m elbow; **~(en)bogenfreiheit** f (fig) elbow room

Elsaß ⚠ ['ɛlzas] **(- od -sses)** nt: **das ~** Alsace

Elster ['ɛlstər] **(-, -n)** f magpie

Eltern ['ɛltərn] pl parents; **~beirat** m (SCH) ≈ PTA (BRIT), parents' council; **~haus** nt home; **e~los** adj parentless

Emaille [e'maljə] **(-s, -s)** nt enamel

emaillieren [ema'jiːrən] vt to enamel

Emanzipation [emantsipatsi'oːn] f emancipation

emanzipieren vt to emancipate

Embryo ['ɛmbryo] **(-s, -s** od **Embryonen)** m embryo

Emi- zW: **~'grant(in)** m(f) emigrant; **~gration** f emigration; **e~grieren** vi to emigrate

Emissionen [emisi'oːnən] fpl emissions

Empfang [ɛm'pfaŋ] **(-(e)s, -̈e)** m reception; (Erhalten) receipt; **in ~ nehmen** to receive; **e~en** (unreg) vt to receive ♦ vi (schwanger

⚠ For information on spelling reform see page 615

werden) to conceive

Empfäng- [ɛmˈpfɛŋ] *zW:* **~er** (**-s, -**) *m*
receiver; *(COMM)* addressee, consignee;
~erabschnitt *m* receipt slip; **e~lich** *adj*
receptive, susceptible; **~nis** (**-, -se**) *f*
conception; **~nisverhütung** *f*
contraception

Empfangs- *zW:* **~bestätigung** *f*
acknowledgement; **~dame** *f* receptionist;
~schein *m* receipt; **~zimmer** *nt* reception
room

empfehlen [ɛmˈpfeːlən] *(unreg) vt* to
recommend ♦ *vr* to take one's leave;
~swert *adj* recommendable

Empfehlung *f* recommendation

empfiehlst *etc* [ɛmˈpfiːlst] *vb siehe*
empfehlen

empfind- [ɛmˈpfɪnt] *zW:* **~en** [-dən] *(unreg)*
vt to feel; **~lich** *adj* sensitive; *(Stelle)* sore;
(reizbar) touchy; **~sam** *adj* sentimental;
E~ung [-dʊŋ] *f* feeling, sentiment

empfohlen *etc* [ɛmˈpfoːlən] *vb siehe*
empfehlen

empor [ɛmˈpoːr] *adv* up, upwards

empören [ɛmˈpøːrən] *vt* to make indignant;
to shock ♦ *vr* to become indignant; **~d** *adj*
outrageous

Emporkömmling [ɛmˈpoːrkœmlɪŋ] *m*
upstart, parvenu

Empörung *f* indignation

emsig [ˈɛmzɪç] *adj* diligent, busy

End- [ˈɛnt] *in zW* final; **~e** (**-s, -n**) *nt* end;
am ~e at the end; *(schließlich)* in the end;
am ~e sein to be at the end of one's
tether; **~e Dezember** at the end of
December; **zu ~e sein** to be finished;
e~en *vi* to end; **e~gültig** [ˈɛnt-] *adj* final,
definite

Endivie [ɛnˈdiːviə] *f* endive

End- *zW:* **e~lich** *adj* final; *(MATH)* finite
♦ *adv* finally; **e~lich!** at last!; **komm e~lich!**
come on!; **e~los** *adj* endless, infinite;
~spiel *nt* final(s); **~spurt** *m (SPORT)* final
spurt; **~station** *f* terminus; **~ung** *f* ending

Energie [enɛrˈgiː] *f* energy; **~bedarf** *m*
energy requirement; **e~los** *adj* lacking in
energy, weak; **~verbrauch** *m* energy

consumption; **~versorgung** *f* supply of
energy; **~wirtschaft** *f* energy industry

energisch [eˈnɛrgɪʃ] *adj* energetic

eng [ɛŋ] *adj* narrow; *(Kleidung)* tight; *(fig:
Horizont)* narrow, limited; *(Freundschaft,
Verhältnis)* close; **~ an etw** *dat* close to sth

Engagement [ãgaʒəˈmãː] (**-s, -s**) *nt*
engagement; *(Verpflichtung)* commitment

engagieren [ãgaˈʒiːrən] *vt* to engage ♦ *vr*
to commit o.s.

Enge [ˈɛŋə] *f (auch fig)* narrowness; *(Land~)*
defile; *(Meer~)* straits *pl*; **jdn in die ~
treiben** to drive sb into a corner

Engel [ˈɛŋəl] (**-s, -**) *m* angel; **e~haft** *adj*
angelic

England [ˈɛŋlant] *nt* England;
Engländer(in) *m(f)* Englishman(-woman);
englisch *adj* English

Engpaß ⚠ *m* defile, pass; *(fig, Verkehr)*
bottleneck

en gros [ãˈgro] *adv* wholesale

engstirnig [ˈɛŋʃtɪrnɪç] *adj* narrow-minded

Enkel [ˈɛŋkəl] (**-s, -**) *m* grandson; **~in** *f*
granddaughter; **~kind** *nt* grandchild

enorm [eˈnɔrm] *adj* enormous

Ensemble [ãˈsãbəl] (**-s, -s**) *nt* company,
ensemble

entbehr- [ɛntˈbeːr] *zW:* **~en** *vt* to do
without, to dispense with; **~lich** *adj*
superfluous; **E~ung** *f* deprivation

entbinden [ɛntˈbɪndən] *(unreg) vt (+gen)* to
release (from); *(MED)* to deliver ♦ *vi (MED)*
to give birth; **Entbindung** *f* release;
confinement; **Entbindungsheim** *nt*
maternity hospital

entdeck- [ɛntˈdɛk] *zW:* **~en** *vt* to discover;
E~er (**-s, -**) *m* discoverer; **E~ung** *f*
discovery

Ente [ˈɛntə] *f* duck; *(fig)* canard, false report

enteignen [ɛntˈʔaɪɡnən] *vt* to expropriate;
(Besitzer) to dispossess

enterben [ɛntˈʔɛrbən] *vt* to disinherit

entfallen [ɛntˈfalən] *(unreg) vi* to drop, to
fall; *(wegfallen)* to be dropped; **jdm ~**
(vergessen) to slip sb's memory; **auf jdn ~**
to be allotted to sb

entfalten [ɛntˈfaltən] *vt* to unfold; *(Talente)*

⚠ *Informationen zur Rechtschreibreform Seite 615*

to develop ♦ *vr* to open; (*Mensch*) to develop one's potential; **Entfaltung** *f* unfolding; (*von Talenten*) development

entfern- [ɛnt'fɛrn] *zW:* **~en** *vt* to remove; (*hinauswerfen*) to expel ♦ *vr* to go away, to withdraw; **~t** *adj* distant; **weit davon ~t sein, etw zu tun** to be far from doing sth; **E~ung** *f* distance; (*Wegschaffen*) removal

entfremden [ɛnt'frɛmdən] *vt* to estrange, to alienate; **Entfremdung** *f* alienation, estrangement

entfrosten [ɛnt'frɔstən] *vt* to defrost

Entfroster (**-s, -**) *m* (*AUT*) defroster

entführ- [ɛnt'fy:r] *zW:* **~en** *vt* to carry off, to abduct; to kidnap; **E~er** *m* kidnapper; **E~ung** *f* abduction; kidnapping

entgegen [ɛnt'ge:gən] *präp +dat* contrary to, against ♦ *adv* towards; **~bringen** (*unreg*) *vt* to bring; **jdm etw ~bringen** (*fig*) to show sb sth; **~gehen** (*unreg*) *vi +dat* to go to meet, to go towards; **~gesetzt** *adj* opposite; (*widersprechend*) opposed; **~halten** (*unreg*) *vt* (*fig*) to object; **E~kommen** *nt* obligingness; **~kommen** (*unreg*) *vi +dat* to approach; to meet; (*fig*) to accommodate; **~kommend** *adj* obliging; **~nehmen** (*unreg*) *vt* to receive, to accept; **~sehen** (*unreg*) *vi +dat* to await; **~setzen** *vt* to oppose; **~treten** (*unreg*) *vi +dat* to step up to; (*fig*) to oppose, to counter; **~wirken** *vi +dat* to counteract

entgegnen [ɛnt'ge:gnən] *vt* to reply, to retort

entgehen [ɛnt'ge:ən] (*unreg*) *vi* (*fig*): **jdm ~** to escape sb's notice; **sich** *dat* **etw ~ lassen** to miss sth

Entgelt [ɛnt'gɛlt] (**-(e)s, -e**) *nt* compensation, remuneration

entgleisen [ɛnt'glaızən] *vi* (*EISENB*) to be derailed; (*fig: Person*) to misbehave; **~ lassen** to derail

entgräten [ɛnt'grɛːtən] *vt* to fillet, to bone

Enthaarungscreme [ɛnt'ha:rʊŋs-] *f* hair-removing cream

enthalten [ɛnt'haltən] (*unreg*) *vt* to contain ♦ *vr:* **sich (von etw) ~** to abstain (from sth), to refrain (from sth)

enthaltsam [ɛnt'haltza:m] *adj* abstinent, abstemious

enthemmen [ɛnt'hɛmən] *vt:* **jdn ~** to free sb from his inhibitions

enthüllen [ɛnt'hʏlən] *vt* to reveal, to unveil

Enthusiasmus [ɛntuzi'asmʊs] *m* enthusiasm

entkommen [ɛnt'kɔmən] (*unreg*) *vi:* **~ (aus** *od +dat*) to get away (from), to escape (from)

entkräften [ɛnt'krɛftən] *vt* to weaken, to exhaust; (*Argument*) to refute

entladen [ɛnt'la:dən] (*unreg*) *vt* to unload; (*ELEK*) to discharge ♦ *vr* (*ELEK: Gewehr*) to discharge; (*Ärger etc*) to vent itself

entlang [ɛnt'laŋ] *adv* along; **~ dem Fluß, den Fluß ~** along the river; **~gehen** (*unreg*) *vi* to walk along

entlarven [ɛnt'larfən] *vt* to unmask, to expose

entlassen [ɛnt'lasən] (*unreg*) *vt* to discharge; (*Arbeiter*) to dismiss; **Entlassung** *f* discharge; dismissal

entlasten [ɛnt'lastən] *vt* to relieve; (*Achse*) to relieve the load on; (*Angeklagten*) to exonerate; (*Konto*) to clear

Entlastung *f* relief; (*COMM*) crediting

Entlastungszug *m* relief train

entlegen [ɛnt'le:gən] *adj* remote

entlocken [ɛnt'lɔkən] *vt:* **(jdm etw) ~** to elicit (sth from sb)

entmutigen [ɛnt'mu:tıgən] *vt* to discourage

entnehmen [ɛnt'ne:mən] (*unreg*) *vt* (*+dat*) to take out (of), to take (from); (*folgern*) to infer (from)

entreißen [ɛnt'raısən] (*unreg*) *vt:* **jdm etw ~** to snatch sth (away) from sb

entrichten [ɛnt'rıçtən] *vt* to pay

entrosten [ɛnt'rɔstən] *vt* to remove rust from

entrümpeln [ɛnt'rʏmpəln] *vt* to clear out

entrüst- [ɛnt'rʏst] *zW:* **~en** *vt* to incense, to outrage ♦ *vr* to be filled with indignation; **~et** *adj* indignant, outraged; **E~ung** *f* indignation

entschädigen [ɛnt'ʃɛːdıgən] *vt* to compensate; **Entschädigung** *f*

⚠ *For information on spelling reform see page 615*

compensation

entschärfen [ɛnt'ʃɛrfən] vt to defuse; (Kritik) to tone down

Entscheid [ɛnt'ʃait] **(-(e)s, -e)** m decision; **e~en** [-dən] (unreg) vt, vi, vr to decide; **e~end** adj decisive; (Stimme) casting; **~ung** f decision

entschieden [ɛnt'ʃiːdən] adj decided; (entschlossen) resolute; **E~heit** f firmness, determination

entschließen [ɛnt'ʃliːsən] (unreg) vr to decide

entschlossen [ɛnt'ʃlɔsən] adj determined, resolute; **E~heit** f determination

Entschluß ⚠ [ɛnt'ʃlus] m decision; **e~freudig** ⚠ adj decisive; **~kraft** ⚠ f determination, decisiveness

entschuldigen [ɛnt'ʃʊldɪgən] vt to excuse ♦ vr to apologize

Entschuldigung f apology; (Grund) excuse; **jdn um ~ bitten** to apologize to sb; **~!** excuse me; (Verzeihung) sorry

entsetz- [ɛnt'zɛts] zW: **~en** vt to horrify; (MIL) to relieve ♦ vr to be horrified od appalled; **E~en (-s)** nt horror, dismay; **~lich** adj dreadful, appalling; **~t** adj horrified

Entsorgung [ɛnt'zɔrgʊŋ] f (von Kraftwerken, Chemikalien) (waste) disposal

entspannen [ɛnt'ʃpanən] vt, vr (Körper) to relax; (POL: Lage) to ease

Entspannung f relaxation, rest; (POL) détente; **~spolitik** f policy of détente

entsprechen [ɛnt'ʃprɛçən] (unreg) vi +dat to correspond to; (Anforderungen, Wünschen) to meet, to comply with; **~d** adj appropriate ♦ adv accordingly

entspringen [ɛnt'ʃprɪŋən] (unreg) vi (+dat) to spring (from)

entstehen [ɛnt'ʃteːən] (unreg) vi: **~ (aus** od **durch)** to arise (from), to result (from)

Entstehung f genesis, origin

entstellen [ɛnt'ʃtɛlən] vt to disfigure; (Wahrheit) to distort

entstören [ɛnt'ʃtøːrən] vt (RAD) to eliminate interference from

enttäuschen [ɛnt'tɔʏʃən] vt to disappoint;

Enttäuschung f disappointment

entwaffnen [ɛnt'vafnən] vt (lit, fig) to disarm

entwässern [ɛnt'vɛsərn] vt to drain; **Entwässerung** f drainage

entweder [ɛnt've:dər] konj either

entwenden [ɛnt'vɛndən] (unreg) vt to purloin, to steal

entwerfen [ɛnt'vɛrfən] (unreg) vt (Zeichnung) to sketch; (Modell) to design; (Vortrag, Gesetz etc) to draft

entwerten [ɛnt've:rtən] vt to devalue; (stempeln) to cancel

Entwerter (-s, -) m ticket punching machine

entwickeln [ɛnt'vɪkəln] vt, vr (auch PHOT) to develop; (Mut, Energie) to show (o.s.), to display (o.s.)

Entwicklung [ɛnt'vɪkluŋ] f development; (PHOT) developing

Entwicklungs- zW: **~hilfe** f aid for developing countries; **~land** nt developing country

entwöhnen [ɛnt'vø:nən] vt to wean; (Süchtige): **(einer Sache** dat od **von etw) ~** to cure of (sth)

Entwöhnung f weaning; cure, curing

entwürdigend [ɛnt'vʏrdɪgənt] adj degrading

Entwurf [ɛnt'vʊrf] m outline, design; (Vertrags~, Konzept) draft

entziehen [ɛnt'tsi:ən] (unreg) vt (+dat) to withdraw (from), to take away (from); (Flüssigkeit) to draw (from), to extract (from) ♦ vr (+dat) to escape (from); (jds Kenntnis) to be outside od beyond; (der Pflicht) to shirk (from)

Entziehung f withdrawal; **~sanstalt** f drug addiction/alcoholism treatment centre; **~skur** f treatment for drug addiction/alcoholism

entziffern [ɛnt'tsɪfərn] vt to decipher; to decode

entzücken [ɛnt'tsʏkən] vt to delight; **E~ (-s)** nt delight; **~d** adj delightful, charming

entzünden [ɛnt'tsʏndən] vt to light, to set light to; (fig, MED) to inflame; (Streit) to

⚠ Informationen zur Rechtschreibreform Seite 615

spark off ♦ vr (*auch fig*) to catch fire; (*Streit*) to start; (*MED*) to become inflamed

Entzündung f (*MED*) inflammation

entzwei [ɛnt'tsvaɪ] *adv* broken; in two; **~brechen** (*unreg*) *vt*, *vi* to break in two; **~en** *vt* to set at odds ♦ *vr* to fall out; **~gehen** (*unreg*) *vi* to break (in two)

Enzian ['entsia:n] (**-s, -e**) *m* gentian

Epidemie [epide'mi:] f epidemic

Epilepsie [epile'psi:] f epilepsy

Episode [epi'zo:də] f episode

Epoche [e'pɔxə] f epoch; **e~machend** △ *adj* epoch-making

Epos ['e:pɔs] (**-s, Epen**) *nt* epic (poem)

er [e:r] (*nom*) *pron* he; it

erarbeiten [ɛr'arbaɪtən] *vt* to work for, to acquire; (*Theorie*) to work out

erbarmen [ɛr'barmən] *vr* (+*gen*) to have pity *od* mercy (on); **E~** (**-s**) *nt* pity

erbärmlich [ɛr'bɛrmlɪç] *adj* wretched, pitiful; **E~keit** f wretchedness

erbarmungslos [ɛr'barmʊŋslo:s] *adj* pitiless, merciless

erbau- [ɛr'baʊ] *zW*: **~en** *vt* to build, to erect; (*fig*) to edify; **E~er** (**-s, -**) *m* builder; **~lich** *adj* edifying

Erbe¹ ['ɛrbə] (**-n, -n**) *m* heir

Erbe² ['ɛrbə] *nt* inheritance; (*fig*) heritage

erben *vt* to inherit

erbeuten [ɛr'bɔytən] *vt* to carry off; (*MIL*) to capture

Erb- [ɛrb] *zW*: **~faktor** *m* gene; **~folge** f (line of) succession; **~in** f heiress

erbittern [ɛr'bɪtərn] *vt* to embitter; (*erzürnen*) to incense

erbittert [ɛr'bɪtərt] *adj* (*Kampf*) fierce, bitter

erblassen [ɛr'blasən] *vi* to (turn) pale

erblich ['ɛrplɪç] *adj* hereditary

erblinden [ɛr'blɪndən] *vi* to go blind

erbrechen [ɛr'brɛçən] (*unreg*) *vt*, *vr* to vomit

Erbschaft f inheritance, legacy

Erbse ['ɛrpsə] f pea

Erbstück *nt* heirloom

Erd- ['e:rd] *zW*: **~achse** f earth's axis; **~atmosphäre** f earth's atmosphere; **~beben** *nt* earthquake; **~beere** f strawberry; **~boden** *m* ground; **~e** f earth;

zu ebener **~e** at ground level; **e~en** *vt* (*ELEK*) to earth

erdenklich [ɛr'dɛŋklɪç] *adj* conceivable

Erd- *zW*: **~gas** *nt* natural gas; **~geschoß** △ *nt* ground floor; **~kunde** f geography; **~nuß** △ f peanut; **~öl** *nt* (mineral) oil

erdrosseln [ɛr'drɔsəln] *vt* to strangle, to throttle

erdrücken [ɛr'drykən] *vt* to crush

Erd- *zW*: **~rutsch** *m* landslide; **~teil** *m* continent

erdulden [ɛr'dʊldən] *vt* to endure, to suffer

ereignen [ɛr'aɪgnən] *vr* to happen

Ereignis [ɛr'aɪgnɪs] (**-ses, -se**) *nt* event; **e~los** *adj* uneventful; **e~reich** *adj* eventful

ererbt [ɛr'ɛrpt] *adj* (*Haus*) inherited; (*Krankheit*) hereditary

erfahren [ɛr'fa:rən] (*unreg*) *vt* to learn, to find out; (*erleben*) to experience ♦ *adj* experienced

Erfahrung f experience; **e~sgemäß** *adv* according to experience

erfassen [ɛr'fasən] *vt* to seize; (*fig*: *einbeziehen*) to include, to register; (*verstehen*) to grasp

erfind- [ɛr'fɪnd] *zW*: **~en** (*unreg*) *vt* to invent; **E~er** (**-s, -**) *m* inventor; **~erisch** *adj* inventive; **E~ung** f invention

Erfolg [ɛr'fɔlk] (**-(e)s, -e**) *m* success; (*Folge*) result; **e~en** [-gən] *vi* to follow; (*sich ergeben*) to result; (*stattfinden*) to take place; (*Zahlung*) to be effected; **e~los** *adj* unsuccessful; **~losigkeit** f lack of success; **e~reich** *adj* successful; **e~versprechend** △ *adj* promising

erforderlich *adj* requisite, necessary

erfordern [ɛr'fɔrdərn] *vt* to require, to demand

erforschen [ɛr'fɔrʃən] *vt* (*Land*) to explore; (*Problem*) to investigate; (*Gewissen*) to search; **Erforschung** f exploration; investigation; searching

erfreuen [ɛr'frɔyən] *vr*: **sich ~ an** +*dat* to enjoy ♦ *vr* to delight; **sich einer Sache** *gen* **~** to enjoy sth

erfreulich [ɛr'frɔylɪç] *adj* pleasing, gratifying; **~erweise** *adv* happily, luckily

△ *For information on spelling reform see page 615*

erfrieren [ɛr'fri:rən] (*unreg*) *vi* to freeze (to death); (*Glieder*) to get frostbitten; (*Pflanzen*) to be killed by frost

erfrischen [ɛr'frɪʃən] *vt* to refresh; **Erfrischung** *f* refreshment

Erfrischungs- *zW:* **~getränk** *nt* (liquid) refreshment; **~raum** *m* snack bar, cafeteria

erfüllen [ɛr'fʏlən] *vt* (*Raum etc*) to fill; (*fig: Bitte etc*) to fulfil ♦ *vr* to come true

ergänzen [ɛr'gɛntsən] *vt* to supplement, to complete ♦ *vr* to complement one another; **Ergänzung** *f* completion; (*Zusatz*) supplement

ergeben [ɛr'ge:bən] (*unreg*) *vt* to yield, to produce ♦ *vr* to surrender; (*folgen*) to result ♦ *adj* devoted, humble

Ergebnis [ɛr'ge:pnɪs] (**-ses, -se**) *nt* result; **e~los** *adj* without result, fruitless

ergehen [ɛr'ge:ən] (*unreg*) *vi* to be issued, to go out ♦ *vi unpers:* **es ergeht ihm gut/ schlecht** he's faring *od* getting on well/ badly ♦ *vr:* **sich in etw** *dat* **~** to indulge in sth; **etw über sich ~ lassen** to put up with sth

ergiebig [ɛr'gi:bɪç] *adj* productive

Ergonomie [ɛrgono'mi:] *f* ergonomics *sg*

Ergonomik [ɛrgo'no:mɪk] *f* = **Ergonomie**

ergreifen [ɛr'graɪfən] (*unreg*) *vt* (*auch fig*) to seize; (*Beruf*) to take up; (*Maßnahmen*) to resort to; (*rühren*) to move; **~d** *adj* moving, touching

ergriffen [ɛr'grɪfən] *adj* deeply moved

Erguß △ [ɛr'gus] *m* discharge; (*fig*) outpouring, effusion

erhaben [ɛr'ha:bən] *adj* raised, embossed; (*fig*) exalted, lofty; **über etw** *akk* **~ sein** to be above sth

erhalten [ɛr'haltən] (*unreg*) *vt* to receive; (*bewahren*) to preserve, to maintain; **gut ~** in good condition

erhältlich [ɛr'hɛltlɪç] *adj* obtainable, available

Erhaltung *f* maintenance, preservation

erhärten [ɛr'hɛrtən] *vt* to harden; (*These*) to substantiate, to corroborate

erheben [ɛr'he:bən] (*unreg*) *vt* to raise; (*Protest, Forderungen*) to make; (*Fakten*) to ascertain, to establish ♦ *vr* to rise (up)

erheblich [ɛr'he:plɪç] *adj* considerable

erheitern [ɛr'haɪtərn] *vt* to amuse, to cheer (up)

Erheiterung *f* exhilaration; **zur allgemeinen ~** to everybody's amusement

erhitzen [ɛr'hɪtsən] *vt* to heat ♦ *vr* to heat up; (*fig*) to become heated

erhoffen [ɛr'hɔfən] *vt* to hope for

erhöhen [ɛr'hø:ən] *vt* to raise; (*verstärken*) to increase

erhol- [ɛr'ho:l] *zW:* **~en** *vr* to recover; (*entspannen*) to have a rest; **~sam** *adj* restful; **E~ung** *f* recovery; relaxation, rest; **~ungsbedürftig** *adj* in need of a rest, run-down; **E~ungsgebiet** *nt* ≈ holiday area; **E~ungsheim** *nt* convalescent home

erhören [ɛr'hø:rən] *vt* (*Gebet etc*) to hear; (*Bitte etc*) to yield to

erinnern [ɛr'ɪnarn] *vt:* **~ (an +***akk*) to remind (of) ♦ *vr:* **sich (an** *akk* **etw) ~** to remember (sth)

Erinnerung *f* memory; (*Andenken*) reminder

erkältet [ɛr'kɛltət] *adj* with a cold; **~ sein** to have a cold

Erkältung *f* cold

erkennbar *adj* recognizable

erkennen [ɛr'kɛnən] (*unreg*) *vt* to recognize; (*sehen, verstehen*) to see

erkennt- *zW:* **~lich** *adj:* **sich ~lich zeigen** to show one's appreciation; **E~lichkeit** *f* gratitude; (*Geschenk*) token of one's gratitude; **E~nis** (**-, -se**) *f* knowledge; (*das Erkennen*) recognition; (*Einsicht*) insight; **zur E~nis kommen** to realize

Erkennung *f* recognition

Erkennungszeichen *nt* identification

Erker ['ɛrkər] (**-s, -**) *m* bay

erklär- [ɛr'klɛ:r] *zW:* **~bar** *adj* explicable; **~en** *vt* to explain; **~lich** *adj* (*verständlich*) understandable; **E~ung** *f* explanation; (*Aussage*) declaration

erkranken [ɛr'kraŋkən] *vi* to fall ill; **Erkrankung** *f* illness

erkund- [ɛr'kʊnd] *zW:* **~en** *vt* to find out, to ascertain; (*bes MIL*) to reconnoitre, to scout; **~igen** *vr*: **sich ~igen (nach)** to inquire (about); **E~igung** *f* inquiry; **E~ung** *f* reconnaissance, scouting

erlahmen [ɛr'laːmən] *vi* to tire; *(nachlassen)* to flag, to wane

erlangen [ɛr'laŋən] *vt* to attain, to achieve

Erlaß △ [ɛr'las] **(-sses, -lässe)** *m* decree; *(Aufhebung)* remission

erlassen *(unreg) vt (Verfügung)* to issue; *(Gesetz)* to enact; *(Strafe)* to remit; **jdm etw ~** to release sb from sth

erlauben [ɛr'laʊbən] *vt*: **(jdm etw) ~** to allow *od* permit (sb (to do) sth) ♦ *vr* to permit o.s., to venture

Erlaubnis [ɛr'laʊpnɪs] **(-, -se)** *f* permission; *(Schriftstück)* permit

erläutern [ɛr'lɔʏtərn] *vt* to explain; **Erläuterung** *f* explanation

erleben [ɛr'leːbən] *vt* to experience; *(Zeit)* to live through; *(miterleben)* to witness; *(noch miterleben)* to live to see

Erlebnis [ɛr'leːpnɪs] **(-ses, -se)** *nt* experience

erledigen [ɛr'leːdɪɡən] *vt* to take care of, to deal with; *(Antrag etc)* to process; *(umg: erschöpfen)* to wear out; *(: ruinieren)* to finish; *(: umbringen)* to do in

erleichtern [ɛr'laɪçtərn] *vt* to make easier; *(fig: Last)* to lighten; *(lindern, beruhigen)* to relieve; **Erleichterung** *f* facilitation; lightening; relief

erleiden [ɛr'laɪdən] *(unreg) vt* to suffer, to endure

erlernen [ɛr'lɛrnən] *vt* to learn, to acquire

erlesen [ɛr'leːzən] *adj* select, choice

erleuchten [ɛr'lɔʏçtən] *vt* to illuminate; *(fig)* to inspire

Erleuchtung *f (Einfall)* inspiration

Erlös [ɛr'løːs] **(-es, -e)** *m* proceeds *pl*

erlösen [ɛr'løːzən] *vt* to redeem, to save; **Erlösung** *f* release; *(REL)* redemption

ermächtigen [ɛr'mɛçtɪɡən] *vt* to authorize, to empower; **Ermächtigung** *f* authorization; authority

ermahnen [ɛr'maːnən] *vt* to exhort, to admonish; **Ermahnung** *f* admonition, exhortation

ermäßigen [ɛr'mɛsɪɡən] *vt* to reduce; **Ermäßigung** *f* reduction

ermessen [ɛr'mɛsən] *(unreg) vt* to estimate, to gauge; **E~ (-s)** *nt* estimation; discretion; **in jds E~ liegen** to lie within sb's discretion

ermitteln [ɛr'mɪtəln] *vt* to determine; *(Täter)* to trace ♦ *vi*: **gegen jdn ~** to investigate sb

Ermittlung [ɛr'mɪtlʊŋ] *f* determination; *(Polizei~)* investigation

ermöglichen [ɛr'møːɡlɪçən] *vt (+dat)* to make possible (for)

ermorden [ɛr'mɔrdən] *vt* to murder

ermüden [ɛr'myːdən] *vt, vi* to tire; *(TECH)* to fatigue; **~d** *adj* tiring; *(fig)* wearisome

Ermüdung *f* fatigue

ermutigen [ɛr'muːtɪɡən] *vt* to encourage

ernähr- [ɛr'nɛːr] *zW*: **~en** *vt* to feed, to nourish; *(Familie)* to support ♦ *vr* to support o.s., to earn a living; **sich ~en von** to live on; **E~er (-s, -)** *m* breadwinner; **E~ung** *f* nourishment; nutrition; *(Unterhalt)* maintenance

ernennen [ɛr'nɛnən] *(unreg) vt* to appoint; **Ernennung** *f* appointment

erneu- [ɛr'nɔʏ] *zW*: **~ern** *vt* to renew; to restore; to renovate; **E~erung** *f* renewal; restoration; renovation; **~t** *adj* renewed, fresh ♦ *adv* once more

ernst [ɛrnst] *adj* serious; **E~ (-es)** *m* seriousness; **das ist mein E~** I'm quite serious; **im E~** in earnest; **E~ machen mit etw** to put sth into practice; **E~fall** *m* emergency; **~gemeint** △ *adj* meant in earnest, serious; **~haft** *adj* serious; **E~haftigkeit** *f* seriousness; **~lich** *adj* serious

Ernte ['ɛrntə] *f* harvest; **e~n** *vt* to harvest; *(Lob etc)* to earn

ernüchtern [ɛr'nyçtərn] *vt* to sober up; *(fig)* to bring down to earth

Erober- [ɛr'oːbər] *zW*: **~er (-s, -)** *m* conqueror; **e~n** *vt* to conquer; **~ung** *f* conquest

eröffnen [ɛr'œfnən] *vt* to open ♦ *vr* to present itself; **jdm etw ~** to disclose sth to sb

△ *For information on spelling reform see page 615*

Eröffnung f opening
erörtern [ɛrˈˈœrtərn] vt to discuss
Erotik [eˈroːtɪk] f eroticism; **erotisch** adj erotic

erpress- [ɛrˈprɛs] zW: **~en** vt (Geld etc) to extort; (Mensch) to blackmail; **E~er (-s, -)** m blackmailer; **E~ung** f extortion; blackmail

erprobt [ɛrˈproːpt] adj (Gerät, Medikamente) proven, tested

erraten [ɛrˈraːtən] (unreg) vt to guess

erreg- [ɛrˈreːg] zW: **~en** vt to excite; (ärgern) to infuriate; (hervorrufen) to arouse, to provoke ♦ vr to get excited od worked up; **E~er (-s, -)** m causative agent; **E~ung** f excitement

erreichbar adj accessible, within reach
erreichen [ɛrˈraɪçən] vt to reach; (Zweck) to achieve; (Zug) to catch
errichten [ɛrˈrɪçtən] vt to erect, to put up; (gründen) to establish, to set up
erringen [ɛrˈrɪŋən] (unreg) vt to gain, to win
erröten [ɛrˈrøːtən] vi to blush, to flush
Errungenschaft [ɛrˈrʊŋənʃaft] f achievement; (umg: Anschaffung) acquisition

Ersatz [ɛrˈzats] (-es) m substitute; replacement; (Schaden~) compensation; (MIL) reinforcements pl; **~dienst** m (MIL) alternative service; **~reifen** m (AUT) spare tyre; **~teil** nt spare (part)

erschaffen [ɛrˈʃafən] (unreg) vt to create
erscheinen [ɛrˈʃaɪnən] (unreg) vi to appear; **Erscheinung** f appearance; (Geist) apparition; (Gegebenheit) phenomenon; (Gestalt) figure
erschießen [ɛrˈʃiːsən] (unreg) vt to shoot (dead)
erschlagen [ɛrˈʃlaːgən] (unreg) vt to strike dead
erschöpf- [ɛrˈʃœpf] zW: **~en** vt to exhaust; **~end** adj exhaustive, thorough; **E~ung** f exhaustion
erschrecken [ɛrˈʃrɛkən] vt to startle, to frighten ♦ vi to be frightened od startled; **~d** adj alarming, frightening
erschrocken [ɛrˈʃrɔkən] adj frightened, startled

erschüttern [ɛrˈʃʏtərn] vt to shake; (fig) to move deeply; **Erschütterung** f shaking; shock
erschweren [ɛrˈʃveːrən] vt to complicate
erschwinglich adj within one's means
ersetzen [ɛrˈzɛtsən] vt to replace; **jdm Unkosten** etc **~** to pay sb's expenses etc
ersichtlich [ɛrˈzɪçtlɪç] adj evident, obvious
ersparen [ɛrˈʃpaːrən] vt (Ärger etc) to spare; (Geld) to save
Ersparnis (-, -se) f saving

erst [eːrst] adv 1 first; **mach erst mal die Arbeit fertig** finish your work first; **wenn du das erst mal hinter dir hast** once you've got that behind you
2 (nicht früher als, nur) only; (nicht bis) not till; **erst gestern** only yesterday; **erst morgen** not until tomorrow; **erst als** only when, not until; **wir fahren erst später** we're not going until later; **er ist (gerade) erst angekommen** he's only just arrived
3: **wäre er doch erst zurück!** if only he were back!

erstatten [ɛrˈʃtatən] vt (Kosten) to (re)pay; **Anzeige** etc **gegen jdn ~** to report sb; **Bericht ~** to make a report
Erstattung f (von Kosten) refund
Erstaufführung [ˈeːrstˈaʊffyːrʊŋ] f first performance
erstaunen [ɛrˈʃtaʊnən] vt to astonish ♦ vi to be astonished; **E~ (-s)** nt astonishment
erstaunlich adj astonishing
erst- [ˈeːrst] zW: **E~ausgabe** f first edition; **~beste(r, s)** adj first that comes along; **~e(r, s)** adj first
erstechen [ɛrˈʃtɛçən] (unreg) vt to stab (to death)
erstehen [ɛrˈʃteːən] (unreg) vt to buy ♦ vi to (a)rise
erstens [ˈeːrstəns] adv firstly, in the first place
ersticken [ɛrˈʃtɪkən] vt (auch fig) to stifle; (Mensch) to suffocate; (Flammen) to smother ♦ vi (Mensch) to suffocate; (Feuer)

to be smothered; **in Arbeit ~** to be snowed under with work

erst- *zW:* **~klassig** *adj* first-class; **~malig** *adj* first; **~mals** *adv* for the first time

erstrebenswert [ɛr'ʃtreːbənsveːrt] *adj* desirable, worthwhile

erstrecken [ɛr'ʃtrɛkən] *vr* to extend, to stretch

ersuchen [ɛr'zuːxən] *vt* to request

ertappen [ɛr'tapən] *vt* to catch, to detect

erteilen [ɛr'taɪlən] *vt* to give

Ertrag [ɛr'traːk] **(-(e)s, -̈e)** *m* yield; (*Gewinn*) proceeds *pl*

ertragen [ɛr'traːgən] (*unreg*) *vt* to bear, to stand

erträglich [ɛr'trɛːklɪç] *adj* tolerable, bearable

ertrinken [ɛr'trɪŋkən] (*unreg*) *vi* to drown; **E~** **(-s)** *nt* drowning

erübrigen [ɛr'lyːbrɪgən] *vt* to spare ♦ *vr* to be unnecessary

erwachen [ɛr'vaxən] *vi* to awake

erwachsen [ɛr'vaksən] *adj* grown-up; **E~e(r)** *f(m)* adult; **E~enbildung** *f* adult education

erwägen [ɛr'vɛːgən] (*unreg*) *vt* to consider; **Erwägung** *f* consideration

erwähn- [ɛr'vɛːn] *zW:* **~en** *vt* to mention; **~enswert** *adj* worth mentioning; **E~ung** *f* mention

erwärmen [ɛr'vɛrmən] *vt* to warm, to heat ♦ *vr* to get warm, to warm up; **sich ~ für** to warm to

Erwarten *nt:* **über meinen/unseren** *usw* **~** beyond my/our *etc* expectations; **wider ~** contrary to expectations

erwarten [ɛr'vartən] *vt* to expect; (*warten auf*) to wait for; **etw kaum ~ können** to be hardly able to wait for sth

Erwartung *f* expectation

erwartungsgemäß *adv* as expected

erwartungsvoll *adj* expectant

erwecken [ɛr'vɛkən] *vt* to rouse, to awake; **den Anschein ~** to give the impression

Erweis [ɛr'vaɪs] **(-es, -e)** *m* proof; **e~en** (*unreg*) *vt* to prove ♦ *vr:* **sich e~en (als)** to prove (to be); **jdm einen Gefallen/Dienst e~en** to do sb a favour/service

Erwerb [ɛr'vɛrp] **(-(e)s, -e)** *m* acquisition; (*Beruf*) trade; **e~en** [-bən] (*unreg*) *vt* to acquire

erwerbs- *zW:* **~los** *adj* unemployed; **E~quelle** *f* source of income; **~tätig** *adj* (gainfully) employed

erwidern [ɛr'viːdərn] *vt* to reply; (*vergelten*) to return

erwischen [ɛr'vɪʃən] (*umg*) *vt* to catch, to get

erwünscht [ɛr'vʏnʃt] *adj* desired

erwürgen [ɛr'vʏrgən] *vt* to strangle

Erz [eːrts] **(-es, -e)** *nt* ore

erzähl- [ɛr'tsɛːl] *zW:* **~en** *vt* to tell ♦ *vi:* **sie kann gut ~en** she's a good story-teller; **E~er** **(-s, -)** *m* narrator; **E~ung** *f* story, tale

Erzbischof *m* archbishop

erzeug- [ɛr'tsɔʏg] *zW:* **~en** *vt* to produce; (*Strom*) to generate; **E~nis** **(-ses, -se)** *nt* product, produce; **E~ung** *f* production, generation

erziehen [ɛr'tsiːən] (*unreg*) *vt* to bring up; (*bilden*) to educate, to train; **Erzieher(in)** **(-s, -)** *m(f)* (*Berufsbezeichnung*) teacher; (*in Kindergarten*) nursery school teacher; **Erziehung** *f* bringing up; (*Bildung*) education; **Erziehungsbeihilfe** *f* educational grant; **Erziehungs- berechtigte(r)** *f(m)* parent; guardian

erzielen [ɛr'tsiːlən] *vt* to achieve, to obtain; (*Tor*) to score

erzwingen [ɛr'tsvɪŋən] (*unreg*) *vt* to force, to obtain by force

es [ɛs] (*nom, akk*) *pron* it

Esel ['eːzəl] **(-s, -)** *m* donkey, ass

Eskalation [ɛskalatsi'oːn] *f* escalation

eß- ['ɛs] *zW:* **~bar** △ *adj* eatable, edible; **E~besteck** △ *nt* knife, fork and spoon; **E~ecke** △ *f* dining area

essen ['ɛsən] (*unreg*) *vt, vi* to eat; **E~** **(-s, -)** *nt* meal; food

Essig ['ɛsɪç] **(-s, -e)** *m* vinegar

Eß- *zW:* **~kastanie** △ *f* sweet chestnut; **~löffel** △ *m* tablespoon; **~tisch** △ *m* dining table; **~waren** △ *pl* foodstuffs, provisions; **~zimmer** △ *nt* dining room

△ *For information on spelling reform see page 615*

etablieren [eta'bli:rən] *vr* to become established; to set up in business

Etage [e'ta:ʒə] *f* floor, storey; ~**nbetten** *pl* bunk beds; ~**nwohnung** *f* flat

Etappe [e'tapə] *f* stage

Etat [e'ta:] (**-s, -s**) *m* budget

etc *abk* (= *et cetera*) etc

Ethik ['e:tɪk] *f* ethics *sg*; **ethisch** *adj* ethical

Etikett [eti'kɛt] (**-(e)s, -e**) *nt* label; tag; ~**e** *f* etiquette, manners *pl*

etliche ['ɛtlɪçə] *pron pl* some, quite a few; ~**s** *pron* a thing or two

Etui [ɛt'vi:] (**-s, -s**) *nt* case

etwa ['ɛtva] *adv* (*ungefähr*) about; (*vielleicht*) perhaps; (*beispielsweise*) for instance; **nicht** ~ by no means; ~**ig** ['ɛtvaɪç] *adj* possible

etwas *pron* something; anything; (*ein wenig*) a little ♦ *adv* a little

euch [ɔʏç] *pron* (*akk von* **ihr**) you; yourselves; (*dat von* **ihr**) (to) you

euer ['ɔʏər] *pron* (*gen von* **ihr**) of you ♦ *adj* your

Eule ['ɔʏlə] *f* owl

eure ['ɔʏrə] *adj f siehe* **euer**

eure(r, s) ['ɔʏrə(r, s)] *pron* yours; ~**rseits** *adv* on your part; ~**s** *adj nt siehe* **euer**; ~**sgleichen** *pron* people like you; ~**twegen** (*für euch*) for your sakes; (*wegen euch*) on your account; ~**twillen** *adv*: **um** ~**twillen** = **euretwegen**

eurige ['ɔʏrɪgə] *pron*: **der/die/das** ~ yours

Euro- *zW*: ~**pa** [ɔʏ'ro:pa] *nt* Europe; ~**päer(in)** [ɔʏro'pɛ:ər(ɪn)] *m(f)* European; **e~päisch** *adj* European; ~**pameister** [ɔʏ'ro:pa-] *m* European champion; ~**paparlament** *nt* European Parliament; ~**scheck** *m* (*FIN*) eurocheque

Euter ['ɔʏtər] (**-s, -**) *nt* udder

ev. *abk* = **evangelisch**

evakuieren [evaku'i:rən] *vt* to evacuate

evangelisch [evaŋ'ge:lɪʃ] *adj* Protestant

Evangelium [evaŋ'ge:liʊm] *nt* gospel

eventuell [evɛntu'ɛl] *adj* possible ♦ *adv* possibly, perhaps

evtl. *abk* = **eventuell**

EWG [e:ve:'ge:] (**-**) *f abk* (= *Europäische Wirtschaftsgemeinschaft*) EEC, Common Market

ewig ['e:vɪç] *adj* eternal; **E~keit** *f* eternity

exakt [ɛ'ksakt] *adj* exact

Examen [ɛ'ksa:mən] (**-s, -** *od* **Examina**) *nt* examination

Exemplar [ɛksɛm'pla:r] (**-s, -e**) *nt* specimen; (*Buch~*) copy; **e~isch** *adj* exemplary

Exil [ɛ'ksi:l] (**-s, -e**) *nt* exile

Existenz [ɛksɪs'tɛnts] *f* existence; (*Unterhalt*) livelihood, living; (*pej: Mensch*) character; ~**minimum** (**-s**) *nt* subsistence level

existieren [ɛksɪs'ti:rən] *vi* to exist

exklusiv [ɛksklu'zi:f] *adj* exclusive; ~**e** *adv* exclusive of, not including ♦ *präp* +*gen* exclusive of, not including

exotisch [ɛ'kso:tɪʃ] *adj* exotic

Expedition [ɛkspeditsi'o:n] *f* expedition

Experiment [ɛksperi'mɛnt] *nt* experiment; **e~ell** [-'tɛl] *adj* experimental; **e~ieren** [-'ti:rən] *vi* to experiment

Experte [ɛks'pɛrtə] (**-n, -n**) *m* expert, specialist

Expertin *f* expert, specialist

explo- [ɛksplo] *zW*: ~**dieren** [-'di:rən] *vi* to explode; **E~sion** [-zi'o:n] *f* explosion; ~**siv** [-'zi:f] *adj* explosive

Export [ɛks'pɔrt] (**-(e)s, -e**) *m* export; ~**eur** [-'tø:r] *m* exporter; ~**handel** *m* export trade; **e~ieren** [-'ti:rən] *vt* to export; ~**land** *nt* exporting country

Expreß- [ɛks'prɛs] *zW*: ~**gut** ⚠ *nt* express goods *pl*, express freight; ~**zug** ⚠ *m* express (train)

extra ['ɛkstra] *adj inv* (*umg: gesondert*) separate; (*besondere*) extra ♦ *adv* (*gesondert*) separately; (*speziell*) specially; (*absichtlich*) on purpose; (*vor Adjektiven, zusätzlich*) extra; **E~** (**-s, -s**) *nt* extra; **E~ausgabe** *f* special edition; ~**blatt** *nt* special edition

Extrakt [ɛks'trakt] (**-(e)s, -e**) *m* extract

extravagant [ɛkstrava'gant] *adj* extravagant

extrem [ɛks'tre:m] *adj* extreme; ~**istisch** [-'mɪstɪʃ] *adj* (*POL*) extremist; **E~itäten** [-mi'tɛ:tən] *pl* extremities

exzentrisch [ɛks'tsɛntrɪʃ] *adj* eccentric

EZ *nt abk* = **Einzelzimmer**

⚠ *Informationen zur Rechtschreibreform Seite 615*

F, f

Fa. *abk* (= *Firma*) firm; (*in Briefen*) Messrs
Fabel ['fa:bəl] (-, -n) *f* fable; **f~haft** *adj* fabulous, marvellous
Fabrik [fa'bri:k] *f* factory; **~ant** [-'kant] *m* (*Hersteller*) manufacturer; (*Besitzer*) industrialist; **~arbeiter** *m* factory worker; **~at** [-'ka:t] (**-(e)s, -e**) *nt* manufacture, product; **~gelände** *nt* factory site
Fach [fax] (**-(e)s, ¨er**) *nt* compartment; (*Sachgebiet*) subject; **ein Mann vom ~** an expert; **~arbeiter** *m* skilled worker; **~arzt** *m* (medical) specialist; **~ausdruck** *m* technical term
Fächer ['fɛçər] (**-s, -**) *m* fan
Fach- *zW*: **~geschäft** *nt* specialist shop; **~hochschule** *f* technical college; **~kraft** *f* skilled worker, trained employee; **f~kundig** *adj* expert, specialist; **f~lich** *adj* professional; expert; **~mann** (*pl* **-leute**) *m* specialist; **f~männisch** *adj* professional; **~schule** *f* technical college; **f~simpeln** *vi* to talk shop; **~werk** *nt* timber frame
Fackel ['fakəl] (**-, -n**) *f* torch
fad(e) [fa:t, 'fa:də] *adj* insipid; (*langweilig*) dull
Faden ['fa:dən] (**-s, ¨**) *m* thread; **f~scheinig** *adj* (*auch fig*) threadbare
fähig ['fɛ:ɪç] *adj*: **~ (zu** *od* **+gen)** capable (of); able (to); **F~keit** *f* ability
fahnden ['fa:ndən] *vi*: **~ nach** to search for; **Fahndung** *f* search
Fahndungsliste *f* list of wanted criminals, wanted list
Fahne ['fa:nə] *f* flag, standard; **eine ~ haben** (*umg*) to smell of drink; **~nflucht** *f* desertion
Fahr- *zW*: **~ausweis** *m* ticket; **~bahn** *f* carriageway (*BRIT*), roadway
Fähre ['fɛ:rə] *f* ferry
fahren ['fa:rən] (*unreg*) *vt* to drive; (*Rad*) to ride; (*befördern*) to drive, to take; (*Rennen*) to drive in ♦ *vi* (*sich bewegen*) to go; (*Schiff*) to sail; (*abfahren*) to leave; **mit dem Auto/**

Zug ~ to go *od* travel by car/train; **mit der Hand ~ über** *+akk* to pass one's hand over
Fahr- *zW*: **~er(in)** (**-s, -**) *m(f)* driver; **~erflucht** *f* hit-and-run; **~gast** *m* passenger; **~geld** *nt* fare; **~karte** *f* ticket; **~kartenausgabe** *f* ticket office; **~kartenautomat** *m* ticket machine; **~kartenschalter** *m* ticket office; **f~lässig** *adj* negligent; **f~lässige Tötung** manslaughter; **~lehrer** *m* driving instructor; **~plan** *m* timetable; **f~planmäßig** *adj* scheduled; **~preis** *m* fare; **~prüfung** *f* driving test; **~rad** *nt* bicycle; **~radweg** *m* cycle lane; **~schein** *m* ticket; **~scheinentwerter** *m* (automatic) ticket stamping machine
Fährschiff ['fɛ:rʃɪf] *nt* ferry(boat)
Fahr- *zW*: **~schule** *f* driving school; **~spur** *f* lane; **~stuhl** *m* lift (*BRIT*), elevator (*US*)
Fahrt [fa:rt] (**-, -en**) *f* journey; (*kurz*) trip; (*AUT*) drive; (*Geschwindigkeit*) speed; **gute ~!** have a good journey
Fährte ['fɛ:rtə] *f* track, trail
Fahr- *zW*: **~kosten** *pl* travelling expenses; **~richtung** *f* course, direction
Fahrzeit *f* time for the journey
Fahrzeug *nt* vehicle; **~brief** *m* log book; **~papiere** *pl* vehicle documents
fair [fɛ:r] *adj* fair
Fakt [fakt] (**-(e)s, -en**) *m* fact
Faktor ['faktɔr] *m* factor
Fakultät [fakul'tɛ:t] *f* faculty
Falke ['falkə] (**-n, -n**) *m* falcon
Fall [fal] (**-(e)s, ¨e**) *m* (*Sturz*) fall; (*Sachverhalt, JUR, GRAM*) case; **auf jeden ~, auf alle Fälle** in any case; (*bestimmt*) definitely; **auf keinen ~!** no way!
Falle *f* trap
fallen (*unreg*) *vi* to fall; **etw ~ lassen** to drop sth
fällen ['fɛlən] *vt* (*Baum*) to fell; (*Urteil*) to pass
fallenlassen △ (*unreg*) *vt* (*Bemerkung*) to make; (*Plan*) to abandon, to drop
fällig ['fɛlɪç] *adj* due
falls [fals] *adv* in case, if
Fallschirm *m* parachute; **~springer** *m*

△ *For information on spelling reform see page 615*

parachutist

falsch [falʃ] *adj* false; (*unrichtig*) wrong

fälschen ['fɛlʃən] *vt* to forge

fälsch- *zW*: **~lich** *adj* false; **~licherweise** *adv* mistakenly; **F~ung** *f* forgery

Falte ['faltə] *f* (*Knick*) fold, crease; (*Haut~*) wrinkle; (*Rock~*) pleat; **f~n** *vt* to fold; (*Stirn*) to wrinkle

faltig ['faltɪç] *adj* (*Hände, Haut*) wrinkled; (*zerknittert: Rock*) creased

familiär [famili'ɛːr] *adj* familiar

Familie [fa'miːliə] *f* family

Familien- *zW*: **~betrieb** *m* family business; **~kreis** *m* family circle; **~mitglied** *nt* member of the family; **~name** *m* surname; **~stand** *m* marital status

Fanatiker [fa'naːtikər] (**-s, -**) *m* fanatic; **fanatisch** *adj* fanatical

fand *etc* [fant] *vb siehe* **finden**

Fang [faŋ] (**-(e)s, -e**) *m* catch; (*Jagen*) hunting; (*Kralle*) talon, claw; **f~en** (*unreg*) *vt* to catch ♦ *vr* to get caught; (*Flugzeug*) to level out; (*Mensch: nicht fallen*) to steady o.s.; (*fig*) to compose o.s.; (*in Leistung*) to get back on form

Farb- ['farb] *zW*: **~abzug** *m* colour print; **~aufnahme** *f* colour photograph; **~band** *nt* typewriter ribbon; **~e** *f* colour; (*zum Malen etc*) paint; (*Stoffarbe*) dye; **f~echt** *adj* colourfast

färben ['fɛrbən] *vt* to colour; (*Stoff, Haar*) to dye

farben- ['farbən] *zW*: **~blind** *adj* colour-blind; **~freudig** *adj* colourful; **~froh** *adj* colourful, gay

Farb- *zW*: **~fernsehen** *nt* colour television; **~film** *m* colour film; **~foto** *nt* colour photograph; **f~ig** *adj* coloured; **~ige(r)** *f(m)* coloured (person); **~kasten** *m* paintbox; **f~lich** *adj* colour; **f~los** *adj* colourless; **~stift** *m* coloured pencil; **~stoff** *m* dye; **~ton** *m* hue, tone

Färbung ['fɛrbʊŋ] *f* colouring; (*Tendenz*) bias

Farn [farn] (**-(e)s, -e**) *m* fern; bracken

Fasan [fa'zaːn] (**-(e)s, -e(n)**) *m* pheasant

Fasching ['faʃɪŋ] (**-s, -e** *od* **-s**) *m* carnival

Faschismus [fa'ʃɪsmʊs] *m* fascism

Faschist *m* fascist

Faser ['faːzər] (**-, -n**) *f* fibre; **f~n** *vi* to fray

Faß ⚠ [fas] (**-sses, Fässer**) *nt* vat, barrel; (*für Öl*) drum; **Bier vom ~** draught beer

Fassade [fa'saːdə] *f* façade

fassen ['fasən] *vt* (*ergreifen*) to grasp, to take; (*inhaltlich*) to hold; (*Entschluß etc*) to take; (*verstehen*) to understand; (*Ring etc*) to set; (*formulieren*) to formulate, to phrase ♦ *vr* to calm down; **nicht zu ~** unbelievable

Fassung ['fasʊŋ] *f* (*Umrahmung*) mounting; (*Lampen~*) socket; (*Wortlaut*) version; (*Beherrschung*) composure; **jdn aus der ~ bringen** to upset sb; **f~slos** *adj* speechless

fast [fast] *adv* almost, nearly

fasten ['fastən] *vi* to fast; **F~zeit** *f* Lent

Fastnacht *f* Shrove Tuesday; carnival

faszinieren [fastsi'niːrən] *vt* to fascinate

fatal [fa'taːl] *adj* fatal; (*peinlich*) embarrassing

faul [faʊl] *adj* rotten; (*Person*) lazy; (*Ausreden*) lame; **daran ist etwas ~** there's something fishy about it; **~en** *vi* to rot; **~enzen** *vi* to idle; **F~enzer** (**-s, -**) *m* idler, loafer; **F~heit** *f* laziness; **~ig** *adj* putrid

Faust ['faʊst] (**-, Fäuste**) *f* fist; **auf eigene ~** off one's own bat; **~handschuh** *m* mitten

Favorit [favo'riːt] (**-en, -en**) *m* favourite

Fax [faks] (**-, -(e)**) *nt* fax

faxen ['faksən] *vt* to fax; **jdm etw ~** to fax sth to sb

FCKW *m abk* (= *Fluorchlorkohlenwasserstoff*) CFC

Februar ['feːbruaːr] (**-(s), -e**) *m* February

fechten ['fɛçtən] (*unreg*) *vi* to fence

Feder ['feːdər] (**-, -n**) *f* feather; (*Schreib~*) pen nib; (*TECH*) spring; **~ball** *m* shuttlecock; **~bett** *nt* continental quilt; **~halter** *m* penholder, pen; **f~leicht** *adj* light as a feather; **f~n** *vi* (*nachgeben*) to be springy; (*sich bewegen*) to bounce ♦ *vt* to spring; **~ung** *f* (*AUT*) suspension

Fee [feː] *f* fairy

fegen ['feːgən] *vt* to sweep

fehl [feːl] *adj*: **~ am Platz** *od* **Ort** out of

place; **F~betrag** m deficit; **~en** vi to be wanting od missing; (abwesend sein) to be absent; **etw ~t jdm** sb lacks sth; **du ~st mir** I miss you; **was ~t ihm?** what's wrong with him?; **F~er** (**-s, -**) m mistake, error; (Mangel, Schwäche) fault; **~erfrei** adj faultless; without any mistakes; **~erhaft** adj incorrect; faulty; **~erlos** adj flawless, perfect; **F~geburt** f miscarriage; **~gehen** (unreg) vi to go astray; **F~griff** m blunder; **F~konstruktion** f badly designed thing; **~schlagen** (unreg) vi to fail; **F~start** m (SPORT) false start; **F~zündung** f (AUT) misfire, backfire

Feier ['faɪər] (**-, -n**) f celebration; **~abend** m time to stop work; **~abend machen** to stop, to knock off; **jetzt ist ~abend!** that's enough!; **f~lich** adj solemn; **~lichkeit** f solemnity; **~lichkeiten** pl (Veranstaltungen) festivities; **f~n** vt, vi to celebrate; **~tag** m holiday

feig(e) [faɪk, 'faɪgə] adj cowardly

Feige ['faɪgə] f fig

Feigheit f cowardice

Feigling m coward

Feile ['faɪlə] f file

feilschen ['faɪlʃən] vi to haggle

fein [faɪn] adj fine; (vornehm) refined; (Gehör etc) keen; **~!** great!

Feind [faɪnt] (**-(e)s, -e**) m enemy; **f~lich** adj hostile; **~schaft** f enmity; **f~selig** adj hostile

Fein- zW: **f~fühlig** adj sensitive; **~gefühl** nt delicacy, tact; **~heit** f fineness; refinement; keenness; **~kostgeschäft** nt delicatessen (shop); **~schmecker** (**-s, -**) m gourmet; **~wäsche** f delicate clothing (when washing); **~waschmittel** nt mild detergent

Feld [fɛlt] (**-(e)s, -er**) nt field; (SCHACH) square; (SPORT) pitch; **~herr** m commander; **~stecher** (**-s, -**) m binoculars pl; **~weg** m path; **~zug** m (fig) campaign

Felge ['fɛlgə] f (wheel) rim

Fell [fɛl] (**-(e)s, -e**) nt fur; coat; (von Schaf) fleece; (von toten Tieren) skin

Fels [fɛls] (**-en, -en**) m rock; (Klippe) cliff

Felsen ['fɛlzən] (**-s, -**) m = **Fels**; **f~fest** adj

firm

feminin [femi'niːn] adj feminine

Fenster ['fɛnstər] (**-s, -**) nt window; **~bank** f windowsill; **~laden** m shutter; **~leder** nt chamois (leather); **~scheibe** f windowpane

Ferien ['feːriən] pl holidays, vacation sg (US); **~ haben** to be on holiday; **~bungalow** [-bʊŋgalo] (**-s, -s**) m holiday bungalow; **~haus** nt holiday home; **~kurs** m holiday course; **~lager** nt holiday camp; **~reise** f holiday; **~wohnung** f holiday apartment

Ferkel ['fɛrkəl] (**-s, -**) nt piglet

fern [fɛrn] adj, adv far-off, distant; **~ von hier** a long way (away) from here; **der F~e Osten** the Far East; **F~bedienung** f remote control; **F~e** f distance; **~er** adj further ♦ adv further; (weiterhin) in future; **F~gespräch** nt trunk call; **F~glas** nt binoculars pl; **~halten** △ (unreg) vt, vr to keep away; **F~licht** nt (AUT) full beam; **F~rohr** nt telescope; **F~ruf** m (förmlich) telephone number; **F~schreiben** nt telex; **F~sehapparat** m television set; **F~sehen** (**-s**) nt television; **im F~sehen** on television; **~sehen** (unreg) vi to watch television; **F~seher** m television; **F~sehturm** m television tower; **F~sprecher** m telephone; **F~steuerung** f remote control; **F~straße** f ≈ 'A' road (BRIT), highway (US); **F~verkehr** m long-distance traffic

Ferse ['fɛrzə] f heel

fertig ['fɛrtɪç] adj (bereit) ready; (beendet) finished; (gebrauchs~) ready-made; **~bringen** △ (unreg) vt (fähig sein) to be capable of; **F~gericht** nt precooked meal; **F~haus** nt kit house, prefab; **F~keit** f skill; **~machen** △ vt (beenden) to finish; (umg: Person) to finish; (: körperlich) to exhaust; (: moralisch) to get down ♦ vr to get ready; **~stellen** △ vt to complete

Fessel ['fɛsəl] (**-, -n**) f fetter; **f~n** vt to fetter; (mit Fesseln) to fetter; (fig) to spellbind; **f~nd** adj fascinating, captivating

Fest (**-(e)s, -e**) nt party; festival; **frohes ~!** Happy Christmas!

△ For information on spelling reform see page 615

fest [fest] *adj* firm; (*Nahrung*) solid; (*Gehalt*) regular ♦ *adv* (*schlafen*) soundly; **~e Kosten** fixed cost; **~angestellt** ⚠ *adj* permanently employed; **~binden** (*unreg*) *vt* to tie, to fasten; **~bleiben** (*unreg*) *vi* to stand firm; **F~essen** *nt* banquet; **~halten** (*unreg*) *vt* to seize, to hold fast; (*Ereignis*) to record ♦ *vr*: **sich ~halten (an** +*dat*) to hold on (to); **~igen** *vt* to strengthen; **F~igkeit** *f* strength; **F~ival** ['festɪval] (**-s, -s**) *nt* festival; **F~land** *nt* mainland; **~legen** *vt* to fix ♦ *vr* to commit o.s.; **~lich** *adj* festive; **~liegen** (*unreg*) *vi* (*feststehen: Termin*) to be confirmed, to be fixed; (*Termin etc*) to fix; **F~machen** *vt* to fasten; (*Termin etc*) to fix; **F~nahme** *f* arrest; **~nehmen** (*unreg*) *vt* to arrest; **F~preis** *m* (*COMM*) fixed price; **F~rede** *f* address; **~setzen** *vt* to fix, to settle; **F~spiele** *pl* (*Veranstaltung*) festival *sg*; **~stehen** (*unreg*) *vi* to be certain; **~stellen** *vt* to establish; (*sagen*) to remark; **F~tag** *m* feast day, holiday; **F~ung** *f* fortress; **F~wochen** *pl* festival *sg*

Fett [fet] (**-(e)s, -e**) *nt* fat, grease

fett *adj* fat; (*Essen etc*) greasy; (*TYP*) bold; **~arm** *adj* low fat; **~en** *vt* to grease; **F~fleck** *m* grease stain; **~ig** *adj* greasy, fatty

Fetzen ['fetsən] (**-s, -**) *m* scrap

feucht [fɔʏçt] *adj* damp; (*Luft*) humid; **F~igkeit** *f* dampness; humidity; **F~igkeitscreme** *f* moisturizing cream

Feuer ['fɔʏər] (**-s, -**) *nt* fire; (*zum Rauchen*) a light; (*fig: Schwung*) spirit; **~alarm** *nt* fire alarm; **f~fest** *adj* fireproof; **~gefahr** *f* danger of fire; **f~gefährlich** *adj* inflammable; **~leiter** *f* fire escape ladder; **~löscher** (**-s, -**) *m* fire extinguisher; **~melder** (**-s, -**) *m* fire alarm; **f~n** *vt, vi* (*auch fig*) to fire; **~stein** *m* flint; **~treppe** *f* fire escape; **~wehr** (**-, -en**) *f* fire brigade; **~wehrauto** *nt* fire engine; **~wehrmann** *m* fireman; **~werk** *nt* fireworks *pl*; **~zeug** *nt* (*cigarette*) lighter

Fichte ['fɪçtə] *f* spruce, pine

Fieber ['fiːbər] (**-s, -**) *nt* fever, temperature; **f~haft** *adj* feverish; **~thermometer** *nt*

thermometer; **fiebrig** *adj* (*Erkältung*) feverish

fiel *etc* [fiːl] *vb siehe* **fallen**

fies [fiːs] (*umg*) *adj* nasty

Figur [fiˈguːr] (**-, -en**) *f* figure; (*Schach~*) chessman, chess piece

Filet [fiˈleː] (**-s, -s**) *nt* (*KOCH*) fillet

Filiale [filiˈaːlə] *f* (*COMM*) branch

Film [fɪlm] (**-(e)s, -e**) *m* film; **~aufnahme** *f* shooting; **f~en** *vt, vi* to film; **~kamera** *f* cine camera

Filter ['fɪltər] (**-s, -**) *m* filter; **f~n** *vt* to filter; **~papier** *nt* filter paper; **~zigarette** *f* tipped cigarette

Filz [fɪlts] (**-es, -e**) *m* felt; **f~en** *vt* (*umg*) to frisk ♦ *vi* (*Wolle*) to mat; **~stift** *m* felt-tip pen

Finale [fiˈnaːlə] (**-s, -(s)**) *nt* finale; (*SPORT*) final(s)

Finanz [fiˈnants] *f* finance; **~amt** *nt* Inland Revenue office; **~beamte(r)** *m* revenue officer; **f~iell** [-tsiˈɛl] *adj* financial; **f~ieren** [-ˈtsiːrən] *vt* to finance; **f~kräftig** *adj* financially strong; **~minister** *m* Chancellor of the Exchequer (*BRIT*), Minister of Finance

Find- ['fɪnd] *zW*: **f~en** (*unreg*) *vt* to find; (*meinen*) to think ♦ *vr* to be (found); (*sich fassen*) to compose o.s.; **ich f~e nichts dabei, wenn ...** I don't see what's wrong if ...; **das wird sich f~en** things will work out; **~er** (**-s, -**) *m* finder; **~erlohn** *m* reward (*for sb who finds sth*); **f~ig** *adj* resourceful

fing *etc* [fɪŋ] *vb siehe* **fangen**

Finger ['fɪŋər] (**-s, -**) *m* finger; **~abdruck** *m* fingerprint; **~nagel** *m* fingernail; **~spitze** *f* fingertip

fingiert *adj* made-up, fictitious

Fink ['fɪŋk] (**-en, -en**) *m* finch

Finn- [fɪn] *zW*: **~e** (**-n, -n**) *m* Finn; **~in** *f* Finn; **f~isch** *adj* Finnish; **~land** *nt* Finland

finster ['fɪnstər] *adj* dark, gloomy; (*verdächtig*) dubious; (*verdrossen*) grim; (*Gedanke*) dark; **F~nis** (**-**) *f* darkness, gloom

Firma ['fɪrma] (**-, -men**) *f* firm

Firmen- ['fɪrmən] *zW*: **~inhaber** *m* owner of firm; **~schild** *nt* (shop) sign; **~wagen**

m company car; **~zeichen** *nt* trademark

Fisch [fɪʃ] (**-(e)s, -e**) *m* fish; **~e** *pl* (*ASTROL*) Pisces *sg*; **f~en** *vt, vi* to fish; **~er** (**-s, -**) *m* fisherman; **~erei** *f* fishing, fishery; **~fang** *m* fishing; **~geschäft** *nt* fishmonger's (shop); **~gräte** *f* fishbone; **~stäbchen** [-ʃtɛːpçən] *nt* fish finger (*BRIT*), fish stick (*US*)

fit [fɪt] *adj* fit; '**Fitneß** ⚠ (**-, -**) *f* (physical) fitness

fix [fɪks] *adj* fixed; (*Person*) alert, smart; **~ und fertig** finished; (*erschöpft*) done in; **~ieren** [fɪˈksiːrən] *vt* to fix; (*anstarren*) to stare at

flach [flax] *adj* flat; (*Gefäß*) shallow

Fläche [ˈflɛçə] *f* area; (*Ober~*) surface

Flachland *nt* lowland

flackern [ˈflakərn] *vi* to flare, to flicker

Flagge [ˈflagə] *f* flag; **f~n** *vi* to fly a flag

flämisch [ˈflɛːmɪʃ] *adj* (*LING*) Flemish

Flamme [ˈflamə] *f* flame

Flandern [ˈflandərn] *nt* Flanders

Flanke [ˈflaŋkə] *f* flank; (*SPORT: Seite*) wing

Flasche [ˈflaʃə] *f* bottle; (*umg: Versager*) wash-out

Flaschen- *zW*: **~bier** *nt* bottled beer; **~öffner** *m* bottle opener; **~zug** *m* pulley

flatterhaft *adj* flighty, fickle

flattern [ˈflatərn] *vi* to flutter

flau [flaʊ] *adj* weak, listless; (*Nachfrage*) slack; **jdm ist ~** sb feels queasy

Flaum [flaʊm] (**-(e)s**) *m* (*Feder*) down; (*Haare*) fluff

flauschig [ˈflaʊʃɪç] *adj* fluffy

Flaute [ˈflaʊtə] *f* calm; (*COMM*) recession

Flechte [ˈflɛçtə] *f* plait; (*MED*) dry scab; (*BOT*) lichen; **f~n** (*unreg*) *vt* to plait; (*Kranz*) to twine

Fleck [flɛk] (**-(e)s, -e**) *m* spot; (*Schmutz~*) stain; (*Stofffleck*) patch; (*Makel*) blemish; **nicht vom ~ kommen** (*auch fig*) not to get any further; **vom ~ weg** straight away

Flecken (**-s, -**) *m* = **Fleck**; **f~los** *adj* spotless; **~mittel** *nt* stain remover; **~wasser** *nt* stain remover

fleckig *adj* spotted; stained

Fledermaus [ˈfleːdərmaʊs] *f* bat

Flegel [ˈfleːgəl] (**-s, -**) *m* (*Mensch*) lout;

f~haft *adj* loutish, unmannerly; **~jahre** *pl* adolescence *sg*

flehen [ˈfleːən] *vi* to implore; **~tlich** *adj* imploring

Fleisch [flaɪʃ] (**-(e)s**) *nt* flesh; (*Essen*) meat; **~brühe** *f* beef tea, meat stock; **~er** (**-s, -**) *m* butcher; **~erei** *f* butcher's (shop); **f~ig** *adj* fleshy; **f~los** *adj* meatless, vegetarian

Fleiß [flaɪs] (**-es**) *m* diligence, industry; **f~ig** *adj* diligent, industrious

fletschen [ˈflɛtʃən] *vt* (*Zähne*) to show

flexibel [flɛˈksiːbəl] *adj* flexible

Flicken [ˈflɪkən] (**-s, -**) *m* patch; **f~** *vt* to mend

Flieder [ˈfliːdər] (**-s, -**) *m* lilac

Fliege [ˈfliːgə] *f* fly; (*Kleidung*) bow tie; **f~n** (*unreg*) *vt, vi* to fly; **auf jdn/etw f~n** (*umg*) to be mad about sb/sth; **~npilz** *m* toadstool; **~r** (**-s, -**) *m* flier, airman

fliehen [ˈfliːən] (*unreg*) *vi* to flee

Fliese [ˈfliːzə] *f* tile

Fließ- [ˈfliːs] *zW*: **~band** *nt* production *od* assembly line; **f~en** (*unreg*) *vi* to flow; **f~end** *adj* flowing; (*Rede, Deutsch*) fluent; (*Übergänge*) smooth

flimmern [ˈflɪmərn] *vi* to glimmer

flink [flɪŋk] *adj* nimble, lively

Flinte [ˈflɪntə] *f* rifle; shotgun

Flitterwochen *pl* honeymoon *sg*

flitzen [ˈflɪtsən] *vi* to flit

Flocke [ˈflɔkə] *f* flake

flog *etc* [floːk] *vb siehe* **fliegen**

Floh [floː] (**-(e)s, ̈e**) *m* flea; **~markt** *m* flea market

florieren [floˈriːrən] *vi* to flourish

Floskel [ˈflɔskəl] (**-, -n**) *f* set phrase

Floß [floːs] (**-es, ̈e**) *nt* raft, float

floß *etc* ⚠ *vb siehe* **fließen**

Flosse [ˈflɔsə] *f* fin

Flöte [ˈfløːtə] *f* flute; (*Block~*) recorder

flott [flɔt] *adj* lively; (*elegant*) smart; (*NAUT*) afloat; **F~e** *f* fleet, navy

Fluch [fluːx] (**-(e)s, ̈e**) *m* curse; **f~en** *vi* to curse, to swear

Flucht [flʊxt] (**-, -en**) *f* flight; (*Fenster~*) row; (*Zimmer~*) suite; **f~artig** *adj* hasty

flücht- [ˈflʏçt] *zW*: **~en** *vi, vr* to flee, to

⚠ *For information on spelling reform see page 615*

escape; **~ig** *adj* fugitive; (*vergänglich*) transitory; (*oberflächlich*) superficial; (*eilig*) fleeting; **F~igkeitsfehler** *m* careless slip; **F~ling** *m* fugitive, refugee

Flug [fluːk] **(-(e)s, "-e)** *m* flight; **~blatt** *nt* pamphlet

Flügel [ˈflyːgəl] **(-s, -)** *m* wing; (*MUS*) grand piano

Fluggast *m* airline passenger

Flug- *zW:* **~gesellschaft** *f* airline (company); **~hafen** *m* airport; **~lärm** *m* aircraft noise; **~linie** *f* airline; **~plan** *m* flight schedule; **~platz** *m* airport; (*klein*) airfield; **~reise** *f* flight; **~schein** *m* (*Ticket*) plane ticket; (*Pilotenschein*) pilot's licence; **~steig** [-ʃtaɪk] **(-(e)s, -e)** *m* gate; **~verbindung** *f* air connection; **~verkehr** *m* air traffic; **~zeug** *nt* (aero)plane, airplane (*US*); **~zeugentführung** *f* hijacking of a plane; **~zeughalle** *f* hangar; **~zeugträger** *m* aircraft carrier

Flunder [ˈflʊndər] **(-, -n)** *f* flounder

flunkern [ˈflʊŋkərn] *vi* to fib, to tell stories

Fluor [ˈfluːɔr] **(-s)** *nt* fluorine

Flur [fluːr] **(-(e)s, -e)** *m* hall; (*Treppen~*) staircase

Fluß △ [flʊs] **(-sses, "-sse)** *m* river; (*Fließen*) flow

flüssig [ˈflʏsɪç] *adj* liquid; **F~keit** *f* liquid; (*Zustand*) liquidity; **~machen** △ *vt* (*Geld*) to make available

flüstern [ˈflʏstərn] *vt, vi* to whisper

Flut [fluːt] **(-, -en)** *f* (*auch fig*) flood; (*Gezeiten*) high tide; **f~en** *vi* to flood; **~licht** *nt* floodlight

Fohlen [ˈfoːlən] **(-s, -)** *nt* foal

Föhn [føːn] **(-(e)s, -e)** *m* (*warmer Fallwind*) föhn

Folge [ˈfɔlgə] *f* series, sequence; (*Fortsetzung*) instalment; (*Auswirkung*) result; **in rascher ~** in quick succession; **etw zur ~ haben** to result in sth; **~n haben** to have consequences; **einer Sache** *dat* **~ leisten** to comply with sth; **f~n** *vi +dat* to follow; (*gehorchen*) to obey; **jdm f~n können** (*fig*) to follow *od* understand sb; **f~nd** *adj* following; **f~ndermaßen** *adv* as follows, in

the following way; **f~rn** *vt:* **f~rn (aus)** to conclude (from); **~rung** *f* conclusion

folglich [ˈfɔlklɪç] *adv* consequently

folgsam [ˈfɔlkzaːm] *adj* obedient

Folie [ˈfoːliə] *f* foil

Folklore [ˈfɔlkloːər] *f* folklore

Folter [ˈfɔltər] **(-, -n)** *f* torture; (*Gerät*) rack; **f~n** *vt* to torture

Fön △ [føːn] **(-(e)s, -e)** ® *m* hair dryer

Fondue [fõdyː] **(-s, -s** *od* **-, -s)** *nt od f* (*KOCH*) fondue

fönen △ *vt* to (blow) dry

Fontäne [fɔnˈtɛːnə] *f* fountain

Förder- [ˈfœrdər] *zW:* **~band** *nt* conveyor belt; **~korb** *m* pit cage; **f~lich** *adj* beneficial

fordern [ˈfɔrdərn] *vt* to demand

fördern [ˈfœrdərn] *vt* to promote; (*unterstützen*) to help; (*Kohle*) to extract

Forderung [ˈfɔrdəruŋ] *f* demand

Förderung [ˈfœrdəruŋ] *f* promotion; help; extraction

Forelle [foˈrɛlə] *f* trout

Form [fɔrm] **(-, -en)** *f* shape; (*Gestaltung*) form; (*Guß~*) mould; (*Back~*) baking tin; **in ~ sein** to be in good form *od* shape; **in ~ von** in the shape of

Formali'tät *f* formality

Format [fɔrˈmaːt] **(-(e)s, -e)** *nt* format; (*fig*) distinction

formbar *adj* malleable

Formblatt *nt* form

Formel **(-, -n)** *f* formula

formell [fɔrˈmɛl] *adj* formal

formen *vt* to form, to shape

Formfehler *m* faux pas, gaffe; (*JUR*) irregularity

formieren [fɔrˈmiːrən] *vt* to form ♦ *vr* to form up

förmlich [ˈfœrmlɪç] *adj* formal; (*umg*) real; **F~keit** *f* formality

formlos *adj* shapeless; (*Benehmen etc*) informal

Formular [fɔrmuˈlaːr] **(-s, -e)** *nt* form

formulieren [fɔrmuˈliːrən] *vt* to formulate

forsch [fɔrʃ] *adj* energetic, vigorous

forsch- *zW:* **~en** *vi:* **~en (nach)** to search

(for); (*wissenschaftlich*) to (do) research;
~end adj searching; **F~er** (**-s, -**) m
research scientist; (*Naturforscher*) explorer;
F~ung f research

Forst [fɔrst] (**-(e)s, -e**) m forest

Förster ['fœrstər] (**-s, -**) m forester; (*für Wild*)
gamekeeper

fort [fɔrt] adv away; (*verschwunden*) gone;
(*vorwärts*) on; **und so ~** and so on; **in
einem ~** on and on; **~bestehen** (*unreg*)
vi to survive; **~bewegen** vt, vr to move
away; **~bilden** vr to continue one's
education; **~bleiben** (*unreg*) vi to stay
away; **F~dauer** f continuance; **~fahren**
(*unreg*) vi to depart; (*fortsetzen*) to go on, to
continue; **~führen** vt to continue, to carry
on; **~gehen** (*unreg*) vi to go away;
~geschritten adj advanced; **~pflanzen** vr
to reproduce; **F~pflanzung** f reproduction

fort- zW: **~schaffen** vt to remove;
~schreiten (*unreg*) vi to advance

Fortschritt ['fɔrtʃrɪt] m advance; **~e
machen** to make progress; **f~lich** adj
progressive

fort- zW: **~setzen** vt to continue;
F~setzung f continuation; (*folgender Teil*)
instalment; **F~setzung folgt** to be
continued; **~während** adj incessant,
continual

Foto ['foːto] (**-s, -s**) nt photo(graph);
~apparat m camera; **~'graf** m
photographer; **~gra'fie** f photography;
(*Bild*) photograph; **f~gra'fieren** vt to
photograph ♦ vi to take photographs;
~kopie f photocopy

Fr. abk (= *Frau*) Mrs, Ms

Fracht [fraxt] (**-, -en**) f freight; (*NAUT*)
cargo; (*Preis*) carriage; **~ zahlt Empfänger**
(*COMM*) carriage forward; **~er** (**-s, -**) m
freighter, cargo boat; **~gut** nt freight

Frack [frak] (**-(e)s, ̈e**) m tails pl

Frage ['fraːgə] (**-, -n**) f question; **etw in ~
stellen** to question sth; **jdm eine ~ stellen**
to ask sb a question, to put a question to
sb; **nicht in ~ kommen** to be out of the
question; **~bogen** m questionnaire; **f~n** vt,
vi to ask; **~zeichen** nt question mark

fraglich adj questionable, doubtful

fraglos adv unquestionably

Fragment [fra'gmɛnt] nt fragment

fragwürdig ['fraːkvʏrdɪç] adj questionable,
dubious

Fraktion [fraktsi'oːn] f parliamentary party

frankieren [fraŋ'kiːrən] vt to stamp, to
frank

franko ['fraŋko] adv post-paid; carriage paid

Frankreich ['fraŋkraɪç] (**-s**) nt France

Franzose [fran'tsoːzə] m Frenchman;
Französin [fran'tsøːzɪn] f Frenchwoman;
französisch adj French

Frau [frau] (**-, -en**) f woman; (*Ehe~*) wife;
(*Anrede*) Mrs, Ms; **~ Doktor** Doctor

Frauen- zW: **~arzt** m gynaecologist;
~bewegung f feminist movement; **~haus**
nt women's refuge; **~zimmer** nt female,
broad (*US*)

Fräulein ['frɔʏlaɪn] nt young lady; (*Anrede*)
Miss, Ms

fraulich ['fraulɪç] adj womanly

frech [frɛç] adj cheeky, impudent; **F~heit** f
cheek, impudence

frei [fraɪ] adj free; (*Stelle, Sitzplatz*) free,
vacant; (*Mitarbeiter*) freelance; (*unbekleidet*)
bare; **sich** dat **einen Tag ~ nehmen** to
take a day off; **von etw ~ sein** to be free of
sth; **im F~en** in the open air; **~ sprechen**
to talk without notes; **~ Haus** (*COMM*)
carriage paid; **~er Wettbewerb** (*COMM*)
fair/open competition; **F~bad** nt open-air
swimming pool; **~bekommen** (*unreg*) vt:
einen Tag ~bekommen to get a day off;
~beruflich adj self-employed; **~gebig** adj
generous; **~halten** (*unreg*) vt to keep free;
~händig adv (*fahren*) with no hands;
F~heit f freedom; **~heitlich** adj liberal;
F~heitsstrafe f prison sentence; **F~karte**
f free ticket; **~lassen** (*unreg*) vt to (set)
free; **~legen** vt to expose; **~lich** adv
certainly, admittedly; **ja ~lich** yes of course;
F~lichtbühne f open-air theatre;
F~lichtmuseum nt open-air museum;
~machen vt (*Post*) to frank ♦ vr to arrange

⚠ *For information on spelling reform see page 615*

to be free; (*entkleiden*) to undress; **Tage ~machen** to take days off; **~sprechen** (*unreg*) *vt:* **~sprechen (von)** to acquit (of); **F~spruch** *m* acquittal; **~stehen** (*unreg*) *vi:* **es steht dir ~, das zu tun** you're free to do that ♦ *vt* (*leerstehen: Wohnung, Haus*) to lie/stand empty; **~stellen** *vt:* **jdm etw ~stellen** to leave sth (up) to sb; **F~stoß** *m* free kick

Freitag *m* Friday; **~s** *adv* on Fridays

frei- *zW:* **~willig** *adj* voluntary; **F~zeit** *f* spare *od* free time; **F~zeitpark** *m* amusement park; **F~zeitzentrum** *nt* leisure centre; **~zügig** *adj* liberal, broad-minded; (*mit Geld*) generous

fremd [fremt] *adj* (*unvertraut*) strange; (*ausländisch*) foreign; (*nicht eigen*) someone else's; **etw ist jdm ~** sth is foreign to sb; **~artig** *adj* strange; **F~enführer** ['fremdən-] *m* (tourist) guide; **F~enverkehr** *m* tourism; **F~enverkehrsamt** *nt* tourist board; **F~enzimmer** *nt* guest room; **F~körper** *m* foreign body; **~ländisch** *adj* foreign; **F~sprache** *f* foreign language; **F~wort** *nt* foreign word

Frequenz [fre'kvɛnts] *f* (*RAD*) frequency

fressen ['frɛsən] (*unreg*) *vt, vi* to eat

Freude ['frɔʏdə] *f* joy, delight

freudig *adj* joyful, happy

freuen ['frɔʏən] *vt unpers* to make happy *od* pleased ♦ *vr* to be glad *od* happy; **freut mich!** pleased to meet you; **sich auf etw** *akk* **~** to look forward to sth; **sich über etw** *akk* **~** to be pleased about sth

Freund [frɔʏnt] (**-(e)s, -e**) *m* friend; boyfriend; **~in** [-dɪn] *f* friend; girlfriend; **f~lich** *adj* kind, friendly; **f~licherweise** *adv* kindly; **~lichkeit** *f* friendliness, kindness; **~schaft** *f* friendship; **f~schaftlich** *adj* friendly

Frieden ['fri:dən] (**-s, -**) *m* peace; **im ~** in peacetime

Friedens- *zW:* **~schluß** ⚠ *m* peace agreement; **~vertrag** *m* peace treaty; **~zeit** *f* peacetime

fried- ['fri:t] *zW:* **~fertig** *adj* peaceable; **F~hof** *m* cemetery; **~lich** *adj* peaceful

frieren ['fri:rən] (*unreg*) *vt, vi* to freeze; **ich friere, es friert mich** I'm freezing, I'm cold

Frikadelle [frika'dɛlə] *f* rissole

Frikassee [frika'se:] (**-s, -s**) *nt* (*KOCH*) fricassee

frisch [frɪʃ] *adj* fresh; (*lebhaft*) lively; **~ gestrichen!** wet paint!; **sich ~ machen** to freshen (o.s.) up; **F~e** *f* freshness; liveliness; **F~haltefolie** *f* cling film

Friseur [fri'zø:r] *m* hairdresser

Friseuse [fri'zø:zə] *f* hairdresser

frisieren [fri'zi:rən] *vt* to do (one's hair); (*fig: Abrechnung*) to fiddle, to doctor ♦ *vr* to do one's hair

Frisiersalon *m* hairdressing salon

frißt ⚠ *etc* [frɪst] *vb siehe* **fressen**

Frist [frɪst] (**-, -en**) *f* period; (*Termin*) deadline; **f~gerecht** *adj* within the stipulated time *od* period; **f~los** *adj* (*Entlassung*) instant

Frisur [fri'zu:r] *f* hairdo, hairstyle

frivol [fri'vo:l] *adj* frivolous

froh [fro:] *adj* happy, cheerful; **ich bin ~, daß ...** I'm glad that ...

fröhlich ['frø:lɪç] *adj* merry, happy; **F~keit** *f* merriness, gaiety

fromm [frɔm] *adj* pious, good; (*Wunsch*) idle; **Frömmigkeit** ['frœmɪçkaɪt] *f* piety

Fronleichnam [fro:n'laɪçna:m] (**-(e)s**) *m* Corpus Christi

Front [frɔnt] (**-, -en**) *f* front; **f~al** [frɔn'ta:l] *adj* frontal

fror *etc* [fro:r] *vb siehe* **frieren**

Frosch [frɔʃ] (**-(e)s, ̈e**) *m* frog; (*Feuerwerk*) squib; **~mann** *m* frogman; **~schenkel** *m* frog's leg

Frost [frɔst] (**-(e)s, ̈e**) *m* frost; **~beule** *f* chilblain

frösteln ['frœstəln] *vi* to shiver

frostig *adj* frosty

Frostschutzmittel *nt* antifreeze

Frottier(hand)tuch [frɔ'ti:r(hant)tu:x] *nt* towel

Frucht [fruxt] (**-, ̈e**) *f* (*auch fig*) fruit; (*Getreide*) corn; **f~bar** *adj* fruitful, fertile; **~barkeit** *f* fertility; **f~ig** *adj* (*Geschmack*) fruity; **f~los** *adj* fruitless; **~saft** *m* fruit juice

früh [fry:] *adj, adv* early; **heute ~** this morning; **F~aufsteher (-s, -)** *m* early riser; **F~e** *f* early morning; **~er** *adj* earlier; *(ehemalig)* former ♦ *adv* formerly; **~er war das anders** that used to be different; **~estens** *adv* at the earliest; **F~jahr** *nt* spring; **F~ling** *m* spring; **~reif** *adj* precocious; **F~stück** *nt* breakfast; **~stücken** *vi* to (have) breakfast; **F~stücksbüfett** *nt* breakfast buffet; **~zeitig** *adj* early; *(pej)* untimely

frustrieren [frus'tri:rən] *vt* to frustrate

Fuchs [fuks] **(-es, ¨e)** *m* fox; **f~en** *(umg)* *vt* to rile, to annoy; **f~teufelswild** *adj* hopping mad

Fuge ['fu:gə] *f* joint; *(MUS)* fugue

fügen ['fy:gən] *vt* to place, to join ♦ *vr:* **sich ~ (in** +*akk*) to be obedient (to); *(anpassen)* to adapt oneself (to) ♦ *vr unpers* to happen

fühl- *zW:* **~bar** *adj* perceptible, noticeable; **~en** *vt, vi, vr* to feel; **F~er (-s, -)** *m* feeler

fuhr *etc* [fu:r] *vb siehe* **fahren**

führen ['fy:rən] *vt* to lead; *(Geschäft)* to run; *(Name)* to bear; *(Buch)* to keep ♦ *vi* to lead ♦ *vr* to behave

Führer ['fy:rər] **(-s, -)** *m* leader; *(Fremden~)* guide; **~schein** *m* driving licence

Führung ['fy:ruŋ] *f* leadership; *(eines Unternehmens)* management; *(MIL)* command; *(Benehmen)* conduct; *(Museums~)* conducted tour; **~szeugnis** *nt* certificate of good conduct

Fülle ['fʏlə] *f* wealth, abundance; **f~n** *vt* to fill; *(KOCH)* to stuff ♦ *vr* to fill (up)

Füll- *zW:* **~er (-s, -)** *m* fountain pen; **~federhalter** *m* fountain pen; **~ung** *f* filling; *(Holzfüllung)* panel

fummeln ['fuməln] *(umg)* *vi* to fumble

Fund [funt] **(-(e)s, -e)** *m* find

Fundament [funda'mɛnt] *nt* foundation; **fundamen'tal** *adj* fundamental

Fund- *zW:* **~büro** *nt* lost property office, lost and found *(US)*; **~grube** *f (fig)* treasure trove

fundiert [fun'di:rt] *adj* sound

fünf [fʏnf] *num* five; **~hundert** *num* five hundred; **~te(r, s)** *adj* fifth; **F~tel (-s, -)** *nt*

fifth; **~zehn** *num* fifteen; **~zig** *num* fifty

Funk [funk] **(-s)** *m* radio, wireless; **~e (-ns, -n)** *m (auch fig)* spark; **f~eln** *vi* to sparkle; **~en (-s, e)** *m (auch fig)* spark; **f~en** *vi (durch Funk)* to signal, to radio; *(umg: richtig funktionieren)* to work ♦ *vt (Funken sprühen)* to shower with sparks; **~er (-s, -)** *m* radio operator; **~gerät** *nt* radio set; **~rufempfänger** *m* pager, paging device; **~streife** *f* police radio patrol; **~telefon** *nt* cellphone

Funktion [funktsi'o:n] *f* function; **f~ieren** [-'ni:rən] *vi* to work, to function

für [fy:r] *präp* +*akk* for; **was ~** what kind *od* sort of; **das F~ und Wider** the pros and cons *pl*; **Schritt ~ Schritt** step by step

Furche ['furçə] *f* furrow

Furcht [furçt] **(-)** *f* fear; **f~bar** *adj* terrible, frightful

fürchten ['fʏrçtən] *vt* to be afraid of, to fear ♦ *vr:* **sich ~ (vor** +*dat*) to be afraid (of)

fürchterlich *adj* awful

furchtlos *adj* fearless

füreinander [fy:r|ai'nandər] *adv* for each other

Furnier [fur'ni:r] **(-s, -e)** *nt* veneer

fürs [fy:rs] = **für das**

Fürsorge ['fy:rzɔrgə] *f* care; *(Sozial~)* welfare; **~r(in) (-s, -)** *m(f)* welfare worker; **~unterstützung** *f* social security, welfare benefit *(US)*; **fürsorglich** *adj* attentive, caring

Fürsprache *f* recommendation; *(um Gnade)* intercession

Fürsprecher *m* advocate

Fürst [fʏrst] **(-en, -en)** *m* prince; **~entum** *nt* principality; **~in** *f* princess; **f~lich** *adj* princely

Fuß [fu:s] **(-es, ¨e)** *m* foot; *(von Glas, Säule etc)* base; *(von Möbel)* leg; **zu ~** on foot; **~ball** *m* football; **~ballplatz** *m* football pitch; **~ballspiel** *nt* football match; **~ballspieler** *m* footballer; **~boden** *m* floor; **~bremse** *f (AUT)* footbrake; **~ende** *nt* foot; **~gänger(in) (-s, -)** *m(f)* pedestrian; **~gängerzone** *f* pedestrian precinct; **~nagel** *m* toenail; **~note** *f*

⚠ *For information on spelling reform see page 615*

footnote; **~spur** f footprint; **~tritt** m kick;
(*Spur*) footstep; **~weg** m footpath
Futter ['fʊtər] (**-s, -**) nt fodder, feed; (*Stoff*)
lining; **~al** [-'raːl] (**-s, -e**) nt case
füttern ['fʏtərn] vt to feed; (*Kleidung*) to line
Futur [fu'tuːr] (**-s, -e**) nt future

G, g

g *abk* = **Gramm**
gab *etc* [gaːp] *vb siehe* **geben**
Gabe ['gaːbə] f gift
Gabel ['gaːbəl] (**-, -n**) f fork; **~ung** f fork
gackern ['gakərn] vi to cackle
gaffen ['gafən] vi to gape
Gage ['gaːʒə] f fee; salary
gähnen ['gɛːnən] vi to yawn
Galerie [galə'riː] f gallery
Galgen ['galgən] (**-s, -**) m gallows *sg*; **~frist**
f respite; **~humor** m macabre humour
Galle ['galə] f gall; (*Organ*) gall bladder;
~nstein m gallstone
gammeln ['gaməln] (*umg*) vi to bum
around; **Gammler(in)** (**-s, -**) (*pej*) m(f)
layabout, loafer (*inf*)
Gang [gaŋ] (**-(e)s, ⁻e**) m walk; (*Boten~*)
errand; (*~art*) gait; (*Abschnitt eines Vorgangs*)
operation; (*Essens~, Ablauf*) course; (*Flur etc*)
corridor; (*Durch~*) passage; (*TECH*) gear; **in ~
bringen** to start up; (*fig*) to get off the
ground; **in ~ sein** to be in operation; (*fig*)
to be under way
gang *adj*: **~ und gäbe** usual, normal
gängig ['gɛŋɪç] *adj* common, current; (*Ware*)
in demand, selling well
Gangschaltung f gears *pl*
Ganove [ga'noːvə] (**-n, -n**) (*umg*) m crook
Gans [gans] (**-, ⁻e**) f goose
Gänse- ['gɛnzə] *zW*: **~blümchen** nt daisy;
~füßchen (*umg*) nt (*Anführungszeichen*)
inverted commas; **~haut** f goose pimples
pl; **~marsch** m: **im ~marsch** in single file;
~rich (**-s, -e**) m gander
ganz [gants] *adj* whole; (*vollständig*)
complete ♦ *adv* quite; (*völlig*) completely; **~
Europa** all Europe; **sein ~es Geld** all his

money; **~ und gar nicht** not at all; **es
sieht ~ so aus** it really looks like it; **aufs
G~e gehen** to go for the lot
gänzlich ['gɛntslɪç] *adj* complete, entire
♦ *adv* completely, entirely
Ganztagsschule f all-day school
gar [gaːr] *adj* cooked, done ♦ *adv* quite; **~
nicht/nichts/keiner** not/nothing/nobody
at all; **~ nicht schlecht** not bad at all
Garage [ga'raːʒə] f garage
Garantie [garan'tiː] f guarantee; **g~ren** vt
to guarantee; **er kommt g~rt** he's
guaranteed to come
Garbe ['garbə] f sheaf
Garde ['gardə] f guard
Garderobe [gardə'roːbə] f wardrobe;
(*Abgabe*) cloakroom; **~nfrau** f cloakroom
attendant
Gardine [gar'diːnə] f curtain
garen ['gaːrən] vt, vi to cook
gären ['gɛːrən] (*unreg*) vi to ferment
Garn [garn] (**-(e)s, -e**) nt thread; yarn (*auch
fig*)
Garnele [gar'neːlə] f shrimp, prawn
garnieren [gar'niːrən] vt to decorate;
(*Speisen, fig*) to garnish
Garnison [garni'zoːn] (**-, -en**) f garrison
Garnitur [garni'tuːr] f (*Satz*) set;
(*Unterwäsche*) set of (matching) underwear;
erste ~ (*fig*) top rank; **zweite ~** (*fig*)
second rate
garstig ['garstɪç] *adj* nasty, horrid
Garten ['gartən] (**-s, ⁻**) m garden; **~arbeit** f
gardening; **~gerät** nt gardening tool;
~lokal nt beer garden; **~tür** f garden gate
Gärtner(in) ['gɛrtnər(ɪn)] (**-s, -**) m(f)
gardener; **~ei** [-'raɪ] f nursery;
(*Gemüsegärtnerei*) market garden (*BRIT*),
truck farm (*US*)
Gärung ['gɛːrʊŋ] f fermentation
Gas [gaːs] (**-es, -e**) nt gas; **~ geben** (*AUT*) to
accelerate, to step on the gas; **~hahn** m
gas tap; **~herd** m gas cooker; **~kocher** m
gas cooker; **~leitung** f gas pipe; **~pedal**
nt accelerator, gas pedal
Gasse ['gasə] f lane, alley
Gast [gast] (**-es, ⁻e**) m guest; (*in Lokal*)

⚠ *Informationen zur Rechtschreibreform Seite 615*

patron; **bei jdm zu ~ sein** to be sb's guest; **~arbeiter(in)** *m(f)* foreign worker

Gäste- ['gɛstə] *zW:* **~buch** *nt* visitors' book, guest book; **~zimmer** *nt* guest *od* spare room

Gast- *zW:* **g~freundlich** *adj* hospitable; **~geber (-s, -)** *m* host; **~geberin** *f* hostess; **~haus** *nt* hotel, inn; **~hof** *m* hotel, inn; **g~ieren** [-'tiːrən] *vi* (THEAT) to (appear as a) guest; **g~lich** *adj* hospitable; **~rolle** *f* guest role; **~spiel** *nt* (THEAT) guest performance; **~stätte** *f* restaurant; pub; **~wirt** *m* innkeeper; **~wirtschaft** *f* hotel, inn

Gaswerk *nt* gasworks *sg*

Gaszähler *m* gas meter

Gatte ['gatə] **(-n, -n)** *m* husband, spouse

Gattin *f* wife, spouse

Gattung ['gatʊŋ] *f* genus; kind

Gaudi ['gaʊdi] (*umg:* SÜDD, ÖSTERR) *nt od f* fun

Gaul [gaʊl] **(-(e)s, Gäule)** *m* horse; nag

Gaumen ['gaʊmən] **(-s, -)** *m* palate

Gauner ['gaʊnər] **(-s, -)** *m* rogue; **~ei** [-'raɪ] *f* swindle

geb. *abk* = **geboren**

Gebäck [gə'bɛk] **(-(e)s, -e)** *nt* pastry

gebacken [gə'bakən] *adj* baked; (*gebraten*) fried

Gebälk [gə'bɛlk] **(-(e)s)** *nt* timberwork

Gebärde [gə'bɛːrdə] *f* gesture; **g~n** *vr* to behave

gebären [gə'bɛːrən] (*unreg*) *vt* to give birth to, to bear

Gebärmutter *f* uterus, womb

Gebäude [gə'bɔʏdə] **(-s, -)** *nt* building; **~komplex** *m* (building) complex

geben ['geːbən] (*unreg*) *vt, vi* to give; (*Karten*) to deal ♦ *vb unpers:* **es gibt** there is/are; there will be ♦ *vr* (*sich verhalten*) to behave, to act; (*aufhören*) to abate; **jdm etw ~** to give sb sth *od* sth to sb; **was gibt's?** what's up?; **was gibt es im Kino?** what's on at the cinema?; **sich geschlagen ~** to admit defeat; **das wird sich schon ~** that'll soon sort itself out

Gebet [gə'beːt] **(-(e)s, -e)** *nt* prayer

gebeten [gə'beːtən] *vb siehe* **bitten**

Gebiet [gə'biːt] **(-(e)s, -e)** *nt* area; (*Hoheits~*) territory; (*fig*) field; **g~en** (*unreg*) *vt* to command, to demand; **g~erisch** *adj* imperious

Gebilde [gə'bɪldə] **(-s, -)** *nt* object

gebildet *adj* cultured, educated

Gebirge [gə'bɪrgə] **(-s, -)** *nt* mountain chain

Gebiß △ [gə'bɪs] **(-sses, -sse)** *nt* teeth *pl*; (*künstlich*) dentures *pl*

gebissen *vb siehe* **beißen**

geblieben [gə'bliːbən] *vb siehe* **bleiben**

geblümt [gə'blyːmt] *adj* (*Kleid, Stoff, Tapete*) floral

geboren [gə'boːrən] *adj* born; (*Frau*) née

geborgen [gə'bɔrgən] *adj* secure, safe

Gebot [gə'boːt] **(-(e)s, -e)** *nt* command; (*REL*) commandment; (*bei Auktion*) bid

geboten [gə'boːtən] *vb siehe* **bieten**

Gebr. *abk* (= *Gebrüder*) Bros.

gebracht [gə'braxt] *vb siehe* **bringen**

gebraten [gə'braːtən] *adj* fried

Gebrauch [gə'braʊx] **(-(e)s, Gebräuche)** *m* use; (*Sitte*) custom; **g~en** *vt* to use

gebräuchlich [gə'brɔʏçlɪç] *adj* usual, customary

Gebrauchs- *zW:* **~anweisung** *f* directions *pl* for use; **g~fertig** *adj* ready for use; **~gegenstand** *m* commodity

gebraucht [gə'braʊxt] *adj* used; **G~wagen** *m* secondhand *od* used car

gebrechlich [gə'brɛçlɪç] *adj* frail

Gebrüder [gə'bryːdər] *pl* brothers

Gebrüll [gə'brʏl] **(-(e)s)** *nt* roaring

Gebühr [gə'byːr] **(-, -en)** *f* charge, fee; **nach ~** fittingly; **über ~** unduly; **g~en** *vi:* **jdm g~en** to be sb's due *od* due to sb ♦ *vr* to be fitting; **g~end** *adj* fitting, appropriate ♦ *adv* fittingly, appropriately

Gebühren- *zW:* **~einheit** *f* (TEL) unit; **~erlaß** △ *m* remission of fees; **~ermäßigung** *f* reduction of fees; **g~frei** *adj* free of charge; **~ordnung** *f* scale of charges, tariff; **g~pflichtig** *adj* subject to a charge

gebunden [gə'bʊndən] *vb siehe* **binden**

Geburt [gə'buːrt] **(-, -en)** *f* birth

Geburtenkontrolle *f* birth control

⚠ *For information on spelling reform see page 615*

Geburtenregelung f birth control

gebürtig [gə'byrtɪç] adj born in, native of; **~e Schweizerin** native of Switzerland

Geburts- zW: **~anzeige** f birth notice; **~datum** nt date of birth; **~jahr** nt year of birth; **~ort** m birthplace; **~tag** m birthday; **~urkunde** f birth certificate

Gebüsch [gə'byʃ] (-(e)s, -e) nt bushes pl

gedacht [gə'daxt] vb siehe **denken**

Gedächtnis [gə'dɛçtnɪs] (-ses, -se) nt memory; **~feier** f commemoration

Gedanke [gə'daŋkə] (-ns, -n) m thought; **sich über etw** akk **~n machen** to think about sth

Gedanken- zW: **~austausch** m exchange of ideas; **g~los** adj thoughtless; **~strich** m dash; **~übertragung** f thought transference, telepathy

Gedeck [gə'dɛk] (-(e)s, -e) nt cover(ing); (Speisenfolge) menu; **ein ~ auflegen** to lay a place

gedeihen [gə'daɪən] (unreg) vi to thrive, to prosper

Gedenken nt: **zum ~ an jdn** in memory of sb

gedenken [gə'dɛŋkən] (unreg) vi +gen (beabsichtigen) to intend; (sich erinnern) to remember

Gedenk- zW: **~feier** f commemoration; **~minute** f minute's silence; **~stätte** f memorial; **~tag** m remembrance day

Gedicht [gə'dɪçt] (-(e)s, -e) nt poem

gediegen [gə'diːgən] adj (good) quality; (Mensch) reliable, honest

Gedränge [gə'drɛŋə] (-s) nt crush, crowd

gedrängt adj compressed; **~ voll** packed

gedrückt [gə'drʏkt] adj (deprimiert) low, depressed

gedrungen [gə'drʊŋən] adj thickset, stocky

Geduld [gə'dʊlt] f patience; **g~en** [gə'dʊldən] vr to be patient; **g~ig** adj patient, forbearing; **~sprobe** f trial of (one's) patience

gedurft [gə'dʊrft] vb siehe **dürfen**

geehrt [gə'|eːrt] adj: **Sehr ~e Frau X!** Dear Mrs X

geeignet [gə'|aɪgnət] adj suitable

Gefahr [gə'faːr] (-, -en) f danger; **~ laufen, etw zu tun** to run the risk of doing sth; **auf eigene ~** at one's own risk

gefährden [gə'fɛːrdən] vt to endanger

Gefahren- zW: **~quelle** f source of danger; **~zulage** f danger money

gefährlich [gə'fɛːrlɪç] adj dangerous

Gefährte [gə'fɛːrtə] (-n, -n) m companion; (Lebenspartner) partner

Gefährtin [gə'fɛːrtɪn] f (female) companion; (Lebenspartner) (female) partner

Gefälle [gə'fɛlə] (-s, -) nt gradient, incline

Gefallen[1] [gə'falən] (-s, -) m favour

Gefallen[2] [gə'falən] (-s) nt pleasure; **an etw** dat **~ finden** to derive pleasure from sth

gefallen pp von **fallen** ♦ vi: **jdm ~** to please sb; **er/es gefällt mir** I like him/it; **das gefällt mir an ihm** that's one thing I like about him; **sich** dat **etw ~ lassen** to put up with sth

gefällig [gə'fɛlɪç] adj (hilfsbereit) obliging; (erfreulich) pleasant; **G~keit** f favour; helpfulness; **etw aus G~keit tun** to do sth out of the goodness of one's heart

gefangen [gə'faŋən] adj captured; (fig) captivated; **G~e(r)** f(m) prisoner, captive; **~halten** △ (unreg) vt to keep prisoner; **G~nahme** f capture; **~nehmen** △ (unreg) vt to take prisoner; **G~schaft** f captivity

Gefängnis [gə'fɛŋnɪs] (-ses, -se) nt prison; **~strafe** f prison sentence; **~wärter** m prison warder; **~zelle** f prison cell

Gefäß [gə'fɛːs] (-es, -e) nt vessel; (auch ANAT) container

gefaßt △ [gə'fast] adj composed, calm; **auf etw** akk **~ sein** to be prepared od ready for sth

Gefecht [gə'fɛçt] (-(e)s, -e) nt fight; (MIL) engagement

Gefieder [gə'fiːdər] (-s, -) nt plumage, feathers pl

gefleckt [gə'flɛkt] adj spotted, mottled

geflogen [gə'floːgən] vb siehe **fliegen**

geflossen [gə'flɔsən] vb siehe **fließen**

Geflügel [gə'flyːgəl] (-s) nt poultry

Gefolgschaft [gə'fɔlkʃaft] f following

gefragt [gə'fra:kt] *adj* in demand

gefräßig [gə'frɛːsɪç] *adj* voracious

Gefreite(r) [gə'fraɪtə(r)] *m* lance corporal; (*NAUT*) able seaman; (*AVIAT*) aircraftman

Gefrierbeutel *m* freezer bag

gefrieren [gə'friːrən] (*unreg*) *vi* to freeze

Gefrier- *zW*: **~fach** *nt* icebox; **~fleisch** *nt* frozen meat; **g~getrocknet** [-gətrɔknət] *adj* freeze-dried; **~punkt** *m* freezing point; **~schutzmittel** *nt* antifreeze; **~truhe** *f* deep-freeze

gefroren [gə'froːrən] *vb siehe* **frieren**

Gefühl [gə'fyːl] (-(e)s, -e) *nt* feeling; **etw im ~ haben** to have a feel for sth; **g~los** *adj* unfeeling

gefühls- *zW*: **~betont** *adj* emotional; **G~duselei** [-duːzə'laɪ] *f* over-sentimentality; **~mäßig** *adj* instinctive

gefüllt [gə'fʏlt] *adj* (*KOCH*) stuffed

gefunden [gə'fʊndən] *vb siehe* **finden**

gegangen [gə'gaŋən] *vb siehe* **gehen**

gegeben [gə'geːbən] *vb siehe* **geben** ♦ *adj* given; **zu ~er Zeit** in good time

gegebenenfalls [gə'geːbənənfals] *adv* if need be

SCHLÜSSELWORT

gegen ['geːgən] *präp +akk* **1** against; **nichts gegen jdn haben** to have nothing against sb; **X gegen Y** (*SPORT, JUR*) X versus Y; **ein Mittel gegen Schnupfen** something for colds

2 (*in Richtung auf*) towards; **gegen Osten** to(wards) the east; **gegen Abend** towards evening; **gegen einen Baum fahren** to drive into a tree

3 (*ungefähr*) round about; **gegen 3 Uhr** around 3 o'clock

4 (*gegenüber*) towards; (*ungefähr*) around; **gerecht gegen alle** fair to all

5 (*im Austausch für*) for; **gegen bar** for cash; **gegen Quittung** against a receipt

6 (*verglichen mit*) compared with

Gegenangriff *m* counter-attack

Gegenbeweis *m* counter-evidence

Gegend ['geːgənt] (-, -en) *f* area, district

Gegen- *zW*: **g~ei'nander** *adv* against one another; **~fahrbahn** *f* oncoming carriageway; **~frage** *f* counter-question; **~gewicht** *nt* counterbalance; **~gift** *nt* antidote; **~leistung** *f* service in return; **~maßnahme** *f* countermeasure; **~mittel** *nt* antidote, cure; **~satz** *m* contrast; **~sätze überbrücken** to overcome differences; **g~sätzlich** *adj* contrary, opposite; (*widersprüchlich*) contradictory; **g~seitig** *adj* mutual, reciprocal; **sich g~seitig helfen** to help each other; **~spieler** *m* opponent; **~sprechanlage** *f* (two-way) intercom; **~stand** *m* object; **~stimme** *f* vote against; **~stoß** *m* counterblow; **~stück** *nt* counterpart; **~teil** *nt* opposite; **im ~teil** on the contrary; **g~teilig** *adj* opposite, contrary

gegenüber [ge:gən'|yːbər] *präp +dat* opposite; (*zu*) to(wards); (*angesichts*) in the face of ♦ *adv* opposite; **G~ (-s, -)** *nt* person opposite; **~liegen** (*unreg*) *vr* to face each other; **~stehen** (*unreg*) *vr* to be opposed (to each other); **~stellen** *vt* to confront; (*fig*) to contrast; **G~stellung** *f* confrontation; (*fig*) contrast; **~treten** (*unreg*) *vi +dat* to face

Gegen- *zW*: **~verkehr** *m* oncoming traffic; **~vorschlag** *m* counterproposal; **~wart** *f* present; **g~wärtig** *adj* present ♦ *adv* at present; **das ist mir nicht mehr g~wärtig** that has slipped my mind; **~wert** *m* equivalent; **~wind** *m* headwind; **g~zeichnen** *vt, vi* to countersign

gegessen [gə'gɛsən] *vb siehe* **essen**

Gegner ['geːgnər] (-s, -) *m* opponent; **g~isch** *adj* opposing

gegr. *abk* (= *gegründet*) est.

gegrillt [gə'grɪlt] *adj* grilled

Gehackte(s) [gə'haktə(s)] *nt* mince(d meat)

Gehalt¹ [gə'halt] (-(e)s, -e) *m* content

Gehalt² [gə'halt] (-(e)s, -̈er) *nt* salary

Gehalts- *zW*: **~empfänger** *m* salary earner; **~erhöhung** *f* salary increase; **~zulage** *f* salary increment

gehaltvoll [gə'haltfɔl] *adj* (*nahrhaft*) nutritious

gehässig [gə'hɛsɪç] *adj* spiteful, nasty

Gehäuse [gə'hɔyzə] (**-s, -**) *nt* case; casing; (*von Apfel etc*) core

Gehege [gə'he:gə] (**-s, -**) *nt* reserve; (*im Zoo*) enclosure

geheim [gə'haɪm] *adj* secret; **G~dienst** *m* secret service, intelligence service; **~halten** ⚠ (*unreg*) *vt* to keep secret; **G~nis** (**-ses, -se**) *nt* secret; mystery; **~nisvoll** *adj* mysterious; **G~polizei** *f* secret police

gehemmt [gə'hɛmt] *adj* inhibited, self-conscious

gehen ['ge:ən] (*unreg*) *vt, vi* to go; (*zu Fuß ~*) to walk ♦ *vb unpers*: **wie geht es (dir)?** how are you *od* things?; **~ nach** (*Fenster*) to face; **mir/ihm geht es gut** I'm/he's (doing) fine; **geht das?** is that possible?; **geht's noch?** can you manage?; **es geht** not too bad, O.K.; **das geht nicht** that's not on; **es geht um etw** sth is concerned, it's about sth

gehenlassen ⚠ (*unreg*) *vr* (*unbeherrscht sein*) to lose control (of o.s.) ♦ *vt* to let/ leave alone; **laß mich gehen!** leave me alone!

geheuer [gə'hɔyər] *adj*: **nicht ~** eerie; (*fragwürdig*) dubious

Gehilfe [gə'hɪlfə] (**-n, -n**) *m* assistant; **Gehilfin** *f* assistant

Gehirn [gə'hɪrn] (**-(e)s, -e**) *nt* brain; **~erschütterung** *f* concussion; **~hautentzündung** *f* meningitis

gehoben [gə'ho:bən] *pp von* **heben** ♦ *adj* (*Position*) elevated; high

geholfen [gə'hɔlfən] *vb siehe* **helfen**

Gehör [gə'hø:r] (**-(e)s**) *nt* hearing; **musikalisches ~** ear; **~ finden** to gain a hearing; **jdm ~ schenken** to give sb a hearing

gehorchen [gə'hɔrçən] *vi +dat* to obey

gehören [gə'hø:rən] *vi* to belong ♦ *vr unpers* to be right *od* proper

gehörig *adj* proper; **~ zu** *od +dat* belonging to; part of

gehörlos *adj* deaf

gehorsam [gə'ho:rza:m] *adj* obedient; **G~** (**-s**) *m* obedience

Geh- ['ge:-] *zW:* **~steig** *m* pavement, sidewalk (*US*); **~weg** *m* pavement, sidewalk (*US*)

Geier ['gaɪər] (**-s, -**) *m* vulture

Geige ['gaɪgə] *f* violin; **~r** (**-s, -**) *m* violinist

geil [gaɪl] *adj* randy (*BRIT*), horny (*US*)

Geisel ['gaɪzəl] (**-, -n**) *f* hostage

Geist [gaɪst] (**-(e)s, -er**) *m* spirit; (*Gespenst*) ghost; (*Verstand*) mind

geisterhaft *adj* ghostly

Geistes- *zW:* **g~abwesend** *adj* absent-minded; **~blitz** *m* brainwave; **~gegenwart** *f* presence of mind; **g~krank** *adj* mentally ill; **~kranke(r)** *f(m)* mentally ill person; **~krankheit** *f* mental illness; **~wissenschaften** *pl* the arts; **~zustand** *m* state of mind

geist- *zW:* **~ig** *adj* intellectual; mental; (*Getränke*) alcoholic; **~ig behindert** mentally handicapped; **~lich** *adj* spiritual, religious; clerical; **G~liche(r)** *m* clergyman; **G~lichkeit** *f* clergy; **~los** *adj* uninspired, dull; **~reich** *adj* clever; witty; **~voll** *adj* intellectual; (*weise*) wise

Geiz [gaɪts] (**-es**) *m* miserliness, meanness; **g~en** *vi* to be miserly; **~hals** *m* miser; **g~ig** *adj* miserly, mean; **~kragen** *m* miser

gekannt [gə'kant] *vb siehe* **kennen**

gekonnt [gə'kɔnt] *adj* skilful ♦ *vb siehe* **können**

gekünstelt [gə'kʏnstəlt] *adj* artificial, affected

Gel [ge:l] (**-s, -e**) *nt* gel

Gelächter [gə'lɛçtər] (**-s, -**) *nt* laughter

geladen [gə'la:dən] *adj* loaded; (*ELEK*) live; (*fig*) furious

gelähmt [gə'lɛ:mt] *adj* paralysed

Gelände [gə'lɛndə] (**-s, -**) *nt* land, terrain; (*von Fabrik, Sport~*) grounds *pl*; (*Bau~*) site; **~lauf** *m* cross-country race

Geländer [gə'lɛndər] (**-s, -**) *nt* railing; (*Treppen~*) banister(s)

gelangen [gə'laŋən] *vi*: **~ (an** *+akk od* **zu)** to reach; (*erwerben*) to attain; **in jds Besitz** *akk* **~** to come into sb's possession

gelangweilt [gə'laŋvaɪlt] *adj* bored

gelassen [gə'lasən] *adj* calm, composed; **G~heit** *f* calmness, composure

⚠ *Informationen zur Rechtschreibreform Seite 615*

Gelatine [ʒelaˈtiːnə] f gelatine

geläufig [gəˈlɔyfɪç] adj (üblich) common; **das ist mir nicht ~** I'm not familiar with that

gelaunt [gəˈlaʊnt] adj: **schlecht/gut ~** in a bad/good mood; **wie ist er ~?** what sort of mood is he in?

gelb [gɛlp] adj yellow; (Ampellicht) amber; **~lich** adj yellowish; **G~sucht** f jaundice

Geld [gɛlt] nt (-(e)s, -er) money; **etw zu ~ machen** to sell sth off; **~anlage** f investment; **~automat** m cash dispenser; **~beutel** m purse; **~börse** f purse; **~geber** (-s, -) m financial backer; **g~gierig** adj avaricious; **~schein** m banknote; **~schrank** m safe, strongbox; **~strafe** f fine; **~stück** nt coin; **~wechsel** m exchange (of money)

Gelee [ʒeˈleː] nt (-s, -s) od m jelly

gelegen [gəˈleːɡən] adj situated; (passend) convenient, opportune ♦ vb siehe **liegen**; **etw kommt jdm ~** sth is convenient for sb

Gelegenheit [gəˈleːɡənhaɪt] f opportunity; (Anlaß) occasion; **bei jeder ~** at every opportunity; **~sarbeit** f casual work; **~skauf** m bargain

gelegentlich [gəˈleːɡəntlɪç] adj occasional ♦ adv occasionally; (bei Gelegenheit) some time (or other) ♦ präp +gen on the occasion of

gelehrt [gəˈleːrt] adj learned; **G~e(r)** f(m) scholar; **G~heit** f scholarliness

Geleise [gəˈlaɪzə] (-s, -) nt = Gleis

Geleit [gəˈlaɪt] nt (-(e)s, -e) escort; **g~en** vt to escort

Gelenk [gəˈlɛŋk] nt (-(e)s, -e) joint; **g~ig** adj supple

gelernt [gəˈlɛrnt] adj skilled

Geliebte(r) [gəˈliːptə(r)] f(m) sweetheart, beloved

geliehen [gəˈliːən] vb siehe **leihen**

gelind(e) [gəˈlɪnd(ə)] adj mild, light; (fig: Wut) fierce; **gelinde gesagt** to put it mildly

gelingen [gəˈlɪŋən] (unreg) vi to succeed; **es ist mir gelungen, etw zu tun** I succeeded in doing sth

geloben [gəˈloːbən] vt, vi to vow, to swear

gelten [ˈgɛltən] (unreg) vt (wert sein) to be worth ♦ vi (gültig sein) to be valid; (erlaubt sein) to be allowed ♦ vb unpers: **es gilt, etw zu tun** it is necessary to do sth; **jdm viel/wenig ~** to mean a lot/not to mean much to sb; **was gilt die Wette?** what do you bet?; **etw ~ lassen** to accept sth; **als** od **für etw ~** to be considered to be sth; **jdm** od **für jdn ~** (betreffen) to apply to od for sb; **~d** adj prevailing; **etw ~d machen** to assert sth; **sich ~d machen** to make itself/o.s. felt

Geltung [ˈgɛltʊŋ] f: **~ haben** to have validity; **sich/etw** dat **~ verschaffen** to establish one's position/the position of sth; **etw zur ~ bringen** to show sth to its best advantage; **zur ~ kommen** to be seen/heard etc to its best advantage

Geltungsbedürfnis nt desire for admiration

Gelübde [gəˈlʏpdə] (-s, -) nt vow

gelungen [gəˈlʊŋən] adj successful

gemächlich [gəˈmɛːçlɪç] adj leisurely

Gemahl [gəˈmaːl] (-(e)s, -e) m husband; **~in** f wife

Gemälde [gəˈmɛːldə] (-s, -) nt picture, painting

gemäß [gəˈmɛːs] präp +dat in accordance with ♦ adj (+dat) appropriate (to)

gemäßigt adj moderate; (Klima) temperate

gemein [gəˈmaɪn] adj common; (niederträchtig) mean; **etw ~ haben (mit)** to have sth in common (with)

Gemeinde [gəˈmaɪndə] f district, community; (Pfarr~) parish; (Kirchen~) congregation; **~steuer** f local rates pl; **~verwaltung** f local administration; **~wahl** f local election

Gemein- zW: **g~gefährlich** adj dangerous to the public; **~heit** f commonness; mean thing to do/to say; **g~nützig** adj charitable; **g~nütziger Verein** non-profit-making organization; **g~sam** adj joint, common (auch MATH) ♦ adv together, jointly; **g~same Sache mit jdm machen** to be in cahoots with sb; **etw g~sam haben** to have sth in common; **~samkeit**

⚠ For information on spelling reform see page 615

f community, having in common; **~schaft** *f* community; **in ~schaft mit** jointly *od* together with; **g~schaftlich** *adj* = **gemeinsam**; **~schaftsarbeit** *f* teamwork; team effort; **~sinn** *m* public spirit

Gemenge [gə'mɛŋə] **(-s, -)** *nt* mixture; (*Hand~*) scuffle

gemessen [gə'mɛsən] *adj* measured

Gemetzel [gə'mɛtsəl] **(-s, -)** *nt* slaughter, carnage, butchery

Gemisch [gə'mɪʃ] **(-es, -e)** *nt* mixture; **g~t** *adj* mixed

gemocht [gə'mɔxt] *vb siehe* **mögen**

Gemse △ ['gɛmzə] *f* chamois

Gemurmel [gə'murməl] **(-s)** *nt* murmur(ing)

Gemüse [gə'my:zə] **(-s, -)** *nt* vegetables *pl*; **~garten** *m* vegetable garden; **~händler** *m* greengrocer

gemußt △ [gə'must] *vb siehe* **müssen**

gemustert [gə'mustərt] *adj* patterned

Gemüt [gə'my:t] **(-(e)s, -er)** *nt* disposition, nature; person; **sich** *dat* **etw zu ~e führen** (*umg*) to indulge in sth; **die ~er erregen** to arouse strong feelings; **g~lich** *adj* comfortable, cosy; (*Person*) good-natured; **~lichkeit** *f* comfortableness, cosiness; amiability

Gemüts- *zW:* **~mensch** *m* sentimental person; **~ruhe** *f* composure; **~zustand** *m* state of mind

Gen [ge:n] **(-s, -e)** *nt* gene

genannt [gə'nant] *vb siehe* **nennen**

genau [gə'nau] *adj* exact, precise ♦ *adv* exactly, precisely; **etw ~ nehmen** to take sth seriously; **~genommen** △ *adv* strictly speaking; **G~igkeit** *f* exactness, accuracy; **~so** *adv* just the same; **~so gut** just as good

genehm [gə'ne:m] *adj* agreeable, acceptable; **~igen** *vt* to approve, to authorize; **sich** *dat* **etw ~igen** to indulge in sth; **G~igung** *f* approval, authorization; (*Schriftstück*) permit

General [gene'ra:l] **(-s, -e** *od* **-̈e)** *m* general; **~direktor** *m* director general; **~konsulat** *nt* consulate general; **~probe** *f* dress

rehearsal; **~streik** *m* general strike; **g~überholen** *vt* to overhaul thoroughly; **~versammlung** *f* general meeting

Generation [generatsi'o:n] *f* generation

Generator [gene'ra:tɔr] *m* generator, dynamo

generell [genə'rɛl] *adj* general

genesen [ge'ne:zən] (*unreg*) *vi* to convalesce, to recover; **Genesung** *f* recovery, convalescence

genetisch [ge'ne:tɪʃ] *adj* genetic

Genf ['gɛnf] *nt* Geneva; **der ~er See** Lake Geneva

genial [geni'a:l] *adj* brilliant

Genick [gə'nɪk] **(-(e)s, -e)** *nt* (back of the) neck

Genie [ʒe'ni:] **(-s, -s)** *nt* genius

genieren [ʒe'ni:rən] *vt* to bother ♦ *vr* to feel awkward *od* self-conscious

genieß- *zW:* **~bar** *adj* edible; drinkable; **~en** (*unreg*) *vt* to enjoy; to eat; to drink; **G~er (-s, -)** *m* epicure; pleasure lover; **~erisch** *adj* appreciative ♦ *adv* with relish

genommen [gə'nɔmən] *vb siehe* **nehmen**

Genosse [gə'nɔsə] **(-n, -n)** *m* (*bes POL*) comrade, companion; **~nschaft** *f* cooperative (association)

Genossin *f* (*bes POL*) comrade, companion

Gentechnik ['ge:nteçnɪk] *f* genetic engineering

genug [gə'nu:k] *adv* enough

Genüge [gə'ny:gə] *f:* **jdm/etw ~ tun** *od* **leisten** to satisfy sb/sth; **g~n** *vi* (+*dat*) to be enough (for); **g~nd** *adj* sufficient

genügsam [gə'ny:kza:m] *adj* modest, easily satisfied; **G~keit** *f* moderation

Genugtuung [gə'nu:ktu:ʊŋ] *f* satisfaction

Genuß △ [gə'nus] **(-sses, -̈sse)** *m* pleasure; (*Zusichnehmen*) consumption; **in den ~ von etw kommen** to receive the benefit of sth; **genüßlich** △ [gə'nʏslɪç] *adv* with relish

Genußmittel △ *pl* (semi-)luxury items

geöffnet [gə'œfnət] *adj* open

Geograph △ [geo'gra:f] **(-en, -en)** *m* geographer; **Geogra'phie** △ *f* geography; **g~isch** △ *adj* geographical

Geologe [geo'lo:gə] (**-n, -n**) *m* geologist; **Geolo'gie** *f* geology

Geometrie [geome'tri:] *f* geometry

Gepäck [gə'pɛk] (**-(e)s**) *nt* luggage, baggage; **~abfertigung** *f* luggage office; **~annahme** *f* luggage office; **~aufbewahrung** *f* left-luggage office (*BRIT*), baggage check (*US*); **~aufgabe** *f* luggage office, (*AVIAT*) luggage reclaim; **~netz** *nt* luggage rack; **~träger** *m* porter; (*Fahrrad*) carrier; **~versicherung** *f* luggage insurance; **~wagen** *m* luggage van (*BRIT*), baggage car (*US*)

gepflegt [gə'pfle:kt] *adj* well-groomed; (*Park etc*) well looked after

Gerade [gə'ra:də] *f* straight line; **g~|aus** *adv* straight ahead; **g~he'raus** *adv* straight out, bluntly; **g~stehen** (*unreg*) *vi*: **für jdn/etw g~stehen** to be answerable for sb's (actions)/sth; **g~wegs** *adv* direct, straight; **g~zu** *adv* (*beinahe*) virtually, almost

---

SCHLÜSSELWORT

gerade [gə'ra:də] *adj* straight; (*aufrecht*) upright; **eine gerade Zahl** an even number

♦ *adv* **1** (*genau*) just, exactly; (*speziell*) especially; **gerade deshalb** that's just *od* exactly why; **das ist es ja gerade!** that's just it!; **gerade du** you especially; **warum gerade ich?** why me (of all people)?; **jetzt gerade nicht!** not now!; **gerade neben** right next to

2 (*eben, soeben*) just; **er wollte gerade aufstehen** he was just about to get up; **gerade erst** only just; **gerade noch** (only) just

---

gerannt [gə'rant] *vb siehe* **rennen**

Gerät [gə're:t] (**-(e)s, -e**) *nt* device; (*Werkzeug*) tool; (*SPORT*) apparatus; (*Zubehör*) equipment *no pl*

geraten [gə'ra:tən] (*unreg*) *vi* (*gedeihen*) to thrive; (*gelingen*): **(jdm) ~** to turn out well (for sb); **gut/schlecht ~** to turn out well/

badly; **an jdn ~** to come across sb; **in etw** *akk* **~** to get into sth; **nach jdm ~** to take after sb

Geratewohl [gəra:tə'vo:l] *nt*: **aufs ~** on the off chance; (*bei Wahl*) at random

geräuchert [gə'rɔyçərt] *adj* smoked

geräumig [gə'rɔymɪç] *adj* roomy

Geräusch [gə'rɔyʃ] (**-(e)s, -e**) *nt* sound, noise; **g~los** *adj* silent

gerben ['gɛrbən] *vt* to tan

gerecht [gə'rɛçt] *adj* just, fair; **jdm/etw ~ werden** to do justice to sb/sth; **G~igkeit** *f* justice, fairness

Gerede [gə're:də] (**-s**) *nt* talk, gossip

geregelt [gə're:gəlt] *adj* (*Arbeit*) steady, regular; (*Mahlzeiten*) regular, set

gereizt [gə'raɪtst] *adj* irritable; **G~heit** *f* irritation

Gericht [gə'rɪçt] (**-(e)s, -e**) *nt* court; (*Essen*) dish; **mit jdm ins ~ gehen** (*fig*) to judge sb harshly; **das Jüngste ~** the Last Judgement; **g~lich** *adj* judicial, legal ♦ *adv* judicially, legally

Gerichts- *zW*: **~barkeit** *f* jurisdiction; **~hof** *m* court (of law); **~kosten** *pl* (legal) costs; **~medizin** *f* forensic medicine; **~saal** *m* courtroom; **~verfahren** *nt* legal proceedings *pl*; **~verhandlung** *f* trial; **~vollzieher** *m* bailiff

gerieben [gə'ri:bən] *adj* grated; (*umg: schlau*) smart, wily ♦ *vb siehe* **reiben**

gering [gə'rɪŋ] *adj* slight, small; (*niedrig*) low; (*Zeit*) short; **~fügig** *adj* slight, trivial; **~schätzig** *adj* disparaging

geringste(r, s) *adj* slightest, least; **~nfalls** *adv* at the very least

gerinnen [gə'rɪnən] (*unreg*) *vi* to congeal; (*Blut*) to clot; (*Milch*) to curdle

Gerippe [gə'rɪpə] (**-s, -**) *nt* skeleton

gerissen [gə'rɪsən] *adj* wily, smart

geritten [gə'rɪtən] *vb siehe* **reiten**

gern(e) ['gɛrn(ə)] *adv* willingly, gladly; **~ haben, ~ mögen** to like; **etwas ~ tun** to like doing something; **ich möchte ~ ...** I'd like ...; **ja, ~** yes, please; yes, I'd like to; **~ geschehen** it's a pleasure

gerochen [gə'rɔxən] *vb siehe* **riechen**

⚠ *For information on spelling reform see page 615*

Geröll [gəˈrœl] (**-(e)s, -e**) *nt* scree

Gerste [ˈgɛrstə] *f* barley; **~nkorn** *nt* (*im Auge*) stye

Geruch [gəˈrʊx] (**-(e)s, ̈-e**) *m* smell, odour; **g~los** *adj* odourless

Gerücht [gəˈrʏçt] (**-(e)s, -e**) *nt* rumour

geruhsam [gəˈruːzaːm] *adj* (*Leben*) peaceful; (*Nacht, Zeit*) peaceful, restful; (*langsam: Arbeitsweise, Spaziergang*) leisurely

Gerümpel [gəˈrʏmpəl] (**-s**) *nt* junk

Gerüst [gəˈrʏst] (**-(e)s, -e**) *nt* (*Bau~*) scaffold(ing); frame

gesalzen [gəˈzaltsən] *pp von* **salzen** ♦ *adj* (*umg: Preis, Rechnung*) steep

gesamt [gəˈzamt] *adj* whole, entire; (*Kosten*) total; (*Werke*) complete; **im ~en** all in all; **~deutsch** *adj* all-German; **G~eindruck** *m* general impression; **G~heit** *f* totality, whole; **G~schule** *f* ≈ comprehensive school

---

GESAMTSCHULE

The **Gesamtschule** *is a comprehensive school for pupils of different abilities. Traditionally pupils go to either a* **Gymnasium**, **Realschule** *or* **Hauptschule**, *depending on ability. The* **Gesamtschule** *seeks to avoid the elitism of many* **Gymnasien**. *However, these schools are still very controversial, with many parents still preferring the traditional education system.*

---

gesandt [gəˈzant] *vb siehe* **senden**

Gesandte(r) [gəˈzantə(r)] *m* envoy

Gesandtschaft [gəˈzantʃaft] *f* legation

Gesang [gəˈzaŋ] (**-(e)s, ̈-e**) *m* song; (*Singen*) singing; **~buch** *nt* (*REL*) hymn book

Gesäß [gəˈzɛːs] (**-es, -e**) *nt* seat, bottom

Geschäft [gəˈʃɛft] (**-(e)s, -e**) *nt* business; (*Laden*) shop; (*Geschäftsabschluß*) deal; **g~ig** *adj* active, busy; (*pej*) officious; **g~lich** *adj* commercial ♦ *adv* on business

Geschäfts- *zW:* **~bedingungen** *pl* terms *pl* of business; **~bericht** *m* financial report; **~frau** *f* businesswoman; **~führer** *m* manager; (*Klub*) secretary; **~geheimnis** *nt* trade secret; **~jahr** *nt* financial year; **~lage** *f* business conditions *pl*; **~mann** *m* businessman; **g~mäßig** *adj* businesslike; **~partner** *m* business partner; **~reise** *f* business trip; **~schluß** ⚠ *m* closing time; **~stelle** *f* office, place of business; **g~tüchtig** *adj* business-minded; **~viertel** *nt* business quarter; shopping centre; **~wagen** *m* company car; **~zeit** *f* business hours *pl*

geschehen [gəˈʃeːən] (*unreg*) *vi* to happen; **es war um ihn ~** that was the end of him

gescheit [gəˈʃait] *adj* clever

Geschenk [gəˈʃɛŋk] (**-(e)s, -e**) *nt* present, gift

Geschichte [gəˈʃɪçtə] *f* story; (*Sache*) affair; (*Historie*) history

geschichtlich *adj* historical

Geschick [gəˈʃɪk] (**-(e)s, -e**) *nt* aptitude; (*Schicksal*) fate; **~lichkeit** *f* skill, dexterity; **g~t** *adj* skilful

geschieden [gəˈʃiːdən] *adj* divorced

geschienen [gəˈʃiːnən] *vb siehe* **scheinen**

Geschirr [gəˈʃɪr] (**-(e)s, -e**) *nt* crockery; pots and pans *pl*; (*Pferde~*) harness; **~spülmaschine** *f* dishwasher; **~spülmittel** *nt* washing-up liquid; **~tuch** *nt* dish cloth

Geschlecht [gəˈʃlɛçt] (**-(e)s, -er**) *nt* sex; (*GRAM*) gender; (*Gattung*) race; family; **g~lich** *adj* sexual

Geschlechts- *zW:* **~krankheit** *f* venereal disease; **~teil** *nt* genitals *pl*; **~verkehr** *m* sexual intercourse

geschlossen [gəˈʃlɔsən] *adj* shut ♦ *vb siehe* **schließen**

Geschmack [gəˈʃmak] (**-(e)s, ̈-e**) *m* taste; **nach jds ~** to sb's taste; **~ finden an etw** *dat* to (come to) like sth; **g~los** *adj* tasteless; (*fig*) in bad taste; **~ssinn** *m* sense of taste; **g~voll** *adj* tasteful

geschmeidig [gəˈʃmaidɪç] *adj* supple; (*formbar*) malleable

Geschnetzelte(s) [gəˈʃnɛtsəltə(s)] *nt* (*KOCH*) strips of meat stewed to produce a thick sauce

---

⚠ *Informationen zur Rechtschreibreform Seite 615*

geschnitten [gə'ʃnɪtən] *vb siehe* **schneiden**

Geschöpf [gə'ʃœpf] **(-(e)s, -e)** *nt* creature

Geschoß ⚠ [gə'ʃɔs] **(-sses, -sse)** *nt* (*MIL*) projectile, missile; (*Stockwerk*) floor

geschossen [gə'ʃɔsən] *vb siehe* **schießen**

geschraubt [gə'ʃraupt] *adj* stilted, artificial

Geschrei [gə'ʃraɪ] **(-s)** *nt* cries *pl*, shouting; (*fig: Aufheben*) noise, fuss

geschrieben [gə'ʃriːbən] *vb siehe* **schreiben**

Geschütz [gə'ʃʏts] **(-es, -e)** *nt* gun, cannon; **ein schweres ~ auffahren** (*fig*) to bring out the big guns

geschützt *adj* protected

Geschw. *abk siehe* **Geschwister**

Geschwätz [gə'ʃvɛts] **(-es)** *nt* chatter, gossip; **g~ig** *adj* talkative

geschweige [gə'ʃvaɪɡə] *adv*: ~ **(denn)** let alone, not to mention

geschwind [gə'ʃvɪnt] *adj* quick, swift; **G~igkeit** [-dɪçkaɪt] *f* speed, velocity; **G~igkeitsbeschränkung** *f* speed limit; **G~igkeitsüberschreitung** *f* exceeding the speed limit

Geschwister [gə'ʃvɪstər] *pl* brothers and sisters

geschwommen [gə'ʃvɔmən] *vb siehe* **schwimmen**

Geschwulst [gə'ʃvʊlst] **(-, ̈-e)** *f* swelling; growth, tumour

geschwungen [gə'ʃvʊŋən] *pp von* **schwingen** ♦ *adj* curved, arched

Geschwür [gə'ʃvyːr] **(-(e)s, -e)** *nt* ulcer

Gesell- [gə'zɛl] *zW*: ~e **(-n, -n)** *m* fellow; (*Handwerksgeselle*) journeyman; **g~ig** *adj* sociable; ~**igkeit** *f* sociability; ~**schaft** *f* society; (*Begleitung, COMM*) company; (*Abendgesellschaft etc*) party; **g~schaftlich** *adj* social; ~**schaftsordnung** *f* social structure; ~**schaftsschicht** *f* social stratum

gesessen [gə'zɛsən] *vb siehe* **sitzen**

Gesetz [gə'zɛts] **(-es, -e)** *nt* law; ~**buch** *nt* statute book; ~**entwurf** *m* (draft) bill; ~**gebung** *f* legislation; **g~lich** *adj* legal, lawful; **g~licher Feiertag** statutory holiday; **g~los** *adj* lawless; **g~mäßig** *adj* lawful; **g~t** *adj* (*Mensch*) sedate; **g~widrig** *adj* illegal, unlawful

Gesicht [gə'zɪçt] **(-(e)s, -er)** *nt* face; **das zweite ~** second sight; **das ist mir nie zu ~ gekommen** I've never laid eyes on that

Gesichts- *zW*: ~**ausdruck** *m* (facial) expression; ~**creme** *f* face cream; ~**farbe** *f* complexion; ~**punkt** *m* point of view; ~**wasser** *nt* face lotion; ~**züge** *pl* features

Gesindel [gə'zɪndəl] **(-s)** *nt* rabble

gesinnt [gə'zɪnt] *adj* disposed, minded

Gesinnung [gə'zɪnʊŋ] *f* disposition; (*Ansicht*) views *pl*

gesittet [gə'zɪtət] *adj* well-mannered

Gespann [gə'ʃpan] **(-(e)s, -e)** *nt* team; (*umg*) couple

gespannt *adj* tense, strained; (*begierig*) eager; **ich bin ~, ob** I wonder if *od* whether; **auf etw/jdn ~ sein** to look forward to sth/meeting sb

Gespenst [gə'ʃpɛnst] **(-(e)s, -er)** *nt* ghost, spectre

gesperrt [gə'ʃpɛrt] *adj* closed off

Gespött [gə'ʃpœt] **(-(e)s)** *nt* mockery; **zum ~ werden** to become a laughing stock

Gespräch [gə'ʃprɛːç] **(-(e)s, -e)** *nt* conversation; discussion(s); (*Anruf*) call; **g~ig** *adj* talkative

gesprochen [gə'ʃprɔxən] *vb siehe* **sprechen**

gesprungen [gə'ʃprʊŋən] *vb siehe* **springen**

Gespür [gə'ʃpyːr] **(-s)** *nt* feeling

Gestalt [gə'ʃtalt] **(-, -en)** *f* form, shape; (*Person*) figure; **in ~ von** in the form of; ~ **annehmen** to take shape; **g~en** *vt* (*formen*) to shape, to form; (*organisieren*) to arrange, to organize ♦ *vr*: **sich g~en (zu)** to turn out (to be); ~**ung** *f* formation; organization

gestanden [gə'ʃtandən] *vb siehe* **stehen**

Geständnis [gə'ʃtɛntnɪs] **(-ses, -se)** *nt* confession

Gestank [gə'ʃtaŋk] **(-(e)s)** *m* stench

gestatten [gə'ʃtatən] *vt* to permit, to allow; ~ **Sie?** may I?; **sich** *dat* ~, **etw zu tun** to take the liberty of doing sth

Geste ['ɡɛstə] *f* gesture

⚠ *For information on spelling reform see page 615*

gestehen [gə'ʃteːən] (*unreg*) *vt* to confess
Gestein [gə'ʃtaɪn] (-(e)s, -e) *nt* rock
Gestell [gə'ʃtɛl] (-(e)s, -e) *nt* frame; (*Regal*) rack, stand
gestern ['gɛstərn] *adv* yesterday; ~ **abend/morgen** yesterday evening/morning
Gestirn [gə'ʃtɪrn] (-(e)s, -e) *nt* star; (*Sternbild*) constellation
gestohlen [gə'ʃtoːlən] *vb siehe* **stehlen**
gestorben [gə'ʃtɔrbən] *vb siehe* **sterben**
gestört [gə'ʃtøːrt] *adj* disturbed
gestreift [gə'ʃtraɪft] *adj* striped
gestrichen [gə'ʃtrɪçən] *adj* cancelled
gestrig [gɛstrɪç] *adj* yesterday's
Gestrüpp [gə'ʃtrʏp] (-(e)s, -e) *nt* undergrowth
Gestüt [gə'ʃtyːt] (-(e)s, -e) *nt* stud farm
Gesuch [gə'zuːx] (-(e)s, -e) *nt* petition; (*Antrag*) application; **g~t** *adj* (*COMM*) in demand; wanted; (*fig*) contrived
gesund [gə'zʊnt] *adj* healthy; **wieder ~ werden** to get better; **G~heit** *f* health(iness); **G~heit!** bless you!; ~**heitlich** *adj* health *attrib*, physical ♦ *adv*: **wie geht es Ihnen ~heitlich?** how's your health?; ~**heitsschädlich** *adj* unhealthy; **G~heitswesen** *nt* health service; **G~heitszustand** *m* state of health
gesungen [gə'zʊŋən] *vb siehe* **singen**
getan [gə'taːn] *vb siehe* **tun**
Getöse [gə'tøːzə] (-s) *nt* din, racket
Getränk [gə'trɛŋk] (-(e)s, -e) *nt* drink; ~**ekarte** *f* wine list
getrauen [gə'traʊən] *vr* to dare, to venture
Getreide [gə'traɪdə] (-s, -) *nt* cereals *pl*, grain; ~**speicher** *m* granary
getrennt [gə'trɛnt] *adj* separate
Getriebe [gə'triːbə] (-s, -) *nt* (*Leute*) bustle; (*AUT*) gearbox
getrieben *vb siehe* **treiben**
getroffen [gə'trɔfən] *vb siehe* **treffen**
getrost [gə'troːst] *adv* without any bother
getrunken [gə'trʊŋkən] *vb siehe* **trinken**
Getue [gə'tuːə] (-s) *nt* fuss
geübt [gə'yːpt] *adj* experienced
Gewächs [gə'vɛks] (-es, -e) *nt* growth; (*Pflanze*) plant

gewachsen [gə'vaksən] *adj*: **jdm/etw ~ sein** to be sb's equal/equal to sth
Gewächshaus *nt* greenhouse
gewagt [gə'vaːkt] *adj* daring, risky
gewählt [gə'vɛːlt] *adj* (*Sprache*) refined, elegant
Gewähr [gə'vɛːr] (-) *f* guarantee; **keine ~ übernehmen für** to accept no responsibility for; **g~en** *vt* to grant; (*geben*) to provide; **g~leisten** *vt* to guarantee
Gewahrsam [gə'vaːrzaːm] (-s, -e) *m* safekeeping; (*Polizei~*) custody
Gewalt [gə'valt] (-, -en) *f* power; (*große Kraft*) force; (~*taten*) violence; **mit aller ~** with all one's might; ~**anwendung** *f* use of force; **g~ig** *adj* tremendous; (*Irrtum*) huge; ~**marsch** *m* forced march; **g~sam** *adj* forcible; **g~tätig** *adj* violent
Gewand [gə'vant] (-(e)s, ̈er) *nt* gown, robe
gewandt [gə'vant] *adj* deft, skilful; (*erfahren*) experienced; **G~heit** *f* dexterity, skill
gewann *etc* [gə'van] *vb siehe* **gewinnen**
Gewässer [gə'vɛsər] (-s, -) *nt* waters *pl*
Gewebe [gə'veːbə] (-s, -) *nt* (*Stoff*) fabric; (*BIOL*) tissue
Gewehr [gə'veːr] (-(e)s, -e) *nt* gun; rifle; ~**lauf** *m* rifle barrel
Geweih [gə'vaɪ] (-(e)s, -e) *nt* antlers *pl*
Gewerb- [gə'vɛrp] *zW*: ~**e** (-s, -) *nt* trade, occupation; **Handel und ~e** trade and industry; ~**eschule** *f* technical school; ~**ezweig** *m* line of trade
Gewerkschaft [gə'vɛrkʃaft] *f* trade union; ~**ler** (-s, -) *m* trade unionist; ~**sbund** *m* trade unions federation
gewesen [gə'veːzən] *pp von* **sein**
Gewicht [gə'vɪçt] (-(e)s, -e) *nt* weight; (*fig*) importance
gewieft [gə'viːft] *adj* shrewd, cunning
gewillt [gə'vɪlt] *adj* willing, prepared
Gewimmel [gə'vɪməl] (-s) *nt* swarm
Gewinde [gə'vɪndə] (-s, -) *nt* (*Kranz*) wreath; (*von Schraube*) thread
Gewinn [gə'vɪn] (-(e)s, -e) *m* profit; (*bei Spiel*) winnings *pl*; **etw mit ~ verkaufen** to sell sth at a profit; **~- und Verlust-**

rechnung (COMM) profit and loss account; **~beteiligung** f profit-sharing; **g~bringend** ⚠ adj profitable; **g~en** (unreg) vt to win; (erwerben) to gain; (Kohle, Öl) to extract ♦ vi to win; (profitieren) to gain; **an etw** dat **g~en** to gain (in) sth; **g~end** adj (Lächeln, Aussehen) winning, charming; **~er(in)** (-s, -) m(f) winner; **~spanne** f profit margin; **~ung** f winning, gaining; (von Kohle etc) extraction

Gewirr [gə'vɪr] (-(e)s, -e) nt tangle; (von Straßen) maze

gewiß ⚠ [gə'vɪs] adj certain ♦ adv certainly

Gewissen [gə'vɪsən] (-s, -) nt conscience; **g~haft** adj conscientious; **g~los** adj unscrupulous

Gewissens- zW: **~bisse** pl pangs of conscience, qualms; **~frage** f matter of conscience; **~konflikt** m moral conflict

gewissermaßen [gəvɪsər'maːsən] adv more or less, in a way

Gewißheit ⚠ [gə'vɪshaɪt] f certainty

Gewitter [gə'vɪtər] (-s, -) nt thunderstorm; **g~n** unpers: **es g~t** there's a thunderstorm

gewitzt [gə'vɪtst] adj shrewd, cunning

gewogen [gə'voːɡən] adj (+dat) well-disposed (towards)

gewöhnen [gə'vøːnən] vt: **jdn an etw** akk ~ to accustom sb to sth; (erziehen zu) to teach sb sth ♦ vr: **sich an etw** akk ~ to get used of accustomed to sth

Gewohnheit [gə'voːnhaɪt] f habit; (Brauch) custom; **aus ~** from habit; **zur ~ werden** to become a habit

Gewohnheits- zW: **~mensch** m creature of habit; **~recht** nt common law

gewöhnlich [gə'vøːnlɪç] adj usual; ordinary; (pej) common; **wie ~** as usual

gewohnt [gə'voːnt] adj usual; **etw ~ sein** to be used to sth

Gewöhnung f: ~ **(an** +akk) getting accustomed (to)

Gewölbe [gə'vœlbə] (-s, -) nt vault

gewollt [gə'vɔlt] adj affected, artificial

gewonnen [gə'vɔnən] vb siehe **gewinnen**

geworden [gə'vɔrdən] vb siehe **werden**

geworfen [gə'vɔrfən] vb siehe **werfen**

Gewühl [gə'vyːl] (-(e)s) nt throng

Gewürz [gə'vvrts] (-es, -e) nt spice, seasoning; **g~t** adj spiced

gewußt ⚠ [gə'vʊst] vb siehe **wissen**

Gezeiten [gə'tsaɪtən] pl tides

gezielt [gə'tsiːlt] adj with a particular aim in mind, purposeful; (Kritik) pointed

gezogen [gə'tsoːɡən] vb siehe **ziehen**

Gezwitscher [gə'tsvɪtʃər] (-s) nt twitter(ing), chirping

gezwungen [gə'tsvʊŋən] adj forced; **~ermaßen** adv of necessity

ggf abk von **gegebenenfalls**

gibst etc [giːpst] vb siehe **geben**

Gicht [gɪçt] (-) f gout

Giebel ['giːbəl] (-s, -) m gable; **~dach** nt gable(d) roof; **~fenster** nt gable window

Gier [giːr] (-) f greed; **g~ig** adj greedy

gießen ['giːsən] (unreg) vt to pour; (Blumen) to water; (Metall) to cast; (Wachs) to mould

Gießkanne f watering can

Gift [gɪft] (-(e)s, -e) nt poison; **g~ig** adj poisonous; (fig: boshaft) venomous; **~müll** m toxic waste; **~stoff** m toxic substance; **~zahn** m fang

ging etc [gɪŋ] vb siehe **gehen**

Gipfel ['gɪpfəl] (-s, -) m summit, peak; (fig: Höhepunkt) height; **g~n** vi to culminate; **~treffen** nt summit (meeting)

Gips [gɪps] (-es, -e) m plaster; (MED) plaster (of Paris); **~abdruck** m plaster cast; **g~en** vt to plaster; **~verband** m plaster (cast)

Giraffe [gi'rafə] f giraffe

Girlande [gɪr'landə] f garland

Giro ['ʒiːro] (-s, -s) nt giro; **~konto** nt current account

Gitarre [gi'tarə] f guitar

Gitter ['gɪtər] (-s, -) nt grating, bars pl; (für Pflanzen) trellis; (Zaun) railing(s); **~bett** nt cot; **~fenster** nt barred window; **~zaun** m railing(s)

Glanz [glants] (-es) m shine, lustre; (fig) splendour

glänzen ['glɛntsən] vi to shine (also fig), to gleam ♦ vt to polish; **~d** adj shining; (fig) brilliant

⚠ For information on spelling reform see page 615

Glanz- *zW:* **~leistung** *f* brilliant achievement; **g~los** *adj* dull; **~zeit** *f* heyday

Glas [glaːs] **(-es, ⁻er)** *nt* glass; **~er (-s, -)** *m* glazier; **~faser** *f* fibreglass; **g~ieren** [glaˈziːrən] *vt* to glaze; **g~ig** *adj* glassy; **~scheibe** *f* pane; **~ur** [glaˈzuːr] *f* glaze; (*KOCH*) icing

glatt [glat] *adj* smooth; (*rutschig*) slippery; (*Absage*) flat; (*Lüge*) downright; **Glätte** *f* smoothness; slipperiness

Glatteis *nt* (black) ice; **jdn aufs ~ führen** (*fig*) to take sb for a ride

glätten *vt* to smooth out

Glatze [ˈglatsə] *f* bald head; **eine ~ bekommen** to go bald

Glaube [ˈglaubə] **(-ns, -n)** *m:* **~ (an** +*akk*) faith (in); belief (in); **g~n** *vt, vi* to believe; to think; **jdm g~n** to believe sb; **an etw** *akk* **g~n** to believe in sth; **daran g~n müssen** (*umg*) to be for it

glaubhaft [ˈglaubhaft] *adj* credible

gläubig [ˈglɔybɪç] *adj* (*REL*) devout; (*vertrauensvoll*) trustful; **G~e(r)** *f(m)* believer; **die G~en** the faithful; **G~er (-s, -)** *m* creditor

glaubwürdig [ˈglaubvyrdɪç] *adj* credible; (*Mensch*) trustworthy; **G~keit** *f* credibility; trustworthiness

gleich [glaɪç] *adj* equal; (*identisch*) (the) same, identical ♦ *adv* equally; (*sofort*) straight away; (*bald*) in a minute; **es ist mir ~** it's all the same to me; **2 mal 2 ~ 4** 2 times 2 is *od* equals 4; **~ groß** the same size; **~ nach/an** right after/at; **~altrig** *adj* of the same age; **~artig** *adj* similar; **~bedeutend** *adj* synonymous; **G~berechtigung** *f* equal rights *pl*; **~bleibend** ⚠ *adj* constant; **~en** (*unreg*) *vi:* **jdm/etw ~en** to be like sb/sth ♦ *vr* to be alike; **~falls** *adv* likewise; **danke ~falls!** the same to you; **G~förmigkeit** *f* uniformity; **~gesinnt** ⚠ *adj* like-minded; **G~gewicht** *nt* equilibrium, balance; **~gültig** *adj* indifferent; (*unbedeutend*) unimportant; **G~gültigkeit** *f* indifference; **G~heit** *f* equality; **~kommen** (*unreg*) *vi* +*dat* to be

equal to; **~mäßig** *adj* even, equal; **~sam** *adv* as it were; **G~schritt** *m:* **im G~schritt gehen** to walk in step; **~stellen** *vt* (*rechtlich etc*) to treat as (an) equal; **G~strom** *m* (*ELEK*) direct current; **~tun** (*unreg*) *vi:* **es jdm ~tun** to match sb; **G~ung** *f* equation; **~viel** *adv* no matter; **~wertig** *adj* (*Geld*) of the same value; (*Gegner*) evenly matched; **~zeitig** *adj* simultaneous

Gleis [glaɪs] **(-es, -e)** *nt* track, rails *pl*; (*Bahnsteig*) platform

gleiten [ˈglaɪtən] (*unreg*) *vi* to glide; (*rutschen*) to slide

Gleitzeit *f* flex(i)time

Gletscher [ˈglɛtʃər] **(-s, -)** *m* glacier; **~spalte** *f* crevasse

Glied [gliːt] **(-(e)s, -er)** *nt* member; (*Arm, Bein*) limb; (*von Kette*) link; (*MIL*) rank(s); **g~ern** [-dərn] *vt* to organize, to structure; **~erung** *f* structure, organization

glimmen [ˈglɪmən] (*unreg*) *vi* to glow, to gleam

glimpflich [ˈglɪmpflɪç] *adj* mild, lenient; **~ davonkommen** to get off lightly

glitschig [ˈglɪtʃɪç] *adj* (*Fisch, Weg*) slippery

glitzern [ˈglɪtsərn] *vi* to glitter; to twinkle

global [gloˈbaːl] *adj* global

Globus [ˈgloːbus] **(- *od* -ses, Globen *od* -se)** *m* globe

Glocke [ˈglɔkə] *f* bell; **etw an die große ~ hängen** (*fig*) to shout sth from the rooftops

Glocken- *zW:* **~blume** *f* bellflower; **~geläut** *nt* peal of bells; **~spiel** *nt* chime(s); (*MUS*) glockenspiel; **~turm** *m* bell tower

Glosse [ˈglɔsə] *f* comment

glotzen [ˈglɔtsən] (*umg*) *vi* to stare

Glück [glyk] **(-(e)s)** *nt* luck, fortune; (*Freude*) happiness; **~ haben** to be lucky; **viel ~!** good luck!; **zum ~** fortunately; **g~en** *vi* to succeed; **es g~te ihm, es zu bekommen** he succeeded in getting it

gluckern [ˈglukərn] *vi* to glug

glück- *zW:* **~lich** *adj* fortunate; (*froh*) happy; **~licherweise** *adv* fortunately; **~'selig** *adj* blissful

⚠ *Informationen zur Rechtschreibreform Seite 615*

Glücks- zW: **~fall** m stroke of luck; **~kind** nt lucky person; **~sache** f matter of luck; **~spiel** nt game of chance

Glückwunsch m congratulations pl, best wishes pl

Glüh- ['glyː] zW: **~birne** f light bulb; **g~en** vi to glow; **~wein** m mulled wine; **~würmchen** nt glow-worm

Glut [gluːt] (-, **-en**) f (Röte) glow; (Feuers~) fire; (Hitze) heat; (fig) ardour

GmbH [geːʔɛmbeːˈhaː] f abk (= Gesellschaft mit beschränkter Haftung) limited company, Ltd

Gnade ['gnaːdə] f (Gunst) favour; (Erbarmen) mercy; (Milde) clemency

Gnaden- zW: **~frist** f reprieve, respite; **g~los** adj merciless; **~stoß** m coup de grâce

gnädig ['gnɛːdɪç] adj gracious; (voll Erbarmen) merciful

Gold [gɔlt] (-(e)s) nt gold; **g~en** adj golden; **~fisch** m goldfish; **~grube** f goldmine; **g~ig** ['gɔldɪç] (umg) adj (fig: allerliebst) sweet, adorable; **~regen** m laburnum; **~schmied** m goldsmith

Golf¹ [gɔlf] (-(e)s, **-e**) m gulf

Golf² [gɔlf] (-s) nt golf; **~platz** m golf course; **~schläger** m golf club

Golfstrom m Gulf Stream

Gondel ['gɔndəl] (-, **-n**) f gondola; (Seilbahn) cable car

gönnen ['gœnən] vt: **jdm etw ~** not to begrudge sb sth; **sich** dat **etw ~** to allow o.s. sth

Gönner (-s, **-**) m patron; **g~haft** adj patronizing

Gosse ['gɔsə] f gutter

Gott [gɔt] (-es, **¨er**) m god; **mein ~!** for heaven's sake!; **um ~es willen!** for heaven's sake!; **grüß ~!** hello; **~ sei Dank!** thank God!; **~heit** f deity

Göttin ['gœtɪn] f goddess

göttlich adj divine

gottlos adj godless

Götze ['gœtsə] (-n, **-n**) m idol

Grab [graːp] (-(e)s, **¨er**) nt grave; **g~en** ['graːbən] (unreg) vt to dig; **~en** (-s, **¨**) m ditch; (MIL) trench; **~stein** m gravestone

Grad [graːt] (-(e)s, **-e**) m degree

Graf [graːf] (-en, **-en**) m count, earl

Gram [graːm] (-(e)s) m grief, sorrow

grämen ['grɛːmən] vr to grieve

Gramm [gram] (-s, **-e**) nt gram(me)

Grammatik [graˈmatɪk] f grammar

Granat [graˈnaːt] (-(e)s, **-e**) m (Stein) garnet

Granate f (MIL) shell; (Hand~) grenade

Granit [graˈniːt] (-s, **-e**) m granite

Graphiker(in) ['graːfɪkər(ɪn)] (-s, **-**) m(f) graphic designer

graphisch ['graːfɪʃ] adj graphic

Gras [graːs] (-es, **¨er**) nt grass; **g~en** ['graːzən] vi to graze; **~halm** m blade of grass

grassieren [graˈsiːrən] vi to be rampant, to rage

gräßlich ⚠ ['grɛslɪç] adj horrible

Grat [graːt] (-(e)s, **-e**) m ridge

Gräte ['grɛːtə] f fishbone

gratis ['graːtɪs] adj, adv free (of charge); **G~probe** f free sample

Gratulation [gratulatsiˈoːn] f congratulation(s)

gratulieren [gratuˈliːrən] vi: **jdm ~ (zu etw)** to congratulate sb (on sth); **(ich) gratuliere!** congratulations!

grau [grau] adj grey

Grauen (-s) nt horror; **g~** vi unpers: **es graut jdm vor etw** sb dreads sth, sb is afraid of sth ♦ vr: **sich g~ vor** to dread, to have a horror of; **g~haft** adj horrible

grauhaarig adj grey-haired

grausam ['grauzaːm] adj cruel; **G~keit** f cruelty

Grausen ['grauzən] (-s) nt horror; **g~** vb = **grauen**

gravieren [graˈviːrən] vt to engrave; **~d** adj grave

graziös [gratsiˈøːs] adj graceful

greifbar adj tangible, concrete; **in ~er Nähe** within reach

greifen ['graifən] (unreg) vt to seize; to grip; **nach etw ~** to reach for sth; **um sich ~** (fig) to spread; **zu etw ~** (fig) to turn to sth

Greis [grais] (-es, **-e**) m old man; **g~enhaft**

⚠ For information on spelling reform see page 615

adj senile; **~in** *f* old woman

grell [grɛl] *adj* harsh

Grenz- ['grɛnts] *zW:* **~beamte(r)** *m* frontier official; **~e** *f* boundary; (*Staatsgrenze*) frontier; (*Schranke*) limit; **g~en** *vi:* **g~en (an** +*akk*) to border (on); **g~enlos** *adj* boundless; **~fall** *m* borderline case; **~kontrolle** *f* border control; **~übergang** *m* frontier crossing

Greuel ⚠ ['grɔʏəl] (**-s, -**) *m* horror, revulsion; **etw ist jdm ein ~** sb loathes sth; **greulich** ⚠ *adj* horrible

Griech- ['griːç] *zW:* **~e** (**-n, -n**) *m* Greek; **~enland** *nt* Greece; **~in** *f* Greek; **g~isch** *adj* Greek

griesgrämig ['griːsgrɛːmɪç] *adj* grumpy

Grieß [griːs] (**-es, -e**) *m* (KOCH) semolina

Griff [grɪf] (**-(e)s, -e**) *m* grip; (*Vorrichtung*) handle; **g~bereit** *adj* handy

Grill [grɪl] *m* grill; **~e** *f* cricket; **g~en** *vt* to grill; **~fest** *nt* barbecue party

Grimasse [grɪ'masə] *f* grimace

grimmig ['grɪmɪç] *adj* furious; (*heftig*) fierce, severe

grinsen ['grɪnzən] *vi* to grin

Grippe ['grɪpə] *f* influenza, flu

grob [groːp] *adj* coarse, gross; (*Fehler, Verstoß*) gross; **G~heit** *f* coarseness; coarse expression

grölen ['grøːlən] (*pej*) *vt* to bawl, to bellow

Groll [grɔl] (**-(e)s**) *m* resentment; **g~en** *vi* (*Donner*) to rumble; **g~en (mit** *od* +*dat*) to bear ill will (towards)

groß [groːs] *adj* big, large; (*hoch*) tall; (*fig*) great ♦ *adv* greatly; **im ~en und ganzen** on the whole; **g~artig** *adj* great, splendid; **G~aufnahme** *f* (CINE) close-up; **G~britannien** *nt* Great Britain

Größe ['grøːsə] *f* size; (*Höhe*) height; (*fig*) greatness

Groß- *zW:* **~einkauf** *m* bulk purchase; **~eltern** *pl* grandparents; **g~enteils** *adv* mostly; **~format** *nt* large size; **~handel** *m* wholesale trade; **~händler** *m* wholesaler; **~macht** *f* great power; **~mutter** *f* grandmother; **~rechner** *m* mainframe (computer); **g~schreiben** (*unreg*) *vt* to

write in block capitals; **bei jdm g~schreiben werden** to be high on sb's list of priorities; **g~spurig** *adj* pompous; **~stadt** *f* city, large town

größte(r, s) [grøːstə(r, s)] *adj superl von* **groß**; **~nteils** *adv* for the most part

Groß- *zW:* **g~tun** (*unreg*) *vi* to boast; **~vater** *m* grandfather; **g~ziehen** (*unreg*) *vt* to raise; **g~zügig** *adj* generous; (*Planung*) on a large scale

grotesk [gro'tɛsk] *adj* grotesque

Grotte ['grɔtə] *f* grotto

Grübchen ['gryːpçən] *nt* dimple

Grube ['gruːbə] *f* pit; mine

grübeln ['gryːbəln] *vi* to brood

Gruft [gruft] (**-, ̈e**) *f* tomb, vault

grün [gryːn] *adj* green; **der ~e Punkt** green spot symbol on recyclable packaging; **G~anlage** *f* park

---

GRÜNER PUNKT

ⓘ The **grüner Punkt** is a green spot which appears on packaging that should be kept separate from normal household refuse to be recycled through the recycling company, DSD (Duales System Deutschland). The recycling is financed by licences bought by the packaging manufacturer from DSD. These costs are often passed on to the consumer.

Grund [grunt] (**-(e)s, ̈e**) *m* ground; (*von See, Gefäß*) bottom; (*fig*) reason; **im ~e genommen** basically; **~ausbildung** *f* basic training; **~besitz** *m* land(ed property), real estate; **~buch** *nt* land register

gründen ['grʏndən] *vt* to found ♦ *vr:* **sich ~ (auf** +*dat*) to be based (on); **~ auf** +*akk* to base on

Gründer (**-s, -**) *m* founder

Grund- *zW:* **~gebühr** *f* basic charge; **~gesetz** *nt* constitution; **~lage** *f* foundation; **g~legend** *adj* fundamental

gründlich *adj* thorough

Grund- *zW:* **g~los** *adj* groundless; **~regel** *f* basic rule; **~riß** ⚠ *m* plan; (*fig*) outline; **~satz** *m* principle; **g~sätzlich** *adj*

⚠ *Informationen zur Rechtschreibreform Seite 615*

fundamental; (*Frage*) of principle ♦ *adv*
fundamentally; (*prinzipiell*) on principle;
~schule *f* elementary school; **~stein** *m*
foundation stone; **~stück** *nt* estate; plot

GRUNDSCHULE

ⓘ The **Grundschule** *is a primary school
which children attend for 4 years from
the age of 6 to 10. There are no formal
examinations in the* **Grundschule** *but
parents receive a report on their child's
progress twice a year. Many children attend
a* **Kindergarten** *from 3-6 years before
going to the* **Grundschule**, *though no
formal instruction takes place in the*
Kindergarten.

Grundwasser *nt* ground water
Grünstreifen *m* central reservation
grunzen ['grʊntsən] *vi* to grunt
Gruppe ['grʊpə] *f* group; **~nermäßigung** *f*
group reduction; **g~nweise** *adv* in groups
gruppieren [grʊ'piːrən] *vt, vr* to group
gruselig *adj* creepy
gruseln ['gruːzəln] *vi unpers*: **es gruselt jdm
vor etw** sth gives sb the creeps ♦ *vr* to
have the creeps
Gruß [gruːs] (**-es, ¨e**) *m* greeting; (*MIL*)
salute; **viele Grüße** best wishes; **mit
freundlichen Grüßen** yours sincerely;
Grüße an +*akk* regards to
grüßen ['gryːsən] *vt* to greet; (*MIL*) to salute;
jdn von jdm ~ to give sb sb's regards;
jdn ~ lassen to send sb one's regards
gucken ['gʊkən] *vi* to look
gültig ['gʏltɪç] *adj* valid; **G~keit** *f* validity
Gummi ['gʊmi] (**-s, -s**) *nt od m* rubber;
(*~harze*) gum; **~band** *nt* rubber *od* elastic
band; (*Hosenband*) elastic; **~bärchen** *nt* ≈
jelly baby (*BRIT*), ≈ gum drop (*US*); **~baum** *m* rubber plant;
g~eren [gʊ'miːrən] *vt* to gum; **~stiefel** *m*
rubber boot
günstig ['gʏnstɪç] *adj* convenient;
(*Gelegenheit*) favourable; **das habe ich ~
bekommen** it was a bargain
Gurgel ['gʊrɡəl] (**-, -n**) *f* throat; **g~n** *vi* to
gurgle; (*im Mund*) to gargle

Gurke ['gʊrkə] *f* cucumber; **saure ~** pickled
cucumber, gherkin
Gurt [gʊrt] (**-(e)s, -e**) *m* belt
Gürtel ['gʏrtəl] (**-s, -**) *m* belt; (*GEOG*) zone;
~reifen *m* radial tyre
GUS *f abk* (= *Gemeinschaft unabhängiger
Staaten*) CIS
Guß △ [gʊs] (**-sses, Güsse**) *m* casting;
(*Regen~*) downpour; (*KOCH*) glazing;
~eisen △ *nt* cast iron

SCHLÜSSELWORT
---

gut *adj* good; **alles Gute** all the best; **also
gut** all right then
♦ *adv* well; **gut schmecken** to taste good;
gut, aber ... OK, but ...; **(na) gut, ich
komme** all right, I'll come; **gut drei
Stunden** a good three hours; **das kann
gut sein** that may well be; **laß es gut sein**
that'll do

Gut [guːt] (**-(e)s, ¨er**) *nt* (*Besitz*) possession;
Güter *pl* (*Waren*) goods; **~achten** (**-s, -**) *nt*
(expert) opinion; **~achter** (**-s, -**) *m* expert;
g~artig *adj* good-natured; (*MED*) benign;
g~bürgerlich *adj* (*Küche*) (good) plain;
~dünken *nt*: **nach ~dünken** at one's
discretion
Güte ['gyːtə] *f* goodness, kindness; (*Qualität*)
quality
Güter- *zW*: **~abfertigung** *f* (*EISENB*) goods
office; **~bahnhof** *m* goods station;
~wagen *m* goods waggon (*BRIT*), freight
car (*US*); **~zug** *m* goods train (*BRIT*), freight
train (*US*)
Gütezeichen *nt* quality mark; ≈ kite mark
gut- *zW*: **~gehen** △ (*unreg*) *vi unpers* to
work, to come off; **es geht jdm ~** sb's
doing fine; **~gemeint** △ *adj* well meant;
~gläubig *adj* trusting; **G~haben** (**-s**) *nt*
credit; **~heißen** (*unreg*) *vt* to approve (of)
gütig ['gyːtɪç] *adj* kind
Gut- *zW*: **g~mütig** *adj* good-natured;
~schein *m* voucher; **g~schreiben** (*unreg*)
vt to credit; **~schrift** *f* (*Betrag*) credit;
g~tun △ (*unreg*) *vi*: **jdm g~tun** to do sb
good; **g~willig** *adj* willing

△ *For information on spelling reform see page 615*

Gymnasium [gʏmˈnaːziʊm] *nt* grammar school (*BRIT*), high school (*US*)

GYMNASIUM

ⓘ The **Gymnasium** is a selective secondary school. After nine years of study pupils sit the Abitur so they can go on to higher education. Pupils who successfully complete six years at a **Gymnasium** automatically gain the mittlere Reife.

Gymnastik [gʏmˈnastɪk] *f* exercises *pl*, keep fit

H, h

Haag [haːk] *m*: **Den ~** the Hague
Haar [haːr] (*-(e)s, -e*) *nt* hair; **um ein ~** nearly; **an den ~en herbeigezogen** (*umg: Vergleich*) very far-fetched; **~bürste** *f* hairbrush; **h~en** *vi, vr* to lose hair; **~esbreite** *f*: **um ~esbreite** by a hair's-breadth; **~festiger** (*-s, -*) *m* (hair) setting lotion; **h~genau** *adv* precisely; **h~ig** *adj* hairy; (*fig*) nasty, **~klammer** *f* hairgrip; **~nadel** *f* hairpin; **h~scharf** *adv* (*beobachten*) very sharply; (*daneben*) by a hair's breadth; **~schnitt** *m* haircut; **~spange** *f* hair slide; **h~sträubend** *adj* hair-raising; **~teil** *nt* hairpiece; **~waschmittel** *nt* shampoo
Habe [ˈhaːbə] (*-*) *f* property
haben [ˈhaːbən] (*unreg*) *vt, vb aux* to have; **Hunger/Angst ~** to be hungry/afraid; **woher hast du das?** where did you get that from?; **was hast du denn?** what's the matter (with you)?; **du hast zu schweigen** you're to be quiet; **ich hätte gern** I would like; **H~** (*-s, -*) *nt* credit
Habgier *f* avarice; **h~ig** *adj* avaricious
Habicht [ˈhaːbɪçt] (*-s, -e*) *m* hawk
Habseligkeiten [ˈhaːpzeːlɪçkaɪtən] *pl* belongings
Hachse [ˈhaksə] *f* (*KOCH*) knuckle
Hacke [ˈhakə] *f* hoe; (*Ferse*) heel; **h~n** *vt* to hack, to chop; (*Erde*) to hoe
Hackfleisch *nt* mince, minced meat
Hafen [ˈhaːfən] (*-s, ̈-*) *m* harbour, port; **~arbeiter** *m* docker; **~rundfahrt** *f* boat trip round the harbour; **~stadt** *f* port
Hafer [ˈhaːfər] (*-s, -*) *m* oats *pl*; **~flocken** *pl* rolled oats; **~schleim** *m* gruel
Haft [haft] (*-*) *f* custody; **h~bar** *adj* liable, responsible; **~befehl** *m* warrant (for arrest); **h~en** *vi* to stick, to cling; **h~en für** to be liable *od* responsible for; **h~enbleiben** △ (*unreg*) *vi*: **h~enbleiben (an** +*dat*) to stick (to); **Häftling** *m* prisoner; **~pflicht** *f* liability; **~pflichtversicherung** *f* (*AUT*) third party insurance; **~schalen** *pl* contact lenses; **~ung** *f* liability; **~ungsbeschränkung** *f* limitation of liability
Hagebutte [ˈhaːgəbʊtə] *f* rose hip
Hagel [ˈhaːgəl] (*-s*) *m* hail; **h~n** *vi unpers* to hail
hager [ˈhaːgər] *adj* gaunt
Hahn [haːn] (*-(e)s, ̈-e*) *m* cock; (*Wasser~*) tap, faucet (*US*)
Hähnchen [ˈhɛːnçən] *nt* cockerel; (*KOCH*) chicken
Hai(fisch) [ˈhaɪ(fɪʃ)] (*-(e)s, -e*) *m* shark
häkeln [ˈhɛːkəln] *vt* to crochet
Haken [ˈhaːkən] (*-s, -*) *m* hook; (*fig*) catch; **~kreuz** *nt* swastika; **~nase** *f* hooked nose
halb [halp] *adj* half; **~ eins** half past twelve; **ein ~es Dutzend** half a dozen; **H~dunkel** *nt* semi-darkness
halber [ˈhalbər] *präp* +*gen* (*wegen*) on account of; (*für*) for the sake of
Halb- *zW*: **~heit** *f* half-measure; **h~ieren** *vt* to halve; **~insel** *f* peninsula; **~jahr** *nt* six months; (*auch: COMM*) half-year; **h~jährlich** *adj* half-yearly; **~kreis** *m* semicircle; **~leiter** *m* semiconductor; **~mond** *m* half-moon; (*fig*) crescent; **h~offen** △ *adj* half-open; **~pension** *f* half-board; **~rechts** (*-, -*) *m* (*SPORT*) inside right; **~schuh** *m* shoe; **h~tags** *adv*: **h~tags arbeiten** to work part-time, to work mornings/afternoons; **h~wegs** *adv* halfway; **h~wegs besser** more or less

better; ~**zeit** f (SPORT) half; (Pause) half-time

Halde ['haldə] f (Kohlen) heap

half [half] vb siehe **helfen**

Hälfte ['hɛlftə] f half

Halfter ['halftər] (-s, -) m od nt (für Tiere) halter

Halle ['halə] f hall; (AVIAT) hangar; **h~n** vi to echo, to resound; ~**bad** nt indoor swimming pool

hallo [ha'lo:] excl hello

Halluzination [halutsinatsi'o:n] f hallucination

Halm [halm] (-(e)s, -e) m blade; stalk

Halogenlampe [halo'ge:nlampə] f halogen lamp

Hals [hals] (-es, ~e) m neck; (Kehle) throat; ~ **über Kopf** in a rush; ~**band** nt (von Hund) collar; ~**kette** f necklace; ~-**Nasen-Ohren-Arzt** m ear, nose and throat specialist; ~**schmerzen** pl sore throat sg; ~**tuch** nt scarf

Halt [halt] (-(e)s, -e) m stop; (fester ~) hold; (innerer ~) stability; **h~** excl stop!, halt!; **h~bar** adj durable; (Lebensmittel) non-perishable; (MIL, fig) tenable; ~**barkeit** f durability; (non-)perishability

halten ['haltən] (unreg) vt to keep; (fest~) to hold; (fig) vi to hold; (frisch bleiben) to keep; (stoppen) to stop ♦ vr (frisch bleiben) to keep; (sich behaupten) to hold out; ~ **für** to regard o.s.; ~ **von** to think of; **an sich ~** to restrain o.s.; **sich rechts/links ~** to keep to the right/left

Halte- zW: ~**stelle** f stop; ~**verbot** nt: **hier ist ~verbot** there's no waiting here

Halt- zW: **h~los** adj unstable; **h~machen** △ vi to stop; ~**ung** f posture; (fig) attitude; (Selbstbeherrschung) composure

Halunke [ha'luŋkə] (-n, -n) m rascal

hämisch ['hɛ:mɪʃ] adj malicious

Hammel ['haməl] (-s, ~ od -) m wether; ~**fleisch** nt mutton

Hammer ['hamər] (-s, ~) m hammer

hämmern ['hɛmərn] vt, vi to hammer

Hämorrhoiden △ [hɛmɔro'i:dən] pl haemorrhoids

Hamster ['hamstər] (-s, -) m hamster; ~**ei** [-'raɪ] f hoarding; **h~n** vi to hoard

Hand [hant] (-, ~e) f hand; ~**arbeit** f manual work; (Nadelarbeit) needlework; ~**ball** m (SPORT) handball; ~**bremse** f handbrake; ~**buch** nt handbook, manual

Händedruck ['hɛndədruk] m handshake

Handel ['handəl] (-s) m trade; (Geschäft) transaction

Handeln ['handəln] (-s) nt action

handeln vi to trade; (agieren) to act ♦ vr unpers: **sich ~ um** to be a question of, to be about; ~ **von** to be about

Handels- zW: ~**bilanz** f balance of trade; ~**kammer** f chamber of commerce; ~**reisende(r)** m commercial traveller; ~**schule** f business school; **h~üblich** adj customary; (Preis) going attrib; ~**vertreter** m sales representative

Hand- zW: ~**feger** (-s, -) m hand brush; **h~fest** adj hefty; **h~gearbeitet** adj handmade; ~**gelenk** nt wrist; ~**gemenge** nt scuffle; ~**gepäck** nt hand luggage; **h~geschrieben** adj handwritten; **h~greiflich** adj palpable; **h~greiflich werden** to become violent; ~**griff** m flick of the wrist; **h~haben** vt insep to handle

Händler ['hɛndlər] (-s, -) m trader, dealer

handlich ['hantlɪç] adj handy

Handlung ['handluŋ] f act(ion); (in Buch) plot; (Geschäft) shop

Hand- zW: ~**schelle** f handcuff; ~**schrift** f handwriting; (Text) manuscript; ~**schuh** m glove; ~**stand** m (SPORT) handstand; ~**tasche** f handbag; ~**tuch** nt towel; ~**umdrehen** nt: **im ~umdrehen** in the twinkling of an eye; ~**werk** nt trade, craft; ~**werker** (-s, -) m craftsman, artisan; ~**werkzeug** nt tools pl

Handy ['hɛndi] (-s, -s) nt mobile (telephone)

Hanf [hanf] (-(e)s) m hemp

Hang [haŋ] (-(e)s, ~e) m inclination; (Ab~) slope

Hänge- ['hɛŋə] in zW hanging; ~**brücke** f suspension bridge; ~**matte** f hammock

hängen ['hɛŋən] (unreg) vi to hang ♦ vt:

△ For information on spelling reform see page 615

etw (an etw *akk*) **~** to hang sth (on sth);
~ an +*dat* (*fig*) to be attached to; **sich ~ an**
+*akk* to hang on to, to cling to; **~bleiben**
⚠ (*unreg*) *vi* to be caught; (*fig*) to remain,
to stick; **~bleiben an** +*dat* to catch *od* get
caught on; **~lassen** ⚠ (*unreg*) *vt*
(*vergessen*) to leave; **den Kopf ~lassen** to
get downhearted

Hannover [ha'noːfɐ] **(-s)** *nt* Hanover
hänseln ['hɛnzəln] *vt* to tease
Hansestadt ['hanzəʃtat] *f* Hanse town
hantieren [han'tiːrən] *vi* to work, to be
busy; **mit etw ~** to handle sth
hapern ['haːpɐn] *vi unpers*: **es hapert an**
etw *dat* there is a lack of sth
Happen ['hapən] **(-s, -)** *m* mouthful
Harfe ['harfə] *f* harp
Harke ['harkə] *f* rake; **h~n** *vt, vi* to rake
harmlos ['harmloːs] *adj* harmless; **H~igkeit**
f harmlessness
Harmonie [harmo'niː] *f* harmony; **h~ren** *vi*
to harmonize
harmonisch [har'moːnɪʃ] *adj* harmonious
Harn ['harn] **(-(e)s, -e)** *m* urine; **~blase** *f*
bladder
Harpune [har'puːnə] *f* harpoon
harren ['harən] *vi*: **~ (auf** +*akk*) to wait (for)
hart [hart] *adj* hard; (*fig*) harsh
Härte ['hɛrtə] *f* hardness; (*fig*) harshness
hart- *zW*: **~gekocht** ⚠ *adj* hard-boiled;
~herzig *adj* hard-hearted; **~näckig** *adj*
stubborn
Harz [haːrts] **(-es, -e)** *nt* resin
Haschee [ha'ʃeː] **(-s, -s)** *nt* hash
Haschisch ['haʃɪʃ] **(-)** *nt* hashish
Hase ['haːzə] **(-n, -n)** *m* hare
Haselnuß ⚠ ['haːzəlnʊs] *f* hazelnut
Hasenscharte *f* harelip
Haß ⚠ [has] **(-sses)** *m* hate, hatred
hassen ['hasən] *vt* to hate
häßlich ⚠ ['hɛslɪç] *adj* ugly; (*gemein*) nasty;
H~keit ⚠ *f* ugliness; nastiness
Hast [hast] *f* haste
hast *vb siehe* **haben**
hasten *vi* to rush
hastig *adj* hasty
hat [hat] *vb siehe* **haben**

hatte *etc* ['hatə] *vb siehe* **haben**
Haube ['haʊbə] *f* hood; (*Mütze*) cap; (*AUT*)
bonnet, hood (*US*)
Hauch [haʊx] **(-(e)s, -e)** *m* breath; (*Luft~*)
breeze; (*fig*) trace; **h~dünn** *adj* extremely
thin
Haue ['haʊə] *f* hoe, pick; (*umg*) hiding; **h~n**
⚠ (*unreg*) *vt* to hew, to cut; (*umg*) to thrash
Haufen ['haʊfən] **(-s, -)** *m* heap; (*Leute*)
crowd; **ein ~ (x)** (*umg*) loads *od* a lot (of x);
auf einem ~ in one heap
häufen ['hɔʏfən] *vt* to pile up ♦ *vr* to
accumulate
haufenweise *adv* in heaps; in droves; **etw**
~ haben to have piles of sth
häufig ['hɔʏfɪç] *adj* frequent ♦ *adv*
frequently; **H~keit** *f* frequency
Haupt [haʊpt] **(-(e)s, Häupter)** *nt* head;
(*Ober~*) chief ♦ *in zW* main; **~bahnhof** *m*
central station; **h~beruflich** *adv* as one's
main occupation; **~darsteller(in)** *m(f)*
leading actor (actress); **~fach** *nt* (*SCH, UNIV*)
main subject, major (*US*); **~gericht** *nt*
(*KOCH*) main course
Häuptling ['hɔʏptlɪŋ] *m* chief(tain)
Haupt- *zW*: **~mann** (*pl* **-leute**) *m* (*MIL*)
captain; **~person** *f* central figure;
~quartier *nt* headquarters *pl*; **~rolle** *f*
leading part; **~sache** *f* main thing;
h~sächlich *adj* chief ♦ *adv* chiefly;
~saison *f* high season, peak season;
~schule *f* ≈ secondary school; **~stadt** *f*
capital; **~straße** *f* main street;
~verkehrszeit *f* rush-hour, peak traffic
hours *pl*

HAUPTSCHULE

---

i *The* **Hauptschule** *is a non-selective*
school which pupils may attend after the
Grundschule. *They complete five years of*
study and most go on to do some vocational
training.

Haus [haʊs] **(-es, Häuser)** *nt* house; **nach**
~e home; **zu ~e** at home; **~apotheke** *f*
medicine cabinet; **~arbeit** *f* housework;
(*SCH*) homework; **~arzt** *m* family doctor;

⚠ *Informationen zur Rechtschreibreform Seite 615*

~**aufgabe** f (SCH) homework;
~**besitzer(in)** m(f) house owner; ~**besuch**
m (von Arzt) house call; ~**durchsuchung** f
police raid; **h~eigen** adj belonging to a/
the hotel/firm

Häuser- ['hɔyzər] zW: ~**block** m block (of
houses); ~**makler** m estate agent (BRIT),
real estate agent (US)

Haus- zW: ~**flur** m hallway; ~**frau** f
housewife; **h~gemacht** adj home-made;
~**halt** m household; (POL) budget;
h~halten △ (unreg) vi (sparen) to
economize; ~**hälterin** f housekeeper;
~**haltsgeld** nt housekeeping (money);
~**haltsgerät** nt domestic appliance; ~**herr**
m host; (Vermieter) landlord; **h~hoch** adv:
h~hoch verlieren to lose by a mile

hausieren [hau'zi:rən] vi to peddle

Hausierer (-s, -) m pedlar (BRIT), peddler
(US)

häuslich ['hɔyslɪç] adj domestic

Haus- zW: ~**meister** m caretaker, janitor;
~**nummer** f street number; ~**ordnung** f
house rules pl; ~**putz** m house cleaning;
~**schlüssel** m front door key; ~**schuh** m
slipper; ~**tier** nt pet; ~**tür** f front door;
~**wirt** m landlord; ~**wirtschaft** f domestic
science; ~**zelt** nt frame tent

Haut [haut] (-, **Häute**) f skin; (Tier~) hide;
~**creme** f skin cream; **h~eng** adj skin-
tight; ~**farbe** f complexion; ~**krebs** m skin
cancer

Haxe ['haksə] f = **Hachse**

Hbf. abk = **Hauptbahnhof**

Hebamme ['he:p|amə] f midwife

Hebel ['he:bəl] (-s, -) m lever

heben ['he:bən] (unreg) vt to raise, to lift

Hecht [hɛçt] (-(e)s, -e) m pike

Heck [hɛk] (-(e)s, -e) nt stern; (von Auto)
rear

Hecke ['hɛkə] f hedge

Heckenschütze m sniper

Heckscheibe f rear window

Heer [he:r] (-(e)s, -e) nt army

Hefe ['he:fə] f yeast

Heft ['hɛft] (-(e)s, -e) nt exercise book;
(Zeitschrift) number; (von Messer) haft;

h~en vt: **h~en (an** +akk) to fasten (to);
(nähen) to tack ((on) to); **etw an etw** akk
h~en to fasten sth to sth; ~**er** (-s, -) m
folder

heftig adj fierce, violent; **H~keit** f
fierceness, violence

Heft- zW: ~**klammer** f paper clip;
~**pflaster** nt sticking plaster; ~**zwecke** f
drawing pin

hegen ['he:gən] vt (Wild, Bäume) to care for,
to tend; (fig, geh: empfinden: Wunsch) to
cherish; (: Mißtrauen) to feel

Hehl [he:l] m od nt: **kein(en) ~ aus etw
machen** to make no secret of sth; ~**er** (-s,
-) m receiver (of stolen goods), fence

Heide[1] ['haidə] (-n, -n) m heathen, pagan

Heide[2] ['haidə] f heath, moor; ~**kraut** nt
heather

Heidelbeere f bilberry

Heidentum nt paganism

Heidin f heathen, pagan

heikel ['haikəl] adj awkward, thorny

Heil [hail] (-(e)s) nt well-being; (Seelen~)
salvation; **h~** adj in one piece, intact;
~**and** (-(e)s, -e) m saviour; **h~bar** adj
curable; **h~en** vt to cure ♦ vi to heal;
h~froh adj very relieved

heilig ['hailiç] adj holy; **H~abend** m
Christmas Eve; **H~e(r)** f(m) saint; ~**en** vt to
sanctify, to hallow; **H~enschein** m halo;
H~keit f holiness; ~ **sprechen** △ (unreg)
vt to canonize; **H~tum** nt shrine;
(Gegenstand) relic

Heil- zW: **h~los** adj unholy; (fig) hopeless;
~**mittel** nt remedy; ~**praktiker(in)** m(f)
non-medical practitioner; **h~sam** adj (fig)
salutary; ~**sarmee** f Salvation Army; ~**ung**
f cure

Heim [haim] (-(e)s, -e) nt home; **h~** adv
home

Heimat ['haima:t] (-, -en) f home (town/
country etc); ~**land** nt homeland; **h~lich**
adj native, home attrib; (Gefühle) nostalgic;
h~los adj homeless; ~**ort** m home town/
area

Heim- zW: ~**computer** m home computer;
h~fahren (unreg) vi to drive home; ~**fahrt**

△ For information on spelling reform see page 615

f journey home; **h~gehen** (*unreg*) *vi* to go home; (*sterben*) to pass away; **h~isch** *adj* (*gebürtig*) native; **sich h~isch fühlen** to feel at home; **~kehr** (-, -en) *f* homecoming; **h~kehren** *vi* to return home; **h~lich** *adj* secret; **~lichkeit** *f* secrecy; **~reise** *f* journey home; **~spiel** *nt* (*SPORT*) home game; **h~suchen** *vt* to afflict; (*Geist*) to haunt; **~trainer** *m* exercise bike; **h~tückisch** *adj* malicious; **~weg** *m* way home; **~weh** *nt* homesickness; **~werker** (-s, -) *m* handyman; **h~zahlen** *vt*: **jdm etw h~zahlen** to pay sb back for sth
Heirat ['haɪraːt] (-, -en) *f* marriage; **h~en** *vt* to marry ♦ *vi* to marry, to get married ♦ *vr* to get married; **~santrag** *m* proposal
heiser ['haɪzər] *adj* hoarse; **H~keit** *f* hoarseness
heiß [haɪs] *adj* hot; **~e(s) Eisen** (*umg*) hot potato; **~blütig** *adj* hot-blooded
heißen ['haɪsən] (*unreg*) *vi* to be called; (*bedeuten*) to mean ♦ *vt* to command; (*nennen*) to name ♦ *vi unpers*: **es heißt** it says; it is said; **das heißt** that is (to say)
Heiß- *zW*: **~hunger** *m* ravenous hunger; **h~laufen** (*unreg*) *vi*, *vr* to overheat
heiter ['haɪtər] *adj* cheerful; (*Wetter*) bright; **H~keit** *f* cheerfulness; (*Belustigung*) amusement
Heiz- ['haɪts] *zW*: **h~bar** *adj* heated; (*Raum*) with heating; **h~en** *vt* to heat; **~körper** *m* radiator; **~öl** *nt* fuel oil; **~sonne** *f* electric fire; **~ung** *f* heating
hektisch ['hɛktɪʃ] *adj* hectic
Held [hɛlt] (-en, -en) *m* hero; **h~enhaft** *adj* heroic; **~in** *f* heroine
helfen ['hɛlfən] (*unreg*) *vi* to help; (*nützen*) to be of use ♦ *vb unpers*: **es hilft nichts, du mußt ...** it's no use, you'll have to ...; **jdm (bei etw) ~** to help sb (with sth); **sich** *dat* **zu ~ wissen** to be resourceful
Helfer (-s, -) *m* helper, assistant; **~shelfer** *m* accomplice
hell [hɛl] *adj* clear, bright; (*Farbe, Bier*) light; **~blau** *adj* light blue; **~blond** *adj* ash blond; **H~e** (-) *f* clearness, brightness; **~hörig** *adj* (*Wand*) paper-thin; **~hörig**

werden (*fig*) to prick up one's ears; **H~seher** *m* clairvoyant; **~wach** *adj* wide-awake
Helm ['hɛlm] (-(e)s, -e) *m* (*auf Kopf*) helmet
Hemd [hɛmt] (-(e)s, -en) *nt* shirt; (*Unter~*) vest; **~bluse** *f* blouse
hemmen ['hɛmən] *vt* to check, to hold up; **gehemmt sein** to be inhibited;
Hemmung *f* check; (*PSYCH*) inhibition; **hemmungslos** *adj* unrestrained, without restraint
Hengst [hɛŋst] (-es, -e) *m* stallion
Henkel ['hɛŋkəl] (-s, -) *m* handle
Henker (-s, -) *m* hangman
Henne ['hɛnə] *f* hen

SCHLÜSSELWORT
---

her [heːr] *adv* **1** (*Richtung*): **komm her zu mir** come here (to me); **von England her** from England; **von weit her** from a long way away; **her damit!** hand it over!; **wo hat er das her?** where did he get that from?

2 (*Blickpunkt*): **von der Form her** as far as the form is concerned

3 (*zeitlich*): **das ist 5 Jahre her** that was 5 years ago; **wo bist du her?** where do you come from?; **ich kenne ihn von früher her** I know him from before

---

herab [hɛ'rap] *adv* down(ward(s)); **~hängen** (*unreg*) *vi* to hang down; **~lassen** (*unreg*) *vt* to let down ♦ *vr* to condescend; **~lassend** *adj* condescending; **~setzen** *vt* to lower, to reduce; (*fig*) to belittle, to disparage
heran [hɛ'ran] *adv*: **näher ~!** come up closer!; **~ zu mir!** come up to me!; **~bringen** (*unreg*) *vt*: **~bringen (an** +*akk*) to bring up (to); **~fahren** (*unreg*) *vi*: **~fahren (an** +*akk*) to drive up (to); **~kommen** (*unreg*) *vi*: **(an jdn/etw) ~kommen** to approach (sb/sth), to come near (to sb/sth); **~machen** *vr*: **sich an jdn ~machen** to make up to sb; **~treten** (*unreg*) *vi*: **mit etw an jdn ~treten** to approach sb with sth; **~wachsen** (*unreg*) *vi* to grow up;

⚠ *Informationen zur Rechtschreibreform Seite 615*

~ziehen (*unreg*) *vt* to pull nearer; (*aufziehen*) to raise; (*ausbilden*) to train; **jdn zu etw ~ziehen** to call upon sb to help in sth

herauf [hɛˈraʊf] *adv* up(ward(s)), up here; **~beschwören** (*unreg*) *vt* to conjure up, to evoke; **~bringen** (*unreg*) *vt* to bring up; **~setzen** *vt* (*Preise, Miete*) to raise, put up

heraus [hɛˈraʊs] *adv* out; **~bekommen** (*unreg*) *vt* to get out; (*fig*) to find *od* figure out; **~bringen** (*unreg*) *vt* to bring out; (*Geheimnis*) to elicit; **~finden** (*unreg*) *vt* to find out; **~fordern** *vt* to challenge; **H~forderung** *f* challenge; provocation; **~geben** (*unreg*) *vt* to hand over; (*zurückgeben*) to give back; (*Buch*) to edit; (*veröffentlichen*) to publish; **H~geber** (**-s, -**) *m* editor; (*Verleger*) publisher; **~gehen** (*unreg*) *vi*: **aus sich ~gehen** to come out of one's shell; **~halten** (*unreg*) *vr*: **sich aus etw ~halten** to keep out of sth; **~hängen**[1] *vt* to hang out; **~hängen**[2] (*unreg*) *vi* to hang out; **~holen** *vt*: **~holen (aus)** to get out (of); **~kommen** (*unreg*) *vi* to come out; **dabei kommt nichts ~** nothing will come of it; **~nehmen** (*unreg*) *vt* to remove (from), take out (of); **sich** *dat* **etw ~nehmen** to take liberties; **~reißen** (*unreg*) *vt* to tear out; to pull out; **~rücken** *vt* (*Geld*) to fork out, to hand over; **mit etw ~rücken** (*fig*) to come out with sth; **~stellen** *vr*: **sich ~stellen (als)** to turn out (to be); **~suchen** *vt*: **sich** *dat* **jdn/etw ~suchen** to pick sb/sth out; **~ziehen** (*unreg*) *vt* to pull out, to extract

herb [hɛrp] *adj* (slightly) bitter, acid; (*Wein*) dry; (*fig: schmerzlich*) bitter

herbei [hɛrˈbaɪ] *adv* (over) here; **~führen** *vt* to bring about; **~schaffen** *vt* to procure

herbemühen [ˈhɛːrbəmyːən] *vr* to take the trouble to come

Herberge [ˈhɛrbɛrgə] *f* shelter; hostel, inn

Herbergsmutter *f* warden

Herbergsvater *m* warden

herbitten (*unreg*) *vt* to ask to come (here)

Herbst [hɛrpst] (**-(e)s, -e**) *m* autumn, fall

(*US*); **h~lich** *adj* autumnal

Herd [heːrt] (**-(e)s, -e**) *m* cooker; (*fig, MED*) focus, centre

Herde [ˈheːrdə] *f* herd; (*Schaf~*) flock

herein [hɛˈraɪn] *adv* in (here), here; **~!** come in!; **~bitten** (*unreg*) *vt* to ask in; **~brechen** (*unreg*) *vi* to set in; **~bringen** (*unreg*) *vt* to bring in; **~fallen** (*unreg*) *vi* to be caught, to be taken in; **~fallen auf** +*akk* to fall for; **~kommen** (*unreg*) *vi* to come in; **~lassen** (*unreg*) *vt* to admit; **~legen** *vt*: **jdn ~legen** to take sb in; **~platzen** (*umg*) *vi* to burst in

Her- *zW*: **~fahrt** *f* journey here; **h~fallen** (*unreg*) *vi*: **h~fallen über** +*akk* to fall upon; **~gang** *m* course of events; **h~geben** (*unreg*) *vt* to give, to hand (over); **sich zu etw h~geben** to lend one's name to sth; **h~gehen** (*unreg*) *vi*: **hinter jdm h~gehen** to follow sb; **es geht hoch h~** there are a lot of goings-on; **h~halten** (*unreg*) *vt* to hold out; **h~halten müssen** (*umg*) to have to suffer; **h~hören** *vi* to listen

Hering [ˈheːrɪŋ] (**-s, -e**) *m* herring

her- [hɛr] *zW*: **~kommen** (*unreg*) *vi* to come; **komm mal ~!** come here!; **~kömmlich** *adj* traditional; **H~kunft** (**-, -künfte**) *f* origin; **H~kunftsland** *nt* country of origin; **H~kunftsort** *m* place of origin; **~laufen** (*unreg*) *vi*: **~laufen hinter** +*dat* to run after

hermetisch [hɛrˈmeːtɪʃ] *adj* hermetic ♦ *adv* hermetically

her'nach *adv* afterwards

Heroin [heroˈiːn] (**-s**) *nt* heroin

Herr [hɛr] (**-(e)n, -en**) *m* master; (*Mann*) gentleman; (*REL*) Lord; (*vor Namen*) Mr.; **mein ~!** sir!; **meine ~en!** gentlemen!

Herren- *zW*: **~haus** *nt* mansion; **~konfektion** *f* menswear; **h~los** *adj* ownerless; **~toilette** *f* men's toilet *od* restroom (*US*)

herrichten [ˈhɛrrɪçtən] *vt* to prepare

Herr- *zW*: **~in** *f* mistress; **h~isch** *adj* domineering; **h~lich** *adj* marvellous, splendid; **~lichkeit** *f* splendour, magnificence; **~schaft** *f* power, rule; (*Herr und Herrin*) master and mistress; **meine**

⚠ *For information on spelling reform see page 615*

~schaften! ladies and gentlemen!

herrschen ['hɛrʃən] *vi* to rule; (*bestehen*) to prevail, to be

Herrscher(in) (-s, -) *m(f)* ruler

her- *zW:* **~rühren** *vi* to arise, to originate; **~sagen** *vt* to recite; **~stellen** *vt* to make, to manufacture; **H~steller (-s, -)** *m* manufacturer; **H~stellung** *f* manufacture

herüber [he'ry:bər] *adv* over (here), across

herum [he'rʊm] *adv* about, (a)round; **um etw ~** around sth; **~führen** *vt* to show around; **~gehen** (*unreg*) *vi* to walk about; **um etw ~gehen** to walk *od* go round sth; **~kommen** (*unreg*) *vi* (*um Kurve etc*) to come round, to turn (round); **~kriegen** (*umg*) *vt* to bring *od* talk around; **~lungern** (*umg*) *vi* to hang about *od* around; **~sprechen** (*unreg*) *vr* to get around, to be spread; **~treiben** *vi*, *vr* to drift about; **~ziehen** *vi*, *vr* to wander about

herunter [he'rʊntər] *adv* downward(s), down (there); **~gekommen** *adj* run-down; **~kommen** (*unreg*) *vi* to come down; (*fig*) to come down in the world; **~machen** *vt* to take down; (*schimpfen*) to have a go at

hervor [hɛr'foːr] *adv* out, forth; **~bringen** (*unreg*) *vt* to produce, (*Wort*) to utter; **~gehen** (*unreg*) *vi* to emerge, to result; **~heben** (*unreg*) *vt* to stress; (*als Kontrast*) to set off; **~ragend** *adj* (*fig*) excellent; **~rufen** (*unreg*) *vt* to cause, to give rise to; **~treten** (*unreg*) *vi* to come out (from behind/between/below); (*Adern*) to be prominent

Herz [hɛrts] (**-ens, -en**) *nt* heart; (*KARTEN*) hearts *pl*; **~anfall** *m* heart attack; **~fehler** *m* heart defect; **h~haft** *adj* hearty

herziehen ['hɛːrtsiːən] (*unreg*) *vi:* **über jdn/etw ~** (*umg: auch fig*) to pull sb/sth to pieces (*inf*)

Herz- *zW:* **~infarkt** *m* heart attack; **~klopfen** *nt* palpitation; **h~lich** *adj* cordial; **h~lichen Glückwunsch** congratulations *pl*; **h~liche Grüße** best wishes; **h~los** *adj* heartless

Herzog ['hɛrtsoːk] (**-(e)s, ̈-e**) *m* duke; **~tum** *nt* duchy

Herz- *zW:* **~schlag** *m* heartbeat; (*MED*)

heart attack; **~stillstand** *m* cardiac arrest; **h~zerreißend** *adj* heartrending

Hessen ['hɛsən] (**-s**) *nt* Hesse

hessisch *adj* Hessian

Hetze ['hɛtsə] *f* (*Eile*) rush; **h~n** *vt* to hunt; (*verfolgen*) to chase ♦ *vi* (*eilen*) to rush; **jdn/etw auf jdn/etw h~n** to set sb/sth on sb/sth; **h~n gegen** to stir up feeling against; **h~n zu** to agitate for

Heu [hɔy] (**-(e)s**) *nt* hay; **Geld wie ~** stacks of money

Heuch- ['hɔyç] *zW:* **~elei** [-ə'laɪ] *f* hypocrisy; **h~eln** *vt* to pretend, to feign ♦ *vi* to be hypocritical; **~ler(in) (-s, -)** *m(f)* hypocrite; **h~lerisch** *adj* hypocritical

heulen ['hɔylən] *vi* to howl; to cry

Heurige(r) ['hɔyrɪgə(r)] *m* new wine

Heu- *zW:* **~schnupfen** *m* hay fever; **'~schrecke** *f* grasshopper; locust

heute ['hɔytə] *adv* today; **~ abend/früh** this evening/morning

heutig ['hɔytɪç] *adj* today's

heutzutage ['hɔyttsutaːgə] *adv* nowadays

Hexe ['hɛksə] *f* witch; **h~n** *vi* to practise witchcraft; **ich kann doch nicht h~n** I can't work miracles; **~nschuß** △ *m* lumbago; **~'rei** *f* witchcraft

Hieb [hiːp] (**-(e)s, -e**) *m* blow; (*Wunde*) cut, gash; (*Stichelei*) cutting remark; **~e bekommen** to get a thrashing

hielt *etc* [hiːlt] *vb siehe* **halten**

hier [hiːr] *adv* here; **~auf** *adv* thereupon; (*danach*) after that; **~behalten** △ (*unreg*) *vt* to keep here; **~bei** *adv* herewith, enclosed; **~bleiben** △ (*unreg*) *vi* to stay here; **~durch** *adv* by this means; (*örtlich*) through here; **~her** *adv* this way, here; **~hin** *adv* here; **~lassen** △ (*unreg*) *vt* to leave here; **~mit** *adv* hereby; **~nach** *adv* hereafter; **~von** *adv* about this, hereof; **~zulande** △ *adv* in this country

hiesig ['hiːzɪç] *adj* of this place, local

hieß *etc* [hiːs] *vb siehe* **heißen**

Hilfe ['hɪlfə] *f* help; aid; **Erste ~** first aid; **~!** help!

Hilf- *zW:* **h~los** *adj* helpless; **~losigkeit** *f* helplessness; **h~reich** *adj* helpful

Hilfs- *zW:* **~arbeiter** *m* labourer; **h~bedürftig** *adj* needy; **h~bereit** *adj* ready to help; **~kraft** *f* assistant, helper

hilfst [hɪlfst] *vb siehe* **helfen**

Himbeere ['hɪmbeːrə] *f* raspberry

Himmel ['hɪməl] **(-s, -)** *m* sky; (*REL, auch fig*) heaven; **~bett** *nt* four-poster bed; **h~blau** *adj* sky-blue; **~fahrt** *f* Ascension; **~srichtung** *f* direction

himmlisch ['hɪmlɪʃ] *adj* heavenly

SCHLÜSSELWORT

hin [hɪn] *adv* **1** (*Richtung*): **hin und zurück** there and back; **hin und her** to and fro; **bis zur Mauer hin** up to the wall; **wo ist er hin?** where has he gone?; **Geld hin, Geld her** money or no money

2 (*auf ... hin*): **auf meine Bitte hin** at my request; **auf seinen Rat hin** on the basis of his advice

3: mein Glück ist hin my happiness has gone

hinab [hɪ'nap] *adv* down; **~gehen** (*unreg*) *vi* to go down; **~sehen** (*unreg*) *vi* to look down

hinauf [hɪ'nauf] *adv* up; **~arbeiten** *vr* to work one's way up; **~steigen** (*unreg*) *vi* to climb

hinaus [hɪ'naus] *adv* out; **~gehen** (*unreg*) *vi* to go out; **~gehen über** +*akk* to exceed; **~laufen** (*unreg*) *vi* to run out; **~laufen auf** +*akk* to come to, to amount to; **~schieben** (*unreg*) *vt* to put off, to postpone; **~werfen** (*unreg*) *vt* (*Gegenstand, Person*) to throw out; **~wollen** *vi* to want to go out; **~wollen auf** +*akk* to drive at, to get at

Hinblick ['hɪnblɪk] *m:* **in** *od* **im ~ auf** +*akk* in view of

hinder- ['hɪndər] *zW:* **~lich** *adj:* **~lich sein** to be a hindrance *od* nuisance; **~n** *vt* to hinder, to hamper; **jdn an etw** *dat* **~n** to prevent sb from doing sth; **H~nis (-ses, -se)** *nt* obstacle; **H~nisrennen** *nt* steeplechase

hindeuten ['hɪndɔytən] *vi:* **~ auf** +*akk* to point to

hindurch [hɪn'durç] *adv* through; across; (*zeitlich*) through(out)

hinein [hɪ'naɪn] *adv* in; **~fallen** (*unreg*) *vi* to fall in; **~fallen in** +*akk* to fall into; **~gehen** (*unreg*) *vi* to go in; **~gehen in** +*akk* to go into, to enter; **~geraten** (*unreg*) *vi:* **~geraten in** +*akk* to get into; **~passen** *vi* to fit in; **~passen in** +*akk* to fit into; (*fig*) to fit in with; **~steigern** *vr* to get worked up; **~versetzen** *vr:* **sich ~versetzen in** +*akk* to put o.s. in the position of; **~ziehen** (*unreg*) *vt* to pull in ♦ *vi* to go in

hin- ['hɪn] *zW:* **~fahren** (*unreg*) *vi* to go; to drive ♦ *vt* to take; to drive; **H~fahrt** *f* journey there; **~fallen** (*unreg*) *vi* to fall (down); **~fällig** *adj* frail; (*fig: ungültig*) invalid; **H~flug** *m* outward flight; **H~gabe** *f* devotion; **~geben** (*unreg*) *vr* +*dat* to give o.s. up to, to devote o.s. to; **~gehen** (*unreg*) *vi* to go; (*Zeit*) to pass; **~halten** (*unreg*) *vt* to hold out; (*warten lassen*) to put off, to stall

hinken ['hɪŋkən] *vi* to limp; (*Vergleich*) to be unconvincing

hinkommen (*unreg*) *vi* (*an Ort*) to arrive

hin- ['hɪn] *zW:* **~legen** *vt* to put down ♦ *vr* to lie down; **~nehmen** (*unreg*) *vt* (*fig*) to put up with, to take; **H~reise** *f* journey out; **~reißen** (*unreg*) *vt* to carry away, to enrapture; **sich ~reißen lassen, etw zu tun** to get carried away and do sth; **~richten** *vt* to execute; **H~richtung** *f* execution; **~setzen** *vt* to put down ♦ *vr* to sit down; **~sichtlich** *präp* +*gen* with regard to; **~stellen** *vt* to put (down) ♦ *vr* to place o.s.

hinten ['hɪntən] *adv* at the back; behind; **~herum** *adv* round the back; (*fig*) secretly

hinter ['hɪntər] *präp* (+*dat od akk*) behind; (*: nach*) after; **~ jdm hersein** to be after sb; **H~achse** *f* rear axle; **H~bliebene(r)** *f(m)* surviving relative; **~e(r, s)** *adj* rear, back; **~einander** *adv* one after the other; **H~gedanke** *m* ulterior motive; **~gehen** (*unreg*) *vt* to deceive; **H~grund** *m* background; **H~halt** *m* ambush; **~hältig**

⚠ *For information on spelling reform see page 615*

adj underhand, sneaky; **~her** *adv* afterwards, after; **H~hof** *m* backyard; **H~kopf** *m* back of one's head; **~'lassen** (*unreg*) *vt* to leave; **~'legen** *vt* to deposit; **H~list** *f* cunning, trickery; (*Handlung*) trick, dodge; **~listig** *adj* cunning, crafty; **H~mann** *m* person behind; **H~rad** *nt* back wheel; **H~radantrieb** *m* (*AUT*) rear wheel drive; **~rücks** *adv* from behind; **H~tür** *f* back door; (*fig: Ausweg*) loophole; **~'ziehen** (*unreg*) *vt* (*Steuern*) to evade

hinüber [hɪˈnyːbər] *adv* across, over; **~gehen** (*unreg*) *vi* to go over *od* across

hinunter [hɪˈnʊntər] *adv* down; **~bringen** (*unreg*) *vt* to take down; **~schlucken** *vt* (*auch fig*) to swallow; **~steigen** (*unreg*) *vi* to descend

Hinweg [ˈhɪnveːk] *m* journey out

hinweghelfen [hɪnˈvɛk-] (*unreg*) *vi*: **jdm über etw** *akk* **~** to help sb to get over sth

hinwegsetzen [hɪnˈvɛk-] *vr*: **sich ~ über** +*akk* to disregard

hin- [ˈhɪn] *zW*: **H~weis** (**-es, -e**) *m* (*Andeutung*) hint; (*Anweisung*) instruction; (*Verweis*) reference; **~weisen** (*unreg*) *vi*: **~weisen auf** +*akk* (*anzeigen*) to point to; (*sagen*) to point out, to refer to; **~werfen** (*unreg*) *vt* to throw down; **~ziehen** (*unreg*) *vr* (*fig*) to drag on

hinzu [hɪnˈtsuː] *adv* in addition; **~fügen** *vt* to add; **~kommen** (*unreg*) *vi* (*Mensch*) to arrive, to turn up; (*Umstand*) to ensue

Hirn [hɪrn] (**-(e)s, -e**) *nt* brain(s); **~gespinst** (**-(e)s, -e**) *nt* fantasy

Hirsch [hɪrʃ] (**-(e)s, -e**) *m* stag

Hirt [hɪrt] (**-en, -en**) *m* herdsman; (*Schaf~, fig*) shepherd

hissen [ˈhɪsən] *vt* to hoist

Historiker [hɪsˈtoːrikər] (**-s, -**) *m* historian

historisch [hɪsˈtoːrɪʃ] *adj* historical

Hitze [ˈhɪtsə] (**-**) *f* heat; **h~beständig** *adj* heat-resistant; **h~frei** *adj*: **h~frei haben** to have time off school because of excessively hot weather; **~welle** *f* heat wave

hitzig [ˈhɪtsɪç] *adj* hot-tempered; (*Debatte*) heated

Hitzkopf *m* hothead

Hitzschlag *m* heatstroke

hl. *abk von* **heilig**

H-Milch [ˈhaːmɪlç] *f* long-life milk

Hobby [ˈhɔbi] (**-s, -s**) *nt* hobby

Hobel [ˈhoːbəl] (**-s, -**) *m* plane; **~bank** *f* carpenter's bench; **h~n** *vt*, *vi* to plane; **~späne** *pl* wood shavings

Hoch (**-s, -s**) *nt* (*Ruf*) cheer; (*MET*) anticyclone

hoch [hoːx] (*attrib* **hohe(r, s)**) *adj* high; **~achten** △ *vt* to respect; **H~achtung** *f* respect, esteem; **~achtungsvoll** *adv* yours faithfully; **H~amt** *nt* high mass; **~arbeiten** *vr* to work one's way up; **H~betrieb** *m* intense activity; (*COMM*) peak time; **H~burg** *f* stronghold; **H~deutsch** *nt* High German; **~dotiert** △ *adj* highly paid; **H~druck** *m* high pressure; **H~ebene** *f* plateau; **H~form** *f* top form; **H~gebirge** *nt* high mountains *pl*; **H~glanz** *m* (*PHOT*) high gloss print; **etw auf H~glanz bringen** to make sth sparkle like new; **~halten** (*unreg*) *vt* to hold up; (*fig*) to uphold, to cherish; **H~haus** *nt* multi-storey building; **~heben** (*unreg*) *vt* to lift (up); **H~konjunktur** *f* boom; **H~land** *nt* highlands *pl*; **~leben** *vi*: **jdn ~leben lassen** to give sb three cheers; **H~mut** *m* pride; **~mütig** *adj* proud, haughty; **~näsig** *adj* stuck-up, snooty; **H~ofen** *m* blast furnace; **~prozentig** *adj* (*Alkohol*) strong; **H~rechnung** *f* projection; **H~saison** *f* high season; **H~schule** *f* college; university; **H~sommer** *m* middle of summer; **H~spannung** *f* high tension; **H~sprung** *m* high jump

höchst [høːçst] *adv* highly, extremely

Hochstapler [ˈhoːxstaːplər] (**-s, -**) *m* swindler

höchste(r, s) *adj* highest; (*äußerste*) extreme

Höchst- *zW*: **h~ens** *adv* at the most; **~geschwindigkeit** *f* maximum speed; **h~persönlich** *adv* in person; **~preis** *m* maximum price; **h~wahrscheinlich** *adv* most probably

Hoch- *zW*: **~verrat** *m* high treason;

~**wasser** nt high water; (Überschwemmung) floods pl

Hochzeit ['hɔxtsaɪt] (-, -en) f wedding; ~**sreise** f honeymoon

hocken ['hɔkən] vi, vr to squat, to crouch

Hocker (-s, -) m stool

Höcker ['hœkər] (-s, -) m hump

Hoden ['hoːdən] (-s, -) m testicle

Hof [hoːf] (-(e)s, -e) m (Hinter~) yard; (Bauern~) farm; (Königs~) court

hoff- ['hɔf] zW: ~**en** vi: ~**en (auf** +akk) to hope (for); ~**entlich** adv I hope, hopefully; **H~nung** f hope

Hoffnungs- zW: **h~los** adj hopeless; ~**losigkeit** f hopelessness; **h~voll** adj hopeful

höflich ['høːflɪç] adj polite, courteous; **H~keit** f courtesy, politeness

hohe(r, s) ['hoːə(r, s)] adj attrib siehe **hoch**

Höhe ['høːə] f height; (Anhöhe) hill

Hoheit ['hoːhaɪt] f (POL) sovereignty; (Titel) Highness

Hoheits- zW: ~**gebiet** nt sovereign territory; ~**gewässer** nt territorial waters pl

Höhen- ['høːən] zW: ~**luft** f mountain air; ~**messer** (-s, -) m altimeter; ~**sonne** f sun lamp; ~**unterschied** m difference in altitude

Höhepunkt m climax

höher adj, adv higher

hohl [hoːl] adj hollow

Höhle ['høːlə] f cave, hole; (Mund~) cavity; (fig, ZOOL) den

Hohlmaß nt measure of volume

Hohn [hoːn] (-(e)s) m scorn

höhnisch ['høːnɪʃ] adj scornful, taunting

holen ['hoːlən] vt to get, to fetch; (Atem) to take; **jdn/etw ~ lassen** to send for sb/sth

Holland ['hɔlant] nt Holland; **Holländer** ['hɔlɛndər] m Dutchman; **holländisch** adj Dutch

Hölle ['hœlə] f hell

höllisch ['hœlɪʃ] adj hellish, infernal

holperig ['hɔlpərɪç] adj rough, bumpy

Holunder [ho'lundər] (-s, -) m elder

Holz [hɔlts] (-es, -er) nt wood

hölzern ['hœltsərn] adj (auch fig) wooden

Holz- zW: ~**fäller** (-s, -) m lumberjack, woodcutter; **h~ig** adj woody; ~**kohle** f charcoal; ~**schuh** m clog; ~**weg** m (fig) wrong track; ~**wolle** f fine wood shavings pl

Homöopathie [homøopa'tiː] f homeopathy

homosexuell [homozeksu'ɛl] adj homosexual

Honig ['hoːnɪç] (-s, -e) m honey; ~**melone** f (BOT, KOCH) honeydew melon; ~**wabe** f honeycomb

Honorar [hono'raːr] (-s, -e) nt fee

Hopfen ['hɔpfən] (-s, -) m hops pl

hopsen ['hɔpsən] vi to hop

Hörapparat m hearing aid

hörbar adj audible

horchen ['hɔrçən] vi to listen; (pej) to eavesdrop

Horde ['hɔrdə] f horde

hör- ['høːr] zW: ~**en** vt, vi to hear; **Musik/Radio ~en** to listen to music/the radio; **H~er** (-s, -) m hearer; (RAD) listener; (UNIV) student; (Telefonhörer) receiver; **H~funk** (-s) m radio; ~**geschädigt** [-gəʃɛːdɪçt] adj hearing-impaired

Horizont [hori'tsɔnt] (-(e)s, -e) m horizon; **h~al** [-'taːl] adj horizontal

Hormon [hɔr'moːn] (-s, -e) nt hormone

Hörmuschel f (TEL) earpiece

Horn [hɔrn] (-(e)s, -er) nt horn; ~**haut** f horny skin

Hornisse [hɔr'nɪsə] f hornet

Horoskop [horo'skoːp] (-s, -e) nt horoscope

Hörspiel nt radio play

Hort [hɔrt] (-(e)s, -e) m (SCH) day centre for schoolchildren whose parents are at work

horten ['hɔrtən] vt to hoard

Hose ['hoːzə] f trousers pl, pants pl (US)

Hosen- zW: ~**anzug** m trouser suit; ~**rock** m culottes pl; ~**tasche** f (trouser) pocket; ~**träger** m braces pl (BRIT), suspenders pl (US)

Hostie ['hɔstiə] f (REL) host

Hotel [ho'tɛl] (-s, -s) nt hotel; ~**ier** [hoteli'eː] (-s, -s) m hotelkeeper, hotelier; ~**verzeichnis** nt hotel register

⚠ For information on spelling reform see page 615

Hubraum ['hu:p-] m (AUT) cubic capacity
hübsch [hypʃ] adj pretty, nice
Hubschrauber ['hu:pʃraubər] (-s, -) m helicopter
Huf ['hu:f] (-(e)s, -e) m hoof; ~**eisen** nt horseshoe
Hüft- ['hyft] zW: ~**e** f hip; ~**gürtel** m girdle; ~**halter** (-s, -) m girdle
Hügel ['hy:gəl] (-s, -) m hill; **h**~**ig** adj hilly
Huhn [hu:n] (-(e)s, ̈-er) nt hen; (KOCH) chicken
Hühner- ['hy:nər] zW: ~**auge** nt corn; ~**brühe** f chicken broth
Hülle ['hylə] f cover(ing); wrapping; **in** ~ **und Fülle** galore; **h**~**n** vt: **h**~**n (in** +akk) to cover (with); to wrap (in)
Hülse ['hylzə] f husk, shell; ~**nfrucht** f pulse
human [hu'ma:n] adj humane; ~**itär** adj humanitarian; **H**~**ität** f humanity
Hummel ['huməl] (-, -n) f bumblebee
Hummer ['humər] (-s, -) m lobster
Humor [hu'mo:r] (-s, -e) m humour; ~ **haben** to have a sense of humour; ~**ist** [-'rɪst] m humorist; **h**~**voll** adj humorous
humpeln ['humpəln] vi to hobble
Humpen ['humpən] (-s, -) m tankard
Hund [hunt] (-(e)s, -e) m dog
Hunde- ['hundə] zW: ~**hütte** f (dog) kennel; **h**~**müde** (umg) adj dog-tired
hundert ['hundərt] num hundred; **H**~**'jahrfeier** f centenary; ~**prozentig** adj, adv one hundred per cent
Hundesteuer f dog licence fee
Hündin ['hyndɪn] f bitch
Hunger ['huŋər] (-s) m hunger; ~ **haben** to be hungry; **h**~**n** vi to starve; ~**snot** f famine
hungrig ['huŋrɪç] adj hungry
Hupe ['hu:pə] f horn; **h**~**n** vi to hoot, to sound one's horn
hüpfen ['hypfən] vi to hop; to jump
Hürde ['hyrdə] f hurdle; (für Schafe) pen; ~**nlauf** m hurdling
Hure ['hu:rə] f whore
hurtig ['hurtɪç] adj brisk, quick ♦ adv briskly, quickly
huschen ['huʃən] vi to flit; to scurry

Husten ['hu:stən] (-s) m cough; **h**~ vi to cough; ~**anfall** m coughing fit; ~**bonbon** m od nt cough drop; ~**saft** m cough mixture
Hut[1] [hu:t] (-(e)s, ̈-e) m hat
Hut[2] [hu:t] (-) f care; **auf der** ~ **sein** to be on one's guard
hüten ['hy:tən] vt to guard ♦ vr to watch out; **sich** ~, **zu** to take care not to; **sich** ~ **(vor)** to beware (of), to be on one's guard (against)
Hütte ['hytə] f hut; cottage; (Eisen~) forge
Hütten- zW: ~**käse** m (KOCH) cottage cheese; ~**schuh** m slipper sock
Hydrant [hy'drant] m hydrant
hydraulisch [hy'draulɪʃ] adj hydraulic
Hygiene [hygi'e:nə] (-) f hygiene
hygienisch [hygi'e:nɪʃ] adj hygienic
Hymne ['hymnə] f hymn; anthem
Hypno- [hyp'no:] zW: ~**se** f hypnosis; **h**~**tisch** adj hypnotic; ~**tiseur** [-ti'zø:r] m hypnotist; **h**~**ti'sieren** vt to hypnotize
Hypothek [hypo'te:k] (-, -en) f mortgage
Hypothese [hypo'te:zə] f hypothesis
Hysterie [hyste'ri:] f hysteria
hysterisch [hys'te:rɪʃ] adj hysterical

I, i

ICE [i:tse:'e:] m abk = **Intercity-Expreßzug**
Ich (-(s), -(s)) nt self; (PSYCH) ego
ich [ɪç] pron I; ~ **bin's!** it's me!
Ideal [ide'a:l] (-s, -e) nt ideal; **i**~ adj ideal; **i**~**istisch** [-'lɪstɪʃ] adj idealistic
Idee [i'de:, pl i'de:ən] f idea
identifizieren [idɛntifi'tsi:rən] vt to identify
identisch [i'dɛntɪʃ] adj identical
Identität [idɛnti'tɛ:t] f identity
Ideo- [ideo] zW: ~**loge** [-'lo:gə] (-n, -n) m ideologist; ~**logie** [-lo'gi:] f ideology; **i**~**logisch** [-'lo:gɪʃ] adj ideological
Idiot [idi'o:t] (-en, -en) m idiot; **i**~**isch** adj idiotic
idyllisch [i'dylɪʃ] adj idyllic
Igel ['i:gəl] (-s, -) m hedgehog
ignorieren [ɪgno'ri:rən] vt to ignore

⚠ Informationen zur Rechtschreibreform Seite 615

ihm [i:m] (*dat von* **er, es**) *pron* (to) him; (to) it

ihn [i:n] (*akk von* **er, es**) *pron* him; it; **~en** (*dat von* **sie** *pl*) *pron* (to) them; **I~en** (*dat von* **Sie** *pl*) *pron* (to) you

---
SCHLÜSSELWORT
---

ihr [i:r] *pron* 1 (*nom pl*) you; **ihr seid es** it's you
2 (*dat von sie*) to her; **gib es ihr** give it to her; **er steht neben ihr** he is standing beside her
♦ *possessiv pron* 1 (*sg*) her; (: *bei Tieren, Dingen*) its; **ihr Mann** her husband
2 (*pl*) their; **die Bäume und ihre Blätter** the trees and their leaves

---

ihr(e) [i:r] *adj* (*sg*) her, its; (*pl*) their; **Ihr(e)** *adj* your

ihre(r, s) *pron* (*sg*) hers, its; (*pl*) theirs; **I~(r, s)** *pron* yours; **~r** (*gen von sie sg/pl*) *pron* of her/them; **I~r** (*gen von Sie*) *pron* of you; **~rseits** *adv* for her/their part; **~sgleichen** *pron* people like her/them; (*von Dingen*) others like it; **~twegen** *adv* (*für sie*) for her/its/their sake; (*wegen ihr*) on her/its/their account; **~twillen** *adv*: **um ~twillen** = **ihretwegen**

ihrige [ˈiːrɪɡə] *pron*: **der/die/das ~** hers; its; theirs

illegal [ˈɪlegaːl] *adj* illegal

Illusion [ɪluziˈoːn] *f* illusion

illusorisch [ɪluˈzoːrɪʃ] *adj* illusory

illustrieren [ɪlʊsˈtriːrən] *vt* to illustrate

Illustrierte *f* magazine

im [ɪm] = **in dem**

Imbiß △ [ˈɪmbɪs] (**-sses, -sse**) *m* snack; **~stube** △ *f* snack bar

imitieren [imiˈtiːrən] *vt* to imitate

Imker [ˈɪmkər] (**-s, -**) *m* beekeeper

immatrikulieren [ɪmatrikuˈliːrən] *vi, vr* to register

immer [ˈɪmər] *adv* always; **~ wieder** again and again; **~ noch** still; **~ noch nicht** still not; **für ~** forever; **~ wenn ich ...** every time I ...; **~ schöner/trauriger** more and more beautiful/sadder and sadder; **was/**

wer (auch) ~ whatever/whoever; **~hin** *adv* all the same; **~zu** *adv* all the time

Immobilien [ɪmoˈbiːliən] *pl* real estate *sg*; **~makler** *m* estate agent (*BRIT*), realtor (*US*)

immun [ɪˈmuːn] *adj* immune; **I~ität** [-iˈtɛːt] *f* immunity; **I~system** *nt* immune system

Imperfekt [ˈɪmpɛrfɛkt] (**-s, -e**) *nt* imperfect (tense)

Impf- [ˈɪmpf] *zW*: **impfen** *vt* to vaccinate; **~stoff** *m* vaccine, serum; **~ung** *f* vaccination

imponieren [ɪmpoˈniːrən] *vi* +*dat* to impress

Import [ɪmˈpɔrt] (**-(e)s, -e**) *m* import; **~eur** *m* importer; **i~ieren** *vt* to import

imposant [ɪmpoˈzant] *adj* imposing

impotent [ˈɪmpotɛnt] *adj* impotent

imprägnieren [ɪmprɛˈɡniːrən] *vt* to (water)proof

improvisieren [ɪmproviˈziːrən] *vt, vi* to improvise

Impuls [ɪmˈpʊls] (**-es, -e**) *m* impulse; **impulsiv** [-ˈziːf] *adj* impulsive

imstande △ [ɪmˈʃtandə] *adj*: **~ sein** to be in a position; (*fähig*) to be able

---
SCHLÜSSELWORT
---

in [ɪn] *präp* +*akk* 1 (*räumlich: wohin?*) in, into; **in die Stadt** into town; **in die Schule gehen** to go to school
2 (*zeitlich*): **bis ins 20. Jahrhundert** into *od* up to the 20th century
♦ *präp* +*dat* 1 (*räumlich: wo*) in; **in der Stadt** in town; **in der Schule sein** to be at school
2 (*zeitlich: wann*): **in diesem Jahr** this year; (*in jenem Jahr*) in that year; **heute in zwei Wochen** two weeks today

---

Inanspruchnahme [ɪnˈʔanʃpruxnaːmə] *f* (+*gen*) demands *pl* (on)

Inbegriff [ˈɪnbəɡrɪf] *m* embodiment, personification; **i~en** *adv* included

indem [ɪnˈdeːm] *konj* while; **~ man etw macht** (*dadurch*) by doing sth

Inder(in) [ˈɪndər(ɪn)] *m(f)* Indian

△ *For information on spelling reform see page 615*

indes(sen) [ɪn'dɛs(ən)] *adv* however; (*inzwischen*) meanwhile ♦ *konj* while

Indianer(in) [ɪndi'aːnər(ɪn)] (**-s, -**) *m(f)* American Indian, native American; **indianisch** *adj* Red Indian

Indien ['ɪndiən] *nt* India

indirekt ['ɪndirɛkt] *adj* indirect

indisch ['ɪndɪʃ] *adj* Indian

indiskret ['ɪndɪskreːt] *adj* indiscreet

indiskutabel ['ɪndɪskutaːbəl] *adj* out of the question

individuell [ɪndividu'ɛl] *adj* individual

Individuum [ɪndi'viːduɔm] (**-s, -en**) *nt* individual

Indiz [ɪn'diːts] (**-es, -ien**) *nt* (*JUR*) clue; **~ (für)** sign (of)

industrialisieren [ɪndʊstriali'ziːrən] *vt* to industrialize

Industrie [ɪndʊs'triː] *f* industry ♦ *in zW* industrial; **~gebiet** *nt* industrial area; **~- und Handelskammer** *f* chamber of commerce; **~zweig** *m* branch of industry

ineinander [ɪnʔaɪ'nandər] *adv* in(to) one another *od* each other

Infarkt [ɪn'farkt] (**-(e)s, -e**) *m* coronary (thrombosis)

Infektion [ɪnfɛktsi'oːn] *f* infection; **~skrankheit** *f* infectious disease

Infinitiv ['ɪnfinitiːf] (**-s, -e**) *m* infinitive

infizieren [ɪnfi'tsiːrən] *vt* to infect ♦ *vr*: **sich (bei jdm) ~** to be infected (by sb)

Inflation [ɪnflatsi'oːn] *f* inflation

inflationär [ɪnflatsio'nɛːr] *adj* inflationary

infolge [ɪn'fɔlgə] *präp +gen* as a result of, owing to; **~dessen** [-'dɛsən] *adv* consequently

Informatik [ɪnfɔr'maːtɪk] *f* information studies *pl*

Information [ɪnfɔrmatsi'oːn] *f* information *no pl*

informieren [ɪnfɔr'miːrən] *vt* to inform ♦ *vr*: **sich ~ (über +akk)** to find out (about)

Ingenieur [ɪnʒeni'øːr] *m* engineer; **~schule** *f* school of engineering

Ingwer ['ɪŋvər] (**-s**) *m* ginger

Inh. *abk* (= *Inhaber*) prop.; (= *Inhalt*) contents

Inhaber(in) ['ɪnhaːbər(ɪn)] (**-s, -**) *m(f)* owner; (*Haus~*) occupier; (*Lizenz~*) licensee, holder; (*FIN*) bearer

inhaftieren [ɪnhaf'tiːrən] *vt* to take into custody

inhalieren [ɪnha'liːrən] *vt, vi* to inhale

Inhalt ['ɪnhalt] (**-(e)s, -e**) *m* contents *pl*; (*eines Buchs etc*) content; (*MATH*) area; volume; **i~lich** *adj* as regards content

Inhalts- *zW*: **~angabe** *f* summary; **~verzeichnis** *nt* table of contents

inhuman ['ɪnhumaːn] *adj* inhuman

Initiative [initsia'tiːvə] *f* initiative

inklusive [ɪnklu'ziːvə] *präp +gen* inclusive of ♦ *adv* inclusive

Inkrafttreten [ɪn'krafttreːtən] (**-s**) *nt* coming into force

Inland ['ɪnlant] (**-(e)s**) *nt* (*GEOG*) inland; (*POL, COMM*) home (country); **~flug** *m* domestic flight

inmitten [ɪn'mɪtən] *präp +gen* in the middle of; **~ von** amongst

innehaben ['ɪnhaːbən] (*unreg*) *vt* to hold

innen ['ɪnən] *adv* inside; **I~architekt** *m* interior designer; **I~einrichtung** *f* (interior) furnishings *pl*; **I~hof** *m* inner courtyard; **I~minister** *m* minister of the interior, Home Secretary (*BRIT*); **I~politik** *f* domestic policy; **~politisch** *adj* (*Entwicklung, Lage*) internal, domestic; **I~stadt** *f* town/city centre

inner- ['ɪnər] *zW*: **~e(r, s)** *adj* inner; (*im Körper, inländisch*) internal; **I~e(s)** *nt* inside; (*Mitte*) centre; (*fig*) heart; **I~eien** [-'raɪən] *pl* innards; **~halb** *adv* within; (*räumlich*) inside ♦ *präp +gen* within; inside; **~lich** *adj* internal; (*geistig*) inward; **~ste(r, s)** *adj* innermost; **I~ste(s)** *nt* heart

innig ['ɪnɪç] *adj* (*Freundschaft*) close

inoffiziell ['ɪnʔɔfitsiɛl] *adj* unofficial

ins [ɪns] = **in das**

Insasse ['ɪnzasə] (**-n, -n**) *m* (*Anstalt*) inmate; (*AUT*) passenger

Insassenversicherung *f* passenger insurance

insbesondere [ɪnsbə'zɔndərə] *adv* (e)specially

Inschrift ['ɪnʃrɪft] *f* inscription

Insekt [ɪn'zɛkt] **(-(e)s, -en)** *nt* insect

Insektenschutzmittel *nt* insect repellent

Insel ['ɪnzəl] **(-, -n)** *f* island

Inser- *zW*: **~at** [ɪnzeˈraːt] **(-(e)s, -e)** *nt* advertisement; **~ent** [ɪnzeˈrɛnt] *m* advertiser; **i~ieren** [ɪnzeˈriːrən] *vt, vi* to advertise

insgeheim [ɪnsgəˈhaɪm] *adv* secretly

insgesamt [ɪnsgəˈzamt] *adv* altogether, all in all

insofern [ɪnzoˈfɛrn] *adv* in this respect ♦ *konj* if; *(deshalb)* (and) so; **~ als** in so far as

insoweit [ɪnzoˈvaɪt] = **insofern**

Installateur [ɪnstalaˈtøːr] *m* electrician; plumber

Instandhaltung [ɪnˈʃtanthaltʊŋ] *f* maintenance

inständig [ɪnˈʃtɛndɪç] *adj* urgent

Instandsetzung [ɪnˈʃtant-] *f* overhaul; *(eines Gebäudes)* restoration

Instanz [ɪnˈstants] *f* authority; *(JUR)* court

Instinkt [ɪnˈstɪŋkt] **(-(e)s, -e)** *m* instinct; **instinktiv** [-ˈtiːf] *adj* instinctive

Institut [ɪnstiˈtuːt] **(-(e)s, -e)** *nt* institute

Instrument [ɪnstruˈmɛnt] *nt* instrument

Intell- [ɪntɛl] *zW*: **i~ektuell** [-ɛktuˈɛl] *adj* intellectual; **i~igent** [-iˈgɛnt] *adj* intelligent; **~igenz** [-iˈgɛnts] *f* intelligence; *(Leute)* intelligentsia *pl*

Intendant [ɪntɛnˈdant] *m* director

intensiv [ɪntɛnˈziːf] *adj* intensive; **Intensivstation** *f* intensive care unit

Intercity- [ɪntərˈsɪti] *zW*: **~-Expreßzug** ⚠ *m* high-speed train; **~-Zug** *m* intercity (train); **~-Zuschlag** *m* intercity supplement

Interess- *zW*: **i~ant** [ɪntəreˈsant] *adj* interesting; **i~anterweise** *adv* interestingly enough; **~e** [ɪntəˈresə] **(-s, -n)** *nt* interest; **~e haben an** +*dat* to be interested in; **~ent** [ɪntəreˈsɛnt] *m* interested party; **i~ieren** [ɪntəreˈsiːrən] *vt* to interest ♦ *vr*: **sich i~ieren für** to be interested in

intern [ɪnˈtɛrn] *adj* *(Angelegenheiten, Regelung)* internal; *(Besprechung)* private

Internat [ɪntɛrˈnaːt] **(-(e)s, -e)** *nt* boarding school

inter- [ɪntɛr] *zW*: **~national** [-natsioˈnaːl] *adj* international; **~pretieren** [-preˈtiːrən] *vt* to interpret; **I~vall** [-ˈval] **(-s, -e)** *nt* interval; **I~view** [-ˈvjuː] **(-s, -s)** *nt* interview; **~viewen** [-ˈvjuːən] *vt* to interview

intim [ɪnˈtiːm] *adj* intimate; **I~ität** *f* intimacy

intolerant ['ɪntolerant] *adj* intolerant

Intrige [ɪnˈtriːgə] *f* intrigue, plot

Invasion [ɪnvaˈzioːn] *f* invasion

Inventar [ɪnvɛnˈtaːr] **(-s, -e)** *nt* inventory

Inventur [ɪnvɛnˈtuːr] *f* stocktaking; **~ machen** to stocktake

investieren [ɪnvɛsˈtiːrən] *vt* to invest

inwie- [ɪnviˈ] *zW*: **~fern** *adv* how far, to what extent; **~weit** *adv* how far, to what extent

inzwischen [ɪnˈtsvɪʃən] *adv* meanwhile

Irak [iˈraːk] **(-s)** *m*: **der ~** Iraq; **i~isch** *adj* Iraqi

Iran [iˈraːn] **(-s)** *m*: **der ~** Iran; **i~isch** *adj* Iranian

irdisch ['ɪrdɪʃ] *adj* earthly

Ire ['iːrə] **(-n, -n)** *m* Irishman

irgend ['ɪrgənt] *adv* at all; **wann/was/wer ~** whenever/whatever/whoever; **~ jemand / etwas** somebody/something; anybody/ anything; **~ein(e, s)** *adj* some, any; **~einmal** *adv* sometime or other; *(fragend)* ever; **~wann** *adv* sometime; **~wie** *adv* somehow; **~wo** *adv* somewhere; anywhere; **~wohin** *adv* somewhere; anywhere

Irin ['iːrɪn] *f* Irishwoman

Irland ['ɪrlant] **(-s)** *nt* Ireland

Ironie [iroˈniː] *f* irony; **ironisch** [iˈroːnɪʃ] *adj* ironic(al)

irre ['ɪrə] *adj* crazy, mad; **I~(r)** *f(m)* lunatic; **~führen** *vt* to mislead; **~machen** *vt* to confuse; **~n** *vi* to be mistaken; *(umherirren)* to wander, to stray ♦ *vr* to be mistaken; **I~nanstalt** *f* lunatic asylum

Irr- *zW*: **~garten** *m* maze; **i~ig** ['ɪrɪç] *adj* incorrect, wrong; **i~itieren** *vt* *(verwirren)* to confuse; *(ärgern)* to irritate; *(stören)* to

⚠ *For information on spelling reform see page 615*

annoy; **i~sinnig** adj mad, crazy; (umg) terrific; **~tum** (-s, -tümer) m mistake, error; **i~tümlich** adj mistaken

Island ['i:slant] (-s) nt Iceland

Isolation [izolatsi'o:n] f isolation; (ELEK) insulation

Isolier- [izo'li:r] zW: **~band** nt insulating tape; **i~en** vt to isolate; (ELEK) to insulate; **~station** f (MED) isolation ward; **~ung** f isolation; (ELEK) insulation

Israel ['israe:l] (-s) nt Israel; **~i** [-'e:li] (-s, -s) m Israeli; **i~isch** adj Israeli

ißt ⚠ [ist] vb siehe **essen**

ist [ist] vb siehe **sein**

Italien [i'ta:liən] (-s) nt Italy; **~er(in)** (-s) m(f) Italian; **i~isch** adj Italian

i.V. abk = **in Vertretung**

J, j

ja [ja:] adv 1 yes; **haben Sie das gesehen? - ja** did you see it? - yes(, I did); **ich glaube ja** (yes) I think so
2 (fragend) really?; **ich habe gekündigt - ja?** I've quit - have you?; **du kommst, ja?** you're coming, aren't you?
3: **sei ja vorsichtig** be careful; **Sie wissen ja, daß ...** as you know, ...; **tu das ja nicht!** don't do that!; **ich habe es ja gewußt** I just knew it!; **ja, also ...** well you see ...

Jacht [jaxt] (-, -en) f yacht

Jacke ['jakə] f jacket; (Woll~) cardigan

Jackett [ʒa'kɛt] (-s, -s od -e) nt jacket

Jagd [ja:kt] (-, -en) f hunt; (Jagen) hunting; **~beute** f kill; **~flugzeug** nt fighter; **~hund** m hunting dog

jagen ['ja:gən] vi to hunt; (eilen) to race ♦ vt to hunt; (weg~) to drive (off); (verfolgen) to chase

Jäger ['jɛ:gər] (-s, -) m hunter; **~schnitzel** nt (KOCH) pork in a spicy sauce with mushrooms

jäh [jɛ:] adj sudden, abrupt; (steil) steep, precipitous

Jahr [ja:r] (-(e)s, -e) nt year; **j~elang** adv for years

Jahres- zW: **~abonnement** nt annual subscription; **~abschluß** ⚠ m end of the year; (COMM) annual statement of account; **~beitrag** m annual subscription; **~karte** f yearly season ticket; **~tag** m anniversary; **~wechsel** m turn of the year; **~zahl** f date; year; **~zeit** f season

Jahr- zW: **~gang** m age group; (von Wein) vintage; **~'hundert** (-s, -e) nt century; **jährlich** ['jɛ:rlɪç] adj, adv yearly; **~markt** m fair; **~tausend** nt millennium; **~'zehnt** nt decade

Jähzorn ['jɛ:tsɔrn] m sudden anger; hot temper; **j~ig** adj hot-tempered

Jalousie [ʒalu'zi:] f venetian blind

Jammer ['jamər] (-s) m misery; **es ist ein ~, daß ...** it is a crying shame that ...

jämmerlich ['jɛmərlɪç] adj wretched, pathetic

jammern vi to wail ♦ vt unpers: **es jammert jdn** it makes sb feel sorry

Januar ['janua:r] (-(s), -e) m January

Japan ['ja:pan] (-s) nt Japan; **~er(in)** [-'pa:nər(ɪn)] (-s) m(f) Japanese; **j~isch** adj Japanese

jäten ['jɛ:tən] vt: **Unkraut ~** to weed

jauchzen ['jaʊxtsən] vi to rejoice

jaulen ['jaʊlən] vi to howl

jawohl [ja'vo:l] adv yes (of course)

Jawort ['ja:vɔrt] nt consent

Jazz [dʒæz] (-) m Jazz

je [je:] adv 1 (jemals) ever; **hast du so was je gesehen?** did you ever see anything like it?
2 (jeweils) every, each; **sie zahlten je 3 Mark** they paid 3 marks each
♦ konj 1: **je nach** depending on; **je nachdem** it depends; **je nachdem, ob ...** depending on whether ...
2: **je eher, desto** od **um so besser** the

sooner the better

Jeans [dʒi:nz] *pl* jeans
jede(r, s) ['je:də(r, s)] *adj* every, each ♦ *pron* everybody; (~ *einzelne*) each; **ohne ~ x** without any x
jedenfalls *adv* in any case
jedermann *pron* everyone
jederzeit *adv* at any time
jedesmal △ *adv* every time, each time
jedoch [je'dɔx] *adv* however
jeher ['je:he:r] *adv*: **von/seit ~** always
jemals ['je:ma:ls] *adv* ever
jemand ['je:mant] *pron* somebody; anybody
jene(r, s) ['je:nə(r, s)] *adj* that ♦ *pron* that one
jenseits ['je:nzaits] *adv* on the other side ♦ *präp +gen* on the other side of, beyond
Jenseits *nt*: **das ~** the hereafter, the beyond
jetzig ['jetsɪç] *adj* present
jetzt [jetst] *adv* now
jeweilig *adj* respective
jeweils *adv*: **~ zwei zusammen** two at a time; **zu ~ 5 DM** at 5 marks each; **~ das erste** the first each time
Jh. *abk = Jahrhundert*
Job [dʒɔp] **(-s, -s)** *m* (*umg*) job; **j~ben** ['dʒɔbən] *vi* (*umg*) to work
Jockei ['dʒɔke] **(-s, -s)** *m* jockey
Jod [jo:t] **(-(e)s)** *nt* iodine
jodeln ['jo:dəln] *vi* to yodel
joggen ['dʒɔgən] *vi* to jog
Joghurt △ ['jo:gʊrt] **(-s, -s)** *m od nt* yogurt
Johannisbeere [jo'hanɪsbe:rə] *f* redcurrant; **schwarze ~** blackcurrant
johlen ['jo:lən] *vi* to yell
jonglieren [ʒõ'gli:rən] *vi* to juggle
Journal- [ʒʊrnal] *zW*: **~ismus** [-'lɪsmʊs] *m* journalism; **~ist(in)** [-'lɪst(ɪn)] *m(f)* journalist; **journa'listisch** *adj* journalistic
Jubel ['ju:bəl] **(-s)** *m* rejoicing; **j~n** *vi* to rejoice
Jubiläum [jubi'lɛ:ʊm] **(-s, Jubiläen)** *nt* anniversary; jubilee
jucken ['jʊkən] *vi* to itch ♦ *vt*: **es juckt mich am Arm** my arm is itching

Juckreiz ['jʊkraits] *m* itch
Jude ['ju:də] **(-n, -n)** *m* Jew
Juden- *zW*: **~tum (-)** *nt* Judaism; Jewry; **~verfolgung** *f* persecution of the Jews
Jüdin ['jy:dɪn] *f* Jewess
jüdisch ['jy:dɪʃ] *adj* Jewish
Jugend ['ju:gənt] **(-)** *f* youth; **j~frei** *adj* (*CINE*) U (*BRIT*), G (*US*), suitable for children; **~herberge** *f* youth hostel; **~herbergsausweis** *m* youth hostelling card; **j~lich** *adj* youthful; **~liche(r)** *f(m)* teenager, young person
Jugoslaw- [jugo'sla:v] *zW*: **~ien (-s)** *nt* Yugoslavia; **j~isch** *adj* Yugoslavian
Juli ['ju:li] **(-(s), -s)** *m* July
jun. *abk (= junior)* jr.
jung [jʊŋ] *adj* young; **J~e (-n, -n)** *m* boy, lad ♦ *nt* young animal; **J~en** *pl* (*von Tier*) young *pl*
Jünger ['jyŋər] **(-s, -)** *m* disciple
jünger *adj* younger
Jung- *zW*: **~frau** *f* virgin; (*ASTROL*) Virgo; **~geselle** *m* bachelor; **~gesellin** *f* unmarried woman
jüngst [jʏŋst] *adv* lately, recently; **~e(r, s)** *adj* youngest; (*neueste*) latest
Juni ['ju:ni] **(-(s), -s)** *m* June
Junior ['ju:niɔr] **(-s, -en)** *m* junior
Jurist [ju'rɪst] *m* jurist, lawyer; **j~isch** *adj* legal
Justiz [jʊs'ti:ts] **(-)** *f* justice; **~beamte(r)** *m* judicial officer; **~irrtum** *m* miscarriage of justice; **~minister** *m* ≈ Lord (High) Chancellor (*BRIT*), ≈ Attorney General (*US*)
Juwel [ju've:l] **(-s, -en)** *nt od m* jewel
Juwelier [juve'li:r] **(-s, -e)** *m* jeweller; **~geschäft** *nt* jeweller's (shop)
Jux [jʊks] **(-es, -e)** *m* joke, lark

K, k

Kabarett [kaba'ret] **(-s, -e od -s)** *nt* cabaret; **~ist** [-'tɪst] *m* cabaret artiste
Kabel ['ka:bəl] **(-s, -)** *nt* (*ELEK*) wire; (*stark*) cable; **~fernsehen** *nt* cable television
Kabeljau ['ka:bəljau] **(-s, -e od -s)** *m* cod

Kabine [ka'bi:nə] f cabin; (*Zelle*) cubicle
Kabinenbahn f cable railway
Kabinett [kabi'nɛt] (**-s, -e**) nt (*POL*) cabinet
Kachel ['kaxəl] (**-, -n**) f tile; **k~n** vt to tile; **~ofen** m tiled stove
Käfer ['kɛːfər] (**-s, -**) m beetle
Kaffee ['kafe] (**-s, -s**) m coffee; **~haus** nt café; **~kanne** f coffeepot; **~löffel** m coffee spoon
Käfig ['kɛːfɪç] (**-s, -e**) m cage
kahl [ka:l] adj bald; **~geschoren** △ adj shaven, shorn; **~köpfig** adj bald-headed
Kahn [ka:n] (**-(e)s, ¨e**) m boat, barge
Kai [kaɪ] (**-s, -e** od **-s**) m quay
Kaiser ['kaɪzər] (**-s, -**) m emperor; **~in** f empress; **k~lich** adj imperial; **~reich** nt empire; **~schnitt** m (*MED*) Caesarian (section)
Kakao [ka'ka:o] (**-s, -s**) m cocoa
Kaktee [kak'te:(ə)] (**-, -n**) f cactus
Kaktus ['kaktʊs] (**-, -teen**) m cactus
Kalb [kalp] (**-(e)s, ¨er**) nt calf; **k~en** ['kalbən] vi to calve; **~fleisch** nt veal; **~sleder** nt calf(skin)
Kalender [ka'lɛndər] (**-s, -**) m calendar; (*Taschen~*) diary
Kaliber [ka'li:bər] (**-s, -**) nt (*auch fig*) calibre
Kalk [kalk] (**-(e)s, -e**) m lime; (*BIOL*) calcium; **~stein** m limestone
kalkulieren [kalku'li:rən] vt to calculate
Kalorie [kalo'ri:] f calorie
kalt [kalt] adj cold; **mir ist (es) ~** I am cold; **~bleiben** △ (*unreg*) vi to remain unmoved; **~blütig** adj cold-blooded; (*ruhig*) cool
Kälte ['kɛltə] (**-**) f cold; coldness; **~grad** m degree of frost od below zero; **~welle** f cold spell
kalt- zW: **~herzig** adj cold-hearted; **~schnäuzig** adj cold, unfeeling; **~stellen** vt to chill; (*fig*) to leave out in the cold
kam etc [ka:m] vb siehe **kommen**
Kamel [ka'me:l] (**-(e)s, -e**) nt camel
Kamera ['kamera] (**-, -s**) f camera
Kamerad [kamə'ra:t] (**-en, -en**) m comrade, friend; **~schaft** f comradeship; **k~schaftlich** adj comradely

Kameramann (**-(e)s, -männer**) m cameraman
Kamille [ka'mɪlə] f camomile; **~ntee** m camomile tea
Kamin [ka'mi:n] (**-s, -e**) m (*außen*) chimney; (*innen*) fireside, fireplace; **~kehrer** (**-s, -**) m chimney sweep
Kamm [kam] (**-(e)s, ¨e**) m comb; (*Berg~*) ridge; (*Hahnen~*) crest
kämmen ['kɛmən] vt to comb ♦ vr to comb one's hair
Kammer ['kamər] (**-, -n**) f chamber; small bedroom; **~diener** m valet
Kampagne [kam'panjə] f campaign
Kampf [kampf] (**-(e)s, ¨e**) m fight, battle; (*Wettbewerb*) contest; (*fig: Anstrengung*) struggle; **k~bereit** adj ready for action
kämpfen ['kɛmpfən] vi to fight
Kämpfer (**-s, -**) m fighter, combatant
Kampf- zW: **~handlung** f action; **k~los** adj without a fight; **~richter** m (*SPORT*) referee; (*TENNIS*) umpire; **~stoff** m: **chemischer/biologischer ~stoff** chemical/biological weapon
Kanada ['kanada] (**-s**) nt Canada; **Ka'nadier(in)** (**-s, -**) m(f) Canadian; **ka'nadisch** adj Canadian
Kanal [ka'na:l] (**-s, Kanäle**) m (*Fluß*) canal; (*Rinne, Ärmel~*) channel; (*für Abfluß*) drain; **~inseln** pl Channel Islands; **~isation** [-izatsi'o:n] f sewage system; **~tunnel** m: **der ~tunnel** the Channel Tunnel
Kanarienvogel [ka'na:riənfo:gəl] m canary
kanarisch [ka'na:rɪʃ] adj: **K~e Inseln** Canary Islands, Canaries
Kandi- [kandi] zW: **~dat** [-'da:t] (**-en, -en**) m candidate; **~datur** [-da'tu:r] f candidature, candidacy; **k~dieren** [-'di:rən] vi to stand, to run
Kandis(zucker) ['kandɪs(tsʊkər)] (**-**) m candy
Känguruh △ ['kɛŋguru] (**-s, -s**) nt kangaroo
Kaninchen [ka'ni:nçən] nt rabbit
Kanister [ka'nɪstər] (**-s, -**) m can, canister
Kännchen ['kɛnçən] nt pot
Kanne ['kanə] f (*Krug*) jug; (*Kaffee~*) pot;

(Milch~) churn; (Gieβ~) can
kannst etc [kanst] vb siehe **können**
Kanone [ka'no:nə] f gun; (HIST) cannon; (fig: Mensch) ace
Kante ['kantə] f edge
Kantine [kan'ti:nəl] f canteen
Kanton [kan'to:n] (-s, -e) m canton

KANTON

i Kanton is the term for a state or region of Switzerland. Under the Swiss constitution the **Kantone** enjoy considerable autonomy. The Swiss **Kantone** are Aargau, Appenzell, Basel, Bern, Fribourg, Geneva, Glarus, Graubünden, Luzern, Neuchâtel, St. Gallen, Schaffhausen, Schwyz, Solothurn, Ticino, Thurgau, Unterwalden, Uri, Valais, Vaud, Zug and Zürich.

Kanu ['ka:nu] (-s, -s) nt canoe
Kanzel ['kantsəl] (-, -n) f pulpit
Kanzler ['kantslər] (-s, -) m chancellor
Kap [kap] (-s, -s) nt cape (GEOG)
Kapazität [kapatsi'tɛ:t] f capacity; (Fachmann) authority
Kapelle [ka'pɛlə] f (Gebäude) chapel; (MUS) band
kapieren [ka'pi:rən] (umg) vt, vi to get, to understand
Kapital [kapi'ta:l] (-s, -e od -ien) nt capital; ~anlage f investment; ~ismus [-'lɪsmʊs] m capitalism; ~ist [-'lɪst] m capitalist; k~istisch adj capitalist
Kapitän [kapi'tɛ:n] (-s, -e) m captain
Kapitel [ka'pɪtəl] (-s, -) nt chapter
Kapitulation [kapitulatsi'o:n] f capitulation
kapitulieren [kapitu'li:rən] vi to capitulate
Kappe ['kapə] f cap; (Kapuze) hood
kappen vt to cut
Kapsel ['kapsəl] (-, -n) f capsule
kaputt [ka'pʊt] (umg) adj kaput, broken; (Person) exhausted, finished; **am Auto ist etwas ~** there's something wrong with the car; ~gehen (unreg) vi to break; (Schuhe) to fall apart; (Firma) to go bust; (Stoff) to wear out; (sterben) to cop it

(umg); ~machen vt to break; (Mensch) to exhaust, to wear out
Kapuze [ka'pu:tsə] f hood
Karamel △ [kara'mɛl] (-s) m caramel; ~bonbon △ m od nt toffee
Karate [ka'ra:tə] (-s) nt karate
Karawane [kara'va:nə] f caravan
Kardinal [kardi'na:l] (-s, **Kardinäle**) m cardinal; ~zahl f cardinal number
Karfreitag [ka:r'fraita:k] m Good Friday
karg [kark] adj (Landschaft, Boden) barren; (Lohn) meagre
kärglich ['kɛrklɪç] adj poor, scanty
Karibik [ka'ri:bɪk] (-) f: **die ~** the Caribbean
karibisch [ka'ri:bɪʃ] adj: **K~e Inseln** Caribbean Islands
kariert [ka'ri:rt] adj (Stoff) checked; (Papier) squared
Karies ['ka:ries] (-) f caries
Karikatur [karika'tu:r] f caricature; ~ist [-'rɪst] m cartoonist
Karneval ['karnəval] (-s, -e od -s) m carnival

KARNEVAL

i Karneval is the time immediately before Lent when people gather to eat, drink and generally have fun before the fasting begins. **Rosenmontag**, the day before Shrove Tuesday, is the most important day of **Karneval** on the Rhine. Most firms take a day's holiday on that day to enjoy the celebrations. In South Germany and Austria **Karneval** is called Fasching.

Karo ['ka:ro] (-s, -s) nt square; (KARTEN) diamonds
Karosserie [karɔsə'ri:] f (AUT) body(work)
Karotte [ka'rɔtə] f carrot
Karpfen ['karpfən] (-s, -) m carp
Karre ['karə] f cart, barrow
Karren (-s, -) m cart, barrow
Karriere [kari'ɛ:rə] f career; ~ **machen** to get on, to get to the top; ~macher (-s, -) m careerist
Karte ['kartə] f card; (Land~) map; (Speise~) menu; (Eintritts~, Fahr~) ticket; **alles auf**

⚠ For information on spelling reform see page 615

eine ~ setzen to put all one's eggs in one basket

Kartei [kar'taɪ] f card index; **~karte** f index card

Kartell [kar'tɛl] (-s, -e) nt cartel

Karten- zW: **~spiel** nt card game; pack of cards; **~telefon** nt cardphone; **~vorverkauf** m advance booking office

Kartoffel [kar'tɔfəl] (-, -n) f potato; **~brei** m mashed potatoes pl; **~mus** nt mashed potatoes pl; **~püree** nt mashed potatoes pl; **~salat** m potato salad

Karton [kar'tõ:] (-s, -s) m cardboard; (*Schachtel*) cardboard box; **k~iert** [karto'niːrt] adj hardback

Karussell [karʊ'sɛl] (-s, -s) nt roundabout (*BRIT*), merry-go-round

Karwoche ['kaːrvɔxə] f Holy Week

Käse ['kɛːzə] (-s, -) m cheese; **~glocke** f cheese (plate) cover; **~kuchen** m cheesecake

Kaserne [ka'zɛrnə] f barracks pl; **~nhof** m parade ground

Kasino [ka'ziːno] (-s, -s) nt club; (*MIL*) officers' mess; (*Spiel~*) casino

Kaskoversicherung ['kasko-] f (*Teilkasko*) ≈ third party, fire and theft insurance; (*Vollkasko*) ≈ fully comprehensive insurance

Kasse ['kasə] f (*Geldkasten*) cashbox; (*in Geschäft*) till, cash register; cash desk, checkout; (*Kino~, Theater~ etc*) box office; ticket office; (*Kranken~*) health insurance; (*Spar~*) savings bank; **~ machen** to count the money; **getrennte ~ führen** to pay separately; **an der ~** (*in Geschäft*) at the desk; **gut bei ~ sein** to be in the money

Kassen- zW: **~arzt** m panel doctor (*BRIT*); **~bestand** m cash balance; **~patient** m panel patient (*BRIT*); **~prüfung** f audit; **~sturz** m: **~sturz machen** to check one's money; **~zettel** m receipt

Kassette [ka'sɛtə] f small box; (*Tonband, PHOT*) cassette; (*Bücher~*) case

Kassettenrecorder (-s, -) m cassette recorder

kassieren [ka'siːrən] vt to take ♦ vi: **darf ich ~?** would you like to pay now?

Kassierer [ka'siːrər] (-s, -) m cashier; (*von Klub*) treasurer

Kastanie [kas'taːniə] f chestnut; (*Baum*) chestnut tree

Kasten ['kastən] (-s, ˝) m (*auch SPORT*) box; case; (*Truhe*) chest

kastrieren [kas'triːrən] vt to castrate

Katalog [kata'loːk] (-(e)s, -e) m catalogue

Katalysator [kataly'zaːtɔr] m catalyst; (*AUT*) catalytic converter

katastrophal [katastro'faːl] adj catastrophic

Katastrophe [kata'stroːfə] f catastrophe, disaster

Kat-Auto ['kat|aʊto] nt car fitted with a catalytic converter

Kategorie [katego'riː] f category

kategorisch [kate'goːrɪʃ] adj categorical

Kater ['kaːtər] (-s, -) m tomcat; (*umg*) hangover

kath. abk (= *katholisch*) Cath.

Kathedrale [kate'draːlə] f cathedral

Katholik [kato'liːk] (-en, -en) m Catholic

katholisch [ka'toːlɪʃ] adj Catholic

Kätzchen ['kɛtsçən] nt kitten

Katze ['katsə] f cat; **für die Katz** (*umg*) in vain, for nothing

Katzen- zW: **~auge** nt cat's eye; (*Fahrrad*) rear light; **~sprung** (*umg*) m stone's throw; short journey

Kauderwelsch ['kaʊdərvɛlʃ] (-(s)) nt jargon; (*umg*) double Dutch

kauen ['kaʊən] vt, vi to chew

kauern ['kaʊərn] vi to crouch down; (*furchtsam*) to cower

Kauf [kaʊf] (-(e)s, Käufe) m purchase, buy; (*Kaufen*) buying; **ein guter ~** a bargain; **etw in ~ nehmen** to put up with sth; **k~en** vt to buy

Käufer(in) ['kɔʏfər(ɪn)] (-s, -) m(f) buyer

Kauf- zW: **~frau** f businesswoman; **~haus** nt department store; **~kraft** f purchasing power

käuflich ['kɔʏflɪç] adj purchasable, for sale; (*pej*) venal ♦ adv: **~ erwerben** to purchase

Kauf- zW: **k~lustig** adj interested in buying; **~mann** (*pl* **-leute**) m businessman; shopkeeper; **k~männisch** adj commercial;

⚠ *Informationen zur Rechtschreibreform Seite 615*

k~männischer Angestellter office worker; **~preis** m purchase price; **~vertrag** m bill of sale

Kaugummi ['kaʊɡʊmi] m chewing gum

Kaulquappe ['kaʊlkvapə] f tadpole

kaum [kaʊm] adv hardly, scarcely

Kaution [kaʊtsi'oːn] f deposit; (JUR) bail

Kauz [kaʊts] (**-es, Käuze**) m owl; (fig) queer fellow

Kavalier [kava'liːr] (**-s, -e**) m gentleman, cavalier; **~sdelikt** nt peccadillo

Kaviar ['kaːviar] m caviar

keck [kɛk] adj daring, bold

Kegel ['keːɡəl] (**-s, -**) m skittle; (MATH) cone; **~bahn** f skittle alley; bowling alley; **k~n** vi to play skittles

Kehle ['keːlə] f throat

Kehlkopf m larynx

Kehre ['keːrə] f turn(ing), bend; **k~n** vt, vi (wenden) to turn; (mit Besen) to sweep; **sich an etw** dat **nicht k~n** not to heed sth

Kehricht ['keːrɪçt] (**-s**) m sweepings pl

Kehrseite f reverse, other side; wrong side; bad side

kehrtmachen vi to turn about, to about-turn

keifen ['kaɪfən] vi to scold, to nag

Keil [kaɪl] (**-(e)s, -e**) m wedge; (MIL) arrowhead; **~riemen** m (AUT) fan belt

Keim [kaɪm] (**-(e)s, -e**) m bud; (MED, fig) germ; **k~en** vi to germinate; **k~frei** adj sterile; **~zelle** f (fig) nucleus

kein [kaɪn] adj no, not ... any; **~e(r, s)** pron no one, nobody; none; **~erlei** adj attrib no ... whatsoever

keinesfalls adv on no account

keineswegs adv by no means

keinmal adv not once

Keks [keːks] (**-es, -e**) m od nt biscuit

Kelch [kɛlç] (**-(e)s, -e**) m cup, goblet, chalice

Kelle ['kɛlə] f (Suppen~) ladle; (Maurer~) trowel

Keller ['kɛlər] (**-s, -**) m cellar

Kellner(in) ['kɛlnər(ɪn)] (**-s, -**) m(f) waiter(-tress)

keltern ['kɛltərn] vt to press

kennen ['kɛnən] (unreg) vt to know; **~lernen** △ vt to get to know; **sich ~lernen** to get to know each other; (zum erstenmal) to meet

Kenner (**-s, -**) m connoisseur

kenntlich adj distinguishable, discernible; **etw ~ machen** to mark sth

Kenntnis (**-, -se**) f knowledge no pl; **etw zur ~ nehmen** to note sth; **von etw ~ nehmen** to take notice of sth; **jdn in ~ setzen** to inform sb

Kenn- zW: **~zeichen** nt mark, characteristic; **k~zeichnen** vt insep to characterize; **~ziffer** f reference number

kentern ['kɛntərn] vi to capsize

Keramik [ke'raːmɪk] (**-, -en**) f ceramics pl, pottery

Kerbe ['kɛrbə] f notch, groove

Kerker ['kɛrkər] (**-s, -**) m prison

Kerl [kɛrl] (**-s, -e**) m chap, bloke (BRIT), guy

Kern [kɛrn] (**-(e)s, -e**) m (Obst~) pip, stone; (Nuß~) kernel; (Atom~) nucleus; (fig) heart, core; **~energie** f nuclear energy; **~forschung** f nuclear research; **~frage** f central issue; **k~gesund** adj thoroughly healthy, fit as a fiddle; **k~ig** adj (kraftvoll) robust; (Ausspruch) pithy; **~kraftwerk** nt nuclear power station; **k~los** adj seedless, without pips; **~physik** f nuclear physics sg; **~spaltung** f nuclear fission; **~waffen** pl nuclear weapons

Kerze ['kɛrtsə] f candle; (Zünd~) plug; **k~ngerade** adj straight as a die; **~nständer** m candle holder

keß △ [kɛs] adj saucy

Kessel ['kɛsəl] (**-s, -**) m kettle; (von Lokomotive etc) boiler; (GEOG) depression; (MIL) encirclement

Kette ['kɛtə] f chain; **k~n** vt to chain; **~nrauchen** (**-s**) nt chain smoking; **~nreaktion** f chain reaction

Ketzer ['kɛtsər] (**-s, -**) m heretic

keuchen ['kɔʏçən] vi to pant, to gasp

Keuchhusten m whooping cough

Keule ['kɔʏlə] f club; (KOCH) leg

keusch [kɔʏʃ] adj chaste; **K~heit** f chastity

kfm. abk = **kaufmännisch**

△ For information on spelling reform see page 615

Kfz [ka:|ɛf'tsɛt] *nt abk* = **Kraftfahrzeug**
KG [ka:'ge:] (-, -s) *f abk*
(= *Kommanditgesellschaft*) limited partnership
kg *abk* = **Kilogramm**
kichern ['kɪçərn] *vi* to giggle
kidnappen ['kɪtnɛpən] *vt* to kidnap
Kiefer¹ ['ki:fər] (-s, -) *m* jaw
Kiefer² ['ki:fər] (-, -n) *f* pine; ~**nzapfen** *m* pine cone
Kiel [ki:l] (-(e)s, -e) *m* (*Feder*~) quill; (*NAUT*) keel
Kieme ['ki:mə] *f* gill
Kies [ki:s] (-es, -e) *m* gravel
Kilo ['ki:lo] *nt* kilo; ~**gramm** [kilo'gram] *nt* kilogram; ~**meter** [kilo'me:tər] *m* kilometre; ~**meterzähler** *m* milometer
Kind [kɪnt] (-(e)s, -er) *nt* child; **von ~ auf** from childhood
Kinder- ['kɪndər] *zW*: ~**betreuung** *f* crèche; ~**ei** [-'rai] *f* childishness; ~**garten** *m* nursery school, playgroup; ~**gärtnerin** *f* nursery school teacher; ~**geld** *nt* child benefit (*BRIT*); ~**heim** *nt* children's home; ~**krippe** *f* crèche; ~**lähmung** *f* poliomyelitis; k~**leicht** *adj* childishly easy; k~**los** *adj* childless; ~**mädchen** *nt* nursemaid; k~**reich** *adj* with a lot of children; ~**sendung** *f* (*RAD, TV*) children's programme; ~**sicherung** *f* (*AUT*) childproof safety catch; ~**spiel** *nt* (*fig*) child's play; ~**tagesstätte** *f* day nursery; ~**wagen** *m* pram, baby carriage (*US*); ~**zimmer** *nt* (*für Kinder*) children's room; (*für Säugling*) nursery

KINDERGARTEN

i *A* **Kindergarten** *is a nursery school for children aged between 3 and 6 years. The children sing and play but do not receive any formal instruction. Most Kindergärten are financed by the town or the church with parents paying a monthly contribution towards the cost.*

Kind- *zW*: ~**heit** *f* childhood; k~**isch** *adj* childish; k~**lich** *adj* childlike

Kinn [kɪn] (-(e)s, -e) *nt* chin; ~**haken** *m* (*BOXEN*) uppercut
Kino ['ki:no] (-s, -s) *nt* cinema; ~**besucher** *m* cinema-goer; ~**programm** *nt* film programme
Kiosk [ki'ɔsk] (-(e)s, -e) *m* kiosk
Kippe ['kɪpə] *f* cigarette end; (*umg*) fag; **auf der ~ stehen** (*fig*) to be touch and go
kippen *vi* to topple over, to overturn ♦ *vt* to tilt
Kirch- ['kɪrç] *zW*: ~**e** *f* church; ~**enlied** *nt* hymn; ~**ensteuer** *f* church tax; ~**gänger** (-s, -) *m* churchgoer; ~**hof** *m* churchyard; k~**lich** *adj* ecclesiastical
Kirmes ['kɪrmɛs] (-, -sen) *f* fair
Kirsche ['kɪrʃə] *f* cherry
Kissen ['kɪsən] (-s, -) *nt* cushion; (*Kopf*~) pillow; ~**bezug** *m* pillowslip
Kiste ['kɪstə] *f* box; chest
Kitsch [kɪtʃ] (-(e)s) *m* kitsch; k~**ig** *adj* kitschy
Kitt [kɪt] (-(e)s, -e) *m* putty
Kittel (-s, -) *m* overall, smock
kitten *vt* to putty; (*fig: Ehe etc*) to cement
kitzelig ['kɪtsəlɪç] *adj* (*auch fig*) ticklish
kitzeln *vi* to tickle
Kiwi ['ki:vi] (-, -s) *f* (*BOT, KOCH*) kiwi fruit
KKW [ka:ka:'ve:] *nt abk* = **Kernkraftwerk**
Klage ['kla:gə] *f* complaint; (*JUR*) action; k~**n** *vi* (*wehklagen*) to lament, to wail; (*sich beschweren*) to complain; (*JUR*) to take legal action
Kläger(in) ['klɛ:gər(ɪn)] (-s, -) *m(f)* plaintiff
kläglich ['klɛ:klɪç] *adj* wretched
klamm [klam] *adj* (*Finger*) numb; (*feucht*) damp
Klammer ['klamər] (-, -n) *f* clamp; (*in Text*) bracket; (*Büro*~) clip; (*Wäsche*~) peg; (*Zahn*~) brace; k~**n** *vr*: **sich k~n an** +*akk* to cling to
Klang [klaŋ] (-(e)s, ¨e) *m* sound; k~**voll** *adj* sonorous
Klappe ['klapə] *f* valve; (*Ofen*~) damper; (*umg: Mund*) trap; k~**n** *vi* (*Geräusch*) to click; (*Sitz etc*) to tip ♦ *vt* to tip ♦ *vb unpers* to work
Klapper ['klapər] (-, -n) *f* rattle; k~**ig** *adj*

run-down, worn-out; **k~n** vi to clatter, to rattle; **~schlange** f rattlesnake; **~storch** m stork

Klapp- zW: **~messer** nt jackknife; **~rad** nt collapsible bicycle; **~stuhl** m folding chair; **~tisch** m folding table

Klaps [klaps] (-es, -e) m slap

klar [klaːr] adj clear; (NAUT) ready for sea; (MIL) ready for action; **sich** dat **im ~en sein über** +akk to be clear about; **ins ~e kommen** to get clear; **(na) ~!** of course!

Kläranlage f purification plant

klären ['klɛːrən] vt (Flüssigkeit) to purify; (Probleme) to clarify ♦ vr to clear (itself) up

Klarheit f clarity

Klarinette [klariˈnɛtə] f clarinet

klar- zW: **~legen** vt to clear up, to explain; **~machen** vt (Schiff) to get ready for sea; **jdm etw ~machen** to make sth clear to sb; **~sehen** △ (unreg) vi to see clearly; **K~sichtfolie** f transparent film; **~stellen** vt to clarify

Klärung ['klɛːrʊŋ] f (von Flüssigkeit) purification; (von Probleme) clarification

klarwerden △ (unreg) vr: **sich** dat **(über etw** akk**) ~** to get (sth) clear in one's mind

Klasse ['klasə] f class; (SCH) class, form

klasse (umg) adj smashing

Klassen- zW: **~arbeit** f test; **~gesellschaft** f class society; **~lehrer** m form master; **k~los** adj classless; **~sprecher(in)** m(f) form prefect; **~zimmer** nt classroom

klassifizieren [klasifiˈtsiːrən] vt to classify

Klassik ['klasɪk] f (Zeit) classical period; (Stil) classicism; **~er** (-s, -) m classic

klassisch adj (auch fig) classical

Klatsch [klatʃ] (-(e)s, -e) m smack, crack; (Gerede) gossip; **~base** f gossip, scandalmonger; **~e** (umg) f crib; **k~en** vi (Geräusch) to clash; (reden) to gossip; (applaudieren) to applaud, to clap ♦ vt: **jdm Beifall k~en** to applaud sb; **~mohn** m (corn) poppy; **k~naß** △ adj soaking wet

Klaue ['klaʊə] f claw; (umg: Schrift) scrawl; **k~n** (umg) vt to pinch

Klausel ['klaʊzəl] (-, -n) f clause

Klausur [klaʊˈzuːr] f seclusion; **~arbeit** f examination paper

Klavier [klaˈviːr] (-s, -e) nt piano

Kleb- ['kleːb] zW: **k~en** ['kleːbən] vt, vi: **k~en (an** +akk**)** to stick (to); **k~rig** adj sticky; **~stoff** m glue; **~streifen** m adhesive tape

kleckern ['klɛkərn] vi to make a mess ♦ vt to spill

Klecks [klɛks] (-es, -e) m blot, stain

Klee [kleː] (-s) m clover; **~blatt** nt cloverleaf; (fig) trio

Kleid [klaɪt] (-(e)s, -er) nt garment; (Frauen~) dress; **~er** pl (Kleidung) clothes; **k~en** ['klaɪdən] vt to clothe, to dress; to suit ♦ vr to dress

Kleider- ['klaɪdər] zW: **~bügel** m coat hanger; **~bürste** f clothes brush; **~schrank** m wardrobe

Kleid- zW: **k~sam** adj flattering; **~ung** f clothing; **~ungsstück** nt garment

klein [klaɪn] adj little, small; **K~e(r, s)** mf little one; **K~format** nt small size; **im K~format** small-scale; **K~geld** nt small change; **~hacken** △ vt to chop up, to mince; **K~igkeit** f trifle; **K~kind** nt infant; **K~kram** m details pl; **~laut** adj dejected, quiet; **~lich** adj petty, paltry; **K~od** ['klaɪnoːt] (-s, -odien) nt gem, jewel; treasure; **~schneiden** △ (unreg) vt to chop up; **K~stadt** f small town; **~städtisch** adj provincial; **~stmöglich** adj smallest possible

Kleister ['klaɪstər] (-s, -) m paste

Klemme ['klɛmə] f clip; (MED) clamp; (fig) jam; **k~n** vt (festhalten) to jam; (quetschen) to pinch, to nip ♦ vr to catch o.s.; (sich hineinzwängen) to squeeze o.s. ♦ vi (Tür) to stick, to jam; **sich hinter jdn/etw k~n** to get on to sb/down to sth

Klempner ['klɛmpnər] (-s, -) m plumber

Klerus ['kleːrʊs] (-) m clergy

Klette ['klɛtə] f burr

Kletter- ['klɛtər] zW: **~er** (-s, -) m climber; **k~n** vi to climb; **~pflanze** f creeper

Klient(in) [kliˈɛnt(ɪn)] m(f) client

Klima ['kliːma] (-s, -s od -te) nt climate;

△ For information on spelling reform see page 615

~**anlage** *f* air conditioning; ~**wechsel** *m* change of air

klimpern ['klɪmpərn] (*umg*) *vi* (*mit Münzen, Schlüsseln*) to jingle; (*auf Klavier*) to plonk (away)

Klinge ['klɪŋə] *f* blade; sword

Klingel ['klɪŋəl] (-, -n) *f* bell; ~**beutel** *m* collection bag; **k~n** *vi* to ring

klingen ['klɪŋən] (*unreg*) *vi* to sound; (*Gläser*) to clink

Klinik ['kliːnɪk] *f* hospital, clinic

Klinke ['klɪŋkə] *f* handle

Klippe ['klɪpə] *f* cliff; (*im Meer*) reef; (*fig*) hurdle

klipp und klar ['klɪp|ʊntklaːr] *adj* clear and concise

klirren ['klɪrən] *vi* to clank, to jangle; (*Gläser*) to clink; ~**de Kälte** biting cold

Klischee [klɪ'ʃeː] (-s, -s) *nt* (*Druckplatte*) plate, block; (*fig*) cliché; ~**vorstellung** *f* stereotyped idea

Klo [kloː] (-s, -s) (*umg*) *nt* loo (*BRIT*), john (*US*)

Kloake [klo'aːkə] *f* sewer

klobig ['kloːbɪç] *adj* clumsy

Klopapier (*umg*) *nt* loo paper (*BRIT*)

klopfen ['klɔpfən] *vi* to knock; (*Herz*) to thump ♦ *vt* to beat; **es klopft** somebody's knocking; **jdm auf die Schulter ~** to tap sb on the shoulder

Klopfer (-s, -) *m* (*Teppich~*) beater; (*Tür~*) knocker

Klops [klɔps] (-es, -e) *m* meatball

Klosett [klo'zɛt] (-s, -e *od* -s) *nt* lavatory, toilet; ~**papier** *nt* toilet paper

Kloß [kloːs] (-es, ̈e) *m* (*im Hals*) lump; (*KOCH*) dumpling

Kloster ['kloːstər] (-s, ̈) *nt* (*Männer~*) monastery; (*Frauen~*) convent; **klösterlich** ['kløːstərlɪç] *adj* monastic; convent *cpd*

Klotz [klɔts] (-es, ̈e) *m* log; (*Hack~*) block; **ein ~ am Bein** (*fig*) a drag, a millstone round (sb's) neck

Klub [klʊp] (-s, -s) *m* club; ~**sessel** *m* easy chair

Kluft [klʊft] (-, ̈e) *f* cleft, gap; (*GEOG*) gorge, chasm

klug [kluːk] *adj* clever, intelligent; **K~heit** *f* cleverness, intelligence

Klumpen ['klʊmpən] (-s, -) *m* (*Erd~*) clod; (*Blut~*) clot; (*Gold~*) nugget; (*KOCH*) lump

km *abk* = **Kilometer**

knabbern ['knabərn] *vt, vi* to nibble

Knabe ['knaːbə] (-n, -n) *m* boy

Knäckebrot ['knɛkəbroːt] *nt* crispbread

knacken ['knakən] *vt, vi* (*auch fig*) to crack

Knacks [knaks] (-es, -e) *m* crack; (*fig*) defect

Knall [knal] (-(e)s, -e) *m* bang; (*Peitschen~*) crack; ~ **und Fall** (*umg*) unexpectedly; ~**bonbon** *nt* cracker; **k~en** *vi* to bang; to crack; **k~rot** *adj* bright red

knapp [knap] *adj* tight; (*Geld*) scarce; (*Sprache*) concise; **eine ~e Stunde** just under an hour; ~ **unter/neben** just under/ by; **K~heit** *f* tightness; scarcity; conciseness

knarren ['knarən] *vi* to creak

Knast [knast] (-(e)s) (*umg*) *m* (*Haftstrafe*) porridge (*inf*), time (*inf*); (*Gefängnis*) slammer (*inf*), clink (*inf*)

knattern ['knatərn] *vi* to rattle; (*Maschinengewehr*) to chatter

Knäuel ['knɔʏəl] (-s, -) *m od nt* (*Woll~*) ball; (*Menschen~*) knot

Knauf [knaʊf] (-(e)s, **Knäufe**) *m* knob; (*Schwert~*) pommel

Knebel ['kneːbəl] (-s, -) *m* gag

kneifen ['knaɪfən] (*unreg*) *vt* to pinch ♦ *vi* to pinch; (*sich drücken*) to back out; **vor etw ~** to dodge sth

Kneipe ['knaɪpə] (*umg*) *f* pub

kneten ['kneːtən] *vt* to knead; (*Wachs*) to mould

Knick [knɪk] (-(e)s, -e) *m* (*Sprung*) crack; (*Kurve*) bend; (*Falte*) fold; **k~en** *vt, vi* (*springen*) to crack; (*brechen*) to break; (*Papier*) to fold; **geknickt sein** to be downcast

Knicks [knɪks] (-es, -e) *m* curtsey

Knie [kniː] (-s, -) *nt* knee; ~**beuge** *f* knee bend; ~**bundhose** *m* knee breeches; ~**gelenk** *nt* knee joint; ~**kehle** *f* back of the knee; **k~n** *vi* to kneel; ~**scheibe** *f*

⚠ *Informationen zur Rechtschreibreform Seite 615*

kneecap; ~strumpf *m* knee-length sock
Kniff [knɪf] **(-(e)s, -e)** *m* (*fig*) trick, knack;
  k~elig *adj* tricky
knipsen ['knɪpsən] *vt* (*Fahrkarte*) to punch;
  (*PHOT*) to take a snap of, to snap ♦ *vi* to
  take a snap *od* snaps
Knirps [knɪrps] **(-es, -e)** *m* little chap;
  (® *Schirm*) telescopic umbrella
knirschen ['knɪrʃən] *vi* to crunch; **mit den**
  Zähnen ~ to grind one's teeth
knistern ['knɪstərn] *vi* to crackle
Knitter- [knɪtər] *zW*: **~falte** *f* crease; **k~frei**
  adj non-crease; **k~n** *vi* to crease
Knoblauch ['kno:plaʊx] **(-(e)s)** *m* garlic;
  ~zehe *f* (*KOCH*) clove of garlic
Knöchel ['knœçəl] **(-s, -)** *m* knuckle; (*Fuß~*)
  ankle
Knochen ['knɔxən] **(-s, -)** *m* bone; **~bruch**
  m fracture; **~gerüst** *nt* skeleton; **~mark** *nt*
  bone marrow
knöchern ['knœçərn] *adj* bone
knochig ['knɔxɪç] *adj* bony
Knödel ['knø:dəl] **(-s, -)** *m* dumpling
Knolle ['knɔlə] *f* tuber
Knopf [knɔpf] **(-(e)s, ¨e)** *m* button;
  (*Kragen~*) stud
knöpfen ['knœpfən] *vt* to button
Knopfloch *nt* buttonhole
Knorpel ['knɔrpəl] **(-s, -)** *m* cartilage, gristle;
  k~ig *adj* gristly
Knospe ['knɔspə] *f* bud
Knoten ['kno:tən] **(-s, -)** *m* knot; (*BOT*)
  node; (*MED*) lump; **k~** *vt* to knot; **~punkt**
  m junction
Knüller ['knʏlər] **(-s, -)** (*umg*) *m* hit;
  (*Reportage*) scoop
knüpfen ['knʏpfən] *vt* to tie; (*Teppich*) to
  knot; (*Freundschaft*) to form
Knüppel ['knʏpəl] **(-s, -)** *m* cudgel;
  (*Polizei~*) baton, truncheon; (*AVIAT*)
  (joy)stick
knurren ['knʊrən] *vi* (*Hund*) to snarl, to
  growl; (*Magen*) to rumble; (*Mensch*) to
  mutter
knusperig ['knʊspərɪç] *adj* crisp; (*Keks*)
  crunchy
k.o. [ka:'o:] *adj* knocked out; (*fig*) done in

Koalition [koalitsi'o:n] *f* coalition
Kobold ['ko:bɔlt] **(-(e)s, -e)** *m* goblin, imp
Koch [kɔx] **(-(e)s, ¨e)** *m* cook; **~buch** *nt*
  cook(ery) book; **k~en** *vt, vi* to cook;
  (*Wasser*) to boil; **~er (-s, -)** *m* stove,
  cooker; **~gelegenheit** *f* cooking facilities
  pl
Köchin ['kœçɪn] *f* cook
Koch- *zW*: **~löffel** *m* kitchen spoon;
  ~nische *f* kitchenette; **~platte** *f* hotplate;
  ~salz *nt* cooking salt; **~topf** *m* saucepan,
  pot
Köder ['kø:dər] **(-s, -)** *m* bait, lure
ködern *vt* (*Tier*) to trap with bait; (*Person*)
  to entice, to tempt
Koexistenz [koɛksɪs'tɛnts] *f* coexistence
Koffein [kɔfe'i:n] **(-s)** *nt* caffeine; **k~frei** *adj*
  decaffeinated
Koffer ['kɔfər] **(-s, -)** *m* suitcase; (*Schrank~*)
  trunk; **~kuli** *m* (luggage) trolley; **~radio** *nt*
  portable radio; **~raum** *m* (*AUT*) boot (*BRIT*),
  trunk (*US*)
Kognak ['kɔnjak] **(-s, -s)** *m* brandy, cognac
Kohl [ko:l] **(-(e)s, -e)** *m* cabbage
Kohle ['ko:lə] *f* coal; (*Holz~*) charcoal; (*CHEM*)
  carbon; **~hydrat (-(e)s, -e)** *nt*
  carbohydrate
Kohlen- *zW*: **~dioxyd (-(e)s, -e)** *nt* carbon
  dioxide; **~händler** *m* coal merchant,
  coalman; **~säure** *f* carbon dioxide; **~stoff**
  m carbon
Kohlepapier *nt* carbon paper
Koje ['ko:jə] *f* cabin; (*Bett*) bunk
Kokain [koka'i:n] **(-s)** *nt* cocaine
kokett [ko'kɛt] *adj* coquettish, flirtatious
Kokosnuß ⚠ ['ko:kɔsnʊs] *f* coconut
Koks [ko:ks] **(-es, -e)** *m* coke
Kolben ['kɔlbən] **(-s, -)** *m* (*Gewehr~*) rifle
  butt; (*Keule*) club; (*CHEM*) flask; (*TECH*)
  piston; (*Mais~*) cob
Kolik ['ko:lik] *f* colic, the gripes *pl*
Kollaps [kɔ'laps] **(-es, -e)** *m* collapse
Kolleg [kɔl'e:k] **(-s, -s** *od* **-ien)** *nt* lecture
  course; **~e** [kɔ'le:gə] **(-n, -n)** *m* colleague;
  ~in *f* colleague; **~ium** *nt* working party;
  (*SCH*) staff
Kollekte [kɔ'lɛktə] *f* (*REL*) collection

⚠ *For information on spelling reform see page 615*

kollektiv [kɔlɛk'tiːf] *adj* collective
Köln [kœln] (**-s**) *nt* Cologne
Kolonie [kolo'niː] *f* colony
kolonisieren [koloni'ziːrən] *vt* to colonize
Kolonne [ko'lɔnə] *f* column; *(von Fahrzeugen)* convoy
Koloß ⚠ [ko'lɔs] (**-sses, -sse**) *m* colossus; **kolo'ssal** *adj* colossal
Kölsch [kœlʃ] (**-, -**) *nt (Bier)* ≈ (strong) lager
Kombi- ['kɔmbi] *zW:* **~nation** [-natsi'oːn] *f* combination; *(Vermutung)* conjecture; *(Hemdhose)* combinations *pl*; **k~nieren** [-'niːrən] *vt* to combine ♦ *vi* to deduce, to work out; *(vermuten)* to guess; **~wagen** *m* station wagon; **~zange** *f* (pair of) pliers *pl*
Komet [ko'meːt] (**-en, -en**) *m* comet
Komfort [kɔm'foːr] (**-s**) *m* luxury
Komik ['koːmɪk] *f* humour, comedy; **~er** (**-s, -**) *m* comedian
komisch ['koːmɪʃ] *adj* funny
Komitee [komi'teː] (**-s, -s**) *nt* committee
Komma ['kɔma] (**-s, -s** *od* **-ta**) *nt* comma; **2 ~ 3** 2 point 3
Kommand- [ko'mand] *zW:* **~ant** [-'dant] *m* commander, commanding officer; **k~ieren** [-'diːrən] *vt, vi* to command; **~o** (**-s, -s**) *nt* command, order; *(Truppe)* detachment, squad; **auf ~o** to order
kommen ['kɔmən] *(unreg) vi* to come; *(näher~)* to approach; *(passieren)* to happen; *(gelangen, geraten)* to get; *(Blumen, Zähne, Tränen etc)* to appear; *(in die Schule, das Zuchthaus etc)* to go; **~ lassen** to send for; **das kommt in den Schrank** that goes in the cupboard; **zu sich ~** to come round *od* to; **zu etw ~** to acquire sth; **um etw ~** to lose sth; **nichts auf jdn/etw ~ lassen** to have nothing said against sb/sth; **jdm frech ~** to get cheeky with sb; **auf jeden vierten kommt ein Platz** there's one place for every fourth person; **wer kommt zuerst?** who's first?; **unter ein Auto ~** to be run over by a car; **wie hoch kommt das?** what does that cost?; **komm gut nach Hause!** safe journey (home); **~den Sonntag** next Sunday; **K~** (**-s**) *nt* coming
Kommentar [kɔmen'taːr] *m* commentary;

kein ~ no comment; **k~los** *adj* without comment
Kommentator [kɔmɛn'taːtɔr] *m (TV)* commentator
kommentieren [kɔmɛn'tiːrən] *vt* to comment on
kommerziell [kɔmɛrtsi'ɛl] *adj* commercial
Kommilitone [kɔmili'toːnə] (**-n, -n**) *m* fellow student
Kommissar [kɔmɪ'saːr] *m* police inspector
Kommission [kɔmɪsi'oːn] *f (COMM)* commission; *(Ausschuß)* committee
Kommode [kɔ'moːdə] *f* (chest of) drawers
kommunal [kɔmu'naːl] *adj* local; *(von Stadt auch)* municipal
Kommune [kɔ'muːnə] *f* commune
Kommunikation [kɔmunikatsi'oːn] *f* communication
Kommunion [kɔmuni'oːn] *f* communion
Kommuniqué ⚠ [kɔmyni'keː] (**-s, -s**) *nt* communiqué
Kommunismus [kɔmu'nɪsmʊs] *m* communism
Kommunist(in) [kɔmu'nɪst(ɪn)] *m(f)* communist; **k~isch** *adj* communist
kommunizieren [kɔmuni'tsiːrən] *vi* to communicate
Komödie [ko'møːdiə] *f* comedy
Kompagnon [kɔmpan'jõː] (**-s, -s**) *m (COMM)* partner
kompakt [kɔm'pakt] *adj* compact
Kompanie [kɔmpa'niː] *f* company
Kompaß ⚠ ['kɔmpas] (**-sses, -sse**) *m* compass
kompatibel [kɔmpa'tiːbəl] *adj* compatible
kompetent [kɔmpe'tɛnt] *adj* competent
Kompetenz *f* competence, authority
komplett [kɔm'plɛt] *adj* complete
Komplex [kɔm'plɛks] (**-es, -e**) *m (Gebäude~)* complex
Komplikation [kɔmplikatsi'oːn] *f* complication
Kompliment [kɔmpli'mɛnt] *nt* compliment
Komplize [kɔm'pliːtsə] (**-n, -n**) *m* accomplice
kompliziert [kɔmpli'tsiːrt] *adj* complicated
komponieren [kɔmpo'niːrən] *vt* to

compose

Komponist [kɔmpo'nɪst(ɪn)] *m* composer

Komposition [kɔmpozitsi'o:n] *f* composition

Kompost [kɔm'pɔst] (**-(e)s, -e**) *m* compost

Kompott [kɔm'pɔt] (**-(e)s, -e**) *nt* stewed fruit

Kompromiß △ [kɔmpro'mɪs] (**-sses, -sse**) *m* compromise; **k~bereit** △ *adj* willing to compromise

Kondens- [kɔn'dɛns] *zW:* **~ation** [kɔndɛnzatsi'o:n] *f* condensation; **k~ieren** [kɔndɛn'zi:rən] *vt* to condense; **~milch** *f* condensed milk

Kondition [kɔnditsi'o:n] *f* (*COMM, FIN*) condition; (*Durchhaltevermögen*) stamina; (*körperliche Verfassung*) physical condition, state of health

Konditionstraining [kɔnditsi'o:nstre:nɪŋ] *nt* fitness training

Konditor [kɔn'di:tɔr] *m* pastry cook; **~ei** [-'raɪ] *f* café; cake shop

Kondom [kɔn'do:m] (**-s, -e**) *nt* condom

Konferenz [kɔnfe'rɛnts] *f* conference, meeting

Konfession [kɔnfesi'o:n] *f* (religious) denomination; **k~ell** [-'nɛl] *adj* denominational; **k~slos** *adj* non-denominational

Konfirmand [kɔnfɪr'mant] *m* candidate for confirmation

Konfirmation [kɔnfɪrmatsi'o:n] *f* (*REL*) confirmation

konfirmieren [kɔnfɪr'mi:rən] *vt* to confirm

konfiszieren [kɔnfɪs'tsi:rən] *vt* to confiscate

Konfitüre [kɔnfi'ty:rə] *f* jam

Konflikt [kɔn'flɪkt] (**-(e)s, -e**) *m* conflict

konfrontieren [kɔnfrɔn'ti:rən] *vt* to confront

konfus [kɔn'fu:s] *adj* confused

Kongreß △ [kɔn'grɛs] (**-sses, -sse**) *m* congress; **~zentrum** △ *nt* conference centre

Kongruenz [kɔngru'ɛnts] *f* agreement, congruence

König ['kø:nɪç] (**-(e)s, -e**) *m* king; **~in** ['kø:nɪgɪn] *f* queen; **k~lich** *adj* royal;

~reich *nt* kingdom

Konjugation [kɔnjugatsi'o:n] *f* conjugation

konjugieren [kɔnju'gi:rən] *vt* to conjugate

Konjunktion [kɔnjʊŋktsi'o:n] *f* conjunction

Konjunktiv ['kɔnjʊŋkti:f] (**-s, -e**) *m* subjunctive

Konjunktur [kɔnjʊŋk'tu:r] *f* economic situation; (*Hoch~*) boom

konkret [kɔn'kre:t] *adj* concrete

Konkurrent(in) [kɔnkʊ'rɛnt(ɪn)] *m(f)* competitor

Konkurrenz [kɔnkʊ'rɛnts] *f* competition; **k~fähig** *adj* competitive; **~kampf** *m* competition; rivalry, competitive situation

konkurrieren [kɔnkʊ'ri:rən] *vi* to compete

Konkurs [kɔn'kʊrs] (**-es, -e**) *m* bankruptcy

Können (**-s**) *nt* ability

SCHLÜSSELWORT

können ['kœnən] (*pt* **konnte**, *pp* **gekonnt** *od* (*als Hilfsverb*) **können**) *vt, vi* 1 to be able to; **ich kann es machen** I can do it, I am able to do it; **ich kann es nicht machen** I can't do it, I'm not able to do it; **ich kann nicht ...** I can't ..., I cannot ...; **ich kann nicht mehr** I can't go on

2 (*wissen, beherrschen*) to know; **können Sie Deutsch?** can you speak German?; **er kann gut Englisch** he speaks English well; **sie kann keine Mathematik** she can't do mathematics

3 (*dürfen*) to be allowed to; **kann ich gehen?** can I go?; **könnte ich ...?** could I ...?; **kann ich mit?** (*umg*) can I come with you?

4 (*möglich sein*): **Sie könnten recht haben** you may be right; **das kann sein** that's possible; **kann sein** maybe

Könner *m* expert

konnte etc ['kɔntə] *vb siehe* **können**

konsequent [kɔnze'kvɛnt] *adj* consistent

Konsequenz [kɔnze'kvɛnts] *f* consistency; (*Folgerung*) conclusion

Konserv- [kɔn'zɛrv] *zW:* **k~ativ** [-a'ti:f] *adj* conservative; **~ative** [-a'ti:və] *f(m)* (*POL*) conservative; **~e** *f* tinned food;

△ *For information on spelling reform see page 615*

~enbüchse *f* tin, can; **k~ieren** [-'vi:rən] *vt* to preserve; ~**ierung** *f* preservation; ~**ierungsstoff** *m* preservatives

Konsonant [kɔnzo'nant] *m* consonant

konstant [kɔn'stant] *adj* constant

konstru- *zW:* ~**ieren** [kɔnstru'i:rən] *vt* to construct; **K~kteur** [kɔnstrʊk'tø:r] *m* designer; **K~ktion** [kɔnstrʊktsi'o:n] *f* construction; ~**ktiv** [kɔnstrʊk'ti:f] *adj* constructive

Konsul ['kɔnzʊl] (-s, -n) *m* consul; ~**at** [-'la:t] *nt* consulate

konsultieren [kɔnzʊl'ti:rən] *vt* to consult

Konsum [kɔn'zu:m] (-s) *m* consumption; ~**artikel** *m* consumer article; ~**ent** [-'mɛnt] *m* consumer; **k~ieren** [-'mi:rən] *vt* to consume

Kontakt [kɔn'takt] (-(e)s, -e) *m* contact; **k~arm** *adj* unsociable; **k~freudig** *adj* sociable; ~**linsen** *pl* contact lenses

kontern ['kɔntərn] *vt, vi* to counter

Kontinent [kɔnti'nɛnt] *m* continent

Kontingent [kɔntɪŋ'gɛnt] (-(e)s, -e) *nt* quota; (*Truppen~*) contingent

kontinuierlich [kɔntinu'i:rlıç] *adj* continuous

Konto ['kɔnto] (-s, Konten) *nt* account; ~**auszug** *m* statement (of account); ~**inhaber(in)** *m(f)* account holder; ~**stand** *m* balance

Kontra ['kɔntra] (-s, -s) *nt* (*KARTEN*) double; **jdm ~ geben** (*fig*) to contradict sb; ~**baß** △ *m* double bass; ~**hent** *m* (*COMM*) contracting party; ~**punkt** *m* counterpoint

Kontrast [kɔn'trast] (-(e)s, -e) *m* contrast

Kontroll- [kɔn'trɔl] *zW:* ~**e** *f* control, supervision; (*Paßkontrolle*) passport control; ~**eur** [-'lø:r] *m* inspector; **k~ieren** [-'li:rən] *vt* to control, to supervise; (*nachprüfen*) to check

Konvention [kɔnvɛntsi'o:n] *f* convention; **k~ell** [-'nɛl] *adj* conventional

Konversation [kɔnvɛrzatsi'o:n] *f* conversation; ~**slexikon** *nt* encyclop(a)edia

Konvoi ['kɔnvɔy] (-s, -s) *m* convoy

Konzentration [kɔntsentratsi'o:n] *f* concentration

Konzentrationslager *nt* concentration camp

konzentrieren [kɔntsen'tri:rən] *vt, vr* to concentrate

konzentriert *adj* concentrated ♦ *adv* (*zuhören, arbeiten*) intently

Konzern [kɔn'tsɛrn] (-s, -e) *m* combine

Konzert [kɔn'tsɛrt] (-(e)s, -e) *nt* concert; (*Stück*) concerto; ~**saal** *m* concert hall

Konzession [kɔntsesi'o:n] *f* licence; (*Zugeständnis*) concession

Konzil [kɔn'tsi:l] (-s, -e *od* -ien) *nt* council

kooperativ [ko|opera'ti:f] *adj* cooperative

koordinieren [ko|ɔrdi'ni:rən] *vt* to coordinate

Kopf [kɔpf] (-(e)s, ⸚e) *m* head; ~**haut** *f* scalp; ~**hörer** *m* headphones *pl*; ~**kissen** *nt* pillow; **k~los** *adj* panic-stricken; **k~rechnen** *vi* to do mental arithmetic; ~**salat** *m* lettuce; ~**schmerzen** *pl* headache *sg*; ~**sprung** *m* header, dive; ~**stand** *m* headstand; ~**stütze** *f* (*im Auto etc*) headrest, head restraint; ~**tuch** *nt* headscarf; ~**weh** *nt* headache; ~**zerbrechen** *nt:* **jdm ~zerbrechen machen** to be a headache for sb

Kopie [ko'pi:] *f* copy; **k~ren** *vt* to copy

Kopiergerät *nt* photocopier

Koppel¹ ['kɔpəl] (-, -n) *f* (*Weide*) enclosure

Koppel² ['kɔpəl] (-s, -) *m* (*Gürtel*) belt

koppeln *vt* to couple

Koppelung *f* coupling

Koralle [ko'ralə] *f* coral

Korb [kɔrp] (-(e)s, ⸚e) *m* basket; **jdm einen ~ geben** (*fig*) to turn sb down; ~**ball** *m* basketball; ~**stuhl** *m* wicker chair

Kord [kɔrt] (-(e)s, -e) *m* corduroy

Kordel ['kɔrdəl] (-, -n) *f* cord, string

Kork [kɔrk] (-(e)s, -e) *m* cork; ~**en** (-s, -) *m* stopper, cork; ~**enzieher** (-s, -) *m* corkscrew

Korn [kɔrn] (-(e)s, ⸚er) *nt* corn, grain; (*Gewehr*) sight

Körper ['kœrpər] (-s, -) *m* body; ~**bau** *m* build; **k~behindert** *adj* disabled; ~**geruch** *m* body odour; ~**gewicht** *nt* weight;

~**größe** f height; **k~lich** adj physical; ~**pflege** f personal hygiene; ~**schaft** f corporation; ~**schaftssteuer** f corporation tax; ~**teil** m part of the body; ~**verletzung** f bodily od physical injury

korpulent [kɔrpuˈlɛnt] adj corpulent

korrekt [kɔˈrɛkt] adj correct; **K~ur** [-ˈtuːr] f (eines Textes) proofreading; (Text) proof; (SCH) marking, correction

Korrespond- [kɔrɛspɔnd] zW: ~**ent(in)** [-ˈdɛnt(ɪn)] m(f) correspondent; ~**enz** [-ˈdɛnts] f correspondence; **k~ieren** [-ˈdiːrən] vi to correspond

Korridor [ˈkɔridoːr] (-s, -e) m corridor

korrigieren [kɔriˈgiːrən] vt to correct

Korruption [kɔruptsiˈoːn] f corruption

Kose- [ˈkoːzə] zW: ~**form** f pet form; ~**name** m pet name; ~**wort** nt term of endearment

Kosmetik [kɔsˈmeːtɪk] f cosmetics pl; ~**erin** f beautician

kosmetisch adj cosmetic; (Chirurgie) plastic

kosmisch [ˈkɔsmɪʃ] adj cosmic

Kosmo- [kɔsmo] zW: ~**naut** [-ˈnaut] (-en, -en) m cosmonaut; **k~politisch** adj cosmopolitan; ~**s** (-) m cosmos

Kost [kɔst] (-) f (Nahrung) food; (Verpflegung) board; **k~bar** adj precious; (teuer) costly, expensive; ~**barkeit** f preciousness; costliness, expensiveness; (Wertstück) valuable

Kosten pl cost(s); (Ausgaben) expenses; **auf ~ von** at the expense of; **k~** vt to cost; (versuchen) to taste ♦ vi to taste; **was kostet ...?** what does ... cost?, how much is ...?; ~**anschlag** m estimate; **k~los** adj free (of charge)

köstlich [ˈkœstlɪç] adj precious; (Einfall) delightful; (Essen) delicious; **sich ~ amüsieren** to have a marvellous time

Kostprobe f taste; (fig) sample

kostspielig adj expensive

Kostüm [kɔsˈtyːm] (-s, -e) nt costume; (Damen~) suit; ~**fest** nt fancy-dress party; **k~ieren** [kɔstyˈmiːrən] vt, vr to dress up; ~**verleih** m costume agency

Kot [koːt] (-(e)s) m excrement

Kotelett [kɔtəˈlɛt] (-(e)s, -e od -s) nt cutlet, chop; ~**en** pl (Bart) sideboards

Köter [ˈkøːtər] (-s, -) m cur

Kotflügel m (AUT) wing

kotzen [ˈkɔtsən] (umg!) vi to puke (umg), to throw up (umg)

Krabbe [ˈkrabə] f shrimp; **k~ln** vi to crawl

Krach [krax] (-(e)s, -s od -e) m crash; (andauernd) noise; (umg: Streit) quarrel, argument; **k~en** vi to crash; (beim Brechen) to crack ♦ vr (umg) to argue, to quarrel

krächzen [ˈkrɛçtsən] vi to croak

Kraft [kraft] (-, ⁺e) f strength; power; force; (Arbeits~) worker; **in ~ treten** to come into force; **k~** präp +gen by virtue of; ~**fahrer** m (motor) driver; ~**fahrzeug** nt motor vehicle; ~**fahrzeugbrief** m logbook; ~**fahrzeugsteuer** f ≈ road tax; ~**fahrzeugversicherung** f car insurance

kräftig [ˈkrɛftɪç] adj strong; ~**en** vt to strengthen

Kraft- zW: **k~los** adj weak; powerless; (JUR) invalid; ~**probe** f trial of strength; ~**stoff** m fuel; **k~voll** adj vigorous; ~**werk** nt power station

Kragen [ˈkraːgən] (-s, -) m collar; ~**weite** f collar size

Krähe [ˈkrɛːə] f crow; **k~n** vi to crow

Kralle [ˈkralə] f claw; (Vogel~) talon; **k~n** vt to clutch; (krampfhaft) to claw

Kram [kraːm] (-(e)s) m stuff, rubbish; **k~en** vi to rummage; ~**laden** (pej) m small shop

Krampf [krampf] (-(e)s, ⁺e) m cramp; (zuckend) spasm; ~**ader** f varicose vein; **k~haft** adj convulsive; (fig: Versuche) desperate

Kran [kraːn] (-(e)s, ⁺e) m crane; (Wasser~) tap, faucet (US)

krank [kraŋk] adj ill, sick; **K~e(r)** f(m) sick person, invalid; patient; ~**en** vi: **an etw** dat ~**en** (fig) to suffer from sth

kränken [ˈkrɛŋkən] vt to hurt

Kranken- zW: ~**geld** nt sick pay; ~**gymnastik** f physiotherapy; ~**haus** nt hospital; ~**kasse** f health insurance; ~**pfleger** m nursing orderly; ~**schein** m

⚠ *For information on spelling reform see page 615*

health insurance card; **~schwester** *f* nurse; **~versicherung** *f* health insurance; **~wagen** *m* ambulance

Krank- *zW:* **k~haft** *adj* diseased; (*Angst etc*) morbid; **~heit** *f* illness; disease; **~heitserreger** *m* disease-causing agent

kränklich ['krɛŋklɪç] *adj* sickly

Kränkung *f* insult, offence

Kranz [krants] (**-es, -e**) *m* wreath, garland

kraß △ [kras] *adj* crass

Krater ['kra:tər] (**-s, -**) *m* crater

Kratz- ['krats] *zW:* **~bürste** *f* (*fig*) crosspatch; **k~en** *vt, vi* to scratch; **~er** (**-s, -**) *m* scratch; (*Werkzeug*) scraper

Kraul [kraʊl] (**-s**) *nt* crawl; **~ schwimmen** to do the crawl; **k~en** *vi* (*schwimmen*) to do the crawl ♦ *vt* (*streicheln*) to fondle

kraus [kraʊs] *adj* crinkly; (*Haar*) frizzy; (*Stirn*) wrinkled

Kraut [kraʊt] (**-(e)s, Kräuter**) *nt* plant; (*Gewürz*) herb; (*Gemüse*) cabbage

Krawall [kra'val] (**-s, -e**) *m* row, uproar

Krawatte [kra'vatə] *f* tie

kreativ [krea'ti:f] *adj* creative

Krebs [kre:ps] (**-es, -e**) *m* crab; (*MED, ASTROL*) cancer; **k~krank** *adj* suffering from cancer

Kredit [kre'di:t] (**-(e)s, -e**) *m* credit; **~institut** *nt* bank; **~karte** *f* credit card

Kreide ['kraɪdə] *f* chalk; **k~bleich** *adj* as white as a sheet

Kreis [kraɪs] (**-es, -e**) *m* circle; (*Stadt~ etc*) district; **im ~ gehen** (*auch fig*) to go round in circles

kreischen ['kraɪʃən] *vi* to shriek, to screech

Kreis- *zW:* **~el** ['kraɪzəl] (**-s, -**) *m* top; (*Kreisverkehr*) roundabout (*BRIT*), traffic circle (*US*); **k~en** ['kraɪzən] *vi* to spin; **~lauf** *m* (*MED*) circulation; (*fig: der Natur etc*) cycle; **~säge** *f* circular saw; **~stadt** *f* county town; **~verkehr** *m* roundabout traffic

Krematorium [krema'to:riʊm] *nt* crematorium

Kreml ['kre:ml] (**-s**) *m* Kremlin

krepieren [kre'pi:rən] (*umg*) *vi* (*sterben*) to die, to kick the bucket

Krepp [krɛp] (**-s, -s** *od* **-e**) *m* crepe;

~(p)apier *nt* crepe paper

Kresse ['krɛsə] *f* cress

Kreta ['kre:ta] (**-s**) *nt* Crete

Kreuz [krɔʏts] (**-es, -e**) *nt* cross; (*ANAT*) small of the back; (*KARTEN*) clubs; **k~en** *vt, vr* to cross ♦ *vi* (*NAUT*) to cruise; **~er** (**-s, -**) *m* (*Schiff*) cruiser; **~fahrt** *f* cruise; **~feuer** *nt* (*fig*): **ins ~feuer geraten** to be under fire from all sides; **~gang** *m* cloisters *pl*; **k~igen** *vt* to crucify; **~igung** *f* crucifixion; **~ung** *f* (*Verkehrskreuzung*) crossing, junction; (*Züchten*) cross; **~verhör** *nt* cross-examination; **~weg** *m* crossroads; (*REL*) Way of the Cross; **~worträtsel** *nt* crossword puzzle; **~zug** *m* crusade

Kriech- ['kri:ç] *zW:* **k~en** (*unreg*) *vi* to crawl, to creep; (*pej*) to grovel, to crawl; **~er** (**-s, -**) *m* crawler; **~spur** *f* crawler lane; **~tier** *nt* reptile

Krieg [kri:k] (**-(e)s, -e**) *m* war

kriegen ['kri:gən] (*umg*) *vt* to get

Kriegs- *zW:* **~erklärung** *f* declaration of war; **~fuß** *m:* **mit jdm/etw auf ~fuß stehen** to be at loggerheads with sb/to have difficulties with sth; **~gefangene(r)** *m* prisoner of war; **~gefangenschaft** *f* captivity; **~gericht** *nt* court-martial; **~schiff** *nt* warship; **~verbrecher** *m* war criminal; **~versehrte(r)** *m* person disabled in the war; **~zustand** *m* state of war

Krim [krɪm] (**-**) *f* Crimea

Krimi ['kri:mi] (**-s, -s**) (*umg*) *m* thriller

Kriminal- [krimi'na:l] *zW:* **~beamte(r)** *m* detective; **~i'tät** *f* criminality; **~'polizei** *f* ≈ Criminal Investigation Department (*BRIT*), Federal Bureau of Investigation (*US*); **~ro'man** *m* detective story

kriminell [krimi'nɛl] *adj* criminal; **K~e(r)** *m* criminal

Krippe ['krɪpə] *f* crib; (*Kinder~*) crèche

Krise ['kri:zə] *f* crisis; **k~ln** *vi:* **es k~lt** there's a crisis

Kristall [krɪs'tal] (**-s, -e**) *m* crystal ♦ *nt* (*Glas*) crystal

Kriterium [kri'te:riʊm] *nt* criterion

Kritik [kri'ti:k] *f* criticism; (*Zeitungs~*) review, write-up; **~er** ['kri:tikər] (**-s, -**) *m* critic;

k~los *adj* uncritical

kritisch ['kri:tɪʃ] *adj* critical

kritisieren [kriti'zi:rən] *vt, vi* to criticize

kritzeln ['krɪtsəln] *vt, vi* to scribble, to scrawl

Kroatien [kro'a:tsiən] *nt* Croatia

Krokodil [kroko'di:l] (**-s, -e**) *nt* crocodile

Krokus ['kro:kus] (**-, -** *od* **-se**) *m* crocus

Krone ['kro:nə] *f* crown; (*Baum~*) top

krönen ['krø:nən] *vt* to crown

Kron- *zW:* **~korken** *m* bottle top; **~leuchter** *m* chandelier; **~prinz** *m* crown prince

Krönung ['krø:nʊŋ] *f* coronation

Kropf [krɔpf] (**-(e)s, ¨e**) *m* (*MED*) goitre; (*von Vogel*) crop

Kröte ['krø:tə] *f* toad

Krücke ['krʏkə] *f* crutch

Krug [kru:k] (**-(e)s, ¨e**) *m* jug; (*Bier~*) mug

Krümel ['kry:məl] (**-s, -**) *m* crumb; **k~n** *vt, vi* to crumble

krumm [krʊm] *adj* (*auch fig*) crooked; (*kurvig*) curved; **~beinig** *adj* bandy-legged; **~lachen** (*umg*) *vr* to laugh o.s. silly; **~nehmen** ⚠ (*unreg*) (*umg*) *vt:* **jdm etw ~nehmen** to take sth amiss

Krümmung ['krʏmʊŋ] *f* bend, curve

Krüppel ['krʏpəl] (**-s, -**) *m* cripple

Kruste ['krʊstə] *f* crust

Kruzifix [krutsi'fɪks] (**-es, -e**) *nt* crucifix

Kübel ['ky:bəl] (**-s, -**) *m* tub; (*Eimer*) pail

Kubikmeter [ku'bi:kme:tər] *m* cubic metre

Küche ['kʏçə] *f* kitchen; (*Kochen*) cooking, cuisine

Kuchen ['ku:xən] (**-s, -**) *m* cake; **~form** *f* baking tin; **~gabel** *f* pastry fork

Küchen- *zW:* **~herd** *m* cooker, stove; **~schabe** *f* cockroach; **~schrank** *m* kitchen cabinet

Kuckuck ['kʊkʊk] (**-s, -e**) *m* cuckoo; **~suhr** *f* cuckoo clock

Kugel ['ku:gəl] (**-, -n**) *f* ball; (*MATH*) sphere; (*MIL*) bullet; (*Erd~*) globe; (*SPORT*) shot; **k~förmig** *adj* spherical; **~lager** *nt* ball bearing; **k~rund** *adj* (*Gegenstand*) round; (*umg: Person*) tubby; **~schreiber** *m* ballpoint (pen), Biro ®; **k~sicher** *adj* bulletproof; **~stoßen** (**-s**) *nt* shot put

Kuh [ku:] (**-, ¨e**) *f* cow

kühl [ky:l] *adj* (*auch fig*) cool; **K~anlage** *f* refrigeration plant; **K~e** (**-**) *f* coolness; **~en** *vt* to cool; **K~er** (**-s, -**) *m* (*AUT*) radiator; **K~erhaube** *f* (*AUT*) bonnet (*BRIT*), hood (*US*); **K~raum** *m* cold storage chamber; **K~schrank** *m* refrigerator; **K~truhe** *f* freezer; **K~ung** *f* cooling; **K~wasser** *nt* radiator water

kühn [ky:n] *adj* bold, daring; **K~heit** *f* boldness

Kuhstall *m* byre, cattle shed

Küken ['ky:kən] (**-s, -**) *nt* chicken

kulant [ku'lant] *adj* obliging

Kuli ['ku:li] (**-s, -s**) *m* coolie; (*umg: Kugelschreiber*) Biro ®

Kulisse [ku'lɪsə] *f* scenery

kullern ['kʊlərn] *vi* to roll

Kult [kʊlt] (**-(e)s, -e**) *m* worship, cult; **mit etw einen ~ treiben** to make a cult out of sth

kultivieren [kʊlti'vi:rən] *vt* to cultivate

kultiviert *adj* cultivated, refined

Kultur [kʊl'tu:r] *f* culture; civilization; (*des Bodens*) cultivation; **~banause** (*umg*) *m* philistine, low-brow; **~beutel** *m* toilet bag; **k~ell** [-u'rɛl] *adj* cultural; **~ministerium** *nt* ministry of education and the arts

Kümmel ['kʏməl] (**-s, -**) *m* caraway seed; (*Branntwein*) kümmel

Kummer ['kʊmər] (**-s**) *m* grief, sorrow

kümmerlich ['kʏmərlɪç] *adj* miserable, wretched

kümmern ['kʏmərn] *vt* to concern ♦ *vr:* **sich um jdn ~** to look after sb; **das kümmert mich nicht** that doesn't worry me; **sich um etw ~** to see to sth

Kumpel ['kʊmpəl] (**-s, -**) (*umg*) *m* mate

kündbar ['kʏntba:r] *adj* redeemable, recallable; (*Vertrag*) terminable

Kunde¹ ['kʊndə] (**-n, -n**) *m* customer

Kunde² ['kʊndə] *f* (*Botschaft*) news

Kunden- *zW:* **~dienst** *m* after-sales service; **~konto** *nt* charge account; **~nummer** *f* customer number

Kund- *zW:* **k~geben** (*unreg*) *vt* to announce; **~gebung** *f* announcement;

⚠ *For information on spelling reform see page 615*

(*Versammlung*) rally

Künd- ['kʏnd] *zW:* **k~igen** *vi* to give in one's notice ♦ *vt* to cancel; **jdm k~igen** to give sb his notice; **die Stellung/Wohnung k~igen** to give notice that one is leaving one's job/house; **jdm die Stellung/Wohnung k~igen** to give sb notice to leave his/her job/house; **~igung** *f* notice; **~igungsfrist** *f* period of notice; **~igungsschutz** *m* protection against wrongful dismissal

Kundin *f* customer

Kundschaft *f* customers *pl*, clientele

künftig ['kʏnftɪç] *adj* future ♦ *adv* in future

Kunst [kʊnst] (-, ̈e) *f* art; (*Können*) skill; **das ist doch keine ~** it's easy; **~dünger** *m* artificial manure; **~faser** *f* synthetic fibre; **~fertigkeit** *f* skilfulness; **~gegenstand** *m* art object; **~gerecht** *adj* skilful; **~geschichte** *f* history of art; **~gewerbe** *nt* arts and crafts *pl*; **~griff** *m* trick, knack; **~händler** *m* art dealer

Künstler(in) ['kʏnstlər(ɪn)] (-s, -) *m(f)* artist; **k~isch** *adj* artistic; **~name** *m* pseudonym

künstlich ['kʏnstlɪç] *adj* artificial

Kunst- *zW:* **~sammler** (-s, -) *m* art collector; **~seide** *f* artificial silk; **~stoff** *m* synthetic material; **~stück** *nt* trick; **~turnen** *nt* gymnastics *sg*; **k~voll** *adj* artistic; **~werk** *nt* work of art

kunterbunt ['kʊntərbʊnt] *adj* higgledy-piggledy

Kupfer ['kʊpfər] (-s) *nt* copper; **k~n** *adj* copper

Kuppe ['kʊpə] *f* (*Berg~*) top; (*Finger~*) tip

Kuppel (-, -n) *f* dome; **k~n** *vi* (*JUR*) to procure; (*AUT*) to declutch ♦ *vt* to join

Kupplung *f* coupling; (*AUT*) clutch

Kur [ku:r] (-, -en) *f* cure, treatment

Kür [ky:r] (-, -en) *f* (*SPORT*) free exercises *pl*

Kurbel ['kʊrbəl] (-, -n) *f* crank, winder; (*AUT*) starting handle; **~welle** *f* crankshaft

Kürbis ['kʏrbɪs] (-ses, -se) *m* pumpkin; (*exotisch*) gourd

Kurgast *m* visitor (to a health resort)

kurieren [ku'ri:rən] *vt* to cure

kurios [kuri'o:s] *adj* curious, odd; **K~ität** *f*

curiosity

Kurort *m* health resort

Kurs [kʊrs] (-es, -e) *m* course; (*FIN*) rate; **~buch** *nt* timetable; **k~ieren** [kʊr'zi:rən] *vi* to circulate; **k~iv** [kʊr'zi:f] *adv* in italics; **~us** ['kʊrzʊs] (-, **Kurse**) *m* course; **~wagen** *m* (*EISENB*) through carriage

Kurtaxe [-taksə] (-, -n) *f* visitors' tax (at health resort or spa)

Kurve ['kʊrvə] *f* curve; (*Straßen~*) curve, bend; **kurvig** *adj* (*Straße*) bendy

kurz [kʊrts] *adj* short; **~ gesagt** in short; **zu ~ kommen** to come off badly; **den kürzeren ziehen** to get the worst of it; **K~arbeit** *f* short-time work; **~ärm(e)lig** *adj* short-sleeved

Kürze ['kʏrtsə] *f* shortness, brevity; **k~n** *vt* to cut short; (*in der Länge*) to shorten; (*Gehalt*) to reduce

kurz- *zW:* **~erhand** *adv* on the spot; **~fristig** *adj* short-term; **K~geschichte** *f* short story; **~halten** (*unreg*) *vt* to keep short; **~lebig** *adj* short-lived

kürzlich ['kʏrtslɪç] *adv* lately, recently

Kurz- *zW:* **~schluß** ⚠ *m* (*ELEK*) short circuit; **k~sichtig** *adj* short-sighted

Kürzung *f* (*eines Textes*) abridgement; (*eines Theaterstück, des Gehalts*) cut

Kurzwelle *f* short wave

kuscheln ['kʊʃəln] *vr* to snuggle up

Kusine [ku'zi:nə] *f* cousin

Kuß ⚠ [kʊs] (-sses, ̈sse) *m* kiss

küssen ['kʏsən] *vt, vr* to kiss

Küste ['kʏstə] *f* coast, shore

Küstenwache *f* coastguard

Küster ['kʏstər] (-s, -) *m* sexton, verger

Kutsche ['kʊtʃə] *f* coach, carriage; **~r** (-s, -) *m* coachman

Kutte ['kʊtə] *f* habit

Kuvert [ku'vert] (-s, -e *od* -s) *nt* envelope; cover

KZ *nt abk von* **Konzentrationslager**

⚠ *Informationen zur Rechtschreibreform Seite 615*

L, I

I. *abk* = **Liter**

labil [laˈbiːl] *adj* (*MED: Konstitution*) delicate

Labor [laˈboːr] (**-s, -e** *od* **-s**) *nt* lab; **~ant(in)** *m(f)* lab(oratory) assistant

Labyrinth [labyˈrɪnt] (**-s, -e**) *nt* labyrinth

Lache [ˈlaxə] *f* (*Flüssigkeit*) puddle; (*von Blut, Benzin etc*) pool

lächeln [ˈlɛçəln] *vi* to smile; **L~** (**-s**) *nt* smile

lachen [ˈlaxən] *vi* to laugh

lächerlich [ˈlɛçərlɪç] *adj* ridiculous

Lachgas *nt* laughing gas

lachhaft *adj* laughable

Lachs [laks] (**-es, -e**) *m* salmon

Lack [lak] (**-(e)s, -e**) *m* lacquer, varnish; (*von Auto*) paint; **l~ieren** [laˈkiːrən] *vt* to varnish; (*Auto*) to spray; **~ierer** [laˈkiːrər] (**-s, -**) *m* varnisher

Laden [ˈlaːdən] (**-s, ⁐**) *m* shop; (*Fenster~*) shutter

laden [ˈlaːdən] (*unreg*) *vt* (*Lasten*) to load; (*JUR*) to summon; (*einladen*) to invite

Laden- *zW:* **~dieb** *m* shoplifter; **~diebstahl** *m* shoplifting; **~schluß** △ *m* closing time; **~tisch** *m* counter

Laderaum *m* freight space; (*AVIAT, NAUT*) hold

Ladung [ˈlaːdʊŋ] *f* (*Last*) cargo, load; (*Beladen*) loading; (*JUR*) summons; (*Einladung*) invitation; (*Spreng~*) charge

Lage [ˈlaːgə] *f* position, situation; (*Schicht*) layer; **in der ~ sein** to be in a position

Lageplan *m* ground plan

Lager [ˈlaːgər] (**-s, -**) *nt* camp; (*COMM*) warehouse; (*Schlaf~*) bed; (*von Tier*) lair; (*TECH*) bearing; **~bestand** *m* stocks *pl*; **~feuer** *nt* campfire; **~haus** *nt* warehouse, store

lagern [ˈlaːgərn] *vi* (*Dinge*) to be stored; (*Menschen*) to camp ♦ *vt* to store; (*betten*) to lay down; (*Maschine*) to bed

Lagune [laˈguːnə] *f* lagoon

lahm [laːm] *adj* lame; **~en** *vi* to be lame

lähmen [ˈlɛːmən] *vt* to paralyse

lahmlegen [ˈlaːmleːgən] *vt* to paralyse

Lähmung *f* paralysis

Laib [laɪp] (**-s, -e**) *m* loaf

Laie [ˈlaɪə] (**-n, -n**) *m* layman; **l~nhaft** *adj* amateurish

Laken [ˈlaːkən] (**-s, -**) *nt* sheet

Lakritze [laˈkrɪtsə] *f* liquorice

lallen [ˈlalən] *vt, vi* to slur; (*Baby*) to babble

Lamelle [laˈmɛlə] *f* lamella; (*ELEK*) lamina; (*TECH*) plate

Lametta [laˈmɛta] (**-s**) *nt* tinsel

Lamm [lam] (**-(e)s, ⁐er**) *nt* lamb

Lampe [ˈlampə] *f* lamp

Lampen- *zW:* **~fieber** *nt* stage fright; **~schirm** *m* lampshade

Lampion [lampiˈoː] (**-s, -s**) *m* Chinese lantern

Land [lant] (**-(e)s, ⁐er**) *nt* land; (*Nation, nicht Stadt*) country; (*Bundes~*) state; **auf dem ~e** (in the country); **~besitz** *m* landed property; **~ebahn** *f* runway; **l~en** [ˈlandən] *vt, vi* to land

---

LAND

ⓘ A **Land** (*plural* **Länder**) is a member state of the **BRD** and of Austria. There are 16 **Länder** in Germany, namely Baden-Württemberg, Bayern, Berlin, Brandenburg, Bremen, Hamburg, Hessen, Mecklenburg-Vorpommern, Niedersachsen, Nordrhein-Westfalen, Rheinland-Pfalz, Saarland, Sachsen, Sachsen-Anhalt, Schleswig-Holstein and Thüringen. Each **Land** has its own parliament and constitution. The 9 **Länder** of Austria are Vorarlberg, Tirol, Salzburg, Oberösterreich, Niederösterreich, Kärnten, Steiermark, Burgenland and Wien.

Landes- [ˈlandəs] *zW:* **~farben** *pl* national colours; **~innere(s)** *nt* inland region; **~sprache** *f* national language; **l~üblich** *adj* customary; **~verrat** *m* high treason; **~währung** *f* national currency; **l~weit** *adj* nationwide

Land- *zW:* **~haus** *nt* country house;

⚠ *For information on spelling reform see page 615*

~**karte** f map; ~**kreis** m administrative region; **l~läufig** adj customary
ländlich ['lɛntlɪç] adj rural
Land- zW: ~**schaft** f countryside; (*KUNST*) landscape; ~**schaftsschutzgebiet** nt nature reserve; ~**sitz** m country seat; ~**straße** f country road; ~**streicher (-s, -)** m tramp; ~**strich** m region
Landung ['landʊŋ] f landing; ~**sbrücke** f jetty, pier
Land- zW: ~**weg** m: **etw auf dem ~weg befördern** to transport sth by land; ~**wirt** m farmer; ~**wirtschaft** f agriculture; ~**zunge** f spit
lang [laŋ] adj long; (*Mensch*) tall; ~**atmig** adj long-winded; ~**e** adv for a long time; (*dauern, brauchen*) a long time
Länge ['lɛŋə] f length; (*GEOG*) longitude
langen ['laŋən] vi (*ausreichen*) to do, to suffice; (*fassen*) ~ **(nach)** to reach (for) ♦ vt: **jdm etw** ~ to hand od pass sb sth; **es langt mir** I've had enough
Längengrad m longitude
Längenmaß nt linear measure
lang- zW: **L~eweile** f boredom; ~**fristig** adj long-term; ~**jährig** (*Freundschaft, Gewohnheit*) long-standing; **L~lauf** m (*SKI*) cross-country skiing
länglich adj longish
längs [lɛŋs] präp (+gen od dat) along ♦ adv lengthwise
lang- zW: ~**sam** adj slow; **L~samkeit** f slowness; **L~schläfer(in)** m(f) late riser
längst [lɛŋst] adv: **das ist ~ fertig** that was finished a long time ago, that has been finished for a long time; ~**e(r, s)** adj longest
lang- zW: ~**weilen** vt to bore ♦ vr to be bored; ~**weilig** adj boring, tedious; **L~welle** f long wave; ~**wierig** adj lengthy, long-drawn-out
Lanze ['lantsə] f lance
Lappalie [la'paːliə] f trifle
Lappen ['lapən] (**-s, -**) m cloth, rag; (*ANAT*) lobe
läppisch ['lɛpɪʃ] adj foolish
Lapsus ['lapsʊs] (**-, -**) m slip

Laptop ['lɛptɔp] (**-s, -s**) m laptop (computer)
Lärche ['lɛrçə] f larch
Lärm [lɛrm] (**-(e)s**) m noise; **l~en** vi to be noisy, to make a noise
Larve ['larfə] f (*BIOL*) larva
lasch [laʃ] adj slack
Laser ['leːzər] (**-s, -**) m laser

SCHLÜSSELWORT

---

lassen ['lasən] (*pt* **ließ**, *pp* **gelassen** *od* (*als Hilfsverb*) **lassen**) vt **1** (*unterlassen*) to stop; (*momentan*) to leave; **laß das (sein)!** don't (do it)!; (*hör auf*) stop it!; **laß mich!** leave me alone; **lassen wir das!** let's leave it; **er kann das Trinken nicht lassen** he can't stop drinking
2 (*zurücklassen*) to leave; **etw lassen, wie es ist** to leave sth (just) as it is
3 (*überlassen*): **jdn ins Haus lassen** to let sb into the house
♦ vi: **laß mal, ich mache das schon** leave it, I'll do it
♦ *Hilfsverb* **1** (*veranlassen*): **etw machen lassen** to have *od* get sth done; **sich** *dat* **etw schicken lassen** to have sth sent (to one)
2 (*zulassen*): **jdn etw wissen lassen** to let sb know sth; **das Licht brennen lassen** to leave the light on; **jdn warten lassen** to keep sb waiting; **das läßt sich machen** that can be done
3: **laß uns gehen** let's go

---

lässig ['lɛsɪç] adj casual; **L~keit** f casualness
Last [last] (**-, -en**) f load, burden; (*NAUT, AVIAT*) cargo; (*meist pl: Gebühr*) charge; **jdm zur ~ fallen** to be a burden to sb; ~**auto** nt lorry, truck; **l~en** vi: **l~en auf** +dat to weigh on; ~**enaufzug** m goods lift od elevator (*US*)
Laster ['lastər] (**-s, -**) nt vice
lästern ['lɛstərn] vt, vi (*Gott*) to blaspheme; (*schlecht sprechen*) to mock
Lästerung f jibe; (*Gottes~*) blasphemy
lästig ['lɛstɪç] adj troublesome, tiresome
Last- zW: ~**kahn** m barge; ~**kraftwagen**

⚠ *Informationen zur Rechtschreibreform Seite 615*

m heavy goods vehicle; **~schrift** *f* debit;
~wagen *m* lorry, truck; **~zúg** *m* articulated
lorry
Latein [la'taɪn] **(-s)** *nt* Latin; **~amerika** *nt*
Latin America
latent [la'tɛnt] *adj* latent
Laterne [la'tɛrnə] *f* lantern; (*Straßen~*) lamp,
light; **~npfahl** *m* lamppost
latschen ['laːtʃən] (*umg*) *vi* (*gehen*) to
wander, to go; (*lässig*) to slouch
Latte ['latə] *f* lath; (*SPORT*) goalpost; (*quer*)
crossbar
Latzhose ['latshoːzə] *f* dungarees *pl*
lau [lau] *adj* (*Nacht*) balmy; (*Wasser*)
lukewarm
Laub [laup] **(-(e)s)** *nt* foliage; **~baum** *m*
deciduous tree; **~frosch** *m* tree frog;
~säge *f* fretsaw
Lauch [laux] **(-(e)s, -e)** *m* leek
Lauer ['lauər] *f*: **auf der ~ sein** *od* **liegen** to
lie in wait; **l~n** *vi* to lie in wait; (*Gefahr*) to
lurk
Lauf [lauf] **(-(e)s, Läufe)** *m* run; (*Wett~*)
race; (*Entwicklung, ASTRON*) course;
(*Gewehr~*) barrel; **einer Sache** *dat* **ihren ~
lassen** to let sth take its course; **~bahn** *f*
career
laufen ['laufən] (*unreg*) *vt, vi* to run; (*umg:
gehen*) to walk; **~d** *adj* running; (*Monat,
Ausgaben*) current; **auf dem ~den sein/
halten** to be/keep up to date; **am ~den
Band** (*fig*) continuously
Läufer ['lɔyfər] **(-s, -)** *m* (*Teppich, SPORT*)
runner; (*Fußball*) half-back; (*Schach*) bishop
Lauf- *zW*: **~masche** *f* run, ladder (*BRIT*);
~paß △ **: jdm den ~paß geben** (*umg*)
to send sb packing (*inf*); **~stall** *m* playpen;
~steg *m* catwalk; **~werk** *nt* (*COMPUT*) disk
drive
Lauge ['laugə] *f* soapy water; (*CHEM*) alkaline
solution
Laune ['launə] *f* mood, humour; (*Einfall*)
caprice; (*schlechte*) temper; **l~nhaft** *adj*
capricious, changeable
launisch *adj* moody; bad-tempered
Laus [laus] **(-, Läuse)** *f* louse
lauschen ['lauʃən] *vi* to eavesdrop, to listen

in
lauschig ['lauʃɪç] *adj* snug
lausig ['lauzɪç] (*umg: pej*) *adj* measly; (*Kälte*)
perishing
laut [laut] *adj* loud ♦ *adv* loudly; (*lesen*) aloud
♦ *präp* (+*gen od dat*) according to; **L~**
(-(e)s, -e) *m* sound
Laute ['lautə] *f* lute
lauten ['lautən] *vi* to say; (*Urteil*) to be
läuten ['lɔytən] *vt, vi* to ring, to sound
lauter ['lautər] *adj* (*Wasser*) clear, pure;
(*Wahrheit, Charakter*) honest ♦ *adj inv*
(*Freude, Dummheit etc*) sheer ♦ *adv* nothing
but, only
laut- *zW*: **~hals** *adv* at the top of one's
voice; **~los** *adj* noiseless, silent; **L~schrift** *f*
phonetics *pl*; **L~sprecher** *m* loudspeaker;
~stark *adj* vociferous; **L~stärke** *f* (*RAD*)
volume
lauwarm ['lauvarm] *adj* (*auch fig*) lukewarm
Lavendel [la'vɛndəl] **(-s, -)** *m* lavender
Lawine [la'viːnə] *f* avalanche; **~ngefahr** *f*
danger of avalanches
lax [laks] *adj* lax
Lazarett [latsa'rɛt] **(-(e)s, -e)** *nt* (*MIL*)
hospital, infirmary
leasen ['liːzən] *vt* to lease
Leben **(-s, -)** *nt* life
leben ['leːbən] *vt, vi* to live; **~d** *adj* living;
~dig [le'bɛndɪç] *adj* living, alive; (*lebhaft*)
lively; **L~digkeit** *f* liveliness
Lebens- *zW*: **~art** *f* way of life;
~erwartung *f* life expectancy; **l~fähig** *adj*
able to live; **~freude** *f* zest for life;
~gefahr *f*: **~gefahr!** danger!; **in ~gefahr**
dangerously ill; **l~gefährlich** *adj*
dangerous; (*Verletzung*) critical;
~haltungskosten *pl* cost of living *sg*;
~jahr *nt* year of life; **l~länglich** *adj* (*Strafe*)
for life; **~lauf** *m* curriculum vitae; **~mittel**
pl food *sg*; **~mittelgeschäft** *nt* grocer's
(shop); **~mittelvergiftung** *f* (*MED*) food
poisoning; **l~müde** *adj* tired of life;
~retter *m* lifesaver; **~standard** *m*
standard of living; **~unterhalt** *m*
livelihood; **~versicherung** *f* life insurance;
~wandel *m* way of life; **~weise** *f* lifestyle,

way of life; **l~wichtig** *adj* vital, essential;
~zeichen *nt* sign of life
Leber ['le:bər] (-, -n) *f* liver; **~fleck** *m* mole;
~tran *m* cod-liver oil; **~wurst** *f* liver
sausage
Lebewesen *nt* creature
leb- ['le:p] *zW:* **~haft** *adj* lively, vivacious;
L~kuchen *m* gingerbread; **~los** *adj* lifeless
Leck [lɛk] (-(e)s, -e) *nt* leak; **l~** *adj* leaky,
leaking; **l~en** *vi* (*Loch haben*) to leak;
(*schlecken*) to lick ♦ *vt* to lick
lecker ['lɛkər] *adj* delicious, tasty; **L~bissen**
m dainty morsel
Leder ['le:dər] (-s, -) *nt* leather; **~hose** *f*
lederhosen; **l~n** *adj* leather; **~waren** *pl*
leather goods
ledig ['le:dɪç] *adj* single; **einer Sache** *gen* **~
sein** to be free of sth; **~lich** *adv* merely,
solely
leer [le:r] *adj* empty; vacant; **~ machen** to
empty; **L~e** (-) *f* emptiness; **~en** *vt, vr* to
empty; **L~gewicht** *nt* weight when empty;
L~gut *nt* empties *pl*; **L~lauf** *m* neutral;
~stehend ⚠ *adj* empty; **L~ung** *f*
emptying; (*Post*) collection
legal [le'ga:l] *adj* legal, lawful; **~i'sieren** *vt*
to legalize
legen ['le:gən] *vt* to lay, to put, to place; (*Ei*)
to lay ♦ *vr* to lie down; (*fig*) to subside
Legende [le'gɛndə] *f* legend
leger [le'ʒe:r] *adj* casual
Legierung [le'gi:rʊŋ] *f* alloy
Legislative [legɪsla'ti:və] *f* legislature
legitim [legi'ti:m] *adj* legitimate
legitimieren [legiti'mi:rən] *vt* to legitimate
♦ *vr* to prove one's identity
Lehm [le:m] (-(e)s, -e) *m* loam; **l~ig** *adj*
loamy
Lehne ['le:nə] *f* arm; back; **l~n** *vt, vr* to lean
Lehnstuhl *m* armchair
Lehr- *zW:* **~amt** *nt* teaching profession;
~buch *nt* textbook
Lehre ['le:rə] *f* teaching, doctrine; (*beruflich*)
apprenticeship; (*moralisch*) lesson; (*TECH*)
gauge; **l~n** *vt* to teach
Lehrer(in) (-s, -) *m(f)* teacher; **~zimmer**
nt staff room

Lehr- *zW:* **~gang** *m* course; **~jahre** *pl*
apprenticeship *sg*; **~kraft** *f* (*förmlich*)
teacher; **~ling** *m* apprentice; **~plan** *m*
syllabus; **l~reich** *adj* instructive; **~stelle** *f*
apprenticeship; **~zeit** *f* apprenticeship
Leib [laɪp] (-(e)s, -er) *m* body; **halt ihn mir
vom ~!** keep him away from me!; **l~haftig**
adj personified; (*Teufel*) incarnate; **l~lich**
adj bodily; (*Vater etc*) own; **~schmerzen** *pl*
stomach pains; **~wache** *f* bodyguard
Leiche ['laɪçə] *f* corpse; **~nhalle** *f* mortuary;
~nwagen *m* hearse
Leichnam ['laɪçnaːm] (-(e)s, -e) *m* corpse
leicht [laɪçt] *adj* (*einfach*) easy;
L~athletik *f* athletics *sg*; **~fallen** ⚠
(*unreg*) *vi:* **jdm ~fallen** to be easy for sb;
~fertig *adj* frivolous; **~gläubig** *adj* gullible,
credulous; **~hin** *adv* lightly; **L~igkeit** *f*
easiness; **mit L~igkeit** with ease;
~machen ⚠ *vt:* **es sich** *dat* **~machen** to
make things easy for o.s.; **L~sinn** *m*
carelessness; **~sinnig** *adj* careless
Leid [laɪt] (-(e)s) *nt* grief, sorrow; **l~** *adj:*
etw l~ haben *od* **sein** to be tired of sth; **es
tut mir/ihm l~** I am/he is sorry; **er/das
tut mir l~** I am sorry for him/it; **l~en**
(*unreg*) *vt* to suffer; (*erlauben*) to permit ♦ *vi*
to suffer; **jdn/etw nicht l~en können** not
to be able to stand sb/sth; **~en** [ˈlaɪdən]
(-s, -) *nt* suffering; (*Krankheit*) complaint;
~enschaft *f* passion; **l~enschaftlich** *adj*
passionate
leider ['laɪdər] *adv* unfortunately; **ja, ~** yes,
I'm afraid so; **~ nicht** I'm afraid not
leidig ['laɪdɪç] *adj* worrying, troublesome
leidlich [ˈlaɪtlɪç] *adj* tolerable ♦ *adv* tolerably
Leid- *zW:* **~tragende(r)** *f(m)* bereaved;
(*Benachteiligter*) one who suffers; **~wesen**
nt: **zu jds ~wesen** to sb's disappointment
Leier ['laɪər] (-, -n) *f* lyre; (*fig*) old story;
~kasten *m* barrel organ
Leihbibliothek *f* lending library
Leihbücherei *f* lending library
leihen [ˈlaɪən] (*unreg*) *vt* to lend; **sich** *dat*
etw ~ to borrow sth
Leih- *zW:* **~gebühr** *f* hire charge; **~haus**
nt pawnshop; **~wagen** *m* hired car

⚠ *Informationen zur Rechtschreibreform Seite 615*

Leim [laim] (-(e)s, -e) *m* glue; **l~en** *vt* to glue

Leine ['lainə] *f* line, cord; (*Hunde~*) leash, lead

Leinen *nt* linen; **l~** *adj* linen

Leinwand *f* (*KUNST*) canvas; (*CINE*) screen

leise ['laizə] *adj* quiet; (*sanft*) soft, gentle

Leiste ['laistə] *f* ledge; (*Zier~*) strip; (*ANAT*) groin

leisten ['laistən] *vt* (*Arbeit*) to do; (*Gesellschaft*) to keep; (*Ersatz*) to supply; (*vollbringen*) to achieve; **sich** *dat* **etw ~ können** to be able to afford sth

Leistung *f* performance; (*gute*) achievement; **~sdruck** *m* pressure; **l~sfähig** *adj* efficient

Leitartikel *m* leading article

Leitbild *nt* model

leiten ['laitən] *vt* to lead; (*Firma*) to manage; (*in eine Richtung*) to direct; (*ELEK*) to conduct

Leiter¹ ['laitər] (-s, -) *m* leader, head; (*ELEK*) conductor

Leiter² ['laitər] (-, -n) *f* ladder

Leitfaden *m* guide

Leitplanke *f* crash barrier

Leitung *f* (*Führung*) direction; (*CINE, THEAT etc*) production; (*von Firma*) management; directors *pl*; (*Wasser~*) pipe; (*Kabel*) cable; **eine lange ~ haben** to be slow on the uptake

Leitungs- *zW*: **~draht** *m* wire; **~rohr** *nt* pipe; **~wasser** *nt* tap water

Lektion [lɛktsi'oːn] *f* lesson

Lektüre [lɛk'tyːrə] *f* (*Lesen*) reading; (*Lesestoff*) reading matter

Lende ['lɛndə] *f* loin; **~nstück** *nt* fillet

lenk- ['lɛŋk] *zW*: **~bar** *adj* (*Fahrzeug*) steerable; (*Kind*) manageable; **~en** *vt* to steer; (*Kind*) to guide; (*Blick, Aufmerksamkeit*): **~en** (**auf** +*akk*) to direct (at); **L~rad** *nt* steering wheel; **L~radschloß** △ *nt* steering (wheel) lock; **L~stange** *f* handlebars *pl*; **L~ung** *f* steering

Lepra ['leːpra] (-) *f* leprosy

Lerche ['lɛrçə] *f* lark

lernbegierig *adj* eager to learn

lernen ['lɛrnən] *vt* to learn

lesbar ['leːsbaːr] *adj* legible

Lesbierin ['lɛsbiərɪn] *f* lesbian

lesbisch ['lɛsbɪʃ] *adj* lesbian

Lese ['leːzə] *f* (*Wein*) harvest

Lesebrille *f* reading glasses

Lesebuch *nt* reading book, reader

lesen (*unreg*) *vt, vi* to read; (*ernten*) to gather, to pick

Leser(in) (-s, -) *m(f)* reader; **~brief** *m* reader's letter; **l~lich** *adj* legible

Lesezeichen *nt* bookmark

Lesung *f* (*PARL*) reading

letzte(r, s) ['lɛtstə(r, s)] *adj* last; (*neueste*) latest; **zum ~nmal** for the last time; **~ns** *adv* lately; **~re(r, s)** *adj* latter

Leuchte ['lɔʏçtə] *f* lamp, light; **l~n** *vi* to shine, to gleam; **~r** (-s, -) *m* candlestick

Leucht- *zW*: **~farbe** *f* fluorescent colour; **~rakete** *f* flare; **~reklame** *f* neon sign; **~röhre** *f* strip light; **~turm** *m* lighthouse

leugnen ['lɔʏgnən] *vt* to deny

Leukämie [lɔʏkɛ'miː] *f* leukaemia

Leukoplast [lɔʏko'plast] (®; -(e)s, -e) *nt* Elastoplast ®

Leumund ['lɔʏmʊnt] (-(e)s, -e) *m* reputation

Leumundszeugnis *nt* character reference

Leute ['lɔʏtə] *pl* people *pl*

Leutnant ['lɔʏtnant] (-s, -s *od* -e) *m* lieutenant

leutselig ['lɔʏtzeːlɪç] *adj* amiable

Lexikon ['lɛksikɔn] (-s, **Lexiken** *od* **Lexika**) *nt* encyclop(a)edia

Libelle [li'bɛlə] *f* dragonfly; (*TECH*) spirit level

liberal [libe'raːl] *adj* liberal; **L~e(r)** *f(m)* liberal

Licht [lɪçt] (-(e)s, -er) *nt* light; **~bild** *nt* photograph; (*Dia*) slide; **~blick** *m* cheering prospect; **l~empfindlich** *adj* sensitive to light; **l~en** *vt* to clear; (*Anker*) to weigh ♦ *vr* to clear up; (*Haar*) to thin; **l~erloh** *adv*: **l~erloh brennen** to be ablaze; **~hupe** *f* flashing of headlights; **~jahr** *nt* light year; **~maschine** *f* dynamo; **~schalter** *m* light switch; **~schutzfaktor** *m* protection factor

Lichtung f clearing, glade

Lid [liːt] (-(e)s, -er) nt eyelid; **~schatten** m eyeshadow

lieb [liːp] adj dear; **das ist ~ von dir** that's kind of you; **~äugeln** ['liːbɔygəln] vi insep: **mit etw ~äugeln** to have one's eye on sth; **mit dem Gedanken ~äugeln, etw zu tun** to toy with the idea of doing sth

Liebe ['liːbə] f love; **l~bedürftig** adj: **l~bedürftig sein** to need love; **l~n** vt to love; to like

liebens- zW: **~wert** adj loveable; **~würdig** adj kind; **~würdigerweise** adv kindly; **L~würdigkeit** f kindness

lieber ['liːbər] adv rather, preferably; **ich gehe ~ nicht** I'd rather not go; *siehe auch* **gern; lieb**

Liebes- zW: **~brief** m love letter; **~kummer** m: **~kummer haben** to be lovesick; **~paar** nt courting couple, lovers pl

liebevoll adj loving

lieb- [liːp] zW: **~gewinnen** ⚠ (unreg) vt to get fond of; **~haben** ⚠ (unreg) vt to be fond of; **L~haber (-s, -)** m lover; **L~habe'rei** f hobby; **~kosen** ['liːpkoːzən] vt insep to caress; **~lich** adj lovely, charming; **L~ling** m darling; **L~lings-** in zW favourite; **~los** adj unloving; **L~schaft** f love affair

Lied [liːt] (-(e)s, -er) nt song; (REL) hymn; **~erbuch** ['liːdər-] nt songbook; hymn book

liederlich ['liːdərlɪç] adj slovenly; (Lebenswandel) loose, immoral; **L~keit** f slovenliness; immorality

lief etc [liːf] vb siehe **laufen**

Lieferant [liːfəˈrant] m supplier

Lieferbedingungen pl terms of delivery

liefern ['liːfərn] vt to deliver; (versorgen mit) to supply; (Beweis) to produce

Liefer- zW: **~schein** m delivery note; **~termin** m delivery date; **~ung** f delivery; supply; **~wagen** m van; **~zeit** f delivery period

Liege ['liːgə] f bed

liegen ['liːgən] (unreg) vi to lie; (sich befinden) to be; **mir liegt nichts/viel daran**

it doesn't matter to me/it matters a lot to me; **es liegt bei Ihnen, ob ...** it's up to you whether ...; **Sprachen ~ mir nicht** languages are not my line; **woran liegt es?** what's the cause?; **~bleiben** ⚠ (unreg) vi (im Bett) to stay in bed; (nicht aufstehen) to stay lying down; (vergessen werden) to be left (behind); **~lassen** ⚠ (unreg) vt (vergessen) to leave behind

Liege- zW: **~sitz** m (AUT) reclining seat; **~stuhl** m deck chair; **~wagen** m (EISENB) couchette

Lift [lɪft] (-(e)s, -e od -s) m lift

Likör [liˈkøːr] (-s, -e) m liqueur

lila ['liːla] adj inv purple, lilac; **L~ (-s, -s)** nt (Farbe) purple, lilac

Lilie ['liːliə] f lily

Limonade [limoˈnaːdə] f lemonade

Limone [liˈmoːnə] f lime

Linde ['lɪndə] f lime tree, linden

lindern ['lɪndərn] vt to alleviate, to soothe; **Linderung** f alleviation

Lineal [lineˈaːl] (-s, -e) nt ruler

Linie ['liːniə] f line

Linien- zW: **~blatt** nt ruled sheet; **~flug** m scheduled flight; **~richter** m linesman

linieren [liˈniːrən] vt to line

Linke ['lɪŋkə] f left side; left hand; (POL) left

linkisch adj awkward, gauche

links [lɪŋks] adv left; to od on the left; **~ von mir** on od to my left; **L~händer(in) (-s, -)** m(f) left-handed person; **L~kurve** f left-hand bend; **L~verkehr** m driving on the left

Linoleum [liˈnoːleʊm] (-s) nt lino(leum)

Linse ['lɪnzə] f lentil; (optisch) lens sg

Lippe ['lɪpə] f lip; **~nstift** m lipstick

lispeln ['lɪspəln] vi to lisp

Lissabon ['lɪsabɔn] (-s) nt Lisbon

List [lɪst] (-, -en) f cunning; trick, ruse

Liste ['lɪstə] f list

listig ['lɪstɪç] adj cunning, sly

Liter ['liːtər] (-s, -) nt od m litre

literarisch [liteˈraːrɪʃ] adj literary

Literatur [literaˈtuːr] f literature

Litfaßsäule ⚠ ['lɪtfasˌzɔylə] f advertising pillar

Liturgie [litʊrˈgiː] *f* liturgy
liturgisch [liˈtʊrgɪʃ] *adj* liturgical
Litze [ˈlɪtsə] *f* braid; (*ELEK*) flex
Lizenz [liˈtsɛnts] *f* licence
Lkw [ɛlkaːˈveː] (**-(s), -(s)**) *m abk =* **Lastkraftwagen**
Lob [loːp] (**-(e)s**) *nt* praise
Lobby [ˈlɔbi] *f* lobby
loben [ˈloːbən] *vt* to praise; **~swert** *adj* praiseworthy
löblich [ˈløːplɪç] *adj* praiseworthy, laudable
Loch [lɔx] (**-(e)s, "-er**) *nt* hole; **l~en** *vt* to punch holes in; **~er** (**-s, -**) *m* punch
löcherig [ˈlœçərɪç] *adj* full of holes
Lochkarte *f* punch card
Lochstreifen *m* punch tape
Locke [ˈlɔkə] *f* lock, curl; **l~n** *vt* to entice; (*Haare*) to curl; **~nwickler** (**-s, -**) *m* curler
locker [ˈlɔkər] *adj* loose; **~lassen** (*unreg*) *vi:* **nicht ~lassen** not to let up; **~n** *vt* to loosen
lockig [ˈlɔkɪç] *adj* curly
lodern [ˈloːdərn] *vi* to blaze
Löffel [ˈlœfəl] (**-s, -**) *m* spoon
löffeln *vt* to spoon
Loge [ˈloːʒə] *f* (*THEAT*) box; (*Freimaurer*) (masonic) lodge; (*Pförtner~*) office
Logik [ˈloːgɪk] *f* logic
logisch [ˈloːgɪʃ] *adj* logical
Logopäde [logoˈpɛːdə] (**-n, -n**) *m* speech therapist
Lohn [loːn] (**-(e)s, "-e**) *m* reward; (*Arbeits~*) pay, wages *pl*; **~büro** *nt* wages office; **~empfänger** *m* wage earner
lohnen [ˈloːnən] *vr unpers* to be worth it ♦ *vt:* (**jdm etw**) **~** to reward (sb for sth); **~d** *adj* worthwhile
Lohn- *zW:* **~erhöhung** *f* pay rise; **~steuer** *f* income tax; **~steuerkarte** *f* (income) tax card; **~streifen** *m* pay slip; **~tüte** *f* pay packet
Lokal [loˈkaːl] (**-(e)s, -e**) *nt* pub(lic house)
lokal *adj* local; **~i'sieren** *vt* to localize
Lokomotive [lokomoˈtiːvə] *f* locomotive
Lokomotivführer *m* engine driver
Lorbeer [ˈlɔrbeːr] (**-s, -en**) *m* (*auch fig*) laurel; **~blatt** *nt* (*KOCH*) bay leaf

Los [loːs] (**-es, -e**) *nt* (*Schicksal*) lot, fate; (*Lotterie~*) lottery ticket
los [loːs] *adj* (*locker*) loose; **~!** go on!; **etw ~ sein** to be rid of sth; **was ist ~?** what's the matter?; **dort ist nichts/viel ~** there's nothing/a lot going on there; **etw ~ haben** (*umg*) to be clever; **~binden** (*unreg*) *vt* to untie
Löschblatt [ˈlœʃblat] *nt* sheet of blotting paper
löschen [ˈlœʃən] *vt* (*Feuer, Licht*) to put out, to extinguish; (*Durst*) to quench; (*COMM*) to cancel; (*COMPUT*) to delete; (*Tonband*) to erase; (*Fracht*) to unload ♦ *vi* (*Feuerwehr*) to put out a fire; (*Tinte*) to blot
Lösch- *zW:* **~fahrzeug** *nt* fire engine; fire boat; **~gerät** *nt* fire extinguisher; **~papier** *nt* blotting paper
lose [ˈloːzə] *adj* loose
Lösegeld *nt* ransom
losen [ˈloːzən] *vi* to draw lots
lösen [ˈløːzən] *vt* to loosen; (*Rätsel etc*) to solve; (*Verlobung*) to call off; (*CHEM*) to dissolve; (*Partnerschaft*) to break up; (*Fahrkarte*) to buy ♦ *vr* (*aufgehen*) to come loose; (*Zucker etc*) to dissolve; (*Problem, Schwierigkeit*) to (re)solve itself
los- *zW:* **~fahren** (*unreg*) *vi* to leave; **~gehen** (*unreg*) *vi* to set out; (*anfangen*) to start; (*Bombe*) to go off; **auf jdn ~gehen** to go for sb; **~kaufen** *vt* (*Gefangene, Geißeln*) to pay ransom for; **~kommen** (*unreg*) *vi:* **von etw ~kommen** to get away from sth; **~lassen** (*unreg*) *vt* (*Seil*) to let go of; (*Schimpfe*) to let loose; **~laufen** (*unreg*) *vi* to run off
löslich [ˈløːslɪç] *adj* soluble; **L~keit** *f* solubility
los- *zW:* **~lösen** *vt:* (**sich**) **~lösen** to free (o.s.); **~machen** *vt* to loosen; (*Boot*) to unmoor *vr* to get away; **~schrauben** *vt* to unscrew
Losung [ˈloːzʊŋ] *f* watchword, slogan
Lösung [ˈløːzʊŋ] *f* (*Lockermachen*) loosening; (*eines Rätsels, CHEM*) solution; **~smittel** *nt* solvent
los- *zW:* **~werden** (*unreg*) *vt* to get rid of;

⚠ *For information on spelling reform see page 615*

~ziehen (*unreg*) (*umg*) *vi* (*sich aufmachen*) to set off

Lot [lo:t] (**-(e)s, -e**) *nt* plumbline; **im ~** vertical; (*fig*) on an even keel

löten ['lø:tən] *vt* to solder

Lothringen ['lo:trɪŋən] (**-s**) *nt* Lorraine

Lotse ['lo:tsə] (**-n, -n**) *m* pilot; (*AVIAT*) air traffic controller; **l~n** *vt* to pilot; (*umg*) to lure

Lotterie [lɔtə'ri:] *f* lottery

Lotto ['lɔto] (**-s, -s**) *nt* national lottery; **~zahlen** *pl* winning lottery numbers

Löwe ['lø:və] (**-n, -n**) *m* lion; (*ASTROL*) Leo; **~nanteil** *m* lion's share; **~nzahn** *m* dandelion

loyal [loa'ja:l] *adj* loyal; **L~ität** *f* loyalty

Luchs [lʊks] (**-es, -e**) *m* lynx

Lücke ['lʏkə] *f* gap

Lücken- *zW:* **~büßer** (**-s, -**) *m* stopgap; **l~haft** *adj* full of gaps; (*Versorgung, Betreuung etc*) inadequate; **l~los** *adj* complete

Luft [lʊft] (**-, ̈-e**) *f* air; (*Atem*) breath; **in der ~ liegen** to be in the air; **jdn wie ~ behandeln** to ignore sb; **~angriff** *m* air raid; **~ballon** *m* balloon; **~blase** *f* air bubble; **l~dicht** *adj* airtight; **~druck** *m* atmospheric pressure

lüften ['lʏftən] *vt* to air; (*Hut*) to lift, to raise ♦ *vi* to let some air in

Luft- *zW:* **~fahrt** *f* aviation; **~fracht** *f* air freight; **l~gekühlt** *adj* air-cooled; **~gewehr** *nt* air rifle, airgun; **l~ig** *adj* (*Ort*) breezy; (*Raum*) airy; (*Kleider*) summery; **~kissenfahrzeug** *nt* hovercraft; **~kurort** *m* health resort; **l~leer** *adj:* **l~leerer Raum** vacuum; **~linie** *f:* **in der ~linie** as the crow flies; **~loch** *nt* air hole; (*AVIAT*) air pocket; **~matratze** *f* Lilo ® (*BRIT*), air mattress; **~pirat** *m* hijacker; **~post** *f* airmail; **~pumpe** *f* air pump; **~röhre** *f* (*ANAT*) windpipe; **~schlange** *f* streamer; **~schutzkeller** *m* air-raid shelter; **~verkehr** *m* air traffic; **~verschmutzung** *f* air pollution; **~waffe** *f* air force; **~zug** *m* draught

Lüge ['ly:gə] *f* lie; **jdn/etw ~n strafen** to give the lie to sb/sth; **l~n** (*unreg*) *vi* to lie

Lügner(in) (**-s, -**) *m(f)* liar

Luke ['lu:kə] *f* dormer window; hatch

Lump [lʊmp] (**-en, -en**) *m* scamp, rascal

Lumpen ['lʊmpən] (**-s, -**) *m* rag

lumpen ['lʊmpən] *vi:* **sich nicht ~ lassen** not to be mean

lumpig ['lʊmpɪç] *adj* shabby

Lupe ['lu:pə] *f* magnifying glass; **unter die ~ nehmen** (*fig*) to scrutinize

Lust [lʊst] (**-, ̈-e**) *f* joy, delight; (*Neigung*) desire; **~ haben zu** *od* **auf etw** *akk***/etw zu tun** to feel like sth/doing sth

lüstern ['lʏstərn] *adj* lustful, lecherous

lustig ['lʊstɪç] *adj* (*komisch*) amusing, funny; (*fröhlich*) cheerful

Lust- *zW:* **l~los** *adj* unenthusiastic; **~mord** *m* sex(ual) murder; **~spiel** *nt* comedy

lutschen ['lʊtʃən] *vt, vi* to suck; **am Daumen ~** to suck one's thumb

Lutscher (**-s, -**) *m* lollipop

luxuriös [lʊksuri'ø:s] *adj* luxurious

Luxus ['lʊksʊs] (**-**) *m* luxury; **~artikel** *pl* luxury goods; **~hotel** *nt* luxury hotel

Luzern [lu'tsɛrn] (**-s**) *nt* Lucerne

Lymphe ['lʏmfə] *f* lymph

lynchen ['lʏnçən] *vt* to lynch

Lyrik ['ly:rɪk] *f* lyric poetry; **~er** (**-s, -**) *m* lyric poet

lyrisch ['ly:rɪʃ] *adj* lyrical

M, m

m *abk* = **Meter**

Machart *f* make

machbar *adj* feasible

SCHLÜSSELWORT

machen ['maxən] *vt* **1** to do; (*herstellen, zubereiten*) to make; **was machst du da?** what are you doing (there)?; **das ist nicht zu machen** that can't be done; **das Radio leiser machen** to turn the radio down; **aus Holz gemacht** made of wood

2 (*verursachen, bewirken*) to make; **jdm Angst machen** to make sb afraid; **das**

macht die Kälte it's the cold that does that

3 (*ausmachen*) to matter; **das macht nichts** that doesn't matter; **die Kälte macht mir nichts** I don't mind the cold

4 (*kosten, ergeben*) to be; **3 und 5 macht 8** 3 and 5 is *od* are 8; **was** *od* **wieviel macht das?** how much does that make?

5: was macht die Arbeit? how's the work going?; **was macht dein Bruder?** how is your brother doing?; **das Auto machen lassen** to have the car done; **mach's gut!** take care!; (*viel Glück*) good luck!

♦ *vi*: **mach schnell!** hurry up!; **Schluß machen** to finish (off); **mach schon!** come on!; **das macht müde** it makes you tired; **in etw** *dat* **machen** to be *od* deal in sth ♦ *vr* to come along (nicely); **sich an etw** *akk* **machen** to set about sth; **sich verständlich machen** to make o.s. understood; **sich** *dat* **viel aus jdm/etw machen** to like sb/sth

Macht [maxt] (-, **-̈e**) *f* power; **~haber (-s, -)** *m* ruler

mächtig ['mɛçtɪç] *adj* powerful, mighty; (*umg: ungeheuer*) enormous

Macht- *zW*: **m~los** *adj* powerless; **~probe** *f* trial of strength; **~wort** *nt*: **ein ~wort sprechen** to exercise one's authority

Mädchen ['mɛːtçən] *nt* girl; **m~haft** *adj* girlish; **~name** *m* maiden name

Made ['maːdə] *f* maggot

madig ['maːdɪç] *adj* maggoty; **jdm etw ~ machen** to spoil sth for sb

mag *etc* [maːk] *vb siehe* **mögen**

Magazin [maga'tsiːn] (-s, -e) *nt* magazine

Magen ['maːgən] (-s, - *od* **-̈**) *m* stomach; **~geschwür** *nt* (*MED*) stomach ulcer; **~schmerzen** *pl* stomachache *sg*

mager ['maːgər] *adj* lean; (*dünn*) thin; **M~keit** *f* leanness; thinness

Magie [ma'giː] *f* magic

magisch ['maːgɪʃ] *adj* magical

Magnet [ma'gneːt] (-s *od* **-en, -en**) *m* magnet; **m~isch** *adj* magnetic; **~nadel** *f* magnetic needle

mähen ['mɛːən] *vt, vi* to mow

Mahl [maːl] (-(e)s, -e) *nt* meal; **m~en** (*unreg*) *vt* to grind; **~zeit** *f* meal ♦ *excl* enjoy your meal

Mahnbrief *m* reminder

Mähne ['mɛːnə] *f* mane

mahn- ['maːn] *zW*: **~en** *vt* to remind; (*warnend*) to warn; (*wegen Schuld*) to demand payment from; **M~mal** *nt* memorial; **M~ung** *f* reminder; admonition, warning

Mai [mai] (-(e)s, -e) *m* May; **~glöckchen** *nt* lily of the valley

Mailand ['mailant] *nt* Milan

mailändisch *adj* Milanese

Mais [mais] (-es, -e) *m* maize, corn (*US*); **~kolben** *m* corncob; **~mehl** *nt* (*KOCH*) corn meal

Majestät [majɛs'tɛːt] *f* majesty; **m~isch** *adj* majestic

Major [ma'joːr] (-s, -e) *m* (*MIL*) major; (*AVIAT*) squadron leader

Majoran [majo'raːn] (-s, -e) *m* marjoram

makaber [ma'kaːbər] *adj* macabre

Makel ['maːkəl] (-s, -) *m* blemish; (*moralisch*) stain; **m~los** *adj* immaculate, spotless

mäkeln ['mɛːkəln] *vi* to find fault

Makler(in) ['maːklər(ɪn)] (-s, -) *m(f)* broker

Makrele [ma'kreːlə] *f* mackerel

Mal [maːl] (-(e)s, -e) *nt* mark, sign; (*Zeitpunkt*) time; **m~** *adv* times; (*umg*) *siehe* **einmal** ♦ *suffix*: **-m~** -times

malen *vt, vi* to paint

Maler (-s, -) *m* painter; **Male'rei** *f* painting; **m~isch** *adj* picturesque

Malkasten *m* paintbox

Mallorca [ma'lɔrka] (-s) *nt* Majorca

malnehmen (*unreg*) *vt, vi* to multiply

Malz [malts] (-es) *nt* malt; **~bier** *nt* (*KOCH*) malt beer; **~bonbon** *nt* cough drop; **~kaffee** *m* malt coffee

Mama ['mama:] (-, -s) (*umg*) *f* mum(my) (*BRIT*), mom(my) (*US*)

Mami ['mami] (-, -s) = **Mama**

Mammut ['mamʊt] (-s, -e *od* -s) *nt* mammoth

man [man] *pron* one, you; **~ sagt, ...** they

⚠ *For information on spelling reform see page 615*

od people say ...; **wie schreibt ~ das?** how do you write it?, how is it written?

Manager(in) [ˈmɛnɪdʒər(ɪn)] **(-s, -)** *m(f)* manager

manch [manç] *(unver)* *pron* many a

manche(r, s) [ˈmançə(r, s)] *adj* many a; *(pl: einige)* a number of ♦ *pron* some

mancherlei [mançərˈlaɪ] *adj inv* various ♦ *pron inv* a variety of things

manchmal *adv* sometimes

Mandant(in) [manˈdant(ɪn)] *m(f) (JUR)* client

Mandarine [mandaˈriːnə] *f* mandarin, tangerine

Mandat [manˈdaːt] **(-(e)s, -e)** *nt* mandate

Mandel [ˈmandəl] **(-, -n)** *f* almond; *(ANAT)* tonsil; **~entzündung** *f (MED)* tonsillitis

Manege [maˈnɛːʒə] *f* ring, arena

Mangel [ˈmaŋəl] **(-s, ")** *m* lack; *(Knappheit)* shortage; *(Fehler)* defect, fault; **~ an** +*dat* shortage of; **~erscheinung** *f* deficiency symptom; **m~haft** *adj* poor; *(fehlerhaft)* defective, faulty; **m~n** *vi unpers:* **es m~t jdm an etw** *dat* sb lacks sth ♦ *vt (Wäsche)* to mangle

mangels *präp* +*gen* for lack of

Manie [maˈniː] *f* mania

Manier [maˈniːr] **(-)** *f* manner; style; *(pej)* mannerism; **~en** *pl (Umgangsformen)* manners; **m~lich** *adj* well-mannered

Manifest [maniˈfɛst] **(-es, -e)** *nt* manifesto

Maniküre [maniˈkyːrə] *f* manicure

manipulieren [manipuˈliːrən] *vt* to manipulate

Manko [ˈmaŋko] **(-s, -s)** *nt* deficiency; *(COMM)* deficit

Mann [man] **(-(e)s, "er)** *m* man; *(Ehe~)* husband; *(NAUT)* hand; **seinen ~ stehen** to hold one's own

Männchen [ˈmɛnçən] *nt* little man; *(Tier)* male

Mannequin [manəˈkɛ̃ː] **(-s, -s)** *nt* fashion model

männlich [ˈmɛnlɪç] *adj (BIOL)* male; *(fig, GRAM)* masculine

Mannschaft *f (SPORT, fig)* team; *(AVIAT, NAUT)* crew; *(MIL)* other ranks *pl*

Manöver [maˈnøːvər] **(-s, -)** *nt* manoeuvre

manövrieren [manøˈvriːrən] *vt, vi* to manoeuvre

Mansarde [manˈzardə] *f* attic

Manschette [manˈʃɛtə] *f* cuff; *(TECH)* collar; sleeve; **~nknopf** *m* cufflink

Mantel [ˈmantəl] **(-s, ")** *m* coat; *(TECH)* casing, jacket

Manuskript [manuˈskrɪpt] **(-(e)s, -e)** *nt* manuscript

Mappe [ˈmapə] *f* briefcase; *(Akten~)* folder

Märchen [ˈmɛːrçən] *nt* fairy tale; **m~haft** *adj* fabulous; **~prinz** *m* Prince Charming

Margarine [margaˈriːnə] *f* margarine

Margerite [margəˈriːtə] *f (BOT)* marguerite

Marienkäfer [maˈriːənkɛːfər] *m* ladybird

Marine [maˈriːnə] *f* navy; **m~blau** *adj* navy blue

marinieren [mariˈniːrən] *vt* to marinate

Marionette [marioˈnɛtə] *f* puppet

Mark¹ [mark] **(-, -)** *f (Münze)* mark

Mark² [mark] **(-(e)s)** *nt (Knochen~)* marrow; **jdm durch ~ und Bein gehen** to go right through sb

markant [marˈkant] *adj* striking

Marke [ˈmarkə] *f* mark; *(Warensorte)* brand; *(Fabrikat)* make; *(Rabatt~, Brief~)* stamp; *(Essen~)* ticket; *(aus Metall etc)* token, disc

Markenartikel *m* proprietary article

markieren [marˈkiːrən] *vt* to mark; *(umg)* to act ♦ *vi (umg)* to act it

Markierung *f* marking

Markise [marˈkiːzə] *f* awning

Markstück *nt* one-mark piece

Markt [markt] **(-(e)s, "e)** *m* market; **~forschung** *f* market research; **~lücke** *f (COMM)* opening, gap in the market; **~platz** *m* market place; **m~üblich** *adj (Preise, Mieten)* standard, usual; **~wert** *m (COMM)* market value; **~wirtschaft** *f* market economy

Marmelade [marməˈlaːdə] *f* jam

Marmor [ˈmarmɔr] **(-s, -e)** *m* marble; **m~ieren** [-ˈriːrən] *vt* to marble

Marokko [maˈrɔko] **(-s)** *nt* Morocco

Marone [maˈroːnə] **(-, -n** *od* **Maroni)** *f* chestnut

Marotte [maˈrɔtə] *f* fad, quirk

Marsch[1] [marʃ] (-, -en) f marsh
Marsch[2] [marʃ] (-(e)s, -e) m march
♦ *excl* march!; ~**befehl** m marching orders
pl; m~**bereit** adj ready to move; m~**ieren**
[mar'ʃi:rən] vi to march
Märtyrer(in) ['mɛrtyrər(ɪn)] (-s, -) m(f)
martyr
März [mɛrts] (-(es), -e) m March
Marzipan [martsi'pa:n] (-s, -e) nt marzipan
Masche ['maʃə] f mesh; (Strick~) stitch; **das
ist die neueste ~** that's the latest thing;
~**ndraht** m wire mesh; m~**nfest** adj run-
resistant
Maschine [ma'ʃi:nə] f machine; (Motor)
engine; (Schreib~) typewriter; m~**ll**
[maʃi'nɛl] adj machine(-); mechanical
Maschinen- zW: ~**bauer** m mechanical
engineer; ~**gewehr** nt machine gun;
~**pistole** f submachine gun; ~**schaden** m
mechanical fault; ~**schlosser** m fitter;
~**schrift** f typescript
maschineschreiben ⚠ (unreg) vi to
type
Maschinist [maʃi'nɪst] m engineer
Maser ['ma:zər] (-, -n) f (von Holz) grain; ~**n**
pl (MED) measles sg
Maske ['maskə] f mask; ~**nball** m fancy-
dress ball
maskieren [mas'ki:rən] vt to mask;
(verkleiden) to dress up ♦ vr to disguise o.s.;
to dress up
Maskottchen [mas'kɔtçən] nt (lucky)
mascot
Maß[1] [ma:s] (-es, -e) nt measure;
(Mäßigung) moderation; (Grad) degree,
extent
Maß[2] [ma:s] (-, -(e)) f litre of beer
Massage [ma'sa:ʒə] f massage
Maßanzug m made-to-measure suit
Maßarbeit f (fig) neat piece of work
Masse ['masə] f mass
Maßeinheit f unit of measurement
Massen- zW: ~**artikel** m mass-produced
article; ~**grab** nt mass grave; m~**haft** adj
loads of; ~**medien** pl mass media pl;
~**veranstaltung** f mass meeting;
m~**weise** adv on a large scale

Masseur [ma'sø:r] m masseur; ~**in** f
masseuse
maßgebend adj authoritative
maßhalten ⚠ (unreg) vi to exercise
moderation
massieren [ma'si:rən] vt to massage; (MIL)
to mass
massig ['masɪç] adj massive; (umg) massive
amount of
mäßig ['mɛ:sɪç] adj moderate; ~**en**
['mɛ:sɪgən] vt to restrain, to moderate;
M~keit f moderation
Massiv (-s, -e) nt massif
massiv [ma'si:f] adj solid; (fig) heavy, rough
Maß- zW: ~**krug** m tankard; m~**los** adj
extreme; ~**nahme** f measure, step; ~**stab**
m rule, measure; (fig) standard; (GEOG)
scale; m~**voll** adj moderate
Mast [mast] (-(e)s, -e(n)) m mast; (ELEK)
pylon
mästen ['mɛstən] vt to fatten
Material [materi'a:l] (-s, -ien) nt material(s);
~**fehler** m material defect; ~**ismus**
[-'lɪsmʊs] m materialism; m~**istisch** [-'lɪstɪʃ]
adj materialistic
Materie [ma'te:riə] f matter, substance
materiell [materi'ɛl] adj material
Mathematik [matema'ti:k] f mathematics
sg; ~**er(in)** [mate'ma:tikər(ɪn)] (-s, -) m(f)
mathematician
mathematisch [mate'ma:tɪʃ] adj
mathematical
Matjeshering ['matjəshe:rɪŋ] m (KOCH)
young herring
Matratze [ma'tratsə] f mattress
Matrixdrucker ['ma:trɪks-] m dot-matrix
printer
Matrose [ma'tro:zə] (-n, -n) m sailor
Matsch [matʃ] (-(e)s) m mud; (Schnee~)
slush; m~**ig** adj muddy; slushy
matt [mat] adj weak; (glanzlos) dull; (PHOT)
matt; (SCHACH) mate
Matte ['matə] f mat
Mattscheibe f (TV) screen
Mauer ['mauər] (-, -n) f wall; m~**n** vi to
build; to lay bricks ♦ vt to build
Maul [maul] (-(e)s, Mäuler) nt mouth;

⚠ For information on spelling reform see page 615

m~en (*umg*) *vi* to grumble; ~esel *m* mule;
~korb *m* muzzle; ~sperre *f* lockjaw;
~tasche *f* (*KOCH*) pasta envelopes stuffed
and used in soup; ~tier *nt* mule; ~wurf *m*
mole

Maurer ['maʊrər] (**-s, -**) *m* bricklayer

Maus [maʊs] (**-, Mäuse**) *f* (*auch COMPUT*)
mouse

Mause- ['maʊzə] *zW*: ~falle *f* mousetrap;
m~n *vi* to catch mice ♦ *vt* (*umg*) to pinch;
m~tot *adj* stone dead

Maut- ['maʊt] *zW*: ~gebühr *f* toll (charge);
~straße *f* toll road

maximal [maksi'maːl] *adj* maximum ♦ *adv*
at most

Mayonnaise [majɔ'nɛːzə] *f* mayonnaise

Mechan- [me'çaːn] *zW*: ~ik *f* mechanics *sg*;
(*Getriebe*) mechanics *pl*; ~iker (**-s, -**) *m*
mechanic, engineer; m~isch *adj*
mechanical; ~ismus *m* mechanism

meckern ['mɛkərn] *vi* to bleat; (*umg*) to moan

Medaille [me'daljə] *f* medal

Medaillon [medal'jõː] (**-s, -s**) *nt* (*Schmuck*)
locket

Medikament [medika'mɛnt] *nt* medicine

Meditation [meditatsi'oːn] *f* meditation

meditieren [medi'tiːrən] *vi* to meditate

Medizin [medi'tsiːn] (**-, -en**) *f* medicine;
m~isch *adj* medical

Meer [meːr] (**-(e)s, -e**) *nt* sea; ~enge *f*
straits *pl*; ~esfrüchte *pl* seafood *sg*;
~esspiegel *m* sea level; ~rettich *m*
horseradish; ~schweinchen *nt* guinea-pig

Mehl [meːl] (**-(e)s, -e**) *nt* flour; m~ig *adj*
floury; ~schwitze *f* (*KOCH*) roux; ~speise
f (*KOCH*) flummery

mehr [meːr] *adj, adv* more; ~deutig *adj*
ambiguous; ~ere *adj* several; ~eres *pron*
several things; ~fach *adj* multiple;
(*wiederholt*) repeated; M~fahrtenkarte *f*
multi-journey ticket; M~heit *f* majority;
~malig *adj* repeated; ~mals *adv*
repeatedly; ~stimmig *adj* for several
voices; ~stimmig singen to harmonize;
M~wertsteuer *f* value added tax;
M~zahl *f* majority; (*GRAM*) plural

Mehrzweck- *in zW* multipurpose

meiden ['maɪdən] (*unreg*) *vt* to avoid

Meile ['maɪlə] *f* mile; ~nstein *m* milestone;
m~nweit *adj* for miles

mein(e) [maɪn] *adj* my; ~e(r, s) *pron* mine

Meineid ['maɪnaɪt] *m* perjury

meinen ['maɪnən] *vi* to think ♦ *vt* to think;
(*sagen*) to say; (*sagen wollen*) to mean; das
will ich ~ I should think so

mein- *zW*: ~erseits *adv* for my part;
~etwegen *adv* (*für mich*) for my sake;
(*wegen mir*) on my account; (*von mir aus*) as
far as I'm concerned; I don't care *od* mind;
~etwillen *adv*: um ~etwillen for my sake,
on my account

Meinung ['maɪnʊŋ] *f* opinion; ganz meine
~ I quite agree; jdm die ~ sagen to give
sb a piece of one's mind

Meinungs- *zW*: ~austausch *m* exchange
of views; ~umfrage *f* opinion poll;
~verschiedenheit *f* difference of opinion

Meise ['maɪzə] *f* tit(mouse)

Meißel ['maɪsəl] (**-s, -**) *m* chisel

meist [maɪst] *adj* most ♦ *adv* mostly; am
~en the most; ~ens *adv* generally, usually

Meister ['maɪstər] (**-s, -**) *m* master; (*SPORT*)
champion; m~haft *adj* masterly; m~n *vt*
(*Schwierigkeiten etc*) to overcome, conquer;
~schaft *f* mastery; (*SPORT*) championship;
~stück *nt* masterpiece; ~werk *nt*
masterpiece

Melancholie [melaŋko'liː] *f* melancholy;
melancholisch [melaŋ'koːlɪʃ] *adj*
melancholy

Melde- ['mɛldə] *zW*: ~frist *f* registration
period; m~n *vt* to report ♦ *vr* to report;
(*SCH*) to put one's hand up; (*freiwillig*) to
volunteer; (*auf etw, am Telefon*) to answer;
sich m~n bei to report to; to register with;
sich zu Wort m~n to ask to speak;
~pflicht *f* obligation to register with the
police; ~schluß △ *m* closing date;
~stelle *f* registration office

Meldung ['mɛldʊŋ] *f* announcement;
(*Bericht*) report

meliert [me'liːrt] *adj* (*Haar*) greying; (*Wolle*)
flecked

melken ['mɛlkən] (*unreg*) *vt* to milk

Melodie [melo'di:] f melody, tune
melodisch [me'lo:dɪʃ] adj melodious, tuneful
Melone [me'lo:nə] f melon; (Hut) bowler (hat)
Membran [mɛm'bra:n] (-, -en) f (TECH) diaphragm
Memoiren [memo'a:rən] pl memoirs
Menge ['mɛŋə] f quantity; (Menschen~) crowd; (große Anzahl) lot (of); **m~n** vt to mix ♦ vr: **sich m~n** in +akk to meddle with; **~nlehre** f (MATH) set theory; **~nrabatt** m bulk discount
Mensch [mɛnʃ] (-en, -en) m human being, man; person ♦ excl hey!; **kein ~** nobody
Menschen- zW: **~affe** m (ZOOL) ape; **m~freundlich** adj philanthropical; **~kenner** m judge of human nature; **m~leer** adj deserted; **m~möglich** adj humanly possible; **~rechte** pl human rights; **m~unwürdig** adj beneath human dignity; **~verstand** m: **gesunder ~verstand** common sense
Mensch- zW: **~heit** f humanity, mankind; **m~lich** adj human; (human) humane; **~lichkeit** f humanity
Menstruation [mɛnstruatsi'o:n] f menstruation
Mentalität [mɛntali'tɛ:t] f mentality
Menü [me'ny:] (-s, -s) nt (auch COMPUT) menu
Merk- ['mɛrk] zW: **~blatt** nt instruction sheet od leaflet; **m~en** vt to notice; **sich dat etw m~en** to remember sth; **m~lich** adj noticeable; **~mal** nt sign, characteristic; **m~würdig** adj odd
meßbar ⚠ ['mɛsba:r] adj measurable
Meßbecher ⚠ m measuring jug
Messe ['mɛsə] f fair; (ECCL) mass; **~gelände** nt exhibition centre; **~halle** f pavilion at a fair
messen (unreg) vt to measure ♦ vr to compete
Messer (-s, -) nt knife; **~spitze** f knife point; (in Rezept) pinch
Messestand m stall at a fair
Meßgerät ⚠ nt measuring device, gauge

Messing ['mɛsɪŋ] (-s) nt brass
Metall [me'tal] (-s, -e) nt metal; **m~isch** adj metallic
Meter ['me:tər] (-s, -) nt od m metre; **~maß** nt tape measure
Methode [me'to:də] f method; **methodisch** adj methodical
Metropole [metro'po:lə] f metropolis
Metzger ['mɛtsgər] (-s, -) m butcher; **~ei** [-'rai] f butcher's (shop)
Meute ['mɔytə] f pack; **~'rei** f mutiny; **m~rn** vi to mutiny
miauen [mi'auən] vi to miaow
mich [mɪç] (akk von ich) pron me; myself
Miene ['mi:nə] f look, expression
mies [mi:s] (umg) adj lousy
Miet- ['mi:t] zW: **~auto** nt hired car; **~e** f rent; **zur ~e wohnen** to live in rented accommodation; **m~en** vt to rent; (Auto) to hire; **~er(in)** (-s, -) m(f) tenant; **~shaus** nt tenement, block of (rented) flats; **~vertrag** m lease
Migräne [mi'grɛ:nə] f migraine
Mikro- [mikro] zW: **~fon** [-'fo:n] (-s, -e) nt microphone; **~phon** ⚠ [-'fo:n] (-s, -e) nt microphone; **~skop** [-'sko:p] (-s, -e) nt microscope; **m~skopisch** adj microscopic; **~wellenherd** m microwave (oven)
Milch [mɪlç] (-) f milk; **~glas** nt frosted glass; **m~ig** adj milky; **~kaffee** m white coffee; **~mann** (pl **-männer**) m milkman; **~mixgetränk** nt (KOCH) milkshake; **~pulver** nt powdered milk; **~straße** f Milky Way; **~zahn** m milk tooth
mild [mɪlt] adj mild; (Richter) lenient; (freundlich) kind, charitable; **M~e** f mildness; leniency; **~ern** vt to mitigate, to soften; (Schmerz) to alleviate; **~ernde Umstände** extenuating circumstances
Milieu [mili'ø:] (-s, -s) nt background, environment; **m~geschädigt** adj maladjusted
Mili- [mili] zW: **m~tant** [-'tant] adj militant; **~tär** [-'tɛ:r] (-s) nt military, army; **~'tärgericht** nt military court; **m~'tärisch** adj military
Milli- ['mili] zW: **~ardär** [-ar'dɛ:r] m

multimillionaire; **~arde** [-'ardə] *f* milliard;
billion (*bes US*); **~meter** *m* millimetre;
~meterpapier *nt* graph paper
Million [mɪli'oːn] (**-, -en**) *f* million; **~är**
[-o'nɛːr] *m* millionaire
Milz [mɪlts] (**-, -en**) *f* spleen
Mimik ['miːmɪk] *f* mime
Mimose [mi'moːzə] *f* mimosa; (*fig*) sensitive
person
minder ['mɪndər] *adj* inferior ♦ *adv* less;
M~heit *f* minority; **~jährig** *adj* minor;
M~jährige(r) *f(m)* minor; **~n** *vt, vr* to
decrease, to diminish; **M~ung** *f* decrease;
~wertig *adj* inferior;
M~wertigkeitskomplex *m* inferiority
complex
Mindest- ['mɪndəst] *zW:* **~alter** *nt*
minimum age; **~betrag** *m* minimum
amount; **m~e(r, s)** *adj* least; **zum m~en** at
least; **m~ens** *adv* at least;
~haltbarkeitsdatum *nt* best-before date;
~lohn *m* minimum wage; **~maß** *nt*
minimum
Mine ['miːnə] *f* mine; (*Bleistift~*) lead;
(*Kugelschreiber~*) refill
Mineral [mine'raːl] (**-s, -e** *od* **-ien**) *nt*
mineral; **m~isch** *adj* mineral; **~wasser** *nt*
mineral water
Miniatur [minia'tuːr] *f* miniature
Mini- *zW:* **~golf** ['mɪnɪɡɔlf] *nt* miniature
golf, crazy golf; **m~mal** [mini'maːl] *adj*
minimal; **~mum** ['miːnɪmʊm] *nt* minimum;
~rock *m* miniskirt
Minister [mi'nɪstər] (**-s, -**) *m* minister;
m~iell *adj* ministerial; **~ium** *nt* ministry;
~präsident *m* prime minister
Minus ['miːnʊs] (**-, -**) *nt* deficit
minus *adv* minus; **M~zeichen** *nt* minus
sign
Minute [mi'nuːtə] *f* minute
Minze ['mɪntsə] *f* mint
mir [miːr] (*dat von* **ich**) *pron* (to) me; **~
nichts, dir nichts** just like that
Misch- ['mɪʃ] *zW:* **~brot** *nt* bread made
from more than one kind of flour; **~ehe** *f*
mixed marriage; **m~en** *vt* to mix; **~ling** *m*
half-caste; **~ung** *f* mixture

miserabel [mizə'raːbəl] (*umg*) *adj* (*Essen,
Film*) dreadful
Miß- ['mɪs] *zW:* **~behagen** ⚠ *nt*
discomfort, uneasiness; **~bildung** ⚠ *f*
deformity; **m~'billigen** ⚠ *vt insep* to
disapprove of; **~brauch** ⚠ *m* abuse;
(*falscher Gebrauch*) misuse; **m~'brauchen**
⚠ *vt insep* to abuse; **jdn zu** *od* **für etw
m~brauchen** to use sb for *od* to do sth;
~erfolg ⚠ *m* failure; **~fallen** ⚠ (**-s**) *nt*
displeasure; **m~'fallen** ⚠ (*unreg*) *vi insep:*
jdm m~fallen to displease sb; **~geschick**
⚠ *nt* misfortune; **m~glücken** ⚠
[mɪs'ɡlʏkən] *vi insep* to fail; **jdm m~glückt
etw** sb does not succeed with sth; **~griff**
⚠ *m* mistake; **~gunst** ⚠ *f* envy;
m~günstig ⚠ *adj* envious; **m~'handeln**
⚠ *vt insep* to ill-treat; **~'handlung** ⚠ *f* ill-
treatment
Mission [mɪsi'oːn] *f* mission; **~ar(in)** *m(f)*
missionary
Miß- *zW:* **~klang** ⚠ *m* discord; **~kredit** ⚠
m discredit; **m~lingen** ⚠ [mɪs'lɪŋən]
(*unreg*) *vi insep* to fail; **~mut** ⚠ *m*
sullenness; **m~mutig** ⚠ *adj* sullen;
m~'raten ⚠ (*unreg*) *vi insep* to turn out
badly ♦ *adj* ill-bred; **~stand** ⚠ *m* bad state
of affairs; abuse; **m~'trauen** ⚠ *vi insep* to
mistrust; **~trauen** ⚠ (**-s**) *nt* distrust,
suspicion; **~trauensantrag** ⚠ *m* (*POL*)
motion of no confidence; **m~trauisch** ⚠
adj distrustful, suspicious; **~verhältnis** ⚠
nt disproportion; **~verständnis** ⚠ *nt*
misunderstanding; **m~verstehen** ⚠
(*unreg*) *vt insep* to misunderstand;
~wirtschaft ⚠ *f* mismanagement
Mist [mɪst] (**-(e)s**) *m* dung; dirt; (*umg*)
rubbish
Mistel (**-, -n**) *f* mistletoe
Misthaufen *m* dungheap
mit [mɪt] *präp +dat* with; (*mittels*) by ♦ *adv*
along, too; **~ der Bahn** by train; **~ 10
Jahren** at the age of 10; **wollen Sie ~?** do
you want to come along?
Mitarbeit ['mɪtarbait] *f* cooperation; **m~en**
vi to cooperate, to collaborate; **~er(in)**
m(f) collaborator; co-worker ♦ *pl* (*Personal*)

⚠ *Informationen zur Rechtschreibreform Seite 615*

staff

Mit- *zW:* **~bestimmung** *f* participation in decision-making; **m~bringen** (*unreg*) *vt* to bring along

miteinander [mɪtaɪˈnandər] *adv* together, with one another

miterleben *vt* to see, to witness

Mitesser [ˈmɪtɛsər] **(-s, -)** *m* blackhead

mitfahr- *zW:* **~en** *vi* to accompany; (*auf Reise auch*) to travel with; **M~gelegenheit** *f* lift; **M~zentrale** *f* agency for arranging lifts

mitfühlend *adj* sympathetic, compassionate

Mit- *zW:* **m~geben** (*unreg*) *vt* to give; **~gefühl** *nt* sympathy; **m~gehen** (*unreg*) *vi* to go/come along; **m~genommen** *adj* done in, in a bad way; **~gift** *f* dowry

Mitglied [ˈmɪtgliːt] *nt* member; **~sbeitrag** *m* membership fee; **~schaft** *f* membership

Mit- *zW:* **m~halten** (*unreg*) *vi* to keep up; **m~helfen** (*unreg*) *vi* to help; **~hilfe** *f* help, assistance; **m~hören** *vt* to listen in to; **m~kommen** (*unreg*) *vi* to come along; (*verstehen*) to keep up, to follow; **~läufer** *m* hanger-on; (*POL*) fellow traveller

Mitleid *nt* compassion; (*Erbarmen*) compassion; **m~ig** *adj* sympathetic; **m~slos** *adj* pitiless, merciless

Mit- *zW:* **m~machen** *vt* to join in, to take part in; **~mensch** *m* fellow man; **m~nehmen** (*unreg*) *vt* to take along/away; (*anstrengen*) to wear out, to exhaust; **zum ~nehmen** to take away; **m~reden** *vi*: **bei etw m~reden** to have a say in sth; **m~reißen** (*unreg*) *vt* to carry away/along; (*fig*) to thrill, captivate

mitsamt [mɪtˈzamt] *präp +dat* together with

Mitschuld *f* complicity; **m~ig** *adj*: **m~ig (an +*dat*)** implicated (in); (*an Unfall*) partly responsible (for)

Mit- *zW:* **~schüler(in)** *m(f)* schoolmate; **m~spielen** *vi* to join in, to take part; **~spieler(in)** *m(f)* partner

Mittag [ˈmɪtaːk] **(-(e)s, -e)** *m* midday, lunchtime; **(zu) ~ essen** to have lunch; **m~** ⚠ *adv* at lunchtime *od* noon; **~essen** *nt*

lunch, dinner

mittags *adv* at lunchtime *od* noon; **~pause** *f* lunch break; **M~schlaf** *m* early afternoon nap, siesta

Mittäter(in) [ˈmɪtɛːtər(ɪn)] *m(f)* accomplice

Mitte [ˈmɪtə] **(-)** *f* middle; (*POL*) centre; **aus unserer ~** from our midst

mitteilen [ˈmɪttaɪlən] *vt*: **jdm etw ~** to inform sb of sth, to communicate sth to sb

Mitteilung *f* communication

Mittel [ˈmɪtəl] **(-s -)** *nt* means; method; (*MATH*) average; (*MED*) medicine; **ein ~ zum Zweck** a means to an end; **~alter** *nt* Middle Ages *pl*; **m~alterlich** *adj* mediaeval; **~ding** *nt* cross; **~europa** *nt* Central Europe; **~gebirge** *nt* low mountain range; **m~mäßig** *adj* mediocre, middling; **~mäßigkeit** *f* mediocrity; **~meer** *nt* Mediterranean; **~ohrentzündung** *f* inflammation of the middle ear; **~punkt** *m* centre; **~stand** *m* middle class; **~streifen** *m* central reservation; **~stürmer** *m* centre-forward; **~weg** *m* middle course; **~welle** *f* (*RAD*) medium wave

mitten [ˈmɪtən] *adv* in the middle; **~ auf der Straße/in der Nacht** in the middle of the street/night

Mitternacht [ˈmɪtərnaxt] *f* midnight

mittlere(r, s) [ˈmɪtlərə(r, s)] *adj* middle; (*durchschnittlich*) medium, average; **~ Reife** ≈ O-levels

---

MITTLERE REIFE

ⓘ The **mittlere Reife** *is the standard certificate gained at a* **Realschule** *or* **Gymnasium** *on successful completion of 6 years' education there. If a pupil at a* **Realschule** *attains good results in several subjects he is allowed to enter the 11th class of a* **Gymnasium** *to study for the* **Abitur**.

---

mittlerweile [ˈmɪtlərvaɪlə] *adv* meanwhile

Mittwoch [ˈmɪtvɔx] **(-(e)s, -e)** *m* Wednesday; **m~s** *adv* on Wednesdays

mitunter [mɪtˈʊntər] *adv* occasionally, sometimes

⚠ *For information on spelling reform see page 615*

Mit- *zW:* **m~verantwortlich** *adj* jointly responsible; **m~wirken** *vi:* **m~wirken (bei)** to contribute (to); *(THEAT)* to take part (in); **~wirkung** *f* contribution; participation

Möbel ['møːbəl] *pl* furniture *sg;* **~wagen** *m* furniture *od* removal van

mobil [mo'biːl] *adj* mobile; *(MIL)* mobilized; **M~iar** [mobili'aːr] *(-s, -e) nt* furnishings *pl;* **M~machung** *f* mobilization; **M~telefon** *nt* mobile phone

möblieren [møˈbliːrən] *vt* to furnish; **möbliert wohnen** to live in furnished accommodation

möchte *etc* ['mϙçtə] *vb siehe* **mögen**

Mode ['moːdə] *f* fashion

Modell [mo'dɛl] *(-s, -e) nt* model; **m~ieren** [-'liːrən] *vt* to model

Modenschau *f* fashion show

moderig ['moːdərɪç] *adj (Keller)* musty; *(Luft)* stale

modern [mo'dɛrn] *adj* modern; *(modisch)* fashionable; **~i'sieren** *vt* to modernize

Mode- *zW:* **~schmuck** *m* fashion jewellery; **~schöpfer(in)** *m(f)* fashion designer; **~wort** *nt* fashionable word, buzz word

modisch ['moːdɪʃ] *adj* fashionable

Mofa ['moːfa] *(-s, -s) nt* small moped

mogeln ['moːgəln] *(umg) vi* to cheat

SCHLÜSSELWORT

---

mögen ['møːgən] *(pt* mochte, *pp* gemocht *od (als Hilfsverb)* mögen) *vt, vi* to like; **magst du/mögen Sie ihn?** do you like him?; **ich möchte ...** I would like ..., I'd like ...; **er möchte in die Stadt** he'd like to go into town; **ich möchte nicht, daß du ...** I wouldn't like you to ...; **ich mag nicht mehr** I've had enough

♦ *Hilfsverb* to like to; *(wollen)* to want; **möchtest du etwas essen?** would you like something to eat?; **sie mag nicht bleiben** she doesn't want to stay; **das mag wohl sein** that may well be; **was mag das heißen?** what might that mean?; **Sie möchten zu Hause anrufen** could you please call home?

---

möglich ['møːklɪç] *adj* possible; **~erweise** *adv* possibly; **M~keit** *f* possibility; **nach M~keit** if possible; **~st** *adv* as ... as possible

Mohn [moːn] *(-(e)s, -e) m (~blume)* poppy; *(~samen)* poppy seed

Möhre ['møːrə] *f* carrot

Mohrrübe ['moːrɹyːbə] *f* carrot

mokieren [mo'kiːrən] *vr:* **sich ~ über** *+akk* to make fun of

Mole ['moːlə] *f (harbour)* mole

Molekül [mole'kyːl] *(-s, -e) nt* molecule

Molkerei [mɔlkə'raɪ] *f* dairy

Moll [mɔl] *(-, -) nt (MUS)* minor (key)

mollig *adj* cosy; *(dicklich)* plump

Moment [mo'mɛnt] *(-(e)s, -e) m* moment ♦ *nt* factor; **im ~** at the moment; **~ (mal)!** just a moment; **m~an** [-'taːn] *adj* momentary ♦ *adv* at the moment

Monarch [mo'narç] *(-en, -en) m* monarch; **~ie** [monar'çiː] *f* monarchy

Monat ['moːnat] *(-(e)s, -e) m* month; **m~elang** *adv* for months; **m~lich** *adj* monthly

Monats- *zW:* **~gehalt** *nt:* **das dreizehnte ~gehalt** Christmas bonus *(of one month's salary);* **~karte** *f* monthly ticket

Mönch [mϙnç] *(-(e)s, -e) m* monk

Mond [moːnt] *(-(e)s, -e) m* moon; **~finsternis** *f* eclipse of the moon; **m~hell** *adj* moonlit; **~landung** *f* moon landing; **~schein** *m* moonlight

Mono- [mono] *in zW* mono; **~log** [-'loːk] *(-s, -e) m* monologue; **~pol** [-'poːl] *(-s, -e) nt* monopoly; **m~polisieren** [-poli'ziːrən] *vt* to monopolize; **m~ton** [-'toːn] *adj* monotonous; **~tonie** [-to'niː] *f* monotony

Montag ['moːntaːk] *(-(e)s, -e) m* Monday

Montage [mɔn'taːʒə] *f (PHOT etc)* montage; *(TECH)* assembly; *(Einbauen)* fitting

Monteur [mɔn'tøːr] *m* fitter

montieren [mɔn'tiːrən] *vt* to assemble

Monument [monu'mɛnt] *nt* monument; **m~al** [-'taːl] *adj* monumental

Moor [moːr] *(-(e)s, -e) nt* moor

Moos [moːs] *(-es, -e) nt* moss

Moped ['moːpɛt] *(-s, -s) nt* moped

⚠ *Informationen zur Rechtschreibreform Seite 615*

Moral [mo'ra:l] (-, -en) *f* morality; (*einer Geschichte*) moral; **m~isch** *adj* moral

Morast [mo'rast] (-(e)s, -e) *m* morass, mire; **m~ig** *adj* boggy

Mord [mɔrt] (-(e)s, -e) *m* murder; **~anschlag** *m* murder attempt

Mörder(in) ['mœrdər] (-s, -) *m(f)* murderer (murderess)

mörderisch *adj* (*fig: schrecklich*) terrible, dreadful ♦ *adv* (*umg: entsetzlich*) terribly, dreadfully

Mord- *zW*: **~kommission** *f* murder squad; **~glück** (*umg*) *nt* amazing luck; **m~smäßig** (*umg*) *adj* terrific, enormous; **~verdacht** *m* suspicion of murder

morgen ['mɔrgən] *adv* tomorrow; **~ früh** tomorrow morning; **M~** (-s, -) *m* morning; **M~mantel** *m* dressing gown; **M~rock** *m* dressing gown; **M~röte** *f* dawn; **~s** *adv* in the morning

morgig ['mɔrgɪç] *adj* tomorrow's; **der ~e Tag** tomorrow

Morphium ['mɔrfiʊm] *nt* morphine

morsch [mɔrʃ] *adj* rotten

Morsealphabet ['mɔrzəlalfabe:t] *nt* Morse code

morsen *vi* to send a message by Morse code

Mörtel ['mœrtəl] (-s, -) *m* mortar

Mosaik [moza'i:k] (-s, -en *od* -e) *nt* mosaic

Moschee [mɔ'ʃe:] (-, -n) *f* mosque

Moskito [mɔs'ki:to] (-s, -s) *m* mosquito

Most [mɔst] (-(e)s, -e) *m* (unfermented) fruit juice; (*Apfelwein*) cider

Motel [mo'tel] (-s, -s) *nt* motel

Motiv [mo'ti:f] (-s, -e) *nt* motive; (*MUS*) theme; **~ation** [-vatsi'o:n] *f* motivation; **m~ieren** [moti'vi:rən] *vt* to motivate

Motor ['mo:tɔr, *pl* mo'to:rən] (-s, -en) *m* engine; (*bes ELEK*) motor; **~boot** *nt* motorboat; **~haube** *f* (*von Auto*) bonnet (*BRIT*), hood (*US*); **m~isieren** *vt* to motorize; **~öl** *nt* engine oil; **~rad** *nt* motorcycle; **~roller** *m* (motor) scooter; **~schaden** *m* engine trouble *od* failure

Motte ['mɔtə] *f* moth; **~nkugel** *f* mothball(s)

Motto ['mɔto] (-s, -s) *nt* motto

Möwe ['mø:və] *f* seagull

Mücke ['mʏkə] *f* midge, gnat; **~nstich** *m* midge *od* gnat bite

müde ['my:də] *adj* tired

Müdigkeit ['my:dɪçkait] *f* tiredness

Muffel (-s, -) (*umg*) *m* killjoy, sourpuss

muffig *adj* (*Luft*) musty

Mühe ['my:ə] *f* trouble, pains *pl*; **mit Müh und Not** with great difficulty; **sich** *dat* **~ geben** to go to a lot of trouble; **m~los** *adj* without trouble, easy; **m~voll** *adj* laborious, arduous

Mühle ['my:lə] *f* mill; (*Kaffee~*) grinder

Müh- *zW*: **~sal** (-, -e) *f* tribulation; **m~sam** *adj* arduous, troublesome; **m~selig** *adj* arduous, laborious

Mulde ['mʊldə] *f* hollow, depression

Mull [mʊl] (-(e)s, -e) *m* thin muslin

Müll [mʏl] (-(e)s) *m* refuse; **~abfuhr** *f* rubbish disposal; (*Leute*) dustmen *pl*; **~abladeplatz** *m* rubbish dump

Mullbinde *f* gauze bandage

Müll- *zW*: **~eimer** *m* dustbin, garbage can (*US*); **~haufen** *m* rubbish heap; **~schlucker** (-s, -) *m* garbage disposal unit; **~tonne** *f* dustbin; **~verbrennungsanlage** *f* incinerator

mulmig ['mʊlmɪç] *adj* rotten; (*umg*) dodgy; **jdm ist ~** sb feels funny

multiplizieren [mʊltipli'tsi:rən] *vt* to multiply

Mumie ['mu:miə] *f* mummy

Mumm [mʊm] (-s) (*umg*) *m* gumption, nerve

Mumps [mʊmps] (-) *m od f* (*MED*) mumps

München ['mʏnçən] (-s) *nt* Munich

Mund [mʊnt] (-(e)s, ̈er) *m* mouth; **~art** *f* dialect

münden ['mʏndən] *vi*: **~ in** +*akk* to flow into

Mund- *zW*: **m~faul** *adj* taciturn; **~geruch** *m* bad breath; **~harmonika** *f* mouth organ

mündig ['mʏndɪç] *adj* of age; **M~keit** *f* majority

mündlich ['mʏntlɪç] *adj* oral

⚠ *For information on spelling reform see page 615*

Mundstück *nt* mouthpiece; (*Zigaretten~*) tip

Mündung ['mʏndʊŋ] *f* (*von Fluß*) mouth; (*Gewehr*) muzzle

Mund- *zW:* **~wasser** *nt* mouthwash; **~werk** *nt:* **ein großes ~werk haben** to have a big mouth; **~winkel** *m* corner of the mouth

Munition [munitsi'oːn] *f* ammunition; **~slager** *nt* ammunition dump

munkeln ['mʊŋkəln] *vi* to whisper, to mutter

Münster ['mʏnstər] (**-s, -**) *nt* minster

munter ['mʊntər] *adj* lively

Münze ['mʏntsə] *f* coin; **m~n** *vt* to coin, to mint

Münzfernsprecher ['mʏntsfɛrnʃprɛçər] *m* callbox (*BRIT*), pay phone

mürb(e) ['mʏrb(ə)] *adj* (*Gestein*) crumbly; (*Holz*) rotten; (*Gebäck*) crisp; **jdn mürbe machen** to wear sb down; **M~eteig** ['mʏrbətaɪç] *m̃* shortcrust pastry

murmeln ['mʊrməln] *vt, vi* to murmur, to mutter

murren ['mʊrən] *vi* to grumble, to grouse

mürrisch ['mʏrɪʃ] *adj* sullen

Mus [muːs] (**-es, -e**) *nt* purée

Muschel ['mʊʃəl] (**-, -n**) *f* mussel; (*~schale*) shell; (*Telefon~*) receiver

Muse ['muːzə] *f* muse

Museum [mu'zeːʊm] (**-s, Museen**) *nt* museum

Musik [mu'ziːk] *f* music; (*Kapelle*) band; **m~alisch** [-ka:lɪʃ] *adj* musical; **~ant(in)** [-'kant(ɪn)] (**-en, -en**) *m(f)* musician; **~box** *f* jukebox; **~er** (**-s, -**) *m* musician; **~hochschule** *f* college of music; **~instrument** *nt* musical instrument

musisch ['muːzɪʃ] *adj* (*Mensch*) artistic

musizieren [muzi'tsiːrən] *vi* to make music

Muskat [mʊs'kaːt] (**-(e)s, -e**) *m* nutmeg

Muskel ['mʊskəl] (**-s, -n**) *m* muscle; **~kater** *m:* **~kater haben** to be stiff

Muskulatur [mʊskula'tuːr] *f* muscular system

muskulös [mʊsku'løːs] *adj* muscular

Müsli ['myːsli] (**-s, -**) *nt* (*KOCH*) muesli

Muß △ [mʊs] (**-**) *nt* necessity, must

Muße ['muːsə] (**-**) *f* leisure

SCHLÜSSELWORT

---

müssen ['mʏsən] (*pt* **mußte**, *pp* **gemußt** *od* (*als Hilfsverb*) **müssen**) *vi* **1** (*Zwang*) must (*nur im Präsens*), to have to; **ich muß es tun** I must do it, I have to do it; **ich mußte es tun** I had to do it; **er muß es nicht tun** he doesn't have to do it; **muß ich?** must I?, do I have to?; **wann müßt ihr zur Schule?** when do you have to go to school?; **er hat gehen müssen** he (has) had to go; **muß das sein?** is that really necessary?; **ich muß mal** (*umg*) I need the toilet

2 (*sollen*): **das mußt du nicht tun!** you oughtn't to *od* shouldn't do that; **Sie hätten ihn fragen müssen** you should have asked him

3: **es muß geregnet haben** it must have rained; **es muß nicht wahr sein** it needn't be true

---

müßig ['myːsɪç] *adj* idle

Muster ['mʊstər] (**-s, -**) *nt* model; (*Dessin*) pattern; (*Probe*) sample; **m~gültig** *adj* exemplary; **m~n** *vt* (*Tapete*) to pattern; (*fig, MIL*) to examine; (*Truppen*) to inspect; **~ung** *f* (*von Stoff*) pattern; (*MIL*) inspection

Mut [muːt] *m* courage; **nur ~!** cheer up!; **jdm ~ machen** to encourage sb; **m~ig** *adj* courageous; **m~los** *adj* discouraged, despondent

mutmaßlich ['muːtmaːslɪç] *adj* presumed ♦ *adv* probably

Mutprobe *f* test *od* trial of courage

Mutter¹ ['mʊtər] (**-, ⸚**) *f* mother

Mutter² ['mʊtər] (**-, Muttern**) *f* (*Schrauben~*) nut

mütterlich ['mʏtərlɪç] *adj* motherly; **~erseits** *adv* on the mother's side

Mutter- *zW:* **~liebe** *f* motherly love; **~mal** *nt* birthmark; **~milch** *f* mother's milk; **~schaft** *f* motherhood, maternity; **~schutz** *m* maternity regulations; **'m~'seelena|llein** *adj* all alone;

△ *Informationen zur Rechtschreibreform Seite 615*

~**sprache** f native language; ~**tag** m Mother's Day

Mutti ['mʊti] (-, -s) f mum(my) (BRIT), mom(my) (US)

mutwillig ['muːtvɪlɪç] adj malicious, deliberate

Mütze ['mʏtsə] f cap

MwSt abk (= Mehrwertsteuer) VAT

mysteriös [mʏsteriˈøːs] adj mysterious

Mythos ['myːtɔs] (-, **Mythen**) m myth

N, n

na [na] excl well; ~ **gut** okay then

Nabel ['naːbəl] (-s, -) m navel; ~**schnur** f umbilical cord

SCHLÜSSELWORT

nach [naːx] präp +dat **1** (örtlich) to; **nach Berlin** to Berlin; **nach links/rechts** (to the) left/right; **nach oben/hinten** up/back

2 (zeitlich) after; **einer nach dem anderen** one after the other; **nach Ihnen!** after you!; **zehn (Minuten) nach drei** ten (minutes) past three

3 (gemäß) according to; **nach dem Gesetz** according to the law; **dem Namen nach** judging by his/her name; **nach allem, was ich weiß** as far as I know

♦ adv: **ihm nach!** after him!; **nach und nach** gradually, little by little; **nach wie vor** still

nachahmen ['naːxʔaːmən] vt to imitate

Nachbar(in) ['naxbaːr(ɪn)] (-s, -n) m(f) neighbour; ~**haus** nt: **im ~haus** next door; **n~lich** adj neighbourly; ~**schaft** f neighbourhood; ~**staat** m neighbouring state

nach- zW: ~**bestellen** vt: **50 Stück ~bestellen** to order another 50; **N~bestellung** f (COMM) repeat order; **N~bildung** f imitation, copy; ~**blicken** vi to gaze after; ~**datieren** vt to postdate

nachdem [naːxˈdeːm] konj after; (weil) since; **je ~ (ob)** it depends (whether)

nachdenken (unreg) vi: ~ **über** +akk to think about; **N~** (-s) nt reflection, meditation

nachdenklich adj thoughtful, pensive

Nachdruck ['naːxdrʊk] m emphasis; (TYP) reprint, reproduction

nachdrücklich ['naːxdrʏklɪç] adj emphatic

nacheinander [naːxʔaɪˈnandər] adv one after the other

nachempfinden ['naːxʔɛmpfɪndən] (unreg) vt: **jdm etw ~** to feel sth with sb

Nacherzählung ['naːxʔɛrtsɛːlʊŋ] f reproduction (of a story)

Nachfahr ['naːxfaːr] (-s, -en) m descendant

Nachfolge ['naːxfɔlgə] f succession; **n~n** vi +dat to follow; ~**r(in)** (-s, -) m(f) successor

nachforschen vt, vi to investigate

Nachforschung f investigation

Nachfrage ['naːxfraːgə] f inquiry; (COMM) demand; **n~n** vi to inquire

nach- zW: ~**füllen** vt to refill; ~**geben** (unreg) vi to give way, to yield; **N~gebühr** f (POST) excess postage

nachgehen ['naːxgeːən] (unreg) vi (+dat) to follow; (erforschen) to inquire (into); (Uhr) to be slow

Nachgeschmack ['naːxgəʃmak] m aftertaste

nachgiebig ['naːxgiːbɪç] adj soft, accommodating; **N~keit** f softness

nachhaltig ['naːxhaltɪç] adj lasting; (Widerstand) persistent

nachhelfen ['naːxhɛlfən] (unreg) vi +dat to assist, to help

nachher [naːxˈheːr] adv afterwards

Nachhilfeunterricht ['naːxhɪlfəʔʊntərrɪçt] m extra tuition

nachholen ['naːxhoːlən] vt to catch up with; (Versäumtes) to make up for

Nachkomme ['naːxkɔmə] (-, -n) m descendant

nachkommen (unreg) vi to follow; (einer Verpflichtung) to fulfil; **N~schaft** f descendants pl

Nachkriegszeit ['naːxkriːkstsaɪt] f postwar period

Nach- zW: ~**laß** ⚠ (-**lasses, -lässe**) m

⚠ For information on spelling reform see page 615

(COMM) discount, rebate; (*Erbe*) estate; **n~lassen** (unreg) vt (*Strafe*) to remit; (*Summe*) to take off; (*Schulden*) to cancel ♦ vi to decrease, to ease off; (*Sturm*) to die down, to ease off; (*schlechter werden*) to deteriorate; **er hat n~gelassen** he has got worse; **n~lässig** adj negligent, careless

nachlaufen ['naːxlaʊfən] (unreg) vi +dat to run after, to chase

nachlösen ['naːxløːzən] vi (*Zuschlag*) to pay on the train, pay at the other end; (*zur Weiterfahrt*) to pay the supplement

nachmachen ['naːxmaxən] vt to imitate, to copy; (*fälschen*) to counterfeit

Nachmittag ['naːxmɪtaːk] m afternoon; **am ~** in the afternoon; **n~s** adv in the afternoon

Nach- zW: **~nahme** f cash on delivery; **per ~nahme** C.O.D.; **~name** m surname; **~porto** nt excess postage

nachprüfen ['naːxpryːfən] vt to check, to verify

nachrechnen ['naːxrɛçnən] vt to check

nachreichen ['naːxraɪçən] vt (*Unterlagen*) to hand in later

Nachricht ['naːxrɪçt] (-, -en) f (piece of) news; (*Mitteilung*) message; **~en** pl (*Neuigkeiten*) news

Nachrichten- zW: **~agentur** f news agency; **~dienst** m (MIL) intelligence service; **~sprecher(in)** m(f) newsreader; **~technik** f telecommunications sg

Nachruf ['naːxruːf] m obituary

nachsagen ['naːxzaːgən] vt to repeat; **jdm etw ~** to say sth of sb

Nachsaison ['naːxzɛzõ] f off-season

nachschicken ['naːxʃɪkən] vt to forward

nachschlagen ['naːxʃlaːgən] (unreg) vt to look up

Nachschlagewerk nt reference book

Nachschlüssel m duplicate key

Nachschub ['naːxʃuːp] m supplies pl; (*Truppen*) reinforcements pl

nachsehen ['naːxzeːən] (unreg) vt (*prüfen*) to check ♦ vi (*erforschen*) to look and see; **jdm etw ~** to forgive sb sth; **das N~ haben** to come off worst

Nachsendeantrag m application to have one's mail forwarded

nachsenden ['naːxzɛndən] (unreg) vt to send on, to forward

nachsichtig adj indulgent, lenient

nachsitzen ['naːxzɪtsən] (unreg) vi: **~ (müssen)** (SCH) to be kept in

Nachspeise ['naːxʃpaɪzə] f dessert, sweet, pudding

Nachspiel ['naːxʃpiːl] nt epilogue; (*fig*) sequel

nachsprechen ['naːxʃprɛçən] (unreg) vt: **(jdm) ~** to repeat (after sb)

nächst [neːçst] präp +dat (*räumlich*) next to; (*außer*) apart from; **~beste(r, s)** adj first that comes along; (*zweitbeste*) next best; **N~e(r)** f(m) neighbour; **~e(r, s)** adj next; (*nächstgelegen*) nearest

nachstellen ['naːxʃtɛlən] vt (TECH: *neu einstellen*) to adjust

nächst- zW: **N~enliebe** f love for one's fellow men; **~ens** adv shortly, soon; **~liegend** adj nearest; (*fig*) obvious; **~möglich** adj next possible

Nacht [naxt] (-, ¨e) f night; **~dienst** m night shift

Nachteil ['naːxtaɪl] m disadvantage; **n~ig** adj disadvantageous

Nachthemd nt (Herren~) nightshirt; (Damen~) nightdress

Nachtigall ['naxtɪgal] (-, -en) f nightingale

Nachtisch ['naːxtɪʃ] m = **Nachspeise**

Nachtklub m night club

Nachtleben nt nightlife

nächtlich ['nɛçtlɪç] adj nightly

Nachtlokal nt night club

Nach- zW: **~trag** (-(e)s, -träge) m supplement; **n~tragen** (unreg) vt to carry; (*zufügen*) to add; **jdm etw n~tragen** to hold sth against sb; **n~träglich** adj later, subsequent; additional ♦ adv later, subsequently; additionally; **n~trauern** vi: **jdm/etw n~trauern** to mourn the loss of sb/sth

Nacht- zW: **n~s** adv at *od* by night; **~schicht** f nightshift; **~schwester** f night nurse; **~tarif** m off-peak tariff; **~tisch** m bedside table; **~wächter** *m* night watchman

Nach- *zW:* **~untersuchung** *f* checkup; **n~wachsen** (*unreg*) *vi* to grow again; **~wahl** *f* (*POL*) ≈ by-election

Nachweis ['na:xvaɪs] (**-es, -e**) *m* proof; **n~bar** *adj* provable, demonstrable; **n~en** (*unreg*) *vt* to prove; **jdm etw n~en** to point sth out to sb; **n~lich** *adj* evident, demonstrable

nach- *zW:* **~wirken** *vi* to have after-effects; **N~wirkung** *f* aftereffect; **N~wort** *nt* epilogue; **N~wuchs** *m* offspring; (*beruflich etc*) new recruits *pl;* **~zahlen** *vt, vi* to pay extra; **N~zahlung** *f* additional payment; (*zurückdatiert*) back pay; **~ziehen** (*unreg*) *vt* (*hinter sich herziehen: Bein*) to drag; **N~zügler (-s, -)** *m* straggler

Nacken ['nakən] (**-s, -**) *m* nape of the neck

nackt [nakt] *adj* naked; (*Tatsachen*) plain, bare; **N~badestrand** *m* nudist beach; **N~heit** *f* nakedness

Nadel ['na:dəl] (**-, -n**) *f* needle; (*Steck~*) pin; **~öhr** *nt* eye of a needle; **~wald** *m* coniferous forest

Nagel ['na:gəl] (**-s, ̈-**) *m* nail; **~bürste** *f* nailbrush; **~feile** *f* nailfile; **~lack** *m* nail varnish *od* polish (*BRIT*); **n~n** *vt, vi* to nail; **n~neu** *adj* brand-new; **~schere** *f* nail scissors *pl*

nagen ['na:gən] *vt, vi* to gnaw

Nagetier ['na:gəti:r] *nt* rodent

nah(e) ['na:(ə)] *adj* (*räumlich*) near(by); (*Verwandte*) near; (*Freunde*) close; (*zeitlich*) near, close ♦ *adv* near(by); near, close; (*verwandt*) closely ♦ *präp +dat* near (to), close to; **der Nahe Osten** the Near East; **Nahaufnahme** *f* close-up

Nähe ['nɛ:ə] (**-**) *f* nearness, proximity; (*Umgebung*) vicinity; **in der ~** close by; at hand; **aus der ~** from close to

nahe- *zW:* **~bei** *adv* nearby; **~gehen** △ (*unreg*) *vi* (+*dat*) to grieve; **~kommen** △ (*unreg*) *vi* (+*dat*) to get close (to); **~legen** △ *vt:* **jdm etw ~legen** to suggest sth to sb; **~liegen** △ (*unreg*) *vi* to be obvious; **~liegend** △ *adj* obvious; **~n** *vi, vr* to

approach, to draw near

nähen ['nɛ:ən] *vt, vi* to sew

näher *adj, adv* nearer; (*Erklärung, Erkundigung*) more detailed; **N~e(s)** *nt* details *pl,* particulars *pl*

Naherholungsgebiet *nt* recreational area (*close to a town*)

näherkommen △ (*unreg*) *vi, vr* to get closer

nähern *vr* to approach

nahe- *zW:* **~stehen** △ (*unreg*) *vi* (+*dat*) to be close (to); **einer Sache ~stehen** to sympathize with sth; **~stehend** △ *adj* close; **~treten** △ (*unreg*) *vi:* **jdm (zu) ~treten** to offend sb; **~zu** *adv* nearly

Nähgarn *nt* thread

Nahkampf *m* hand-to-hand fighting

Nähkasten *m* sewing basket, workbox

nahm *etc* [na:m] *vb siehe* **nehmen**

Nähmaschine *f* sewing machine

Nähnadel *f* needle

nähren ['nɛ:rən] *vt* to feed ♦ *vr* (*Person*) to feed o.s.; (*Tier*) to feed

nahrhaft ['na:rhaft] *adj* nourishing, nutritious

Nahrung ['na:rʊŋ] *f* food; (*fig auch*) sustenance

Nahrungs- *zW:* **~mittel** *nt* foodstuffs *pl;* **~mittelindustrie** *f* food industry; **~suche** *f* search for food

Nährwert *m* nutritional value

Naht [na:t] (**-, ̈-e**) *f* seam; (*MED*) suture; (*TECH*) join; **n~los** *adj* seamless; **n~los ineinander übergehen** to follow without a gap

Nah- *zW:* **~verkehr** *m* local traffic; **~verkehrszug** *m* local train; **~ziel** *nt* immediate objective

Name ['na:mə] (**-ns, -n**) *m* name; **im ~n von** on behalf of; **n~ns** *adv* by the name of; **~nstag** *m* name day, saint's day; **n~ntlich** *adj* by name ♦ *adv* particularly, especially

---

NAMENSTAG

---

i In Catholic areas of Germany the **Namenstag** is often a more important celebration than a birthday. This is the day

---

△ *For information on spelling reform see page 615*

dedicated to the saint after whom a person is called, and on that day the person receives presents and invites relatives and friends round to celebrate.

namhaft ['na:mhaft] *adj* (*berühmt*) famed, renowned; (*beträchtlich*) considerable; **~ machen** to name

nämlich ['nɛ:mlɪç] *adv* that is to say, namely; (*denn*) since

nannte *etc* ['nantə] *vb siehe* **nennen**

Napf [napf] **(-(e)s, ⸚e)** *m* bowl, dish

Narbe ['narbə] *f* scar; **narbig** *adj* scarred

Narkose [nar'ko:zə] *f* anaesthetic

Narr [nar] **(-en, -en)** *m* fool; **n~en** *vt* to fool; **Närrin** ['nɛrɪn] *f* fool; **närrisch** *adj* foolish, crazy

Narzisse [nar'tsɪsə] *f* narcissus; daffodil

naschen ['naʃən] *vt, vi* to nibble; (*heimlich kosten*) to pinch a bit

naschhaft *adj* sweet-toothed

Nase ['na:zə] *f* nose

Nasen- *zW:* **~bluten (-s)** *nt* nosebleed; **~loch** *nt* nostril; **~tropfen** *pl* nose drops

naseweis *adj* pert, cheeky; (*neugierig*) nosey

Nashorn ['na:shɔrn] *nt* rhinoceros

naß △ [nas] *adj* wet

Nässe ['nɛsə] **(-)** *f* wetness; **n~n** *vt* to wet

naßkalt △ *adj* wet and cold

Naßrasur △ *f* wet shave

Nation [natsi'o:n] *f* nation

national [natsio'na:l] *adj* national; **N~feiertag** *m* national holiday; **N~hymne** *f* national anthem; **~isieren** [-i'zi:rən] *vt* to nationalize; **N~ismus** [-'lɪsmʊs] *m* nationalism; **~istisch** [-'lɪstɪʃ] *adj* nationalistic; **N~i'tät** *f* nationality; **N~mannschaft** *f* national team; **N~sozialismus** *m* national socialism

Natron ['na:trɔn] **(-s)** *nt* soda

Natter ['natər] **(-, -n)** *f* adder

Natur [na'tu:r] *f* nature; (*körperlich*) constitution; **~ell** **(-s, -e)** *nt* disposition; **~erscheinung** *f* natural phenomenon *od* event; **n~farben** *adj* natural coloured; **n~gemäß** *adj* natural; **~gesetz** *nt* law of nature; **n~getreu** *adj* true to life; **~katastrophe** *f* natural disaster

natürlich [na'ty:rlɪç] *adj* natural ♦ *adv* naturally; **ja, ~!** yes, of course; **N~keit** *f* naturalness

Natur- *zW:* **~park** *m* ≈ national park; **~produkt** *nt* natural product; **n~rein** *adj* natural, pure; **~schutz** *m* nature conservation; **unter ~schutz stehen** to be legally protected; **~schutzgebiet** *nt* nature reserve; **~wissenschaft** *f* natural science; **~wissenschaftler(in)** *m(f)* scientist

nautisch ['naʊtɪʃ] *adj* nautical

Nazi ['na:tsi] **(-s, -s)** *m* Nazi

NB *abk* (= *nota bene*) nb

n.Chr. *abk* (= *nach Christus*) A.D.

Nebel ['ne:bəl] **(-s, -)** *m* fog, mist; **n~ig** *adj* foggy, misty; **~scheinwerfer** *m* fog lamp

neben ['ne:bən] *präp* (+*akk od dat*) next to; (+*dat:* *außer*) apart from, besides; **~an** [ne:bən'|an] *adv* next door; **N~anschluß** △ *m* (*TEL*) extension; **N~ausgang** *m* side exit; **~bei** [ne:bən'baɪ] *adv* at the same time; (*außerdem*) additionally; (*beiläufig*) incidentally; **N~beruf** *m* second job; **N~beschäftigung** *f* second job; **N~buhler(in)** **(-s, -)** *m(f)* rival; **~einander** [ne:bən|aɪ'nandər] *adv* side by side; **~einanderlegen** △ *vt* to put next to each other; **N~eingang** *m* side entrance; **N~fach** *nt* subsidiary subject; **N~fluß** △ *m* tributary; **N~gebäude** *nt* annexe; **N~geräusch** *nt* (*RAD*) atmospherics *pl*, interference; **~her** [ne:bən'he:r] *adv* (*zusätzlich*) besides; (*gleichzeitig*) at the same time; (*daneben*) alongside; **N~kosten** *pl* extra charges, extras; **N~produkt** *nt* by-product; **N~sache** *f* trifle, side issue; **~sächlich** *adj* minor, peripheral; **N~saison** *f* low season; **N~straße** *f* side street; **N~verdienst** *m* secondary income; **N~wirkung** *f* side effect; **N~zimmer** *nt* adjoining room

neblig ['ne:blɪç] *adj* foggy, misty

Necessaire △ [nese'sɛ:r] **(-s, -s)** *nt* (*Näh~*) needlework box; (*Nagel~*) manicure case

necken ['nɛkən] vt to tease

Neckerei [nɛkə'raɪ] f teasing

Neffe ['nɛfə] (-n, -n) m nephew

negativ ['ne:gati:f] adj negative; **N~** (-s, -e) nt (PHOT) negative

Neger ['ne:gər] (-s, -) m negro; ~in f negress

nehmen ['ne:mən] (unreg) vt to take; **jdn zu sich ~** to take sb in; **sich ernst ~** to take o.s. seriously; **nimm dir doch bitte** please help yourself

Neid [naɪt] (-(e)s) m envy; ~**er** (-s, -) m envier; **n~isch** ['naɪdɪʃ] adj envious, jealous

neigen ['naɪgən] vt to incline, to lean; (Kopf) to bow ♦ vi: **zu etw ~** to tend to sth

Neigung f (des Geländes) slope; (Tendenz) tendency, inclination; (Vorliebe) liking; (Zuneigung) affection

nein [naɪn] adv no

Nektarine [nɛkta'ri:nə] f (Frucht) nectarine

Nelke ['nɛlkə] f carnation, pink; (Gewürz) clove

Nenn- ['nɛn] zW: **n~en** (unreg) vt to name; (mit Namen) to call; **wie n~t man ...?** what do you call ...?; ~**enswert** adj worth mentioning; ~**er** (-s, -) m denominator; ~**wert** m nominal value; (COMM) par

Neon ['ne:ɔn] (-s) nt neon; ~**licht** nt neon light; ~**röhre** f neon tube

Nerv [nɛrf] (-s, -en) m nerve; **jdm auf die ~en gehen** to get on sb's nerves; **n~enaufreibend** adj nerve-racking; ~**enbündel** nt bundle of nerves; ~**enheilanstalt** f mental home; **n~enkrank** adj mentally ill; ~**ensäge** (umg) f pain (in the neck) (umg); ~**ensystem** nt nervous system; ~**enzusammenbruch** m nervous breakdown; **n~lich** adj (Belastung) affecting the nerves; **n~ös** [nɛr'vø:s] adj nervous; ~**osi'tät** f nervousness; **n~tötend** adj nerve-racking; (Arbeit) soul-destroying

Nerz [nɛrts] (-es, -e) m mink

Nessel ['nɛsəl] (-, -n) f nettle

Nest [nɛst] (-(e)s, -er) nt nest; (umg: Ort) dump

nett [nɛt] adj nice; (freundlich) nice, kind; ~**erweise** adv kindly

netto ['nɛto:] adv net

Netz [nɛts] (-es, -e) nt net; (Gepäck~) rack; (Einkaufs~) string bag; (Spinnen~) web; (System) network; **jdm ins ~ gehen** (fig) to fall into sb's trap; ~**anschluß** m mains connection; ~**haut** f retina

neu [nɔy] adj new; (Sprache, Geschichte) modern; **seit ~estem** (since) recently; **die ~esten Nachrichten** the latest news; ~ **schreiben** to rewrite, to write again; **N~anschaffung** f new purchase od acquisition; ~**artig** adj new kind of; **N~bau** m new building; **N~e(r)** f(m) the new man/woman; ~**erdings** adv (kürzlich) (since) recently; (von neuem) again; **N~erscheinung** f (Buch) new publication; (Schallplatte) new release; **N~erung** f innovation, new departure; **N~gier** f curiosity; ~**gierig** adj curious; **N~heit** f newness; novelty; **N~igkeit** f news sg; **N~jahr** nt New Year; ~**lich** adv recently, the other day; **N~ling** m novice; **N~mond** m new moon

neun [nɔyn] num nine; ~**zehn** num nineteen; ~**zig** num ninety

neureich adj nouveau riche; **N~e(r)** f(m) nouveau riche

neurotisch adj neurotic

Neuseeland [nɔy'ze:lant] nt New Zealand; **Neuseeländer(in)** [nɔy'ze:lɛndər(ɪn)] m(f) New Zealander

neutral [nɔy'tra:l] adj neutral; ~**i'sieren** vt to neutralize

Neutrum ['nɔytrʊm] (-s, -a od -en) nt neuter

Neu- zW: ~**wert** m purchase price; **n~wertig** adj (as) new, not used; ~**zeit** f modern age; **n~zeitlich** adj modern, recent

---

SCHLÜSSELWORT

---

nicht [nɪçt] adv **1** (Verneinung) not; **er ist es nicht** it's not him, it isn't him; **er raucht nicht** (gerade) he isn't smoking; (gewöhnlich) he doesn't smoke; **ich kann das nicht - ich auch nicht** I can't do it -

⚠ For information on spelling reform see page 615

neither *od* nor can I; **es regnet nicht mehr** it's not raining any more

2 (*Bitte, Verbot*): **nicht!** don't!, no!; **nicht berühren!** do not touch!; **nicht doch!** don't!

3 (*rhetorisch*): **du bist müde, nicht (wahr)?** you're tired, aren't you?; **das ist schön, nicht (wahr)?** it's nice, isn't it?

4: was du nicht sagst! the things you say!

Nichtangriffspakt [nɪçt'|angrɪfspakt] *m* non-aggression pact

Nichte ['nɪçtə] *f* niece

nichtig ['nɪçtɪç] *adj* (*ungültig*) null, void; (*wertlos*) futile; **N~keit** *f* nullity, invalidity; (*Sinnlosigkeit*) futility

Nichtraucher(in) *m(f)* non-smoker

nichts [nɪçts] *pron* nothing; **für ~ und wieder ~** for nothing at all; **N~** (-) *nt* nothingness; (*pej: Person*) nonentity

Nichtschwimmer *m* non-swimmer

nichts- *zW:* **~desto'weniger** *adv* nevertheless; **N~nutz** (**-es, -e**) *m* good-for-nothing; **~nutzig** *adj* worthless, useless; **~sagend** ⚠ *adj* meaningless; **N~tun** (-s) *nt* idleness

Nichtzutreffende(s) *nt:* **~s (bitte) streichen!** (please) delete where appropriate

Nickel ['nɪkəl] (**-s**) *nt* nickel

nicken ['nɪkən] *vi* to nod

Nickerchen ['nɪkərçən] *nt* nap

nie [niː] *adv* never; **~ wieder** *od* **mehr** never again; **~ und nimmer** never ever

nieder ['niːdər] *adj* low; (*gering*) inferior ♦ *adv* down; **N~gang** *m* decline; **~gedrückt** *adj* (*deprimiert*) dejected, depressed; **~gehen** (*unreg*) *vi* to descend; (*AVIAT*) to come down; (*Regen*) to fall; (*Boxer*) to go down; **~geschlagen** *adj* depressed, dejected; **N~lage** *f* defeat; **N~lande** *pl* Netherlands; **N~länder(in)** *m(f)* Dutchman(-woman); **~ländisch** *adj* Dutch; **~lassen** (*unreg*) *vr* (*sich setzen*) to sit down; (*an Ort*) to settle (down); (*Arzt, Rechtsanwalt*) to set up a practice; **N~lassung** *f* settlement; (*COMM*) branch;

~legen *vt* to lay down; (*Arbeit*) to stop; (*Amt*) to resign; **N~sachsen** *nt* Lower Saxony; **N~schlag** *m* (*MET*) precipitation; rainfall; **~schlagen** (*unreg*) *vt* (*Gegner*) to beat down; (*Gegenstand*) to knock down; (*Augen*) to lower; (*Aufstand*) to put down ♦ *vr* (*CHEM*) to precipitate; **~trächtig** *adj* base, mean; **N~trächtigkeit** *f* meanness, baseness; outrage; **N~ung** *f* (*GEOG*) depression; (*Mündungsgebiet*) flats *pl*

niedlich ['niːtlɪç] *adj* sweet, cute

niedrig ['niːdrɪç] *adj* low; (*Stand*) lowly, humble; (*Gesinnung*) mean

niemals ['niːmaːls] *adv* never

niemand ['niːmant] *pron* nobody, no one

Niemandsland ['niːmantslant] *nt* no-man's-land

Niere ['niːrə] *f* kidney

nieseln ['niːzəln] *vi* to drizzle

niesen ['niːzən] *vi* to sneeze

Niete ['niːtə] *f* (*TECH*) rivet; (*Los*) blank; (*Reinfall*) flop; (*Mensch*) failure; **n~n** *vt* to rivet

---

ST. NIKOLAUS

ⓘ On December 6th, St. Nikolaus visits German children to reward those who have been good by filling shoes they have left out with sweets and small presents.

Nikotin [niko'tiːn] (**-s**) *nt* nicotine

Nilpferd [niːl-] *nt* hippopotamus

Nimmersatt ['nɪmərzat] (**-(e)s, -e**) *m* glutton

nimmst *etc* [nɪmst] *vb siehe* **nehmen**

nippen ['nɪpən] *vt, vi* to sip

nirgend- ['nɪrgənt] *zW:* **~s** *adv* nowhere; **~wo** *adv* nowhere; **~wohin** *adv* nowhere

Nische ['niːʃə] *f* niche

nisten ['nɪstən] *vi* to nest

Niveau [ni'voː] (**-s, -s**) *nt* level

Nixe ['nɪksə] *f* water nymph

nobel ['noːbəl] *adj* (*großzügig*) generous; (*elegant*) posh (*inf*)

SCHLÜSSELWORT

noch [nɔx] *adv* **1** (*weiterhin*) still; **noch nicht**

⚠ *Informationen zur Rechtschreibreform Seite 615*

not yet; **noch nie** never (yet); **noch immer** *od* **immer noch** still; **bleiben Sie doch noch** stay a bit longer

2 (*in Zukunft*) still, yet; **das kann noch passieren** that might still happen; **er wird noch kommen** he'll come (yet)

3 (*nicht später als*): **noch vor einer Woche** only a week ago; **noch am selben Tag** the very same day; **noch im 19. Jahrhundert** as late as the 19th century; **noch heute** today

4 (*zusätzlich*): **wer war noch da?** who else was there?; **noch einmal** once more, again; **noch dreimal** three more times; **noch einer** another one

5 (*bei Vergleichen*): **noch größer** even bigger; **das ist noch besser** that's better still; **und wenn es noch so schwer ist** however hard it is

6: **Geld noch und noch** heaps (and heaps) of money; **sie hat noch und noch versucht, ...** she tried again and again to ...

♦ *konj*: **weder A noch B** neither A nor B

noch- *zW*: **~mal** ['nɔxmaːl] *adv* again, once more; **~malig** ['nɔxmaːlɪç] *adj* repeated; **~mals** *adv* again, once more

Nominativ ['noːminatiːf] (**-s, -e**) *m* nominative

nominell [nomiˈnɛl] *adj* nominal

Nonne ['nɔnə] *f* nun

Nord(en) ['nɔrd(ən)] (**-s**) *m* north

Nordirland *nt* Northern Ireland

nordisch *adj* northern

nördlich ['nœrtlɪç] *adj* northerly, northern
♦ *präp +gen* (to the) north of; **~ von** (to the) north of

Nord- *zW*: **~pol** *m* North Pole; **~rhein-Westfalen** *nt* North Rhine-Westphalia; **~see** *f* North Sea; **n~wärts** *adv* northwards

nörgeln ['nœrgəln] *vi* to grumble; **Nörgler** (**-s, -**) *m* grumbler

Norm [nɔrm] (**-, -en**) *f* norm; (*Größenvorschrift*) standard; **n~al** [nɔrˈmaːl] *adj* normal; **~al(benzin)** *nt* ≈ 2-star petrol

(*BRIT*), regular petrol (*US*); **n~alerweise** *adv* normally; **n~ali'sieren** *vt* to normalize
♦ *vr* to return to normal

normen *vt* to standardize

Norwegen ['nɔrveːgən] *nt* Norway; **norwegisch** *adj* Norwegian

Nostalgie [nɔstalˈgiː] *f* nostalgia

Not [noːt] (**-, ¨e**) *f* need; (*Mangel*) want; (*Mühe*) trouble; (*Zwang*) necessity; **zur ~** if necessary; (*gerade noch*) just about

Notar [noˈtaːr] (**-s, -e**) *m* notary; **n~i'ell** *adj* notarial

Not- *zW*: **~arzt** *m* emergency doctor; **~ausgang** *m* emergency exit; **~behelf** (**-s, -e**) *m* makeshift; **~bremse** *f* emergency brake; **~dienst** *m* (*Bereitschaftsdienst*) emergency service; **n~dürftig** *adj* scanty; (*behelfsmäßig*) makeshift

Note ['noːtə] *f* note; (*SCH*) mark (*BRIT*), grade (*US*)

Noten- *zW*: **~blatt** *nt* sheet of music; **~schlüssel** *m* clef; **~ständer** *m* music stand

Not- *zW*: **~fall** *m* (case of) emergency; **n~falls** *adv* if need be; **n~gedrungen** *adj* necessary, unavoidable; **etw n~gedrungen machen** to be forced to do sth

notieren [noˈtiːrən] *vt* to note; (*COMM*) to quote

Notierung *f* (*COMM*) quotation

nötig ['nøːtɪç] *adj* necessary; **etw ~ haben** to need sth; **~en** [-gən] *vt* to compel, to force; **~enfalls** *adv* if necessary

Notiz [noˈtiːts] (**-, -en**) *f* note; (*Zeitungs~*) item; **~ nehmen** to take notice; **~block** *m* notepad; **~buch** *nt* notebook

Not- *zW*: **~lage** *f* crisis, emergency; **n~landen** *vi* to make a forced *od* emergency landing; **n~leidend** ⚠ *adj* needy; **~lösung** *f* temporary solution; **~lüge** *f* white lie

notorisch [noˈtoːrɪʃ] *adj* notorious

Not- *zW*: **~ruf** *m* emergency call; **~rufsäule** *f* emergency telephone; **~stand** *m* state of emergency; **~unterkunft** *f* emergency accommodation; **~verband** *m* emergency

⚠ *For information on spelling reform see page 615*

dressing; ~**wehr** (-) *f* self-defence;
n~wendig *adj* necessary; ~**wendigkeit** *f*
necessity

Novelle [noˈvɛlə] *f* short novel; (*JUR*)
amendment

November [noˈvɛmbər] (-**s**, -) *m* November

Nu [nuː] *m*: **im ~** in an instant

Nuance [nyˈãːsə] *f* nuance

nüchtern [ˈnʏçtərn] *adj* sober; (*Magen*)
empty; (*Urteil*) prudent; **N~heit** *f* sobriety

Nudel [ˈnuːdəl] (-, -**n**) *f* noodle; ~**n** *pl*
(*Teigwaren*) pasta *sg*; (*in Suppe*) noodles

Null [nʊl] (-, -**en**) *f* nought, zero; (*pej:
Mensch*) washout; **n~** *num* zero; (*Fehler*)
no; **n~ Uhr** midnight; **n~ und nichtig** null
and void; ~**punkt** *m* zero; **auf dem ~punkt**
at zero

numerieren ⚠ [numeˈriːrən] *vt* to number

numerisch [nuˈmeːrɪʃ] *adj* numerical

Nummer [ˈnʊmər] (-, -**n**) *f* number; (*Größe*)
size; ~**nschild** *nt* (*AUT*) number *od* license
(*US*) plate

nun [nuːn] *adv* now ♦ *excl* well; **das ist ~
mal so** that's the way it is

nur [nuːr] *adv* just, only; **wo bleibt er ~?**
(just) where is he?

Nürnberg [ˈnʏrnbɛrk] (-**s**) *nt* Nuremberg

Nuß ⚠ [nʊs] (-, **Nüsse**) *f* nut; ~**baum** ⚠
m walnut tree; ~**knacker** ⚠ (-**s**, -) *m*
nutcracker

nutz [nʊts] *adj*: **zu nichts ~ sein** to be no
use for anything; ~**bringend** *adj*
(*Verwendung*) profitable

nütze [ˈnʏtsə] *adj* = **nutz**

Nutzen (-**s**) *m* usefulness; (*Gewinn*) profit;
von ~ useful; **n~** *vi* to be of use ♦ *vt*: **etw
zu etw n~** to use sth for sth; **was nutzt
es?** what's the use?, what use is it?

nützen *vi*, *vt* = **nutzen**

nützlich [ˈnʏtslɪç] *adj* useful; **N~keit** *f*
usefulness

Nutz- *zW*: **n~los** *adj* useless; ~**losigkeit** *f*
uselessness; ~**nießer** (-**s**, -) *m* beneficiary

Nylon [ˈnaɪlɔn] (-(**s**)) *nt* nylon

O, o

Oase [oˈaːzə] *f* oasis

ob [ɔp] *konj* if, whether; **~ das wohl wahr
ist?** can that be true?; **und ~!** you bet!

obdachlos *adj* homeless

Obdachlose(r) *f(m)* homeless person;
~**nasyl** *nt* shelter for the homeless

Obduktion [ɔpdʊktsiˈoːn] *f* post-mortem

obduzieren [ɔpduˈtsiːrən] *vt* to do a post-
mortem on

O-Beine [ˈoːbaɪnə] *pl* bow *od* bandy legs

oben [ˈoːbən] *adv* above; (*in Haus*) upstairs;
nach ~ up; **von ~** down; **~ ohne** topless;
jdn von ~ bis unten ansehen to look sb
up and down; ~**an** *adv* at the top; ~**auf**
adv up above, on the top ♦ *adj* (*munter*) in
form; ~**drein** *adv* into the bargain;
~**erwähnt** ⚠ *adj* above-mentioned;
~**genannt** ⚠ *adj* above-mentioned

Ober [ˈoːbər] (-**s**, -) *m* waiter; **die ~en** *pl*
(*umg*) the bosses; (*ECCL*) the superiors;
~**arm** *m* upper arm; ~**arzt** *m* senior
physician; ~**aufsicht** *f* supervision;
~**bayern** *nt* Upper Bavaria; ~**befehl** *m*
supreme command; ~**befehlshaber** *m*
commander-in-chief; ~**bekleidung** *f* outer
clothing; ~'**bürgermeister** *m* lord mayor;
~**deck** *nt* upper *od* top deck; **o~e(r, s)** *adj*
upper; ~**fläche** *f* surface; **o~flächlich** *adj*
superficial; ~**geschoß** ⚠ *nt* upper storey;
o~halb *adv* above ♦ *präp* +*gen* above;
~**haupt** *nt* head, chief; ~**haus** *nt* (*POL*)
upper house, House of Lords (*BRIT*);
~**hemd** *nt* shirt; ~**herrschaft** *f* supremacy,
sovereignty; ~**in** *f* matron; (*ECCL*) Mother
Superior; ~**kellner** *m* head waiter; ~**kiefer**
m upper jaw; ~**körper** *m* upper part of
body; ~**leitung** *f* direction; (*ELEK*) overhead
cable; ~**licht** *nt* skylight; ~**lippe** *f* upper
lip; ~**schenkel** *m* thigh; ~**schicht** *f* upper
classes *pl*; ~**schule** *f* grammar school
(*BRIT*), high school (*US*); ~**schwester** *f*
(*MED*) matron

Oberst [ˈoːbərst] (-**en** *od* -**s**, -**en** *od* -**e**) *m* colonel; **o~e(r, s)** *adj* very top, topmost

Ober- *zW:* **~stufe** *f* upper school; **~teil** *nt* upper part; **~weite** *f* bust/chest measurement

obgleich [ɔp'glaiç] *konj* although

Obhut ['ɔphu:t] (-) *f* care, protection; **in jds ~ sein** to be in sb's care

obig ['o:biç] *adj* above

Objekt [ɔp'jɛkt] (-(e)s, -e) *nt* object; **~iv** [-'ti:f] (-s, -e) *nt* lens; **o~iv** *adj* objective; **~ivi'tät** *f* objectivity

Oblate [o'bla:tə] *f* (*Gebäck*) wafer; (*ECCL*) host

obligatorisch [ɔbliga'to:rɪʃ] *adj* compulsory, obligatory

Obrigkeit ['o:brɪçkaɪt] *f* (*Behörden*) authorities *pl*, administration; (*Regierung*) government

obschon [ɔp'ʃo:n] *konj* although

Observatorium [ɔpzɛrva'to:riʊm] *nt* observatory

obskur [ɔps'ku:r] *adj* obscure; (*verdächtig*) dubious

Obst [o:pst] (-(e)s) *nt* fruit; **~baum** *m* fruit tree; **~garten** *m* orchard; **~händler** *m* fruiterer, fruit merchant; **~kuchen** *m* fruit tart

obszön [ɔps'tsø:n] *adj* obscene; **O~i'tät** *f* obscenity

obwohl [ɔp'vo:l] *konj* although

Ochse ['ɔksə] (-n, -n) *m* ox; **o~n** (*umg*) *vt*, *vi* to cram, to swot (*BRIT*)

Ochsenschwanzsuppe *f* oxtail soup

Ochsenzunge *f* oxtongue

öd(e) ['ø:d(ə)] *adj* (*Land*) waste, barren; (*fig*) dull; **Öde** *f* desert, waste(land); (*fig*) tedium

oder ['o:dər] *konj* or; **das stimmt, ~?** that's right, isn't it?

Ofen ['o:fən] (-s, ¨) *m* oven; (*Heiz~*) fire, heater; (*Kohlen~*) stove; (*Hoch~*) furnace; (*Herd*) cooker, stove; **~rohr** *nt* stovepipe

offen ['ɔfən] *adj* open; (*aufrichtig*) frank; (*Stelle*) vacant; **~ gesagt** to be honest; **~bar** *adj* obvious; **~baren** [ɔfən'ba:rən] *vt* to reveal, to manifest; **O~'barung** *f* (*REL*) revelation; **~bleiben** △ (*unreg*) *vi* (*Fenster*)

to stay open; (*Frage, Entscheidung*) to remain open; **~halten** △ (*unreg*) *vt* to keep open; **O~heit** *f* candour, frankness; **~herzig** *adj* candid, frank; (*Kleid*) revealing; **~kundig** *adj* well-known; (*klar*) evident; **~lassen** △ (*unreg*) *vt* to leave open; **~sichtlich** *adj* evident, obvious

offensiv [ɔfɛn'zi:f] *adj* offensive; **O~e** [-'zi:və] *f* offensive

offenstehen △ (*unreg*) *vi* to be open; (*Rechnung*) to be unpaid; **es steht Ihnen offen, es zu tun** you are at liberty to do it

öffentlich ['œfəntlɪç] *adj* public; **Ö~keit** *f* (*Leute*) public; (*einer Versammlung etc*) public nature; **in aller Ö~keit** in public; **an die Ö~keit dringen** to reach the public ear

offiziell [ɔfitsi'ɛl] *adj* official

Offizier [ɔfi'tsi:r] (-s, -e) *m* officer; **~skasino** *nt* officers' mess

öffnen ['œfnən] *vt*, *vr* to open; **jdm die Tür ~** to open the door for sb

Öffner ['œfnər] (-s, -) *m* opener

Öffnung ['œfnʊŋ] *f* opening; **~szeiten** *pl* opening times

oft [ɔft] *adv* often

öfter ['œftər] *adv* more often *od* frequently; **~s** *adv* often, frequently

oh [o:] *excl* oh; **~ je!** oh dear

OHG *abk* (= *Offene Handelsgesellschaft*) general partnership

ohne ['o:nə] *präp* +*akk* without ♦ *konj* without; **das ist nicht ~** (*umg*) it's not bad; **~ weiteres** without a second thought; (*sofort*) immediately; **~ zu fragen** without asking; **~ daß er es wußte** without him knowing it; **~dies** [o:nə'di:s] *adv* anyway; **~gleichen** [o:nə'glaiçən] *adj* unsurpassed, without equal; **~hin** [o:nə'hɪn] *adv* anyway, in any case

Ohnmacht ['o:nmaxt] *f* faint; (*fig*) impotence; **in ~ fallen** to faint

ohnmächtig ['o:nmɛçtɪç] *adj* in a faint, unconscious; (*fig*) weak, impotent; **sie ist ~** she has fainted

Ohr [o:r] (-(e)s, -en) *nt* ear

Öhr [ø:r] (-(e)s, -e) *nt* eye

Ohren- *zW:* **~arzt** *m* ear specialist;

△ *For information on spelling reform see page 615*

o~betäubend *adj* deafening; ~schmalz *nt* earwax; ~schmerzen *pl* earache *sg*

Ohr- *zW*: ~feige *f* slap on the face; box on the ears; o~feigen *vt*: jdn o~feigen to slap sb's face; to box sb's ears; ~läppchen *nt* ear lobe; ~ring *m* earring; ~wurm *m* earwig; (*MUS*) catchy tune

Öko- [øko] *zW*: ~laden *m* wholefood shop; ö~logisch [-'lo:gɪʃ] *adj* ecological; ö~nomisch [-'no:mɪʃ] *adj* economical

Oktober [ɔk'to:bər] (-s, -) *m* October; ~fest *nt* Munich beer festival

OKTOBERFEST

i The annual beer festival, the **Oktoberfest**, takes place in Munich at the end of September in a huge area where beer tents and various amusements are set up. People sit at long wooden tables, drink beer from enormous beer mugs, eat pretzels and listen to brass bands. It is a great attraction for tourists and locals alike.

ökumenisch [øku'me:nɪʃ] *adj* ecumenical

Öl [ø:l] (-(e)s, -e) *nt* oil; ~baum *m* olive tree; ö~en *vt* to oil; (*TECH*) to lubricate; ~farbe *f* oil paint; ~feld *nt* oilfield; ~film *m* film of oil; ~heizung *f* oil-fired central heating; ö~ig *adj* oily; ~industrie *f* oil industry

oliv [o'li:f] *adj* olive-green; O~e *f* olive

Öl- *zW*: ~meßstab △ *m* dipstick; ~sardine *f* sardine; ~stand *m* oil level; ~standanzeiger *m* (*AUT*) oil gauge; ~tanker *m* oil tanker; ~ung *f* lubrication; oiling; (*ECCL*) anointment; die Letzte ~ung Extreme Unction; ~wechsel *m* oil change

Olymp- [o'lʏmp] *zW*: ~iade [olʏmpi'a:də] *f* Olympic Games *pl*; ~iasieger(in) [-iazi:gər(ɪn)] *m(f)* Olympic champion; ~iateilnehmer(in) *m(f)* Olympic competitor; o~isch *adj* Olympic

Ölzeug *nt* oilskins *pl*

Oma ['o:ma] (-, -s) (*umg*) *f* granny

Omelett [ɔm(ə)'let] (-(e)s, -s) *nt* omelet(te)

ominös [omi'nø:s] *adj* (*unheilvoll*) ominous

Omnibus ['ɔmnibʊs] *m* (omni)bus

Onanie [ona'ni:] *f* masturbation; o~ren *vi* to masturbate

Onkel ['ɔŋkəl] (-s, -) *m* uncle

Opa ['o:pa] (-s, -s) (*umg*) *m* grandpa

Oper ['o:pər] (-, -n) *f* opera; opera house

Operation [operatsi'o:n] *f* operation; ~ssaal *m* operating theatre

Operette [ope'retə] *f* operetta

operieren [ope'ri:rən] *vt* to operate on ♦ *vi* to operate

Opern- *zW*: ~glas *nt* opera glasses *pl*; ~haus *nt* opera house

Opfer ['ɔpfər] (-s, -) *nt* sacrifice; (*Mensch*) victim; o~n *vt* to sacrifice; ~ung *f* sacrifice

opponieren [ɔpo'ni:rən] *vi*: gegen jdn/etw ~ to oppose sb/sth

Opportunist [ɔpɔrtu'nɪst] *m* opportunist

Opposition [ɔpozitsi'o:n] *f* opposition; o~ell *adj* opposing

Optik ['ɔptɪk] *f* optics *sg*; ~er (-s, -) *m* optician

optimal [ɔpti'ma:l] *adj* optimal, optimum

Optimismus [ɔpti'mɪsmʊs] *m* optimism

Optimist [ɔpti'mɪst] *m* optimist; o~isch *adj* optimistic

optisch ['ɔptɪʃ] *adj* optical

Orakel [o'ra:kəl] (-s, -) *nt* oracle

oral [o'ra:l] *adj* (*MED*) oral

Orange [o'rã:ʒə] *f* orange; o~ *adj* orange; ~ade [orã'ʒa:də] *f* orangeade; ~at [orã'ʒa:t] (-s, -e) *nt* candied peel

Orchester [ɔr'kestər] (-s, -) *nt* orchestra

Orchidee [ɔrçi'de:ə] *f* orchid

Orden ['ɔrdən] (-s, -) *m* (*ECCL*) order; (*MIL*) decoration; ~sschwester *f* nun

ordentlich ['ɔrdəntlɪç] *adj* (*anständig*) decent, respectable; (*geordnet*) tidy, neat; (*umg: annehmbar*) not bad; (: *tüchtig*) real, proper ♦ *adv* properly; ~er Professor (full) professor; O~keit *f* respectability; tidiness, neatness

ordinär [ɔrdi'nɛ:r] *adj* common, vulgar

ordnen ['ɔrdnən] *vt* to order, to put in order

Ordner (-s, -) *m* steward; (*COMM*) file

Ordnung *f* order; (*Ordnen*) ordering; (*Geordnetsein*) tidiness; ~ machen to tidy up; in ~! okay!

Ordnungs- *zW:* **o~gemäß** *adj* proper, according to the rules; **o~liebend** *adj* orderly, methodical; **~strafe** *f* fine; **o~widrig** *adj* contrary to the rules, irregular; **~widrigkeit** [-vɪdrɪçkaɪt] *f* infringement *(of law or rule);* **~zahl** *f* ordinal number

Organ [ɔr'gaːn] **(-s, -e)** *nt* organ; *(Stimme)* voice; **~isation** [-izatsi'oːn] *f* organization; **~isator** [i'zaːtɔr] *m* organizer; **o~isch** *adj* organic; **o~isieren** [-i'ziːrən] *vt* to organize, to arrange; *(umg: beschaffen)* to acquire ♦ *vr* to organize; **~ismus** [-'nɪsmʊs] *m* organism; **~ist** [-'nɪst] *m* organist; **~spende** *f* organ donation; **~spenderausweis** *m* donor card

Orgasmus [ɔr'gasmʊs] *m* orgasm

Orgel ['ɔrgəl] **(-, -n)** *f* organ

Orgie ['ɔrgiə] *f* orgy

Orient ['oːriɛnt] **(-s)** *m* Orient, east; **o~alisch** [-'taːlɪʃ] *adj* oriental

orientieren *zW:* **~en** [-'tiːrən] *vt (örtlich)* to locate; *(fig)* to inform ♦ *vr* to find one's way *od* bearings; to inform o.s.; **O~ung** [-'tiːrʊŋ] *f* orientation; *(fig)* information; **O~ungssinn** *m* sense of direction; **O~ungsstufe** *f* period during which pupils are selected for different schools

---

ORIENTIERUNGSSTUFE

i *The Orientierungsstufe is the name given to the first two years spent in a Realschule or Gymnasium, during which a child is assessed as to his or her suitability for that type of school. At the end of two years it may be decided to transfer the child to a school more suited to his or her ability.*

---

original [origi'naːl] *adj* original; **O~ (-s, -e)** *nt* original; **O~fassung** *f* original version; **O~i'tät** *f* originality

originell [origi'nɛl] *adj* original

Orkan [ɔr'kaːn] **(-(e)s, -e)** *m* hurricane; **o~artig** *adj (Wind)* gale-force; *(Beifall)* thunderous

Ornament [ɔrna'mɛnt] *nt* decoration, ornament; **o~al** [-'taːl] *adj* decorative, ornamental

Ort [ɔrt] **(-(e)s, -e** *od* **⁻er)** *m* place; **an ~ und Stelle** on the spot; **o~en** *vt* to locate

ortho- [ɔrto] *zW:* **~dox** [-'dɔks] *adj* orthodox; **O~graphie** ⚠ [-graːˈfiː] *f* spelling, orthography; **~'graphisch** ⚠ *adj* orthographic; **O~päde** [-'pɛːdə] **(-n, -n)** *m* orthopaedist; **O~pädie** [-pɛ'diː] *f* orthopaedics *sg;* **~'pädisch** *adj* orthopaedic

örtlich ['œrtlɪç] *adj* local; **Ö~keit** *f* locality

ortsansässig *adj* local

Ortschaft *f* village, small town

Orts- *zW:* **o~fremd** *adj* non-local; **~gespräch** *nt* local (phone)call; **~name** *m* place name; **~netz** *nt (TEL)* local telephone exchange area; **~tarif** *m (TEL)* tariff for local calls; **~zeit** *f* local time

Ortung *f* locating

Öse ['øːzə] *f* loop, eye

Ost|asien [ɔs'taːziən] *nt* Eastern Asia

Osten ['ɔstən] **(-s)** *m* east

Oster- ['oːstər] *zW:* **~ei** *nt* Easter egg; **~fest** *nt* Easter; **~glocke** *f* daffodil; **~hase** *m* Easter bunny; **~montag** *m* Easter Monday; **~n (-s, -)** *nt* Easter

Österreich ['øːstəraɪç] **(-s)** *nt* Austria; **~er(in) (-s, -)** *m(f)* Austrian; **ö~isch** *adj* Austrian

Ostküste *f* east coast

östlich ['œstlɪç] *adj* eastern, easterly

Ostsee *f:* **die ~** the Baltic (Sea)

Ouvertüre [uver'tyːrə] *f* overture

oval [o'vaːl] *adj* oval

Ovation [ovatsi'oːn] *f* ovation

Oxyd [ɔ'ksyːt] **(-(e)s, -e)** *nt* oxide; **o~ieren** *vt, vi* to oxidize; **~ierung** *f* oxidization

Ozean ['oːtseaːn] **(-s, -e)** *m* ocean; **~dampfer** *m* (ocean-going) liner

Ozon [o'tsoːn] **(-s)** *nt* ozone; **~loch** *nt* ozone hole; **~schicht** *f* ozone layer

⚠ *For information on spelling reform see page 615*

P, p

Paar [pa:r] (**-(e)s, -e**) *nt* pair; (*Ehe~*) couple; **ein p~** a few; **p~en** *vt, vr* to couple; (*Tiere*) to mate; **~lauf** *m* pair skating; **p~mal** △ *adv*: **ein p~mal** a few times; **~ung** *f* combination; mating; **p~weise** *adv* in pairs; in couples

Pacht [paxt] (**-, -en**) *f* lease; **p~en** *vt* to lease

Pächter ['pɛçtər] (**-s, -**) *m* leaseholder, tenant

Pack¹ [pak] (**-(e)s, -e** *od* **¨e**) *m* bundle, pack

Pack² [pak] (**-(e)s, -e**) *nt* (*pej*) mob, rabble

Päckchen ['pɛkçən] *nt* small package; (*Zigaretten*) packet; (*Post~*) small parcel

Pack- *zW*: **p~en** *vt* to pack; (*fassen*) to grasp, to seize; (*umg: schaffen*) to manage; (*fig: fesseln*) to grip; **~en** (**-s, -**) *m* bundle; (*fig: Menge*) heaps of; **~esel** *m* (*auch fig*) packhorse; **~papier** *nt* brown paper, wrapping paper; **~ung** *f* packet; (*Pralinenpackung etc*) box; (*MED*) compress; **~ungsbeilage** *f* enclosed instructions *pl* for use

Pädagog- [pɛda'go:g] *zW*: **~e** (**-n, -n**) *m* teacher; **~ik** *f* education; **p~isch** *adj* educational, pedagogical

Paddel ['padəl] (**-s, -**) *nt* paddle; **~boot** *nt* canoe; **p~n** *vi* to paddle

Page ['pa:ʒə] (**-n, -n**) *m* page

Paket [pa'ke:t] (**-(e)s, -e**) *nt* packet; (*Post~*) parcel; **~karte** *f* dispatch note; **~post** *f* parcel post; **~schalter** *m* parcels counter

Pakt [pakt] (**-(e)s, -e**) *m* pact

Palast [pa'last] (**-es, Paläste**) *m* palace

Palästina [palɛ'sti:na] (**-s**) *nt* Palestine

Palme ['palmə] *f* palm (tree)

Pampelmuse ['pampəlmu:zə] *f* grapefruit

panieren [pa'ni:rən] *vt* (*KOCH*) to bread

Paniermehl [pa'ni:rme:l] *nt* breadcrumbs *pl*

Panik ['pa:nɪk] *f* panic

panisch ['pa:nɪʃ] *adj* panic-stricken

Panne ['panə] *f* (*AUT etc*) breakdown; (*Mißgeschick*) slip; **~nhilfe** *f* breakdown service

panschen ['panʃən] *vi* to splash about ♦ *vt* to water down

Pantoffel [pan'tɔfəl] (**-s, -n**) *m* slipper

Pantomime [panto'mi:mə] *f* mime

Panzer ['pantsər] (**-s, -**) *m* armour; (*Platte*) armour plate; (*Fahrzeug*) tank; **~glas** *nt* bulletproof glass; **p~n** *vt* to armour ♦ *vr* (*fig*) to arm o.s.

Papa [pa'pa:] (**-s, -s**) (*umg*) *m* dad, daddy

Papagei [papa'gai] (**-s, -en**) *m* parrot

Papier [pa'pi:r] (**-s, -e**) *nt* paper; (*Wert~*) security; **~fabrik** *f* paper mill; **~geld** *nt* paper money; **~korb** *m* wastepaper basket; **~taschentuch** *nt* tissue

Papp- ['pap] *zW*: **~deckel** *m* cardboard; **~e** *f* cardboard; **~el** (**-, -n**) *f* poplar; **p~en** (*umg*) *vt, vi* to stick; **p~ig** *adj* sticky

Paprika ['paprika] (**-s, -s**) *m* (*Gewürz*) paprika; (*~schote*) pepper

Papst [pa:pst] (**-(e)s, ¨e**) *m* pope

päpstlich ['pɛ:pstlɪç] *adj* papal

Parabel [pa'ra:bəl] (**-, -n**) *f* parable; (*MATH*) parabola

Parabolantenne [para'bo:lantenə] *f* satellite dish

Parade [pa'ra:də] *f* (*MIL*) parade, review; (*SPORT*) parry

Paradies [para'di:s] (**-es, -e**) *nt* paradise; **p~isch** *adj* heavenly

Paradox [para'dɔks] (**-es, -e**) *nt* paradox; **p~** *adj* paradoxical

Paragraph △ [para'gra:f] (**-en, -en**) *m* paragraph; (*JUR*) section

parallel [para'le:l] *adj* parallel; **P~e** *f* parallel

Parasit [para'zi:t] (**-en, -en**) *m* (*auch fig*) parasite

parat [pa'ra:t] *adj* ready

Pärchen ['pɛ:rçən] *nt* couple

Parfüm [par'fy:m] (**-s, -s** *od* **-e**) *nt* perfume; **~erie** [-ə'ri:] *f* perfumery; **p~frei** *adj* non-perfumed; **p~ieren** *vt* to scent, to perfume

parieren [pa'ri:rən] *vt* to parry ♦ *vi* (*umg*) to obey

Paris [pa'ri:s] (**-**) *nt* Paris; **~er** *adj* Parisian ♦ *m* Parisian; **~erin** *f* Parisian

Park [park] (-s, -s) m park; ~**anlage** f park; (um Gebäude) grounds pl; **p~en** vt, vi to park; ~**ett** (-(e)s, -e) nt parquet (floor); (THEAT) stalls pl; ~**gebühr** f parking fee; ~**haus** nt multi-storey car park; ~**lücke** f parking space; ~**platz** m parking place; car park, parking lot (US); ~**scheibe** f parking disc; ~**schein** m car park ticket; ~**uhr** f parking meter; ~**verbot** nt parking ban

Parlament [parla'mɛnt] nt parliament; ~**arier** [-'taːriər] (-s, -) m parliamentarian; **p~arisch** [-'taːrɪʃ] adj parliamentary

Parlaments- zW: ~**beschluß** ⚠ m vote of parliament; ~**mitglied** nt member of parliament; ~**sitzung** f sitting of parliament)

Parodie [paro'diː] f parody; **p~ren** vt to parody

Parole [pa'roːlə] f password; (Wahlspruch) motto

Partei [par'tai] f party; ~ **ergreifen für jdn** to take sb's side; **p~isch** adj partial, bias(s)ed; **p~los** adj neutral, impartial; ~**mitglied** nt party member; ~**programm** nt (party) manifesto; ~**tag** m party conference

Parterre [par'tɛr] (-s, -s) nt ground floor; (THEAT) stalls pl

Partie [par'tiː] f part; (Spiel) game; (Ausflug) outing; (Mann, Frau) catch; (COMM) lot; **mit von der ~ sein** to join in

Partizip [parti'tsiːp] (-s, -ien) nt participle

Partner(in) ['partnər(ɪn)] (-s, -) m(f) partner; ~**schaft** f partnership; (von Städten) twinning; **p~schaftlich** adj as partners; ~**stadt** f twin town

Party ['paːrti] (-, -s od **Parties**) f party

Paß ⚠ [pas] (-sses, ˙sse) m pass; (Ausweis) passport

passabel [pa'saːbəl] adj passable, reasonable

Passage [pa'saːʒə] f passage

Passagier [pasa'ʒiːr] (-s, -e) m passenger; ~**flugzeug** nt airliner

Paßamt ⚠ nt passport office

Passant [pa'sant] m passer-by

Paßbild ⚠ nt passport photograph

passen ['pasən] vi to fit; (Farbe) to go; (auf Frage, KARTEN, SPORT) to pass; **das paßt mir nicht** that doesn't suit me; ~ **zu** (Farbe, Kleider) to go with; **er paßt nicht zu dir** he's not right for you; ~**d** adj suitable; (zusammenpassend) matching; (angebracht) fitting; (Zeit) convenient

passier- [pa'siːr] zW: ~**bar** adj passable; ~**en** vt to pass; (durch Sieb) to strain ♦ vi to happen; **P~schein** m pass, permit

Passion [pasi'oːn] f passion; **p~iert** [-'niːrt] adj enthusiastic, passionate; ~**sspiel** nt Passion Play

passiv ['pasiːf] adj passive; **P~** (-s, -e) nt passive; **P~a** pl (COMM) liabilities; **P~i'tät** f passiveness; **P~rauchen** nt passive smoking

Paß- zW: ~**kontrolle** ⚠ f passport control; ~**stelle** ⚠ f passport office; ~**straße** ⚠ f (mountain) pass

Paste ['pastə] f paste

Pastete [pas'teːtə] f pie

pasteurisieren [pastøri'ziːrən] vt to pasteurize

Pastor ['pastɔr] m vicar; pastor, minister

Pate ['paːtə] (-n, -n) m godfather; ~**kind** nt godchild

Patent [pa'tɛnt] (-(e)s, -e) nt patent; (MIL) commission; **p~** adj clever; ~**amt** nt patent office

Patentante f godmother

patentieren [patɛn'tiːrən] vt to patent

Patentinhaber m patentee

pathetisch [pa'teːtɪʃ] adj emotional; bombastic

Pathologe [pato'loːgə] (-n, -n) m pathologist

pathologisch adj pathological

Pathos ['paːtɔs] (-) nt emotiveness, emotionalism

Patient(in) [patsi'ɛnt(ɪn)] m(f) patient

Patin ['paːtɪn] f godmother

Patriot [patri'oːt] (-en, -en) m patriot; **p~isch** adj patriotic; ~**ismus** [-'tɪsmʊs] m patriotism

Patrone [pa'troːnə] f cartridge

Patrouille [pa'trʊljə] f patrol

⚠ For information on spelling reform see page 615

patrouillieren [patrʊlˈjiːrən] *vi* to patrol

patsch [patʃ] *excl* splash; **P~e** (*umg*) *f* (*Bedrängnis*) mess, jam; **~en** *vi* to smack, to slap; (*im Wasser*) to splash; **~naß** ⚠ *adj* soaking wet

patzig [ˈpatsɪç] (*umg*) *adj* cheeky, saucy

Pauke [ˈpaʊkə] *f* kettledrum; **auf die ~ hauen** to live it up

pauken *vt* (*intensiv lernen*) to swot up (*inf*) ♦ *vi* to swot (*inf*), cram (*inf*)

pausbäckig [ˈpaʊsbɛkɪç] *adj* chubby-cheeked

pauschal [paʊˈʃaːl] *adj* (*Kosten*) inclusive; (*Urteil*) sweeping; **P~e** *f* flat rate; **P~gebühr** *f* flat rate; **P~preis** *m* all-in price; **P~reise** *f* package tour; **P~summe** *f* lump sum

Pause [ˈpaʊzə] *f* break; (*THEAT*) interval; (*Innehalten*) pause; (*Kopie*) tracing

pausen *vt* to trace; **~los** *adj* non-stop; **P~zeichen** *nt* call sign; (*MUS*) rest

Pauspapier [ˈpaʊspapiːr] *nt* tracing paper

Pavillon [ˈpavɪljõ] (**-s, -s**) *m* pavilion

Pazif- [paˈtsiːf] *zW:* **~ik** (**-s**) *m* Pacific; **p~istisch** *adj* pacifist

Pech [pɛç] (**-s, -e**) *nt* pitch; (*fig*) bad luck; **~ haben** to be unlucky; **p~schwarz** *adj* pitch-black; **~strähne** (*umg*) *m* unlucky patch; **~vogel** (*umg*) *m* unlucky person

Pedal [peˈdaːl] (**-s, -e**) *nt* pedal

Pedant [peˈdant] *m* pedant; **~e'rie** *f* pedantry; **p~isch** *adj* pedantic

Pediküre [pediˈkyːrə] *f* (*Fußpflege*) pedicure

Pegel [ˈpeːgəl] (**-s, -**) *m* water gauge; **~stand** *m* water level

peilen [ˈpaɪlən] *vt* to get a fix on

Pein [paɪn] (**-**) *f* agony, pain; **p~igen** *vt* to torture; (*plagen*) to torment; **p~lich** *adj* (*unangenehm*) embarrassing, awkward, painful; (*genau*) painstaking

Peitsche [ˈpaɪtʃə] *f* whip; **p~n** *vt* to whip; (*Regen*) to lash

Pelle [ˈpɛlə] *f* skin; **p~n** *vt* to skin, to peel

Pellkartoffeln *pl* jacket potatoes

Pelz [pɛlts] (**-es, -e**) *m* fur

Pendel [ˈpɛndəl] (**-s, -**) *nt* pendulum; **p~n** *vi* (*Zug, Fähre etc*) to operate a shuttle service; (*Mensch*) to commute; **~verkehr** *m* shuttle traffic; (*für Pendler*) commuter traffic

Pendler [ˈpɛndlər] (**-s, -**) *m* commuter

penetrant [peneˈtrant] *adj* sharp; (*Person*) pushing

Penis [ˈpeːnɪs] (**-, -se**) *m* penis

pennen [ˈpɛnən] (*umg*) *vi* to kip

Penner (*umg: pej*) *m* (*Landstreicher*) tramp

Pension [penziˈoːn] *f* (*Geld*) pension; (*Ruhestand*) retirement; (*für Gäste*) boarding od guesthouse; **~är(in)** [-ˈnɛːr(ɪn)] (**-s, -e**) *m(f)* pensioner; **p~ieren** *vt* to pension off; **p~iert** *adj* retired; **~ierung** *f* retirement; **~sgast** *m* boarder, paying guest

Pensum [ˈpɛnzʊm] (**-s, Pensen**) *nt* quota; (*SCH*) curriculum

per [pɛr] *präp +akk* by, per; (*pro*) per; (*bis*) by

Perfekt [ˈpɛrfɛkt] (**-(e)s, -e**) *nt* perfect; **p~** *adj* perfect

perforieren [pɛrfoˈriːrən] *vt* to perforate

Pergament [pɛrgaˈmɛnt] *nt* parchment; **~papier** *nt* greaseproof paper

Periode [periˈoːdə] *f* period; **periodisch** *adj* periodic; (*dezimal*) recurring

Perle [ˈpɛrlə] *f* (*auch fig*) pearl; **p~n** *vi* to sparkle; (*Tropfen*) to trickle

Perl- [ˈpɛrl] *zW:* **~mutt** (**-s**) *nt* mother-of-pearl; **~wein** *m* sparkling wine

perplex [pɛrˈplɛks] *adj* dumbfounded

Person [pɛrˈzoːn] (**-, -en**) *f* person; **ich für meine ~ ...** personally I ...

Personal [pɛrzoˈnaːl] (**-s**) *nt* personnel; (*Bedienung*) servants *pl*; **~ausweis** *m* identity card; **~computer** *m* personal computer; **~ien** [-iən] *pl* particulars; **~mangel** *m* undermanning; **~pronomen** *nt* personal pronoun

personell [pɛrzoˈnɛl] *adj* (*Veränderungen*) personnel

Personen- *zW:* **~aufzug** *m* lift, elevator (*US*); **~kraftwagen** *m* private motorcar; **~schaden** *m* injury to persons; **~zug** *m* stopping train; passenger train

personifizieren [pɛrzonifiˈtsiːrən] *vt* to personify

persönlich [pɛrˈzøːnlɪç] *adj* personal ♦ *adv* in person; personally; **P~keit** *f* personality

⚠ *Informationen zur Rechtschreibreform Seite 615*

Perspektive [pɛrspɛk'tiːvə] f perspective

Perücke [pe'rykə] f wig

pervers [pɛr'vɛrs] adj perverse

Pessimismus [pɛsi'mɪsmus] m pessimism

Pessimist [pɛsi'mɪst] m pessimist; **p~isch** adj pessimistic (US)

Pest [pɛst] (-) f plague

Petersilie [petar'ziːliə] f parsley

Petroleum [pe'troːleʊm] (-s) nt paraffin, kerosene (US)

Pfad [pfaːt] (-(e)s, -e) m path; **~finder** (-s, -) m boy scout; **~finderin** f girl guide

Pfahl [pfaːl] (-(e)s, "-e) m post, stake

Pfand [pfant] (-(e)s, "-er) nt pledge, security; (Flaschen~) deposit; (im Spiel) forfeit; **~brief** m bond

pfänden ['pfɛndən] vt to seize, to distrain

Pfänderspiel nt game of forfeits

Pfandflasche f returnable bottle

Pfandschein m pawn ticket

Pfändung ['pfɛndʊŋ] f seizure, distraint

Pfanne ['pfanə] f (frying) pan

Pfannkuchen m pancake; (Berliner) doughnut

Pfarr- ['pfar] zW: **~ei** f parish; **~er** (-s, -) m priest; (evangelisch) vicar; minister; **~haus** nt vicarage; manse

Pfau [pfaʊ] (-(e)s, -en) m peacock; **~enauge** nt peacock butterfly

Pfeffer ['pfɛfər] (-s, -) m pepper; **~kuchen** m gingerbread; **~minz** (-es, -e) nt peppermint; **~mühle** f pepper mill; **p~n** vt to pepper; (umg: werfen) to fling; **gepfefferte Preise/Witze** steep prices/ spicy jokes

Pfeife ['pfaɪfə] f whistle; (Tabak~, Orgel~) pipe; **p~n** (unreg) vt, vi to whistle; **~r** (-s, -) m piper

Pfeil [pfaɪl] (-(e)s, -e) m arrow

Pfeiler ['pfaɪlər] (-s, -) m pillar, prop; (Brücken~) pier

Pfennig ['pfɛnɪç] (-(e)s, -e) m pfennig (hundredth part of a mark)

Pferd [pfeːrt] (-(e)s, -e) nt horse

Pferde- ['pfeːrdə] zW: **~rennen** nt horse race; horse racing; **~schwanz** m (Frisur) ponytail; **~stall** m stable

Pfiff [pfɪf] (-(e)s, -e) m whistle

Pfifferling ['pfɪfərlɪŋ] m yellow chanterelle (mushroom); **keinen ~ wert** not worth a thing

pfiffig adj sly, sharp

Pfingsten ['pfɪŋstən] (-, -) nt Whitsun (BRIT), Pentecost

Pfirsich ['pfɪrzɪç] (-s, -e) m peach

Pflanz- ['pflants] zW: **~e** f plant; **p~en** vt to plant; **~enfett** nt vegetable fat; **p~lich** adj vegetable; **~ung** f plantation

Pflaster ['pflastər] (-s, -) nt plaster; (Straße) pavement; **p~n** vt to pave; **~stein** m paving stone

Pflaume ['pflaʊmə] f plum

Pflege ['pfleːgə] f care; (von Idee) cultivation; (Kranken~) nursing; **in ~ sein** (Kind) to be fostered out; **p~bedürftig** adj needing care; **~eltern** pl foster parents; **~heim** nt nursing home; **~kind** nt foster child; **p~leicht** adj easy-care; **~mutter** f foster mother; **p~n** vt to look after; (Kranke) to nurse; (Beziehungen) to foster; **~r** (-s, -) m orderly; male nurse; **~rin** f nurse, attendant; **~vater** m foster father

Pflicht [pflɪçt] (-, -en) f duty; (SPORT) compulsory section; **p~bewußt** △ adj conscientious; **~fach** nt (SCH) compulsory subject; **~gefühl** nt sense of duty; **p~gemäß** adj dutiful ♦ adv as in duty bound; **~versicherung** f compulsory insurance

pflücken ['pflʏkən] vt to pick; (Blumen) to pick, to pluck

Pflug [pfluːk] (-(e)s, "-e) m plough

pflügen ['pflyːgən] vt to plough

Pforte ['pfɔrtə] f gate; door

Pförtner ['pfœrtnər] (-s, -) m porter, doorkeeper, doorman

Pfosten ['pfɔstən] (-s, -) m post

Pfote ['pfoːtə] f paw; (umg: Schrift) scrawl

Pfropfen (-s, -) m (Flaschen~) stopper; (Blut~) clot

pfui [pfʊi] excl ugh!

Pfund [pfʊnt] (-(e)s, -e) nt pound

pfuschen ['pfʊʃən] (umg) vi to be sloppy; **jdm ins Handwerk ~** to interfere in sb's

△ *For information on spelling reform see page 615*

business

Pfuscher ['pfuʃər] (**-s, -**) (*umg*) *m* sloppy worker; (*Kur~*) quack; **~ei** (*umg*) *f* sloppy work; quackery

Pfütze ['pfʏtsə] *f* puddle

Phänomen [fɛnoˈmeːn] (**-s, -e**) *nt* phenomenon; **p~al** [-ˈnaːl] *adj* phenomenal

Phantasie △ [fantaˈziː] *f* imagination; **p~los** △ *adj* unimaginative; **p~ren** △ *vi* to fantasize; **p~voll** △ *adj* imaginative

phantastisch △ [fanˈtastɪʃ] *adj* fantastic

Phase ['faːzə] *f* phase

Philologie [filoloˈgiː] *f* philology

Philosoph [filoˈzoːf] (**-en, -en**) *m* philosopher; **~ie** [-ˈfiː] *f* philosophy; **p~isch** *adj* philosophical

phlegmatisch [flɛˈgmaːtɪʃ] *adj* lethargic

Phonetik [foˈneːtɪk] *f* phonetics *sg*

phonetisch *adj* phonetic

Phosphor ['fɔsfɔr] (**-s**) *m* phosphorus

Photo *etc* ['foːto] (**-s, -s**) *nt* = **Foto** *etc*

Phrase ['fraːzə] *f* phrase; (*pej*) hollow phrase

pH-Wert [peːˈhaːveːrt] *m* pH-value

Physik [fyˈziːk] *f* physics *sg*; **p~alisch** [-ˈkaːlɪʃ] *adj* of physics; **~er(in)** ['fyːzɪkər(ɪn)] (**-s, -**) *m(f)* physicist

Physiologie [fyzioloˈgiː] *f* physiology

physisch ['fyːzɪʃ] *adj* physical

Pianist(in) [piaˈnɪst(ɪn)] *m(f)* pianist

Pickel ['pɪkəl] (**-s, -**) *m* pimple; (*Werkzeug*) pickaxe; (*Berg~*) ice axe; **p~ig** *adj* pimply, spotty

picken ['pɪkən] *vi* to pick, to peck

Picknick ['pɪknɪk] (**-s, -e** *od* **-s**) *nt* picnic; **~ machen** to have a picnic

piepen ['piːpən] *vi* to chirp

piepsen ['piːpsən] *vi* to chirp

Piepser (*umg*) *m* pager, paging device

Pier [piːər] (**-s, -s** *od* **-e**) *m od* **f** pier

Pietät [pieˈtɛːt] *f* piety, reverence; **p~los** *adj* impious, irreverent

Pigment [pɪgˈmɛnt] *nt* pigment

Pik [piːk] (**-s, -s**) *nt* (*KARTEN*) spades

pikant [piˈkant] *adj* spicy, piquant; (*anzüglich*) suggestive

Pilger ['pɪlgər] (**-s, -**) *m* pilgrim; **~fahrt** *f* pilgrimage

Pille ['pɪlə] *f* pill

Pilot [piˈloːt] (**-en, -en**) *m* pilot

Pilz [pɪlts] (**-es, -e**) *m* fungus; (*eßbar*) mushroom; (*giftig*) toadstool; **~krankheit** *f* fungal disease

Pinguin ['pɪŋguiːn] (**-s, -e**) *m* penguin

Pinie ['piːniə] *f* pine

pinkeln ['pɪŋkəln] (*umg*) *vi* to pee

Pinnwand ['pɪnvant] *f* noticeboard

Pinsel ['pɪnzəl] (**-s, -**) *m* paintbrush

Pinzette [pɪnˈtsɛtə] *f* tweezers *pl*

Pionier [pioˈniːr] (**-s, -e**) *m* pioneer; (*MIL*) sapper, engineer

Pirat [piˈraːt] (**-en, -en**) *m* pirate

Piste ['pɪstə] *f* (*SKI*) run, piste; (*AVIAT*) runway

Pistole [pɪsˈtoːlə] *f* pistol

Pizza ['pɪtsa] (**-, -s**) *f* pizza

Pkw [peːkaːˈveː] (**-(s), -(s)**) *m abk* = **Personenkraftwagen**

plädieren [plɛˈdiːrən] *vi* to plead

Plädoyer [plɛdoaˈjeː] (**-s, -s**) *nt* speech for the defence; (*fig*) plea

Plage ['plaːgə] *f* plague; (*Mühe*) nuisance; **~geist** *m* pest, nuisance; **p~n** *vt* to torment ♦ *vr* to toil, to slave

Plakat [plaˈkaːt] (**-(e)s, -e**) *nt* placard; poster

Plan [plaːn] (**-(e)s, ̈-e**) *m* plan; (*Karte*) map

Plane *f* tarpaulin

planen *vt* to plan; (*Mord etc*) to plot

Planer (**-s, -**) *m* planner

Planet [plaˈneːt] (**-en, -en**) *m* planet

planieren [plaˈniːrən] *vt* to plane, to level

Planke ['plaŋkə] *f* plank

plan- ['plaːn] *zW*: **~los** *adj* (*Vorgehen*) unsystematic; (*Umherlaufen*) aimless; **~mäßig** *adj* according to plan; systematic; (*EISENB*) scheduled

Planschbecken ['planʃbɛkən] *nt* paddling pool

planschen ['planʃən] *vi* to splash

Plansoll (**-s**) *nt* output target

Plantage [planˈtaːʒə] *f* plantation

Planung *f* planning

Planwirtschaft *f* planned economy

plappern ['plapərn] *vi* to chatter

plärren ['plɛrən] *vi* (*Mensch*) to cry, to whine; (*Radio*) to blare

△ *Informationen zur Rechtschreibreform Seite 615*

Plasma ['plasma] (**-s, Plasmen**) *nt* plasma
Plastik[1] ['plastɪk] *f* sculpture
Plastik[2] ['plastɪk] (**-s**) *nt* (*Kunststoff*) plastic;
~**beutel** *m* plastic bag, carrier bag; ~**folie**
f plastic film
plastisch ['plastɪʃ] *adj* plastic; **stell dir das**
~ **vor!** just picture it!
Platane [pla'taːnə] *f* plane (tree)
Platin ['plaːtiːn] (**-s**) *nt* platinum
platonisch [pla'toːnɪʃ] *adj* platonic
platsch [platʃ] *excl* splash; ~**en** *vi* to splash
plätschern ['plɛtʃərn] *vi* to babble
platschnaß △ *adj* drenched
platt [plat] *adj* flat; (*umg: überrascht*)
flabbergasted; (*fig: geistlos*) flat, boring;
~**deutsch** *adj* low German; **P~e** *f*
(*Speisenplatte, PHOT, TECH*) plate;
(*Steinplatte*) flag; (*Kachel*) tile; (*Schallplatte*)
record; **P~enspieler** *m* record player;
P~enteller *m* turntable
Platz [plats] (**-es, ¨e**) *m* place; (*Sitz~*) seat;
(*Raum*) space, room; (*in Stadt*) square;
(*Sport~*) playing field; ~ **nehmen** to take a
seat; **jdm ~ machen** to make room for sb;
~**angst** *f* claustrophobia; ~**anweiser(in)**
(**-s, -**) *m(f)* usher(ette)
Plätzchen ['plɛtsçən] *nt* spot; (*Gebäck*)
biscuit
Platz- *zW:* **p~en** *vi* to burst; (*Bombe*) to
explode; **vor Wut p~en** (*umg*) to be
bursting with anger; ~**karte** *f* seat
reservation; ~**mangel** *m* lack of space;
~**patrone** *f* blank cartridge; ~**regen** *m*
downpour; ~**reservierung** [-rezervi:rʊŋ] *f*
seat reservation; ~**wunde** *f* cut
Plauderei [plaʊdə'raɪ] *f* chat, conversation;
(*RAD*) talk
plaudern ['plaʊdərn] *vi* to chat, to talk
plausibel [plaʊ'ziːbəl] *adj* plausible
plazieren △ [pla'tsiːrən] *vt* to place ♦ *vr*
(*SPORT*) to be placed; (*TENNIS*) to be seeded
Pleite ['plaɪtə] *f* bankruptcy; (*umg: Reinfall*)
flop; ~ **machen** to go bust; **p~** (*umg*) *adj*
broke
Plenum ['pleːnʊm] (**-s**) *nt* plenum
Plombe ['plɔmbə] *f* lead seal; (*Zahn~*) filling
plombieren [plɔm'biːrən] *vt* to seal; (*Zahn*)

to fill
plötzlich ['plœtslɪç] *adj* sudden ♦ *adv*
suddenly
plump [plʊmp] *adj* clumsy; (*Hände*) coarse;
(*Körper*) shapeless; ~**sen** (*umg*) *vi* to plump
down, to fall
Plunder ['plʊndər] (**-s**) *m* rubbish
plündern ['plʏndərn] *vt* to plunder; (*Stadt*)
to sack ♦ *vi* to plunder; **Plünderung** *f*
plundering, sack, pillage
Plural ['pluːraːl] (**-s, -e**) *m* plural; **p~istisch**
adj pluralistic
Plus [plʊs] (**-, -**) *nt* plus; (*FIN*) profit; (*Vorteil*)
advantage; **p~** *adv* plus
Plüsch [plyːʃ] (**-(e)s, -e**) *m* plush
Plus- [plʊs] *zW:* ~**pol** *m* (*ELEK*) positive pole;
~**punkt** *m* point; (*fig*) point in sb's favour
Plutonium [plu'toːniʊm] (**-s**) *nt* plutonium
PLZ *abk* = **Postleitzahl**
Po [poː] (**-s, -s**) (*umg*) *m* bottom, bum
Pöbel ['pøːbəl] (**-s**) *m* mob, rabble; ~**ei** *f*
vulgarity; **p~haft** *adj* low, vulgar
pochen ['pɔxən] *vi* to knock; (*Herz*) to
pound; **auf etw** *akk* ~ (*fig*) to insist on sth
Pocken ['pɔkən] *pl* smallpox *sg*
Podium ['poːdiʊm] *nt* podium;
~**sdiskussion** *f* panel discussion
Poesie [poe'ziː] *f* poetry
Poet [po'eːt] (**-en, -en**) *m* poet; **p~isch** *adj*
poetic
Pointe [po'ɛ̃ːtə] *f* point
Pokal [po'kaːl] (**-s, -e**) *m* goblet; (*SPORT*)
cup; ~**spiel** *nt* cup tie
pökeln ['pøːkəln] *vt* to pickle, to salt
Poker ['poːkər] (**-s**) *nt od m* poker
Pol [poːl] (**-s, -e**) *m* pole; **p~ar** *adj* polar;
~**arkreis** *m* Arctic circle
Pole ['poːlə] (**-n, -n**) *m* Pole
polemisch [po:le:mɪʃ] *adj* polemical
Polen ['poːlən] (**-s**) *nt* Poland
Police [po'liːs(ə)] *f* insurance policy
Polier [po'liːr] (**-s, -e**) *m* foreman
polieren *vt* to polish
Poliklinik [poli'kliːnɪk] *f* outpatients
(department) *sg*
Polin *f* Pole
Politik [poli'tiːk] *f* politics *sg*; (*eine bestimmte*)

△ *For information on spelling reform see page 615*

policy; **~er(in)** [poli'ti:kər(ın)] **(-s, -)** *m(f)* politician
politisch [po'li:tıʃ] *adj* political
Politur [poli'tu:r] *f* polish
Polizei [poli'tsaı] *f* police; **~beamte(r)** *m* police officer; **p~lich** *adj* police; **sich p~lich melden** to register with the police; **~revier** *nt* police station; **~staat** *m* police state; **~streife** *f* police patrol; **~stunde** *f* closing time; **~wache** *f* police station
Polizist(in) [poli'tsıst(ın)] **(-en, -en)** *m(f)* policeman(-woman)
Pollen ['pɔlən] **(-s, -)** *m* pollen; **~flug** *m* pollen count
polnisch ['pɔlnıʃ] *adj* Polish
Polohemd ['po:lohemt] *nt* polo shirt
Polster ['pɔlstər] **(-s, -)** *nt* cushion; *(Polsterung)* upholstery; *(in Kleidung)* padding; *(fig: Geld)* reserves *pl*; **~er (-s, -)** *m* upholsterer; **~möbel** *pl* upholstered furniture *sg*; **p~n** *vt* to upholster; to pad
Polterabend ['pɔltəra:bənt] *m* party on eve of wedding
poltern *vi* *(Krach machen)* to crash; *(schimpfen)* to rant
Polyp [po'ly:p] **(-en, -en)** *m* polyp; *(umg)* cop; **~en** *pl* *(MED)* adenoids
Pomade [po'ma:də] *f* pomade
Pommes frites [pɔm'frıt] *pl* chips, French fried potatoes
Pomp [pɔmp] **(-(e)s)** *m* pomp; **p~ös** *adj* *(Auftritt, Fest, Haus)* ostentatious, showy
Pony ['pɔni] **(-s, -s)** *nt* *(Pferd)* pony ♦ *m* *(Frisur)* fringe
Popmusik ['pɔpmuzi:k] *f* pop music
Popo [po'po:] **(-s, -s)** *(umg)* *m* bottom, bum
poppig ['pɔpıç] *adj* *(Farbe etc)* gaudy
populär [popu'lɛ:r] *adj* popular
Popularität [populari'tɛ:t] *f* popularity
Pore ['po:rə] *f* pore
Pornographie ⚠ [pɔrnogra'fi:] *f* pornography; **pornographisch** ⚠ [pɔrno'gra:fıʃ] *adj* pornographic
porös [po'rø:s] *adj* porous
Porree ['pɔre] **(-s, -s)** *m* leek
Portal [pɔr'ta:l] **(-s, -e)** *nt* portal
Portefeuille [pɔrt(ə)'fø:j] *nt* *(POL, FIN)*

portfolio
Portemonnaie ⚠ [pɔrtmɔ'ne:] **(-s, -s)** *nt* purse
Portier [pɔr'tie:] **(-s, -s)** *m* porter
Portion [pɔrtsi'o:n] *f* portion, helping; *(umg: Anteil)* amount
Porto ['pɔrto] **(-s, -s)** *nt* postage; **p~frei** *adj* post-free, (postage) prepaid
Porträt [pɔr'trɛ:] **(-s, -s)** *nt* = **Porträt**; **p~ieren** *vt* = **porträtieren**
Porträt [pɔr'trɛ:] **(-s, -s)** *nt* portrait; **p~ieren** *vt* to paint, to portray
Portugal ['pɔrtugal] **(-s)** *nt* Portugal; **Portugiese (-n, -n)** *m* Portuguese; **Portu'giesin** *f* Portuguese; **portu'giesisch** *adj* Portuguese
Porzellan [pɔrtse'la:n] **(-s, -e)** *nt* china, porcelain; *(Geschirr)* china
Posaune [po'zaunə] *f* trombone
Pose ['po:zə] *f* pose
Position [pozitsi'o:n] *f* position
positiv ['po:ziti:f] *adj* positive; **P~ (-s, -e)** *nt* *(PHOT)* positive
possessiv ['pɔsɛsi:f] *adj* possessive; **P~pronomen (-s, -e)** *nt* possessive pronoun
possierlich [pɔ'si:rlıç] *adj* funny
Post [pɔst] **(-, -en)** *f* post (office); *(Briefe)* mail; **~amt** *nt* post office; **~anweisung** *f* postal order, money order; **~bote** *m* postman; **~en (-s, -)** *m* post, position; *(COMM)* item; *(auf Liste)* entry; *(MIL)* sentry; *(Streikposten)* picket; **~er (-s, -(s))** *nt* poster; **~fach** *nt* post office box; **~karte** *f* postcard; **p~lagernd** *adv* poste restante *(BRIT)*, general delivery *(US)*; **~leitzahl** *f* postal code; **~scheckkonto** *nt* postal giro account; **~sparbuch** *nt* post office savings book; **~sparkasse** *f* post office savings bank; **~stempel** *m* postmark; **p~wendend** *adv* by return of post; **~wertzeichen** *nt* postage stamp
potent [po'tɛnt] *adj* potent; **P~ial** ⚠ **(-s, -e)** *nt* potential; **~iell** ⚠ *adj* potential
Potenz [po'tɛnts] *f* power; *(eines Mannes)* potency
Pracht [praxt] **(-)** *f* splendour, magnificence;

prächtig ['prɛçtɪç] adj splendid
Prachtstück nt showpiece
prachtvoll adj splendid, magnificent
Prädikat [predi'ka:t] (-(e)s, -e) nt title; (GRAM) predicate; (Zensur) distinction
prägen ['prɛ:gən] vt to stamp; (Münze) to mint; (Ausdruck) to coin; (Charakter) to form
prägnant [prɛ'gnant] adj precise, terse
Prägung ['prɛ:gʊŋ] f minting; forming; (Eigenart) character, stamp
prahlen ['pra:lən] vi to boast, to brag; **Prahle'rei** f boasting
Praktik ['praktɪk] f practice; **p~abel** [-'ka:bəl] adj practicable; **~ant(in)** [-'kant(ɪn)] m(f) trainee; **~um** (-s, **Praktika** od **Praktiken**) nt practical training
praktisch ['praktɪʃ] adj practical, handy; **~er Arzt** general practitioner
praktizieren [praktɪ'tsi:rən] vt, vi to practise
Praline [pra'li:nə] f chocolate
prall [pral] adj firmly rounded; (Segel) taut; (Arme) plump; (Sonne) blazing; **~en** vi to bounce, to rebound; (Sonne) to blaze
Prämie ['prɛ:miə] f premium; (Belohnung) award, prize; **p~ren** vt to give an award to
Präparat [prepa'ra:t] (-(e)s, -e) nt (BIOL) preparation; (MED) medicine
Präposition [prepozitsi'o:n] f preposition
Prärie [prɛ'ri:] f prairie
Präsens ['prɛ:zɛns] (-) nt present tense
präsentieren [prɛzɛn'ti:rən] vt to present
Präservativ [prɛzɛrva'ti:f] (-s, -e) nt contraceptive
Präsident(in) [prɛzi'dɛnt(ɪn)] m(f) president; **~schaft** f presidency
Präsidium [prɛ'zi:diʊm] nt presidency, chair(manship); (Polizei~) police headquarters pl
prasseln ['prasəln] vi (Feuer) to crackle; (Hagel) to drum; (Wörter) to rain down
Praxis ['praksɪs] (-, **Praxen**) f practice; (Behandlungsraum) surgery; (von Anwalt) office
Präzedenzfall [prɛtse'dɛnts-] m precedent
präzis [prɛ'tsi:s] adj precise; **P~ion** [prɛtsizi'o:n] f precision
predigen ['pre:dɪgən] vt, vi to preach;

Prediger (-s, -) m preacher
Predigt ['pre:dɪçt] (-, -en) f sermon
Preis [praɪs] (-es, -e) m price; (Sieges~) prize; **um keinen ~** not at any price; **p~bewußt** △ adj price-conscious
Preiselbeere f cranberry
preis- ['praɪz] zW: **~en** (unreg) vi to praise; **~geben** (unreg) vt to abandon; (opfern) to sacrifice; (zeigen) to expose; **~gekrönt** adj prizewinning; **P~gericht** nt jury; **~günstig** adj inexpensive; **P~lage** f price range; **~lich** adj (Lage, Unterschied) price, in price; **P~liste** f price list; **P~richter** m judge (in a competition); **P~schild** nt price tag; **P~träger(in)** m(f) prizewinner; **~wert** adj inexpensive
Prell- [prɛl] zW: **~bock** m buffers pl; **p~en** vt to bump; (fig) to cheat, to swindle; **~ung** f bruise
Premiere [prəmi'e:rə] f premiere
Premierminister [prəmi'e:mɪnɪstər] m prime minister, premier
Presse ['prɛsə] f press; **~agentur** f press agency; **~freiheit** f freedom of the press; **p~n** vt to press
Preßluft △ ['prɛslʊft] f compressed air; **~bohrer** △ m pneumatic drill
Prestige [prɛs'ti:ʒə] (-s) nt prestige
prickeln ['prɪkəln] vt, vi to tingle; to tickle
Priester ['pri:stər] (-s, -) m priest
prima [pri:ma] adj inv first-class, excellent
primär [pri'mɛ:r] adj primary
Primel ['pri:məl] (-, -n) f primrose
primitiv [primi'ti:f] adj primitive
Prinz [prɪnts] (-en, -en) m prince; **~essin** f princess
Prinzip [prɪn'tsi:p] (-s, -ien) nt principle; **p~iell** [-i'ɛl] adj, adv on principle; **p~ienlos** adj unprincipled
Priorität [priori'tɛ:t] f priority
Prise ['pri:zə] f pinch
Prisma ['prɪsma] (-s, **Prismen**) nt prism
privat [pri'va:t] adj private; **P~besitz** m private property; **P~fernsehen** nt commercial television; **P~patient(in)** m(f) private patient; **P~schule** f public school
Privileg [privi'le:k] (-(e)s, -ien) nt privilege

△ For information on spelling reform see page 615

Pro [pro:] (-) *nt* pro
pro *präp +akk* per
Probe ['pro:bə] *f* test; (*Teststück*) sample; (*THEAT*) rehearsal; **jdn auf die ~ stellen** to put sb to the test; **~exemplar** *nt* specimen copy; **~fahrt** *f* test drive; **p~n** *vt* to try; (*THEAT*) to rehearse; **p~weise** *adv* on approval; **~zeit** *f* probation period
probieren [pro'bi:rən] *vt* to try; (*Wein, Speise*) to taste, to sample ♦ *vi* to try; to taste
Problem [pro'ble:m] (-s, -e) *nt* problem; **~atik** [-'ma:tɪk] *f* problem; **p~atisch** [-'ma:tɪʃ] *adj* problematic; **p~los** *adj* problem-free
Produkt [pro'dʊkt] (-(e)s, -e) *nt* product; (*AGR*) produce *no pl*; **~ion** [prodʊktsi'o:n] *f* production; output; **p~iv** [-'ti:f] *adj* productive; **~ivi'tät** *f* productivity
Produzent [produ'tsɛnt] *m* manufacturer; (*Film*) producer
produzieren [produ'tsi:rən] *vt* to produce
Professor [pro'fɛsɔr] *m* professor
Profi ['pro:fi] (-s, -s) *m* (*umg, SPORT*) pro
Profil [pro'fi:l] (-s, -e) *nt* profile; (*fig*) image
Profit [pro'fi:t] (-(e)s, -e) *m* profit; **p~ieren** *vi*: **p~ieren (von)** to profit (from)
Prognose [pro'gno:zə] *f* prediction, prognosis
Programm [pro'gram] (-s, -e) *nt* programme; (*COMPUT*) program; **p~ieren** [-'mi:rən] *vt* to programme; (*COMPUT*) to program; **~ierer(in)** (-s, -) *m(f)* programmer
progressiv [progrɛ'si:f] *adj* progressive
Projekt [pro'jɛkt] (-(e)s, -e) *nt* project; **~or** [pro'jɛktɔr] *m* projector
proklamieren [prokla'mi:rən] *vt* to proclaim
Prokurist(in) [proku'rɪst(ɪn)] *m(f)* ≈ company secretary
Prolet [pro'le:t] (-en, -en) *m* prole, pleb; **~arier** [-'ta:riər] (-s, -) *m* proletarian
Prolog [pro'lo:k] (-(e)s, -e) *m* prologue
Promenade [promə'na:də] *f* promenade
Promille [pro'mɪlə] (-(s), -) *nt* alcohol level
prominent [promi'nɛnt] *adj* prominent

Prominenz [promi'nɛnts] *f* VIPs *pl*
Promotion [promotsi'o:n] *f* doctorate, Ph.D.
promovieren [promo'vi:rən] *vi* to do a doctorate *od* Ph.D.
prompt [prɔmpt] *adj* prompt
Pronomen [pro'no:mɛn] (-s, -) *nt* pronoun
Propaganda [propa'ganda] (-) *f* propaganda
Propeller [pro'pɛlər] (-s, -) *m* propeller
Prophet [pro'fe:t] (-en, -en) *m* prophet
prophezeien [profe'tsaɪən] *vt* to prophesy; **Prophezeiung** *f* prophecy
Proportion [proportsi'o:n] *f* proportion; **p~al** [-'na:l] *adj* proportional
proportioniert [proportsio'ni:rt] *adj*: **gut/ schlecht ~** well-/badly-proportioned
Prosa ['pro:za] (-) *f* prose; **p~isch** [pro'za:ɪʃ] *adj* prosaic
prosit ['pro:zɪt] *excl* cheers
Prospekt [pro'spɛkt] (-(e)s, -e) *m* leaflet, brochure
prost [pro:st] *excl* cheers
Prostituierte [prostitu'i:rtə] *f* prostitute
Prostitution [prostitutsi'o:n] *f* prostitution
Protest [pro'tɛst] (-(e)s, -e) *m* protest; **~ant(in)** [protɛs'tant(ɪn)] *m(f)* Protestant; **p~antisch** [protɛs'tantɪʃ] *adj* Protestant; **p~ieren** [protɛs'ti:rən] *vi* to protest
Prothese [pro'te:zə] *f* artificial limb; (*Zahn~*) dentures *pl*
Protokoll [proto'kɔl] (-s, -e) *nt* register; (*von Sitzung*) minutes *pl*; (*diplomatisch*) protocol; (*Polizei~*) statement; **p~ieren** [-'li:rən] *vt* to take down in the minutes
protzen ['prɔtsən] *vi* to show off
Proviant [provi'ant] (-s, -e) *m* provisions *pl*, supplies *pl*
Provinz [pro'vɪnts] (-, -en) *f* province; **p~i'ell** *adj* provincial
Provision [provizi'o:n] *f* (*COMM*) commission
provisorisch [provi'zo:rɪʃ] *adj* provisional
Provokation [provokatsi'o:n] *f* provocation
provozieren [provo'tsi:rən] *vt* to provoke
Prozedur [protse'du:r] *f* procedure; (*pej*) carry-on

⚠ *Informationen zur Rechtschreibreform Seite 615*

Prozent [pro'tsɛnt] (-(e)s, -e) nt per cent, percentage; **~satz** m percentage; **p~ual** [-u'a:l] adj percentage cpd; as a percentage

Prozeß △ [pro'tsɛs] (-sses, -sse) m trial, case

Prozession [protsɛsi'o:n] f procession

prüde ['pry:də] adj prudish; **P~rie** [-'ri:] f prudery

Prüf- ['pry:f] zW: **p~en** vt to examine, to test; (nachprüfen) to check; **~er** (-s, -) m examiner; **~ling** m examinee; **~ung** f examination; checking; **~ungsausschuß** △ m examining board

Prügel ['pry:gəl] (-s, -) m cudgel ♦ pl (Schläge) beating; **~ei** f fight; **p~n** vt to beat ♦ vr to fight; **~strafe** f corporal punishment

Prunk [prʊŋk] (-(e)s) m pomp, show; **p~voll** adj splendid, magnificent

PS [pe:'ɛs] abk (= Pferdestärke) H.P.

Psych- ['psyç] zW: **~iater** [-i'a:tər] (-s, -) m psychiatrist; **p~iatrisch** adj (MED) psychiatric; **p~isch** adj psychological; **~oanalyse** [-o|ana'ly:zə] f psychoanalysis; **~ologe** (-n, -n) m psychologist; **~olo'gie** f psychology; **p~ologisch** adj psychological; **~otherapeut(in)** (-en, -en) m(f) psychotherapist

Pubertät [puber'tɛ:t] f puberty

Publikum ['pu:blikʊm] (-s) nt audience; (SPORT) crowd

publizieren [publi'tsi:rən] vt to publish, to publicize

Pudding ['pʊdɪŋ] (-s, -e od -s) m blancmange

Pudel ['pu:dəl] (-s) m poodle

Puder ['pu:dər] (-s, -) m powder; **~dose** f powder compact; **p~n** vt to powder; **~zucker** m icing sugar

Puff¹ [pʊf] (-s, -e) m (Wäsche~) linen basket; (Sitz~) pouf

Puff² [pʊf] (-s, ¨e) (umg) m (Stoß) push

Puff³ [pʊf] (-s, -) (umg) m od nt (Bordell) brothel

Puffer (-s, -) m buffer

Pullover [pʊ'lo:vər] (-s, -) m pullover, jumper

Puls [pʊls] (-es, -e) m pulse; **~ader** f artery; **p~ieren** vi to throb, to pulsate

Pult [pʊlt] (-(e)s, -e) nt desk

Pulver ['pʊlfər] (-s, -) nt powder; **p~ig** adj powdery; **~schnee** m powdery snow

pummelig ['pʊməlɪç] adj chubby

Pumpe ['pʊmpə] f pump; **p~n** vt to pump; (umg) to lend; to borrow

Punkt [pʊŋkt] (-(e)s, -e) m point; (bei Muster) dot; (Satzzeichen) full stop; **p~ieren** [-'ti:rən] vt to dot; (MED) to aspirate

pünktlich ['pʏŋktlɪç] adj punctual; **P~keit** f punctuality

Punktsieg m victory on points

Punktzahl f score

Punsch [pʊnʃ] (-(e)s, -e) m punch

Pupille [pu'pɪlə] f pupil

Puppe ['pʊpə] f doll; (Marionette) puppet; (Insekten~) pupa, chrysalis

Puppen- zW: **~spieler** m puppeteer; **~stube** f doll's house; **~theater** nt puppet theatre

pur [pu:r] adj pure; (völlig) sheer; (Whisky) neat

Püree [py're:] (-s, -s) nt mashed potatoes pl

Purzelbaum ['pʊrtsəlbaʊm] m somersault

purzeln ['pʊrtsəln] vi to tumble

Puste ['pu:stə] (-) (umg) f puff; (fig) steam; **p~n** vi to puff, to blow

Pute ['pu:tə] f turkey hen; **~r** (-s, -) m turkey cock

Putsch [pʊtʃ] (-(e)s, -e) m revolt, putsch

Putz [pʊts] (-es) m (Mörtel) plaster, roughcast

putzen vt to clean; (Nase) to wipe, to blow ♦ vr to clean o.s.; to dress o.s. up

Putz- zW: **~frau** f charwoman; **p~ig** adj quaint, funny; **~lappen** m cloth

Puzzle ['pasəl] (-s, -s) nt jigsaw

PVC nt abk PVC

Pyjama [pi'dʒa:ma] (-s, -s) m pyjamas pl

Pyramide [pyra'mi:də] f pyramid

Pyrenäen [pyre'nɛ:ən] pl Pyrenees

△ For information on spelling reform see page 615

Q, q

Quacksalber ['kvakzalbər] (**-s**, **-**) *m* quack (doctor)

Quader ['kva:dər] (**-s**, **-**) *m* square stone; (*MATH*) cuboid

Quadrat [kva'dra:t] (**-(e)s**, **-e**) *nt* square; **q~isch** *adj* square; **~meter** *m* square metre

quaken ['kva:kən] *vi* to croak; (*Ente*) to quack

quäken ['kvɛ:kən] *vi* to screech

Qual [kva:l] (**-**, **-en**) *f* pain, agony; (*seelisch*) anguish

quälen ['kvɛ:lən] *vt* to torment ♦ *vr* to struggle; (*geistig*) to torment o.s.

Quälerei [kvɛ:lə'raɪ] *f* torture, torment

Qualifikation [kvalifikatsi'o:n] *f* qualification

qualifizieren [kvalifi'tsi:rən] *vt* to qualify; (*einstufen*) to label ♦ *vr* to qualify

Qualität [kvali'tɛ:t] *f* quality; **~sware** *f* article of high quality

Qualle ['kvalə] *f* jellyfish

Qualm [kvalm] (**-(e)s**) *m* thick smoke; **q~en** *vt*, *vi* to smoke

qualvoll ['kva:lfɔl] *adj* excruciating, painful, agonizing

Quant- ['kvant] *zW*: **~ität** [-i'tɛ:t] *f* quantity; **q~itativ** [-ita'ti:f] *adj* quantitative; **~um** (**-s**) *nt* quantity, amount

Quarantäne [karan'tɛ:nə] *f* quarantine

Quark [kvark] (**-s**) *m* curd cheese

Quartal [kvar'ta:l] (**-s**, **-e**) *nt* quarter (year)

Quartier [kvar'ti:r] (**-s**, **-e**) *nt* accommodation; (*MIL*) quarters *pl*; (*Stadt~*) district

Quarz [kva:rts] (**-es**, **-e**) *m* quartz

quasseln ['kvasəln] (*umg*) *vi* to natter

Quatsch [kvatʃ] (**-es**) *m* rubbish; **q~en** *vi* to chat, to natter

Quecksilber ['kvɛkzɪlbər] *nt* mercury

Quelle ['kvɛlə] *f* spring; (*eines Flusses*) source; **q~n** (*unreg*) *vi* (*hervorquellen*) to pour *od* gush forth; (*schwellen*) to swell

quer [kve:r] *adv* crossways, diagonally; (*rechtwinklig*) at right angles; **~ auf dem Bett** across the bed; **Q~flöte** *f* flute; **Q~format** *nt* (*PHOT*) oblong format; **Q~schnitt** *m* cross-section; **~schnittsgelähmt** *adj* paralysed below the waist; **Q~straße** *f* intersecting road

quetschen ['kvɛtʃən] *vt* to squash, to crush; (*MED*) to bruise

Quetschung *f* bruise, contusion

quieken ['kvi:kən] *vi* to squeak

quietschen ['kvi:tʃən] *vi* to squeak

Quintessenz ['kvɪntɛsɛnts] *f* quintessence

Quirl [kvɪrl] (**-(e)s**, **-e**) *m* whisk

quitt [kvɪt] *adj* quits, even

Quitte *f* quince

quittieren [kvɪ'ti:rən] *vt* to give a receipt for; (*Dienst*) to leave

Quittung *f* receipt

Quiz [kvɪs] (**-**, **-**) *nt* quiz

quoll *etc* [kvɔl] *vb siehe* **quellen**

Quote ['kvo:tə] *f* number, rate

R, r

Rabatt [ra'bat] (**-(e)s**, **-e**) *m* discount

Rabattmarke *f* trading stamp

Rabe ['ra:bə] (**-n**, **-n**) *m* raven

rabiat [rabi'a:t] *adj* furious

Rache ['raxə] (**-**) *f* revenge, vengeance

Rachen (**-s**, **-**) *m* throat

rächen ['rɛçən] *vt* to avenge, to revenge ♦ *vr* to take (one's) revenge; **das wird sich ~** you'll pay for that

Rad [ra:t] (**-(e)s**, **-er**) *nt* wheel; (*Fahr~*) bike

Radar ['ra:da:r] (**-s**) *m od nt* radar; **~falle** *f* speed trap; **~kontrolle** *f* radar-controlled speed trap

Radau [ra'dau] (**-s**) (*umg*) *m* row

radeln ['ra:dəln] (*umg*) *vi* to cycle

radfahr- *zW*: **~en** ⚠ (*unreg*) *vi* to cycle; **R~er(in)** *m(f)* cyclist; **R~weg** *m* cycle track *od* path

Radier- [ra'di:r] *zW*: **~en** *vt* to rub out, to erase; (*KUNST*) to etch; **~gummi** *m* rubber, eraser; **~ung** *f* etching

⚠ *Informationen zur Rechtschreibreform Seite 615*

Radieschen [ra'di:sçən] *nt* radish

radikal [radi'ka:l] *adj* radical

Radio ['ra:dio] (**-s, -s**) *nt* radio, wireless; **r~ak'tiv** *adj* radioactive; **~aktivi'tät** *f* radioactivity; **~apparat** *m* radio, wireless set

Radius ['ra:diʊs] (**-, Radien**) *m* radius

Rad- *zW*: **~kappe** *f* (AUT) hub cap; **~ler(in)** (*umg*) *m(f)* cyclist; **~rennen** *nt* cycle race; cycle racing; **~sport** *m* cycling; **~weg** *m* cycleway

raffen ['rafən] *vt* to snatch, to pick up; (*Stoff*) to gather (up); (*Geld*) to pile up, to rake in

raffi'niert *adj* crafty, cunning

ragen ['ra:gən] *vi* to tower, to rise

Rahm [ra:m] (**-s**) *m* cream

Rahmen (**-s, -**) *m* frame(work); **im ~ des Möglichen** within the bounds of possibility; **r~** *vt* to frame

Rakete [ra'ke:tə] *f* rocket; **~nstützpunkt** *m* missile base

rammen ['ramən] *vt* to ram

Rampe ['rampə] *f* ramp; **~nlicht** *nt* (THEAT) footlights *pl*

ramponieren [rampo'ni:rən] (*umg*) *vt* to damage

Ramsch [ramʃ] (**-(e)s, -e**) *m* junk

ran [ran] (*umg*) *adv* = **heran**

Rand [rant] (**-(e)s, ̈er**) *m* edge; (*von Brille, Tasse etc*) rim; (*Hut~*) brim; (*auf Papier*) margin; (*Schmutz~, unter Augen*) ring; (*fig*) verge, brink; **außer ~ und Band** wild; **am ~e bemerkt** mentioned in passing

randalieren [randa'li:rən] *vi* to (go on the) rampage

Rang [raŋ] (**-(e)s, ̈e**) *m* rank; (*Stand*) standing; (*Wert*) quality; (THEAT) circle

Rangier- [rãʒi:r] *zW*: **~bahnhof** *m* marshalling yard; **r~en** *vt* (EISENB) to shunt, to switch (*US*) ♦ *vi* to rank, to be classed; **~gleis** *nt* siding

Ranke ['raŋkə] *f* tendril, shoot

ranzig ['rantsɪç] *adj* rancid

Rappen ['rapən] *m* (FIN) rappen, centime

rar [ra:r] *adj* rare; **sich ~ machen** (*umg*) to keep o.s. to o.s.; **R~i'tät** *f* rarity

(*Sammelobjekt*) curio

rasant [ra'zant] *adj* quick, rapid

rasch [raʃ] *adj* quick

rascheln *vi* to rustle

Rasen ['ra:zən] (**-s, -**) *m* lawn; grass

rasen *vi* to rave; (*schnell*) to race; **~d** *adj* furious; **~de Kopfschmerzen** a splitting headache

Rasenmäher (**-s, -**) *m* lawnmower

Rasier- [ra'zi:r] *zW*: **~apparat** *m* shaver; **~creme** *f* shaving cream; **r~en** *vt*, *vr* to shave; **~klinge** *f* razor blade; **~messer** *nt* razor; **~pinsel** *m* shaving brush; **~schaum** *m* shaving foam; **~seife** *f* shaving soap *od* stick; **~wasser** *nt* shaving lotion

Rasse ['rasə] *f* race; (*Tier~*) breed; **~hund** *m* thoroughbred dog

rasseln ['rasəln] *vi* to clatter

Rassen- *zW*: **~haß** △ *m* race *od* racial hatred; **~trennung** *f* racial segregation

Rassismus [ra'sɪsmʊs] *m* racism

Rast [rast] (**-, -en**) *f* rest; **r~en** *vi* to rest; **~hof** *m* (AUT) service station; **r~los** *adj* tireless; (*unruhig*) restless; **~platz** *m* (AUT) layby; **~stätte** *f* (AUT) service station

Rasur [ra'zu:r] *f* shaving

Rat [ra:t] (**-(e)s, -schläge**) *m* advice *no pl*; **ein ~** a piece of advice; **jdn zu ~e ziehen** to consult sb; **keinen ~ wissen** not to know what to do

Rate *f* instalment

raten (*unreg*) *vt*, *vi* to guess; (*empfehlen*): **jdm ~** to advise sb

Ratenzahlung *f* hire purchase

Ratgeber (**-s, -**) *m* adviser

Rathaus *nt* town hall

ratifizieren [ratifi'tsi:rən] *vt* to ratify

Ration [ratsi'o:n] *f* ration; **r~al** [-'na:l] *adj* rational; **r~ali'sieren** *vt* to rationalize; **r~ell** [-'nɛl] *adj* efficient; **r~ieren** [-'ni:rən] *vt* to ration

Rat- *zW*: **r~los** *adj* at a loss, helpless; **r~sam** *adj* advisable; **~schlag** *m* (piece of) advice

Rätsel ['rɛ:tsəl] (**-s, -**) *nt* puzzle; (*Wort~*) riddle; **r~haft** *adj* mysterious; **es ist mir r~haft** it's a mystery to me

△ *For information on spelling reform see page 615*

Ratte ['ratə] f rat; **~nfänger** (-s, -) m ratcatcher

rattern ['ratərn] vi to rattle, to clatter

Raub [raop] (-(e)s) m robbery; (*Beute*) loot, booty; **~bau** m ruthless exploitation; **r~en** ['raobən] vt to rob; (*Mensch*) to kidnap, to abduct

Räuber ['rɔybər] (-s, -) m robber

Raub- zW: **~mord** m robbery with murder; **~tier** nt predator; **~überfall** m robbery with violence; **~vogel** m bird of prey

Rauch [raox] (-(e)s) m smoke; **r~en** vt, vi to smoke; **~er(in)** (-s, -) m(f) smoker; **~erabteil** nt (*EISENB*) smoker; **räuchern** vt to smoke, to cure; **~fleisch** nt smoked meat; **r~ig** adj smoky

rauf [raof] (*umg*) adv = **herauf; hinauf**

raufen vt (*Haare*) to pull out ♦ vi, vr to fight; **Raufe'rei** f brawl, fight

rauh △ [rao] adj rough, coarse; (*Wetter*) harsh; **R~reif** △ m hoarfrost

Raum [raom] (-(e)s, **Räume**) m space; (*Zimmer, Platz*) room; (*Gebiet*) area

räumen ['rɔymən] vt to clear; (*Wohnung, Platz*) to vacate; (*wegbringen*) to shift, to move; (*in Schrank etc*) to put away

Raum- zW: **~fähre** f space shuttle; **~fahrt** f space travel; **~inhalt** m cubic capacity, volume

räumlich ['rɔymlıç] adj spatial; **R~keiten** pl premises

Raum- zW: **~pflegerin** f cleaner; **~schiff** nt spaceship; **~schiffahrt** △ f space travel

Räumung ['rɔymoŋ] f vacating, evacuation; clearing (away)

Räumungs- zW: **~arbeiten** pl clearance operations; **~verkauf** m clearance sale; (*bei Geschäftsaufgabe*) closing down sale

raunen ['raonən] vt, vi to whisper

Raupe ['raopə] f caterpillar; (*Raupenkette*) (caterpillar) track

raus [raos] (*umg*) adv = **heraus; hinaus**

Rausch [raoʃ] (-(e)s, **Räusche**) m intoxication

rauschen vi (*Wasser*) to rush; (*Baum*) to rustle; (*Radio etc*) to hiss; (*Mensch*) to sweep, to sail; **~d** adj (*Beifall*) thunderous;

(*Fest*) sumptuous

Rauschgift nt drug; **~süchtige(r)** f(m) drug addict

räuspern ['rɔyspərn] vr to clear one's throat

Razzia ['ratsia] (-, **Razzien**) f raid

Reagenzglas [rea'gentsglaːs] nt test tube

reagieren [rea'giːrən] vi: **~ (auf** +*akk*) to react (to)

Reakt- zW: **~ion** [reaktsi'oːn] f reaction; **r~io'när** adj reactionary; **~or** [re'aktɔr] m reactor

real [re'aːl] adj real, material

reali'sieren vt (*verwirklichen: Pläne*) to carry out

Realismus [rea'lısmos] m realism

rea'listisch adj realistic

Realschule f secondary school

REALSCHULE
---

i The **Realschule** is one of the secondary schools a German schoolchild may attend after the **Grundschule**. On the successful completion of six years of schooling in the **Realschule** pupils gain the **mittlere Reife** and usually go on to vocational training or further education.

Rebe ['reːbə] f vine

rebellieren [rebe'liːrən] vi to rebel; **Rebelli'on** f rebellion; **re'bellisch** adj rebellious

Rebhuhn ['rɛphuːn] nt (*KOCH, ZOOL*) partridge

Rechen ['rɛçən] (-s, -) m rake

Rechen- zW: **~fehler** m miscalculation; **~maschine** f calculating machine; **~schaft** f account; **für etw ~schaft ablegen** to account for sth; **~schieber** m slide rule

Rech- ['rɛç] zW: **r~nen** vt, vi to calculate; **jdn/etw r~nen zu** to count sb/sth among; **r~nen mit** to reckon with; **r~nen auf** +*akk* to count on; **~nen** nt arithmetic; **~ner** (-s, -) m calculator; (*COMPUT*) computer; **~nung** f calculation(s); (*COMM*) bill, check (*US*); **jdm/etw ~nung tragen** to take sb/sth into account; **~nungsbetrag** m total amount

△ *Informationen zur Rechtschreibreform Seite 615*

of a bill/invoice); **~nungsjahr** nt financial year; **~nungsprüfer** m auditor

Recht [rɛçt] (**-(e)s, -e**) nt right; (JUR) law; **mit ~** rightly, justly; **von ~s wegen** by rights

recht adj right ♦ adv (vor Adjektiv) really, quite; **das ist mir ~** that suits me; **jetzt erst ~** now more than ever; **~ haben** to be right; **jdm ~ geben** to agree with sb

Rechte f right (hand); (POL) Right; **r~(r, s)** adj right; (POL) right-wing; **ein ~r** a right-winger; **~(s)** nt right thing; **etwas/nichts ~s** something/nothing proper

recht- zW: **~eckig** adj rectangular; **~fertigen** vt insep to justify ♦ vr insep to justify o.s.; **R~fertigung** f justification; **~haberisch** (pej) adj (Mensch) opinionated; **~lich** adj (gesetzlich: Gleichstellung, Anspruch) legal; **~los** adj with no rights; **~mäßig** adj legal, lawful

rechts [rɛçts] adv on/to the right; **R~anwalt** m lawyer, barrister; **R~anwältin** f lawyer, barrister

Rechtschreibung f spelling

Rechts- zW: **~fall** m (law) case; **~händer** (**-s, -**) m right-handed person; **r~kräftig** adj valid, legal; **~kurve** f right-hand bend; **r~verbindlich** adj legally binding; **~verkehr** m driving on the right; **r~widrig** adj illegal; **~wissenschaft** f jurisprudence

rechtwinklig adj right-angled

rechtzeitig adj timely ♦ adv in time

Reck [rɛk] (**-(e)s, -e**) nt horizontal bar; **r~en** vt, vr to stretch

recyceln [riːˈsaɪkəln] vt to recycle; **Recycling** [riːˈsaɪklɪŋ] (**-s**) nt recycling

Redakteur [redakˈtøːr] m editor

Redaktion [redakˈtsɪoːn] f editing; (Leute) editorial staff; (Büro) editorial office(s)

Rede [ˈreːdə] f speech; (Gespräch) talk; **jdn zur ~ stellen** to take sb to task; **~freiheit** f freedom of speech; **r~gewandt** adj eloquent; **r~n** vi to talk, to speak ♦ vt to say; (Unsinn etc) to talk; **~nsart** f set phrase

redlich [ˈreːtlɪç] adj honest

Redner (**-s, -**) m speaker, orator

redselig [ˈreːtzeːlɪç] adj talkative, loquacious

reduzieren [reduˈtsiːrən] vt to reduce

Reede [ˈreːdə] f protected anchorage; **~r** (**-s, -**) m shipowner; **~'rei** f shipping line od firm

reell [reˈɛl] adj fair, honest; (MATH) real

Refer- zW: **~at** [refeˈraːt] (**-(e)s, -e**) nt report; (Vortrag) paper; (Gebiet) section; **~ent** [refeˈrɛnt] m speaker; (Berichterstatter) reporter; (Sachbearbeiter) expert; **r~ieren** [refeˈriːrən] vi: **r~ieren über** +akk to speak od talk on

reflektieren [reflɛkˈtiːrən] vt (Licht) to reflect

Reflex [reˈflɛks] (**-es, -e**) m reflex; **r~iv** [-ˈksiːf] adj (GRAM) reflexive

Reform [reˈfɔrm] (**-, -en**) f reform; **~ati'on** f reformation; **~ationstag** m Reformation Day; **~haus** nt health food shop; **r~ieren** [-ˈmiːrən] vt to reform

Regal [reˈɡaːl] (**-s, -e**) nt (book)shelves pl, bookcase; stand, rack

rege [ˈreːɡə] adj (lebhaft: Treiben) lively; (wach, lebendig: Geist) keen

Regel [ˈreːɡəl] (**-, -n**) f rule; (MED) period; **r~mäßig** adj regular; **~mäßigkeit** f regularity; **r~n** vt to regulate, to control; (Angelegenheit) to settle ♦ vr: **sich von selbst r~n** to take care of itself; **r~recht** adj regular, proper, thorough; **~ung** f regulation; settlement; **r~widrig** adj irregular, against the rules

Regen [ˈreːɡən] (**-s, -**) m rain; **~bogen** m rainbow; **~bogenpresse** f tabloids pl

regenerierbar [regeneˈriːrbaːr] adj renewable

Regen- zW: **~mantel** m raincoat, mac(kintosh); **~schauer** m shower (of rain); **~schirm** m umbrella; **~wald** m (GEOG) rainforest; **~wurm** m earthworm; **~zeit** f rainy season

Regie [reˈʒiː] f (Film etc) direction; (THEAT) production

Regier- [reˈɡiːr] zW: **r~en** vt, vi to govern, to rule; **~ung** f government; (Monarchie) reign; **~ungssitz** m seat of government; **~ungswechsel** m change of government;

⚠ For information on spelling reform see page 615

~**ungszeit** f period in government; (*von König*) reign

Regiment [regi'mɛnt] (-**s, -er**) nt regiment

Region [regi'oːn] f region

Regisseur [reʒɪˈsøːr] m director; (*THEAT*) (stage) producer

Register [re'gɪstər] (-**s, -**) nt register; (*in Buch*) table of contents, index

registrieren [regɪs'triːrən] vt to register

Regler ['reːglər] (-**s, -**) m regulator, governor

reglos ['reːkloːs] adj motionless

regnen ['reːgnən] vt unpers to rain

regnerisch adj rainy

regulär [regu'lɛːr] adj regular

regulieren [regu'liːrən] vt to regulate; (*COMM*) to settle

Regung ['reːgʊŋ] f motion; (*Gefühl*) feeling, impulse; r~**slos** adj motionless

Reh [reː] (-**(e)s, -e**) nt deer, roe; ~**bock** m roebuck; ~**kitz** nt fawn

Reib- ['raib] *zW:* ~**e** f grater; ~**eisen** nt grater; r~**en** (*unreg*) vt to rub; (*KOCH*) to grate; ~**fläche** f rough surface; ~**ung** f friction; r~**ungslos** adj smooth

Reich (-**(e)s, -e**) nt empire, kingdom; (*fig*) realm; **das Dritte** ~ the Third Reich

reich [raɪç] adj rich

reichen vi to reach; (*genügen*) to be enough *od* sufficient ♦ vt to hold out; (*geben*) to pass, to hand; (*anbieten*) to offer; **jdm** ~ to be enough *od* sufficient for sb

reich- *zW:* ~**haltig** adj ample, rich; ~**lich** adj ample, plenty of; R~**tum** (-**s**) m wealth; R~**weite** f range

Reif (-**(e)s, -e**) m (*Ring*) ring, hoop

reif [raɪf] adj ripe; (*Mensch, Urteil*) mature

Reife (-) f ripeness; maturity; r~**n** vi to mature; to ripen

Reifen (-**s, -**) m ring, hoop; (*Fahrzeug~*) tyre; ~**druck** m tyre pressure; ~**panne** f puncture

Reihe ['raɪə] f row; (*von Tagen etc, umg: Anzahl*) series *sg*; **der** ~ **nach** in turn; **er ist an der** ~ it's his turn; **an die** ~ **kommen** to have one's turn

Reihen- *zW:* ~**folge** f sequence;

alphabetische ~**folge** alphabetical order; ~**haus** nt terraced house

reihum [raɪˈʔʊm] adv: **es geht/wir machen das** ~ we take turns

Reim [raɪm] (-**(e)s, -e**) m rhyme; r~**en** vt to rhyme

rein[1] [raɪn] (*umg*) adv = **herein; hinein**

rein[2] [raɪn] adj pure; (*sauber*) clean ♦ adv purely; **etw ins** ~**e schreiben** to make a fair copy of sth; **etw ins** ~**e bringen** to clear up sth; R~**fall** (*umg*) m let-down; R~**gewinn** m net profit; R~**heit** f purity; cleanness; ~**igen** vt to clean; (*Wasser*) to purify; R~**igung** f cleaning; purification; (*Geschäft*) cleaner's; **chemische R~igung** dry cleaning; dry cleaner's; R~**igungsmittel** nt cleansing agent; ~**rassig** adj pedigree; R~**schrift** f fair copy

Reis [raɪs] (-**es, -e**) m rice

Reise ['raɪzə] f journey; (*Schiffs~*) voyage; ~**n** pl (*Herumreisen*) travels; **gute** ~! have a good journey; ~**apotheke** f first-aid kit; ~**büro** nt travel agency; r~**fertig** adj ready to start; ~**führer** m guide(book); (*Mensch*) travel guide; ~**gepäck** nt luggage; ~**gesellschaft** f party of travellers; ~**kosten** pl travelling expenses; ~**leiter** m courier; ~**lektüre** f reading matter for the journey; r~**n** vi to travel; r~**n nach** to go to; ~**nde(r)** f(m) traveller; ~**paß** ⚠ m passport; ~**proviant** m food and drink for the journey; ~**route** f route, itinerary; ~**ruf** m personal message; ~**scheck** m traveller's cheque; ~**veranstalter** m tour operator; ~**versicherung** f travel insurance; ~**ziel** nt destination

Reißbrett nt drawing board

reißen ['raɪsən] (*unreg*) vt to tear; (*ziehen*) to pull, to drag; (*Witz*) to crack ♦ vi to tear; to pull, to drag; **etw an sich** ~ to snatch sth up; (*fig*) to take over sth; **sich um etw** ~ to scramble for sth; ~**d** adj (*Fluß*) raging; (*WIRTS: Verkauf*) rapid

Reiß- *zW:* ~**verschluß** ⚠ m zip(per), zip fastener; ~**zwecke** m drawing pin (*BRIT*), thumbtack (*US*)

⚠ *Informationen zur Rechtschreibreform Seite 615*

Reit- ['raɪt] *zW*: **r~en** (*unreg*) *vt, vi* to ride; **~er (-s, -)** *m* rider; (*MIL*) cavalryman, trooper; **~erin** *f* rider; **~hose** *f* riding breeches *pl*; **~pferd** *nt* saddle horse; **~stiefel** *m* riding boot; **~weg** *n* bridle path; **~zeug** *nt* riding outfit

Reiz [raɪts] **(-es, -e)** *m* stimulus; (*angenehm*) charm; (*Verlockung*) attraction; **r~bar** *adj* irritable; **~barkeit** *f* irritability; **r~en** *vt* to stimulate; (*unangenehm*) to irritate; (*verlocken*) to appeal to, to attract; **r~end** *adj* charming; **r~voll** *adj* attractive

rekeln ['re:kəln] *vr* to stretch out; (*lümmeln*) to lounge *od* loll about

Reklamation [reklamatsi'o:n] *f* complaint

Reklame [re'kla:mə] *f* advertising; advertisement; **~ machen für etw** to advertise sth

rekonstruieren [rekɔnstru'i:rən] *vt* to reconstruct

Rekord [re'kɔrt] **(-(e)s, -e)** *m* record; **~leistung** *f* record performance

Rektor ['rɛktɔr] *m* (*UNIV*) rector, vice-chancellor; (*SCH*) headteacher (*BRIT*), principal (*US*); **~at** [-'ra:t] **(-(e)s, -e)** *nt* rectorate, vice-chancellorship; headship; (*Zimmer*) rector's *etc* office

Relais [rə'lɛ:] **(-, -)** *nt* relay

relativ [rela'ti:f] *adj* relative; **R~ität** [relativi'tɛ:t] *f* relativity

relevant [rele'vant] *adj* relevant

Relief [reli'ɛf] **(-s, -s)** *nt* relief

Religion [religi'o:n] *f* religion

religiös [religi'ø:s] *adj* religious

Reling ['re:lɪŋ] **(-, -s)** *f* (*NAUT*) rail

Remoulade [remu'la:də] *f* remoulade

Rendezvous [rãde'vu:] **(-, -)** *nt* rendezvous

Renn- ['rɛn] *zW*: **~bahn** *f* racecourse; (*AUT*) circuit, race track; **r~en** (*unreg*) *vt, vi* to run, to race; **~en (-s, -)** *nt* running; (*Wettbewerb*) race; **~fahrer** *m* racing driver; **~pferd** *nt* racehorse; **~wagen** *m* racing car

renommiert [renɔ'mi:rt] *adj* renowned

renovieren [reno'vi:rən] *vt* to renovate; **Renovierung** *f* renovation

rentabel [rɛn'ta:bəl] *adj* profitable, lucrative

Rentabilität [rɛntabili'tɛ:t] *f* profitability

Rente ['rɛntə] *f* pension

Rentenversicherung *f* pension scheme

rentieren [rɛn'ti:rən] *vr* to pay, to be profitable

Rentner(in) ['rɛntnər(ɪn)] **(-s, -)** *m(f)* pensioner

Reparatur [repara'tu:r] *f* repairing; repair; **~werkstatt** *f* repair shop; (*AUT*) garage

reparieren [repa'ri:rən] *vt* to repair

Reportage [repɔr'ta:ʒə] *f* (on-the-spot) report; (*TV, RAD*) live commentary *od* coverage

Reporter [re'pɔrtər] **(-s, -)** *m* reporter, commentator

repräsentativ [reprɛzɛnta'ti:f] *adj* (*stellvertretend, typisch: Menge, Gruppe*) representative; (*beeindruckend: Haus, Auto etc*) impressive

repräsentieren [reprɛzɛn'ti:rən] *vt* (*Staat, Firma*) to represent; (*darstellen: Wert*) to constitute ♦ *vi* (*gesellschaftlich*) to perform official duties

Repressalie [reprɛ'sa:liə] *f* reprisal

Reprivatisierung [reprivati'zi:rʊŋ] *f* denationalization

Reproduktion [reprodʊktsi'o:n] *f* reproduction

reproduzieren [reprodu'tsi:rən] *vt* to reproduce

Reptil [rɛp'ti:l] **(-s, -ien)** *nt* reptile

Republik [repu'bli:k] *f* republic; **r~anisch** *adj* republican

Reservat [rezɛr'va:t] **(-(e)s, -e)** *nt* reservation

Reserve [re'zɛrvə] *f* reserve; **~rad** *nt* (*AUT*) spare wheel; **~spieler** *m* reserve; **~tank** *m* reserve tank

reservieren [rezɛr'vi:rən] *vt* to reserve

Reservoir [rezɛrvo'a:r] **(-s, -e)** *nt* reservoir

Residenz [rezi'dɛnts] *f* residence, seat

resignieren [rezi'gni:rən] *vi* to resign

resolut [rezo'lu:t] *adj* resolute

Resonanz [rezo'nants] *f* resonance; (*fig*) response

Resozialisierung [rezotsiali'zi:rʊŋ] *f* rehabilitation

⚠ *For information on spelling reform see page 615*

Respekt [re'ʃpɛkt] **(-(e)s)** *m* respect;
r~ieren [-'tiːrən] *vt* to respect; **r~los** *adj*
disrespectful; **r~voll** *adj* respectful
Ressort [re'soːr] **(-s, -s)** *nt* department
Rest [rɛst] **(-(e)s, -e)** *m* remainder, rest;
(Über~) remains *pl*
Restaurant [rɛsto'rãː] **(-s, -s)** *nt* restaurant
restaurieren [rɛstau'riːrən] *vt* to restore
Rest- *zW:* **~betrag** *m* remainder,
outstanding sum; **r~lich** *adj* remaining;
r~los *adj* complete
Resultat [rezɔl'taːt] **(-(e)s, -e)** *nt* result
Retorte [re'tɔrtə] *f* retort
Retouren [re'tuːrən] *pl* (COMM) returns
retten ['rɛtən] *vt* to save, to rescue
Retter(in) *m(f)* rescuer
Rettich ['rɛtɪç] **(-s, -e)** *m* radish
Rettung *f* rescue; *(Hilfe)* help; **seine letzte
~** his last hope
Rettungs- *zW:* **~boot** *nt* lifeboat; **~dienst**
m rescue service; **r~los** *adj* hopeless; **~ring**
m lifebelt, life preserver *(US)*; **~wagen** *m*
ambulance
retuschieren [retu'ʃiːrən] *vt* (PHOT) to
retouch
Reue ['rɔyə] **(-)** *f* remorse; *(Bedauern)* regret;
r~n *vt:* **es reut ihn** he regrets (it) *od* is
sorry (about it)
Revanche [re'vãːʃə] *f* revenge; *(SPORT)*
return match
revanchieren [revã'ʃiːrən] *vr* (sich rächen)
to get one's own back, to have one's
revenge; *(erwidern)* to reciprocate, to return
the compliment
Revier [re'viːr] **(-s, -e)** *nt* district; *(Jagd~)*
preserve; *(Polizei~)* police station; beat
Revolte [re'vɔltə] *f* revolt
revol'tieren *vi* (gegen jdn/etw) to rebel
Revolution [revolutsi'oːn] *f* revolution; **~är**
[-'nɛːr] **(-s, -e)** *m* revolutionary; **r~ieren**
[-'niːrən] *vt* to revolutionize
Rezept [re'tsɛpt] **(-(e)s, -e)** *nt* recipe; *(MED)*
prescription; **r~frei** *adj* available without
prescription; **~ion** *f* reception; **r~pflichtig**
adj available only on prescription
R-Gespräch ['ɛrɡəʃprɛːç] *nt* reverse charge
call *(BRIT)*, collect call *(US)*

Rhabarber [ra'barbər] **(-s)** *m* rhubarb
Rhein [raɪn] **(-s)** *m* Rhine; **r~isch** *adj*
Rhenish
Rheinland-Pfalz *nt* (GEOG) Rheinland-
Pfalz, Rhineland-Palatinate
Rhesusfaktor ['reːzusfaktɔr] *m* rhesus
factor
rhetorisch [re'toːrɪʃ] *adj* rhetorical
Rheuma ['rɔyma] **(-s)** *nt* rheumatism;
r~tisch [-'maːtɪʃ] *adj* rheumatic
rhythmisch ['rytmɪʃ] *adj* rhythmical
Rhythmus ['rytmus] *m* rhythm
richt- ['rɪçt] *zW:* **~en** *vt* to direct; *(Waffe)* to
aim; *(einstellen)* to adjust; *(instandsetzen)* to
repair; *(zurechtmachen)* to prepare;
(bestrafen) to pass judgement on ♦ *vr:* **sich
~en nach** to go by; **~en an** *+akk* to direct
at; *(fig)* to direct to; **~en auf** *+akk* to aim
at; **R~er(in)** **(-s, -)** *m(f)* judge; **~erlich** *adj*
judicial; **R~geschwindigkeit** *f*
recommended speed
richtig *adj* right, correct; *(echt)* proper ♦ *adv*
(umg: sehr) really; **bin ich hier ~?** am I in
the right place?; **der/die R~e** the right
one/person; **das R~e** the right thing;
R~keit *f* correctness; **~stellen** ⚠ *vt* to
correct
Richt- *zW:* **~linie** *f* guideline; **~preis** *m*
recommended price
Richtung *f* direction; tendency, orientation
rieb *etc* [riːp] *vb siehe* **reiben**
riechen ['riːçən] *(unreg)* *vt, vi* to smell; **an
etw** *dat* **~** to smell sth; **nach etw ~** to
smell of sth; **ich kann das/ihn nicht ~**
(umg) I can't stand it/him
rief *etc* [riːf] *vb siehe* **rufen**
Riegel ['riːɡəl] **(-s, -)** *m* bolt; *(Schokolade
usw)* bar
Riemen ['riːmən] **(-s, -)** *m* strap; *(Gürtel,
TECH)* belt; *(NAUT)* oar
Riese ['riːzə] **(-n, -n)** *m* giant
rieseln *vi* to trickle; *(Schnee)* to fall gently
Riesen- *zW:* **~erfolg** *m* enormous success;
r~groß *adj* colossal, gigantic, huge; **~rad**
nt big wheel
riesig ['riːzɪç] *adj* enormous, huge, vast
riet *etc* [riːt] *vb siehe* **raten**

⚠ *Informationen zur Rechtschreibreform Seite 615*

Riff [rɪf] (-(e)s, -e) nt reef

Rille ['rɪlə] f groove

Rind [rɪnt] (-(e)s, -er) nt ox; cow; cattle pl; (KOCH) beef

Rinde ['rɪndə] f rind; (Baum~) bark; (Brot~) crust

Rind- ['rɪnt] zW: ~**fleisch** nt beef; ~**vieh** nt cattle pl; (umg) blockhead, stupid oaf

Ring [rɪŋ] (-(e)s, -e) m ring; ~**buch** nt ring binder; **r~en** (unreg) vi to wrestle; ~**en** (-s) nt wrestling; ~**finger** m ring finger; ~**kampf** m wrestling bout; ~**richter** m referee; **r~s** adv: **r~s um** round; **r~sherum** adv round about; ~**straße** f ring road; **r~sum** adv (rundherum) round about; (überall) all round; **r~sumher** = **ringsum**

Rinn- ['rɪn] zW: ~**e** f gutter, drain; **r~en** (unreg) vi to run, to trickle; ~**stein** m gutter

Rippchen ['rɪpçən] nt small rib; cutlet

Rippe ['rɪpə] f rib

Risiko ['riːziko] (-s, -s od **Risiken**) nt risk

riskant [rɪs'kant] adj risky, hazardous

riskieren [rɪs'kiːrən] vt to risk

Riß ⚠ [rɪs] (-sses, -sse) m tear; (in Mauer, Tasse etc) crack; (in Haut) scratch; (TECH) design

rissig ['rɪsɪç] adj torn; cracked; scratched

Ritt [rɪt] (-(e)s, -e) m ride

ritt etc vb siehe **reiten**

Ritter (-s, -) m knight; **r~lich** adj chivalrous

Ritze ['rɪtsə] f crack, chink

Rivale [ri'vaːlə] (-n, -n) m rival

Rivalität [rivali'tɛːt] f rivalry

Robbe ['rɔbə] f seal

Roboter ['rɔbɔtər] (-s, -) m robot

robust [ro'bʊst] adj (kräftig: Mensch, Gesundheit) robust

roch etc [rɔx] vb siehe **riechen**

Rock [rɔk] (-(e)s, ̈e) m skirt; (Jackett) jacket; (Uniform~) tunic

Rodel ['roːdəl] (-s, -) m toboggan; ~**bahn** f toboggan run; **r~n** vi to toboggan

Rogen ['roːgən] (-s, -) m roe, spawn

Roggen ['rɔgən] (-s, -) m rye; ~**brot** nt (KOCH) rye bread

roh [roː] adj raw; (Mensch) coarse, crude;

R~**bau** m shell of a building; R~**material** nt raw material; R~**öl** nt crude oil

Rohr [roːr] (-(e)s, -e) nt pipe, tube; (BOT) cane; (Schilf) reed; (Gewehr~) barrel; ~**bruch** m burst pipe

Röhre ['røːrə] f tube, pipe; (RAD etc) valve; (Back~) oven

Rohr- zW: ~**leitung** f pipeline; ~**zucker** m cane sugar

Rohstoff m raw material

Rokoko ['rɔkoko] (-s) nt rococo

Roll- zW: ~**(l)aden** ⚠ m shutter; ~**bahn** f (AVIAT) runway

Rolle ['rɔlə] f roll; (THEAT, soziologisch) role; (Garn~ etc) reel, spool; (Walze) roller; (Wäsche~) mangle; **keine ~ spielen** not to matter; **eine (wichtige) ~ spielen bei** to play a (major) part od role in; **r~n** vt, vi to roll; (AVIAT) to taxi; ~**r** (-s, -) m scooter; (Welle) roller

Roll- zW: ~**kragen** m rollneck, polo neck; ~**mops** m pickled herring; ~**schuh** m roller skate; ~**stuhl** m wheelchair; ~**stuhlfahrer(in)** m(f) wheelchair user; ~**treppe** f escalator

Rom [roːm] (-s) nt Rome

Roman [ro'maːn] (-s, -e) m novel; ~**tik** f romanticism; ~**tiker** [ro'mantɪkər] (-s, -) m romanticist; **r~tisch** [ro'mantɪʃ] adj romantic; ~**ze** [ro'mantsə] f romance

Römer ['røːmər] (-s, -) m wineglass; (Mensch) Roman

römisch ['røːmɪʃ] adj Roman; ~**-katholisch** adj (REL) Roman Catholic

röntgen ['rœntgən] vt to X-ray; R~**bild** nt X-ray; R~**strahlen** pl X-rays

rosa ['roːza] adj inv pink, rose(-coloured)

Rose ['roːzə] f rose

Rosen- zW: ~**kohl** m Brussels sprouts pl; ~**kranz** m rosary; ~**montag** m Monday before Ash Wednesday

rosig ['roːzɪç] adj rosy

Rosine [ro'ziːnə] f raisin, currant

Roß ⚠ [rɔs] (-sses, -sse) nt horse, steed; ~**kastanie** ⚠ f horse chestnut

Rost [rɔst] (-(e)s, -e) m rust; (Gitter) grill, gridiron; (Bett~) springs pl; ~**braten** m

⚠ For information on spelling reform see page 615

roast(ed) meat, roast; **r~en** vi to rust

rösten ['rø:stən] vt to roast; to toast; to grill

Rost- zW: **r~frei** adj rust-free; rustproof; stainless; **r~ig** adj rusty; **~schutz** m rust-proofing

rot [ro:t] adj red; **in den ~en Zahlen** in the red

Röte ['rø:tə] (-) f redness; **~ln** pl German measles sg; **r~n** vt, vr to redden

rothaarig adj red-haired

rotieren [ro'ti:rən] vi to rotate

Rot- zW: **~kehlchen** nt robin; **~stift** m red pencil; **~wein** m red wine

Rouge [ru:ʒ] nt blusher

Roulade [ru'la:də] f (KOCH) beef olive

Route ['ru:tə] f route

Routine [ru'ti:nə] f experience; routine

Rübe ['ry:bə] f turnip; **gelbe ~** carrot; **rote ~** beetroot (BRIT), beet (US)

rüber ['ry:bər] (umg) adv = herüber; hinüber

Rubrik [ru'bri:k] f heading; (Spalte) column

Ruck [rʊk] (-(e)s, -e) m jerk, jolt

Rück- ['rʏk] zW: **~antwort** f reply, answer; **r~bezüglich** adj reflexive

Rücken ['rʏkən] (-s, -) m back; (Berg~) ridge

rücken vt, vi to move

Rücken- zW: **~mark** nt spinal cord; **~schwimmen** nt backstroke

Rück- zW: **~erstattung** f return, restitution; **~fahrkarte** f return (ticket); **~fahrt** f return journey; **~fall** m relapse; **r~fällig** adj relapsing; **r~fällig werden** to relapse; **~flug** m return flight; **~frage** f question; **r~fragen** vi to check, to inquire (further); **~gabe** f return; **~gaberecht** nt right of return; **~gang** m decline, fall; **r~gängig** adj: **etw r~gängig machen** to cancel sth; **~grat** (-(e)s, -e) nt spine, backbone; **~halt** m (Unterstützung) backing, support; **~kehr** (-, -en) f return; **~licht** nt back light; **r~lings** adv from behind; backwards; **~nahme** f taking back; **~porto** nt return postage; **~reise** f return journey; (NAUT) home voyage; **~reiseverkehr** m homebound traffic; **~ruf** m recall

Rucksack ['rʊkzak] m rucksack;

~tourist(in) m(f) backpacker

Rück- zW: **~schau** f reflection; **~schlag** m (plötzliche Verschlechterung) setback; **~schluß** ⚠ m conclusion; **~schritt** m retrogression; **r~schrittlich** adj reactionary; retrograde; **~seite** f back; (von Münze etc) reverse; **~sicht** f consideration; **~sicht nehmen auf** +akk to show consideration for; **r~sichtslos** adj inconsiderate; (Fahren) reckless; (unbarmherzig) ruthless; **r~sichtsvoll** adj considerate; **~sitz** m back seat; **~spiegel** m (AUT) rear-view mirror; **~spiel** nt return match; **~sprache** f further discussion od talk; **~stand** m arrears pl; **r~ständig** adj backward, out-of-date; (Zahlungen) in arrears; **~strahler** (-s, -) m rear reflector; **~tritt** m resignation; **~trittbremse** f pedal brake; **~vergütung** f repayment; (COMM) refund; **~versicherung** f reinsurance; **r~wärtig** adj rear; **r~wärts** adv backward(s), back; **~wärtsgang** m (AUT) reverse gear; **~weg** m return journey, way back; **r~wirkend** adj retroactive; **~wirkung** f reaction; retroactive effect; **~zahlung** f repayment; **~zug** m retreat

Rudel ['ru:dəl] (-s, -) nt pack; herd

Ruder ['ru:dər] (-s, -) nt oar; (Steuer) rudder; **~boot** nt rowing boat; **r~n** vt, vi to row

Ruf [ru:f] (-(e)s, -e) m call, cry; (Ansehen) reputation; **r~en** (unreg) vt, vi to call; to cry; **~name** m usual (first) name; **~nummer** f (tele)phone number; **~säule** f (an Autobahn) emergency telephone; **~zeichen** nt (RAD) call sign; (TEL) ringing tone

rügen ['ry:gən] vt to rebuke

Ruhe ['ru:ə] (-) f rest; (Ungestörtheit) peace, quiet; (Gelassenheit, Stille) calm; (Schweigen) silence; **jdn in ~ lassen** to leave sb alone; **sich zur ~ setzen** to retire; **~!** be quiet!, silence!; **r~n** vi to rest; **~pause** f break; **~stand** m retirement; **~stätte** f: **letzte ~stätte** final resting place; **~störung** f breach of the peace; **~tag** m (von Geschäft) closing day

ruhig ['ru:ɪç] adj quiet; (bewegungslos) still;

(*Hand*) steady; (*gelassen, friedlich*) calm; (*Gewissen*) clear; **kommen Sie ~ herein** just come on in; **tu das ~** feel free to do that
Ruhm [ruːm] (**-(e)s**) *m* fame, glory
rühmen ['ryːmən] *vt* to praise ♦ *vr* to boast
Rühr- [ryːr] *zW*: **~ei** *nt* scrambled egg; **r~en** *vt, vr* (*auch fig*) to move, to stir ♦ *vi*: **r~en von** to come *od* stem from; **r~en an** +*akk* to touch; (*fig*) to touch on; **r~end** *adj* touching, moving; **r~selig** *adj* sentimental, emotional; **~ung** *f* emotion
Ruin [ruˈiːn] (**-s, -e**) *m* ruin; **~e** *f* ruin; **r~ieren** [-'niːrən] *vt* to ruin
rülpsen ['rʏlpsən] *vi* to burp, to belch
Rum [rom] (**-s, -s**) *m* rum
Rumän- [ruˈmɛːn] *zW*: **~ien** (**-s**) *nt* Ro(u)mania; **r~isch** *adj* Ro(u)manian
Rummel ['roməl] (**-s**) (*umg*) *m* hubbub; (*Jahrmarkt*) fair; **~platz** *m* fairground, fair
Rumpf [rompf] (**-(e)s, ̈-e**) *m* trunk, torso; (*AVIAT*) fuselage; (*NAUT*) hull
rümpfen ['rʏmpfən] *vt* (*Nase*) to turn up
rund [ront] *adj* round ♦ *adv* (*etwa*) around; **~ um etw** round sth; **R~brief** *m* circular; **R~e** [ˈrondə] *f* round; (*in Rennen*) lap; (*Gesellschaft*) circle; **R~fahrt** *f* (round) trip
Rundfunk ['rontfoŋk] (**-(e)s**) *m* broadcasting; **im ~** on the radio; **~gerät** *nt* wireless set; **~sendung** *f* broadcast, radio programme
Rund- *zW*: **r~heraus** *adv* straight out, bluntly; **r~herum** *adv* round about; all round; **r~lich** *adj* plump, rounded; **~reise** *f* round trip; **~schreiben** *nt* (*COMM*) circular; **~(wander)weg** *m* circular path *od* route
runter ['rontər] (*umg*) *adv* = **herunter; hinunter**
Runzel ['rontsəl] (**-, -n**) *f* wrinkle; **r~ig** *adj* wrinkled; **r~n** *vt* to wrinkle; **die Stirn r~n** to frown
rupfen ['ropfən] *vt* to pluck
ruppig ['ropıç] *adj* rough, gruff
Rüsche ['ryːʃə] *f* frill
Ruß [ruːs] (**-es**) *m* soot
Russe ['rosə] (**-n, -n**) *m* Russian
Rüssel ['rʏsəl] (**-s, -**) *m* snout; (*Elefanten~*)

trunk
rußig ['ruːsıç] *adj* sooty
Russin ['rosın] *f* Russian
russisch *adj* Russian
Rußland ⚠ ['roslant] (**-s**) *nt* Russia
rüsten ['rʏstən] *vt* to prepare ♦ *vi* to prepare; (*MIL*) to arm ♦ *vr* to prepare (o.s.); to arm o.s.
rüstig ['rʏstıç] *adj* sprightly, vigorous
Rüstung ['rʏstoŋ] *f* preparation; arming; (*Ritter~*) armour; (*Waffen etc*) armaments *pl*; **~skontrolle** *f* arms control
Rute ['ruːtə] *f* rod
Rutsch [rotʃ] (**-(e)s, -e**) *m* slide; (*Erd~*) landslide; **~bahn** *f* slide; **r~en** *vi* to slide; (*ausrutschen*) to slip; **r~ig** *adj* slippery
rütteln ['rʏtəln] *vt, vi* to shake, to jolt

S, s

S. *abk* (= *Seite*) p.; = **Schilling**
s. *abk* (= *siehe*) see
Saal [zaːl] (**-(e)s, Säle**) *m* hall; room
Saarland ['zaːrlant] *nt*: **das ~** the Saar(land)
Saat [zaːt] (**-, -en**) *f* seed; (*Pflanzen*) crop; (*Säen*) sowing
Säbel ['zɛːbəl] (**-s, -**) *m* sabre, sword
Sabotage [zaboˈtaːʒə] *f* sabotage
Sach- [zax] *zW*: **~bearbeiter** *m* specialist; **s~dienlich** *adj* relevant, helpful; **~e** *f* thing; (*Angelegenheit*) affair, business; (*Frage*) matter; (*Pflicht*) task; **zur ~e** to the point; **s~kundig** *adj* expert; **s~lich** *adj* matter-of-fact; objective; (*Irrtum, Angabe*) factual
sächlich ['zɛxlıç] *adj* neuter
Sachschaden *m* material damage
Sachsen ['zaksən] (**-s**) *nt* Saxony
sächsisch ['zɛksıʃ] *adj* Saxon
sacht(e) ['zaxt(ə)] *adv* softly, gently
Sachverständige(r) *f(m)* expert
Sack [zak] (**-(e)s, ̈-e**) *m* sack; **~gasse** *f* cul-de-sac, dead-end street (*US*)
Sadismus [zaˈdısmos] *m* sadism
Sadist [zaˈdıst] *m* sadist

⚠ *For information on spelling reform see page 615*

säen ['zɛːən] *vt, vi* to sow

Safe(r) Sex ⚠ *m* safe sex

Saft [zaft] **(-(e)s, ⸚e)** *m* juice; (*BOT*) sap; **s~ig** *adj* juicy; **s~los** *adj* dry

Sage ['zaːgə] *f* saga

Säge ['zɛːgə] *f* saw; **~mehl** *nt* sawdust

sagen ['zaːgən] *vt, vi* to say; (*mitteilen*) **jdm ~** to tell sb; **• Sie ihm, daß ...** tell him ...

sägen *vt, vi* to saw

sagenhaft *adj* legendary; (*umg*) great, smashing

sah *etc* [zaː] *vb siehe* **sehen**

Sahne ['zaːnə] **(-)** *f* cream

Saison [zɛˈzõː] **(-, -s)** *f* season

Saite ['zaɪtə] *f* string

Sakko ['zako] **(-s, -s)** *m od nt* jacket

Sakrament [zakraˈmɛnt] *nt* sacrament

Sakristei [zakrɪsˈtaɪ] *f* sacristy

Salat [zaˈlaːt] **(-(e)s, -e)** *m* salad; (*Kopf~*) lettuce; **~soße** *f* salad dressing

Salbe ['zalbə] *f* ointment

Salbei ['zalbaɪ] **(-s** *od* **-)** *m od f* sage

Saldo ['zaldo] **(-s, Salden)** *m* balance

Salmiak [zalmiˈak] **(-s)** *m* sal ammoniac; **~geist** *m* liquid ammonia

Salmonellenvergiftung [zalmoˈnɛlən-] *f* salmonella (poisoning)

salopp [zaˈlɔp] *adj* casual

Salpeter [zalˈpeːtər] **(-s)** *m* saltpetre; **~säure** *f* nitric acid

Salz [zalts] **(-es, -e)** *nt* salt; **s~en** (*unreg*) *vt* to salt; **s~ig** *adj* salty; **~kartoffeln** *pl* boiled potatoes; **~säure** *f* hydrochloric acid; **~streuer** *m* salt cellar; **~wasser** *nt* (*Meerwasser*) salt water

Samen ['zaːmən] **(-s, -)** *m* seed; (*ANAT*) sperm

Sammel- ['zaməl] *zW:* **~band** *m* anthology; **~fahrschein** *m* multi-journey ticket; (*für mehrere Personen*) group ticket

sammeln ['zaməln] *vt* to collect **•** *vr* to assemble, to gather; (*konzentrieren*) to concentrate

Sammlung ['zamlʊŋ] *f* collection; assembly, gathering; concentration

Samstag ['zamstaːk] *m* Saturday; **s~s** *adv* (on) Saturdays

Samt [zamt] **(-(e)s, -e)** *m* velvet; **~** *präp* +*dat* (along) with, together with; **~ und sonders** each and every one (of them)

sämtlich ['zɛmtlɪç] *adj* all (the), entire

Sand [zant] **(-(e)s, -e)** *m* sand

Sandale [zanˈdaːlə] *f* sandal

Sand- *zW:* **~bank** *f* sandbank; **s~ig** ['zandɪç] *adj* sandy; **~kasten** *m* sandpit; **~kuchen** *m* Madeira cake; **~papier** *nt* sandpaper; **~stein** *m* sandstone; **s~strahlen** *vt, vi insep* to sandblast; **~strand** *m* sandy beach

sandte *etc* ['zantə] *vb siehe* **senden**

sanft [zanft] *adj* soft, gentle; **~mütig** *adj* gentle, meek

sang *etc* [zaŋ] *vb siehe* **singen**

Sänger(in) ['zɛŋər(ɪn)] **(-s, -)** *m(f)* singer

Sani- *zW:* **s~eren** [zaˈniːrən] *vt* to redevelop; (*Betrieb*) to make financially sound **•** *vr* to line one's pockets; to become financially sound; **s~tär** [zaniˈtɛːr] *adj* sanitary; **s~täre Anlagen** sanitation *sg*; **~täter** [zaniˈtɛːtər] **(-s, -)** *m* first-aid attendant; (*MIL*) (medical) orderly

sanktionieren [zaŋktsioˈniːrən] *vt* to sanction

Sardelle [zarˈdɛlə] *f* anchovy

Sardine [zarˈdiːnə] *f* sardine

Sarg [zark] **(-(e)s, ⸚e)** *m* coffin

Sarkasmus [zarˈkasmʊs] *m* sarcasm

saß *etc* [zaːs] *vb siehe* **sitzen**

Satan ['zaːtan] **(-s, -e)** *m* Satan; devil

Satellit [zateˈliːt] **(-en, -en)** *m* satellite; **~enfernsehen** *nt* satellite television

Satire [zaˈtiːrə] *f* satire; **satirisch** *adj* satirical

satt [zat] *adj* full; (*Farbe*) rich, deep; **jdn/etw ~ sein** *od* **haben** to be fed up with sb/sth; **sich ~ hören/sehen an** +*dat* to hear/see enough of sth; **sich ~ essen** to eat one's fill; **~ machen** to be filling

Sattel ['zatəl] **(-s, ⸚)** *m* saddle; (*Berg*) ridge; **s~n** *vt* to saddle; **~schlepper** *m* articulated lorry

sättigen ['zɛtɪgən] *vt* to satisfy; (*CHEM*) to saturate

Satz [zats] **(-es, ⸚e)** *m* (*GRAM*) sentence;

⚠ *Informationen zur Rechtschreibreform Seite 615*

(*Neben~, Adverbial~*) clause; (*Theorem*) theorem; (*MUS*) movement; (*TENNIS, Briefmarken etc*) set; (*Kaffee*) grounds *pl*; (*COMM*) rate; (*Sprung*) jump; ~**teil** *m* part of a sentence; ~**ung** *f* (*Statut*) statute, rule; ~**zeichen** *nt* punctuation mark

Sau [zau] (-, **Säue**) *f* sow; (*umg*) dirty pig

sauber ['zaubər] *adj* clean; (*ironisch*) fine; ~**halten** △ (*unreg*) *vt* to keep clean; **S~keit** *f* cleanness (*einer Person*) cleanliness

säuberlich ['zɔybərlıç] *adv* neatly

säubern *vt* to clean; (*POL etc*) to purge; **Säuberung** *f* cleaning; purge

Sauce ['zo:sə] *f* sauce, gravy

sauer ['zauər] *adj* sour; (*CHEM*) acid; (*umg*) cross; **saurer Regen** acid rain; **S~braten** *m* braised beef marinated in vinegar

Sauerei [zauə'rai] (*umg*) *f* rotten state of affairs, scandal; (*Schmutz etc*) mess; (*Unanständigkeit*) obscenity

Sauerkraut *nt* sauerkraut, pickled cabbage

säuerlich ['zɔyərlıç] *adj* (*Geschmack*) sour; (*mißvergnügt: Gesicht*) dour

Sauer- *zW*: ~**milch** *f* sour milk; ~**rahm** *m* (*KOCH*) sour cream; ~**stoff** *m* oxygen; ~**teig** *m* leaven

saufen ['zaufən] (*unreg*) (*umg*) *vt, vi* to drink, to booze; **Säufer** (-s, -) (*umg*) *m* boozer

saugen ['zaugən] (*unreg*) *vt, vi* to suck

säugen ['zɔygən] *vt* to suckle

Sauger ['zaugər] (-s, -) *m* dummy, comforter (*US*); (*auf Flasche*) teat

Säugetier ['zɔygə-] *nt* mammal

Säugling *m* infant, baby

Säule ['zɔylə] *f* column, pillar

Saum [zaum] (-(e)s, **Säume**) *m* hem; (*Naht*) seam

säumen ['zɔymən] *vt* to hem; to seam ♦ *vi* to delay, to hesitate

Sauna ['zauna] (-, -s) *f* sauna

Säure ['zɔyrə] *f* acid

sausen ['zauzən] *vi* to blow; (*umg: eilen*) to rush; (*Ohren*) to buzz; **etw ~ lassen** (*umg*) not to bother with sth

Saxophon △ [zakso'fo:n] (-s, -e) *nt* saxophone

SB *abk* = **Selbstbedienung**

S-Bahn *f abk* (= *Schnellbahn*) high speed railway; (= *Stadtbahn*) suburban railway

schaben ['ʃa:bən] *vt* to scrape

schäbig ['ʃɛ:bıç] *adj* shabby

Schablone [ʃa'blo:nə] *f* stencil; (*Muster*) pattern; (*fig*) convention

Schach [ʃax] (-s, -s) *nt* chess; (*Stellung*) check; ~**brett** *nt* chessboard; ~**figur** *f* chessman; **s~'matt** *adj* checkmate; ~**spiel** *nt* game of chess

Schacht [ʃaxt] (-(e)s, ¨e) *m* shaft

Schachtel (-, -n) *f* box

schade ['ʃa:də] *adj* a pity *od* shame ♦ *excl*: (**wie**) ~! (what a) pity *od* shame; **sich** *dat* **zu ~ sein für etw** to consider o.s. too good for sth

Schädel ['ʃɛ:dəl] (-s, -) *m* skull; ~**bruch** *m* fractured skull

Schaden ['ʃa:dən] (-s, ¨) *m* damage; (*Verletzung*) injury; (*Nachteil*) disadvantage; **s~** *vi +dat* to hurt; **einer Sache s~** to damage sth; ~**ersatz** *m* compensation, damages *pl*; ~**freude** *f* malicious glee; **s~froh** *adj* (*Mensch, Lachen*) gloating; ~**sfall** *m*: **im ~sfall** in the event of a claim

schadhaft ['ʃa:thaft] *adj* faulty, damaged

schäd- ['ʃɛ:t] *zW*: ~**igen** ['ʃɛdıgən] *vt* to damage; (*Person*) to do harm to, to harm; ~**lich** *adj*: ~**lich (für)** harmful (to); **S~lichkeit** *f* harmfulness; **S~ling** *m* pest

Schadstoff ['ʃa:tʃtɔf] *m* harmful substance; **s~arm** *adj*: **s~arm sein** to contain a low level of harmful substances

Schaf [ʃa:f] (-(e)s, -e) *nt* sheep

Schäfer ['ʃɛ:fər] (-s, -e) *m* shepherd; ~**hund** *m* Alsatian (dog) (*BRIT*), German shepherd (dog) (*US*)

Schaffen ['ʃafən] (-s) *nt* (creative) activity

schaffen¹ ['ʃafən] (*unreg*) *vt* to create; (*Platz*) to make

schaffen² ['ʃafən] *vt* (*erreichen*) to manage, to do; (*erledigen*) to finish; (*Prüfung*) to pass; (*transportieren*) to take ♦ *vi* (*umg: arbeiten*) to work; **sich** *dat* **etw ~** to get o.s. sth; **sich an etw** *dat* **zu ~ machen** to busy o.s. with sth

△ *For information on spelling reform see page 615*

Schaffner(in) ['ʃafnər(ɪn)] **(-s, -)** *m(f)* (*Bus~*) conductor(-tress); (*EISENB*) guard

Schaft [ʃaft] **(-(e)s, ⸚e)** *m* shaft; (*von Gewehr*) stock; (*von Stiefel*) leg; (*BOT*) stalk; tree trunk

Schal [ʃaːl] **(-s, -e** *od* **-s)** *m* scarf

schal *adj* flat; (*fig*) insipid

Schälchen ['ʃɛːlçən] *nt* cup, bowl

Schale ['ʃaːlə] *f* skin; (*abgeschält*) peel; (*Nuß~, Muschel~, Ei~*) shell; (*Geschirr*) dish, bowl

schälen ['ʃɛːlən] *vt* to peel; to shell ♦ *vr* to peel

Schall [ʃal] **(-(e)s, -e)** *m* sound; **~dämpfer** **(-s, -)** *m* (*AUT*) silencer; **s~dicht** *adj* soundproof; **s~en** *vi* to (re)sound; **s~end** *adj* resounding, loud; **~mauer** *f* sound barrier; **~platte** *f* (gramophone) record

Schalt- ['ʃalt] *zW*: **~bild** *nt* circuit diagram; **~brett** *nt* switchboard; **s~en** *vt* to switch, to turn ♦ *vi* (*AUT*) to change (gear); (*umg: begreifen*) to catch on; **~er** **(-s, -)** *m* counter; (*an Gerät*) switch; **~erbeamte(r)** *m* counter clerk; **~erstunden** *pl* hours of business; **~hebel** *m* switch; (*AUT*) gear lever; **~jahr** *nt* leap year; **~ung** *f* switching; (*ELEK*) circuit; (*AUT*) gear change

Scham [ʃaːm] **(-)** *f* shame; (*~gefühl*) modesty; (*Organe*) private parts *pl*

schämen ['ʃɛːmən] *vr* to be ashamed

schamlos *adj* shameless

Schande ['ʃandə] **(-)** *f* disgrace

schändlich ['ʃɛntlɪç] *adj* disgraceful, shameful

Schändung ['ʃɛndʊŋ] *f* violation, defilement

Schanze ['ʃantsə] *f* (*Sprung~*) ski jump

Schar [ʃaːr] **(-, -en)** *f* band, company; (*Vögel*) flock; (*Menge*) crowd; **in ~en** in droves; **s~en** *vr* to assemble, to rally

scharf [ʃarf] *adj* sharp; (*Essen*) hot, spicy; (*Munition*) live; **~ nachdenken** to think hard; **auf etw** *akk* **~ sein** (*umg*) to be keen on sth

Schärfe ['ʃɛrfə] *f* sharpness; (*Strenge*) rigour; **s~n** *vr* to sharpen

Scharf- *zW*: **s~machen** (*umg*) *vt* to stir

up; **~richter** *m* executioner; **~schütze** *m* marksman, sharpshooter; **s~sinnig** *adj* astute, shrewd

Scharlach ['ʃarlax] **(-s, -e)** *m* (*~fieber*) scarlet fever

Scharnier [ʃar'niːr] **(-s, -e)** *nt* hinge

scharren ['ʃarən] *vt, vi* to scrape, to scratch

Schaschlik ['ʃaʃlɪk] **(-s, -s)** *m od nt* (shish) kebab

Schatten ['ʃatən] **(-s, -)** *m* shadow; **~riß** △ *m* silhouette; **~seite** *f* shady side, dark side

schattieren [ʃa'tiːrən] *vt, vi* to shade

schattig ['ʃatɪç] *adj* shady

Schatulle [ʃa'tʊlə] *f* casket; (*Geld~*) coffer

Schatz [ʃats] **(-es, ⸚e)** *m* treasure; (*Person*) darling

schätz- [ʃɛts] *zW*: **~bar** *adj* assessable; **S~chen** *nt* darling, love; **~en** *vt* (*abschätzen*) to estimate; (*Gegenstand*) to value; (*würdigen*) to value, to esteem; (*vermuten*) to reckon; **S~ung** *f* estimate; estimation; valuation; **nach meiner S~ung ...** I reckon that ...

Schau [ʃaʊ] **(-)** *f* show; (*Ausstellung*) display, exhibition; **etw zur ~ stellen** to make a show of sth, to show sth off; **~bild** *nt* diagram

Schauder ['ʃaʊdər] **(-s, -)** *m* shudder; (*wegen Kälte*) shiver; **s~haft** *adj* horrible; **s~n** *vi* to shudder; to shiver

schauen ['ʃaʊən] *vi* to look

Schauer ['ʃaʊər] **(-s, -)** *m* (*Regen~*) shower; (*Schreck*) shudder; **~geschichte** *f* horror story; **s~lich** *adj* horrific, spine-chilling

Schaufel ['ʃaʊfəl] **(-, -n)** *f* shovel; (*NAUT*) paddle; (*TECH*) scoop; **s~n** *vt* to shovel, to scoop

Schau- *zW*: **~fenster** *nt* shop window; **~fensterbummel** *m* window shopping (expedition); **~kasten** *m* showcase

Schaukel ['ʃaʊkəl] **(-, -n)** *f* swing; **s~n** *vi* to swing, to rock; **~pferd** *nt* rocking horse; **~stuhl** *m* rocking chair

Schaulustige(r) ['ʃaʊlʊstɪɡə(r)] *f(m)* onlooker

Schaum [ʃaʊm] **(-(e)s, Schäume)** *m* foam;

(*Seifen~*) lather; **~bad** *nt* bubble bath

schäumen ['ʃɔymən] *vi* to foam

Schaum- *zW:* **~festiger (-s, -)** *m* mousse; **~gummi** *m* foam (rubber); **s~ig** *adj* frothy, foamy; **~stoff** *m* foam material; **~wein** *m* sparkling wine

Schauplatz *m* scene

schaurig ['ʃaurɪç] *adj* horrific, dreadful

Schauspiel *nt* spectacle; (*THEAT*) play; **~er(in)** *m(f)* actor (actress); **s~ern** *vi insep* to act; **~haus** *nt* theatre

Scheck [ʃɛk] **(-s, -s)** *m* cheque; **~gebühr** *f* encashment fee; **~heft** *nt* cheque book; **~karte** *f* cheque card

scheffeln ['ʃɛfəln] *vt* to amass

Scheibe ['ʃaibə] *f* disc; (*Brot etc*) slice; (*Glas~*) pane; (*MIL*) target

Scheiben- *zW:* **~bremse** *f* (*AUT*) disc brake; **~wischer** *m* (*AUT*) windscreen wiper

Scheide ['ʃaidə] *f* sheath; (*Grenze*) boundary; (*ANAT*) vagina; **s~n** (*unreg*) *vt* to separate; (*Ehe*) to dissolve ♦ *vi* to depart; to part; **sich s~n lassen** to get a divorce

Scheidung *f* (*Ehe~*) divorce

Schein [ʃain] **(-(e)s, -e)** *m* light; (*Anschein*) appearance; (*Geld*) (bank)note; (*Bescheinigung*) certificate; **zum ~** in pretence; **s~bar** *adj* apparent; **s~en** (*unreg*) *vi* to shine; (*Anschein haben*) to seem; **s~heilig** *adj* hypocritical; **~werfer (-s, -)** *m* floodlight; spotlight; (*Suchscheinwerfer*) searchlight; (*AUT*) headlamp

Scheiß- ['ʃais] (*umg*) *in zW* bloody

Scheiße ['ʃaisə] **(-)** (*umg*) *f* shit

Scheitel ['ʃaitəl] **(-s, -)** *m* top; (*Haar~*) parting; **s~n** *vt* to part

scheitern ['ʃaitərn] *vi* to fail

Schelle ['ʃɛlə] *f* small bell; **s~n** *vi* to ring

Schellfisch ['ʃɛlfɪʃ] *m* haddock

Schelm [ʃɛlm] **(-(e)s, -e)** *m* rogue; **s~isch** *adj* mischievous, roguish

Schelte ['ʃɛltə] *f* scolding; **s~n** (*unreg*) *vt* to scold

Schema ['ʃeːma] **(-s, -s** *od* **-ta)** *nt* scheme, plan; (*Darstellung*) schema; **nach ~** quite mechanically; **s~tisch** [ʃeˈmaːtɪʃ] *adj*

schematic; (*pej*) mechanical

Schemel ['ʃeːməl] **(-s, -)** *m* (foot)stool

Schenkel ['ʃɛŋkəl] **(-s, -)** *m* thigh

schenken ['ʃɛŋkən] *vt* (*auch fig*) to give; (*Getränk*) to pour; **sich** *dat* **etw ~** (*umg*) to skip sth; **das ist geschenkt!** (*billig*) that's a giveaway!; (*nichts wert*) that's worthless!

Scherbe ['ʃɛrbə] *f* broken piece, fragment; (*archäologisch*) potsherd

Schere ['ʃeːrə] *f* scissors *pl*; (*groß*) shears *pl*; **s~n** (*unreg*) *vt* to cut; (*Schaf*) to shear; (*kümmern*) to bother ♦ *vr* to care; **scher dich zum Teufel!** get lost!; **~'rei** (*umg*) *f* bother, trouble

Scherz [ʃɛrts] **(-es, -e)** *m* joke; fun; **~frage** *f* conundrum; **s~haft** *adj* joking, jocular

Scheu [ʃɔy] **(-)** *f* shyness; (*Angst*) fear; (*Ehrfurcht*) awe; **s~** *adj* shy; **s~en** *vr*: **sich s~en vor** +*dat* to be afraid of, to shrink from ♦ *vt* to shun ♦ *vi* (*Pferd*) to shy

scheuern ['ʃɔyərn] *vt* to scour, to scrub

Scheune ['ʃɔynə] *f* barn

Scheusal ['ʃɔyzaːl] **(-s, -e)** *nt* monster

scheußlich ['ʃɔyslɪç] *adj* dreadful, frightful

Schi [ʃiː] *m* = **Ski**

Schicht [ʃɪçt] **(-, -en)** *f* layer; (*Klasse*) class, level; (*in Fabrik etc*) shift; **~arbeit** *f* shift work; **s~en** *vt* to layer, to stack

schick [ʃɪk] *adj* stylish, chic

schicken *vt* to send ♦ *vr*: **sich ~ (in** +*akk*) to resign o.s. (to) ♦ *vb unpers* (*anständig sein*) to be fitting

schicklich *adj* proper, fitting

Schicksal **(-s, -e)** *nt* fate; **~sschlag** *m* great misfortune, blow

Schieb- ['ʃiːb] *zW:* **~edach** *nt* (*AUT*) sun roof; **s~en** (*unreg*) *vt* (*auch Drogen*) to push; (*Schuld*) to put ♦ *vi* to push; **~etür** *f* sliding door; **~ung** *f* fiddle

Schieds- ['ʃiːts] *zW:* **~gericht** *nt* court of arbitration; **~richter** *m* referee; umpire; (*Schlichter*) arbitrator

schief [ʃiːf] *adj* crooked; (*Ebene*) sloping; (*Turm*) leaning; (*Winkel*) oblique; (*Blick*) funny; (*Vergleich*) distorted ♦ *adv* crooked(ly); (*ansehen*) askance; **etw ~ stellen** to slope sth

⚠ *For information on spelling reform see page 615*

Schiefer [ˈʃiːfər] **(-s, -)** m slate

schiefgehen ⚠ (unreg) (umg) vi to go wrong

schielen [ˈʃiːlən] vi to squint; **nach etw ~** (fig) to eye sth

schien etc [ʃiːn] vb siehe **scheinen**

Schienbein nt shinbone

Schiene [ˈʃiːnə] f rail; (MED) splint; **s~n** vt to put in splints

schier [ʃiːr] adj (fig) sheer ♦ adv nearly, almost

Schieß- [ˈʃiːs] zW: **~bude** f shooting gallery; **s~en** (unreg) vt to shoot; (Ball) to kick; (Geschoß) to fire ♦ vi to shoot; (Salat etc) to run to seed; **s~en auf** +akk to shoot at; **~e'rei** f shooting incident, shoot-out; **~pulver** nt gunpowder; **~scharte** f embrasure

Schiff [ʃɪf] **(-(e)s, -e)** nt ship, vessel; (Kirchen~) nave; **s~bar** adj (Fluß) navigable; **~bruch** m shipwreck; **s~brüchig** adj shipwrecked; **~chen** nt small boat; (Weben) shuttle; (Mütze) forage cap; **~er (-s, -)** m bargeman, boatman; **~(f)ahrt** ⚠ f shipping; (Reise) voyage

Schikane [ʃiˈkaːnə] f harassment; dirty trick; **mit allen ~n** with all the trimmings

schikanieren [ʃikaˈniːrən] vt to harass, to torment

Schild¹ [ʃɪlt] **(-(e)s, -e)** m shield; **etw im ~e führen** to be up to sth

Schild² [ʃɪlt] **(-(e)s, -er)** nt sign; nameplate; (Etikett) label

Schilddrüse f thyroid gland

schildern [ˈʃɪldərn] vt to depict, to portray

Schildkröte f tortoise; (Wasser~) turtle

Schilf [ʃɪlf] **(-(e)s, -e)** nt (Pflanze) reed; (Material) reeds pl, rushes pl; **~rohr** nt (Pflanze) reed

schillern [ˈʃɪlərn] vi to shimmer; **~d** adj iridescent

Schilling [ˈʃɪlɪŋ] m schilling

Schimmel [ˈʃɪməl] **(-s, -)** m mould; (Pferd) white horse; **s~ig** adj mouldy; **s~n** vi to get mouldy

Schimmer [ˈʃɪmər] **(-s)** m (Lichtsein) glimmer; (Glanz) shimmer; **s~n** vi to glimmer, to shimmer

Schimpanse [ʃɪmˈpanzə] **(-n, -n)** m chimpanzee

schimpfen [ˈʃɪmpfən] vt to scold ♦ vi to curse, to complain; to scold

Schimpfwort nt term of abuse

schinden [ˈʃɪndən] (unreg) vt to maltreat, to drive too hard ♦ vr: **sich ~ (mit)** to sweat and strain (at), to toil away (at); **Eindruck ~** (umg) to create an impression

Schinde'rei f grind, drudgery

Schinken [ˈʃɪŋkən] **(-s, -)** m ham

Schirm [ʃɪrm] **(-(e)s, -e)** m (Regen~) umbrella; (Sonnen~) parasol, sunshade; (Wand~, Bild~) screen; (Lampen~) (lamp)shade; (Mützen~) peak; (Pilz~) cap; **~mütze** f peaked cap; **~ständer** m umbrella stand

schizophren [ʃitsoˈfreːn] adj schizophrenic

Schlacht [ʃlaxt] **(-, -en)** f battle; **s~en** vt to slaughter, to kill; **~er (-s, -)** m butcher; **~feld** nt battlefield; **~hof** m slaughterhouse, abattoir; **~schiff** nt battleship; **~vieh** nt animals kept for meat; beef cattle

Schlaf [ʃlaːf] **(-(e)s)** m sleep; **~anzug** m pyjamas pl

Schläfe f (ANAT) temple

schlafen [ˈʃlaːfən] (unreg) vi to sleep; **~ gehen** to go to bed; **S~zeit** f bedtime

schlaff [ʃlaf] adj slack; (energielos) limp; (erschöpft) exhausted

Schlaf- zW: **~gelegenheit** f sleeping accommodation; **~lied** nt lullaby; **s~los** adj sleepless; **~losigkeit** f sleeplessness, insomnia; **~mittel** nt sleeping pill

schläfrig [ˈʃlɛːfriç] adj sleepy

Schlaf- zW: **~saal** m dormitory; **~sack** m sleeping bag; **~tablette** f sleeping pill; **~wagen** m sleeping car, sleeper; **s~wandeln** vi insep to sleepwalk; **~zimmer** nt bedroom

Schlag [ʃlaːk] **(-(e)s, ¨e)** m (auch fig) blow; (auch MED) stroke; (Puls~, Herz~) beat; (ELEK) shock; (Blitz~) bolt, stroke; (Autotür) car door; (umg: Portion) helping; (Art) kind, type; **Schläge** pl (Tracht Prügel) beating sg;

⚠ Informationen zur Rechtschreibreform Seite 615

mit einem ~ all at once; **~ auf ~** in rapid succession; **~ader** f artery; **~anfall** m stroke; **s~artig** adj sudden, without warning; **~baum** m barrier; **s~en** ['ʃlaːgən] (unreg) vt, vi to strike, to hit; (wiederholt schlagen, besiegen) to beat; (Glocke) to ring; (Stunde) to strike; (Sahne) to whip; (Schlacht) to fight ♦ vi to fight; **nach jdm s~en** (fig) to take after sb; **sich gut s~en** (fig) to do well; **~er** ['ʃlaːgər] (-s, -) m (auch fig) hit

Schläger ['ʃlɛːgər] m brawler; (SPORT) bat; (TENNIS etc) racket; (GOLF) club; hockey stick; (Waffe) rapier; **Schläge'rei** f fight, punch-up

Schlagersänger(in) m(f) pop singer

Schlag- zW: **s~fertig** adj quick-witted; **~fertigkeit** f ready wit, quickness of repartee; **~loch** nt pothole; **~obers** (ÖSTERR) nt = **Schlagsahne**; **~sahne** f (whipped) cream; **~seite** f (NAUT) list; **~wort** nt slogan, catch phrase; **~zeile** f headline; **~zeug** nt percussion; drums pl; **~zeuger** (-s, -) m drummer

Schlamassel [ʃlaˈmasəl] (-s, -) (umg) m mess

Schlamm [ʃlam] (-(e)s, -e) m mud; **s~ig** adj muddy

Schlamp- ['ʃlamp] zW: **~e** (umg) f slut; **s~en** (umg) vi to be sloppy; **~e'rei** f disorder, untidiness; sloppy work; **s~ig** (umg) adj (Mensch, Arbeit) sloppy, messy

Schlange ['ʃlaŋə] f snake; (Menschen~) queue (BRIT), line-up (US); **~ stehen** to (form a) queue, to line up

schlängeln ['ʃlɛŋəln] vr (Schlange) to wind; (Weg) to wind, twist; (Fluß) to meander

Schlangen- zW: **~biß** ⚠ m snake bite; **~gift** nt snake venom; **~linie** f wavy line

schlank [ʃlaŋk] adj slim, slender; **S~heit** f slimness, slenderness; **S~heitskur** f diet

schlapp [ʃlap] adj limp; (locker) slack; **S~e** (umg) f setback

Schlaraffenland [ʃlaˈrafənlant] nt land of milk and honey

schlau [ʃlaʊ] adj crafty, cunning

Schlauch [ʃlaʊx] (-(e)s, Schläuche) m hose; (in Reifen) inner tube; (umg: Anstrengung) grind; **~boot** nt rubber dinghy; **s~en** (umg) vt to tell on, to exhaust

Schläue ['ʃlɔʏə] (-) f cunning

Schlaufe ['ʃlaʊfə] f loop; (Aufhänger) hanger

Schlauheit f cunning

schlecht [ʃlɛçt] adj bad ♦ adv badly; **~ gelaunt** in a bad mood; **~ und recht** after a fashion; **jdm ist ~** sb feels sick od bad; **~gehen** ⚠ (unreg) vi unpers: **jdm geht es ~** sb is in a bad way; **S~igkeit** f badness; bad deed; **~machen** ⚠ vt to run down

schlecken ['ʃlɛkən] vt, vi to lick

Schlegel ⚠ ['ʃleːgəl] (-s, -) m (drum)stick; (Hammer) mallet, hammer; (KOCH) leg

schleichen ['ʃlaɪçən] (unreg) vi to creep, to crawl; **~d** adj gradual; creeping

Schleichwerbung f (COMM) plug

Schleier ['ʃlaɪər] (-s, -) m veil; **s~haft** (umg) adj: **jdm s~haft sein** to be a mystery to sb

Schleif- ['ʃlaɪf] zW: **~e** f loop; (Band) bow; **s~en**[1] vt, vi to drag; **s~en**[2] (unreg) vt to grind; (Edelstein) to cut; **~stein** m grindstone

Schleim [ʃlaɪm] (-(e)s, -e) m slime; (MED) mucus; (KOCH) gruel; **~haut** f (ANAT) mucous membrane; **s~ig** adj slimy

Schlemm- ['ʃlɛm] zW: **s~en** vi to feast; **~er** (-s, -) m gourmet; **~e'rei** f gluttony, feasting

schlendern ['ʃlɛndərn] vi to stroll

schlenkern ['ʃlɛŋkərn] vt, vi to swing, to dangle

Schlepp- ['ʃlɛp] zW: **~e** f train; **s~en** vt to drag; (Auto, Schiff) to tow; (tragen) to lug; **s~end** adj dragging, slow; **~er** (-s, -) m tractor; (Schiff) tug

Schlesien ['ʃleːziən] (-s) nt (GEOG) Silesia

Schleuder ['ʃlɔʏdər] (-, -n) f catapult; (Wäsche~) spin-drier; (Butter~ etc) centrifuge; **~gefahr** f risk of skidding; **„Achtung ~gefahr"** "slippery road ahead"; **s~n** vt to hurl; (Wäsche) to spin-dry ♦ vi (AUT) to skid; **~preis** m give-away price; **~sitz** m (AVIAT) ejector seat; (fig) hot seat; **~ware** f cheap od cut-price goods pl

⚠ For information on spelling reform see page 615

schleunigst ['ʃlɔynɪçst] *adv* straight away

Schleuse ['ʃlɔyzə] *f* lock; (*Schleusentor*) sluice

schlicht [ʃlɪçt] *adj* simple, plain; **~en** *vt* (*glätten*) to smooth, to dress; (*Streit*) to settle; **S~er (-s, -)** *m* mediator, arbitrator; **S~ung** *f* settlement; arbitration

Schlick [ʃlɪk] **(-(e)s, -e)** *m* mud; (*Öl~*) slick

schlief *etc* [ʃliːf] *vb siehe* **schlafen**

Schließ- ['ʃliːs] *zW:* **s~en** (*unreg*) *vt* to close, to shut; (*beenden*) to close; (*Freundschaft, Bündnis, Ehe*) to enter into; (*folgern*): **s~en (aus)** to infer (from) ♦ *vi, vr* to close, to shut; **etw in sich s~en** to include sth; **~fach** *nt* locker; **s~lich** *adv* finally; **s~lich doch** after all

Schliff [ʃlɪf] **(-(e)s, -e)** *m* cut(ting); (*fig*) polish

schlimm [ʃlɪm] *adj* bad; **~er** *adj* worse; **~ste(r, s)** *adj* worst; **~stenfalls** *adv* at (the) worst

Schlinge ['ʃlɪŋə] *f* loop; (*bes Henkers~*) noose; (*Falle*) snare; (*MED*) sling; **s~n** (*unreg*) *vt* to wind; (*essen*) to bolt, to gobble ♦ *vi* (*essen*) to bolt one's food, to gobble

Schlingel **(-s, -)** *m* rascal

schlingern *vi* to roll

Schlips [ʃlɪps] **(-es, -e)** *m* tie

Schlitten ['ʃlɪtən] **(-s, -)** *m* sledge, sleigh; **~fahren (-s)** *nt* tobogganing

schlittern ['ʃlɪtərn] *vi* to slide

Schlittschuh ['ʃlɪtʃuː] *m* skate; **~ laufen** to skate; **~bahn** *f* skating rink; **~läufer(in)** *m(f)* skater

Schlitz [ʃlɪts] **(-es, -e)** *m* slit; (*für Münze*) slot; (*Hosen~*) flies *pl*; **s~äugig** *adj* slant-eyed

Schloß ⚠ [ʃlɔs] **(-sses, ⁻sser)** *nt* lock; (*an Schmuck etc*) clasp; (*Bau*) castle; chateau

schloß ⚠ *etc vb siehe* **schließen**

Schlosser ['ʃlɔsər] **(-s, -)** *m* fitter; (*Auto~*) fitter; (*für Schlüssel etc*) locksmith

Schlosserei [-'raɪ] *f* metal (working) shop

Schlot [ʃloːt] **(-(e)s, -e)** *m* chimney; (*NAUT*) funnel

schlottern ['ʃlɔtərn] *vi* to shake, to tremble;

(*Kleidung*) to be baggy

Schlucht [ʃlʊxt] **(-, -en)** *f* gorge, ravine

schluchzen ['ʃlʊxtsən] *vi* to sob

Schluck [ʃlʊk] **(-(e)s, -e)** *m* swallow; (*Menge*) drop; **~auf (-s, -s)** *m* hiccups *pl*; **s~en** *vt, vi* to swallow

schludern ['ʃluːdərn] *vi* to skimp, to do sloppy work

schlug *etc* [ʃluːk] *vb siehe* **schlagen**

Schlummer ['ʃlʊmər] **(-s)** *m* slumber; **s~n** *vi* to slumber

Schlund [ʃlʊnt] **(-(e)s, ⁻e)** *m* gullet; (*fig*) jaw

schlüpfen ['ʃlʏpfən] *vi* to slip; (*Vogel etc*) to hatch (out)

Schlüpfer ['ʃlʏpfər] **(-s, -)** *m* panties *pl*, knickers *pl*

schlüpfrig ['ʃlʏpfrɪç] *adj* slippery; (*fig*) lewd; **S~keit** *f* slipperiness; (*fig*) lewdness

schlurfen ['ʃlʊrfən] *vi* to shuffle

schlürfen ['ʃlʏrfən] *vt, vi* to slurp

Schluß ⚠ [ʃlʊs] **(-sses, ⁻sse)** *m* end; (*Schlußfolgerung*) conclusion; **am ~** at the end; **~ machen mit** to finish with

Schlüssel ['ʃlʏsəl] **(-s, -)** *m* (*auch fig*) key; (*Schrauben~*) spanner, wrench; (*MUS*) clef; **~bein** *nt* collarbone; **~blume** *f* cowslip, primrose; **~bund** *m* bunch of keys; **~dienst** *m* key cutting service; **~loch** *nt* keyhole; **~position** *f* key position; **~wort** *nt* keyword

schlüssig ['ʃlʏsɪç] *adj* conclusive

Schluß- *zW:* **~licht** ⚠ *nt* taillight; (*fig*) tailender; **~strich** ⚠ *m* (*fig*) final stroke; **~verkauf** ⚠ *m* clearance sale

schmächtig ['ʃmɛçtɪç] *adj* slight

schmackhaft ['ʃmakhaft] *adj* tasty

schmal [ʃmaːl] *adj* narrow; (*Person, Buch etc*) slender, slim; (*karg*) meagre

schmälern ['ʃmɛːlərn] *vt* to diminish; (*fig*) to belittle

Schmalfilm *m* cine film

Schmalz [ʃmalts] **(-es, -e)** *nt* dripping, lard; (*fig*) sentiment, schmaltz; **s~ig** *adj* (*fig*) schmaltzy

schmarotzen [ʃma'rɔtsən] *vi* to sponge; (*BOT*) to be parasitic; **Schmarotzer (-s, -)**

m parasite; sponger

Schmarren ['ʃmarən] (**-s, -**) *m* (ÖSTERR) small piece of pancake; (*fig*) rubbish, tripe

schmatzen ['ʃmatsən] *vi* to smack one's lips; to eat noisily

schmecken ['ʃmɛkən] *vt, vi* to taste; **es schmeckt ihm** he likes it

Schmeichel- ['ʃmaɪçəl] *zW:* **~ei** [-'laɪ] *f* flattery; **s~haft** *adj* flattering; **s~n** *vi* to flatter

schmeißen ['ʃmaɪsən] (*unreg*) (*umg*) *vt* to throw, to chuck

Schmeißfliege *f* bluebottle

Schmelz [ʃmɛlts] (**-es, -e**) *m* enamel; (*Glasur*) glaze; (*von Stimme*) melodiousness; **s~en** (*unreg*) *vt* to melt; (*Erz*) to smelt ♦ *vi* to melt; **~punkt** *m* melting point; **~wasser** *nt* melted snow

Schmerz [ʃmɛrts] (**-es, -en**) *m* pain; (*Trauer*) grief; **s~empfindlich** *adj* sensitive to pain; **s~en** *vt, vi* to hurt; **~ensgeld** *nt* compensation; **s~haft** *adj* painful; **s~lich** *adj* painful; **s~los** *adj* painless; **~mittel** *nt* painkiller; **~tablette** *f* painkiller

Schmetterling ['ʃmɛtərlɪŋ] *m* butterfly

schmettern ['ʃmɛtərn] *vt* (*werfen*) to hurl; (*TENNIS: Ball*) to smash; (*singen*) to belt out (*inf*)

Schmied [ʃmiːt] (**-(e)s, -e**) *m* blacksmith; **~e** ['ʃmiːdə] *f* smithy, forge; **~eeisen** *nt* wrought iron; **s~en** *vt* to forge; (*Pläne*) to devise, to concoct

schmiegen ['ʃmiːɡən] *vt* to press, to nestle ♦ *vr:* **sich ~ (an** +*akk*) to cuddle up (to), to nestle (up to)

Schmier- ['ʃmiːr] *zW:* **~e** *f* grease; (*THEAT*) greasepaint, make-up; **s~en** *vt* to smear; (*ölen*) to lubricate, to grease; (*bestechen*) to bribe; (*schreiben*) to scrawl ♦ *vi* (*schreiben*) to scrawl; **~fett** *nt* grease; **~geld** *nt* bribe; **s~ig** *adj* greasy; **~seife** *f* soft soap

Schminke ['ʃmɪŋkə] *f* make-up; **s~n** *vt, vr* to make up

schmirgeln ['ʃmɪrɡəln] *vt* to sand (down)

Schmirgelpapier *nt* emery paper

schmollen ['ʃmɔlən] *vi* to sulk, to pout

Schmorbraten *m* stewed *od* braised meat

schmoren ['ʃmoːrən] *vt* to stew, to braise

Schmuck [ʃmʊk] (**-(e)s, -e**) *m* jewellery; (*Verzierung*) decoration

schmücken ['ʃmʏkən] *vt* to decorate

Schmuck- *zW:* **s~los** *adj* unadorned, plain; **~sachen** *pl* jewels, jewellery *sg*

Schmuggel ['ʃmʊɡəl] (**-s**) *m* smuggling; **s~n** *vt, vi* to smuggle

Schmuggler (**-s, -**) *m* smuggler

schmunzeln ['ʃmʊntsəln] *vi* to smile benignly

schmusen ['ʃmuːzən] (*umg*) *vi* (*zärtlich sein*) to cuddle, to canoodle (*inf*)

Schmutz [ʃmʊts] (**-es**) *m* dirt, filth; **~fink** *m* filthy creature; **~fleck** *m* stain; **s~ig** *adj* dirty

Schnabel ['ʃnaːbəl] (**-s, ¨**) *m* beak, bill; (*Ausguß*) spout

Schnalle ['ʃnalə] *f* buckle, clasp; **s~n** *vt* to buckle

Schnapp- ['ʃnap] *zW:* **s~en** *vt* to grab, to catch ♦ *vi* to snap; **~schloß** △ *nt* spring lock; **~schuß** △ *m* (*PHOT*) snapshot

Schnaps [ʃnaps] (**-es, ¨e**) *m* spirits *pl*; schnapps

schnarchen ['ʃnarçən] *vi* to snore

schnattern ['ʃnatərn] *vi* (*Gänse*) to gabble; (*Ente*) to quack

schnauben ['ʃnaʊbən] *vi* to snort ♦ *vr* to blow one's nose

schnaufen ['ʃnaʊfən] *vi* to puff, to pant

Schnauze *f* snout, muzzle; (*Ausguß*) spout; (*umg*) gob

Schnecke ['ʃnɛkə] *f* snail; **~nhaus** *nt* snail's shell

Schnee [ʃneː] (**-s**) *m* snow; (*Ei~*) beaten egg white; **~ball** *m* snowball; **~flocke** *f* snowflake; **s~frei** *adj* free of snow; **~gestöber** *nt* snowstorm; **~glöckchen** *nt* snowdrop; **~grenze** *f* snow line; **~kette** *f* (*AUT*) snow chain; **~mann** *m* snowman; **~pflug** *m* snowplough; **~regen** *m* sleet; **~schmelze** *f* thaw; **~wehe** *f* snowdrift

Schneide ['ʃnaɪdə] *f* edge; (*Klinge*) blade; **s~n** (*unreg*) *vt* to cut; (*kreuzen*) to cross, to intersect with ♦ *vr* to cut o.s.; (*Linien*) to cross, to intersect; **s~nd** *adj* cutting; **~r** (**-s, -**) *m*

△ *For information on spelling reform see page 615*

tailor; **~rei** f (*Geschäft*) tailor's; **~rin** f dressmaker; **s~rn** vt to make ♦ vi to be a tailor; **~zahn** m incisor

schneien ['ʃnaɪən] vi unpers to snow

Schneise ['ʃnaɪzə] f clearing

schnell [ʃnɛl] adj quick, fast ♦ adv quick, quickly, fast; **S~hefter (-s, -)** m loose-leaf binder; **S~igkeit** f speed; **S~imbiß** ⚠ m (*Lokal*) snack bar; **S~kochtopf** m (*Dampfkochtopf*) pressure cooker; **S~reinigung** f dry cleaner's; **~stens** adv as quickly as possible; **S~straße** f expressway; **S~zug** m fast *od* express train

schneuzen ⚠ ['ʃnɔʏtsən] vr to blow one's nose

schnippeln ['ʃnɪpəln] (*umg*) vt: **~ (an** +*dat*) to snip (at)

schnippisch ['ʃnɪpɪʃ] adj sharp-tongued

Schnitt (-(e)s, -e) m cut(ting); (*~punkt*) intersection; (*Quer~*) (cross) section; (*Durch~*) average; (*~muster*) pattern; (*an Buch*) edge; (*umg: Gewinn*) profit

schnitt etc vb siehe **schneiden**

Schnitt- zW: **~blumen** pl cut flowers; **~e** f slice; (*belegt*) sandwich; **~fläche** f section; **~lauch** m chive; **~punkt** m (point of) intersection; **~stelle** f (COMPUT) interface; **~wunde** f cut

Schnitz- ['ʃnɪts] zW: **~arbeit** f wood carving; **~el (-s, -)** nt chip; (*KOCH*) escalope; **s~en** vt to carve; **~er (-s, -)** m carver; (*umg*) blunder; **~e'rei** f carving, carved woodwork

schnodderig ['ʃnɔdərɪç] (*umg*) adj snotty

Schnorchel ['ʃnɔrçəl] (-s, -) m snorkel

Schnörkel ['ʃnœrkəl] (-s, -) m flourish; (*ARCHIT*) scroll

schnorren ['ʃnɔrən] vt, vi to cadge

schnüffeln ['ʃnʏfəln] vi to sniff

Schnüffler (-s, -) m snooper

Schnuller ['ʃnʊlər] (-s, -) m dummy, comforter (*US*)

Schnupfen ['ʃnʊpfən] (-s, -) m cold

schnuppern ['ʃnʊpərn] vi to sniff

Schnur [ʃnuːr] (-, ̈e) f string, cord; (*ELEK*) flex

schnüren ['ʃnyːrən] vt to tie

schnurgerade adj straight (as a die)

Schnurrbart ['ʃnʊrbaːrt] m moustache

schnurren ['ʃnʊrən] vi to purr; (*Kreisel*) to hum

Schnürschuh m lace-up (shoe)

Schnürsenkel m shoelace

schnurstracks adv straight (away)

Schock [ʃɔk] (-(e)s, -e) m shock

schockieren [ʃɔ'kiːrən] vt to shock, to outrage

Schöffe ['ʃœfə] (-n, -n) m lay magistrate; **Schöffin** f lay magistrate

Schokolade [ʃoko'laːdə] f chocolate

Scholle ['ʃɔlə] f clod; (*Eis~*) ice floe; (*Fisch*) plaice

SCHLÜSSELWORT

---

schon [ʃoːn] adv 1 (*bereits*) already; **er ist schon da** he's there already, he's already there; **ist er schon da?** is he there yet?; **warst du schon einmal da?** have you ever been there?; **ich war schon einmal da** I've been there before; **das war schon immer so** that has always been the case; **schon oft** often; **hast du schon gehört?** have you heard?

2 (*bestimmt*) all right; **du wirst schon sehen** you'll see (all right); **das wird schon noch gut** that'll be OK

3 (*bloß*) just; **allein schon das Gefühl ...** just the very feeling ...; **schon der Gedanke** the very thought; **wenn ich das schon höre** I only have to hear that

4 (*einschränkend*): **ja schon, aber ...** yes (well), but ...

5: **schon möglich** possible; **schon gut!** OK!; **du weißt schon** you know; **komm schon!** come on!

---

schön [ʃøːn] adj beautiful; (*nett*) nice; **~e Grüße** best wishes; **~e Ferien** have a nice holiday; **~en Dank** (many) thanks

schonen ['ʃoːnən] vt to look after ♦ vr to take it easy; **~d** adj careful, gentle

Schön- zW: **~heit** f beauty; **~heitsfehler** m blemish, flaw; **~heitsoperation** f

---

⚠ *Informationen zur Rechtschreibreform Seite 615*

cosmetic surgery

Schonkost (-) f light diet; (*Spezialdiät*) special diet

schönmachen vr to make o.s. look nice

Schon- zW: **~ung** f good care; (*Nachsicht*) consideration; (*Forst*) plantation of young trees; **s~ungslos** adj unsparing, harsh; **~zeit** f close season

Schöpf- ['fœpf] zW: **s~en** vt to scoop, to ladle; (*Mut*) to summon up; (*Luft*) to breathe in; **~er** (-s, -) m creator; **s~erisch** adj creative; **~kelle** f ladle; **~ung** f creation

Schorf [fɔrf] (-(e)s, -e) m scab

Schornstein ['fɔrnʃtain] m chimney; (*NAUT*) funnel; **~feger** (-s, -) m chimney sweep

Schoß [fo:s] (-es, -̈e) m lap; (*Rock~*) coat tail

schoß etc △ vb siehe **schießen**

Schoßhund m pet dog, lapdog

Schote ['fo:tə] f pod

Schotte ['fɔtə] m Scot, Scotsman

Schotter ['fɔtər] (-s) m broken stone, road metal; (*EISENB*) ballast

Schott- [fɔt] zW: **~in** f Scot, Scotswoman; **s~isch** adj Scottish, Scots; **~land** nt Scotland

schraffieren [fra'fi:rən] vt to hatch

schräg [frɛːk] adj slanting, not straight; etw ~ **stellen** to put sth at an angle; ~ **gegenüber** diagonally opposite; **S~e** ['frɛːgə] f slant; **S~strich** m oblique stroke

Schramme ['framə] f scratch; **s~n** vt to scratch

Schrank [fraŋk] (-(e)s, -̈e) m cupboard; (*Kleider~*) wardrobe; **~e** f barrier; **~koffer** m trunk

Schraube ['fraubə] f screw; **s~n** vt to screw; **~nschlüssel** m spanner; **~nzieher** (-s, -) m screwdriver

Schraubstock ['fraupʃtɔk] m (*TECH*) vice

Schreck [frɛk] (-(e)s, -e) m terror; fright; **~en** (-s, -) m terror; fright; **s~en** vt to frighten, to scare; **~gespenst** nt spectre, nightmare; **s~haft** adj jumpy, easily frightened; **s~lich** adj terrible, dreadful

Schrei [frai] (-(e)s, -e) m scream; (*Ruf*) shout

Schreib- ['fraib] zW: **~block** m writing pad; **s~en** (*unreg*) vt, vi to write; (*buchstabieren*) to spell; **~en** (-s, -) nt letter, communication; **s~faul** adj bad about writing letters; **~kraft** f typist; **~maschine** f typewriter; **~papier** nt notepaper; **~tisch** m desk; **~ung** f spelling; **~waren** pl stationery sg; **~weise** f spelling; way of writing; **~zentrale** f typing pool; **~zeug** nt writing materials pl

schreien ['fraiən] (*unreg*) vt, vi to scream; (*rufen*) to shout; **~d** adj (*fig*) glaring; (*Farbe*) loud

Schrein [frain] (-(e)s, -e) m shrine

Schreiner ['frainər] (-s, -) m joiner; (*Zimmermann*) carpenter; (*Möbel~*) cabinetmaker; **~ei** [-'rai] f joiner's workshop

schreiten ['fraitən] (*unreg*) vi to stride

schrieb etc [fri:p] vb siehe **schreiben**

Schrift [frift] (-, -en) f writing; handwriting; (*~art*) script; (*Gedrucktes*) pamphlet, work; **~deutsch** nt written German; **~führer** m secretary; **s~lich** adj written ♦ adv in writing; **~sprache** f written language; **~steller(in)** (-s, -) m(f) writer; **~stück** nt document; **~wechsel** m correspondence

schrill [fril] adj shrill

Schritt [frit] (-(e)s, -e) m step; (*Gangart*) walk; (*Tempo*) pace; (*von Hose*) crutch; ~ **fahren** to drive at walking pace; **~macher** (-s, -) m pacemaker; **~(t)empo** △ nt: im **~(t)empo** at a walking pace

schroff [frɔf] adj steep; (*zackig*) jagged; (*fig*) brusque

schröpfen ['frœpfən] vt (*fig*) to fleece

Schrot [fro:t] (-(e)s, -e) m od nt (*Blei*) (small) shot; (*Getreide*) coarsely ground grain, groats pl; **~flinte** f shotgun

Schrott [frɔt] (-(e)s, -e) m scrap metal; **~haufen** m scrap heap; **s~reif** adj ready for the scrap heap

schrubben ['frubən] vt to scrub

Schrubber (-s, -) m scrubbing brush

schrumpfen ['frumpfən] vi to shrink; (*Apfel*) to shrivel

Schub- ['fu:b] zW: **~fach** nt drawer; **~karren** m wheelbarrow; **~lade** f drawer

△ *For information on spelling reform see page 615*

Schubs [ʃuːps] **(-es, -e)** (*umg*) *m* shove (*inf*), push

schüchtern ['ʃʏçtərn] *adj* shy; **S~heit** *f* shyness

Schuft [ʃʊft] **(-(e)s, -e)** *m* scoundrel

schuften (*umg*) *vi* to graft, to slave away

Schuh [ʃuː] **(-(e)s, -e)** *m* shoe; **~band** *nt* shoelace; **~creme** *f* shoe polish; **~größe** *f* shoe size; **~löffel** *m* shoehorn; **~macher** (**-s, -**) *m* shoemaker

Schul- *zW*: **~arbeit** *f* homework (*no pl*); **~aufgaben** *pl* homework *sg*; **~besuch** *m* school attendance; **~buch** *nt* school book

Schuld [ʃʊlt] **(-, -en)** *f* guilt; (*FIN*) debt; (*Verschulden*) fault; **s~** *adj*: **s~ sein** *od* **haben (an** +*dat*) to be to blame (for); **er ist** *od* **hat s~** it's his fault; **jdm s~ geben** to blame sb; **s~en** ['ʃʊldən] *vt* to owe; **s~enfrei** *adj* free from debt; **~gefühl** *nt* feeling of guilt; **s~ig** *adj* guilty; (*gebührend*) due; **s~ig an etw** *dat* **sein** to be guilty of sth; **jdm etw s~ig sein** to owe sb sth; **jdm etw s~ig bleiben** not to provide sb with sth; **s~los** *adj* innocent, without guilt; **~ner** (**-s, -**) *m* debtor; **~schein** *m* promissory note, IOU

Schule ['ʃuːlə] *f* school; **s~n** *vt* to train, to school

Schüler(in) ['ʃyːlər(ın)] **(-s, -)** *m(f)* pupil; **~austausch** *m* school *od* student exchange; **~ausweis** *m* (school) student card

Schul- *zW*: **~ferien** *pl* school holidays; **s~frei** *adj*: **s~freier Tag** holiday; **s~frei sein** to be a holiday; **~hof** *m* playground; **~jahr** *nt* school year; **~kind** *nt* schoolchild; **s~pflichtig** *adj* of school age; **~schiff** *nt* (*NAUT*) training ship; **~stunde** *f* period, lesson; **~tasche** *f* school bag

Schulter ['ʃʊltər] **(-, -n)** *f* shoulder; **~blatt** *nt* shoulder blade; **s~n** *vt* to shoulder

Schulung *f* education, schooling

Schulzeugnis *nt* school report

Schund [ʃʊnt] **(-(e)s)** *m* trash, garbage

Schuppe ['ʃʊpə] *f* scale; **~n** *pl* (*Haarschuppen*) dandruff *sg*

Schuppen (**-s, -**) *m* shed

schuppig ['ʃʊpıç] *adj* scaly

Schur [ʃuːr] **(-, -en)** *f* shearing

schüren ['ʃyːrən] *vt* to rake; (*fig*) to stir up

schürfen ['ʃʏrfən] *vt, vi* to scrape, to scratch; (*MIN*) to prospect

Schurke ['ʃʊrkə] **(-n, -n)** *m* rogue

Schurwolle *f*: **"reine ~"** "pure new wool"

Schürze ['ʃʏrtsə] *f* apron

Schuß ⚠ [ʃʊs] **(-sses, ⁻sse)** *m* shot; (*WEBEN*) woof; **~bereich** ⚠ *m* effective range

Schüssel ['ʃʏsəl] **(-, -n)** *f* bowl

Schuß- *zW*: **~linie** ⚠ *f* line of fire; **~verletzung** ⚠ *f* bullet wound; **~waffe** ⚠ *f* firearm

Schuster ['ʃuːstər] **(-s, -)** *m* cobbler, shoemaker

Schutt [ʃʊt] **(-(e)s)** *m* rubbish; (*Bau~*) rubble

Schüttelfrost *m* shivering

schütteln ['ʃʏtəln] *vt, vr* to shake

schütten ['ʃʏtən] *vt* to pour; (*Zucker, Kies etc*) to tip; (*ver~*) to spill ♦ *vi unpers* to pour (down)

Schutthalde *f* dump

Schutthaufen *m* heap of rubble

Schutz [ʃʊts] **(-es)** *m* protection; (*Unterschlupf*) shelter; **jdn in ~ nehmen** to stand up for sb; **~anzug** *m* overalls *pl*; **~blech** *nt* mudguard

Schütze ['ʃʏtsə] **(-n, -n)** *m* gunman; (*Gewehr~*) rifleman; (*Scharf~, Sport~*) marksman; (*ASTROL*) Sagittarius

schützen ['ʃʏtsən] *vt* to protect; **~ vor** +*dat od* **gegen** to protect from

Schützenfest *nt* fair featuring shooting matches

Schutz- *zW*: **~engel** *m* guardian angel; **~gebiet** *nt* protectorate; (*Naturschutzgebiet*) reserve; **~hütte** *f* shelter, refuge; **~impfung** *f* immunisation

Schützling ['ʃʏtslıŋ] *m* protégé(e); (*bes Kind*) charge

Schutz- *zW*: **s~los** *adj* defenceless; **~mann** *m* policeman; **~patron** *m* patron saint

Schwaben ['ʃvaːbən] *nt* Swabia; **schwäbisch** *adj* Swabian

schwach [ʃvax] *adj* weak, feeble
Schwäche [ˈʃvɛçə] *f* weakness; **s~n** *vt* to weaken
Schwachheit *f* weakness
schwächlich *adj* weakly, delicate
Schwächling *m* weakling
Schwach- *zW*: **~sinn** *m* imbecility; **s~sinnig** *adj* mentally deficient; (*Idee*) idiotic; **~strom** *m* weak current
Schwächung [ˈʃvɛçʊŋ] *f* weakening
Schwager [ˈʃvaːɡər] (**-s**, ¨) *m* brother-in-law; **Schwägerin** *f* sister-in-law
Schwalbe [ˈʃvalbə] *f* swallow
Schwall [ʃval] (**-(e)s**, **-e**) *m* surge; (*Worte*) flood, torrent
Schwamm [ʃvam] (**-(e)s**, ¨e) *m* sponge; (*Pilz*) fungus
schwamm *etc vb siehe* **schwimmen**
schwammig *adj* spongy; (*Gesicht*) puffy
Schwan [ʃvaːn] (**-(e)s**, ¨e) *m* swan
schwanger [ˈʃvaŋər] *adj* pregnant; **S~schaft** *f* pregnancy
schwanken *vi* to sway; (*taumeln*) to stagger, to reel; (*Preise, Zahlen*) to fluctuate; (*zögern*) to hesitate, to vacillate
Schwankung *f* fluctuation
Schwanz [ʃvants] (**-es**, ¨e) *m* tail
schwänzen [ˈʃvɛntsən] (*umg*) *vt* to skip, to cut ♦ *vi* to play truant
Schwarm [ʃvarm] (**-(e)s**, ¨e) *m* swarm; (*umg*) heart-throb, idol
schwärm- [ˈʃvɛrm] *zW*: **~en** *vi* to swarm; **~en für** to be mad *od* wild about; **S~erei** [-əˈraɪ] *f* enthusiasm; **~erisch** *adj* impassioned, effusive
Schwarte [ˈʃvartə] *f* hard skin; (*Speck~*) rind
schwarz [ʃvarts] *adj* black; **~es Brett** notice board; **ins S~e treffen** (*auch fig*) to hit the bull's eye; **in den ~en Zahlen** in the black; **S~arbeit** *f* illicit work, moonlighting; **S~brot** *nt* black bread; **S~e(r)** *f(m)* black (man/woman)
Schwärze [ˈʃvɛrtsə] *f* blackness; (*Farbe*) blacking; (*Drucker~*) printer's ink; **s~n** *vt* to blacken
Schwarz- *zW*: **s~fahren** (*unreg*) *vi* to travel without paying; to drive without a

licence; **~handel** *m* black market (trade); **~markt** *m* black market; **s~sehen** (*unreg*) (*umg*) *vi* to see the gloomy side of things; **~wald** *m* Black Forest; **s~weiß** *adj* black and white
schwatzen [ˈʃvatsən] *vi* to chatter
schwätzen [ˈʃvɛtsən] *vi* to chatter
Schwätzer [ˈʃvɛtsər] (**-s**, **-**) *m* gasbag
schwatzhaft *adj* talkative, gossipy
Schwebe [ˈʃveːbə] *f*: **in der ~** (*fig*) in abeyance; **~bahn** *f* overhead railway; **s~n** *vi* to drift, to float; (*hoch*) to soar
Schwed- [ˈʃveːd] *zW*: **~e** *m* Swede; **~en** *nt* Sweden; **~in** *f* Swede; **s~isch** *adj* Swedish
Schwefel [ˈʃveːfəl] (**-s**) *m* sulphur; **s~ig** *adj* sulphurous; **~säure** *f* sulphuric acid
Schweig- [ˈʃvaɪɡ] *zW*: **~egeld** *nt* hush money; **~en** (**-s**) *nt* silence; **s~en** (*unreg*) *vi* to be silent; to stop talking; **~epflicht** *f* pledge of secrecy; (*von Anwalt*) requirement of confidentiality; **s~sam** [ˈʃvaɪkzaːm] *adj* silent, taciturn; **~samkeit** *f* taciturnity, quietness
Schwein [ʃvaɪn] (**-(e)s**, **-e**) *nt* pig; (*umg*) (good) luck
Schweine- *zW*: **~fleisch** *nt* pork; **~'rei** *f* mess; (*Gemeinheit*) dirty trick; **~stall** *m* pigsty
schweinisch *adj* filthy
Schweinsleder *nt* pigskin
Schweiß [ʃvaɪs] (**-es**) *m* sweat, perspiration; **s~en** *vt*, *vi* to weld; **~er** (**-s**, **-**) *m* welder; **~füße** *pl* sweaty feet; **~naht** *f* weld
Schweiz [ʃvaɪts] *f* Switzerland; **~er(in)** *m(f)* Swiss; **s~erisch** *adj* Swiss
schwelgen [ˈʃvɛlɡən] *vi* to indulge
Schwelle [ˈʃvɛlə] *f* (*auch fig*) threshold; doorstep; (*EISENB*) sleeper (*BRIT*), tie (*US*)
schwellen (*unreg*) *vi* to swell
Schwellung *f* swelling
Schwemme [ˈʃvɛmə] *f* (*WIRTS*: *Überangebot*) surplus
Schwenk- [ˈʃvɛŋk] *zW*: **s~bar** *adj* swivel-mounted; **s~en** *vt* to swing; (*Fahne*) to wave; (*abspülen*) to rinse ♦ *vi* to turn, to swivel; (*MIL*) to wheel; **~ung** *f* turn; wheel
schwer [ʃveːr] *adj* heavy; (*schwierig*) difficult,

⚠ *For information on spelling reform see page 615*

hard; (*schlimm*) serious, bad ♦ *adv* (*sehr*)
very (much); (*verletzt etc*) seriously, badly;
S~arbeiter *m* manual worker, labourer;
S~behinderte(r) *f(m)* seriously
handicapped person; **S~e** *f* weight,
heaviness; (*PHYS*) gravity; **~elos** *adj*
weightless; (*Kammer*) zero-G; **~erziehbar**
⚠ *adj* difficult (to bring up); **~fallen** ⚠
(*unreg*) *vi*: **jdm ~fallen** to be difficult for sb;
~fällig *adj* ponderous; **S~gewicht** *nt*
heavyweight; (*fig*) emphasis; **~hörig** *adj*
hard of hearing; **S~industrie** *f* heavy
industry; **S~kraft** *f* gravity; **S~kranke(r)**
f(m) person who is seriously ill; **~lich** *adv*
hardly; **~machen** ⚠ *vt*: **jdm/sich etw**
~machen to make sth difficult for sb/o.s.;
~mütig *adj* melancholy; **~nehmen** ⚠
(*unreg*) *vt* to take to heart; **S~punkt** *m*
centre of gravity; (*fig*) emphasis, crucial
point
Schwert [ʃveːrt] (-(e)s, -er) *nt* sword; **~lilie**
f iris
schwer- *zW*: **~tun** ⚠ (*unreg*) *vi*: **sich** *dat*
od akk **~tun** to have difficulties;
S~verbrecher(in) *m(f)* criminal, serious
offender; **~verdaulich** ⚠ *adj* indigestible,
heavy; **~verletzt** ⚠ *adj* badly injured;
S~verletzte(r) *f(m)* serious casualty; (*bei*
Unfall usw auch) seriously injured person;
~wiegend *adj* weighty, important
Schwester [ʃvɛstər] (-, -n) *f* sister; (*MED*)
nurse; **s~lich** *adj* sisterly
Schwieger- [ʃviːgər] *zW*: **~eltern** *pl*
parents-in-law; **~mutter** *f* mother-in-law;
~sohn *m* son-in-law; **~tochter** *f*
daughter-in-law; **~vater** *m* father-in-law
schwierig [ʃviːrɪç] *adj* difficult, hard;
S~keit *f* difficulty
Schwimm- [ʃvɪm] *zW*: **~bad** *nt* swimming
baths *pl*; **~becken** *nt* swimming pool;
s~en (*unreg*) *vi* to swim; (*treiben, nicht*
sinken) to float; (*fig: unsicher sein*) to be all
at sea; **~er** (-s, -) *m* swimmer; (*Angeln*)
float; **~erin** *f* (female) swimmer; **~lehrer**
m swimming instructor; **~weste** *f* life
jacket
Schwindel [ʃvɪndəl] (-s) *m* giddiness; dizzy

spell; (*Betrug*) swindle, fraud; (*Zeug*) stuff;
s~frei *adj*: **s~frei sein** to have a good
head for heights; **s~n** (*umg*) *vi* (*lügen*) to
fib; **jdm s~t es** sb feels dizzy
schwinden [ʃvɪndən] (*unreg*) *vi* to
disappear; (*sich verringern*) to decrease;
(*Kräfte*) to decline
Schwindler [ʃvɪndlər] *m* swindler; (*Lügner*)
liar
schwindlig *adj* dizzy; **mir ist ~** I feel dizzy
Schwing- [ʃvɪŋ] *zW*: **s~en** (*unreg*) *vt* to
swing; (*Waffe etc*) to brandish ♦ *vi* to swing;
(*vibrieren*) to vibrate; (*klingen*) to sound;
~tür *f* swing door(s); **~ung** *f* vibration;
(*PHYS*) oscillation
Schwips [ʃvɪps] (-es, -e) *m*: **einen ~ haben**
to be tipsy
schwirren [ʃvɪrən] *vi* to buzz
schwitzen [ʃvɪtsən] *vi* to sweat, to perspire
schwören [ʃvøːrən] (*unreg*) *vt, vi* to swear
schwul [ʃvuːl] (*umg*) *adj* gay, queer
schwül [ʃvyːl] *adj* sultry, close; **S~e** (-) *f*
sultriness
Schwule(r) (*umg*) *f(m)* gay (man/woman)
Schwung [ʃvʊŋ] (-(e)s, ⁻e) *m* swing;
(*Triebkraft*) momentum; (*fig: Energie*) verve,
energy; (*umg: Menge*) batch; **s~haft** *adj*
brisk, lively; **s~voll** *adj* vigorous
Schwur [ʃvuːr] (-(e)s, ⁻e) *m* oath; **~gericht**
nt court with a jury
sechs [zɛks] *num* six; **~hundert** *num* six
hundred; **~te(r, s)** *adj* sixth; **S~tel** (-s, -)
nt sixth
sechzehn [zɛçtseːn] *num* sixteen
sechzig [zɛçtsɪç] *num* sixty
See¹ [zeː] (-, -n) *f* sea
See² [zeː] (-s, -n) *m* lake
See- [zeː] *zW*: **~bad** *nt* seaside resort;
~hund *m* seal; **~igel** [ˈzeːiːɡəl] *m* sea
urchin; **s~krank** *adj* seasick; **~krankheit** *f*
seasickness; **~lachs** *m* rock salmon
Seele [ˈzeːlə] *f* soul; **s~nruhig** *adv* calmly
Seeleute [ˈzeːlɔʏtə] *pl* seamen
Seel- *zW*: **s~isch** *adj* mental; **~sorge** *f*
pastoral duties *pl*; **~sorger** (-s, -) *m*
clergyman
See- *zW*: **~macht** *f* naval power; **~mann**

⚠ *Informationen zur Rechtschreibreform Seite 615*

(*pl* **-leute**) *m* seaman, sailor; **~meile** *f* nautical mile; **~möwe** *f* (*ZOOL*) seagull; **~not** *f* distress; **~räuber** *m* pirate; **~rose** *f* water lily; **~stern** *m* starfish; **s~tüchtig** *adj* seaworthy; **~weg** *m* sea route; **auf dem ~weg** by sea; **~zunge** *f* sole

Segel ['ze:gəl] (**-s, -**) *nt* sail; **~boot** *nt* yacht; **~fliegen (-s)** *nt* gliding; **~flieger** *m* glider pilot; **~flugzeug** *nt* glider; **s~n** *vt, vi* to sail; **~schiff** *nt* sailing vessel; **~sport** *m* sailing; **~tuch** *nt* canvas

Segen ['ze:gən] (**-s, -**) *m* blessing

Segler ['ze:glər] (**-s, -**) *m* sailor, yachtsman

segnen ['ze:gnən] *vt* to bless

Seh- ['ze:-] *zW*: **s~behindert** *adj* partially sighted; **s~en** (*unreg*) *vt, vi* to see; (*in bestimmter Richtung*) to look; **mal s~en(, ob ...)** let's see (if ...); **siehe Seite 5** see page 5; **s~enswert** *adj* worth seeing; **~enswürdigkeiten** *pl* sights (of a town); **~fehler** *m* sight defect

Sehne ['ze:nə] *f* sinew; (*an Bogen*) string

sehnen *vr*: **sich ~ nach** to long *od* yearn for

sehnig *adj* sinewy

Sehn- *zW*: **s~lich** *adj* ardent; **~sucht** *f* longing; **s~süchtig** *adj* longing

sehr [ze:r] *adv* very; (*mit Verben*) a lot, (very) much; **zu ~** too much; **~ geehrte(r) ...** dear ...

seicht [zaiçt] *adj* (*auch fig*) shallow

Seide ['zaidə] *f* silk; **s~n** *adj* silk; **~npapier** *nt* tissue paper

seidig ['zaidiç] *adj* silky

Seife ['zaifə] *f* soap

Seifen- *zW*: **~lauge** *f* soapsuds *pl*; **~schale** *f* soap dish; **~schaum** *m* lather

seihen ['zaiən] *vt* to strain, to filter

Seil [zail] (**-(e)s, -e**) *nt* rope; cable; **~bahn** *f* cable railway; **~hüpfen (-s)** *nt* skipping; **~springen (-s)** *nt* skipping; **~tänzer(in)** *m(f)* tightrope walker

---

sein [zain] (*pt* **war**, *pp* **gewesen**) *vi* 1 to be; **ich bin** I am; **du bist** you are; **er/sie/es ist** he/she/it is; **wir sind/ihr seid/sie sind** we/you/they are; **wir waren** we were; **wir sind gewesen** we have been

2: **seien Sie nicht böse** don't be angry; **sei so gut und ...** be so kind as to ...; **das wäre gut** that would *od* that'd be a good thing; **wenn ich Sie wäre** if I were *od* was you; **das wär's** that's all, that's it; **morgen bin ich in Rom** tomorrow I'll *od* I will *od* I shall be in Rome; **waren Sie mal in Rom?** have you ever been to Rome?

3: **wie ist das zu verstehen?** how is that to be understood?; **er ist nicht zu ersetzen** he cannot be replaced; **mit ihr ist nicht zu reden** you can't talk to her

4: **mir ist kalt** I'm cold; **was ist?** what's the matter?, what is it?; **ist was?** is something the matter?; **es sei denn, daß ...** unless ...; **wie dem auch sei** be that as it may; **wie wäre es mit ...?** how *od* what about ...?; **laß das sein!** stop that!

---

sein(e) ['zainə] *adj* his; its; **~e(r, s)** *pron* his; its; **~er** (*gen von* **er**) *pron* of him; **~erseits** *adv* for his part; **~erzeit** *adv* in those days, formerly; **~esgleichen** *pron* people like him; **~etwegen** *adv* (*für ihn*) for his sake; (*wegen ihm*) on his account; (*von ihm aus*) as far as he is concerned; **~etwillen** *adv*: **um ~etwillen** = **seinetwegen**; **~ige** *pron*: **der/die/das ~ige** his

seit [zait] *präp +dat* since ♦ *konj* since; **er ist ~ einer Woche hier** he has been here for a week; **~ langem** for a long time; **~dem** [zait'de:m] *adv, konj* since

Seite ['zaitə] *f* side; (*Buch~*) page; (*MIL*) flank

Seiten- *zW*: **~ansicht** *f* side view; **~hieb** *m* (*fig*) passing shot, dig; **s~s** *präp +gen* on the part of; **~schiff** *nt* aisle; **~sprung** *m* extramarital escapade; **~stechen** *nt* (a) stitch; **~straße** *f* side road; **~streifen** *m* verge; (*der Autobahn*) hard shoulder

seither [zait'he:r] *adv, konj* since (then)

seit- *zW*: **~lich** *adj* on one *od* the side; side *cpd*; **~wärts** *adv* sidewards

Sekretär [zekre'tε:r] *m* secretary; (*Möbel*) bureau

Sekretariat [zekretari'a:t] (**-(e)s, -e**) *nt*

⚠ *For information on spelling reform see page 615*

secretary's office, secretariat
Sekretärin f secretary
Sekt [zɛkt] (-(e)s, -e) m champagne
Sekte ['zɛktə] f sect
Sekunde [ze'kʊndə] f second
selber ['zɛlbər] = **selbst**
Selbst [zɛlpst] (-) nt self

SCHLÜSSELWORT

selbst [zɛlpst] pron 1: **ich/er/wir selbst** I
myself/he himself/we ourselves; **sie ist die
Tugend selbst** she's virtue itself; **er braut
sein Bier selbst** he brews his own beer;
wie geht's? - gut, und selbst? how are
things? - fine, and yourself?
2 (*ohne Hilfe*) alone, on my/his/one's *etc*
own; **von selbst** by itself; **er kam von
selbst** he came of his own accord
♦ adv even; **selbst wenn** even if; **selbst
Gott** even God (himself)

---

selbständig ⚠ ['zɛlpʃtɛndɪç] adj
independent; **S~keit** ⚠ f independence
Selbst- zW: **~auslöser** m (PHOT) delayed-
action shutter release; **~bedienung** f self-
service; **~befriedigung** f masturbation;
~beherrschung f self-control;
~bestimmung f (POL) self-determination;
~beteiligung f (VERSICHERUNG: bei Kosten)
(voluntary) excess; **s~bewußt** ⚠ adj
(self-)confident; **~bewußtsein** ⚠ nt self-
confidence; **~erhaltung** f self-preservation;
~erkenntnis f self-knowledge; **s~gefällig**
adj smug, self-satisfied; **s~gemacht** ⚠ adj
home-made; **~gespräch** nt conversation
with o.s.; **~kostenpreis** m cost price;
s~los adj unselfish, selfless; **~mord** m
suicide; **~mörder(in)** m(f) suicide;
s~mörderisch adj suicidal; **s~sicher** adj
self-assured; **s~süchtig** adj (Mensch)
selfish; **~versorger** (-s, -) m (im Urlaub etc)
self-caterer; **s~verständlich**
['zɛlpstfɛrʃtɛntlɪç] adj obvious ♦ adv naturally;
ich halte das für s~verständlich I take
that for granted; **~verteidigung** f self-
defence; **~vertrauen** nt self-confidence;
~verwaltung f autonomy, self-

government
selig ['ze:lɪç] adj happy, blissful; (REL)
blessed; (tot) late; **S~keit** f bliss
Sellerie ['zɛləri:] (-s, -(s) od -, -) m od f
celery
selten ['zɛltən] adj rare ♦ adv seldom, rarely;
S~heit f rarity
Selterswasser ['zɛltərsvasər] nt soda water
seltsam ['zɛltza:m] adj strange, curious;
S~keit f strangeness
Semester [ze'mɛstər] (-s, -) nt semester;
~ferien pl vacation sg
Semi- [zemi] in zW semi-; **~kolon** [-'ko:lɔn]
(-s, -s) nt semicolon
Seminar [zemi'na:r] (-s, -e) nt seminary;
(Kurs) seminar; (UNIV: Ort) department
building
Semmel ['zɛməl] (-, -n) f roll
Senat [ze'na:t] (-(e)s, -e) m senate, council
Sende- ['zɛndə] zW: **~bereich** m
transmission range; **~folge** f (Serie) series;
s~n (unreg) vt to send; (RAD, TV) to
transmit, to broadcast ♦ vi to transmit, to
broadcast; **~r** (-s, -) m station; (Anlage)
transmitter; **~reihe** f series (of broadcasts)
Sendung ['zɛndʊŋ] f consignment;
(Aufgabe) mission; (RAD, TV) transmission;
(Programm) programme
Senf [zɛnf] (-(e)s, -e) m mustard
senil [ze'ni:l] (pej) adj senile
Senior(in) ['ze:nior(ɪn)] (-s, -en) m(f)
(Mensch im Rentenalter) (old age) pensioner
Seniorenheim [zeni'o:rənhaɪm] nt old
people's home
Senk- ['zɛŋk] zW: **~blei** nt plumb; **~e** f
depression; **s~en** vt to lower ♦ vr to sink,
to drop gradually; **s~recht** adj vertical,
perpendicular; **~rechte** f perpendicular;
~rechtstarter m (AVIAT) vertical take-off
plane; (fig) high-flyer
Sensation [zɛnzatsi'o:n] f sensation; **s~ell**
[-'nɛl] adj sensational
sensibel [zɛn'zi:bəl] adj sensitive
sentimental [zɛntimɛn'ta:l] adj sentimental;
S~ität f sentimentality
separat [zepa'ra:t] adj separate
September [zɛp'tɛmbər] (-(s), -) m

⚠ *Informationen zur Rechtschreibreform Seite 615*

September

Serie ['zeːriə] f series

serien- zW: **~mäßig** adj standard; **S~mörder(in)** m(f) serial killer; **~weise** adv in series

seriös [zeri'øːs] adj serious, bona fide

Service¹ [zɛr'viːs] (-(s), -) nt (Geschirr) set, service

Service² (-, -s) m service

servieren [zɛr'viːrən] vt, vi to serve

Serviererin [zɛr'viːrərɪn] f waitress

Serviette [zɛr'vi'ɛtə] f napkin, serviette

Servo- ['zɛrvo] zW: **~bremse** f (AUT) servo(-assisted) brake; **~lenkung** f (AUT) power steering

Sessel ['zɛsəl] (-s, -) m armchair; **~lift** m chairlift

seßhaft ['zɛshaft] adj settled; (ansässig) resident

setzen ['zɛtsən] vt to put, to set; (Baum etc) to plant; (Segel, TYP) to set ♦ vr to settle; (Person) to sit down ♦ vi (springen) to leap; (wetten) to bet

Setz- ['zɛts] zW: **~er** (-s, -) m (TYP) compositor; **~ling** m young plant

Seuche ['zɔʏçə] f epidemic; **~ngebiet** nt infected area

seufzen ['zɔʏftsən] vt, vi to sigh

Seufzer ['zɔʏftsər] (-s, -) m sigh

Sex [zɛks] (-(es)) m sex; **~ualität** [-uali'tɛt] f sex, sexuality; **~ualkunde** [zɛksu'aːl-] f (SCH) sex education; **s~uell** [-u'ɛl] adj sexual

sezieren [ze'tsiːrən] vt to dissect

Shampoo [ʃam'puː] (-s, -s) nt shampoo

Sibirien [zi'biːriən] nt Siberia

┌─────────────────────┐
│ *SCHLÜSSELWORT* │
└─────────────────────┘

sich [zɪç] pron 1 (akk): **er/sie/es ... sich** he/she/it ... himself/herself/itself; **sie** pl/**man ... sich** they/one ... themselves/oneself; **Sie ... sich** you ... yourself/yourselves pl; **sich wiederholen** to repeat oneself/itself

2 (dat): **er/sie/es ... sich** he/she/it ... to himself/herself/itself; **sie** pl/**man ... sich** they/one ... to themselves/oneself; **Sie ...**

sich you ... to yourself/yourselves pl; **sie hat sich einen Pullover gekauft** she bought herself a jumper; **sich die Haare waschen** to wash one's hair

3 (mit Präposition): **haben Sie Ihren Ausweis bei sich?** do you have your pass on you?; **er hat nichts bei sich** he's got nothing on him; **sie bleiben gern unter sich** they keep themselves to themselves

4 (einander) each other, one another; **sie bekämpfen sich** they fight each other od one another

5: **dieses Auto fährt sich gut** this car drives well; **hier sitzt es sich gut** it's good to sit here

└─────────────────────┘

Sichel ['zɪçəl] (-, -n) f sickle; (Mond~) crescent

sicher ['zɪçər] adj safe; (gewiß) certain; (zuverlässig) secure, reliable; (selbst~) confident; **vor jdm/etw ~ sein** to be safe from sb/sth; **ich bin nicht ~** I'm not sure od certain; **~ nicht** surely not; **aber ~!** of course!; **~gehen** (unreg) vi to make sure

Sicherheit ['zɪçərhaɪt] f safety; (auch FIN) security; (Gewißheit) certainty; (Selbst~) confidence

Sicherheits- zW: **~abstand** m safe distance; **~glas** nt safety glass; **~gurt** m safety belt; **s~halber** adv for safety; to be on the safe side; **~nadel** f safety pin; **~schloß** △ nt safety lock; **~vorkehrung** f safety precaution

sicher- zW: **~lich** adv certainly, surely; **~n** vt to secure; (schützen) to protect; (Waffe) to put the safety catch on; **jdm etw ~n** to secure sth for sb; **sich** dat **etw ~n** to secure sth (for o.s.); **~stellen** vt to impound; **S~ung** f (Sichern) securing; (Vorrichtung) safety device; (an Waffen) safety catch; (ELEK) fuse; **S~ungskopie** f back-up copy

Sicht [zɪçt] (-) f sight; (Aussicht) view; **auf od nach ~** (FIN) at sight; **auf lange ~** on a long-term basis; **s~bar** adj visible; **s~en** vt to sight; (auswählen) to sort out; **s~lich** adj evident, obvious; **~verhältnisse** pl visibility sg; **~vermerk** m visa; **~weite** f

△ *For information on spelling reform see page 615*

visibility

sickern ['zɪkərn] vi to trickle, to seep

Sie [ziː] (nom, akk) pron you

sie [ziː] pron (sg: nom) she, it; (: akk) her, it; (pl: nom) they; (: akk) them

Sieb [ziːp] (-(e)s, -e) nt sieve; (KOCH) strainer; **s~en** ['ziːbən] vt to sift; (Flüssigkeit) to strain

sieben² num seven; **~hundert** num seven hundred; **S~sachen** pl belongings

siebte(r, s) ['ziːptə(r, s)] adj seventh; **S~l** (-s, -) nt seventh

siebzehn ['ziːptseːn] num seventeen

siebzig ['ziːptsɪç] num seventy

siedeln ['ziːdəln] vi to settle

sieden ['ziːdən] vt, vi to boil, to simmer

Siedepunkt m boiling point

Siedler (-s, -) m settler

Siedlung f settlement; (Häuser~) housing estate

Sieg [ziːk] (-(e)s, -e) m victory

Siegel ['ziːgəl] (-s, -) nt seal; **~ring** m signet ring

Sieg- zW: **s~en** vi to be victorious; (SPORT) to win; **~er** (-s, -) m victor; (SPORT etc) winner; **s~reich** adj victorious

siehe etc ['ziːə] vb siehe **sehen**

siezen ['ziːtsən] vt to address as "Sie"

Signal [zɪ'gnaːl] (-s, -e) nt signal

Silbe ['zɪlbə] f syllable

Silber ['zɪlbər] (-s) nt silver; **~hochzeit** f silver wedding (anniversary); **s~n** adj silver; **~papier** nt silver paper

Silhouette [zilu'ɛtə] f silhouette

Silvester [zɪl'vɛstər] (-s, -) nt New Year's Eve, Hogmanay (SCOTTISH); **~abend** m = **Silvester**

SILVESTER

ⓘ **Silvester** is the German word for New Year's Eve. Although not an official holiday most businesses close early and shops shut at midday. Most Germans celebrate in the evening, and at midnight they let off fireworks; the revelry usually lasts until the early hours of the morning.

---

simpel ['zɪmpəl] adj simple

Sims [zɪms] (-es, -e) nt od m (Kamin~) mantelpiece; (Fenster~) (window)sill

simulieren [zimu'liːrən] vt to simulate; (vortäuschen) to feign ♦ vi to feign illness

simultan [zimʊl'taːn] adj simultaneous

Sinfonie [zɪnfoˈniː] f symphony

singen ['zɪŋən] (unreg) vt, vi to sing

Singular ['zɪŋgulaːr] m singular

Singvogel ['zɪŋfoːgəl] m songbird

sinken ['zɪŋkən] (unreg) vi to sink; (Preise etc) to fall, to go down

Sinn [zɪn] (-(e)s, -e) m mind; (Wahrnehmungs~) sense; (Bedeutung) sense, meaning; **~ für etw** sense of sth; **von ~en sein** to be out of one's mind; **es hat keinen ~** there's no point; **~bild** nt symbol; **s~en** (unreg) vi to ponder; **auf etw** akk **s~en** to contemplate sth; **~estäuschung** f illusion; **s~gemäß** adj faithful; (Wiedergabe) in one's own words; **s~ig** adj clever; **s~lich** adj sensual, sensuous; (Wahrnehmung) sensory; **~lichkeit** f sensuality; **s~los** adj senseless; meaningless; **~losigkeit** f senselessness; meaninglessness; **s~voll** adj meaningful; (vernünftig) sensible

Sintflut ['zɪntfluːt] f Flood

Sippe ['zɪpə] f clan, kin

Sippschaft ['zɪpʃaft] (pej) f relations pl, tribe; (Bande) gang

Sirene [ziˈreːnə] f siren

Sirup ['ziːrʊp] (-s, -e) m syrup

Sitt- ['zɪt] zW: **~e** f custom; **~en** pl (Sittlichkeit) morals; **~enpolizei** f vice squad; **s~sam** adj modest, demure

Situation [zituatsiˈoːn] f situation

Sitz [zɪts] (-es, -e) m seat; **der Anzug hat einen guten ~** the suit is a good fit; **s~en** (unreg) vi to sit; (Bemerkung, Schlag) to strike home, to tell; (Gelerntes) to have sunk in; **s~en bleiben** to remain seated; **s~enbleiben** △ (unreg) vi (SCH) to have to repeat a year; **auf etw** dat **s~enbleiben** to be lumbered with sth; **s~end** adj (Tätigkeit) sedentary; **s~enlassen** △ (unreg) vt (SCH)

△ *Informationen zur Rechtschreibreform Seite 615*

to make (sb) repeat a year; (*Mädchen*) to jilt; (*Wartenden*) to stand up; **etw auf sich dat s~enlassen** to take sth lying down; **~gelegenheit** f place to sit down; **~platz** m seat; **~streik** m sit-down strike; **~ung** f meeting

Sizilien [zi'tsi:liən] nt Sicily

Skala ['ska:la] (-, **Skalen**) f scale

Skalpell [skal'pɛl] (-s, -e) nt scalpel

Skandal [skan'da:l] (-s, -e) m scandal; **s~ös** [-'lø:s] adj scandalous

Skandinav- [skandi'na:v] zW: **~ien** nt Scandinavia; **~ier(in)** m(f) Scandinavian; **s~isch** adj Scandinavian

Skelett [ske'lɛt] (-(e)s, -e) nt skeleton

Skepsis ['skɛpsɪs] (-) f scepticism

skeptisch ['skɛptɪʃ] adj sceptical

Ski [ʃi:] (-s, **-er**) m ski; **~ laufen** od **fahren** to ski; **~fahrer** m skier; **~gebiet** nt ski(ing) area; **~läufer** m skier; **~lehrer** m ski instructor; **~lift** m ski-lift; **~springen** nt ski-jumping; **~stock** m ski-pole

Skizze ['skɪtsə] f sketch

skizzieren [skɪ'tsi:rən] vt, vi to sketch

Sklave ['skla:və] (-n, -n) m slave; **~'rei** f slavery; **Sklavin** f slave

Skonto ['skɔnto] (-s, -s) m od nt discount

Skorpion [skɔrpi'o:n] (-s, -e) m scorpion; (*ASTROL*) Scorpio

Skrupel ['skru:pəl] (-s, -) m scruple; **s~los** adj unscrupulous

Skulptur [skʊlp'tu:r] f (*Gegenstand*) sculpture

S-Kurve ['ɛskʊrvə] f S-bend

Slip [slɪp] (-s, -s) m (under)pants; **~einlage** f panty liner

Slowakei [slova'kaɪ] f: **die ~** Slovakia

Slowenien [slo've:niən] nt Slovenia

Smaragd [sma'rakt] (-(e)s, -e) m emerald

Smoking ['smo:kɪŋ] (-s, -s) m dinner jacket

SCHLÜSSELWORT

so [zo:] adv **1** (*sosehr*) so; **so groß/schön** *etc* so big/nice *etc*; **so groß/schön wie ...** as big/nice as ...; **das hat ihn so geärgert, daß ...** that annoyed him so much that ...; **so einer wie ich** somebody like me; **na so**

was! well, well!
2 (*auf diese Weise*) like this; **mach es nicht so** don't do it like that; **so oder so** in one way or the other; **und so weiter** and so on; **... oder so was** ... or something like that; **das ist gut** so that's fine
3 (*umg: umsonst*): **ich habe es so bekommen** I got it for nothing
♦ *konj*: **so daß** so that; **so wie es jetzt ist** as things are at the moment
♦ *excl*: **so?** really?; **so, das wär's** so, that's it then

---

s.o. abk = siehe oben

Söckchen ['zœkçən] nt ankle socks

Socke ['zɔkə] f sock

Sockel ['zɔkəl] (-s, -) m pedestal, base

Sodawasser ['zo:davasər] nt soda water

Sodbrennen ['zo:tbrɛnən] (-s, -) nt heartburn

soeben [zo'|e:bən] adv just (now)

Sofa ['zo:fa] (-s, -s) nt sofa

sofern [zo'fɛrn] konj if, provided (that)

sofort [zo'fɔrt] adv immediately, at once; **~ig** adj immediate

Sog [zo:k] (-(e)s, -e) m (*Strömung*) undertow

sogar [zo'ga:r] adv even

sogenannt △ ['zo:gənant] adj so-called

sogleich [zo'glaɪç] adv straight away, at once

Sohle ['zo:lə] f sole; (*Tal~ etc*) bottom; (*MIN*) level

Sohn [zo:n] (-(e)s, ¨e) m son

Solar- [zo'la:r] in zW solar; **~zelle** f solar cell

solch [zɔlç] pron such; **ein ~e(r, s) ...** such a ...

Soldat [zɔl'da:t] (-en, -en) m soldier

Söldner ['zœldnər] (-s, -) m mercenary

solidarisch [zoli'da:rɪʃ] adj in od with solidarity; **sich ~ erklären** to declare one's solidarity

Solidari'tät f solidarity

solid(e) [zo'li:d(ə)] adj solid; (*Leben, Person*) respectable

Solist(in) [zo'lɪst(ɪn)] m(f) soloist

Soll [zɔl] (-(s), -(s)) nt (*FIN*) debit (side);

△ *For information on spelling reform see page 615*

(Arbeitsmenge) quota, target

SCHLÜSSELWORT

sollen ['zɔlən] *(pt* **sollte,** *pp* **gesollt** *od (als Hilfsverb)* **sollen)** *Hilfsverb* **1** *(Pflicht, Befehl)* to be supposed to; **du hättest nicht gehen sollen** you shouldn't have gone, you oughtn't to have gone; **soll ich?** shall I?; **soll ich dir helfen?** shall I help you?; **sag ihm, er soll warten** tell him he's to wait; **was soll ich machen?** what should I do? **2** *(Vermutung)*: **sie soll verheiratet sein** she's said to be married; **was soll das heißen?** what's that supposed to mean?; **man sollte glauben, daß ...** you would think that ...; **sollte das passieren, ...** if that should happen ...

♦ *vt, vi:* **was soll das?** what's all this?; **das sollst du nicht** you shouldn't do that; **was soll's?** what the hell!

Solo ['zo:lo] *(-s, -s* od **Soli)** *nt* solo
somit [zo'mit] *konj* and so, therefore
Sommer ['zɔmər] *(-s, -)* m summer; **s~lich** *adj* summery; summer; **~reifen** m normal tyre; **~schlußverkauf** ⚠ m summer sale; **~sprossen** *pl* freckles
Sonde ['zɔndə] f probe
Sonder- ['zɔndər] *in zW* special; **~angebot** *nt* special offer; **s~bar** *adj* strange, odd; **~fahrt** f special trip; **~fall** m special case; **s~lich** *adj* particular; *(außergewöhnlich)* remarkable; *(eigenartig)* peculiar; **~marke** f special issue stamp; **s~n** *konj* but ♦ *vt* to separate; **nicht nur ...,** **s~n auch** not only ..., but also; **~preis** m special reduced price; **~zug** m special train
Sonnabend ['zɔn|a:bənt] m Saturday
Sonne ['zɔnə] f sun; **s~n** *vr* to sun o.s.
Sonnen- *zW:* **~aufgang** m sunrise; **s~baden** *vi* to sunbathe; **~brand** m sunburn; **~brille** f sunglasses *pl;* **~creme** f suntan lotion; **~energie** f solar energy, solar power; **~finsternis** f solar eclipse; **~kollektor** m solar panel; **~schein** m sunshine; **~schirm** m parasol, sunshade; **~schutzfaktor** m protection factor;

~stich m sunstroke; **~uhr** f sundial; **~untergang** m sunset; **~wende** f solstice
sonnig ['zɔnɪç] *adj* sunny
Sonntag ['zɔnta:k] m Sunday
sonst [zɔnst] *adv* otherwise; *(mit pron, in Fragen)* else; *(zu anderer Zeit)* at other times, normally ♦ *konj* otherwise; **~ noch etwas?** anything else?; **~ nichts** nothing else; **~ig** *adj* other; **~jemand** ⚠ *pron* anybody (at all); **~wo** ⚠ *adv* somewhere else; **~woher** ⚠ *adv* from somewhere else; **~wohin** ⚠ *adv* somewhere else
sooft [zo'ɔft] *konj* whenever
Sopran [zo'pra:n] *(-s, -e)* m soprano
Sorge ['zɔrgə] f care, worry
sorgen *vi:* **für jdn ~** to look after sb ♦ *vr:* **sich ~ (um)** to worry (about); **für etw ~** to take care of *od* see to sth; **~frei** *adj* carefree; **~voll** *adj* troubled, worried
Sorgerecht *nt* custody (of a child)
Sorg- [zɔrk] *zW:* **~falt** *(-)* f care(fulness); **s~fältig** *adj* careful; **s~los** *adj* careless; *(ohne Sorgen)* carefree; **s~sam** *adj* careful
Sorte ['zɔrtə] f sort; *(Waren~)* brand; **~n** *pl* *(FIN)* foreign currency *sg*
sortieren [zɔr'ti:rən] *vt* to sort (out)
Sortiment [zɔrti'mɛnt] *nt* assortment
sosehr [zo'ze:r] *konj* as much as
Soße ['zo:sə] f sauce; *(Braten~)* gravy
soufflieren [zu'fli:rən] *vt, vi* to prompt
Souterrain [zutɛ'rɛ:] *(-s, -s)* *nt* basement
souverän [zuva'rɛ:n] *adj* sovereign; *(überlegen)* superior
so- *zW:* **~viel** [zo'fi:l] *konj:* **~viel ich weiß** as far as I know ♦ *pron:* **~viel (wie)** as much as; **rede nicht ~viel** don't talk so much; **~weit** [zo'vait] *konj* as far as ♦ *adj:* **~weit sein** to be ready; **~weit wie** *od* **als möglich** as far as possible; **ich bin ~weit zufrieden** by and large I'm quite satisfied; **~wenig** [zo've:nɪç] *konj* little as ♦ *pron:* **~wenig (wie)** as little (as); **~wie** [zo'vi:] *konj (sobald)* as soon as; *(ebenso)* as well as; **~wieso** [zovi'zo:] *adv* anyway
sowjetisch [zɔ'vjɛtɪʃ] *adj* Soviet
Sowjetunion f Soviet Union
sowohl [zo'vo:l] *konj:* **~ ... als** *od* **wie auch**

⚠ *Informationen zur Rechtschreibreform Seite 615*

both

sozial [zotsi'aːl] adj social; **S~abgaben** pl national insurance contributions; **S~arbeiter(in)** m(f) social worker; **S~demokrat** m social democrat; **~demokratisch** adj social democratic; **S~hilfe** f income support (BRIT), welfare (aid) (US); **~isieren** vt to socialize; **S~ismus** [-'lɪsmʊs] m socialism; **S~ist** [-'lɪst] m socialist; **~istisch** adj socialist; **S~politik** f social welfare policy; **S~produkt** nt (net) national product; **S~staat** m welfare state; **S~versicherung** f national insurance (BRIT), social security (US); **S~wohnung** f council flat

soziologisch [zotsio'loːgɪʃ] adj sociological

sozusagen [zotsu'zaːgən] adv so to speak

Spachtel ['ʃpaxtəl] (-s, -) m spatula

spähen ['ʃpeːən] vi to peep, to peek

Spalier [ʃpa'liːr] (-s, -e) nt (Gerüst) trellis; (Leute) guard of honour

Spalt [ʃpalt] (-(e)s, -e) m crack; (Tür~) chink; (fig: Kluft) split; **~e** f crack, fissure; (Gletscherspalte) crevasse; (in Text) column; **s~en** vt, vr (auch fig) to split; **~ung** f splitting

Span [ʃpaːn] (-(e)s, -e) m shaving

Spanferkel nt sucking pig

Spange ['ʃpaŋə] f clasp; (Haar~) hair slide; (Schnalle) buckle

Spanien ['ʃpaːniən] nt Spain; **Spanier(in)** m(f) Spaniard; **spanisch** adj Spanish

Spann- ['ʃpan] zW: **~beton** m prestressed concrete; **~bettuch** △ nt fitted sheet; **~e** f (Zeitspanne) space; (Differenz) gap; **s~en** vt (straffen) to tighten, to tauten; (befestigen) to brace ♦ vi to be tight; **s~end** adj exciting, gripping; **~ung** f tension; (ELEK) voltage; (fig) suspense; (unangenehm) tension

Spar- ['ʃpaːr] zW: **~buch** nt savings book; **~büchse** f money box; **s~en** vt, vi to save; **sich** dat **etw s~en** to save o.s. sth; (Bemerkung) to keep sth to o.s.; **mit etw s~en** to be sparing with sth; **an etw** dat **s~en** to economize on sth; **~er** (-s, -) m saver

Spargel ['ʃpargəl] (-s, -) m asparagus

Sparkasse f savings bank

Sparkonto nt savings account

spärlich ['ʃpeːrlɪç] adj meagre; (Bekleidung) scanty

Spar- zW: **~preis** m economy price; **s~sam** adj economical, thrifty; **~samkeit** f thrift, economizing; **~schwein** nt piggy bank

Sparte ['ʃpartə] f field; line of business; (PRESSE) column

Spaß [ʃpaːs] (-es, ¨e) m joke; (Freude) fun; **jdm ~ machen** to be fun (for sb); **viel ~!** have fun!; **s~en** vi to joke; **mit ihm ist nicht zu s~en** you can't take liberties with him; **s~haft** adj funny, droll; **s~ig** adj funny, droll

spät [ʃpeːt] adj, adv late; **wie ~ ist es?** what's the time?

Spaten ['ʃpaːtən] (-s, -) m spade

später adj, adv later

spätestens adv at the latest

Spätvorstellung f late show

Spatz [ʃpats] (-en, -en) m sparrow

spazier- [ʃpa'tsiːr] zW: **~en** vi to stroll, to walk; **~enfahren** △ (unreg) vi to go for a drive; **~engehen** △ (unreg) vi to go for a walk; **S~gang** m walk; **S~stock** m walking stick; **S~weg** m path, walk

Specht [ʃpɛçt] (-(e)s, -e) m woodpecker

Speck [ʃpɛk] (-(e)s, -e) m bacon

Spediteur [ʃpedi'tøːr] m carrier; (Möbel~) furniture remover

Spedition [ʃpeditsi'oːn] f carriage; (Speditionsfirma) road haulage contractor; removal firm

Speer [ʃpeːr] (-(e)s, -e) m spear; (SPORT) javelin

Speiche ['ʃpaɪçə] f spoke

Speichel ['ʃpaɪçəl] (-s) m saliva, spit(tle)

Speicher ['ʃpaɪçər] (-s, -) m storehouse; (Dach~) attic, loft; (Korn~) granary; (Wasser~) tank; (TECH) store; (COMPUT) memory; **s~n** vt to store; (COMPUT) to save

speien ['ʃpaɪən] (unreg) vt, vi to spit; (erbrechen) to vomit; (Vulkan) to spew

△ For information on spelling reform see page 615

Speise [ˈʃpaɪzə] f food; **~eis** [-ˌaɪs] nt ice-cream; **~kammer** f larder, pantry; **~karte** f menu; **s~n** vt to feed; to eat ♦ vi to dine; **~röhre** f gullet, oesophagus; **~saal** m dining room; **~wagen** m dining car

Speku- [ʃpeku] zW: **~lant** m speculator; **~lation** [-latsiˈoːn] f speculation; **s~lieren** [-ˈliːrən] vi (fig) to speculate; **auf etw** akk **s~lieren** to have hopes of sth

Spelunke [ʃpeˈlʊŋkə] f dive

Spende [ˈʃpɛndə] f donation; **s~n** vt to donate, to give; **~r (-s, -)** m donor, donator

spendieren [ʃpɛnˈdiːrən] vt to pay for, to buy; **jdm etw ~** to treat sb to sth, to stand sb sth

Sperling [ˈʃpɛrlɪŋ] m sparrow

Sperma [ˈʃpɛrma] (-s, **Spermen**) nt sperm

Sperr- [ʃpɛr] zW: **~e** f barrier; (Verbot) ban; **s~en** vt to block; (SPORT) to suspend, to bar; (vom Ball) to obstruct; (einschließen) to lock; (verbieten) to ban ♦ vr to baulk to jib(e); **~gebiet** nt prohibited area; **~holz** nt plywood; **s~ig** adj bulky; **~müll** m bulky refuse; **~sitz** m (THEAT) stalls pl; **~stunde** f closing time

Spesen [ˈʃpeːzən] pl expenses

Spezial- [ʃpetsiˈaːl] in zW special; **~gebiet** nt specialist field; **s~i'sieren** vr to specialize; **~i'sierung** f specialization; **~ist** [-ˈlɪst] m specialist; **~i'tät** f speciality

speziell [ʃpetsiˈɛl] adj special

spezifisch [ʃpeˈtsiːfɪʃ] adj specific

Sphäre [ˈsfɛːrə] f sphere

Spiegel [ˈʃpiːɡəl] (-s, -) m mirror; (Wasser~) level; (MIL) tab; **~bild** nt reflection; **s~bildlich** adj reversed; **~ei** nt fried egg; **s~n** vt to mirror, to reflect ♦ vr to be reflected ♦ vi to gleam; (widerspiegeln) to be reflective; **~ung** f reflection

Spiel [ʃpiːl] (-(e)s, -e) nt game; (Schau~) play; (Tätigkeit) play(ing); (KARTEN) deck; (TECH) (free) play; **s~en** vt, vi to play; (um Geld) to gamble; (THEAT) to perform, to act; **s~end** adv easily; **~er (-s, -)** m player; (um Geld) gambler; **~e'rei** f trifling pastime; **~feld** nt pitch, field; **~film** m feature film;

~kasino nt casino; **~plan** m (THEAT) programme; **~platz** m playground; **~raum** m room to manoeuvre, scope; **~regel** f rule; **~sachen** pl toys; **~uhr** f musical box; **~verderber (-s, -)** m spoilsport; **~waren** pl toys; **~zeug** nt toy(s)

Spieß [ʃpiːs] (-es, -e) m spear; (Brat~) spit; **~bürger** m bourgeois; **~er (-s, -)** (umg) m bourgeois; **s~ig** (pej) adj (petit) bourgeois

Spinat [ʃpiˈnaːt] (-(e)s, -e) m spinach

Spind [ʃpɪnt] (-(e)s, -e) m od nt locker

Spinn- [ˈʃpɪn] zW: **~e** f spider; **s~en** (unreg) vt, vi to spin; (umg) to talk rubbish; (verrückt sein) to be crazy od mad; **~e'rei** f spinning mill; **~rad** nt spinning wheel; **~webe** f cobweb

Spion [ʃpiˈoːn] (-s, -e) m spy; (in Tür) spyhole; **~age** [ʃpioˈnaːʒə] f espionage; **s~ieren** [ʃpioˈniːrən] vi to spy; **~in** f (female) spy

Spirale [ʃpiˈraːlə] f spiral

Spirituosen [ʃpirituˈoːzən] pl spirits

Spiritus [ˈʃpiːritʊs] (-, -se) m (methylated) spirit

Spital [ʃpiˈtaːl] (-s, ̈er) nt hospital

spitz [ʃpɪts] adj pointed; (Winkel) acute; (fig: Zunge) sharp; (: Bemerkung) caustic

Spitze f point, tip; (Berg~) peak; (Bemerkung) taunt, dig; (erster Platz) lead, top; (meist pl: Gewebe) lace

Spitzel (-s, -) m police informer

spitzen vt to sharpen

Spitzenmarke f brand leader

spitzfindig adj (over)subtle

Spitzname m nickname

Splitter [ˈʃplɪtər] (-s, -) m splinter

sponsern [ˈʃpɔnzərn] vt to sponsor

spontan [ʃpɔnˈtaːn] adj spontaneous

Sport [ʃpɔrt] (-(e)s, -e) m sport; (fig) hobby; **~lehrer(in)** m(f) games od P.E. teacher; **~ler(in) (-s, -)** m(f) sportsman(-woman); **s~lich** adj sporting; (Mensch) sporty; **~platz** m playing od sports field; **~schuh** m (Turnschuh) training shoe, trainer; **~stadion** nt sports stadium; **~verein** m sports club; **~wagen** m sports car

Spott [ʃpɔt] (-(e)s) m mockery, ridicule;

⚠ *Informationen zur Rechtschreibreform Seite 615*

s~billig adj dirt-cheap; **s~en** vi to mock; **s~en** (über +akk) to ridicule
spöttisch ['ʃpœtɪʃ] adj mocking
sprach etc [ʃpraːx] vb siehe **sprechen**
Sprach- zW: **s~begabt** adj good at languages; **~e** f language; **~enschule** f language school; **~fehler** m speech defect; **~führer** m phrasebook; **~gefühl** nt feeling for language; **~kenntnisse** pl linguistic proficiency sg; **~kurs** m language course; **~labor** nt language laboratory; **s~lich** adj linguistic; **s~los** adj speechless
sprang etc [ʃpraŋ] vb siehe **springen**
Spray [spreː] (-s, -s) m od nt spray
Sprech- ['ʃprɛç] zW: **~anlage** f intercom; **s~en** (unreg) vi to speak, to talk ♦ vt to say; (Sprache) to speak; (Person) to speak to; **mit jdm s~en** to speak to sb; **das spricht für ihn** that's a point in his favour; **~er(in)** (-s, -) m(f) speaker; (für Gruppe) spokesman(-woman); (RAD, TV) announcer; **~stunde** f consultation (hour); (doctor's) surgery; **~stundenhilfe** f (doctor's) receptionist; **~zimmer** nt consulting room, surgery, office (US)
spreizen ['ʃpraɪtsən] vt (Beine) to open, to spread; (Finger, Flügel) to spread
Spreng- etc ['ʃprɛŋ] zW: **s~en** vt to sprinkle; (mit Sprengstoff) to blow up; (Gestein) to blast; (Versammlung) to break up; **~stoff** m explosive(s)
sprichst etc [ʃprɪçst] vb siehe **sprechen**
Sprichwort nt proverb; **sprichwörtlich** adj proverbial
Spring- ['ʃprɪŋ] zW: **~brunnen** m fountain; **s~en** (unreg) vi to jump; (Glas) to crack; (mit Kopfsprung) to dive; **~er** (-s, -) m jumper; (Schach) knight
Sprit [ʃprɪt] (-(e)s, -e) (umg) m juice, gas
Spritz- ['ʃprɪts] zW: **~e** f syringe; injection; (an Schlauch) nozzle; **s~en** vt to spray; (MED) to inject ♦ vi to splash; (herausspritzen) to spurt; (MED) to give injections; **~pistole** f spray gun; **~tour** f (umg) spin
spröde ['ʃprøːdə] adj brittle; (Person) reserved, coy

Sprosse ['ʃprɔsə] f rung
Sprößling ⚠ ['ʃprœslɪŋ] (umg) m (Kind) offspring (pl inv)
Spruch [ʃprʊx] (-(e)s, -̈e) m saying, maxim; (JUR) judgement
Sprudel ['ʃpruːdəl] (-s, -) m mineral water; lemonade; **s~n** vi to bubble; **~wasser** nt (KOCH) sparkling od fizzy mineral water
Sprüh- ['ʃpryː] zW: **~dose** f aerosol (can); **s~en** vi to spray; (fig) to sparkle ♦ vt to spray; **~regen** m drizzle
Sprung [ʃprʊŋ] (-(e)s, -̈e) m jump; (Riß) crack; **~brett** nt springboard; **s~haft** adj erratic; (Aufstieg) rapid; **~schanze** f ski jump
Spucke ['ʃpʊkə] (-) f spit; **s~n** vt, vi to spit
Spuk [ʃpuːk] (-(e)s, -e) m haunting; (fig) nightmare; **s~en** vi (Geist) to walk; **hier s~t es** this place is haunted
Spülbecken ['ʃpyːlbɛkən] nt (in Küche) sink
Spule ['ʃpuːlə] f spool; (ELEK) coil
Spül- ['ʃpyːl] zW: **~e** f (kitchen) sink; **s~en** vt, vi to rinse; (Geschirr) to wash up; (Toilette) to flush; **~maschine** f dishwasher; **~mittel** nt washing-up liquid; **~stein** m sink; **~ung** f rinsing; flush; (MED) irrigation
Spur [ʃpuːr] (-, -en) f trace; (Fuß~, Rad~, Tonband~) track; (Fährte) trail; (Fahr~) lane
spürbar adj noticeable, perceptible
spüren ['ʃpyːrən] vt to feel
spurlos adv without (a) trace
Spurt [ʃpʊrt] (-(e)s, -s od -e) m spurt; **s~en** vi to spurt
sputen etc ['ʃpuːtən] vr to make haste
St. abk = **Stück**; (= Sankt) St.
Staat [ʃtaːt] (-(e)s, -en) m state; (Prunk) show; (Kleidung) finery; **s~enlos** adj stateless; **s~lich** adj state(-); state-run
Staats- zW: **~angehörige(r)** f(m) national; **~angehörigkeit** f nationality; **~anwalt** m public prosecutor; **~bürger** m citizen; **~dienst** m civil service; **~examen** nt (UNIV) state exam(ination); **s~feindlich** adj subversive; **~mann** (pl -männer) m statesman; **~oberhaupt** nt head of state
Stab [ʃtaːp] (-(e)s, -̈e) m rod; (Gitter~) bar;

⚠ For information on spelling reform see page 615

(*Menschen*) staff; **~hochsprung** *m* pole vault

stabil [ʃtaˈbiːl] *adj* stable; (*Möbel*) sturdy; **~i'sieren** *vt* to stabilize

Stachel [ˈʃtaxəl] (**-s, -n**) *m* spike; (*von Tier*) spine; (*von Insekten*) sting; **~beere** *f* gooseberry; **~draht** *m* barbed wire; **s~ig** *adj* prickly; **~schwein** *nt* porcupine

Stadion [ˈʃtaːdiɔn] (**-s, Stadien**) *nt* stadium

Stadium [ˈʃtaːdiʊm] *nt* stage, phase

Stadt [ʃtat] (**-, ¨e**) *f* town; **~autobahn** *f* urban motorway; **~bahn** *f* suburban railway; **~bücherei** *f* municipal library

Städt- [ˈʃtɛt] *zW*: **~ebau** *m* town planning; **~epartnerschaft** *f* town twinning; **~er(in)** (**-s, -**) *m(f)* town dweller; **s~isch** *adj* municipal; (*nicht ländlich*) urban

Stadt- *zW*: **~kern** *m* town centre, city centre; **~mauer** *f* city wall(s); **~mitte** *f* town centre; **~plan** *m* street map; **~rand** *m* outskirts *pl*; **~rat** *m* (*Behörde*) town council, city council; **~rundfahrt** *f* tour of a/the city; **~teil** *m* district, part of town; **~zentrum** *nt* town centre

Staffel [ˈʃtafəl] (**-, -n**) *f* rung; (*SPORT*) relay (team); (*AVIAT*) squadron; **~lauf** *m* (*SPORT*) relay (race); **s~n** *vt* to graduate

Stahl [ʃtaːl] (**-(e)s, ¨e**) *m* steel

stahl *etc vb siehe* **stehlen**

stak *etc* [ʃtaːk] *vb siehe* **stecken**

Stall [ʃtal] (**-(e)s, ¨e**) *m* stable; (*Kaninchen~*) hutch; (*Schweine~*) sty; (*Hühner~*) henhouse

Stamm [ʃtam] (**-(e)s, ¨e**) *m* (*Baum~*) trunk; (*Menschen~*) tribe; (*GRAM*) stem; **~baum** *m* family tree; (*von Tier*) pedigree; **s~eln** *vt, vi* to stammer; **s~en** *vi*: **s~en von** *od* **aus** to come from; **~gast** *m* regular (customer)

stämmig [ˈʃtɛmɪç] *adj* sturdy; (*Mensch*) stocky

Stammtisch [ˈʃtamtɪʃ] *m* table for the regulars

stampfen [ˈʃtampfən] *vt, vi* to stamp; (*stapfen*) to tramp; (*mit Werkzeug*) to pound

Stand [ʃtant] (**-(e)s, ¨e**) *m* position; (*Wasser~, Benzin~ etc*) level; (*Stehen*) standing position; (*Zustand*) state; (*Spiel~*) score; (*Messe~ etc*) stand; (*Klasse*) class;

(*Beruf*) profession

stand *etc vb siehe* **stehen**

Standard [ˈʃtandart] (**-s, -s**) *m* standard

Ständer [ˈʃtɛndər] (**-s, -**) *m* stand

Standes- [ˈʃtandəs] *zW*: **~amt** *nt* registry office; **~beamte(r)** *m* registrar; **s~gemäß** *adj, adv* according to one's social position; **~unterschied** *m* social difference

Stand- *zW*: **s~haft** *adj* steadfast; **s~halten** (*unreg*) *vi*: (**jdm/etw**) **s~halten** to stand firm (against sb/sth), ꞏto resist (sb/sth)

ständig [ˈʃtɛndɪç] *adj* permanent; (*ununterbrochen*) constant, continual

Stand- *zW*: **~licht** *nt* sidelights *pl*, parking lights *pl* (*US*); **~ort** *m* location; (*MIL*) garrison; **~punkt** *m* standpoint; **~spur** *f* hard shoulder

Stange [ˈʃtaŋə] *f* stick; (*Stab*) pole, bar; rod; (*Zigaretten*) carton; **von der ~** (*COMM*) off the peg; **eine ~ Geld** (*umg*) quite a packet

Stapel [ˈʃtaːpəl] (**-s, -**) *m* pile; (*NAUT*) stocks *pl*; **~lauf** *m* launch; **s~n** *vt* to pile (up)

Star¹ [ʃtaːr] (**-(e)s, -e**) *m* starling; (*MED*) cataract

Star² [ʃtaːr] (**-s, -s**) *m* (*Film~ etc*) star

starb *etc* [ʃtarp] *vb siehe* **sterben**

stark [ʃtark] *adj* strong; (*heftig, groß*) heavy; (*Maßangabe*) thick

Stärke [ˈʃtɛrkə] *f* strength; heaviness; thickness; (*KOCH, Wäschestärke*) starch; **s~n** *vt* to strengthen; (*Wäsche*) to starch

Starkstrom *m* heavy current

Stärkung [ˈʃtɛrkʊŋ] *f* strengthening; (*Essen*) refreshment

starr [ʃtar] *adj* stiff; (*unnachgiebig*) rigid; (*Blick*) staring; **~en** *vi* to stare; **~en vor** *od* **von** to be covered in; (*Waffen*) to be bristling with; **S~heit** *f* rigidity; **~köpfig** *adj* stubborn; **S~sinn** *m* obstinacy

Start [ʃtart] (**-(e)s, -e**) *m* start; (*AVIAT*) takeoff; **~automatik** *f* (*AUT*) automatic choke; **~bahn** *f* runway; **s~en** *vt* to start ♦ *vi* to start; to take off; **~er** (**-s, -**) *m* starter; **~erlaubnis** *f* takeoff clearance; **~hilfekabel** *nt* jump leads *pl*

Station [ʃtatsiˈoːn] *f* station; hospital ward; **s~är** [ʃtatsioˈnɛːr] *adj* (*MED*) in-patient *attr*;

s~ieren [-'niːrən] *vt* to station

Statist [ʃtaˈtɪst] *m* extra, supernumerary

Statistik *f* statistics *sg*; **~er (-s, -)** *m* statistician

statistisch *adj* statistical

Stativ [ʃtaˈtiːf] **(-s, -e)** *nt* tripod

statt [ʃtat] *konj* instead of ♦ *präp (+gen od dat)* instead of

Stätte [ˈʃtɛtə] *f* place

statt- *zW*: **~finden** *(unreg) vi* to take place; **~haft** *adj* admissible; **~lich** *adj* imposing, handsome

Statue [ˈʃtaːtuə] *f* statue

Status [ˈʃtaːtʊs] **(-, -)** *m* status

Stau [ʃtaʊ] **(-(e)s, -e)** *m* blockage; *(Verkehrs~)* (traffic) jam

Staub [ʃtaʊp] **(-(e)s)** *m* dust; **s~en** [ˈʃtaʊbən] *vi* to be dusty; **s~ig** *adj* dusty; **s~saugen** *vi* to vacuum, to hoover ®; **~sauger** *m* vacuum cleaner; **~tuch** *nt* duster

Staudamm *m* dam

Staude [ˈʃtaʊdə] *f* shrub

stauen [ˈʃtaʊən] *vt (Wasser)* to dam up; *(Blut)* to stop the flow of ♦ *vr (Wasser)* to become dammed up; *(MED, Verkehr)* to become congested; *(Menschen)* to collect; *(Gefühle)* to build up

staunen [ˈʃtaʊnən] *vi* to be astonished; **S~ (-s)** *nt* amazement

Stausee [ˈʃtaʊzeː] **(-s, -n)** *m* reservoir, man-made lake

Stauung [ˈʃtaʊʊŋ] *f (von Wasser)* damming-up; *(von Blut, Verkehr)* congestion

Std. *abk (= Stunde)* hr.

Steak [ʃteːk] *nt* steak

Stech- [ˈʃtɛç] *zW*: **s~en** *(unreg) vt (mit Nadel etc)* to prick; *(mit Messer)* to stab; *(mit Finger)* to poke; *(Biene etc)* to sting; *(Mücke)* to bite; *(Sonne)* to burn; *(KARTEN)* to take; *(KUNST)* to engrave; *(Torf, Spargel)* to cut; **in See s~en** to put to sea; **~en (-s, -)** *nt (SPORT)* play-off; jump-off; **s~end** *adj* piercing, stabbing; *(Geruch)* pungent; **~uhr** *f* time clock

Steck- [ˈʃtɛk] *zW*: **~brief** *m* "wanted" poster; **~dose** *f* (wall) socket; **s~en** *vt* to put, to insert; *(Nadel)* to stick; *(Pflanzen)* to

plant; *(beim Nähen)* to pin ♦ *vi (auch unreg)* to be; *(festsitzen)* to be stuck; *(Nadeln)* to stick; **s~enbleiben** ⚠ *(unreg) vi* to get stuck; **s~enlassen** ⚠ *(unreg) vt* to leave in; **~enpferd** *nt* hobby-horse; **~er (-s, -)** *m* plug; **~nadel** *f* pin

Steg [ʃteːk] **(-(e)s, -e)** *m* small bridge; *(Anlege~)* landing stage; **~reif** *m*: **aus dem ~reif** just like that

stehen [ˈʃteːən] *(unreg) vi* to stand; *(sich befinden)* to be; *(in Zeitung)* to say; *(still~)* to have stopped ♦ *vi unpers*: **es steht schlecht um jdn/etw** things are bad for sb/sth; **zu jdm/etw ~** to stand by sb/sth; **jdm ~** to suit sb; **wie steht's?** how are things?; *(SPORT)* what's the score?; **~bleiben** ⚠ *(unreg) vi* to remain standing; **~bleiben** ⚠ *(unreg) vi (Uhr)* to stop; *(Fehler)* to stay as it is; **~lassen** ⚠ *(unreg) vt* to leave; *(Bart)* to grow

Stehlampe [ˈʃteːlampə] *f* standard lamp

stehlen [ˈʃteːlən] *(unreg) vt* to steal

Stehplatz [ˈʃteːplats] *m* standing place

steif [ʃtaɪf] *adj* stiff; **S~heit** *f* stiffness

Steig- [ˈʃtaɪk] *zW*: **~bügel** *m* stirrup; **s~en** [ˈʃtaɪɡən] *(unreg) vi* to rise; *(klettern)* to climb; **s~en in** +*akk*/**auf** +*akk* to get in/on; **s~ern** *vt* to raise; *(GRAM)* to compare ♦ *vi (Auktion)* to bid ♦ *vr* to increase; **~erung** *f* raising; *(GRAM)* comparison; **~ung** *f* incline, gradient, rise

steil [ʃtaɪl] *adj* steep; **S~küste** *f* steep coast; *(Klippen)* cliffs *pl*

Stein [ʃtaɪn] **(-(e)s, -e)** *m* stone; *(in Uhr)* jewel; **~bock** *m (ASTROL)* Capricorn; **~bruch** *m* quarry; **s~ern** *adj* (made of) stone; *(fig)* stony; **~gut** *nt* stoneware; **s~ig** [ˈʃtaɪnɪç] *adj* stony; **s~igen** *vt* to stone; **~kohle** *f* mineral coal; **~zeit** *f* Stone Age

Stelle [ˈʃtɛlə] *f* place; *(Arbeit)* post, job; *(Amt)* office; **an Ihrer/meiner ~** in your/my place

stellen *vt* to put; *(Uhr etc)* to set; *(zur Verfügung ~)* to supply; *(fassen: Dieb)* to apprehend ♦ *vr (sich aufstellen)* to stand; *(sich einfinden)* to present o.s.; *(bei Polizei)* to give o.s. up; *(vorgeben)* to pretend (to

⚠ *For information on spelling reform see page 615*

be); **sich zu etw ~** to have an opinion of sth

Stellen- *zW:* **~angebot** *nt* offer of a post; (*in Zeitung*) "vacancies"; **~anzeige** *f* job advertisement; **~gesuch** *nt* application for a post; **~vermittlung** *f* employment agency

Stell- *zW:* **~ung** *f* position; (*MIL*) line; **~ung nehmen zu** to comment on; **~ungnahme** *f* comment; **s~vertretend** *adj* deputy, acting; **~vertreter** *m* deputy

Stelze ['ʃtɛltsə] *f* stilt

stemmen ['ʃtɛmən] *vt* to lift (up); (*drücken*) to press; **sich ~ gegen** (*fig*) to resist, to oppose

Stempel ['ʃtɛmpəl] (**-s, -**) *m* stamp; (*BOT*) pistil; **~kissen** *nt* ink pad; **s~n** *vt* to stamp; (*Briefmarke*) to cancel; **s~n gehen** (*umg*) to be *od* go on the dole

Stengel ⚠ ['ʃtɛŋəl] (**-s, -**) *m* stalk

Steno- [ʃteno] *zW:* **~gramm** [-'gram] *nt* shorthand report; **~graphie** ⚠ [-gra'fiː] *f* shorthand; **s~graphieren** ⚠ [-gra'fiːrən] *vt, vi* to write (in) shorthand; **~typist(in)** [-ty'pɪst(ɪn)] *m(f)* shorthand typist

Stepp- ['ʃtɛp] *zW:* **~decke** *f* quilt; **~e** *f* prairie; steppe; **s~en** *vt* to stitch ♦ *vi* to tap-dance

Sterb- ['ʃtɛrb] *zW:* **~efall** *m* death; **~ehilfe** *f* euthanasia; **s~en** (*unreg*) *vi* to die; **s~lich** ['ʃtɛrplɪç] *adj* mortal; **~lichkeit** *f* mortality; **~lichkeitsziffer** *f* death rate

stereo- ['steːreo] *in zW* stereo(-); **S~anlage** *f* stereo (system); **~typ** [ʃtereo'tyːp] *adj* stereotype

steril [ʃteˈriːl] *adj* sterile; **~isieren** *vt* to sterilize; **S~isierung** *f* sterilization

Stern [ʃtɛrn] (**-(e)s, -e**) *m* star; **~bild** *nt* constellation; **~schnuppe** *f* meteor, falling star; **~stunde** *f* historic moment; **~zeichen** *nt* sign of the zodiac

stet [ʃteːt] *adj* steady; **~ig** *adj* constant, continual; **~s** *adv* continually, always

Steuer¹ ['ʃtɔʏər] (**-s, -**) *nt* (*NAUT*) helm; (*~ruder*) rudder; (*AUT*) steering wheel

Steuer² ['ʃtɔʏər] (**-, -n**) *f* tax; **~berater(in)** *m(f)* tax consultant

Steuerbord *nt* (*NAUT, AVIAT*) starboard

Steuer- ['ʃtɔʏər] *zW:* **~erklärung** *f* tax return; **s~frei** *adj* tax-free; **~freibetrag** *m* tax allowance; **~klasse** *f* tax group; **~knüppel** *m* control column; (*AVIAT, COMPUT*) joystick; **~mann** (*pl* **-männer** *od* **-leute**) *m* helmsman; **s~n** *vt, vi* to steer; (*Flugzeug*) to pilot; (*Entwicklung, Tonstärke*) to control; **s~pflichtig** [-pflɪçtɪç] *adj* taxable; **~rad** *nt* steering wheel; **~ung** *f* (*auch AUT*) steering; piloting; control; (*Vorrichtung*) controls *pl*; **~zahler** (**-s, -**) *m* taxpayer

Steward ['stjuːərt] (**-s, -s**) *m* steward; **~eß** ⚠ ['stjuːərdɛs] (**-, -essen**) *f* stewardess; air hostess

Stich [ʃtɪç] (**-(e)s, -e**) *m* (*Insekten~*) sting; (*Messer~*) stab; (*beim Nähen*) stitch; (*Färbung*) tinge; (*KARTEN*) trick; (*ART*) engraving; **jdn im ~ lassen** to leave sb in the lurch; **s~eln** *vi* (*fig*) to jibe; **s~haltig** *adj* sound, tenable; **~probe** *f* spot check; **~wahl** *f* final ballot; **~wort** *nt* cue; (*in Wörterbuch*) headword; (*für Vortrag*) note

sticken ['ʃtɪkən] *vt, vi* to embroider

Sticke'rei *f* embroidery

stickig *adj* stuffy, close

Stickstoff *m* nitrogen

Stief- ['ʃtiːf] *in zW* step

Stiefel ['ʃtiːfəl] (**-s, -**) *m* boot

Stief- *zW:* **~kind** *nt* stepchild; (*fig*) Cinderella; **~mutter** *f* stepmother; **~mütterlich** *nt* pansy; **s~mütterlich** *adj* (*fig*): **jdn/etw s~mütterlich behandeln** to pay little attention to sb/sth; **~vater** *m* stepfather

stiehlst *etc* [ʃtiːlst] *vb siehe* **stehlen**

Stiel [ʃtiːl] (**-(e)s, -e**) *m* handle; (*BOT*) stalk

Stier (**-(e)s, -e**) *m* bull; (*ASTROL*) Taurus

stieren *vi* to stare

Stierkampf *m* bullfight

Stierkämpfer *m* bullfighter

Stift [ʃtɪft] (**-(e)s, -e**) *m* peg; (*Nagel*) tack; (*Farb~*) crayon; (*Blei~*) pencil ♦ *nt* (charitable) foundation; (*ECCL*) religious institution; **s~en** *vt* to found; (*Unruhe*) to cause; (*spenden*) to contribute; **~er(in)** (**-s,**

⚠ *Informationen zur Rechtschreibreform Seite 615*

-) *m(f)* founder; **~ung** *f* donation; (*Organisation*) foundation; **~zahn** *m* post crown

Stil [ʃtiːl] (-(e)s, -e) *m* style

still [ʃtɪl] *adj* quiet; (*unbewegt*) still; (*heimlich*) secret; **S~er Ozean** Pacific; **S~e** *f* stillness, quietness; **in aller S~e** quietly; **~en** *vt* to stop; (*befriedigen*) to satisfy; (*Säugling*) to breast-feed; **~halten** (*unreg*) *vi* to keep still; **~(l)egen** △ *vt* to close down; **~schweigen** (*unreg*) *vi* to be silent; **S~schweigen** *nt* silence; **~schweigend** *adj* silent; (*Einverständnis*) tacit ♦ *adv* silently; tacitly; **S~stand** *m* standstill

Stimm- ['ʃtɪm] *zW:* **~bänder** *pl* vocal cords; **s~berechtigt** *adj* entitled to vote; **~e** *f* voice; (*Wahlstimme*) vote; **s~en** *vt* (*MUS*) to tune ♦ *vi* to be right; **das s~te ihn traurig** that made him feel sad; **s~en für/gegen** to vote for/against; **s~t so!** that's right; **~enmehrheit** *f* majority (of votes); **~enthaltung** *f* abstention; **~gabel** *f* tuning fork; **~recht** *nt* right to vote; **~ung** *f* mood; atmosphere; **s~ungsvoll** *adj* enjoyable; full of atmosphere; **~zettel** *m* ballot paper

stinken ['ʃtɪŋkən] (*unreg*) *vi* to stink

Stipendium [ʃtiˈpɛndiʊm] *nt* grant

stirbst *etc* [ʃtɪrpst] *vb siehe* **sterben**

Stirn [ʃtɪrn] (-, -en) *f* forehead, brow; (*Frechheit*) impudence; **~band** *nt* headband; **~höhle** *f* sinus

stöbern ['ʃtøːbərn] *vi* to rummage

stochern ['ʃtɔxərn] *vi* to poke (about)

Stock¹ [ʃtɔk] (-(e)s, -̈e) *m* stick; (*BOT*) stock

Stock² [ʃtɔk] (-(e)s, - *od* **Stockwerke**) *m* storey

stocken *vi* to stop, to pause; **~d** *adj* halting

Stockung *f* stoppage

Stockwerk *nt* storey, floor

Stoff [ʃtɔf] (-(e)s, -e) *m* (*Gewebe*) material, cloth; (*Materie*) matter; (*von Buch etc*) subject (matter); **s~lich** *adj* material; **~tier** *nt* soft toy; **~wechsel** *m* metabolism

stöhnen ['ʃtøːnən] *vi* to groan

Stollen ['ʃtɔlən] (-s, -) *m* (*MIN*) gallery;

(*KOCH*) cake eaten at Christmas; (*von Schuhen*) stud

stolpern ['ʃtɔlpərn] *vi* to stumble, to trip

Stolz [ʃtɔlts] (-es) *m* pride; **s~** *adj* proud; **s~ieren** [ʃtɔlˈtsiːrən] *vi* to strut

stopfen ['ʃtɔpfən] *vt* (*hinein~*) to stuff; (*voll~*) to fill (up); (*nähen*) to darn ♦ *vi* (*MED*) to cause constipation

Stopfgarn *nt* darning thread

Stoppel ['ʃtɔpəl] (-, -n) *f* stubble

Stopp- ['ʃtɔp] *zW:* **s~en** *vt* to stop; (*mit Uhr*) to time ♦ *vi* to stop; **~schild** *nt* stop sign; **~uhr** *f* stopwatch

Stöpsel ['ʃtœpsəl] (-s, -) *m* plug; (*für Flaschen*) stopper

Storch [ʃtɔrç] (-(e)s, -̈e) *m* stork

Stör- ['ʃtøːr] *zW:* **s~en** *vt* to disturb; (*behindern, RADIO*) to interfere with ♦ *vr:* **sich an etw** *dat* **s~en** to let sth bother one; **s~end** *adj* disturbing, annoying; **~enfried** (-(e)s, -e) *m* troublemaker

stornieren [ʃtɔrˈniːrən] *vt* (*Auftrag*) to cancel; (*Buchung*) to reverse

Stornogebühr ['ʃtɔrno-] *f* cancellation fee

störrisch ['ʃtœrɪʃ] *adj* stubborn, perverse

Störung *f* disturbance; interference

Stoß [ʃtoːs] (-es, -̈e) *m* (*Schub*) push; (*Schlag*) blow; knock; (*mit Schwert*) thrust; (*mit Fuß*) kick; (*Erd~*) shock; (*Haufen*) pile; **~dämpfer** (-s, -) *m* shock absorber; **s~en** (*unreg*) *vt* (*mit Druck*) to shove, to push; (*mit Schlag*) to knock, to bump; (*mit Fuß*) to kick; (*Schwert etc*) to thrust; (*anstoßen: Kopf etc*) to bump ♦ *vr* to get a knock ♦ *vi:* **s~en an** *od* **auf** +*akk* to bump into; (*finden*) to come across; (*angrenzen*) to be next to; **sich s~en an** +*dat* (*fig*) to take exception to; **~stange** *f* (*AUT*) bumper

stottern ['ʃtɔtərn] *vt, vi* to stutter

Str. *abk* (= *Straße*) St.

Straf- ['ʃtraːf] *zW:* **~anstalt** *f* penal institution; **~arbeit** *f* (*SCH*) punishment; lines *pl*; **s~bar** *adj* punishable; **~e** *f* punishment; (*JUR*) penalty; (*Gefängnisstrafe*) sentence; (*Geldstrafe*) fine; **s~en** *vt* to punish

straff [ʃtraf] *adj* tight; (*streng*) strict; (*Stil etc*)

△ *For information on spelling reform see page 615*

concise; (*Haltung*) erect; **~en** *vt* to tighten, to tauten

Strafgefangene(r) *f(m)* prisoner, convict

Strafgesetzbuch *nt* penal code

sträflich ['ʃtrɛːflɪç] *adj* criminal

Sträfling *m* convict

Straf- *zW:* **~porto** *nt* excess postage (charge); **~predigt** *f* telling-off; **~raum** *m* (*SPORT*) penalty area; **~recht** *nt* criminal law; **~stoß** *m* (*SPORT*) penalty (kick); **~tat** *f* punishable act; **~zettel** *m* ticket

Strahl [ʃtraːl] **(-s, -en)** *m* ray, beam; (*Wasser~*) jet; **s~en** *vi* to radiate; (*fig*) to beam; **~ung** *f* radiation

Strähne ['ʃtrɛːnə] *f* strand

stramm [ʃtram] *adj* tight; (*Haltung*) erect; (*Mensch*) robust

strampeln ['ʃtrampəln] *vi* to kick (about), to fidget

Strand [ʃtrant] **(-(e)s, ¨e)** *m* shore; (*mit Sand*) beach; **~bad** *nt* open-air swimming pool, lido; **s~en** ['ʃtrandən] *vi* to run aground; (*fig: Mensch*) to fail; **~gut** *nt* flotsam; **~korb** *m* beach chair

Strang [ʃtraŋ] **(-(e)s, ¨e)** *m* cord, rope; (*Bündel*) skein

Strapaz- *zW:* **~e** [ʃtra'paːtsə] *f* strain, exertion; **s~ieren** [ʃtrapa'tsiːrən] *vt* (*Material*) to treat roughly, to punish; (*Mensch, Kräfte*) to wear out, to exhaust; **s~ierfähig** *adj* hard-wearing; **s~iös** [ʃtrapatsi'øːs] *adj* exhausting, tough

Straße ['ʃtraːsə] *f* street, road

Straßen- *zW:* **~bahn** *f* tram, streetcar (*US*); **~glätte** *f* slippery road surface; **~karte** *f* road map; **~kehrer (-s, -)** *m* roadsweeper; **~sperre** *f* roadblock; **~verkehr** *m* (road) traffic; **~verkehrsordnung** *f* highway code

Strateg- [ʃtra'teːg] *zW:* **~e** **(-n, -n)** *m* strategist; **~ie** [ʃtrate'giː] *f* strategy; **s~isch** *adj* strategic

sträuben ['ʃtrɔybən] *vt* to ruffle ♦ *vr* to bristle; (*Mensch*): **sich (gegen etw) ~** to resist (sth)

Strauch [ʃtraux] **(-(e)s, Sträucher)** *m* bush, shrub

Strauß¹ [ʃtraus] **(-es, Sträuße)** *m* bunch; bouquet

Strauß² [ʃtraus] **(-es, -e)** *m* ostrich

Streb- [ʃtreːb] *zW:* **s~en** *vi* to strive, to endeavour; **s~en nach** to strive for; **~er (-s, -)** (*pej*) *m* pusher, climber; (*SCH*) swot (*BRIT*)

Strecke ['ʃtrɛkə] *f* stretch; (*Entfernung*) distance; (*EISENB, MATH*) line; **s~n** *vt* to stretch; (*Waffen*) to lay down; (*KOCH*) to eke out ♦ *vr* to stretch (o.s.)

Streich [ʃtraɪç] **(-(e)s, -e)** *m* trick, prank; (*Hieb*) blow; **s~eln** *vt* to stroke; **s~en** (*unreg*) *vt* (*berühren*) to stroke; (*auftragen*) to spread; (*anmalen*) to paint; (*durchstreichen*) to delete; (*nicht genehmigen*) to cancel ♦ *vi* (*berühren*) to brush; (*schleichen*) to prowl; **~holz** *nt* match; **~instrument** *nt* string instrument

Streif- [ʃtraɪf] *zW:* **~e** *f* patrol; **s~en** *vt* (*leicht berühren*) to brush against, to graze; (*Blick*) to skim over; (*Thema, Problem*) to touch on; (*abstreifen*) to take off ♦ *vi* (*gehen*) to roam; **~en (-s, -)** *m* (*Linie*) stripe; (*Stück*) strip; (*Film*) film; **~enwagen** *m* patrol car; **~schuß** ⚠ *m* graze, grazing shot; **~zug** *m* scouting trip

Streik [ʃtraɪk] **(-(e)s, -s)** *m* strike; **~brecher (-s, -)** *m* blackleg, strikebreaker; **s~en** *vi* to strike; **~posten** *m* (strike) picket

Streit [ʃtraɪt] **(-(e)s, -e)** *m* argument; dispute; **s~en** (*unreg*) *vi, vr* to argue; to dispute; **~frage** *f* point at issue; **s~ig** *adj:* **jdm etw s~ig machen** to dispute sb's right to sth; **~igkeiten** *pl* quarrel *sg*, dispute *sg*; **~kräfte** *pl* (*MIL*) armed forces

streng [ʃtrɛŋ] *adj* severe; (*Lehrer, Maßnahme*) strict; (*Geruch etc*) sharp; **S~e (-)** *f* severity, strictness, sharpness; **~genommen** ⚠ *adv* strictly speaking; **~gläubig** *adj* orthodox, strict; **~stens** *adv* strictly

Streß ⚠ [ʃtrɛs] **(-sses, -sse)** *m* stress

stressen *vt* to put under stress

streuen ['ʃtrɔyən] *vt* to strew, to scatter, to spread

Strich [ʃtrɪç] **(-(e)s, -e)** *m* (*Linie*) line; (*Feder~, Pinsel~*) stroke; (*von Geweben*) nap;

(*von Fell*) pile; **auf den ~ gehen** (*umg*) to walk the streets; **jdm gegen den ~ gehen** to rub sb up the wrong way; **einen ~ machen durch** to cross out; (*fig*) to foil; **~kode** *m* (*auf Waren*) bar code; **~mädchen** *nt* streetwalker; **s~weise** *adv* here and there

Strick [ʃtrɪk] (**-(e)s, -e**) *m* rope; **s~en** *vt, vi* to knit; **~jacke** *f* cardigan; **~leiter** *f* rope ladder; **~nadel** *f* knitting needle; **~waren** *pl* knitwear *sg*

strikt [strɪkt] *adj* strict

strittig [ʃtrɪtɪç] *adj* disputed, in dispute

Stroh [ʃtroː] (**-(e)s**) *nt* straw; **~blume** *f* everlasting flower; **~dach** *nt* thatched roof; **~halm** *m* (drinking) straw

Strom [ʃtroːm] (**-(e)s, ⸚e**) *m* river; (*fig*) stream; (*ELEK*) current; **s~abwärts** *adv* downstream; **s~aufwärts** *adv* upstream; **~ausfall** *m* power failure

strömen [ʃtrøːmən] *vi* to stream, to pour

Strom- *zW:* **~kreis** *m* circuit; **s~linienförmig** *adj* streamlined; **~sperre** *f* power cut

Strömung [ʃtrøːmʊŋ] *f* current

Strophe [ʃtroːfə] *f* verse

strotzen [ʃtrɔtsən] *vi:* **~ vor** *od* **von** to abound in, to be full of

Strudel [ʃtruːdəl] (**-s, -**) *m* whirlpool, vortex; (*KOCH*) strudel

Struktur [ʃtrʊkˈtuːr] *f* structure

Strumpf [ʃtrʊmpf] (**-(e)s, ⸚e**) *m* stocking; **~band** *nt* garter; **~hose** *f* (pair of) tights

Stube [ʃtuːbə] *f* room

Stuben- *zW:* **~arrest** *m* confinement to one's room; (*MIL*) confinement to quarters; **~hocker** (*umg*) *m* stay-at-home; **s~rein** *adj* house-trained

Stuck [ʃtʊk] (**-(e)s**) *m* stucco

Stück [ʃtʏk] (**-(e)s, -e**) *nt* piece; (*etwas*) bit; (*THEAT*) play; **~chen** *nt* little piece; **~lohn** *m* piecework wages *pl*; **s~weise** *adv* bit by bit, piecemeal; (*COMM*) individually

Student(in) [ʃtuˈdɛnt(ɪn)] *m(f)* student; **s~isch** *adj* student, academic

Studie [ʃtuːdiə] *f* study

Studienfahrt *f* study trip

studieren [ʃtuˈdiːrən] *vt, vi* to study

Studio [ʃtuːdio] (**-s, -s**) *nt* studio

Studium [ʃtuːdiʊm] *nt* studies *pl*

Stufe [ʃtuːfə] *f* step; (*Entwicklungs~*) stage; **s~nweise** *adv* gradually

Stuhl [ʃtuːl] (**-(e)s, ⸚e**) *m* chair; **~gang** *m* bowel movement

stülpen [ʃtʏlpən] *vt* (*umdrehen*) to turn upside down; (*bedecken*) to put

stumm [ʃtʊm] *adj* silent; (*MED*) dumb

Stummel [ʃtʊməl] (**-s, -**) *m* stump; (*Zigaretten~*) stub

Stummfilm *m* silent film

Stümper [ʃtʏmpər] (**-s, -**) *m* incompetent, duffer; **s~haft** *adj* bungling, incompetent; **s~n** *vi* to bungle

Stumpf [ʃtʊmpf] (**-(e)s, ⸚e**) *m* stump; **s~** *adj* blunt; (*teilnahmslos, glanzlos*) dull; (*Winkel*) obtuse; **~sinn** *m* tediousness; **s~sinnig** *adj* dull

Stunde [ʃtʊndə] *f* hour; (*SCH*) lesson

stunden *vt:* **jdm etw ~** to give sb time to pay sth; **S~geschwindigkeit** *f* average speed per hour; **S~kilometer** *pl* kilometres per hour; **~lang** *adj* for hours; **S~lohn** *m* hourly wage; **S~plan** *m* timetable; **~weise** *adj* by the hour; every hour

stündlich [ʃtʏntlɪç] *adj* hourly

Stups [ʃtʊps] (**-es, -e**) (*umg*) *m* push; **~nase** *f* snub nose

stur [ʃtuːr] *adj* obstinate, pigheaded

Sturm [ʃtʊrm] (**-(e)s, ⸚e**) *m* storm, gale; (*MIL etc*) attack, assault

stürm- [ʃtʏrm] *zW:* **~en** *vi* (*Wind*) to blow hard, to rage; (*rennen*) to storm ♦ *vt* (*MIL, fig*) to storm ♦ *vb unpers:* **es ~t** there's a gale blowing; **S~er** (**-s, -**) *m* (*SPORT*) forward, striker; **~isch** *adj* stormy

Sturmwarnung *f* gale warning

Sturz [ʃtʊrts] (**-es, ⸚e**) *m* fall; (*POL*) overthrow

stürzen [ʃtʏrtsən] *vt* (*werfen*) to hurl; (*POL*) to overthrow; (*umkehren*) to overturn ♦ *vr* to rush; (*hinein~*) to plunge ♦ *vi* to fall; (*AVIAT*) to dive; (*rennen*) to dash

Sturzflug *m* nose dive

⚠ *For information on spelling reform see page 615*

Sturzhelm m crash helmet

Stute ['ʃtuːtə] f mare

Stützbalken m brace, joist

Stütze ['ʃtʏtsə] f support; help

stutzen ['ʃtʊtsən] vt to trim; (Ohr, Schwanz) to dock; (Flügel) to clip ♦ vi to hesitate; to become suspicious

stützen vt (auch fig) to support; (Ellbogen etc) to prop up

stutzig adj perplexed, puzzled; (mißtrauisch) suspicious

Stützpunkt m point of support; (von Hebel) fulcrum; (MIL, fig) base

Styropor [ʃtyroˈpoːr] (®; -s) nt polystyrene

s.u. abk = siehe unten

Subjekt [zʊpˈjɛkt] (-(e)s, -e) nt subject; **s~iv** [-ˈtiːf] adj subjective; **~ivi'tät** f subjectivity

Subsidiarität f subsidiarity

Substantiv [zʊpstanˈtiːf] (-s, -e) nt noun

Substanz [zʊpˈstants] f substance

subtil [zʊpˈtiːl] adj subtle

subtrahieren [zʊptraˈhiːrən] vt to subtract

subtropisch ['zʊptroːpɪʃ] adj subtropical

Subvention [zʊpvɛntsiˈoːn] f subsidy; **s~ieren** vt to subsidize

Such- ['zuːx] zW: **~aktion** f search; **~e** f search; **s~en** vt to look (for), to seek; (versuchen) to try ♦ vi to seek, to search; **~er** (-s, -) m seeker, searcher; (PHOT) viewfinder

Sucht [zʊxt] (-, ¨e) f mania; (MED) addiction, craving

süchtig ['zʏçtɪç] adj addicted; **S~e(r)** f(m) addict

Süd- ['zyːt] zW: **~en** ['zyːdən] (-s) m south; **~früchte** pl Mediterranean fruit sg; **s~lich** adj southern; **s~lich von** (to the) south of; **~pol** m South Pole; **s~wärts** adv southwards

süffig ['zʏfɪç] adj (Wein) pleasant to the taste

süffisant [zʏfiˈzant] adj smug

suggerieren [zʊgeˈriːrən] vt to suggest

Sühne ['zyːnə] f atonement, expiation; **s~n** vt to atone for, to expiate

Sultan ['zʊltan] (-s, -e) m sultan; **~ine** [zʊltaˈniːnə] f sultana

Sülze ['zʏltsə] f brawn

Summe ['zʊmə] f sum, total

summen vt, vi to buzz; (Lied) to hum

Sumpf [zʊmpf] (-(e)s, ¨e) m swamp, marsh; **s~ig** adj marshy

Sünde ['zʏndə] f sin; **~nbock** (umg) m scapegoat; **~r(in)** (-s, -) m(f) sinner; **sündigen** vi to sin

Super ['zuːpar] (-s) nt (Benzin) four star (petrol) (BRIT), premium (US); **~lativ** [-latiːf] (-s, -e) m superlative; **~macht** f superpower; **~markt** m supermarket

Suppe ['zʊpə] f soup; **~nteller** m soup plate

süß [zyːs] adj sweet; **S~e** (-) f sweetness; **~en** vt to sweeten; **S~igkeit** f sweetness; (Bonbon etc) sweet (BRIT), candy (US); **~lich** adj sweetish; (fig) sugary; **~sauer** adj (Gurke) pickled; (Sauce etc) sweet-and-sour; **S~speise** f pudding, sweet; **S~stoff** m sweetener; **S~waren** pl confectionery (sing); **S~wasser** nt fresh water

Symbol [zymˈboːl] (-s, -e) nt symbol; **s~isch** adj symbolic(al)

Symmetrie [zymeˈtriː] f symmetry

symmetrisch [zyˈmeːtrɪʃ] adj symmetrical

Sympathie [zympaˈtiː] f liking, sympathy; **sympathisch** [zymˈpaːtɪʃ] adj likeable; **er ist mir sympathisch** I like him; **sympathi'sieren** vi to sympathize

Symphonie [zymfoˈniː] f (MUS) symphony

Symptom [zympˈtoːm] (-s, -e) nt symptom; **s~atisch** [zymptoˈmaːtɪʃ] adj symptomatic

Synagoge [zynaˈgoːgə] f synagogue

synchron [zynˈkroːn] adj synchronous; **~i'sieren** vt to synchronize; (Film) to dub

Synonym [zynoˈnyːm] (-s, -e) nt synonym; **s~** adj synonymous

Synthese [zynˈteːzə] f synthesis

synthetisch adj synthetic

System [zysˈteːm] (-s, -e) nt system; **s~atisch** [zysteˈmaːtɪʃ] adj systematic; **s~ati'sieren** vt to systematize

Szene ['stseːnə] f scene; **~rie** [stsenəˈriː] f scenery

⚠ *Informationen zur Rechtschreibreform Seite 615*

T, t

t *abk* (= *Tonne*) t

Tabak ['ta:bak] (**-s, -e**) *m* tobacco

Tabell- [ta'bɛl] *zW*: **t~arisch** [tabɛ'la:rɪʃ] *adj* tabular; **~e** *f* table

Tablett [ta'blɛt] *nt* tray; **~e** *f* tablet, pill

Tabu [ta'bu:] *nt* taboo; **t~** *adj* taboo

Tachometer [taxo'me:tər] (**-s, -**) *m* (AUT) speedometer

Tadel ['ta:dəl] (**-s, -**) *m* censure; scolding; (*Fehler*) fault, blemish; **t~los** *adj* faultless, irreproachable; **t~n** *vt* to scold

Tafel ['ta:fəl] (**-, -n**) *f* (*auch* MATH) table; (*Anschlag~*) board; (*Wand~*) blackboard; (*Schiefer~*) slate; (*Gedenk~*) plaque; (*Illustration*) plate; (*Schalt~*) panel; (*Schokolade etc*) bar

Tag [ta:k] (**-(e)s, -e**) *m* day; daylight; **unter/über ~e** (MIN) underground/on the surface; **an den ~ kommen** to come to light; **guten ~!** good morning/afternoon!; **t~aus** *adv*: **t~aus, tagein** day in, day out; **~dienst** *m* day duty

Tage- ['ta:gə] *zW*: **~buch** ['ta:gəbu:x] *nt* diary, journal; **~geld** *nt* daily allowance; **t~lang** *adv* for days; **t~n** *vi* to sit, to meet ♦ *vb unpers*: **es tagt** dawn is breaking

Tages- *zW*: **~ablauf** *m* course of the day; **~anbruch** *m* dawn; **~fahrt** *f* day trip; **~karte** *f* menu of the day; (*Fahrkarte*) day ticket; **~licht** *nt* daylight; **~ordnung** *f* agenda; **~zeit** *f* time of day; **~zeitung** *f* daily (paper)

täglich ['tɛ:klɪç] *adj, adv* daily

tagsüber ['ta:ks|y:bər] *adv* during the day

Tagung *f* conference

Taille ['taljə] *f* waist

Takt [takt] (**-(e)s, -e**) *m* tact; (MUS) time; **~gefühl** *nt* tact

Taktik *f* tactics *pl*; **taktisch** *adj* tactical

Takt- *zW*: **t~los** *adj* tactless; **~losigkeit** *f* tactlessness; **~stock** *m* (conductor's) baton; **t~voll** *adj* tactful

Tal [ta:l] (**-(e)s, -̈er**) *nt* valley

Talent [ta'lɛnt] (**-(e)s, -e**) *nt* talent; **t~iert** [talɛn'ti:rt] *adj* talented, gifted

Talisman ['ta:lɪsman] (**-s, -e**) *m* talisman

Talsohle *f* bottom of a valley

Talsperre *f* dam

Tampon ['tampɔn] (**-s, -s**) *m* tampon

Tandem ['tandɛm] (**-s, -s**) *nt* tandem

Tang [taŋ] (**-(e)s, -e**) *m* seaweed

Tank [taŋk] (**-s, -s**) *m* tank; **~anzeige** *f* fuel gauge; **t~en** *vi* to fill up with petrol (BRIT) *od* gas (US); (AVIAT) to (re)fuel; **~er** (**-s, -**) *m* tanker; **~schiff** *nt* tanker; **~stelle** *f* petrol (BRIT) *od* gas (US) station; **~wart** *m* petrol pump (BRIT) *od* gas station (US) attendant

Tanne ['tanə] *f* fir

Tannen- *zW*: **~baum** *m* fir tree; **~zapfen** *m* fir cone

Tante ['tantə] *f* aunt

Tanz [tants] (**-es, -̈e**) *m* dance; **t~en** *vt, vi* to dance

Tänzer(in) ['tɛntsər(ɪn)] (**-s, -**) *m(f)* dancer

Tanzfläche *f* (dance) floor

Tanzschule *f* dancing school

Tapete [ta'pe:tə] *f* wallpaper; **~nwechsel** *m* (*fig*) change of scenery

tapezieren [tape'tsi:rən] *vt* to (wall)paper; **Tapezierer** [tape'tsi:rər] (**-s, -**) *m* (interior) decorator

tapfer ['tapfər] *adj* brave; **T~keit** *f* courage, bravery

Tarif [ta'ri:f] (**-s, -e**) *m* tariff, (scale of) fares *od* charges; **~lohn** *m* standard wage rate; **~verhandlungen** *pl* wage negotiations; **~zone** *f* fare zone

Tarn- ['tarn] *zW*: **t~en** *vt* to camouflage; (*Person, Absicht*) to disguise; **~ung** *f* camouflaging; disguising

Tasche ['taʃə] *f* pocket; handbag

Taschen- *in zW* pocket; **~buch** *nt* paperback; **~dieb** *m* pickpocket; **~geld** *nt* pocket money; **~lampe** *f* (electric) torch, flashlight (US); **~messer** *nt* penknife; **~tuch** *nt* handkerchief

Tasse ['tasə] *f* cup

Tastatur [tasta'tu:r] *f* keyboard

Taste ['tastə] *f* push-button control; (*an Schreibmaschine*) key; **t~n** *vt* to feel, to touch ♦ *vi* to feel, to grope ♦ *vr* to feel one's way

Tat [ta:t] (-, -en) *f* act, deed, action; **in der ~** indeed, as a matter of fact; **t~** *etc vb siehe* **tun**; **~bestand** *m* facts *pl* of the case; **t~enlos** *adj* inactive

Tät- ['tɛːt] *zW:* **~er(in)** (-s, -) *m(f)* perpetrator, culprit; **t~ig** *adj* active; **in einer Firma t~ig sein** to work for a firm; **~igkeit** *f* activity; (*Beruf*) occupation; **t~lich** *adj* violent; **~lichkeit** *f* violence; **~lichkeiten** *pl* (*Schläge*) blows

tätowieren [tɛto'viːrən] *vt* to tattoo

Tatsache *f* fact

tatsächlich *adj* actual ♦ *adv* really

Tau¹ [tau] (-(e)s, -e) *nt* rope

Tau² [tau] (-(e)s) *m* dew

taub [taup] *adj* deaf; (*Nuß*) hollow

Taube ['taubə] *f* dove; pigeon; **~nschlag** *m* dovecote; **hier geht es zu wie in einem ~nschlag** it's a hive of activity here

taub- *zW:* **T~heit** *f* deafness; **~stumm** *adj* deaf-and-dumb

Tauch- [taux] *zW:* **t~en** *vt* to dip ♦ *vi* to dive; (*NAUT*) to submerge; **~er** (-s, -) *m* diver; **~eranzug** *m* diving suit; **~erbrille** *f* diving goggles *pl*; **~sieder** (-s, -) *m* immersion coil (*for boiling water*)

tauen ['tauən] *vt, vi* to thaw ♦ *vb unpers:* **es taut** it's thawing

Tauf- ['tauf] *zW:* **~becken** *nt* font; **~e** *f* baptism; **t~en** *vt* to christen, to baptize; **~pate** *m* godfather; **~patin** *f* godmother; **~schein** *m* certificate of baptism

taug- ['taug] *zW:* **~en** *vi* to be of use; **~en für** to do for, to be good for; **nicht ~en** to be no good *od* useless; **T~enichts** (-es, -e) *m* good-for-nothing; **~lich** ['tauklɪç] *adj* suitable; (*MIL*) fit (for service)

Taumel ['tauməl] (-s) *m* dizziness; (*fig*) frenzy; **t~n** *vi* to reel, to stagger

Tausch [tauʃ] (-(e)s, -e) *m* exchange; **t~en** *vt* to exchange, to swap

täuschen ['tɔyʃən] *vt* to deceive ♦ *vi* to be deceptive ♦ *vr* to be wrong; **~d** *adj* deceptive

Tauschhandel *m* barter

Täuschung *f* deception; (*optisch*) illusion

tausend ['tauzənt] *num* (a) thousand

Tauwetter *nt* thaw

Taxi ['taksi] (-(s), -(s)) *nt* taxi; **~fahrer** *m* taxi driver; **~stand** *m* taxi rank

Tech- [tɛç] *zW:* **~nik** *f* technology; (*Methode, Kunstfertigkeit*) technique; **~niker** (-s, -) *m* technician; **t~nisch** *adj* technical; **~nolo'gie** *f* technology; **t~no'logisch** *adj* technological

Tee [te:] (-s, -s) *m* tea; **~beutel** *m* tea bag; **~kanne** *f* teapot; **~löffel** *m* teaspoon

Teer [te:r] (-(e)s, -e) *m* tar; **t~en** *vt* to tar

Teesieb *nt* tea strainer

Teich [taɪç] (-(e)s, -e) *m* pond

Teig [taɪk] (-(e)s, -e) *m* dough; **t~ig** ['taɪgɪç] *adj* doughy; **~waren** *pl* pasta *sg*

Teil [taɪl] (-(e)s, -e) *m od nt* part; (*Anteil*) share; (*Bestand~*) component; **zum ~** partly; **t~bar** *adj* divisible; **~betrag** *m* instalment; **~chen** *nt* (atomic) particle; **t~en** *vt, vr* to divide; (*mit jdm*) to share; **t~haben** (*unreg*) *vi:* **t~haben an** +*dat* to share in; **~haber** (-s, -) *m* partner; **~kaskoversicherung** *f* third party, fire and theft insurance; **t~möbliert** *adj* partially furnished; **~nahme** *f* participation; (*Mitleid*) sympathy; **t~nahmslos** *adj* disinterested, apathetic; **t~nehmen** (*unreg*) *vi:* **t~nehmen an** +*dat* to take part in; **~nehmer** (-s, -) *m* participant; **t~s** *adv* partly; **~ung** *f* division; **t~weise** *adv* partially, in part; **~zahlung** *f* payment by instalments; **~zeitarbeit** *f* part-time work

Teint [tɛ̃ː] (-s, -s) *m* complexion

Telefax ['te:lefaks] *nt* fax

Telefon [tele'fo:n] (-s, -e) *nt* telephone; **~anruf** *m* (tele)phone call; **~at** [telefo'na:t] (-(e)s, -e) *nt* (tele)phone call; **~buch** *nt* telephone directory; **~hörer** *m* (telephone) receiver; **t~ieren** *vi* to telephone; **t~isch** [-ɪʃ] *adj* telephone; (*Benachrichtigung*) by telephone; **~ist(in)** [telefo'nɪst(ɪn)] *m(f)* telephonist; **~karte** *f* phonecard; **~nummer** *f* (tele)phone number; **~zelle** *f* telephone kiosk, callbox; **~zentrale** *f* telephone exchange

Telegraf [tele'gra:f] **(-en, -en)** *m* telegraph; **~enmast** *m* telegraph pole; **~ie** [-'fi:] *f* telegraphy; **t~ieren** [-'fi:rən] *vt, vi* to telegraph, to wire

Telegramm [tele'gram] **(-s, -e)** *nt* telegram, cable; **~adresse** *f* telegraphic address

Tele- *zW:* **~objektiv** ['te:le|ɔpjekti:f] *nt* telephoto lens; **t~pathisch** [tele'pa:tɪʃ] *adj* telepathic; **~skop** [tele'sko:p] **(-s, -e)** *nt* telescope

Teller ['tɛlər] **(-s, -)** *m* plate; **~gericht** *nt* (*KOCH*) one-course meal

Tempel ['tɛmpəl] **(-s, -)** *m* temple

Temperament [tempera'mɛnt] *nt* temperament; (*Schwung*) vivacity, liveliness; **t~voll** *adj* high-spirited, lively

Temperatur [tempera'tu:r] *f* temperature

Tempo[1] ['tɛmpo] **(-s, Tempi)** *nt* (*MUS*) tempo

Tempo[2] ['tɛmpo] **(-s, -s)** *nt* speed, pace; **~!** get a move on!; **~limit** [-lɪmɪt] **(-s, -s)** *nt* speed limit; **t~taschentuch** ® *nt* tissue

Tendenz [tɛn'dɛnts] *f* tendency; (*Absicht*) intention; **t~iös** [-i'ø:s] *adj* biased, tendentious

tendieren [tɛn'di:rən] *vi:* **~ zu** to show a tendency to, to incline towards

Tennis ['tɛnɪs] **(-)** *nt* tennis; **~ball** *m* tennis ball; **~platz** *m* tennis court; **~schläger** *m* tennis racket; **~schuh** *m* tennis shoe; **~spieler(in)** *m(f)* tennis player

Tenor [te'no:r] **(-s, ̈-e)** *m* tenor

Teppich ['tɛpɪç] **(-s, -e)** *m* carpet; **~boden** *m* wall-to-wall carpeting

Termin [tɛr'mi:n] **(-s, -e)** *m* (*Zeitpunkt*) date; (*Frist*) time limit, deadline; (*Arzt~ etc*) appointment; **~kalender** *m* diary, appointments book; **~planer** *m* personal organizer

Terrasse [tɛ'rasə] *f* terrace

Terrine [tɛ'ri:nə] *f* tureen

territorial [tɛritori'a:l] *adj* territorial

Territorium [tɛri'to:riɔm] *nt* territory

Terror ['tɛrɔr] **(-s)** *m* terror; reign of terror; **t~isieren** [tɛrori'zi:rən] *vt* to terrorize;

~ismus [-'rɪsmʊs] *m* terrorism; **~ist** [-'rɪst] *m* terrorist

Tesafilm ['te:zafɪlm] ® *m* Sellotape ® (*BRIT*), Scotch tape ® (*US*)

Tessin [tɛ'si:n] **(-s)** *nt:* **das ~** Ticino

Test [tɛst] **(-s, -s)** *m* test

Testament [tɛsta'mɛnt] *nt* will, testament; (*REL*) Testament; **t~arisch** [-'ta:rɪʃ] *adj* testamentary

Testamentsvollstrecker *m* executor (of a will)

testen *vt* to test

Tetanus ['te:tanʊs] **(-)** *m* tetanus; **~impfung** *f* (anti-)tetanus injection

teuer ['tɔʏər] *adj* dear, expensive; **T~ung** *f* increase in prices; **T~ungszulage** *f* cost of living bonus

Teufel ['tɔʏfəl] **(-s, -)** *m* devil; **teuflisch** *adj* fiendish, diabolical

Text [tɛkst] **(-(e)s, -e)** *m* text; (*Lieder~*) words *pl*; **t~en** *vi* to write the words

textil [tɛks'ti:l] *adj* textile; **T~ien** *pl* textiles; **T~industrie** *f* textile industry; **T~waren** *pl* textiles

Textverarbeitung *f* word processing

Theater [te'a:tər] **(-s, -)** *nt* theatre; (*umg*) fuss; **~ spielen** (*auch fig*) to playact; **~besucher** *m* playgoer; **~kasse** *f* box office; **~stück** *nt* (stage) play

Theke ['te:kə] *f* (*Schanktisch*) bar; (*Ladentisch*) counter

Thema ['te:ma] **(-s, Themen** *od* **-ta)** *nt* theme, topic, subject

Themse ['tɛmzə] *f* Thames

Theo- [teo] *zW:* **~loge** [-'lo:gə] **(-n, -n)** *m* theologian; **~logie** [-lo'gi:] *f* theology; **t~logisch** [-'lo:gɪʃ] *adj* theological; **~retiker** [-'re:tikər] **(-s, -)** *m* theorist; **t~retisch** [-'re:tɪʃ] *adj* theoretical; **~rie** [-'ri:] *f* theory

Thera- [tera] *zW:* **~peut** [-'pɔʏt] **(-en, -en)** *m* therapist; **t~peutisch** [-'pɔʏtɪʃ] *adj* therapeutic; **~pie** [-'pi:] *f* therapy

Therm- *zW:* **~albad** [tɛr'ma:lba:t] *nt* thermal bath; thermal spa; **~odrucker** [tɛrmo-] *m* thermal printer; **~ometer** [tɛrmo'me:tər] **(-s, -)** *nt* thermometer;

⚠ *For information on spelling reform see page 615*

~osflasche ['tɛrmɔsflaʃə] ® f Thermos ® flask

These ['te:zə] f thesis

Thrombose [trɔm'bo:zə] f thrombosis

Thron [tro:n] (-(e)s, -e) m throne; **t~en** vi to sit enthroned; (fig) to sit in state; **~folge** f succession (to the throne); **~folger(in)** (-s, -) m(f) heir to the throne

Thunfisch ⚠ ['tu:nfɪʃ] m tuna

Thüringen ['ty:rɪŋən] (-s) nt Thuringia

Thymian ['ty:mia:n] (-s, -e) m thyme

Tick [tɪk] (-(e)s, -s) m tic; (Eigenart) quirk; (Fimmel) craze

ticken vi to tick

tief [ti:f] adj deep; (~sinnig) profound; (Ausschnitt, Preis, Ton) low; **T~** (-s, -s) nt (MET) depression; **T~druck** m low pressure; **T~e** f depth; **T~ebene** f plain; **T~enschärfe** f (PHOT) depth of focus; **T~garage** f underground garage; **~gekühlt** ⚠ adj frozen; **~greifend** ⚠ adj far-reaching; **T~kühlfach** nt deepfreeze compartment; **T~kühlkost** f (deep) frozen food; **T~kühltruhe** f deep-freeze, freezer; **T~punkt** m low point; (fig) low ebb; **T~schlag** m (BOXEN, fig) blow below the belt; **~schürfend** ⚠ adj profound; **T~see** f deep sea; **~sinnig** adj profound; melancholy; **T~stand** m low level; **T~stwert** m minimum od lowest value

Tier [ti:r] (-(e)s, -e) nt animal; **~arzt** m vet(erinary surgeon); **~garten** m zoo(logical gardens pl); **~heim** nt cat/dog home; **t~isch** adj animal; (auch fig) brutish; (fig: Ernst etc) deadly; **~kreis** m zodiac; **~kunde** f zoology; **t~liebend** adj fond of animals; **~park** m zoo; **~quälerei** [-kvɛ:lə'raɪ] f cruelty to animals; **~schutzverein** m society for the prevention of cruelty to animals

Tiger(in) ['ti:gər(ɪn)] (-s, -) m(f) tiger(-gress)

tilgen ['tɪlgən] vt to erase; (Sünden) to expiate; (Schulden) to pay off

Tinte ['tɪntə] f ink

Tintenfisch m cuttlefish

Tip ⚠ [tɪp] m tip; **t~pen** vt, vi to tap, to touch; (umg: schreiben) to type; (im Lotto

etc) to bet (on); **auf jdn t~pen** (umg: raten) to tip sb, to put one's money on sb (fig)

Tipp- ['tɪp] zW: **~fehler** (umg) m typing error; **t~topp** (umg) adj tip-top; **~zettel** m (pools) coupon

Tirol [ti'ro:l] nt the Tyrol; **~er(in)** m(f) Tyrolean; **t~isch** adj Tyrolean

Tisch [tɪʃ] (-(e)s, -e) m table; **bei ~** at table; **vor/nach ~** before/after eating; **unter den ~ fallen** (fig) to be dropped; **~decke** f tablecloth; **~ler** (-s, -) m carpenter, joiner; **~lerei** f joiner's workshop; (Arbeit) carpentry, joinery; **t~lern** vi to do carpentry etc; **~rede** f after-dinner speech; **~tennis** nt table tennis; **~tuch** nt tablecloth

Titel ['ti:təl] (-s, -) m title; **~bild** nt cover (picture); (von Buch) frontispiece; **~rolle** f title role; **~seite** f cover; (Buchtitelseite) title page; **~verteidiger** m defending champion, title holder

Toast [to:st] (-(e)s, -s od -e) m toast; **~brot** nt bread for toasting; **~er** (-s, -) m toaster

tob- ['to:b] zW: **~en** vi to rage; (Kinder) to romp about; **~süchtig** adj maniacal

Tochter ['tɔxtər] (-, ⸚) f daughter; **~gesellschaft** f subsidiary (company)

Tod [to:t] (-(e)s, -e) m death; **t~ernst** adj deadly serious ♦ adv in dead earnest

Todes- ['to:dəs] zW: **~angst** [-aŋst] f mortal fear; **~anzeige** f obituary (notice); **~fall** m death; **~strafe** f death penalty; **~ursache** f cause of death; **~urteil** nt death sentence; **~verachtung** f utter disgust

todkrank adj dangerously ill

tödlich ['tø:tlɪç] adj deadly, fatal

tod- zW: **~müde** adj dead tired; **~schick** (umg) adj smart, classy; **~sicher** (umg) adj absolutely od dead certain; **T~sünde** f deadly sin

Toilette [toa'lɛtə] f toilet, lavatory; (Frisiertisch) dressing table

Toiletten- zW: **~artikel** pl toiletries, toilet articles; **~papier** nt toilet paper; **~tisch** m dressing table

toi, toi, toi ['tɔy'tɔy'tɔy] excl touch wood

tolerant [tole'rant] adj tolerant

⚠ *Informationen zur Rechtschreibreform Seite 615*

Toleranz [tole'rants] f tolerance

tolerieren [tole'riːrən] vt to tolerate

toll [tɔl] adj mad; (Treiben) wild; (umg) terrific; **~en** vi to romp; **T~kirsche** f deadly nightshade; **~kühn** adj daring; **T~wut** f rabies

Tomate [to'maːtə] f tomato; **~nmark** nt tomato purée

Ton¹ [toːn] (-(e)s, -e) m (Erde) clay

Ton² [toːn] (-(e)s, ⸚e) m (Laut) sound; (MUS) note; (Redeweise) tone; (Farb~, Nuance) shade; (Betonung) stress; **t~angebend** adj leading; **~art** f (musical) key; **~band** nt tape; **~bandgerät** nt tape recorder

tönen ['tøːnən] vi to sound ♦ vt to shade; (Haare) to tint

tönern ['tøːnərn] adj clay

Ton- zW: **~fall** m intonation; **~film** m sound film; **~leiter** f (MUS) scale; **t~los** adj soundless

Tonne ['tɔnə] f barrel; (Maß) ton

Ton- zW: **~taube** f clay pigeon; **~waren** pl pottery sg, earthenware sg

Topf [tɔpf] (-(e)s, ⸚e) m pot; **~blume** f pot plant

Töpfer ['tœpfər] (-s, -) m potter; **~ei** [-'rai] f piece of pottery; potter's workshop; **~scheibe** f potter's wheel

topographisch ⚠ [topo'graːfɪʃ] adj topographic

Tor¹ [toːr] (-en, -en) m fool

Tor² [toːr] (-(e)s, -e) nt gate; (SPORT) goal; **~bogen** m archway

Torf [tɔrf] (-(e)s) m peat

Torheit f foolishness; foolish deed

töricht ['tøːrɪçt] adj foolish

torkeln ['tɔrkəln] vi to stagger, to reel

Torte ['tɔrtə] f cake; (Obst~) flan, tart

Tortur [tɔr'tuːr] f ordeal

Torwart [toːr] (-(e)s, -e) m goalkeeper

tosen ['toːzən] vi to roar

tot [toːt] adj dead

total [to'taːl] adj total; **~itär** [totali'tɛːr] adj totalitarian; **T~schaden** m (AUT) complete write-off

Tote(r) f(m) dead person

töten ['tøːtən] vt, vi to kill

Toten- zW: **~bett** nt death bed; **t~blaß** ⚠ adj deathly pale, white as a sheet; **~kopf** m skull; **~schein** m death certificate; **~stille** f deathly silence

tot- zW: **~fahren** (unreg) vt to run over; **~geboren** ⚠ adj stillborn; **~lachen** (umg) vr to laugh one's head off

Toto ['toːto] (-s, -s) m od nt pools pl; **~schein** m pools coupon

tot- zW: **T~schlag** m manslaughter; **~schlagen** (unreg) vt (auch fig) to kill; **~schweigen** (unreg) vt to hush up; **~stellen** vr to pretend to be dead

Tötung ['tøːtʊŋ] f killing

Toupet [tu'peː] (-s, -s) nt toupee

toupieren [tu'piːrən] vt to backcomb

Tour [tuːr] (-, -en) f tour, trip; (Umdrehung) revolution; (Verhaltensart) way; **in einer ~** incessantly; **~ismus** [tu'rɪsmʊs] m tourism; **~ist** [tu'rɪst] m tourist; **~istenklasse** f tourist class; **~nee** [tʊr'neː] (-, -n) f (THEAT etc) tour; **auf ~nee gehen** to go on tour

Trab [traːp] (-(e)s) m trot

Trabantenstadt f satellite town

traben ['traːbən] vi to trot

Tracht [traxt] (-, -en) f (Kleidung) costume, dress; **eine ~ Prügel** a sound thrashing; **t~en** vi: **t~en (nach)** to strive (for); **jdm nach dem Leben t~en** to seek to kill sb; **danach t~en, etw zu tun** to strive od endeavour to do sth

trächtig ['trɛçtɪç] adj (Tier) pregnant

Tradition [traditsi'oːn] f tradition; **t~ell** [-'nɛl] adj traditional

traf etc [traːf] vb siehe **treffen**

Tragbahre f stretcher

tragbar adj (Gerät) portable; (Kleidung) wearable; (erträglich) bearable

träge ['trɛːgə] adj sluggish, slow; (PHYS) inert

tragen ['traːgən] (unreg) vt to carry; (Kleidung, Brille) to wear; (Namen, Früchte) to bear; (erdulden) to endure ♦ vi (schwanger sein) to be pregnant; (Eis) to hold; **sich mit einem Gedanken ~** to have an idea in mind; **zum T~ kommen** to have an effect

⚠ For information on spelling reform see page 615

Träger ['trɛːgər] (**-s, -**) *m* carrier; wearer; bearer; (*Ordens~*) holder; (*an Kleidung*) (shoulder) strap; (*Körperschaft etc*) sponsor

Tragetasche *f* carrier bag

Tragfläche *f* (*AVIAT*) wing

Tragflügelboot *nt* hydrofoil

Trägheit ['trɛːkhaɪt] *f* laziness; (*PHYS*) inertia

Tragik ['traːgɪk] *f* tragedy; **tragisch** *adj* tragic

Tragödie [tra'gøːdiə] *f* tragedy

Tragweite *f* range; (*fig*) scope

Train- ['trɛːn] *zW:* **~er** (**-s, -**) *m* (*SPORT*) trainer, coach; (*Fußball*) manager; **t~ieren** [trɛˈniːrən] *vt, vi* to train; (*Mensch*) to train, to coach; (*Übung*) to practise; **~ing** (**-s, -s**) *nt* training; **~ingsanzug** *m* track suit

Traktor ['traktɔr] *m* tractor; (*von Drucker*) tractor feed

trällern ['trɛlərn] *vt, vi* to trill, to sing

Tram [tram] (**-, -s**) *f* tram

trampeln ['trampəln] *vt, vi* to trample, to stamp

trampen ['trɛmpən] *vi* to hitch-hike

Tramper(in) [trɛmpər(ɪn)] (**-s, -**) *m(f)* hitch-hiker

Tran [traːn] (**-(e)s, -e**) *m* train oil, blubber

tranchieren [trãˈʃiːrən] *vt* to carve

Träne ['trɛːnə] *f* tear; **t~n** *vi* to water; **~ngas** *nt* teargas

trank *etc* [traŋk] *vb siehe* **trinken**

tränken ['trɛŋkən] *vt* (*Tiere*) to water

Trans- *zW:* **~formator** [transfɔrˈmaːtɔr] *m* transformer; **~istor** [tranˈzɪstɔr] *m* transistor; **~itverkehr** [tranˈzɪtfɛrkeːr] *m* transit traffic; **~itvisum** *nt* transit visa; **t~parent** *adj* transparent; **~parent** (**-(e)s, -e**) *nt* (*Bild*) transparency; (*Spruchband*) banner; **~plantation** [transplantatsiˈoːn] *f* transplantation; (*Hauttransplantation*) graft(ing)

Transport [transˈpɔrt] (**-(e)s, -e**) *m* transport; **t~ieren** [transpɔrˈtiːrən] *vt* to transport; **~kosten** *pl* transport charges, carriage *sg*; **~mittel** *nt* means *sg* of transportation; **~unternehmen** *nt* carrier

Traube ['traʊbə] *f* grape; bunch (of grapes); **~nzucker** *m* glucose

trauen ['traʊən] *vi:* **jdm/etw ~** to trust sb/sth ♦ *vr* to dare ♦ *vt* to marry

Trauer ['traʊər] (**-**) *f* sorrow; (*für Verstorbenen*) mourning; **~fall** *m* death, bereavement; **~feier** *f* funeral service; **~kleidung** *f* mourning; **t~n** *vi* to mourn; **um jdn t~n** to mourn (for) sb; **~rand** *m* black border; **~spiel** *nt* tragedy

traulich ['traʊlɪç] *adj* cosy, intimate

Traum [traʊm] (**-(e)s, Träume**) *m* dream

Trauma (**-s, -men**) *nt* trauma

träum- ['trɔʏm] *zW:* **~en** *vt, vi* to dream; **T~er** (**-s, -**) *m* dreamer; **T~e'rei** *f* dreaming; **~erisch** *adj* dreamy

traumhaft *adj* dreamlike; (*fig*) wonderful

traurig ['traʊrɪç] *adj* sad; **T~keit** *f* sadness

Trau- ['traʊ] *zW:* **~ring** *m* wedding ring; **~schein** *m* marriage certificate; **~ung** *f* wedding ceremony; **~zeuge** *m* witness (to a marriage); **~zeugin** *f* witness (to a marriage)

treffen ['trɛfən] (*unreg*) *vt* to strike, to hit; (*Bemerkung*) to hurt; (*begegnen*) to meet; (*Entscheidung etc*) to make; (*Maßnahmen*) to take ♦ *vi* to hit ♦ *vr* to meet; **er hat es gut getroffen** he did well; **~ auf** *+akk* to come across, to meet with; **es traf sich, daß ...** it so happened that ...; **es trifft sich gut** it's convenient; **wie es so trifft** as these things happen; **T~** (**-s, -**) *nt* meeting; **~d** *adj* pertinent, apposite

Treffer (**-s, -**) *m* hit; (*Tor*) goal; (*Los*) winner

Treffpunkt *m* meeting place

Treib- ['traɪb] *zW:* **~eis** *nt* drift ice; **t~en** (*unreg*) *vt* to drive; (*Studien etc*) to pursue; (*Sport*) to do, to go in for ♦ *vi* (*Schiff etc*) to drift; (*Pflanzen*) to sprout; (*KOCH: aufgehen*) to rise; (*Tee, Kaffee*) to be diuretic; **~haus** *nt* greenhouse; **~hauseffekt** *m* greenhouse effect; **~hausgas** *nt* greenhouse gas; **~stoff** *m* fuel

trenn- ['trɛn] *zW:* **~bar** *adj* separable; **~en** *vt* to separate; (*teilen*) to divide ♦ *vr* to separate; **sich ~en von** to part with; **T~ung** *f* separation; **T~wand** *f* partition (wall)

Trepp- ['trɛp] *zW:* **t~ab** *adv* downstairs;

t~auf *adv* upstairs; ~e *f* stair(case);
~engeländer *nt* banister; ~enhaus *nt*
staircase
Tresor [tre'zo:r] (-s, -e) *m* safe
Tretboot *nt* pedalo, pedal boat
treten ['tre:tən] (*unreg*) *vi* to step; (*Tränen,
Schweiß*) to appear ♦ *vt* (*mit Fußtritt*) to kick;
(*nieder~*) to tread, to trample; ~ **nach** to
kick at; ~ **in** +*akk* to step in(to); **in
Verbindung ~** to get in contact; **in
Erscheinung ~** to appear
treu [trɔy] *adj* faithful, true; **T~e** (-) *f* loyalty,
faithfulness; **T~händer** (-s, -) *m* trustee;
T~handanstalt *f* trustee organization;
T~handgesellschaft *f* trust company;
~herzig *adj* innocent; ~los *adj* faithless

TREUHANDANSTALT

i The **Treuhandanstalt** was the
organization set up in 1990 to take over
the nationally-owned companies of the
former **DDR**, break them down into smaller
units and privatize them. It was based in
Berlin and had nine branches. Many
companies were closed down by the
Treuhandanstalt because of their outdated
equipment and inability to compete with
Western firms which resulted in rising
unemployment. Having completed its initial
task, the **Treuhandanstalt** was closed
down in 1995.

Tribüne [tri'by:nə] *f* grandstand; (*Redner~*)
platform
Trichter ['trɪçtər] (-s, -) *m* funnel; (*in Boden*)
crater
Trick [trɪk] (-s, -e *od* -s) *m* trick; ~film *m*
cartoon
Trieb [tri:p] (-(e)s, -e) *m* urge, drive;
(*Neigung*) inclination; (*an Baum etc*) shoot;
t~ *etc vb siehe* **treiben**; ~kraft *f* (*fig*) drive;
~täter *m* sex offender; ~werk *nt* engine
triefen ['tri:fən] *vi* to drip
triffst *etc* [trɪfst] *vb siehe* **treffen**
triftig ['trɪftɪç] *adj* good, convincing
Trikot [tri'ko:] (-s, -s) *nt* vest; (*SPORT*) shirt
Trimester [tri'mɛstər] (-s, -) *nt* term

trimmen ['trɪmən] *vr* to do keep fit
exercises
trink- ['trɪŋk] *zW:* ~bar *adj* drinkable; ~en
(*unreg*) *vt, vi* to drink; **T~er** (-s, -) *m*
drinker; **T~geld** *nt* tip; **T~halle** *f*
refreshment kiosk; **T~wasser** *nt* drinking
water
Tripper ['trɪpər] (-s, -) *m* gonorrhoea
Tritt [trɪt] (-(e)s, -e) *m* step; (*Fuß~*) kick;
~brett *nt* (*EISENB*) step; (*AUT*) running
board
Triumph [tri'ʊmf] (-(e)s, -e) *m* triumph;
~bogen *m* triumphal arch; t~ieren
[triʊm'fi:rən] *vi* to triumph; (*jubeln*) to exult
trocken ['trɔkən] *adj* dry; **T~element** *nt*
dry cell; **T~haube** *f* hair dryer; **T~heit** *f*
dryness; ~legen *vt* (*Sumpf*) to drain;
(*Kind*) to put a clean nappy on; **T~milch** *f*
dried milk; **T~rasur** *f* dry shave, electric
shave
trocknen ['trɔknən] *vt, vi* to dry
Trödel ['trø:dəl] (-s) (*umg*) *m* junk; ~markt
m flea market; t~n (*umg*) *vi* to dawdle
Trommel ['trɔməl] (-, -n) *f* drum; ~fell *nt*
eardrum; t~n *vt, vi* to drum
Trompete [trɔm'pe:tə] *f* trumpet; ~r (-s, -)
m trumpeter
Tropen ['tro:pən] *pl* tropics; ~helm *m* sun
helmet
tröpfeln ['trœpfəln] *vi* to drop, to trickle
Tropfen ['trɔpfən] (-s, -) *m* drop; t~ *vt, vi*
to drip ♦ *vb unpers*: **es tropft** a few
raindrops are falling; t~weise *adv* in drops
Tropfsteinhöhle *f* stalactite cave
tropisch ['tro:pɪʃ] *adj* tropical
Trost [tro:st] (-es) *m* consolation, comfort
trösten ['trø:stən] *vt* to console, to comfort
trost- *zW:* ~los *adj* bleak; (*Verhältnisse*)
wretched; **T~preis** *m* consolation prize;
~reich *adj* comforting
Trott [trɔt] (-(e)s, -e) *m* trot; (*Routine*)
routine; ~el (-s, -) (*umg*) *m* fool, dope;
t~en *vi* to trot
Trotz [trɔts] (-es) *m* pigheadedness; **etw
aus ~ tun** to do sth just to show them;
jdm zum ~ in defiance of sb; t~ *präp*
(+*gen od dat*) in spite of; t~dem *adv*

⚠ *For information on spelling reform see page 615*

nevertheless, all the same ♦ *konj* although; **t~en** *vi* (+*dat*) to defy; (*der Kälte, Klima etc*) to withstand; (*der Gefahr*) to brave; (*trotzig sein*) to be awkward; **t~ig** *adj* defiant, pigheaded; **~kopf** *m* obstinate child

trüb [try:p] *adj* dull; (*Flüssigkeit, Glas*) cloudy; (*fig*) gloomy

Trubel ['tru:bəl] (**-s**) *m* hurly-burly

trüb- *zW:* **~en** ['try:bən] *vt* to cloud ♦ *vr* to become clouded; **T~heit** *f* dullness; cloudiness; gloom; **T~sal** (**-, -e**) *f* distress; **~selig** *adj* sad, melancholy; **T~sinn** *m* depression; **~sinnig** *adj* depressed, gloomy

Trüffel ['tryfəl] (**-, -n**) *f* truffle

trug *etc* [tru:k] *vb siehe* **tragen**

trügen ['try:gən] (*unreg*) *vt* to deceive ♦ *vi* to be deceptive

trügerisch *adj* deceptive

Trugschluß ⚠ ['tru:gʃlʊs] *m* false conclusion

Truhe ['tru:ə] *f* chest

Trümmer ['trʏmər] *pl* wreckage *sg*; (*Bau~*) ruins; **~haufen** *m* heap of rubble

Trumpf [trʊmpf] (**-(e)s, ̈e**) *m* (*auch fig*) trump; **t~en** *vt, vi* to trump

Trunk [trʊŋk] (**-(e)s, ̈e**) *m* drink; **t~en** *adj* intoxicated; **~enheit** *f* intoxication; **~enheit am Steuer** drunken driving; **~sucht** *f* alcoholism

Trupp [trʊp] (**-s, -s**) *m* troop; **~e** *f* troop; (*Waffengattung*) force; (*Schauspieltruppe*) troupe; **~en** *pl* (MIL) troops; **~enübungsplatz** *m* training area

Truthahn ['tru:tha:n] *m* turkey

Tschech- ['tʃɛç] *zW:* **~e** *m* Czech; **~ien** (**-s**) *nt* the Czech Republic; **~in** *f* Czech; **t~isch** *adj* Czech; **~oslowakei** [-oslova'kaɪ] *f:* **die ~oslowakei** Czechoslovakia; **t~oslowakisch** [-oslo'va:kɪʃ] *adj* Czechoslovak(ian)

tschüs ⚠ [tʃʏs] *excl* cheerio

T-Shirt ['ti:ʃə:t] *nt* T-shirt

Tube ['tu:bə] *f* tube

Tuberkulose [tuberku'lo:zə] *f* tuberculosis

Tuch [tu:x] (**-(e)s, ̈er**) *nt* cloth; (*Hals~*) scarf; (*Kopf~*) headscarf; (*Hand~*) towel

tüchtig ['tʏçtɪç] *adj* efficient, (cap)able;

(*umg: kräftig*) good, sound; **T~keit** *f* efficiency, ability

Tücke ['tʏkə] *f* (*Arglist*) malice; (*Trick*) trick; (*Schwierigkeit*) difficulty, problem

tückisch ['tʏkɪʃ] *adj* treacherous; (*böswillig*) malicious

Tugend ['tu:gənt] (**-, -en**) *f* virtue; **t~haft** *adj* virtuous

Tülle *f* spout

Tulpe ['tʊlpə] *f* tulip

Tumor ['tu:mɔr] (**-s, -e**) *m* tumour

Tümpel ['tʏmpəl] (**-s, -**) *m* pool, pond

Tumult [tu'mʊlt] (**-(e)s, -e**) *m* tumult

tun [tu:n] (*unreg*) *vt* (*machen*) to do; (*legen*) to put ♦ *vi* to act ♦ *vr:* **es tut sich etwas/ viel** something/a lot is happening; **jdm etw ~** (*antun*) to do sth to sb; **etw tut es auch** sth will do; **das tut nichts** that doesn't matter; **das tut nichts zur Sache** that's neither here nor there; **so ~, als ob** to act as if

tünchen ['tʏnçən] *vt* to whitewash

Tunke ['tʊŋkə] *f* sauce; **t~n** *vt* to dip, to dunk

tunlichst ['tu:nlɪçst] *adv* if at all possible; **~ bald** as soon as possible

Tunnel ['tʊnəl] (**-s, -s** *od* **-**) *m* tunnel

Tupfen ['tʊpfən] (**-s, -**) *m* dot, spot; **t~** *vt, vi* to dab; (*mit Farbe*) to dot

Tür [ty:r] (**-, -en**) *f* door

Turbine [tʊr'bi:nə] *f* turbine

Türk- [tʏrk] *zW:* **~e** *m* Turk; **~ei** [tʏr'kaɪ] *f:* **die ~ei** Turkey; **~in** *f* Turk

Türkis [tʏr'ki:s] (**-es, -e**) *m* turquoise; **t~** *adj* turquoise

türkisch ['tʏrkɪʃ] *adj* Turkish

Türklinke *f* doorknob, door handle

Turm [tʊrm] (**-(e)s, ̈e**) *m* tower; (*Kirch~*) steeple; (*Sprung~*) diving platform; (SCHACH) castle, rook

türmen ['tʏrmən] *vr* to tower up ♦ *vt* to heap up ♦ *vi* (*umg*) to scarper, to bolt

Turn- ['tʊrn] *zW:* **t~en** *vi* to do gymnastic exercises ♦ *vt* to perform; **~en** (**-s**) *nt* gymnastics; (*SCH*) physical education, P.E.; **~er(in)** (**-s, -**) *m(f)* gymnast; **~halle** *f* gym(nasium); **~hose** *f* gym shorts *pl*

Turnier [tʊrˈniːr] (-s, -e) *nt* tournament
Turn- *zW*: ~**schuh** *m* gym shoe; ~**verein** *m* gymnastics club; ~**zeug** *nt* gym things *pl*
Tusche [ˈtʊʃə] *f* Indian ink
tuscheln [ˈtʊʃəln] *vt, vi* to whisper
Tuschkasten *m* paintbox
Tüte [ˈtyːtə] *f* bag
tuten [ˈtuːtən] *vi* (AUT) to hoot (BRIT), to honk (US)
TÜV [tʏf] (-s, -s) *m abk* (= *Technischer Überwachungsverein*) ≈ MOT
Typ [tyːp] (-s, -en) *m* type; ~**e** *f* (TYP) type
Typhus [ˈtyːfʊs] (-) *m* typhoid (fever)
typisch [ˈtyːpɪʃ] *adj*: ~ (**für**) typical (of)
Tyrann [tyˈran] (-en, -en) *m* tyrant; ~**ei** [-ˈnaɪ] *f* tyranny; **t~isch** *adj* tyrannical; **t~i'sieren** *vt* to tyrannize

U, u

u.a. *abk* = **unter anderem**
U-Bahn [ˈuːbaːn] *f* underground, tube
übel [ˈyːbəl] *adj* bad; (*moralisch*) bad, wicked; **jdm ist** ~ sb feels sick; **Ü~** (-s, -) *nt* evil; (*Krankheit*) disease; ~**gelaunt** ⚠ *adj* bad-tempered; **Ü~keit** *f* nausea; ~**nehmen** ⚠ (*unreg*) *vt*: **jdm eine Bemerkung** *etc* ~**nehmen** to be offended at sb's remark *etc*
üben [ˈyːbən] *vt, vi* to exercise, to practise

SCHLÜSSELWORT

über [ˈyːbər] *präp +dat* **1** (*räumlich*) over, above; **zwei Grad über Null** two degrees above zero
2 (*zeitlich*) over; **über der Arbeit einschlafen** to fall asleep over one's work
♦ *präp +akk* **1** (*räumlich*) over; (*hoch über auch*) above; (*quer über auch*) across
2 (*zeitlich*) over; **über Weihnachten** over Christmas; **über kurz oder lang** sooner or later
3 (*mit Zahlen*): **Kinder über 12 Jahren** children over *od* above 12 years of age; **ein Scheck über 200 Mark** a cheque for 200 marks
4 (*auf dem Wege*) via; **nach Köln über Aachen** to Cologne via Aachen; **ich habe es über die Auskunft erfahren** I found out from information
5 (*betreffend*) about; **ein Buch über ...** a book about *od* on ...; **über jdn/etw lachen** to laugh about *od* at sb/sth
6: **Macht über jdn haben** to have power over sb; **sie liebt ihn über alles** she loves him more than everything
♦ *adv* over; **über und über** over and over; **den ganzen Tag über** all day long; **jdm in etw** *dat* **über sein** to be superior to sb in sth

überall [yːbərˈʔal] *adv* everywhere; ~**'hin** *adv* everywhere
überanstrengen [yːbərˈʔanʃtrɛŋən] *vt insep* to overexert ♦ *vr insep* to overexert o.s.
überarbeiten [yːbərˈʔarbaɪtən] *vt insep* to revise, to rework ♦ *vr insep* to overwork (o.s.)
überaus [ˈyːbərʔaʊs] *adv* exceedingly
überbelichten [ˈyːbərbəlɪçtən] *vt* (PHOT) to overexpose
über'bieten (*unreg*) *vt insep* to outbid; (*übertreffen*) to surpass; (*Rekord*) to break
Überbleibsel [ˈyːbərblaɪpsəl] (-s, -) *nt* residue, remainder
Überblick [ˈyːbərblɪk] *m* view; (*fig: Darstellung*) survey, overview; (*Fähigkeit*): ~ (**über** +*akk*) grasp (of), overall view (of); **ü~en** [-ˈblɪkən] *vt insep* to survey
überbring- [yːbərˈbrɪŋ] *zW*: ~**en** (*unreg*) *vt insep* to deliver, to hand over; **Ü~er** (-s, -) *m* bearer
überbrücken [yːbərˈbrʏkən] *vt insep* to bridge (over)
überbuchen [ˈyːbərbuːxən] *vt insep* to overbook
über'dauern *vt insep* to outlast
über'denken (*unreg*) *vt insep* to think over
überdies [yːbərˈdiːs] *adv* besides
überdimensional [ˈyːbərdimɛnzionaːl] *adj* oversize
Überdruß ⚠ [ˈyːbərdrʊs] (-sses) *m* weariness; **bis zum** ~ ad nauseam

⚠ *For information on spelling reform see page 615*

überdurchschnittlich ['y:bərdʊrçʃnɪtlɪç] *adj* above-average ♦ *adv* exceptionally

übereifrig ['y:bər|aifrɪç] *adj* over-keen

übereilt [y:bər'|ailt] *adj* (over)hasty, premature

überein- [y:bər'|ain] *zW*: **~ander** [y:bər|ai'nandər] *adv* one upon the other; (*sprechen*) about each other; **~kommen** (*unreg*) *vi* to agree; **Ü~kunft (-, -künfte)** *f* agreement; **~stimmen** *vi* to agree; **Ü~stimmung** *f* agreement

überempfindlich ['y:bər|ɛmpfɪntlɪç] *adj* hypersensitive

überfahren [y:bər'fa:rən] (*unreg*) *vt insep* (*AUT*) to run over; (*fig*) to walk all over

Überfahrt ['y:bərfa:rt] *f* crossing

Überfall ['y:bərfal] *m* (*Bank~, MIL*) raid; (*auf jdn*) assault; **ü~en** [-'falən] (*unreg*) *vt insep* to attack; (*Bank*) to raid; (*besuchen*) to drop in on, to descend on

überfällig ['y:bərfɛlɪç] *adj* overdue

überfliegen [y:bər'fli:gən] (*unreg*) *vt insep* to fly over, to overfly; (*Buch*) to skim through

Überfluß ⚠ ['y:bərflʊs] *m*: **~ (an +*dat*)** (super)abundance (of), excess (of)

überflüssig ['y:bərflʏsɪç] *adj* superfluous

überfordern *vt insep* to demand too much of, (*Kräfte etc*) to overtax

überführen *vt insep* (*Leiche etc*) to transport; (*Täter*) to have convicted

Überführung *f* transport; conviction; (*Brücke*) bridge, overpass

überfüllt *adj* (*Schulen, Straßen*) overcrowded; (*Kurs*) oversubscribed

Übergabe ['y:bərga:bə] *f* handing over; (*MIL*) surrender

Übergang ['y:bərgaŋ] *m* crossing; (*Wandel, Überleitung*) transition

Übergangs- *zW*: **~lösung** *f* provisional solution, stopgap; **~zeit** *f* transitional period

übergeben (*unreg*) *vt insep* to hand over; (*MIL*) to surrender ♦ *vr insep* to be sick

übergehen ['y:bərge:ən] (*unreg*) *vi* (*Besitz*) to pass; (*zum Feind etc*) to go over, to defect; **~ in** +*akk* to turn into; **über'gehen** (*unreg*) *vt insep* to pass over, to omit

Übergewicht ['y:bərgəvɪçt] *nt* excess weight; (*fig*) preponderance

überglücklich ['y:bərglʏklɪç] *adj* overjoyed

Übergröße ['y:bərgrø:sə] *f* oversize

überhaupt [y:bər'haupt] *adv* at all; (*im allgemeinen*) in general; (*besonders*) especially; **~ nicht/keine** not/none at all

überheblich [y:bər'he:plɪç] *adj* arrogant; **Ü~keit** *f* arrogance

über'holen *vt insep* to overtake; (*TECH*) to overhaul

über'holt *adj* out-of-date, obsolete

Überholverbot [y:bər'ho:lfɛrbo:t] *nt* restriction on overtaking

über'hören *vt insep* not to hear; (*absichtlich*) to ignore

überirdisch ['y:bər|ɪrdɪʃ] *adj* supernatural, unearthly

über'laden (*unreg*) *vt insep* to overload ♦ *adj* (*fig*) cluttered

über'lassen (*unreg*) *vt insep*: **jdm etw ~** to leave sth to sb ♦ *vr insep*: **sich einer Sache** *dat* **~** to give o.s. over to sth

über'lasten *vt insep* to overload; (*Mensch*) to overtax

überlaufen ['y:bərlaufən] (*unreg*) *vi* (*Flüssigkeit*) to flow over; (*zum Feind etc*) to go over, to defect; **~ sein** to be inundated *od* besieged; **über'laufen** (*unreg*) *vt insep* (*Schauer etc*) to come over

über'leben *vt insep* to survive; **Über'lebende(r)** *f(m)* survivor

über'legen *vt insep* to consider ♦ *adj* superior; **ich muß es mir ~** I'll have to think about it; **Über'legenheit** *f* superiority

Über'legung *f* consideration, deliberation

über'liefern *vt insep* to hand down, to transmit

Überlieferung *f* tradition

überlisten [y:bər'lɪstən] *vt insep* to outwit

überm ['y:bərm] = **über dem**

Übermacht ['y:bərmaxt] *f* superior force, superiority; **übermächtig** *adj* superior (in strength); (*Gefühl etc*) overwhelming

übermäßig ['y:bərmɛ:sɪç] *adj* excessive

Übermensch ['y:bərmɛnʃ] *m* superman;

ü~lich adj superhuman
übermitteln [y:bɐrˈmɪtəln] vt insep to convey
übermorgen [ˈy:bɐrmɔrɡən] adv the day after tomorrow
Übermüdung [y:bɐrˈmy:dʊŋ] f fatigue, overtiredness
Übermut [ˈy:bɐrmu:t] m exuberance
übermütig [ˈy:bɐrmy:tɪç] adj exuberant, high-spirited; **~ werden** to get overconfident
übernächste(r, s) [ˈy:bɐrnɛːçstə(r, s)] adj (Jahr) next but one
übernacht- [y:bɐrˈnaxt] zW: **~en** vi insep: **(bei jdm) ~en** to spend the night (at sb's place); **Ü~ung** f overnight stay; **Ü~ung mit Frühstück** bed and breakfast; **Ü~ungsmöglichkeit** f overnight accommodation no pl
Übernahme [ˈy:bɐrna:mə] f taking over od on, acceptance
über'nehmen (unreg) vt insep to take on, to accept; (Amt, Geschäft) to take over ♦ vr insep to take on too much
über'prüfen vt insep to examine, to check
überqueren [y:bɐrˈkve:rən] vt insep to cross
überragen [y:bɐrˈra:ɡən] vt insep to tower above; (fig) to surpass
überraschen [y:bɐrˈraʃən] vt insep to surprise
Überraschung f surprise
überreden [y:bɐrˈre:dən] vt insep to persuade
überreichen [y:bɐrˈraɪçən] vt insep to present, to hand over
'**Überrest** m remains, remnants
überrumpeln [y:bɐrˈrʊmpəln] vt insep to take by surprise
überrunden [y:bɐrˈrʊndən] vt insep to lap
übers [ˈy:bɐrs] = **über das**
Überschall- [ˈy:bɐrʃal] zW: **~flugzeug** nt supersonic jet; **~geschwindigkeit** f supersonic speed
über'schätzen vt insep to overestimate
'**überschäumen** vi (Bier) to foam over, bubble over; (Temperament) to boil over
Überschlag [ˈy:bɐrʃla:k] m (FIN) estimate;

(SPORT) somersault; **ü~en** [-ˈʃla:ɡən] (unreg) vt insep (berechnen) to estimate; (auslassen: Seite) to omit ♦ vr insep to somersault; (Stimme) to crack; (AVIAT) to loop the loop; '**überschlagen** (unreg) vt (Beine) to cross ♦ vi (Wellen) to break; (Funken) to flash
überschnappen [ˈy:bɐrʃnapən] vi (Stimme) to crack; (umg: Mensch) to flip one's lid
über'schneiden (unreg) vr insep (auch fig) to overlap; (Linien) to intersect
über'schreiben (unreg) vt insep to provide with a heading; **jdm etw ~** to transfer od make over sth to sb
über'schreiten (unreg) vt insep to cross over; (fig) to exceed; (verletzen) to transgress
Überschrift [ˈy:bɐrʃrɪft] f heading, title
Überschuß ⚠ [ˈy:bɐrʃʊs] m: **~ (an** +dat) surplus (of); **überschüssig** adj surplus, excess
über'schütten vt insep: **jdn / etw mit etw ~** to pour sth over sb/sth; **jdn mit etw ~** (fig) to shower sb with sth
überschwemmen [y:bɐrˈʃvemən] vt insep to flood
Überschwemmung f flood
überschwenglich [ˈy:bɐrʃvɛŋlɪç] adj effusive
Übersee [ˈy:bɐrze:] f: **nach / in ~** overseas; **ü~isch** adj overseas
über'sehen (unreg) vt insep to look (out) over; (fig: Folgen) to see, to get an overall view of; (: nicht beachten) to overlook
über'senden (unreg) vt insep to send, to forward
übersetz- zW: **~en** [y:bɐrˈzetsən] vt insep to translate; '**übersetzen** vi to cross; **Ü~er(in)** [-ˈzetsɐr(ɪn)] (-s, -) m(f) translator; **Ü~ung** [-ˈzetsʊŋ] f translation; (TECH) gear ratio
Übersicht [ˈy:bɐrzɪçt] f overall view; (Darstellung) survey; **ü~lich** adj clear; (Gelände) open; **~lichkeit** f clarity, lucidity
übersiedeln [ˈy:bɐrzi:dəln] vi sep to move; **über'siedeln** vi to move
über'spannt adj eccentric; (Idee) wild, crazy

⚠ For information on spelling reform see page 615

überspitzt [y:bər'ʃpɪtst] *adj* exaggerated

über'springen (*unreg*) *vt insep* to jump over; (*fig*) to skip

überstehen [y:bər'ʃte:ən] (*unreg*) *vt insep* to overcome, to get over; (*Winter etc*) to survive, to get through; '**überstehen** (*unreg*) *vi insep* to project

über'steigen (*unreg*) *vt insep* to climb over; (*fig*) to exceed

über'stimmen *vt insep* to outvote

Überstunden ['y:bərʃtʊndən] *pl* overtime *sg*

über'stürzen *vt insep* to rush ♦ *vr insep* to follow (one another) in rapid succession

überstürzt *adj* (over)hasty

Übertrag ['y:bərtra:k] (**-(e)s, -träge**) *m* (COMM) amount brought forward; **ü~bar** [-'tra:kba:r] *adj* transferable; (MED) infectious; **ü~en** [-'tra:gən] (*unreg*) *vt insep* to transfer; (RAD) to broadcast; (*übersetzen*) to render; (*Krankheit*) to transmit ♦ *vr insep* to spread ♦ *adj* figurative; **ü~en auf** +*akk* to transfer to; **jdm etw ü~en** to assign sth to sb; **sich ü~en auf** +*akk* to spread to; **~ung** [-'tra:gʊŋ] *f* transfer(ence); (RAD) broadcast; rendering; transmission

über'treffen (*unreg*) *vt insep* to surpass

über'treiben (*unreg*) *vt insep* to exaggerate; **Übertreibung** *f* exaggeration

übertreten [y:bər'tre:tən] (*unreg*) *vt insep* to cross; (*Gebot etc*) to break; '**übertreten** (*unreg*) *vi* (*über Linie, Gebiet*) to step (over); (SPORT) to overstep; (*zu anderem Glauben*) to be converted; '**übertreten (in** +*akk*) (POL) to go over (to)

Über'tretung *f* violation, transgression

übertrieben [y:bər'tri:bən] *adj* exaggerated, excessive

übervölkert [y:bər'fœlkərt] *adj* overpopulated

übervoll ['y:bərfɔl] *adj* overfull

übervorteilen [y:bər'fɔrtailən] *vt insep* to dupe, to cheat

über'wachen *vt insep* to supervise; (*Verdächtigen*) to keep under surveillance; **Überwachung** *f* supervision; surveillance

überwältigen [y:bər'vɛltɪgən] *vt insep* to overpower; **~d** *adj* overwhelming

überweisen [y:bər'vaɪzən] (*unreg*) *vt insep* to transfer

Überweisung *f* transfer; **~sauftrag** *m* (credit) transfer order

über'wiegen (*unreg*) *vi insep* to predominate; **~d** *adj* predominant

über'winden [y:bər'vɪndən] (*unreg*) *vt insep* to overcome ♦ *vr insep* to make an effort, to bring o.s. (to do sth)

Überwindung *f* effort, strength of mind

Überzahl ['y:bərtsa:l] *f* superiority, superior numbers *pl*; **in der ~ sein** to be numerically superior

überzählig ['y:bərtse:lɪç] *adj* surplus

über'zeugen *vt insep* to convince; **~d** *adj* convincing

Überzeugung *f* conviction

überziehen [y:bər'tsi:ən] (*unreg*) *vt* to put on; **über'ziehen** *vt insep* to cover; (*Konto*) to overdraw

Überziehungskredit *m* overdraft provision

Überzug ['y:bərtsu:k] *m* cover; (*Belag*) coating

üblich ['y:plɪç] *adj* usual

U-Boot ['u:bo:t] *nt* submarine

übrig ['y:brɪç] *adj* remaining; **für jdn etwas ~ haben** (*umg*) to be fond of sb; **die ~en** the others; **das ~e** the rest; **im ~en** besides; **~bleiben** △ (*unreg*) *vi* to remain, to be left (over); **~ens** ['y:brɪgəns] *adv* besides; (*nebenbei bemerkt*) by the way; **~lassen** △ (*unreg*) *vt* to leave (over)

Übung ['y:bʊŋ] *f* practice; (*Turn~, Aufgabe etc*) exercise; **~ macht den Meister** practice makes perfect

Ufer ['u:fər] (**-s, -**) *nt* bank; (*Meeres~*) shore

Uhr [u:r] (**-, -en**) *f* clock; (*Armband~*) watch; **wieviel ~ ist es?** what time is it?; **1 ~** 1 o'clock; **20 ~** 8 o'clock, 20.00 (twenty hundred) hours; **~(arm)band** *nt* watch strap; **~band** *nt* watch strap; **~macher** (**-s, -**) *m* watchmaker; **~werk** *nt* clockwork; works of a watch; **~zeiger** *m* hand; **~zeigersinn** *m*: **im ~zeigersinn** clockwise; **entgegen dem ~zeigersinn** anticlockwise; **~zeit** *f* time (of day)

Uhu ['u:hu] (**-s, -s**) *m* eagle owl
UKW [u:ka:'ve:] *abk* (= *Ultrakurzwelle*) VHF
ulkig ['ʊlkɪç] *adj* funny
Ulme ['ʊlmə] *f* elm
Ultimatum [ʊlti'ma:tʊm] (**-s, Ultimaten**) *nt* ultimatum
Ultra- ['ʊltra] *zW*: **~schall** *m* (*PHYS*) ultrasound; **u~violett** *adj* ultraviolet

---
SCHLÜSSELWORT
---

um [ʊm] *präp +akk* **1** (*um herum*) (a)round; **um Weihnachten** around Christmas; **er schlug um sich** he hit about him
2 (*mit Zeitangabe*) at; **um acht (Uhr)** at eight (o'clock)
3 (*mit Größenangabe*) by; **etw um 4 cm kürzen** to shorten sth by 4 cm; **um 10% teurer** 10% more expensive; **um vieles besser** better by far; **um nichts besser** not in the least bit better; **um so besser** so much the better
4: **der Kampf um den Titel** the battle for the title; **um Geld spielen** to play for money; **Stunde um Stunde** hour after hour; **Auge um Auge** an eye for an eye
♦ *präp +gen*: **um ... willen** for the sake of ...; **um Gottes willen** for goodness *od* (*stärker*) God's sake
♦ *konj*: **um ... zu** (in order) to ...; **zu klug, um zu ...** too clever to ...; **um so besser/ schlimmer** so much the better/worse
♦ *adv* **1** (*ungefähr*) about; **um (die) 30 Leute** about *od* around 30 people
2 (*vorbei*): **die 2 Stunden sind um** the two hours are up

---

umändern ['ʊm|ɛndərn] *vt* to alter
Umänderung *f* alteration
umarbeiten ['ʊm|arbaɪtən] *vt* to remodel; (*Buch etc*) to revise, to rework
umarmen [ʊm'|armən] *vt insep* to embrace
Umbau ['ʊmbaʊ] (**-(e)s, -e** *od* **-ten**) *m* reconstruction, alteration(s); **u~en** *vt* to rebuild, to reconstruct
umbilden ['ʊmbɪldən] *vt* to reorganize; (*POL: Kabinett*) to reshuffle
umbinden ['ʊmbɪndən] (*unreg*) *vt* (*Krawatte*

etc) to put on
umblättern ['ʊmblɛtərn] *vt* to turn over
umblicken ['ʊmblɪkən] *vr* to look around
umbringen ['ʊmbrɪŋən] (*unreg*) *vt* to kill
umbuchen ['ʊmbu:xən] *vi* to change one's reservation/flight *etc* ♦ *vt* to change
umdenken ['ʊmdɛŋkən] (*unreg*) *vi* to adjust one's views
umdrehen ['ʊmdre:ən] *vt* to turn (round); (*Hals*) to wring ♦ *vr* to turn (round)
Um'drehung *f* revolution; rotation
umeinander [ʊm|aɪ'nandər] *adv* round one another; (*füreinander*) for one another
umfahren ['ʊmfa:rən] (*unreg*) *vt* to run over; **um'fahren** (*unreg*) *vt insep* to drive round; to sail round
umfallen ['ʊmfalən] (*unreg*) *vi* to fall down *od* over
Umfang ['ʊmfaŋ] *m* extent; (*von Buch*) size; (*Reichweite*) range; (*Fläche*) area; (*MATH*) circumference; **u~reich** *adj* extensive; (*Buch etc*) voluminous
um'fassen *vt insep* to embrace; (*umgeben*) to surround; (*enthalten*) to include; **~d** *adj* comprehensive, extensive
umformen ['ʊmfɔrmən] *vi* to transform
Umfrage ['ʊmfra:gə] *f* poll
umfüllen ['ʊmfʏlən] *vt* to transfer; (*Wein*) to decant
umfunktionieren ['ʊmfʊŋktsioni:rən] *vt* to convert, to transform
Umgang ['ʊmgaŋ] *m* company; (*mit jdm*) dealings *pl*; (*Behandlung*) way of behaving
umgänglich ['ʊmgɛŋlɪç] *adj* sociable
Umgangs- *zW*: **~formen** *pl* manners; **~sprache** *f* colloquial language
umgeben [ʊm'ge:bən] (*unreg*) *vt insep* to surround
Umgebung *f* surroundings *pl*; (*Milieu*) environment; (*Personen*) people in one's circle
umgehen ['ʊmge:ən] (*unreg*) *vi* to go (a)round; **im Schlosse ~** to haunt the castle; **mit jdm grob** *etc* **~** to treat sb roughly *etc*; **mit Geld sparsam ~** to be careful with one's money; **um'gehen** *vt insep* to bypass; (*MIL*) to outflank; (*Gesetz*

⚠ *For information on spelling reform see page 615*

etc) to circumvent; (*vermeiden*) to avoid;
'**umgehend** *adj* immediate

Um'gehung *f* bypassing; outflanking;
circumvention; avoidance; **~sstraße** *f*
bypass

umgekehrt ['ʊmgəkeːrt] *adj* reverse(d);
(*gegenteilig*) opposite ♦ *adv* the other way
around; **und ~** and vice versa

umgraben ['ʊmgraːbən] (*unreg*) *vt* to dig up

Umhang ['ʊmhaŋ] *m* wrap, cape

umhauen ['ʊmhaʊən] *vt* to fell; (*fig*) to
bowl over

umher [ʊm'heːr] *adv* about, around;
~gehen (*unreg*) *vi* to walk about; **~ziehen**
(*unreg*) *vi* to wander from place to place

umhinkönnen [ʊm'hɪnkœnən] (*unreg*) *vi*:
ich kann nicht umhin, das zu tun I can't
help doing it

umhören ['ʊmhøːrən] *vr* to ask around

Umkehr ['ʊmkeːr] (-) *f* turning back;
(*Änderung*) change; **u~en** *vi* to turn back
♦ *vt* to turn round, to reverse; (*Tasche etc*)
to turn inside out; (*Gefäß etc*) to turn
upside down

umkippen ['ʊmkɪpən] *vt* to tip over ♦ *vi* to
overturn; (*umg: Mensch*) to keel over; (*fig:
Meinung ändern*) to change one's mind

Umkleide- ['ʊmklaɪdə] *zW*: **~kabine** *f* (*im
Schwimmbad*) (changing) cubicle; **~raum** *m*
changing *od* dressing room

umkommen ['ʊmkɔmən] (*unreg*) *vi* to die,
to perish; (*Lebensmittel*) to go bad

Umkreis ['ʊmkraɪs] *m* neighbourhood; **im ~
von** within a radius of

Umlage ['ʊmlaːgə] *f* share of the costs

Umlauf ['ʊmlaʊf] *m* (*Geld~*) circulation; (*von
Gestirn*) revolution; **~bahn** *f* orbit

Umlaut ['ʊmlaʊt] *m* umlaut

umlegen ['ʊmleːgən] *vt* to put on; (*verlegen*)
to move, to shift; (*Kosten*) to share out;
(*umkippen*) to tip over; (*umg: töten*) to
bump off

umleiten ['ʊmlaɪtən] *vt* to divert

Umleitung *f* diversion

umliegend ['ʊmliːgənt] *adj* surrounding

um'randen *vt insep* to border, to edge

umrechnen ['ʊmreçnən] *vt* to convert

Umrechnung *f* conversion; **~skurs** *m* rate
of exchange

um'reißen (*unreg*) *vt insep* to outline, to
sketch

Umriß ⚠ ['ʊmrɪs] *m* outline

umrühren ['ʊmryːrən] *vt, vi* to stir

ums [ʊms] = **um das**

Umsatz ['ʊmzats] *m* turnover; **~steuer** *f*
sales tax

umschalten ['ʊmʃaltən] *vt* to switch

umschauen *vr* to look round

Umschlag ['ʊmʃlaːk] *m* cover; (*Buch~ auch*)
jacket; (*MED*) compress; (*Brief~*) envelope;
(*Wechsel*) change; (*von Hose*) turn-up; **u~en**
[-gən] (*unreg*) *vi* to change; (*NAUT*) to
capsize ♦ *vt* to knock over; (*Ärmel*) to turn
up; (*Seite*) to turn over; (*Waren*) to transfer;
~platz *m* (*COMM*) distribution centre

umschreiben ['ʊmʃraɪbən] (*unreg*) *vt*
(*neuschreiben*) to rewrite; (*übertragen*) to
transfer; **~ auf** +*akk* to transfer to;
um'schreiben (*unreg*) *vt insep* to
paraphrase; (*abgrenzen*) to define

umschulen ['ʊmʃuːlən] *vt* to retrain; (*Kind*)
to send to another school

Umschweife ['ʊmʃvaɪfə] *pl*: **ohne ~** without
beating about the bush, straight out

Umschwung ['ʊmʃvʊŋ] *m* change
(around), revolution

umsehen ['ʊmzeːən] (*unreg*) *vr* to look
around *od* about; (*suchen*): **sich ~ (nach)** to
look out (for)

umseitig ['ʊmzaɪtɪç] *adv* overleaf

umsichtig ['ʊmzɪçtɪç] *adj* cautious, prudent

umsonst [ʊm'zɔnst] *adv* in vain; (*gratis*) for
nothing

umspringen ['ʊmʃprɪŋən] (*unreg*) *vi* to
change; (*Wind auch*) to veer; **mit jdm ~** to
treat sb badly

Umstand ['ʊmʃtant] *m* circumstance;
Umstände *pl* (*fig: Schwierigkeiten*) fuss; **in
anderen Umständen sein** to be pregnant;
Umstände machen to go to a lot of
trouble; **unter Umständen** possibly

umständlich ['ʊmʃtɛntlɪç] *adj* (*Methode*)
cumbersome, complicated; (*Ausdrucksweise,
Erklärung*) long-winded; (*Mensch*)

⚠ *Informationen zur Rechtschreibreform Seite 615*

ponderous

Umstandskleid nt maternity dress

Umstehende(n) ['ʊmʃteːəndə(n)] pl bystanders

umsteigen ['ʊmʃtaɪɡən] (unreg) vi (EISENB) to change

umstellen ['ʊmʃtɛlən] vt (an anderen Ort) to change round, to rearrange; (TECH) to convert ♦ vr to adapt (o.s.); **sich auf etw** akk ~ to adapt to sth; **um'stellen** vt insep to surround

Umstellung ['ʊmʃtɛlʊŋ] f change; (Umgewöhnung) adjustment; (TECH) conversion

umstimmen ['ʊmʃtɪmən] vt (MUS) to retune; **jdn** ~ to make sb change his mind

umstoßen ['ʊmʃtoːsən] (unreg) vt to overturn; (Plan etc) to change, to upset

umstritten [ʊm'ʃtrɪtən] adj disputed

Umsturz ['ʊmʃtʊrts] m overthrow

umstürzen ['ʊmʃtyrtsən] vt (umwerfen) to overturn ♦ vi to collapse, to fall down; (Wagen) to overturn

Umtausch ['ʊmtaʊʃ] m exchange; **u~en** vt to exchange

Umverpackung ['ʊmfɛrpakʊŋ] f packaging

umwandeln ['ʊmvandəln] vt to change, to convert; (ELEK) to transform

umwechseln ['ʊmvɛksəln] vt to change

Umweg ['ʊmveːk] m detour, roundabout way

Umwelt ['ʊmvɛlt] f environment; **u~freundlich** adj not harmful to the environment, environment-friendly; **u~schädlich** adj ecologically harmful; **~schutz** m environmental protection; **~schützer** m environmentalist; **~verschmutzung** f environmental pollution

umwenden ['ʊmvɛndən] (unreg) vt, vr to turn (round)

umwerfen ['ʊmvɛrfən] (unreg) vt to upset, to overturn; (fig: erschüttern) to upset, to throw; **~d** (umg) fantastic

umziehen ['ʊmtsiːən] (unreg) vt, vr to change ♦ vi to move

Umzug ['ʊmtsuːk] m procession;

(Wohnungs~) move, removal

unab- ['ʊn|ap] zW: **~änderlich** adj irreversible, unalterable; **~hängig** adj independent; **U~hängigkeit** f independence; **~kömmlich** adj indispensable; **zur Zeit ~kömmlich** not free at the moment; **~lässig** adj incessant, constant; **~sehbar** adj immeasurable; (Folgen) unforeseeable; (Kosten) incalculable; **~sichtlich** adj unintentional; **~'wendbar** adj inevitable

unachtsam ['ʊn|axtzaːm] adj careless; **U~keit** f carelessness

unan- ['ʊn|an] zW: **~'fechtbar** adj indisputable; **~gebracht** adj uncalled-for; **~gemessen** adj inadequate; **~genehm** adj unpleasant; **U~nehmlichkeit** f inconvenience; **U~nehmlichkeiten** pl (Ärger) trouble sg; **~sehnlich** adj unsightly; **~ständig** adj indecent, improper

unappetitlich ['ʊn|apetiːtlɪç] adj unsavoury

Unart ['ʊn|aːrt] f bad manners pl; (Angewohnheit) bad habit; **u~ig** adj naughty, badly behaved

unauf- ['ʊn|aʊf] zW: **~fällig** adj unobtrusive; (Kleidung) inconspicuous; **~'findbar** adj not to be found; **~gefordert** adj unasked ♦ adv spontaneously; **~haltsam** adj irresistible; **~'hörlich** adj incessant, continuous; **~merksam** adj inattentive; **~richtig** adj insincere

unaus- ['ʊn|aʊs] zW: **~geglichen** adj unbalanced; **~'sprechlich** adj inexpressible; **~'stehlich** adj intolerable

unbarmherzig ['ʊnbarmhɛrtsɪç] adj pitiless, merciless

unbeabsichtigt ['ʊnbə|apzɪçtɪçt] adj unintentional

unbeachtet ['ʊnbə|axtət] adj unnoticed, ignored

unbedenklich ['ʊnbədɛŋklɪç] adj (Plan) unobjectionable

unbedeutend ['ʊnbədɔʏtənt] adj insignificant, unimportant; (Fehler) slight

unbedingt ['ʊnbədɪŋt] adj unconditional ♦ adv absolutely; **mußt du ~ gehen?** do you really have to go?

⚠ For information on spelling reform see page 615

unbefangen [ˈʊnbəfaŋən] *adj* impartial, unprejudiced; (*ohne Hemmungen*) uninhibited; **U~heit** *f* impartiality; uninhibitedness

unbefriedigend [ˈʊnbəfriːdɪgənd] *adj* unsatisfactory

unbefriedigt [ˈʊnbəfriːdɪçt] *adj* unsatisfied, dissatisfied

unbefugt [ˈʊnbəfuːkt] *adj* unauthorized

unbegreiflich [ʊnbəˈgraɪflɪç] *adj* inconceivable

unbegrenzt [ˈʊnbəgrɛntst] *adj* unlimited

unbegründet [ˈʊnbəgrʏndət] *adj* unfounded

Unbehagen [ˈʊnbəhaːgən] *nt* discomfort; **unbehaglich** *adj* uncomfortable; (*Gefühl*) uneasy

unbeholfen [ˈʊnbəhɔlfən] *adj* awkward, clumsy

unbekannt [ˈʊnbəkant] *adj* unknown

unbekümmert [ˈʊnbəkʏmərt] *adj* unconcerned

unbeliebt [ˈʊnbəliːpt] *adj* unpopular

unbequem [ˈʊnbəkveːm] *adj* (*Stuhl*) uncomfortable; (*Mensch*) bothersome; (*Regelung*) inconvenient

unberechenbar [ʊnbəˈrɛçənbaːr] *adj* incalculable; (*Mensch, Verhalten*) unpredictable

unberechtigt [ˈʊnbərɛçtɪçt] *adj* unjustified; (*nicht erlaubt*) unauthorized

unberührt [ˈʊnbərʏːrt] *adj* untouched, intact; **sie ist noch ~** she is still a virgin

unbescheiden [ˈʊnbəʃaɪdən] *adj* presumptuous

unbeschreiblich [ʊnbəˈʃraɪplɪç] *adj* indescribable

unbeständig [ˈʊnbəʃtɛndɪç] *adj* (*Mensch*) inconstant; (*Wetter*) unsettled; (*Lage*) unstable

unbestechlich [ʊnbəˈʃtɛçlɪç] *adj* incorruptible

unbestimmt [ˈʊnbəʃtɪmt] *adj* indefinite; (*Zukunft auch*) uncertain

unbeteiligt [ʊnbəˈtaɪlɪçt] *adj* unconcerned, indifferent

unbeweglich [ˈʊnbəveːklɪç] *adj* immovable

unbewohnt [ˈʊnbəvoːnt] *adj* uninhabited; (*Wohnung*) unoccupied

unbewußt ⚠ [ˈʊnbəvʊst] *adj* unconscious

unbezahlt [ˈʊnbətsaːlt] *adj* (*Rechnung*) outstanding, unsettled; (*Urlaub*) unpaid

unbrauchbar [ˈʊnbraʊxbaːr] *adj* (*Arbeit*) useless; (*Gerät auch*) unusable

und [ʊnt] *konj* and; **~ so weiter** and so on

Undank [ˈʊndaŋk] *m* ingratitude; **u~bar** *adj* ungrateful

undefinierbar [ʊndefiˈniːrbaːr] *adj* indefinable

undenkbar [ʊnˈdɛŋkbaːr] *adj* inconceivable

undeutlich [ˈʊndɔʏtlɪç] *adj* indistinct

undicht [ˈʊndɪçt] *adj* leaky

Unding [ˈʊndɪŋ] *nt* absurdity

undurch- [ˈʊndʊrç] *zW:* **~führbar** [-ˈfyːrbaːr] *adj* impracticable; **~lässig** [-ˈlɛsɪç] *adj* waterproof, impermeable; **~sichtig** [-ˈzɪçtɪç] *adj* opaque; (*fig*) obscure

uneben [ˈʊnˌeːbən] *adj* uneven

unecht [ˈʊnˌɛçt] *adj* (*Schmuck*) fake; (*vorgetäuscht: Freundlichkeit*) false

unehelich [ˈʊnˌeːəlɪç] *adj* illegitimate

uneinig [ˈʊnˌaɪnɪç] *adj* divided; **~ sein** to disagree; **U~keit** *f* discord, dissension

uneins [ˈʊnˌaɪns] *adj* at variance, at odds

unempfindlich [ˈʊnˌɛmpfɪntlɪç] *adj* insensitive; (*Stoff*) practical

unendlich [ʊnˈʔɛntlɪç] *adj* infinite

unent- [ˈʊnˌɛnt] *zW:* **~behrlich** [-ˈbeːrlɪç] *adj* indispensable; **~geltlich** [-gɛltlɪç] *adj* free (of charge); **~schieden** [-ˈʃiːdən] *adj* undecided; **~schieden enden** (*SPORT*) to end in a draw; **~schlossen** [-ˈʃlɔsən] *adj* undecided; irresolute; **~wegt** [-ˈveːkt] *adj* unswerving; (*unaufhörlich*) incessant

uner- [ˈʊnˌeɾ] *zW:* **~bittlich** [-ˈbɪtlɪç] *adj* unyielding, inexorable; **~fahren** [-faːrən] *adj* inexperienced; **~freulich** [-frɔʏlɪç] *adj* unpleasant; **~gründlich** *adj* unfathomable; **~hört** [-høːrt] *adj* unheard-of; (*Bitte*) outrageous; **~läßlich** ⚠ [-ˈlɛslɪç] *adj* indispensable; **~laubt** *adj* unauthorized; **~meßlich** ⚠ *adj* immeasurable, immense; **~reichbar** *adj* (*Ziel*) unattainable; (*Ort*) inaccessible; (*telefonisch*) unobtainable;

⚠ *Informationen zur Rechtschreibreform Seite 615*

~schöpflich [-ˈʃœpflɪç] *adj* inexhaustible; **~schwinglich** [-ˈʃvɪŋlɪç] *adj* (*Preis*) exorbitant; too expensive; **~träglich** [-ˈtrɛːklɪç] *adj* unbearable; (*Frechheit*) insufferable; **~wartet** *adj* unexpected; **~wünscht** *adj* undesirable, unwelcome

unfähig [ˈʊnfɛːɪç] *adj* incapable, incompetent; **zu etw ~ sein** to be incapable of sth; **U~keit** *f* incapacity; incompetence

unfair [ˈʊnfɛːr] *adj* unfair

Unfall [ˈʊnfal] *m* accident; **~flucht** *f* hit-and-run (driving); **~schaden** *m* damages *pl*; **~station** *f* emergency ward; **~stelle** *f* scene of the accident; **~versicherung** *f* accident insurance

unfaßbar ⚠ [ʊnˈfasbaːr] *adj* inconceivable

unfehlbar [ʊnˈfeːlbaːr] *adj* infallible ♦ *adv* inevitably; **U~keit** *f* infallibility

unförmig [ˈʊnfœrmɪç] *adj* (*formlos*) shapeless

unfrei [ˈʊnfraɪ] *adj* not free, unfree; (*Paket*) unfranked; **~willig** *adj* involuntary, against one's will

unfreundlich [ˈʊnfrɔʏntlɪç] *adj* unfriendly; **U~keit** *f* unfriendliness

Unfriede(n) [ˈʊnfriːdə(n)] *m* dissension, strife

unfruchtbar [ˈʊnfrʊxtbaːr] *adj* infertile; (*Gespräche*) unfruitful; **U~keit** *f* infertility; unfruitfulness

Unfug [ˈʊnfuːk] (**-s**) *m* (*Benehmen*) mischief; (*Unsinn*) nonsense; **grober ~** (*JUR*) gross misconduct; malicious damage

Ungar(in) [ˈʊŋɡar(ɪn)] *m(f)* Hungarian; **u~isch** *adj* Hungarian; **~n** *nt* Hungary

ungeachtet [ˈʊŋɡəˈaxtət] *präp +gen* notwithstanding

ungeahnt [ˈʊŋɡəˈaːnt] *adj* unsuspected, undreamt-of

ungebeten [ˈʊŋɡəbeːtən] *adj* uninvited

ungebildet [ˈʊŋɡəbɪldət] *adj* uneducated; uncultured

ungedeckt [ˈʊŋɡədɛkt] *adj* (*Scheck*) uncovered

Ungeduld [ˈʊŋɡədʊlt] *f* impatience; **u~ig** [-dɪç] *adj* impatient

ungeeignet [ˈʊŋɡəˈaɪɡnət] *adj* unsuitable

ungefähr [ˈʊŋɡəfɛːr] *adj* rough, approximate; **das kommt nicht von ~** that's hardly surprising

ungefährlich [ˈʊŋɡəfɛːrlɪç] *adj* not dangerous, harmless

ungehalten [ˈʊŋɡəhaltən] *adj* indignant

ungeheuer [ˈʊŋɡəhɔʏər] *adj* huge ♦ *adv* (*umg*) enormously; **U~** (**-s, -**) *nt* monster; **~lich** [-ˈhɔʏərlɪç] *adj* monstrous

ungehörig [ˈʊŋɡəhøːrɪç] *adj* impertinent, improper

ungehorsam [ˈʊŋɡəhoːrzaːm] *adj* disobedient

Ungehorsam *m* disobedience

ungeklärt [ˈʊŋɡəklɛːrt] *adj* not cleared up; (*Rätsel*) unsolved

ungeladen [ˈʊŋɡəlaːdən] *adj* not loaded; (*Gast*) uninvited

ungelegen [ˈʊŋɡəleːɡən] *adj* inconvenient

ungelernt [ˈʊŋɡəlɛrnt] *adj* unskilled

ungelogen [ˈʊŋɡəloːɡən] *adv* really, honestly

ungemein [ˈʊŋɡəmaɪn] *adj* uncommon

ungemütlich [ˈʊŋɡəmyːtlɪç] *adj* uncomfortable; (*Person*) disagreeable

ungenau [ˈʊŋɡənaʊ] *adj* inaccurate; **U~igkeit** *f* inaccuracy

ungenießbar [ˈʊŋɡəniːsbaːr] *adj* inedible; undrinkable; (*umg*) unbearable

ungenügend [ˈʊŋɡənyːɡənt] *adj* insufficient, inadequate

ungepflegt [ˈʊŋɡəpfleːkt] *adj* (*Garten etc*) untended; (*Person*) unkempt; (*Hände*) neglected

ungerade [ˈʊŋɡəraːdə] *adj* uneven, odd

ungerecht [ˈʊŋɡərɛçt] *adj* unjust; **~fertigt** *adj* unjustified; **U~igkeit** *f* injustice, unfairness

ungern [ˈʊŋɡɛrn] *adv* unwillingly, reluctantly

ungeschehen [ˈʊŋɡəʃeːən] *adj*: **~ machen** to undo

Ungeschicklichkeit [ˈʊŋɡəʃɪklɪçkaɪt] *f* clumsiness

ungeschickt *adj* awkward, clumsy

ungeschminkt [ˈʊŋɡəʃmɪŋkt] *adj* without make-up; (*fig*) unvarnished

ungesetzlich [ˈʊŋɡəzɛtslɪç] *adj* illegal

⚠ *For information on spelling reform see page 615*

ungestört ['ʊngəʃtøːrt] *adj* undisturbed

ungestraft ['ʊngəʃtraːft] *adv* with impunity

ungestüm ['ʊngəʃtyːm] *adj* impetuous; tempestuous

ungesund ['ʊngəzʊnt] *adj* unhealthy

ungetrübt ['ʊngətryːpt] *adj* clear; *(fig)* untroubled; *(Freude)* unalloyed

Ungetüm ['ʊngətyːm] (-(e)s, -e) *nt* monster

ungewiß △ ['ʊngəvɪs] *adj* uncertain; **U~heit** △ *f* uncertainty

ungewöhnlich ['ʊngəvøːnlɪç] *adj* unusual

ungewohnt ['ʊngəvoːnt] *adj* unaccustomed

Ungeziefer ['ʊngətsiːfər] (-s) *nt* vermin

ungezogen ['ʊngətsoːgən] *adj* rude, impertinent; **U~heit** *f* rudeness, impertinence

ungezwungen ['ʊngətsvʊŋən] *adj* natural, unconstrained

unglaublich [ʊn'glaʊplɪç] *adj* incredible

ungleich ['ʊnglaɪç] *adj* dissimilar; unequal ♦ *adv* incomparably; **~artig** *adj* different; **U~heit** *f* dissimilarity; inequality; **~mäßig** *adj* irregular, uneven

Unglück ['ʊnglʏk] (-(e)s, -e) *nt* misfortune; *(Pech)* bad luck; *(Unglücksfall)* calamity, disaster; *(Verkehrs~)* accident; **u~lich** *adj* unhappy; *(erfolglos)* unlucky; *(unerfreulich)* unfortunate; **u~licherweise** [-'vaɪtsə] *adv* unfortunately; **~sfall** *m* accident, calamity

ungültig ['ʊngʏltɪç] *adj* invalid; **U~keit** *f* invalidity

ungünstig ['ʊngʏnstɪç] *adj* unfavourable

ungut ['ʊnguːt] *adj* *(Gefühl)* uneasy; **nichts für ~** no offence

unhaltbar ['ʊnhaltbaːr] *adj* untenable

Unheil ['ʊnhaɪl] *nt* evil; *(Unglück)* misfortune; **~ anrichten** to cause mischief; **u~bar** *adj* incurable

unheimlich ['ʊnhaɪmlɪç] *adj* weird, uncanny ♦ *adv* *(umg)* tremendously

unhöflich ['ʊnhøːflɪç] *adj* impolite; **U~keit** *f* impoliteness

unhygienisch ['ʊnhygieːnɪʃ] *adj* unhygienic

Uni ['ʊni] (-, -s) *(umg)* *f* university

Uniform [uni'fɔrm] *f* uniform; **u~iert** [-'miːrt] *adj* uniformed

uninteressant ['ʊn|ɪnteresant] *adj* uninteresting

Uni- *zW:* **~versität** [univerzi'tɛːt] *f* university; **~versum** [uni'verzʊm] (-s) *nt* universe

unkenntlich ['ʊnkɛntlɪç] *adj* unrecognizable

Unkenntnis ['ʊnkɛntnɪs] *f* ignorance

unklar ['ʊnklaːr] *adj* unclear; **im ~en sein über** +*akk* to be in the dark about; **U~heit** *f* unclarity; *(Unentschiedenheit)* uncertainty

unklug ['ʊnkluːk] *adj* unwise

Unkosten ['ʊnkɔstən] *pl* expense(s); **~beitrag** *m* contribution to costs *od* expenses

Unkraut ['ʊnkraʊt] *nt* weed; weeds *pl*

unkündbar ['ʊnkʏntbaːr] *adj* *(Stelle)* permanent; *(Vertrag)* binding

unlauter ['ʊnlaʊtər] *adj* unfair

unleserlich ['ʊnleːzərlɪç] *adj* illegible

unlogisch ['ʊnloːgɪʃ] *adj* illogical

unlösbar [ʊn'løːsbar] *adj* insoluble

Unlust ['ʊnlʊst] *f* lack of enthusiasm

Unmenge ['ʊnmɛŋə] *f* tremendous number, hundreds *pl*

Unmensch ['ʊnmɛnʃ] *m* ogre, brute; **u~lich** *adj* inhuman, brutal; *(ungeheuer)* awful

unmerklich [ʊn'mɛrklɪç] *adj* imperceptible

unmißverständlich △ ['ʊnmɪsfɛrʃtɛntlɪç] *adj* unmistakable

unmittelbar ['ʊnmɪtəlbaːr] *adj* immediate

unmodern ['ʊnmodɛrn] *adj* old-fashioned

unmöglich ['ʊnmøːklɪç] *adj* impossible; **U~keit** *f* impossibility

unmoralisch ['ʊnmoraːlɪʃ] *adj* immoral

Unmut ['ʊnmuːt] *m* ill humour

unnachgiebig ['ʊnnaːxgiːbɪç] *adj* unyielding

unnahbar [ʊn'naːbaːr] *adj* unapproachable

unnötig ['ʊnnøːtɪç] *adj* unnecessary

unnütz ['ʊnnʏts] *adj* useless

unordentlich ['ʊnɔrdəntlɪç] *adj* untidy

Unordnung ['ʊnɔrdnʊŋ] *f* disorder

unparteiisch ['ʊnpartaɪʃ] *adj* impartial; **U~e(r)** *f(m)* umpire; *(FUSSBALL)* referee

unpassend ['ʊnpasənt] *adj* inappropriate; *(Zeit)* inopportune

unpäßlich △ ['ʊnpɛslɪç] *adj* unwell

unpersönlich ['ʊnpɛrzøːnlɪç] *adj*

impersonal

unpolitisch ['ʊnpoliːtɪʃ] *adj* apolitical

unpraktisch ['ʊnpraktɪʃ] *adj* unpractical

unpünktlich ['ʊnpʏŋktlɪç] *adj* unpunctual

unrationell ['ʊnratsionɛl] *adj* inefficient

unrealistisch ['ʊnrealɪstɪʃ] *adj* unrealistic

unrecht ['ʊnrɛçt] *adj* wrong; **U~** *nt* wrong; **zu U~** wrongly; **U~ haben** to be wrong; **~mäßig** *adj* unlawful, illegal

unregelmäßig ['ʊnreːɡəlmɛːsɪç] *adj* irregular; **U~keit** *f* irregularity

unreif ['ʊnraif] *adj* (*Obst*) unripe; (*fig*) immature

unrentabel ['ʊnrɛnta:bəl] *adj* unprofitable

unrichtig ['ʊnrɪçtɪç] *adj* incorrect, wrong

Unruhe ['ʊnru:ə] *f* unrest; **~stifter** *m* troublemaker

unruhig ['ʊnru:ɪç] *adj* restless

uns [ʊns] (*akk, dat von* **wir**) *pron* us; ourselves

unsachlich ['ʊnzaxlɪç] *adj* not to the point, irrelevant

unsagbar [ʊn'za:kba:r] *adj* indescribable

unsanft ['ʊnzanft] *adj* rough

unsauber ['ʊnzaʊbər] *adj* unclean, dirty; (*fig*) crooked; (*MUS*) fuzzy

unschädlich ['ʊnʃɛ:tlɪç] *adj* harmless; **jdn/ etw ~ machen** to render sb/sth harmless

unscharf ['ʊnʃarf] *adj* indistinct; (*Bild etc*) out of focus, blurred

unscheinbar ['ʊnʃainba:r] *adj* insignificant; (*Aussehen, Haus etc*) unprepossessing

unschlagbar [ʊn'ʃla:kba:r] *adj* invincible

unschön ['ʊnʃø:n] *adj* (*häßlich: Anblick*) ugly, unattractive; (*unfreundlich: Benehmen*) unpleasant, ugly

Unschuld ['ʊnʃʊlt] *f* innocence; **u~ig** [-dɪç] *adj* innocent

unselbständig ⚠ ['ʊnzɛlpʃtɛndɪç] *adj* dependent, over-reliant on others

unser(e) ['ʊnzər(ə)] *adj* our; **~e(r, s)** *pron* ours; **~einer** *pron* people like us; **~eins** *pron* = **unsereiner**; **~erseits** *adv* on our part; **~twegen** *adv* (*für uns*) for our sake; (*wegen uns*) on our account; **~twillen** *adv*: **um ~twillen** = **unsertwegen**

unsicher ['ʊnzɪçər] *adj* uncertain; (*Mensch*) insecure; **U~heit** *f* uncertainty; insecurity

unsichtbar ['ʊnzɪçtba:r] *adj* invisible

Unsinn ['ʊnzɪn] *m* nonsense; **u~ig** *adj* nonsensical

Unsitte ['ʊnzɪtə] *f* deplorable habit

unsozial ['ʊnzotsia:l] *adj* (*Verhalten*) antisocial

unsportlich ['ʊnʃpɔrtlɪç] *adj* not sporty; unfit; (*Verhalten*) unsporting

unsre ['ʊnzrə] = **unsere**

unsterblich ['ʊnʃtɛrplɪç] *adj* immortal

Unstimmigkeit ['ʊnʃtɪmɪçkait] *f* inconsistency; (*Streit*) disagreement

unsympathisch ['ʊnzʏmpatɪʃ] *adj* unpleasant; **er ist mir ~** I don't like him

untätig ['ʊntɛ:tɪç] *adj* idle

untauglich ['ʊntaʊklɪç] *adj* unsuitable; (*MIL*) unfit

unteilbar [ʊn'tailba:r] *adj* indivisible

unten ['ʊntən] *adv* below; (*im Haus*) downstairs; (*an der Treppe etc*) at the bottom; **nach ~** down; **~ am Berg** *etc* at the bottom of the mountain *etc*; **ich bin bei ihm ~ durch** (*umg*) he's through with me

unter ['ʊntər] *präp +dat* **1** (*räumlich, mit Zahlen*) under; (*drunter*) underneath, below; **unter 18 Jahren** under 18 years **2** (*zwischen*) among(st); **sie waren unter sich** they were by themselves; **einer unter ihnen** one of them; **unter anderem** among other things

♦ *präp +akk* under, below

Unterarm ['ʊntar|arm] *m* forearm

unter- *zW*: **~belichten** *vt* (*PHOT*) to underexpose; **U~bewußtsein** ⚠ *nt* subconscious; **~bezahlt** *adj* underpaid

unterbieten [ʊntar'bi:tən] (*unreg*) *vt insep* (*COMM*) to undercut; (*Rekord*) to lower

unterbrechen [ʊntar'brɛçən] (*unreg*) *vt insep* to interrupt

Unterbrechung *f* interruption

unterbringen ['ʊntarbrɪŋən] (*unreg*) *vt* (*in Koffer*) to stow; (*in Zeitung*) to place;

(*Person: in Hotel etc*) to accommodate, to put up

unterdessen [ʊntər'dɛsən] *adv* meanwhile

Unterdruck ['ʊntərdrʊk] *m* low pressure

unterdrücken [ʊntər'drʏkən] *vt insep* to suppress; (*Leute*) to oppress

untere(r, s) ['ʊntərə(r, s)] *adj* lower

untereinander [ʊntəraɪ'nandər] *adv* with each other; among themselves *etc*

unterentwickelt ['ʊntərʔɛntvɪkəlt] *adj* underdeveloped

unterernährt ['ʊntərʔɛrnɛːrt] *adj* undernourished, underfed

Unterernährung *f* malnutrition

Unter'führung *f* subway, underpass

Untergang ['ʊntərgaŋ] *m* (down)fall, decline; (*NAUT*) sinking; (*von Gestirn*) setting

unter'geben *adj* subordinate

untergehen ['ʊntərgeːən] (*unreg*) *vi* to go down; (*Sonne auch*) to set; (*Staat*) to fall; (*Volk*) to perish; (*Welt*) to come to an end; (*im Lärm*) to be drowned

Untergeschoß ⚠ ['ʊntərgəʃɔs] *nt* basement

'Untergewicht *nt* underweight

unter'gliedern *vt insep* to subdivide

Untergrund ['ʊntərgrʊnt] *m* foundation; (*POL*) underground; **~bahn** *f* underground, tube, subway (*US*)

unterhalb ['ʊntərhalp] *präp +gen* below ♦ *adv* below; **~ von** below

Unterhalt ['ʊntərhalt] *m* maintenance; **u~en** (*unreg*) *vt insep* to maintain; (*belustigen*) to entertain ♦ *vr insep* to talk; (*sich belustigen*) to enjoy o.s.; **u~sam** *adj* (*Abend, Person*) entertaining, amusing; **~ung** *f* maintenance; (*Belustigung*) entertainment, amusement; (*Gespräch*) talk

Unterhändler ['ʊntərhɛntlər] *m* negotiator

Unter- *zW*: **~hemd** *nt* vest, undershirt (*US*); **~hose** *f* underpants *pl*; **~kiefer** *m* lower jaw

unterkommen ['ʊntərkɔmən] (*unreg*) *vi* to find shelter; to find work; **das ist mir noch nie untergekommen** I've never met with that

unterkühlt [ʊntər'kyːlt] *adj* (*Körper*) affected

by hypothermia

Unterkunft ['ʊntərkʊnft] (*-, -künfte*) *f* accommodation

Unterlage ['ʊntərlaːgə] *f* foundation; (*Beleg*) document; (*Schreib~ etc*) pad

unter'lassen (*unreg*) *vt insep* (*versäumen*) to fail to do; (*sich enthalten*) to refrain from

unterlaufen [ʊntər'laufən] (*unreg*) *vi insep* to happen ♦ *adj*: **mit Blut ~** suffused with blood; (*Augen*) bloodshot

unterlegen ['ʊntərleːgən] *vt* to lay *od* put under; **unter'legen** *adj* inferior; (*besiegt*) defeated

Unterleib ['ʊntərlaɪp] *m* abdomen

unter'liegen (*unreg*) *vi insep* (+*dat*) to be defeated *od* overcome (by); (*unterworfen sein*) to be subject (to)

Untermiete ['ʊntərmiːtə] *f*: **zur ~ wohnen** to be a subtenant *od* lodger; **~r(in)** *m(f)* subtenant, lodger

unter'nehmen (*unreg*) *vt insep* to undertake; **Unter'nehmen** (*-s, -*) *nt* undertaking, enterprise (*auch COMM*)

Unternehmer [ʊntər'neːmər] (*-s, -*) *m* entrepreneur, businessman

'unterordnen ['ʊntərʔɔrdnən] *vr* +*dat* to submit o.s. (to), to give o.s. second place to

Unterredung [ʊntər'reːdʊŋ] *f* discussion, talk

Unterricht ['ʊntərrɪçt] (*-(e)s, -e*) *m* instruction, lessons *pl*; **u~en** [ʊntər'rɪçtən] *vt insep* to teach; (*SCH*) to instruct; (*SCH*) to teach ♦ *vr insep*: **sich u~en (über** +*akk*) to inform o.s. (about), to obtain information (about); **~sfach** *nt* subject (on school *etc* curriculum)

Unterrock ['ʊntərrɔk] *m* petticoat, slip

unter'sagen *vt insep* to forbid; **jdm etw ~** to forbid sb to do sth

Untersatz ['ʊntərzats] *m* coaster, saucer

unter'schätzen *vt insep* to underestimate

unter'scheiden (*unreg*) *vt insep* to distinguish ♦ *vr insep* to differ

Unter'scheidung *f* (*Unterschied*) distinction; (*Unterscheiden*) differentiation

Unterschied ['ʊntərʃiːt] (*-(e)s, -e*) *m*

difference, distinction; **im ~ zu** as distinct from; **u~lich** adj varying, differing; (*diskriminierend*) discriminatory

unterschiedslos adv indiscriminately

unter'schlagen (*unreg*) vt insep to embezzle; (*verheimlichen*) to suppress

Unter'schlagung f embezzlement

Unterschlupf ['ʊntərʃlʊpf] (-(e)s, -schlüpfe) m refuge

unter'schreiben (*unreg*) vt insep to sign

Unterschrift ['ʊntərʃrɪft] f signature

Unterseeboot ['ʊntərze:bo:t] nt submarine

Untersetzer ['ʊntərzetsər] m tablemat; (*für Gläser*) coaster

untersetzt [ʊntərzetst] adj stocky

unterste(r, s) ['ʊntərstə(r, s)] adj lowest, bottom

unterstehen [ʊntər'ʃte:ən] (*unreg*) vi insep (+dat) to be under ♦ vr insep to dare; **'unterstehen** (*unreg*) vi to shelter

unterstellen [ʊntər'ʃtelən] vt insep to subordinate; (*fig*) to impute ♦ vt (*Auto*) to garage, to park ♦ vr to take shelter

unter'streichen (*unreg*) vt insep (*auch fig*) to underline

Unterstufe ['ʊntərʃtu:fə] f lower grade

unter'stützen vt insep to support

Unter'stützung f support, assistance

unter'suchen vt insep (*MED*) to examine; (*Polizei*) to investigate

Unter'suchung f examination; investigation, inquiry; **~sausschuß** △ m committee of inquiry; **~shaft** f imprisonment on remand

Untertasse ['ʊntərtasə] f saucer

untertauchen ['ʊntərtauxən] vi to dive; (*fig*) to disappear, to go underground

Unterteil ['ʊntərtail] nt od m lower part, bottom; **u~en** [ʊntər'tailən] vt insep to divide up

Untertitel ['ʊntərti:təl] m subtitle

Unterwäsche ['ʊntərveʃə] f underwear

unterwegs [ʊntər've:ks] adv on the way

unter'werfen (*unreg*) vt insep to subject; (*Volk*) to subjugate ♦ vr insep (+dat) to submit (to)

unter'zeichnen vt insep to sign

unter'ziehen (*unreg*) vt insep to subject ♦ vr insep (+dat) to undergo; (*einer Prüfung*) to take

untragbar [ʊn'tra:kba:r] adj unbearable, intolerable

untreu ['ʊntrɔy] adj unfaithful; **U~e** f unfaithfulness

untröstlich [ʊn'trø:stlɪç] adj inconsolable

unüberlegt ['ʊnʔy:bərle:kt] adj ill-considered ♦ adv without thinking

unübersichtlich adj (*Gelände*) broken; (*Kurve*) blind

unumgänglich [ʊnʔʊm'gɛŋlɪç] adj indispensable, vital; absolutely necessary

ununterbrochen ['ʊnʔʊntərbrɔxən] adj uninterrupted

unver- ['ʊnfɛr] zW: **~änderlich** [-'ɛndərlɪç] adj unchangeable; **~antwortlich** [-'antvɔrtlɪç] adj irresponsible; (*unentschuldbar*) inexcusable; **~besserlich** adj incorrigible; **~bindlich** adj not binding; (*Antwort*) curt ♦ adv (*COMM*) without obligation; **~bleit** adj (*Benzin usw*) unleaded; **ich fahre ~bleit** I use unleaded; **~blümt** [-'bly:mt] adj plain, blunt ♦ adv plainly, bluntly; **~daulich** adj indigestible; **~einbar** adj incompatible; **~fänglich** [-'fɛŋlɪç] adj harmless; **~froren** adj impudent; **~geßlich** △ adj (*Tag, Erlebnis*) unforgettable; **~hofft** [-'hɔft] adj unexpected; **~meidlich** [-'maitlɪç] adj unavoidable; **~mutet** adj unexpected; **~nünftig** [-'nʏnftɪç] adj foolish; **~schämt** adj impudent; **U~schämtheit** f impudence, insolence; **~sehrt** adj uninjured; **~söhnlich** [-'zø:nlɪç] adj irreconcilable; **~ständlich** [-'ʃtɛntlɪç] adj unintelligible; **~träglich** adj quarrelsome; (*Meinungen, MED*) incompatible; **~zeihlich** adj unpardonable; **~züglich** [-'tsy:klɪç] adj immediate

unvollkommen ['ʊnfɔlkɔmən] adj imperfect

unvollständig adj incomplete

unvor- ['ʊnfo:r] zW: **~bereitet** adj unprepared; **~eingenommen** adj unbiased; **~hergesehen** [-hɛr'ge:ze:ən] adj unforeseen; **~sichtig** [-zɪçtɪç] adj careless, imprudent; **~stellbar** [-'ʃtɛlbaːr] *adj* inconceivable; **~teilhaft** *adj* disadvantageous

unwahr ['ʊnvaːr] *adj* untrue; **~scheinlich** *adj* improbable, unlikely ♦ *adv* (*umg*) incredibly

unweigerlich [ʊn'vaɪgərlɪç] *adj* unquestioning ♦ *adv* without fail

Unwesen ['ʊnveːzən] *nt* nuisance; (*Unfug*) mischief; **sein ~ treiben** to wreak havoc

unwesentlich *adj* inessential, unimportant; **~ besser** marginally better

Unwetter ['ʊnvɛtər] *nt* thunderstorm

unwichtig ['ʊnvɪçtɪç] *adj* unimportant

unwider- ['ʊnviːdər] *zW*: **~legbar** *adj* irrefutable; **~ruflich** *adj* irrevocable; **~stehlich** *adj* irresistible

unwill- ['ʊnvɪl] *zW*: **U~e(n)** *m* indignation; **~ig** *adj* indignant; (*widerwillig*) reluctant; **~kürlich** [-kyːrlɪç] *adj* involuntary ♦ *adv* instinctively; (*lachen*) involuntarily

unwirklich ['ʊnvɪrklɪç] *adj* unreal

unwirksam ['ʊnvɪrkzaːm] *adj* (*Mittel, Methode*) ineffective

unwirtschaftlich ['ʊnvɪrtʃaftlɪç] *adj* uneconomical

unwissen- ['ʊnvɪsən] *zW*: **~d** *adj* ignorant; **U~heit** *f* ignorance; **~tlich** *adv* unknowingly, unwittingly

unwohl ['ʊnvoːl] *adj* unwell, ill; **U~sein (-s)** *nt* indisposition

unwürdig ['ʊnvʏrdɪç] *adj* unworthy

unzählig [ʊn'tsɛːlɪç] *adj* innumerable, countless

unzer- [ʊntsɛr] *zW*: **~brechlich** *adj* unbreakable; **~störbar** *adj* indestructible; **~trennlich** *adj* inseparable

Unzucht ['ʊntsʊxt] *f* sexual offence

unzüchtig ['ʊntsʏçtɪç] *adj* immoral; lewd

unzu- ['ʊntsu] *zW*: **~frieden** *adj* dissatisfied; **U~friedenheit** *f* discontent; **~länglich** *adj* inadequate; **~lässig** *adj* inadmissible; **~rechnungsfähig** *adj* irresponsible; **~treffend** *adj* incorrect; **~verlässig** *adj* unreliable

unzweideutig ['ʊntsvaɪdɔʏtɪç] *adj* unambiguous

⚠ *Informationen zur Rechtschreibreform Seite 615*

üppig ['ʏpɪç] *adj* (*Frau*) curvaceous; (*Busen*) full, ample; (*Essen*) sumptuous; (*Vegetation*) luxuriant, lush

Ur- ['uːr] *in zW* original

uralt ['uːr|alt] *adj* ancient, very old

Uran [u'raːn] (**-s**) *nt* uranium

Ur- *zW*: **~aufführung** *f* first performance; **~einwohner** *m* original inhabitant; **~enkel(in)** *m(f)* great-grandchild, great-grandson(-daughter); **~großeltern** *pl* great-grandparents; **~heber (-s, -)** *m* originator; (*Autor*) author; **~heberrecht** *nt* copyright

Urin [u'riːn] (**-s, -e**) *m* urine

Urkunde ['uːrkʊndə] *f* document, deed

Urlaub ['uːrlaʊp] (**-(e)s, -e**) *m* holiday(s *pl*) (*BRIT*), vacation (*US*); (*MIL etc*) leave; **~er** [-'laʊbər] (**-s, -**) *m* holiday-maker (*BRIT*), vacationer (*US*); **~sort** *m* holiday resort; **~szeit** *f* holiday season

Urne ['ʊrnə] *f* urn

Ursache ['uːrzaxə] *f* cause; **keine ~** that's all right

Ursprung ['uːrʃprʊŋ] *m* origin, source; (*von Fluß*) source

ursprünglich ['uːrʃprʏŋlɪç] *adj* original ♦ *adv* originally

Ursprungsland *nt* country of origin

Urteil ['ʊrtaɪl] (**-s, -e**) *nt* opinion; (*JUR*) sentence, judgement; **u~en** *vi* to judge; **~sspruch** *m* sentence, verdict

Urwald *m* jungle

Urzeit *f* prehistoric times *pl*

USA [uːʔɛs'ʔaː] *pl abk* (= *Vereinigte Staaten von Amerika*) USA

usw. *abk* (= *und so weiter*) etc

Utensilien [utɛn'ziːliən] *pl* utensils

Utopie [uto'piː] *f* pipe dream

utopisch [u'toːpɪʃ] *adj* utopian

V, v

vag(e) [va:k, 'va:gə] *adj* vague

Vagina [va'gi:na] (-, **Vaginen**) *f* vagina

Vakuum ['va:kuʊm] (-s, **Vakua** *od* **Vakuen**) *nt* vacuum

Vampir [vam'pi:r] (-s, -e) *m* vampire

Vanille [va'nɪljə] (-) *f* vanilla

Variation [variatsi'o:n] *f* variation

variieren [vari'i:rən] *vt*, *vi* to vary

Vase ['va:zə] *f* vase

Vater ['fa:tər] (-s, ⸚) *m* father; ~**land** *nt* native country; Fatherland

väterlich ['fɛ:tərlɪç] *adj* fatherly

Vaterschaft *f* paternity

Vaterunser (-s, -) *nt* Lord's prayer

Vati ['fa:ti] *m* daddy

v.Chr. *abk* (= *vor Christus*) B.C.

Vegetarier(in) [vege'ta:riər(ɪn)] (-s, -) *m(f)* vegetarian

vegetarisch [vege'ta:rɪʃ] *adj* vegetarian

Veilchen ['faɪlçən] *nt* violet

Vene ['ve:nə] *f* vein

Ventil [ven'ti:l] (-s, -e) *nt* valve

Ventilator [venti'la:tɔr] *m* ventilator

verab- [fer'ap] *zW:* ~**reden** *vt* to agree, to arrange ♦ *vr:* **sich mit jdm ~reden** to arrange to meet sb; **mit jdm ~redet sein** to have arranged to meet sb; **V~redung** *f* arrangement; (*Treffen*) appointment; ~**scheuen** *vt* to detest, to abhor; ~**schieden** *vt* (*Gäste*) to say goodbye to; (*entlassen*) to discharge; (*Gesetz*) to pass ♦ *vr* to take one's leave; **V~schiedung** *f* leave-taking; discharge; passing

ver- [fer] *zW:* ~**achten** *vt* to despise; ~**ächtlich** [-'ɛçtlɪç] *adj* contemptuous; (*verachtenswert*) contemptible; **jdn ~ächtlich machen** to run sb down; **V~achtung** *f* contempt

verallgemeinern [fer|algə'maɪnərn] *vt* to generalize; **Verallgemeinerung** *f* generalization

veralten [fer'altən] *vi* to become obsolete *od* out-of-date

Veranda [ve'randa] (-, **Veranden**) *f* veranda

veränder- [fer'|ɛndər] *zW:* ~**lich** *adj* changeable; ~**n** *vt*, *vr* to change, to alter; **V~ung** *f* change, alteration

veran- [fer'|an] *zW:* ~**lagt** *adj* with a ... nature; **V~lagung** *f* disposition; ~**lassen** *vt* to cause; **Maßnahmen ~lassen** to take measures; **sich ~laßt sehen** to feel prompted; ~**schaulichen** *vt* to illustrate; ~**schlagen** *vt* to estimate; ~**stalten** *vt* to organize, to arrange; **V~stalter** (-s, -) *m* organizer; **V~staltung** *f* (*Veranstalten*) organizing; (*Konzert etc*) event, function

verantwort- [fer'|antvɔrt] *zW:* ~**en** *vt* to answer for ♦ *vr* to justify o.s.; ~**lich** *adj* responsible; **V~ung** *f* responsibility; ~**ungsbewußt** ⚠ *adj* responsible; ~**ungslos** *adj* irresponsible

verarbeiten [fer'|arbaɪtən] *vt* to process; (*geistig*) to assimilate; **etw zu etw ~** to make sth into sth; **Verarbeitung** *f* processing; assimilation

verärgern [fer'|ɛrgərn] *vt* to annoy

verausgaben [fer'|ausga:bən] *vr* to run out of money; (*fig*) to exhaust o.s.

Verb [verp] (-s, -en) *nt* verb

Verband [fer'bant] (-(e)s, ⸚e) *m* (MED) bandage, dressing; (*Bund*) association, society; (MIL) unit; ~**skasten** *m* medicine chest, first-aid box; ~**szeug** *nt* bandage

verbannen [fer'banən] *vt* to banish

verbergen [fer'bergən] *vt*, *vr:* **(sich) ~ (vor +dat)** to hide (from)

verbessern [fer'bɛsərn] *vt*, *vr* to improve; (*berichtigen*) to correct (o.s.)

Verbesserung *f* improvement; correction

verbeugen [fer'bɔygən] *vr* to bow

Verbeugung *f* bow

ver'biegen (*unreg*) *vi* to bend

ver'bieten (*unreg*) *vt* to forbid; **jdm etw ~** to forbid sb to do sth

verbilligen [fer'bilɪgən] *vt* to reduce the cost of; (*Preis*) to reduce

ver'binden (*unreg*) *vt* to connect; (*kombinieren*) to combine; (MED) to bandage ♦ *vt* (*auch CHEM*) to combine, to join; **jdm die Augen ~** to blindfold sb

⚠ *For information on spelling reform see page 615*

verbindlich [fɛrˈbɪntlɪç] *adj* binding; (*freundlich*) friendly

Ver'bindung *f* connection; (*Zusammensetzung*) combination; (*CHEM*) compound; (*UNIV*) club

verbissen [fɛrˈbɪsən] *adj* (*Kampf*) bitter; (*Gesichtsausdruck*) grim

ver'bitten (*unreg*) *vt*: **sich** *dat* **etw ~** not to tolerate sth, not to stand for sth

Verbleib [fɛrˈblaɪp] (**-(e)s**) *m* whereabouts; **v~en** (*unreg*) *vi* to remain

verbleit [fɛrˈblaɪt] *adj* (*Benzin*) leaded

verblüffen [fɛrˈblʏfən] *vt* to stagger, to amaze; **Verblüffung** *f* stupefaction

ver'blühen *vi* to wither, to fade

ver'bluten *vi* to bleed to death

verborgen [fɛrˈbɔrgən] *adj* hidden

Verbot [fɛrˈboːt] (**-(e)s, -e**) *nt* prohibition, ban; **v~en** *adj* forbidden; **Rauchen v~en!** no smoking; **~sschild** *nt* prohibitory sign

Verbrauch [fɛrˈbraʊx] (**-(e)s**) *m* consumption; **v~en** *vt* to use up; **~er** (**-s, -**) *m* consumer; **v~t** *adj* used up, finished; (*Luft*) stale; (*Mensch*) worn-out

Verbrechen [fɛrˈbrɛçən] (**-s, -**) *nt* crime

Verbrecher [fɛrˈbrɛçər] (**-s, -**) *m* criminal; **v~isch** *adj* criminal

ver'breiten *vt, vr* to spread; **sich über etw** *akk* **~** to expound on sth

verbreitern [fɛrˈbraɪtərn] *vt* to broaden

Verbreitung *f* spread(ing), propagation

verbrenn- [fɛrˈbrɛn] *zW*: **~bar** *adj* combustible; **~en** (*unreg*) *vt* to burn; (*Leiche*) to cremate; **V~ung** *f* burning; (*in Motor*) combustion; (*von Leiche*) cremation; **V~ungsmotor** *m* internal combustion engine

verbringen [fɛrˈbrɪŋən] (*unreg*) *vt* to spend

verbrühen [fɛrˈbryːən] *vt* to scald

verbuchen [fɛrˈbuːxən] *vt* (*FIN*) to register; (*Erfolg*) to enjoy; (*Mißerfolg*) to suffer

verbunden [fɛrˈbʊndən] *adj* connected; **jdm ~ sein** to be obliged *od* indebted to sb; „**falsch ~**" (*TEL*) "wrong number"

verbünden [fɛrˈbʏndən] *vr* to ally o.s.; **Verbündete(r)** *f(m)* ally

ver'bürgen *vr*: **sich ~ für** to vouch for

ver'büßen *vt*: **eine Strafe ~** to serve a sentence

Verdacht [fɛrˈdaxt] (**-(e)s**) *m* suspicion

verdächtig [fɛrˈdɛçtɪç] *adj* suspicious, suspect; **~en** [fɛrˈdɛçtɪgən] *vt* to suspect

verdammen [fɛrˈdamən] *vt* to damn, to condemn; **verdammt!** damn!

verdammt (*umg*) *adj, adv* damned; **~ noch mal!** damn!, dammit!

ver'dampfen *vi* to vaporize, to evaporate

ver'danken *vt*: **jdm etw ~** to owe sb sth

verdau- [fɛrˈdaʊ] *zW*: **~en** *vt* (*auch fig*) to digest; **~lich** *adj* digestible; **das ist schwer ~lich** that is hard to digest; **V~ung** *f* digestion

Verdeck [fɛrˈdɛk] (**-(e)s, -e**) *nt* (*AUT*) hood; (*NAUT*) deck; **v~en** *vt* to cover (up); (*verbergen*) to hide

Verderb- [fɛrˈdɛrp] *zW*: **~en** [-ˈdɛrbən] (**-s**) *nt* ruin; **v~en** (*unreg*) *vt* to spoil; (*schädigen*) to ruin; (*moralisch*) to corrupt ♦ *vi* (*Essen*) to spoil, to rot; (*Mensch*) to go to the bad; **es mit jdm v~en** to get into sb's bad books; **v~lich** *adj* (*Einfluß*) pernicious; (*Lebensmittel*) perishable

verdeutlichen [fɛrˈdɔytlɪçən] *vt* to make clear

ver'dichten *vt, vr* to condense

ver'dienen *vt* to earn; (*moralisch*) to deserve

Ver'dienst (**-(e)s, -e**) *m* earnings *pl* ♦ *nt* merit; (*Leistung*): **~ (um)** service (to)

verdient [fɛrˈdiːnt] *adj* well-earned; (*Person*) deserving of esteem; **sich um etw ~ machen** to do a lot for sth

verdoppeln [fɛrˈdɔpəln] *vt* to double

verdorben [fɛrˈdɔrbən] *adj* spoilt; (*geschädigt*) ruined; (*moralisch*) corrupt

verdrängen [fɛrˈdrɛŋən] *vt* to oust, to displace (*auch PHYS*); (*PSYCH*) to repress

ver'drehen *vt* (*auch fig*) to twist; (*Augen*) to roll; **jdm den Kopf ~** (*fig*) to turn sb's head

verdrießlich [fɛrˈdriːslɪç] *adj* peevish, annoyed

Verdruß △ [fɛrˈdrʊs] (**-sses, -sse**) *m* annoyance, worry

△ *Informationen zur Rechtschreibreform Seite 615*

verdummen [fɛrˈdʊmən] *vt* to make stupid
♦ *vi* to grow stupid
verdunkeln [fɛrˈdʊŋkəln] *vt* to darken; (*fig*)
to obscure ♦ *vr* to darken
Verdunk(e)lung *f* blackout; (*fig*)
obscuring
verdünnen [fɛrˈdʏnən] *vt* to dilute
verdunsten [fɛrˈdʊnstən] *vi* to evaporate
verdursten [fɛrˈdʊrstən] *vi* to die of thirst
verdutzt [fɛrˈdʊtst] *adj* nonplussed, taken
aback
verehr- [fɛrˈʔeːr] *zW:* **~en** *vt* to venerate, to
worship (*auch REL*); **jdm etw ~en** to present
sb with sth; **V~er(in)** (**-s, -**) *m(f)* admirer,
worshipper (*auch REL*); **~t** *adj* esteemed;
V~ung *f* respect; (*REL*) worship
Verein [fɛrˈʔaɪn] (**-(e)s, -e**) *m* club,
association; **v~bar** *adj* compatible;
v~baren *vt* to agree upon; **~barung** *f*
agreement; **v~en** *vt* (*Menschen, Länder*) to
unite; (*Prinzipien*) to reconcile; **mit v~ten
Kräften** having pooled resources, having
joined forces; **~te Nationen** United
Nations; **v~fachen** *vt* to simplify;
v~heitlichen [-haɪtlɪçən] *vt* to standardize;
v~igen *vt, vr* to unite; **~igung** *f* union;
(*Verein*) association; **v~t** *adj* united; **v~zelt**
adj isolated
ver'eitern *vi* to suppurate, to fester
verengen [fɛrˈʔɛŋən] *vr* to narrow
vererb- [fɛrˈʔɛrb] *zW:* **~en** *vt* to bequeath;
(*BIOL*) to transmit ♦ *vr* to be hereditary;
V~ung *f* bequeathing; (*BIOL*) transmission;
(*Lehre*) heredity
verewigen [fɛrˈʔeːvɪgən] *vt* to immortalize
♦ *vr* (*umg*) to immortalize o.s.
ver'fahren (*unreg*) *vi* to act ♦ *vr* to get lost
♦ *adj* tangled; **~ mit** to deal with;
Ver'fahren (**-s, -**) *nt* procedure; (*TECH*)
process; (*JUR*) proceedings *pl*
Verfall [fɛrˈfal] (**-(e)s**) *m* decline; (*von Haus*)
dilapidation; (*FIN*) expiry; **v~en** (*unreg*) *vi* to
decline; (*Haus*) to be falling down; (*FIN*) to
lapse; **v~en in** +*akk* to lapse into; **v~en auf**
+*akk* to hit upon; **einem Laster v~en sein**
to be addicted to a vice; **~sdatum** *nt*
expiry date; (*der Haltbarkeit*) sell-by date

ver'färben *vr* to change colour
verfassen [fɛrˈfasən] *vt* (*Rede*) to prepare,
work out
Verfasser(in) [fɛrˈfasər(ɪn)] (**-s, -**) *m(f)*
author, writer
Verfassung *f* (*auch POL*) constitution
Verfassungs- *zW:* **~gericht** *nt*
constitutional court; **v~widrig** *adj*
unconstitutional
ver'faulen *vi* to rot
ver'fehlen *vt* to miss; **etw für verfehlt
halten** to regard sth as mistaken
verfeinern [fɛrˈfaɪnərn] *vt* to refine
ver'filmen *vt* to film
verflixt [fɛrˈflɪkst] (*umg*) *adj* damned, damn
ver'fluchen *vt* to curse
verfolg- [fɛrˈfɔlg] *zW:* **~en** *vt* to pursue;
(*gerichtlich*) to prosecute; (*grausam, bes POL*)
to persecute; **V~er** (**-s, -**) *m* pursuer;
V~ung *f* pursuit; prosecution; persecution
verfrüht [fɛrˈfryːt] *adj* premature
verfüg- [fɛrˈfyːg] *zW:* **~bar** *adj* available;
~en *vt* to direct, to order ♦ *vr* to proceed
♦ *vi:* **~en über** +*akk* to have at one's
disposal; **V~ung** *f* direction, order; **zur
V~ung** at one's disposal; **jdm zur V~ung
stehen** to be available to sb
verführ- [fɛrˈfyːr] *zW:* **~en** *vt* to tempt;
(*sexuell*) to seduce; **V~er** *m* tempter;
seducer; **~erisch** *adj* seductive; **V~ung** *f*
seduction; (*Versuchung*) temptation
ver'gammeln (*umg*) *vi* to go to seed;
(*Nahrung*) to go off
vergangen [fɛrˈgaŋən] *adj* past; **V~heit** *f*
past
vergänglich [fɛrˈgɛŋlɪç] *adj* transitory
vergasen [fɛrˈgaːzən] *vt* (*töten*) to gas
Vergaser (**-s, -**) *m* (*AUT*) carburettor
vergaß *etc* [fɛrˈgaːs] *vb siehe* **vergessen**
vergeb- [fɛrˈgeːb] *zW:* **~en** (*unreg*) *vt*
(*verzeihen*) to forgive; (*weggeben*) to give
away; **jdm etw ~en** to forgive sb (for) sth;
~ens *adv* in vain; **~lich** [fɛrˈgeːplɪç] *adv* in
vain ♦ *adj* vain, futile; **V~ung** *f* forgiveness
ver'gehen (*unreg*) *vi* to pass by *od* away
♦ *vr* to commit an offence; **jdm vergeht
etw** sb loses sth; **sich an jdm ~** to

⚠ *For information on spelling reform see page 615*

(sexually) assault sb; **Ver'gehen** (-s, -) *nt* offence

ver'gelten (*unreg*) *vt*: **jdm etw ~** to pay sb back for sth, to repay sb for sth

Ver'geltung *f* retaliation, reprisal

vergessen (*unreg*) *vt* to forget; **V~heit** *f* oblivion

vergeßlich ⚠ [fɛr'gɛslɪç] *adj* forgetful; **V~keit** ⚠ *f* forgetfulness

vergeuden [fɛr'gɔydən] *vt* to squander, to waste

vergewaltigen [fɛrgə'valtɪgən] *vt* to rape; (*fig*) to violate

Vergewaltigung *f* rape

vergewissern [fɛrgə'vɪsərn] *vr* to make sure

ver'gießen (*unreg*) *vt* to shed

vergiften [fɛr'gɪftən] *vt* to poison

Vergiftung *f* poisoning

Vergißmeinnicht ⚠ [fɛr'gɪsmaɪnnɪçt] (-(e)s, -e) *nt* forget-me-not

vergißt ⚠ *etc* [fɛr'gɪst] *vb siehe* **vergessen**

Vergleich [fɛr'glaɪç] (-(e)s, -e) *m* comparison; (*JUR*) settlement; **im ~ mit** *od* **zu** compared with *od* to; **v~bar** *adj* comparable; **v~en** (*unreg*) *vt* to compare ♦ *vr* to reach a settlement

vergnügen [fɛr'gny:gən] *vr* to enjoy *od* amuse o.s.; **V~** (-s, -) *nt* pleasure; **viel V~!** enjoy yourself!

vergnügt [fɛr'gny:kt] *adj* cheerful

Vergnügen *f* pleasure, amusement; **~spark** *m* amusement park

vergolden [fɛr'gɔldən] *vt* to gild

ver'graben *vt* to bury

ver'greifen (*unreg*) *vr*: **sich an jdm ~** to lay hands on sb; **sich an etw ~** to misappropriate sth; **sich im Ton ~** to say the wrong thing

vergriffen [fɛr'grɪfən] *adj* (*Buch*) out of print; (*Ware*) out of stock

vergrößern [fɛr'grøːsərn] *vt* to enlarge; (*mengenmäßig*) to increase; (*Lupe*) to magnify

Vergrößerung *f* enlargement; increase; magnification

Vergrößerungsglas *nt* magnifying glass

Vergünstigung [fɛr'gʏnstɪgʊŋ] *f* concession, privilege

Vergütung *f* compensation

verhaften [fɛr'haftən] *vt* to arrest

Verhaftung *f* arrest

ver'halten (*unreg*) *vr* to be, to stand; (*sich benehmen*) to behave ♦ *vt* to hold *od* keep back; (*Schritt*) to check; **sich ~ (zu)** (*MATH*) to be in proportion (to); **V~** (-s) *nt* behaviour

Verhältnis [fɛr'hɛltnɪs] (-ses, -se) *nt* relationship; (*MATH*) proportion, ratio; **~se** *pl* (*Umstände*) conditions; **über seine ~se leben** to live beyond one's means; **v~mäßig** *adj* relative, comparative ♦ *adv* relatively, comparatively

verhandeln [fɛr'handəln] *vi* to negotiate; (*JUR*) to hold proceedings ♦ *vt* to discuss; (*JUR*) to hear; **über etw** *akk* **~** to negotiate sth *od* about sth

Verhandlung *f* negotiation; (*JUR*) proceedings *pl*; **~sbasis** *f* (*FIN*) basis for negotiations

ver'hängen *vt* (*fig*) to impose, to inflict

Verhängnis [fɛr'hɛŋnɪs] (-ses, -se) *nt* fate, doom; **jdm zum ~ werden** to be sb's undoing; **v~voll** *adj* fatal, disastrous

verharmlosen [fɛr'harmloːzən] *vt* to make light of, to play down

verhärten [fɛr'hɛrtən] *vr* to harden

verhaßt ⚠ [fɛr'hast] *adj* odious, hateful

verhauen [fɛr'hauən] (*unreg*) (*umg*) *vt* (*verprügeln*) to beat up

verheerend [fɛr'heːrənt] *adj* disastrous, devastating

verheimlichen [fɛr'haɪmlɪçən] *vt*: **jdm etw ~** to keep sth secret from sb

verheiratet [fɛr'haɪraːtət] *adj* married

ver'helfen (*unreg*) *vi*: **jdm ~ zu** to help sb to get

ver'hindern *vt* to prevent; **verhindert sein** to be unable to make it

verhöhnen [fɛr'høːnən] *vt* to mock, to sneer at

Verhör [fɛr'høːr] (-(e)s, -e) *nt* interrogation; (*gerichtlich*) (cross-)examination; **v~en** *vt* to interrogate; to (cross-)examine ♦ *vr* to misunderstand, to mishear

⚠ *Informationen zur Rechtschreibreform Seite 615*

ver'hungern *vi* to starve, to die of hunger
ver'hüten *vt* to prevent, to avert
Ver'hütung *f* prevention; **~smittel** *nt* contraceptive
verirren [fɛrˈʔɪrən] *vr* to go astray
ver'jagen *vt* to drive away *od* out
verkalken [fɛrˈkalkən] *vi* to calcify; (*umg*) to become senile
Verkauf [fɛrˈkaʊf] *m* sale; **v~en** *vt* to sell
Verkäufer(in) [fɛrˈkɔʏfər(ɪn)] (**-s, -**) *m(f)* seller; salesman(-woman); (*in Laden*) shop assistant
verkaufsoffen *adj*: **~er Samstag** *Saturday when the shops stay open all day*
Verkehr [fɛrˈkeːr] (**-s, -e**) *m* traffic; (*Umgang, bes sexuell*) intercourse; (*Umlauf*) circulation; **v~en** *vi* (*Fahrzeug*) to ply, to run ♦ *vt, vr* to turn, to transform; **v~en mit** (*besuchen*) to associate with; **bei jdm v~en** (*besuchen*) to visit sb regularly
Verkehrs- *zW*: **~ampel** *f* traffic lights *pl*; **~aufkommen** *nt* volume of traffic; **~beruhigung** *f* traffic calming; **~delikt** *nt* traffic offence; **~funk** *m* radio traffic service; **v~günstig** *adj* convenient; **~mittel** *nt* means of transport; **~schild** *nt* road sign; **~stau(ung)** *f* traffic jam, stoppage; **~unfall** *m* traffic accident; **~verein** *m* tourist information office; **~zeichen** *nt* traffic sign
verkehrt *adj* wrong; (*umgekehrt*) the wrong way round
ver'kennen (*unreg*) *vt* to misjudge, not to appreciate
ver'klagen *vt* to take to court
verkleiden [fɛrˈklaɪdən] *vr* to disguise (o.s.); (*sich kostümieren*) to get dressed up ♦ *vt* (*Wand*) to cover
Verkleidung *f* disguise; (*ARCHIT*) wainscoting
verkleinern [fɛrˈklaɪnərn] *vt* to make smaller, to reduce in size
ver'kneifen (*umg*) *vt*: **sich** *dat* **etw ~** (*Lachen*) to stifle sth; (*Schmerz*) to hide sth; (*sich versagen*) to do without sth
verknüpfen [fɛrˈknʏpfən] *vt* to tie (up), to knot; (*fig*) to connect

ver'kommen (*unreg*) *vi* to deteriorate, to decay; (*Mensch*) to go downhill, to come down in the world ♦ *adj* (*moralisch*) dissolute, depraved
verkörpern [fɛrˈkœrpərn] *vt* to embody, to personify
verkraften [fɛrˈkraftən] *vt* to cope with
ver'kriechen (*unreg*) *vr* to creep away, to creep into a corner
verkrüppelt [fɛrˈkrʏpəlt] *adj* crippled
ver'kühlen *vr* to get a chill
ver'kümmern *vi* to waste away
verkünden [fɛrˈkʏndən] *vt* to proclaim; (*Urteil*) to pronounce
verkürzen [fɛrˈkʏrtsən] *vt* to shorten; (*Wort*) to abbreviate; **sich** *dat* **die Zeit ~** to while away the time
Verkürzung *f* shortening; abbreviation
verladen [fɛrˈlaːdən] (*unreg*) *vt* (*Waren, Vieh*) to load; (*Truppen*) to embark, entrain, enplane
Verlag [fɛrˈlaːk] (**-(e)s, -e**) *m* publishing firm
verlangen [fɛrˈlaŋən] *vt* to demand; to desire ♦ *vi*: **~ nach** to ask for, to desire; **~ Sie Herrn X** ask for Mr X; **V~** (**-s, -**) *nt*: **V~ (nach)** desire (for); **auf jds V~ (hin)** at sb's request
verlängern [fɛrˈlɛŋərn] *vt* to extend; (*länger machen*) to lengthen
Verlängerung *f* extension; (*SPORT*) extra time; **~sschnur** *f* extension cable
verlangsamen [fɛrˈlaŋzaːmən] *vt, vr* to decelerate, to slow down
Verlaß △ [fɛrˈlas] *m*: **auf ihn / das ist kein ~** he/it cannot be relied upon
ver'lassen (*unreg*) *vt* to leave ♦ *vr*: **sich ~ auf** *+akk* to depend on ♦ *adj* desolate; (*Mensch*) abandoned
verläßlich △ [fɛrˈlɛslɪç] *adj* reliable
Verlauf [fɛrˈlaʊf] *m* course; **v~en** (*unreg*) *vi* (*zeitlich*) to pass; (*Farben*) to run ♦ *vr* to get lost; (*Menschenmenge*) to disperse
ver'lauten *vi*: **etw ~ lassen** to disclose sth; **wie verlautet** as reported
ver'legen *vt* to move; (*verlieren*) to mislay; (*Buch*) to publish ♦ *vr*: **sich auf etw** *akk* **~** to take up *od* to sth ♦ *adj* embarrassed;

△ *For information on spelling reform see page 615*

nicht ~ um never at a loss for;
Ver'legenheit f embarrassment; (*Situation*) difficulty, scrape

Verleger [fɛr'le:gər] (**-s, -**) m publisher

Verleih [fɛr'laɪ] (**-(e)s, -e**) m hire service; **v~en** (*unreg*) vt to lend; (*Kraft, Anschein*) to confer, to bestow; (*Preis, Medaille*) to award; **~ung** f lending; bestowal; award

ver'leiten vt to lead astray; **~ zu** to talk into, to tempt into

ver'lernen vt to forget, to unlearn

ver'lesen (*unreg*) vt to read out; (*aussondern*) to sort out ♦ vr to make a mistake in reading

verletz- [fɛr'lɛts] zW: **~en** vt (*auch fig*) to injure, to hurt; (*Gesetz etc*) to violate; **~end** adj (*fig: Worte*) hurtful; **~lich** adj vulnerable, sensitive; **V~te(r)** f(m) injured person; **V~ung** f injury; (*Verstoß*) violation, infringement

verleugnen [fɛr'lɔʏgnən] vt (*Herkunft, Glauben*) to belie; (*Menschen*) to disown

verleumden [fɛr'lɔʏmdən] vt to slander; **Verleumdung** f slander, libel

ver'lieben vr: **sich ~ (in** +akk) to fall in love (with)

verliebt [fɛr'li:pt] adj in love

verlieren [fɛr'li:rən] (*unreg*) vt, vi to lose ♦ vr to get lost

Verlierer m loser

verlob- [fɛr'lo:b] zW: **~en** vr: **sich ~en (mit)** to get engaged (to); **V~te(r)** [fɛr'lo:ptə(r)] f(m) fiancé m, fiancée f; **V~ung** f engagement

ver'locken vt to entice, to lure

Ver'lockung f temptation, attraction

verlogen [fɛr'lo:gən] adj untruthful

verlor etc vb siehe **verlieren**

verloren [fɛr'lo:rən] adj lost; (*Eier*) poached ♦ vb siehe **verlieren**; **etw ~ geben** to give sth up for lost; **~gehen** ⚠ (*unreg*) vi to get lost

verlosen [fɛr'lo:zən] vt to raffle, to draw lots for; **Verlosung** f raffle, lottery

Verlust [fɛr'lʊst] (**-(e)s, -e**) m loss; (*MIL*) casualty

ver'machen vt to bequeath, to leave

Vermächtnis [fɛr'mɛçtnɪs] (**-ses, -se**) nt legacy

Vermählung [fɛr'mɛ:lʊŋ] f wedding, marriage

vermarkten [fɛr'marktən] vt (*COMM: Artikel*) to market

vermehren [fɛr'me:rən] vt, vr to multiply; (*Menge*) to increase

Vermehrung f multiplying; increase

ver'meiden (*unreg*) vt to avoid

vermeintlich [fɛr'maɪntlɪç] adj supposed

Vermerk [fɛr'mɛrk] (**-(e)s, -e**) m note; (*in Ausweis*) endorsement; **v~en** vt to note

ver'messen (*unreg*) vt to survey ♦ adj presumptuous, bold; **V~heit** f presumptuousness; recklessness

Ver'messung f survey(ing)

vermiet- [fɛr'mi:t] zW: **~en** vt to let, to rent (out); (*Auto*) to hire out, to rent; **V~er(in)** (**-s, -**) m(f) landlord(-lady); **V~ung** f letting, renting (out); (*von Autos*) hiring (out)

vermindern [fɛr'mɪndərn] vt, vr to lessen, to decrease; (*Preise*) to reduce

Verminderung f reduction

ver'mischen vt, vr to mix, to blend

vermissen [fɛr'mɪsən] vt to miss

vermitt- [fɛr'mɪt] zW: **~eln** vi to mediate ♦ vt (*Gespräch*) to connect; **jdm etw ~eln** to help sb to obtain sth; **V~ler** (**-s, -**) m (*Schlichter*) agent, mediator; **V~lung** f procurement; (*Stellenvermittlung*) agency; (*TEL*) exchange; (*Schlichtung*) mediation; **V~lungsgebühr** f commission

ver'mögen (*unreg*) vt to be capable of; **~ zu** to be able to; **V~** (**-s, -**) nt wealth; (*Fähigkeit*) ability; **ein V~ kosten** to cost a fortune; **~d** adj wealthy

vermuten [fɛr'mu:tən] vt to suppose, to guess; (*argwöhnen*) to suspect

vermutlich adj supposed, presumed ♦ adv probably

Vermutung f supposition; suspicion

vernachlässigen [fɛr'na:xlɛsɪgən] vt to neglect

ver'nehmen (*unreg*) vt to perceive, to hear; (*erfahren*) to learn; (*JUR*) to

⚠ *Informationen zur Rechtschreibreform Seite 615*

(cross-)examine; **dem V~ nach** from what I/we *etc* hear

Vernehmung *f* (cross-)examination

verneigen [fɛr'naɪɡən] *vr* to bow

verneinen [fɛr'naɪnən] *vt* (*Frage*) to answer in the negative; (*ablehnen*) to deny; (*GRAM*) to negate; **~d** *adj* negative

Verneinung *f* negation

vernichten [fɛr'nɪçtən] *vt* to annihilate, to destroy; **~d** *adj* (*fig*) crushing; (*Blick*) withering; (*Kritik*) scathing

Vernunft [fɛr'nʊnft] (-) *f* reason, understanding

vernünftig [fɛr'nʏnftɪç] *adj* sensible, reasonable

veröffentlichen [fɛr'œfəntlɪçən] *vt* to publish; **Veröffentlichung** *f* publication

verordnen [fɛr'ɔrdnən] *vt* (*MED*) to prescribe

Verordnung *f* order, decree; (*MED*) prescription

ver'pachten *vt* to lease (out)

ver'packen *vt* to pack

Ver'packung *f* packing, wrapping; **~smaterial** *nt* packing, wrapping

ver'passen *vt* to miss; **jdm eine Ohrfeige ~** (*umg*) to give sb a clip round the ear

verpfänden [fɛr'pfɛndən] *vt* (*Besitz*) to mortgage

ver'pflanzen *vt* to transplant

ver'pflegen *vt* to feed, to cater for

Ver'pflegung *f* feeding, catering; (*Kost*) food; (*in Hotel*) board

verpflichten [fɛr'pflɪçtən] *vt* to oblige, to bind; (*anstellen*) to engage ♦ *vr* to undertake; (*MIL*) to sign on ♦ *vi* to carry obligations; **jdm zu Dank verpflichtet sein** to be obliged to sb

Verpflichtung *f* obligation, duty

verpönt [fɛr'pø:nt] *adj* disapproved (of), taboo

ver'prügeln (*umg*) *vt* to beat up, to do over

Verputz [fɛr'pʊts] *m* plaster, roughcast; **v~en** *vt* to plaster; (*umg: Essen*) to put away

Verrat [fɛr'ra:t] (-(e)s) *m* treachery; (*POL*) treason; **v~en** (*unreg*) *vt* to betray; (*Geheimnis*) to divulge ♦ *vr* to give o.s. away

Verräter [fɛr'rɛ:tər] (-s, -) *m* traitor(-tress); **v~isch** *adj* treacherous

ver'rechnen *vt*: **~ mit** to set off against ♦ *vr* to miscalculate

Verrechnungsscheck [fɛr'rɛçnʊŋsʃɛk] *m* crossed cheque

verregnet [fɛr're:ɡnət] *adj* spoilt by rain, rainy

ver'reisen *vi* to go away (on a journey)

verrenken [fɛr'rɛŋkən] *vt* to contort; (*MED*) to dislocate; **sich** *dat* **den Knöchel ~** to sprain one's ankle

ver'richten *vt* to do, to perform

verriegeln [fɛr'ri:ɡəln] *vt* to bolt up, to lock

verringern [fɛr'rɪŋərn] *vt* to reduce ♦ *vr* to diminish

Verringerung *f* reduction; lessening

ver'rinnen (*unreg*) *vi* to run out *od* away; (*Zeit*) to elapse

ver'rosten *vi* to rust

verrotten [fɛr'rɔtən] *vi* to rot

ver'rücken *vt* to move, to shift

verrückt [fɛr'rʏkt] *adj* crazy, mad; **V~e(r)** *f(m)* lunatic; **V~heit** *f* madness, lunacy

Verruf [fɛr'ru:f] *m*: **in ~ geraten/bringen** to fall/bring into disrepute; **v~en** *adj* notorious, disreputable

Vers [fɛrs] (-es, -e) *m* verse

ver'sagen *vt*: **jdm/sich etw ~** to deny sb/o.s. sth ♦ *vi* to fail; **V~** (-s) *nt* failure

ver'salzen (*unreg*) *vt* to put too much salt in; (*fig*) to spoil

ver'sammeln *vt, vr* to assemble, to gather

Ver'sammlung *f* meeting, gathering

Versand [fɛr'zant] (-(e)s) *m* forwarding; dispatch; (*~abteilung*) dispatch department; **~haus** *nt* mail-order firm

versäumen [fɛr'zɔymən] *vt* to miss; (*unterlassen*) to neglect, to fail

ver'schaffen *vt*: **jdm/sich etw ~** to get *od* procure sth for sb/o.s.

verschämt [fɛr'ʃɛ:mt] *adj* bashful

verschandeln [fɛr'ʃandəln]·(*umg*) *vt* to

⚠ *For information on spelling reform see page 615*

spoil
verschärfen [fɛrˈʃɛrfən] *vt* to intensify;
(*Lage*) to aggravate ♦ *vr* to intensify; to
become aggravated

ver'schätzen *vr* to be out in one's
reckoning

ver'schenken *vt* to give away

verscheuchen [fɛrˈʃɔyçən] *vt* (*Tiere*) to
chase off *od* away

ver'schicken *vt* to send off

ver'schieben (*unreg*) *vt* to shift; (*EISENB*) to
shunt; (*Termin*) to postpone

verschieden [fɛrˈʃiːdən] *adj* different; (*pl:
mehrere*) various; **sie sind ~ groß** they are
of different sizes; **~tlich** *adv* several times

verschimmeln [fɛrˈʃɪməln] *vi*
(*Nahrungsmittel*) to go mouldy

verschlafen [fɛrˈʃlaːfən] (*unreg*) *vt* to sleep
through; (*fig: versäumen*) to miss ♦ *vi, vr* to
oversleep ♦ *adj* sleepy

Verschlag [fɛrˈʃlaːk] *m* shed; **v~en** [-gən]
(*unreg*) *vt* to board up ♦ *adj* cunning; **jdm
den Atem v~en** to take sb's breath away;
an einen Ort v~en werden to wind up in
a place

verschlechtern [fɛrˈʃlɛçtərn] *vt* to make
worse ♦ *vr* to deteriorate, to get worse;
Verschlechterung *f* deterioration

Verschleiß [fɛrˈʃlaɪs] (**-es, -e**) *m* wear and
tear; **v~en** (*unreg*) *vt* to wear out

ver'schleppen *vt* to carry off, to abduct;
(*Krankheit*) to protract; (*zeitlich*) to drag out

ver'schleudern *vt* to squander; (*COMM*)
to sell dirt-cheap

verschließbar *adj* lockable

verschließen [fɛrˈʃliːsən] (*unreg*) *vt* to
close; to lock ♦ *vr*: **sich einer Sache** *dat* **~**
to close one's mind to sth

verschlimmern [fɛrˈʃlɪmərn] *vt* to make
worse, to aggravate ♦ *vr* to get worse, to
deteriorate

verschlingen [fɛrˈʃlɪŋən] (*unreg*) *vt* to
devour, to swallow up; (*Fäden*) to twist

verschlossen [fɛrˈʃlɔsən] *adj* locked; (*fig*)
reserved; **V~heit** *f* reserve

ver'schlucken *vt* to swallow ♦ *vr* to choke

Verschluß ⚠ [fɛrˈʃlʊs] *m* lock; (*von Kleid*

etc) fastener; (*PHOT*) shutter; (*Stöpsel*) plug

verschlüsseln [fɛrˈʃlʏsəln] *vt* to encode

verschmieren [fɛrˈʃmiːrən] *vt* (*verstreichen:
Gips, Mörtel*) to apply, spread on; (*schmutzig
machen: Wand etc*) to smear

verschmutzen [fɛrˈʃmʊtsən] *vt* to soil;
(*Umwelt*) to pollute

verschneit [fɛrˈʃnaɪt] *adj* snowed up,
covered in snow

verschollen [fɛrˈʃɔlən] *adj* lost, missing

ver'schonen *vt*: **jdn mit etw ~** to spare
sb sth

verschönern [fɛrˈʃøːnərn] *vt* to decorate;
(*verbessern*) to improve

ver'schreiben (*unreg*) *vt* (*MED*) to
prescribe ♦ *vr* to make a mistake (in
writing); **sich einer Sache** *dat* **~** to devote
o.s. to sth

verschreibungspflichtig *adj*
(*Medikament*) available on prescription only

verschrotten [fɛrˈʃrɔtən] *vt* to scrap

verschuld- [fɛrˈʃʊld] *zW*: **~en** *vt* to be
guilty of; **V~en** (**-s**) *nt* fault, guilt; **~et** *adj*
in debt; **V~ung** *f* fault; (*Geld*) debts *pl*

ver'schütten *vt* to spill; (*zuschütten*) to fill;
(*unter Trümmern*) to bury

ver'schweigen (*unreg*) *vt* to keep secret;
jdm etw ~ to keep sth from sb

verschwend- [fɛrˈʃvɛnd] *zW*: **~en** *vt* to
squander; **V~er** (**-s, -**) *m* spendthrift;
~erisch *adj* wasteful, extravagant; **V~ung**
f waste; extravagance

verschwiegen [fɛrˈʃviːgən] *adj* discreet;
(*Ort*) secluded; **V~heit** *f* discretion;
seclusion

ver'schwimmen (*unreg*) *vi* to grow hazy,
to become blurred

ver'schwinden (*unreg*) *vi* to disappear, to
vanish; **V~** (**-s**) *nt* disappearance

verschwitzt [fɛrˈʃvɪtst] *adj* (*Mensch*) sweaty

verschwommen [fɛrˈʃvɔmən] *adj* hazy,
vague

verschwör- [fɛrˈʃvøːr] *zW*: **~en** (*unreg*) *vr*
to plot, to conspire; **V~ung** *f* conspiracy,
plot

ver'sehen (*unreg*) *vt* to supply, to provide;
(*Pflicht*) to carry out; (*Amt*) to fill; (*Haushalt*)

⚠ *Informationen zur Rechtschreibreform Seite 615*

to keep ♦ *vr* (*fig*) to make a mistake; **ehe er (es) sich ~ hatte ...** before he knew it ...; **V~ (-s, -)** *nt* oversight; **aus V~** by mistake; **~lich** *adv* by mistake

Versehrte(r) [fɛr'zeːrtə(r)] *f(m)* disabled person

ver'senden (*unreg*) *vt* to forward, to dispatch

ver'senken *vt* to sink ♦ *vr*: **sich ~ in** +*akk* to become engrossed in

versessen [fɛr'zɛsən] *adj*: **~ auf** +*akk* mad about

ver'setzen *vt* to transfer; (*verpfänden*) to pawn; (*umg*) to stand up ♦ *vr*: **sich in jdn** *od* **in jds Lage ~** to put o.s. in sb's place; **jdm einen Tritt/Schlag ~** to kick/hit sb; **etw mit etw ~** to mix sth with sth; **jdn in gute Laune ~** to put sb in a good mood

Ver'setzung *f* transfer

verseuchen [fɛr'zɔyçən] *vt* to contaminate

versichern [fɛr'zɪçərn] *vt* to assure; (*mit Geld*) to insure

Versicherung *f* assurance; insurance

Versicherungs- *zW*: **~gesellschaft** *f* insurance company; **~karte** *f* insurance card; **die grüne ~karte** the green card; **~police** *f* insurance policy

ver'sinken (*unreg*) *vi* to sink

versöhnen [fɛr'zøːnən] *vt* to reconcile ♦ *vr* to become reconciled

Versöhnung *f* reconciliation

ver'sorgen *vt* to provide, to supply; (*Familie etc*) to look after

Ver'sorgung *f* provision; (*Unterhalt*) maintenance; (*Altersversorgung etc*) benefit, assistance

verspäten [fɛr'ʃpeːtən] *vr* to be late

verspätet *adj* (*Zug, Abflug, Ankunft*) late; (*Glückwünsche*) belated

Verspätung *f* delay; **~ haben** to be late

ver'sperren *vt* to bar, to obstruct

verspielt [fɛr'ʃpiːlt] *adj* (*Kind, Tier*) playful

ver'spotten *vt* to ridicule, to scoff at

ver'sprechen (*unreg*) *vt* to promise; **sich** *dat* **etw von etw ~** to expect sth from sth; **V~ (-s, -)** *nt* promise

verstaatlichen [fɛr'ʃtaːtlɪçən] *vt* to nationalize

Verstand [fɛr'ʃtant] *m* intelligence; mind; **den ~ verlieren** to go out of one's mind; **über jds ~ gehen** to go beyond sb

verständig [fɛr'ʃtɛndɪç] *adj* sensible; **~en** [fɛr'ʃtɛndɪgən] *vt* to inform ♦ *vr* to communicate; (*sich einigen*) to come to an understanding; **V~ung** *f* communication; (*Benachrichtigung*) informing; (*Einigung*) agreement

verständ- [fɛr'ʃtɛnt] *zW*: **~lich** *adj* understandable, comprehensible; **V~lichkeit** *f* clarity, intelligibility; **V~nis (-ses, -se)** *nt* understanding; **~nislos** *adj* uncomprehending; **~nisvoll** *adj* understanding, sympathetic

verstärk- [fɛr'ʃtɛrk] *zW*: **~en** *vt* to strengthen; (*Ton*) to amplify; (*erhöhen*) to intensify ♦ *vr* to intensify; **V~er (-s, -)** *m* amplifier; **V~ung** *f* strengthening; (*Hilfe*) reinforcements *pl*; (*von Ton*) amplification

verstauchen [fɛr'ʃtauxən] *vt* to sprain

verstauen [fɛr'ʃtauən] *vt* to stow away

Versteck [fɛr'ʃtɛk] **(-(e)s, -e)** *nt* hiding (place); **v~en** *vt, vr* to hide; **v~t** *adj* hidden

ver'stehen (*unreg*) *vt* to understand ♦ *vr* to get on; **das versteht sich (von selbst)** that goes without saying

versteigern [fɛr'ʃtaɪgərn] *vt* to auction; **Versteigerung** *f* auction

verstell- [fɛr'ʃtɛl] *zW*: **~bar** *adj* adjustable, variable; **~en** *vt* to move, to shift; (*Uhr*) to adjust; (*versperren*) to block; (*fig*) to disguise ♦ *vr* to pretend, to put on an act; **V~ung** *f* pretence

versteuern [fɛr'ʃtɔyərn] *vt* to pay tax on

verstimmt [fɛr'ʃtɪmt] *adj* out of tune; (*fig*) cross, put out; (*Magen*) upset

ver'stopfen *vt* to block, to stop up; (*MED*) to constipate

Ver'stopfung *f* obstruction; (*MED*) constipation

verstorben [fɛr'ʃtɔrbən] *adj* deceased, late

verstört [fɛr'ʃtøːrt] *adj* (*Mensch*) distraught

Verstoß [fɛr'ʃtoːs] *m*: **~ (gegen)** infringement (of), violation (of); **v~en** (*unreg*) *vt* to disown, to reject ♦ *vi*: **v~en**

gegen to offend against

ver'streichen (*unreg*) *vt* to spread ♦ *vi* to elapse

ver'streuen *vt* to scatter (about)

verstümmeln [fɛr'ʃtʏməln] *vt* to maim, to mutilate (*auch fig*)

verstummen [fɛr'ʃtʊmən] *vi* to go silent; (*Lärm*) to die away

Versuch [fɛr'zuːx] (*-(e)s, -e*) *m* attempt; (*SCI*) experiment; **v~en** *vt* to try; (*verlocken*) to tempt ♦ *vr*: **sich an etw v~en** to try one's hand at sth; **~skaninchen** *nt* (*fig*) guinea-pig; **~ung** *f* temptation

vertagen [fɛr'taːgən] *vt, vi* to adjourn

ver'tauschen *vt* to exchange; (*versehentlich*) to mix up

verteidig- [fɛr'taɪdɪg] *zW*: **~en** *vt* to defend; **V~er** (*-s, -*) *m* defender; (*JUR*) defence counsel; **V~ung** *f* defence

ver'teilen *vt* to distribute; (*Rollen*) to assign; (*Salbe*) to spread

Verteilung *f* distribution, allotment

vertiefen [fɛr'tiːfən] *vt* to deepen ♦ *vr*: **sich in etw** *akk* **~** to become engrossed *od* absorbed in sth

Vertiefung *f* depression

vertikal [vɛrti'kaːl] *adj* vertical

vertilgen [fɛr'tɪlgən] *vt* to exterminate; (*umg*) to eat up, to consume

vertonen [fɛr'toːnən] *vt* to set to music

Vertrag [fɛr'traːk] (*-(e)s, ⁻e*) *m* contract, agreement; (*POL*) treaty; **v~en** (*unreg*) *vt* to tolerate, to stand ♦ *vr* to get along; (*sich aussöhnen*) to become reconciled; **v~lich** *adj* contractual

verträglich [fɛr'trɛːklɪç] *adj* good-natured, sociable; (*Speisen*) easily digested; (*MED*) easily tolerated; **V~keit** *f* sociability; good nature; digestibility

Vertrags- *zW*: **~bruch** *m* breach of contract; **~händler** *m* appointed retailer; **~partner** *m* party to a contract; **~werkstatt** *f* appointed repair shop; **v~widrig** *adj* contrary to contract

vertrauen [fɛr'traʊən] *vi*: **jdm ~** to trust sb; **~ auf** +*akk* to rely on; **V~** (*-s*) *nt* confidence; **~erweckend** ⚠ *adj* inspiring

trust; **~svoll** *adj* trustful; **~swürdig** *adj* trustworthy

vertraulich [fɛr'traʊlɪç] *adj* familiar; (*geheim*) confidential

vertraut [fɛr'traʊt] *adj* familiar; **V~heit** *f* familiarity

ver'treiben (*unreg*) *vt* to drive away; (*aus Land*) to expel; (*COMM*) to sell; (*Zeit*) to pass

vertret- [fɛr'treːt] *zW*: **~en** (*unreg*) *vt* to represent; (*Ansicht*) to hold, to advocate; **sich** *dat* **die Beine ~en** to stretch one's legs; **V~er** (*-s, -*) *m* representative; (*Verfechter*) advocate; **V~ung** *f* representation; advocacy

Vertrieb [fɛr'triːp] (*-(e)s, -e*) *m* marketing (department)

ver'trocknen *vi* to dry up

ver'trösten *vt* to put off

vertun [fɛr'tuːn] (*unreg*) *vt* to waste ♦ *vr* (*umg*) to make a mistake

vertuschen [fɛr'tʊʃən] *vt* to hush *od* cover up

verübeln [fɛr'|yːbəln] *vt*: **jdm etw ~** to be cross *od* offended with sb on account of sth

verüben [fɛr'|yːbən] *vt* to commit

verun- [fɛr'|ʊn] *zW*: **~glimpfen** *vt* to disparage; **~glücken** *vi* to have an accident; **tödlich ~glücken** to be killed in an accident; **~reinigen** *vt* to soil; (*Umwelt*) to pollute; **~sichern** *vt* to rattle; **~treuen** [-trɔɪən] *vt* to embezzle

verur- [fɛr'|uːr] *zW*: **~sachen** *vt* to cause; **~teilen** [-taɪlən] *vt* to condemn; **V~teilung** *f* condemnation; (*JUR*) sentence

verviel- [fɛr'fiːl] *zW*: **~fachen** *vt* to multiply; **~fältigen** *vt* to duplicate, to copy; **V~fältigung** *f* duplication, copying

vervollkommnen [fɛr'fɔlkɔmnən] *vt* to perfect

vervollständigen [fɛr'fɔlʃtɛndɪgən] *vt* to complete

ver'wackeln *vt* (*Foto*) to blur

ver'wählen *vr* (*TEL*) to dial the wrong number

verwahren [fɛr'vaːrən] *vt* to keep, to lock away ♦ *vr* to protest

⚠ *Informationen zur Rechtschreibreform Seite 615*

verwalt- [fɛr'valt] zW: **~en** vt to manage; to administer; **V~er (-s, -)** m manager; (*Vermögensverwalter*) trustee; **V~ung** f administration; management

ver'wandeln vt to change, to transform ♦ vr to change; to be transformed; **Ver'wandlung** f change, transformation

verwandt [fɛr'vant] adj: **~ (mit)** related (to); **V~e(r)** f(m) relative, relation; **V~schaft** f relationship; (*Menschen*) relations pl

ver'warnen vt to caution

Ver'warnung f caution

ver'wechseln vt: **~ mit** to confuse with; to mistake for; **zum V~ ähnlich** as like as two peas

Ver'wechslung f confusion, mixing up

Verwehung [fɛr've:ʊŋ] f snowdrift; sand drift

verweichlicht [fɛr'vaɪçlɪçt] adj effeminate, soft

ver'weigern vt: **jdm etw ~** to refuse sb sth; **den Gehorsam/die Aussage ~** to refuse to obey/testify

Ver'weigerung f refusal

Verweis [fɛr'vaɪs] (**-es, -e**) m reprimand, rebuke; (*Hinweis*) reference; **v~en** (*unreg*) vt to refer; **jdn von der Schule v~en** to expel sb (from school); **jdn des Landes v~en** to deport od expel sb

ver'welken vi to fade

verwend- [fɛr'vɛnd] zW: **~bar** [-'vɛntbaːr] adj usable; **~en** (*unreg*) vt to use; (*Mühe, Zeit, Arbeit*) to spend ♦ vr to intercede; **V~ung** f use

ver'werfen (*unreg*) vt to reject

verwerflich [fɛr'vɛrflɪç] adj reprehensible

ver'werten vt to utilize

Ver'wertung f utilization

verwesen [fɛr've:zən] vi to decay

ver'wickeln vt to tangle (up); (*fig*) to involve ♦ vr to get tangled (up); **jdn in etw** akk **~** to involve sb in sth; **sich in etw** akk **~** to get involved in sth

verwickelt [fɛr'vɪkəlt] adj (*Situation, Fall*) difficult, complicated

verwildern [fɛr'vɪldərn] vi to run wild

verwirklichen [fɛr'vɪrklɪçən] vt to realize, to

put into effect

Verwirklichung f realization

verwirren [fɛr'vɪrən] vt to tangle (up); (*fig*) to confuse

Verwirrung f confusion

verwittern [fɛr'vɪtərn] vi to weather

verwitwet [fɛr'vɪtvət] adj widowed

verwöhnen [fɛr'vøːnən] vt to spoil

verworren [fɛr'vɔrən] adj confused

verwundbar [fɛr'vʊntbaːr] adj vulnerable

verwunden [fɛr'vʊndən] vt to wound

verwunder- [fɛr'vʊndər] zW: **~lich** adj surprising; **V~ung** f astonishment

Verwundete(r) f(m) injured person

Verwundung f wound, injury

ver'wünschen vt to curse

verwüsten [fɛr'vyːstən] vt to devastate

verzagen [fɛr'tsaːgən] vi to despair

ver'zählen vr to miscount

verzehren [fɛr'tseːrən] vt to consume

ver'zeichnen vt to list; (*Niederlage, Verlust*) to register

Verzeichnis [fɛr'tsaɪçnɪs] (**-ses, -se**) nt list, catalogue; (*in Buch*) index

verzeih- [fɛr'tsaɪ] zW: **~en** (*unreg*) vt, vi to forgive; **jdm etw ~en** to forgive sb for sth; **~lich** adj pardonable; **V~ung** f forgiveness, pardon; **V~ung!** sorry!, excuse me!

verzichten [fɛr'tsɪçtən] vi: **~ auf** +akk to forgo, to give up

ver'ziehen (*unreg*) vi to move ♦ vt to put out of shape; (*Kind*) to spoil; (*Pflanzen*) to thin out ♦ vr to go out of shape; (*Gesicht*) to contort; (*verschwinden*) to disappear; **das Gesicht ~** to pull a face

verzieren [fɛr'tsiːrən] vt to decorate, to ornament

Verzierung f decoration

verzinsen [fɛr'tsɪnzən] vt to pay interest on

ver'zögern vt to delay

Ver'zögerung f delay, time lag; **~staktik** f delaying tactics pl

verzollen [fɛr'tsɔlən] vt to pay duty on

Verzug [fɛr'tsuːk] m delay

verzweif- [fɛr'tsvaɪf] zW: **~eln** vi to despair; **~elt** adj desperate; **V~lung** f despair

Veto ['ve:to] (**-s, -s**) nt veto

Vetter ['fɛtər] (**-s, -n**) *m* cousin
vgl. *abk* (= *vergleiche*) cf.
v.H. *abk* (= *vom Hundert*) p.c.
vibrieren [vi'briːrən] *vi* to vibrate
Video ['viːdeo] *nt* video; **~gerät** *nt* video
recorder; **~recorder** *m* video recorder
Vieh [fiː] (**-(e)s**) *nt* cattle *pl*;
bestial **v~isch** *adj*
viel [fiːl] *adj* a lot of, much ♦ *adv* a lot,
much; **~e** *pron pl* a lot of, many; **~**
zuwenig much too little; **~erlei** *adj* a
great variety of; **~es** *pron* a lot; **~fach** *adj*,
adv many times; **auf ~fachen Wunsch** at
the request of many people; **V~falt** (**-**) *f*
variety; **~fältig** *adj* varied, many-
sided
vielleicht [fi'laɪçt] *adv* perhaps
viel- *zW:* **~mal(s)** *adv* many times; **danke**
~mals many thanks; **~mehr** *adv* rather, on
the contrary; **~sagend** △ *adj* significant;
~seitig *adj* many-sided; **~versprechend**
△ *adj* promising
vier [fiːr] *num* four; **V~eck** (**-(e)s, -e**) *nt*
four-sided figure; (*gleichseitig*) square;
~eckig *adj* four-sided; square;
V~taktmotor *m* four-stroke engine; **~te(r,**
s) ['fiːrtə(r, s)] *adj* fourth; **V~tel** ['fɪrtəl] (**-s,**
-) *nt* quarter; **V~teljahr** *nt* quarter;
~teljährlich *adj* quarterly; **~teln** *vt* to
divide into four; (*Kuchen usw*) to divide into
quarters; **V~telstunde** *f* quarter of an
hour; **~zehn** ['fɪrtseːn] *num* fourteen; **in**
~zehn Tagen in a fortnight; **~zehntägig**
adj fortnightly; **~zig** ['fɪrtsɪç] *num* forty
Villa ['vɪla] (**-, Villen**) *f* villa
violett [vio'lɛt] *adj* violet
Violin- [vio'liːn] *zW:* **~e** *f* violin;
~schlüssel *m* treble clef
virtuell [vɪrtu'ɛl] *adj* (*COMPUT*) virtual; **~e**
Realität virtual reality
Virus ['viːrʊs] (**-, Viren**) *m od nt* (*auch*
COMPUT) virus
Visa ['viːza] *pl von* **Visum**
vis-à-vis [viza'viː] *adv* opposite
Visen ['viːzən] *pl von* **Visum**
Visier [vi'ziːr] (**-s, -e**) *nt* gunsight; (*am Helm*)
visor

Visite [vi'ziːtə] *f* (*MED*) visit; **~nkarte** *f*
visiting card
Visum ['viːzʊm] (**-s, Visa** *od* **Visen**) *nt* visa
vital [vi'taːl] *adj* lively, full of life, vital
Vitamin [vita'miːn] (**-s, -e**) *nt* vitamin
Vogel ['foːgəl] (**-s, ̈**) *m* bird; **einen ~**
haben (*umg*) to have bats in the belfry;
jdm den ~ zeigen (*umg*) to tap one's
forehead (*meaning that one thinks sb stupid*);
~bauer *nt* birdcage; **~perspektive** *f*
bird's-eye view; **~scheuche** *f* scarecrow
Vokabel [vo'kaːbəl] (**-, -n**) *f* word
Vokabular [vokabu'laːr] (**-s, -e**) *nt*
vocabulary
Vokal [vo'kaːl] (**-s, -e**) *m* vowel
Volk [fɔlk] (**-(e)s, ̈er**) *nt* people; nation
Völker- ['fœlkər] *zW:* **~recht** *nt*
international law; **~rechtlich** *adj*
according to international law;
~verständigung *f* international
understanding

VOLKSHOCHSCHULE

i The **Volkshochschule** (*VHS*) is an
institution which offers Adult Education
classes. No set qualifications are necessary
to attend. For a small fee adults can attend
both vocational and non-vocational classes
in the day-time or evening.

Volks- *zW:* **~entscheid** *m* referendum;
~fest *nt* fair; **~hochschule** *f* adult
education classes *pl*; **~lied** *nt* folksong;
~republik *f* people's republic; **~schule** *f*
elementary school; **~tanz** *m* folk dance;
~vertreter(in) *m(f)* people's
representative; **~wirtschaft** *f* economics
sg
voll [fɔl] *adj* full; **etw ~ machen** to fill sth
up; **~ und ganz** completely; **jdn für ~**
nehmen (*umg*) to take sb seriously; **~auf**
adv amply; **V~bart** *m* full beard;
V~beschäftigung *f* full employment;
~bringen (*unreg*) *vt insep* to accomplish;
~enden *vt insep* to finish, to complete;
~endet *adj* (*vollkommen*) completed;
~ends ['fɔlɛnts] *adv* completely;

V~|**endung** f completion
Volleyball ['vɔlibal] m volleyball
Vollgas nt: **mit ~** at full throttle; **~ geben**
to step on it
völlig ['fœlɪç] adj complete ♦ adv completely
voll- zW: **~jährig** adj of age;
V~**kaskoversicherung** ['fɔlkaskofɛrzɪçərʊŋ]
f fully comprehensive insurance;
~'**kommen** adj perfect; V~'**kommenheit**
f perfection; V~**kornbrot** nt wholemeal
bread; V~**macht** (-, -en) f authority, full
powers pl; V~**milch** f (KOCH) full-cream
milk; V~**mond** m full moon; V~**pension** f
full board; ~'**strecken** vt insep to execute;
~'**strecken** vt insep to execute;
~**tanken** ⚠ vt, vi to fill up;
V~**waschmittel** nt detergent;
V~**wertkost** f wholefood; ~**zählig**
['fɔlʃtɛndɪç] adj complete; in full number;
~'**ziehen** (unreg) vt insep to carry out ♦ vr
insep to happen; V~'**zug** m execution
Volumen [voˈluːmən] (-s, - od **Volumina**) nt
volume
vom [fɔm] = **von dem**

von [fɔn] präp +dat **1** (Ausgangspunkt) from;
von ... bis from ... to; **von morgens bis**
abends from morning till night; **von ...**
nach ... from ... to ...; **von ... an** from ...;
von ... aus from ...; **von dort aus** from
there; **etw von sich aus tun** to do sth of
one's own accord; **von mir aus** (umg) if
you like, I don't mind; **von wo/wann ...?**
where/when ... from?
2 (Ursache, im Passiv) by; **ein Gedicht von**
Schiller a poem by Schiller; **nett von dir**
nice of you; **jeweils zwei von zehn** two out of
every ten
3 (als Genitiv) of; **ein Freund von mir** a
friend of mine; **nett von dir** nice of you;
jeweils zwei von zehn two out of every
ten
4 (über) about; **er erzählte vom Urlaub** he
talked about his holiday
5: von wegen! (umg) no way!

voneinander adv from each other

vor [foːr] präp +dat **1** (räumlich) in front of;
vor der Kirche links abbiegen turn left
before the church
2 (zeitlich) before; **ich war vor ihm da** I
was there before him; **vor 2 Tagen** 2 days
ago; **5 (Minuten) vor 4** 5 (minutes) to 4;
vor kurzem a little while ago
3 (Ursache) with; **vor Wut/Liebe** with
rage/love; **vor Hunger sterben** to die of
hunger; **vor lauter Arbeit** because of work
4: vor allem, vor allen Dingen most of all
♦ präp +akk (räumlich) in front of
♦ adv: **vor und zurück** backwards and
forwards

Vorabend ['foːrˌʔaːbənt] m evening before,
eve
voran [foˈran] adv before, ahead; **mach ~!**
get on with it!; ~**gehen** (unreg) vi to go
ahead; **einer Sache** dat ~**gehen** to
precede sth; ~**kommen** (unreg) vi to come
along, to make progress
Voranschlag ['foːrˌʔanʃlaːk] m estimate
Vorarbeiter ['foːrˌʔarbaitər] m foreman
voraus [foˈraus] adv ahead; (zeitlich) in
advance; **jdm ~ sein** to be ahead of sb; **im**
~ in advance; ~**gehen** (unreg) vi to go
(on) ahead; (fig) to precede; ~**haben**
(unreg) vt: **jdm etw ~haben** to have the
edge on sb in sth; V~**sage** f prediction;
~**sagen** vt to predict; ~**sehen** (unreg) vt
to foresee; ~**setzen** vt to assume;
~**gesetzt, daß ...** provided that ...;
V~**setzung** f requirement, prerequisite;
V~**sicht** f foresight; **aller V~sicht nach** in
all probability; ~**sichtlich** adv probably
Vorbehalt ['foːrbəhalt] (-(e)s, -e) m
reservation, proviso; v~**en** (unreg) vt:
sich/jdm etw v~en to reserve sth (for
o.s.)/for sb; v~**los** adj unconditional ♦ adv
unconditionally
vorbei [fɔrˈbai] adv by, past; **das ist ~**
that's over; ~**gehen** (unreg) vi to pass by,
to go past; ~**kommen** (unreg) vi: **bei jdm**
~**kommen** to drop in od call in on sb

⚠ *For information on spelling reform see page 615*

vor- *zW:* **~belastet** ['fo:rbəlastət] *adj (fig)* handicapped; **~bereiten** *vt* to prepare; **V~bereitung** *f* preparation; **V~bestellung** *f* advance order; *(von Platz, Tisch etc)* advance booking; **~bestraft** ['fo:rbəʃtra:ft] *adj* previously convicted, with a record

vorbeugen ['fo:rbɔygən] *vt, vr* to lean forward ♦ *vi +dat* to prevent; **~d** *adj* preventive

Vorbeugung *f* prevention; **zur ~ gegen** for the prevention of

Vorbild ['fo:rbɪlt] *nt* model; **sich** *dat* **jdn zum ~ nehmen** to model o.s. on sb; **v~lich** *adj* model, ideal

vorbringen ['fo:rbrɪŋən] *(unreg) vt* to advance, to state

Vorder- ['fɔrdər] *zW:* **~achse** *f* front axle; **v~e(r, s)** *adj* front; **~grund** *m* foreground; **~mann** *(pl* **-männer)** *m* man in front; **jdn auf ~mann bringen** *(umg)* to get sb to shape up; **~seite** *f* front (side); **v~ste(r, s)** *adj* front

vordrängen ['fo:rdrɛŋən] *vr* to push to the front

voreilig ['fo:raɪlɪç] *adj* hasty, rash

voreinander [fo:raɪˈnandər] *adv (räumlich)* in front of each other

voreingenommen ['fo:raɪngənɔmən] *adj* biased; **V~heit** *f* bias

vorenthalten ['fo:rɛnthaltən] *(unreg) vt:* **jdm etw ~** to withhold sth from sb

vorerst ['fo:reːrst] *adv* for the moment *od* present

Vorfahr ['fo:rfa:r] *(-en, -en) m* ancestor

vorfahren *(unreg) vi* to drive (on) ahead; *(vors Haus etc)* to drive up

Vorfahrt *f (AUT)* right of way; **~ achten!** give way!

Vorfahrts- *zW:* **~regel** *f* right of way; **~schild** *nt* give way sign; **~straße** *f* major road

Vorfall ['fo:rfal] *m* incident; **v~en** *(unreg) vi* to occur

vorfinden ['fo:rfɪndən] *(unreg) vt* to find

Vorfreude ['fo:rfrɔydə] *f* (joyful) anticipation

vorführen ['fo:rfy:rən] *vt* to show, to display; **dem Gericht ~** to bring before the court

Vorgabe ['fo:rga:bə] *f (SPORT)* start, handicap ♦ *in zW (COMPUT)* default

Vorgang ['fo:rgaŋ] *m* course of events; *(bes SCI)* process

Vorgänger(in) ['fo:rgɛŋər(ɪn)] *(-s, -) m(f)* predecessor

vorgeben ['fo:rge:bən] *(unreg) vt* to pretend, to use as a pretext; *(SPORT)* to give an advantage *od* a start of

vorgefertigt ['fo:rgəfɛrtɪçt] *adj* prefabricated

vorgehen ['fo:rge:ən] *(unreg) vi (voraus)* to go (on) ahead; *(nach vorn)* to go up front; *(handeln)* to act, to proceed; *(Uhr)* to be fast; *(Vorrang haben)* to take precedence; *(passieren)* to go on

Vorgehen *(-s) nt* action

Vorgeschichte ['fo:rgəʃɪçtə] *f* past history

Vorgeschmack ['fo:rgəʃmak] *m* foretaste

Vorgesetzte(r) ['fo:rgəzɛtstə(r)] *f(m)* superior

vorgestern ['fo:rgɛstərn] *adv* the day before yesterday

vorhaben ['fo:rha:bən] *(unreg) vt* to intend; **hast du schon was vor?** have you got anything on?; **V~ (-s, -)** *nt* intention

vorhalten ['fo:rhaltən] *(unreg) vt* to hold *od* put up ♦ *vi* to last; **jdm etw ~** *(fig)* to reproach sb for sth

vorhanden [fo:rˈhandən] *adj* existing; *(erhältlich)* available

Vorhang ['fo:rhaŋ] *m* curtain

Vorhängeschloß ⚠ ['fo:rhɛŋəʃlɔs] *nt* padlock

vorher [fo:rˈhe:r] *adv* before(hand); **~bestimmen** *vt (Schicksal)* to preordain; **~gehen** *(unreg) vi* to precede; **~ig** *adj* previous

Vorherrschaft ['fo:rhɛrʃaft] *f* predominance, supremacy

vorherrschen ['fo:rhɛrʃən] *vi* to predominate

vorher- [fo:rˈhe:r] *zW:* **V~sage** *f* forecast; **~sagen** *vt* to forecast, to predict; **~sehbar** *adj* predictable; **~sehen** *(unreg)*

⚠ *Informationen zur Rechtschreibreform Seite 615*

vt to foresee

vorhin [fo:r'hɪn] *adv* not long ago, just now;
~ein ⚠ *adv*: **im ~ein** beforehand

vorig ['fo:rɪç] *adj* previous, last

Vorkämpfer(in) ['fo:rkɛmpfər(ɪn)] *m(f)*
pioneer

Vorkaufsrecht ['fo:rkaufsrɛçt] *nt* option to
buy

Vorkehrung ['fo:rke:rʊŋ] *f* precaution

vorkommen ['fo:rkɔmən] (*unreg*) *vi* to
come forward; (*geschehen, sich finden*) to
occur; (*scheinen*) to seem (to be); **sich** *dat*
dumm *etc* **~** to feel stupid *etc*; **V~ (-s, -)**
nt occurrence

Vorkriegs- ['fo:rkri:ks] *in zW* prewar

Vorladung ['fo:rla:dʊŋ] *f* summons *sg*

Vorlage ['fo:rla:gə] *f* model, pattern;
(*Gesetzes~*) bill; (*SPORT*) pass

vorlassen ['fo:rlasən] (*unreg*) *vt* to admit;
(*vorgehen lassen*) to allow to go in front

vorläufig ['fo:rlɔyfɪç] *adj* temporary,
provisional

vorlaut ['fo:rlaut] *adj* impertinent, cheeky

vorlesen ['fo:rle:zən] (*unreg*) *vt* to read (out)

Vorlesung *f* (*UNIV*) lecture

vorletzte(r, s) ['fo:rlɛtstə(r, s)] *adj* last but
one

Vorliebe ['fo:rli:bə] *f* preference, partiality

vorliebnehmen ⚠ [fo:r'li:pne:mən]
(*unreg*) *vi*: **~ mit** to make do with

vorliegen ['fo:rli:gən] (*unreg*) *vi* to be
(here); **etw liegt jdm vor** sb has sth; **~d**
adj present, at issue

vormachen ['fo:rmaxən] *vt*: **jdm etw ~** to
show sb how to do sth; (*fig*) to fool sb; to
have sb on

Vormachtstellung ['fo:rmaxtʃtɛlʊŋ] *f*
supremacy, hegemony

Vormarsch ['fo:rmarʃ] *m* advance

vormerken ['fo:rmɛrkən] *vt* to book

Vormittag ['fo:rmɪta:k] *m* morning; **v~s** *adv*
in the morning, before noon

vorn [fɔrn] *adv* in front; **von ~ anfangen** to
start at the beginning; **nach ~** to the front

Vorname ['fo:rna:mə] *m* first name,
Christian name

vorne ['fɔrnə] *adv* = **vorn**

vornehm ['fo:rne:m] *adj* distinguished;
refined; elegant

vornehmen (*unreg*) *vt* (*fig*) to carry out;
sich *dat* **etw ~** to start on sth; (*beschließen*)
to decide to do sth; **sich** *dat* **jdn ~** to tell
sb off

vornherein ['fɔrnhɛraɪn] *adv*: **von ~** from
the start

Vorort ['fo:rɔrt] *m* suburb

Vorrang ['fo:rraŋ] *m* precedence, priority;
v~ig *adj* of prime importance, primary

Vorrat ['fo:rra:t] *m* stock, supply

vorrätig ['fo:rrɛ:tɪç] *adj* in stock

Vorratskammer *f* pantry

Vorrecht ['fo:rrɛçt] *nt* privilege

Vorrichtung ['fo:rrɪçtʊŋ] *f* device,
contrivance

vorrücken ['fo:rrʏkən] *vi* to advance ♦ *vt* to
move forward

Vorsaison ['fo:rzɛzõ:] *f* early season

Vorsatz ['fo:rzats] *m* intention; (*JUR*) intent;
einen ~ fassen to make a resolution

vorsätzlich ['fo:rzɛtslɪç] *adj* intentional; (*JUR*)
premeditated ♦ *adv* intentionally

Vorschau ['fo:rʃau] *f* (*RAD, TV*) (programme)
preview; (*Film*) trailer

Vorschlag ['fo:rʃla:k] *m* suggestion,
proposal; **v~en** (*unreg*) *vt* to suggest, to
propose

vorschreiben ['fo:rʃraɪbən] (*unreg*) *vt* to
prescribe, to specify

Vorschrift ['fo:rʃrɪft] *f* regulation(s); rule(s);
(*Anweisungen*) instruction(s); **Dienst nach ~**
work-to-rule; **v~smäßig** *adj* as per
regulations/instructions

Vorschuß ⚠ ['fo:rʃʊs] *m* advance

vorsehen ['fo:rze:ən] (*unreg*) *vt* to provide
for, to plan ♦ *vr* to take care, to be careful
♦ *vi* to be visible

Vorsehung *f* providence

Vorsicht ['fo:rzɪçt] *f* caution, care; **~!** look
out!, take care!; (*auf Schildern*) caution!,
danger!; **~, Stufe!** mind the step!; **v~ig** *adj*
cautious, careful; **v~shalber** *adv* just in
case

Vorsilbe ['fo:rzɪlbə] *f* prefix

vorsingen ['fo:rzɪŋən] *vt* (*vor Zuhörern*) to

⚠ *For information on spelling reform see page 615*

sing (to); (*in Prüfung, für Theater etc*) to audition (for) ♦ *vi* to sing

Vorsitz ['foːrzɪts] *m* chair(manship); **~ende(r)** *f(m)* chairman(-woman)

Vorsorge ['foːrzɔrgə] *f* precaution(s), provision(s); **v~n** *vi*: **v~n für** to make provision(s) for; **~untersuchung** *f* check-up

vorsorglich ['foːrzɔrklɪç] *adv* as a precaution

Vorspeise ['foːrʃpaɪzə] *f* hors d'oeuvre, appetizer

Vorspiel ['foːrʃpiːl] *nt* prelude

vorspielen *vt*: **jdm etw ~** (*MUS*) to play sth for *od* to sb ♦ *vi* (*zur Prüfung etc*) to play for *od* to sb

vorsprechen ['foːrʃprɛçən] (*unreg*) *vt* to say out loud, to recite ♦ *vi*: **bei jdm ~** to call on sb

Vorsprung ['foːrʃprʊŋ] *m* projection, ledge; (*fig*) advantage, start

Vorstadt ['foːrʃtat] *f* suburbs *pl*

Vorstand ['foːrʃtant] *m* executive committee; (*COMM*) board (of directors); (*Person*) director, manager

vorstehen ['foːrʃteːən] (*unreg*) *vi* to project; **einer Sache** *dat* **~** (*fig*) to be the head of sth

vorstell- ['foːrʃtɛl] *zW*: **~bar** *adj* conceivable; **~en** *vt* to put forward; (*bekannt machen*) to introduce; (*darstellen*) to represent; **~en vor** +*akk* to put in front of; **sich** *dat* **etw ~en** to imagine sth; **V~ung** *f* (*Bekanntmachen*) introduction; (*THEAT etc*) performance; (*Gedanke*) idea, thought

vorstoßen ['foːrʃtoːsən] (*unreg*) *vi* (*ins Unbekannte*) to venture (forth)

Vorstrafe ['foːrʃtraːfə] *f* previous conviction

Vortag ['foːrtaːk] *m*: **am ~ einer Sache** *gen* on the day before sth

vortäuschen ['foːrtɔʏʃən] *vt* to feign, to pretend

Vorteil ['foːrtaɪl] (**-s, -e**) *m*: **~ (gegenüber)** advantage (over); **im ~ sein** to have the advantage; **v~haft** *adj* advantageous

Vortrag ['foːrtraːk] (**-(e)s, Vorträge**) *m* talk,

lecture; **v~en** [-gən] (*unreg*) *vt* to carry forward; (*fig*) to recite; (*Rede*) to deliver; (*Lied*) to perform; (*Meinung etc*) to express

vortreten ['foːrtreːtən] (*unreg*) *vi* to step forward; (*Augen etc*) to protrude

vorüber [fo'ryːbər] *adv* past, over; **~gehen** (*unreg*) *vi* to pass (by); **~gehen an** +*dat* (*fig*) to pass over; **~gehend** *adj* temporary, passing

Vorurteil ['foːrʔʊrtaɪl] *nt* prejudice

Vorverkauf ['foːrfɛrkaʊf] *m* advance booking

Vorwahl ['foːrvaːl] *f* preliminary election; (*TEL*) dialling code

Vorwand ['foːrvant] (**-(e)s, Vorwände**) *m* pretext

vorwärts ['foːrvɛrts] *adv* forward; **V~gang** *m* (*AUT etc*) forward gear; **~gehen** △ (*unreg*) *vi* to progress; **~kommen** △ (*unreg*) *vi* to get on, to make progress

Vorwäsche *f* prewash

vorweg [foːr'vɛk] *adv* in advance; **~nehmen** (*unreg*) *vt* to anticipate

vorweisen ['foːrvaɪzən] (*unreg*) *vt* to show, to produce

vorwerfen ['foːrvɛrfən] (*unreg*) *vt*: **jdm etw ~** to reproach sb for sth, to accuse sb of sth; **sich** *dat* **nichts vorzuwerfen haben** to have nothing to reproach o.s. with

vorwiegend ['foːrviːgənt] *adj* predominant ♦ *adv* predominantly

vorwitzig ['foːrvɪtsɪç] *adj* (*Mensch, Bemerkung*) cheeky

Vorwort ['foːrvɔrt] (**-(e)s, -e**) *nt* preface

Vorwurf ['foːrvʊrf] *m* reproach; **jdm/sich Vorwürfe machen** to reproach sb/o.s.; **v~svoll** *adj* reproachful

vorzeigen ['foːrtsaɪgən] *vt* to show, to produce

vorzeitig ['foːrtsaɪtɪç] *adj* premature

vorziehen ['foːrtsiːən] (*unreg*) *vt* to pull forward; (*Gardinen*) to draw; (*lieber haben*) to prefer

Vorzimmer ['foːrtsɪmər] *nt* (*Büro*) outer office

Vorzug ['foːrtsuːk] *m* preference; (*gute Eigenschaft*) merit, good quality; (*Vorteil*)

advantage

vorzüglich [foːrˈtsyːklɪç] adj excellent

Vorzugspreis m special discount price

vulgär [vʊlˈgɛːr] adj vulgar

Vulkan [vʊlˈkaːn] (-s, -e) m volcano

W, w

Waage [ˈvaːgə] f scales pl; (*ASTROL*) Libra; **w~recht** adj horizontal

Wabe [ˈvaːbə] f honeycomb

wach [vax] adj awake; (*fig*) alert; **W~e** f guard, watch; **W~e halten** to keep watch; **W~e stehen** to stand guard; **~en** vi to be awake; (*Wache halten*) to guard

Wachs [vaks] (-es, -e) nt wax

wachsam [ˈvaxzaːm] adj watchful, vigilant, alert

wachsen (*unreg*) vi to grow

Wachstuch [ˈvakstuːx] nt oilcloth

Wachstum [ˈvakstuːm] (-s) nt growth

Wächter [ˈvɛçtər] (-s, -) m guard, warden, keeper; (*Parkplatz~*) attendant

wackel- [ˈvakəl] zW: **~ig** adj shaky, wobbly; **W~kontakt** m loose connection; **~n** vi to shake; (*fig: Position*) to be shaky

wacker [ˈvakər] adj valiant, stout ♦ adv well, bravely

Wade [ˈvaːdə] f (*ANAT*) calf

Waffe [ˈvafə] f weapon

Waffel [ˈvafəl] (-, -n) f waffle; wafer

Waffen- zW: **~schein** m gun licence; **~stillstand** m armistice, truce

Wagemut [ˈvaːgəmuːt] m daring

wagen [ˈvaːgən] vt to venture, to dare

Wagen [ˈvaːgən] (-s, -) m vehicle; (*Auto*) car; (*EISENB*) carriage; (*Pferde~*) cart; **~heber** (-s, -) m jack

Waggon ⚠ [vaˈgõː] (-s, -s) m carriage; (*Güter~*) goods van, freight truck (*US*)

Wagnis [ˈvaːknɪs] (-ses, -se) nt risk

Wahl [vaːl] (-, -en) f choice; (*POL*) election; **zweite ~** (*COMM*) seconds pl

wähl- [ˈvɛːl] zW: **~bar** adj eligible; **~en** vt, vi to choose; (*POL*) to elect, to vote (for); (*TEL*) to dial; **W~er(in)** (-s, -) m(f) voter;

~erisch adj fastidious, particular

Wahl- zW: **~fach** nt optional subject; **~gang** m ballot; **~kabine** f polling booth; **~kampf** m election campaign; **~kreis** m constituency; **~lokal** nt polling station; **w~los** adv at random; **~recht** nt franchise; **~spruch** m motto; **~urne** f ballot box

Wahn [vaːn] (-(e)s) m delusion; folly; **~sinn** m madness; **w~sinnig** adj insane, mad ♦ adv (*umg*) incredibly

wahr [vaːr] adj true

wahren vt to maintain, to keep

während [ˈvɛːrənt] präp +gen during ♦ konj while; **~dessen** adv meanwhile

wahr- zW: **~haben** (*unreg*) vt: **etw nicht ~haben wollen** to refuse to admit sth; **~haft** adv (*tatsächlich*) truly; **~haftig** [vaːrˈhaftɪç] adj true, real ♦ adv really; **W~heit** f truth; **~nehmen** (*unreg*) vt to perceive, to observe; **W~nehmung** f perception; **~sagen** vi to prophesy, to tell fortunes; **W~sager(in)** (-s, -) m(f) fortune teller; **~scheinlich** [vaːrˈʃaɪnlɪç] adj probable ♦ adv probably; **W~'scheinlichkeit** f probability; **aller W~scheinlichkeit nach** in all probability

Währung [ˈvɛːrʊŋ] f currency

Wahrzeichen nt symbol

Waise [ˈvaɪzə] f orphan; **~nhaus** nt orphanage

Wald [valt] (-(e)s, ¨er) m wood(s); (*groß*) forest; **~brand** m forest fire; **~sterben** nt *trees dying due to pollution*

Wales [weɪlz] (-) nt Wales

Wal(fisch) [ˈvaːl(fɪʃ)] (-(e)s, -e) m whale

Waliser [vaˈliːzər] (-s, -) m Welshman; **Waliserin** [vaˈliːzərɪn] f Welsh woman; **walisisch** [vaˈliːzɪʃ] adj Welsh

Walkman [ˈwɔːkman] ®; (-s, **Walkmen**) m Walkman ®, personal stereo

Wall [val] (-(e)s, ¨e) m embankment; (*Bollwerk*) rampart

Wallfahr- zW: **~er(in)** m(f) pilgrim; **~t** f pilgrimage

Walnuß ⚠ [ˈvalnʊs] f walnut

Walroß ⚠ [ˈvalrɔs] nt walrus

Walze [ˈvaltsə] f (*Gerät*) cylinder; (*Fahrzeug*)

⚠ *For information on spelling reform see page 615*

roller; **w~n** *vt* to roll (out)

wälzen ['vɛltsən] *vt* to roll (over); (*Bücher*) to hunt through; (*Probleme*) to deliberate on ♦ *vr* to wallow; (*vor Schmerzen*) to roll about; (*im Bett*) to toss and turn

Walzer ['valtsər] (**-s, -**) *m* waltz

Wand [vant] (**-, ̈e**) *f* wall; (*Trenn~*) partition; (*Berg~*) precipice

Wandel ['vandəl] (**-s**) *m* change; **w~bar** *adj* changeable, variable; **w~n** *vt, vr* to change ♦ *vi* (*gehen*) to walk

Wander- ['vandər] *zW*: **~er** (**-s, -**) *m* hiker, rambler; **~karte** *f* map of country walks; **w~n** *vi* to hike; (*Blick*) to wander; (*Gedanken*) to stray; **~schaft** *f* travelling; **~ung** *f* walk, hike; **~weg** *m* trail, walk

Wandlung *f* change, transformation

Wange ['vaŋə] *f* cheek

wanken ['vaŋkən] *vi* to stagger; (*fig*) to waver

wann [van] *adv* when

Wanne ['vanə] *f* tub

Wanze ['vantsə] *f* bug

Wappen ['vapən] (**-s, -**) *nt* coat of arms, crest; **~kunde** *f* heraldry

war *etc* [va:r] *vb siehe* **sein**

Ware ['va:rə] *f* ware

Waren- *zW*: **~haus** *nt* department store; **~lager** *nt* stock, store; **~muster** *nt* trade sample; **~probe** *f* sample; **~sendung** *f* trade sample (*sent by post*); **~zeichen** *nt*: **(eingetragenes) ~zeichen** (registered) trademark

warf *etc* [va:rf] *vb siehe* **werfen**

warm [varm] *adj* warm; (*Essen*) hot

Wärm- ['vɛrm] *zW*: **~e** *f* warmth; **w~en** *vt, vr* to warm (up), to heat (up); **~flasche** *f* hot-water bottle

Warn- ['varn] *zW*: **~blinkanlage** *f* (*AUT*) hazard warning lights *pl*; **~dreieck** *nt* warning triangle; **w~en** *vt* to warn; **~ung** *f* warning

warten ['vartən] *vi*: **~ (auf +akk)** to wait (for); **auf sich ~ lassen** to take a long time

Wärter(in) ['vɛrtər(ɪn)] (**-s, -**) *m(f)* attendant

Warte- ['vartə] *zW*: **~saal** *m* (*EISENB*) waiting room; **~zimmer** *nt* waiting room

Wartung *f* servicing; service; **~ und Instandhaltung** maintenance

warum [va'rʊm] *adv* why

Warze ['vartsə] *f* wart

was [vas] *pron* what; (*umg: etwas*) something; **~ für (ein) ...** what sort of ...

waschbar *adj* washable

Waschbecken *nt* washbasin

Wäsche ['vɛʃə] *f* wash(ing); (*Bett~*) linen; (*Unter~*) underclothing

waschecht *adj* colourfast; (*fig*) genuine

Wäsche- *zW*: **~klammer** *f* clothes peg (*BRIT*), clothespin (*US*); **~leine** *f* washing line (*BRIT*)

waschen ['vaʃən] (*unreg*) *vt, vi* to wash ♦ *vr* to (have a) wash; **sich** *dat* **die Hände ~** to wash one's hands

Wäsche'rei *f* laundry

Wasch- *zW*: **~gelegenheit** *f* washing facilities; **~küche** *f* laundry room; **~lappen** *m* face flannel, washcloth (*US*); (*umg*) sissy; **~maschine** *f* washing machine; **~mittel** *nt* detergent, washing powder; **~pulver** *nt* detergent, washing powder; **~raum** *m* washroom; **~salon** *m* Launderette ®

Wasser ['vasər] (**-s, -**) *nt* water; **~ball** *m* water polo; **w~dicht** *adj* waterproof; **~fall** *m* waterfall; **~farbe** *f* watercolour; **~hahn** *m* tap, faucet (*US*); **~kraftwerk** *nt* hydroelectric power station; **~leitung** *f* water pipe; **~mann** *m* (*ASTROL*) Aquarius

wässern ['vɛsərn] *vt, vi* to water

Wasser- *zW*: **w~scheu** *adj* afraid of (the) water; **~ski** ['vasərʃi:] *nt* water-skiing; **~stoff** *m* hydrogen; **~waage** *f* spirit level; **~zeichen** *nt* watermark

wäßrig ⚠ ['vɛsrɪç] *adj* watery

Watt [vat] (**-(e)s, -en**) *nt* mud flats *pl*

Watte *f* cotton wool, absorbent cotton (*US*)

WC ['ve:'tse:] (**-s, -s**) *nt abk* (= water closet) W.C.

Web- ['ve:b] *zW*: **w~en** (*unreg*) *vt* to weave; **~er** (**-s, -**) *m* weaver; **~e'rei** *f* (*Betrieb*) weaving mill; **~stuhl** *m* loom

Wechsel ['vɛksəl] (**-s, -**) *m* change; (*COMM*) bill of exchange; **~geld** *nt* change; **w~haft**

adj (*Wetter*) variable; **~jahre** *pl* change of life *sg*; **~kurs** *m* rate of exchange; **w~n** *vt* to change; (*Blicke*) to exchange ♦ *vi* to change; to vary; (*Geldwechseln*) to have change; **~strom** *m* alternating current; **~stube** *f* bureau de change; **~wirkung** *f* interaction

Weck- ['vɛk] *zW:* **~dienst** *m* alarm call service; **w~en** *vt* to wake (up); to call; **~er** (**-s, -**) *m* alarm clock

wedeln ['ve:dəln] *vi* (*mit Schwanz*) to wag; (*mit Fächer etc*) to wave

weder ['ve:dər] *konj* neither; **~ ... noch ...** neither ... nor ....

Weg [ve:k] (**-(e)s, -e**) *m* way; (*Pfad*) path; (*Route*) route; **sich auf den ~ machen** to be on one's way; **jdm aus dem ~ gehen** to keep out of sb's way

weg [vɛk] *adv* away, off; **über etw** *akk* **~ sein** to be over sth; **er war schon ~** he had already left; **Finger ~!** hands off!

wegbleiben (*unreg*) *vi* to stay away

wegen ['ve:gən] *präp* +*gen* (*umg:* +*dat*) because of

weg- ['vɛk] *zW:* **~fallen** (*unreg*) *vi* to be left out; (*Ferien, Bezahlung*) to be cancelled; (*aufhören*) to cease; **~gehen** (*unreg*) *vi* to go away; to leave; **~lassen** (*unreg*) *vt* to leave out; **~laufen** (*unreg*) *vi* to run away *od* off; **~legen** *vt* to put aside; **~machen** (*umg*) *vt* to get rid of; **~müssen** (*unreg*) (*umg*) *vi* to have to go; **~nehmen** (*unreg*) *vt* to take away; **~tun** (*unreg*) *vt* to put away; **W~weiser** [ve:k-] (**-s, -**) *m* road sign, signpost; **~werfen** (*unreg*) *vt* to throw away

weh [ve:] *adj* sore; **~ tun** to hurt, to be sore; **jdm/sich ~ tun** to hurt sb/o.s.; **~(e)** *excl:* **~(e), wenn du ...** woe betide you if ...; **o ~!** oh dear!; **~e!** just you dare!

wehen *vt, vi* to blow; (*Fahnen*) to flutter

weh- *zW:* **~leidig** *adj* whiny, whining; **~mütig** *adj* melancholy

Wehr [ve:r] (**-, -en**) *f:* **sich zur ~ setzen** to defend o.s.; **~dienst** *m* military service; **~dienstverweigerer** *m* ≈ conscientious objector; **w~en** *vr* to defend o.s.; **w~los**

adj defenceless; **~pflicht** *f* compulsory military service; **w~pflichtig** *adj* liable for military service

---
WEHRDIENST

🛈 **Wehrdienst** is military service which is still compulsory in Germany. All young men receive their call-up papers at 18 and all those pronounced physically fit are required to spend 10 months in the **Bundeswehr**. Conscientious objectors are allowed to do **Zivildienst** as an alternative, after attending a hearing and presenting their case.

Weib [vaip] (**-(e)s, -er**) *nt* woman, female; wife; **~chen** *nt* female; **w~lich** *adj* feminine

weich [vaiç] *adj* soft; **W~e** *f* (*EISENB*) points *pl*; **~en** (*unreg*) *vi* to yield, to give way; **W~heit** *f* softness; **~lich** *adj* soft, namby-pamby

Weide ['vaidə] *f* (*Baum*) willow; (*Gras*) pasture; **w~n** *vi* to graze ♦ *vr:* **sich an etw** *dat* **w~n** to delight in sth

weigern ['vaigərn] *vr* to refuse

Weigerung ['vaigərʊŋ] *f* refusal

Weihe ['vaiə] *f* consecration; (*Priester~*) ordination; **w~n** *vt* to consecrate; to ordain

Weihnacht- *zW:* **~en** (**-**) *nt* Christmas; **w~lich** *adj* Christmas *cpd*

Weihnachts- *zW:* **~abend** *m* Christmas Eve; **~lied** *nt* Christmas carol; **~mann** *m* Father Christmas, Santa Claus; **~markt** *m* Christmas fair; **~tag** *m* Christmas Day; **zweiter ~tag** Boxing Day

---
WEIHNACHTSMARKT

🛈 The **Weihnachtsmarkt** is a market held in most large towns in Germany in the weeks prior to Christmas. People visit it to buy presents, toys and Christmas decorations, and to enjoy the festive atmosphere. Traditional Christmas food and drink can also be consumed there, for example, **Lebkuchen** and **Glühwein**.

⚠ *For information on spelling reform see page 615*

Weihwasser *nt* holy water

weil [vaɪl] *konj* because

Weile ['vaɪlə] (-) *f* while, short time

Wein [vaɪn] (-(e)s, -e) *m* wine; (*Pflanze*) vine; **~bau** *m* cultivation of vines; **~berg** *m* vineyard; **~bergschnecke** *f* snail; **~brand** *m* brandy

weinen *vt, vi* to cry; **das ist zum W~** it's enough to make you cry *od* weep

Wein- *zW:* **~glas** *nt* wine glass; **~karte** *f* wine list; **~lese** *f* vintage; **~probe** *f* wine-tasting; **~rebe** *f* vine; **w~rot** *adj* burgundy, claret, wine-red; **~stock** *m* vine; **~stube** *f* wine bar; **~traube** *f* grape

weise ['vaɪzə] *adj* wise

Weise *f* manner, way; (*Lied*) tune; **auf diese ~** in this way

weisen (*unreg*) *vt* to show

Weisheit ['vaɪshaɪt] *f* wisdom; **~szahn** *m* wisdom tooth

weiß [vaɪs] *adj* white ♦ *vb siehe* **wissen**; **W~bier** *nt* weissbier (*light, fizzy beer made using top-fermentation yeast*); **W~brot** *nt* white bread; **~en** *vt* to whitewash; **W~glut** *f* (*TECH*) incandescence; **jdn bis zur W~glut bringen** (*fig*) to make sb see red; **W~kohl** *m* (white) cabbage; **W~wein** *m* white wine; **W~wurst** *f* veal sausage

weit [vaɪt] *adj* wide; (*Begriff*) broad; (*Reise, Wurf*) long ♦ *adv* far; **wie ~ ist es ...?** how far is it ...?; **in ~er Ferne** in the far distance; **das geht zu ~** that's going too far; **~aus** *adv* by far; **~blickend** ⚠ *adj* far-seeing; **W~e** *f* width; (*Raum*) space; (*von Entfernung*) distance; **~en** *vt, vr* to widen

weiter ['vaɪtər] *adj* wider; broader; farther (away); (*zusätzlich*) further ♦ *adv* further; **ohne ~es** without further ado; just like that; **~ nichts/niemand** nothing/nobody else; **~arbeiten** *vi* to go on working; **~bilden** *vr* to continue one's education; **~empfehlen** (*unreg*) *vt* to recommend (to others); **W~fahrt** *f* continuation of the journey; **~führen** *vi* (*Straße*) to lead on (to) ♦ *vt* (*fortsetzen*) to continue, carry on; **~gehen** (*unreg*) *vi* to go on; **~hin** *adv:* **etw ~hin tun** to go on doing sth; **~kommen**

(*unreg*) *vi* (*fig: mit Arbeit*) to make progress; **~leiten** *vt* to pass on; **~machen** *vt, vi* to continue

weit- *zW:* **~gehend** *adj* considerable ♦ *adv* largely; **~läufig** *adj* (*Gebäude*) spacious; (*Erklärung*) lengthy; (*Verwandter*) distant; **~reichend** ⚠ *adj* long-range; (*fig*) far-reaching; **~schweifig** *adj* long-winded; **~sichtig** *adj* (*MED*) long-sighted; (*fig*) far-sighted; **W~sprung** *m* long jump; **~verbreitet** ⚠ *adj* widespread

Weizen ['vaɪtsən] (-s, -) *m* wheat

┌─────────────────────────────┐
│ *SCHLÜSSELWORT* │
└─────────────────────────────┘

welche(r, s) *interrogativ pron* which; **welcher von beiden?** which (one) of the two?; **welchen hast du genommen?** which (one) did you take?; **welche eine ...!** what a ...!; **welche Freude!** what joy! ♦ *indef pron* some; (*in Fragen*) any; **ich habe welche** I have some; **haben Sie welche?** do you have any? ♦ *relativ pron* (*bei Menschen*) who; (*bei Sachen*) which, that; **welche(r, s) auch immer** whoever/whichever/whatever

welk [vɛlk] *adj* withered; **~en** *vi* to wither

Welle ['vɛlə] *f* wave; (*TECH*) shaft

Wellen- *zW:* **~bereich** *m* waveband; **~länge** *f* (*auch fig*) wavelength; **~linie** *f* wavy line; **~sittich** *m* budgerigar

Welt [vɛlt] (-, -en) *f* world; **~all** *nt* universe; **~anschauung** *f* philosophy of life; **w~berühmt** *adj* world-famous; **~krieg** *m* world war; **w~lich** *adj* worldly; (*nicht kirchlich*) secular; **~macht** *f* world power; **~meister** *m* world champion; **~raum** *m* space; **~reise** *f* trip round the world; **~stadt** *f* metropolis; **w~weit** *adj* world-wide

wem [ve:m] (*dat von* **wer**) *pron* to whom

wen [ve:n] (*akk von* **wer**) *pron* whom

Wende ['vɛndə] *f* turn; (*Veränderung*) change; **~kreis** *m* (*GEOG*) tropic; (*AUT*) turning circle; **~ltreppe** *f* spiral staircase; **w~n** (*unreg*) *vt, vi, vr* to turn; **sich an jdn w~n** to go/come to sb

wendig ['vɛndɪç] *adj* (*Auto etc*)
manœuvrable; (*fig*) agile

Wendung *f* turn; (*Rede~*) idiom

wenig ['ve:nɪç] *adj, adv* little; ~**e** *pron pl* few
pl; ~**er** *adj* less; (*mit pl*) fewer ♦ *adv* less;
~**ste(r, s)** *adj* least; **am** ~**sten** least;
~**stens** *adv* at least

┌─ *SCHLÜSSELWORT* ─┐

wenn [vɛn] *konj* **1** (*falls, bei Wünschen*) if;
wenn auch ..., selbst wenn ... even if ...;
wenn ich doch ... if only I ...
2 (*zeitlich*) when; **immer wenn** whenever

└─────────────┘

wennschon ['vɛnʃo:n] *adv*: **na** ~ so what?;
~, **dennschon!** in for a penny, in for a
pound

wer [ve:r] *pron* who

Werbe- ['vɛrbə] *zW*: ~**fernsehen** *nt*
commercial television; ~**geschenk** *nt* gift
(*from company*); (*zu Gekauftem*) free gift;
w~n (*unreg*) *vt* to win; (*Mitglied*) to recruit
♦ *vi* to advertise; **um jdn/etw w~n** to try to
win sb/sth; **für jdn/etw w~n** to promote
sb/sth

Werbung *f* advertising; (*von Mitgliedern*)
recruitment; ~ **um jdn/etw** promotion of
sb/sth

Werdegang ['ve:rdəgaŋ] *m* (*Laufbahn*)
development; (*beruflich*) career

┌─ *SCHLÜSSELWORT* ─┐

werden ['ve:rdən] (*pt* **wurde**, *pp* **geworden**
od (*bei Passiv*) **worden**) *vi* to become; **was
ist aus ihm/aus der Sache geworden?**
what became of him/it?; **es ist nichts/gut
geworden** it came to nothing/turned out
well; **es wird Nacht/Tag** it's getting dark/
light; **mir wird kalt** I'm getting cold; **mir
wird schlecht** I feel ill; **Erster werden** to
come *od* be first; **das muß anders werden**
that'll have to change; **rot/zu Eis werden**
to turn red/to ice; **was willst du** (*mal*)
werden? what do you want to be?; **die
Fotos sind gut geworden** the photos have
come out nicely
♦ *als Hilfsverb* **1** (*bei Futur*): **er wird es tun**

he will *od* he'll do it; **er wird das nicht tun**
he will not *od* he won't do it; **es wird
gleich regnen** it's going to rain
2 (*bei Konjunktiv*): **ich würde ...** I would ...;
er würde gern ... he would *od* he'd like to
...; **ich würde lieber ...** I would *od* I'd
rather ...
3 (*bei Vermutung*): **sie wird in der Küche
sein** she will be in the kitchen
4 (*bei Passiv*): **gebraucht werden** to be
used; **er ist erschossen worden** he has *od*
he's been shot; **mir wurde gesagt, daß ...**
I was told that ...

└─────────────┘

werfen ['vɛrfən] (*unreg*) *vt* to throw

Werft [vɛrft] (-, -en) *f* shipyard, dockyard

Werk [vɛrk] (-(e)s, -e) *nt* work; (*Tätigkeit*)
job; (*Fabrik, Mechanismus*) works *pl*; **ans** ~
gehen to set to work; ~**statt** (-, -**stätten**) *f*
workshop; (*AUT*) garage; ~**tag** *m* working
day; **w~tags** *adv* on working days;
w~tätig *adj* working; ~**zeug** *nt* tool

Wermut ['ve:rmu:t] (-(e)s) *m* wormwood;
(*Wein*) vermouth

Wert [ve:rt] (-(e)s, -e) *m* worth; (*FIN*) value;
~ **legen auf** +*akk* to attach importance to;
es hat doch keinen ~ it's useless; **w~** *adj*
worth; (*geschätzt*) dear; worthy; **das ist
nichts/viel w~** it's not worth anything/it's
worth a lot; **das ist es/er mir w~** it's/he's
worth that to me; ~**angabe** *f* declaration
of value; ~**brief** *m* registered letter
(*containing sth of value*); **w~en** *vt* to rate;
~**gegenstände** *mpl* valuables; **w~los** *adj*
worthless; ~**papier** *nt* security; **w~voll** *adj*
valuable

Wesen ['ve:zən] (-s, -) *nt* (*Geschöpf*) being;
(*Natur, Charakter*) nature; **w~tlich** *adj*
significant; (*beträchtlich*) considerable

weshalb [vɛs'halp] *adv* why

Wespe ['vɛspə] *f* wasp

wessen ['vɛsən] (*gen von* **wer**) *pron* whose

Weste ['vɛstə] *f* waistcoat, vest (*US*); (*Woll~*)
cardigan

West- *zW*: ~**en** (-s) *m* west; ~**europa** *nt*
Western Europe; **w~lich** *adj* western ♦ *adv*
to the west

⚠ *For information on spelling reform see page 615*

weswegen [vɛsˈveːgən] *adv* why

wett [vɛt] *adj* even; **W~bewerb** *m* competition; **W~e** *f* bet, wager; **~en** *vt, vi* to bet

Wetter [ˈvɛtər] (**-s, -**) *nt* weather; **~bericht** *m* weather report; **~dienst** *m* meteorological service; **~lage** *f* (weather) situation; **~vorhersage** *f* weather forecast; **~warte** *f* weather station

Wett- *zW:* **~kampf** *m* contest; **~lauf** *m* race; **w~machen** *vt* to make good

wichtig [ˈvɪçtɪç] *adj* important; **W~keit** *f* importance

wickeln [ˈvɪkəln] *vt* to wind; (*Haare*) to set; (*Kind*) to change; **jdn/etw in etw** *akk* **~** to wrap sb/sth in sth

Wickelraum *m* mothers' (and babies') room

Widder [ˈvɪdər] (**-s, -**) *m* ram; (*ASTROL*) Aries

wider [ˈviːdər] *präp +akk* against; **~'fahren** (*unreg*) *vi* to happen; **~'legen** *vt* to refute

widerlich [ˈviːdərlɪç] *adj* disgusting, repulsive

wider- [ˈviːdər] *zW:* **~rechtlich** *adj* unlawful; **W~rede** *f* contradiction; **~'rufen** (*unreg*) *vt insep* to retract; (*Anordnung*) to revoke; (*Befehl*) to countermand; **~'setzen** *vr insep:* **sich jdm/etw ~setzen** to oppose sb/sth

widerspenstig [ˈviːdərʃpɛnstɪç] *adj* wilful

wider- [ˈviːdər] *zW:* **~spiegeln** *vt* (*Entwicklung, Erscheinung*) to mirror, reflect ♦ *vr* to be reflected; **~'sprechen** (*unreg*) *vi insep:* **jdm ~sprechen** to contradict sb

Widerspruch [ˈviːdərʃprʊx] *m* contradiction; **w~slos** *adv* without arguing

Widerstand [ˈviːdərʃtant] *m* resistance

Widerstands- *zW:* **~bewegung** *f* resistance (movement); **w~fähig** *adj* resistant, tough; **w~los** *adj* unresisting; **wider'stehen** (*unreg*) *vi insep:* **jdm/etw ~** to withstand sb/sth

wider- [ˈviːdər] *zW:* **~wärtig** *adj* nasty, horrid; **W~wille** *m:* **W~wille (gegen)** aversion (to); **~willig** *adj* unwilling, reluctant

widmen [ˈvɪtmən] *vt* to dedicate; to devote

♦ *vr* to devote o.s.

widrig [ˈviːdrɪç] *adj* (*Umstände*) adverse

SCHLÜSSELWORT
---

wie [viː] *adv* how; **wie groß/schnell?** how big/fast?; **wie wär's?** how about it?; **wie ist er?** what's he like?; **wie gut du das kannst!** you're very good at it; **wie bitte?** pardon?; (*entrüstet*) I beg your pardon!; **und wie!** and how!

♦ *konj* **1** (*bei Vergleichen*): **so schön wie ...** as beautiful as ...; **wie ich schon sagte** as I said; **wie du** like you; **singen wie ein ...** to sing like a ...; **wie (zum Beispiel)** such as (for example)

2 (*zeitlich*): **wie er das hörte, ging er** when he heard that he left; **er hörte, wie der Regen fiel** he heard the rain falling

---

wieder [ˈviːdər] *adv* again; **~ da sein** to be back (again); **gehst du schon ~?** are you off again?; **~ ein(e) ...** another ...; **W~aufbau** *m* rebuilding; **~aufbereiten** ⚠ *vt sep* to recycle; **~aufnehmen** ⚠ (*unreg*) *vt* to resume; **~erkennen** ⚠ (*unreg*) *vt* to recognize; **W~gabe** *f* reproduction; **~geben** (*unreg*) *vt* (*zurückgeben*) to return; (*Erzählung etc*) to repeat; (*Gefühle etc*) to convey; **~gutmachen** ⚠ *vt* to make up for; (*Fehler*) to put right; **W~'gutmachung** *f* reparation; **~'herstellen** ⚠ *vt* to restore; **~'holen** *vt insep* to repeat; **W~'holung** *f* repetition; **W~hören** *nt:* **auf W~hören** (*TEL*) goodbye; **W~kehr** (**-**) *f* return; (*von Vorfall*) repetition, recurrence; **~sehen** ⚠ (*unreg*) *vt* to see again; **auf W~sehen** goodbye; **~um** *adv* again; (*andererseits*) on the other hand; **~vereinigen** ⚠ *vt* to reunite; (*POL*) to reunify; **W~vereinigung** *f* (*POL*) reunification; **~verwerten** ⚠ *vt sep* to recycle; **W~wahl** *f* re-election

Wiege [ˈviːgə] *f* cradle; **w~n¹** *vt* (*schaukeln*) to rock

wiegen² (*unreg*) *vt, vi* (*Gewicht*) to weigh

Wien [viːn] *nt* Vienna

Wiese [ˈviːzə] *f* meadow

⚠ *Informationen zur Rechtschreibreform Seite 615*

Wiesel ['vi:zəl] (**-s, -**) nt weasel
wieso [vi:'zo:] adv why
wieviel ⚠ [vi:'fi:l] adj how much; ~
Menschen how many people; **~mal** adv
how often; **~te(r, s)** adj: **zum ~ten Mal?**
how many times?; **den W~ten haben wir?**
what's the date?; **an ~ter Stelle?** in what
place?; **der ~te Besucher war er?** how
many visitors were there before him?
wieweit [vi:'vait] adv to what extent
wild [vilt] adj wild; **W~** (**-(e)s**) nt game;
W~e(r) ['vildə(r)] f(m) savage; **~ern** vi to
poach; **~'fremd** (umg) adj quite strange od
unknown; **W~heit** f wildness; **W~leder** nt
suede; **W~nis** (**-, -se**) f wilderness;
W~schwein nt (wild) boar
will etc [vil] vb siehe **wollen**
Wille ['vilə] (**-ns, -n**) m will; **w~n** präp +gen:
um ... w~n for the sake of ...; **w~nsstark**
adj strong-willed
will- zW: **~ig** adj willing; **W~kommen**
[vil'kɔmən] (**-s, -**) nt welcome; **~kommen**
adj welcome; **jdn ~kommen heißen** to
welcome sb; **~kürlich** adj arbitrary;
(Bewegung) voluntary
wimmeln ['viməln] vi: **~ (von)** to swarm
(with)
wimmern ['vimərn] vi to whimper
Wimper ['vimpər] (**-, -n**) f eyelash
Wimperntusche f mascara
Wind [vint] (**-(e)s, -e**) m wind; **~beutel** m
cream puff; (fig) rake; **~e** f (TECH) winch,
windlass; (BOT) bindweed; **~el** ['vindəl] (**-,
-n**) f nappy, diaper (US); **w~en** vi unpers to
be windy ♦ vt (unreg) to wind; (Kranz) to
weave; (entwinden) to twist ♦ vr (unreg) to
wind; (Person) to writhe; **~energie** f wind
energy; **w~ig** ['vindiç] adj windy; (fig)
dubious; **~jacke** f windcheater; **~mühle** f
windmill; **~pocken** pl chickenpox sg;
~schutzscheibe f (AUT) windscreen (BRIT),
windshield (US); **~stärke** f wind force;
w~still adj (Tag) still, windless; (Platz)
sheltered; **~stille** f calm; **~stoß** m gust of
wind
Wink [viŋk] (**-(e)s, -e**) m (mit Hand) wave;
(mit Kopf) nod; (Hinweis) hint

Winkel ['viŋkəl] (**-s, -**) m (MATH) angle;
(Gerät) set square; (in Raum) corner
winken ['viŋkən] vt, vi to wave
winseln ['vinzəln] vi to whine
Winter ['vintər] (**-s, -**) m winter; **w~fest** adj
(Pflanze) hardy; **~garten** m conservatory;
w~lich adj wintry; **~reifen** m winter tyre;
~sport m winter sports pl
Winzer ['vintsər] (**-s, -**) m vine grower
winzig ['vintsiç] adj tiny
Wipfel ['vipfəl] (**-s, -**) m treetop
wir [vi:r] pron we; **~ alle** all of us, we all
Wirbel ['virbəl] (**-s, -**) m whirl, swirl; (Trubel)
hurly-burly; (Aufsehen) fuss; (ANAT) vertebra;
w~n vi to whirl, to swirl; **~säule** f spine
wird [virt] vb siehe **werden**
wirfst etc [virfst] vb siehe **werfen**
wirken ['virkən] vi to have an effect;
(erfolgreich sein) to work; (scheinen) to seem
♦ vt (Wunder) to work
wirklich ['virkliç] adj real ♦ adv really;
W~keit f reality
wirksam ['virkza:m] adj effective
Wirkstoff m (biologisch, chemisch, pflanzlich)
active substance
Wirkung ['virkuŋ] f effect; **w~slos** adj
ineffective; **w~slos bleiben** to have no
effect; **w~svoll** adj effective
wirr [vir] adj confused, wild; **W~warr** (**-s**) m
disorder, chaos
wirst [virst] vb siehe **werden**
Wirt(in) [virt(in)] (**-(e)s, -e**) m(f)
landlord(lady); **~schaft** f (Gaststätte) pub;
(Haushalt) housekeeping; (eines Landes)
economy; (umg: Durcheinander) mess;
w~schaftlich adj economical; (POL)
economic
Wirtschafts- zW: **~krise** f economic
crisis; **~politik** f economic policy; **~prüfer**
m chartered accountant; **~wunder** nt
economic miracle
Wirtshaus nt inn
wischen ['vi∫ən] vt to wipe
Wischer (**-s, -**) m (AUT) wiper
Wißbegier(de) ⚠ ['visbəgi:r(də)] f thirst
for knowledge; **w~ig** ⚠ adj inquisitive,
eager for knowledge

⚠ For information on spelling reform see page 615

wissen ['vɪsən] (*unreg*) *vt* to know; **was weiß ich!** I don't know!; **W~** (**-s**) *nt* knowledge; **W~schaft** *f* science; **W~schaftler(in)** (**-s, -**) *m(f)* scientist; **~schaftlich** *adj* scientific; **~swert** *adj* worth knowing

wittern ['vɪtərn] *vt* to scent; (*fig*) to suspect

Witterung *f* weather; (*Geruch*) scent

Witwe ['vɪtvə] *f* widow; **~r** (**-s, -**) *m* widower

Witz [vɪts] (**-es, -e**) *m* joke; **~bold** (**-(e)s, -e**) *m* joker, wit; **w~ig** *adj* funny

wo [vo:] *adv* where; (*umg: irgendwo*) somewhere; **im Augenblick, ~ ...** the moment (that) ...; **die Zeit, ~ ...** the time when ...; **~anders** [vo:ʔandərs] *adv* elsewhere; **~bei** [-'baɪ] *adv* (*relativ*) by/with which; (*interrogativ*) what ... in/by/with

Woche ['vɔxə] *f* week

Wochen- *zW:* **~ende** *nt* weekend; **w~lang** *adj, adv* for weeks; **~markt** *m* weekly market; **~schau** *f* newsreel

wöchentlich ['vœçəntlɪç] *adj, adv* weekly

wodurch [vo:'dʊrç] *adv* (*relativ*) through which; (*interrogativ*) what ... through

wofür [vo:'fy:r] *adv* (*relativ*) for which; (*interrogativ*) what ... for

wog *etc* [vo:k] *vb siehe* **wiegen**

wo- [vo:] *zW:* **~'gegen** *adv* (*relativ*) against which; (*interrogativ*) what ... against; **~her** [-'he:r] *adv* where ... from; **~hin** [-'hɪn] *adv* where ... to

---
SCHLÜSSELWORT
---

wohl [vo:l] *adv* **1**: **sich wohl fühlen** (*zufrieden*) to feel happy; (*gesundheitlich*) to feel well; **wohl oder übel** whether one likes it or not

2 (*wahrscheinlich*) probably; (*gewiß*) certainly; (*vielleicht*) perhaps; **sie ist wohl zu Hause** she's probably at home; **das ist doch wohl nicht dein Ernst!** surely you're not serious!; **das mag wohl sein** that may well be; **ob das wohl stimmt?** I wonder if that's true; **er weiß das sehr wohl** he knows that perfectly well

Wohl [vo:l] (**-(e)s**) *nt* welfare; **zum ~!** cheers!; **w~auf** *adv* well; **~behagen** *nt* comfort; **~fahrt** *f* welfare; **~fahrtsstaat** *m* welfare state; **w~habend** *adj* wealthy; **w~ig** *adj* contented, comfortable; **w~schmeckend** *adj* delicious; **~stand** *m* prosperity; **~standsgesellschaft** *f* affluent society; **~tat** *f* relief; act of charity; **~täter(in)** *m(f)* benefactor; **w~tätig** *adj* charitable; **~tätigkeits-** *zW* charity, charitable; **w~verdient** *adj* well-earned, well-deserved; **w~weislich** *adv* prudently; **~wollen** (**-s**) *nt* good will; **w~wollend** *adj* benevolent

wohn- ['vo:n] *zW:* **~en** *vi* to live; **W~gemeinschaft** *f* (*Menschen*) people sharing a flat; **~haft** *adj* resident; **W~heim** *nt* (*für Studenten*) hall of residence; (*für Senioren*) home; (*bes für Arbeiter*) hostel; **~lich** *adj* comfortable; **W~mobil** (**-s, -e**) *nt* camper; **W~ort** *m* domicile; **W~sitz** *m* place of residence; **W~ung** *f* house; (*Etagenwohnung*) flat, apartment (*US*); **W~wagen** *m* caravan; **W~zimmer** *nt* living room

wölben ['vœlbən] *vt, vr* to curve

Wolf [vɔlf] (**-(e)s, ¨e**) *m* wolf

Wolke ['vɔlkə] *f* cloud; **~nkratzer** *m* skyscraper

wolkig ['vɔlkɪç] *adj* cloudy

Wolle ['vɔlə] *f* wool; **w~n¹** *adj* woollen

SCHLÜSSELWORT
---

wollen² ['vɔlən] (*pt* **wollte**, *pp* **gewollt** *od* (*als Hilfsverb*) **wollen**) *vt, vi* to want; **ich will nach Hause** I want to go home; **er will nicht** he doesn't want to; **er wollte das nicht** he didn't want it; **wenn du willst** if you like; **ich will, daß du mir zuhörst** I want you to listen to me

♦ *Hilfsverb:* **er will ein Haus kaufen** he wants to buy a house; **ich wollte, ich wäre ...** I wish I were ...; **etw gerade tun wollen** to be going to do sth

---

wollüstig ['vɔlʏstɪç] *adj* lusty, sensual

wo- *zW:* **~mit** *adv* (*relativ*) with which;

(*interrogativ*) what ... with; **~möglich** *adv* probably, I suppose; **~nach** *adv* (*relativ*) after/for which; (*interrogativ*) what ... for/ after; **~ran** *adv* (*relativ*) on/at which; (*interrogativ*) what ... on/at; **~rauf** *adv* (*relativ*) on which; (*interrogativ*) what ... on; **~raus** *adv* (*relativ*) from/out of which; (*interrogativ*) what ... from/out of; **~rin** *adv* (*relativ*) in which; (*interrogativ*) what ... in

Wort [vɔrt] **(-(e)s, "er** *od* **-e)** *nt* word; **jdn beim ~ nehmen** to take sb at his word; **mit anderen ~en** in other words; **w~brüchig** *adj* not true to one's word

Wörterbuch ['vœrtɐbuːx] *nt* dictionary

Wort- *zW:* **~führer** *m* spokesman; **w~karg** *adj* taciturn; **~laut** *m* wording

wörtlich ['vœrtlɪç] *adj* literal

Wort- *zW:* **w~los** *adj* mute; **w~reich** *adj* wordy, verbose; **~schatz** *m* vocabulary; **~spiel** *nt* play on words, pun

wo- *zW:* **~rüber** *adv* (*relativ*) over/about which; (*interrogativ*) what ... over/about; **~rum** *adv* (*relativ*) about/round which; (*interrogativ*) what ... about/round; **~runter** *adv* (*relativ*) under which; (*interrogativ*) what ... under; **~von** *adv* (*relativ*) from which; (*interrogativ*) what ... from; **~vor** *adv* (*relativ*) in front of/before which; (*interrogativ*) in front of/before what; of what; **~zu** *adv* (*relativ*) to/for which; (*interrogativ*) what ... for/to; (*warum*) why

Wrack [vrak] **(-(e)s, -s)** *nt* wreck

Wucher ['vuːxɐ] **(-s)** *m* profiteering; **~er (-s, -)** *m* profiteer; **w~isch** *adj* profiteering; **w~n** *vi* (*Pflanzen*) to grow wild; **~ung** *f* (*MED*) growth, tumour

Wuchs [vuːks] **(-es)** *m* (*Wachstum*) growth; (*Statur*) build

Wucht [vʊxt] **(-)** *f* force

wühlen ['vyːlən] *vi* to scrabble; (*Tier*) to root; (*Maulwurf*) to burrow; (*umg: arbeiten*) to slave away ♦ *vt* to dig

Wulst [vʊlst] **(-es, "e)** *m* bulge; (*an Wunde*) swelling

wund [vʊnt] *adj* sore, raw; **W~e** *f* wound

Wunder ['vʊndɐ] **(-s, -)** *nt* miracle; **es ist kein ~** it's no wonder; **w~bar** *adj*

wonderful, marvellous; **~kerze** *f* sparkler; **~kind** *nt* infant prodigy; **w~lich** *adj* odd, peculiar; **w~n** *vr* to be surprised ♦ *vt* to surprise; **sich w~n über** +*akk* to be surprised at; **w~schön** *adj* beautiful; **w~voll** *adj* wonderful

Wundstarrkrampf ['vʊntʃtarkrampf] *m* tetanus, lockjaw

Wunsch [vʊnʃ] **(-(e)s, "e)** *m* wish

wünschen ['vʏnʃən] *vt* to wish; **sich** *dat* **etw ~** to want sth, to wish for sth; **~swert** *adj* desirable

wurde *etc* ['vʊrdə] *vb siehe* **werden**

Würde ['vʏrdə] *f* dignity; (*Stellung*) honour; **w~voll** *adj* dignified

würdig ['vʏrdɪç] *adj* worthy; (*würdevoll*) dignified; **~en** *vt* to appreciate

Wurf [vʊrf] **(-s, "e)** *m* throw; (*Junge*) litter

Würfel ['vʏrfəl] **(-s, -)** *m* dice; (*MATH*) cube; **~becher** *m* (dice) cup; **w~n** *vi* to play dice ♦ *vt* to dice; **~zucker** *m* lump sugar

würgen ['vʏrgən] *vt, vi* to choke

Wurm [vʊrm] **(-(e)s, "er)** *m* worm; **w~stichig** *adj* worm-ridden

Wurst [vʊrst] **(-, "e)** *f* sausage; **das ist mir ~** (*umg*) I don't care, I don't give a damn

Würstchen ['vʏrstçən] *nt* sausage

Würze ['vʏrtsə] *f* seasoning, spice

Wurzel ['vʊrtsəl] **(-, -n)** *f* root

würzen ['vʏrtsən] *vt* to season, to spice

würzig *adj* spicy

wusch *etc* [vʊʃ] *vb siehe* **waschen**

wußte *etc* ⚠ ['vʊstə] *vb siehe* **wissen**

wüst [vyːst] *adj* untidy, messy; (*ausschweifend*) wild; (*öde*) waste; (*umg: heftig*) terrible; **W~e** *f* desert

Wut [vuːt] **(-)** *f* rage, fury; **~anfall** *m* fit of rage

wüten ['vyːtən] *vi* to rage; **~d** *adj* furious, mad

⚠ *For information on spelling reform see page 615*

X, x

X-Beine ['ıksbaınə] *pl* knock-knees
x-beliebig [ıksbə'li:bıç] *adj* any (whatever)
xerokopieren [kseroko'pi:rən] *vt* to xerox, to photocopy
x-mal ['ıksma:l] *adv* any number of times, n times
Xylophon △ [ksylo'fo:n] **(-s, -e)** *nt* xylophone

Y, y

Yacht **(-, -en)** *f siehe* **Jacht**
Ypsilon ['ypsilɔn] **(-(s), -s)** *nt* the letter Y

Z, z

Zacke ['tsakə] *f* point; (*Berg~*) jagged peak; (*Gabel~*) prong; (*Kamm~*) tooth
zackig ['tsakıç] *adj* jagged; (*umg*) smart; (*Tempo*) brisk
zaghaft ['tsa:khaft] *adj* timid
zäh [tse:] *adj* tough; (*Mensch*) tenacious; (*Flüssigkeit*) thick; (*schleppend*) sluggish; **Z~igkeit** *f* toughness; tenacity
Zahl [tsa:l] **(-, -en)** *f* number; **z~bar** *adj* payable; **z~en** *vt, vi* to pay; **z~en bitte!** the bill please!
zählen ['tse:lən] *vt, vi* to count; **~ auf** +*akk* to count on; **~ zu** to be numbered among
Zahlenschloß △ *nt* combination lock
Zähler ['tse:lər] **(-s, -)** *m* (*TECH*) meter; (*MATH*) numerator
Zahl- *zW:* **z~los** *adj* countless; **z~reich** *adj* numerous; **~tag** *m* payday; **~ung** *f* payment; **~ungsanweisung** *f* giro transfer order; **z~ungsfähig** *adj* solvent; **~wort** *nt* numeral
zahm [tsa:m] *adj* tame
zähmen ['tse:mən] *vt* to tame; (*fig*) to curb
Zahn [tsa:n] **(-(e)s, ¨e)** *m* tooth; **~arzt** *m* dentist; **~ärztin** *f* (female) dentist;

~bürste *f* toothbrush; **~fleisch** *nt* gums *pl*; **~pasta** *f* toothpaste; **~rad** *nt* cog(wheel); **~schmerzen** *pl* toothache *sg*; **~stein** *m* tartar; **~stocher** **(-s, -)** *m* toothpick
Zange ['tsaŋə] *f* pliers *pl*; (*Zucker~ etc*) tongs *pl*; (*Beiß~, ZOOL*) pincers *pl*; (*MED*) forceps *pl*
zanken ['tsaŋkən] *vi, vr* to quarrel
zänkisch ['tseŋkıʃ] *adj* quarrelsome
Zäpfchen ['tsepfçən] *nt* (*ANAT*) uvula; (*MED*) suppository
Zapfen ['tsapfən] **(-s, -)** *m* plug; (*BOT*) cone; (*Eis~*) icicle
zappeln ['tsapəln] *vi* to wriggle; to fidget
zart [tsart] *adj* (*weich, leise*) soft; (*Fleisch*) tender; (*fein, schwächlich*) delicate; **Z~heit** *f* softness; tenderness; delicacy
zärtlich ['tse:rtlıç] *adj* tender, affectionate
Zauber ['tsaubər] **(-s, -)** *m* magic; (*~bann*) spell; **~ei** [-'raı] *f* magic; **~er** **(-s, -)** *m* magician; conjuror; **z~haft** *adj* magical, enchanting; **~künstler** *m* conjuror; **~kunststück** *nt* conjuring trick; **z~n** *vi* to conjure, to practise magic
zaudern ['tsaudərn] *vi* to hesitate
Zaum [tsaum] **(-(e)s, Zäume)** *m* bridle; **etw im ~ halten** to keep sth in check
Zaun [tsaun] **(-(e)s, Zäune)** *m* fence
z.B. *abk* (= *zum Beispiel*) e.g.
Zebra ['tse:bra] *nt* zebra; **~streifen** *m* zebra crossing
Zeche ['tseçə] *f* (*Rechnung*) bill; (*Bergbau*) mine
Zeh [tse:] **(-s, -en)** *m* toe
Zehe [tse:ə] *f* toe; (*Knoblauch~*) clove
zehn [tse:n] *num* ten; **~te(r, s)** *adj* tenth; **Z~tel (-s, -)** *nt* tenth (part)
Zeich- ['tsaıç] *zW:* **~en (-s, -)** *nt* sign; **z~nen** *vt* to draw; (*kennzeichnen*) to mark; (*unterzeichnen*) to sign ♦ *vi* to draw; to sign; **~ner (-s, -)** *m* artist; **technischer ~ner** draughtsman; **~nung** *f* drawing; (*Markierung*) markings *pl*
Zeige- ['tsaıgə] *zW:* **~finger** *m* index finger; **z~n** *vt* to show ♦ *vi* to point ♦ *vr* to show o.s.; **z~n auf** +*akk* to point to; to point at; **es wird sich z~n** time will tell; **es zeigte**

sich, daß ... it turned out that ...; **~r (-s, -)** m pointer; (*Uhrzeiger*) hand

Zeile ['tsaɪlə] f line; (*Häuser~*) row

Zeit [tsaɪt] **(-, -en)** f time; (*GRAM*) tense; **zur ~** at the moment; **sich** *dat* **~ lassen** to take one's time; **von ~ zu ~** from time to time; **~alter** nt age; **~ansage** f (*TEL*) speaking clock; **~arbeit** f (*COMM*) temporary job; **z~gemäß** adj in keeping with the times; **~genosse** m contemporary; **z~ig** adj early; **z~lich** adj temporal; **~lupe** f slow motion; **z~raubend** adj time-consuming; **~raum** m period; **~rechnung** f time, era; **nach/vor unserer ~rechnung** A.D./B.C.; **~schrift** f periodical; **~ung** f newspaper; **~vertreib** m pastime, diversion; **z~weilig** adj temporary; **z~weise** adv for a time; **~wort** nt verb

Zelle ['tsɛlə] f cell; (*Telefon~*) callbox

Zellstoff m cellulose

Zelt [tsɛlt] **(-(e)s, -e)** nt tent; **z~en** vi to camp; **~platz** m camp site

Zement [tse'mɛnt] **(-(e)s, -e)** m cement; **z~ieren** vt to cement

zensieren [tsɛn'ziːrən] vt to censor; (*SCH*) to mark

Zensur [tsɛn'zuːr] f censorship; (*SCH*) mark

Zentimeter [tsɛnti'meːtər] m od nt centimetre

Zentner ['tsɛntnər] **(-s, -)** m hundredweight

zentral [tsɛn'traːl] adj central; **Z~e** f central office; (*TEL*) exchange; **Z~heizung** f central heating

Zentrum ['tsɛntrʊm] **(-s, Zentren)** nt centre

zerbrechen [tsɛr'brɛçən] (*unreg*) vt, vi to break

zerbrechlich adj fragile

zer'drücken vt to squash, to crush; (*Kartoffeln*) to mash

Zeremonie [tseremo'niː] f ceremony

Zerfall [tsɛr'fal] m decay; **z~en** (*unreg*) vi to disintegrate, to decay; (*sich gliedern*) **z~en (in** +*akk*) to fall (into)

zer'gehen (*unreg*) vi to melt, to dissolve

zerkleinern [tsɛr'klaɪnərn] vt to reduce to small pieces

zerlegbar [tsɛr'leːkbaːr] adj able to be dismantled

zerlegen [tsɛr'leːgən] vt to take to pieces; (*Fleisch*) to carve; (*Satz*) to analyse

zermürben [tsɛr'mʏrbən] vt to wear down

zerquetschen [tsɛr'kvɛtʃən] vt to squash

zer'reißen (*unreg*) vt to tear to pieces ♦ vi to tear, to rip

zerren ['tsɛrən] vt to drag ♦ vi: **~ (an** +*dat*) to tug (at)

zer'rinnen (*unreg*) vi to melt away

zerrissen [tsɛr'rɪsən] adj torn, tattered; **Z~heit** f tattered state; (*POL*) disunion, discord; (*innere Zerrissenheit*) disintegration

Zerrung f (*MED*): **eine ~** pulled muscle

zerrütten [tsɛr'rʏtən] vt to wreck, to destroy

zer'schlagen (*unreg*) vt to shatter, to smash ♦ vr to fall through

zer'schneiden (*unreg*) vt to cut up

zer'setzen vt, vr to decompose, to dissolve

zer'springen (*unreg*) vi to shatter, to burst

Zerstäuber [tsɛr'ʃtɔybər] **(-s, -)** m atomizer

zerstören [tsɛr'ʃtøːrən] vt to destroy

Zerstörung f destruction

zerstreu- [tsɛr'ʃtrɔy] zW: **~en** vt to disperse, to scatter; (*unterhalten*) to divert; (*Zweifel etc*) to dispel ♦ vr to disperse, to scatter; to be dispelled; **~t** adj scattered; (*Mensch*) absent-minded; **Z~theit** f absent-mindedness; **Z~ung** f dispersion; (*Ablenkung*) diversion

zerstückeln [tsɛr'ʃtʏkəln] vt to cut into pieces

zer'teilen vt to divide into parts

Zertifikat [tsɛrtifi'kaːt] **(-(e)s, -e)** nt certificate

zer'treten (*unreg*) vt to crush underfoot

zertrümmern [tsɛr'trʏmərn] vt to shatter; (*Gebäude etc*) to demolish

Zettel ['tsɛtəl] **(-s, -)** m piece of paper, slip; (*Notiz~*) note; (*Formular*) form

Zeug [tsɔyk] **(-(e)s, -e)** (*umg*) nt stuff; (*Ausrüstung*) gear; **dummes ~** (stupid) nonsense; **das ~ haben zu** to have the makings of; **sich ins ~ legen** to put one's shoulder to the wheel

Zeuge ['tsɔygə] **(-n, -n)** m witness; **z~n** vi to

⚠ *For information on spelling reform see page 615*

bear witness, to testify ♦ *vt* (*Kind*) to father; **es zeugt von ...** it testifies to ...; **~naussage** *f* evidence; **Zeugin** ['tsɔygɪn] *f* witness

Zeugnis ['tsɔygnɪs] (**-ses, -se**) *nt* certificate; (*SCH*) report; (*Referenz*) reference; (*Aussage*) evidence, testimony; **~ geben von** to be evidence of, to testify to

z.H(d). *abk* (= *zu Händen*) attn.

Zickzack ['tsɪktsak] (**-(e)s, -e**) *m* zigzag

Ziege ['tsiːgə] *f* goat

Ziegel ['tsiːgəl] (**-s, -**) *m* brick; (*Dach~*) tile

ziehen ['tsiːən] (*unreg*) *vt* to draw; (*zerren*) to pull; (*SCHACH etc*) to move; (*züchten*) to rear ♦ *vi* to draw; (*umziehen, wandern*) to move; (*Rauch, Wolke etc*) to drift; (*reißen*) to pull ♦ *vb unpers*: **es zieht** there is a draught, it's draughty ♦ *vr* (*Gummi*) to stretch; (*Grenze etc*) to run; (*Gespräche*) to be drawn out; **etw nach sich ~** to lead to sth, to entail sth

Ziehung ['tsiːʊŋ] *f* (*Los~*) drawing

Ziel [tsiːl] (**-(e)s, -e**) *nt* (*einer Reise*) destination; (*SPORT*) finish; (*MIL*) target; (*Absicht*) goal; **z~bewußt** △ *adj* decisive; **z~en** *vi*: **z~en (auf** +*akk*) to aim (at); **z~los** *adj* aimless; **~scheibe** *f* target; **z~strebig** *adj* purposeful

ziemlich ['tsiːmlɪç] *adj* quite a; fair ♦ *adv* rather; quite a bit

zieren ['tsiːrən] *vr* to act coy

zierlich ['tsiːrlɪç] *adj* dainty

Ziffer ['tsɪfər] (**-, -n**) *f* figure, digit; **~blatt** *nt* dial, clock-face

zig [tsɪk] (*umg*) *adj* umpteen

Zigarette [tsiga'rɛtə] *f* cigarette

Zigaretten- *zW*: **~automat** *m* cigarette machine; **~schachtel** *f* cigarette packet; **~spitze** *f* cigarette holder

Zigarre [tsi'garə] *f* cigar

Zigeuner(in) [tsi'gɔynər(ɪn)] (**-s, -**) *m(f)* gipsy

Zimmer ['tsɪmər] (**-s, -**) *nt* room; **~lautstärke** *f* reasonable volume; **~mädchen** *nt* chambermaid; **~mann** *m* carpenter; **z~n** *vt* to make (from wood); **~nachweis** *m* accommodation office;

~pflanze *f* indoor plant; **~service** *m* room service

zimperlich ['tsɪmpərlɪç] *adj* squeamish; (*pingelig*) fussy, finicky

Zimt [tsɪmt] (**-(e)s, -e**) *m* cinnamon

Zink [tsɪŋk] (**-(e)s**) *nt* zinc

Zinn [tsɪn] (**-(e)s**) *nt* (*Element*) tin; (*in ~waren*) pewter; **~soldat** *m* tin soldier

Zins [tsɪns] (**-es, -en**) *m* interest; **~eszins** *m* compound interest; **~fuß** *m* rate of interest; **z~los** *adj* interest-free; **~satz** *m* rate of interest

Zipfel ['tsɪpfəl] (**-s, -**) *m* corner; (*spitz*) tip; (*Hemd~*) tail; (*Wurst~*) end

zirka ['tsɪrka] *adv* (round) about

Zirkel ['tsɪrkəl] (**-s, -**) *m* circle; (*MATH*) pair of compasses

Zirkus ['tsɪrkʊs] (**-, -se**) *m* circus

zischen ['tsɪʃən] *vi* to hiss

Zitat [tsi'taːt] (**-(e)s, -e**) *nt* quotation, quote

zitieren [tsi'tiːrən] *vt* to quote

Zitrone [tsi'troːnə] *f* lemon; **~nlimonade** *f* lemonade; **~nsaft** *m* lemon juice

zittern ['tsɪtərn] *vi* to tremble

zivil [tsi'viːl] *adj* civil; (*Preis*) moderate; **Z~** (**-s**) *nt* plain clothes *pl*; (*MIL*) civilian clothing; **Z~courage** *f* courage of one's convictions; **Z~dienst** *m* community service; **Z~isation** *f* civilization; **Z~isationskrankheit** *f* disease peculiar to civilization; **~i'sieren** *vt* to civilize

┌─────────────────────────────┐
│ **ZIVILDIENST** │
└─────────────────────────────┘

i *A young German has to complete his 13 months' Zivildienst or service to the community if he has opted out of military service as a conscientious objector. This is usually done in a hospital or old people's home. About 18% of young Germans choose to do this as an alternative to the* **Wehrdienst.**

Zivilist [tsivi'lɪst] *m* civilian

zögern ['tsøːgərn] *vi* to hesitate

Zoll [tsɔl] (**-(e)s, ¨e**) *m* customs *pl*; (*Abgabe*) duty; **~abfertigung** *f* customs clearance; **~amt** *nt* customs office; **~beamte(r)** *m* customs official; **~erklärung** f customs declaration; **z~frei** adj duty-free; **~kontrolle** f customs check; **z~pflichtig** adj liable to duty, dutiable

Zone ['tso:nə] f zone

Zoo [tso:] (**-s, -s**) m zoo; **~loge** [tsoo'lo:gə] (**-n, -n**) m zoologist; **~lo'gie** f zoology; **z~'logisch** adj zoological

Zopf [tsɔpf] (**-(e)s, œe**) m plait; pigtail; **alter ~** antiquated custom

Zorn [tsɔrn] (**-(e)s**) m anger; **z~ig** adj angry

zottig ['tsɔtɪç] adj shaggy

z.T. abk = **zum Teil**

SCHLÜSSELWORT

zu [tsu:] präp +dat **1** (örtlich) to; **zum Bahnhof/Arzt gehen** to go to the station/doctor; **zur Schule/Kirche gehen** to go to school/church; **sollen wir zu euch gehen?** shall we go to your place?; **sie sah zu ihm hin** she looked towards him; **zum Fenster herein** through the window; **zu meiner Linken** to od on my left

2 (zeitlich) at; **zu Ostern** at Easter; **bis zum 1. Mai** until May 1st; (nicht später als) by May 1st; **zu meiner Zeit** in my time

3 (Zusatz) with; **Wein zum Essen trinken** to drink wine with one's meal; **sich zu jdm setzen** to sit down beside sb; **setz dich doch zu uns** (come and) sit with us; **Anmerkungen zu etw** notes on sth

4 (Zweck) for; **Wasser zum Waschen** water for washing; **Papier zum Schreiben** paper to write on; **etw zum Geburtstag bekommen** to get sth for one's birthday

5 (Veränderung) into; **zu etw werden** to turn into sth; **jdn zu etw machen** to make sb (into) sth; **zu Asche verbrennen** to burn to ashes

6 (mit Zahlen): **3 zu 2** (SPORT) 3-2; **das Stück zu 2 Mark** at 2 marks each; **zum ersten Mal** for the first time

7: **zu meiner Freude** to my joy etc; **zum Glück** luckily; **zu Fuß** on foot; **es ist zum Weinen** it's enough to make you cry

♦ konj to; **etw zu essen** sth to eat; **um besser sehen zu können** in order to see

better; **ohne es zu wissen** without knowing it; **noch zu bezahlende Rechnungen** bills that are still to be paid

♦ adv **1** (allzu) too; **zu sehr** too much

2 (örtlich) toward(s); **er kam auf mich zu** he came up to me

3 (geschlossen) shut, closed; **die Geschäfte haben zu** the shops are closed; **„auf/zu"** (Wasserhahn etc) "on/off"

4 (umg: los): **nur zu!** just keep on!; **mach zu!** hurry up!

---

zualler- [tsu'|alər] zW: **~erst** [-'|e:rst] adv first of all; **~letzt** [-'letst] adv last of all

Zubehör ['tsu:bəhø:r] (**-(e)s, -e**) nt accessories pl

zubereiten ['tsu:bəraitən] vt to prepare

zubilligen ['tsu:bɪlɪgən] vt to grant

zubinden ['tsu:bɪndən] (unreg) vt to tie up

zubringen ['tsu:brɪŋən] (unreg) vt (Zeit) to spend

Zubringer (**-s, -**) m (Straße) approach od slip road

Zucchini [tsʊ'ki:ni:] pl (BOT, KOCH) courgette (BRIT), zucchini (US)

Zucht [tsʊxt] (**-, -en**) f (von Tieren) breeding; (von Pflanzen) cultivation; (Rasse) breed; (Erziehung) raising; (Disziplin) discipline

züchten ['tsʏçtən] vt (Tiere) to breed; (Pflanzen) to cultivate, to grow; **Züchter** (**-s, -**) m breeder; grower

Zuchthaus nt prison, penitentiary (US)

züchtigen ['tsʏçtɪgən] vt to chastise

Züchtung f (Zuchtart, Sorte: von Tier) breed; (: von Pflanze) variety

zucken ['tsʊkən] vi to jerk, to twitch; (Strahl etc) to flicker ♦ vt (Schultern) to shrug

Zucker ['tsʊkər] (**-s, -**) m sugar; (MED) diabetes; **~guß** △ m icing; **z~krank** adj diabetic; **~krankheit** f (MED) diabetes; **z~n** vt to sugar; **~rohr** nt sugar cane; **~rübe** f sugar beet

Zuckung ['tsʊkʊŋ] f convulsion, spasm; (leicht) twitch

zudecken ['tsu:dekən] vt to cover (up)

zudem [tsu'de:m] adv in addition (to this)

zudringlich ['tsu:drɪŋlɪç] adj forward,

△ For information on spelling reform see page 615

pushing, obtrusive

zudrücken ['tsuːdrʏkən] *vt* to close; **ein Auge ~** to turn a blind eye

zueinander [tsuˌaɪˈnandər] *adv* to one other; (*in Verbindung*) together

zuerkennen ['tsuː|ɛrkɛnən] (*unreg*) *vt* to award; **jdm etw ~** to award sth to sb, to award sb sth

zuerst [tsuˈ|eːrst] *adv* first; (*zu Anfang*) at first; **~ einmal** first of all

Zufahrt ['tsuːfaːrt] *f* approach; **~sstraße** *f* approach road; (*von Autobahn etc*) slip road

Zufall ['tsuːfal] *m* chance; (*Ereignis*) coincidence; **durch ~** by accident; **so ein ~** what a coincidence; **z~en** (*unreg*) *vi* to close, to shut; (*Anteil, Aufgabe*) to fall

zufällig ['tsuːfɛlɪç] *adj* chance ♦ *adv* by chance; (*in Frage*) by any chance

Zuflucht ['tsuːflʊxt] *f* recourse; (*Ort*) refuge

zufolge [tsuˈfɔlgə] *präp* (*+dat od gen*) judging by; (*laut*) according to

zufrieden [tsuˈfriːdən] *adj* content(ed), satisfied; **~geben** △ (*unreg*) *vr* to be content *od* satisfied (with); **~stellen** △ *vt* to satisfy

zufrieren ['tsuːfriːrən] (*unreg*) *vi* to freeze up *od* over

zufügen ['tsuːfyːgən] *vt* to add; (*Leid etc*): **(jdm) etw ~** to cause (sb) sth

Zufuhr ['tsuːfuːr] (*-, -en*) *f* (*Herbeibringen*) supplying; (*MET*) influx

Zug [tsuːk] (*-(e)s, ⁼e*) *m* (*EISENB*) train; (*Luft~*) draught; (*Ziehen*) pull(ing); (*Gesichts~*) feature; (*SCHACH etc*) move; (*Schrift~*) stroke; (*Atem~*) breath; (*Charakter~*) trait; (*an Zigarette*) puff, pull, drag; (*Schluck*) gulp; (*Menschengruppe*) procession; (*von Vögeln*) flight; (*MIL*) platoon; **etw in vollen Zügen genießen** to enjoy sth to the full

Zu- ['tsuː] *zW*: **~gabe** *f* extra; (*in Konzert etc*) encore; **~gang** *m* access, approach; **z~gänglich** *adj* accessible; (*Mensch*) approachable

zugeben ['tsuːgeːbən] (*unreg*) *vt* (*beifügen*) to add, to throw in; (*zugestehen*) to admit; (*erlauben*) to permit

zugehen ['tsuːgeːən] (*unreg*) *vi* (*schließen*) to shut; **es geht dort seltsam zu** there are strange goings-on there; **auf jdn/etw ~** to walk towards sb/sth; **dem Ende ~** to be finishing

Zugehörigkeit ['tsuːgəhøːrɪçkaɪt] *f*: **~ (zu)** membership (of), belonging (to)

Zügel ['tsyːgəl] (*-s, -*) *m* rein(s); (*fig*) curb; **z~n** *vt* to curb; (*Pferd*) to rein in

zuge- ['tsuːgə] *zW*: **Z~ständnis** (*-ses, -se*) *nt* concession; **~stehen** (*unreg*) *vt* to admit; (*Rechte*) to concede

Zugführer *m* (*EISENB*) guard

zugig ['tsuːgɪç] *adj* draughty

zügig ['tsyːgɪç] *adj* speedy, swift

zugreifen ['tsuːgraɪfən] (*unreg*) *vi* to seize *od* grab at; (*helfen*) to help; (*beim Essen*) to help o.s.

Zugrestaurant *nt* dining car

zugrunde △ [tsuˈgrʊndə] *adv*: **~ gehen** to collapse; (*Mensch*) to perish; **einer Sache** *dat* **etw ~ legen** to base sth on sth; **einer Sache** *dat* **~ liegen** to be based on sth; **~ richten** to ruin, to destroy

zugunsten △ [tsuˈgʊnstən] *präp* (*+gen od dat*) in favour of

zugute [tsuˈguːtə] *adv*: **jdm etw ~ halten** to concede sth to sb; **jdm ~ kommen** to be of assistance to sb

Zugvogel *m* migratory bird

zuhalten ['tsuːhaltən] (*unreg*) *vt* to keep closed ♦ *vi*: **auf jdn/etw ~** to make a beeline for sb/sth

Zuhälter ['tsuːhɛltər] (*-s, -*) *m* pimp

Zuhause [tsuˈhaʊzə] (*-*) *nt* home

zuhören ['tsuːhøːrən] *vi* to listen

Zuhörer (*-s, -*) *m* listener

zukleben ['tsuːkleːbən] *vt* to paste up

zukommen ['tsuːkɔmən] (*unreg*) *vi* to come up; **auf jdn ~** to come up to sb; **jdm etw ~ lassen** to give sb sth; **etw auf sich ~ lassen** to wait and see; **jdm ~** (*sich gehören*) to be fitting for sb

Zukunft ['tsuːkʊnft] (*-, Zukünfte*) *f* future; **zukünftig** ['tsuːkʏnftɪç] *adj* future ♦ *adv* in future; **mein zukünftiger Mann** my husband to be

△ *Informationen zur Rechtschreibreform Seite 615*

Zulage ['tsu:la:gə] f bonus

zulassen ['tsu:lasən] (*unreg*) vt (*hereinlassen*) to admit; (*erlauben*) to permit; (*Auto*) to license; (*umg: nicht öffnen*) to (keep) shut

zulässig ['tsu:lɛsɪç] adj permissible, permitted

Zulassung f (*amtlich*) authorization; (*von Kfz*) licensing

zulaufen ['tsu:laʊfən] (*unreg*) vi (*subj: Mensch*): ~ **auf jdn/etw** to run up to sb/ sth; (: *Straße*): ~ **auf** to lead towards

zuleide ⚠ [tsu:laɪdə] adv: **jdm etw ~ tun** od harm sb

zuletzt [tsu:lɛtst] adv finally, at last

zuliebe [tsu:li:bə] adv: **jdm ~** to please sb

zum [tsʊm] = **zu dem**; ~ **dritten Mal** for the third time; ~ **Scherz** as a joke; ~ **Trinken** for drinking

zumachen ['tsu:maxən] vt to shut; (*Kleidung*) to do up, to fasten ♦ vi to shut; (*umg*) to hurry up

zu- zW: ~**mal** [tsu:'ma:l] konj especially (as); ~**meist** [tsu:'maɪst] adv mostly; ~**mindest** [tsu:'mɪndəst] adv at least

zumut- zW: ~**bar** ['tsu:mu:tba:r] adj reasonable; ~**e** ⚠ adv: **wie ist ihm ~e?** how does he feel?; ~**en** ['tsu:mu:tən] vt: **(jdm) etw ~en** to expect od ask sth (of sb); **Z~ung** ['tsu:mu:tʊŋ] f unreasonable expectation od demand, impertinence

zunächst [tsu:nɛ:çst] adv first of all; ~ **einmal** to start with

Zunahme ['tsu:na:mə] f increase

Zuname ['tsu:na:mə] m surname

Zünd- [tsʏnd] zW: **z~en** vi (*Feuer*) to light, to ignite; (*Motor*) to fire; (*begeistern*): **bei jdm z~en** to fire sb (with enthusiasm); **z~end** adj fiery; ~**er** (**-s, -**) m fuse; (*MIL*) detonator; ~**holz** ['tsʏnt-] nt match; ~**kerze** f (*AUT*) spark(ing) plug; ~**schloß** ⚠ nt ignition lock; ~**schlüssel** m ignition key; ~**schnur** f fuse wire; ~**stoff** m (*fig*) inflammatory stuff; ~**ung** f ignition

zunehmen ['tsu:ne:mən] (*unreg*) vi to increase, to grow; (*Mensch*) to put on weight

Zuneigung ['tsu:naɪgʊŋ] f affection

Zunft [tsʊnft] (**-, ⁻e**) f guild

zünftig ['tsʏnftɪç] adj proper, real; (*Handwerk*) decent

Zunge ['tsʊŋə] f tongue

zunichte [tsu:'nɪçtə] adv: ~ **machen** to ruin, to destroy; ~ **werden** to come to nothing

zunutze ⚠ [tsu:'nʊtsə] adv: **sich** dat **etw ~ machen** to make use of sth

zuoberst [tsu:'o:bərst] adv at the top

zupfen ['tsʊpfən] vt to pull, to pick, to pluck; (*Gitarre*) to pluck

zur [tsu:r] = **zu der**

zurechnungsfähig ['tsu:rɛçnʊŋsfɛ:ɪç] adj responsible, accountable

zurecht- [tsu:'rɛçt] zW: ~**finden** (*unreg*) vr to find one's way (about); ~**kommen** (*unreg*) vi to (be able to) cope, to manage; ~**legen** vt to get ready; (*Ausrede etc*) to have ready; ~**machen** vt to prepare ♦ vr to get ready; ~**weisen** (*unreg*) vt to reprimand

zureden ['tsu:re:dən] vi: **jdm ~** to persuade od urge sb

zurück [tsu:'rʏk] adv back; ~**behalten** (*unreg*) vt to keep back; ~**bekommen** (*unreg*) vt to get back; ~**bleiben** (*unreg*) vi (*Mensch*) to remain behind; (*nicht nachkommen*) to fall behind, to lag; (*Schaden*) to remain; ~**bringen** (*unreg*) vt to bring back; ~**fahren** (*unreg*) vi to travel back; (*vor Schreck*) to recoil, to start ♦ vt to drive back; ~**finden** (*unreg*) vi to find one's way back; ~**fordern** vt to demand back; ~**führen** vt to lead back; **etw auf etw** akk ~**führen** to trace sth back to sth; ~**geben** (*unreg*) vt to give back; (*antworten*) to retort with; ~**geblieben** adj retarded; ~**gehen** (*unreg*) vi to go back; (*fallen*) to go down, to fall; (*zeitlich*): ~**gehen (auf** +akk) to date back (to); ~**gezogen** adj retired, withdrawn; ~**halten** (*unreg*) vt to hold back; (*Mensch*) to restrain; (*hindern*) to prevent ♦ vr (*reserviert sein*) to be reserved; (*im Essen*) to hold back; ~**haltend** adj reserved; **Z~haltung** f reserve; ~**kehren** vi to return; ~**kommen** (*unreg*) vi to come back; **auf etw** akk ~**kommen** to return to sth; **~lassen** (*unreg*) *vt* to leave behind; **~legen** *vt* to put back; (*Geld*) to put by; (*reservieren*) to keep back; (*Strecke*) to cover; **~nehmen** (*unreg*) *vt* to take back; **~stellen** *vt* to put back, to replace; (*aufschieben*) to put off, to postpone; (*Interessen*) to defer; (*Ware*) to keep; **~treten** (*unreg*) *vi* to step back; (*vom Amt*) to retire; **gegenüber etw** *od* **hinter etw** *dat* **~treten** to diminish in importance in view of sth; **~weisen** (*unreg*) *vt* to turn down; (*Mensch*) to reject; **~zahlen** *vt* to repay, to pay back; **~ziehen** (*unreg*) *vt* to pull back; (*Angebot*) to withdraw ♦ *vr* to retire

Zuruf ['tsu:ruf] *m* shout, cry

Zusage ['tsu:za:gə] *f* promise; (*Annahme*) consent; **z~n** *vt* to promise ♦ *vi* to accept; **jdm z~n** (*gefallen*) to agree with *od* please sb

zusammen [tsu'zamən] *adv* together; **Z~arbeit** *f* cooperation; **~arbeiten** *vi* to cooperate; **~beißen** (*unreg*) *vt* (*Zähne*) to clench; **~brechen** (*unreg*) *vi* to collapse; (*Mensch auch*) to break down; **~bringen** (*unreg*) *vt* to bring *od* get together; (*Geld*) to get; (*Sätze*) to put together; **Z~bruch** *m* collapse; **~fassen** *vt* to summarize; (*vereinigen*) to unite; **Z~fassung** *f* summary, résumé; **~fügen** *vt* to join (together), to unite; **~halten** (*unreg*) *vi* to stick together; **Z~hang** *m* connection; **im/aus dem Z~hang** in/out of context; **~hängen** (*unreg*) *vi* to be connected *od* linked; **~kommen** (*unreg*) *vi* to meet, to assemble; (*sich ereignen*) to occur at once *od* together; **~legen** *vt* to put together; (*stapeln*) to pile up; (*falten*) to fold; (*verbinden*) to combine, to unite; (*Termine, Fest*) to amalgamate; (*Geld*) to collect; **~nehmen** (*unreg*) *vt* to summon up ♦ *vr* to pull o.s. together; **alles ~genommen** all in all; **~passen** *vi* to go well together, to match; **~schließen** (*unreg*) *vt, vr* to join (together); **Z~schluß** △ *m* amalgamation; **~schreiben** (*unreg*) *vt* to write as one word; (*Bericht*) to put together; **Z~sein** (**-s**) *nt* get-together;

~setzen *vt* to put together ♦ *vr* (*Stoff*) to be composed of; (*Menschen*) to get together; **Z~setzung** *f* composition; **~stellen** *vt* to put together; to compile; **Z~stoß** *m* collision; **~stoßen** (*unreg*) *vi* to collide; **~treffen** (*unreg*) *vi* to coincide; (*Menschen*) to meet; **Z~treffen** *nt* coincidence; meeting; **~zählen** *vt* to add up; **~ziehen** (*unreg*) *vt* (*verengern*) to draw together; (*vereinigen*) to bring together; (*addieren*) to add up ♦ *vr* to shrink; (*sich bilden*) to form, to develop

zusätzlich ['tsu:zɛtslɪç] *adj* additional ♦ *adv* in addition

zuschauen ['tsu:ʃauən] *vi* to watch, to look on; **Zuschauer(in)** (**-s, -**) *m(f)* spectator ♦ *pl* (*THEAT*) audience *sg*

zuschicken ['tsu:ʃɪkən] *vt*: **(jdm etw) ~** to send *od* to forward (sth to sb)

Zuschlag ['tsu:ʃla:k] *m* extra charge, surcharge; **z~en** (*unreg*) *vt* (*Tür*) to slam; (*Ball*) to hit; (*bei Auktion*) to knock down; (*Steine etc*) to knock into shape ♦ *vi* (*Fenster, Tür*) to shut; (*Mensch*) to hit, to punch; **~karte** *f* (*EISENB*) surcharge ticket; **z~pflichtig** *adj* subject to surcharge

zuschneiden ['tsu:ʃnaidən] (*unreg*) *vt* to cut out; to cut to size

zuschrauben ['tsu:ʃraubən] *vt* to screw down *od* up

zuschreiben ['tsu:ʃraibən] (*unreg*) *vt* (*fig*) to ascribe, to attribute; (*COMM*) to credit

Zuschrift ['tsu:ʃrɪft] *f* letter, reply

zuschulden △ [tsu'ʃʊldən] *adv*: **sich** *dat* **etw ~ kommen lassen** to make o.s. guilty of sth

Zuschuß △ ['tsu:ʃʊs] *m* subsidy, allowance

zusehen ['tsu:ze:ən] (*unreg*) *vi* to watch; (*dafür sorgen*) to take care; **jdm/etw ~** to watch sb/sth; **~ds** *adv* visibly

zusenden ['tsu:zɛndən] (*unreg*) *vt* to send on, to send on

zusichern ['tsu:zɪçərn] *vt*: **jdm etw ~** to assure sb of sth

zuspielen ['tsu:ʃpi:lən] *vt, vi* to pass

zuspitzen ['tsu:ʃpɪtsən] *vt* to sharpen ♦ *vr* (*Lage*) to become critical

△ *Informationen zur Rechtschreibreform Seite 615*

zusprechen ['tsu:ʃprɛçən] (unreg) vt (zuerkennen) to award ♦ vi to speak; **jdm etw ~** to award sb sth od sth to sb; **jdm Trost ~** to comfort sb; **dem Essen/ Alkohol ~** to eat/drink a lot

Zustand ['tsu:ʃtant] m state, condition; **z~e** ⚠ [tsu:ʃtandə] adv: **z~e bringen** to bring about; **z~e kommen** to come about

zuständig ['tsu:ʃtɛndɪç] adj responsible; **Z~keit** f competence, responsibility

zustehen ['tsu:ʃte:ən] (unreg) vi: **jdm ~** to be sb's right

zustellen ['tsu:ʃtɛlən] vt (verstellen) to block; (Post etc) to send

Zustellung f delivery

zustimmen ['tsu:ʃtɪmən] vi to agree

Zustimmung f agreement, consent

zustoßen ['tsu:ʃto:sən] (unreg) vi (fig) to happen

zutage ⚠ [tsu:'ta:gə] adv: **~ bringen** to bring to light; **~ treten** to come to light

Zutaten ['tsu:ta:tən] pl ingredients

zuteilen ['tsu:taɪlən] vt (Arbeit, Rolle) to designate, assign; (Aktien, Wohnung) to allocate

zutiefst [tsu:'ti:fst] adv deeply

zutragen ['tsu:tra:gən] (unreg) vt to bring; (Klatsch) to tell ♦ vr to happen

zutrau- ['tsu:trau] zW: **Z~en (-s)** nt: **Z~en (zu)** trust (in); **~en** vt: **jdm etw ~en** to credit sb with sth; **~lich** adj trusting, friendly

zutreffen ['tsu:trɛfən] (unreg) vi to be correct; to apply; **~d** adj (richtig) accurate; **Z~des bitte unterstreichen** please underline where applicable

Zutritt ['tsu:trɪt] m access, admittance

Zutun ['tsu:tu:n] (-s) nt assistance

zuverlässig ['tsu:fɛrlɛsɪç] adj reliable; **Z~keit** f reliability

zuversichtlich ['tsu:fɛrzɪçtlɪç] adj confident

zuviel ⚠ [tsu:'fi:l] adv too much

zuvor [tsu:'fo:r] adv before, previously; **~kommen** (unreg) vi +dat to anticipate; **jdm ~kommen** to beat sb to it; **~kommend** adj obliging, courteous

Zuwachs ['tsu:vaks] (-es) m increase,

growth; (umg) addition; **z~en** (unreg) vi to become overgrown; (Wunde) to heal (up)

zuwege ⚠ [tsu:'ve:gə] adv: **etw ~ bringen** to accomplish sth

zuweilen [tsu:'vaɪlən] adv at times, now and then

zuweisen ['tsu:vaɪzən] (unreg) vt to assign, to allocate

zuwenden ['tsu:vɛndən] (unreg) vt (+dat) to turn (towards) ♦ vr: **sich jdm/etw ~** to devote o.s. to sb/sth; to turn to sb/sth

zuwenig ⚠ [tsu:'ve:nɪç] adv too little

zuwider [tsu:'vi:dər] adv: **etw ist jdm ~** sb loathes sth, sb finds sth repugnant; **~handeln** vi: **einer Sache** dat **~handeln** to act contrary to sth; **einem Gesetz ~handeln** to contravene a law

zuziehen ['tsu:tsi:ən] (unreg) vt (schließen: Vorhang) to draw, to close; (herbeirufen: Experten) to call in ♦ vi to move in, to come; **sich** dat **etw ~** (Krankheit) to catch sth; (Zorn) to incur sth

zuzüglich ['tsu:tsy:klɪç] präp +gen plus, with the addition of

Zwang [tsvaŋ] (-(e)s, -̈e) m compulsion, coercion

zwängen ['tsvɛŋən] vt, vr to squeeze

zwanglos adj informal

Zwangs- zW: **~arbeit** f forced labour; (Strafe) hard labour; **~lage** f predicament, tight corner; **z~läufig** adj necessary, inevitable

zwanzig ['tsvantsɪç] num twenty

zwar [tsva:r] adv to be sure, indeed; **das ist ~ ..., aber ...** that may be ... but ...; **und ~ am Sonntag** on Sunday to be precise; **und ~ so schnell, daß ...** in fact so quickly that ...

Zweck [tsvɛk] (-(e)s, -e) m purpose, aim; **es hat keinen ~** there's no point; **z~dienlich** adj practical; expedient

Zwecke f hobnail; (Heft~) drawing pin, thumbtack (US)

Zweck- zW: **z~los** adj pointless; **z~mäßig** adj suitable, appropriate; **z~s** präp +gen for the purpose of

zwei [tsvaɪ] num two; **Z~bettzimmer** nt

⚠ For information on spelling reform see page 615

twin room; **~deutig** *adj* ambiguous; (*unanständig*) suggestive; **~erlei** *adj*: **~erlei Stoff** two different kinds of material; **~erlei Meinung** of differing opinions; **~fach** *adj* double

Zweifel ['tsvaɪfəl] (**-s, -**) *m* doubt; **z~haft** *adj* doubtful, dubious; **z~los** *adj* doubtless; **z~n** *vi*: (**an etw** *dat*) **z~n** to doubt (sth)

Zweig [tsvaɪk] (**-(e)s, -e**) *m* branch; **~stelle** *f* branch (office)

zwei- *zW*: **~hundert** *num* two hundred; **Z~kampf** *m* duel; **~mal** *adv* twice; **~sprachig** *adj* bilingual; **~spurig** *adj* (*AUT*) two-lane; **~stimmig** *adj* for two voices

zweit [tsvaɪt] *adv*: **zu ~** together; (*bei mehreren Paaren*) in twos

zweitbeste(r, s) *adj* second best

zweite(r, s) *adj* second

zweiteilig ['tsvaɪtaɪlɪç] *adj* (*Gruppe*) two-piece; (*Fernsehfilm*) two-part; (*Kleidung*) two-piece

zweit- *zW*: **~ens** *adv* secondly; **~größte(r, s)** *adj* second largest; **~klassig** *adj* second-class; **~letzte(r, s)** *adj* last but one, penultimate; **~rangig** *adj* second-rate

Zwerchfell ['tsvɛrçfɛl] *nt* diaphragm

Zwerg [tsvɛrk] (**-(e)s, -e**) *m* dwarf

Zwetsch(g)e ['tsvɛtʃ(g)ə] *f* plum

Zwieback ['tsvi:bak] (**-(e)s, -e**) *m* rusk

Zwiebel ['tsvi:bəl] (**-, -n**) *f* onion; (*Blumen~*) bulb

Zwie- ['tsvi:] *zW*: **z~lichtig** *adj* shady, dubious; **z~spältig** *adj* (*Gefühle*)

conflicting; (*Charakter*) contradictory; **~tracht** *f* discord, dissension

Zwilling ['tsvɪlɪŋ] (**-s, -e**) *m* twin; **~e** *pl* (*ASTROL*) Gemini

zwingen ['tsvɪŋən] (*unreg*) *vt* to force; **~d** *adj* (*Grund etc*) compelling

zwinkern ['tsvɪŋkərn] *vi* to blink; (*absichtlich*) to wink

Zwirn [tsvɪrn] (**-(e)s, -e**) *m* thread

zwischen ['tsvɪʃən] *präp* (+*akk od dat*) between; **Z~bemerkung** *f* (incidental) remark; **Z~ding** *nt* cross; **~durch** *adv* in between; (*räumlich*) here and there; **Z~ergebnis** *nt* intermediate result; **Z~fall** *m* incident; **Z~frage** *f* question; **Z~handel** *m* middlemen *pl*; middleman's trade; **Z~landung** *f* (*AVIAT*) stopover; **~menschlich** *adj* interpersonal; **Z~raum** *m* space; **Z~ruf** *m* interjection; **Z~stecker** *m* adaptor (plug); **Z~zeit** *f* interval; **in der Z~zeit** in the interim, meanwhile

zwitschern ['tsvɪtʃərn] *vt, vi* to twitter, to chirp

zwo [tsvo:] *num* two

zwölf [tsvœlf] *num* twelve

Zyklus ['tsy:klʊs] (**-, Zyklen**) *m* cycle

Zylinder [tsi'lɪndər] (**-s, -**) *m* cylinder; (*Hut*) top hat

Zyniker ['tsy:nikər(ɪn)] (**-s, -**) *m* cynic

zynisch ['tsy:nɪʃ] *adj* cynical

Zypern ['tsy:pərn] *nt* Cyprus

Zyste ['tsʏstə] *f* cyst

z.Z(t). *abk* = **zur Zeit**

PUZZLES AND
WORDGAMES

PUZZLES AND WORDGAMES

Introduction

We are delighted that you have decided to invest in this Collins Pocket Dictionary! Whether you intend to use it in school, at home, on holiday or at work, we are sure that you will find it very useful.

In the pages which follow you will find explanations and wordgames (not too difficult!) designed to give you practice in exploring the dictionary's contents and in retrieving information for a variety of purposes. Answers are provided at the end. If you spend a little time on these pages you should be able to use your dictionary more efficiently and effectively. Have fun!

Supplement by
Roy Simon
reproduced by kind permission of
Tayside Region Education Department

HOW INFORMATION IS PRESENTED IN YOUR DICTIONARY

A great deal of information is packed into your Collins Pocket Dictionary using colour, various typefaces, sizes of type, symbols, abbreviations and brackets. The purpose of this section is to acquaint you with the conventions used in presenting information.

Headwords

A headword is the word you look up in a dictionary. Headwords are listed in alphabetical order throughout the dictionary. They are printed in colour so that they stand out clearly from all the other words on the dictionary page.

Note that at the top of each page a headword appears. This is a guide to the alphabetical order of words on the page. It is there to help you scan through the dictionary more quickly to find the word you want.

The German alphabet consists of the same 26 letters as the English alphabet, plus the letter ß, which is used in some words instead of ss. Although certain letters in the German alphabet take umlaut (ä, ö, ü), this does not affect the order of words in the German-English section of the dictionary.

A Dictionary Entry

An entry is made up of a headword and all the information about that headword. Entries will be short or long depending on how frequently a word is used in either English or German and how many meanings it has. Inevitably, the fuller the dictionary entry the more care is needed in sifting through it to find the information you require.

Meanings

The translations of a headword are given in ordinary type. Where there is more than one meaning or usage, a semi-colon separates one from the other.

abladen ['aplaːdən] (*unreg*) *vt* to unload
Ablage ['aplaːɡə] *f* (*für Akten*) tray; (*für Kleider*) cloakroom
ablassen ['aplasən] (*unreg*) *vt* (*Wasser, Dampf*) to let off; (*vom Preis*) to knock off
♦ *vi*: **von etw ~** to give sth up, to abandon sth

brünett [bryˈnɛt] *adj* brunette, dark-haired
Brunnen ['brʊnən] (**-s, -**) *m* fountain; (*tief*)

Bude ['buːdə] *f* booth, stall; (*umg*) digs *pl* (*BRIT*)

Ohnmacht ['oːnmaxt] *f* faint; (*fig*) impotence; **in ~ fallen** to faint
ohnmächtig ['oːnmɛçtɪç] *adj* in a faint, unconscious; (*fig*) weak, impotent; **sie ist ~** she has fainted
Ohr [oːr] (**-(e)s, -en**) *nt* ear
Öhr [øːr] (**-(e)s, -e**) *nt* eye

Gurt [ɡʊrt] (**-(e)s, -e**) *m* belt

klar- *zW*: **~legen** *vt* to clear up, to explain; **~machen** *vt* (*Schiff*) to get ready for sea; **jdm etw ~machen** to make sth clear to sb; **~sehen** △ (*unreg*) *vi* to see clearly; **K~sichtfolie** *f* transparent film; **~stellen**

Zug [tsuːk] (**-(e)s, ¨e**) *m* (*EISENB*) train; (*Luft~*) draught; (*Ziehen*) pull(ing); (*Gesichts~*) feature; (*SCHACH etc*) move; (*Schrift~*) stroke; (*Atem~*) breath; (*Charakter~*) trait; (*an Zigarette*) puff, pull, drag; (*Schluck*) gulp; (*Menschengruppe*) procession; (*von Vögeln*) flight; (*MIL*) platoon; **etw in vollen Zügen genießen** to enjoy sth to the full

279

In addition, you will often find other words appearing in *italics* in brackets before the translations. These either give some notion of the contexts in which the headword might appear (as with 'scharf' opposite – 'scharfes Essen', 'scharfe Munition', etc.) or else they provide synonyms (as with 'fremd' opposite – 'unvertraut', 'ausländisch', etc.).

Phonetic Spellings

In square brackets immediately after most headwords you will find the phonetic spelling of the word – i.e. its pronunciation. The phonetic transcription of German and English vowels and consonants is given on page xii near the front of your dictionary.

Additional Information About Headwords

Information about the usage or form of certain headwords is given in brackets between the phonetics and the translation or translations. Have a look at the entries for 'KG', 'Filiale', 'löschen' and 'Bruch' opposite.

This information is usually given in abbreviated form. A helpful list of abbreviations is given on pages viii to x at the front of your dictionary.

You should be particularly careful with colloquial words or phrases. Words labelled '(*umg*)' would not normally be used in formal speech, while those labelled '(*umg!*)' would be considered offensive.

Careful consideration of such style labels will provide indications as to the degree of formality and appropriateness of a word and could help you avoid many an embarrassing situation when using German!

Expressions in which the Headword Appears

An entry will often feature certain common expressions in which the headword appears. These expressions are in **bold** type but in black as opposed to colour. A swung dash (-) is used instead of repeating a headword in an entry. 'Schikane' and 'man' opposite illustrate this point.

Related Words

In the Pocket Dictionary words related to certain headwords are sometimes given at the end of an entry, as with 'Lohn' and 'accept' opposite. These are easily picked out as they are also in colour. To help you find these words, they are placed in alphabetical order after the headword to which they belong – see 'acceptable', 'acceptance' etc. opposite.

scharf [ʃarf] *adj* sharp; *(Essen)* hot, spicy; *(Munition)* live; **~ nachdenken** to think hard; **auf etw** *akk* **~ sein** *(umg)* to be keen on sth

fremd [frɛmt] *adj (unvertraut)* strange; *(ausländisch)* foreign; *(nicht eigen)* someone else's; **etw ist jdm ~** sth is foreign to sb; **~artig** *adj* strange; **F~enführer** ['frɛmdən-]

gänzlich ['gɛntslɪç] *adj* complete, entire
♦ *adv* completely, entirely

KG [kaːˈgeː] **(-, -s)** *f abk* **(= Kommanditgesellschaft)** limited partnership

Filiale [filiˈaːlə] *f (COMM)* branch

Teufel ['tɔʏfəl] **(-s, -)** *m* devil; **teuflisch** *adj* fiendish, diabolical

löschen ['lœʃən] *vt (Feuer, Licht)* to put out, to extinguish; *(Durst)* to quench; *(COMM)* to cancel; *(COMPUT)* to delete; *(Tonband)* to erase; *(Fracht)* to unload ♦ *vi (Feuerwehr)* to put out a fire; *(Tinte)* to blot

Bruch [brʊx] **(-(e)s, ⁼e)** *m* breakage; *(zerbrochene Stelle)* break; *(fig)* split, breach; *(MED: Eingeweide~)* rupture, hernia; *(Bein~ etc)* fracture; *(MATH)* fraction

schenken ['ʃɛŋkən] *vt (auch fig)* to give; *(Getränk)* to pour; **sich** *dat* **etw ~** *(umg)* to skip sth; **das ist geschenkt!** *(billig)* that's a giveaway!; *(nichts wert)* that's worthless!

Bombenerfolg *(umg) m* smash hit

Arsch [arʃ] **(-es, ⁼e)** *(umg!) m* arse *(BRIT!)*, ass *(US!)*

Schikane [ʃiˈkaːnə] *f* harassment; dirty trick; **mit allen ~n** with all the trimmings

man [man] *pron* one, you; **~ sagt, ...** they *od* people say ...; **wie schreibt ~ das?** how do you write it?, how is it written?

Lohn [loːn] **(-(e)s, ⁼e)** *m* reward; *(Arbeits~)* pay, wages *pl*; **~büro** *nt* wages office; **~empfänger** *m* wage earner

accept [əkˈsɛpt] *vt (take)* annehmen; *(agree to)* akzeptieren; **~able** *adj* annehmbar; **~ance** *n* Annahme *f*

'Key' Words

Your Collins Pocket Dictionary gives special status to certain German and English words which can be looked on as 'key' words in each language. These are words which have many different usages. 'Werden', 'alle(r, s)' and 'sich' opposite are typical examples in German. You are likely to become familiar with them in your day-to-day language studies.

There will be occasions, however, when you want to check on a particular usage. Your dictionary can be very helpful here. Note how different parts of speech and different usages are clearly indicated by a combination of lozenges (♦) and numbers. In addition, further guides to usage are given in italics in brackets in the language of the user who needs them.

werden ['ve:rdən] (*pt* **wurde,** *pp* **geworden** *od* (*bei Passiv*) **worden**) *vi* to become; **was ist aus ihm/aus der Sache geworden?** what became of him/it?; **es ist nichts/gut geworden** it came to nothing/turned out well; **es wird Nacht/Tag** it's getting dark/ light; **mir wird kalt** I'm getting cold; **mir wird schlecht** I feel ill; **Erster werden** to come *od* be first; **das muß anders werden** that'll have to change; **rot/zu Eis werden** to turn red/to ice; **was willst du (mal) werden?** what do you want to be?; **die Fotos sind gut geworden** the photos have come out nicely

♦ *als Hilfsverb* **1** (*bei Futur*): **er wird es tun** he will *od* he'll do it; **er wird das nicht tun** he will not *od* he won't do it; **es wird gleich regnen** it's going to rain

2 (*bei Konjunktiv*): **ich würde ...** I would ...; **er würde gern ...** he would *od* he'd like to ...; **ich würde lieber ...** I would *od* I'd rather ...

3 (*bei Vermutung*): **sie wird in der Küche sein** she will be in the kitchen

4 (*bei Passiv*): **gebraucht werden** to be used; **er ist erschossen worden** he has *od* he's been shot; **mir wurde gesagt, daß ...** I was told that ...

alle(r, s) ['alə(r,s)] *adj* **1** (*sämtliche*) all; **wir alle** all of us; **alle Kinder waren da** all the children were there; **alle Kinder mögen ...** all children like ...; **alle beide** both of us/ them; **sie kamen alle** they all came; **alles Gute** all the best; **alles in allem** all in all **2** (*mit Zeit- oder Maßangaben*) every; **alle vier Jahre** every four years; **alle fünf Meter** every five metres

♦ *pron* everything; **alles was er sagt** everything he says, all that he says

♦ *adv* (*zu Ende, aufgebraucht*) finished; **die Milch ist alle** the milk's all gone, there's no milk left; **etw alle machen** to finish sth up

sich [zɪç] *pron* **1** (*akk*): **er/sie/es ... sich** he/she/it ... himself/herself/itself; **sie** *pl/* **man ... sich** they/one ... themselves/ oneself; **Sie ... sich** you ... yourself/ yourselves *pl*; **sich wiederholen** to repeat oneself/itself

2 (*dat*): **er/sie/es ... sich** he/she/it ... to himself/herself/itself; **sie** *pl/***man ... sich** they/one ... to themselves/oneself; **Sie ... sich** you ... to yourself/yourselves *pl*; **sie hat sich einen Pullover gekauft** she bought herself a jumper; **sich die Haare waschen** to wash one's hair

3 (*mit Präposition*): **haben Sie Ihren Ausweis bei sich?** do you have your pass on you?; **er hat nichts bei sich** he's got nothing on him; **sie bleiben gern unter sich** they keep themselves to themselves

4 (*einander*) each other, one another; **sie bekämpfen sich** they fight each other *od* one another

5: dieses Auto fährt sich gut this car drives well; **hier sitzt es sich gut** it's good to sit here

WORDGAME 1
HEADWORDS

Study the following sentences. In each sentence a wrong word spelt very similarly to the correct word has deliberately been put in and the sentence doesn't make sense. This word is shaded each time. Write out the correct word, which you will find in your dictionary near the wrong word.

> Example   Raufen verboten
>
> ['Raufen' (= 'to pull out') is the wrong word and
> should be replaced by 'rauchen' (= 'to smoke')]

1. Hast du das Buch schon gekonnt?

2. Ich habe ein paar VW-Akten gekauft.

3. Wir waren gestern im Kilo.

4. Sollen wir die Theaterkarten schon kauen?

5. Unser Nachbar hat einen kleinen schwarzen Puder.

6. Ich zähle heute die Rechnung.

7. Der Student muß sich für den Kurs einschreiten.

8. Das neue Restaurant ist gar nicht über.

9. Gans viele Leute standen am Unfallort.

10. Ich habe meiner Tanne einen Brief geschrieben.

WORDGAME 2

DICTIONARY ENTRIES

Complete the crossword below by looking up the English words in the list and finding the correct German translations. There is a slight catch, however! All the English words can be translated several ways into German, but only one translation will fit correctly into each part of the crossword. So look carefully through the entries in the English-German section of your dictionary.

1. FAIR

2. CATCH

3. LEARN

4. FALL

5. HIT

6. HARD

7. CALF

8. PLACE

9. HOLD

10. PLACE

11. TRACK

12. HOME

WORDGAME 3

FINDING MEANINGS

In this list there are eight pairs of words that have some sort of connection with each other. For example, 'Diplom' (= 'diploma') and 'Student' (='student') are linked. Find the other pairs by looking up the words in your dictionary.

1. Morgenrock
2. Handtasche
3. Bett
4. Kirche
5. Fisch
6. Nest
7. Diplom
8. Lederwaren
9. Hausschuhe
10. Glockengeläut
11. Student
12. Decke
13. Elster
14. Buch
15. Schuppe
16. Regal

WORDGAME 4
SYNONYMS

Complete the crossword by supplying synonyms of the words below. You will sometimes find the words you are looking for in italics in brackets in the entries for the words in the list. Sometimes you will have to turn to the English-German section for help.

1. Art
2. probieren
3. Feuer
4. sich ereignen
5. Arroganz

6. namhaft
7. Ladung
8. Plan
9. begegnen
10. Neigung

WORDGAME 5

SPELLING

You will often use your dictionary to check spellings. The person who has compiled this list of ten German words has made <u>three</u> spelling mistakes. Find the three words which have been misspelt and write them out correctly.

1. nachsehen
2. nacht
3. Nagetier
4. Name
5. Nature
6. neuriech
7. Nickerchen
8. Nimmersatt
9. nördlich
10. nötig

WORDGAME 6
ANTONYMS

Complete the crossword by supplying ANTONYMS (i.e. opposites) in German of the words below. Use your dictionary to help.

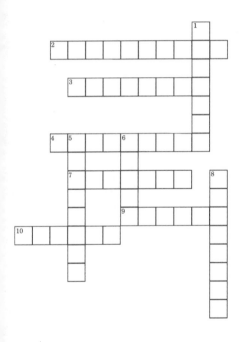

1. gestehen
2. enthüllen
3. unschuldig
4. kaufen
5. verbieten
6. Reichtum
7. ruhig
8. ankommen
9. ängstlich
10. schmutzig

WORDGAME 7
PHONETIC SPELLINGS

The phonetic transcriptions of ten German words are given below. If you study page xii near the front of your dictionary you should be able to work out what the words are.

1. frika'dɛlə
2. ʃpuːr
3. faɪn
4. 'lyːgə
5. 'ʃtaxəl
6. 'naʊtɪʃ
7. gə'vœlbə
8. 'kɔʏçən
9. 'møːgən
10. 'glaʊbvʏrdɪç

WORDGAME 8

EXPRESSIONS IN WHICH THE HEADWORD APPEARS

If you look up the headword 'Satz' in the German-English section of your dictionary you will find that the word can have many meanings. Study the entry carefully and translate the following sentences into English.

1. Der Satz ist viel zu lang.

2. Unterstreicht jeden Satz, der mit einer Konjunktion beginnt.

3. Den Satz von Pythagoras kennt jeder.

4. Das Orchester hat den letzten Satz ganz ausgezeichnet gespielt.

5. Steffi Graf hat in der Meisterschaft keinen Satz verloren.

6. Der ganze Satz war in der Tasse.

7. Bei Lieferungen ins Ausland gilt ein anderer Satz.

8. Sie hat vor lauter Begeisterung einen großen Satz gemacht.

WORDGAME 9
RELATED WORDS

Fill in the blanks in the pairs of sentences below. The missing words are related to the headwords on the left. Choose the correct "relative" each time. You will find it in your dictionary near the headword provided.

HEADWORD	RELATED WORDS
Stellung	1. Ich habe die Uhr auf halb sechs _____. 2. Das Auto steht an der gleichen_____.
Hoffnung	3. _____bleibt das Wetter so. 4. Sie_____, daß sie bald wieder gesund ist.
Betrug	5. Von ihm lassen wir uns nicht mehr_____. 6. Er ist als_____bekannt.
sprechen	7. Hat er schon mit seiner Mutter_____? 8. Das Buch wurde in fünf _____übersetzt.
Student	9. Er hat letztes Semester mit dem_____ begonnen. 10. Sie _____Medizin.
kurz	11. Ich habe_____noch mit ihm gesprochen. 12. Der Rock muß_____werden.

WORDGAME 10

'KEY' WORDS

Study carefully the entry 'machen' in your dictionary and find translations for the following:

1. what are you doing (there)?

2. it's the cold that does that

3. that doesn't matter

4. I don't mind the cold

5. 3 and 5 are 8

6. to have the car done

7. how's the work going?

8. hurry up!

9. to set about sth

10. to turn the radio down

THE DICTIONARY AND GRAMMAR

While it is true that a dictionary can never be a substitute for a detailed grammar book, it nevertheless provides a great deal of grammatical information. If you know how to extract this information you will be able to use German more accurately both in speech and in writing.

The Collins Pocket Dictionary presents grammatical information as follows.

Parts of Speech

Parts of speech are given in italics immediately after the phonetic spellings of headwords. Abbreviated forms are used. Abbreviations can be checked on pages viii to x.

Changes in parts of speech within an entry – for example, from adjective to pronoun to adverb, or from noun to intransitive verb to transitive verb – are indicated by means of lozenges (♦), as with the German 'alle(r, s)' and the English 'fast' opposite.

German Nouns

The gender of each noun in the German-English section of the dictionary is indicated in the following way:

m = Maskulinum
f = Femininum
nt = Neutrum

You will occasionally see 'm od nt' or 'm od f' beside an entry. This indicates that the noun can be either masculine or neuter (see 'Knäuel' opposite or masculine or feminine (see 'Sellerie' opposite).

Feminine forms of nouns are shown, as with 'Schaffner(in)' opposite. This is marked $m(f)$ to show that the feminine form has the ending '-in'. Nouns which have the ending '-(r)', like 'Angeklagte(r)' opposite, are formed from adjectives and are marked $f(m)$ to show that they can be either masculine or feminine. Their spelling changes in the same way as adjectives, depending on their article and position in the sentence.

prosit ['pro:zɪt] *excl* cheers

leiten ['laɪtən] *vt* to lead; (*Firma*) to manage; (*in eine Richtung*) to direct; (*ELEK*) to conduct

alle(r, s) ['alə(r,s)] *adj* **1** (*sämtliche*) all; **wir alle** all of us; **alle Kinder waren da** all the children were there; **alle Kinder mögen ...** all children like ...; **sie kamen alle** they all came; **alles Gute** all the best; **alles in allem** all in all **2** (*mit Zeit- oder Maßangaben*) every; **alle vier Jahre** every four years; **alle fünf Meter** every five metres
♦ *pron* everything; **alles was er sagt** everything he says, all that he says
♦ *adv* (*zu Ende, aufgebraucht*) finished; **die Milch ist alle** the milk's all gone, there's no milk left; **etw alle machen** to finish sth up

fast [fʊːst] *adj* schnell; (*firm*) fest ♦ *adv* schnell; fest ♦ *n* Fasten *nt* ♦ *vi* fasten; **to be ~** (*clock*) vorgehen

Knäuel ['knɔʏəl] (**-s**, **-**) *m od nt* (*Woll~*) ball; (*Menschen~*) knot

Sellerie ['zɛləriː] (**-s**, **-(s)** *od* **-**, **-**) *m od f* celery

Schaffner(in) ['ʃafnər(ɪn)] (**-s**, **-**) *m(f)* (*Bus~*) conductor(-tress); (*EISENB*) guard

Angeklagte(r) ['angəklaːktə(r)] *f(m)* accused

295

So many things depend on you knowing the correct gender of a German noun – whether you use 'er', 'sie' or 'es' to translate 'it'; whether you use 'er' or 'es' to translate 'he', 'sie' or 'es' to translate 'she'; the spelling of adjectives etc. If you are in any doubt as to the gender of a noun, it is always best to check it in your dictionary.

Genitive singular and nominative plural forms of many nouns are also given (see 'Bube' and 'Scheitel' opposite). A list of regular noun endings is given on page xi and nouns which have these forms will not show genitive singular and nominative plural at the headword (see 'Rasur' and 'Forelle' opposite). Nouns formed from two or more words do not have genitive singular and nominative plural shown if the last element appears in the dictionary as a headword. For example, if you want to know how to decline 'Backenzahn', you will find the necessary information at 'Zahn'.

Adjectives

Adjectives are given in the form used when they come after a verb. If the adjective comes before a noun, the spelling changes, depending on the gender of the noun and on the article (if any), which comes before the adjective. Compare 'der Hund ist schwarz' with 'der schwarze Hund'. If you find an unfamiliar adjective in a text and want to look it up in the dictionary, you will have to decide what spelling changes have been made before you can know how it will appear in the dictionary.

Some adjectives are never used after a verb. In these cases, the dictionary shows all the possible nominative singular endings.

Adverbs

German adverbs come in three main types.

Some are just adjectives in their after-verb form, used as adverbs. Sometimes the meaning is similar to the meaning of the adjective (see 'laut'), sometimes it is rather different (see 'richtig').

Some adverbs are formed by adding '-weise', '-sweise' or '-erweise' to the adjective.

Other adverbs are not considered to be derived from particular adjectives.

In your dictionary, adjective-adverbs may be shown by a change of part of speech or by the mention 'adj, adv' at the beginning of the entry.

Fuß [fuːs] (-es, -̈e) *m* foot; (*von Glas, Säule etc*) base; (*von Möbel*) leg; **zu ~** on foot;

Stube ['ʃtuːbə] *f* room

Mädchen ['mɛːtçən] *nt* girl; **m~haft** *adj* girlish; **~name** *m* maiden name

Rasur [ra'zuːr] *f* shaving

Forelle [fo'rɛlə] *f* trout

schwarz [ʃvarts] *adj* black; **~es Brett** notice board; **ins S~e treffen** (*auch fig*) to hit the bull's eye; **in den ~en Zahlen** in the black; **S~arbeit** *f* illicit work, moonlighting; **S~brot** *nt* black bread; **S~e(r)** *f(m)* black (man/woman)

laut [laut] *adj* loud ♦ *adv* loudly; (*lesen*) aloud ♦ *präp* (+*gen od dat*) according to; **L~** (-(e)s, -e) *m* sound

richtig *adj* right, correct; (*echt*) proper ♦ *adv* (*umg: sehr*) really; **bin ich hier ~?** am I in the right place?; **der/die R~e** the right one/person; **das R~e** the right thing; **R~keit** *f* correctness; **~stellen** △ *vt* to correct

leider ['laɪdər] *adv* unfortunately; **ja, ~** yes, I'm afraid so; **~ nicht** I'm afraid not

oben ['oːbən] *adv* above; (*in Haus*) upstairs; **nach ~** up; **von ~** down; **~ ohne** topless;

Bube ['buːbə] (-n, -n) *m* (*Schurke*) rogue; (*KARTEN*) jack

Scheitel ['ʃaɪtəl] (-s, -) *m* top; (*Haar~*) parting; **s~n** *vt* to part

Backenzahn *m* molar

Zahn [tsaːn] (-(e)s, -̈e) *m* tooth; **~arzt** *m* dentist; **~ärztin** *f* (female) dentist; **~bürste** *f* toothbrush; **~fleisch** *nt* gums *pl*; **~pasta** *f* toothpaste; **~rad** *nt* cog(wheel);

besondere(r, s) [bə'zɔndərə(r, s)] *adj* special; (*eigen*) particular; (*gesondert*) separate; (*eigentümlich*) peculiar

letzte(r, s) ['lɛtstə(r, s)] *adj* last; (*neueste*) latest; **zum ~nmal** for the last time; **~ns** *adv* lately; **~re(r, s)** *adj* latter

nett [nɛt] *adj* nice; (*freundlich*) nice, kind; **~erweise** *adv* kindly

glück- *zW:* **~lich** *adj* fortunate; (*froh*) happy; **~licherweise** *adv* fortunately; **~'selig** *adj* blissful

Adjective-plus-ending adverbs will usually appear as subentries.

Adverbs like 'oben' and 'leider' will usually appear as separate headwords.

Where a word in your text seems to be an adverb but does not appear in the dictionary, you should be able to work out a translation from the word it is related to, once you have found that in the dictionary.

Information about Verbs

A major problem facing language learners is that the form of a verb will change according to the subject and/or the tense being used. A typical German verb can take on many different forms – too many to list in a dictionary entry.

Yet, although verbs are listed in your dictionary in their infinitive forms only, this does not mean that the dictionary is of limited value when it comes to handling the verb system of the German language. On the contrary, it contains much valuable information.

First of all, your dictionary will help you with the meanings of unfamiliar verbs. If you came across the word 'füllt' in a text and looked it up in your dictionary you wouldn't find it. What you must do is assume that it is part of a verb and look for the infinitive form. Thus you will deduce that 'füllt' is a form of the verb 'füllen'. You now have the basic meaning of the word you are concerned with – something to do with English verb 'fill' – and this should be enough to help you understand the text you are reading.

It is usually an easy task to make the connection between the form of a verb and the infinitive. For example, 'füllten', 'füllst', 'füllte' and 'gefüllt' are all recognizable as parts of the infinitive 'füllen'. However, sometimes it is less obvious – for example, 'hilft', 'halfen' and 'geholfen' are all parts of 'helfen'. The only real solution to this problem is to learn the various forms of the main German irregular verbs.

And this is the second source of help offered by your dictionary as far as verbs are concerned. The irregular verb lists on pages 611 to 615 at the back of the Collins Pocket Dictionary provide the main forms of the main tenses of the basic irregular verbs. (Verbs which consist of a basic verb with prefix usually follow the rules for the basic verb.) Consider the verb 'sehen' below where the following information is given:

infinitive	present indicative (2nd, 3rd sg)	imperfect	past participle
sehen	siehst, sieht	sah	gesehen

In order to make maximum use of the information contained in these pages, a good working knowledge of the various rules affecting German verbs is required. You will acquire this in the course of your German studies and your Collins dictionary will serve as a useful 'aide-mémoire'. If you happen to forget how to form the second person singular form of the Past Tense of 'sehen' (i.e. how to translate 'You saw'), there will be no need to panic – your dictionary contains the information!

In addition, the main parts of the most common irregular verbs are listed in the body of the dictionary.

WORDGAME 11

PARTS OF SPEECH

In each sentence below a word has been shaded. Put a tick in the appropriate box to indicate the **part of speech** each time.

SENTENCE	Noun	Adj	Adv	Verb
1. Das Essen ist fertig.				
2. Er hat kein Recht dazu.				
3. Warum fahren wir nicht in die Stadt zum Essen?				
4. Ich gehe nicht mit essen.				
5. Rauchen ist strengstens verboten.				
6. Gehen Sie geradeaus und dann die erste Straße links.				
7. Das war aber ein interessanter Vortrag.				
8. Die Schauspielerin trug ein herrliches Kleid.				
9. Hast du schon von deiner Freundin gehört?				
10. Es ist immer noch recht sommerlich.				

WORDGAME 12

MEANING CHANGING WITH GENDER

Some German nouns change meaning according to their gender. Look at the pairs of sentences below and fill in the blanks with either 'ein, einen, eine' or 'der, den, die, das'.

1. Ist das _____ erste Band der Schillerausgabe?

    _____ Band ist nicht lang genug.

2. _____ Mark ist in letzter Zeit wieder gestiegen.

    Der Metzger löst _____ Mark aus den Knochen.

3. Was kostet _____ Bund Petersilie?

    _____ Bund an der Hose ist zu weit.

4. _____ Tau lag noch auf den Wiesen.

    Der Mann konnte _____ Tau nicht heben.

5. Wie steht mir _____ Hut?

    Wir müssen wirklich auf _____ Hut sein.

6. Hinter dem Haus steht _____ Kiefer.

    Er hat sich _____ Kiefer gebrochen.

WORDGAME 13

ADJECTIVES

Try to work out how the adjectives in the following phrases will appear in the dictionary. Write your answer beside the phrase, then check in the dictionary.

1. ein englisches Buch

2. der rote Traktor

3. letzte Nacht

4. mein kleiner Bruder

5. eine lange Reise

6. guter Käse

7. das alte Trikot

8. schwarzes Brot

9. die große Kommode

10. ein heftiger Schlag

11. der siebte Sohn

12. die neuen Nachbarn

WORDGAME 14
VERB TENSES

Use your dictionary to help you fill in the blanks in the table below.
(Remember the important pages at the back of your dictionary.)

INFINITIVE	PRESENT TENSE	IMPERFECT	PERFECT TENSE
sehen		ich	
schlafen	du		
sein			ich
schlagen		ich	
anrufen			ich
abfahren	er		
studieren			ich
haben		ich	
anfangen	du		
waschen	er		
werden		ich	
nehmen			ich

WORDGAME 15
PAST PARTICIPLES

Use your dictionary to find the past participle of these verbs.

INFINITIVE	PAST PARTICIPLE
singen	
beißen	
bringen	
frieren	
reiben	
gewinnen	
helfen	
geschehen	
liegen	
lügen	
schneiden	
kennen	
mögen	
wissen	
können	

WORDGAME 16
IDENTIFYING INFINITIVES

In the sentences below you will see various German verbs shaded. Use your dictionary to help you find the INFINITIVE form of each verb.

1. Leider habe ich Ihren Namen vergessen.

2. Bitte ruf mich doch morgen früh mal an.

3. Er ist um 16 Uhr angekommen.

4. Sie hielt an ihrem Argument fest.

5. Wir waren im Sommer in Italien.

6. Ich würde gerne kommen, wenn ich nur könnte.

7. Die Maschine flog über den Nordpol.

8. Ich würde es ja machen, aber ich habe keine Zeit.

9. Wohin fährst du diesen Winter zum Skilaufen?

10. Wen habt ihr sonst noch eingeladen?

11. Er hat deinen Brief erst gestern bekommen.

12. Liest du das Buch nicht zu Ende?

13. Meine Mutter ist letztes Jahr gestorben.

14. Er hat den Zettel aus Versehen weggeworfen.

15. Ich nahm ihn jeden Tag mit nach Hause.

MORE ABOUT MEANING

In this section we will consider some of the problems associated with using a bilingual dictionary.

Overdependence on your dictionary

That the dictionary is an invaluable tool for the language learner is beyond dispute. Nevertheless, it is possible to become overdependent on your dictionary, turning to it in an almost automatic fashion every time you come up against a new German word or phrase. Tackling an unfamiliar text in this way will turn reading in German into an extremely tedious activity. If you stop to look up every new word you may actually be *hindering* your ability to read in German – you are so concerned with the individual words that you pay no attention to the text as a whole and to the context which gives them meaning. It is therefore important to develop appropriate reading skills – using clues such as titles, headlines, illustrations, etc., understanding relations within a sentence, etc. to predict or infer what a text is about.

A detailed study of the development of reading skills is not within the scope of this supplement; we are concerned with knowing how to use a dictionary, which is only one of several important skills involved in reading. Nevertheless, it may be instructive to look at one example. You see the following text in a German newspaper and are interested in working out what it is about.

Contextual clues here include the word in large type which you would probably recognize as a German name, something that looks like a date below, and the name and address at the bottom. Some 'form' words such as 'wir', 'sind', 'und' and 'Tochter' will be familiar to you from your general studies in German. Given that we are dealing with

> *Wir sind glüklich*
> *über die Geburt*
> *unserer Tochter*
>
> ## Julia
>
> am 5. November 1997
>
> *Christine und Artur Landgraf*
> *Vacher Straße 50 B, Köln*

a newspaper, you will probably have worked out by now that this could be an announcement placed in the 'Personal Column'.

So you have used a series of cultural, contextual and word-formation clues to get you to the point where you have understood that Christine and Artur Landgraf have placed this notice in the 'Personal Column' of the newspaper and that something happened to Julia on 5 November 1997. And you have reached this point *without* opening your dictionary once. Common sense and your knowledge of newspaper contents in this country might suggest that this must be an announcement of someone's birth or death. Thus 'glücklich' ('happy') and 'Geburt' ('birth') become the only words that you might have to look up in order to confirm that this is indeed a birth announcement.

When learning German we are helped by the fact that some German and English words look and sound alike and have exactly the same meaning. Such words are called 'COGNATES' i.e. words derived from the same root. Many words come from a common Latin root. Other words are the same or nearly the same in both languages because the German language has borrowed a word from English or vice versa. The dictionary should not be necessary where cognates are concerned – provided you know the English word that the German word resembles!

Words With More Than One Meaning

The need to examine with care *all* the information contained in a dictionary entry must be stressed. This is particularly important with the many German words which have more than one meaning. For example, the German 'Zeit' can mean 'grammatical tense' as well as 'time'. How you translated the word would depend on the context in which you found it.

Similarly, if you were trying to translate a phrase such as 'sich vor etwas drücken', you would have to look through the whole entry for 'drücken' to get the right translation. If you restricted your search to the first couple of lines of the entry and saw that the first meaning given is 'press', you might be tempted to assume that the idiom meant 'to press o.s. in front of sth'. But if you examined the entry closely you would see that 'sich vor etwas drücken' means 'to get out of (doing) sth', as in the sentence 'Sie drückt sich immer vor dem Abwasch'.

The same need for care applies when you are using the English-German section of your dictionary to translate a word from English into German. Watch out in particular for the lozenges indicating changes in parts of speech.

If you want to translate 'You can't fool me', the capital letters at 'Narr' and 'Närrin' will remind you that these words are nouns. But watch what you are doing with the verbs or you could end up with a mistranslation like 'Sie können mich nicht herumalbern'!

fool [fuːl] n Narr m, Närrin f ♦ vt (deceive) hereinlegen ♦ vi (also: ~ around) (herum)albern; **~hardy** adj tollkühn; **~ish** adj albern; **~proof** adj idiotensicher

Phrasal Verbs

Another potential source of difficulty is English phrasal verbs. These consist of a common verb ('go', 'make', etc.) plus an adverb and/or a preposition to give English expressions such as 'to take after', 'to make out', etc. Entries for such verbs tend to be fairly full; therefore close examination of the contents is required. Note how these verbs appear in colour within the entry.

make [meɪk] (pt, pp **made**) vt machen; (appoint) ernennen (zu); (cause to do sth) veranlassen; (reach) erreichen; (in time) schaffen; (earn) verdienen ♦ n Marke f; **to ~ sth happen** etw geschehen lassen; **to ~ it** es schaffen; **what time do you ~ it?** wie spät hast du es?; **to ~ do with** auskommen mit; **~ for** vi gehen/fahren nach; **~ out** vt (write out) ausstellen; (understand) verstehen; **~ up** vt machen; (face) schminken; (quarrel) beilegen; (story etc) erfinden ♦ vi sich versöhnen; **~ up for** vt wiedergutmachen ⚠; (COMM) vergüten; **~-believe** n Phantasie ⚠ f; **~r** n (COMM) Hersteller m; **~shift** adj behelfsmäßig, Not-; **~-up** n Schminke f, Make-up nt; **~-up remover** n Make-up-Entferner m;

False Friends

Some German and English words have similar forms *and* meanings. There are, however, German words which *look* like English words but have a completely *different* meaning. For example, 'blank' in German means 'bright'; 'Probe' means 'rehearsal'; 'bilden' means 'to educate'. This can easily lead to serious mistranslations.

Sometimes the meaning of the German word is close to the English. For example, 'die Chips' are 'potato crisps' rather than 'chips'; 'der Hund' means a dog of any sort, not just a 'hound'. But some German words have two meanings, one the same as the English, the other completely different! 'Golf' can mean 'gulf' as well as 'golf'; 'senden' can mean 'to send' but can also mean 'to transmit/broadcast'.

Such words are often referred to as 'false friends'. You will have to look at the context in which they appear in order to arrive at the correct meaning. If they seem to fit with the sense of the passage as a whole, it will probably not be necessary to look them up. If they don't make sense, however, you may be dealing with 'false friends'.

WORDGAME 17

WORDS IN CONTEXT

Study the sentences below. Translations of the underlined words are given at the bottom. Match the number of the sentence and the letter of the translation correctly each time.

1. Sprich bitte lauter, ich kann dich nicht hören.

2. Er hört den ganzen Tag Radio.

3. Kannst du das Licht ausmachen, wenn du ins Bett gehst?

4. Können wir heute schon einen Termin ausmachen?

5. Seine Frau saß am Steuer, als der Unfall passierte.

6. Ich muß dieses Jahr viel Steuern nachzahlen.

7. Die Nachfrage nach japanischen Autos ist groß.

8. Aufgrund meiner Nachfrage konnte ich dann doch etwas erfahren.

9. Das Haus wird auf meinen Namen umgeschrieben.

10. Das Referat mußt du völlig umschreiben.

11. Sind die Äpfel schon reif?

12. Für ihr Alter wirkt sie schon ziemlich reif.

a. demand
b. transferred
c. turn off
d. hear
e. ripe
f. inquiry
g. mature
h. rewrite
i. steering wheel
j. listens to
k. agree
l. tax

WORDGAME 18

FALSE FRIENDS

Look at the advertisements below. The words which have been shaded resemble English words but have different meanings here. Find a correct translation for each word in the context.

Reformhaus
Neustr. 23
Sonderangebot:
Vollkornbrot 2, 78 DM

1

2

Hotel Olympia

Alle Zimmer mit Dusche/WC
Gemütliche Atmosphäre
Bitte Prospekt anfordern

Heinrichstraße 51 –
7000 STUTTGART 25
Tel. 0711/21 56 93

3

KP- Chef Italiens fliegt
morgen nach New York

4

W. Meinzer   Lebensmittel
Heute Chips
im
Sonderangebot

5

Der Mann im Smoking

6

Clinton
will wieder Präsident der USA werden

7

Nach der Jahrtausendwende erst mit 65 in Rente

8

Europaparlament

Fraktions-Flanke abdecken

9

Reise sorgenfrei mit diesen Drei

Reisescheck
Devisen
Sparkassenbuch

BEZIRKSSPARKASSE HAUSACH
Hauptstr. 14

WORDGAME 19

WORDS WITH MORE THAN ONE MEANING

Look at the advertisements and headlines below. The words which have been shaded can have more than one meaning. Use your dictionary to help you work out the correct translation in the context.

1

Landespräsident tritt zurück

2

Vermögen:

Vom kleinen zum großen Geld

3

Ich weiß, wie ich
Schmerzen schnell los werde

Parazetamol
Aus Ihrer Apotheke

4

Heinrich Wohnmobile GmbH

Spezialisten bieten
günstige Preise

5

Hotel Restaurant
Seeberger

Alle Preise inklusive
Bedienung

Marktplatz 12
Loßburg   Telefon (07165) 33 14

6

Müsli – Riegel

von Cadbury

– gibt Kraft und Energie!

7

Hotel - Pension Miramar

Behagliche Atmosphäre
Günstige Nachsaisonpreise

Strandstr. 6,
24340 Eckernförde
Telefon (04269) 29 51

8

Das Blatt
Finanz- und
Wirtschaftszeitung

HAVE FUN WITH YOUR DICTIONARY

Here are some word games for you to try. You will find your dictionary helpful as you attempt the activities.

WORDGAME 20
CODED WORDS

In the boxes below the letters of eight German words have been replaced by numbers. A number represents the same letter each time.

Try to crack the code and find the eight words. If you need help, use your dictionary.

Here is a clue: all the words you are looking for have something to do with TRANSPORT.

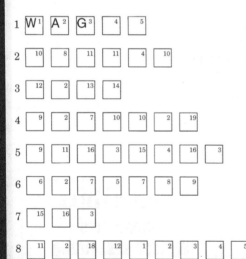

1 W¹ A² G³ ⬜⁴ ⬜⁵

2 ⬜¹⁰ ⬜⁸ ⬜¹¹ ⬜¹¹ ⬜⁴ ⬜¹⁰

3 ⬜¹² ⬜² ⬜¹³ ⬜¹⁴

4 ⬜⁹ ⬜² ⬜⁷ ⬜¹⁰ ⬜¹⁰ ⬜² ⬜¹⁹

5 ⬜⁹ ⬜¹¹ ⬜¹⁶ ⬜³ ⬜¹⁵ ⬜⁴ ⬜¹⁶ ⬜³

6 ⬜⁶ ⬜² ⬜⁷ ⬜⁵ ⬜⁷ ⬜⁸ ⬜⁹

7 ⬜¹⁵ ⬜¹⁶ ⬜³

8 ⬜¹¹ ⬜² ⬜¹⁸ ⬜¹² ⬜¹ ⬜² ⬜³ ⬜⁴ ⬜⁵

WORDGAME 21

BEHEADED WORDS

If you 'behead' certain German words, i.e. take away their first letter, you are left with another German word. For example, if you behead 'Kleider' (= 'clothes'), you get 'leider' (= 'unfortunately'), and 'dort' (= 'there') gives 'Ort' (= 'place').

The following words have their heads chopped off, i.e. the first letter has been removed. Use your dictionary to help you form a new German word by adding one letter to the start of each word below. Write down the new German word and its meaning.

1. ragen (= to tower)

2. tollen (= to romp)

3. nie (= never)

4. Rand (= edge)

5. oben (= above)

6. ich (= I)

7. Rad (= wheel)

8. innen (= inside)

9. raten (= to guess)

10. indisch (= Indian)

11. eigen (=own)

12. eben (= level)

13. Ohr (= ear)

14. pur (= pure)

WORDGAME 22

CROSSWORD

Complete this crossword by looking up the words listed below in the English-German section of your dictionary. Remember to read through the entry carefully to find the word that will fit.

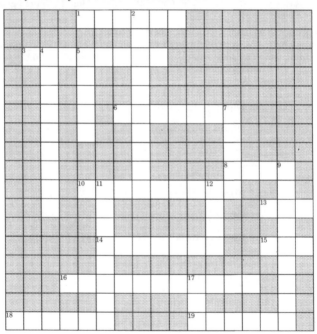

1. Heavily	6. Sad
2. Tearful	7. Smooth
3. Meal	8. Deaf
4. To record	9. To reassure
5. Mood	10. (A piece of) news
11. To start up (a car)	15. Clock
12. Tap	16. To dirty
13. Place	17. Day
14. To withdraw	18. To fold
	19. Profit

WORDGAME 23

There are twelve German words hidden in the grid below. Each word is made up of five letters but has been split into two parts.

Find the German words. Each group of letters can only be used once.

Use your dictionary to help you.

Re	ten	cke	er	Lad	Na
rbe	Sch	tr	Sip	eh	wei
unt	en	He	am	ank	pe
ren	be	ne	cht	se	ben

WORDGAME 24

Here is a list of German words for things you will find in the kitchen. Unfortunately, they have all been jumbled up. Try to work out what each word is and put the word in the boxes on the right. You will see that there are six shaded boxes below. With the six letters in the shaded boxes make up <u>another</u> German word for an object you can find in the kitchen.

1. CSIHT
Die Kinder decken den____

2. DERH
Die Kasserolle steht auf dem ____

3. RSNAHKC
Ist die Kaffeekanne in diesem ____ ?

4. SAETS
Sie gießt den Tee in die____

5. SRIGHCRE
Das____ liegt im Spülbecken

6. HKRÜHNSKCLA
Hol die Milch aus dem ____ heraus

The word you are looking for is:

318

WORDGAME 25

Take the four letters given each time and put them in the four empty boxes in the centre of each grid. Arrange them in such a way that you form four six-letter words. Use your dictionary to check the words.

ANSWERS

WORDGAME 1

1	gekannt	6	zahle
2	Aktien	7	einschreiben
3	Kino	8	übel
4	kaufen	9	Ganz
5	Pudel	10	Tante

WORDGAME 2

1	gerecht	7	Wade
2	erreichen	8	Ort
3	erfahren	9	fassen
4	Herbst	10	Stelle
5	treffen	11	Gleis
6	schwer	12	Heim

WORDGAME 3

Morgenrock+Hausschuhe
Handtasche+Lederwaren
Bett+Decke
Kirchturm+Glockengeläut
Fisch+Schuppe
Nest+Elster
Diplom+Student
Buch+Regal

WORDGAME 4

1	Weise *or* Sorte	6	berühmt
2	versuchen	7	Last
3	Brand	8	Karte
4	passieren	9	treffen
5	Überheblichkeit	10	Tendenz

WORDGAME 5

2 Nacht	5 Natur	6 neureich

WORDGAME 6

1	leugnen	6	Armut
2	verstecken	7	lärmend
3	schuldig	8	abreisen
4	verkaufen	9	tapfer
5	erlauben	10	sauber

WORDGAME 7

1	Frikadelle	6	nautisch
2	Spur	7	Gewölbe
3	fein	8	keuchen
4	Lüge	9	mögen
5	Stachel	10	glaubwürdig

WORDGAME 8

1 The sentence is much too long.
2 Underline every clause which starts with a conjunction.
3 Everybody knows Pythagoras' theorem.
4 The orchestra performed the last movement really well.
5 Steffi Graf hasn't lost a set in the championships.
6 All the grounds were in the cup.
7 For deliveries abroad there is a different rate.
8 She jumped for joy.

WORDGAME 9

1	gestellt	7	gesprochen
2	Stelle	8	Sprachen
3	hoffentlich	9	Studium
4	hofft	10	studiert
5	betrügen	11	kürzlich
6	Betrüger	12	gekürzt

WORDGAME 11

1	adj	6	adv
2	noun	7	adj
3	noun	8	verb
4	verb	9	verb
5	adv	10	adj

WORDGAME 12

1 der/das
2 die/das
3 das (*or* ein)/der
4 der/das
5 der/der
6 eine/den

WORDGAME 13

1	englisch	7	alt
2	rot	8	schwarz
3	letzte(r, s)	9	groß
4	klein	10	heftig
5	lang	11	siebte(r, s)
6	gut	12	neu

WORDGAME 14

ich sah
du schläfst
ich bin gewesen
ich schlug
ich habe angerufen
er fährt ab
ich habe studiert
ich hatte
du fängst an
er wäscht
ich wurde
ich habe genommen

WORDGAME 15

gesungen	gelegen
gebissen	gelogen
gebracht	geschnitten
gefroren	gekannt
gerieben	gemocht
gewonnen	gewußt
geholfen	gekonnt
geschehen	

WORDGAME 16

1	vergessen	9	fahren
2	anrufen	10	einladen
3	ankommen	11	bekommen
4	festhalten	12	lesen
5	sein	13	sterben
6	können	14	wegwerfen
7	fliegen	15	mitnehmen
8	werden		

WORDGAME 17

1	d	5	i	9	b
2	j	6	l	10	h
3	c	7	a	11	e
4	k	8	f	12	g

WORDGAME 18

1 health food shop
2 brochure
3 boss
4 crisps
5 dinner jacket
6 wants
7 pension
8 parliamentary party
9 foreign currency

WORDGAME 19

1 resigns
2 wealth
3 know
4 offer
5 service
6 bar
7 guesthouse
8 newspaper

WORDGAME 20

1 Wagen
2 Roller
3 Taxi
4 Fahrrad
5 Flugzeug
6 Bahnhof
7 Zug
8 Lastwagen

WORDGAME 21

1 tragen (= to carry); fragen (= to ask)
2 Stollen (= gallery)
3 Knie (= knee)
4 Brand (= fire)
5 loben (= to praise)
6 dich (= you); sich (= oneself); mich (= me)
7 Grad (= degree)
8 sinnen (= to ponder); rinnen (= to trickle)
9 braten (= to roast)
10 kindisch (= childish)
11 zeigen (= to show); neigen (= to incline)
12 geben (= to give); leben (= to live); neben (= next to); beben (= to tremble); heben (= to raise); weben (= to weave)
13 Rohr (= pipe, tube)
14 Spur (= race)

WORDGAME 22

1 schwer
2 weinerlich
3 Mahlzeit
4 aufnehmen
5 Laune
6 traurig
7 glatt
8 taub
9 beruhigen
10 Nachricht
11 anlassen
12 Hahn
13 Ort
14 abheben
15 Uhr
16 beschmutzen
17 Tag
18 falten
19 gewinn

WORDGAME 23

1	Recht	7	neben
2	Laden	8	Sippe
3	Hecke	9	unter
4	ehren	10	Scham
5	beten	11	weise
6	Narbe	12	trank

WORDGAME 24

1	Tisch	4	Tasse
2	Herd	5	Geschirr
3	Schrank	6	Kühlschrank

Hidden word – KESSEL

WORDGAME 25

ENGLISH-GERMAN DICTIONARY

WÖRTERBUCH ENGLISCH-DEUTSCH

ENGLISH – GERMAN
ENGLISCH – DEUTSCH

A, a

A [eɪ] n (MUS) A nt; **~ road** Hauptverkehrsstraße f

---KEYWORD---

a [eɪ, ə] (before vowel or silent h: an) indef art **1** ein; eine; **a woman** eine Frau; **a book** ein Buch; **an eagle** ein Adler; **she's a doctor** sie ist Ärztin

2 (instead of the number „one") ein, eine; **a year ago** vor einem Jahr; **a hundred/thousand** etc **pounds** (ein) hundert/(ein) tausend etc Pfund

3 (in expressing ratios, prices etc) pro; **3 a day/week** 3 pro Tag/Woche, 3 am Tag/in der Woche; **10 km an hour** 10 km pro Stunde/in der Stunde

---

A.A. n abbr = **Alcoholics Anonymous**; (BRIT) **Automobile Association**

A.A.A. (US) n abbr = **American Automobile Association**

aback [ə'bæk] adv: **to be taken ~** verblüfft sein

abandon [ə'bændən] vt (give up) aufgeben; (desert) verlassen ♦ n Hingabe f

abate [ə'beɪt] vi nachlassen, sich legen

abattoir ['æbətwɑːr] (BRIT) n Schlachthaus nt

abbey ['æbɪ] n Abtei f

abbot ['æbət] n Abt m

abbreviate [ə'briːvɪeɪt] vt abkürzen; **abbreviation** [əbriːvɪ'eɪʃən] n Abkürzung f

abdicate ['æbdɪkeɪt] vt aufgeben ♦ vi abdanken

abdomen ['æbdəmən] n Unterleib m

abduct [æb'dʌkt] vt entführen

aberration [æbə'reɪʃən] n (geistige) Verwirrung f

abet [ə'bet] vt see **aid**

abeyance [ə'beɪəns] n: **in ~** in der Schwebe; (disuse) außer Kraft

abide [ə'baɪd] vt vertragen; leiden; **~ by** vt sich halten an +acc

ability [ə'bɪlɪtɪ] n (power) Fähigkeit f; (skill) Geschicklichkeit f

abject ['æbdʒekt] adj (liar) übel; (poverty) größte(r, s); (apology) zerknirscht

ablaze [ə'bleɪz] adj in Flammen

able ['eɪbl] adj geschickt, fähig; **to be ~ to do sth** etw tun können; **~-bodied** ['eɪbl'bɔdɪd] adj kräftig; (seaman) Voll-; **ably** ['eɪblɪ] adv geschickt

abnormal [æb'nɔːməl] adj regelwidrig, abnorm

aboard [ə'bɔːd] adv, prep an Bord +gen

abode [ə'bəud] n: **of no fixed ~** ohne festen Wohnsitz

abolish [ə'bɔlɪʃ] vt abschaffen; **abolition** [æbə'lɪʃən] n Abschaffung f

abominable [ə'bɔmɪnəbl] adj scheußlich

aborigine [æbə'rɪdʒɪnɪ] n Ureinwohner m

abort [ə'bɔːt] vt abtreiben; fehlgebären; **~ion** [ə'bɔːʃən] n Abtreibung f; (miscarriage) Fehlgeburt f; **~ive** adj mißlungen ⚠

abound [ə'baund] vi im Überfluß ⚠ vorhanden sein; **to ~ in** Überfluß haben an +dat

---KEYWORD---

about [ə'baut] adv **1** (approximately) etwa, ungefähr; **about a hundred/thousand** etc etwa hundert/tausend etc; **at about 2 o'clock** etwa um 2 Uhr; **I've just about finished** ich bin gerade fertig

2 (referring to place) herum, umher; **to leave things lying about** Sachen herumliegen lassen; **to run/walk** etc **about** herumrennen/gehen etc

3: to be about to do sth im Begriff sein, etw zu tun; **he was about to go to bed** er wollte gerade ins Bett gehen

⚠ For information on spelling reform see page 615

♦ *prep* **1** (*relating to*) über +*acc*; **a book about London** ein Buch über London; **what is it about?** worum geht es?; (*book etc*) wovon handelt es?; **we talked about it** wir haben darüber geredet; **what** or **how about doing this?** wollen wir das machen? **2** (*referring to place*) um (... herum); **to walk about the town** in der Stadt herumgehen; **her clothes were scattered about the room** ihre Kleider waren über das ganze Zimmer verstreut

about-turn [ə'baut'tɜːn] *n* Kehrtwendung *f*
above [ə'bʌv] *adv* oben ♦ *prep* über; **~ all** vor allem; **~ board** *adj* offen, ehrlich
abrasive [ə'breɪzɪv] *adj* Abschleif-; (*personality*) zermürbend, aufreibend
abreast [ə'brɛst] *adv* nebeneinander; **to keep ~ of** Schritt halten mit
abroad [ə'brɔːd] *adv* (*be*) im Ausland; (*go*) ins Ausland
abrupt [ə'brʌpt] *adj* (*sudden*) abrupt, jäh; (*curt*) schroff; **~ly** *adv* abrupt
abscess ['æbsɪs] *n* Geschwür *nt*
abscond [əb'skɒnd] *vi* flüchten, sich davonmachen
abseil ['æbseɪl] *vi* (*also*: **~ down**) sich abseilen
absence ['æbsəns] *n* Abwesenheit *f*
absent ['æbsənt] *adj* abwesend, nicht da; (*lost in thought*) geistesabwesend; **~-minded** *adj* zerstreut
absolute ['æbsəluːt] *adj* absolut; (*power*) unumschränkt; (*rubbish*) vollkommen, rein; **~ly** [æbsə'luːtlɪ] *adv* absolut, vollkommen; **~ly!** ganz bestimmt!
absolve [əb'zɒlv] *vt* entbinden; freisprechen
absorb [əb'zɔːb] *vt* aufsaugen, absorbieren; (*fig*) ganz in Anspruch nehmen, fesseln; **to be ~ed in a book** in ein Buch vertieft sein; **~ent cotton** (*US*) *n* Verbandwatte *f*; **~ing** *adj* aufsaugend; (*fig*) packend; **absorption** [əb'sɔːpʃən] *n* Aufsaugung *f*, Absorption *f*; (*fig*) Versunkenheit *f*
abstain [əb'steɪn] *vi* (*in vote*) sich enthalten; **to ~ from** (*keep from*) sich enthalten +*gen*
abstemious [əb'stiːmɪəs] *adj* enthaltsam

abstinence ['æbstɪnəns] *n* Enthaltsamkeit *f*
abstract ['æbstrækt] *adj* abstrakt
absurd [əb'sɜːd] *adj* absurd
abundance [ə'bʌndəns] *n*: **~ (of)** Überfluß ⚠ *m* (an +*dat*); **abundant** [ə'bʌndənt] *adj* reichlich
abuse [*n* ə'bjuːs, *vb* ə'bjuːz] *n* (*rude language*) Beschimpfung *f*; (*ill usage*) Mißbrauch ⚠ *m*; (*bad practice*) (Amts)mißbrauch ⚠ *m* ♦ *vt* (*misuse*) mißbrauchen ⚠; **abusive** [ə'bjuːsɪv] *adj* beleidigend, Schimpf-
abysmal [ə'bɪzməl] *adj* scheußlich; (*ignorance*) bodenlos
abyss [ə'bɪs] *n* Abgrund *m*
AC *abbr* (= *alternating current*) Wechselstrom *m*
academic [ækə'dɛmɪk] *adj* akademisch; (*theoretical*) theoretisch ♦ *n* Akademiker(in) *m(f)*
academy [ə'kædəmɪ] *n* (*school*) Hochschule *f*; (*society*) Akademie *f*
accelerate [æk'sɛləreɪt] *vi* schneller werden; (*AUT*) Gas geben ♦ *vt* beschleunigen; **acceleration** [æksɛlə'reɪʃən] *n* Beschleunigung *f*; **accelerator** [æk'sɛləreɪtəʳ] *n* Gas(pedal) *nt*
accent ['æksənt] *n* Akzent *m*, Tonfall *m*; (*mark*) Akzent *m*; (*stress*) Betonung *f*
accept [ək'sɛpt] *vt* (*take*) annehmen; (*agree to*) akzeptieren; **~able** *adj* annehmbar; **~ance** *n* Annahme *f*
access ['æksɛs] *n* Zugang *m*; **~ible** [æk'sɛsəbl] *adj* (*easy to approach*) zugänglich; (*within reach*) (leicht) erreichbar
accessory [æk'sɛsərɪ] *n* Zubehörteil *nt*; **toilet accessories** Toilettenartikel *pl*
accident ['æksɪdənt] *n* Unfall *m*; (*coincidence*) Zufall *m*; **by ~** zufällig; **~al** [æksɪ'dɛntl] *adj* unbeabsichtigt; **~ally** [æksɪ'dɛntəlɪ] *adv* zufällig; **~ insurance** *n* Unfallversicherung *f*; **~-prone** *adj*: **to be ~-prone** zu Unfällen neigen
acclaim [ə'kleɪm] *vt* zujubeln +*dat* ♦ *n* Beifall *m*
acclimatize [ə'klaɪmətaɪz] *vt*: **to become ~d (to)** sich gewöhnen (an +*acc*), sich akklimatisieren (in +*dat*)

⚠ *Informationen zur Rechtschreibreform Seite 615*

accommodate [əˈkɔmədeɪt] vt
unterbringen; (hold) Platz haben für;
(oblige) (aus)helfen +dat
accommodating [əˈkɔmədeɪtɪŋ] adj
entgegenkommend
accommodation [əkɔməˈdeɪʃən] (US
accommodations) n Unterkunft f
accompany [əˈkʌmpənɪ] vt begleiten
accomplice [əˈkʌmplɪs] n Helfershelfer m,
Komplize m
accomplish [əˈkʌmplɪʃ] vt (fulfil)
durchführen; (finish) vollenden; (aim)
erreichen; ~**ed** adj vollendet,
ausgezeichnet; ~**ment** n (skill) Fähigkeit f;
(completion) Vollendung f; (feat) Leistung f
accord [əˈkɔːd] n Übereinstimmung f ♦ vt
gewähren; **of one's own** ~ freiwillig; ~**ing**
to nach, laut +gen; ~**ance** n: **in** ~**ance with**
in Übereinstimmung mit; ~**ingly** adv
danach, dementsprechend
accordion [əˈkɔːdɪən] n Akkordeon nt
accost [əˈkɔst] vt ansprechen
account [əˈkaunt] n (bill) Rechnung f;
(narrative) Bericht m; (report)
Rechenschaftsbericht m; (in bank) Konto nt;
(importance) Geltung f; ~**s** npl (FIN) Bücher
pl; **on** ~ auf Rechnung; **of no** ~ ohne
Bedeutung; **on no** ~ keinesfalls; **on** ~ **of**
wegen; **to take into** ~ berücksichtigen; ~
for vt fus (expenditure) Rechenschaft
ablegen für; **how do you** ~ **for that?** wie
erklären Sie (sich) das?; ~**able** adj
verantwortlich; ~**ancy** [əˈkauntənsɪ] n
Buchhaltung f; ~**ant** [əˈkauntənt] n
Wirtschaftsprüfer(in) m(f); ~ **number** n
Kontonummer f
accumulate [əˈkjuːmjuleɪt] vt ansammeln
♦ vi sich ansammeln
accuracy [ˈækjurəsɪ] n Genauigkeit f
accurate [ˈækjurɪt] adj genau; ~**ly** adv
genau, richtig
accusation [ækjuˈzeɪʃən] n Anklage f,
Beschuldigung f
accuse [əˈkjuːz] vt anklagen, beschuldigen;
~**d** n Angeklagte(r) mf
accustom [əˈkʌstəm] vt: **to** ~ **sb (to sth)**
jdn (an etw acc) gewöhnen; ~**ed** adj
gewohnt

ace [eɪs] n As △ nt; (inf) As △ nt, Kanone f
ache [eɪk] n Schmerz m ♦ vi (be sore)
schmerzen, weh tun
achieve [əˈtʃiːv] vt zustande △ bringen;
(aim) erreichen; ~**ment** n Leistung f; (act)
Erreichen nt
acid [ˈæsɪd] n Säure f ♦ adj sauer, scharf; ~
rain n saure(r) Regen m
acknowledge [əkˈnɔlɪdʒ] vt (receipt)
bestätigen; (admit) zugeben; ~**ment** n
Anerkennung f; (letter)
Empfangsbestätigung f
acne [ˈæknɪ] n Akne f
acorn [ˈeɪkɔːn] n Eichel f
acoustic [əˈkuːstɪk] adj akustisch; ~**s** npl
Akustik f
acquaint [əˈkweɪnt] vt vertraut machen; **to**
be ~**ed with sb** mit jdm bekannt sein;
~**ance** n (person) Bekannte(r) f(m);
(knowledge) Kenntnis f
acquire [əˈkwaɪəʳ] vt erwerben; **acquisition**
[ækwɪˈzɪʃən] n Errungenschaft f; (act) Erwerb
m
acquit [əˈkwɪt] vt (free) freisprechen; **to** ~
o.s. well sich bewähren; ~**tal** n Freispruch
m
acre [ˈeɪkəʳ] n Morgen m
acrid [ˈækrɪd] adj (smell, taste) bitter; (smoke)
beißend
acrobat [ˈækrəbæt] n Akrobat m
across [əˈkrɔs] prep über +acc ♦ adv hinüber,
herüber; **he lives** ~ **the river** er wohnt auf
der anderen Seite des Flusses; **ten metres**
~ zehn Meter breit; **he lives** ~ **from us** er
wohnt uns gegenüber; **to run / swim** ~
hinüberlaufen/schwimmen
acrylic [əˈkrɪlɪk] adj Acryl-
act [ækt] n (deed) Tat f; (JUR) Gesetz nt;
(THEAT) Akt m; (: item) Nummer f ♦ vi (take
action) handeln; (behave) sich verhalten;
(pretend) vorgeben; (THEAT) spielen ♦ vt (in
play) spielen; **to** ~ **as** fungieren als; ~**ing**
adj stellvertretend ♦ n Schauspielkunst f;
(performance) Aufführung f
action [ˈækʃən] n (deed) Tat f; Handlung f;
(motion) Bewegung f; (way of working)

△ For information on spelling reform see page 615

Funktionieren *nt*; (*battle*) Einsatz *m*, Gefecht *nt*; (*lawsuit*) Klage *f*, Prozeß △ *m*; **out of ~** (*person*) nicht einsatzfähig; (*thing*) außer Betrieb; **to take ~** etwas unternehmen; **~ replay** *n* (*TV*) Wiederholung *f*

activate [ˈæktɪveɪt] *vt* (*mechanism*) betätigen; (*CHEM, PHYS*) aktivieren

active [ˈæktɪv] *adj* (*brisk*) rege, tatkräftig; (*working*) aktiv; (*GRAM*) aktiv, Tätigkeits-; **~ly** *adv* aktiv; (*dislike*) offen

activity [ækˈtɪvɪtɪ] *n* Aktivität *f*; (*doings*) Unternehmungen *pl*; (*occupation*) Tätigkeit *f*; **~ holiday** *n* Aktivurlaub *m*

actor [ˈæktəʳ] *n* Schauspieler *m*

actress [ˈæktrɪs] *n* Schauspielerin *f*

actual [ˈæktjuəl] *adj* wirklich; **~ly** *adv* tatsächlich; **~ly no** eigentlich nicht

acumen [ˈækjumən] *n* Scharfsinn *m*

acute [əˈkjuːt] *adj* (*severe*) heftig, akut; (*keen*) scharfsinnig

ad [æd] *n abbr* = **advertisement**

A.D. *adv abbr* (= *Anno Domini*) n. Chr.

adamant [ˈædəmənt] *adj* eisern; hartnäckig

adapt [əˈdæpt] *vt* anpassen ♦ *vi*: **to ~ (to)** sich anpassen (an +*acc*); **~able** [ædæpˈteɪʃən] *n* (*THEAT etc*) Bearbeitung *f*; (*adjustment*) Anpassung *f*; **~er** *n* (*ELEC*) Zwischenstecker *m*; **~or** *n* (*ELEC*) = **adapter**

add [æd] *vt* (*join*) hinzufügen; (*numbers: also*: **~ up**) addieren; **~ up** *vi* (*make sense*) stimmen; **~ up to** *vt fus* ausmachen

adder [ˈædəʳ] *n* Kreuzotter *f*, Natter *f*

addict [ˈædɪkt] *n* Süchtige(r) *f(m)*; **~ed** [əˈdɪktɪd] *adj*: **~ed to** -süchtig; **~ion** [əˈdɪkʃən] *n* Sucht *f*; **~ive** [əˈdɪktɪv] *adj*: **to be ~ive** süchtig machen

addition [əˈdɪʃən] *n* Anhang *m*, Addition *f*; (*MATH*) Addition *f*, Zusammenzählen *nt*; **in ~** zusätzlich, außerdem; **~al** *adj* zusätzlich, weiter

additive [ˈædɪtɪv] *n* Zusatz *m*

address [əˈdrɛs] *n* Adresse *f*; (*speech*) Ansprache *f* ♦ *vt* (*letter*) adressieren; (*speak to*) ansprechen; (*make speech to*) eine Ansprache halten an +*acc*

adept [ˈædɛpt] *adj* geschickt; **to be ~ at** gut

sein in +*dat*

adequate [ˈædɪkwɪt] *adj* angemessen

adhere [ədˈhɪəʳ] *vi*: **to ~ to** haften an +*dat*; (*fig*) festhalten an +*dat*

adhesive [ədˈhiːzɪv] *adj* klebend; Kleb(e)- ♦ *n* Klebstoff *m*; **~ tape** *n* (*BRIT*) Klebestreifen *m*; (*US*) Heftpflaster *nt*

ad hoc [ædˈhɔk] *adj* (*decision, committee*) Ad-hoc- ♦ *adv* ad hoc

adjacent [əˈdʒeɪsənt] *adj* benachbart; **~ to** angrenzend an +*acc*

adjective [ˈædʒɛktɪv] *n* Adjektiv *nt*, Eigenschaftswort *nt*

adjoining [əˈdʒɔɪnɪŋ] *adj* benachbart, Neben-

adjourn [əˈdʒɜːn] *vt* vertagen ♦ *vi* abbrechen

adjudicate [əˈdʒuːdɪkeɪt] *vi* entscheiden, ein Urteil fällen

adjust [əˈdʒʌst] *vt* (*alter*) anpassen; (*put right*) regulieren, richtigstellen △ ♦ *vi* sich anpassen; **~able** *adj* verstellbar

ad-lib [ædˈlɪb] *vt, vi* improvisieren ♦ *adv*: **ad lib** aus dem Stegreif

administer [ədˈmɪnɪstəʳ] *vt* (*manage*) verwalten; (*dispense*) ausüben; (*justice*) sprechen; (*medicine*) geben; **administration** [ədmɪnɪsˈtreɪʃən] *n* Verwaltung *f*; (*POL*) Regierung *f*; **administrative** [ədˈmɪnɪstrətɪv] *adj* Verwaltungs-; **administrator** [ədˈmɪnɪstreɪtəʳ] *n* Verwaltungsbeamte(r) *f(m)*

Admiralty [ˈædmərəltɪ] (*BRIT*) *n* Admiralität *f*

admiration [ædməˈreɪʃən] *n* Bewunderung *f*

admire [ədˈmaɪəʳ] *vt* (*respect*) bewundern; (*love*) verehren; **~r** *n* Bewunderer *m*

admission [ədˈmɪʃən] *n* (*entrance*) Einlaß △ *m*; (*fee*) Eintritt(spreis *m*) *m*; (*confession*) Geständnis *nt*, Eingeständnis(preis) *m*

admit [ədˈmɪt] *vt* (*let in*) einlassen; (*confess*) gestehen; (*accept*) anerkennen; **~tance** *n* Zulassung *f*; **~tedly** *adv* zugegebenermaßen

admonish [ədˈmɔnɪʃ] *vt* ermahnen

ad nauseam [ædˈnɔːsɪæm] *adv* (*repeat, talk*) endlos

ado [əˈduː] n: **without more ~** ohne weitere Umstände

adolescence [ædəʊˈlesns] n Jugendalter nt; **adolescent** [ædəʊˈlesnt] adj jugendlich ♦ n Jugendliche(r) f(m)

adopt [əˈdɒpt] vt (child) adoptieren; (idea) übernehmen; **~ion** [əˈdɒpʃən] n Adoption f; Übernahme f

adore [əˈdɔːʳ] vt anbeten; verehren

adorn [əˈdɔːn] vt schmücken

Adriatic [eɪdrɪˈætɪk] n: **the ~ (Sea)** die Adria

adrift [əˈdrɪft] adv Wind und Wellen preisgegeben

adult [ˈædʌlt] n Erwachsene(r) f(m)

adultery [əˈdʌltərɪ] n Ehebruch m

advance [ədˈvɑːns] n (progress) Vorrücken nt; (money) Vorschuß ⚠ m ♦ vt (move forward) vorrücken; (money) vorschießen; (argument) vorbringen ♦ vi vorwärtsgehen ⚠; **in ~** im voraus; **~ booking** n Vorverkauf m; **~d** adj (ahead) vorgerückt; (modern) fortgeschritten; (study) für Fortgeschrittene

advantage [ədˈvɑːntɪdʒ] n Vorteil m; **to have an ~ over sb** jdm gegenüber im Vorteil sein; **to take ~ of** (misuse) ausnutzen; (profit from) Nutzen ziehen aus; **~ous** [ædvənˈteɪdʒəs] adj vorteilhaft

advent [ˈædvənt] n Ankunft f; **A~** Advent m

adventure [ədˈventʃəʳ] n Abenteuer nt; **adventurous** adj abenteuerlich, waghalsig

adverb [ˈædvɜːb] n Adverb nt, Umstandswort nt

adversary [ˈædvəsərɪ] n Gegner m

adverse [ˈædvɜːs] adj widrig; **adversity** [ədˈvɜːsɪtɪ] n Widrigkeit f, Mißgeschick ⚠ nt

advert [ˈædvɜːt] n Anzeige f; **~ise** [ˈædvətaɪz] vt werben für ♦ vi annoncieren; **to ~ise for sth** etw (per Anzeige) suchen; **~isement** [ədˈvɜːtɪsmənt] n Anzeige f, Inserat nt; **~iser** n (in newspaper etc) Inserent m; **~ising** n Werbung f

advice [ədˈvaɪs] n Rat(schlag) m

advisable [ədˈvaɪzəbl] adj ratsam

advise [ədˈvaɪz] vt: **to ~ (sb)** (jdm) raten; **~dly** [ədˈvaɪzɪdlɪ] adv (deliberately) bewußt

⚠; **~r** n Berater m; **advisory** [ədˈvaɪzərɪ] adj beratend, Beratungs-

advocate [vb ˈædvəkeɪt, n ˈædvəkət] vt vertreten ♦ n Befürworter(in) m(f)

Aegean [iːˈdʒiːən] n: **the ~ (Sea)** die Ägäis

aerial [ˈeərɪəl] n Antenne f ♦ adj Luft-

aerobics [eəˈrəʊbɪks] n Aerobic nt

aerodynamic [ˈeərəʊdaɪˈnæmɪk] adj aerodynamisch

aeroplane [ˈeərəpleɪn] n Flugzeug nt

aerosol [ˈeərəsɒl] n Aerosol nt; Sprühdose f

aesthetic [iːsˈθetɪk] adj ästhetisch

afar [əˈfɑːʳ] adv: **from ~** aus der Ferne

affable [ˈæfəbl] adj umgänglich

affair [əˈfeəʳ] n (concern) Angelegenheit f; (event) Ereignis nt; (love ~) Verhältnis nt; **~s** npl (business) Geschäfte pl

affect [əˈfekt] vt (influence) (ein)wirken auf +acc; (move deeply) bewegen; **this change doesn't ~ us** diese Änderung betrifft uns nicht; **~ed** adj affektiert, gekünstelt

affection [əˈfekʃən] n Zuneigung f; **~ate** adj liebevoll

affiliated [əˈfɪlɪeɪtɪd] adj angeschlossen

affinity [əˈfɪnɪtɪ] n (attraction) gegenseitige Anziehung f; (relationship) Verwandtschaft f

affirmative [əˈfɜːmətɪv] adj bestätigend

afflict [əˈflɪkt] vt quälen, heimsuchen

affluence [ˈæfluəns] n (wealth) Wohlstand m; **affluent** adj wohlhabend, Wohlstands-

afford [əˈfɔːd] vt sich dat leisten; (yield) bieten, einbringen

afield [əˈfiːld] adv: **far ~** weit fort

afloat [əˈfləʊt] adj: **to be ~** schwimmen

afoot [əˈfʊt] adv im Gang

afraid [əˈfreɪd] adj ängstlich; **to be ~ of** Angst haben vor +dat; **to be ~ to do sth** sich scheuen, etw zu tun; **I am ~ I have ...** ich habe leider ...; **I'm ~ so/not** leider/ leider nicht; **I am ~ that ...** ich fürchte(, daß) ...

afresh [əˈfreʃ] adv von neuem

Africa [ˈæfrɪkə] n Afrika nt; **~n** adj afrikanisch ♦ n Afrikaner(in) m(f)

after [ˈɑːftəʳ] prep nach; (following, seeking) hinter ... dat ... her; (in imitation) nach, im Stil von ♦ adv: **soon ~** bald danach ♦ conj

⚠ *For information on spelling reform see page 615*

nachdem; **what are you ~?** was wollen Sie?; **~ he left** nachdem er gegangen war; **~ you!** nach Ihnen!; **~ all** letzten Endes; **~ having shaved** als er sich rasiert hatte; **~effects** *npl* Nachwirkungen *pl*; **~math** *n* Auswirkungen *pl*; **~noon** *n* Nachmittag *m*; **~s** (*inf*) *n* (*dessert*) Nachtisch *m*; **~sales service** (*BRIT*) *n* Kundendienst *m*; **~shave (lotion)** *n* Rasierwasser *nt*; **~sun** *n* Aftersunlotion *f*; **~thought** *n* nachträgliche(r) Einfall *m*; **~wards** *adv* danach, nachher

again [ə'gɛn] *adv* wieder, noch einmal; (*besides*) außerdem, ferner; **~ and ~** immer wieder

against [ə'gɛnst] *prep* gegen

age [eɪdʒ] *n* (*of person*) Alter *nt*; (*in history*) Zeitalter *nt* ♦ *vi* altern, alt werden ♦ *vt* älter machen; **to come of ~** mündig werden; **20 years of ~** 20 Jahre alt; **it's been ~s since ...** es ist ewig her, seit ...

aged¹ [eɪdʒd] *adj* ... Jahre alt, -jährig

aged² [eɪdʒɪd] *adj* (*elderly*) betagt ♦ *npl*: **the ~** die Alten *pl*

age group *n* Altersgruppe *f*

age limit *n* Altersgrenze *f*

agency [eɪdʒənsɪ] *n* Agentur *f*; Vermittlung *f*; (*CHEM*) Wirkung *f*; **through** *or* **by the ~ of ...** mit Hilfe von ...

agenda [ə'dʒɛndə] *n* Tagesordnung *f*

agent [eɪdʒənt] *n* (*COMM*) Vertreter *m*; (*spy*) Agent *m*

aggravate [ægrəveɪt] *vt* (*make worse*) verschlimmern; (*irritate*) reizen

aggregate [ægrɪgɪt] *n* Summe *f*

aggression [ə'grɛʃən] *n* Aggression *f*;

aggressive [ə'grɛsɪv] *adj* aggressiv

aghast [ə'gɑːst] *adj* entsetzt

agile [ædʒaɪl] *adj* flink, agil; (*mind*) rege

agitate [ædʒɪteɪt] *vt* rütteln; **to ~ for** sich stark machen für

AGM *n abbr* (= *annual general meeting*) JHV *f*

ago [ə'gəʊ] *adv*: **two days ~** vor zwei Tagen; **not long ~** vor kurzem; **it's so long ~** es ist schon so lange her

agog [ə'gɒg] *adj* gespannt

agonizing [ægənaɪzɪŋ] *adj* quälend

agony [ægənɪ] *n* Qual *f*; **to be in ~** Qualen leiden

agree [ə'griː] *vt* (*date*) vereinbaren ♦ *vi* (*have same opinion, correspond*) übereinstimmen; (*consent*) zustimmen; (*be in harmony*) sich vertragen; **to ~ to sth** einer Sache *dat* zustimmen; **to ~ that ...** (*admit*) zugeben, daß ...; **to ~ to do sth** sich bereit erklären, etw zu tun; **garlic doesn't ~ with me** Knoblauch vertrage ich nicht; **I ~** einverstanden, ich stimme zu; **to ~ on sth** sich auf etw *acc* einigen; **~able** *adj* (*pleasing*) liebenswürdig; (*willing to consent*) einverstanden; **~d** *adj* vereinbart; **~ment** *n* (*agreeing*) Übereinstimmung *f*; (*contract*) Vereinbarung *f*, Vertrag *m*; **to be in ~ment** übereinstimmen

agricultural [ægrɪ'kʌltʃərəl] *adj* landwirtschaftlich, Landwirtschafts-

agriculture [ægrɪkʌltʃəʳ] *n* Landwirtschaft *f*

aground [ə'graʊnd] *adv*: **to run ~** auf Grund laufen

ahead [ə'hɛd] *adv* vorwärts; **to be ~** voraus sein; **~ of time** der Zeit voraus; **go right** *or* **straight ~** gehen Sie geradeaus; fahren Sie geradeaus

aid [eɪd] *n* (*assistance*) Hilfe *f*, Unterstützung *f*; (*person*) Hilfe *f*; (*thing*) Hilfsmittel *nt* ♦ *vt* unterstützen, helfen +*dat*; **in ~ of** zugunsten +*gen*; **to ~ and abet sb** jdm Beihilfe leisten

aide [eɪd] *n* (*person*) Gehilfe *m*; (*MIL*) Adjutant *m*

AIDS [eɪdz] *n abbr* (= *acquired immune deficiency syndrome*) Aids *nt*; **AIDS-related** aidsbedingt

ailing [eɪlɪŋ] *adj* kränkelnd

ailment [eɪlmənt] *n* Leiden *nt*

aim [eɪm] *vt* (*gun, camera*) richten ♦ *vi* (*with gun: also*: **take ~**) zielen; (*intend*) beabsichtigen ♦ *n* (*intention*) Absicht *f*, Ziel *nt*; (*pointing*) Zielen *nt*, Richten *nt*; **to ~ at sth** auf etw *dat* richten; (*fig*) etw anstreben; **to ~ to do sth** vorhaben, etw zu tun; **~less** *adj* ziellos; **~lessly** *adv* ziellos

ain't [eɪnt] (*inf*) = **am not**; **are not**; **is not**; **has not**; **have not**

⚠ *Informationen zur Rechtschreibreform Seite 615*

air [ɛəʳ] n Luft f; (manner) Miene f, Anschein m; (MUS) Melodie f ♦ vt lüften; (fig) an die Öffentlichkeit bringen ♦ cpd Luft-; **by ~** (travel) auf dem Luftweg; **to be on the ~** (RADIO, TV: programme) gesendet werden; **~bed** (BRIT) n Luftmatratze f; **~-conditioned** adj mit Klimaanlage; **~-conditioning** n Klimaanlage f; **~craft** n Flugzeug nt, Maschine f; **~craft carrier** n Flugzeugträger m; **~field** n Flugplatz m; **~ force** f Luftwaffe f; **~ freshener** n Raumspray nt; **~gun** n Luftgewehr nt; **~ hostess** (BRIT) n Stewardeß △ f; **~ letter** (BRIT) n Luftpostbrief m; **~lift** n Luftbrücke f; **~line** n Luftverkehrsgesellschaft f; **~liner** n Verkehrsflugzeug nt; **~lock** n Luftblase f; **~mail** n: **by ~mail** mit Luftpost; **~ miles** npl ≈ Flugkilometer m; **~plane** (US) n Flugzeug nt; **~port** n Flughafen m, Flugplatz m; **~ raid** n Luftangriff m; **~sick** adj luftkrank; **~space** n Luftraum m; **~strip** n Landestreifen m; **~ terminal** n Terminal m; **~tight** adj luftdicht; **~ traffic controller** n Fluglotse m; **~y** adj luftig; (manner) leichtfertig

aisle [aɪl] n Gang m; **~ seat** n Sitz m am Gang

ajar [əˈdʒɑːʳ] adv angelehnt; einen Spalt offen

alarm [əˈlɑːm] n (warning) Alarm m; (bell etc) Alarmanlage f; (anxiety) Sorge f ♦ vt erschrecken; **~ call** n (in hotel etc) Weckruf m; **~ clock** n Wecker m

Albania [ælˈbeɪnɪə] n Albanien nt

albeit [ɔːlˈbiːɪt] conj obgleich

album [ˈælbəm] n Album nt

alcohol [ˈælkəhɒl] n Alkohol m; **~-free** adj alkoholfrei; **~ic** [ælkəˈhɒlɪk] adj (drink) alkoholisch ♦ n Alkoholiker(in) m(f); **~ism** n Alkoholismus m

alert [əˈlɜːt] adj wachsam ♦ n Alarm m ♦ vt alarmieren; **to be on the ~** wachsam sein

Algeria [ælˈdʒɪərɪə] n Algerien nt

alias [ˈeɪlɪəs] adv alias ♦ n Deckname m

alibi [ˈælɪbaɪ] n Alibi nt

alien [ˈeɪlɪən] n Ausländer m ♦ adj (foreign) ausländisch; (strange) fremd; **~ to** fremd

+dat; **~ate** vt entfremden

alight [əˈlaɪt] adj brennend; (of building) in Flammen ♦ vi (descend) aussteigen; (bird) sich setzen

align [əˈlaɪn] vt ausrichten

alike [əˈlaɪk] adj gleich, ähnlich ♦ adv gleich, ebenso; **to look ~** sich dat ähnlich sehen

alimony [ˈælɪmənɪ] n Unterhalt m, Alimente pl

alive [əˈlaɪv] adj (living) lebend; (lively) lebendig, aufgeweckt; **~ (with)** (full of) voll (von), wimmelnd (von)

KEYWORD

---

all [ɔːl] adj alle(r, s); **all day/night** den ganzen Tag/die ganze Nacht; **all men are equal** alle Menschen sind gleich; **all five came** alle fünf kamen; **all the books/food** die ganzen Bücher/das ganze Essen; **all the time** die ganze Zeit (über); **all his life** sein ganzes Leben (lang)

♦ pron 1 alles; **I ate it all, I ate all of it** ich habe alles gegessen; **all of us/the boys went** wir gingen alle/alle Jungen gingen; **we all sat down** wir setzten uns alle

2 (in phrases): **above all** vor allem; **after all** schließlich; **at all: not at all** (in answer to question) überhaupt nicht; (in answer to thanks) gern geschehen; **I'm not at all tired** ich bin überhaupt nicht müde; **anything at all will do** es ist egal, welche(r, s); **all in all** alles in allem

♦ adv ganz; **all alone** ganz allein; **it's not as hard as all that** so schwer ist es nun auch wieder nicht; **all the more/the better** um so mehr/besser; **all but** fast; **the score is 2 all** es steht 2 zu 2

---

allay [əˈleɪ] vt (fears) beschwichtigen

all clear n Entwarnung f

allegation [ælɪˈɡeɪʃən] n Behauptung f

allege [əˈledʒ] vt (declare) behaupten; (falsely) vorgeben; **~dly** adv angeblich

allegiance [əˈliːdʒəns] n Treue f

allergic [əˈlɜːdʒɪk] adj: **~ (to)** allergisch (gegen)

allergy [ˈælədʒɪ] n Allergie f

△ For information on spelling reform see page 615

alleviate [əˈliːvɪeɪt] vt lindern
alley [ˈælɪ] n Gasse f, Durchgang m
alliance [əˈlaɪəns] n Bund m, Allianz f
allied [ˈælaɪd] adj vereinigt; (powers) alliiert;
~ **(to)** verwandt (mit)
all: ~**-in** (BRIT) adj, adv (charge) alles
inbegriffen, Gesamt-; ~**-night** adj (café,
cinema) die ganze Nacht geöffnet, Nacht-
allocate [ˈæləkeɪt] vt zuteilen
allot [əˈlɒt] vt zuteilen; ~**ment** n (share)
Anteil m; (plot) Schrebergarten m
all-out [ˈɔːlaʊt] adj total; **all out** adv mit
voller Kraft
allow [əˈlaʊ] vt (permit) erlauben, gestatten;
(grant) bewilligen; (deduct) abziehen;
(concede): **to** ~ **that ...** annehmen, daß ...;
to ~ **sb sth** jdm etw erlauben, jdm etw
gestatten; **to** ~ **sb to do sth** jdm erlauben
or gestatten, etw zu tun; ~ **for** vt fus
berücksichtigen, einplanen; ~**ance** n
Beihilfe f; **to make** ~**ances for**
berücksichtigen
alloy [ˈælɔɪ] n Metallegierung f
all: ~ **right** adv (well) gut; (correct) richtig;
(as answer) okay; ~**-round** adj (sportsman)
allseitig, Allround-; (view) Rundum-; ~**-time**
adj (record, high) ... aller Zeiten, Höchst-
allude [əˈluːd] vi: **to** ~ **to** hinweisen auf +acc,
anspielen auf +acc
alluring [əˈljʊərɪŋ] adj verlockend
ally [n ˈælaɪ, vb əˈlaɪ] n Verbündete(r) f(m);
(POL) Alliierte(r) f(m) ♦ vr: **to** ~ **o.s. with**
sich verbünden mit
almighty [ɔːlˈmaɪtɪ] adj allmächtig
almond [ˈɑːmənd] n Mandel f
almost [ˈɔːlməʊst] adv fast, beinahe
alms [ɑːmz] npl Almosen nt
alone [əˈləʊn] adj, adv allein; **to leave sth**
~ etw sein lassen; **let** ~ ... geschweige
denn ...
along [əˈlɒŋ] prep entlang, längs ♦ adv
(onward) vorwärts, weiter; ~ **with**
zusammen mit; **he was limping** ~ er
humpelte einher; all ~ (all the time) die
ganze Zeit; ~**side** adv (walk) nebenher;
(come) nebendran; (be) daneben ♦ prep
(walk, compared with) neben +dat; (come)

neben +acc; (be) entlang, neben +dat; (of
ship) längsseits +gen
aloof [əˈluːf] adj zurückhaltend ♦ adv fern; **to**
stand ~ abseits stehen
aloud [əˈlaʊd] adv laut
alphabet [ˈælfəbet] n Alphabet nt; ~**ical**
[ælfəˈbetɪkl] adj alphabetisch
alpine [ˈælpaɪn] adj alpin, Alpen-
Alps [ælps] npl: **the** ~ die Alpen pl
already [ɔːlˈredɪ] adv schon, bereits
alright [ˈɔːlraɪt] (BRIT) adv = **all right**
Alsatian [ælˈseɪʃən] n (dog) Schäferhund m
also [ˈɔːlsəʊ] adv auch, außerdem
altar [ˈɔːltəʳ] n Altar m
alter [ˈɔːltəʳ] vt ändern; (dress) umändern;
~**ation** [ɔːltəˈreɪʃən] n Änderung f;
Umänderung f; (to building) Umbau m
alternate [adj ɔlˈtɜːnɪt, vb ˈɔːltəːneɪt] adj
abwechselnd ♦ vi abwechseln; **on** ~ **days**
jeden zweiten Tag
alternating [ˈɔːltəːneɪtɪŋ] adj: ~ **current**
Wechselstrom m; **alternative** [ɒlˈtɜːnətɪv]
adj andere(r, s) ♦ n Alternative f;
alternative medicine Alternativmedizin f;
alternatively adv im anderen Falle;
alternatively one could ... oder man
könnte ...; **alternator** [ˈɔːltəneɪtəʳ] n (AUT)
Lichtmaschine f
although [ɔːlˈðəʊ] conj obwohl
altitude [ˈæltɪtjuːd] n Höhe f
alto [ˈæltəʊ] n Alt m
altogether [ɔːltəˈgeðəʳ] adv (on the whole)
im ganzen genommen; (entirely) ganz und
gar
aluminium [æljuˈmɪnɪəm] (BRIT) n
Aluminium nt
aluminum [əˈluːmɪnəm] (US) n Aluminium
nt
always [ˈɔːlweɪz] adv immer
Alzheimer's (disease) [ˈæltshaɪməz-] n
(MED) Alzheimerkrankheit f
am [æm] see **be**
a.m. adv abbr (= ante meridiem) vormittags
amalgamate [əˈmælgəmeɪt] vi (combine)
sich vereinigen ♦ vt (mix) amalgamieren
amass [əˈmæs] vt anhäufen
amateur [ˈæmətəʳ] n Amateur m; (pej)

Amateur *m*, Stümper *m*; **~ish** *(pej) adj*
dilettantisch, stümperhaft

amaze [ə'meɪz] *vt* erstaunen; **to be ~d (at)**
erstaunt sein (über); **~ment** *n* höchste(s)
Erstaunen *nt*; **amazing** *adj* höchst
erstaunlich

Amazon ['æməzən] *n (GEOG)* Amazonas *m*

ambassador [æm'bæsədə*r*] *n* Botschafter *m*

amber ['æmbə*r*] *n* Bernstein *m*; **at ~** *(BRIT:
AUT)* auf Gelb

ambiguous [æm'bɪgjuəs] *adj* zweideutig;
(not clear) unklar

ambition [æm'bɪʃən] *n* Ehrgeiz *m*;
ambitious *adj* ehrgeizig

amble ['æmbl] *vi (usu: ~ along)* schlendern

ambulance ['æmbjuləns] *n* Krankenwagen
m; **~ man** *(irreg)* Sanitäter *m*

ambush ['æmbuʃ] *n* Hinterhalt *m* ♦ *vt* (aus
dem Hinterhalt) überfallen

amenable [ə'mi:nəbl] *adj* gefügig; **~ (to)**
(reason) zugänglich (+*dat*); *(flattery)*
empfänglich (für)

amend [ə'mɛnd] *vt (law etc)* abändern,
ergänzen; **to make ~s** etw
wiedergutmachen; **~ment** *n* Abänderung *f*

amenities [ə'mi:nɪtɪz] *npl* Einrichtungen *pl*

America [ə'mɛrɪkə] *n* Amerika *nt*; **~n** *adj*
amerikanisch ♦ *n* Amerikaner(in) *m(f)*

amiable ['eɪmɪəbl] *adj* liebenswürdig

amicable ['æmɪkəbl] *adj* freundschaftlich;
(settlement) gütlich

amid(st) [ə'mɪd(st)] *prep* mitten in *or* unter
+*dat*

amiss [ə'mɪs] *adv*: **to take sth ~** etw
übelnehmen ⚠; **there's something ~** da
stimmt irgend etwas nicht

ammonia [ə'məunɪə] *n* Ammoniak *nt*

ammunition [æmju'nɪʃən] *n* Munition *f*

amnesia [æm'ni:zɪə] *n* Gedächtnisverlust *m*

amnesty ['æmnɪstɪ] *n* Amnestie *f*

amok [ə'mɔk] *adv*: **to run ~** Amok laufen

among(st) [ə'mʌŋ(st)] *prep* unter

amoral [æ'mɔrəl] *adj* unmoralisch

amorous ['æmərəs] *adj* verliebt

amount [ə'maunt] *n (of money)* Betrag *m*; *(of
water, sand)* Menge *f* ♦ *vi*: **to ~ to** *(total)*
sich belaufen auf +*acc*; **a great ~ of time/**

energy ein großer Aufwand an Zeit/
Energie *(dat)*; **this ~s to treachery** das
kommt Verrat gleich; **he won't ~ to much**
aus ihm wird nie was

amp(ere) [æmp(εə*r*)] *n* Ampere *nt*

amphibian [æm'fɪbɪən] *n* Amphibie *f*

ample ['æmpl] *adj (portion)* reichlich; *(dress)*
weit, groß; **~ time** genügend Zeit

amplifier ['æmplɪfaɪə*r*] *n* Verstärker *m*

amuse [ə'mju:z] *vt (entertain)* unterhalten;
(make smile) belustigen; **~ment** *n (feeling)*
Unterhaltung *f*; *(recreation)* Zeitvertreib *m*;
~ment arcade *n* Spielhalle *f*; **~ment
park** *n* Vergnügungspark *m*

an [æn, ən] *see* **a**

anaemia [ə'ni:mɪə] *n* Anämie *f*; **anaemic**
adj blutarm

anaesthetic [ænɪs'θɛtɪk] *n*
Betäubungsmittel *nt*; **under ~** unter
Narkose; **anaesthetist** [æ'ni:sθɪtɪst] *n*
Anästhesist(in) *m(f)*

analgesic [ænæl'dʒi:sɪk] *n*
schmerzlindernde(s) Mittel *nt*

analog(ue) ['ænəlɔg] *adj* Analog-

analogy [ə'nælədʒɪ] *n* Analogie *f*

analyse ['ænəlaɪz] *(BRIT) vt* analysieren

analyses [ə'næləsi:z] *(BRIT) npl of* **analysis**

analysis [ə'næləsɪs] *(pl* **analyses**) *n* Analyse
f

analyst ['ænəlɪst] *n* Analytiker(in) *m(f)*

analytic(al) [ænə'lɪtɪk(l)] *adj* analytisch

analyze ['ænəlaɪz] *(US) vt =* **analyse**

anarchy ['ænəkɪ] *n* Anarchie *f*

anatomy [ə'nætəmɪ] *n (structure)*
anatomische(r) Aufbau *m*; *(study)* Anatomie
f

ancestor ['ænsɪstə*r*] *n* Vorfahr *m*

anchor ['æŋkə*r*] *n* Anker *m* ♦ *vi (also: to
drop ~)* ankern, vor Anker gehen ♦ *vt*
verankern; **to weigh ~** den Anker lichten

anchovy ['æntʃəvɪ] *n* Sardelle *f*

ancient ['eɪnʃənt] *adj* alt; *(car etc)* uralt

ancillary [æn'sɪlərɪ] *adj* Hilfs-

and [ænd] *conj* und; **~ so on** und so weiter;
try ~ come versuche zu kommen; **better ~
better** immer besser

Andes ['ændi:z] *npl*: **the ~** die Anden *pl*

⚠ *For information on spelling reform see page 615*

anemia etc [əˈniːmɪə] (US) n = **anaemia** etc

anesthetic etc [ænɪsˈθetɪk] (US) n = **anaesthetic** etc

anew [əˈnjuː] adv von neuem

angel [ˈeɪndʒəl] n Engel m

anger [ˈæŋgəʳ] n Zorn m ♦ vt ärgern

angina [ænˈdʒaɪnə] n Angina f

angle [ˈæŋgl] n Winkel m; (point of view) Standpunkt m

angler [ˈæŋgləʳ] n Angler m

Anglican [ˈæŋglɪkən] adj anglikanisch ♦ n Anglikaner(in) m(f)

angling [ˈæŋglɪŋ] n Angeln nt

angrily [ˈæŋgrɪlɪ] adv ärgerlich, böse

angry [ˈæŋgrɪ] adj ärgerlich, ungehalten, böse; (wound) entzündet; **to be ~ with sb** auf jdn böse sein; **to be ~ at sth** über etw acc verärgert sein

anguish [ˈæŋgwɪʃ] n Qual f

angular [ˈæŋgjʊləʳ] adj eckig, winkelförmig; (face) kantig

animal [ˈænɪməl] n Tier nt; (living creature) Lebewesen nt ♦ adj tierisch

animate [vb ˈænɪmeɪt, adj ˈænɪmɪt] vt beleben ♦ adj lebhaft; **~d** adj lebendig; (film) Zeichentrick-

animosity [ænɪˈmɒsɪtɪ] n Feindseligkeit f, Abneigung f

aniseed [ˈænɪsiːd] n Anis m

ankle [ˈæŋkl] n (Fuß)knöchel m; **~ sock** n Söckchen nt

annex [n ˈæneks, vb əˈneks] n (BRIT: also: **~e**) Anbau m ♦ vt anfügen; (POL) annektieren, angliedern

annihilate [əˈnaɪəleɪt] vt vernichten

anniversary [ænɪˈvɜːsərɪ] n Jahrestag m

announce [əˈnauns] vt ankündigen, anzeigen; **~ment** n Ankündigung f; (official) Bekanntmachung f; **~r** n Ansager(in) m(f)

annoy [əˈnɔɪ] vt ärgern; **don't get ~ed!** reg' dich nicht auf!; **~ance** n Ärgernis nt, Störung f; **~ing** adj ärgerlich; (person) lästig

annual [ˈænjʊəl] adj jährlich; (salary) Jahres- ♦ n (plant) einjährige Pflanze f; (book) Jahrbuch nt; **~ly** adv jährlich

annul [əˈnʌl] vt aufheben, annullieren

annum [ˈænəm] n see **per**

anonymous [əˈnɒnɪməs] adj anonym

anorak [ˈænəræk] n Anorak m, Windjacke f

anorexia [ænəˈreksɪə] n (MED) Magersucht f

another [əˈnʌðəʳ] adj, pron (different) ein(e) andere(r, s); (additional) noch eine(r, s); see also **one**

answer [ˈɑːnsəʳ] n Antwort f ♦ vi antworten; (on phone) sich melden ♦ vt (person) antworten +dat; (letter, question) beantworten; (telephone) gehen an +acc, abnehmen; (door) öffnen; **in ~ to your letter** in Beantwortung Ihres Schreibens; **to ~ the phone** ans Telefon gehen; **to ~ the bell** or **the door** aufmachen; **~ back** vi frech sein; **~ for sth** vi fus: **to ~ for sth** für etw verantwortlich sein; **~able** adj: **to be ~able to sb for sth** jdm gegenüber für etw verantwortlich sein; **~ing machine** n Anrufbeantworter m

ant [ænt] n Ameise f

antagonism [ænˈtægənɪzəm] n Antagonismus m

antagonize [ænˈtægənaɪz] vt reizen

Antarctic [æntˈɑːktɪk] adj antarktisch ♦ n: **the ~** die Antarktis

antelope [ˈæntɪləʊp] n Antilope f

antenatal [ˈæntɪˈneɪtl] adj vor der Geburt; **~ clinic** n Sprechstunde f für werdende Mütter

antenna [ænˈtenə] n (BIOL) Fühler m; (RAD) Antenne f

antennae [ænˈteniː] npl of **antenna**

anthem [ˈænθəm] n Hymne f; **national ~** Nationalhymne f

anthology [ænˈθɒlədʒɪ] n Gedichtsammlung f, Anthologie f

anti- [ˈæntɪ] prefix Gegen-, Anti-

anti-aircraft [ˈæntɪˈeəkrɑːft] adj Flugabwehr-

antibiotic [ˈæntɪbaɪˈɒtɪk] n Antibiotikum nt

antibody [ˈæntɪbɒdɪ] n Antikörper m

anticipate [ænˈtɪsɪpeɪt] vt (expect: trouble, question) erwarten, rechnen mit; (look forward to) sich freuen auf +acc; (do first) vorwegnehmen; (foresee) ahnen, vorhersehen; **anticipation** [æntɪsɪˈpeɪʃən] n Erwartung f; (foreshadowing)

⚠ *Informationen zur Rechtschreibreform Seite 615*

Vorwegnahme f

anticlimax ['æntɪ'klaɪmæks] n Ernüchterung f

anticlockwise ['æntɪ'klɔkwaɪz] adv entgegen dem Uhrzeigersinn

antics ['æntɪks] npl Possen pl

anti: ~**cyclone** n Hoch nt, Hochdruckgebiet nt; ~**dote** n Gegenmittel nt; ~**freeze** n Frostschutzmittel nt; ~**histamine** n Antihistamin nt

antiquated ['æntɪkweɪtɪd] adj antiquiert

antique [æn'ti:k] n Antiquität f ♦ adj antik; (old-fashioned) altmodisch; ~ **shop** n Antiquitätenladen m; **antiquity** [æn'tɪkwɪtɪ] n Altertum nt

antiseptic [æntɪ'septɪk] n Antiseptikum nt ♦ adj antiseptisch

antisocial ['æntɪ'səʊʃəl] adj (person) ungesellig; (law) unsozial

antlers ['æntləz] npl Geweih nt

anus ['eɪnəs] n After m

anvil ['ænvɪl] n Amboß ⚠ m

anxiety [æŋ'zaɪətɪ] n Angst f; (worry) Sorge f; **anxious** ['æŋkʃəs] adj ängstlich; (worried) besorgt; **to be anxious to do sth** etw unbedingt tun wollen

KEYWORD

any ['enɪ] adj **1** (in questions etc): **have you any butter?** haben Sie (etwas) Butter?; **have you any children?** haben Sie Kinder?; **if there are any tickets left** falls noch Karten da sind
2 (with negative): **I haven't any money/ books** ich habe kein Geld/keine Bücher
3 (no matter which) jede(r, s) (beliebige); **any colour (at all)** jede beliebige Farbe; **choose any book you like** nehmen Sie ein beliebiges Buch
4 (in phrases): **in any case** in jedem Fall; **any day now** jeden Tag; **at any moment** jeden Moment; **at any rate** auf jeden Fall
♦ pron **1** (in questions etc): **have you got any?** haben Sie welche?; **can any of you sing?** kann (irgend)einer von euch singen?
2 (with negative): **I haven't any (of them)** ich habe keinen/keines (davon)

3 (no matter which one(s)): **take any of those books (you like)** nehmen Sie irgendeines dieser Bücher
♦ adv **1** (in questions etc): **do you want any more soup/sandwiches?** möchten Sie noch Suppe/Brote?; **are you feeling any better?** fühlen Sie sich etwas besser?
2 (with negative): **I can't hear him any more** ich kann ihn nicht mehr hören

anybody ['enɪbɒdɪ] pron (no matter who) jede(r); (in questions etc) (irgend) jemand, (irgend)eine(r); (with negative): **I can't see ~** ich kann niemanden sehen

anyhow ['enɪhaʊ] adv (at any rate): **I shall go ~** ich gehe sowieso; (haphazardly): **do it ~** machen Sie es, wie Sie wollen

anyone ['enɪwʌn] pron = **anybody**

KEYWORD

anything ['enɪθɪŋ] pron **1** (in questions etc) (irgend) etwas; **can you see anything?** können Sie etwas sehen?
2 (with negative): **I can't see anything** ich kann nichts sehen
3 (no matter what): **you can say anything you like** Sie können sagen, was Sie wollen; **anything will do** irgend etwas(, wird genügen), irgendeine(r, s) (wird genügen); **he'll eat anything** er ißt alles

anyway ['enɪweɪ] adv (at any rate) auf jeden Fall; (besides): **~, I couldn't come even if I wanted to** jedenfalls könnte ich nicht kommen, selbst wenn ich wollte; **why are you phoning, ~?** warum rufst du überhaupt an?

anywhere ['enɪweə'] adv (in questions etc) irgendwo; (: with direction) irgendwohin; (no matter where) überall; (: with direction) überallhin; (with negative): **I can't see him ~** ich kann ihn nirgendwo or nirgends sehen; **can you see him ~?** siehst du ihn irgendwo?; **put the books down ~** leg die Bücher irgendwohin

apart [ə'pɑ:t] adv (parted) auseinander; (away) beiseite, abseits; **10 miles ~** 10

⚠ *For information on spelling reform see page 615*

Meilen auseinander; **to take ~** auseinandernehmen; **~ from** prep außer

apartheid [əˈpɑːteɪt] n Apartheid f

apartment [əˈpɑːtmənt] (US) n Wohnung f; **~ building** (US) n Wohnhaus nt

apathy [ˈæpəθɪ] n Teilnahmslosigkeit f, Apathie f

ape [eɪp] n (Menschen)affe m ♦ vt nachahmen

aperitif [əˈperɪtiːf] n Aperitif m

aperture [ˈæpətʃuə] n Öffnung f; (PHOT) Blende f

APEX [ˈeɪpeks] n abbr (AVIAT: = advance purchase excursion) APEX (im voraus reservierte(r) Fahrkarte/Flugschein zu reduzierten Preisen)

apex [ˈeɪpeks] n Spitze f

apiece [əˈpiːs] adv pro Stück; (per person) pro Kopf

apologetic [əpɒləˈdʒetɪk] adj entschuldigend; **to be ~** sich sehr entschuldigen

apologize [əˈpɒlədʒaɪz] vi: **to ~ (for sth to sb)** sich (für etw bei jdm) entschuldigen; **apology** n Entschuldigung f

apostle [əˈpɒsl] n Apostel m

apostrophe [əˈpɒstrəfɪ] n Apostroph m

appal [əˈpɔːl] vt erschrecken; **~ling** adj schrecklich

apparatus [æpəˈreɪtəs] n Gerät nt

apparel [əˈpærəl] (US) n Kleidung f

apparent [əˈpærənt] adj offenbar; **~ly** adv anscheinend

apparition [æpəˈrɪʃən] n (ghost) Erscheinung f, Geist m

appeal [əˈpiːl] vi dringend ersuchen; (JUR) Berufung einlegen ♦ n Aufruf m; (JUR) Berufung f; **to ~ for** dringend bitten um; **to ~ to** sich wenden an +acc; (to public) appellieren an +acc; **it doesn't ~ to me** es gefällt mir nicht; **~ing** adj ansprechend

appear [əˈpɪə] vi (come into sight) erscheinen; (be seen) auftauchen; (seem) scheinen; **it would ~ that ...** anscheinend ...; **~ance** n (coming into sight) Erscheinen nt; (outward show) Äußere(s) nt

appease [əˈpiːz] vt beschwichtigen

appendices [əˈpendɪsiːz] npl of **appendix**

appendicitis [əpendɪˈsaɪtɪs] n Blinddarmentzündung f

appendix [əˈpendɪks] (pl appendices) n (in book) Anhang m; (MED) Blinddarm m

appetite [ˈæpɪtaɪt] n Appetit m; (fig) Lust f

appetizer [ˈæpɪtaɪzə] n Appetitanreger m; **appetizing** [ˈæpɪtaɪzɪ] adj appetitanregend

applaud [əˈplɔːd] vi Beifall klatschen, applaudieren ♦ vt Beifall klatschen +dat; **applause** [əˈplɔːz] n Beifall m, Applaus m

apple [ˈæpl] n Apfel m; **~ tree** n Apfelbaum m

appliance [əˈplaɪəns] n Gerät nt

applicable [əˈplɪkəbl] adj anwendbar; (in forms) zutreffend

applicant [ˈæplɪkənt] n Bewerber(in) m(f)

application [æplɪˈkeɪʃən] n (request) Antrag m; (for job) Bewerbung f; (putting into practice) Anwendung f; (hard work) Fleiß m; **~ form** n Bewerbungsformular nt

applied [əˈplaɪd] adj angewandt

apply [əˈplaɪ] vi (be suitable) zutreffen; (ask): **to ~ (to)** sich wenden (an +acc); (request): **to ~ for** sich melden für +acc ♦ vt (place on) auflegen; (cream) auftragen; (put into practice) anwenden; **to ~ for sth** sich um etw bewerben; **to ~ o.s. to sth** sich bei etw anstrengen

appoint [əˈpɔɪnt] vt (to office) ernennen, berufen; (settle) festsetzen; **~ment** n (meeting) Verabredung f; (at hairdresser etc) Bestellung f; (in business) Termin m; (choice for a position) Ernennung f; (UNIV) Berufung f

appraisal [əˈpreɪzl] n Beurteilung f

appreciable [əˈpriːʃəbl] adj (perceptible) merklich; (able to be estimated) abschätzbar

appreciate [əˈpriːʃeɪt] vt (value) zu schätzen wissen; (understand) einsehen ♦ vi (increase in value) im Wert steigen; **appreciation** [əprɪʃɪˈeɪʃən] n Wertschätzung f; (COMM) Wertzuwachs m; **appreciative** [əˈpriːʃɪətɪv] adj (showing thanks) dankbar; (showing liking) anerkennend

apprehend [æprɪˈhend] vt (arrest)

⚠ *Informationen zur Rechtschreibreform Seite 615*

festnehmen; (*understand*) erfassen

apprehension [æprɪ'henʃən] n Angst f

apprehensive [æprɪ'hensɪv] adj furchtsam

apprentice [ə'prentɪs] n Lehrling m; **~ship** n Lehrzeit f

approach [ə'prəʊtʃ] vi sich nähern ♦ vt herantreten an +acc; (*problem*) herangehen an +acc ♦ n Annäherung f; (*to problem*) Ansatz m; (*path*) Zugang m, Zufahrt f; **~able** adj zugänglich

appropriate [adj ə'prəʊprɪɪt, vb ə'prəʊprɪeɪt] adj angemessen; (*remark*) angebracht ♦ vt (*take for o.s.*) sich aneignen; (*set apart*) bereitstellen

approval [ə'pruːvəl] n (*show of satisfaction*) Beifall m; (*permission*) Billigung f; **on ~** (COMM) bei Gefallen

approve [ə'pruːv] vt, vi billigen; **I don't ~ of it/him** ich halte nichts davon/von ihm; **~d school** (BRIT) n Erziehungsheim nt

approximate [adj ə'prɒksɪmɪt, vb ə'prɒksɪmeɪt] adj annähernd, ungefähr ♦ vt nahekommen △ +dat; **~ly** adv rund, ungefähr

apricot ['eɪprɪkɒt] n Aprikose f

April ['eɪprəl] n April m; **~ Fools' Day** n der erste April

apron ['eɪprən] n Schürze f

apt [æpt] adj (*suitable*) passend; (*able*) begabt; (*likely*): **to be ~ to do sth** dazu neigen, etw zu tun

aptitude ['æptɪtjuːd] n Begabung f

aqualung ['ækwəlʌŋ] n Unterwasseratmungsgerät nt

aquarium [ə'kweərɪəm] n Aquarium nt

Aquarius [ə'kweərɪəs] n Wassermann m

aquatic [ə'kwætɪk] adj Wasser-

Arab ['ærəb] n Araber(in) m(f)

Arabia [ə'reɪbɪə] n Arabien nt; **~n** adj arabisch

Arabic ['ærəbɪk] adj arabisch ♦ n Arabisch nt

arable ['ærəbl] adj bebaubar, Kultur-

arbitrary ['ɑːbɪtrərɪ] adj willkürlich

arbitration [ɑːbɪ'treɪʃən] n Schlichtung f

arc [ɑːk] n Bogen m

arcade [ɑː'keɪd] n Säulengang m; (*with video games*) Spielhalle f

arch [ɑːtʃ] n Bogen m ♦ vt überwölben; (*back*) krumm machen

archaeologist [ɑːkɪ'ɒlədʒɪst] n Archäologe m

archaeology [ɑːkɪ'ɒlədʒɪ] n Archäologie f

archaic [ɑː'keɪɪk] adj altertümlich

archbishop [ɑːtʃ'bɪʃəp] n Erzbischof m

archenemy ['ɑːtʃ'enəmɪ] n Erzfeind m

archeology etc [ɑːkɪ'ɒlədʒɪ] (US) = **archaeology** etc

archery ['ɑːtʃərɪ] n Bogenschießen nt

architect ['ɑːkɪtekt] n Architekt(in) m(f); **~ural** [ɑːkɪ'tektʃərəl] adj architektonisch; **~ure** n Architektur f

archives ['ɑːkaɪvz] npl Archiv nt

archway ['ɑːtʃweɪ] n Bogen m

Arctic ['ɑːktɪk] adj arktisch ♦ n: **the ~** die Arktis

ardent ['ɑːdənt] adj glühend

arduous ['ɑːdjʊəs] adj mühsam

are [ɑː] see **be**

area ['eərɪə] n Fläche f; (*of land*) Gebiet nt; (*part of sth*) Teil m, Abschnitt m

arena [ə'riːnə] n Arena f

aren't [ɑːnt] = **are not**

Argentina [ɑːdʒən'tiːnə] n Argentinien nt; **Argentinian** [ɑːdʒən'tɪnɪən] adj argentinisch ♦ n Argentinier(in) m(f)

arguably ['ɑːgjuːəblɪ] adv wohl

argue ['ɑːgjuː] vi diskutieren; (*angrily*) streiten; **argument** n (*theory*) Argument nt; (*reasoning*) Argumentation f; (*row*) Auseinandersetzung f, Streit m; **to have an argument** sich streiten; **argumentative** [ɑːgjuː'mentətɪv] adj streitlustig

aria ['ɑːrɪə] n Arie f

Aries ['eərɪz] n Widder m

arise [ə'raɪz] (*pt* arose, *pp* arisen) vi aufsteigen; (*get up*) aufstehen; (*difficulties etc*) entstehen; (*case*) vorkommen; **to ~ from sth** sich ergeben von etw; **~n** [ə'rɪzn] pp of **arise**

aristocracy [ærɪs'tɒkrəsɪ] n Adel m, Aristokratie f; **aristocrat** ['ærɪstəkræt] n Adlige(r) f(m), Aristokrat(in) m(f)

arithmetic [ə'rɪθmətɪk] n Rechnen nt, Arithmetik f

△ *For information on spelling reform see page 615*

arm [ɑːm] *n* Arm *m*; (*branch of military service*) Zweig *m* ♦ *vt* bewaffnen; **~s** *npl* (*weapons*) Waffen *pl*

armaments ['ɑːməmənts] *npl* Ausrüstung *f*

armchair ['ɑːmtʃeəʳ] *n* Lehnstuhl *m*

armed [ɑːmd] *adj* (*forces*) Streit-, bewaffnet; **~ robbery** *n* bewaffnete(r) Raubüberfall *m*

armistice ['ɑːmɪstɪs] *n* Waffenstillstand *m*

armour ['ɑːməʳ] (*US* **armor**) *n* (*knight's*) Rüstung *f*; (*MIL*) Panzerplatte *f*; **~ed car** *n* Panzerwagen *m*

armpit ['ɑːmpɪt] *n* Achselhöhle *f*

armrest ['ɑːmrest] *n* Armlehne *f*

army ['ɑːmɪ] *n* Armee *f*, Heer *nt*; (*host*) Heer *nt*

aroma [ə'rəumə] *n* Duft *m*, Aroma *nt*; **~therapy** [ərəumə'θerəpɪ] *n* Aromatherapie *f*; **~tic** [ærə'mætɪk] *adj* aromatisch, würzig

arose [ə'rəuz] *pt of* **arise**

around [ə'raund] *adv* ringsherum; (*almost*) ungefähr ♦ *prep* um ... herum; **is he ~?** ist er hier?

arrange [ə'reɪndʒ] *vt* (*time, meeting*) festsetzen; (*holidays*) festlegen; (*flowers, hair, objects*) anordnen; **I ~d to meet him** ich habe mit ihm ausgemacht, ihn zu treffen; **it's all ~d** es ist alles arrangiert; **~ment** *n* (*order*) Reihenfolge *f*; (*agreement*) Vereinbarung *f*; **~ments** *npl* (*plans*) Pläne *pl*

array [ə'reɪ] *n* (*collection*) Ansammlung *f*

arrears [ə'rɪəz] *npl* (*of debts*) Rückstand *m*; (*of work*) Unerledigte(s) *nt*; **in ~** im Rückstand

arrest [ə'rest] *vt* (*person*) verhaften; (*stop*) aufhalten ♦ *n* Verhaftung *f*; **under ~** in Haft

arrival [ə'raɪvl] *n* Ankunft *f*

arrive [ə'raɪv] *vi* ankommen; **to ~ at** ankommen in +*dat*, ankommen bei

arrogance ['ærəgəns] *n* Überheblichkeit *f*, Arroganz *f*; **arrogant** ['ærəgənt] *adj* überheblich, arrogant

arrow ['ærəu] *n* Pfeil *m*

arse [ɑːs] (*inf!*) *n* Arsch *m* (*!*)

arsenal ['ɑːsɪnl] *n* Waffenlager *nt*, Zeughaus *nt*

arsenic ['ɑːsnɪk] *n* Arsen *nt*

arson ['ɑːsn] *n* Brandstiftung *f*

art [ɑːt] *n* Kunst *f*; **A~s** *npl* (*UNIV*) Geisteswissenschaften *pl*

artery ['ɑːtərɪ] *n* Schlagader *f*, Arterie *f*

art gallery *n* Kunstgalerie *f*

arthritis [ɑː'θraɪtɪs] *n* Arthritis *f*

artichoke ['ɑːtɪtʃəuk] *n* Artischocke *f*; **Jerusalem ~** Erdartischocke *f*

article ['ɑːtɪkl] *n* (*PRESS, GRAM*) Artikel *m*; (*thing*) Gegenstand *m*, Artikel *m*; (*clause*) Abschnitt *m*, Paragraph ⚠ *m*; **~ of clothing** Kleidungsstück *nt*

articulate [*adj* ɑː'tɪkjulɪt, *vb* ɑː'tɪkjuleɪt] *adj* (*able to express o.s.*) redegewandt; (*speaking clearly*) deutlich, verständlich ♦ *vt* (*connect*) zusammenfügen, gliedern; **to be ~** sich gut ausdrücken können; **~d vehicle** *n* Sattelschlepper *m*

artificial [ɑːtɪ'fɪʃəl] *adj* künstlich, Kunst-; **~ respiration** *n* künstliche Atmung *f*

artisan ['ɑːtɪzæn] *n* gelernte(r) Handwerker *m*

artist ['ɑːtɪst] *n* Künstler(in) *m(f)*; **~ic** [ɑː'tɪstɪk] *adj* künstlerisch; **~ry** *n* künstlerische(s) Können *nt*

art school *n* Kunsthochschule *f*

KEYWORD

as [æz] *conj* **1** (*referring to time*) als; **as the years went by** mit den Jahren; **he came in as I was leaving** als er hereinkam, ging ich gerade; **as from tomorrow** ab morgen

2 (*in comparisons*): **as big as** so groß wie; **twice as big as** zweimal so groß wie; **as much/many as** soviel/so viele wie; **as soon as** sobald

3 (*since, because*) da; **he left early as he had to be home by 10** er ging früher, da er um 10 zu Hause sein mußte

4 (*referring to manner, way*) wie; **do as you wish** mach was du willst; **as she said** wie sie sagte

5 (*concerning*): **as for** *or* **to that** was das betrifft *or* angeht

6: as if *or* **though** als ob

♦ *prep* als; *see also* **long**; **he works as a driver** er arbeitet als Fahrer; *see also* **such**;

⚠ *Informationen zur Rechtschreibreform Seite 615*

he gave it to me as a present er hat es mir als Geschenk gegeben; *see also* **well**

a.s.a.p. *abbr* = **as soon as possible**

asbestos [æz'bestəs] *n* Asbest *m*

ascend [ə'send] *vi* aufsteigen ♦ *vt* besteigen; **ascent** *n* Aufstieg *m*; Besteigung *f*

ascertain [æsə'teɪn] *vt* feststellen

ascribe [ə'skraɪb] *vt*: **to ~ sth to sth /sth to sb** etw einer Sache/jdm etw zuschreiben

ash [æʃ] *n* Asche *f*; (*tree*) Esche *f*

ashamed [ə'ʃeɪmd] *adj* beschämt; **to be ~ of sth** sich für etw schämen

ashen [ˈæʃən] *adj* (*pale*) aschfahl

ashore [əˈʃɔːr] *adv* an Land

ashtray [ˈæʃtreɪ] *n* Aschenbecher *m*

Ash Wednesday *n* Aschermittwoch *m*

Asia [ˈeɪʃə] *n* Asien *nt*; **~n** *adj* asiatisch ♦ *n* Asiat(in) *m(f)*

aside [ə'saɪd] *adv* beiseite

ask [ɑːsk] *vt* fragen; (*permission*) bitten um; **~ him his name** frage ihn nach seinem Namen; **he ~ed to see you** er wollte dich sehen; **to ~ sb to do sth** jdn bitten, etw zu tun; **to ~ sb about sth** jdn nach etw fragen; **to ~ (sb) a question** (jdn) etwas fragen; **to ~ sb out to dinner** jdn zum Essen einladen; **~ after** *vt fus* fragen nach; **~ for** *vt fus* bitten um

askance [ə'skɑːns] *adv*: **to look ~ at sb** jdn schief ansehen

asking price [ˈɑːskɪŋ-] *n* Verkaufspreis *m*

asleep [ə'sliːp] *adj*: **to be ~** schlafen; **to fall ~** einschlafen

asparagus [əs'pærəgəs] *n* Spargel *m*

aspect [ˈæspekt] *n* Aspekt *m*

aspersions [əs'pɜːʃənz] *npl*: **to cast ~ on sb/sth** sich abfällig über jdn/etw äußern

asphyxiation [æsfɪksɪ'eɪʃən] *n* Erstickung *f*

aspirations [əspə'reɪʃənz] *npl*: **to have ~ towards sth** etw anstreben

aspire [əs'paɪər] *vi*: **to ~ to** streben nach

aspirin [ˈæsprɪn] *n* Aspirin *nt*

ass [æs] *n* (*also fig*) Esel *m*; (*US: inf!*) Arsch *m* (!)

assailant [ə'seɪlənt] *n* Angreifer *m*

assassin [ə'sæsɪn] *n* Attentäter(in) *m(f)*;

~ate *vt* ermorden; **~ation** [əsæsɪ'neɪʃən] *n* (geglückte(s)) Attentat *nt*

assault [ə'sɔːlt] *n* Angriff *m* ♦ *vt* überfallen; (*woman*) herfallen über +*acc*

assemble [ə'sembl] *vt* versammeln; (*parts*) zusammensetzen ♦ *vi* sich versammeln; **assembly** *n* (*meeting*) Versammlung *f*; (*construction*) Zusammensetzung *f*, Montage *f*; **assembly line** *n* Fließband *nt*

assent [ə'sent] *n* Zustimmung *f*

assert [ə'sɜːt] *vt* erklären; **~ion** *n* Behauptung *f*

assess [ə'ses] *vt* schätzen; **~ment** *n* Bewertung *f*, Einschätzung *f*; **~or** *n* Steuerberater *m*

asset [ˈæset] *n* Vorteil *m*, Wert *m*; **~s** *npl* (*FIN*) Vermögen *nt*; (*estate*) Nachlaß △ *m*

assign [ə'saɪn] *vt* zuweisen; **~ment** *n* Aufgabe *f*, Auftrag *m*

assimilate [ə'sɪmɪleɪt] *vt* sich aneignen, aufnehmen

assist [ə'sɪst] *vt* beistehen +*dat*; **~ance** *n* Unterstützung *f*, Hilfe *f*; **~ant** *n* Assistent(in) *m(f)*, Mitarbeiter(in) *m(f)*; (*BRIT: also:* **shop ~ant**) Verkäufer(in) *m(f)*

associate [*n* ə'səʊʃɪɪt, *vb* ə'səʊʃɪeɪt] *n* (*partner*) Kollege *m*, Teilhaber *m*; (*member*) außerordentliche(s) Mitglied *nt* ♦ *vt* verbinden ♦ *vi* (*keep company*) verkehren; **association** [əsəʊsɪ'eɪʃən] *n* Verband *m*, Verein *m*; (*PSYCH*) Assoziation *f*; (*link*) Verbindung *f*

assorted [ə'sɔːtɪd] *adj* gemischt

assortment [ə'sɔːtmənt] *n* Sammlung *f*; (*COMM*): **~ (of)** Sortiment *nt* (von), Auswahl *f* (an +*dat*)

assume [ə'sjuːm] *vt* (*take for granted*) annehmen; (*put on*) annehmen, sich geben; **~d name** *n* Deckname *m*

assumption [ə'sʌmpʃən] *n* Annahme *f*

assurance [ə'ʃʊərəns] *n* (*firm statement*) Versicherung *f*; (*confidence*) Selbstsicherheit *f*; (*insurance*) (Lebens)versicherung *f*

assure [ə'ʃʊər] *vt* (*make sure*) sicherstellen; (*convince*) versichern +*dat*; (*life*) versichern

asterisk [ˈæstərɪsk] *n* Sternchen *nt*

asthma [ˈæsmə] *n* Asthma *nt*

△ *For information on spelling reform see page 615*

astonish [ə'stɒnɪʃ] vt erstaunen; **~ment** n Erstaunen nt

astound [ə'staʊnd] vt verblüffen

astray [ə'streɪ] adv in die Irre; auf Abwege; **to go ~** (go wrong) sich vertun; **to lead ~** irreführen

astride [ə'straɪd] adv rittlings ♦ prep rittlings auf

astrologer [əs'trɒlədʒəʳ] n Astrologe m, Astrologin f; **astrology** n Astrologie f

astronaut ['æstrənɔːt] n Astronaut(in) m(f)

astronomer [əs'trɒnəməʳ] n Astronom m

astronomical [æstrə'nɒmɪkl] adj astronomisch; (success) riesig

astronomy [əs'trɒnəmɪ] n Astronomie f

astute [əs'tjuːt] adj scharfsinnig; schlau, gerissen

asylum [ə'saɪləm] n (home) Heim nt; (refuge) Asyl nt

KEYWORD

at [æt] prep **1** (referring to position, direction) an +dat, bei +dat; (with place) in +dat; **at the top** an der Spitze; **at home/school** zu Hause/in der Schule; **at the baker's** beim Bäcker; **to look at sth** auf etw acc blicken; **to throw sth at sb** etw nach jdm werfen

2 (referring to time): **at 4 o'clock** um 4 Uhr; **at night** bei Nacht; **at Christmas** zu Weihnachten; **at times** manchmal

3 (referring to rates, speed etc): **at £1 a kilo** zu £1 pro Kilo; **two at a time** zwei auf einmal; **at 50 km/h** mit 50 km/h

4 (referring to manner): **at a stroke** mit einem Schlag; **at peace** in Frieden

5 (referring to activity): **to be at work** bei der Arbeit sein; **to play at cowboys** Cowboy spielen; **to be good at sth** gut in etw dat sein

6 (referring to cause): **shocked/surprised/annoyed at sth** schockiert/überrascht/verärgert über etw acc; **I went at his suggestion** ich ging auf seinen Vorschlag hin

---

ate [eɪt] pt of **eat**

atheist ['eɪθɪɪst] n Atheist(in) m(f)

Athens ['æθɪnz] n Athen nt

athlete ['æθliːt] n Athlet m, Sportler m

athletic [æθ'letɪk] adj sportlich, athletisch; **~s** n Leichtathletik f

Atlantic [ət'læntɪk] adj atlantisch ♦ n: **the ~ (Ocean)** der Atlantik

atlas ['ætləs] n Atlas m

ATM abbr (= automated teller machine) Geldautomat m

atmosphere ['ætməsfɪəʳ] n Atmosphäre f

atom ['ætəm] n Atom nt; (fig) bißchen △ nt; **~ic** [ə'tɒmɪk] adj atomar, Atom-; **~(ic) bomb** n Atombombe f

atomizer ['ætəmaɪzəʳ] n Zerstäuber m

atone [ə'təʊn] vi sühnen; **to ~ for sth** etw sühnen

atrocious [ə'trəʊʃəs] adj gräßlich △

atrocity [ə'trɒsɪtɪ] n Scheußlichkeit f; (deed) Greueltat △ f

attach [ə'tætʃ] vt (fasten) befestigen; **to be ~ed to sb/sth** an jdm/etw hängen; **to ~ importance etc to sth** Wichtigkeit etc auf etw acc legen, einer Sache dat Wichtigkeit etc beimessen

attaché case [ə'tæʃeɪ] n Aktenkoffer m

attachment [ə'tætʃmənt] n (tool) Zubehörteil nt; (love): **~ (to sb)** Zuneigung f (zu jdm)

attack [ə'tæk] vt angreifen ♦ n Angriff m; (MED) Anfall m; **~er** n Angreifer(in) m(f)

attain [ə'teɪn] vt erreichen; **~ments** npl Kenntnisse pl

attempt [ə'tempt] n Versuch m ♦ vt versuchen; **~ed murder** Mordversuch m

attend [ə'tend] vt (go to) teilnehmen (an +dat); (lectures) besuchen; **to ~ to** (needs) nachkommen +dat; (person) sich kümmern um; **~ance** n (presence) Anwesenheit f; (people present) Besucherzahl f; **good ~ance** gute Teilnahme; **~ant** n (companion) Begleiter(in) m(f); Gesellschafter(in) m(f); (in car park etc) Wächter(in) m(f); (servant) Bedienstete(r) mf ♦ adj begleitend; (fig) damit verbunden

attention [ə'tenʃən] n Aufmerksamkeit f; (care) Fürsorge f; (for machine etc) Pflege f ♦ excl (MIL) Achtung!; **for the ~ of ...** zu

Händen (von) ...

attentive [əˈtɛntɪv] *adj* aufmerksam

attic [ˈætɪk] *n* Dachstube *f*, Mansarde *f*

attitude [ˈætɪtjuːd] *n* (*mental*) Einstellung *f*

attorney [əˈtəːnɪ] *n* (*solicitor*) Rechtsanwalt *m*; **A~ General** *n* Justizminister *m*

attract [əˈtrækt] *vt* anziehen; (*attention*) erregen; **~ion** *n* Anziehungskraft *f*; (*thing*) Attraktion *f*; **~ive** *adj* attraktiv

attribute [*n* ˈætrɪbjuːt, *vb* əˈtrɪbjuːt] *n* Eigenschaft *f*, Attribut *nt* ♦ *vt* zuschreiben

attrition [əˈtrɪʃən] *n*: **war of ~** Zermürbungskrieg *m*

aubergine [ˈəubəʒiːn] *n* Aubergine *f*

auburn [ˈɔːbən] *adj* kastanienbraun

auction [ˈɔːkʃən] *n* (*also*: **sale by ~**) Versteigerung *f*, Auktion *f* ♦ *vt* versteigern; **~eer** [ɔːkʃəˈnɪəʳ] *n* Versteigerer *m*

audacity [ɔːˈdæsɪtɪ] *n* (*boldness*) Wagemut *m*; (*impudence*) Unverfrorenheit *f*

audible [ˈɔːdɪbl] *adj* hörbar

audience [ˈɔːdɪəns] *n* Zuhörer *pl*, Zuschauer *pl*; (*with queen*) Audienz *f*

audiotypist [ˈɔːdɪəuˌtaɪpɪst] *n* Phonotypistin *f*

audiovisual [ˈɔːdɪəuˈvɪzjuəl] *adj* audiovisuell

audit [ˈɔːdɪt] *vt* prüfen

audition [ɔːˈdɪʃən] *n* Probe *f*

auditor [ˈɔːdɪtəʳ] *n* (*accountant*) Rechnungsprüfer(in) *m(f)*, Buchprüfer *m*

auditorium [ɔːdɪˈtɔːrɪəm] *n* Zuschauerraum *m*

augment [ɔːgˈmɛnt] *vt* vermehren

augur [ˈɔːgəʳ] *vi* bedeuten, voraussagen; **this ~s well** das ist ein gutes Omen

August [ˈɔːgəst] *n* August *m*

aunt [ɑːnt] *n* Tante *f*; **~ie** *n* Tantchen *nt*; **~y** *n* = **auntie**

au pair [ˈəuˈpɛəʳ] *n* (*also*: **~ girl**) Au-pair-Mädchen *nt*

aura [ˈɔːrə] *n* Nimbus *m*

auspicious [ɔːsˈpɪʃəs] *adj* günstig; verheißungsvoll

austere [ɔsˈtɪəʳ] *adj* streng; (*room*) nüchtern; **austerity** [ɔsˈtɛrɪtɪ] *n* Strenge *f*; (*POL*) wirtschaftliche Einschränkung *f*

Australia [ɔsˈtreɪlɪə] *n* Australien *nt*; **~n** *adj*

australisch ♦ *n* Australier(in) *m(f)*

Austria [ˈɔstrɪə] *n* Österreich *nt*; **~n** *adj* österreichisch ♦ *n* Österreicher(in) *m(f)*

authentic [ɔːˈθɛntɪk] *adj* echt, authentisch

author [ˈɔːθəʳ] *n* Autor *m*, Schriftsteller *m*; (*beginner*) Urheber *m*, Schöpfer *m*

authoritarian [ɔːθɔrɪˈtɛərɪən] *adj* autoritär

authoritative [ɔːˈθɔrɪtətɪv] *adj* (*account*) maßgeblich; (*manner*) herrisch

authority [ɔːˈθɔrɪtɪ] *n* (*power*) Autorität *f*; (*expert*) Autorität *f*, Fachmann *m*; **the authorities** *npl* (*ruling body*) die Behörden *pl*

authorize [ˈɔːθəraɪz] *vt* bevollmächtigen; (*permit*) genehmigen

auto [ˈɔːtəu] (*US*) *n* Auto *nt*, Wagen *m*

autobiography [ɔːtəbaɪˈɔgrəfɪ] *n* Autobiographie *f*

autograph [ˈɔːtəgrɑːf] *n* (*of celebrity*) Autogramm *nt* ♦ *vt* mit Autogramm versehen

automatic [ɔːtəˈmætɪk] *adj* automatisch ♦ *n* (*gun*) Selbstladepistole *f*; (*car*) Automatik *m*; **~ally** *adv* automatisch

automation [ɔːtəˈmeɪʃən] *n* Automatisierung *f*

automobile [ˈɔːtəməbiːl] (*US*) *n* Auto(mobil) *nt*

autonomous [ɔːˈtɔnəməs] *adj* autonom; **autonomy** *n* Autonomie *f*

autumn [ˈɔːtəm] *n* Herbst *m*

auxiliary [ɔːgˈzɪlɪərɪ] *adj* Hilfs-

Av. *abbr* = **avenue**

avail [əˈveɪl] *vt*: **to ~ o.s. of sth** sich einer Sache *gen* bedienen ♦ *n*: **to no ~** nutzlos

availability [əveɪləˈbɪlɪtɪ] *n* Erhältlichkeit *f*, Vorhandensein *nt*

available [əˈveɪləbl] *adj* erhältlich; zur Verfügung stehend; (*person*) erreichbar, abkömmlich

avalanche [ˈævəlɑːnʃ] *n* Lawine *f*

Ave. *abbr* = **avenue**

avenge [əˈvɛndʒ] *vt* rächen, sühnen

avenue [ˈævənjuː] *n* Allee *f*

average [ˈævərɪdʒ] *n* Durchschnitt *m* ♦ *adj* durchschnittlich, Durchschnitts- ♦ *vt* (*figures*) den Durchschnitt nehmen von;

⚠ *For information on spelling reform see page 615*

(*perform*) durchschnittlich leisten; (*in car etc*) im Schnitt fahren; **on ~** durchschnittlich, im Durchschnitt; **~ out** *vi*: **to ~ out at** im Durchschnitt betragen

averse [ə'vɜːs] *adj*: **to be ~ to doing sth** eine Abneigung dagegen haben, etw zu tun

avert [ə'vɜːt] *vt* (*turn away*) abkehren; (*prevent*) abwehren

aviary ['eɪvɪərɪ] *n* Vogelhaus *nt*

aviation [eɪvɪ'eɪʃən] *n* Luftfahrt *f*, Flugwesen *nt*

avid ['ævɪd] *adj*: **~ (for)** gierig (auf +*acc*)

avocado [ævə'kɑːdəʊ] *n* (*BRIT: also:* **~ pear**) Avocado(birne) *f*

avoid [ə'vɔɪd] *vt* vermeiden

await [ə'weɪt] *vt* erwarten, entgegensehen +*dat*

awake [ə'weɪk] (*pt* **awoke**, *pp* **awoken** *or* **awaked**) *adj* wach ♦ *vt* (auf)wecken ♦ *vi* aufwachen; **to be ~** wach sein; **~ning** *n* Erwachen *nt*

award [ə'wɔːd] *n* (*prize*) Preis *m* ♦ *vt*: **to ~ (sb sth)** (jdm etw) zuerkennen

aware [ə'wɛə*] *adj* bewußt △; **to be ~** sich bewußt sein; **~ness** *n* Bewußtsein △ *nt*

awash [ə'wɒʃ] *adj* überflutet

away [ə'weɪ] *adv* weg, fort; **two hours ~ by car** zwei Autostunden entfernt; **the holiday was two weeks ~** es war noch zwei Wochen bis zum Urlaub; **two kilometres ~** zwei Kilometer entfernt; **~ match** *n* (*SPORT*) Auswärtsspiel *nt*

awe [ɔː] *n* Ehrfurcht *f*; **~-inspiring** *adj* ehrfurchtgebietend △; **~some** *adj* ehrfurchtgebietend △

awful ['ɔːfəl] *adj* (*very bad*) furchtbar; **~ly** *adv* furchtbar, sehr

awhile [ə'waɪl] *adv* eine Weile

awkward ['ɔːkwəd] *adj* (*clumsy*) ungeschickt, linkisch; (*embarrassing*) peinlich

awning ['ɔːnɪŋ] *n* Markise *f*

awoke [ə'wəʊk] *pt of* **awake**; **~n** *pp of* **awake**

awry [ə'raɪ] *adv* schief; **to go ~** (*plans*) schiefgehen

axe [æks] (*US* **ax**) *n* Axt *f*, Beil *nt* ♦ *vt* (*end*

suddenly) streichen

axes[1] ['æksɪz] *npl of* **axe**

axes[2] ['æksɪz] *npl of* **axis**

axis ['æksɪs] (*pl* **axes**) *n* Achse *f*

axle ['æksl] *n* Achse *f*

ay(e) [aɪ] *excl* (*yes*) ja

azalea [ə'zeɪlɪə] *n* Azalee *f*

B, b

B [biː] *n* (*MUS*) H *nt*; **~ road** (*BRIT*) Landstraße *f*

B.A. *n abbr* = **Bachelor of Arts**

babble ['bæbl] *vi* schwätzen

baby ['beɪbɪ] *n* Baby *nt*; **~ carriage** (*US*) *n* Kinderwagen *m*; **~ food** *n* Babynahrung *f*; **~-sit** *vi* Kinder hüten, babysitten; **~-sitter** *n* Babysitter *m*; **~sitting** *n* Babysitten *nt*, Babysitting *nt*; **~ wipe** *n* Ölpflegetuch *nt*

bachelor ['bætʃələ*] *n* Junggeselle *m*; **B~ of Arts** Bakkalaureus *m* der philosophischen Fakultät; **B~ of Science** Bakkalaureus *m* der Naturwissenschaften

back [bæk] *n* (*of person, horse*) Rücken *m*; (*of house*) Rückseite *f*; (*of train*) Ende *nt*; (*FOOTBALL*) Verteidiger *m* ♦ *vt* (*support*) unterstützen; (*wager*) wetten auf +*acc*; (*car*) rückwärts fahren ♦ *vi* (*go backwards*) rückwärts gehen *or* fahren ♦ *adj* hintere(r, s) ♦ *adv* zurück; (*to the rear*) nach hinten; **~ down** *vi* zurückstecken; **~ out** *vi* sich zurückziehen; (*inf*) kneifen; **~ up** *vt* (*support*) unterstützen; (*car*) zurücksetzen; (*COMPUT*) eine Sicherungskopie machen von; **~ache** *n* Rückenschmerzen *pl*; **~bencher** (*BRIT*) *n* Parlamentarier(in) *m(f)*; **~bone** *n* Rückgrat *nt*; (*support*) Rückhalt *m*; **~cloth** *n* Hintergrund *m*; **~date** *vt* rückdatieren; **~drop** *n* (*THEAT*) = **backcloth**; (*background*) Hintergrund *m*; **~fire** *vi* (*plan*) fehlschlagen; (*TECH*) fehlzünden; **~ground** *n* Hintergrund *m*; (*person's education*) Vorbildung *f*; **family ~ground** Familienverhältnisse *pl*; **~hand** *n* (*TENNIS: also:* **~hand stroke**) Rückhand *f*; **~hander** (*BRIT*) *n* (*bribe*) Schmiergeld *nt*; **~ing** *n* ˙

(*support*) Unterstützung *f*; **~lash** *n* (*fig*) Gegenschlag *m*; **~log** *n* (*of work*) Rückstand *m*; **~ number** *n* (*PRESS*) alte Nummer *f*; **~pack** *n* Rucksack *m*; **~packer** *n* Rucksacktourist(in) *m(f)*; **~ pain** *n* Rückenschmerzen *pl*; **~ pay** *n* (Gehalts- or Lohn)nachzahlung *f*; **~ payments** *npl* Zahlungsrückstände *pl*; **~ seat** *n* (*AUT*) Rücksitz *m*; **~side** (*inf*) *n* Hintern *m*; **~stage** *adv* hinter den Kulissen; **~stroke** *n* Rückenschwimmen *nt*; **~up** *adj* (*COMPUT*) Sicherungs- ♦ *n* (*COMPUT*) Sicherungskopie *f*; **~ward** *adj* (*less developed*) zurückgeblieben; (*primitive*) rückständig; **~wards** *adv* rückwärts; **~water** *n* (*fig*) Kaff *nt*; **~yard** *n* Hinterhof *m*

bacon ['beɪkən] *n* Schinkenspeck *m*

bacteria [bæk'tɪərɪə] *npl* Bakterien *pl*

bad [bæd] *adj* schlecht, schlimm; **to go ~** schlecht werden

bade [bæd] *pt of* **bid**

badge [bædʒ] *n* Abzeichen *nt*

badger ['bædʒə'] *n* Dachs *m*

badly ['bædlɪ] *adv* schlecht, schlimm; **~ wounded** schwerverwundet; **he needs it ~** er braucht es dringend; **to be ~ off (for money)** dringend Geld nötig haben

badminton ['bædmɪntən] *n* Federball *m*, Badminton *nt*

bad-tempered ['bæd'tempəd] *adj* schlecht gelaunt

baffle ['bæfl] *vt* (*puzzle*) verblüffen

bag [bæg] *n* (*sack*) Beutel *m*; (*paper*) Tüte *f*; (*hand~*) Tasche *f*; (*suitcase*) Koffer *m*; (*inf: old woman*) alte Schachtel *f* ♦ *vt* (*put in sack*) in einen Sack stecken; (*hunting*) erlegen; **~s of** (*inf: lots of*) eine Menge +*acc*; **~gage** ['bægɪdʒ] *n* Gepäck *nt*; **~ allowance** *n* Freigepäck *nt*; **~ reclaim** *n* Gepäcksausgabe *f*; **~gy** ['bægɪ] *adj* bauschig, sackartig

bagpipes ['bægpaɪps] *npl* Dudelsack *m*

bail [beɪl] *n* (*money*) Kaution *f* ♦ *vt* (*prisoner: usu: grant ~ to*) gegen Kaution freilassen; (*boat: also: ~ out*) ausschöpfen; **on ~** (*prisoner*) gegen Kaution freigelassen; **to ~ sb out** die Kaution für jdn stellen; *see also* bale

bailiff ['beɪlɪf] *n* Gerichtsvollzieher(in) *m(f)*

bait [beɪt] *n* Köder *m* ♦ *vt* mit einem Köder versehen; (*fig*) ködern

bake [beɪk] *vt, vi* backen; **~d beans** gebackene Bohnen *npl*; **~d potatoes** *npl* in der Schale gebackene Kartoffeln *pl*; **~r** *n* Bäcker *m*; **~ry** *n* Bäckerei *f*; **baking** *n* Backen *nt*; **baking powder** *n* Backpulver *nt*

balance ['bæləns] *n* (*scales*) Waage *f*; (*equilibrium*) Gleichgewicht *nt*; (*FIN: state of account*) Saldo *m*; (*difference*) Bilanz *f*; (*amount remaining*) Restbetrag *m* ♦ *vt* (*weigh*) wägen; (*make equal*) ausgleichen; **~ of trade/payments** Handels-/Zahlungsbilanz *f*; **~d** *adj* ausgeglichen; **~ sheet** *n* Bilanz *f*, Rechnungsabschluß ⚠ *m*

balcony ['bælkənɪ] *n* Balkon *m*

bald [bɔːld] *adj* kahl; (*statement*) knapp

bale [beɪl] *n* Ballen *m*; **bale out** *vi* (*from a plane*) abspringen

ball [bɔːl] *n* Ball *m*; **~ bearing** *n* Kugellager *nt*

ballet ['bæleɪ] *n* Ballett *nt*; **~ dancer** *n* Ballettänzer(in) ⚠ *m(f)*; **~ shoe** *n* Ballettschuh *m*

balloon [bə'luːn] *n* (Luft)ballon *m*

ballot ['bælət] *n* (*geheime*) Abstimmung *f*

ballpoint (pen) ['bɔːlpɔɪnt(-)] *n* Kugelschreiber *m*

ballroom ['bɔːlrum] *n* Tanzsaal *m*

Baltic ['bɔːltɪk] *n*: **the ~ (Sea)** die Ostsee

bamboo [bæm'buː] *n* Bambus *m*

ban [bæn] *n* Verbot *nt* ♦ *vt* verbieten

banana [bə'nɑːnə] *n* Banane *f*

band [bænd] *n* Band *nt*; (*group*) Gruppe *f*; (*of criminals*) Bande *f*; (*MUS*) Kapelle *f*, Band *f*; **~ together** *vi* sich zusammentun

bandage ['bændɪdʒ] *n* Verband *m*; (*elastic*) Bandage *f* ♦ *vt* (*cut*) verbinden; (*broken limb*) bandagieren

Bandaid ['bændeɪd] ((Ⓡ) *US*) *n* Heftpflaster *nt*

bandit ['bændɪt] *n* Bandit *m*, Räuber *m*

bandwagon ['bændwægən] *n*: **to jump on the ~** (*fig*) auf den fahrenden Zug

⚠ *For information on spelling reform see page 615*

aufspringen

bandy ['bændɪ] vt wechseln; **~-legged** adj o-beinig

bang [bæŋ] n (explosion) Knall m; (blow) Hieb m ♦ vt, vi knallen

Bangladesh [bæŋglə'deʃ] n Bangladesch nt

bangle ['bæŋgl] n Armspange f

bangs [bæŋz] (US) npl (fringe) Pony m

banish ['bænɪʃ] vt verbannen

banister(s) ['bænɪstə(z)] n(pl) (Treppen)geländer nt

bank [bæŋk] n (raised ground) Erdwall m; (of lake etc) Ufer nt; (FIN) Bank f ♦ vt (tilt: AVIAT) in die Kurve bringen; (money) einzahlen; **~ on** vt fus: **to ~ on sth** mit etw rechnen; **~ account** n Bankkonto nt; **~ card** n Scheckkarte f; **~er** n Bankier m; **~er's card** (BRIT) n = **bank card**; **B~ holiday** (BRIT) n gesetzliche(r) Feiertag m; **~ing** n Bankwesen nt; **~note** n Banknote f; **~ rate** n Banksatz m

---

BANK HOLIDAY

ⓘ   Als **bank holiday** wird in Großbritannien ein gesetzlicher Feiertag bezeichnet, an dem die Banken geschlossen sind. Die meisten dieser Feiertage, abgesehen von Weihnachten und Ostern, fallen auf Montage im Mai und August. An diesen langen Wochenenden (bank holiday weekends) fahren viele Briten in Urlaub, so daß dann auf den Straßen, Flughäfen und bei der Bahn sehr viel Betrieb ist.

---

bankrupt ['bæŋkrʌpt] adj: **to be ~** bankrott sein; **to go ~** Bankrott machen; **~cy** n Bankrott m

bank statement n Kontoauszug m

banned [bænd] adj: **he was ~ from driving** (BRIT) ihm wurde Fahrverbot erteilt

banner ['bænəʳ] n Banner nt

banns [bænz] npl Aufgebot nt

baptism ['bæptɪzəm] n Taufe f

baptize [bæp'taɪz] vt taufen

bar [bɑːʳ] n (rod) Stange f; (obstacle) Hindernis nt; (of chocolate) Tafel f; (of soap) Stück nt; (for food, drink) Buffet nt, Bar f;

(pub) Wirtschaft f; (MUS) Takt(strich) m ♦ vt (fasten) verriegeln; (hinder) versperren; (exclude) ausschließen; **behind ~s** hinter Gittern; **the B~:** **to be called to the B~** als Anwalt zugelassen werden; **~ none** ohne Ausnahme

barbaric [bɑː'bærɪk] adj primitiv, unkultiviert

barbecue ['bɑːbɪkjuː] n Barbecue nt

barbed wire ['bɑːbd-] n Stacheldraht m

barber ['bɑːbəʳ] n Herrenfriseur m

bar code n (COMM) Registrierkode f

bare [bɛəʳ] adj nackt; (trees, country) kahl; (mere) bloß ♦ vt entblößen; **~back** adv ungesattelt; **~faced** adj unverfroren; **~foot** adj, adv barfuß; **~ly** adv kaum, knapp

bargain ['bɑːgɪn] n (sth cheap) günstiger Kauf; (agreement: written) Kaufvertrag m; (: oral) Geschäft nt; **into the ~** obendrein; **~ for** vt: **he got more than he ~ed for** er erlebte sein blaues Wunder

barge [bɑːdʒ] n Lastkahn m; **~ in** vi hereinplatzen; **~ into** vt rennen gegen

bark [bɑːk] n (of tree) Rinde f; (of dog) Bellen nt ♦ vi (dog) bellen

barley ['bɑːlɪ] n Gerste f; **~ sugar** n Malzbonbon nt

bar: **~maid** n Bardame f; **~man** (irreg) n Barkellner m; **~ meal** n einfaches Essen in einem Pub

barn [bɑːn] n Scheune f

barometer [bə'rɔmɪtəʳ] n Barometer nt

baron ['bærən] n Baron m; **~ess** n Baronin f

barracks ['bærəks] npl Kaserne f

barrage ['bærɑːʒ] n (gunfire) Sperrfeuer nt; (dam) Staudamm m; Talsperre f

barrel ['bærəl] n Faß ⚠ nt; (of gun) Lauf m

barren ['bærən] adj unfruchtbar

barricade [bærɪ'keɪd] n Barrikade f ♦ vt verbarrikadieren

barrier ['bærɪəʳ] n (obstruction) Hindernis nt; (fence) Schranke f

barring ['bɑːrɪŋ] prep außer im Falle +gen

barrister ['bærɪstəʳ] (BRIT) n Rechtsanwalt m

barrow ['bærəu] n (cart) Schubkarren m

bartender ['bɑːtendəʳ] (US) n Barmann or -kellner m

barter ['bɑːtəʳ] vt handeln

⚠ *Informationen zur Rechtschreibreform Seite 615*

base [beɪs] n (*bottom*) Boden m, Basis f; (*MIL*) Stützpunkt m ♦ vt gründen; (*opinion, theory*) to be ~d on basieren auf +dat ♦ adj (*low*) gemein; **I'm ~d in London** ich wohne in London; **~ball** ['beɪsbɔːl] n Baseball m; **~ment** ['beɪsmənt] n Kellergeschoß △ nt

bases[1] ['beɪsiːz] npl of **base**

bases[2] ['beɪsiːz] npl of **basis**

bash [bæʃ] (*inf*) vt (heftig) schlagen

bashful ['bæʃful] adj schüchtern

basic ['beɪsɪk] adj grundlegend; **~s** npl: **the ~s** das Wesentliche (sg); **~ally** adv im Grunde

basil ['bæzl] n Basilikum nt

basin ['beɪsn] n (*dish*) Schüssel f; (*for washing, also valley*) Becken nt; (*dock*) (Trocken)becken nt

basis ['beɪsɪs] n (pl **bases**) n Basis f, Grundlage f

bask [bɑːsk] vi: **to ~ in the sun** sich sonnen

basket ['bɑːskɪt] n Korb m; **~ball** n Basketball m

bass [beɪs] n (*MUS, also instrument*) Baß △ m; (*voice*) Baßstimme △ f; **~ drum** n große Trommel

bassoon [bə'suːn] n Fagott nt

bastard ['bɑːstəd] n Bastard m; (*inf!*) Arschloch nt (!)

bat [bæt] n (*SPORT*) Schlagholz nt; Schläger m; (*ZOOL*) Fledermaus f ♦ vt: **he didn't ~ an eyelid** er hat nicht mit der Wimper gezuckt

batch [bætʃ] n (*of letters*) Stoß m; (*of samples*) Satz m

bated ['beɪtɪd] adj: **with ~ breath** mit angehaltenem Atem

bath [bɑːθ] n Bad nt; (~ tub) Badewanne f ♦ vt baden; **to have a ~** baden; see also **baths**

bathe [beɪð] vt, vi baden; **~r** n Badende(r) f(m)

bathing ['beɪðɪŋ] n Baden nt; **~ cap** n Badekappe f; **~ costume** n Badeanzug m; **~ suit** (*US*) n Badeanzug m; **~ trunks** (*BRIT*) npl Badehose f

bath: **~robe** n Bademantel m; **~room** n Bad(ezimmer) nt; **~s** npl (Schwimm)bad nt; **~ towel** n Badetuch nt

baton ['bætən] n (*of police*) Gummiknüppel m; (*MUS*) Taktstock m

batter ['bætə*] vt verprügeln ♦ n Schlagteig m; (*for cake*) Biskuitteig m; **~ed** adj (*hat, pan*) verbeult

battery ['bætəri] n (*ELEC*) Batterie f; (*MIL*) Geschützbatterie f

battery farming n (Hühner- *etc*)batterien pl

battle ['bætl] n Schlacht f; (*small*) Gefecht nt ♦ vi kämpfen; **~field** n Schlachtfeld nt; **~ship** n Schlachtschiff nt

Bavaria [bə'veəriə] n Bayern nt; **~n** adj bay(e)risch ♦ n (*person*) Bayer(in) m(f)

bawdy ['bɔːdɪ] adj unflätig

bawl [bɔːl] vi brüllen

bay [beɪ] n (*of sea*) Bucht f ♦ vi bellen; **to keep at ~** unter Kontrolle halten; **~ window** n Erkerfenster nt

bazaar [bə'zɑː*] n Basar m

B. & B. abbr = **bed and breakfast**

BBC n abbr (= *British Broadcasting Corporation*) BBC f or m

B.C. adv abbr (= *before Christ*) v. Chr.

KEYWORD

be [biː] (pt **was, were**, pp **been**) aux vb **1** (*with present participle: forming continuous tenses*): **what are you doing?** was machst du (gerade)?; **it is raining** es regnet; **I've been waiting for you for hours** ich warte schon seit Stunden auf dich

2 (*with pp: forming passives*): **to be killed** getötet werden; **the thief was nowhere to be seen** der Dieb war nirgendwo zu sehen

3 (*in tag questions*): **it was fun, wasn't it?** es hat Spaß gemacht, nicht wahr?

4 (+*to* +*infin*): **the house is to be sold** das Haus soll verkauft werden; **he's not to open it** er darf es nicht öffnen

♦ vb +complement **1** (*usu*) sein; **I'm tired** ich bin müde; **I'm hot/cold** mir ist heiß/kalt; **he's a doctor** er ist Arzt; **2 and 2 are 4** 2 und 2 ist or sind 4; **she's tall/pretty** sie ist groß/hübsch; **be careful/quiet** sei vorsichtig/ruhig

2 (*of health*): **how are you?** wie geht es

dir?; **he's very ill** er ist sehr krank; **I'm fine now** jetzt geht es mir gut
3 (*of age*): **how old are you?** wie alt bist du?; **I'm sixteen (years old)** ich bin sechzehn (Jahre alt)
4 (*cost*): **how much was the meal?** was *or* wieviel hat das Essen gekostet?; **that'll be £5.75, please** das macht £5.75, bitte
♦ vi 1 (*exist, occur etc*) sein; **is there a God?** gibt es einen Gott?; **be that as it may** wie dem auch sei; **so be it** also gut
2 (*referring to place*) sein; **I won't be here tomorrow** ich werde morgen nicht hier sein
3 (*referring to movement*): **where have you been?** wo bist du gewesen?; **I've been in the garden** ich war im Garten
♦ impers vb 1 (*referring to time, distance, weather*) sein; **it's 5 o'clock** es ist 5 Uhr; **it's 10 km to the village** es sind 10 km bis zum Dorf; **it's too hot/cold** es ist zu heiß/kalt
2 (*emphatic*): **it's me** ich bin's; **it's the postman** es ist der Briefträger

beach [biːtʃ] *n* Strand *m* ♦ vt (*ship*) auf den Strand setzen
beacon ['biːkən] *n* (*signal*) Leuchtfeuer *nt*; (*traffic ~*) Bake *f*
bead [biːd] *n* Perle *f*; (*drop*) Tropfen *m*
beak [biːk] *n* Schnabel *m*
beaker ['biːkər] *n* Becher *m*
beam [biːm] *n* (*of wood*) Balken *m*; (*of light*) Strahl *m*; (*smile*) strahlende(s) Lächeln *nt* ♦ vi strahlen
bean [biːn] *n* Bohne *f*; (*also:* baked ~s) gebackene Bohnen *pl*; ~ **sprouts** *npl* Sojasprossen *pl*
bear [bɛər] (*pt* bore, *pp* borne) *n* Bär *m* ♦ vt (*weight, crops*) tragen; (*tolerate*) ertragen; (*young*) gebären ♦ vi: **to ~ right/left** sich rechts/links halten; ~ **out** vt (*suspicions etc*) bestätigen; ~ **up** vi sich halten
beard [bɪəd] *n* Bart *m*; ~**ed** adj bärtig
bearer ['bɛərər] *n* Träger *m*
bearing ['bɛərɪŋ] *n* (*posture*) Haltung *f*; (*relevance*) Relevanz *f*; (*relation*) Bedeutung

f; (*TECH*) Kugellager *nt*; ~**s** *npl* (*direction*) Orientierung *f*; (*also:* ball ~s) (Kugel)lager *nt*
beast [biːst] *n* Tier *nt*, Vieh *nt*; (*person*) Biest *nt*
beat [biːt] (*pt* beat, *pp* beaten) *n* (*stroke*) Schlag *m*; (*pulsation*) (Herz)schlag *m*; (*police round*) Runde *f*; Revier *nt*; (*MUS*) Takt *m*; Beat *m* ♦ vt, vi schlagen; **to ~ it** abhauen; **off the ~en track** abgelegen; ~ **off** vt abschlagen; ~ **up** vt zusammenschlagen; ~**en** *pp of* beat; ~**ing** *n* Prügel *pl*
beautiful ['bjuːtɪful] adj schön; ~**ly** adv ausgezeichnet
beauty ['bjuːtɪ] *n* Schönheit *f*; ~ **salon** *n* Schönheitssalon *m*; ~ **spot** *n* Schönheitsfleck *m*; (*BRIT: TOURISM*) (besonders) schöne(r) Ort *m*
beaver ['biːvər] *n* Biber *m*
became [bɪˈkeɪm] *pt of* become
because [bɪˈkɒz] *conj* weil ♦ prep: ~ **of** wegen +gen, wegen +dat (*inf*)
beck [bɛk] *n*: **to be at the ~ and call of sb** nach jds Pfeife tanzen
beckon ['bɛkən] vt, vi: **to ~ to sb** jdm ein Zeichen geben
become [bɪˈkʌm] (*irreg: like* come) vi werden ♦ vt werden; (*clothes*) stehen +dat
becoming [bɪˈkʌmɪŋ] adj (*suitable*) schicklich; (*clothes*) kleidsam
bed [bɛd] *n* Bett *nt*; (*of river*) Flußbett △ *nt*; (*foundation*) Schicht *f*; (*in garden*) Beet *nt*; **to go to ~** zu Bett gehen; ~ **and breakfast** *n* Übernachtung *f* mit Frühstück; ~**clothes** *npl* Bettwäsche *f*; ~**ding** *n* Bettzeug *nt*

BED AND BREAKFAST

ℹ **Bed and Breakfast** bedeutet "Übernachtung mit Frühstück", wobei sich dies in Großbritannien nicht auf Hotels, sondern auf kleinere Pensionen, Privathäuser und Bauernhöfe bezieht, wo man wesentlich preisgünstiger übernachten kann als in Hotels. Oft wird für Bed and Breakfast, auch B & B genannt, durch ein entsprechendes Schild geworben.

△ *Informationen zur Rechtschreibreform Seite 615*

bedlam [ˈbedləm] n (uproar) tolle(s) Durcheinander nt

bed linen n Bettwäsche f

bedraggled [brˈdrægld] adj ramponiert

bed: ~ridden adj bettlägerig; **~room** n Schlafzimmer nt; **~side** n: **at the ~side** am Bett; **~sit(ter)** (BRIT) n Einzimmerwohnung f, möblierte(s) Zimmer nt; **~spread** n Tagesdecke f; **~time** n Schlafenszeit f

bee [biː] n Biene f

beech [biːtʃ] n Buche f

beef [biːf] n Rindfleisch nt; **roast ~** Roastbeef nt; **~burger** n Hamburger m

beehive [ˈbiːhaɪv] n Bienenstock m

beeline [ˈbiːlaɪn] n: **to make a ~ for** schnurstracks zugehen auf +acc

been [biːn] pp of **be**

beer [bɪəʳ] n Bier nt

beet [biːt] n (vegetable) Rübe f; (US: also: **red ~**) rote Bete f or Rübe f

beetle [ˈbiːtl] n Käfer m

beetroot [ˈbiːtruːt] (BRIT) n rote Bete f

before [brˈfɔːʳ] prep vor ♦ conj bevor ♦ adv (of time) zuvor; früher; **the week ~** die Woche zuvor or vorher; **I've done it ~** das hab' ich schon mal getan; **~ going** bevor er/sie etc geht/ging; **~ she goes** bevor sie geht; **~hand** adv im voraus

beg [beg] vt, vi (implore) dringend bitten; (alms) betteln

began [brˈgæn] pt of **begin**

beggar [ˈbegəʳ] n Bettler(in) m(f)

begin [brˈgɪn] (pt **began**, pp **begun**) vt, vi anfangen, beginnen; (found) gründen; **to ~ doing** or **to do sth** anfangen or beginnen, etw zu tun; **to ~ with** zunächst (einmal); **~ner** n Anfänger m; **~ning** n Anfang m

begun [brˈgʌn] pp of **begin**

behalf [brˈhɑːf] n: **on ~ of** im Namen +gen; **on my ~** für mich

behave [brˈheɪv] vi sich benehmen; **behaviour** [brˈheɪvjəʳ] (US **behavior**) n Benehmen nt

beheld [brˈheld] pt, pp of **behold**

behind [brˈhaɪnd] prep hinter ♦ adv (late) im Rückstand; (in the rear) hinten ♦ n (inf)

Hinterteil nt; **~ the scenes** (fig) hinter den Kulissen

behold [brˈhəʊld] (irreg: like **hold**) vt erblicken

beige [beɪʒ] adj beige

Beijing [ˈbeɪˈdʒɪŋ] n Peking nt

being [ˈbiːɪŋ] n (existence) (Da)sein nt; (person) Wesen n; **to come into ~** entstehen

Belarus [bɛləˈrus] n Weißrußland △ nt

belated [brˈleɪtɪd] adj verspätet

belch [beltʃ] vi rülpsen ♦ vt (smoke) ausspeien

belfry [ˈbelfrɪ] n Glockenturm m

Belgian [ˈbeldʒən] adj belgisch ♦ n Belgier(in) m(f)

Belgium [ˈbeldʒəm] n Belgien nt

belie [brˈlaɪ] vt Lügen strafen +acc

belief [brˈliːf] n Glaube m; (conviction) Überzeugung f; **~ in sb/sth** Glaube an jdn/etw

believe [brˈliːv] vt glauben +dat; (think) glauben, meinen, denken ♦ vi (have faith) glauben; **to ~ in sth** an etw acc glauben; **~r** n Gläubige(r) f(m)

belittle [brˈlɪtl] vt herabsetzen

bell [bel] n Glocke f

belligerent [brˈlɪdʒərənt] adj (person) streitsüchtig; (country) kriegführend △

bellow [ˈbeləʊ] vt, vi brüllen

bellows [ˈbeləʊz] npl (TECH) Gebläse nt; (for fire) Blasebalg m

belly [ˈbelɪ] n Bauch m

belong [brˈlɒŋ] vi gehören; **to ~ to sb** jdm gehören; **to ~ to a club** etc einem Club etc angehören; **~ings** npl Habe f

beloved [brˈlʌvɪd] adj innig geliebt ♦ n Geliebte(r) f(m)

below [brˈləʊ] prep unter ♦ adv unten

belt [belt] n (band) Riemen m; (round waist) Gürtel m ♦ vt (fasten) mit Riemen befestigen; (inf: beat) schlagen; **~way** (US) n (AUT: ring road) Umgehungsstraße f

bemused [brˈmjuːzd] adj verwirrt

bench [bentʃ] n (seat) Bank f; (workshop) Werkbank f; (judge's seat) Richterbank f; (judges) Richter pl

△ *For information on spelling reform see page 615*

bend [bend] (*pt, pp* bent) *vt* (*curve*) biegen; (*stoop*) beugen ♦ *vi* sich biegen; sich beugen ♦ *n* Biegung *f*; (*BRIT: in road*) Kurve *f*; ~ **down** *or* **over** *vi* sich bücken

beneath [bɪ'ni:θ] *prep* unter ♦ *adv* darunter

benefactor ['benɪfæktər] *n* Wohltäter(in) *m(f)*

beneficial [benɪ'fɪʃəl] *adj* vorteilhaft; (*to health*) heilsam

benefit ['benɪfɪt] *n* (*advantage*) Nutzen *m* ♦ *vt* fördern ♦ *vi*: **to ~ (from)** Nutzen ziehen (aus)

Benelux ['benɪlʌks] *n* Beneluxstaaten *pl*

benevolent [bɪ'nevələnt] *adj* wohlwollend

benign [bɪ'naɪn] *adj* (*person*) gütig; (*climate*) mild

bent [bent] *pt, pp of* **bend** ♦ *n* (*inclination*) Neigung *f* ♦ *adj* (*inf: dishonest*) unehrlich; **to be ~ on** versessen sein auf *+acc*

bequest [bɪ'kwest] *n* Vermächtnis *nt*

bereaved [bɪ'ri:vd] *npl*: **the ~** die Hinterbliebenen *pl*

beret ['bereɪ] *n* Baskenmütze *f*

Berlin [bə:'lɪn] *n* Berlin *nt*

berm [bə:m] (*US*) *n* (*AUT*) Seitenstreifen *m*

berry ['berɪ] *n* Beere *f*

berserk [bə'sə:k] *adj*: **to go ~** wild werden

berth [bə:θ] *n* (*for ship*) Ankerplatz *m*; (*in ship*) Koje *f*; (*in train*) Bett *nt* ♦ *vi* am Kai festmachen ♦ *vi* anlegen

beseech [bɪ'si:tʃ] (*pt, pp* **besought**) *vt* anflehen

beset [bɪ'set] (*pt, pp* **beset**) *vt* bedrängen

beside [bɪ'saɪd] *prep* neben, bei; (*except*) außer; **to be ~ o.s. (with)** außer sich sein (vor *+dat*); **that's ~ the point** das tut nichts zur Sache

besides [bɪ'saɪdz] *prep* außer, neben ♦ *adv* außerdem

besiege [bɪ'si:dʒ] *vt* (*MIL*) belagern; (*surround*) umlagern, bedrängen

besought [bɪ'sɔ:t] *pt, pp of* **beseech**

best [best] *adj* beste(r, s) ♦ *adv* am besten; **the ~ part of** (*quantity*) das meiste *+gen*; **at ~** höchstens; **to make the ~ of it** das Beste daraus machen; **to do one's ~** sein Bestes tun; **to the ~ of my knowledge** meines

Wissens; **to the ~ of my ability** so gut ich kann; **for the ~** zum Besten; **~-before date** *n* Mindesthaltbarkeitsdatum *nt*; **~ man** *n* Trauzeuge *m*

bestow [bɪ'stəu] *vt* verleihen

bet [bet] (*pt, pp* **bet** *or* **betted**) *n* Wette *f* ♦ *vt, vi* wetten

betray [bɪ'treɪ] *vt* verraten

better ['betər] *adj, adv* besser ♦ *vt* verbessern ♦ *n*: **to get the ~ of sb** jdn überwinden; **he thought ~ of it** er hat sich eines Besseren besonnen; **you had ~ leave** Sie gehen jetzt wohl besser; **to get ~** (*MED*) gesund werden; **~ off** *adj* (*richer*) wohlhabender

betting ['betɪŋ] *n* Wetten *nt*; **~ shop** (*BRIT*) *n* Wettbüro *nt*

between [bɪ'twi:n] *prep* zwischen; (*among*) unter ♦ *adv* dazwischen

beverage ['bevərɪdʒ] *n* Getränk *nt*

bevy ['bevɪ] *n* Schar *f*

beware [bɪ'weər] *vt, vi* sich hüten vor *+dat*; **"~ of the dog"** „Vorsicht, bissiger Hund!"

bewildered [bɪ'wɪldəd] *adj* verwirrt

beyond [bɪ'jɔnd] *prep* (*place*) jenseits *+gen*; (*time*) über ... hinaus; (*out of reach*) außerhalb *+gen* ♦ *adv* darüber hinaus; **~ doubt** ohne Zweifel; **~ repair** nicht mehr zu reparieren

bias ['baɪəs] *n* (*slant*) Neigung *f*; (*prejudice*) Vorurteil *nt*; **~(s)ed** *adj* voreingenommen

bib [bɪb] *n* Latz *m*

Bible ['baɪbl] *n* Bibel *f*

bicarbonate of soda [baɪ'kɑ:bənɪt-] *n* Natron *nt*

bicker ['bɪkər] *vi* zanken

bicycle ['baɪsɪkl] *n* Fahrrad *nt*

bid [bɪd] (*pt* **bade** *or* **bid**, *pp* **bid(den)**) *n* (*offer*) Gebot *nt*; (*attempt*) Versuch *m* ♦ *vt, vi* (*offer*) bieten; **to ~ farewell** Lebewohl sagen; **~der** *n* (*person*) Steigerer *m*; **the highest ~der** der Meistbietende; **~ding** *n* (*command*) Geheiß *nt*

bide [baɪd] *vt*: **to ~ one's time** abwarten

bifocals [baɪ'fəuklz] *npl* Bifokalbrille *f*

big [bɪg] *adj* groß; **~ dipper** [-'dɪpər] *n* Achterbahn *f*; **~headed** ['bɪg'hedɪd] *adj* eingebildet

⚠ *Informationen zur Rechtschreibreform Seite 615*

bigot ['bɪgət] n Frömmler m; **~ed** adj bigott; **~ry** n Bigotterie f

big top n Zirkuszelt nt

bike [baɪk] n Rad nt

bikini [bɪ'ki:nɪ] n Bikini m

bile [baɪl] n (BIOL) Galle f

bilingual [baɪ'lɪŋgwəl] adj zweisprachig

bill [bɪl] n (account) Rechnung f; (POL) Gesetzentwurf m; (US: FIN) Geldschein m; **to fit** or **fill the ~** (fig) der/die/das richtige sein; **"post no ~s"** „Plakate ankleben verboten"; **~board** n ['bɪlbɔːd] n Reklameschild nt

billet ['bɪlɪt] n Quartier nt

billfold ['bɪlfəʊld] (US) n Geldscheintasche f

billiards ['bɪljədz] n Billard nt

billion ['bɪljən] n (BRIT) Billion f; (US) Milliarde f

bimbo ['bɪmbəʊ] n (inf: pej) n Puppe f, Häschen nt

bin [bɪn] n Kasten m; (dust~) (Abfall)eimer m

bind [baɪnd] n (pt, pp bound) vt (tie) binden; (tie together) zusammenbinden; (oblige) verpflichten; **~ing** n (Buch)einband m ♦ adj verbindlich

binge [bɪndʒ] n (inf) Sauferei f

bingo ['bɪŋgəʊ] n Bingo nt

binoculars [bɪ'nɒkjʊləz] npl Fernglas nt

bio... [baɪəʊ] prefix: **~chemistry** ♦ n Biochemie f; **~degradable** adj biologisch abbaubar; **~graphy** n Biographie △ f; **~logical** [baɪə'lɒdʒɪkl] adj biologisch; **~logy** [baɪ'ɒlədʒɪ] n Biologie f

birch [bɜːtʃ] n Birke f

bird [bɜːd] n Vogel m; (BRIT: inf: girl) Mädchen nt; **~'s-eye view** n Vogelschau f; **~ watcher** n Vogelbeobachter(in) m(f); **~ watching** n Vogelbeobachten nt

Biro ['baɪərəʊ] ® n Kugelschreiber m

birth [bɜːθ] n Geburt f; **to give ~ to** zur Welt bringen; **~ certificate** n Geburtsurkunde f; **~ control** n Geburtenkontrolle f; **~day** n Geburtstag m; **~day card** n Geburtstagskarte f; **~place** n Geburtsort m; **~ rate** n Geburtenrate f

biscuit ['bɪskɪt] n Keks m

bisect [baɪ'sekt] vt halbieren

bishop ['bɪʃəp] n Bischof m

bit [bɪt] pt of **bite** ♦ n bißchen △, Stückchen nt; (horse's) Gebiß △ nt; (COMPUT) Bit nt; **a ~ tired** etwas müde

bitch [bɪtʃ] n (dog) Hündin f; (unpleasant woman) Weibsstück nt

bite [baɪt] (pt bit, pp bitten) vt, vi beißen ♦ n Biß △ m; (mouthful) Bissen m; **to ~ one's nails** Nägel kauen; **let's have a ~ to eat** laß uns etwas essen

bitten ['bɪtn] pp of **bite**

bitter ['bɪtə'] adj bitter; (memory etc) schmerzlich; (person) verbittert ♦ n (BRIT: beer) dunkle(s) Bier nt; **~ness** f Bitterkeit f

blab [blæb] vi klatschen ♦ vt (also: ~ **out**) ausplaudern

black [blæk] adj schwarz; (night) finster ♦ vt schwärzen; (shoes) wichsen; (eye) blau schlagen; (BRIT: INDUSTRY) boykottieren; **to give sb a ~ eye** jdm ein blaues Auge schlagen; **in the ~** (bank account) in den schwarzen Zahlen; **~ and blue** adj grün und blau; **~berry** n Brombeere f; **~bird** n Amsel f; **~board** n (Wand)tafel f; **~ coffee** n schwarze(r) Kaffee m; **~currant** n schwarze Johannisbeere f; **~en** vt schwärzen; (fig) verunglimpfen; **B~ Forest** n Schwarzwald m; **~ ice** n Glatteis nt; **~leg** (BRIT) n Streikbrecher(in) m(f); **~list** n schwarze Liste f; **~mail** n Erpressung f ♦ vt erpressen; **~ market** n Schwarzmarkt m; **~out** n Verdunklung f; (MED): **to have a ~out** bewußtlos △ werden; **~ pudding** n ≈ Blutwurst f; **B~ Sea** n: **the B~ Sea** das Schwarze Meer; **~ sheep** n schwarze(s) Schaf nt; **~smith** n Schmied m; **~ spot** n (AUT) Gefahrenstelle f; (for unemployment etc) schwer betroffene(s) Gebiet nt

bladder ['blædə'] n Blase f

blade [bleɪd] n (of weapon) Klinge f; (of grass) Halm m; (of oar) Ruderblatt nt

blame [bleɪm] n Tadel m, Schuld f ♦ vt Vorwürfe machen +dat; **to ~ sb for sth** jdm die Schuld an etw dat geben; **he is to ~** er ist daran schuld

bland [blænd] adj mild

blank [blæŋk] adj leer, unbeschrieben; (look)

verdutzt; (*verse*) Blank- ♦ *n* (*space*) Lücke *f*; Zwischenraum *m*; (*cartridge*) Platzpatrone *f*; ~ **cheque** *n* Blankoscheck *m*; (*fig*) Freibrief *m*

blanket ['blæŋkɪt] *n* (Woll)decke *f*

blare [bleəʳ] *vi* (*radio*) plärren; (*horn*) tuten; (*MUS*) schmettern

blasé ['blɑːzeɪ] *adj* blasiert

blast [blɑːst] *n* Explosion *f*; (*of wind*) Windstoß *m* ♦ *vt* (*blow up*) sprengen; ~! (*inf*) verflixt!; ~**off** *n* (*SPACE*) (Raketen)abschuß ⚠ *m*

blatant ['bleɪtənt] *adj* offenkundig

blaze [bleɪz] *n* (*fire*) lodernde(s) Feuer *nt* ♦ *vi* lodern ♦ *vt*: **to ~ a trail** Bahn brechen

blazer ['bleɪzəʳ] *n* Blazer *m*

bleach [bliːtʃ] *n* (*also*: **household ~**) Bleichmittel *nt* ♦ *vt* bleichen; ~**ed** *adj* gebleicht

bleachers ['bliːtʃəz] (*US*) *npl* (*SPORT*) unüberdachte Tribüne *f*

bleak [bliːk] *adj* kahl, rauh ⚠; (*future*) trostlos

bleary-eyed ['blɪərɪˈaɪd] *adj* triefäugig; (*on waking up*) mit verschlafenen Augen

bleat [bliːt] *vi* blöken; (*fig*: *complain*) meckern

bled [bled] *pt*, *pp* of **bleed**

bleed [bliːd] (*pt*, *pp* **bled**) *vi* bluten ♦ *vt* (*draw blood*) zur Ader lassen; **to ~ to death** verbluten

bleeper ['bliːpəʳ] *n* (*of doctor etc*) Funkrufempfänger *m*

blemish ['blemɪʃ] *n* Makel *m* ♦ *vt* verunstalten

blend [blend] *n* Mischung *f* ♦ *vt* mischen ♦ *vi* sich mischen; ~**er** *n* Mixer *m*, Mixgerät *nt*

bless [bles] (*pt*, *pp* **blessed**) *vt* segnen; (*give thanks*) preisen; (*make happy*) glücklich machen; ~ **you!** Gesundheit!; ~**ing** *n* Segen *m*; (*at table*) Tischgebet *nt*; (*happiness*) Wohltat *f*; Segen *m*; (*good wish*) Glück *nt*

blew [bluː] *pt* of **blow**

blimey ['blaɪmɪ] (*BRIT*: *inf*) *excl* verflucht

blind [blaɪnd] *adj* blind; (*corner*) unübersichtlich ♦ *n* (*for window*) Rouleau *nt*

♦ *vt* blenden; ~ **alley** *n* Sackgasse *f*; ~**fold** *n* Augenbinde *f* ♦ *adj*, *adv* mit verbundenen Augen ♦ *vt*: **to ~fold sb** jdm die Augen verbinden; ~**ly** *adv* blind; (*fig*) blindlings; ~**ness** *n* Blindheit *f*; ~ **spot** *n* (*AUT*) tote(r) Winkel *m*; (*fig*) schwache(r) Punkt *m*

blink [blɪŋk] *vi* blinzeln; ~**ers** *npl* Scheuklappen *pl*

bliss [blɪs] *n* (Glück)seligkeit *f*

blister ['blɪstəʳ] *n* Blase *f* ♦ *vi* Blasen werfen

blitz [blɪts] *n* Luftkrieg *m*

blizzard ['blɪzəd] *n* Schneesturm *m*

bloated ['bləʊtɪd] *adj* aufgedunsen; (*inf*: *full*) nudelsatt

blob [blɒb] *n* Klümpchen *nt*

bloc [blɒk] *n* (*POL*) Block *m*

block [blɒk] *n* (*of wood*) Block *m*, Klotz *m*; (*of houses*) Häuserblock *m* ♦ *vt* blockieren; ~**age** *n* Verstopfung *f*; ~**buster** *n* Knüller *m*; ~ **letters** *npl* Blockbuchstaben *pl*; ~ **of flats** (*BRIT*) *n* Häuserblock *m*

bloke [bləʊk] (*BRIT*: *inf*) *n* Kerl *m*, Typ *m*

blond(e) [blɒnd] *adj* blond ♦ *n* Blondine *f*

blood [blʌd] *n* Blut *nt*; ~ **donor** *n* Blutspender *m*; ~ **group** *n* Blutgruppe *f*; ~ **poisoning** *n* Blutvergiftung *f*; ~ **pressure** *n* Blutdruck *m*; ~**shed** *n* Blutvergießen *nt*; ~**shot** *adj* blutunterlaufen; ~ **sports** *npl* Jagdsport, Hahnenkampf *etc*; ~**stained** *adj* blutbefleckt; ~**stream** *n* Blut *nt*, Blutkreislauf *m*; ~ **test** *n* Blutprobe *f*; ~**thirsty** *adj* blutrünstig; ~ **vessel** *n* Blutgefäß *nt*; ~**y** *adj* blutig; (*BRIT*: *inf*) verdammt; ~**y-minded** (*BRIT*: *inf*) *adj* stur

bloom [bluːm] *n* Blüte *f*; (*freshness*) Glanz *m* ♦ *vi* blühen

blossom ['blɒsəm] *n* Blüte *f* ♦ *vi* blühen

blot [blɒt] *n* Klecks *m* ♦ *vt* beklecksen; (*ink*) (ab)löschen; ~ **out** *vt* auslöschen

blotchy ['blɒtʃɪ] *adj* fleckig

blotting paper ['blɒtɪŋ-] *n* Löschpapier *nt*

blouse [blaʊz] *n* Bluse *f*

blow [bləʊ] (*pt* **blew**, *pp* **blown**) *n* Schlag *m* ♦ *vt* blasen ♦ *vi* (*wind*) wehen; **to ~ one's nose** sich *dat* die Nase putzen; ~ **away** *vt* wegblasen; ~ **down** *vt* umwehen; ~ **off**

⚠ *Informationen zur Rechtschreibreform Seite 615*

vt wegwehen ♦ *vi* wegfliegen; **~ out** *vi* ausgehen; **~ over** *vi* vorübergehen; **~ up** *vi* explodieren ♦ *vt* sprengen; **~-dry** *n*: **to have a ~-dry** sich fönen ⚠ lassen ♦ *vt* fönen ⚠; **~lamp** (*BRIT*) *n* Lötlampe *f*; **~n** *pp* of **blow**; **~-out** *n* (*AUT*) geplatzte(r) Reifen *m*; **~torch** *n* = **blowlamp**

blue [bluː] *adj* blau; (*inf: unhappy*) niedergeschlagen; (*obscene*) pornographisch ♦ *n*: **out of the ~** (*fig*) aus heiterem Himmel; **to have the ~s** traurig sein; **~bell** *n* Glockenblume *f*; **~bottle** *n* Schmeißfliege *f*; **~ film** *n* Pornofilm *m*; **~print** *n* (*fig*) Entwurf *m*

bluff [blʌf] *vi* bluffen, täuschen ♦ *n* (*deception*) Bluff *m*; **to call sb's ~** es darauf ankommen lassen

blunder ['blʌndəʳ] *n* grobe(r) Fehler *m*, Schnitzer *m* ♦ *vi* einen groben Fehler machen

blunt [blʌnt] *adj* (*knife*) stumpf; (*talk*) unverblümt ♦ *vt* abstumpfen

blur [bləːʳ] *n* Fleck *m* ♦ *vt* verschwommen machen

blurb [bləːb] *n* Waschzettel *m*

blush [blʌʃ] *vi* erröten

blustery ['blʌstəri] *adj* stürmisch

boar [bɔːʳ] *n* Keiler *m*, Eber *m*

board [bɔːd] *n* (*of wood*) Brett *nt*; (*of card*) Pappe *f*; (*committee*) Ausschuß ⚠ *m*; (*of firm*) Aufsichtsrat *m*; (*SCH*) Direktorium *nt* ♦ *vt* (*train*) einsteigen in *+acc*; (*ship*) an Bord gehen *+gen*; **on ~** (*AVIAT*, *NAUT*) an Bord; **~ and lodging** Unterkunft *f* und Verpflegung; **full/half ~** (*BRIT*) Voll-/Halbpension *f*; **to go by the ~** flachfallen, über Bord gehen; **~ up** *vt* mit Brettern vernageln; **~er** *n* Kostgänger *m*; (*SCH*) Internatsschüler(in) *m(f)*; **~ game** *n* Brettspiel *nt*; **~ing card** *n* (*AVIAT*, *NAUT*) Bordkarte *f*; **~ing house** *n* Pension *f*; **~ing school** *n* Internat *nt*; **~ room** *n* Sitzungszimmer *nt*

boast [bəust] *vi* prahlen ♦ *vt* sich rühmen *+gen* ♦ *n* Großtuerei *f*; Prahlerei *f*; **to ~ about** *or* **of sth** mit etw prahlen

boat [bəut] *n* Boot *nt*; (*ship*) Schiff *nt*; **~er** *n* (*hat*) Kreissäge *f*; **~swain** *n* = **bosun**; **~ train** *n* Zug *m* mit Fährenanschluß ⚠

bob [bɔb] *vi* sich auf und nieder bewegen; **~ up** *vi* auftauchen

bobbin ['bɔbɪn] *n* Spule *f*

bobby ['bɔbi] (*BRIT*: *inf*) *n* Bobby *m*

bobsleigh ['bɔbsleɪ] *n* Bob *m*

bode [bəud] *vi*: **to ~ well/ill** ein gutes/ schlechtes Zeichen sein

bodily ['bɔdɪli] *adj*, *adv* körperlich

body ['bɔdi] *n* Körper *m*; (*dead*) Leiche *f*; (*group*) Mannschaft *f*; (*AUT*) Karosserie *f*; (*trunk*) Rumpf *m*; **~ building** *n* Bodybuilding *nt*; **~guard** *n* Leibwache *f*; **~work** *n* Karosserie *f*

bog [bɔg] *n* Sumpf *m* ♦ *vt*: **to get ~ged down** sich festfahren

boggle ['bɔgl] *vi* stutzen; **the mind ~s** es ist kaum auszumalen

bog-standard *adj* stinknormal (*inf*)

bogus ['bəugəs] *adj* unecht, Schein-

boil [bɔɪl] *vt*, *vi* kochen ♦ *n* (*MED*) Geschwür *nt*; **to come to the** (*BRIT*) or **a** (*US*) **~** zu kochen anfangen; **to ~ down to** (*fig*) hinauslaufen auf *+acc*; **~ over** *vi* überkochen; **~ed egg** *n* (weich)gekochte(s) Ei *nt*; **~ed potatoes** *npl* Salzkartoffeln *pl*; **~er** *n* Boiler *m*; **~er suit** *n* (*BRIT*) Arbeitsanzug *m*; **~ing point** *n* Siedepunkt *m*

boisterous ['bɔɪstərəs] *adj* ungestüm

bold [bəuld] *adj* (*fearless*) unerschrocken; (*handwriting*) fest und klar

bollard ['bɔləd] *n* (*NAUT*) Poller *m*; (*BRIT*: *AUT*) Pfosten *m*

bolt [bəult] *n* Bolzen *m*; (*lock*) Riegel *m* ♦ *adv*: **~ upright** kerzengerade ♦ *vt* verriegeln; (*swallow*) verschlingen ♦ *vi* (*horse*) durchgehen

bomb [bɔm] *n* Bombe *f* ♦ *vt* bombardieren; **~ard** [bɔm'baːd] *vt* bombardieren; **~ardment** [bɔm'baːdmənt] *n* Beschießung *f*; **~ disposal** *n*: **~ disposal unit** Bombenräumkommando *nt*; **~er** *n* Bomber *m*; (*terrorist*) Bombenattentäter(in) *m(f)*; **~ing** *n* Bomben *nt*; **~shell** *n* (*fig*) Bombe *f*

bona fide ['bəunə'faɪdɪ] *adj* echt

bond [bɔnd] n (link) Band nt; (FIN) Schuldverschreibung f

bondage ['bɔndɪdʒ] n Sklaverei f

bone [bəun] n Knochen m; (of fish) Gräte f; (piece of ~) Knochensplitter m ♦ vt die Knochen herausnehmen +dat; (fish) entgräten; ~ **dry** adj (inf) knochentrocken; ~ **idle** adj stinkfaul; ~ **marrow** n (ANAT) Knochenmark nt

bonfire ['bɔnfaɪəʳ] n Feuer nt im Freien

bonnet ['bɔnɪt] n Haube f; (for baby) Häubchen nt; (BRIT: AUT) Motorhaube f

bonus ['bəunəs] n Bonus m; (annual ~) Prämie f

bony ['bəunɪ] adj knochig, knochendürr

boo [buː] vt auspfeifen

booby trap ['buːbɪ-] n Falle f

book [buk] n Buch nt ♦ vt (ticket etc) vorbestellen; (person) verwarnen; ~s npl (COMM) Bücher pl; ~**case** n Bücherregal nt, Bücherschrank m; ~**ing office** (BRIT) (RAIL) Fahrkartenschalter m; (THEAT) Vorverkaufsstelle f; ~**keeping** n Buchhaltung f; ~**let** n Broschüre f; ~**maker** n Buchmacher m; ~**seller** n Buchhändler m; ~**shelf** n Bücherbord nt; ~**shop** ['bukʃɔp], ~**store** n Buchhandlung f

boom [buːm] n (noise) Dröhnen nt; (busy period) Hochkonjunktur f ♦ vi dröhnen

boon [buːn] n Wohltat f, Segen m

boost [buːst] n Auftrieb m; (fig) Reklame f ♦ vt Auftrieb geben; ~**er** n (MED) Wiederholungsimpfung f

boot [buːt] n Stiefel m; (BRIT: AUT) Kofferraum m ♦ vt (kick) einen Fußtritt geben; (COMPUT) laden; **to ~** (in addition) obendrein

booth [buːð] n (at fair) Bude f; (telephone ~) Zelle f; (voting ~) Kabine f

booze [buːz] (inf) n Alkohol m, Schnaps m ♦ vi saufen

border ['bɔːdəʳ] n Grenze f; (edge) Kante f; (in garden) (Blumen)rabatte f ♦ adj Grenz-; **the B~s** Grenzregion zwischen England und Schottland; ~ **on** vt grenzen an +acc; ~**line** n Grenze f; ~**line case** n Grenzfall m

bore [bɔːʳ] pt of **bear** ♦ vt bohren; (weary)

langweilen ♦ n (person) Langweiler m; (thing) langweilige Sache f; (of gun) Kaliber nt; **I am ~d** ich langweile mich; ~**dom** n Langeweile f

boring ['bɔːrɪŋ] adj langweilig

born [bɔːn] adj: **to be ~** geboren werden

borne [bɔːn] pp of **bear**

borough ['bʌrə] n Stadt(gemeinde) f, Stadtbezirk m

borrow ['bɔrəu] vt borgen

Bosnia (and) Herzegovina ['bɔznɪə (ənd) hɜːtsəgəuˈviːnə] n Bosnien und Herzegowina nt; ~**n** n Bosnier(in) m(f) ♦ adj bosnisch

bosom ['buzəm] n Busen m

boss [bɔs] n Chef m, Boß △ m ♦ vt: **to ~ around** or **about** herumkommandieren; ~**y** adj herrisch

bosun ['bəusn] n Bootsmann m

botany ['bɔtənɪ] n Botanik f

botch [bɔtʃ] vt (also: ~ **up**) verpfuschen

both [bəuθ] adj beide(s) ♦ pron beide(s) ♦ adv: ~ **X and Y** sowohl X wie or als auch Y; ~ **(of) the books** beide Bücher; ~ **of us went, we ~ went** wir gingen beide

bother ['bɔðəʳ] vt (pester) quälen ♦ vi (fuss) sich aufregen ♦ n Mühe f, Umstand m; **to ~ doing sth** sich dat die Mühe machen, etw zu tun; **what a ~!** wie ärgerlich!

bottle ['bɔtl] n Flasche f ♦ vt (in Flaschen) abfüllen; ~ **up** vt aufstauen; ~ **bank** n Altglascontainer m; ~**d beer** n Flaschenbier nt; ~**d water** n in Flaschen abgefülltes Wasser; ~**neck** n (also fig) Engpaß △ m; ~ **opener** n Flaschenöffner m

bottom ['bɔtəm] n Boden m; (of person) Hintern m; (riverbed) Flußbett △ nt ♦ adj unterste(r, s)

bough [bau] n Zweig m, Ast m

bought [bɔːt] pt, pp of **buy**

boulder ['bəuldəʳ] n Felsbrocken m

bounce [bauns] vi (person) herumhüpfen; (ball) hochspringen; (cheque) platzen ♦ vt (auf)springen lassen ♦ n (rebound) Aufprall m; ~**r** n Rausschmeißer m

bound [baund] pt, pp of **bind** ♦ n Grenze f; (leap) Sprung m ♦ vi (spring, leap) (auf)springen ♦ *adj* (*obliged*) gebunden, verpflichtet; **out of ~s** Zutritt verboten; **to be ~ to do sth** verpflichtet sein, etw zu tun; **it's ~ to happen** es muß so kommen; **to be ~ for ...** nach ... fahren

boundary ['baundrɪ] *n* Grenze *f*

bouquet ['bukeɪ] *n* Strauß *m*; (*of wine*) Blume *f*

bourgeois ['buəʒwɑ:] *adj* kleinbürgerlich, bourgeois ♦ *n* Spießbürger(in) *m(f)*

bout [baut] *n* (*of illness*) Anfall *m*; (*of contest*) Kampf *m*

bow¹ [bəu] *n* (*ribbon*) Schleife *f*; (*weapon, MUS*) Bogen *m*

bow² [bau] *n* (*with head, body*) Verbeugung *f*; (*of ship*) Bug *m* ♦ *vi* sich verbeugen; (*submit*): **to ~ to** sich beugen +*dat*

bowels ['bauəlz] *npl* (*ANAT*) Darm *m*

bowl [bəul] *n* (*basin*) Schüssel *f*; (*of pipe*) (Pfeifen)kopf *m*; (*wooden ball*) (Holz)kugel *f* ♦ *vt, vi* (die Kugel) rollen

bow-legged ['bəu'legɪd] *adj* o-beinig

bowler ['bəulə*ʳ*] *n* Werfer *m*; (*BRIT: also:* ~ **hat**) Melone *f*

bowling ['bəulɪŋ] *n* Kegeln *nt*; ~ **alley** *n* Kegelbahn *f*; ~ **green** *n* Rasen *m* zum Bowling-Spiel

bowls *n* (*game*) Bowls-Spiel *nt*

bow tie [bəu-] *n* Fliege *f*

box [bɒks] *n* (*also:* **cardboard** ~) Schachtel *f*; (*bigger*) Kasten *m*; (*THEAT*) Loge *f* ♦ *vt* einpacken ♦ *vi* boxen; ~**er** *n* Boxer *m*; ~**er shorts** (*BRIT*) Boxer-Shorts *pl*; ~**ing** *n* (*SPORT*) Boxen *nt*; **B~ing Day** (*BRIT*) *n* zweite(r) Weihnachtsfeiertag *m*; ~**ing gloves** *npl* Boxhandschuhe *pl*; ~**ing ring** *n* Boxring *m*; ~ **office** *n* (Theater)kasse *f*; ~**room** *n* Rumpelkammer *f*

BOXING DAY

ⓘ **Boxing Day** (26.12.) ist ein Feiertag in Großbritannien. Wenn Weihnachten auf ein Wochenende fällt, wird der Feiertag am nächsten darauffolgenden Wochentag nachgeholt. Der Name geht auf einen alten Brauch zurück; früher erhielten Händler und Lieferanten an diesem Tag ein Geschenk,

die sogenannte *Christmas Box*.

boy [bɔɪ] *n* Junge *m*

boycott ['bɔɪkɔt] *n* Boykott *m* ♦ *vt* boykottieren

boyfriend ['bɔɪfrend] *n* Freund *m*

boyish ['bɔɪɪʃ] *adj* jungenhaft

B.R. *n abbr* = **British Rail**

bra [brɑ:] *n* BH *m*

brace [breɪs] *n* (*TECH*) Stütze *f*; (*MED*) Klammer *f* ♦ *vt* stützen; ~**s** *npl* (*BRIT*) Hosenträger *pl*; **to ~ o.s. for sth** (*fig*) sich auf etw *acc* gefaßt machen

bracelet ['breɪslɪt] *n* Armband *nt*

bracing ['breɪsɪŋ] *adj* kräftigend

bracken ['brækən] *n* Farnkraut *nt*

bracket ['brækɪt] *n* Halter *m*, Klammer *f*; (*in punctuation*) Klammer *f*; (*group*) Gruppe *f* ♦ *vt* einklammern; (*fig*) in dieselbe Gruppe einordnen

brag [bræg] *vi* sich rühmen

braid [breɪd] *n* (*hair*) Flechte *f*; (*trim*) Borte *f*

Braille [breɪl] *n* Blindenschrift *f*

brain [breɪn] *n* (*ANAT*) Gehirn *nt*; (*intellect*) Intelligenz *f*, Verstand *m*; (*person*) kluge(r) Kopf *m*; ~**s** *npl* (*intelligence*) Verstand *m*; ~**child** *n* Erfindung *f*; ~**wash** *vt* eine Gehirnwäsche vornehmen bei; ~**wave** *n* Geistesblitz *m*; ~**y** *adj* gescheit

braise [breɪz] *vt* schmoren

brake [breɪk] *n* Bremse *f* ♦ *vt, vi* bremsen; ~ **fluid** *n* Bremsflüssigkeit *f*; ~ **light** *n* Bremslicht *nt*

bramble ['bræmbl] *n* Brombeere *f*

bran [bræn] *n* Kleie *f*; (*food*) Frühstücksflocken *pl*

branch [brɑ:ntʃ] *n* Ast *m*; (*division*) Zweig *m* ♦ *vi* (*also:* ~ **out**: *road*) sich verzweigen

brand [brænd] *n* (*COMM*) Marke *f*, Sorte *f*; (*on cattle*) Brandmal *nt* ♦ *vt* brandmarken; (*COMM*) ein Warenzeichen geben +*dat*

brandish ['brændɪʃ] *vt* (drohend) schwingen

brand-new ['brænd'nju:] *adj* funkelnagelneu

brandy ['brændɪ] *n* Weinbrand *m*, Kognak *m*

brash [bræʃ] *adj* unverschämt

brass [brɑ:s] *n* Messing *nt*; **the ~** (*MUS*) das

⚠ *For information on spelling reform see page 615*

Blech; **~ band** n Blaskapelle f

brassière [ˈbræsiəʳ] n Büstenhalter m

brat [bræt] n Gör nt

bravado [brəˈvɑːdəu] n Tollkühnheit f

brave [breɪv] adj tapfer ♦ vt die Stirn bieten +dat; **~ry** n Tapferkeit f

brawl [brɔːl] n Rauferei f

brawn [brɔːn] n (ANAT) Muskeln pl; (strength) Muskelkraft f

bray [breɪ] vi schreien

brazen [ˈbreɪzn] adj (shameless) unverschämt ♦ vt: **to ~ it out** sich mit Lügen und Betrügen durchsetzen

brazier [ˈbreɪziəʳ] n (of workmen) offene(r) Kohlenofen m

Brazil [brəˈzɪl] n Brasilien nt; **~ian** adj brasilianisch ♦ n Brasilianer(in) m(f)

breach [briːtʃ] n (gap) Lücke f; (MIL) Durchbruch m; (of discipline) Verstoß m (gegen die Disziplin); (of faith) Vertrauensbruch m ♦ vt durchbrechen; **~ of contract** Vertragsbruch m; **~ of the peace** öffentliche Ruhestörung f

bread [bred] n Brot nt; **~ and butter** Butterbrot nt; **~bin** n Brotkasten m; **~ box** (US) n Brotkasten m; **~crumbs** npl Brotkrumen pl; (COOK) Paniermehl nt; **~line** n: **to be on the ~line** sich gerade so durchschlagen

breadth [bretθ] n Breite f

breadwinner [ˈbredwɪnəʳ] n Ernährer m

break [breɪk] (pt broke, pp broken) vt (destroy) (ab- or zer)brechen; (promise) brechen, nicht einhalten ♦ vi (fall apart) auseinanderbrechen ⚠; (collapse) zusammenbrechen; (dawn) anbrechen ♦ n (gap) Lücke f; (chance) Chance f, Gelegenheit f; (fracture) Bruch m; (rest) Pause f; **~ down** vt (figures, data) aufschlüsseln; (undermine) überwinden ♦ vi (car) eine Panne haben; (person) zusammenbrechen; **~ even** vi die Kosten decken; **~ free** vi sich losreißen; **~ in** vt (horse) zureiten ♦ vi (burglar) einbrechen; **~ into** vt fus (house) einbrechen in +acc; **~ loose** vi sich losreißen; **~ off** vi abbrechen; **~ open** vt (door etc) aufbrechen; **~ out** vi

ausbrechen; **to ~ out in spots** Pickel bekommen; **~ up** vi zerbrechen; (fig) sich zerstreuen; (BRIT: SCH) in die Ferien gehen ♦ vt brechen; **~age** n Bruch m, Beschädigung f; **~down** n (TECH) Panne f; (MED: also: **nervous ~down**) Zusammenbruch m; **~down van** (BRIT) n Abschleppwagen m; **~er** n Brecher m

breakfast [ˈbrekfəst] n Frühstück nt

break: **~-in** n Einbruch m; **~ing** n: **~ing and entering** (JUR) Einbruch m; **~through** n Durchbruch m; **~water** n Wellenbrecher m

breast [brest] n Brust f; **~-feed** (irreg: like feed) vt, vi stillen; **~-stroke** n Brustschwimmen nt

breath [breθ] n Atem m; **out of ~** außer Atem; **under one's ~** flüsternd

Breathalyzer [ˈbreθəlaɪzəʳ] ® n Röhrchen nt

breathe [briːð] vt, vi atmen; **~ in** vt, vi einatmen; **~ out** vt, vi ausatmen; **~r** n Verschnaufpause f; **breathing** n Atmung f

breathless [ˈbreθlɪs] adj atemlos

breathtaking [ˈbreθteɪkɪŋ] adj atemberaubend

bred [bred] pt, pp of breed

breed [briːd] (pt, pp bred) vi sich vermehren ♦ vt züchten ♦ n (race) Rasse f, Zucht f; **~ing** n Züchtung f; (upbringing) Erziehung f

breeze [briːz] n Brise f; **breezy** adj windig; (manner) munter

brevity [ˈbrevɪtɪ] n Kürze f

brew [bruː] vt (beer) brauen ♦ vi (storm) sich zusammenziehen; **~ery** n Brauerei f

bribe [braɪb] n Bestechungsgeld nt, Bestechungsgeschenk nt ♦ vt bestechen; **~ry** [ˈbraɪbərɪ] n Bestechung f

bric-a-brac [ˈbrɪkəbræk] n Nippes pl

brick [brɪk] n Backstein m; **~layer** n Maurer m; **~works** n Ziegelei f

bridal [ˈbraɪdl] adj Braut-

bride [braɪd] n Braut f; **~groom** n Bräutigam m; **~smaid** n Brautjungfer f

bridge [brɪdʒ] n Brücke f; (NAUT) Kommandobrücke f; (CARDS) Bridge nt; (ANAT) Nasenrücken m ♦ vt eine Brücke

⚠ *Informationen zur Rechtschreibreform Seite 615*

schlagen über +*acc*; (*fig*) überbrücken

bridle ['braɪdl] *n* Zaum *m* ♦ *vt* (*fig*) zügeln; (*horse*) aufzäumen; **~ path** *n* Reitweg *m*

brief [bri:f] *adj* kurz ♦ *n* (*JUR*) Akten *pl* ♦ *vt* instruieren; **~s** *npl* (*underwear*) Schlüpfer *m*, Slip *m*; **~case** *n* Aktentasche *f*; **~ing** *n* (genaue) Anweisung *f*; **~ly** *adv* kurz

brigadier [brɪɡə'dɪə'] *n* Brigadegeneral *m*

bright [braɪt] *adj* hell; (*cheerful*) heiter; (*idea*) klug; **~en (up)** *vt* [braɪtn-] *vt* aufhellen; (*person*) aufheitern ♦ *vi* sich aufheitern

brilliance ['brɪljəns] *n* Glanz *m*; (*of person*) Scharfsinn *m*

brilliant ['brɪljənt] *adj* glänzend

brim [brɪm] *n* Rand *m*

brine [braɪn] *n* Salzwasser *nt*

bring [brɪŋ] (*pt, pp* **brought**) *vt* bringen; **~ about** *vt* zustande △ bringen; **~ back** *vt* zurückbringen; **~ down** *vt* (*price*) senken; **~ forward** *vt* (*meeting*) vorverlegen; (*COMM*) übertragen; **~ in** *vt* hereinbringen; (*harvest*) einbringen; **~ off** *vt* davontragen; (*success*) erzielen; **~ out** *vt* (*object*) herausbringen; **~ round** *or* **to** *vt* wieder zu sich bringen; **~ up** *vt* aufziehen; (*question*) zur Sprache bringen

brink [brɪŋk] *n* Rand *m*

brisk [brɪsk] *adj* lebhaft

bristle ['brɪsl] *n* Borste *f* ♦ *vi* sich sträuben; **bristling with** strotzend vor +*dat*

Britain ['brɪtən] *n* (*also:* **Great ~**) Großbritannien *nt*

British ['brɪtɪʃ] *adj* britisch ♦ *npl*: **the ~** die Briten *pl*; **~ Isles** *npl*: **the ~ Isles** die Britischen Inseln *pl*; **~ Rail** *n* die Britischen Eisenbahnen

Briton ['brɪtən] *n* Brite *m*, Britin *f*

Brittany ['brɪtənɪ] *n* die Bretagne

brittle ['brɪtl] *adj* spröde

broach [brəʊtʃ] *vt* (*subject*) anschneiden

broad [brɔ:d] *adj* breit; (*hint*) deutlich; (*general*) allgemein; (*accent*) stark; **in ~ daylight** am hellichten Tag; **~cast** (*pt, pp* **broadcast**) *n* Rundfunkübertragung *f* ♦ *vt, vi* übertragen, senden; **~en** *vt* erweitern ♦ *vi* sich erweitern; **~ly** *adv* allgemein gesagt; **~-minded** *adj* tolerant

broccoli ['brɔkəlɪ] *n* Brokkoli *pl*

brochure ['brəʊʃjʊə'] *n* Broschüre *f*

broil [brɔɪl] *vt* (*grill*) grillen

broke [brəʊk] *pt of* **break** ♦ *adj* (*inf*) pleite

broken ['brəʊkn] *pp of* **break** ♦ *adj*: **~ leg** gebrochenes Bein; **in ~ English** in gebrochenem Englisch; **~-hearted** *adj* untröstlich

broker ['brəʊkə'] *n* Makler *m*

brolly ['brɔlɪ] (*BRIT: inf*) *n* Schirm *m*

bronchitis [brɔŋ'kaɪtɪs] *n* Bronchitis *f*

bronze [brɔnz] *n* Bronze *f*

brooch [brəʊtʃ] *n* Brosche *f*

brood [bru:d] *n* Brut *f* ♦ *vi* brüten

brook [bruk] *n* Bach *m*

broom [brum] *n* Besen *m*

Bros. *abbr* = **Brothers**

broth [brɔθ] *n* Suppe *f*, Fleischbrühe *f*

brothel ['brɔθl] *n* Bordell *nt*

brother ['brʌðə'] *n* Bruder *m*; **~-in-law** *n* Schwager *m*

brought [brɔ:t] *pt, pp of* **bring**

brow [brau] *n* (*eye-~*) (Augen)braue *f*; (*forehead*) Stirn *f*; (*of hill*) Bergkuppe *f*

brown [braun] *adj* braun ♦ *n* Braun *nt* ♦ *vt* bräunen; **~ bread** *n* Mischbrot *nt*; **B~ie** *n* Wichtel *m*; **~ paper** *n* Packpapier *nt*; **~ sugar** *n* braune(r) Zucker *m*

browse [brauz] *vi* (*in books*) blättern; (*in shop*) schmökern, herumschauen

bruise [bru:z] *n* Bluterguß △ *m*, blaue(r) Fleck *m* ♦ *vt* einen blauen Fleck geben ♦ *vi* einen blauen Fleck bekommen

brunt [brʌnt] *n* volle Wucht *f*

brush [brʌʃ] *n* Bürste *f*; (*for sweeping*) Handbesen *m*; (*for painting*) Pinsel *m*; (*fight*) kurze(r) Kampf *m* ♦ *vt* (*clean*) bürsten; (*sweep*) fegen; (*usu:* **~ past**, **~ against**) streifen; **~ aside** *vt* abtun; **~ up** *vt* (*knowledge*) auffrischen; **~wood** *n* Gestrüpp *nt*

brusque [bru:sk] *adj* schroff

Brussels ['brʌslz] *n* Brüssel *nt*; **~ sprout** *n* Rosenkohl *m*

brutal ['bru:tl] *adj* brutal

brute [bru:t] *n* (*person*) Scheusal *nt* ♦ *adj*: **by**

△ *For information on spelling reform see page 615*

~ **force** mit roher Kraft

B.Sc. *n abbr* = **Bachelor of Science**

BSE *n abbr* (= *bovine spongiform encephalopathy*) BSE *f*

bubble ['bʌbl] *n* (Luft)blase *f* ♦ *vi* sprudeln; (*with joy*) übersprudeln; ~ **bath** *n* Schaumbad *nt*; ~ **gum** *n* Kaugummi *m or nt*

buck [bʌk] *n* Bock *m*; (*US: inf*) Dollar *m* ♦ *vi* bocken; **to pass the** ~ **(to sb)** die Verantwortung (auf jdn) abschieben; ~ **up** (*inf*) *vi* sich zusammenreißen

bucket ['bʌkɪt] *n* Eimer *m*

BUCKINGHAM PALACE

i **Buckingham Palace** *ist die offizielle Londoner Residenz der britischen Monarchen und liegt am St James Park. Der Palast wurde 1703 für den Herzog von Buckingham erbaut, 1762 von George III gekauft, zwischen 1821 und 1836 von John Nash umgebaut, und Anfang des 20. Jahrhunderts teilweise neu gestaltet. Teile des Buckingham Palace sind heute der Öffentlichkeit zugänglich.*

buckle ['bʌkl] *n* Schnalle *f* ♦ *vt* (an- or zusammen)schnallen ♦ *vi* (*bend*) sich verziehen

bud [bʌd] *n* Knospe *f* ♦ *vi* knospen, keimen

Buddhism ['budɪzəm] *n* Buddhismus *m*; **Buddhist** *adj* buddhistisch ♦ *n* Buddhist(in) *m(f)*

budding ['bʌdɪŋ] *adj* angehend

buddy ['bʌdɪ] (*inf*) *n* Kumpel *m*

budge [bʌdʒ] *vt, vi* (sich) von der Stelle rühren

budgerigar ['bʌdʒərɪgaː*] *n* Wellensittich *m*

budget ['bʌdʒɪt] *n* Budget *nt*; (*POL*) Haushalt *m* ♦ *vi*: **to** ~ **for sth** etw einplanen

budgie ['bʌdʒɪ] *n* = **budgerigar**

buff [bʌf] *adj* (*colour*) lederfarben ♦ *n* (*enthusiast*) Fan *m*

buffalo ['bʌfələu] (*pl* ~ *or* ~**es**) *n* (*BRIT*) Büffel *m*; (*US: bison*) Bison *m*

buffer ['bʌfə*] *n* Puffer *m*; (*COMPUT*) Pufferspeicher *m*; ~ **zone** *n* Pufferzone *f*

buffet[1] ['bʌfɪt] *n* (*blow*) Schlag *m* ♦ *vt* (herum)stoßen

buffet[2] ['bufeɪ] (*BRIT*) *n* (*bar*) Imbißraum △ *m*, Erfrischungsraum *m*; (*food*) (kaltes) Büfett *nt*; ~ **car** (*BRIT*) *n* Speisewagen *m*

bug [bʌg] *n* (*also fig*) Wanze *f* ♦ *vt* verwanzen, das Zimmer ist verwanzt

bugle ['bjuːgl] *n* Jagdhorn *nt*; (*MIL: MUS*) Bügelhorn *nt*

build [bɪld] (*pt, pp* **built**) *vt* bauen ♦ *n* Körperbau *m*; ~ **up** vt aufbauen; ~**er** *n* Bauunternehmer *m*; ~**ing** *n* Gebäude *nt*; ~**ing society** (*BRIT*) *n* Bausparkasse *f*

built [bɪlt] *pt, pp* of **build**; ~**-in** *adj* (*cupboard*) eingebaut; ~**-up area** *n* Wohngebiet *nt*

bulb [bʌlb] *n* (*BOT*) (Blumen)zwiebel *f*; (*ELEC*) Glühlampe *f*, Birne *f*

Bulgaria [bʌlˈgeərɪə] *n* Bulgarien *nt*; ~**n** *adj* bulgarisch ♦ *n* Bulgare *m*, Bulgarin *f*; (*LING*) Bulgarisch *nt*

bulge [bʌldʒ] *n* Wölbung *f* ♦ *vi* sich wölben

bulk [bʌlk] *n* Größe *f*, Masse *f*; (*greater part*) Großteil *m*; **in** ~ (*COMM*) en gros; **the** ~ **of** der größte Teil +*gen*; ~**head** *n* Schott *nt*; ~**y** *adj* (sehr) umfangreich; (*goods*) sperrig

bull [bul] *n* Bulle *m*; (*cattle*) Stier *m*; ~**dog** *n* Bulldogge *f*

bulldozer ['buldəuzə*] *n* Planierraupe *f*

bullet ['bulɪt] *n* Kugel *f*

bulletin ['bulɪtɪn] *n* Bulletin *nt*, Bekanntmachung *f*

bulletproof ['bulɪtpruːf] *adj* kugelsicher

bullfight ['bulfaɪt] *n* Stierkampf *m*; ~**er** *n* Stierkämpfer *m*; ~**ing** *n* Stierkampf *m*

bullion ['buljən] *n* Barren *m*

bullock ['bulək] *n* Ochse *m*

bullring ['bulrɪŋ] *n* Stierkampfarena *f*

bull's-eye ['bulzaɪ] *n* Zentrum *nt*

bully ['bulɪ] *n* Raufbold *m* ♦ *vt* einschüchtern

bum [bʌm] *n* (*inf: backside*) Hintern *m*; (*tramp*) Landstreicher *m*

bumblebee ['bʌmblbiː] *n* Hummel *f*

bump [bʌmp] *n* (*blow*) Stoß *m*; (*swelling*) Beule *f* ♦ *vt, vi* stoßen, prallen; ~ **into** *vt fus* stoßen gegen ♦ *vt* (*person*) treffen; ~**er** *n* (*AUT*) Stoßstange *f* ♦ *adj* (*edition*) dick; (*harvest*) Rekord-

△ *Informationen zur Rechtschreibreform Seite 615*

bumpy ['bʌmpɪ] adj holprig

bun [bʌn] n Korinthenbrötchen nt

bunch [bʌntʃ] n (of flowers) Strauß m; (of keys) Bund m; (of people) Haufen m; **~es** npl (in hair) Zöpfe pl

bundle ['bʌndl] n Bündel nt ♦ vt (also: **~ up**) bündeln

bungalow ['bʌŋgələu] n einstöckige(s) Haus nt, Bungalow m

bungle ['bʌŋgl] vt verpfuschen

bunion ['bʌnjən] n entzündete(r) Fußballen m

bunk [bʌŋk] n Schlafkoje f; **~ beds** npl Etagenbett nt

bunker ['bʌŋkəʳ] n (coal store) Kohlenbunker m; (GOLF) Sandloch nt

bunny ['bʌnɪ] n (also: **~ rabbit**) Häschen nt

bunting ['bʌntɪŋ] n Fahnentuch nt

buoy [bɔɪ] n Boje f; (life~) Rettungsboje f; **~ant** adj (floating) schwimmend; (fig) heiter

burden ['bə:dn] n (weight) Ladung f, Last f; (fig) Bürde f ♦ vt belasten

bureau ['bjuərəu] (pl **~x**) n (BRIT: writing desk) Sekretär m; (US: chest of drawers) Kommode f; (for information etc) Büro nt

bureaucracy [bjuə'rɔkrəsɪ] n Bürokratie f

bureaucrat ['bjuərəkræt] n Bürokrat(in) m(f)

bureaux ['bjuərəuz] npl of **bureau**

burglar ['bə:gləʳ] n Einbrecher m; **~ alarm** n Einbruchssicherung f; **~y** n Einbruch m

burial ['berɪəl] n Beerdigung f

burly ['bə:lɪ] adj stämmig

Burma ['bə:mə] n Birma nt

burn [bə:n] (pt, pp **burned** or **burnt**) vt verbrennen ♦ vi brennen ♦ n Brandwunde f; **~ down** vt, vi abbrennen; **~er** n Brenner m; **~ing** adj brennend; **~t** [bə:nt] pt, pp of **burn**

burrow ['bʌrəu] n (of fox) Bau m; (of rabbit) Höhle f ♦ vt eingraben

bursar ['bə:səʳ] n Kassenverwalter m, Quästor m; **~y** (BRIT) n Stipendium nt

burst [bə:st] (pt, pp **burst**) vt zerbrechen ♦ vi platzen ♦ n Explosion f; (outbreak) Ausbruch m; (in pipe) Bruch(stelle f) m; **to ~ into flames** in Flammen aufgehen; **to ~ into tears** in Tränen ausbrechen; **to ~ out**

laughing in Gelächter ausbrechen; **~ into** vt fus (room etc) platzen in +acc; **~ open** vi aufbrechen

bury ['berɪ] vt vergraben; (in grave) beerdigen

bus [bʌs] n (Auto)bus m, Omnibus m

bush [buʃ] n Busch m; **to beat about the ~** wie die Katze um den heißen Brei herumgehen; **~y** ['buʃɪ] adj buschig

busily ['bɪzɪlɪ] adv geschäftig

business ['bɪznɪs] n Geschäft nt; (concern) Angelegenheit f; **it's none of your ~** es geht dich nichts an; **to mean ~** es ernst meinen; **to be away on ~** geschäftlich verreist sein; **it's my ~ to ...** es ist meine Sache, zu ...; **~like** adj geschäftsmäßig; **~man** (irreg) n Geschäftsmann m; **~ trip** n Geschäftsreise f; **~woman** (irreg) n Geschäftsfrau f

busker ['bʌskəʳ] n (BRIT) Straßenmusikant m

bus: ~ shelter n Wartehäuschen nt; **~ station** n Busbahnhof m; **~ stop** n Bushaltestelle f

bust [bʌst] n Büste f ♦ adj (broken) kaputt(gegangen); (business) pleite; **to go ~** pleite machen

bustle ['bʌsl] n Getriebe nt ♦ vi hasten

bustling ['bʌslɪŋ] adj geschäftig

busy ['bɪzɪ] adj beschäftigt; (road) belebt ♦ vt: **to ~ o.s.** sich beschäftigen; **~body** n Übereifrige(r) mf; **~ signal** (US) n (TEL) Besetztzeichen nt

KEYWORD

but [bʌt] conj **1** (yet) aber; **not X but Y** nicht X sondern Y

2 (however): **I'd love to come, but I'm busy** ich würde gern kommen, bin aber beschäftigt

3 (showing disagreement, surprise etc): **but that's fantastic!** (aber) das ist ja fantastisch!

♦ prep (apart from, except): **nothing but trouble** nichts als Ärger; **no-one but him can do it** niemand außer ihn kann es machen; **but for you/your help** ohne dich/deine Hilfe; **anything but that** alles,

⚠ For information on spelling reform see page 615

nur das nicht

♦ *adv* (*just, only*): **she's but a child** sie ist noch ein Kind; **had I but known** wenn ich es nur gewußt hätte; **I can but try** ich kann es immerhin versuchen; **all but finished** so gut wie fertig

butcher ['butʃəʳ] *n* Metzger *m*; (*murderer*) Schlächter *m* ♦ *vt* schlachten; (*kill*) abschlachten; **~'s (shop)** *n* Metzgerei *f*

butler ['bʌtləʳ] *n* Butler *m*

butt [bʌt] *n* (*cask*) große(s) Faß △ *nt*; (*BRIT: fig: target*) Zielscheibe *f*; (*of gun*) Kolben *m*; (*of cigarette*) Stummel *m* ♦ *vt* (mit dem Kopf) stoßen; **~ in** *vi* sich einmischen

butter ['bʌtəʳ] *n* Butter *f* ♦ *vt* buttern; **~ bean** *n* Wachsbohne *f*; **~cup** *n* Butterblume *f*

butterfly ['bʌtəflaɪ] *n* Schmetterling *m*; (*SWIMMING: also:* **~ stroke**) Butterflystil *m*

buttocks ['bʌtəks] *npl* Gesäß *nt*

button ['bʌtn] *n* Knopf *m* ♦ *vt, vi* (*also:* **~ up**) zuknöpfen

buttress ['bʌtrɪs] *n* Strebepfeiler *m*; Stützbogen *m*

buxom ['bʌksəm] *adj* drall

buy [baɪ] (*pt, pp* **bought**) *vt* kaufen ♦ *n* Kauf *m*; **to ~ sb a drink** jdm einen Drink spendieren; **~er** *n* Käufer(in) *m(f)*

buzz [bʌz] *n* Summen *nt* ♦ *vi* summen; **~er** ['bʌzəʳ] *n* Summer *m*; **~ word** *n* Modewort *nt*

KEYWORD

by [baɪ] *prep* **1** (*referring to cause, agent*) von, durch; **killed by lightning** vom Blitz getötet; **a painting by Picasso** ein Gemälde von Picasso

2 (*referring to method, manner*): **by bus/ car/train** mit dem Bus/Auto/Zug; **to pay by cheque** per Scheck bezahlen; **by moonlight** bei Mondschein; **by saving hard, he ...** indem er eisern sparte, ... er ...

3 (*via, through*) über +*acc*; **he came in by the back door** er kam durch die Hintertür herein

4 (*close to, past*) bei, an +*dat*; **a holiday by**

the sea ein Urlaub am Meer; **she rushed by me** sie eilte an mir vorbei

5 (*not later than*): **by 4 o'clock** bis 4 Uhr; **by this time tomorrow** morgen um diese Zeit; **by the time I got here it was too late** als ich hier ankam, war es zu spät

6 (*during*): **by day** bei Tag

7 (*amount*): **by the kilo/metre** kiloweise/ meterweise; **paid by the hour** stundenweise bezahlt

8 (*MATH, measure*): **to divide by 3** durch 3 teilen; **to multiply by 3** mit 3 malnehmen; **a room 3 metres by 4** ein Zimmer 3 mal 4 Meter; **it's broader by a metre** es ist (um) einem Meter breiter

9 (*according to*) nach; **it's all right by me** von mir aus gern

10: **(all) by oneself** *etc* ganz allein

11: **by the way** übrigens

♦ *adv* **1** *see* **go**; **pass** *etc*

2: **by and by** irgendwann; (*with past tenses*) nach einiger Zeit; **by and large** (*on the whole*) im großen und ganzen

---

bye(-bye) ['baɪ('baɪ)] *excl* (auf) Wiedersehen

by(e)-law ['baɪlɔ:] *n* Verordnung *f*

by-election ['baɪɪlekʃən] (*BRIT*) *n* Nachwahl *f*

bygone ['baɪgɔn] *adj* vergangen ♦ *n*: **let ~s be ~s** laß(t) △ das Vergangene vergangen sein

bypass ['baɪpɑ:s] *n* Umgehungsstraße *f* ♦ *vt* umgehen

by-product ['baɪprɔdʌkt] *n* Nebenprodukt *nt*

bystander ['baɪstændəʳ] *n* Zuschauer *m*

byte [baɪt] *n* (*COMPUT*) Byte *nt*

byword ['baɪwə:d] *n* Inbegriff *m*

C, c

C [si:] *n* (*MUS*) C *nt*

C. *abbr* (= *centigrade*) C

C.A. *abbr* = **chartered accountant**

cab [kæb] *n* Taxi *nt*; (*of train*) Führerstand *m*; (*of truck*) Führersitz *m*

cabaret ['kæbəreɪ] *n* Kabarett *nt*

△ *Informationen zur Rechtschreibreform Seite 615*

cabbage ['kæbɪdʒ] n Kohl(kopf) m

cabin ['kæbɪn] n Hütte f; (NAUT) Kajüte f; (AVIAT) Kabine f; ~ **crew** n (AVIAT) Flugbegleitpersonal nt; ~ **cruiser** n Motorjacht f

cabinet ['kæbɪnɪt] n Schrank m; (for china) Vitrine f; (POL) Kabinett nt; ~-**maker** n Kunsttischler m

cable ['keɪbl] n Drahtseil nt, Tau nt; (TEL) (Leitungs)kabel nt; (telegram) Kabel nt ♦ vt kabeln, telegraphieren ⚠; ~ **car** n Seilbahn f; ~ **television** n Kabelfernsehen nt

cache [kæʃ] n geheime(s) (Waffen)lager nt; geheime(s) (Proviant)lager nt

cackle ['kækl] vi gackern

cacti ['kæktaɪ] npl of **cactus**

cactus ['kæktəs] (pl **cacti**) n Kaktus m, Kaktee f

caddie ['kædɪ] n (GOLF) Golfjunge m; **caddy** ['kædɪ] n = **caddie**

cadet [kə'dɛt] n Kadett m

cadge [kædʒ] vt schmarotzen

Caesarean [sɪ'zɛərɪən] adj: ~ **(section)** Kaiserschnitt m

café ['kæfeɪ] n Café nt, Restaurant nt

cafeteria [kæfɪ'tɪərɪə] n Selbstbedienungsrestaurant nt

caffein(e) ['kæfiːn] n Koffein nt

cage [keɪdʒ] n Käfig m ♦ vt einsperren

cagey ['keɪdʒɪ] adj geheimnistuerisch, zurückhaltend

cagoule [kə'guːl] n Windhemd nt

Cairo ['kaɪərəu] n Kairo nt

cajole [kə'dʒəul] vt überreden

cake [keɪk] n Kuchen m; (of soap) Stück nt; ~d adj verkrustet

calamity [kə'læmɪtɪ] n Unglück nt, (Schicksals)schlag m

calcium ['kælsɪəm] n Kalzium nt

calculate ['kælkjuleɪt] vt berechnen, kalkulieren; **calculating** adj berechnend; **calculation** [kælkju'leɪʃən] n Berechnung f; **calculator** n Rechner m

calendar ['kælɪndər] n Kalender m; ~ **month** n Kalendermonat m

calf [kɑːf] (pl **calves**) n Kalb nt; (also: ~**skin**) Kalbsleder nt; (ANAT) Wade f

calibre ['kælɪbər] (US **caliber**) n Kaliber nt

call [kɔːl] vt rufen; (name) nennen; (meeting) einberufen; (awaken) wecken; (TEL) anrufen ♦ vi (shout) rufen; (visit: also: ~ **in**, ~ **round**) vorbeikommen ♦ n (shout) Ruf m; (TEL) Anruf m; **to be ~ed** heißen; **on** ~ in Bereitschaft; ~ **back** vi (return) wiederkommen; (TEL) zurückrufen; ~ **for** vt fus (demand) erfordern, verlangen; (fetch) abholen; ~ **off** vt (cancel) absagen; ~ **on** vt fus (visit) besuchen; (turn to) bitten; ~ **out** vi rufen; ~ **up** vt (MIL) einberufen; ~**box** (BRIT) n Telefonzelle f; ~**er** n Besucher(in) m(f); (TEL) Anrufer m; ~ **girl** n Callgirl nt; ~-**in** (US) n (phone-in) Phone-in nt; ~**ing** n (vocation) Berufung f; ~**ing card** (US) n Visitenkarte f

callous ['kæləs] adj herzlos

calm [kɑːm] n Ruhe f; (NAUT) Flaute f ♦ vt beruhigen ♦ adj ruhig; (person) gelassen; ~ **down** vi sich beruhigen ♦ vt beruhigen

Calor gas ['kælər-] ® n Propangas nt

calorie ['kælərɪ] n Kalorie f

calves [kɑːvz] npl of **calf**

Cambodia [kæm'bəudɪə] n Kambodscha nt

camcorder ['kæmkɔːdər] n Camcorder m

came [keɪm] pt of **come**

cameo ['kæmɪəu] n Kamee f

camera ['kæmərə] n Fotoapparat m; (CINE, TV) Kamera f; **in** ~ unter Ausschluß der Öffentlichkeit; ~**man** (irreg) n Kameramann m

camouflage ['kæməflɑːʒ] n Tarnung f ♦ vt tarnen

camp [kæmp] n Lager nt ♦ vi zelten, campen ♦ adj affektiert

campaign [kæm'peɪn] n Kampagne f; (MIL) Feldzug m ♦ vi (MIL) Krieg führen; (fig) werben, Propaganda machen; (POL) den Wahlkampf führen

camp: ~ **bed** ['kæmp'bed] (BRIT) n Campingbett nt; ~**er** ['kæmpər] n Camper(in) m(f); (vehicle) Campingwagen m; ~**ing** ['kæmpɪŋ] n: **to go** ~**ing** zelten, Camping machen; ~**ing gas** (US) n Campinggas nt; ~**site** ['kæmpsaɪt] n

Campingplatz *m*

campus ['kæmpəs] *n* Universitätsgelände *nt*, Campus *m*

can[1] [kæn] *n* Büchse *f*, Dose *f*; (*for water*) Kanne *f* ♦ *vt* konservieren, in Büchsen einmachen

---
KEYWORD
---

can[2] [kæn] (*negative* **cannot, can't**, *conditional* **could**) *aux vb* **1** (*be able to, know how to*) können; **I can see you tomorrow, if you like** ich könnte Sie morgen sehen, wenn Sie wollen; **I can swim** ich kann schwimmen; **can you speak German?** sprechen Sie Deutsch?

2 (*may*) können, dürfen; **could I have a word with you?** könnte ich Sie kurz sprechen?

Canada ['kænədə] *n* Kanada *nt*; **Canadian** [kə'neɪdɪən] *adj* kanadisch ♦ *n* Kanadier(in) *m(f)*

canal [kə'næl] *n* Kanal *m*

canapé ['kænəpeɪ] *n* Cocktail- *or* Appetithappen *m*

canary [kə'nɛərɪ] *n* Kanarienvogel *m*

cancel ['kænsəl] *vt* absagen; (*delete*) durchstreichen; (*train*) streichen; **~lation** [kænsə'leɪʃən] *n* Absage *f*; Streichung *f*

cancer ['kænsə*r*] *n* (*ASTROL: Cancer*) Krebs *m*

candid ['kændɪd] *adj* offen, ehrlich

candidate ['kændɪdeɪt] *n* Kandidat(in) *m(f)*

candle ['kændl] *n* Kerze *f*; **~light** *n* Kerzenlicht *nt*; **~stick** *n* (*also:* **~ holder**) Kerzenhalter *m*

candour ['kændə*r*] (*US* **candor**) *n* Offenheit *f*

candy ['kændɪ] *n* Kandis(zucker) *m*; (*US*) Bonbons *pl*; **~floss** (*BRIT*) *n* Zuckerwatte *f*

cane [keɪn] *n* (*BOT*) Rohr *nt*; (*stick*) Stock *m* ♦ *vt* (*BRIT: beat*) schlagen

canine ['keɪnaɪn] *adj* Hunde-

canister ['kænɪstə*r*] *n* Blechdose *f*

cannabis ['kænəbɪs] *n* Hanf *m*, Haschisch *nt*

canned [kænd] *adj* Büchsen-, eingemacht

cannon ['kænən] (*pl* ~ *or* ~**s**) *n* Kanone *f*

cannot ['kænɔt] = **can not**

canny ['kænɪ] *adj* schlau

canoe [kə'nu:] *n* Kanu *nt*; **~ing** *n* Kanusport *m*, Kanufahren *nt*

canon ['kænən] *n* (*clergyman*) Domherr *m*; (*standard*) Grundsatz *m*

can-opener ['kænəupnə*r*] *n* Büchsenöffner *m*

canopy ['kænəpɪ] *n* Baldachin *m*

can't [kænt] = **can not**

cantankerous [kæn'tæŋkərəs] *adj* zänkisch, mürrisch

canteen [kæn'ti:n] *n* Kantine *f*; (*BRIT: of cutlery*) Besteckkasten *m*

canter ['kæntə*r*] *n* Kanter *m* ♦ *vi* in kurzem Galopp reiten

canvas ['kænvəs] *n* Segeltuch *nt*; (*sail*) Segel *nt*; (*for painting*) Leinwand *f*; **under ~** (*camping*) in Zelten

canvass ['kænvəs] *vi* um Stimmen werben; **~ing** *n* Wahlwerbung *f*

canyon ['kænjən] *n* Felsenschlucht *f*

cap [kæp] *n* Mütze *f*; (*of pen*) Kappe *f*; (*of bottle*) Deckel *m* ♦ *vt* (*surpass*) übertreffen; (*SPORT*) aufstellen; (*put limit on*) einen Höchstsatz festlegen für

capability [keɪpə'bɪlɪtɪ] *n* Fähigkeit *f*

capable ['keɪpəbl] *adj* fähig

capacity [kə'pæsɪtɪ] *n* Fassungsvermögen *nt*; (*ability*) Fähigkeit *f*; (*position*) Eigenschaft *f*

cape [keɪp] *n* (*garment*) Cape *nt*, Umhang *m*; (*GEOG*) Kap *nt*

caper ['keɪpə*r*] *n* (*COOK: usu:* ~**s**) Kaper *f*; (*prank*) Kapriole *f*

capital ['kæpɪtl] *n* (~ *city*) Hauptstadt *f*; (*FIN*) Kapital *nt*; (~ *letter*) Großbuchstabe *m*; **~ gains tax** *n* Kapitalertragssteuer *f*; **~ism** *n* Kapitalismus *m*; **~ist** *adj* kapitalistisch ♦ *n* Kapitalist(in) *m(f)*; **~ize** *vi*: **to ~ize on** Kapital schlagen aus; **~ punishment** *n* Todesstrafe *f*

CAPITOL

ⓘ **Capitol** *ist das Gebäude in Washington auf dem Capitol Hill, in dem der Kongreß der USA zusammentritt. Die Bezeichnung wird in vielen amerikanischen Bundesstaaten auch für das Parlamentsgebäude des jeweiligen Staates*

⚠ *Informationen zur Rechtschreibreform Seite 615*

verwendet.

Capricorn ['kæprɪkɔːn] n Steinbock m
capsize [kæp'saɪz] vt, vi kentern
capsule ['kæpsjuːl] n Kapsel f
captain ['kæptɪn] n Kapitän m; (MIL)
  Hauptmann m ♦ vt anführen
caption ['kæpʃən] n (heading) Überschrift f;
  (to picture) Unterschrift f
captivate ['kæptɪveɪt] vt fesseln
captive ['kæptɪv] n Gefangene(r) f(m) ♦ adj
  gefangen(gehalten) △; **captivity**
  [kæp'tɪvɪtɪ] n Gefangenschaft f
capture ['kæptʃəʳ] vt gefangennehmen △;
  (place) erobern; (attention) erregen ♦ n
  Gefangennahme f; (data ~) Erfassung f
car [kɑːʳ] n Auto nt, Wagen m; (RAIL) Wagen
  m
caramel ['kærəməl] n Karamelle f,
  Karamelbonbon △ m or nt; (burnt sugar)
  Karamel △ m
carat ['kærət] n Karat nt
caravan ['kærəvæn] n (BRIT) Wohnwagen m;
  (in desert) Karawane f; **~ning** n Caravaning
  nt, Urlaub m im Wohnwagen; **~ site** (BRIT)
  n Campingplatz m für Wohnwagen
carbohydrate [kɑːbəʊ'haɪdreɪt] n
  Kohlenhydrat nt
carbon ['kɑːbən] n Kohlenstoff m; **~ copy** n
  Durchschlag m; **~ dioxide** n Kohlendioxyd
  nt; **~ monoxide** n Kohlenmonoxyd nt; **~
  paper** n Kohlepapier nt
car boot sale n auf einem Parkplatz
  stattfindender Flohmarkt mit dem
  Kofferraum als Auslage
carburettor [kɑːbju'retəʳ] (US **carburetor**) n
  Vergaser m
carcass ['kɑːkəs] n Kadaver m
card [kɑːd] n Karte f; **~board** n Pappe f; **~
  game** n Kartenspiel nt
cardiac ['kɑːdɪæk] adj Herz-
cardigan ['kɑːdɪgən] n Strickjacke f
cardinal ['kɑːdɪnl] adj: **~ number**
  Kardinalzahl f ♦ n (REL) Kardinal m
card index n Kartei f; (in library) Katalog m
cardphone n Kartentelefon nt
care [kɛəʳ] n (of teeth, car etc) Pflege f; (of

children) Fürsorge f; (carefulness) Sorgfalt f;
  (worry) Sorge f ♦ vi: **to ~ about** sich
  kümmern um; **~ of** bei; **in sb's ~** in jds
  Obhut; **I don't ~** das ist mir egal; **I
  couldn't ~ less** es ist mir doch völlig egal;
  to take ~ aufpassen; **to take ~ of** sorgen
  für; **to take ~ to do sth** sich bemühen, etw
  zu tun; **~ for** vt sorgen für; (like) mögen
career [kə'rɪəʳ] n Karriere f, Laufbahn f ♦ vi
  (also: **~ along**) rasen; **~ woman** (irreg) n
  Karrierefrau f
care: ~free adj sorgenfrei; **~ful** adj
  sorgfältig; **(be) ~ful!** paß auf!; **~fully** adv
  vorsichtig; (methodically) sorgfältig; **~less**
  adj nachlässig; **~lessness** n Nachlässigkeit
  f; **~r** n (MED) Betreuer(in) m(f)
caress [kə'res] n Liebkosung f ♦ vt liebkosen
caretaker ['kɛəteɪkəʳ] n Hausmeister m
car ferry n Autofähre f
cargo ['kɑːgəʊ] (pl **~es**) n Schiffsladung f
car hire n Autovermietung f
Caribbean [kærɪ'biːən] n: **the ~ (Sea)** die
  Karibik
caricature ['kærɪkətjuəʳ] n Karikatur f
caring ['kɛərɪŋ] adj (society, organization)
  sozial eingestellt; (person) liebevoll
carnage ['kɑːnɪdʒ] n Blutbad nt
carnation [kɑː'neɪʃən] n Nelke f
carnival ['kɑːnɪvl] n Karneval m, Fasching
  m; (US: fun fair) Kirmes f
carnivorous [kɑː'nɪvərəs] adj fleischfressend
  △
carol ['kærəl] n: **(Christmas) ~**
  (Weihnachts)lied nt
carp [kɑːp] n (fish) Karpfen m
car park (BRIT) n Parkplatz m; (covered)
  Parkhaus nt
carpenter ['kɑːpɪntəʳ] n Zimmermann m;
  carpentry ['kɑːpɪntrɪ] n Zimmerei f
carpet ['kɑːpɪt] n Teppich m ♦ vt mit einem
  Teppich auslegen; **~ bombing** n
  Flächenbombardierung f; **~ slippers** npl
  Pantoffeln pl; **~ sweeper** ['kɑːpɪtswiːpəʳ] n
  Teppichkehrer m
car phone n (TEL) Autotelefon nt
car rental (US) n Autovermietung f
carriage ['kærɪdʒ] n Kutsche f; (RAIL, of

△ *For information on spelling reform see page 615*

typewriter) Wagen m; (of goods)
Beförderung f; (bearing) Haltung f; ~
return n (on typewriter) Rücklauftaste f;
~way (BRIT) n (part of road) Fahrbahn f
carrier ['kærɪəʳ] n Träger(in) m(f); (COMM)
Spediteur m; ~ **bag** (BRIT) n Tragetasche m
carrot ['kærət] n Möhre f, Karotte f
carry ['kærɪ] vt, vi tragen; (of goods)
away (fig) sich nicht mehr bremsen
können; ~ **on** vi (continue) weitermachen;
(inf: complain) Theater machen; ~ **out** vt
(orders) ausführen; (investigation)
durchführen; **~cot** (BRIT) n Babytragetasche
f; **~-on** (inf) n (fuss) Theater nt
cart [kɑːt] n Wagen m, Karren m ♦ vt
schleppen
cartilage ['kɑːtɪlɪdʒ] n Knorpel m
carton ['kɑːtən] n Karton m; (of milk) Tüte f
cartoon [kɑːˈtuːn] n (PRESS) Karikatur f;
(comic strip) Comics pl; (CINE)
(Zeichen)trickfilm m
cartridge ['kɑːtrɪdʒ] n Patrone f
carve [kɑːv] vt (wood) schnitzen; (stone)
meißeln; (meat) (vor)schneiden; ~ **up** vt
aufschneiden; **carving** ['kɑːvɪŋ] n
Schnitzerei f; **carving knife** n
Tranchiermesser nt
car wash n Autowäsche f
cascade [kæsˈkeɪd] n Wasserfall m ♦ vi
kaskadenartig herabfallen
case [keɪs] n (box) Kasten m; (BRIT: also:
suitcase) Koffer m; (JUR, matter) Fall m; **in** ~
falls, im Falle; **in any** ~ jedenfalls, auf
jeden Fall
cash [kæʃ] n (Bar)geld nt ♦ vt einlösen; ~ **on
delivery** per Nachnahme; ~ **book** n
Kassenbuch nt; ~ **card** n Scheckkarte f; ~
desk (BRIT) n Kasse f; ~ **dispenser** n
Geldautomat m
cashew [kæˈʃuː] n (also: ~ **nut**) Cashewnuß
⚠ f
cash flow n Cash-flow m
cashier [kæˈʃɪəʳ] n Kassierer(in) m(f)
cashmere ['kæʃmɪəʳ] n Kaschmirwolle f
cash register n Registrierkasse f
casing ['keɪsɪŋ] n Gehäuse nt
casino [kəˈsiːnəu] n Kasino nt

casket ['kɑːskɪt] n Kästchen nt; (US: coffin)
Sarg m
casserole ['kæsərəul] n Kasserolle f; (food)
Auflauf m
cassette [kæˈset] n Kassette f; ~ **player** n
Kassettengerät nt
cast [kɑːst] (pt, pp **cast**) vt werfen; (horns)
verlieren; (metal) gießen; (THEAT) besetzen;
(vote) abgeben ♦ n (THEAT) Besetzung f;
(also: **plaster** ~) Gipsverband m; ~ **off** vi
(NAUT) losmachen
castaway ['kɑːstəweɪ] n Schiffbrüchige(r)
f(m)
caste [kɑːst] n Kaste f
caster sugar ['kɑːstə-] (BRIT) n Raffinade f
casting vote ['kɑːstɪŋ-] (BRIT) n
entscheidende Stimme f
cast iron n Gußeisen ⚠ nt
castle ['kɑːsl] n Burg f; Schloß ⚠ nt; (CHESS)
Turm m
castor ['kɑːstəʳ] n (wheel) Laufrolle f
castor oil n Rizinusöl nt
castrate [kæsˈtreɪt] vt kastrieren
casual ['kæʒjul] adj (attitude) nachlässig;
(dress) leger; (meeting) zufällig; (work)
Gelegenheits-; **~ly** adv (dress) zwanglos,
leger; (remark) beiläufig
casualty ['kæʒjultɪ] n Verletzte(r) f(m);
(dead) Tote(r) f(m); (also: ~ **department**)
Unfallstation f
cat [kæt] n Katze f
catalogue ['kætəlɒg] (US **catalog**) n Katalog
m ♦ vt katalogisieren
catalyst ['kætəlɪst] n Katalysator m
catalytic converter [kætəˈlɪtɪk kənˈvɜːtəʳ]
n Katalysator m
catapult ['kætəpʌlt] n Schleuder f
cataract ['kætərækt] n (MED) graue(r) Star m
catarrh [kəˈtɑːʳ] n Katarrh ⚠ m
catastrophe [kəˈtæstrəfɪ] n Katastrophe f
catch [kætʃ] (pt, pp **caught**) vt fangen;
(arrest) fassen; (train) erreichen; (person: by
surprise) ertappen; (also: ~ **up**) einholen ♦ vi
(fire) in Gang kommen; (in branches etc)
hängenbleiben ⚠ n (fish etc) Fang m;
(trick) Haken m; (of lock) Sperrhaken m; **to ~
an illness** sich dat eine Krankheit holen; **to**

~ fire Feuer fangen; **~ on** vi (understand) begreifen; (grow popular) ankommen; **~ up** vi (fig) aufholen; **~ing** ['kætʃɪŋ] adj ansteckend; **~ment area** ['kætʃmənt-] (BRIT) n Einzugsgebiet nt; **~ phrase** n Slogan m; **~y** ['kætʃɪ] adj (tune) eingängig

categoric(al) [kætɪ'gɒrɪk(l)] adj kategorisch

category ['kætɪgərɪ] n Kategorie f

cater ['keɪtər] vi versorgen; **~ for** (BRIT) vt fus (party) ausrichten; (needs) eingestellt sein auf +acc; **~er** n Lieferant(in) m(f) von Speisen und Getränken; **~ing** n Gastronomie f

caterpillar ['kætəpɪlər] n Raupe f; **~ track** ® n Gleiskette f

cathedral [kə'θiːdrəl] n Kathedrale f, Dom m

Catholic ['kæθəlɪk] adj (REL) katholisch ♦ n Katholik(in) m(f); **c~** adj (tastes etc) vielseitig

CAT scan [kæt-] n Computertomographie Δ f

Catseye ['kæts'aɪ] (BRIT: ®) n (AUT) Katzenauge nt

cattle ['kætl] npl Vieh nt

catty ['kætɪ] adj gehässig

caucus ['kɔːkəs] n (POL) Gremium nt; (US: meeting) Sitzung f

caught [kɔːt] pt, pp of **catch**

cauliflower ['kɒlɪflauər] n Blumenkohl m

cause [kɔːz] n Ursache f; (purpose) Sache f ♦ vt verursachen

causeway ['kɔːzweɪ] n Damm m

caustic ['kɔːstɪk] adj ätzend; (fig) bissig

caution ['kɔːʃən] n Vorsicht f; (warning) Verwarnung f ♦ vt verwarnen; **cautious** ['kɔːʃəs] adj vorsichtig

cavalry ['kævəlrɪ] n Kavallerie f

cave [keɪv] n Höhle f; **~ in** vi einstürzen; **~man** (irreg) n Höhlenmensch m

cavern ['kævən] n Höhle f

caviar(e) ['kævɪɑːr] n Kaviar m

cavity ['kævɪtɪ] n Loch nt

cavort [kə'vɔːt] vi umherspringen

C.B. n abbr (= Citizens' Band (Radio)) CB

C.B.I. n abbr (= Confederation of British Industry) ≈ BDI m

cc n abbr = **carbon copy; cubic centimetres**

CD n abbr (= compact disc) CD f

CDI n abbr (= Compact Disk Interactive) CD-I f

CD player n CD-Spieler m

CD-ROM n abbr (= compact disc read-only memory) CD-Rom f

cease [siːs] vi aufhören ♦ vt beenden; **~fire** n Feuereinstellung f; **~less** adj unaufhörlich

cedar ['siːdər] n Zeder f

ceiling ['siːlɪŋ] n Decke f; (fig) Höchstgrenze f

celebrate ['selɪbreɪt] vt, vi feiern; **~d** adj gefeiert; **celebration** [selɪ'breɪʃən] n Feier f

celebrity [sɪ'lebrɪtɪ] n gefeierte Persönlichkeit f

celery ['selərɪ] n Sellerie m or f

celibacy ['selɪbəsɪ] n Zölibat nt or m

cell [sel] n Zelle f; (ELEC) Element nt

cellar ['selər] n Keller m

cello ['tʃeləu] n Cello nt

Cellophane ['seləfeɪn] ® n Cellophan nt ®

cellphone ['selfəun] n Funktelefon nt

cellular ['seljulər] adj zellular

cellulose ['seljuləus] n Zellulose f

Celt [kelt, selt] n Kelte m, Keltin f; **~ic** ['keltɪk, 'seltɪk] adj keltisch

cement [sə'ment] n Zement m ♦ vt zementieren; **~ mixer** n Betonmischmaschine f

cemetery ['semɪtrɪ] n Friedhof m

censor ['sensər] n Zensor m ♦ vt zensieren; **~ship** n Zensur f

censure ['senʃər] vt rügen

census ['sensəs] n Volkszählung f

cent [sent] n (US: coin) Cent m; see also **per cent**

centenary [sen'tiːnərɪ] n Jahrhundertfeier f

center ['sentər] (US) n = **centre**

centigrade ['sentɪgreɪd] adj Celsius

centimetre ['sentɪmiːtər] (US **centimeter**) n Zentimeter m

centipede ['sentɪpiːd] n Tausendfüßler m

central ['sentrəl] adj zentral; **C~ America** n Mittelamerika nt; **~ heating** n

Δ For information on spelling reform see page 615

Zentralheizung *f*; **~ize** *vt* zentralisieren; **~ reservation** (*BRIT*) *n* (*AUT*) Mittelstreifen *m*

centre ['sɛntər] (*US* **center**) *n* Zentrum *nt* ♦ *vt* zentrieren; **~-forward** *n* (*SPORT*) Mittelstürmer *m*; **~-half** *n* (*SPORT*) Stopper *m*

century ['sɛntjʊrɪ] *n* Jahrhundert *nt*

ceramic [sɪ'ræmɪk] *adj* keramisch; **~s** *npl* Keramiken *pl*

cereal ['siːrɪəl] *n* (*grain*) Getreide *nt*; (*at breakfast*) Getreideflocken *pl*

cerebral ['sɛrɪbrəl] *adj* zerebral; (*intellectual*) geistig

ceremony ['sɛrɪmənɪ] *n* Zeremonie *f*; **to stand on ~** förmlich sein

certain ['sɜːtən] *adj* sicher; (*particular*) gewiß ⚠; **for ~** ganz bestimmt; **~ly** *adv* sicher, bestimmt; **~ty** *n* Gewißheit ⚠ *f*

certificate [sə'tɪfɪkɪt] *n* Bescheinigung *f*; (*SCH etc*) Zeugnis *nt*

certified mail ['sɜːtɪfaɪd-] (*US*) *n* Einschreiben *nt*

certified public accountant ['sɜːtɪfaɪd-] (*US*) *n* geprüfte(r) Buchhalter *m*

certify ['sɜːtɪfaɪ] *vt* bescheinigen

cervical ['sɜːvɪkl] *adj* (*smear, cancer*) Gebärmutterhals-

cervix ['sɜːvɪks] *n* Gebärmutterhals *m*

cf. *abbr* (= *compare*) vgl.

CFC *n abbr* (= *chlorofluorocarbon*) FCKW *m*

ch. *abbr* (= *chapter*) Kap.

chafe [tʃeɪf] *vt* scheuern

chaffinch ['tʃæfɪntʃ] *n* Buchfink *m*

chain [tʃeɪn] *n* Kette *f* ♦ *vt* (*also:* **~ up**) anketten; **~ reaction** *n* Kettenreaktion *f*; **~-smoke** *vi* kettenrauchen; **~ store** *n* Kettenladen *m*

chair [tʃɛər] *n* Stuhl *m*; (*arm~*) Sessel *m*; (*UNIV*) Lehrstuhl *m* ♦ *vt* (*meeting*) den Vorsitz führen bei; **~lift** *n* Sessellift *m*; **~man** (*irreg*) *n* Vorsitzende(r) *m*

chalet ['ʃæleɪ] *n* Chalet *nt*

chalk [tʃɔːk] *n* Kreide *f*

challenge ['tʃælɪndʒ] *n* Herausforderung *f* ♦ *vt* herausfordern; (*contest*) bestreiten; **challenging** *adj* (*tone*) herausfordernd; (*work*) anspruchsvoll

chamber ['tʃeɪmbər] *n* Kammer *f*; **~ of commerce** Handelskammer *f*; **~maid** *n* Zimmermädchen *nt*; **~ music** *n* Kammermusik *f*

chamois ['ʃæmwɑː] *n* Gemse ⚠ *f*

champagne [ʃæm'peɪn] *n* Champagner *m*, Sekt *m*

champion ['tʃæmpɪən] *n* (*SPORT*) Meister(in) *m(f)*; (*of cause*) Verfechter(in) *m(f)*; **~ship** *n* Meisterschaft *f*

chance [tʃɑːns] *n* (*luck*) Zufall *m*; (*possibility*) Möglichkeit *f*; (*opportunity*) Gelegenheit *f*, Chance *f*; (*risk*) Risiko *nt* ♦ *adj* zufällig ♦ *vt*: **to ~ it** es darauf ankommen lassen; **by ~** zufällig; **to take a ~** ein Risiko eingehen

chancellor ['tʃɑːnsələr] *n* Kanzler *m*; **C~ of the Exchequer** (*BRIT*) *n* Schatzkanzler *m*

chandelier [ʃændə'lɪər] *n* Kronleuchter *m*

change [tʃeɪndʒ] *vt* ändern; (*replace, COMM: money*) wechseln; (*exchange*) umtauschen; (*transform*) verwandeln ♦ *vi* sich ändern; (*~ trains*) umsteigen; (*~ clothes*) sich umziehen ♦ *n* Veränderung *f*; (*money returned*) Wechselgeld *nt*; (*coins*) Kleingeld *nt*; **to ~ one's mind** es sich *dat* anders überlegen; **to ~ into sth** (*be transformed*) sich in etw *acc* verwandeln; **for a ~** zur Abwechslung; **~able** *adj* (*weather*) wechselhaft; **~ machine** *n* Geldwechselautomat *m*; **~over** *n* Umstellung *f*

changing ['tʃeɪndʒɪŋ] *adj* veränderlich; **~ room** (*BRIT*) *n* Umkleideraum *m*

channel ['tʃænl] *n* (*stream*) Bachbett *nt*; (*NAUT*) Straße *f*; (*TV*) Kanal *m*; (*fig*) Weg *m* ♦ *vt* (*efforts*) lenken; **the (English) C~** der Ärmelkanal; **~-hopping** *n* (*TV*) ständiges Umschalten; **C~ Islands** *npl*: **the C~ Islands** die Kanalinseln *pl*; **C~ Tunnel** *n*: **the C~ Tunnel** der Kanaltunnel

chant [tʃɑːnt] *n* Gesang *m*; (*of fans*) Sprechchor *m* ♦ *vt* intonieren

chaos ['keɪɒs] *n* Chaos *nt*

chap [tʃæp] (*inf*) *n* Kerl *m*

chapel ['tʃæpl] *n* Kapelle *f*

chaperon ['ʃæpərəʊn] *n* Anstandsdame *f*

chaplain ['tʃæplɪn] *n* Kaplan *m*

chapped [tʃæpt] *adj* (*skin, lips*) spröde

⚠ *Informationen zur Rechtschreibreform Seite 615*

chapter ['tʃæptə'] n Kapitel nt

char [tʃɑː'] vt (burn) verkohlen

character ['kærɪktə'] n Charakter m, Wesen nt; (in novel, film) Figur f; **~istic** [kærɪktə'rɪstɪk] adj: **~istic (of sb/sth)** (für jdn/etw) charakteristisch ♦ n Kennzeichen nt; **~ize** vt charakterisieren, kennzeichnen

charade [ʃə'rɑːd] n Scharade f

charcoal ['tʃɑːkəʊl] n Holzkohle f

charge [tʃɑːdʒ] n (cost) Preis m; (JUR) Anklage f; (explosive) Ladung f; (attack) Angriff m ♦ vt (gun, battery) laden; (price) verlangen; (JUR) anklagen; (MIL) angreifen ♦ vi (rush) (an)stürmen; **bank ~s** Bankgebühren pl; **free of ~** kostenlos; **to reverse the ~s** (TEL) ein R-Gespräch führen; **to be in ~ of** verantwortlich sein für; **to take ~** (die Verantwortung) übernehmen; **to ~ sth (up) to sb's account** jdm etw in Rechnung stellen; **~ card** n Kundenkarte f

charitable ['tʃærɪtəbl] adj wohltätig; (lenient) nachsichtig

charity ['tʃærɪtɪ] n (institution) Hilfswerk nt; (attitude) Nächstenliebe f

charm [tʃɑːm] n Charme m; (spell) Bann m; (object) Talisman m ♦ vt bezaubern; **~ing** adj reizend

chart [tʃɑːt] n Tabelle f; (NAUT) Seekarte f ♦ vt (course) abstecken

charter ['tʃɑːtə'] vt chartern ♦ n Schutzbrief m; **~ed accountant** n Wirtschaftsprüfer(in) m(f); **~ flight** n Charterflug m

chase [tʃeɪs] vt jagen, verfolgen ♦ n Jagd f

chasm ['kæzəm] n Kluft f

chassis ['ʃæsɪ] n Fahrgestell nt

chat [tʃæt] vi (also: **have a ~**) plaudern ♦ n Plauderei f; **~ show** (BRIT) n Talkshow f

chatter ['tʃætə'] vi schwatzen; (teeth) klappern ♦ n Geschwätz nt; **~box** n Quasselstrippe f

chatty ['tʃætɪ] adj geschwätzig

chauffeur ['ʃəʊfə'] n Chauffeur m

chauvinist ['ʃəʊvɪnɪst] n (male ~) Chauvi m (inf)

cheap [tʃiːp] adj, adv billig; **~ day return** n

Tagesrückfahrkarte f (zu einem günstigerem Tarif); **~ly** adv billig

cheat [tʃiːt] vt, vi betrügen; (SCH) mogeln ♦ n Betrüger(in) m(f)

check [tʃek] vt (examine) prüfen; (make sure) nachsehen; (control) kontrollieren; (restrain) zügeln; (stop) anhalten ♦ n (examination, restraint) Kontrolle f; (bill) Rechnung f; (pattern) Karo(muster) nt; (US) = **cheque** ♦ adj (pattern, cloth) kariert; **~ in** vi (in hotel, airport) einchecken ♦ vt (luggage) abfertigen lassen; **~ out** vi (of hotel) abreisen; **~ up** vi nachschauen; **~ up on** vt kontrollieren; **~ered** (US) adj = **chequered**; **~ers** (US) n (draughts) Damespiel nt; **~-in (desk)** n Abfertigung f; **~ing account** (US) n (current account) Girokonto nt; **~mate** n Schachmatt nt; **~out** n Kasse f; **~point** n Kontrollpunkt m; **~ room** (US) n (left-luggage office) Gepäckaufbewahrung f; **~up** n (Nach)prüfung f; (MED) (ärztliche) Untersuchung f

cheek [tʃiːk] n Backe f; (fig) Frechheit f; **~bone** n Backenknochen m; **~y** adj frech

cheep [tʃiːp] vi piepsen

cheer [tʃɪə'] n (usu pl) Hurra- or Beifallsruf m ♦ vt zujubeln; (encourage) aufmuntern ♦ vi jauchzen; **~s!** Prost!; **~ up** vi bessere Laune bekommen ♦ vt aufmuntern; **~ up!** nun lach doch mal!; **~ful** adj fröhlich

cheerio [tʃɪərɪ'əʊ] (BRIT) excl tschüs!

cheese [tʃiːz] n Käse m; **~board** n (gemischte) Käseplatte f

cheetah ['tʃiːtə] n Gepard m

chef [ʃef] n Küchenchef m

chemical ['kemɪkl] adj chemisch ♦ n Chemikalie f

chemist ['kemɪst] n (BRIT: pharmacist) Apotheker m, Drogist m; (scientist) Chemiker m; **~ry** n Chemie f; **~'s (shop)** (BRIT) n Apotheke f; Drogerie f

cheque [tʃek] (BRIT) n Scheck m; **~book** n Scheckbuch nt; **~ card** n Scheckkarte f

chequered ['tʃekəd] adj (fig) bewegt

cherish ['tʃerɪʃ] vt (person) ↑lieben; (hope) hegen

⚠ For information on spelling reform see page 615

cherry ['tʃerɪ] n Kirsche f
chess [tʃes] n Schach nt; ~**board** n Schachbrett nt; ~**man** (irreg) n Schachfigur f
chest [tʃest] n (ANAT) Brust f; (box) Kiste f; ~ **of drawers** Kommode f
chestnut ['tʃesnʌt] n Kastanie f
chew [tʃuː] vt, vi kauen; ~**ing gum** n Kaugummi m
chic [ʃiːk] adj schick, elegant
chick [tʃɪk] n Küken nt; (US: inf: girl) Biene f
chicken ['tʃɪkɪn] n Huhn nt; (food) Hähnchen nt; ~ **out** (inf) vi kneifen
chickenpox ['tʃɪkɪnpɒks] n Windpocken pl
chicory ['tʃɪkərɪ] n (in coffee) Zichorie f; (plant) Chicorée △ f
chief [tʃiːf] n (of tribe) Häuptling m; (COMM) Chef m ♦ adj Haupt-; ~ **executive** n Geschäftsführer(in) m(f); ~**ly** adv hauptsächlich
chilblain ['tʃɪlblɛɪn] n Frostbeule f
child [tʃaɪld] n (pl ~**ren**) Kind nt; ~**birth** n Entbindung f; ~**hood** n Kindheit f; ~**ish** adj kindisch; ~**like** adj kindlich; ~ **minder** (BRIT) n Tagesmutter f; ~**ren** ['tʃɪldrən] npl of **child**; ~ **seat** n Kindersitz m
Chile ['tʃɪlɪ] n Chile nt; ~**an** adj chilenisch
chill [tʃɪl] n Kühle f; (MED) Erkältung f ♦ vt (CULIN) kühlen
chilli ['tʃɪlɪ] n Peperoni pl; (meal, spice) Chili m
chilly ['tʃɪlɪ] adj kühl, frostig
chime [tʃaɪm] n Geläut nt ♦ vi ertönen
chimney ['tʃɪmnɪ] n Schornstein m; ~ **sweep** n Schornsteinfeger(in) m(f)
chimpanzee [tʃɪmpæn'ziː] n Schimpanse m
chin [tʃɪn] n Kinn nt
China ['tʃaɪnə] n China nt
china ['tʃaɪnə] n Porzellan nt
Chinese [tʃaɪ'niːz] adj chinesisch ♦ n (inv) Chinese m, Chinesin f; (LING) Chinesisch nt
chink [tʃɪŋk] n (opening) Ritze f; (noise) Klirren nt
chip [tʃɪp] n (of wood etc) Splitter m; (in poker etc; US: crisp) Chip m ♦ vt absplittern; ~**s** npl (BRIT: COOK) Pommes frites pl; ~ **in** vi Zwischenbemerkungen machen

---

CHIP SHOP

ⓘ **Chip shop**, auch fish-and-chip shop, ist die traditionelle britische Imbißbude, in der vor allem fritierte Fischfilets und Pommes frites, aber auch andere einfache Mahlzeiten angeboten werden. Früher wurde das Essen zum Mitnehmen in Zeitungspapier verpackt. Manche chip shops haben auch einen Eßraum.

---

chiropodist [kɪ'rɒpədɪst] (BRIT) n Fußpfleger(in) m(f)
chirp [tʃɜːp] vi zwitschern
chisel ['tʃɪzl] n Meißel m
chit [tʃɪt] n Notiz f
chivalrous ['ʃɪvəlrəs] adj ritterlich; **chivalry** ['ʃɪvəlrɪ] n Ritterlichkeit f
chives [tʃaɪvz] npl Schnittlauch m
chlorine ['klɔːriːn] n Chlor nt
chock-a-block ['tʃɒkə'blɒk] adj vollgepfropft △
chock-full [tʃɒk'ful] adj vollgepfropft △
chocolate ['tʃɒklɪt] n Schokolade f
choice [tʃɔɪs] n Wahl f; (of goods) Auswahl f ♦ adj Qualitäts-
choir ['kwaɪər] n Chor m; ~**boy** n Chorknabe m
choke [tʃəuk] vi ersticken ♦ vt erdrosseln; (block) (ab)drosseln ♦ n (AUT) Starterklappe f
cholera ['kɒlərə] n Cholera f
cholesterol [kə'lestərɒl] n Cholesterin nt
choose [tʃuːz] (pt **chose**, pp **chosen**) vt wählen; **choosy** ['tʃuːzɪ] adj wählerisch
chop [tʃɒp] vt (wood) spalten; (COOK: also: ~ **up**) (zer)hacken ♦ n Hieb m; (COOK) Kotelett nt; ~**s** npl (jaws) Lefzen pl
chopper ['tʃɒpər] n (helicopter) Hubschrauber m
choppy ['tʃɒpɪ] adj (sea) bewegt
chopsticks ['tʃɒpstɪks] npl (Eß)stäbchen △ pl
choral ['kɔːrəl] adj Chor-
chord [kɔːd] n Akkord m
chore [tʃɔːr] n Pflicht f; ~**s** npl (housework) Hausarbeit f

△ Informationen zur Rechtschreibreform Seite 615

choreographer [kɒrɪˈɒɡrəfər] n Choreograph(in) △ m(f)

chorister [ˈkɒrɪstər] n Chorsänger(in) m(f)

chortle [ˈtʃɔːtl] vi glucksen

chorus [ˈkɔːrəs] n Chor m; (in song) Refrain m

chose [tʃəuz] pt of **choose**

chosen [ˈtʃəuzn] pp of **choose**

chowder [ˈtʃaudər] (US) n sämige Fischsuppe f

Christ [kraɪst] n Christus m

christen [ˈkrɪsn] vt taufen; **~ing** n Taufe f

Christian [ˈkrɪstɪən] adj christlich ♦ n Christ(in) m(f); **~ity** [krɪstɪˈænɪtɪ] n Christentum nt; **~ name** n Vorname m

Christmas [ˈkrɪsməs] n Weihnachten pl; **Happy** or **Merry ~!** Frohe or fröhliche Weihnachten!; **~ card** n Weihnachtskarte f; **~ Day** n der erste Weihnachtstag; **~ Eve** n Heiligabend m; **~ tree** n Weihnachtsbaum m

chrome [krəum] n Verchromung f

chromium [ˈkrəumɪəm] n Chrom nt

chronic [ˈkrɒnɪk] adj chronisch

chronicle [ˈkrɒnɪkl] n Chronik f

chronological [krɒnəˈlɒdʒɪkl] adj chronologisch

chubby [ˈtʃʌbɪ] adj rundlich

chuck [tʃʌk] vt werfen; (BRIT: also: **~ up**) hinwerfen; **~ out** vt (person) rauswerfen; (old clothes etc) wegwerfen

chuckle [ˈtʃʌkl] vi in sich hineinlachen

chug [tʃʌg] vi tuckern

chunk [tʃʌŋk] n Klumpen m; (of food) Brocken m

church [tʃɜːtʃ] n Kirche f; **~yard** n Kirchhof m

churn [tʃɜːn] n (for butter) Butterfaß △ nt; (for milk) Milchkanne f; **~ out** (inf) vt produzieren

chute [ʃuːt] n Rutsche f; (rubbish ~) Müllschlucker m

chutney [ˈtʃʌtnɪ] n Chutney nt

CIA (US) n abbr (= Central Intelligence Agency) CIA m

CID (BRIT) n abbr (= Criminal Investigation Department) ≈ Kripo f

cider [ˈsaɪdər] n Apfelwein m

cigar [sɪˈɡɑːr] n Zigarre f

cigarette [sɪɡəˈret] n Zigarette f; **~ case** n Zigarettenetui nt; **~ end** n Zigarettenstummel m

Cinderella [sɪndəˈrelə] n Aschenbrödel nt

cinders [ˈsɪndəz] npl Asche f

cine camera [ˈsɪnɪ-] (BRIT) n Filmkamera f

cine film (BRIT) n Schmalfilm m

cinema [ˈsɪnəmə] n Kino nt

cinnamon [ˈsɪnəmən] n Zimt m

circle [ˈsɜːkl] n Kreis m; (in cinema etc) Rang m ♦ vi kreisen ♦ vt (surround) umgeben; (move round) kreisen um

circuit [ˈsɜːkɪt] n (track) Rennbahn f; (lap) Runde f; (ELEC) Stromkreis m

circular [ˈsɜːkjulər] adj rund ♦ n Rundschreiben nt

circulate [ˈsɜːkjuleɪt] vi zirkulieren ♦ vt in Umlauf setzen; **circulation** [sɜːkjuˈleɪʃən] n (of blood) Kreislauf m; (of newspaper) Auflage f; (of money) Umlauf m

circumcise [ˈsɜːkəmsaɪz] vt beschneiden

circumference [səˈkʌmfərəns] n (Kreis)umfang m

circumspect [ˈsɜːkəmspekt] adj umsichtig

circumstances [ˈsɜːkəmstənsɪz] npl Umstände pl; (financial) Verhältnisse pl

circumvent [sɜːkəmˈvent] vt umgehen

circus [ˈsɜːkəs] n Zirkus m

CIS n abbr (= Commonwealth of Independent States) GUS f

cistern [ˈsɪstən] n Zisterne f; (of W.C.) Spülkasten m

cite [saɪt] vt zitieren, anführen

citizen [ˈsɪtɪzn] n Bürger(in) m(f); **~ship** n Staatsbürgerschaft f

citrus fruit [ˈsɪtrəs-] n Zitrusfrucht f

city [ˈsɪtɪ] n Großstadt f; **the C~** die City, das Finanzzentrum Londons

city technology college n ≈ Technische Fachschule f

civic [ˈsɪvɪk] adj (of town) städtisch; (of citizen) Bürger-; **~ centre** (BRIT) n Stadtverwaltung f

civil [ˈsɪvɪl] adj bürgerlich; (not military) zivil; (polite) höflich; **~ engineer** n Bauingenieur

△ *For information on spelling reform see page 615*

m; **~ian** [sɪ'vɪlɪən] *n* Zivilperson *f* ♦ *adj* zivil, Zivil-

civilization [sɪvɪlaɪ'zeɪʃən] *n* Zivilisation *f*

civilized ['sɪvɪlaɪzd] *adj* zivilisiert

civil: ~ law *n* Zivilrecht *nt*; **~ servant** *n* Staatsbeamte(r) *m*; **C~ Service** *n* Staatsdienst *m*; **~ war** *n* Bürgerkrieg *m*

clad [klæd] *adj*: **~ in** gehüllt in +*acc*

claim [kleɪm] *vt* beanspruchen; (*have opinion*) behaupten ♦ *vi* (*for insurance*) Ansprüche geltend machen ♦ *n* (*demand*) Forderung *f*; (*right*) Anspruch *m*; (*pretension*) Behauptung *f*; **~ant** *n* Antragsteller(in) *m(f)*

clairvoyant [kleə'vɔɪənt] *n* Hellseher(in) *m(f)*

clam [klæm] *n* Venusmuschel *f*

clamber ['klæmbə*] *vi* kraxeln

clammy ['klæmɪ] *adj* klamm

clamour ['klæmə*] *vi*: **to ~ for sth** nach etw verlangen

clamp [klæmp] *n* Schraubzwinge *f* ♦ *vt* einspannen; (*AUT: wheel*) krallen; **~ down on** *vt fus* Maßnahmen ergreifen gegen

clan [klæn] *n* Clan *m*

clandestine [klæn'destɪn] *adj* geheim

clang [klæŋ] *vi* scheppern

clap [klæp] *vi* klatschen ♦ *vt* Beifall klatschen +*dat* ♦ *n* (*of hands*) Klatschen *nt*; (*of thunder*) Donnerschlag *m*; **~ping** *n* Klatschen *nt*

claret ['klærət] *n* rote(r) Bordeaux(wein) *m*

clarify ['klærɪfaɪ] *vt* klären, erklären

clarinet [klærɪ'net] *n* Klarinette *f*

clarity ['klærɪtɪ] *n* Klarheit *f*

clash [klæʃ] *n* (*fig*) Konflikt *m* ♦ *vi* zusammenprallen; (*colours*) sich beißen; (*argue*) sich streiten

clasp [klɑːsp] *n* Griff *m*; (*on jewels, bag*) Verschluß ⚠ *m* ♦ *vt* umklammern

class [klɑːs] *n* Klasse *f* ♦ *vt* einordnen; **~-conscious** *adj* klassenbewußt ⚠

classic ['klæsɪk] *n* Klassiker *m* ♦ *adj* klassisch; **~al** *adj* klassisch

classified ['klæsɪfaɪd] *adj* (*information*) Geheim-; **~ advertisement** *n* Kleinanzeige *f*

classify ['klæsɪfaɪ] *vt* klassifizieren

classmate ['klɑːsmeɪt] *n*

Klassenkamerad(in) *m(f)*

classroom ['klɑːsrʊm] *n* Klassenzimmer *nt*

clatter ['klætə*] *vi* klappern; (*feet*) trappeln

clause [klɔːz] *n* (*JUR*) Klausel *f*; (*GRAM*) Satz *m*

claustrophobia [klɔːstrə'fəʊbɪə] *n* Platzangst *f*

claw [klɔː] *n* Kralle *f* ♦ *vt* (zer)kratzen

clay [kleɪ] *n* Lehm *m*; (*for pots*) Ton *m*

clean [kliːn] *adj* sauber ♦ *vt* putzen; (*clothes*) reinigen; **~ out** *vt* gründlich putzen; **~ up** *vt* aufräumen; **~-cut** *adj* (*person*) adrett; (*clear*) klar; **~er** *n* (*person*) Putzfrau *f*; **~er's** *n* (*also:* **dry ~er's**) Reinigung *f*; **~ing** *n* Putzen *nt*; (*clothes*) Reinigung *f*; **~liness** ['klenlɪnɪs] *n* Reinlichkeit *f*

cleanse [klenz] *vt* reinigen; **~r** *n* (*for face*) Reinigungsmilch *f*

clean-shaven ['kliːn'ʃeɪvn] *adj* glattrasiert ⚠

cleansing department ['klenzɪŋ-] (*BRIT*) *n* Stadtreinigung *f*

clear [klɪə*] *adj* klar; (*road*) frei ♦ *vt* (*road etc*) freimachen; (*obstacle*) beseitigen; (*JUR: suspect*) freisprechen ♦ *vi* klarwerden ⚠; (*fog*) sich lichten ♦ *adv*: **~ of** von ... entfernt; **to ~ the table** den Tisch abräumen; **~ up** *vt* aufräumen; (*solve*) aufklären; **~ance** ['klɪərəns] *n*. (*removal*) Räumung *f*; (*free space*) Lichtung *f*; (*permission*) Freigabe *f*; **~-cut** *adj* (*case*) eindeutig; **~ing** *n* Lichtung *f*; **~ing bank** (*BRIT*) *n* Clearingbank *f*; **~ly** *adv* klar; (*obviously*) eindeutig; **~way** (*BRIT*) *n* (Straße *f* mit) Halteverbot *nt*

cleaver ['kliːvə*] *n* Hackbeil *f*

cleft [kleft] *n* (*in rock*) Spalte *f*

clementine ['kleməntaɪn] *n* (*fruit*) Klementine *f*

clench [klentʃ] *vt* (*teeth*) zusammenbeißen; (*fist*) ballen

clergy ['klɜːdʒɪ] *n* Geistliche(n) *pl*; **~man** (*irreg*) *n* Geistliche(r) *m*

clerical ['klerɪkl] *adj* (*office*) Schreib-, Büro-; (*REL*) geistlich

clerk [klɑːk, (*US*) klɜːrk] *n* (*in office*) Büroangestellte(r) *mf*; (*US: sales person*)

⚠ *Informationen zur Rechtschreibreform Seite 615*

Verkäufer(in) m(f)

clever ['klɛvəʳ] adj klug; (crafty) schlau

cliché ['kliːʃeɪ] n Klischee nt

click [klɪk] vt (tongue) schnalzen mit; (heels) zusammenklappen

client ['klaɪənt] n Klient(in) m(f); **~ele** [kliːɑːnˈtɛl] n Kundschaft f

cliff [klɪf] n Klippe f

climate ['klaɪmɪt] n Klima nt

climax ['klaɪmæks] n Höhepunkt m

climb [klaɪm] vt besteigen ♦ vi steigen, klettern ♦ n Aufstieg m; **~-down** n Abstieg m; **~er** n Bergsteiger(in) m(f); **~ing** n Bergsteigen nt

clinch [klɪntʃ] vt (decide) entscheiden; (deal) festmachen

cling [klɪŋ] (pt, pp clung) vi (clothes) eng anliegen; **to ~ to** sich festklammern an +dat

clinic ['klɪnɪk] n Klinik f; **~al** adj klinisch

clink [klɪŋk] vi klimpern

clip [klɪp] n Spange f; (also: **paper ~**) Klammer f ♦ vt (papers) heften; (hair, hedge) stutzen; **~pers** npl (for hedge) Heckenschere f; (for hair) Haarschneidemaschine f; **~ping** n Ausschnitt m

cloak [kləuk] n Umhang m ♦ vt hüllen; **~room** n (for coats) Garderobe f; (BRIT: W.C.) Toilette f

clock [klɒk] n Uhr f; **~ in** or **on** vi stempeln; **~ off** or **out** vi stempeln; **~wise** adv im Uhrzeigersinn; **~work** n Uhrwerk nt ♦ adj zum Aufziehen

clog [klɒg] n Holzschuh m ♦ vt verstopfen

cloister ['klɔɪstəʳ] n Kreuzgang m

clone [kləun] n Klon m

close¹ [kləus] adj (near) in der Nähe; (friend, connection, print) eng; (relative) nahe; (result) knapp; (examination) eingehend; (weather) schwül; (room) stickig ♦ adv nahe, dicht; **~ by** in der Nähe; **~ at hand** in der Nähe; **to have a ~ shave** (fig) mit knapper Not davonkommen

close² [kləuz] vt (shut) schließen; (end) beenden ♦ vi (shop etc) schließen; (door etc) sich schließen ♦ n Ende nt; **~ down** vi schließen; **~d** adj (shop etc) geschlossen

~d shop n Gewerkschaftszwang m

close-knit ['kləusˈnɪt] adj eng zusammengewachsen

closely ['kləuslɪ] adv eng; (carefully) genau

closet ['klɒzɪt] n Schrank m

close-up ['kləusʌp] n Nahaufnahme f

closure ['kləuʒəʳ] n Schließung f

clot [klɒt] n (of blood) Blutgerinnsel nt; (fool) Blödmann m ♦ vi gerinnen

cloth [klɒθ] n (material) Tuch nt; (rag) Lappen m

clothe [kləuð] vt kleiden

clothes [kləuðz] npl Kleider pl; **~ brush** n Kleiderbürste f; **~ line** n Wäscheleine f; **~ peg**, **~ pin** (US) n Wäscheklammer f

clothing ['kləuðɪŋ] n Kleidung f

clotted cream ['klɒtɪd-] (BRIT) n Sahne aus erhitzter Milch

cloud [klaud] n Wolke f; **~burst** n Wolkenbruch m; **~y** adj bewölkt; (liquid) trüb

clout [klaut] vt hauen

clove [kləuv] n Gewürznelke f; **~ of garlic** Knoblauchzehe f

clover ['kləuvəʳ] n Klee m

clown [klaun] n Clown m ♦ vi (also: **~ about, ~ around**) kaspern

cloying ['klɔɪɪŋ] adj (taste, smell) übersüß

club [klʌb] n (weapon) Knüppel m; (society) Klub m; (also: **golf ~**) Golfschläger m ♦ vt prügeln ♦ vi: **to ~ together** zusammenlegen; **~s** npl (CARDS) Kreuz nt; **~ car** (US) n (RAIL) Speisewagen m; **~ class** n (AVIAT) Club-Klasse f; **~house** n Klubhaus nt

cluck [klʌk] vi glucken

clue [kluː] n Anhaltspunkt m; (in crosswords) Frage f; **I haven't a ~** (ich hab') keine Ahnung

clump [klʌmp] n Gruppe f

clumsy ['klʌmzɪ] adj (person) unbeholfen; (shape) unförmig

clung [klʌŋ] pt, pp of **cling**

cluster ['klʌstəʳ] n (of trees etc) Gruppe f ♦ vi sich drängen, sich scharen

clutch [klʌtʃ] n Griff m; (AUT) Kupplung f ♦ vt sich festklammern an +dat

⚠ For information on spelling reform see page 615

clutter ['klʌtə'] *vt* vollpropfen △; (*desk*) übersäen

CND *n abbr* = **Campaign for Nuclear Disarmament**

Co. *abbr* = **county; company**

c/o *abbr* (= *care of*) c/o

coach [kəʊtʃ] *n* (*bus*) Reisebus *m*; (*horse-drawn*) Kutsche *f*; (*RAIL*) (Personen)wagen *m*; (*trainer*) Trainer *m* ♦ *vt* (*SCH*) Nachhilfeunterricht geben +*dat*; (*SPORT*) trainieren; ~ **trip** *n* Busfahrt *f*

coal [kəʊl] *n* Kohle *f*; ~ **face** *n* Streb *m*

coalition [kəʊə'lɪʃən] *n* Koalition *f*

coalman ['kəʊlmən] (*irreg*) *n* Kohlenhändler *m*

coal mine *n* Kohlenbergwerk *nt*

coarse [kɔːs] *adj* grob; (*fig*) ordinär

coast [kəʊst] *n* Küste *f* ♦ *vi* dahinrollen; (*AUT*) im Leerlauf fahren; ~**al** *adj* Küsten-; ~**guard** *n* Küstenwache *f*; ~**line** *n* Küste(nlinie) *f*

coat [kəʊt] *n* Mantel *m*; (*on animals*) Fell *nt*; (*of paint*) Schicht *f* ♦ *vt* überstreichen; ~**hanger** *n* Kleiderbügel *m*; ~**ing** *n* Überzug *m*; (*of paint*) Schicht *f*; ~ **of arms** *n* Wappen *nt*

coax [kəʊks] *vt* beschwatzen

cob [kɔb] *n see* **corn**

cobbler ['kɔblə'] *n* Schuster *m*

cobbles ['kɔblz] *npl* Pflastersteine *pl*

cobweb ['kɔbweb] *n* Spinnennetz *nt*

cocaine [kə'keɪn] *n* Kokain *nt*

cock [kɔk] *n* Hahn *m* ♦ *vt* (*gun*) entsichern; ~**erel** ['kɔkrəl] *n* junge(r) Hahn *m*; ~**eyed** *adj* (*fig*) verrückt

cockle ['kɔkl] *n* Herzmuschel *f*

cockney ['kɔknɪ] *n* echte(r) Londoner *m*

cockpit ['kɔkpɪt] *n* (*AVIAT*) Pilotenkanzel *f*

cockroach ['kɔkrəʊtʃ] *n* Küchenschabe *f*

cocktail ['kɔkteɪl] *n* Cocktail *m*; ~ **cabinet** *n* Hausbar *f*; ~ **party** *n* Cocktailparty *f*

cocoa ['kəʊkəʊ] *n* Kakao *m*

coconut ['kəʊkənʌt] *n* Kokosnuß △ *f*

cocoon [kə'kuːn] *n* Kokon *m*

cod [kɔd] *n* Kabeljau *m*

C.O.D. *abbr* = **cash on delivery**

code [kəʊd] *n* Kode *m*; (*JUR*) Kodex *m*

cod-liver oil ['kɔdlɪvə-] *n* Lebertran *m*

coercion [kəʊ'ɜːʃən] *n* Zwang *m*

coffee ['kɔfɪ] *n* Kaffee *m*; ~ **bar** (*BRIT*) *n* Café *nt*; ~ **bean** *n* Kaffeebohne *f*; ~ **break** *n* Kaffeepause *f*; ~**pot** *n* Kaffeekanne *f*; ~ **table** *n* Couchtisch *m*

coffin ['kɔfɪn] *n* Sarg *m*

cog [kɔg] *n* (Rad)zahn *m*

cognac ['kɔnjæk] *n* Kognak *m*

coherent [kəʊ'hɪərənt] *adj* zusammenhängend; (*person*) verständlich

coil [kɔɪl] *n* Rolle *f*; (*ELEC*) Spule *f*; (*contraceptive*) Spirale *f* ♦ *vt* aufwickeln

coin [kɔɪn] *n* Münze *f* ♦ *vt* prägen; ~**age** ['kɔɪnɪdʒ] *n* (*word*) Prägung *f*; ~ **box** (*BRIT*) *n* Münzfernsprecher *m*

coincide [kəʊɪn'saɪd] *vi* (*happen together*) zusammenfallen; (*agree*) übereinstimmen; ~**nce** [kəʊ'ɪnsɪdəns] *n* Zufall *m*

coinphone ['kɔɪnfəʊn] *n* Münzfernsprecher *m*

Coke [kəʊk] ® *n* (*drink*) Coca-Cola *f* ®

coke [kəʊk] *n* Koks *m*

colander ['kɔləndə'] *n* Durchschlag *m*

cold [kəʊld] *adj* kalt ♦ *n* Kälte *f*; (*MED*) Erkältung *f*; **I'm ~** mir ist kalt; **to catch ~** sich erkälten; **in ~ blood** kaltblütig; **to give sb the ~ shoulder** jdm die kalte Schulter zeigen; ~**ly** *adv* kalt; ~**-shoulder** *vt* die kalte Schulter zeigen +*dat*; ~ **sore** *n* Erkältungsbläschen *nt*

coleslaw ['kəʊlslɔː] *n* Krautsalat *m*

colic ['kɔlɪk] *n* Kolik *f*

collaborate [kə'læbəreɪt] *vi* zusammenarbeiten

collapse [kə'læps] *vi* (*people*) zusammenbrechen; (*things*) einstürzen ♦ *n* Zusammenbruch *m*; Einsturz *m*; **collapsible** *adj* zusammenklappbar, Klapp-

collar ['kɔlə'] *n* Kragen *m*; ~**bone** *n* Schlüsselbein *nt*

collateral [kə'lætərl] *n* (zusätzliche) Sicherheit *f*

colleague ['kɔliːg] *n* Kollege *m*, Kollegin *f*

collect [kə'lekt] *vt* sammeln; (*BRIT*: *call and pick up*) abholen ♦ *vi* sich sammeln ♦ *adv*:

△ *Informationen zur Rechtschreibreform Seite 615*

to call ~ (*US: TEL*) ein R-Gespräch führen; **~ion** [kə'lekʃən] n Sammlung f; (*REL*) Kollekte f; (*of post*) Leerung f; **~ive** [kə'lektɪv] adj gemeinsam; (*POL*) kollektiv; **~or** [kə'lektə'] n Sammler m; (*tax collector*) (Steuer)einnehmer m

college ['kɒlɪdʒ] n (*UNIV*) College nt; (*TECH*) Fach-, Berufsschule f

collide [kə'laɪd] vi zusammenstoßen

collie ['kɒlɪ] n Collie m

colliery ['kɒlɪərɪ] (*BRIT*) n Zeche f

collision [kə'lɪʒən] n Zusammenstoß m

colloquial [kə'ləʊkwɪəl] adj umgangssprachlich

colon ['kəʊlən] n Doppelpunkt m; (*MED*) Dickdarm m

colonel ['kɜːnl] n Oberst m

colonial [kə'ləʊnɪəl] adj Kolonial-

colonize ['kɒlənaɪz] vt kolonisieren

colony ['kɒlənɪ] n Kolonie f

colour ['kʌlə'] (*US* color) n Farbe f ♦ vt (*also fig*) färben ♦ vi sich verfärben; **~s** npl (*of club*) Fahne f; **~ bar** n Rassenschranke f; **~-blind** adj farbenblind; **~ed** adj farbig; **~ film** n Farbfilm m; **~ful** adj bunt; (*personality*) schillernd; **~ing** n (*complexion*) Gesichtsfarbe f; (*substance*) Farbstoff m; **~ scheme** n Farbgebung f; **~ television** n Farbfernsehen nt

colt [kəʊlt] n Fohlen nt

column ['kɒləm] n Säule f; (*MIL*) Kolonne f; (*of print*) Spalte f; **~ist** ['kɒləmnɪst] n Kolumnist m

coma ['kəʊmə] n Koma nt

comb [kəʊm] n Kamm m ♦ vt kämmen; (*search*) durchkämmen

combat ['kɒmbæt] n Kampf m ♦ vt bekämpfen

combination [kɒmbɪ'neɪʃən] n Kombination f

combine [vb kəm'baɪn, n 'kɒmbaɪn] vt verbinden ♦ vi sich vereinigen ♦ n (*COMM*) Konzern m; **~ (harvester)** n Mähdrescher m

combustion [kəm'bʌstʃən] n Verbrennung f

come [kʌm] (*pt* came, *pp* come) vi kommen; **to ~ undone** aufgehen; **~ about** vi geschehen; **~ across** vt fus (*find*) stoßen auf +acc; **~ away** vi (*person*) weggehen; (*handle etc*) abgehen; **~ back** vi zurückkommen; **~ by** vt fus (*find*): **to ~ by sth** zu etw kommen; **~ down** vi (*price*) fallen; **~ forward** vi (*volunteer*) sich melden; **~ from** vt fus (*result*) kommen von; **where do you ~ from?** wo kommen Sie her?; **I ~ from London** ich komme aus London; **~ in** vi hereinkommen; (*train*) einfahren; **~ in for** vt fus abkriegen; **~ into** vt fus (*inherit*) erben; **~ off** vi (*handle*) abgehen; (*succeed*) klappen; **~ on** vi (*progress*) vorankommen; **~ on!** komm!; (*hurry*) beeil dich!; **~ out** vi herauskommen; **~ round** vi (*MED*) wieder zu sich kommen; **~ to** vi (*MED*) wieder zu sich kommen ♦ vt fus (*bill*) sich belaufen auf +acc; **~ up** vi hochkommen; (*sun*) aufgehen; (*problem*) auftauchen; **~ up against** vt fus (*resistance, difficulties*) stoßen auf +acc; **~ upon** vt fus stoßen auf +acc; **~ up with** vt fus sich einfallen lassen

comedian [kə'miːdɪən] n Komiker m; **comedienne** [kəmiːdɪ'en] n Komikerin f

comedown ['kʌmdaʊn] n Abstieg m

comedy ['kɒmɪdɪ] n Komödie f

comet ['kɒmɪt] n Komet m

comeuppance [kʌm'ʌpəns] n: **to get one's ~** seine Quittung bekommen

comfort ['kʌmfət] n Komfort m; (*consolation*) Trost m ♦ vt trösten; **~able** adj bequem; **~ably** adv (*sit etc*) bequem; (*live*) angenehm; **~ station** (*US*) n öffentliche Toilette f

comic ['kɒmɪk] n Comic(heft) nt; (*comedian*) Komiker m ♦ adj (*also:* **~al**) komisch; **~ strip** n Comic strip m

coming ['kʌmɪŋ] n Kommen nt; **~(s) and going(s)** n(pl) Kommen und Gehen nt

comma ['kɒmə] n Komma nt

command [kə'mɑːnd] n Befehl m; (*control*) Führung f; (*MIL*) Kommando nt; (*mastery*) Beherrschung f ♦ vt befehlen +dat; (*MIL*) kommandieren; (*be able to get*) verfügen über +acc; **~eer** [kəmən'dɪə'] vt requirieren; **~er** n Kommandant m; **~ment** n (*REL*)

⚠ *For information on spelling reform see page 615*

Gebot *nt*

commando [kə'mɑːndəʊ] *n* Kommandotruppe *nt*; (*person*) Mitglied *nt* einer Kommandotruppe

commemorate [kə'mɛməreɪt] *vt* gedenken +*gen*

commence [kə'mɛns] *vt, vi* beginnen

commend [kə'mɛnd] *vt* (*recommend*) empfehlen; (*praise*) loben

commensurate [kə'mɛnʃərɪt] *adj*: ~ **with sth** einer Sache *dat* entsprechend

comment ['kɔmɛnt] *n* Bemerkung *f* ♦ *vi*: **to ~ (on)** sich äußern (zu); **~ary** *n* Kommentar *m*; **~ator** *n* Kommentator *m*; (*TV*) Reporter(in) *m(f)*

commerce ['kɔmɜːs] *n* Handel *m*

commercial [kə'mɜːʃəl] *adj* kommerziell, geschäftlich; (*training*) kaufmännisch ♦ *n* (*TV*) Fernsehwerbung *f*; ~ **break** *n* Werbespot *m*; **~ize** *vt* kommerzialisieren

commiserate [kə'mɪzəreɪt] *vi*: **to ~ with** Mitleid haben mit

commission [kə'mɪʃən] *n* (*act*) Auftrag *m*; (*fee*) Provision *f*; (*body*) Kommission *f* ♦ *vt* beauftragen; (*MIL*) zum Offizier ernennen; (*work of art*) in Auftrag geben; **out of ~** außer Betrieb; **~er** *n* (*POLICE*) Polizeipräsident *m*

commit [kə'mɪt] *vt* (*crime*) begehen; (*entrust*) anvertrauen; **to ~ o.s.** sich festlegen; **~ment** *n* Verpflichtung *f*

committee [kə'mɪtɪ] *n* Ausschuß △ *m*

commodity [kə'mɔdɪtɪ] *n* Ware *f*

common ['kɔmən] *adj* (*cause*) gemeinsam; (*pej*) gewöhnlich; (*widespread*) üblich, häufig ♦ *n* Gemeindeland *nt*; **C~s** *npl* (*BRIT*): **the C~s** das Unterhaus; **~er** *n* Bürgerliche(r) *mf*; ~ **law** *n* Gewohnheitsrecht *nt*; **~ly** *adv* gewöhnlich; **C~ Market** *n* Gemeinsame(r) Markt *m*; **~place** *adj* alltäglich; ~ **room** *n* Gemeinschaftsraum *m*; ~ **sense** *n* gesunde(r) Menschenverstand *m*; **C~wealth** *n*: **the C~wealth** das Commonwealth

commotion [kə'məʊʃən] *n* Aufsehen *nt*

communal ['kɔmjuːnl] *adj* Gemeinde-;

Gemeinschafts-

commune [*n* 'kɔmjuːn, *vb* kə'mjuːn] *n* Kommune *f* ♦ *vi*: **to ~ with** sich mitteilen +*dat*

communicate [kə'mjuːnɪkeɪt] *vt* (*transmit*) übertragen ♦ *vi* (*be in touch*) in Verbindung stehen; (*make self understood*) sich verständigen; **communication** [kəmjuːnɪ'keɪʃən] *n* (*message*) Mitteilung *f*; (*making understood*) Kommunikation *f*; **communication cord** (*BRIT*) *n* Notbremse *f*

communion [kə'mjuːnɪən] *n* (*also*: **Holy C~**) Abendmahl *nt*, Kommunion *f*

communism ['kɔmjunɪzəm] *n* Kommunismus *m*; **communist** ['kɔmjunɪst] *n* Kommunist(in) *m(f)* ♦ *adj* kommunistisch

community [kə'mjuːnɪtɪ] *n* Gemeinschaft *f*; ~ **centre** *n* Gemeinschaftszentrum *nt*; ~ **chest** (*US*) *n* Wohltätigkeitsfonds *m*; ~ **home** (*BRIT*) *n* Erziehungsheim *nt*

commutation ticket [kɔmjuː'teɪʃən-] (*US*) *n* Zeitkarte *f*

commute [kə'mjuːt] *vi* pendeln ♦ *vt* umwandeln; **~r** *n* Pendler *m*

compact [*adj* kəm'pækt, *n* 'kɔmpækt] *adj* kompakt ♦ *n* (*for make-up*) Puderdose *f*; ~ **disc** *n* Compact-disc *f*; ~ **disc player** *n* CD-Spieler *m*

companion [kəm'pænjən] *n* Begleiter(in) *m(f)*; **~ship** *n* Gesellschaft *f*

company ['kʌmpənɪ] *n* Gesellschaft *f*; (*COMM*) Firma *f*, Gesellschaft *f*; **to keep sb ~** jdm Gesellschaft leisten; ~ **secretary** (*BRIT*) *n* ≈ Prokurist(in) *m(f)*

comparable ['kɔmpərəbl] *adj* vergleichbar

comparative [kəm'pærətɪv] *adj* (*relative*) relativ; **~ly** *adv* verhältnismäßig

compare [kəm'pεə^r] *vt* vergleichen ♦ *vi* sich vergleichen lassen; **comparison** [kəm'pærɪsn] *n* Vergleich *m*; **in comparison (with)** im Vergleich (mit *or* zu)

compartment [kəm'pɑːtmənt] *n* (*RAIL*) Abteil *nt*; (*in drawer*) Fach *nt*

compass ['kʌmpəs] *n* Kompaß △ *m*; **~es** *npl* (*MATH etc*: *also*: **pair of ~es**) Zirkel *m*

compassion [kəm'pæʃən] *n* Mitleid *nt*;

~ate *adj* mitfühlend

compatible [kəm'pætɪbl] *adj* vereinbar; (*COMPUT*) kompatibel

compel [kəm'pel] *vt* zwingen

compensate ['kɒmpənseɪt] *vt* entschädigen ♦ *vi*: **to~ for** Ersatz leisten für; **compensation** [kɒmpən'seɪʃən] *n* Entschädigung *f*

compère ['kɒmpeəʳ] *n* Conférencier *m*

compete [kəm'piːt] *vi* (*take part*) teilnehmen; (*vie with*) konkurrieren

competent ['kɒmpɪtənt] *adj* kompetent

competition [kɒmpɪ'tɪʃən] *n* (*contest*) Wettbewerb *m*; (*COMM, rivalry*) Konkurrenz *f*; **competitive** [kəm'petɪtɪv] *adj* Konkurrenz-; (*COMM*) konkurrenzfähig; **competitor** [kəm'petɪtəʳ] *n* (*COMM*) Konkurrent(in) *m(f)*; (*participant*) Teilnehmer(in) *m(f)*

compile [kəm'paɪl] *vt* zusammenstellen

complacency [kəm'pleɪsnsɪ] *n* Selbstzufriedenheit *f*

complacent [kəm'pleɪsnt] *adj* selbstzufrieden

complain [kəm'pleɪn] *vi* sich beklagen; (*formally*) sich beschweren; **~t** *n* Klage *f*; (*formal complaint*) Beschwerde *f*; (*MED*) Leiden *nt*

complement [*n* 'kɒmplɪmənt, *vb* 'kɒmplɪmɛnt] *n* Ergänzung *f*; (*ship's crew etc*) Bemannung *f* ♦ *vt* ergänzen; **~ary** [kɒmplɪ'mentərɪ] *adj* (sich) ergänzend

complete [kəm'pliːt] *adj* (*full*) vollkommen, ganz; (*finished*) fertig ♦ *vt* vervollständigen; (*finish*) beenden; (*fill in: form*) ausfüllen; **~ly** *adv* ganz; **completion** [kəm'pliːʃən] *n* Fertigstellung *f*; (*of contract etc*) Abschluß ⚠ *m*

complex ['kɒmpleks] *adj* kompliziert

complexion [kəm'plekʃən] *n* Gesichtsfarbe *f*; (*fig*) Aspekt *m*

complexity [kəm'pleksɪtɪ] *n* Kompliziertheit *f*

compliance [kəm'plaɪəns] *n* Fügsamkeit *f*, Einwilligung *f*; **in ~ with sth** einer Sache *dat* gemäß

complicate ['kɒmplɪkeɪt] *vt* komplizieren;

~d *adj* kompliziert; **complication** [kɒmplɪ'keɪʃən] *n* Komplikation *f*

compliment [*n* 'kɒmplɪmənt, *vb* 'kɒmplɪmɛnt] *n* Kompliment *nt* ♦ *vt* ein Kompliment machen +*dat*; **~s** *npl* (*greetings*) Grüße *pl*; **to pay sb a ~** jdm ein Kompliment machen; **~ary** [kɒmplɪ'mentərɪ] *adj* schmeichelhaft; (*free*) Frei-, Gratis-

comply [kəm'plaɪ] *vi*: **to ~ with** erfüllen +*acc*; entsprechen +*dat*

component [kəm'pəunənt] *adj* Teil- ♦ *n* Bestandteil *m*

compose [kəm'pəuz] *vt* (*music*) komponieren; (*poetry*) verfassen; **to ~ o.s.** sich sammeln; **~d** *adj* gefaßt ⚠; **~r** *n* Komponist(in) *m(f)*; **composition** *n* (*MUS*) Komposition *f*; (*SCH*) Aufsatz *m*; (*structure*) Zusammensetzung *f*, Aufbau *m*

compost ['kɒmpɒst] *n* Kompost *m*

composure [kəm'pəuʒəʳ] *n* Fassung *f*

compound ['kɒmpaund] *n* (*CHEM*) Verbindung *f*; (*enclosure*) Lager *nt*; (*LING*) Kompositum *nt* ♦ *adj* zusammengesetzt; (*fracture*) kompliziert; **~ interest** *n* Zinseszins *m*

comprehend [kɒmprɪ'hend] *vt* begreifen; **comprehension** *n* Verständnis *nt*

comprehensive [kɒmprɪ'hensɪv] *adj* umfassend ♦ *n* = **comprehensive school**; **~ insurance** *n* Vollkasko *nt*; **~ school** (*BRIT*) *n* Gesamtschule *f*

compress [*vb* kəm'pres, *n* 'kɒmpres] *vt* komprimieren ♦ *n* (*MED*) Kompresse *f*

comprise [kəm'praɪz] *vt* (*also:* **be ~d of**) umfassen, bestehen aus

compromise ['kɒmprəmaɪz] *n* Kompromiß ⚠ *m* ♦ *vt* kompromittieren ♦ *vi* einen Kompromiß ⚠ schließen

compulsion [kəm'pʌlʃən] *n* Zwang *m*; **compulsive** [kəm'pʌlsɪv] *adj* zwanghaft; **compulsory** [kəm'pʌlsərɪ] *adj* obligatorisch

computer [kəm'pjuːtəʳ] *n* Computer *m*, Rechner *m*; **~ game** *n* Computerspiel *nt*; **~-generated** *adj* computergeneriert; **~ize** *vt* (*information*) computerisieren; (*company, accounts*) auf Computer umstellen; **~ programmer** *n* Programmierer(in) *m(f)*; **~**

⚠ *For information on spelling reform see page 615*

programming n Programmieren nt; ~
science n Informatik f; **computing**
[kəm'pju:tɪŋ] n (science) Informatik f; (work)
Computerei f
comrade ['kɔmrɪd] n Kamerad m; (POL)
Genosse m
con [kɔn] vt hereinlegen ♦ n Schwindel nt
concave ['kɔnkeɪv] adj konkav
conceal [kən'si:l] vt (secret) verschweigen;
(hide) verbergen
concede [kən'si:d] vt (grant) gewähren;
(point) zugeben ♦ vi (admit defeat)
nachgeben
conceit [kən'si:t] n Einbildung f; ~ed adj
eingebildet
conceivable [kən'si:vəbl] adj vorstellbar
conceive [kən'si:v] vt (idea) ausdenken;
(imagine) sich vorstellen; (baby) empfangen
♦ vi empfangen
concentrate ['kɔnsəntreɪt] vi sich
konzentrieren ♦ vt konzentrieren; **to ~ on
sth** sich auf etw acc konzentrieren;
concentration [kɔnsən'treɪʃən] n
Konzentration f; **concentration camp** n
Konzentrationslager nt, KZ nt
concept ['kɔnsept] n Begriff m
conception [kən'sepʃən] n (idea)
Vorstellung f; (BIOL) Empfängnis f
concern [kən'sɜ:n] n (affair) Angelegenheit
f; (COMM) Unternehmen nt; (worry) Sorge f
♦ vt (interest) angehen; (be about) handeln
von; (have connection with) betreffen; **to be
~ed (about)** sich Sorgen machen (um);
~ing prep hinsichtlich +gen
concert ['kɔnsət] n Konzert nt
concerted [kən'sɜ:tɪd] adj gemeinsam
concert hall n Konzerthalle f
concertina [kɔnsə'ti:nə] n Handharmonika f
concerto [kən'tʃɜ:təu] n Konzert nt
concession [kən'seʃən] n (yielding)
Zugeständnis nt; **tax ~** Steuerkonzession f
conciliation [kənsɪlɪ'eɪʃən] n Versöhnung f;
(official) Schlichtung f
concise [kən'saɪs] adj präzis
conclude [kən'klu:d] vt (end) beenden;
(treaty) (ab)schließen; (decide) schließen,
folgern; **conclusion** [kən'klu:ʒən] n

(Ab)schluß △ m; (deduction) Schluß △ m;
conclusive [kən'klu:sɪv] adj schlüssig
concoct [kən'kɔkt] vt zusammenbrauen;
~ion [kən'kɔkʃən] n Gebräu nt
concourse ['kɔŋkɔ:s] n (Bahnhofs)halle f,
Vorplatz m
concrete ['kɔŋkri:t] n Beton m ♦ adj konkret
concur [kən'kɜ:] vi übereinstimmen
concurrently [kən'kʌrntlɪ] adv gleichzeitig
concussion [kən'kʌʃən] n
(Gehirn)erschütterung f
condemn [kən'dem] vt (JUR) verurteilen;
(building) abbruchreif erklären
condensation [kɔnden'seɪʃən] n
Kondensation f
condense [kən'dens] vi (CHEM)
kondensieren ♦ vt (fig) zusammendrängen;
~d milk n Kondensmilch f
condescending [kɔndɪ'sendɪŋ] adj
herablassend
condition [kən'dɪʃən] n (state) Zustand m;
(presupposition) Bedingung f ♦ vt (hair etc)
behandeln; (accustom) gewöhnen; **~s** npl
(circumstances) Verhältnisse pl; **on ~ that ...**
unter der Bedingung, daß ...; **~al** adj
bedingt; **~er** n (for hair) Spülung f; (for
fabrics) Weichspüler m
condolences [kən'dəulənsɪz] npl Beileid nt
condom [kən'dəm] n Kondom nt or m
condominium [kɔndə'mɪnɪəm] (US) n
Eigentumswohnung f; (block)
Eigentumsblock m
condone [kən'dəun] vt gutheißen
conducive [kən'dju:sɪv] adj: **~ to** dienlich
+dat
conduct [n 'kɔndʌkt, vb kən'dʌkt] n
(behaviour) Verhalten nt; (management)
Führung f ♦ vt führen; (MUS) dirigieren;
~ed tour n Führung f; **~or** [kən'dʌktər] n
(of orchestra) Dirigent m; (in bus, US: on
train) Schaffner m; (ELEC) Leiter m; **~ress**
[kən'dʌktrɪs] n (in bus) Schaffnerin f
cone [kəun] n (MATH) Kegel m; (for ice cream)
(Waffel)tüte f; (BOT) Tannenzapfen m
confectioner's (shop) [kən'fekʃənəz-] n
Konditorei f
confectionery [kən'fekʃənrɪ] n Süßigkeiten

pl

confer [kən'fɜːʳ] vt (degree) verleihen ♦ vi (discuss) konferieren, verhandeln; **~ence** ['kɒnfərəns] n Konferenz f

confess [kən'fes] vt, vi gestehen; (ECCL) beichten; **~ion** [kən'feʃən] n Geständnis nt; (ECCL) Beichte f; **~ional** n Beichtstuhl m

confide [kən'faɪd] vi: **to ~ in** (sich) anvertrauen +dat

confidence ['kɒnfɪdns] n Vertrauen nt; (assurance) Selbstvertrauen nt; (secret) Geheimnis nt; **in ~** (speak, write) vertraulich; **~ trick** n Schwindel m

confident ['kɒnfɪdənt] adj (sure) überzeugt; (self-assured) selbstsicher

confidential [kɒnfɪ'denʃəl] adj vertraulich

confine [kən'faɪn] vt (limit) beschränken; (lock up) einsperren; **~d** adj (space) eng; **~ment** n (in prison) Haft f; (MED) Wochenbett nt; **~s** ['kɒnfaɪnz] npl Grenzen pl

confirm [kən'fɜːm] vt bestätigen; **~ation** [kɒnfə'meɪʃən] n Bestätigung f; (REL) Konfirmation f; **~ed** adj unverbesserlich; (bachelor) eingefleischt

confiscate ['kɒnfɪskeɪt] vt beschlagnahmen

conflict [n 'kɒnflɪkt, vb kən'flɪkt] n Konflikt m ♦ vi im Widerspruch stehen; **~ing** [kən'flɪktɪŋ] adj widersprüchlich

conform [kən'fɔːm] vi: **to ~ (to)** (things) entsprechen +dat; (people) sich anpassen +dat; (to rules) sich richten (nach)

confound [kən'faʊnd] vt verblüffen; (confuse) durcheinanderbringen ⚠

confront [kən'frʌnt] vt (enemy) entgegentreten +dat; (problems) sich stellen +dat; **to ~ sb with sth** jdn mit etw konfrontieren; **~ation** [kɒnfrən'teɪʃən] n Konfrontation f

confuse [kən'fjuːz] vt verwirren; (sth with sth) verwechseln; **~d** adj verwirrt; **confusing** adj verwirrend; **confusion** [kən'fjuːʒən] n (perplexity) Verwirrung f; (mixing up) Verwechslung f; (tumult) Aufruhr m

congeal [kən'dʒiːl] vi (clot) gerinnen

congenial [kən'dʒiːnɪəl] adj angenehm

congested [kən'dʒestɪd] adj überfüllt

congestion [kən'dʒestʃən] n Stau m

conglomerate [kən'glɒmərɪt] n (COMM, GEOL) Konglomerat nt

conglomeration [kənglɒmə'reɪʃən] n Anhäufung f

congratulate [kən'grætjuleɪt] vt: **to ~ sb (on sth)** jdn (zu etw) beglückwünschen; **congratulations** [kəngrætju'leɪʃənz] npl Glückwünsche pl; **congratulations!** gratuliere!, herzlichen Glückwunsch!

congregate ['kɒŋgrɪgeɪt] vi sich versammeln; **congregation** [kɒŋgrɪ'geɪʃən] n Gemeinde f

congress ['kɒŋgres] n Kongreß ⚠ m; **C~man** (irreg: US) n Mitglied nt des amerikanischen Repräsentantenhauses

conifer ['kɒnɪfəʳ] n Nadelbaum m

conjunction [kən'dʒʌŋkʃən] n Verbindung f; (GRAM) Konjunktion f

conjunctivitis [kəndʒʌŋktɪ'vaɪtɪs] n Bindehautentzündung f

conjure ['kʌndʒəʳ] vi zaubern; **~ up** vt heraufbeschwören; **~r** n Zauberkünstler(in) m(f)

conk out [kɒŋk-] (inf) vi den Geist aufgeben

con man (irreg) n Schwindler m

connect [kə'nekt] vt verbinden; (ELEC) anschließen; **to be ~ed with** ein Beziehung haben zu; (be related to) verwandt sein mit; **~ion** [kə'nekʃən] n Verbindung f; (relation) Zusammenhang m; (ELEC, TEL, RAIL) Anschluß ⚠ m

connive [kə'naɪv] vi: **to ~ at** stillschweigend dulden

connoisseur [kɒnɪ'sɜːʳ] n Kenner m

conquer ['kɒŋkəʳ] vt (feelings) überwinden; (enemy) besiegen; (country) erobern; **~or** n Eroberer m

conquest ['kɒŋkwest] n Eroberung f

cons [kɒnz] npl see **convenience**; **pro**

conscience ['kɒnʃəns] n Gewissen nt

conscientious [kɒnʃɪ'enʃəs] adj gewissenhaft

conscious ['kɒnʃəs] adj bewußt ⚠; (MED) bei Bewußtsein ⚠; **~ness** n Bewußtsein ⚠ nt

⚠ *For information on spelling reform see page 615*

conscript ['kɔnskrɪpt] *n* Wehrpflichtige(r) *m*; **~ion** [kən'skrɪpʃən] *n* Wehrpflicht *f*

consecutive [kən'sekjutɪv] *adj* aufeinanderfolgend △

consensus [kən'sensəs] *n* allgemeine Übereinstimmung *f*

consent [kən'sent] *n* Zustimmung *f* ♦ *vi* zustimmen

consequence ['kɔnsɪkwəns] *n* (*importance*) Bedeutung *f*; (*effect*) Folge *f*

consequently ['kɔnsɪkwəntlɪ] *adv* folglich

conservation [kɔnsə'veɪʃən] *n* Erhaltung *f*; (*nature* ~) Umweltschutz *m*

conservative [kən'sə:vətɪv] *adj* konservativ; **C~** (*BRIT*) *adj* konservativ ♦ *n* Konservative(r) *mf*

conservatory [kən'sə:vətrɪ] *n* (*room*) Wintergarten *m*

conserve [kən'sə:v] *vt* erhalten

consider [kən'sɪdər] *vt* überlegen; (*take into account*) in Betracht ziehen; (*regard as*) halten für; **to ~ doing sth** daran denken, etw zu tun; **~able** [kən'sɪdərəbl] *adj* beträchtlich; **~ably** *adv* beträchtlich; **~ate** [kən'sɪdərɪt] *adj* rücksichtsvoll; **~ation** [kənsɪdə'reɪʃən] *n* Rücksicht(nahme) *f*; (*thought*) Erwägung *f*; **~ing** [kən'sɪdərɪŋ] *prep* in Anbetracht +gen

consign [kən'saɪn] *vt* übergeben; **~ment** *n* Sendung *f*

consist [kən'sɪst] *vi*: **to ~ of** bestehen aus

consistency [kən'sɪstənsɪ] *n* (*of material*) Konsistenz *f*; (*of argument, person*) Konsequenz *f*

consistent [kən'sɪstənt] *adj* (*person*) konsequent; (*argument*) folgerichtig

consolation [kɔnsə'leɪʃən] *n* Trost *m*

console[1] [kən'səul] *vt* trösten

console[2] ['kɔnsəul] *n* Kontrollpult *nt*

consolidate [kən'sɔlɪdeɪt] *vt* festigen

consommé [kən'sɔmeɪ] *n* Fleischbrühe *f*

consonant ['kɔnsənənt] *n* Konsonant *m*, Mitlaut *m*

conspicuous [kən'spɪkjuəs] *adj* (*prominent*) auffällig; (*visible*) deutlich sichtbar

conspiracy [kən'spɪrəsɪ] *n* Verschwörung *f*

conspire [kən'spaɪər] *vi* sich verschwören

constable ['kʌnstəbl] (*BRIT*) *n* Polizist(in) *m(f)*; **chief ~** Polizeipräsident *m*;

constabulary [kən'stæbjulərɪ] *n* Polizei *f*

constant ['kɔnstənt] *adj* (*continuous*) ständig; (*unchanging*) konstant; **~ly** *adv* ständig

constellation [kɔnstə'leɪʃən] *n* Sternbild *nt*

consternation [kɔnstə'neɪʃən] *n* Bestürzung *f*

constipated ['kɔnstɪpeɪtɪd] *adj* verstopft; **constipation** [kɔnstɪ'peɪʃən] *n* Verstopfung *f*

constituency [kən'stɪtjuənsɪ] *n* Wahlkreis *m*

constituent [kən'stɪtjuənt] *n* (*person*) Wähler *m*; (*part*) Bestandteil *m*

constitute ['kɔnstɪtju:t] *vt* (*make up*) bilden; (*amount to*) darstellen

constitution [kɔnstɪ'tju:ʃən] *n* Verfassung *f*; **~al** *adj* Verfassungs-

constraint [kən'streɪnt] *n* Zwang *m*; (*shyness*) Befangenheit *f*

construct [kən'strʌkt] *vt* bauen; **~ion** [kən'strʌkʃən] *n* Konstruktion *f*; (*building*) Bau *m*; **~ive** *adj* konstruktiv

construe [kən'stru:] *vt* deuten

consul ['kɔnsl] *n* Konsul *m*; **~ate** *n* Konsulat *nt*

consult [kən'sʌlt] *vt* um Rat fragen; (*doctor*) konsultieren; (*book*) nachschlagen in +dat; **~ant** *n* (*MED*) Facharzt *m*; (*other specialist*) Gutachter *m*; **~ation** [kɔnsəl'teɪʃən] *n* Beratung *f*; (*MED*) Konsultation *f*; **~ing room** *n* Sprechzimmer *nt*

consume [kən'sju:m] *vt* verbrauchen; (*food*) konsumieren; **~r** *n* Verbraucher *m*; **~r goods** *npl* Konsumgüter *pl*; **~rism** *n* Konsum *m*; **~r society** *n* Konsumgesellschaft *f*

consummate ['kɔnsʌmeɪt] *vt* (*marriage*) vollziehen

consumption [kən'sʌmpʃən] *n* Verbrauch *m*; (*of food*) Konsum *m*

cont. *abbr* (= *continued*) Forts.

contact ['kɔntækt] *n* (*touch*) Berührung *f*; (*connection*) Verbindung *f*; (*person*) Kontakt *m* ♦ *vt* sich in Verbindung setzen mit; **~ lenses** *npl* Kontaktlinsen *pl*

△ *Informationen zur Rechtschreibreform Seite 615*

contagious [kənˈteɪdʒəs] adj ansteckend

contain [kənˈteɪn] vt enthalten; **to ~ o.s.** sich zügeln; **~er** n Behälter m; (transport) Container m

contaminate [kənˈtæmɪneɪt] vt verunreinigen

cont'd abbr (= continued) Forts.

contemplate [ˈkɒntəmpleɪt] vt (look at) (nachdenklich) betrachten; (think about) überdenken; (plan) vorhaben

contemporary [kənˈtempərərɪ] adj zeitgenössisch ♦ n Zeitgenosse m

contempt [kənˈtempt] n Verachtung f; **~ of court** (JUR) Mißachtung △ f des Gerichts; **~ible** adj verachtenswert; **~uous** adj verächtlich

contend [kənˈtend] vt (argue) behaupten ♦ vi kämpfen; **~er** n (for post) Bewerber(in) m(f); (SPORT) Wettkämpfer(in) m(f)

content [adj, vb kənˈtent, n ˈkɒntent] adj zufrieden ♦ vt befriedigen ♦ n (also: **~s**) Inhalt m; **~ed** adj zufrieden

contention [kənˈtenʃən] n (dispute) Streit m; (argument) Behauptung f

contentment [kənˈtentmənt] n Zufriedenheit f

contest [n ˈkɒntest, vb kənˈtest] n (Wett)kampf m ♦ vt (dispute) bestreiten; (JUR) anfechten; (POL) kandidieren in +dat; **~ant** [kənˈtestənt] n Bewerber(in) m(f)

context [ˈkɒntekst] n Zusammenhang m

continent [ˈkɒntɪnənt] n Kontinent m; **the C~** (BRIT) das europäische Festland; **~al** [kɒntɪˈnentl] adj kontinental; **~al breakfast** n kleines Frühstück nt; **~al quilt** (BRIT) n Federbett nt

contingency [kənˈtɪndʒənsɪ] n Möglichkeit f

contingent [kənˈtɪndʒənt] n Kontingent nt

continual [kənˈtɪnjʊəl] adj (endless) fortwährend; (repeated) immer wiederkehrend; **~ly** adv immer wieder

continuation [kəntɪnjʊˈeɪʃən] n Fortsetzung f

continue [kənˈtɪnjuː] vi (person) weitermachen; (thing) weitergehen ♦ vt fortsetzen

continuity [kɒntɪˈnjuːɪtɪ] n Kontinuität f

continuous [kənˈtɪnjuəs] adj ununterbrochen; **~ stationery** n Endlospapier nt

contort [kənˈtɔːt] vt verdrehen; **~ion** [kənˈtɔːʃən] n Verzerrung f

contour [ˈkɒntuəʳ] n Umriß △ m; (also: **~ line**) Höhenlinie f

contraband [ˈkɒntrəbænd] n Schmuggelware f

contraception [kɒntrəˈsepʃən] n Empfängnisverhütung f

contraceptive [kɒntrəˈseptɪv] n empfängnisverhütende(s) Mittel nt ♦ adj empfängnisverhütend

contract [n ˈkɒntrækt, vb kənˈtrækt] n Vertrag m ♦ vi (muscle, metal) sich zusammenziehen ♦ vt zusammenziehen; **to ~ to do sth** (COMM) sich vertraglich verpflichten, etw zu tun; **~ion** [kənˈtrækʃən] n (shortening) Verkürzung f; **~or** [kənˈtræktəʳ] n Unternehmer m

contradict [kɒntrəˈdɪkt] vt widersprechen +dat; **~ion** [kɒntrəˈdɪkʃən] n Widerspruch m

contraflow [ˈkɒntrəfləʊ] n (AUT) Gegenverkehr m

contraption [kənˈtræpʃən] n (inf) Apparat m

contrary¹ [ˈkɒntrərɪ] adj (opposite) entgegengesetzt ♦ n Gegenteil nt; **on the ~** im Gegenteil

contrary² [kənˈtreərɪ] adj (obstinate) widerspenstig

contrast [n ˈkɒntrɑːst, vb kənˈtrɑːst] n Kontrast m ♦ vt entgegensetzen; **~ing** [kənˈtrɑːstɪŋ] adj Kontrast-

contravene [kɒntrəˈviːn] vt verstoßen gegen

contribute [kənˈtrɪbjuːt] vt, vi: **to ~ to** beitragen zu; **contribution** [kɒntrɪˈbjuːʃən] n Beitrag m; **contributor** [kənˈtrɪbjuːtəʳ] n Beitragende(r) f(m)

contrive [kənˈtraɪv] vt ersinnen ♦ vi: **to ~ to do sth** es schaffen, etw zu tun

control [kənˈtrəʊl] vt (direct, test) kontrollieren ♦ n Kontrolle f; **~s** npl (of vehicle) Steuerung f; (of engine) Schalttafel f; **to be in ~ of** (business, office) leiten; (group *of children*) beaufsichtigen; **out of ~** außer Kontrolle; **under ~** unter Kontrolle; **~led substance** *n* verschreibungspflichtiges Medikament; **~ panel** *n* Schalttafel *f*; **~ room** *n* Kontrollraum *m*; **~ tower** *n* (*AVIAT*) Kontrollturm *m*

controversial [kɒntrə'vɜːʃl] *adj* umstritten; **controversy** ['kɒntrəvɜːsɪ] *n* Kontroverse *f*

conurbation [kɒnə'beɪʃən] *n* Ballungsgebiet *nt*

convalesce [kɒnvə'les] *vi* genesen; **~nce** [kɒnvə'lesns] *n* Genesung *f*

convector [kən'vektəʳ] *n* Heizlüfter *m*

convene [kən'viːn] *vt* zusammenrufen ♦ *vi* sich versammeln

convenience [kən'viːnɪəns] *n* Annehmlichkeit *f*; **all modern ~s** or (*BRIT*) **cons** mit allem Komfort; **at your ~** wann es Ihnen paßt

convenient [kən'viːnɪənt] *adj* günstig

convent ['kɒnvənt] *n* Kloster *nt*

convention [kən'venʃən] *n* Versammlung *f*; (*custom*) Konvention *f*; **~al** *adj* konventionell

convent school *n* Klosterschule *f*

converge [kən'vɜːdʒ] *vi* zusammenlaufen

conversant [kən'vɜːsnt] *adj*: **to be ~ with** bewandert sein in +*dat*

conversation [kɒnvə'seɪʃən] *n* Gespräch *nt*; **~al** *adj* Unterhaltungs-

converse [*n* 'kɒnvɜːs, *vb* kən'vɜːs] *n* Gegenteil *nt* ♦ *vi* sich unterhalten

conversion [kən'vɜːʃən] *n* Umwandlung *f*; (*REL*) Bekehrung *f*

convert [*vb* kən'vɜːt, *n* 'kɒnvɜːt] *vt* (*change*) umwandeln; (*REL*) bekehren ♦ *n* Bekehrte(r) *mf*; Konvertit(in) *m(f)*; **~ible** *n* (*AUT*) Kabriolett *nt* ♦ *adj* umwandelbar; (*FIN*) konvertierbar

convex ['kɒnveks] *adj* konvex

convey [kən'veɪ] *vt* (*carry*) befördern; (*feelings*) vermitteln; **~or belt** *n* Fließband *nt*

convict [*vb* kən'vɪkt, *n* 'kɒnvɪkt] *vt* verurteilen ♦ *n* Häftling *m*; **~ion** [kən'vɪkʃən] *n* (*verdict*) Verurteilung *f*; (*belief*) Überzeugung *f*

convince [kən'vɪns] *vt* überzeugen; **~d** *adj*: **~d that** überzeugt davon, daß; **convincing** *adj* überzeugend

convoluted ['kɒnvəluːtɪd] *adj* verwickelt; (*style*) gewunden

convoy ['kɒnvɔɪ] *n* (*of vehicles*) Kolonne *f*; (*protected*) Konvoi *m*

convulse [kən'vʌls] *vt* zusammenzucken lassen; **to be ~d with laughter** sich vor Lachen krümmen; **convulsion** [kən'vʌlʃən] *n* (*esp MED*) Zuckung *f*, Krampf *m*

coo [kuː] *vi* gurren

cook [kuk] *vt*, *vi* kochen ♦ *n* Koch *m*, Köchin *f*; **~ book** *n* Kochbuch *nt*; **~er** *n* Herd *m*; **~ery** *n* Kochkunst *f*; **~ery book** (*BRIT*) *n* = **cook book**; **~ie** (*US*) *n* Plätzchen *nt*; **~ing** *n* Kochen *nt*

cool [kuːl] *adj* kühl ♦ *vt*, *vi* (ab)kühlen; **~ down** *vt*, *vi* (*fig*) (sich) beruhigen; **~ness** *n* Kühle *f*; (*of temperament*) kühle(r) Kopf *m*

coop [kuːp] *n* Hühnerstall *m* ♦ *vt*: **~ up** (*fig*) einpferchen

cooperate [kəu'ɒpəreɪt] *vi* zusammenarbeiten; **cooperation** [kəuɒpə'reɪʃən] *n* Zusammenarbeit *f*

cooperative [kəu'ɒpərətɪv] *adj* hilfsbereit; (*COMM*) genossenschaftlich ♦ *n* (*of farmers*) Genossenschaft *f*; (*~ store*) Konsumladen *m*

coordinate [*v* kəu'ɔːdɪneɪt, *n* kəu'ɔːdɪnət] *vt* koordinieren ♦ *n* (*MATH*) Koordinate *f*; **~s** *npl* (*clothes*) Kombinationen *pl*; **coordination** [kəuɔːdɪ'neɪʃən] *n* Koordination *f*

cop [kɒp] (*inf*) *n* Polyp *m*, Bulle *m*

cope [kəup] *vi*: **to ~ with** fertig werden mit

copious ['kəupɪəs] *adj* reichhaltig

copper ['kɒpəʳ] *n* (*metal*) Kupfer *nt*; (*inf: policeman*) Polyp *m*, Bulle *m*; **~s** *npl* (*money*) Kleingeld *nt*

copse [kɒps] *n* Unterholz *nt*

copy ['kɒpɪ] *n* (*imitation*) Kopie *f*; (*of book etc*) Exemplar *nt*; (*of newspaper*) Nummer *f* ♦ *vt* kopieren, abschreiben; **~right** *n* Copyright *nt*

coral ['kɒrəl] *n* Koralle *f*; **~ reef** *n* Korallenriff *nt*

cord [kɔːd] *n* Schnur *f*; (*ELEC*) Kabel *nt*

⚠ *Informationen zur Rechtschreibreform Seite 615*

cordial ['kɔ:dɪəl] *adj* herzlich ♦ *n* Fruchtsaft *m*

cordon ['kɔ:dn] *n* Absperrkette *f*; ~ **off** *vt* abriegeln

corduroy ['kɔ:dərɔɪ] *n* Kord(samt) *m*

core [kɔ:*] *n* Kern *m* ♦ *vt* entkernen

cork [kɔ:k] *n* (*bark*) Korkrinde *f*; (*stopper*) Korken *m*; **~screw** *n* Korkenzieher *m*

corn [kɔ:n] *n* (*BRIT: wheat*) Getreide *nt*, Korn *nt*; (*US: maize*) Mais *m*; (*on foot*) Hühnerauge *nt*; ~ **on the cob** Maiskolben *m*

corned beef ['kɔ:nd-] *n* Corned Beef *nt*

corner ['kɔ:nə*] *n* Ecke *f*; (*on road*) Kurve *f* ♦ *vt* in die Enge treiben; (*market*) monopolisieren ♦ *vi* (*AUT*) in die Kurve gehen; **~stone** *n* Eckstein *m*

cornet ['kɔ:nɪt] *n* (*MUS*) Kornett *nt*; (*BRIT: of ice cream*) Eistüte *f*

corn: **~flakes** ['kɔ:nfleɪks] *npl* Cornflakes *pl* ℝ; **~flour** ['kɔ:nflauə*] (*BRIT*) *n* Maizena *nt* ℝ; **~starch** ['kɔ:nstɑ:tʃ] (*US*) *n* Maizena *nt* ℝ

corny ['kɔ:nɪ] *adj* (*joke*) blöd(e)

coronary ['kɔrənərɪ] *n* (*also:* ~ **thrombosis**) Herzinfarkt *m*

coronation [kɔrə'neɪʃən] *n* Krönung *f*

coroner ['kɔrənə*] *n* Untersuchungsrichter *m*

corporal ['kɔ:pərl] *n* Obergefreite(r) *m* ♦ *adj*: ~ **punishment** Prügelstrafe *f*

corporate ['kɔ:pərɪt] *adj* gemeinschaftlich, korporativ

corporation [kɔ:pə'reɪʃən] *n* (*of town*) Gemeinde *f*; (*COMM*) Körperschaft *f*, Aktiengesellschaft *f*

corps [kɔ:*] (*pl* ~) *n* (Armee)korps *nt*

corpse [kɔ:ps] *n* Leiche *f*

corral [kə'rɑ:l] *n* Pferch *m*, Korral *m*

correct [kə'rɛkt] *adj* (*accurate*) richtig; (*proper*) korrekt ♦ *vt* korrigieren; **~ion** [kə'rɛkʃən] *n* Berichtigung *f*

correlation [kɔrɪ'leɪʃən] *n* Wechselbeziehung *f*

correspond [kɔrɪs'pɔnd] *vi* (*agree*) übereinstimmen; (*exchange letters*) korrespondieren; **~ence** *n* (*similarity*) Entsprechung *f*; (*letters*) Briefwechsel *m*,

Korrespondenz *f*; **~ence course** *n* Fernkurs *m*; **~ent** *n* (*PRESS*) Berichterstatter *m*

corridor ['kɔrɪdɔ:*] *n* Gang *m*

corroborate [kə'rɔbəreɪt] *vt* bestätigen

corrode [kə'rəud] *vt* zerfressen ♦ *vi* rosten

corrosion [kə'rəuʒən] *n* Korrosion *f*

corrugated ['kɔrəgeɪtɪd] *adj* gewellt; ~ **iron** *n* Wellblech *nt*

corrupt [kə'rʌpt] *adj* korrupt ♦ *vt* verderben; (*bribe*) bestechen; **~ion** [kə'rʌpʃən] *n* Verdorbenheit *f*; (*bribery*) Bestechung *f*

corset ['kɔ:sɪt] *n* Korsett *nt*

Corsica ['kɔ:sɪkə] *n* Korsika *nt*

cosmetics [kɔz'mɛtɪks] *npl* Kosmetika *pl*

cosmic ['kɔzmɪk] *adj* kosmisch

cosmonaut ['kɔzmənɔ:t] *n* Kosmonaut(in) *m(f)*

cosmopolitan [kɔzmə'pɔlɪtn] *adj* international; (*city*) Welt-

cosmos ['kɔzmɔs] *n* Kosmos *m*

cost [kɔst] (*pt, pp* **cost**) *n* Kosten *pl*, Preis *m* ♦ *vt, vi* kosten; **~s** *npl* (*JUR*) Kosten *pl*; **how much does it** ~? wieviel kostet das?; **at all** ~**s** um jeden Preis

co-star ['kəustɑ:*] *n* zweite(r) *or* weitere(r) Hauptdarsteller(in) *m(f)*

cost: **~-effective** *adj* rentabel; **~ly** ['kɔstlɪ] *adj* kostspielig; **~-of-living** ['kɔstəv'lɪvɪŋ] *adj* (*index*) Lebenshaltungskosten-; ~ **price** (*BRIT*) *n* Selbstkostenpreis *m*

costume ['kɔstju:m] *n* Kostüm *nt*; (*fancy dress*) Maskenkostüm *nt*; (*BRIT: also:* **swimming ~**) Badeanzug *m*; ~ **jewellery** *n* Modeschmuck *m*

cosy ['kəuzɪ] (*BRIT*) *adj* behaglich; (*atmosphere*) gemütlich

cot [kɔt] *n* (*BRIT: child's*) Kinderbett(chen) *nt*; (*US: camp bed*) Feldbett *nt*

cottage ['kɔtɪdʒ] *n* kleine(s) Haus *nt*; ~ **cheese** *n* Hüttenkäse *m*; ~ **industry** *n* Heimindustrie *f*; ~ **pie** *n* Auflauf mit Hackfleisch und Kartoffelbrei

cotton ['kɔtn] *n* Baumwolle *f*; (*thread*) Garn *nt*; ~ **on to** (*inf*) *vt* kapieren; ~ **candy** (*US*) *n* Zuckerwatte *f*; ~ **wool** (*BRIT*) *n* Watte *f*

couch [kautʃ] *n* Couch *f*

⚠ *For information on spelling reform see page 615*

couchette [kuːˈʃet] n (on train, boat) Liegewagenplatz m

cough [kɒf] vi husten ♦ n Husten m; ~ **drop** n Hustenbonbon nt

could [kʊd] pt of **can**²

couldn't [ˈkʊdnt] = **could not**

council [ˈkaʊnsl] n (of town) Stadtrat m; ~ **estate** (BRIT) n Siedlung f des sozialen Wohnungsbaus; ~ **house** (BRIT) n Haus nt des sozialen Wohnungsbaus; ~**lor** [ˈkaʊnslər] n Stadtrat m/-rätin f

counsel [ˈkaʊnsl] n (barrister) Anwalt m; (advice) Rat(schlag) m ♦ vt beraten; ~**lor** [ˈkaʊnslər] n Berater m

count [kaʊnt] vt, vi zählen ♦ n (reckoning) Abrechnung f; (nobleman) Graf m; ~ **on** vt zählen auf +acc

countenance [ˈkaʊntɪnəns] n (old) Antlitz nt ♦ vt (tolerate) gutheißen

counter [ˈkaʊntər] n (in shop) Ladentisch m; (in café) Theke f; (in bank, post office) Schalter m ♦ vt entgegnen

counteract [ˈkaʊntərˈækt] vt entgegenwirken +dat

counterfeit [ˈkaʊntəfɪt] n Fälschung f ♦ vt fälschen ♦ adj gefälscht

counterfoil [ˈkaʊntəfɔɪl] n (Kontroll)abschnitt m

counterpart [ˈkaʊntəpaːt] n (object) Gegenstück nt; (person) Gegenüber nt

counterproductive [ˈkaʊntəprəˈdʌktɪv] adj destruktiv

countersign [ˈkaʊntəsaɪn] vt gegenzeichnen

countess [ˈkaʊntɪs] n Gräfin f

countless [ˈkaʊntlɪs] adj zahllos, unzählig

country [ˈkʌntrɪ] n Land nt; ~ **dancing** (BRIT) n Volkstanz m; ~ **house** n Landhaus nt; ~**man** (irreg) n (national) Landsmann m; (rural) Bauer m; ~**side** n Landschaft f

county [ˈkaʊntɪ] n Landkreis m; (BRIT) Grafschaft f

coup [kuː] (pl ~**s**) n Coup m; (also: ~ **d'état**) Staatsstreich m, Putsch m

couple [ˈkʌpl] n Paar nt ♦ vt koppeln; **a ~ of** ein paar

coupon [ˈkuːpɒn] n Gutschein m

coups [kuː] npl of **coup**

courage [ˈkʌrɪdʒ] n Mut m; ~**ous** [kəˈreɪdʒəs] adj mutig

courgette [kuəˈʒet] (BRIT) n Zucchini f

courier [ˈkʊrɪər] n (for holiday) Reiseleiter m; (messenger) Kurier m

course [kɔːs] n (race) Bahn f; (of stream) Lauf m; (golf ~) Platz m; (NAUT, SCH) Kurs m; (in meal) Gang m; **of** ~ natürlich

court [kɔːt] n (royal) Hof m; (JUR) Gericht nt ♦ vt (woman) gehen mit; (danger) herausfordern; **to take to** ~ vor Gericht bringen

courteous [ˈkəːtɪəs] adj höflich

courtesy [ˈkəːtəsɪ] n Höflichkeit f

courtesy bus, courtesy coach n gebührenfreier Bus m

court: ~ **house** (US) n Gerichtsgebäude nt; ~**ier** [ˈkɔːtɪər] n Höfling m; ~ **martial** [ˈkɔːtˈmaːʃəl] (pl ~**s martial**) n Kriegsgericht nt ♦ vt vor ein Kriegsgericht stellen; ~**room** n Gerichtssaal m; ~**s martial** npl of **court martial**; ~**yard** [ˈkɔːtjaːd] n Hof m

cousin [ˈkʌzn] n Cousin m, Vetter m; Kusine f

cove [kəʊv] n kleine Bucht f

covenant [ˈkʌvənənt] n (ECCL) Bund m; (JUR) Verpflichtung f

cover [ˈkʌvər] vt (spread over) bedecken; (shield) abschirmen; (include) sich erstrecken über +acc; (protect) decken; (distance) zurücklegen; (report on) berichten über +acc ♦ n (lid) Deckel m; (for bed) Decke f; (MIL) Bedeckung f; (of book) Einband m; (of magazine) Umschlag m; (insurance) Versicherung f; **to take** ~ (from rain) sich unterstellen; (MIL) in Deckung gehen; **under** ~ (indoors) drinnen; **under** ~ **of** im Schutze +gen; **under separate** ~ (COMM) mit getrennter Post; **to ~ up for sb** jdn decken; ~**age** n (PRESS: reports) Berichterstattung f; (distribution) Verbreitung f; ~ **charge** n Bedienungsgeld nt; ~**ing** n Bedeckung f; ~**ing letter**, ~ **letter** (US) n Begleitbrief m; ~ **note** n (INSURANCE) vorläufige(r) Versicherungsschein m

covert ['kʌvət] *adj* geheim

cover-up ['kʌvərʌp] *n* Vertuschung *f*

cow [kau] *n* Kuh *f* ♦ *vt* einschüchtern

coward ['kauəd] *n* Feigling *m*; **~ice**
['kauədɪs] *n* Feigheit *f*; **~ly** *adj* feige

cower ['kauə'] *vi* kauern

coy [kɔɪ] *adj* schüchtern

coyote [kɔɪ'əutɪ] *n* Präriewolf *m*

cozy ['kəuzɪ] (*US*) *adj* = **cosy**

CPA (*US*) *n abbr* = **certified public
accountant**

crab [kræb] *n* Krebs *m*

crab apple *n* Holzapfel *m*

crack [kræk] *n* Riß △ *m*, Sprung *m*; (*noise*)
Knall *m*; (*drug*) Crack *nt* ♦ *vt* (*break*)
springen lassen; (*joke*) reißen; (*nut, safe*)
knacken; (*whip*) knallen lassen ♦ *vi* springen
♦ *adj* erstklassig; (*troops*) Elite-; **~ down** *vi*:
to ~ down (on) hart durchgreifen (bei); **~
up** *vi* (*fig*) zusammenbrechen

cracked [krækt] *adj* (*glass, plate, ice*)
gesprungen; (*rib, bone*) gebrochen,
angeknackst (*umg*); (*broken*) gebrochen;
(*surface, walls*) rissig; (*inf: mad*)
übergeschnappt

cracker ['krækə'] *n* (*firework*) Knallkörper *m*,
Kracher *m*; (*biscuit*) Keks *m*; (*Christmas ~*)
Knallbonbon *nt*

crackle ['krækl] *vi* knistern; (*fire*) prasseln

cradle ['kreɪdl] *n* Wiege *f*

craft [krɑːft] *n* (*skill*) (Hand- *or*
Kunst)fertigkeit *f*; (*trade*) Handwerk *nt*;
(*NAUT*) Schiff *nt*; **~sman** *n* (*irreg*) *m*
Handwerker *m*; **~smanship** *n* (*quality*)
handwerkliche Ausführung *f*; (*ability*)
handwerkliche(s) Können *nt*

crafty ['krɑːftɪ] *adj* schlau

crag [kræg] *n* Klippe *f*

cram [kræm] *vt* vollstopfen △ ♦ *vi* (*learn*)
pauken; **to ~ sth into sth** etw in etw *acc*
stopfen

cramp [kræmp] *n* Krampf *m* ♦ *vt* (*limit*)
einengen; (*hinder*) hemmen; **~ed** *adj*
(*position*) verkrampft; (*space*) eng

crampon ['kræmpən] *n* Steigeisen *nt*

cranberry ['krænbərɪ] *n* Preiselbeere *f*

crane [kreɪn] *n* (*machine*) Kran *m*; (*bird*)
Kranich *m*

crank [kræŋk] *n* (*lever*) Kurbel *f*; (*person*)
Spinner *m*; **~shaft** *n* Kurbelwelle *f*

cranny ['krænɪ] *n see* **nook**

crash [kræʃ] *n* (*noise*) Krachen *nt*; (*with cars*)
Zusammenstoß *m*; (*with plane*) Absturz *m*;
(*COMM*) Zusammenbruch *m* ♦ *vt* (*plane*)
abstürzen mit ♦ *vi* (*cars*) zusammenstoßen;
(*plane*) abstürzen; (*economy*)
zusammenbrechen; (*noise*) knallen; **~
course** *n* Schnellkurs *m*; **~ helmet** *n*
Sturzhelm *m*; **~ landing** *n* Bruchlandung *f*

crass [kræs] *adj* kraß △

crate [kreɪt] *n* (*also fig*) Kiste *f*

crater ['kreɪtə'] *n* Krater *m*

cravat(e) [krə'væt] *n* Halstuch *nt*

crave [kreɪv] *vt* verlangen nach

crawl [krɔːl] *vi* kriechen; (*baby*) krabbeln ♦ *n*
Kriechen *nt*; (*swim*) Kraul *nt*

crayfish ['kreɪfɪʃ] *n inv* (*freshwater*) Krebs *m*;
(*saltwater*) Languste *f*

crayon ['kreɪən] *n* Buntstift *m*

craze [kreɪz] *n* Fimmel *m*

crazy ['kreɪzɪ] *adj* verrückt

creak [kriːk] *vi* knarren

cream [kriːm] *n* (*from milk*) Rahm *m*, Sahne
f; (*polish, cosmetic*) Creme *f*; (*fig: people*)
Elite *f* ♦ *adj* cremefarbig; **~ cake** *n*
Sahnetorte *f*; **~ cheese** *n* Rahmquark *m*;
~y *adj* sahnig

crease [kriːs] *n* Falte *f* ♦ *vt* falten; (*wrinkle*)
zerknittern ♦ *vi* (*wrinkle up*) knittern; **~d** *adj*
zerknittert, faltig

create [kriː'eɪt] *vt* erschaffen; (*cause*)
verursachen; **creation** [kriː'eɪʃən] *n*
Schöpfung *f*; **creative** *adj* kreativ; **creator**
n Schöpfer *m*

creature ['kriːtʃə'] *n* Geschöpf *nt*

crèche [krɛʃ] *n* Krippe *f*

credence ['kriːdns] *n*: **to lend** *or* **give ~ to
sth** etw *dat* Glauben schenken

credentials [krɪ'denʃlz] *npl*
Beglaubigungsschreiben *nt*

credibility [kredɪ'bɪlɪtɪ] *n* Glaubwürdigkeit *f*

credible ['kredɪbl] *adj* (*person*) glaubwürdig;
(*story*) glaubhaft

credit ['kredɪt] *n* (*also COMM*) Kredit *m* ♦ *vt*

△ *For information on spelling reform see page 615*

Glauben schenken +*dat*; (*COMM*)
gutschreiben; **~s** *npl* (*of film*) Mitwirkende
pl; **~able** *adj* rühmlich; **~ card** *n*
Kreditkarte *f*; **~or** *n* Gläubiger *m*

creed [kri:d] *n* Glaubensbekenntnis *nt*

creek [kri:k] *n* (*inlet*) kleine Bucht *f*; (*US: river*) kleine(r) Wasserlauf *m*

creep [kri:p] (*pt, pp* **crept**) *vi* kriechen; **~er** *n* Kletterpflanze *f*; **~y** *adj* (*frightening*) gruselig

cremate [krɪ'meɪt] *vt* einäschern; **cremation** [krɪ'meɪʃən] *n* Einäscherung *f*; **crematorium** [kremə'tɔ:rɪəm] *n* Krematorium *m*

crêpe [kreɪp] *n* Krepp *m*; **~ bandage** (*BRIT*) *n* Elastikbinde *f*

crept [krept] *pt, pp of* **creep**

crescent ['kresnt] *n* (*of moon*) Halbmond *m*

cress [kres] *n* Kresse *f*

crest [krest] *n* (*of cock*) Kamm *m*; (*of wave*) Wellenkamm *m*; (*coat of arms*) Wappen *nt*

crestfallen ['krestfɔ:lən] *adj* niedergeschlagen

Crete [kri:t] *n* Kreta *nt*

crevice ['krevɪs] *n* Riß ⚠ *m*

crew [kru:] *n* Besatzung *f*, Mannschaft *f*; **~-cut** *n* Bürstenschnitt *m*; **~ neck** *n* runde(r) Ausschnitt *m*

crib [krɪb] *n* (*bed*) Krippe *f* ♦ *vt* (*inf*) spicken

crick [krɪk] *n* Muskelkrampf *m*

cricket ['krɪkɪt] *n* (*insect*) Grille *f*; (*game*) Kricket *nt*

crime [kraɪm] *n* Verbrechen *nt*

criminal ['krɪmɪnl] *n* Verbrecher *m* ♦ *adj* kriminell; (*act*) strafbar

crimson ['krɪmzn] *adj* leuchtend rot

cringe [krɪndʒ] *vi* sich ducken

crinkle ['krɪŋkl] *vt* zerknittern

cripple ['krɪpl] *n* Krüppel *m* ♦ *vt* lahmlegen; (*MED*) verkrüppeln

crises ['kraɪsi:z] *npl of* **crisis**

crisis ['kraɪsɪs] (*pl* **crises**) *n* Krise *f*

crisp [krɪsp] *adj* knusprig; **~s** (*BRIT*) *npl* Chips *pl*

crisscross ['krɪskrɔs] *adj* gekreuzt, Kreuz-

criteria [kraɪ'tɪərɪə] *npl of* **criterion**

criterion [kraɪ'tɪərɪən] (*pl* **criteria**) *n*

Kriterium *nt*

critic ['krɪtɪk] *n* Kritiker(in) *m(f)*; **~al** *adj* kritisch; **~ally** *adv* kritisch; (*ill*) gefährlich; **~ism** ['krɪtɪsɪzəm] *n* Kritik *f*; **~ize** ['krɪtɪsaɪz] *vt* kritisieren

croak [krəuk] *vi* krächzen; (*frog*) quaken

Croatia [krəu'eɪʃə] *n* Kroatien *nt*

crochet ['krəuʃeɪ] *n* Häkelei *f*

crockery ['krɔkərɪ] *n* Geschirr *nt*

crocodile ['krɔkədaɪl] *n* Krokodil *nt*

crocus ['krəukəs] *n* Krokus *m*

croft [krɔft] (*BRIT*) *n* kleine(s) Pachtgut *nt*

crony ['krəunɪ] (*inf*) *n* Kumpel *m*

crook [kruk] *n* (*criminal*) Gauner *m*; (*stick*) Hirtenstab *m*

crooked ['krukɪd] *adj* krumm

crop [krɔp] *n* (*harvest*) Ernte *f*; (*riding ~*) Reitpeitsche *f* ♦ *vt* ernten; **~ up** *vi* passieren

croquette [krə'ket] *n* Krokette *f*

cross [krɔs] *n* Kreuz *nt* ♦ *vt* (*road*) überqueren; (*legs*) übereinander legen; kreuzen ♦ *adj* (*annoyed*) böse; **~ out** *vt* streichen; **~ over** *vi* hinübergehen; **~bar** *n* Querstange *f*; **~-country** (*race*) *n* Geländelauf *m*; **~-examine** *vt* ins Kreuzverhör nehmen; **~-eyed** *adj*: **to be ~-eyed** schielen; **~fire** *n* Kreuzfeuer *nt*; **~ing** *n* (*crossroads*) (Straßen)kreuzung *f*; (*of ship*) Überfahrt *f*; (*for pedestrians*) Fußgängerüberweg *m*; **~ing guard** (*US*) *n* Schülerlotse *m*; **~ purposes** *npl*: **to be at ~ purposes** aneinander vorbeireden; **~-reference** *n* Querverweis *m*; **~roads** *n* Straßenkreuzung *f*; (*fig*) Scheideweg *m*; **~ section** *n* Querschnitt *m*; **~walk** (*US*) *n* Fußgängerüberweg *m*; **~wind** *n* Seitenwind *m*; **~word (puzzle)** *n* Kreuzworträtsel *nt*

crotch [krɔtʃ] *n* Zwickel *m*; (*ANAT*) Unterleib *nt*

crouch [krautʃ] *vi* hocken

crow [krəu] *n* (*bird*) Krähe *f*; (*of cock*) Krähen *nt* ♦ *vi* krähen

crowbar ['krəubɑ:r] *n* Stemmeisen *nt*

crowd [kraud] *n* Menge *f* ♦ *vt* (*fill*) überfüllen ♦ *vi* drängen; **~ed** *adj* überfüllt

⚠ *Informationen zur Rechtschreibreform Seite 615*

crown [kraun] n Krone f; (of head, hat) Kopf m ♦ vt krönen; ~ **jewels** npl Kronjuwelen pl; ~ **prince** n Kronprinz m

crow's-feet ['krəʊzfiːt] npl Krähenfüße pl

crucial ['kruːʃl] adj entscheidend

crucifix ['kruːsɪfɪks] n Kruzifix nt; ~**ion** [kruːsɪ'fɪkʃən] n Kreuzigung f

crude [kruːd] adj (raw) roh; (humour, behaviour) grob; (basic) primitiv; ~ **(oil)** n Rohöl nt

cruel ['kruəl] adj grausam; ~**ty** n Grausamkeit f

cruise [kruːz] n Kreuzfahrt f ♦ vi kreuzen; ~**r** n (MIL) Kreuzer m

crumb [krʌm] n Krume f

crumble ['krʌmbl] vt, vi zerbröckeln; **crumbly** adj krümelig

crumpet ['krʌmpɪt] n Tee(pfann)kuchen m·

crumple ['krʌmpl] vt zerknittern

crunch [krʌntʃ] n: **the ~** (fig) der Knackpunkt ♦ vt knirschen; ~**y** adj knusprig

crusade [kruː'seɪd] n Kreuzzug m

crush [krʌʃ] n Gedränge nt ♦ vt zerdrücken; (rebellion) unterdrücken

crust [krʌst] n Kruste f

crutch [krʌtʃ] n Krücke f

crux [krʌks] n springende(r) Punkt m

cry [kraɪ] vi (shout) schreien; (weep) weinen ♦ n (call) Schrei m; ~ **off** vi (plötzlich) absagen

crypt [krɪpt] n Krypta f

cryptic ['krɪptɪk] adj hintergründig

crystal ['krɪstl] n Kristall m; (glass) Kristallglas nt; (mineral) Bergkristall m; ~-**clear** adj kristallklar

crystallize ['krɪstəlaɪz] vt, vi kristallisieren; (fig) klären

CSA n abbr (= Child Support Agency) Amt zur Regelung von Unterhaltszahlungen für Kinder

CTC (BRIT) n abbr = **city technology college**

cub [kʌb] n Junge(s) nt; (also: **C~ scout**) Wölfling m

Cuba ['kjuːbə] n Kuba nt; ~**n** adj kubanisch ♦ n Kubaner(in) m(f)

cubbyhole ['kʌbɪhəʊl] n Eckchen nt

cube [kjuːb] n Würfel m ♦ vt (MATH) hoch

drei nehmen

cubic ['kjuːbɪk] adj würfelförmig; (centimetre etc) Kubik-; ~ **capacity** n Fassungsvermögen nt

cubicle ['kjuːbɪkl] n Kabine f

cuckoo ['kuku:] n Kuckuck m; ~ **clock** n Kuckucksuhr f

cucumber ['kjuːkʌmbə'] n Gurke f

cuddle ['kʌdl] vt, vi herzen, drücken (inf)

cue [kjuː] n (THEAT) Stichwort nt; (snooker ~) Billardstock m

cuff [kʌf] n (BRIT: of shirt, coat etc) Manschette f; Aufschlag m; (US) = **turn-up**; **off the ~** aus dem Handgelenk; ~**link** n Manschettenknopf m

cuisine [kwɪ'zi:n] n Kochkunst f, Küche f

cul-de-sac ['kʌldəsæk] n Sackgasse f

culinary ['kʌlɪnərɪ] adj Koch-

cull [kʌl] vt (select) auswählen

culminate ['kʌlmɪneɪt] vi gipfeln; **culmination** [kʌlmɪ'neɪʃən] n Höhepunkt m

culottes [kjuː'lɒts] npl Hosenrock m

culpable ['kʌlpəbl] adj schuldig

culprit ['kʌlprɪt] n Täter m

cult [kʌlt] n Kult m

cultivate ['kʌltɪveɪt] vt (AGR) bebauen; (mind) bilden; **cultivation** [kʌltɪ'veɪʃən] n (AGR) Bebauung f; (of person) Bildung f

cultural ['kʌltʃərəl] adj kulturell, Kultur-

culture ['kʌltʃə'] n Kultur f; ~**d** adj gebildet

cumbersome ['kʌmbəsəm] adj (object) sperrig

cumulative ['kjuːmjʊlətɪv] adj gehäuft

cunning ['kʌnɪŋ] n Verschlagenheit f ♦ adj schlau

cup [kʌp] n Tasse f; (prize) Pokal m

cupboard ['kʌbəd] n Schrank m

cup tie (BRIT) n Pokalspiel nt

curate ['kjuərɪt] n (Catholic) Kurat m; (Protestant) Vikar m

curator [kjuə'reɪtə'] n Kustos m

curb [kəːb] vt zügeln ♦ n (on spending etc) Einschränkung f; (US) Bordstein m

curdle ['kəːdl] vi gerinnen

cure [kjuə'] n Heilmittel nt; (process) Heilverfahren nt ♦ vt heilen

curfew ['kəːfjuː] n Ausgangssperre f;

⚠ For information on spelling reform see page 615

Sperrstunde *f*

curio ['kjʊərɪəʊ] *n* Kuriosität *f*

curiosity [kjʊərɪ'ɒsɪtɪ] *n* Neugier *f*

curious ['kjʊərɪəs] *adj* neugierig; (*strange*) seltsam

curl [kɜːl] *n* Locke *f* ♦ *vt* locken ♦ *vi* sich locken; ~ **up** *vi* sich zusammenrollen; (*person*) sich ankuscheln; **~er** *n* Lockenwickler *m*; **~y** ['kɜːlɪ] *adj* lockig

currant ['kʌrnt] *n* Korinthe *f*

currency ['kʌrnsɪ] *n* Währung *f*; **to gain ~** an Popularität gewinnen

current ['kʌrnt] *n* Strömung *f* ♦ *adj* (*expression*) gängig, üblich; (*issue*) neueste; **~ account** (*BRIT*) *n* Girokonto *nt*; **~ affairs** *npl* Zeitgeschehen *nt*; **~ly** *adv* zur Zeit

curricula [kə'rɪkjʊlə] *npl* of **curriculum**

curriculum [kə'rɪkjʊləm] (*pl* **~s** *or* **curricula**) *n* Lehrplan *m*; **~ vitae** [-'viːtaɪ] *n* Lebenslauf *m*

curry ['kʌrɪ] *n* Currygericht *n* ♦ *vt*: **to ~ favour with** sich einschmeicheln bei; **~ powder** *n* Curry(pulver) *nt*

curse [kɜːs] *vi* (*swear*): **to ~ (at)** fluchen (auf *or* über +*acc*) ♦ *vt* (*insult*) verwünschen ♦ *n* Fluch *m*

cursor ['kɜːsəʳ] *n* (*COMPUT*) Cursor *m*

cursory ['kɜːsərɪ] *adj* flüchtig

curt [kɜːt] *adj* schroff

curtail [kɜː'teɪl] *vt* abkürzen; (*rights*) einschränken

curtain ['kɜːtn] *n* Vorhang *m*

curts(e)y ['kɜːtsɪ] *n* Knicks *m* ♦ *vi* knicksen

curve [kɜːv] *n* Kurve *f*; (*of body, vase etc*) Rundung *f* ♦ *vi* sich biegen; (*hips, breasts*) sich runden; (*road*) einen Bogen machen

cushion ['kʊʃən] *n* Kissen *nt* ♦ *vt* dämpfen

custard ['kʌstəd] *n* Vanillesoße *f*

custodian [kʌs'təʊdɪən] *n* Kustos *m*, Verwalter(in) *m(f)*

custody ['kʌstədɪ] *n* Aufsicht *f*; (*police ~*) Haft *f*; **to take into ~** verhaften

custom ['kʌstəm] *n* (*tradition*) Brauch *m*; (*COMM*) Kundschaft *f*; **~ary** *adj* üblich

customer ['kʌstəməʳ] *n* Kunde *m*, Kundin *f*

customized ['kʌstəmaɪzd] *adj* (*car etc*) mit Spezialausrüstung

custom-made ['kʌstəm'meɪd] *adj* speziell angefertigt

customs ['kʌstəmz] *npl* Zoll *m*; **~ duty** *n* Zollabgabe *f*; **~ officer** *n* Zollbeamte(r) *m*, Zollbeamtin *f*

cut [kʌt] (*pt, pp* **cut**) *vt* schneiden; (*wages*) kürzen; (*prices*) heruntersetzen ♦ *vi* schneiden; (*intersect*) sich schneiden ♦ *n* Schnitt *m*; (*wound*) Schnittwunde *f*; (*in income etc*) Kürzung *f*; (*share*) Anteil *m*; **to ~ a tooth** zahnen; **~ down** *vt* (*tree*) fällen; (*reduce*) einschränken; **~ off** *vt* (*also fig*) abschneiden; (*allowance*) sperren; **~ out** *vt* (*shape*) ausschneiden; (*delete*) streichen; **~ up** *vt* (*meat*) aufschneiden; **~back** *n* Kürzung *f*

cute [kjuːt] *adj* niedlich

cuticle ['kjuːtɪkl] *n* Nagelhaut *f*

cutlery ['kʌtlərɪ] *n* Besteck *nt*

cutlet ['kʌtlɪt] *n* (*pork*) Kotelett *nt*; (*veal*) Schnitzel *nt*

cut: **~out** *n* (*cardboard cutout*) Ausschneidemodell *nt*; **~-price, ~-rate** (*US*) *adj* verbilligt; **~throat** *n* Verbrechertyp *m* ♦ *adj* mörderisch

cutting ['kʌtɪŋ] *adj* schneidend ♦ *n* (*BRIT: PRESS*) Ausschnitt *m*; (*: RAIL*) Durchstich *m*

CV *n abbr* = **curriculum vitae**

cwt *abbr* = **hundredweight(s)**

cyanide ['saɪənaɪd] *n* Zyankali *nt*

cyberspace ['saɪbəspeɪs] *n* Cyberspace *m*

cycle ['saɪkl] *n* Fahrrad *nt*; (*series*) Reihe *f* ♦ *vi* radfahren △; **~ hire**, **~ path** *n* (Fahr)radweg *m*; **cycling** *n* Radfahren *nt*; **cyclist** *n* Radfahrer(in) *m(f)*

cyclone ['saɪkləʊn] *n* Zyklon *m*

cygnet ['sɪgnɪt] *n* junge(r) Schwan *m*

cylinder ['sɪlɪndəʳ] *n* Zylinder *m*; (*TECH*) Walze *f*; **~ head gasket** *n* Zylinderkopfdichtung *f*

cymbals ['sɪmblz] *npl* Becken *nt*

cynic ['sɪnɪk] *n* Zyniker(in) *m(f)*; **~al** *adj* zynisch; **~ism** ['sɪnɪsɪzəm] *n* Zynismus *m*

cypress ['saɪprɪs] *n* Zypresse *f*

Cyprus ['saɪprəs] *n* Zypern *nt*

cyst [sɪst] *n* Zyste *f*

△ *Informationen zur Rechtschreibreform Seite 615*

cystitis [sɪsˈtaɪtɪs] n Blasenentzündung f

czar [zɑːʳ] n Zar m

Czech [tʃɛk] adj tschechisch ♦ n Tscheche m, Tschechin f

Czechoslovakia [tʃɛkəsləˈvækɪə] (HIST) n die Tschechoslowakei; **~n** adj tschechoslowakisch ♦ n Tschechoslowake m, Tschechoslowakin f

D, d

D [diː] n (MUS) D nt

dab [dæb] vt (wound, paint) betupfen ♦ n (little bit) bißchen ⚠ nt; (of paint) Tupfer m

dabble [ˈdæbl] vi: **to ~ in sth** in etw dat machen

dad [dæd] n Papa m, Vati m; **~dy** [ˈdædɪ] n Papa m, Vati m; **~dy-long-legs** n Weberknecht m

daffodil [ˈdæfədɪl] n Osterglocke f

daft [dɑːft] (inf) adj blöd(e), doof

dagger [ˈdægəʳ] n Dolch m

daily [ˈdeɪlɪ] adj täglich ♦ n (PRESS) Tageszeitung f; (BRIT: cleaner) Haushaltshilfe f ♦ adv täglich

dainty [ˈdeɪntɪ] adj zierlich

dairy [ˈdɛərɪ] n (shop) Milchgeschäft nt; (on farm) Molkerei f ♦ adj Milch-; **~ farm** n Hof m mit Milchwirtschaft; **~ produce** n Molkereiprodukte pl; **~ products** npl Milchprodukte pl, Molkereiprodukte pl; **~ store** (US) n Milchgeschäft nt

dais [ˈdeɪs] n Podium nt

daisy [ˈdeɪzɪ] n Gänseblümchen nt

dale [deɪl] n Tal nt

dam [dæm] n (Stau)damm m ♦ vt stauen

damage [ˈdæmɪdʒ] n Schaden m ♦ vt beschädigen; **~s** npl (JUR) Schaden(s)ersatz m

damn [dæm] vt verdammen ♦ n (inf): **I don't give a ~** das ist mir total egal ♦ adj (inf: also: **~ed**) verdammt; **~ it!** verflucht!; **~ing** adj vernichtend

damp [dæmp] adj feucht ♦ n Feuchtigkeit f ♦ vt (also: **~en**) befeuchten; (discourage) dämpfen

damson [ˈdæmzən] n Damaszenerpflaume f

dance [dɑːns] n Tanz m ♦ vi tanzen; **~ hall** n Tanzlokal nt; **~r** n Tänzer(in) m(f); **dancing** n Tanzen nt

dandelion [ˈdændɪlaɪən] n Löwenzahn m

dandruff [ˈdændrəf] n (Kopf)schuppen pl

Dane [deɪn] n Däne m, Dänin f

danger [ˈdeɪndʒəʳ] n Gefahr f; **~!** (sign) Achtung!; **to be in ~ of doing sth** Gefahr laufen, etw zu tun; **~ous** adj gefährlich

dangle [ˈdæŋgl] vi baumeln ♦ vt herabhängen lassen

Danish [ˈdeɪnɪʃ] adj dänisch ♦ n Dänisch nt

dare [dɛəʳ] vt herausfordern ♦ vi: **to ~ (to) do sth** es wagen, etw zu tun; **I ~ say** ich würde sagen; **daring** [ˈdɛərɪŋ] adj (audacious) verwegen; (bold) wagemutig; (dress) gewagt ♦ n Mut m

dark [dɑːk] adj dunkel; (fig) düster, trübe; (deep colour) dunkel- ♦ n Dunkelheit f; **to be left in the ~ about** im dunkeln sein über +acc; **after ~** nach Anbruch der Dunkelheit; **~en** vt, vi verdunkeln; **~ glasses** npl Sonnenbrille f; **~ness** n Finsternis nt; **~room** n Dunkelkammer f

darling [ˈdɑːlɪŋ] n Liebling m ♦ adj lieb

darn [dɑːn] vt stopfen

dart [dɑːt] n (weapon) Pfeil m; (in sewing) Abnäher m ♦ vi sausen; **~s** n (game) Pfeilwerfen nt; **~board** n Zielscheibe f

dash [dæʃ] n Sprung m; (mark) (Gedanken)strich m; (small amount) bißchen ⚠ nt ♦ vt (hopes) zunichte machen ♦ vi stürzen; **~ away** vi davonstürzen; **~ off** vi davonstürzen

dashboard [ˈdæʃbɔːd] n Armaturenbrett nt

dashing [ˈdæʃɪŋ] adj schneidig

data [ˈdeɪtə] npl Einzelheiten pl, Daten pl; **~base** n Datenbank f; **~ processing** n Datenverarbeitung f

date [deɪt] n Datum nt; (for meeting etc) Termin m; (with person) Verabredung f; (fruit) Dattel f ♦ vt (letter etc) datieren; (person) gehen mit; **~ of birth** Geburtsdatum nt; **to ~** bis heute; **out of ~** überholt; **up to ~** (clothes) modisch; (report) up-to-date; (with news) auf dem

⚠ *For information on spelling reform see page 615*

laufenden; **~d** *adj* altmodisch; **~ rape** *n* Vergewaltigung *f* nach einem Rendezvous

daub [dɔːb] *vt* beschmieren; (*paint*) schmieren

daughter ['dɔːtər] *n* Tochter *f*; **~-in-law** *n* Schwiegertochter *f*

daunting ['dɔːntɪŋ] *adj* entmutigend

dawdle ['dɔːdl] *vi* trödeln

dawn [dɔːn] *n* Morgendämmerung *f* ♦ *vi* dämmern; (*fig*): **it ~ed on him that ...** es dämmerte ihm, daß ...

day [deɪ] *n* Tag *m*; **the ~ before/after** am Tag zuvor/danach; **the ~ after tomorrow** übermorgen; **the ~ before yesterday** vorgestern; **by ~** am Tage; **~break** *n* Tagesanbruch *m*; **~dream** *vi* mit offenen Augen träumen; **~light** *n* Tageslicht *nt*; **~ return** (*BRIT*) *n* Tagesrückfahrkarte *f*; **~time** *n* Tageszeit *f*; **~-to-~** *adj* alltäglich

daze [deɪz] *vt* betäuben ♦ *n* Betäubung *f*; **in a ~** benommen

dazzle ['dæzl] *vt* blenden

DC *abbr* (= *direct current*) Gleichstrom *m*

D-day ['diːdeɪ] *n* (*HIST*) *Tag der Invasion durch die Alliierten (6.6.44)*; (*fig*) der Tag X

deacon ['diːkən] *n* Diakon *m*

dead [dɛd] *adj* tot; (*without feeling*) gefühllos ♦ *adv* ganz; (*exactly*) genau ♦ *npl*: **the ~** die Toten *pl*; **to shoot sb ~** jdn erschießen; **~ tired** todmüde; **to stop ~** abrupt stehenbleiben; **~en** *vt* (*pain*) abtöten; (*sound*) ersticken; **~ end** *n* Sackgasse *f*; **~ heat** *n* tote(s) Rennen *nt*; **~line** *n* Stichtag *m*; **~lock** *n* Stillstand *m*; **~ loss** (*inf*) *n*: **to be a ~ loss** ein hoffnungsloser Fall sein; **~ly** *adj* tödlich; **~pan** *adj* undurchdringlich; **D~ Sea** *n*: **the D~ Sea** das Tote Meer

deaf [dɛf] *adj* taub; **~en** *vt* taub machen; **~ening** *adj* (*noise*) ohrenbetäubend; (*noise*) lautstark; **~-mute** *n* Taubstumme(r) *mf*; **~ness** *n* Taubheit *f*

deal [diːl] (*pt, pp* **dealt**) *n* Geschäft *nt* ♦ *vt* austeilen; (*CARDS*) geben; **a great ~ of** sehr viel; **~ in** *vt fus* handeln mit; **~ with** *vt fus* (*person*) behandeln; (*subject*) sich befassen mit; (*problem*) in Angriff nehmen; **~er** *n*

(*COMM*) Händler *m*; (*CARDS*) Kartengeber *m*; **~ings** *npl* (*FIN*) Geschäfte *pl*; (*relations*) Beziehungen *pl*; **~t** [dɛlt] *pt, pp of* **deal**

dean [diːn] *n* (*Protestant*) Superintendent *m*; (*Catholic*) Dechant *m*; (*UNIV*) Dekan *m*

dear [dɪər] *adj* lieb; (*expensive*) teuer ♦ *n* Liebling *m* ♦ *excl*: **~ me!** du liebe Zeit!; **D~ Sir** Sehr geehrter Herr!; **D~ John** Lieber John!; **~ly** *adv* (*love*) herzlich; (*pay*) teuer

death [dɛθ] *n* Tod *m*; (*statistic*) Todesfall *m*; **~ certificate** *n* Totenschein *m*; **~ly** *adj* totenähnlich, Toten-; **~ penalty** *n* Todesstrafe *f*; **~ rate** *n* Sterblichkeitsziffer *f*

debar [dɪˈbɑːr] *vt* ausschließen

debase [dɪˈbeɪs] *vt* entwerten

debatable [dɪˈbeɪtəbl] *adj* anfechtbar

debate [dɪˈbeɪt] *n* Debatte *f* ♦ *vt* debattieren, diskutieren; (*consider*) überlegen

debilitating [dɪˈbɪlɪteɪtɪŋ] *adj* schwächend

debit ['dɛbɪt] *n* Schuldposten *m* ♦ *vt* belasten

debris ['dɛbriː] *n* Trümmer *pl*

debt [dɛt] *n* Schuld *f*; **to be in ~** verschuldet sein; **~or** *n* Schuldner *m*

debunk [diːˈbʌŋk] *vt* entlarven

decade ['dɛkeɪd] *n* Jahrzehnt *nt*

decadence ['dɛkədəns] *n* Dekadenz *f*

decaff ['diːkæf] (*inf*) *n* koffeinfreier Kaffee

decaffeinated [diːˈkæfɪneɪtɪd] *adj* koffeinfrei

decanter [dɪˈkæntər] *n* Karaffe *f*

decay [dɪˈkeɪ] *n* Verfall *m*; (*tooth ~*) Karies *m* ♦ *vi* verfallen; (*teeth, meat etc*) faulen; (*leaves etc*) verrotten

deceased [dɪˈsiːst] *adj* verstorben

deceit [dɪˈsiːt] *n* Betrug *m*; **~ful** *adj* falsch

deceive [dɪˈsiːv] *vt* täuschen

December [dɪˈsɛmbər] *n* Dezember *m*

decency ['diːsənsɪ] *n* Anstand *m*

decent ['diːsənt] *adj* (*respectable*) anständig; (*pleasant*) annehmbar

deception [dɪˈsɛpʃən] *n* Betrug *m*

deceptive [dɪˈsɛptɪv] *adj* irreführend

decibel ['dɛsɪbɛl] *n* Dezibel *nt*

decide [dɪˈsaɪd] *vt* entscheiden ♦ *vi* sich entscheiden; **to ~ on sth** etw beschließen; **~d** *adj* entschieden; **~dly** [dɪˈsaɪdɪdlɪ] *adv* entschieden

⚠ *Informationen zur Rechtschreibreform Seite 615*

deciduous [dɪˈsɪdjʊəs] *adj* Laub-

decimal [ˈdesɪməl] *adj* dezimal ♦ *n*
Dezimalzahl *f*; ~ **point** *n* Komma *nt*

decipher [dɪˈsaɪfəʳ] *vt* entziffern

decision [dɪˈsɪʒən] *n* Entscheidung *f*,
Entschluß △ *m*

decisive [dɪˈsaɪsɪv] *adj* entscheidend;
(*person*) entschlossen

deck [dek] *n* (NAUT) Deck *nt*; (*of cards*) Pack
m; ~**chair** *n* Liegestuhl *m*

declaration [dekləˈreɪʃən] *n* Erklärung *f*

declare [dɪˈkleəʳ] *vt* erklären; (CUSTOMS)
verzollen

decline [dɪˈklaɪn] *n* (*decay*) Verfall *m*;
(*lessening*) Rückgang *m* ♦ *vt* (*invitation*)
ablehnen ♦ *vi* (*say no*) ablehnen; (*of
strength*) nachlassen

decode [ˈdiːˈkəʊd] *vt* entschlüsseln; ~**r** *n*
(TV) Decoder *m*

decompose [diːkəmˈpəʊz] *vi* (sich)
zersetzen

décor [ˈdeɪkɔːʳ] *n* Ausstattung *f*

decorate [ˈdekəreɪt] *vt* (*room: paper*)
tapezieren; (: *paint*) streichen; (*adorn*)
(aus)schmücken; (*cake*) verzieren; (*honour*)
auszeichnen; **decoration** [dekəˈreɪʃən] *n* (*of
house*) (Wand)dekoration *f*; (*medal*) Orden
m; **decorator** [ˈdekəreɪtəʳ] *n* Maler *m*,
Anstreicher *m*

decorum [dɪˈkɔːrəm] *n* Anstand *m*

decoy [ˈdiːkɔɪ] *n* Lockvogel *m*

decrease [*n* diːˈkriːs, *vb* diːˈkriːs] *n*
Abnahme *f* ♦ *vt* vermindern ♦ *vi* abnehmen

decree [dɪˈkriː] *n* Erlaß △ *m*; ~ **nisi** *n*
vorläufige(s) Scheidungsurteil *nt*

decrepit [dɪˈkrepɪt] *adj* hinfällig

dedicate [ˈdedɪkeɪt] *vt* widmen; ~**d** *adj*
hingebungsvoll, engagiert; (COMPUT)
dediziert; **dedication** [dedɪˈkeɪʃən] *n*
(*devotion*) Ergebenheit *f*; (*in book*) Widmung
f

deduce [dɪˈdjuːs] *vt*: **to ~ sth (from sth)**
etw (aus etw) ableiten, etw (aus etw)
schließen

deduct [dɪˈdʌkt] *vt* abziehen; ~**ion**
[dɪˈdʌkʃən] *n* (*of money*) Abzug *m*;
(*conclusion*) (Schluß)folgerung △ *f*

deed [diːd] *n* Tat *f*; (*document*) Urkunde *f*

deem [diːm] *vt*: **to ~ sb/sth (to be) sth**
jdn/etw für etw halten

deep [diːp] *adj* tief ♦ *adv*: **the spectators
stood 20 ~** die Zuschauer standen in 20
Reihen hintereinander; **to be 4m ~** 4
Meter tief sein; ~**en** *vt* vertiefen ♦ *vi*
(*darkness*) tiefer werden; ~ **end** *n*: **the ~
end** (*of swimming pool*) das Tiefe; ~**freeze**
n Tiefkühlung *f*; ~**fry** *vt* fritieren △; ~**ly**
adv tief; ~**-sea diving** *n* Tiefseetauchen *nt*;
~**-seated** *adj* tiefsitzend

deer [dɪəʳ] *n* Reh *nt*; ~**skin** *n* Hirsch-/
Rehleder *nt*

deface [dɪˈfeɪs] *vt* entstellen

defamation [defəˈmeɪʃən] *n* Verleumdung *f*

default [dɪˈfɔːlt] *n* Versäumnis *nt*; (COMPUT)
Standardwert *m* ♦ *vi* versäumen; **by ~**
durch Nichterscheinen

defeat [dɪˈfiːt] *n* Niederlage *f* ♦ *vt* schlagen;
~**ist** *adj* defätistisch ♦ *n* Defätist *m*

defect [*n* ˈdiːfekt, *vb* dɪˈfekt] *n* Fehler *m* ♦ *vi*
überlaufen; ~**ive** [dɪˈfektɪv] *adj* fehlerhaft

defence [dɪˈfens] *n* Verteidigung *f*; ~**less**
adj wehrlos

defend [dɪˈfend] *vt* verteidigen; ~**ant** *n*
Angeklagte(r) *m*; ~**er** *n* Verteidiger *m*

defense [dɪˈfens] (US) *n* = **defence**

defensive [dɪˈfensɪv] *adj* defensiv ♦ *n*: **on
the ~** in der Defensive

defer [dɪˈfɜːʳ] *vt* verschieben

deference [ˈdefərəns] *n* Rücksichtnahme *f*

defiance [dɪˈfaɪəns] *n* Trotz *m*,
Unnachgiebigkeit *f*; **in ~ of sth** einer Sache
dat zum Trotz

defiant [dɪˈfaɪənt] *adj* trotzig, unnachgiebig

deficiency [dɪˈfɪʃənsɪ] *n* (*lack*) Mangel *m*;
(*weakness*) Schwäche *f*

deficient [dɪˈfɪʃənt] *adj* mangelhaft

deficit [ˈdefɪsɪt] *n* Defizit *nt*

defile [*vb* dɪˈfaɪl, *n* ˈdiːfaɪl] *vt* beschmutzen
♦ *n* Hohlweg *m*

define [dɪˈfaɪn] *vt* bestimmen; (*explain*)
definieren

definite [ˈdefɪnɪt] *adj* (*fixed*) definitiv; (*clear*)
eindeutig; ~**ly** *adv* bestimmt

definition [defɪˈnɪʃən] *n* Definition *f*

△ *For information on spelling reform see page 615*

deflate [di:'fleɪt] *vt* die Luft ablassen aus

deflect [dɪ'flɛkt] *vt* ablenken

deformity [dɪ'fɔːmɪtɪ] *n* Mißbildung △ *f*

defraud [dɪ'frɔːd] *vt* betrügen

defrost [di:'frɒst] *vt* (*fridge*) abtauen; (*food*) auftauen; **~er** (*US*) *n* (*demister*) Gebläse *nt*

deft [dɛft] *adj* geschickt

defunct [dɪ'fʌŋkt] *adj* verstorben

defuse [di:'fjuːz] *vt* entschärfen

defy [dɪ'faɪ] *vt* (*disobey*) sich widersetzen +*dat*; (*orders, death*) trotzen +*dat*; (*challenge*) herausfordern

degenerate [*v* dɪ'dʒɛnəreɪt, *adj* dɪ'dʒɛnərɪt] *vi* degenerieren ♦ *adj* degeneriert

degrading [dɪ'greɪdɪŋ] *adj* erniedrigend

degree [dɪ'griː] *n* Grad *m*; (*UNIV*) Universitätsabschluß *m*; **by ~s** allmählich; **to some ~** zu einem gewissen Grad

dehydrated [diːhaɪ'dreɪtɪd] *adj* (*person*) ausgetrocknet

de-ice ['diː'aɪs] *vt* enteisen

deign [deɪn] *vi* sich herablassen

deity ['diːɪtɪ] *n* Gottheit *f*

dejected [dɪ'dʒɛktɪd] *adj* niedergeschlagen

delay [dɪ'leɪ] *vt* (*hold back*) aufschieben ♦ *vi* (*linger*) sich aufhalten ♦ *n* Aufschub *m*, Verzögerung *f*; (*of train etc*) Verspätung *f*; **to be ~ed** (*train*) Verspätung haben; **without ~** unverzüglich

delectable [dɪ'lɛktəbl] *adj* köstlich; (*fig*) reizend

delegate [*n* 'dɛlɪgɪt, *vb* 'dɛlɪgeɪt] *n* Delegierte(r) *mf* ♦ *vt* delegieren

delete [dɪ'liːt] *vt* (aus)streichen

deliberate [*adj* dɪ'lɪbərɪt, *vb* dɪ'lɪbəreɪt] *adj* (*intentional*) absichtlich; (*slow*) bedächtig ♦ *vi* (*consider*) überlegen; (*debate*) sich beraten; **~ly** *adv* absichtlich

delicacy ['dɛlɪkəsɪ] *n* Zartheit *f*; (*weakness*) Anfälligkeit *f*; (*food*) Delikatesse *f*

delicate ['dɛlɪkɪt] *adj* (*fine*) fein; (*fragile*) zart; (*situation*) heikel; (*MED*) empfindlich

delicatessen [dɛlɪkə'tɛsn] *n* Feinkostgeschäft *nt*

delicious [dɪ'lɪʃəs] *adj* lecker

delight [dɪ'laɪt] *n* Wonne *f* ♦ *vt* entzücken; **to take ~ in sth** Freude an etw *dat* haben;

~ed *adj*: **~ed (at** *or* **with sth)** entzückt (über +*acc* etw); **~ed to do sth** etw sehr gern tun; **~ful** *adj* entzückend, herrlich

delinquency [dɪ'lɪŋkwənsɪ] *n* Kriminalität *f*

delinquent [dɪ'lɪŋkwənt] *n* Straffällige(r) *mf* ♦ *adj* straffällig

delirious [dɪ'lɪrɪəs] *adj* im Fieberwahn

deliver [dɪ'lɪvəʳ] *vt* (*goods*) (ab)liefern; (*letter*) zustellen; (*speech*) halten; **~y** *n* (Ab)lieferung *f*; (*of letter*) Zustellung *f*; (*of speech*) Vortragsweise *f*; (*MED*) Entbindung *f*; **to take ~y of** in Empfang nehmen

delude [dɪ'luːd] *vt* täuschen

deluge ['dɛljuːdʒ] *n* Überschwemmung *f*; (*fig*) Flut *f* ♦ *vt* (*fig*) überfluten

delusion [dɪ'luːʒən] *n* (Selbst)täuschung *f*

de luxe [də'lʌks] *adj* Luxus-

delve [dɛlv] *vi*: **to ~ into** sich vertiefen in +*acc*

demand [dɪ'mɑːnd] *vt* verlangen ♦ *n* (*request*) Verlangen *nt*; (*COMM*) Nachfrage *f*; **in ~** gefragt; **on ~** auf Verlangen; **~ing** *adj* anspruchsvoll

demean [dɪ'miːn] *vt*: **to ~ o.s.** sich erniedrigen

demeanour [dɪ'miːnəʳ] (*US* **demeanor**) *n* Benehmen *nt*

demented [dɪ'mɛntɪd] *adj* wahnsinnig

demister [diː'mɪstəʳ] *n* (*AUT*) Gebläse *nt*

demo ['dɛməu] (*inf*) *n abbr* (= *demonstration*) Demo *f*

democracy [dɪ'mɒkrəsɪ] *n* Demokratie *f*

democrat ['dɛməkræt] *n* Demokrat *m*; **democratic** [dɛmə'krætɪk] *adj* demokratisch

demolish [dɪ'mɒlɪʃ] *vt* abreißen; (*fig*) vernichten

demolition [dɛmə'lɪʃən] *n* Abbruch *m*

demon ['diːmən] *n* Dämon *m*

demonstrate ['dɛmənstreɪt] *vt, vi* demonstrieren; **demonstration** [dɛmən'streɪʃən] *n* Demonstration *f*; **demonstrator** ['dɛmənstreɪtəʳ] *n* (*POL*) Demonstrant(in) *m(f)*

demote [dɪ'məut] *vt* degradieren

demure [dɪ'mjuəʳ] *adj* ernst

den [dɛn] *n* (*of animal*) Höhle *f*; (*study*) Bude *f*

denatured alcohol [di:'neɪtʃəd-] (*US*) *n* ungenießbar gemachte(r) Alkohol *m*

denial [dɪ'naɪəl] *n* Leugnung *f*; **official ~** Dementi *nt*

denim ['denɪm] *adj* Denim-; **~s** *npl* Denim-Jeans *pl*

Denmark ['denmɑ:k] *n* Dänemark *nt*

denomination [dɪnɒmɪ'neɪʃən] *n* (*ECCL*) Bekenntnis *nt*; (*type*) Klasse *f*; (*FIN*) Wert *m*

denote [dɪ'nəʊt] *vt* bedeuten

denounce [dɪ'naʊns] *vt* brandmarken

dense [dens] *adj* dicht; (*stupid*) schwer von Begriff; **~ly** *adv* dicht; **density** ['densɪtɪ] *n* Dichte *f*; **single/double density disk** Diskette *f* mit einfacher/doppelter Dichte

dent [dent] *n* Delle *f* ♦ *vt* (*also:* **make a ~ in**) einbeulen

dental ['dentl] *adj* Zahn-; **~ surgeon** *n* = **dentist**

dentist ['dentɪst] *n* Zahnarzt(-ärztin) *m(f)*

dentures ['dentʃəz] *npl* Gebiß △ *nt*

deny [dɪ'naɪ] *vt* leugnen; (*officially*) dementieren; (*help*) abschlagen

deodorant [di:'əʊdərənt] *n* Deodorant *nt*

depart [dɪ'pɑ:t] *vi* abfahren; **to ~ from** (*fig: differ from*) abweichen von

department [dɪ'pɑ:tmənt] *n* (*COMM*) Abteilung *f*; (*UNIV*) Seminar *nt*; (*POL*) Ministerium *nt*; **~ store** *n* Warenhaus *nt*

departure [dɪ'pɑ:tʃə] *n* (*of person*) Abreise *f*; (*of train*) Abfahrt *f*; (*of plane*) Abflug *m*; **new ~** Neuerung *f*; **~ lounge** *n* (*at airport*) Abflughalle *f*

depend [dɪ'pend] *vi*: **to ~ on** abhängen von; (*rely on*) angewiesen sein auf +*acc*; **it ~s** es kommt darauf an; **~ing on the result ...** abhängend vom Resultat ...; **~able** *adj* zuverlässig; **~ant** *n* Angehörige(r) *f(m)*; **~ence** *n* Abhängigkeit *f*; **~ent** *adj* abhängig ♦ *n* = **dependant**; **~ent on** abhängig von

depict [dɪ'pɪkt] *vt* schildern

depleted [dɪ'pli:tɪd] *adj* aufgebraucht

deplorable [dɪ'plɔ:rəbl] *adj* bedauerlich

deploy [dɪ'plɔɪ] *vt* einsetzen

depopulation ['di:pɒpju'leɪʃən] *n* Entvölkerung *f*

deport [dɪ'pɔ:t] *vt* deportieren; **~ation** [di:pɔ:'teɪʃən] *n* Abschiebung *f*

deportment [dɪ'pɔ:tmənt] *n* Betragen *nt*

deposit [dɪ'pɒzɪt] *n* (*in bank*) Guthaben *nt*; (*down payment*) Anzahlung *f*; (*security*) Kaution *f*; (*CHEM*) Niederschlag *m* ♦ *vt* (*in bank*) deponieren; (*put down*) niederlegen; **~ account** *n* Sparkonto *nt*

depot ['depəʊ] *n* Depot *nt*

depraved [dɪ'preɪvd] *adj* verkommen

depreciate [dɪ'pri:ʃɪeɪt] *vi* im Wert sinken; **depreciation** [dɪpri:ʃɪ'eɪʃən] *n* Wertminderung *f*

depress [dɪ'pres] *vt* (*press down*) niederdrücken; (*in mood*) deprimieren; **~ed** *adj* deprimiert; **~ion** [dɪ'preʃən] *n* (*mood*) Depression *f*; (*in trade*) Wirtschaftskrise *f*; (*hollow*) Vertiefung *f*; (*MET*) Tief(druckgebiet) *nt*

deprivation [depri'veɪʃən] *n* Not *f*

deprive [dɪ'praɪv] *vt*: **to ~ sb of sth** jdn einer Sache *gen* berauben; **~d** *adj* (*child*) sozial benachteiligt; (*area*) unterentwickelt

depth [depθ] *n* Tiefe *f*; **in the ~s of despair** in tiefster Verzweiflung

deputation [depju'teɪʃən] *n* Abordnung *f*

deputize ['depjutaɪz] *vi*: **to ~ (for sb)** (jdn) vertreten

deputy ['depjutɪ] *adj* stellvertretend ♦ *n* (Stell)vertreter *m*; **~ head** *n* (*BRIT: SCOL*) *n* Konrektor(in) *m(f)*

derail [dɪ'reɪl] *vt*: **to be ~ed** entgleisen; **~ment** *n* Entgleisung *f*

deranged [dɪ'reɪndʒd] *adj* verrückt

derby ['dɑ:rbɪ] (*US*) *n* Melone *f*

derelict ['derɪlɪkt] *adj* verlassen

deride [dɪ'raɪd] *vt* auslachen

derisory [dɪ'raɪsərɪ] *adj* spöttisch

derivative [dɪ'rɪvətɪv] *n* Derivat *nt* ♦ *adj* abgeleitet

derive [dɪ'raɪv] *vt* (*get*) gewinnen; (*deduce*) ableiten ♦ *vi* (*come from*) abstammen

dermatitis [də:mə'taɪtɪs] *n* Hautentzündung *f*

derogatory [dɪ'rɒgətərɪ] *adj* geringschätzig

derrick ['derɪk] *n* Drehkran *m*

descend [dɪ'send] *vt, vi* hinuntersteigen; **to**

~ from abstammen von; **~ant** n Nachkomme m; **descent** [dɪ'sɛnt] n (coming down) Abstieg m; (origin) Abstammung f

describe [dɪs'kraɪb] vt beschreiben

description [dɪs'krɪpʃən] n Beschreibung f; (sort) Art f

descriptive [dɪs'krɪptɪv] adj beschreibend; (word) anschaulich

desecrate ['dɛsɪkreɪt] vt schänden

desert [n 'dɛzət, vb dɪ'zɜːt] n Wüste f ♦ vt verlassen; (temporarily) im Stich lassen ♦ vi (MIL) desertieren; **~s** npl (what one deserves): **to get one's just ~s** seinen gerechten Lohn bekommen; **~er** n Deserteur m; **~ion** [dɪ'zɜːʃən] n (of wife) Verlassen nt; (MIL) Fahnenflucht f; **~ island** n einsame Insel f

deserve [dɪ'zɜːv] vt verdienen; **deserving** adj verdienstvoll

design [dɪ'zaɪn] n (plan) Entwurf m; (planning) Design nt ♦ vt entwerfen

designate [vb 'dɛzɪgneɪt, adj 'dɛzɪgnɪt] vt bestimmen ♦ adj designiert

designer [dɪ'zaɪnəʳ] n Designer(in) m(f); (TECH) Konstrukteur(in) m(f); (fashion ~) Modeschöpfer(in) m(f)

desirable [dɪ'zaɪərəbl] adj wünschenswert

desire [dɪ'zaɪəʳ] n Wunsch m, Verlangen nt ♦ vt (lust) begehren; (ask for) wollen

desk [dɛsk] n Schreibtisch m; (BRIT: in shop, restaurant) Kasse f; **~top publishing** n Desktop-Publishing nt

desolate ['dɛsəlɪt] adj öde; (sad) trostlos; **desolation** [dɛsə'leɪʃən] n Trostlosigkeit f

despair [dɪs'pɛəʳ] n Verzweiflung f ♦ vi: **to ~ (of)** verzweifeln (an +dat)

despatch [dɪs'pætʃ] n, vt = **dispatch**

desperate ['dɛspərɪt] adj verzweifelt; **~ly** adv verzweifelt; **desperation** [dɛspə'reɪʃən] n Verzweiflung f

despicable [dɪs'pɪkəbl] adj abscheulich

despise [dɪs'paɪz] vt verachten

despite [dɪs'paɪt] prep trotz +gen

despondent [dɪs'pɒndənt] adj mutlos

dessert [dɪ'zɜːt] n Nachtisch m; **~spoon** n Dessertlöffel m

destination [dɛstɪ'neɪʃən] n (of person)

(Reise)ziel nt; (of goods) Bestimmungsort m

destiny ['dɛstɪnɪ] n Schicksal nt

destitute ['dɛstɪtjuːt] adj notleidend △

destroy [dɪs'trɔɪ] vt zerstören; **~er** n (NAUT) Zerstörer m

destruction [dɪs'trʌkʃən] n Zerstörung f

destructive [dɪs'trʌktɪv] adj zerstörend

detach [dɪ'tætʃ] vt loslösen; **~able** adj abtrennbar; **~ed** adj (attitude) distanziert; (house) Einzel-; **~ment** n (fig) Abstand m; (MIL) Sonderkommando nt

detail ['diːteɪl] n Einzelheit f, Detail nt ♦ vt (relate) ausführlich berichten; (appoint) abkommandieren; **in ~** im Detail; **~ed** adj detailliert

detain [dɪ'teɪn] vt aufhalten; (imprison) in Haft halten

detect [dɪ'tɛkt] vt entdecken; **~ion** [dɪ'tɛkʃən] n Aufdeckung f; **~ive** n Detektiv m; **~ive story** n Kriminalgeschichte f, Krimi m

détente [deɪ'tɑːnt] n Entspannung f

detention [dɪ'tɛnʃən] n Haft f; (SCH) Nachsitzen nt

deter [dɪ'tɜːʳ] vt abschrecken

detergent [dɪ'tɜːdʒənt] n Waschmittel nt

deteriorate [dɪ'tɪərɪəreɪt] vi sich verschlechtern; **deterioration** [dɪtɪərɪə'reɪʃən] n Verschlechterung f

determination [dɪtəːmɪ'neɪʃən] n Entschlossenheit f

determine [dɪ'tɜːmɪn] vt bestimmen; **~d** adj entschlossen

deterrent [dɪ'tɛrənt] n Abschreckungsmittel nt

detest [dɪ'tɛst] vt verabscheuen

detonate ['dɛtəneɪt] vt explodieren lassen ♦ vi detonieren

detour ['diːtuəʳ] n Umweg m; (US: AUT: diversion) Umleitung f ♦ vt (US: AUT: traffic) umleiten

detract [dɪ'trækt] vi: **to ~ from** schmälern

detriment ['dɛtrɪmənt] n: **to the ~ of** zum Schaden +gen; **~al** [dɛtrɪ'mɛntl] adj schädlich

devaluation [diːvæljuː'eɪʃən] n Abwertung f

devastate ['dɛvəsteɪt] vt verwüsten; (fig: shock): **to be ~d by** niedergeschmettert sein von; **devastating** adj verheerend

develop [dɪ'vɛləp] vt entwickeln; (resources) erschließen ♦ vi sich entwickeln; ~**ing country** n Entwicklungsland nt; ~**ment** n Entwicklung f

deviate ['di:vɪeɪt] vi abweichen

device [dɪ'vaɪs] n Gerät nt

devil ['dɛvl] n Teufel m

devious ['di:vɪəs] adj (means) krumm; (person) verschlagen

devise [dɪ'vaɪz] vt entwickeln

devoid [dɪ'vɔɪd] adj: ~ **of** ohne

devolution [di:və'lu:ʃən] n (POL) Dezentralisierung f

devote [dɪ'vəʊt] vt: **to** ~ **sth (to sth)** etw (einer Sache dat) widmen; ~**d** adj ergeben; ~**e** [dɛvəʊ'ti:] n Anhänger(in) m(f), Verehrer(in) m(f); **devotion** [dɪ'vəʊʃən] n (piety) Andacht f; (loyalty) Ergebenheit f, Hingabe f

devour [dɪ'vauər] vt verschlingen

devout [dɪ'vaut] adj andächtig

dew [dju:] n Tau m

dexterity [dɛks'tɛrɪtɪ] n Geschicklichkeit f

DHSS (BRIT) n abbr = **Department of Health and Social Security**

diabetes [daɪə'bi:ti:z] n Zuckerkrankheit f

diabetic [daɪə'bɛtɪk] adj zuckerkrank; (food) Diabetiker- ♦ n Diabetiker m

diabolical [daɪə'bɔlɪkl] (inf) adj (weather, behaviour) saumäßig

diagnose [daɪəg'nəʊz] vt diagnostizieren

diagnoses [daɪəg'nəʊsi:z] npl of **diagnosis**

diagnosis [daɪəg'nəʊsɪs] n Diagnose f

diagonal [daɪ'ægənl] adj diagonal ♦ n Diagonale f

diagram ['daɪəgræm] n Diagramm nt, Schaubild nt

dial ['daɪəl] n (TEL) Wählscheibe f; (of clock) Zifferblatt nt ♦ vt wählen

dialect ['daɪəlɛkt] n Dialekt m

dialling code ['daɪəlɪŋ-] n Vorwahl f

dialling tone n Amtszeichen nt

dialogue ['daɪəlɔg] n Dialog m

dial tone (US) n = **dialling tone**

diameter [daɪ'æmɪtər] n Durchmesser m

diamond ['daɪəmənd] n Diamant m; ~**s** npl (CARDS) Karo nt

diaper ['daɪəpər] (US) n Windel f

diaphragm ['daɪəfræm] n Zwerchfell nt

diarrhoea [daɪə'ri:ə] (US **diarrhea**) n Durchfall m

diary ['daɪərɪ] n Taschenkalender m; (account) Tagebuch nt

dice [daɪs] n Würfel pl ♦ vt in Würfel schneiden

dictate [dɪk'teɪt] vt diktieren; ~**s** ['dɪkteɪts] npl Gebote pl; **dictation** [dɪk'teɪʃən] n Diktat nt

dictator [dɪk'teɪtər] n Diktator m; ~**ship** [dɪk'teɪtəʃɪp] n Diktatur f

dictionary ['dɪkʃənrɪ] n Wörterbuch nt

did [dɪd] pt of **do**

didn't ['dɪdnt] = **did not**

die [daɪ] vi sterben; **to be dying for sth** etw unbedingt haben wollen; **to be dying to do sth** darauf brennen, etw zu tun; ~ **away** vi schwächer werden; ~ **down** vi nachlassen; ~ **out** vi aussterben

diesel ['di:zl] n (car) Diesel m; ~ **engine** n Dieselmotor m; ~ **oil** n Dieselkraftstoff m

diet ['daɪət] n Nahrung f; (special food) Diät f; (slimming) Abmagerungskur f ♦ vi (also: **be on a** ~) eine Abmagerungskur machen

differ ['dɪfər] vi sich unterscheiden; (disagree) anderer Meinung sein; ~**ence** n Unterschied m; ~**ent** adj anders; (two things) verschieden; ~**entiate** [dɪfə'rɛnʃɪeɪt] vt, vi unterscheiden; ~**ently** adv anders; (from one another) unterschiedlich

difficult ['dɪfɪkəlt] adj schwierig; ~**y** n Schwierigkeit f

diffuse [adj dɪ'fju:s, vb dɪ'fju:z] adj langatmig ♦ vt verbreiten

dig [dɪg] (pt, pp **dug**) vt graben ♦ n (prod) Stoß m; (remark) Spitze f; (archaeological) Ausgrabung f; ~ **in** vi (MIL) sich eingraben; ~ **into** vt fus (savings) angreifen; ~ **up** vt ausgraben; (fig) aufgabeln

digest [vb daɪ'dʒɛst, n 'daɪdʒɛst] vt verdauen ♦ n Auslese f; ~**ion** [dɪ'dʒɛstʃən] n Verdauung f

digit ['dɪdʒɪt] n Ziffer f; (ANAT) Finger m; ~**al** adj digital, Digital-

⚠ For information on spelling reform see page 615

dignified [ˈdɪgnɪfaɪd] adj würdevoll

dignity [ˈdɪgnɪtɪ] n Würde f

digress [daɪˈgres] vi abschweifen

digs [dɪgz] (BRIT: inf) npl Bude f

dilapidated [dɪˈlæpɪdeɪtɪd] adj baufällig

dilate [daɪˈleɪt] vt weiten ♦ vi sich weiten

dilemma [daɪˈlemə] n Dilemma nt

diligent [ˈdɪlɪdʒənt] adj fleißig

dilute [daɪˈluːt] vt verdünnen

dim [dɪm] adj trübe; (stupid) schwer von Begriff ♦ vt verdunkeln; **to ~ one's headlights** (esp US) abblenden

dime [daɪm] (US) n Zehncentstück nt

dimension [daɪˈmenʃən] n Dimension f

diminish [dɪˈmɪnɪʃ] vt, vi verringern

diminutive [dɪˈmɪnjʊtɪv] adj winzig ♦ n Verkleinerungsform f

dimmer [ˈdɪmər] (US) n (AUT) Abblendschalter m; **~s** npl Abblendlicht nt; (sidelights) Begrenzungsleuchten pl

dimple [ˈdɪmpl] n Grübchen nt

din [dɪn] n Getöse nt

dine [daɪn] vi speisen; **~r** n Tischgast m; (RAIL) Speisewagen m

dinghy [ˈdɪŋgɪ] n Dingi nt; **rubber ~** Schlauchboot nt

dingy [ˈdɪndʒɪ] adj armselig

dining car (BRIT) n Speisewagen m

dining room [ˈdaɪnɪŋ-] n Eßzimmer nt; (in hotel) Speisezimmer nt △

dinner [ˈdɪnər] n (lunch) Mittagessen nt; (evening) Abendessen nt; (public) Festessen nt; **~ jacket** n Smoking m; **~ party** n Tischgesellschaft f; **~ time** n Tischzeit f

dinosaur [ˈdaɪnəsɔːr] n Dinosaurier m

dint [dɪnt] n: **by ~ of** durch

diocese [ˈdaɪəsɪs] n Diözese f

dip [dɪp] n (hollow) Senkung f; (bathe) kurze(s) Baden nt ♦ vt eintauchen; (BRIT: AUT) abblenden ♦ vi (slope) sich senken, abfallen

diploma [dɪˈpləʊmə] n Diplom nt

diplomacy [dɪˈpləʊməsɪ] n Diplomatie f

diplomat [ˈdɪpləmæt] n Diplomat(in) m(f); **~ic** [dɪpləˈmætɪk] adj diplomatisch

dip stick n Ölmeßstab △ m

dipswitch [ˈdɪpswɪtʃ] (BRIT) n (AUT)

Abblendschalter m

dire [daɪər] adj schrecklich

direct [daɪˈrekt] adj direkt ♦ vt leiten; (film) die Regie führen +gen; (aim) richten; (order) anweisen; **can you ~ me to ...?** können Sie mir sagen, wo ich zu ... komme?; **~ debit** n (BRIT) Einzugsauftrag m; (transaction) automatische Abbuchung f

direction [dɪˈrekʃən] n Richtung f; (CINE) Regie f; Leitung f; **~s** npl (for use) Gebrauchsanleitung f; (orders) Anweisungen pl; **sense of ~** Orientierungssinn m

directly [dɪˈrektlɪ] adv direkt; (at once) sofort

director [dɪˈrektər] n Direktor m; (of film) Regisseur m

directory [dɪˈrektərɪ] n (TEL) Telefonbuch nt; **~ enquiries**, (US) **~ assistance** (US) n (Fernsprech)auskunft f

dirt [dɜːt] n Schmutz m, Dreck m; **~-cheap** adj spottbillig; **~y** adj schmutzig ♦ vt beschmutzen; **~y trick** n gemeine(r) Trick m

disability [dɪsəˈbɪlɪtɪ] n Körperbehinderung f

disabled [dɪsˈeɪbld] adj körperbehindert

disadvantage [dɪsədˈvɑːntɪdʒ] n Nachteil m

disagree [dɪsəˈgriː] vi nicht übereinstimmen; (quarrel) (sich) streiten; (food): **to ~ with sb** jdm nicht bekommen; **~able** adj unangenehm; **~ment** n (between persons) Streit m; (between things) Widerspruch m

disallow [dɪsəˈlaʊ] vt nicht zulassen

disappear [dɪsəˈpɪər] vi verschwinden; **~ance** n Verschwinden nt

disappoint [dɪsəˈpɔɪnt] vt enttäuschen; **~ed** adj enttäuscht; **~ment** n Enttäuschung f

disapproval [dɪsəˈpruːvəl] n Mißbilligung △ f

disapprove [dɪsəˈpruːv] vi: **to ~ of** mißbilligen △

disarm [dɪsˈɑːm] vt entwaffnen; (POL) abrüsten; **~ament** n Abrüstung f

disarray [dɪsəˈreɪ] n: **to be in ~** (army) in Auflösung (begriffen) sein; (clothes) in unordentlichen Zustand sein

disaster [dɪˈzɑːstər] n Katastrophe f;

disastrous [dɪˈzɑːstrəs] *adj* verhängnisvoll
disband [dɪsˈbænd] *vt* auflösen ♦ *vi* auseinandergehen △
disbelief [ˈdɪsbəˈliːf] *n* Ungläubigkeit *f*
disc [dɪsk] *n* Scheibe *f*; (*record*) (Schall)platte *f*; (COMPUT) = **disk**
discard [dɪsˈkɑːd] *vt* ablegen
discern [dɪˈsɜːn] *vt* erkennen; **~ing** *adj* scharfsinnig
discharge [*vb* dɪsˈtʃɑːdʒh], *n* ˈdɪstʃɑːdʒ] *vt* (*ship*) entladen; (*duties*) nachkommen +*dat*; (*dismiss*) entlassen; (*gun*) abschießen; (JUR) freisprechen ♦ *n* (*of ship, ELEC*) Entladung *f*; (*dismissal*) Entlassung *f*; (MED) Ausfluß △ *m*
disciple [dɪˈsaɪpl] *n* Jünger *m*
discipline [ˈdɪsɪplɪn] *n* Disziplin *f* ♦ *vt* (*train*) schulen; (*punish*) bestrafen
disc jockey *n* Diskjockey *m*
disclaim [dɪsˈkleɪm] *vt* nicht anerkennen
disclose [dɪsˈkləʊz] *vt* enthüllen; **disclosure** [dɪsˈkləʊʒəʳ] *n* Enthüllung *f*
disco [ˈdɪskəʊ] *n abbr* = **discotheque**
discoloured [dɪsˈkʌləd] (US **discolored**) *adj* verfärbt
discomfort [dɪsˈkʌmfət] *n* Unbehagen *nt*
disconcert [dɪskənˈsɜːt] *vt* aus der Fassung bringen
disconnect [dɪskəˈnekt] *vt* abtrennen
discontent [dɪskənˈtent] *n* Unzufriedenheit *f*; **~ed** *adj* unzufrieden
discontinue [dɪskənˈtɪnjuː] *vt* einstellen
discord [ˈdɪskɔːd] *n* Zwietracht *f*; (*noise*) Dissonanz *f*
discotheque [ˈdɪskəʊtek] *n* Diskothek *f*
discount [*n* ˈdɪskaʊnt, *vb* dɪsˈkaʊnt] *n* Rabatt *m* ♦ *vt* außer acht lassen
discourage [dɪsˈkʌrɪdʒ] *vt* entmutigen; (*prevent*) abraten
discourteous [dɪsˈkɜːtɪəs] *adj* unhöflich
discover [dɪsˈkʌvəʳ] *vt* entdecken; **~y** *n* Entdeckung *f*
discredit [dɪsˈkredɪt] *vt* in Verruf bringen
discreet [dɪsˈkriːt] *adj* diskret
discrepancy [dɪsˈkrepənsɪ] *n* Diskrepanz *f*
discriminate [dɪsˈkrɪmɪneɪt] *vi* unterscheiden; **to ~ against** diskriminieren; **discriminating** *adj* anspruchsvoll;

discrimination [dɪskrɪmɪˈneɪʃən] *n* Urteilsvermögen *nt*; (*pej*) Diskriminierung *f*
discuss [dɪsˈkʌs] *vt* diskutieren, besprechen; **~ion** *n* Diskussion *f*, Besprechung *f*
disdain [dɪsˈdeɪn] *n* Verachtung *f*
disease [dɪˈziːz] *n* Krankheit *f*
disembark [dɪsɪmˈbɑːk] *vi* von Bord gehen
disenchanted [ˈdɪsɪnˈtʃɑːntɪd] *adj* desillusioniert
disengage [dɪsɪnˈgeɪdʒ] *vt* (AUT) auskuppeln
disentangle [dɪsɪnˈtæŋgl] *vt* entwirren
disfigure [dɪsˈfɪgəʳ] *vt* entstellen
disgrace [dɪsˈgreɪs] *n* Schande *f* ♦ *vt* Schande bringen über +*acc*; **~ful** *adj* unerhört
disgruntled [dɪsˈgrʌntld] *adj* verärgert
disguise [dɪsˈgaɪz] *vt* verkleiden; (*feelings*) verhehlen ♦ *n* Verkleidung *f*; **in ~** verkleidet, maskiert
disgust [dɪsˈgʌst] *n* Abscheu *f* ♦ *vt* anwidern; **~ed** *adj* angeekelt; (*at sb's behaviour*) empört; **~ing** *adj* widerlich
dish [dɪʃ] *n* Schüssel *f*; (*food*) Gericht *nt*; **to do** *or* **wash the ~es** abwaschen; **~ up** *vt* auftischen; **~ cloth** *n* Spüllappen *m*
dishearten [dɪsˈhɑːtn] *vt* entmutigen
dishevelled [dɪˈʃevəld] *adj* (*hair*) zerzaust; (*clothing*) ungepflegt
dishonest [dɪsˈɒnɪst] *adj* unehrlich
dishonour [dɪsˈɒnəʳ] (US **dishonor**) *n* Unehre *f*; **~able** *adj* unehrenhaft
dishtowel [ˈdɪʃtaʊəl] *n* Geschirrtuch *nt*
dishwasher [ˈdɪʃwɒʃəʳ] *n* Geschirrspülmaschine *f*
disillusion [dɪsɪˈluːʒən] *vt* enttäuschen, desillusionieren
disincentive [dɪsɪnˈsentɪv] *n* Entmutigung *f*
disinfect [dɪsɪnˈfekt] *vt* desinfizieren; **~ant** *n* Desinfektionsmittel *nt*
disintegrate [dɪsˈɪntɪgreɪt] *vi* sich auflösen
disinterested [dɪsˈɪntrəstɪd] *adj* uneigennützig; (*inf*) uninteressiert
disjointed [dɪsˈdʒɔɪntɪd] *adj* unzusammenhängend
disk [dɪsk] *n* (COMPUT) Diskette *f*; **single/ double sided ~** einseitige/beidseitige Diskette; **~ drive** *n* Diskettenlaufwerk *nt*;

△ *For information on spelling reform see page 615*

~ette [dɪsˈket] (*US*) *n* = **disk**

dislike [dɪsˈlaɪk] *n* Abneigung *f* ♦ *vt* nicht leiden können

dislocate [ˈdɪsləkeɪt] *vt* auskugeln

dislodge [dɪsˈlɔdʒ] *vt* verschieben; (*MIL*) aus der Stellung werfen

disloyal [dɪsˈlɔɪəl] *adj* treulos

dismal [ˈdɪzml] *adj* trostlos, trübe

dismantle [dɪsˈmæntl] *vt* demontieren

dismay [dɪsˈmeɪ] *n* Bestürzung *f* ♦ *vt* bestürzen

dismiss [dɪsˈmɪs] *vt* (*employee*) entlassen; (*idea*) von sich weisen; (*send away*) wegschicken; (*JUR*) abweisen; **~al** *n* Entlassung *f*

dismount [dɪsˈmaunt] *vi* absteigen

disobedience [dɪsəˈbiːdɪəns] *n* Ungehorsam *m*; **disobedient** *adj* ungehorsam

disobey [dɪsəˈbeɪ] *vt* nicht gehorchen +*dat*

disorder [dɪsˈɔːdəʳ] *n* (*confusion*) Verwirrung *f*; (*commotion*) Aufruhr *m*; (*MED*) Erkrankung *f*

disorderly [dɪsˈɔːdəlɪ] *adj* (*untidy*) unordentlich; (*unruly*) ordnungswidrig

disorganized [dɪsˈɔːgənaɪzd] *adj* unorganisiert

disorientated [dɪsˈɔːrɪenteɪtɪd] *adj* (*person: after journey*) verwirrt

disown [dɪsˈaun] *vt* (*child*) verstoßen

disparaging [dɪsˈpærɪdʒɪŋ] *adj* geringschätzig

dispassionate [dɪsˈpæʃənət] *adj* objektiv

dispatch [dɪsˈpætʃ] *vt* (*goods*) abschicken, abfertigen ♦ *n* Absendung *f*; (*esp MIL*) Meldung *f*

dispel [dɪsˈpel] *vt* zerstreuen

dispensary [dɪsˈpensərɪ] *n* Apotheke *f*

dispense [dɪsˈpens] *vt* verteilen, austeilen; **~ with** *vt fus* verzichten auf +*acc*; **~r** *n* (*container*) Spender *m*; **dispensing** *adj*: **dispensing chemist** (*BRIT*) Apotheker *m*

dispersal [dɪsˈpɜːsl] *n* Zerstreuung *f*

disperse [dɪsˈpɜːs] *vt* zerstreuen ♦ *vi* sich verteilen

dispirited [dɪsˈpɪrɪtɪd] *adj* niedergeschlagen

displace [dɪsˈpleɪs] *vt* verschieben; **~d**

person *n* Verschleppte(r) *mf*

display [dɪsˈpleɪ] *n* (*of goods*) Auslage *f*; (*of feeling*) Zurschaustellung *f* ♦ *vt* zeigen; (*ostentatiously*) vorführen; (*goods*) ausstellen

displease [dɪsˈpliːz] *vt* mißfallen ⚠ +*dat*

displeasure [dɪsˈpleʒəʳ] *n* Mißfallen ⚠ *nt*

disposable [dɪsˈpəuzəbl] *adj* Wegwerf-; **~ nappy** *n* Papierwindel *f*

disposal [dɪsˈpəuzl] *n* (*of property*) Verkauf *m*; (*throwing away*) Beseitigung *f*; **to be at one's ~** einem zur Verfügung stehen

dispose [dɪsˈpəuz] *vi*: **to ~ of** loswerden; **~d** *adj* geneigt

disposition [dɪspəˈzɪʃən] *n* Wesen *nt*

disproportionate [dɪsprəˈpɔːʃənət] *adj* unverhältnismäßig

disprove [dɪsˈpruːv] *vt* widerlegen

dispute [dɪsˈpjuːt] *n* Streit *m*; (*also: industrial ~*) Arbeitskampf *m* ♦ *vt* bestreiten

disqualify [dɪsˈkwɔlɪfaɪ] *vt* disqualifizieren

disquiet [dɪsˈkwaɪət] *n* Unruhe *f*

disregard [dɪsrɪˈgɑːd] *vt* nicht (be)achten

disrepair [ˈdɪsrɪˈpeəʳ] *n*: **to fall into ~** verfallen

disreputable [dɪsˈrepjutəbl] *adj* verrufen

disrespectful [dɪsrɪˈspektful] *adj* respektlos

disrupt [dɪsˈrʌpt] *vt* stören; (*service*) unterbrechen; **~ion** [dɪsˈrʌpʃən] *n* Störung *f*; Unterbrechung *f*

dissatisfaction [dɪssætɪsˈfækʃən] *n* Unzufriedenheit *f*; **dissatisfied** [dɪsˈsætɪsfaɪd] *adj* unzufrieden

dissect [dɪˈsekt] *vt* zerlegen, sezieren

dissent [dɪˈsent] *n* abweichende Meinung *f*

dissertation [dɪsəˈteɪʃən] *n* wissenschaftliche Arbeit *f*; (*Ph.D.*) Doktorarbeit *f*

disservice [dɪsˈsɜːvɪs] *n*: **to do sb a ~** jdm einen schlechten Dienst erweisen

dissident [ˈdɪsɪdnt] *adj* andersdenkend ⚠ ♦ *n* Dissident *m*

dissimilar [dɪˈsɪmɪləʳ] *adj*: **~ (to sb/sth)** (jdm/etw) unähnlich

dissipate [ˈdɪsɪpeɪt] *vt* (*waste*) verschwenden; (*scatter*) zerstreuen

dissociate [dɪˈsəuʃɪeɪt] *vt* trennen

⚠ *Informationen zur Rechtschreibreform Seite 615*

dissolve [dɪ'zɒlv] vt auflösen ♦ vi sich auflösen

dissuade [dɪ'sweɪd] vt: **to ~ sb from doing sth** jdn davon abbringen, etw zu tun

distance ['dɪstns] n Entfernung f; **in the ~** in der Ferne; **distant** adj entfernt, fern; (with time) fern

distaste [dɪs'teɪst] n Abneigung f; **~ful** adj widerlich

distended [dɪs'tendɪd] adj (stomach) aufgebläht

distil [dɪs'tɪl] vt destillieren; **~lery** n Brennerei f

distinct [dɪs'tɪŋkt] adj (separate) getrennt; (clear) klar, deutlich; **as ~ from** im Unterschied zu; **~ion** [dɪs'tɪŋkʃən] n Unterscheidung f; (eminence) Auszeichnung f; **distinctive** adj bezeichnend

distinguish [dɪs'tɪŋgwɪʃ] vt unterscheiden; **~ed** adj (eminent) berühmt; **~ing** adj bezeichnend

distort [dɪs'tɔ:t] vt verdrehen; (misrepresent) entstellen; **~ion** [dɪs'tɔ:ʃən] n Verzerrung f

distract [dɪs'trækt] vt ablenken; **~ing** adj verwirrend; **~ion** [dɪs'trækʃən] n (distress) Raserei f; (diversion) Zerstreuung f

distraught [dɪs'trɔ:t] adj bestürzt

distress [dɪs'tres] n Not f; (suffering) Qual f ♦ vt quälen; **~ing** adj erschütternd; **~ signal** n Notsignal nt

distribute [dɪs'trɪbju:t] vt verteilen; **distribution** [dɪstrɪ'bju:ʃən] n Verteilung f; **distributor** n Verteiler m

district ['dɪstrɪkt] n (of country) Kreis m; (of town) Bezirk m; **~ attorney** (US) n Oberstaatsanwalt m; **~ nurse** n Kreiskrankenschwester f

distrust [dɪs'trʌst] n Mißtrauen ⚠ nt ♦ vt mißtrauen ⚠ +dat

disturb [dɪs'tɜ:b] vt stören; (agitate) erregen; **~ance** n Störung f; **~ed** adj beunruhigt; **emotionally ~ed** emotional gestört; **~ing** adj beunruhigend

disuse [dɪs'ju:s] n: **to fall into ~** außer Gebrauch kommen; **~d** [dɪs'ju:zd] adj außer Gebrauch; (mine, railway line) stillgelegt

ditch [dɪtʃ] n Graben m ♦ vt (person)

loswerden; (plan) fallenlassen ⚠

dither ['dɪðə*] vi verdattert sein

ditto ['dɪtəu] adv dito, ebenfalls

divan [dɪ'væn] n Liegesofa nt

dive [daɪv] n (into water) Kopfsprung m; (AVIAT) Sturzflug m ♦ vi tauchen; **~r** n Taucher m

diverge [daɪ'və:dʒ] vi auseinandergehen ⚠

diverse [daɪ'və:s] adj verschieden

diversion [daɪ'və:ʃən] n Ablenkung f; (BRIT: AUT) Umleitung f

diversity [daɪ'və:sɪtɪ] n Vielfalt f

divert [daɪ'və:t] vt ablenken; (traffic) umleiten

divide [dɪ'vaɪd] vt teilen ♦ vi sich teilen; **~d highway** (US) n Schnellstraße f

divine [dɪ'vaɪn] adj göttlich

diving ['daɪvɪŋ] n (SPORT) Turmspringen nt; (underwater ~) Tauchen nt; **~ board** n Sprungbrett nt

divinity [dɪ'vɪnɪtɪ] n Gottheit f; (subject) Religion f

division [dɪ'vɪʒən] n Teilung f; (MIL) Division f; (part) Abteilung f; (in opinion) Uneinigkeit f; (BRIT: POL) (Abstimmung f durch) Hammelsprung m

divorce [dɪ'vɔ:s] n (Ehe)scheidung f ♦ vt scheiden; **~d** adj geschieden; **~e** [dɪvɔ:'si:] n Geschiedene(r) f(m)

divulge [daɪ'vʌldʒ] vt preisgeben

DIY (BRIT) n abbr = **do-it-yourself**

dizzy ['dɪzɪ] adj schwindlig

DJ n abbr = **disc jockey**

DNA fingerprinting n genetische Fingerabdrücke pl

KEYWORD

do [du:] (pt **did**, pp **done**) n (inf: party etc) Fete f

♦ aux vb **1** (in negative constructions and questions): **I don't understand** ich verstehe nicht; **didn't you know?** wußtest du das nicht?; **what do you think?** was meinen Sie?

2 (for emphasis, in polite phrases): **she does seem rather tired** sie scheint wirklich sehr müde zu sein; **do sit down/help yourself**

⚠ For information on spelling reform see page 615

setzen Sie sich doch hin/greifen Sie doch zu

3 (*used to avoid repeating vb*): **she swims better than I do** sie schwimmt besser als ich; **she lives in Glasgow - so do I** sie wohnt in Glasgow - ich auch

4 (*in tag questions*): **you like him, don't you?** du magst ihn doch, oder?

♦ *vt* **1** (*carry out, perform etc*) tun, machen; **what are you doing tonight?** was machst du heute abend?; **I've got nothing to do** ich habe nichts zu tun; **to do one's hair/nails** sich die Haare/Nägel machen

2 (*AUT etc*) fahren

♦ *vi* **1** (*act, behave*): **do as I do** mach es wie ich

2 (*get on, fare*): **he's doing well/badly at school** er ist gut/schlecht in der Schule; **how do you do?** guten Tag

3 (*be suitable*) gehen; (*be sufficient*) reichen; **to make do (with)** auskommen mit

do away with *vt* (*kill*) umbringen; (*abolish: law etc*) abschaffen

do up *vt* (*laces, dress, buttons*) zumachen; (*room, house*) renovieren

do with *vt* (*need*) brauchen; (*be connected*) zu tun haben mit

do without *vt, vi* auskommen ohne

---

docile ['dəusaɪl] *adj* gefügig

dock [dɒk] *n* Dock *nt*; (*JUR*) Anklagebank *f* ♦ *vi* ins Dock gehen; **~er** *n* Hafenarbeiter *m*; **~yard** *n* Werft *f*

doctor ['dɒktə'] *n* Arzt *m*, Ärztin *f*; (*UNIV*) Doktor *m* ♦ *vt* (*fig*) fälschen; (*drink etc*) etw beimischen +*dat*; **D~ of Philosophy** *n* Doktor *m* der Philosophie

document ['dɒkjumənt] *n* Dokument *nt*; **~ary** [dɒkju'mentəri] *n* Dokumentarbericht *m*; (*film*) Dokumentarfilm *m* ♦ *adj* dokumentarisch; **~ation** [dɒkjumən'teɪʃən] *n* dokumentarische(r) Nachweis *m*

dodge [dɒdʒ] *n* Kniff *m* ♦ *vt* ausweichen +*dat*

dodgems ['dɒdʒəmz] (*BRIT*) *npl* Autoskooter *m*

doe [dəu] *n* (*roe deer*) Ricke *f*; (*red deer*)

Hirschkuh *f*; (*rabbit*) Weibchen *nt*

does [dʌz] *vb see* **do**; **~n't** = **does not**

dog [dɒg] *n* Hund *m*; **~ collar** *n* Hundehalsband *nt*; (*ECCL*) Kragen *m* des Geistlichen; **~-eared** *adj* mit Eselsohren

dogged ['dɒgɪd] *adj* hartnäckig

dogsbody ['dɒgzbɒdɪ] *n* Mädchen *nt* für alles

doings ['duːɪŋz] *npl* (*activities*) Treiben *nt*

do-it-yourself ['duːɪtjɔː'self] *n* Do-it-yourself *nt*

doldrums ['dɒldrəmz] *npl*: **to be in the ~** (*business*) Flaute haben; (*person*) deprimiert sein

dole [dəul] (*BRIT*) *n* Stempelgeld *nt*; **to be on the ~** stempeln gehen; **~ out** *vt* ausgeben, austeilen

doleful ['dəulful] *adj* traurig

doll [dɒl] *n* Puppe *f* ♦ *vt*: **to ~ o.s. up** sich aufdonnern

dollar ['dɒlə'] *n* Dollar *m*

dolphin ['dɒlfɪn] *n* Delphin △ *m*

dome [dəum] *n* Kuppel *f*

domestic [də'mestɪk] *adj* häuslich; (*within country*) Innen-, Binnen-; (*animal*) Haus-; **~ated** *adj* (*person*) häuslich; (*animal*) zahm

dominant ['dɒmɪnənt] *adj* vorherrschend

dominate ['dɒmɪneɪt] *vt* beherrschen

domineering [dɒmɪ'nɪərɪŋ] *adj* herrisch

dominion [də'mɪnɪən] *n* (*rule*) Regierungsgewalt *f*; (*land*) Staatsgebiet *nt* mit Selbstverwaltung

domino ['dɒmɪnəu] (*pl* **~es**) *n* Dominostein *m*; **~es** *n* (*game*) Domino(spiel) *nt*

don [dɒn] (*BRIT*) *n* akademische(r) Lehrer *m*

donate [də'neɪt] *vt* (*blood, money*) spenden; (*lot of money*) stiften; **donation** [də'neɪʃən] *n* Spende *f*

done [dʌn] *pp of* **do**

donkey ['dɒŋkɪ] *n* Esel *m*

donor ['dəunə'] *n* Spender *m*; **~ card** *n* Organspenderausweis *m*

don't [dəunt] = **do not**

doodle ['duːdl] *vi* kritzeln

doom [duːm] *n* böse(s) Geschick *nt*; (*downfall*) Verderben *nt* ♦ *vt*: **to be ~ed** zum Untergang verurteilt sein; **~sday** *n* der Jüngste Tag

door [dɔ:ʳ] n Tür f; **~bell** n Türklingel f; **~handle** n Türklinke f; **~man** (irreg) n Türsteher m; **~mat** n Fußmatte f; **~step** n Türstufe f; **~way** n Türöffnung f

dope [dəʊp] n (drug) Aufputschmittel nt ♦ vt (horse) dopen

dopey ['dəʊpɪ] (inf) adj bekloppt

dormant ['dɔ:mənt] adj latent

dormitory ['dɔ:mɪtrɪ] n Schlafsaal m

dormouse ['dɔ:maʊs] (pl -mice) n Haselmaus f

DOS [dɒs] n abbr (= disk operating system) DOS nt

dosage ['dəʊsɪdʒ] n Dosierung f

dose [dəʊs] n Dosis f

dosh [dɒʃ] (inf) n (money) Moos nt, Knete f

doss house ['dɒs-] (BRIT) n Bleibe f

dot [dɒt] n Punkt m; **~ted with** übersät mit; **on the ~** pünktlich

dote [dəʊt]: **to ~ on** vt fus vernarrt sein in +acc

dotted line ['dɒtɪd-] n punktierte Linie f

double ['dʌbl] adj, adv doppelt ♦ n Doppelgänger m ♦ vt verdoppeln ♦ vi sich verdoppeln; **~s** npl (TENNIS) Doppel nt; **on** or **at the ~** im Laufschritt; **~ bass** n Kontrabaß △ m; **~ bed** n Doppelbett nt; **~ bend** (BRIT) n S-Kurve f; **~-breasted** adj zweireihig; **~-cross** vt hintergehen; **~-decker** n Doppeldecker m; **~ glazing** (BRIT) n Doppelverglasung f; **~ room** n Doppelzimmer nt

doubly ['dʌblɪ] adv doppelt

doubt [daʊt] n Zweifel m ♦ vt bezweifeln; **~ful** adj zweifelhaft; **~less** adv ohne Zweifel

dough [dəʊ] n Teig m; **~nut** n Berliner m

douse [daʊz] vt (drench) mit Wasser begießen, durchtränken; (extinguish) ausmachen

dove [dʌv] n Taube f

dovetail ['dʌvteɪl] vi (plans) übereinstimmen

dowdy ['daʊdɪ] adj unmodern

down [daʊn] n (fluff) Flaum m; (hill) Hügel m ♦ adv unten; (motion) herunter; hinunter ♦ prep: **to go ~ the street** die Straße hinuntergehen ♦ vt niederschlagen; **~ with X!** nieder mit X!; **~-and-out** n Tramp m; **~-at-heel** adj schäbig; **~cast** adj niedergeschlagen; **~fall** n Sturz m; **~hearted** adj niedergeschlagen; **~hill** adv bergab; **~ payment** n Anzahlung f; **~pour** n Platzregen m; **~right** adj ausgesprochen; **~size** vi (ECON: company) sich verkleinern

┌─────────────────────┐
│ DOWNING STREET │
└─────────────────────┘

ⓘ **Downing Street** *ist die Straße in London, die von Whitehall zum St James Park führt und in der sich der offizielle Wohnsitz des Premierministers (Nr. 10) und des Finanzministers (Nr. 11) befindet. Im weiteren Sinne bezieht sich der Begriff Downing Street auf die britische Regierung.*

Down's syndrome [daʊnz-] n (MED) Down-Syndrom nt

down: **~stairs** adv unten; (motion) nach unten; **~stream** adv flußabwärts △; **~-to-earth** adj praktisch; **~town** adv in der Innenstadt; (motion) in die Innenstadt; **~ under** (BRIT: inf) adv in/nach Australien/Neuseeland; **~ward** adj Abwärts-, nach unten ♦ adv abwärts, nach unten; **~wards** adv abwärts, nach unten

dowry ['daʊrɪ] n Mitgift f

doz. abbr (= dozen) Dtzd.

doze [dəʊz] vi dösen; **~ off** vi einnicken

dozen ['dʌzn] n Dutzend nt; **a ~ books** ein Dutzend Bücher; **~s of** Dutzende von

Dr. abbr = **doctor**; **drive**

drab [dræb] adj düster, eintönig

draft [drɑ:ft] n Entwurf m; (FIN) Wechsel m; (US: MIL) Einberufung f ♦ vt skizzieren; see also **draught**

draftsman ['drɑ:ftsmən] (US) (irreg) n = **draughtsman**

drag [dræg] vt schleppen; (river) mit einem Schleppnetz absuchen ♦ vi sich (dahin)schleppen ♦ n (bore) etwas Blödes; **in ~** als Tunte; **a man in ~** eine Tunte; **~ on** vi sich in die Länge ziehen; **~ and drop** vt (COMPUT) Drag & Drop

△ *For information on spelling reform see page 615*

dragon ['drægn] n Drache m; **~fly**
['drægənflaɪ] n Libelle f
drain [dreɪn] n Abfluß △ m; (fig: burden)
Belastung f ♦ vt ableiten; (exhaust)
erschöpfen ♦ vi (of water) abfließen; **~age**
n Kanalisation f; **~ing board** (US **~board**) n
Ablaufbrett nt; **~pipe** n Abflußrohr △ nt
dram [dræm] n Schluck m
drama ['drɑːmə] n Drama nt; **~tic**
[drə'mætɪk] adj dramatisch; **~tist** ['dræmətɪst]
n Dramatiker m; **~tize** ['dræmətaɪz] vt
(events) dramatisieren; (for TV etc)
bearbeiten
drank [dræŋk] pt of **drink**
drape [dreɪp] vt drapieren; **~s** (US) npl
Vorhänge pl
drastic ['dræstɪk] adj drastisch
draught [drɑːft] (US **draft**) n Zug m; (NAUT)
Tiefgang m; **~s** n Damespiel nt; **on ~** (beer)
vom Faß; **~ beer** n Bier nt vom Faß △;
~board (BRIT) n Zeichenbrett nt
draughtsman ['drɑːftsmən] (irreg) n
technische(r) Zeichner m
draw [drɔː] (pt **drew**, pp **drawn**) vt ziehen;
(crowd) anlocken; (picture) zeichnen;
(money) abheben; (water) schöpfen ♦ vi
(SPORT) unentschieden spielen ♦ n (SPORT)
Unentschieden nt; (lottery) Ziehung f; **~
near** vi näherrücken △; **~ out** vi (train)
ausfahren; (lengthen) sich hinziehen; **~ up**
vi (stop) halten ♦ vt (document) aufsetzen
drawback ['drɔːbæk] n Nachteil m
drawbridge ['drɔːbrɪdʒ] n Zugbrücke f
drawer [drɔːʳ] n Schublade f
drawing ['drɔːɪŋ] n Zeichnung f; Zeichnen
nt; **~ board** n Reißbrett nt; **~ pin** (BRIT) n
Reißzwecke f; **~ room** n Salon m
drawl [drɔːl] n schleppende Sprechweise f
drawn [drɔːn] pp of **draw**
dread [dred] n Furcht f ♦ vt fürchten; **~ful**
adj furchtbar
dream [driːm] (pt, pp **dreamed** or **dreamt**)
n Traum m ♦ vt träumen ♦ vi: **to ~ (about)**
träumen (von); **~er** n Träumer m; **~t**
[dremt] pt, pp of **dream**; **~y** adj verträumt
dreary ['drɪərɪ] adj trostlos, öde
dredge [dredʒ] vt ausbaggern

dregs [dregz] npl Bodensatz m; (fig)
Abschaum m
drench [drentʃ] vt durchnässen
dress [dres] n Kleidung f; (garment) Kleid nt
♦ vt anziehen; (MED) verbinden; **to get ~ed**
sich anziehen; **~ up** vi sich fein machen; **~
circle** (BRIT) n erste(r) Rang m; **~er** n
(furniture) Anrichte f; **~ing** n (MED) Verband
m; (COOK) Soße f; **~ing gown** (BRIT) n
Morgenrock m; **~ing room** n (THEAT)
Garderobe f; (SPORT) Umkleideraum m;
~ing table n Toilettentisch m; **~maker** n
Schneiderin f; **~ rehearsal** n Generalprobe
f
drew [druː] pt of **draw**
dribble ['drɪbl] vi sabbern ♦ vt (ball)
dribbeln
dried [draɪd] adj getrocknet; (fruit) Dörr-,
gedörrte(r, s); **~ milk** n Milchpulver nt
drier ['draɪəʳ] n = **dryer**
drift [drɪft] n Strömung f; (snow~)
Schneewehe f; (fig) Richtung f ♦ vi sich
treiben lassen; **~wood** n Treibholz nt
drill [drɪl] n Bohrer m; (MIL) Drill m ♦ vt
bohren; (MIL) ausbilden ♦ vi: **to ~ (for)**
bohren (nach)
drink [drɪŋk] (pt **drank**, pp **drunk**) n Getränk
nt; (spirits) Drink m ♦ vt, vi trinken; **to have
a ~** etwas trinken; **~er** n Trinker m; **~ing
water** n Trinkwasser nt
drip [drɪp] n Tropfen m ♦ vi tropfen; **~-dry**
adj bügelfrei; **~ping** n Bratenfett nt
drive [draɪv] (pt **drove**, pp **driven**) n Fahrt f;
(road) Einfahrt f; (campaign) Aktion f;
(energy) Schwung m; (SPORT) Schlag m;
(also: **disk ~**) Diskettenlaufwerk nt ♦ vt (car)
fahren; (animals, people, objects) treiben;
(power) antreiben ♦ vi fahren; **left-/right-
hand ~** Links-/Rechtssteuerung f; **to ~ sb
mad** jdn verrückt machen; **~-by shooting**
n Schußwaffenangriff aus einem
vorbeifahrenden Wagen
drivel ['drɪvl] n Faselei f
driven ['drɪvn] pp of **drive**
driver ['draɪvəʳ] n Fahrer m; **~'s license**
(US) n Führerschein m
driveway ['draɪvweɪ] n Auffahrt f; (longer)

Zufahrtsstraße f

driving ['draɪvɪŋ] *adj* (*rain*) stürmisch; ~ **instructor** *n* Fahrlehrer *m*; ~ **lesson** *n* Fahrstunde *f*; ~ **licence** (*BRIT*) *n* Führerschein *m*; ~ **school** *n* Fahrschule *f*; ~ **test** *n* Fahrprüfung *f*

drizzle ['drɪzl] *n* Nieselregen *m* ♦ *vi* nieseln

droll [drəʊl] *adj* drollig

drone [drəʊn] *n* (*sound*) Brummen *nt*; (*bee*) Drohne *f*

drool [druːl] *vi* sabbern

droop [druːp] *vi* (*schlaff*) herabhängen

drop [drɒp] *n* (*of liquid*) Tropfen *m*; (*fall*) Fall *m* ♦ *vt* fallen lassen; (*lower*) senken; (*abandon*) fallenlassen △ ♦ *vi* (*fall*) herunterfallen; ~s *npl* (*MED*) Tropfen *pl*; ~ **off** *vi* (*sleep*) einschlafen ♦ *vt* (*passenger*) absetzen; ~ **out** *vi* (*withdraw*) ausscheiden; ~**-out** *n* Aussteiger *m*; ~**per** *n* Pipette *f*; ~**pings** *npl* Kot *m*

drought [draʊt] *n* Dürre *f*

drove [drəʊv] *pt of* drive

drown [draʊn] *vt* ertränken; (*sound*) übertönen ♦ *vi* ertrinken

drowsy ['draʊzɪ] *adj* schläfrig

drudgery ['drʌdʒərɪ] *n* Plackerei *f*

drug [drʌg] *n* (*MED*) Arznei *f*; (*narcotic*) Rauschgift *n* ♦ *vt* betäuben; ~ **addict** *n* Rauschgiftsüchtige(r) *f(m)*; ~**gist** (*US*) *n* Drogist(in) *m(f)*; ~**store** (*US*) *n* Drogerie *f*

drum [drʌm] *n* Trommel *f* ♦ *vi* trommeln; ~**s** *npl* (*MUS*) Schlagzeug *nt*; ~**mer** *n* Trommler *m*

drunk [drʌŋk] *pp of* drink ♦ *adj* betrunken ♦ *n* (*also:* ~**ard**) Trinker(in) *m(f)*; ~**en** *adj* betrunken

dry [draɪ] *adj* trocken ♦ *vt* (ab)trocknen ♦ *vi* trocknen; ~ **up** *vi* austrocknen ♦ *vt* (*dishes*) abtrocknen; ~ **cleaner's** *n* chemische Reinigung *f*; ~ **cleaning** *n* chemische Reinigung *f*; ~**er** *n* Trockner *m*; (*US: spin-dryer*) (Wäsche)schleuder *f*; ~ **goods store** (*US*) *n* Kurzwarengeschäft *nt*; ~**ness** *n* Trockenheit *f*; ~ **rot** *n* Hausschwamm *m*

DSS (*BRIT*) *n abbr* (= *Department of Social Security*) ≈ Sozialministerium *nt*

DTP *n abbr* (= *desk-top publishing*) DTP *nt*

dual ['djuəl] *adj* doppelt; ~ **carriageway** (*BRIT*) *n* zweispurige Fahrbahn *f*; ~ **nationality** *n* doppelte Staatsangehörigkeit *f*; ~**-purpose** *adj* Mehrzweck-

dubbed [dʌbd] *adj* (*film*) synchronisiert

dubious ['djuːbɪəs] *adj* zweifelhaft

duchess ['dʌtʃɪs] *n* Herzogin *f*

duck [dʌk] *n* Ente *f* ♦ *vi* sich ducken; ~**ling** *n* Entchen *nt*

duct [dʌkt] *n* Röhre *f*

dud [dʌd] *n* Niete *f* ♦ *adj* (*cheque*) ungedeckt

due [djuː] *adj* fällig; (*fitting*) angemessen ♦ *n* Gebühr *f*; (*right*) Recht *nt* ♦ *adv* (*south etc*) genau; ~**s** *npl* (*for club*) Beitrag *m*; (*NAUT*) Gebühren *pl*; ~ **to** wegen *+gen*

duel ['djuəl] *n* Duell *nt*

duet [djuːˈet] *n* Duett *nt*

duffel ['dʌfl] *adj*: ~ **bag** Matchbeutel *m*, Matchsack *m*

dug [dʌg] *pt*, *pp of* dig

duke [djuːk] *n* Herzog *m*

dull [dʌl] *adj* (*colour, weather*) trübe; (*stupid*) schwer von Begriff; (*boring*) langweilig ♦ *vt* abstumpfen

duly ['djuːlɪ] *adv* ordnungsgemäß

dumb [dʌm] *adj* stumm; (*inf: stupid*) doof, blöde; ~**founded** [dʌmˈfaʊndɪd] *adj* verblüfft

dummy ['dʌmɪ] *n* Schneiderpuppe *f*; (*substitute*) Attrappe *f*; (*BRIT: for baby*) Schnuller *m* ♦ *adj* Schein-

dump [dʌmp] *n* Abfallhaufen *m*; (*MIL*) Stapelplatz *m*; (*inf: place*) Nest *nt* ♦ *vt* abladen, auskippen; ~**ing** *n* (*COMM*) Schleuderexport *m*; (*of rubbish*) Schuttabladen *nt*

dumpling ['dʌmplɪŋ] *n* Kloß *m*, Knödel *m*

dumpy ['dʌmpɪ] *adj* pummelig

dunce [dʌns] *n* Dummkopf *m*

dune [djuːn] *n* Düne *f*

dung [dʌŋ] *n* Dünger *m*

dungarees [dʌŋgəˈriːz] *npl* Latzhose *f*

dungeon ['dʌndʒən] *n* Kerker *m*

dupe [djuːp] *n* Gefoppte(r) *m* ♦ *vt* hintergehen, anführen

duplex ['djuːpleks] (*US*) *n* zweistöckige Wohnung *f*

△ *For information on spelling reform see page 615*

duplicate [n 'dju:plɪkət, vb 'dju:plɪkeɪt] n
Duplikat nt ♦ vt verdoppeln; (make copies)
kopieren; **in ~** in doppelter Ausführung

duplicity [dju:'plɪsɪtɪ] n Doppelspiel nt

durable ['djuərəbl] adj haltbar

duration [djuə'reɪʃən] n Dauer f

duress [djuə'rɛs] n: **under ~** unter Zwang

during ['djuərɪŋ] prep während +gen

dusk [dʌsk] n Abenddämmerung f

dust [dʌst] n Staub m ♦ vt abstauben;
(sprinkle) bestäuben; **~bin** (BRIT) n
Mülleimer m; **~er** n Staubtuch nt; **~ jacket**
n Schutzumschlag m; **~man** (BRIT) (irreg) n
Müllmann m; **~y** adj staubig

Dutch [dʌtʃ] adj holländisch, niederländisch
♦ n (LING) Holländisch nt, Niederländisch
nt; **the ~** npl (people) die Holländer pl, die
Niederländer pl; **to go ~** getrennte Kasse
machen; **~man/woman** (irreg) n
Holländer(in) m(f), Niederländer(in) m(f)

dutiful ['dju:tɪful] adj pflichtbewußt △

duty ['dju:tɪ] n Pflicht f; (job) Aufgabe f; (tax)
Einfuhrzoll m; **on ~** im Dienst; **~**
chemist's n Apotheke f im
Bereitschaftsdienst; **~-free** adj zollfrei

duvet ['du:veɪ] (BRIT) n Daunendecke nt

dwarf [dwɔ:f] (pl **dwarves**) n Zwerg m ♦ vt
überragen

dwell [dwɛl] (pt, pp **dwelt**) vi wohnen; **~ on**
vt fus verweilen bei; **~ing** n Wohnung f

dwelt [dwɛlt] pt, pp of **dwell**

dwindle ['dwɪndl] vi schwinden

dye [daɪ] n Farbstoff m ♦ vt färben

dying ['daɪɪŋ] adj (person) sterbend;
(moments) letzt

dyke [daɪk] (BRIT) n (channel) Kanal m;
(barrier) Deich m, Damm m

dynamic [daɪ'næmɪk] adj dynamisch

dynamite ['daɪnəmaɪt] n Dynamit nt

dynamo ['daɪnəməu] n Dynamo m

dyslexia [dɪs'lɛksɪə] n Legasthenie f

E, e

E [i:] n (MUS) E nt

each [i:tʃ] adj jeder/jede/jedes ♦ pron (ein)
jeder/(eine) jede/(ein) jedes; **~ other**
einander, sich; **they have two books ~** sie
haben je 2 Bücher

eager ['i:gər] adj eifrig

eagle ['i:gl] n Adler m

ear [ɪər] n Ohr nt; (of corn) Ähre f; **~ache** n
Ohrenschmerzen pl; **~drum** n Trommelfell
nt

earl [ə:l] n Graf m

earlier ['ə:lɪər] adj, adv früher; **I can't come**
any ~ ich kann nicht früher or eher
kommen

early ['ə:lɪ] adj, adv früh; **~ retirement** n
vorzeitige Pensionierung

earmark ['ɪəmɑ:k] vt vorsehen

earn [ə:n] vt verdienen

earnest ['ə:nɪst] adj ernst; **in ~** im Ernst

earnings ['ə:nɪŋz] npl Verdienst m

ear: ~phones ['ɪəfəunz] npl Kopfhörer pl;
~ring ['ɪərɪŋ] n Ohrring m; **~shot** ['ɪəʃɔt] n
Hörweite f

earth [ə:θ] n Erde f; (BRIT: ELEC) Erdung f ♦ vt
erden; **~enware** n Steingut nt; **~quake** n
Erdbeben nt; **~y** adj roh

earwig ['ɪəwɪg] n Ohrwurm m

ease [i:z] n (simplicity) Leichtigkeit f; (social)
Ungezwungenheit f ♦ vt (pain) lindern;
(burden) erleichtern; **at ~** ungezwungen,
(MIL) rührt euch!; **~ off** or **up** vi
nachlassen

easel ['i:zl] n Staffelei f

easily ['i:zɪlɪ] adv leicht

east [i:st] n Osten m ♦ adj östlich ♦ adv nach
Osten

Easter ['i:stər] n Ostern nt; **~ egg** n Osterei
nt

east: ~erly adj östlich, Ost-; **~ern** adj
östlich; **~ward(s)** adv ostwärts

easy ['i:zɪ] adj (task) einfach; (life) bequem;
(manner) ungezwungen, natürlich ♦ adv
leicht; **~ chair** n Sessel m; **~-going** adj

gelassen; (*lax*) lässig

eat [iːt] (*pt* **ate**, *pp* **eaten**) *vt* essen; (*animals*) fressen; (*destroy*) (zer)fressen ♦ *vi* essen; fressen; **~ away** *vt* zerfressen; **~ into** *vt fus* zerfressen; **~en** *pp of* **eat**

eau de Cologne [ˈəʊdəkəˈləʊn] *n* Kölnisch Wasser *nt*

eaves [iːvz] *npl* Dachrand *m*

eavesdrop [ˈiːvzdrɒp] *vi* lauschen; **to ~ on sb** jdn belauschen

ebb [ɛb] *n* Ebbe *f* ♦ *vi* (*fig: also:* **~ away**) (ab)ebben

ebony [ˈɛbənɪ] *n* Ebenholz *nt*

EC *n abbr* (= *European Community*) EG *f*

eccentric [ɪkˈsɛntrɪk] *adj* exzentrisch ♦ *n* Exzentriker(in) *m(f)*

ecclesiastical [ɪkliːzɪˈæstɪkl] *adj* kirchlich

echo [ˈɛkəʊ] (*pl* **~es**) *n* Echo *nt* ♦ *vt* zurückwerfen; (*fig*) nachbeten ♦ *vi* widerhallen

eclipse [ɪˈklɪps] *n* Finsternis *f* ♦ *vt* verfinstern

ecology [ɪˈkɒlədʒɪ] *n* Ökologie *f*

economic [iːkəˈnɒmɪk] *adj* wirtschaftlich; **~al** *adj* wirtschaftlich; (*person*) sparsam; **~ refugee** *n* Wirtschaftsflüchtling *m*; **~s** *n* Volkswirtschaft *f*

economist [ɪˈkɒnəmɪst] *n* Volkswirt(schaftler) *m*

economize [ɪˈkɒnəmaɪz] *vi* sparen

economy [ɪˈkɒnəmɪ] *n* (*thrift*) Sparsamkeit *f*; (*of country*) Wirtschaft *f*; **~ class** *n* Touristenklasse *f*

ecstasy [ˈɛkstəsɪ] *n* Ekstase *f*; (*drug*) Ecstasy *nt*; **ecstatic** [ɛksˈtætɪk] *adj* hingerissen

ECU [ˈeɪkjuː] *n abbr* (= *European Currency Unit*) ECU *m*

eczema [ˈɛksɪmə] *n* Ekzem *nt*

edge [ɛdʒ] *n* Rand *m*; (*of knife*) Schneide *f* ♦ *vt* (*SEWING*) einfassen; **on ~** (*fig*) = **edgy**; **to ~ away from** langsam abrücken von; **~ways** *adv*: **he couldn't get a word in ~ways** er kam überhaupt nicht zu Wort

edgy [ˈɛdʒɪ] *adj* nervös

edible [ˈɛdɪbl] *adj* eßbar △

edict [ˈiːdɪkt] *n* Erlaß △ *m*

edit [ˈɛdɪt] *vt* redigieren; **~ion** [ɪˈdɪʃən] *n* Ausgabe *f*; **~or** *n* (*of newspaper*) Redakteur

m; (*of book*) Lektor *m*

editorial [ɛdɪˈtɔːrɪəl] *adj* Redaktions- ♦ *n* Leitartikel *m*

educate [ˈɛdjukeɪt] *vt* erziehen, (aus)bilden; **~d** *adj* gebildet; **education** [ɛdjuˈkeɪʃən] *n* (*teaching*) Unterricht *m*; (*system*) Schulwesen *nt*; (*schooling*) Erziehung *f*; Bildung *f*; **educational** *adj* pädagogisch

eel [iːl] *n* Aal *m*

eerie [ˈɪərɪ] *adj* unheimlich

effect [ɪˈfɛkt] *n* Wirkung *f* ♦ *vt* bewirken; **~s** *npl* (*sound, visual*) Effekte *pl*; **in ~** in der Tat; **to take ~** (*law*) in Kraft treten; (*drug*) wirken; **~ive** *adj* wirksam, effektiv; **~ively** *adv* wirksam, effektiv

effeminate [ɪˈfɛmɪnɪt] *adj* weibisch

effervescent [ɛfəˈvɛsnt] *adj* (*also fig*) sprudelnd

efficiency [ɪˈfɪʃənsɪ] *n* Leistungsfähigkeit *f*

efficient [ɪˈfɪʃənt] *adj* tüchtig; (*TECH*) leistungsfähig; (*method*) wirksam

effigy [ˈɛfɪdʒɪ] *n* Abbild *nt*

effort [ˈɛfət] *n* Anstrengung *f*; **~less** *adj* mühelos

effusive [ɪˈfjuːsɪv] *adj* überschwenglich △

e.g. *adv abbr* (= *exempli gratia*) z.B.

egalitarian [ɪgælɪˈtɛərɪən] *adj* Gleichheits-, egalitär

egg [ɛg] *n* Ei *nt*; **~ on** *vt* anstacheln; **~cup** *n* Eierbecher *m*; **~plant** *n* (*esp US*) Aubergine *f*; **~shell** *n* Eierschale *f*

ego [ˈiːgəʊ] *n* Ich *nt*, Selbst *nt*; **~tism** [ˈɛgəʊtɪzəm] *n* Ichbezogenheit *f*; **~tist** [ˈɛgəʊtɪst] *n* Egozentriker *m*

Egypt [ˈiːdʒɪpt] *n* Ägypten *nt*; **~ian** [ɪˈdʒɪpʃən] *adj* ägyptisch ♦ *n* Ägypter(in) *m(f)*

eiderdown [ˈaɪdədaʊn] *n* Daunendecke *f*

eight [eɪt] *num* acht; **~een** *num* achtzehn; **~h** [eɪtθ] *adj* achte(r, s) ♦ *n* Achtel *nt*; **~y** *num* achtzig

Eire [ˈɛərə] *n* Irland *nt*

either [ˈaɪðə*] *conj*: **~ ... or** entweder ... oder ♦ *pron*: **~ of the two** eine(r, s) von beiden ♦ *adj*: **on ~ side** auf beiden Seiten ♦ *adv*: **I don't ~** ich auch nicht; **I don't want ~** ich will keins von beiden

eject [ɪˈdʒɛkt] *vt* ausstoßen, vertreiben

△ *For information on spelling reform see page 615*

eke [iːk] vt: **to ~ out** strecken

elaborate [adj ɪˈlæbərɪt, vb ɪˈlæbəreɪt] adj sorgfältig ausgearbeitet, ausführlich ♦ vt sorgfältig ausarbeiten ♦ vi ausführlich darstellen

elapse [ɪˈlæps] vi vergehen

elastic [ɪˈlæstɪk] n Gummiband nt ♦ adj elastisch; **~ band** (*BRIT*) n Gummiband nt

elated [ɪˈleɪtɪd] adj froh

elation [ɪˈleɪʃən] n gehobene Stimmung f

elbow [ˈɛlbəʊ] n Ellbogen m

elder [ˈɛldə^r] adj älter ♦ n Ältere(r) f(m); **~ly** adj ältere(r, s) ♦ npl: **the ~ly** die Älteren pl; **eldest** [ˈɛldɪst] adj älteste(r, s) ♦ n Älteste(r) f(m)

elect [ɪˈlɛkt] vt wählen ♦ adj zukünftig; **~ion** [ɪˈlɛkʃən] n Wahl f; **~ioneering** [ɪlɛkʃəˈnɪərɪŋ] n Wahlpropaganda f; **~or** n Wähler m; **~oral** adj Wahl-; **~orate** n Wähler pl, Wählerschaft f

electric [ɪˈlɛktrɪk] adj elektrisch, Elektro-; **~al** adj elektrisch; **~ blanket** n Heizdecke f; **~ chair** n elektrische(r) Stuhl m; **~ fire** n elektrische(r) Heizofen m

electrician [ɪlɛkˈtrɪʃən] n Elektriker m

electricity [ɪlɛkˈtrɪsɪtɪ] n Elektrizität f

electrify [ɪˈlɛktrɪfaɪ] vt elektrifizieren; (*fig*) elektrisieren

electrocute [ɪˈlɛktrəkjuːt] vt durch elektrischen Strom töten

electronic [ɪlɛkˈtrɒnɪk] adj elektronisch, Elektronen-; **~ mail** n elektronische(r) Briefkasten m; **~s** n Elektronik f

elegance [ˈɛlɪɡəns] n Eleganz f; **elegant** [ˈɛlɪɡənt] adj elegant

element [ˈɛlɪmənt] n Element nt; **~ary** [ɛlɪˈmɛntərɪ] adj einfach; (*primary*) Grund-

elephant [ˈɛlɪfənt] n Elefant m

elevate [ˈɛlɪveɪt] vt emporheben; **elevation** [ɛlɪˈveɪʃən] n (*height*) Erhebung f; (*ARCHIT*) (Quer)schnitt m; **elevator** (*US*) n Fahrstuhl m, Aufzug m

eleven [ɪˈlɛvn] num elf; **~ses** (*BRIT*) npl ≈ zweite(s) Frühstück nt; **~th** adj elfte(r, s)

elicit [ɪˈlɪsɪt] vt herausbekommen

eligible [ˈɛlɪdʒəbl] adj wählbar; **to be ~ for a pension** pensionsberechtigt sein

eliminate [ɪˈlɪmɪneɪt] vt ausschalten

elite [eɪˈliːt] n Elite f

elm [ɛlm] n Ulme f

elocution [ɛləˈkjuːʃən] n Sprecherziehung f

elongated [ˈiːlɒŋɡeɪtɪd] adj verlängert

elope [ɪˈləʊp] vi entlaufen

eloquence [ˈɛləkwəns] n Beredsamkeit f; **eloquent** adj redegewandt

else [ɛls] adv sonst; **who ~?** wer sonst?; **somebody ~** jemand anders; **or ~** sonst; **~where** adv anderswo, woanders

elude [ɪˈluːd] vt entgehen +dat

elusive [ɪˈluːsɪv] adj schwer faßbar ⚠

emaciated [ɪˈmeɪsɪeɪtɪd] adj abgezehrt

E-mail [ˈiːmeɪl] n abbr (= electronic mail) E-Mail f

emancipation [ɪmænsɪˈpeɪʃən] n Emanzipation f; Freilassung f

embankment [ɪmˈbæŋkmənt] n (*of river*) Uferböschung f; (*of road*) Straßendamm m

embargo [ɪmˈbɑːɡəʊ] (pl **~es**) n Embargo nt

embark [ɪmˈbɑːk] vi sich einschiffen; **~ on** vt fus unternehmen; **~ation** [ɛmbɑːˈkeɪʃən] n Einschiffung f

embarrass [ɪmˈbærəs] vt in Verlegenheit bringen; **~ed** adj verlegen; **~ing** adj peinlich; **~ment** n Verlegenheit f

embassy [ˈɛmbəsɪ] n Botschaft f

embed [ɪmˈbɛd] vt einbetten

embellish [ɪmˈbɛlɪʃ] vt verschönern

embers [ˈɛmbəz] npl Glut(asche) f

embezzle [ɪmˈbɛzl] vt unterschlagen; **~ment** n Unterschlagung f

embitter [ɪmˈbɪtə^r] vt verbittern

embody [ɪmˈbɒdɪ] vt (*ideas*) verkörpern; (*new features*) (in sich) vereinigen

embossed [ɪmˈbɒst] adj geprägt

embrace [ɪmˈbreɪs] vt umarmen; (*include*) einschließen ♦ vi sich umarmen ♦ n Umarmung f

embroider [ɪmˈbrɔɪdə^r] vt (be)sticken; (*story*) ausschmücken; **~y** n Stickerei f

emerald [ˈɛmərəld] n Smaragd m

emerge [ɪˈmɜːdʒ] vi auftauchen; (*truth*) herauskommen; **~nce** n Erscheinen nt

emergency [ɪˈmɜːdʒənsɪ] n Notfall m; **~ cord** (*US*) n Notbremse f; **~ exit** n

⚠ *Informationen zur Rechtschreibreform Seite 615*

Notausgang *m*; **~ landing** *n* Notlandung *f*;
~ services *npl* Notdienste *pl*

emery board ['ɛmərɪ-] *n* Papiernagelfeile *f*

emigrant ['ɛmɪgrənt] *n* Auswanderer *m*

emigrate ['ɛmɪgreɪt] *vi* auswandern;
emigration [ɛmɪ'greɪʃən] *n* Auswanderung *f*

eminence ['ɛmɪnəns] *n* hohe(r) Rang *m*

eminent ['ɛmɪnənt] *adj* bedeutend

emission [ɪ'mɪʃən] *n* Ausströmen *nt*; **~s** *npl*
Emissionen *fpl*

emit [ɪ'mɪt] *vt* von sich *dat* geben

emotion [ɪ'məʊʃən] *n* Emotion *f*, Gefühl *nt*;
~al *adj* (*person*) emotional; (*scene*)
ergreifend

emotive [ɪ'məʊtɪv] *adj* gefühlsbetont

emperor ['ɛmpərər] *n* Kaiser *m*

emphases ['ɛmfəsiːz] *npl of* **emphasis**

emphasis ['ɛmfəsɪs] *n* (*LING*) Betonung *f*;
(*fig*) Nachdruck *m*; **emphasize** ['ɛmfəsaɪz]
vt betonen

emphatic [ɛm'fætɪk] *adj* nachdrücklich;
~ally *adv* nachdrücklich

empire ['ɛmpaɪər] *n* Reich *nt*

empirical [ɛm'pɪrɪkl] *adj* empirisch

employ [ɪm'plɔɪ] *vt* (*hire*) anstellen; (*use*)
verwenden; **~ee** [ɪmplɔɪ'iː] *n* Angestellte(r)
f(m); **~er** *n* Arbeitgeber(in) *m(f)*; **~ment** *n*
Beschäftigung *f*; **~ment agency** *n*
Stellenvermittlung *f*

empower [ɪm'paʊər] *vt*: **to ~ sb to do sth**
jdn ermächtigen, etw zu tun

empress ['ɛmprɪs] *n* Kaiserin *f*

emptiness ['ɛmptɪnɪs] *n* Leere *f*

empty ['ɛmptɪ] *adj* leer ♦ *n* (*bottle*) Leergut
nt ♦ *vt* (*contents*) leeren; (*container*)
ausleeren ♦ *vi* (*water*) abfließen; (*river*)
münden; (*house*) sich leeren; **~-handed**
adj mit leeren Händen

EMU ['iːmjuː] *n abbr* (= *economic and
monetary union*) EWU *f*

emulate ['ɛmjʊleɪt] *vt* nacheifern +*dat*

emulsion [ɪ'mʌlʃən] *n* Emulsion *f*

enable [ɪ'neɪbl] *vt*: **to ~ sb to do sth** es jdm
ermöglichen, etw zu tun

enact [ɪ'nækt] *vt* (*law*) erlassen; (*play*)
aufführen; (*role*) spielen

enamel [ɪ'næməl] *n* Email *nt*; (*of teeth*)
(Zahn)schmelz *m*

encased [ɪn'keɪst] *adj*: **~ in** (*enclosed*)
eingeschlossen in +*dat*; (*covered*) verkleidet
mit

enchant [ɪn'tʃɑːnt] *vt* bezaubern; **~ing** *adj*
entzückend

encircle [ɪn'sɜːkl] *vt* umringen

encl. *abbr* (= *enclosed*) Anl.

enclose [ɪn'kləʊz] *vt* einschließen; **to ~ sth
(in** *or* **with a letter)** etw (einem Brief)
beilegen; **~d** (*in letter*) beiliegend, anbei;
enclosure [ɪn'kləʊʒər] *n* Einfriedung *f*; (*in
letter*) Anlage *f*

encompass [ɪn'kʌmpəs] *vt* (*include*)
umfassen

encore [ɔŋ'kɔːr] *n* Zugabe *f*

encounter [ɪn'kaʊntər] *n* Begegnung *f*;
(*MIL*) Zusammenstoß *m* ♦ *vt* treffen;
(*resistance*) stoßen auf +*acc*

encourage [ɪn'kʌrɪdʒ] *vt* ermutigen;
~ment *n* Ermutigung *f*, Förderung *f*;
encouraging *adj* ermutigend,
vielversprechend △

encroach [ɪn'krəʊtʃ] *vi*: **to ~ (up)on**
eindringen in +*acc*; (*time*) in Anspruch
nehmen

encrusted [ɪn'krʌstɪd] *adj*: **~ with** besetzt
mit

encyclop(a)edia [ɛnsaɪkləʊ'piːdɪə] *n*
Konversationslexikon *nt*

end [ɛnd] *n* Ende *nt*, Schluß △ *m*; (*purpose*)
Zweck *m* ♦ *vt* (*also*: **bring to an ~, put an ~
to**) beenden ♦ *vi* zu Ende gehen; **in the ~**
zum Schluß; **on ~** (*object*) hochkant; **to
stand on ~** (*hair*) zu Berge stehen; **for
hours on ~** stundenlang; **~ up** *vi* landen

endanger [ɪn'deɪndʒər] *vt* gefährden; **~ed
species** *n* eine vom Aussterben bedrohte
Art

endearing [ɪn'dɪərɪŋ] *adj* gewinnend

endeavour [ɪn'dɛvər] (*US* **endeavor**) *n*
Bestrebung *f* ♦ *vi* sich bemühen

ending ['ɛndɪŋ] *n* Ende *nt*

endless ['ɛndlɪs] *adj* endlos

endorse [ɪn'dɔːs] *vt* unterzeichnen;
(*approve*) unterstützen; **~ment** *n* (*AUT*)
Eintrag *m*

△ *For information on spelling reform see page 615*

endow [ɪn'dau] *vt*: **to ~ sb with sth** jdm etw verleihen; (*with money*) jdm etw stiften
endurance [ɪn'djuərəns] *n* Ausdauer *f*
endure [ɪn'djuəʳ] *vt* ertragen ♦ *vi* (*last*) (fort)dauern
enemy ['enəmɪ] *n* Feind *m* ♦ *adj* feindlich
energetic [enə'dʒetɪk] *adj* tatkräftig
energy ['enədʒɪ] *n* Energie *f*.
enforce [ɪn'fɔːs] *vt* durchsetzen
engage [ɪn'geɪdʒ] *vt* (*employ*) einstellen; (*in conversation*) verwickeln; (*TECH*) einschalten ♦ *vi* (*TECH*) ineinandergreifen △; (*clutch*) fassen; **to ~ in** sich beteiligen an +*dat*; **~d** *adj* verlobt; (*BRIT: TEL, toilet*) besetzt; (: *busy*) beschäftigt; **to get ~d** sich verloben; **~d tone** (*BRIT*) *n* (*TEL*) Besetztzeichen *nt*; **~ment** *n* (*appointment*) Verabredung *f*; (*to marry*) Verlobung *f*; (*MIL*) Gefecht *nt*; **~ment ring** *n* Verlobungsring *m*; **engaging** *adj* gewinnend
engender [ɪn'dʒendəʳ] *vt* hervorrufen
engine ['endʒɪn] *n* (*AUT*) Motor *m*; (*RAIL*) Lokomotive *f*; **~ driver** *n* Lok(omotiv)führer(in) *m(f)*
engineer [endʒɪ'nɪəʳ] *n* Ingenieur *m*; (*US: RAIL*) Lok(omotiv)führer(in) *m(f)*; **~ing** [endʒɪ'nɪərɪŋ] *n* Technik *f*
England ['ɪŋglənd] *n* England *nt*
English ['ɪŋglɪʃ] *adj* englisch ♦ *n* (*LING*) Englisch *nt*; **the ~** *npl* (*people*) die Engländer *pl*; **~ Channel** *n*: **the ~ Channel** der Ärmelkanal *m*; **~man/woman** (*irreg*) *n* Engländer(in) *m(f)*
engraving [ɪn'greɪvɪŋ] *n* Stich *m*
engrossed [ɪn'grəust] *adj* vertieft
engulf [ɪn'gʌlf] *vt* verschlingen
enhance [ɪn'hɑːns] *vt* steigern, heben
enigma [ɪ'nɪgmə] *n* Rätsel *nt*; **~tic** [enɪg'mætɪk] *adj* rätselhaft
enjoy [ɪn'dʒɔɪ] *vt* genießen; (*privilege*) besitzen; **to ~ o.s.** sich amüsieren; **~able** *adj* erfreulich; **~ment** *n* Genuß △ *m*, Freude *f*
enlarge [ɪn'lɑːdʒ] *vt* erweitern; (*PHOT*) vergrößern ♦ *vi*: **to ~ on sth** etw weiter ausführen; **~ment** *n* Vergrößerung *f*
enlighten [ɪn'laɪtn] *vt* aufklären; **~ment** *n*:

the **E~ment** (*HIST*) die Aufklärung
enlist [ɪn'lɪst] *vt* gewinnen ♦ *vi* (*MIL*) sich melden
enmity ['enmɪtɪ] *n* Feindschaft *f*
enormity [ɪ'nɔːmɪtɪ] *n* Ungeheuerlichkeit *f*
enormous [ɪ'nɔːməs] *adj* ungeheuer
enough [ɪ'nʌf] *adj, adv* genug; **funnily ~** komischerweise
enquire [ɪn'kwaɪəʳ] *vt, vi* = **inquire**
enrage [ɪn'reɪdʒ] *vt* wütend machen
enrich [ɪn'rɪtʃ] *vt* bereichern
enrol [ɪn'rəul] *vt* einschreiben ♦ *vi* (*register*) sich anmelden; **~ment** *n* (*for course*) Anmeldung *f*
en route [ɔn'ruːt] *adv* unterwegs
ensign ['ensaɪn, 'ensən] *n* (*NAUT*) Flagge *f*; (*MIL*) Fähnrich *m*
enslave [ɪn'sleɪv] *vt* versklaven
ensue [ɪn'sjuː] *vi* folgen, sich ergeben
en suite [ɔnswiːt] *adj*: **room with ~ bathroom** Zimmer *nt* mit eigenem Bad
ensure [ɪn'ʃuəʳ] *vt* garantieren
entail [ɪn'teɪl] *vt* mit sich bringen
entangle [ɪn'tæŋgl] *vt* verwirren, verstricken; **~d** *adj*: **to become ~d (in)** (*in net, rope etc*) sich verfangen (in +*dat*)
enter ['entəʳ] *vt* eintreten in +*dat*, betreten; (*club*) beitreten +*dat*; (*in book*) eintragen ♦ *vi* hereinkommen, hineingehen; **~ for** *vt fus* sich beteiligen an +*dat*; **~ into** *vt fus* (*agreement*) eingehen; (*plans*) eine Rolle spielen bei; **~ (up)on** *vt fus* beginnen
enterprise ['entəpraɪz] *n* (*in person*) Initiative *f*; (*COMM*) Unternehmen *nt*; **enterprising** ['entəpraɪzɪŋ] *adj* unternehmungslustig
entertain [entə'teɪn] *vt* (*guest*) bewirten; (*amuse*) unterhalten; **~er** *n* Unterhaltungskünstler(in) *m(f)*; **~ing** *adj* unterhaltsam; **~ment** *n* Unterhaltung *f*
enthralled [ɪn'θrɔːld] *adj* gefesselt
enthusiasm [ɪn'θuːzɪæzəm] *n* Begeisterung *f*
enthusiast [ɪn'θuːzɪæst] *n* Enthusiast *m*; **~ic** [ɪnθuːzɪ'æstɪk] *adj* begeistert
entice [ɪn'taɪs] *vt* verleiten, locken
entire [ɪn'taɪəʳ] *adj* ganz; **~ly** *adv* ganz,

völlig; **~ty** [ɪn'taɪərətɪ] n: **in its ~ty** in seiner Gesamtheit

entitle [ɪn'taɪtl] vt (allow) berechtigen; (name) betiteln; **~d** adj (book) mit dem Titel; **to be ~d to sth** das Recht auf etw acc haben; **to be ~d to do sth** das Recht haben, etw zu tun

entity ['entɪtɪ] n Ding nt, Wesen nt

entourage [ɒntu'rɑːʒ] n Gefolge nt

entrails ['entreɪlz] npl Eingeweide pl

entrance [n 'entrns, vb ɪn'trɑːns] n Eingang m; (entering) Eintritt m ♦ vt hinreißen; **~ examination** n Aufnahmeprüfung f; **~ fee** n Eintrittsgeld nt; **~ ramp** (US) n (AUT) Einfahrt f

entrant ['entrnt] n (for exam) Kandidat m; (in race) Teilnehmer m

entreat [en'triːt] vt anflehen

entrenched [en'trentʃt] adj (fig) verwurzelt

entrepreneur ['ɒntrəprə'nəːr] n Unternehmer(in) m(f)

entrust [ɪn'trʌst] vt: **to ~ sb with sth** or **sth to sb** jdm etw anvertrauen

entry ['entrɪ] n Eingang m; (THEAT) Auftritt m; (in account) Eintragung f; (in dictionary) Eintrag m; **"no ~"** „Eintritt verboten"; (for cars) „Einfahrt verboten"; **~ form** n Anmeldeformular nt; **~ phone** n Sprechanlage f

enumerate [ɪ'njuːmərɪt] vt aufzählen

enunciate [ɪ'nʌnsɪeɪt] vt aussprechen

envelop [ɪn'veləp] vt einhüllen

envelope ['envələup] n Umschlag m

enviable ['envɪəbl] adj beneidenswert

envious ['envɪəs] adj neidisch

environment [ɪn'vaɪərnmənt] n Umgebung f; (ECOLOGY) Umwelt f; **~al** [ɪnvaɪərn'mentl] adj Umwelt-; **~-friendly** adj umweltfreundlich

envisage [ɪn'vɪzɪdʒ] vt sich dat vorstellen

envoy ['envɔɪ] n Gesandte(r) mf

envy ['envɪ] n Neid m ♦ vt: **to ~ sb sth** jdn um etw beneiden

enzyme ['enzaɪm] n Enzym nt

epic ['epɪk] n Epos nt ♦ adj episch

epidemic [epɪ'demɪk] n Epidemie f

epilepsy ['epɪlepsɪ] n Epilepsie f; **epileptic** [epɪ'leptɪk] adj epileptisch ♦ n Epileptiker(in) m(f)

episode ['epɪsəud] n (incident) Vorfall m; (story) Episode f

epitaph ['epɪtɑːf] n Grabinschrift f

epitome [ɪ'pɪtəmɪ] n Inbegriff m

epitomize [ɪ'pɪtəmaɪz] vt verkörpern

equable ['ekwəbl] adj ausgeglichen

equal ['iːkwl] adj gleich ♦ n Gleichgestellte(r) mf ♦ vt gleichkommen +dat; **~ to the task** der Aufgabe gewachsen; **equality** [iː'kwɒlɪtɪ] n Gleichheit f; (equal rights) Gleichberechtigung f; **~ize** vt gleichmachen ♦ vi (SPORT) ausgleichen; **~izer** n (SPORT) Ausgleich(streffer) m; **~ly** adv gleich

equanimity [ekwə'nɪmɪtɪ] n Gleichmut m

equate [ɪ'kweɪt] vt gleichsetzen

equation [ɪ'kweɪʒən] n Gleichung f

equator [ɪ'kweɪtər] n Äquator m

equestrian [ɪ'kwestrɪən] adj Reit-

equilibrium [iːkwɪ'lɪbrɪəm] n Gleichgewicht nt

equinox ['iːkwɪnɒks] n Tagundnachtgleiche f

equip [ɪ'kwɪp] vt ausrüsten; **to be well ~ped** gut ausgerüstet sein; **~ment** n Ausrüstung f; (TECH) Gerät nt

equitable ['ekwɪtəbl] adj gerecht, billig

equities ['ekwɪtɪz] (BRIT) npl (FIN) Stammaktien pl

equivalent [ɪ'kwɪvələnt] adj gleichwertig, entsprechend ♦ n Äquivalent nt; (in money) Gegenwert m; **~ to** gleichwertig +dat, entsprechend +dat

equivocal [ɪ'kwɪvəkl] adj zweideutig

era ['ɪərə] n Epoche f, Ära f

eradicate [ɪ'rædɪkeɪt] vt ausrotten

erase [ɪ'reɪz] vt ausradieren; (tape) löschen; **~r** n Radiergummi m

erect [ɪ'rekt] adj aufrecht ♦ vt errichten; **~ion** [ɪ'rekʃən] n Errichtung f; (ANAT) Erektion f

ERM n abbr (= Exchange Rate Mechanism) Wechselkursmechanismus m

erode [ɪ'rəud] vt zerfressen; (land)

⚠ For information on spelling reform see page 615

auswaschen
erotic [ɪ'rɒtɪk] *adj* erotisch
err [əːʳ] *vi* sich irren
errand ['erənd] *n* Besorgung *f*
erratic [ɪ'rætɪk] *adj* unberechenbar
erroneous [ɪ'rəʊnɪəs] *adj* irrig
error ['erəʳ] *n* Fehler *m*
erupt [ɪ'rʌpt] *vi* ausbrechen; **~ion** [ɪ'rʌpʃən] *n* Ausbruch *m*
escalate ['eskəleɪt] *vi* sich steigern
escalator ['eskəleɪtəʳ] *n* Rolltreppe *f*
escape [ɪs'keɪp] *n* Flucht *f*; (*of gas*) Entweichen *nt* ♦ *vi* entkommen; (*prisoners*) fliehen; (*leak*) entweichen ♦ *vt* entkommen +*dat*; **escapism** *n* Flucht *f* (vor der Wirklichkeit)
escort [*n* 'eskɔːt, *vb* ɪs'kɔːt] *n* (*person accompanying*) Begleiter *m*; (*guard*) Eskorte *f* ♦ *vt* (*lady*) begleiten; (*MIL*) eskortieren
Eskimo ['eskɪməʊ] *n* Eskimo(frau) *m(f)*
especially [ɪs'peʃlɪ] *adv* besonders
espionage ['espɪənɑːʒ] *n* Spionage *f*
esplanade [esplə'neɪd] *n* Promenade *f*
Esquire [ɪs'kwaɪəʳ] *n*: **J. Brown ~** Herrn J. Brown
essay ['eseɪ] *n* Aufsatz *m*; (*LITER*) Essay *m*
essence ['esns] *n* (*quality*) Wesen *nt*; (*extract*) Essenz *f*
essential [ɪ'senʃl] *adj* (*necessary*) unentbehrlich; (*basic*) wesentlich ♦ *n* Allernötigste(s) *nt*; **~ly** *adv* eigentlich
establish [ɪs'tæblɪʃ] *vt* (*set up*) gründen; (*prove*) nachweisen; **~ed** *adj* anerkannt; (*belief, laws etc*) herrschend; **~ment** *n* (*setting up*) Einrichtung *f*
estate [ɪs'teɪt] *n* Gut *nt*; (*BRIT: housing ~*) Siedlung *f*; (*will*) Nachlaß ⚠ *m*; **~ agent** (*BRIT*) *n* Grundstücksmakler *m*; **~ car** (*BRIT*) *n* Kombiwagen *m*
esteem [ɪs'tiːm] *n* Wertschätzung *f*
esthetic [ɪs'θetɪk] (*US*) *adj* = **aesthetic**
estimate [*n* 'estɪmət, *vb* 'estɪmeɪt] *n* Schätzung *f*; (*of price*) (Kosten)voranschlag *m* ♦ *vt* schätzen; **estimation** [estɪ'meɪʃən] *n* Einschätzung *f*; (*esteem*) Achtung *f*
estranged [ɪs'treɪndʒd] *adj* entfremdet
estuary ['estjʊərɪ] *n* Mündung *f*

etc *abbr* (= *et cetera*) usw
etching ['etʃɪŋ] *n* Kupferstich *m*
eternal [ɪ'tɜːnl] *adj* ewig
eternity [ɪ'tɜːnɪtɪ] *n* Ewigkeit *f*
ether ['iːθəʳ] *n* Äther *m*
ethical ['eθɪkl] *adj* ethisch
ethics ['eθɪks] *n* Ethik *f* ♦ *npl* Moral *f*
Ethiopia [iːθɪ'əʊpɪə] *n* Äthiopien *nt*
ethnic ['eθnɪk] *adj* Volks-, ethnisch; **~ minority** *n* ethnische Minderheit *f*
ethos ['iːθɒs] *n* Gesinnung *f*
etiquette ['etɪket] *n* Etikette *f*
EU *abbr* (= *European Union*) EU *f*
euphemism ['juːfəmɪzəm] *n* Euphemismus *m*
Eurocheque ['jʊərəʊtʃek] *n* Euroscheck *m*
Europe ['jʊərəp] *n* Europa *nt*; **~an** [jʊərə'piːən] *adj* europäisch ♦ *n* Europäer(in) *m(f)*; **~an Community** *n*: **the ~an Community** die Europäische Gemeinschaft
Euro-sceptic ['jʊərəʊskeptɪk] *n* Kritiker der Europäischen Gemeinschaft
evacuate [ɪ'vækjʊeɪt] *vt* (*place*) räumen; (*people*) evakuieren; **evacuation** [ɪvækjʊ'eɪʃən] *n* Räumung *f*; Evakuierung *f*
evade [ɪ'veɪd] *vt* (*escape*) entkommen +*dat*; (*avoid*) meiden; (*duty*) sich entziehen +*dat*
evaluate [ɪ'væljʊeɪt] *vt* bewerten; (*information*) auswerten
evaporate [ɪ'væpəreɪt] *vi* verdampfen ♦ *vt* verdampfen lassen; **~d milk** *n* Kondensmilch *f*
evasion [ɪ'veɪʒən] *n* Umgehung *f*
evasive [ɪ'veɪsɪv] *adj* ausweichend
eve [iːv] *n*: **on the ~ of** am Vorabend +*gen*
even ['iːvn] *adj* eben; gleichmäßig; (*score etc*) unentschieden; (*number*) gerade ♦ *adv*: **~ you** sogar du; **to get ~ with sb** jdm heimzahlen; **~ if** selbst wenn; **~ so** dennoch; **~ though** obwohl; **~ more** noch mehr; **~ out** *vi* sich ausgleichen
evening ['iːvnɪŋ] *n* Abend *m*; **in the ~** abends, am Abend; **~ class** *n* Abendschule *f*; **~ dress** *n* (*man's*) Gesellschaftsanzug *m*; (*woman's*) Abendkleid *nt*
event [ɪ'vent] *n* (*happening*) Ereignis *nt*; (*SPORT*) Disziplin *f*; **in the ~ of** im Falle +*gen*;

~ful adj ereignisreich

eventual [ɪˈventʃuəl] adj (final) schließlich; **~ity** [ɪventʃuˈælɪtɪ] n Möglichkeit f; **~ly** adv am Ende; (given time) schließlich

ever [ˈevəʳ] adv (always) immer; (at any time) je(mals) ♦ conj seit; **~ since** seitdem; **have you ~ seen it?** haben Sie es je gesehen?; **~green** n Immergrün nt; **~lasting** adj immerwährend △

every [ˈevrɪ] adj jede(r, s); **~ other/third day** jeden zweiten/dritten Tag; **~ one of them** alle; **I have ~ confidence in him** ich habe uneingeschränktes Vertrauen in ihn; **we wish you ~ success** wir wünschen Ihnen viel Erfolg; **he's ~ bit as clever as his brother** er ist genauso klug wie sein Bruder; **~ now and then** ab und zu; **~body** pron = **everyone**; **~day** adj (daily) täglich; (commonplace) alltäglich, Alltags-; **~one** pron jeder, alle pl; **~thing** pron alles; **~where** adv überall(hin); (wherever) wohin; **~where you go** wohin du auch gehst

evict [ɪˈvɪkt] vt ausweisen; **~ion** [ɪˈvɪkʃən] n Ausweisung f

evidence [ˈevɪdns] n (sign) Spur f; (proof) Beweis m; (testimony) Aussage f

evident [ˈevɪdnt] adj augenscheinlich; **~ly** adv offensichtlich

evil [ˈiːvl] adj böse ♦ n Böse nt

evocative [ɪˈvɔkətɪv] adj: **to be ~ of sth** an etw acc erinnern

evoke [ɪˈvəuk] vt hervorrufen

evolution [iːvəˈluːʃən] n Entwicklung f; (of life) Evolution f

evolve [ɪˈvɔlv] vt entwickeln ♦ vi sich entwickeln

ewe [juː] n Mutterschaf nt

ex- [eks] prefix Ex-, Alt-, ehemalig

exacerbate [eksˈæsəbeɪt] vt verschlimmern

exact [ɪgˈzækt] adj genau ♦ vt (demand) verlangen; **~ing** adj anspruchsvoll; **~ly** adv genau

exaggerate [ɪgˈzædʒəreɪt] vt, vi übertreiben; **exaggeration** [ɪgzædʒəˈreɪʃən] n Übertreibung f

exalted [ɪgˈzɔːltɪd] adj (position, style) hoch; (person) exaltiert

exam [ɪgˈzæm] n abbr (SCH) = **examination**

examination [ɪgzæmɪˈneɪʃən] n Untersuchung f; (SCH) Prüfung f, Examen nt; (customs) Kontrolle f

examine [ɪgˈzæmɪn] vt untersuchen; (SCH) prüfen; (consider) erwägen; **~r** n Prüfer m

example [ɪgˈzɑːmpl] n Beispiel nt; **for ~** zum Beispiel

exasperate [ɪgˈzɑːspəreɪt] vt zum Verzweifeln bringen; **exasperating** adj ärgerlich, zum Verzweifeln bringend; **exasperation** [ɪgzɑːspəˈreɪʃən] n Verzweiflung f

excavate [ˈekskəveɪt] vt ausgraben; **excavation** [ekskəˈveɪʃən] n Ausgrabung f

exceed [ɪkˈsiːd] vt überschreiten; (hopes) übertreffen; **~ingly** adv äußerst

excel [ɪkˈsel] vi sich auszeichnen; **~lence** [ˈeksələns] n Vortrefflichkeit f; **E~lency** [ˈeksələnsɪ] n: **His E~lency** Seine Exzellenz f; **~lent** [ˈeksələnt] adj ausgezeichnet

except [ɪkˈsept] prep (also: **~ for**, **~ing**) außer +dat ♦ vt ausnehmen; **~ion** [ɪkˈsepʃən] n Ausnahme f; **to take ~ion to** Anstoß nehmen an +dat; **~ional** [ɪkˈsepʃənl] adj außergewöhnlich

excerpt [ˈeksəːpt] n Auszug m

excess [ɪkˈses] n Übermaß nt; **an ~ of** ein Übermaß an +dat; **~ baggage** n Mehrgepäck nt; **~ fare** n Nachlösegebühr f; **~ive** adj übermäßig

exchange [ɪksˈtʃeɪndʒ] n Austausch m; (also: **telephone ~**) Zentrale f ♦ vt (goods) tauschen; (greetings) austauschen; (money, blows) wechseln; **~ rate** n Wechselkurs m

Exchequer [ɪksˈtʃekəʳ] (BRIT) n: **the ~** das Schatzamt

excise [ˈeksaɪz] n Verbrauchssteuer f

excite [ɪkˈsaɪt] vt erregen; **to get ~d** sich aufregen; **~ment** n Aufregung f; **exciting** adj spannend

exclaim [ɪksˈkleɪm] vi ausrufen

exclamation [ekskləˈmeɪʃən] n Ausruf m; **~ mark** n Ausrufezeichen nt

exclude [ɪksˈkluːd] vt ausschließen

exclusion [ɪksˈkluːʒən] n Ausschluß △ m; **~ zone** n Sperrzone f

△ For information on spelling reform see page 615

exclusive [iks'klu:siv] *adj* (*select*) exklusiv; (*sole*) ausschließlich, Allein-; ~ **of** exklusive +*gen*; ~**ly** *adv* nur, ausschließlich

excommunicate [ekskə'mju:nikeit] *vt* exkommunizieren

excrement ['ekskrəmənt] *n* Kot *m*

excruciating [iks'kru:fieitiŋ] *adj* qualvoll

excursion [iks'kə:fən] *n* Ausflug *m*

excusable [iks'kju:zəbl] *adj* entschuldbar

excuse [*n* iks'kju:s, *vb* iks'kju:z] *n* Entschuldigung *f* ♦ *vt* entschuldigen; ~ **me!** entschuldigen Sie!

ex-directory ['eksdi'rektəri] (*BRIT*) *adj*: **to be** ~ nicht im Telefonbuch stehen

execute ['eksikju:t] *vt* (*carry out*) ausführen; (*kill*) hinrichten; **execution** [eksi'kju:fən] *n* Ausführung *f*; (*killing*) Hinrichtung *f*; **executioner** [eksi'kju:fnə*r*] *n* Scharfrichter *m*

executive [ig'zekjutiv] *n* (*COMM*) Geschäftsführer *m*; (*POL*) Exekutive *f* ♦ *adj* Exekutiv-, ausführend

executor [ig'zekjutə*r*] *n* Testamentsvollstrecker *m*

exemplary [ig'zempləri] *adj* musterhaft

exemplify [ig'zemplifai] *vt* veranschaulichen

exempt [ig'zempt] *adj* befreit ♦ *vt* befreien; ~**ion** [ig'zempfən] *n* Befreiung *f*

exercise ['eksəsaiz] *n* Übung *f* ♦ *vt* (*power*) ausüben; (*muscle, patience*) üben; (*dog*) ausführen ♦ *vi* Sport treiben; ~ **bike** *n* Heimtrainer *m*; ~ **book** *n* (Schul)heft *nt*

exert [ig'zə:t] *vt* (*influence*) ausüben; **to ~ o.s.** sich anstrengen; ~**ion** [ig'zə:fən] *n* Anstrengung *f*

exhale [eks'heil] *vt, vi* ausatmen

exhaust [ig'zɔ:st] *n* (*fumes*) Abgase *pl*; (*pipe*) Auspuffrohr *nt* ♦ *vt* erschöpfen; ~**ed** *adj* erschöpft; ~**ion** [ig'zɔ:stfən] *n* Erschöpfung *f*; ~**ive** *adj* erschöpfend

exhibit [ig'zibit] *n* (*JUR*) Beweisstück *nt*; (*ART*) Ausstellungsstück *nt* ♦ *vt* ausstellen; ~**ion** [eksi'bifən] *n* (*ART*) Ausstellung *f*; (*of. temper etc*) Zurschaustellung *f*; ~**ionist** [eksi'bifənist] *n* Exhibitionist *m*

exhilarating [ig'ziləreitiŋ] *adj* erhebend

ex-husband *n* Ehemann *m*

exile ['eksail] *n* Exil *nt*; (*person*) Verbannte(r) *f(m)* ♦ *vt* verbannen

exist [ig'zist] *vi* existieren; ~**ence** *n* Existenz *f*; ~**ing** *adj* bestehend

exit ['eksit] *n* Ausgang *m*; (*THEAT*) Abgang *m* ♦ *vi* (*THEAT*) abtreten; (*COMPUT*) aus einem Programm herausgehen; ~ **poll** *n bei Wahlen unmittelbar nach Verlassen der Wahllokal durchgeführte Umfrage*; ~ **ramp** (*US*) *n* (*AUT*) Ausfahrt *f*

exodus ['eksədəs] *n* Auszug *m*

exonerate [ig'zɔnəreit] *vt* entlasten

exorbitant [ig'zɔ:bitnt] *adj* übermäßig; (*price*) Phantasie- ⚠

exotic [ig'zɔtik] *adj* exotisch

expand [iks'pænd] *vt* ausdehnen ♦ *vi* sich ausdehnen

expanse [iks'pæns] *n* Fläche *f*

expansion [iks'pænfən] *n* Erweiterung *f*

expatriate [eks'pætriət] *n* Ausländer(in) *m(f)*

expect [iks'pekt] *vt* erwarten; (*suppose*) annehmen ♦ *vi*: **to be ~ing** ein Kind erwarten; ~**ancy** *n* Erwartung *f*; ~**ant mother** *n* werdende Mutter *f*; ~**ation** [ekspek'teifən] *n* Hoffnung *f*

expedient [iks'pi:diənt] *adj* zweckdienlich ♦ *n* (Hilfs)mittel *nt*

expedition [ekspə'difən] *n* Expedition *f*

expel [iks'pel] *vt* ausweisen; (*student*) (ver)weisen

expend [iks'pend] *vt* (*effort*) aufwenden; ~**iture** *n* Ausgaben *pl*

expense [iks'pens] *n* Kosten *pl*; ~**s** *npl* (*COMM*) Spesen *pl*; **at the ~ of** auf Kosten von; ~ **account** *n* Spesenkonto *nt*; **expensive** [iks'pensiv] *adj* teuer

experience [iks'piəriəns] *n* (*incident*) Erlebnis *nt*; (*practice*) Erfahrung *f* ♦ *vt* erleben; ~**d** *adj* erfahren

experiment [iks'perimənt] *n* Versuch *m*, Experiment *nt* ♦ *vi* experimentieren; ~**al** [iksperi'mentl] *adj* experimentell

expert ['ekspə:t] *n* Fachmann *m*; (*official*) Sachverständige(r) *m* ♦ *adj* erfahren; ~**ise** [ekspə:'ti:z] *n* Sachkenntnis *f*

expire [iks'paiə*r*] *vi* (*end*) ablaufen; (*ticket*) verfallen; (*die*) sterben; **expiry** *n* Ablauf *m*

explain [ɪks'pleɪn] vt erklären

explanation [ɛksplə'neɪʃən] n Erklärung f; **explanatory** [ɪks'plænətrɪ] adj erklärend

explicit [ɪks'plɪsɪt] adj ausdrücklich

explode [ɪks'pləud] vi explodieren ♦ vt (bomb) sprengen

exploit [n 'ɛksplɔɪt, vb ɪks'plɔɪt] n (Helden)tat f ♦ vt ausbeuten; **~ation** [ɛksplɔɪ'teɪʃən] n Ausbeutung f

exploration [ɛksplə'reɪʃən] n Erforschung f

exploratory [ɪks'plɔrətrɪ] adj Probe-

explore [ɪks'plɔːʳ] vt (travel) erforschen; (search) untersuchen; **~r** n Erforscher m

explosion [ɪks'pləuʒən] n Explosion f; (fig) Ausbruch m

explosive [ɪks'pləusɪv] adj explosiv, Spreng- ♦ n Sprengstoff m

export [vb ɪks'pɔːt, n 'ɛkspɔːt] vt exportieren ♦ n Export m ♦ cpd (trade) Export-; **~er** [ɪks'pɔːtəʳ] n Exporteur m

expose [ɪks'pəuz] vt (to danger etc) aussetzen; (impostor) entlarven; **to ~ sb to sth** jdn einer Sache dat aussetzen; **~d** adj (position) exponiert; **exposure** [ɪks'pəuʒəʳ] n (MED) Unterkühlung f; (PHOT) Belichtung f; **exposure meter** n Belichtungsmesser m

express [ɪks'prɛs] adj ausdrücklich; (speedy) Expreß- ⚠, Eil- ♦ n (RAIL) Schnellzug m ♦ adv (send) per Expreß ⚠ ♦ vt ausdrücken; **to ~ o.s.** sich ausdrücken; **~ion** [ɪks'prɛʃən] n Ausdruck m; **~ive** adj ausdrucksvoll; **~ly** adv ausdrücklich; **~way** (US) n Schnellstraße f

expulsion [ɪks'pʌlʃən] n Ausweisung f

exquisite [ɛks'kwɪzɪt] adj erlesen

extend [ɪks'tɛnd] vt (visit etc) verlängern; (building) ausbauen; (hand) ausstrecken; (welcome) bieten ♦ vi (land) sich erstrecken

extension [ɪks'tɛnʃən] n Erweiterung f; (of building) Anbau m; (TEL) Apparat m

extensive [ɪks'tɛnsɪv] adj (knowledge) umfassend; (use) weitgehend

extent [ɪks'tɛnt] n Ausdehnung f; (fig) Ausmaß nt; **to a certain ~** bis zu einem gewissen Grade; **to such an ~ that ...** dermaßen, daß ...; **to what ~?** inwieweit?

extenuating [ɪks'tɛnjueɪtɪŋ] adj mildernd

exterior [ɛks'tɪərɪəʳ] adj äußere(r, s), Außen- ♦ n Äußere(s) nt

exterminate [ɪks'təːmɪneɪt] vt ausrotten

external [ɛks'təːnl] adj äußere(r, s), Außen-

extinct [ɪks'tɪŋkt] adj ausgestorben; **~ion** [ɪks'tɪŋkʃən] n Aussterben nt

extinguish [ɪks'tɪŋgwɪʃ] vt (aus)löschen

extort [ɪks'tɔːt] vt erpressen; **~ion** [ɪks'tɔːʃən] n Erpressung f; **~ionate** [ɪks'tɔːʃnɪt] adj überhöht, erpresserisch

extra ['ɛkstrə] adj zusätzlich ♦ adv besonders ♦ n (for car etc) Extra nt; (charge) Zuschlag m; (THEAT) Statist m ♦ prefix außer...

extract [v ɪks'trækt, n 'ɛkstrækt] vt (heraus)ziehen ♦ n (from book etc) Auszug m; (COOK) Extrakt m

extracurricular ['ɛkstrəkə'rɪkjuləʳ] adj außerhalb des Stundenplans

extradite ['ɛkstrədaɪt] vt ausliefern

extramarital ['ɛkstrə'mærɪtl] adj außerehelich

extramural ['ɛkstrə'mjuərəl] adj (course) Volkshochschul-

extraordinary [ɪks'trɔːdnrɪ] adj außerordentlich; (amazing) erstaunlich

extravagance [ɪks'trævəgəns] n Verschwendung f; (lack of restraint) Zügellosigkeit f; (an ~) Extravaganz f

extravagant [ɪks'trævəgənt] adj extravagant

extreme [ɪks'triːm] adj (edge) äußerste(r, s), hinterste(r, s); (cold) äußerste(r, s); (behaviour) außergewöhnlich, übertrieben ♦ n Extrem nt; **~ly** adv äußerst, höchst; **extremist** n Extremist(in) m(f)

extremity [ɪks'trɛmɪtɪ] n (end) Spitze f, äußerste(s) Ende nt; (hardship) bitterste Not f; (ANAT) Hand f; Fuß m

extrovert ['ɛkstrəvəːt] n extrovertierte(r) Mensch m

exuberant [ɪg'zjuːbərnt] adj ausgelassen

exude [ɪg'zjuːd] vt absondern

eye [aɪ] n Auge nt; (of needle) Öhr nt ♦ vt betrachten; (up and down) mustern; **to keep an ~ on** aufpassen auf +acc; **~ball** n Augapfel m; **~bath** n Augenbad nt; **~brow** n Augenbraue f; **~brow pencil** n

⚠ For information on spelling reform see page 615

Augenbrauenstift m; **~drops** npl
Augentropfen pl; **~lash** n Augenwimper f;
~lid n Augenlid nt; **~liner** n Eyeliner nt; **~-
opener** n: that was an ~-opener das hat
mir/ihm etc die Augen geöffnet; **~shadow**
n Lidschatten m; **~sight** n Sehkraft f;
~sore n Schandfleck m; **~ witness** n
Augenzeuge m

F, f

F [ɛf] n (MUS) F nt
F. abbr (= Fahrenheit) F
fable ['feɪbl] n Fabel f
fabric ['fæbrɪk] n Stoff m; (fig) Gefüge nt
fabrication [fæbrɪ'keɪʃən] n Erfindung f
fabulous ['fæbjuləs] adj sagenhaft
face [feɪs] n Gesicht nt; (surface) Oberfläche
f; (of clock) Zifferblatt nt ♦ vt (point towards)
liegen nach; (situation, difficulty) sich stellen
+dat; **~ down** (person) mit dem Gesicht
nach unten; (card) mit der Vorderseite nach
unten; **to make** or **pull a ~** das Gesicht
verziehen; **in the ~ of** angesichts +gen; **on
the ~ of it** so, wie es aussieht; **~ to ~** Auge
in Auge; **to ~ up to sth** einer Sache dat ins
Auge sehen; **~ cloth** (BRIT) n Waschlappen
m; **~ cream** n Gesichtscreme f; **~ lift** n
Face-lifting nt; **~ powder** n
(Gesichts)puder m
facet ['fæsɪt] n Aspekt m; (of gem) Facette ⚠
f
facetious [fə'si:ʃəs] adj witzig
face value n Nennwert m; **to take sth at
(its) ~** (fig) etw für bare Münze nehmen
facial ['feɪʃl] adj Gesichts-
facile ['fæsaɪl] adj (easy) leicht
facilitate [fə'sɪlɪteɪt] vt erleichtern
facilities [fə'sɪlɪtɪz] npl Einrichtungen pl;
credit ~ Kreditmöglichkeiten pl
facing ['feɪsɪŋ] adj zugekehrt ♦ prep
gegenüber
facsimile [fæk'sɪmɪlɪ] n Faksimile nt;
(machine) Telekopierer m
fact [fækt] n Tatsache f; **in ~** in der Tat
faction ['fækʃən] n Splittergruppe f

factor ['fæktər] n Faktor m
factory ['fæktərɪ] n Fabrik f
factual ['fæktjuəl] adj sachlich
faculty ['fækəltɪ] n Fähigkeit f; (UNIV)
Fakultät f; (US: teaching staff) Lehrpersonal
nt
fad [fæd] n Tick m; (fashion) Masche f
fade [feɪd] vi (lose colour) verblassen; (dim)
nachlassen; (sound, memory) schwächer
werden; (wilt) verwelken
fag [fæg] (inf) n (cigarette) Kippe f
fail [feɪl] vt (exam) nicht bestehen; (student)
durchfallen lassen; (courage) verlassen;
(memory) im Stich lassen ♦ vi (supplies) zu
Ende gehen; (student) durchfallen; (eyesight)
nachlassen; (light) schwächer werden;
(crop) fehlschlagen; (remedy) nicht wirken;
to ~ to do sth (neglect) es unterlassen, etw
zu tun; (be unable) es nicht schaffen, etw zu
tun; **without ~** unbedingt; **~ing** n
Schwäche f ♦ prep mangels +gen; **~ure**
['feɪljər] n (person) Versager m; (act)
Versagen nt; (TECH) Defekt m
faint [feɪnt] adj schwach ♦ n Ohnmacht f
♦ vi ohnmächtig werden
fair [feər] adj (just) gerecht, fair; (hair) blond;
(skin) hell; (weather) schön; (not very good)
mittelmäßig; (sizeable) ansehnlich ♦ adv
(play) fair ♦ n (COMM) Messe f; (BRIT: fun~)
Jahrmarkt m; **~ly** adv (honestly) gerecht,
fair; (rather) ziemlich; **~ness** n Fairneß ⚠ f
fairy ['feərɪ] n Fee f; **~ tale** n Märchen nt
faith [feɪθ] n Glaube m; (trust) Vertrauen nt;
(sect) Bekenntnis nt; **~ful** adj treu; **~fully**
adv treu; **yours ~fully** (BRIT)
hochachtungsvoll
fake [feɪk] n (thing) Fälschung f; (person)
Schwindler m ♦ adj vorgetäuscht ♦ vt
fälschen
falcon ['fɔːlkən] n Falke m
fall [fɔːl] (pt fell, pp fallen) n Fall m, Sturz m;
(decrease) Fallen nt; (of snow) (Schnee)fall
m; (US: autumn) Herbst m ♦ vi (also fig)
fallen; (night) hereinbrechen; **~s** npl
(water~) Fälle pl; **to ~ flat** platt hinfallen;
(joke) nicht ankommen; **~ back** vi
zurückweichen; **~ back on** vt fus

zurückgreifen auf +*acc*; ~ **behind** *vi*
zurückbleiben; ~ **down** *vi* (*person*)
hinfallen; (*building*) einstürzen; ~ **for** *vt fus*
(*trick*) hereinfallen auf +*acc*; (*person*) sich
verknallen in +*acc*; ~ **in** *vi* (*roof*) einstürzen;
~ **off** *vi* herunterfallen; (*diminish*) sich
vermindern; ~ **out** *vi* sich streiten; (*MIL*)
wegtreten; ~ **through** *vi* (*plan*) ins Wasser
fallen

fallacy ['fæləsɪ] *n* Trugschluß △ *m*

fallen ['fɔːlən] *pp* of **fall**

fallible ['fæləbl] *adj* fehlbar

fallout ['fɔːlaut] *n* radioaktive(r)
Niederschlag *m*; ~ **shelter** *n* Atombunker
m

fallow ['fæləu] *adj* brach(liegend)

false [fɔːls] *adj* falsch; (*artificial*) künstlich;
under ~ pretences unter Vorspiegelung
falscher Tatsachen; ~ **alarm** *n* Fehlalarm
m; ~ **teeth** (*BRIT*) *npl* Gebiß △ *nt*

falter ['fɔːltər] *vi* schwanken; (*in speech*)
stocken

fame [feɪm] *n* Ruhm *m*

familiar [fə'mɪlɪər] *adj* bekannt; (*intimate*)
familiär; **to be ~ with** vertraut sein mit;
~**ize** *vt* vertraut machen

family ['fæmɪlɪ] *n* Familie *f*; (*relations*)
Verwandtschaft *f*; ~ **business** *n*
Familienunternehmen *nt*; ~ **doctor** *n*
Hausarzt *m*

famine ['fæmɪn] *n* Hungersnot *f*

famished ['fæmɪʃt] *adj* ausgehungert

famous ['feɪməs] *adj* berühmt

fan [fæn] *n* (*folding*) Fächer *m*; (*ELEC*)
Ventilator *m*; (*admirer*) Fan *m* ♦ *vt* fächeln;
~ **out** *vi* sich (fächerförmig) ausbreiten

fanatic [fə'nætɪk] *n* Fanatiker(in) *m(f)*

fan belt *n* Keilriemen *m*

fanciful ['fænsɪful] *adj* (*odd*) seltsam;
(*imaginative*) phantasievoll △

fancy ['fænsɪ] *n* (*liking*) Neigung *f*;
(*imagination*) Einbildung *f* ♦ *adj* schick ♦ *vt*
(*like*) gern haben; wollen; (*imagine*) sich
einbilden; **he fancies her** er mag sie; ~
dress *n* Maskenkostüm *nt*; ~**-dress ball** *n*
Maskenball *m*

fang [fæŋ] *n* Fangzahn *m*; (*of snake*) Giftzahn

m

fantastic [fæn'tæstɪk] *adj* phantastisch △

fantasy ['fæntəsɪ] *n* Phantasie △ *f*

far [fɑːr] *adj* weit ♦ *adv* weit entfernt; (*very
much*) weitaus; **by ~** bei weitem; **so ~**
soweit; bis jetzt; **go as ~ as the station**
gehen Sie bis zum Bahnhof; **as ~ as I
know** soweit *or* soviel ich weiß; ~**away** *adj*
weit entfernt

farce [fɑːs] *n* Farce *f*; **farcical** ['fɑːsɪkl] *adj*
lächerlich

fare [feər] *n* Fahrpreis *m*; Fahrgeld *nt*; (*food*)
Kost *f*; **half/full ~** halber/voller Fahrpreis *m*

Far East *n*: **the ~** der Ferne Osten

farewell [feə'wel] *n* Abschied(sgruß) *m*
♦ *excl* lebe wohl!

farm [fɑːm] *n* Bauernhof *m*, Farm *f* ♦ *vt*
bewirtschaften; ~**er** *n* Bauer *m*, Landwirt
m; ~**hand** *n* Landarbeiter *m*; ~**house** *n*
Bauernhaus *nt*; ~**ing** *n* Landwirtschaft *f*;
~**land** *n* Ackerland *nt*; ~**yard** *n* Hof *m*

far-reaching ['fɑː'riːtʃɪŋ] *adj* (*reform, effect*)
weitreichend △

fart [fɑːt] (*infl*) *n* Furz *m* ♦ *vi* furzen

farther ['fɑːðər] *adv* weiter; **farthest**
['fɑːðɪst] *adj* fernste(r, s) ♦ *adv* am weitesten

fascinate ['fæsɪneɪt] *vt* faszinieren;
fascinating *adj* faszinierend; **fascination**
[fæsɪ'neɪʃən] *n* Faszination *f*

fascism ['fæʃɪzəm] *n* Faschismus *m*

fashion ['fæʃən] *n* (*of clothes*) Mode *f*;
(*manner*) Art *f* (*und Weise f*) ♦ *vt* machen;
in ~ in Mode; **out of ~** unmodisch; ~**able**
adj (*clothes*) modisch; (*place*) elegant; ~
show *n* Mode(n)schau *f*

fast [fɑːst] *adj* schnell; (*firm*) fest ♦ *adv*
schnell; fest ♦ *n* Fasten *nt* ♦ *vi* fasten; **to be
~** (*clock*) vorgehen

fasten ['fɑːsn] *vt* (*attach*) befestigen; (*with
rope*) zuschnüren; (*seat belt*) festmachen;
(*coat*) zumachen ♦ *vi* sich schließen lassen;
~**er** *n* Verschluß △ *m*; ~**ing** *n* Verschluß
△ *m*

fast food *n* Fast food *nt*

fastidious [fæs'tɪdɪəs] *adj* wählerisch

fat [fæt] *adj* dick ♦ *n* Fett *nt*

fatal ['feɪtl] *adj* tödlich; (*disastrous*)

△ *For information on spelling reform see page 615*

verhängnisvoll; **~ity** [fəˈtælɪtɪ] n (road death etc) Todesopfer nt; **~ly** adv tödlich

fate [feɪt] n Schicksal nt; **~ful** adj (prophetic) schicksalsschwer; (important) schicksalhaft

father [ˈfɑːðər] n Vater m; (REL) Pater m; **~-in-law** n Schwiegervater m; **~ly** adj väterlich

fathom [ˈfæðəm] n Klafter m ♦ vt ausloten; (fig) ergründen

fatigue [fəˈtiːg] n Ermüdung f

fatten [ˈfætn] vt dick machen; (animals) mästen ♦ vi dick werden

fatty [ˈfætɪ] adj fettig ♦ n (inf) Dickerchen nt

fatuous [ˈfætjuəs] adj albern, affig

faucet [ˈfɔːsɪt] (US) n Wasserhahn m

fault [fɔːlt] n (defect) Defekt m; (ELEC) Störung f; (blame) Schuld f; (GEOG) Verwerfung f; **it's your ~** du bist daran schuld; **to find ~ with (sth/sb)** etwas auszusetzen haben an (etw/jdm); **at ~** im Unrecht; **~less** adj tadellos; **~y** adj fehlerhaft, defekt

fauna [ˈfɔːnə] n Fauna f

favour [ˈfeɪvər] (US **favor**) n (approval) Wohlwollen nt; (kindness) Gefallen m ♦ vt (prefer) vorziehen; **in ~ of** für; zugunsten +gen; **to find ~ with sb** bei jdm Anklang finden; **~able** [ˈfeɪvrəbl] adj günstig; **~ite** [ˈfeɪvrɪt] adj Lieblings- ♦ n (child) Liebling m; (SPORT) Favorit m

fawn [fɔːn] adj rehbraun ♦ n (animal) (Reh)kitz nt ♦ vi: **to ~ (up)on** (fig) katzbuckeln vor +dat

fax [fæks] n (document) Fax nt; (machine) Telefax nt ♦ vt: **to ~ sth to sb** jdm etw faxen

FBI (US) n abbr (= Federal Bureau of Investigation) FBI nt

fear [fɪər] n Furcht f ♦ vt fürchten; **~ful** adj (timid) furchtsam; (terrible) fürchterlich; **~less** adj furchtlos

feasible [ˈfiːzəbl] adj durchführbar

feast [fiːst] n Festmahl nt; (REL: also: **~ day**) Feiertag m ♦ vi: **to ~ (on)** sich gütlich tun (an +dat)

feat [fiːt] n Leistung f

feather [ˈfeðər] n Feder f

feature [ˈfiːtʃər] n (Gesichts)zug m; (important part) Grundzug m; (CINE, PRESS) Feature nt ♦ vt darstellen; (advertising etc) groß herausbringen ♦ vi vorkommen; **featuring X** mit X; **~ film** n Spielfilm m

February [ˈfebruərɪ] n Februar m

fed [fed] pt, pp of **feed**

federal [ˈfedərəl] adj Bundes-

federation [fedəˈreɪʃən] n (society) Verband m; (of states) Staatenbund m

fed up adj: **to be ~ with sth** etw satt haben; **I'm ~** ich habe die Nase voll

fee [fiː] n Gebühr f

feeble [ˈfiːbl] adj (person) schwach; (excuse) lahm

feed [fiːd] (pt, pp **fed**) n (for animals) Futter nt ♦ vt füttern; (support) ernähren; (data) eingeben; **to ~ on** fressen; **~back** n (information) Feedback nt; **~ing bottle** (BRIT) n Flasche f

feel [fiːl] (pt, pp **felt**) n: **it has a soft ~** es fühlt sich weich an ♦ vt (sense) fühlen; (touch) anfassen; (think) meinen ♦ vi (person) sich fühlen; (thing) sich anfühlen; **to get the ~ of sth** sich an etw acc gewöhnen; **I ~ cold** mir ist kalt; **I ~ like a cup of tea** ich habe Lust auf eine Tasse Tee; **~ about** or **around** vi herumsuchen; **~er** n Fühler m; **~ing** n Gefühl nt; (opinion) Meinung f

feet [fiːt] npl of **foot**

feign [feɪn] vt vortäuschen

feline [ˈfiːlaɪn] adj katzenartig

fell [fel] pt of **fall** ♦ vt (tree) fällen

fellow [ˈfeləu] n (man) Kerl m; **~ citizen** n Mitbürger(in) m(f); **~ countryman** (irreg) n Landsmann m; **~ men** npl Mitmenschen pl; **~ship** n (group) Körperschaft f; (friendliness) Kameradschaft f; (scholarship) Forschungsstipendium nt; **~ student** n Kommilitone m, Kommilitonin f

felony [ˈfelənɪ] n schwere(s) Verbrechen nt

felt [felt] pt, pp of **feel** ♦ n Filz m; **~-tip pen** n Filzstift m

female [ˈfiːmeɪl] n (of animals) Weibchen nt ♦ adj weiblich

feminine [ˈfemɪnɪn] adj (LING) weiblich;

(*qualities*) fraulich
feminist ['feminist] *n* Feminist(in) *m(f)*
fence [fens] *n* Zaun *m* ♦ *vt* (*also:* ~ **in**) einzäunen ♦ *vi* fechten; **fencing** ['fensiŋ] *n* Zaun *m*; (*SPORT*) Fechten *nt*
fend [fend] *vi*: **to ~ for o.s.** sich (allein) durchschlagen; **~ off** *vt* abwehren
fender ['fendə*] *n* Kaminvorsetzer *m*; (*US: AUT*) Kotflügel *m*
ferment [*vb* fə'ment, *n* 'fɜ:ment] *vi* (*CHEM*) gären ♦ *n* (*unrest*) Unruhe *f*
fern [fɜ:n] *n* Farn *m*
ferocious [fə'rəuʃəs] *adj* wild, grausam
ferret ['ferit] *n* Frettchen *nt* ♦ *vt*: **to ~ out** aufspüren
ferry ['feri] *n* Fähre *f* ♦ *vt* übersetzen
fertile ['fɜ:tail] *adj* fruchtbar
fertilize ['fɜ:tilaiz] *vt* (*AGR*) düngen; (*BIOL*) befruchten; **~r** *n* (Kunst)dünger *m*
fervent ['fɜ:vənt] *adj* (*admirer*) glühend; (*hope*) innig
fervour ['fɜ:və*] (*US* **fervor**) *n* Leidenschaft *f*
fester ['festə*] *vi* eitern
festival ['festivəl] *n* (*REL etc*) Fest *nt*; (*ART, MUS*) Festspiele *pl*
festive ['festiv] *adj* festlich; **the ~ season** (*Christmas*) die Festzeit; **festivities** [fes'tiviti:z] *npl* Feierlichkeiten *pl*
festoon [fes'tu:n] *vt*: **to ~ with** schmücken mit
fetch [fetʃ] *vt* holen; (*in sale*) einbringen
fetching ['fetʃiŋ] *adj* reizend
fête [feit] *n* Fest *nt*
fetus ['fi:təs] (*esp US*) *n* = **foetus**
feud [fju:d] *n* Fehde *f*
feudal ['fju:dl] *adj* Feudal-
fever ['fi:və*] *n* Fieber *nt*; **~ish** *adj* (*MED*) fiebrig; (*fig*) fieberhaft
few [fju:] *adj* wenig; **a ~** einige; **~er** *adj* weniger; **~est** *adj* wenigste(r,s)
fiancé [fi'ã:ŋsei] *n* Verlobte(r) *m*; **~e** *n* Verlobte *f*
fib [fib] *n* Flunkerei *f* ♦ *vi* flunkern
fibre ['faibə*] (*US* **fiber**) *n* Faser *f*; **~glass** *n* Glaswolle *f*
fickle ['fikl] *adj* unbeständig
fiction ['fikʃən] *n* (*novels*) Romanliteratur *f*;

(*story*) Erdichtung *f*; **~al** *adj* erfunden
fictitious [fik'tiʃəs] *adj* erfunden, fingiert
fiddle ['fidl] *n* Geige *f*; (*trick*) Schwindelei *f* ♦ *vt* (*BRIT: accounts*) frisieren; **~ with** *vt fus* herumfummeln an +*dat*
fidelity [fi'deliti] *n* Treue *f*
fidget ['fidʒit] *vi* zappeln
field [fi:ld] *n* Feld *nt*; (*range*) Gebiet *nt*; **~ marshal** *n* Feldmarschall *m*; **~work** *n* Feldforschung *f*
fiend [fi:nd] *n* Teufel *m*
fierce [fiəs] *adj* wild
fiery ['faiəri] *adj* (*person*) hitzig
fifteen [fif'ti:n] *num* fünfzehn
fifth [fifθ] *adj* fünfte(r, s) ♦ *n* Fünftel *nt*
fifty ['fifti] *num* fünfzig; **~-fifty** *adj, adv* halbe halbe, fifty fifty (*inf*)
fig [fig] *n* Feige *f*
fight [fait] (*pt, pp* **fought**) *n* Kampf *m*; (*brawl*) Schlägerei *f*; (*argument*) Streit *m* ♦ *vt* kämpfen gegen; sich schlagen mit; (*fig*) bekämpfen ♦ *vi* kämpfen; sich schlagen; streiten; **~er** *n* Kämpfer(in) *m(f)*; (*plane*) Jagdflugzeug *nt*; **~ing** *n* Kämpfen *nt*; (*war*) Kampfhandlungen *pl*
figment ['figmənt] *n*: **~ of the imagination** reine Einbildung *f*
figurative ['figjurətiv] *adj* bildlich
figure ['figə*] *n* (*of person*) Figur *f*; (*person*) Gestalt *f*; (*number*) Ziffer *f* ♦ *vt* (*US: imagine*) glauben ♦ *vi* (*appear*) erscheinen; **~ out** *vt* herausbekommen; **~head** *n* (*NAUT, fig*) Galionsfigur *f*; **~ of speech** *n* Redensart *f*
file [fail] *n* (*tool*) Feile *f*; (*dossier*) Akte *f*; (*folder*) Aktenordner *m*; (*COMPUT*) Datei *f*; (*row*) Reihe *f* ♦ *vt* (*metal, nails*) feilen; (*papers*) abheften; (*claim*) einreichen ♦ *vi*: **to ~ in/out** hintereinander hereinkommen/ hinausgehen; **to ~ past** vorbeimarschieren; **filing** ['failiŋ] *n* Ablage *f*; **filing cabinet** *n* Aktenschrank *m*
fill [fil] *vt* füllen; (*occupy*) ausfüllen; (*satisfy*) sättigen ♦ *n*: **to eat one's ~** sich richtig satt essen; **~ in** *vt* (*hole*) (auf)füllen; (*form*) ausfüllen; **~ up** *vt* (*container*) auffüllen; (*form*) ausfüllen ♦ *vi* (*AUT*) tanken
fillet ['filit] *n* Filet *nt*; **~ steak** *n* Filetsteak *nt*

⚠ *For information on spelling reform see page 615*

filling ['fılıŋ] n (COOK) Füllung f; (for tooth) (Zahn)plombe f; ~ **station** n Tankstelle f

film [fılm] n Film m ♦ vt (scene) filmen; ~ **star** n Filmstar m

filter ['fıltə'] n Filter m ♦ vt filtern; ~ **lane** n (BRIT) Abbiegespur f; **~-tipped** adj Filter-

filth [fılθ] n Dreck m; **~y** adj dreckig; (weather) scheußlich

fin [fın] n Flosse f

final ['faınl] adj letzte(r, s) End-; (conclusive) endgültig ♦ n (FOOTBALL etc) Endspiel nt; **~s** npl (UNIV) Abschlußexamen ⚠ nt; (SPORT) Schlußrunde ⚠ f

finale [fı'nɑːlı] n (MUS) Finale nt

final: **~ist** n (SPORT) Schlußrunden- teilnehmer ⚠ m; **~ize** vt endgültige Form geben +dat; abschließen; **~ly** adv (lastly) zuletzt; (eventually) endlich; (irrevocably) endgültig

finance [faı'næns] n Finanzwesen nt ♦ vt finanzieren; **~s** npl (funds) Finanzen pl; **financial** [faı'nænʃəl] adj Finanz-; finanziell

find [faınd] (pt, pp **found**) vt finden ♦ n Fund m; **to ~ sb guilty** jdn für schuldig erklären; ~ **out** vt herausfinden; **~ings** npl (JUR) Ermittlungsergebnis nt; (of report) Befund m

fine [faın] adj fein; (good) gut; (weather) schön ♦ adv (well) gut; (small) klein ♦ n (JUR) Geldstrafe f ♦ vt (JUR) mit einer Geldstrafe belegen; ~ **arts** npl schöne(n) Künste pl

finger ['fıŋgə'] n Finger m ♦ vt befühlen; **~nail** n Fingernagel m; **~print** n Fingerabdruck m; **~tip** n Fingerspitze f

finicky ['fınıkı] adj pingelig

finish ['fınıʃ] n Ende nt; (SPORT) Ziel nt; (of object) Verarbeitung f; (of paint) Oberflächenwirkung f ♦ vt beenden; (book) zu Ende lesen ♦ vi aufhören; (SPORT) ans Ziel kommen; **to be ~ed with sth** fertig sein mit etw; **to ~ doing sth** mit etw fertig werden; ~ **off** vt (complete) fertigmachen ⚠; (kill) den Gnadenstoß geben +dat; (knock out) erledigen (umg); ~ **up** vt (food) aufessen; (drink) austrinken ♦ vi (end up) enden; **~ing line** n Ziellinie f; **~ing school** n Mädchenpensionat nt

finite ['faınaıt] adj endlich, begrenzt

Finland ['fınlənd] n Finnland nt

Finn [fın] n Finne m, Finnin f; **~ish** adj finnisch ♦ n (LING) Finnisch nt

fir [fəː'] n Tanne f

fire ['faıə'] n Feuer nt; (in house etc) Brand m ♦ vt (gun) abfeuern; (imagination) entzünden; (dismiss) hinauswerfen ♦ vi (AUT) zünden; **to be on** ~ brennen; ~ **alarm** n Feueralarm m; **~arm** n Schußwaffe ⚠ f; ~ **brigade** (BRIT) n Feuerwehr f; ~ **department** (US) n Feuerwehr f; ~ **engine** n Feuerwehrauto nt; ~ **escape** n Feuerleiter f; ~ **extinguisher** n Löschgerät nt; **~man** (irreg) n Feuerwehrmann m; **~place** n Kamin m; **~side** n Kamin m; ~ **station** n Feuerwehrwache f; **~wood** n Brennholz nt; **~works** npl Feuerwerk nt; **firing squad** n Exekutionskommando nt

firm [fəːm] adj fest ♦ n Firma f; **~ly** ['fəːmlı] adv (grasp, speak) fest; (push, tug) energisch; (decide) endgültig

first [fəːst] adj erste(r, s) ♦ adv zuerst; (arrive) als erste(r); (happen) zum erstenmal ⚠ ♦ n (person: in race) Erste(r) mf; (UNIV) Eins f; (AUT) erste(r) Gang m; **at** ~ zuerst; ~ **of all** zu allererst; ~ **aid** n Erste Hilfe f; **~-aid kit** n Verbandskasten m; **~-class** adj erstklassig; (travel) erster Klasse; **~-hand** adj aus erster Hand; ~ **lady** (US) n First Lady f; **~ly** adv erstens; ~ **name** n Vorname m; **~- rate** adj erstklassig

fiscal ['fıskl] adj Finanz-

fish [fıʃ] n inv Fisch m ♦ vi fischen; angeln; **to go ~ing** angeln gehen; (in sea) fischen gehen; **~erman** (irreg) n Fischer m; ~ **farm** n Fischzucht f; ~ **fingers** (BRIT) npl Fischstäbchen pl; **~ing boat** n Fischerboot nt; **~ing line** n Angelschnur f; **~ing rod** n Angel(rute) f; **~ing tackle** n (for sport) Angelgeräte pl; **~monger's (shop)** n Fischhändler m; ~ **slice** n Fischvorlegemesser nt; ~ **sticks** (US) npl = **fish fingers**

fishy ['fıʃı] (inf) adj (suspicious) faul

fission ['fıʃən] n Spaltung f

fissure ['fıʃə'] n Riß ⚠ m

⚠ Informationen zur Rechtschreibreform Seite 615

fist [fɪst] n Faust f

fit [fɪt] adj (MED) gesund; (SPORT) in Form, fit; (suitable) geeignet ♦ vt passen +dat; (insert, attach) einsetzen ♦ vi passen; (in space, gap) hineinpassen ♦ n (of clothes) Sitz m; (MED, of anger) Anfall m; (of laughter) Krampf m; **by ~s and starts** (move) ruckweise; (work) unregelmäßig; **~ in** vi hineinpassen; (fig: person) passen; **~ out** vt (also: **~ up**) ausstatten; **~ful** adj (sleep) unruhig; **~ment** n Einrichtungsgegenstand m; **~ness** n (suitability) Eignung f; (MED) Gesundheit f; (SPORT) Fitneß ⚠ f; **~ted carpet** n Teppichboden m; **~ted kitchen** n Einbauküche f; **~ter** n (TECH) Monteur m; **~ting** adj passend ♦ n (of dress) Anprobe f; (piece of equipment) (Ersatz)teil nt; **~tings** npl (equipment) Zubehör nt; **~ting room** n Anproberaum m

five [faɪv] num fünf; **~r** (inf) n (BRIT) Fünf-Pfund-Note f; (US) Fünf-Dollar-Note f

fix [fɪks] vt befestigen; (settle) festsetzen; (repair) reparieren ♦ n: **in a ~** in der Klemme; **~ up** vt (meeting) arrangieren; **to ~ sb up with sth** jdm etw acc verschaffen; **~ation** [fɪk'seɪʃən] n Fixierung f; **~ed** [fɪkst] adj fest; **~ture** ['fɪkstʃər] n Installationsteil m; (SPORT) Spiel nt

fizzy ['fɪzɪ] adj Sprudel-, sprudelnd

flabbergasted ['flæbəgɑːstɪd] (inf) adj platt

flabby ['flæbɪ] adj wabbelig

flag [flæg] n Fahne f ♦ vi (strength) nachlassen; (spirit) erlahmen; **~ down** vt anhalten; **~pole** ['flægpəul] n Fahnenstange f

flair [fleər] n Talent nt

flak [flæk] n Flakfeuer nt

flake [fleɪk] n (of snow) Flocke f; (of rust) Schuppe f ♦ vi (also: **~ off**) abblättern

flamboyant [flæm'bɔɪənt] adj extravagant

flame [fleɪm] n Flamme f

flamingo [flə'mɪŋgəu] n Flamingo m

flammable ['flæməbl] adj brennbar

flan [flæn] (BRIT) n Obsttorte f

flank [flæŋk] n Flanke f ♦ vt flankieren

flannel ['flænl] n Flanell m; (BRIT: also: face ~) Waschlappen m; (: inf) Geschwafel nt;

~s npl (trousers) Flanellhose f

flap [flæp] n Klappe f; (inf: crisis) (helle) Aufregung f ♦ vt (wings) schlagen mit ♦ vi flattern

flare [fleər] n (signal) Leuchtsignal nt; (in skirt etc) Weite f; **~ up** vi aufflammen; (fig) aufbrausen; (revolt) (plötzlich) ausbrechen

flash [flæʃ] n Blitz m; (also: **news ~**) Kurzmeldung f; (PHOT) Blitzlicht nt ♦ vt aufleuchten lassen ♦ vi aufleuchten; **in a ~** im Nu; **~ by** or **past** vi vorbeirasen; **~back** n Rückblende f; **~bulb** n Blitzlichtbirne f; **~ cube** n Blitzwürfel m; **~light** n Blitzlicht nt

flashy ['flæʃɪ] (pej) adj knallig

flask [flɑːsk] n (CHEM) Kolben m; (also: **vacuum ~**) Thermosflasche f ®

flat [flæt] adj flach; (dull) matt; (MUS) erniedrigt; (beer) schal; (tyre) platt ♦ n (BRIT: rooms) Wohnung f; (MUS) b nt; (AUT) Platte(r) m; **to work ~ out** auf Hochtouren arbeiten; **~ly** adv glatt; **~-screen** adj (TV, COMPUT) mit flachem Bildschirm; **~ten** vt (also: **~ten out**) ebnen

flatter ['flætər] vt schmeicheln +dat; **~ing** adj schmeichelhaft; **~y** n Schmeichelei f

flatulence ['flætjuləns] n Blähungen pl

flaunt [flɔːnt] vt prunken mit

flavour ['fleɪvər] (US **flavor**) n Geschmack m ♦ vt würzen; **~ed** adj: **strawberry-~ed** mit Erdbeergeschmack; **~ing** n Würze f

flaw [flɔː] n Fehler m; **~less** adj einwandfrei

flax [flæks] n Flachs m; **~en** adj flachsfarben

flea [fliː] n Floh m

fleck [flek] n (mark) Fleck m; (pattern) Tupfen m

fled [fled] pt, pp of **flee**

flee [fliː] (pt, pp **fled**) vi fliehen ♦ vt fliehen vor +dat; (country) fliehen aus

fleece [fliːs] n Vlies nt ♦ vt (inf) schröpfen

fleet [fliːt] n Flotte f

fleeting ['fliːtɪŋ] adj flüchtig

Flemish ['flemɪʃ] adj flämisch

flesh [fleʃ] n Fleisch nt; **~ wound** n Fleischwunde f

flew [fluː] pt of **fly**

flex [fleks] n Kabel nt ♦ vt beugen; **~ibility**

⚠ For information on spelling reform see page 615

[fleksɪ'bɪlɪtɪ] n Biegsamkeit f; (fig) Flexibilität f; **~ible** adj biegsam; (plans) flexibel

flick [flɪk] n leichte(r) Schlag m ♦ vt leicht schlagen; **~ through** vt fus durchblättern

flicker ['flɪkəʳ] n Flackern nt ♦ vi flackern

flier ['flaɪəʳ] n Flieger m

flight [flaɪt] n Flug m; (fleeing) Flucht f; (also: **~ of steps**) Treppe f; **to take ~** die Flucht ergreifen; **~ attendant** (US) n Steward(eß) ⚠ m(f); **~ deck** n Flugdeck nt

flimsy ['flɪmzɪ] adj (thin) hauchdünn; (excuse) fadenscheinig

flinch [flɪntʃ] vi: **to ~ (away from)** zurückschrecken (vor +dat)

fling [flɪŋ] (pt, pp flung) vt schleudern

flint [flɪnt] n Feuerstein m

flip [flɪp] vt werfen

flippant ['flɪpənt] adj schnippisch

flipper ['flɪpəʳ] n Flosse f

flirt [flɜːt] vi flirten ♦ n: **he/she is a ~** er/sie flirtet gern

flit [flɪt] vi flitzen

float [fləut] n (FISHING) Schwimmer m; (esp in procession) Plattformwagen m ♦ vi schwimmen; (in air) schweben ♦ vt (COMM) gründen; (currency) floaten

flock [flɒk] n (of sheep, REL) Herde f; (of birds) Schwarm m

flog [flɒg] vt prügeln; (inf: sell) verkaufen

flood [flʌd] n Überschwemmung f; (fig) Flut f ♦ vt überschwemmen; **~ing** n Überschwemmung f; **~light** n Flutlicht nt

floor [flɔːʳ] n (Fuß)boden m; (storey) Stock m ♦ vt (person) zu Boden schlagen; **ground ~** (BRIT) Erdgeschoß ⚠ nt; **first ~** (BRIT) erste(r) Stock m; (US) Erdgeschoß ⚠ nt; **~board** n Diele f; **~ show** n Kabarettvorstellung f

flop [flɒp] n Plumps m; (failure) Reinfall m ♦ vi (fail) durchfallen

floppy ['flɒpɪ] adj hängend; **~ (disk)** n (COMPUT) Diskette f

flora ['flɔːrə] n Flora f; **~l** adj Blumen-

florist ['flɒrɪst] n Blumenhändler(in) m(f); **~'s (shop)** n Blumengeschäft nt

flotation [fləu'teɪʃən] n (FIN) Auflegung f

flounce [flauns] n Volant m

flounder ['flaundəʳ] vi (fig) ins Schleudern kommen ♦ n (ZOOL) Flunder f

flour ['flauəʳ] n Mehl nt

flourish ['flʌrɪʃ] vi blühen; gedeihen ♦ n (waving) Schwingen nt; (of trumpets) Tusch m, Fanfare f

flout [flaut] vt mißachten ⚠

flow [fləu] n Fließen nt; (of sea) Flut f ♦ vi fließen; **~ chart** n Flußdiagramm ⚠ nt

flower ['flauəʳ] n Blume f ♦ vi blühen; **~ bed** n Blumenbeet nt; **~pot** n Blumentopf m; **~y** adj (style) blumenreich

flown [fləun] pp of **fly**

flu [fluː] n Grippe f

fluctuate ['flʌktjueɪt] vi schwanken; **fluctuation** [flʌktju'eɪʃən] n Schwankung f

fluency ['fluːənsɪ] n Flüssigkeit f

fluent ['fluːənt] adj fließend; **~ly** adv fließend

fluff [flʌf] n Fussel f; **~y** adj flaumig

fluid ['fluːɪd] n Flüssigkeit f ♦ adj flüssig; (fig: plans) veränderbar

fluke [fluːk] n (inf) Dusel m

flung [flʌŋ] pt, pp of **fling**

fluoride ['fluəraɪd] n Fluorid nt; **~ toothpaste** n Fluorzahnpasta f

flurry ['flʌrɪ] n (of snow) Gestöber nt; (of activity) Aufregung f

flush [flʌʃ] n Erröten nt; (of excitement) Glühen nt ♦ vt (aus)spülen ♦ vi erröten ♦ adj glatt; **~ out** vt aufstöbern; **~ed** adj rot

flustered ['flʌstəd] adj verwirrt

flute [fluːt] n Querflöte f

flutter ['flʌtəʳ] n Flattern nt ♦ vi flattern

flux [flʌks] n: **in a state of ~** im Fluß ⚠

fly [flaɪ] (pt flew, pp flown) n (insect) Fliege f; (on trousers: also: **flies**) (Hosen)schlitz m ♦ vt fliegen ♦ vi fliegen; (flee) fliehen; (flag) wehen; **~ away** or **off** vi (bird, insect) wegfliegen; **~-drive** n: **~-drive holiday** Fly & Drive-Urlaub m; **~ing** n Fliegen nt ♦ adj: **with ~ing colours** mit fliegenden Fahnen; **~ing start** n gute(r) Start m; **~ing visit** n Stippvisite f; **~ing saucer** n fliegende Untertasse f; **~over** (BRIT) n Überführung f; **~sheet** n (for tent) Regendach nt

⚠ *Informationen zur Rechtschreibreform Seite 615*

foal [fəul] n Fohlen nt

foam [fəum] n Schaum m ♦ vi schäumen; ~ **rubber** n Schaumgummi m

fob [fɔb] vt: **to ~ sb off with sth** jdm etw andrehen; (with promise) jdn mit etw abspeisen

focal ['fəukl] adj Brenn-; ~ **point** n (of room, activity) Mittelpunkt m

focus ['fəukəs] (pl **~es**) n Brennpunkt m ♦ vt (attention) konzentrieren; (camera) scharf einstellen ♦ vi: **to ~ (on)** sich konzentrieren (auf +acc); **in ~** scharf eingestellt; **out of ~** unscharf

fodder ['fɔdəʳ] n Futter nt

foe [fəu] n Feind m

foetus ['fi:təs] (US **fetus**) n Fötus m

fog [fɔg] n Nebel m; **~gy** adj neblig; ~ **lamp** (BRIT), ~ **light** (US) n (AUT) Nebelscheinwerfer m

foil [fɔil] vt vereiteln ♦ n (metal, also fig) Folie f; (FENCING) Florett nt

fold [fəuld] n (bend, crease) Falte f; (AGR) Pferch m ♦ vt falten; ~ **up** vt (map etc) zusammenfalten ♦ vi (business) eingehen; **~er** n Schnellhefter m; **~ing** adj (chair etc) Klapp-

foliage ['fəulɪdʒ] n Laubwerk nt

folk [fəuk] npl Leute pl ♦ adj Volks-; **~s** npl (family) Leute pl; **~lore** ['fəuklɔ:ʳ] n (study) Volkskunde f; (tradition) Folklore f; ~ **song** n Volkslied nt; (modern) Folksong m

follow ['fɔləu] vt folgen +dat; (fashion) mitmachen ♦ vi folgen; ~ **up** vt verfolgen; **~er** n Anhänger(in) m(f); **~ing** adj folgend ♦ n (people) Gefolgschaft f; **~-on call** n weiteres Gespräch in einer Telefonzelle um Guthaben zu verbrauchen

folly ['fɔlɪ] n Torheit f

fond [fɔnd] adj: **to be ~ of** gern haben

fondle ['fɔndl] vt streicheln

font [fɔnt] n Taufbecken nt

food [fu:d] n Essen nt; (fodder) Futter nt; ~ **mixer** n Küchenmixer m; ~ **poisoning** n Lebensmittelvergiftung f; ~ **processor** n Küchenmaschine f; **~stuffs** npl Lebensmittel pl

fool [fu:l] n Narr m, Närrin f ♦ vt (deceive) hereinlegen ♦ vi (also: ~ **around**) (herum)albern; **~hardy** adj tollkühn; **~ish** adj albern; **~proof** adj idiotensicher

foot [fut] (pl **feet**) n Fuß m ♦ vt (bill) bezahlen; **on ~** zu Fuß

footage ['futɪdʒ] n (CINE) Filmmaterial nt

football ['futbɔ:l] n Fußball m; (game: BRIT) Fußball m; (: US) Football m; ~ **player** n (BRIT: also: **~er**) Fußballspieler m, Fußballer m; (US) Footballer m

FOOTBALL POOLS

i Football Pools, umgangssprachlich auch the pools genannt, ist das in Großbritannien sehr beliebte Fußballtoto, bei dem auf die Ergebnisse der samstäglichen Fußballspiele gewettet wird. Teilnehmer schicken ihren ausgefüllten Totoschein vor den Spielen an die Totogesellschaft und vergleichen nach den Spielen die Ergebnisse mit ihrem Schein. Die Gewinne können sehr hoch sein und gelegentlich Millionen von Pfund betragen.

foot: **~brake** n Fußbremse f; **~bridge** n Fußgängerbrücke f; **~hills** npl Ausläufer pl; **~hold** n Halt m; **~ing** n Halt m; (fig) Verhältnis nt; **~lights** npl Rampenlicht nt; **~man** (irreg) n Bedienstete(r) m; **~note** n Fußnote f; **~path** n Fußweg m; **~print** n Fußabdruck m; **~sore** adj fußkrank; **~step** n Schritt m; **~wear** n Schuhzeug nt

KEYWORD

for [fɔːʳ] prep **1** für; **is this for me?** ist das für mich?; **the train for London** der Zug nach London; **he went for the paper** er ging die Zeitung holen; **give it to me – what for?** gib es mir – warum?

2 (because of) wegen; **for this reason** aus diesem Grunde

3 (referring to distance): **there are roadworks for 5 km** die Baustelle ist 5 km lang; **we walked for miles** wir sind meilenweit gegangen

4 (referring to time) seit; (: with future sense) für; **he was away for 2 years** er war zwei

⚠ For information on spelling reform see page 615

Jahre lang weg

5 (+*infin clauses*): **it is not for me to decide** das kann ich nicht entscheiden; **for this to be possible ...** damit dies möglich wird/ wurde ...

6 (*in spite of*) trotz +*gen or (inf) dat* ; **for all his complaints** obwohl er sich ständig beschwert

♦ *conj* denn

---

forage ['fɒrɪdʒ] *n* (Vieh)futter *nt*

foray ['fɒreɪ] *n* Raubzug *m*

forbad(e) [fə'bæd] *pt of* **forbid**

forbid [fə'bɪd] (*pt* **forbad(e)**, *pp* **forbidden**) *vt* verbieten; ~**ding** *adj* einschüchternd

force [fɔːs] *n* Kraft *f*; (*compulsion*) Zwang *m* ♦ *vt* zwingen; (*lock*) aufbrechen; **the F~s** *npl* (*BRIT*) die Streitkräfte; **in ~** (*rule*) gültig; (*group*) in großer Stärke; ~**d** *adj* (*smile*) gezwungen; (*landing*) Not-; ~**feed** *vt* zwangsernähren; ~**ful** *adj* (*speech*) kraftvoll; (*personality*) resolut

forceps ['fɔːseps] *npl* Zange *f*

forcibly ['fɔːsəblɪ] *adv* zwangsweise

ford [fɔːd] *n* Furt *f* ♦ *vt* durchwaten

fore [fɔː] *n*: **to the ~** in den Vordergrund; ~**arm** ['fɔːrɑːm] *n* Unterarm *m*; ~**boding** [fɔː'bəʊdɪŋ] *n* Vorahnung *f*; ~**cast** ['fɔːkɑːst] (*irreg: like* **cast**) *n* Vorhersage *f* ♦ *vt* voraussagen; ~**court** ['fɔːkɔːt] *n* (*of garage*) Vorplatz *m*; ~**fathers** ['fɔːfɑːðəz] *npl* Vorfahren *pl*; ~**finger** ['fɔːfɪŋgə'] *n* Zeigefinger *m*; ~**front** ['fɔːfrʌnt] *n* Spitze *f*

forego [fɔː'gəʊ] (*irreg: like* **go**) *vt* verzichten auf +*acc*

fore: ~**gone** ['fɔːgɒn] *adj*: **it's a ~gone conclusion** es steht von vornherein fest; ~**ground** ['fɔːgraund] *n* Vordergrund *m*; ~**head** ['fɒrɪd] *n* Stirn *f*

foreign ['fɒrɪn] *adj* Auslands-; (*accent*) ausländisch; (*trade*) Außen-; (*body*) Fremd-; ~**er** *n* Ausländer(in) *m(f)*; ~ **exchange** *n* Devisen *pl*; **F~ Office** (*BRIT*) *n* Außenministerium *nt*; **F~ Secretary** (*BRIT*) *n* Außenminister *m*

fore [fɔː]: ~**leg** *n* Vorderbein *nt*; ~**man** (*irreg*) *n* Vorarbeiter *m*; ~**most** *adj* erste(r,

s) ♦ *adv*: **first and ~most** vor allem

forensic [fə'rɛnsɪk] *adj* gerichtsmedizinisch

fore ['fɔː-]: ~**runner** *n* Vorläufer *m*; ~**see** [fɔː'siː] (*irreg: like* **see**) *vt* vorhersehen; ~**seeable** *adj* absehbar; ~**shadow** [fɔː'ʃædəʊ] *vt* andeuten; ~**sight** ['fɔːsaɪt] *n* Voraussicht *f*

forest ['fɒrɪst] *n* Wald *m*

forestall [fɔː'stɔːl] *vt* zuvorkommen +*dat*

forestry ['fɒrɪstrɪ] *n* Forstwirtschaft *f*

foretaste ['fɔːteɪst] *n* Vorgeschmack *m*

foretell [fɔː'tɛl] (*irreg: like* **tell**) *vt* vorhersagen

forever [fə'rɛvə'] *adv* für immer

foreword ['fɔːwɜːd] *n* Vorwort *nt*

forfeit ['fɔːfɪt] *n* Einbuße *f* ♦ *vt* verwirken

forgave [fə'geɪv] *pt of* **forgive**

forge [fɔːdʒ] *n* Schmiede *f* ♦ *vt* fälschen; (*iron*) schmieden; ~ **ahead** *vi* Fortschritte machen; ~**d** *adj* gefälscht; ~**d banknotes** Blüten (*inf*) *pl*; ~**r** *n* Fälscher *m*; ~**ry** *n* Fälschung *f*

forget [fə'get] (*pt* **forgot**, *pp* **forgotten**) *vt, vi* vergessen; ~**ful** *adj* vergeßlich ⚠; ~**-me-not** *n* Vergißmeinnicht ⚠ *nt*

forgive [fə'gɪv] (*pt* **forgave**, *pp* **forgiven**) *vt* verzeihen; **to ~ sb (for sth)** jdm (etw) verzeihen; ~**ness** *n* Verzeihung *f*

forgot [fə'gɒt] *pt of* **forget**; ~**ten** *pp of* **forget**

fork [fɔːk] *n* Gabel *f*; (*in road*) Gabelung *f* ♦ *vi* (*road*) sich gabeln; ~ **out** (*inf*) *vt* (*pay*) blechen; ~**-lift truck** *n* Gabelstapler *m*

forlorn [fə'lɔːn] *adj* (*person*) verlassen; (*hope*) vergeblich

form [fɔːm] *n* Form *f*; (*type*) Art *f*; (*figure*) Gestalt *f*; (*SCH*) Klasse *f*; (*bench*) (Schul)bank *f*; (*document*) Formular *nt* ♦ *vt* formen; (*be part of*) bilden

formal ['fɔːməl] *adj* formell; (*occasion*) offiziell; ~**ly** *adv* (*ceremoniously*) formell; (*officially*) offiziell

format ['fɔːmæt] *n* Format *nt* ♦ *vt* (*COMPUT*) formatieren; ~**ion** [fɔː'meɪʃən] *n* Bildung *f*; (*AVIAT*) Formation *f*

formative ['fɔːmətɪv] *adj* (*years*) formend

former ['fɔːmə'] *adj* früher; (*opposite of latter*) erstere(r, s); ~**ly** *adv* früher

⚠ *Informationen zur Rechtschreibreform Seite 615*

formidable ['fɔ:mɪdəbl] *adj* furchtbar

formula ['fɔ:mjulə] (*pl* **~e** or **~s**) *n* Formel *f*; **~e** *f* ['fɔ:mjuli:] *npl of* **formula**; **~te** ['fɔ:mjuleɪt] *vt* formulieren

fort [fɔ:t] *n* Feste *f*, Fort *nt*

forte ['fɔ:tɪ] *n* Stärke *f*, starke Seite *f*

forth [fɔ:θ] *adv*: **and so ~** und so weiter; **~coming** *adj* kommend; (*character*) entgegenkommend; **~right** *adj* offen; **~with** *adv* umgehend

fortify ['fɔ:tɪfaɪ] *vt* (ver)stärken; (*protect*) befestigen

fortitude ['fɔ:tɪtju:d] *n* Seelenstärke *f*

fortnight ['fɔ:tnaɪt] (*BRIT*) *n* vierzehn Tage *pl*; **~ly** (*BRIT*) *adj* zweiwöchentlich ♦ *adv* alle vierzehn Tage

fortress ['fɔ:trɪs] *n* Festung *f*

fortunate ['fɔ:tʃənɪt] *adj* glücklich; **~ly** *adv* glücklicherweise, zum Glück

fortune ['fɔ:tʃən] *n* Glück *nt*; (*money*) Vermögen *nt*; **~-teller** *n* Wahrsager(in) *m(f)*

forty ['fɔ:tɪ] *num* vierzig

forum ['fɔ:rəm] *n* Forum *nt*

forward ['fɔ:wəd] *adj* vordere(r, s); (*movement*) Vorwärts-; (*person*) vorlaut; (*planning*) Voraus- ♦ *adv* vorwärts ♦ *n* (*SPORT*) Stürmer *m* ♦ *vt* (*send*) schicken; (*help*) fördern; **~s** *adv* vorwärts

fossil ['fɔsl] *n* Fossil *nt*, Versteinerung *f*

foster ['fɔstəʳ] *vt* (*talent*) fördern; **~ child** *n* Pflegekind *nt*; **~ mother** *n* Pflegemutter *f*

fought [fɔ:t] *pt, pp of* **fight**

foul [faul] *adj* schmutzig; (*language*) gemein; (*weather*) schlecht ♦ *n* (*SPORT*) Foul *nt* ♦ *vt* (*mechanism*) blockieren; (*SPORT*) foulen; **~ play** *n* (*SPORT*) Foulspiel *nt*; (*LAW*) Verbrechen *nt*

found [faund] *pt, pp of* **find** ♦ *vt* gründen; **~ation** [faun'deɪʃən] *n* (*act*) Gründung *f*; (*fig*) Fundament *nt*; (*also:* **~ation cream**) Grundierungscreme *f*; **~ations** *npl* (*of house*) Fundament *nt*; **~er** ['faundəʳ] *n* Gründer(in) *m(f)* ♦ *vi* sinken

foundry ['faundrɪ] *n* Gießerei *f*

fountain ['fauntɪn] *n* (Spring)brunnen *m*; **~ pen** *n* Füllfederhalter *m*

four [fɔ:ʳ] *num* vier; **on all ~s** auf allen vieren; **~-poster** *n* Himmelbett *nt*; **~some** *n* Quartett *nt*; **~teen** *num* vierzehn; **~teenth** *adj* vierzehnte(r, s); **~th** *adj* vierte(r, s)

fowl [faul] *n* Huhn *nt*; (*food*) Geflügel *nt*

fox [fɔks] *n* Fuchs *m* ♦ *vt* täuschen

foyer ['fɔɪeɪ] *n* Foyer *nt*, Vorhalle *f*

fraction ['frækʃən] *n* (*MATH*) Bruch *m*; (*part*) Bruchteil *m*

fracture ['fræktʃəʳ] *n* (*MED*) Bruch *m* ♦ *vt* brechen

fragile ['frædʒaɪl] *adj* zerbrechlich

fragment ['frægmənt] *n* Bruchstück *nt*; (*small part*) Splitter *m*

fragrance ['freɪgrəns] *n* Duft *m*; **fragrant** ['freɪgrənt] *adj* duftend

frail [freɪl] *adj* schwach, gebrechlich

frame [freɪm] *n* Rahmen *m*; (*of spectacles: also:* **~s**) Gestell *nt*; (*body*) Gestalt *f* ♦ *vt* einrahmen; **to ~ sb** (*inf: incriminate*) jdm etwas anhängen; **~ of mind** Verfassung *f*; **~work** *n* Rahmen *m*; (*of society*) Gefüge *nt*

France [frɑ:ns] *n* Frankreich *nt*

franchise ['fræntʃaɪz] *n* (*POL*) (aktives) Wahlrecht *nt*; (*COMM*) Lizenz *f*

frank [fræŋk] *adj* offen ♦ *vt* (*letter*) frankieren; **~ly** *adv* offen gesagt

frantic ['fræntɪk] *adj* verzweifelt

fraternal [frə'tə:nl] *adj* brüderlich

fraternity [frə'tə:nɪtɪ] *n* (*club*) Vereinigung *f*; (*spirit*) Brüderlichkeit *f*; (*US: SCH*) Studentenverbindung *f*

fraternize ['frætənaɪz] *vi* fraternisieren

fraud [frɔ:d] *n* (*trickery*) Betrug *m*; (*person*) Schwindler(in) *m(f)*; **~ulent** ['frɔ:djulənt] *adj* betrügerisch

fraught [frɔ:t] *adj*: **~ with** voller +*gen*

fray [freɪ] *vt, vi* ausfransen; **tempers were ~ed** die Gemüter waren erhitzt

freak [fri:k] *n* Monstrosität *f* ♦ *cpd* (*storm etc*) anormal

freckle ['frekl] *n* Sommersprosse *f*

free [fri:] *adj* frei; (*loose*) lose; (*liberal*) freigebig ♦ *vt* (*set ~*) befreien; (*unblock*) freimachen; **~ (of charge)** gratis, umsonst; **for ~** gratis, umsonst; **~dom** ['fri:dəm] *n*

⚠ *For information on spelling reform see page 615*

Freiheit f; **F~fone** ® n: **call F~fone 0800 ...** rufen Sie gebührenfrei 0800 ... an; **~-for-all** n (fight) allgemeine(s) Handgemenge nt; **~ gift** n Geschenk nt; **~ kick** n Freistoß m; **~lance** adj frei; (artist) freischaffend; **~ly** adv frei; (admit) offen; **F~post** ® n ≈ Gebühr zahlt Empfänger; **~-range** adj (hen) Farmhof-; (eggs) Land-; **~ trade** n Freihandel m; **~way** (US) n Autobahn f; **~wheel** vi im Freilauf fahren; **~ will** n: **of one's own ~ will** aus freien Stücken

freeze [friːz] (pt **froze**, pp **frozen**) vi gefrieren; (feel cold) frieren ♦ vt (also fig) einfrieren ♦ n (fig, FIN) Stopp m; **~r** n Tiefkühltruhe f; (in fridge) Gefrierfach nt; **freezing** adj eisig; (freezing cold) eiskalt; **freezing point** n Gefrierpunkt m

freight [freɪt] n Fracht f; **~ train** n Güterzug m

French [frɛntʃ] adj französisch ♦ n (LING) Französisch nt; **the ~** npl (people) die Franzosen pl; **~ bean** n grüne Bohne f; **~ fried potatoes** (BRIT) npl Pommes frites pl; **~ fries** (US) npl Pommes frites pl; **~ horn** n (MUS) (Wald)horn nt; **~ kiss** n Zungenkuß ⚠ m; **~ loaf** n Baguette f; **~man/woman** (irreg) n Franzose m/Französin f; **~ window** n Verandatür f

frenzy ['frɛnzɪ] n Raserei f

frequency ['friːkwənsɪ] n Häufigkeit f; (PHYS) Frequenz f

frequent [adj 'friːkwənt, vb frɪ'kwɛnt] adj häufig ♦ vt (regelmäßig) besuchen; **~ly** adv (often) häufig, oft

fresh [frɛʃ] adj frisch; **~en** vi (also: **~en up**) (sich) auffrischen; (person) sich frisch machen; **~er** (inf: BRIT) n (UNIV) Erstsemester nt; **~ly** adv gerade; **~man** (irreg) n (US) = **fresher**; **~ness** n Frische f; **~water** adj (fish) Süßwasser-

fret [frɛt] vi sich dat Sorgen machen

friar ['fraɪəʳ] n Klosterbruder m

friction ['frɪkʃən] n (also fig) Reibung f

Friday ['fraɪdɪ] n Freitag m

fridge [frɪdʒ] (BRIT) n Kühlschrank m

fried [fraɪd] adj gebraten

friend [frɛnd] n Freund(in) m(f); **~ly** adj freundlich; (relations) freundschaftlich; **~ly fire** n Beschuß ⚠ m durch die eigene Seite; **~ship** n Freundschaft f

frieze [friːz] n Fries m

frigate ['frɪgɪt] n Fregatte f

fright [fraɪt] n Schrecken m; **to take ~** es mit der Angst zu tun bekommen; **~en** vt erschrecken; **to be ~ened** Angst haben; **~ening** adj schrecklich; **~ful** (inf) adj furchtbar

frigid ['frɪdʒɪd] adj frigide

frill [frɪl] n Rüsche f

fringe [frɪndʒ] n Besatz m; (BRIT: of hair) Pony m; (fig) Peripherie f; **~ benefits** npl zusätzliche Leistungen pl

Frisbee ['frɪzbɪ] ® n Frisbee ® nt

frisk [frɪsk] vt durchsuchen

frisky ['frɪskɪ] adj lebendig, ausgelassen

fritter ['frɪtəʳ] vt: **to ~ away** vergeuden

frivolous ['frɪvələs] adj frivol

frizzy ['frɪzɪ] adj kraus

fro [frəʊ] adv see **to**

frock [frɔk] n Kleid nt

frog [frɔg] n Frosch m; **~man** (irreg) n Froschmann m

frolic ['frɔlɪk] vi ausgelassen sein

KEYWORD

from [frɔm] prep 1 (indicating starting place) von; (indicating origin etc) aus +dat; **a letter/telephone call from my sister** ein Brief/Anruf von meiner Schwester; **where do you come from?** woher kommen Sie?; **to drink from the bottle** aus der Flasche trinken

2 (indicating time) von ... an; (: past) seit; **from one o'clock to** or **until** or **till two** von ein Uhr bis zwei; **from January (on)** ab Januar

3 (indicating distance) von ... (entfernt)

4 (indicating price, number etc) ab +dat; **from £10** ab £10; **there were from 20 to 30 people** es waren zwischen 20 und 30 Leute da

5 (indicating difference): **he can't tell red from green** er kann nicht zwischen rot und

⚠ *Informationen zur Rechtschreibreform Seite 615*

grün unterscheiden; **to be different from sb/sth** anders sein als jd/etw
6 (*because of, based on*): **from what he says** aus dem, was er sagt; **weak from hunger** schwach vor Hunger

front [frʌnt] *n* Vorderseite *f*; (*of house*) Fassade *f*; (*promenade: also:* **sea ~**) Strandpromenade *f*; (*MIL, POL, MET*) Front *f*; (*fig: appearances*) Fassade *f* ♦ *adj* (*forward*) vordere(r, s), Vorder-; (*first*) vorderste(r, s); **in ~** vorne; **in ~ of** vor; **~age** ['frʌntɪdʒ] *n* Vorderfront *f*; **~ door** *n* Haustür *f*; **~ier** ['frʌntɪəʳ] *n* Grenze *f*; **~ page** *n* Titelseite *f*; **~ room** (*BRIT*) *n* Wohnzimmer *nt*; **~-wheel drive** *n* Vorderradantrieb *m*

frost [frɔst] *n* Frost *m*; **~bite** *n* Erfrierung *f*; **~ed** *adj* (*glass*) Milch-; **~y** *adj* frostig

froth [frɔθ] *n* Schaum *m*

frown [fraun] *n* Stirnrunzeln *nt* ♦ *vi* die Stirn runzeln

froze [frʌuz] *pt of* **freeze**

frozen ['frʌuzn] *pp of* **freeze**

frugal ['fru:gl] *adj* sparsam, bescheiden

fruit [fru:t] *n inv* (*as collective*) Obst *nt*; (*particular*) Frucht *f*; **~ful** *adj* fruchtbar; **~ion** [fru:'ɪʃən] *n*: **to come to ~ion** in Erfüllung gehen; **~ juice** *n* Fruchtsaft *m*; **~ machine** (*BRIT*) *n* Spielautomat *m*; **~ salad** *n* Obstsalat *m*

frustrate [frʌs'treɪt] *vt* vereiteln; **~d** *adj* gehemmt; (*PSYCH*) frustriert

fry [fraɪ] (*pt, pp* **fried**) *vt* braten ♦ *npl*: **small ~** kleine Fische *pl*; **~ing pan** *n* Bratpfanne *f*

ft. *abbr* = **foot**; **feet**

fuddy-duddy ['fʌdɪdʌdɪ] *n* altmodische(r) Kauz *m*

fudge [fʌdʒ] *n* Fondant *m*

fuel ['fjuəl] *n* Treibstoff *m*; (*for heating*) Brennstoff *m*; (*for lighter*) Benzin *nt*; **~ oil** *n* (*diesel fuel*) Heizöl *nt*; **~ tank** *n* Tank *m*

fugitive ['fju:dʒɪtɪv] *n* Flüchtling *m*

fulfil [ful'fɪl] *vt* (*duty*) erfüllen; (*promise*) einhalten; **~ment** *n* Erfüllung *f*

full [ful] *adj* (*box, bottle, price*) voll; (*person: satisfied*) satt; (*member, power, employment*)

Voll-; (*complete*) vollständig, Voll-; (*speed*) höchste(r, s); (*skirt*) weit ♦ *adv*: **~ well** sehr wohl; **in ~** vollständig; **a ~ two hours** volle zwei Stunden; **~-length** *adj* (*lifesize*) lebensgroß; **a ~-length photograph** eine Ganzaufnahme; **~ moon** *n* Vollmond *m*; **~-scale** *adj* (*attack*) General-; (*drawing*) in Originalgröße; **~ stop** *n* Punkt *m*; **~-time** *adj* (*job*) Ganztags- ♦ *adv* (*work*) ganztags ♦ *n* (*SPORT*) Spielschluß *nt*; **~y** *adv* völlig; **~y fledged** *adj* (*also fig*) flügge; **~y licensed** *adj* (*hotel, restaurant*) mit voller Schankkonzession *or* -erlaubnis

fumble ['fʌmbl] *vi*: **to ~** (**with**) herumfummeln (an +*dat*)

fume [fju:m] *vi* qualmen; (*fig*) kochen (*inf*); **~s** *npl* (*of fuel, car*) Abgase *pl*

fumigate ['fju:mɪgeɪt] *vt* ausräuchern

fun [fʌn] *n* Spaß *m*; **to make ~ of** sich lustig machen über +*acc*

function ['fʌŋkʃən] *n* Funktion *f*; (*occasion*) Veranstaltung *f* ♦ *vi* funktionieren; **~al** *adj* funktionell

fund [fʌnd] *n* (*money*) Geldmittel *pl*, Fonds *m*; (*store*) Vorrat *m*; **~s** *npl* (*resources*) Mittel *pl*

fundamental [fʌndə'mentl] *adj* fundamental, grundlegend

funeral ['fju:nərəl] *n* Beerdigung *f*; **~ parlour** *n* Leichenhalle *f*; **~ service** *n* Trauergottesdienst *m*

funfair ['fʌnfeəʳ] (*BRIT*) *n* Jahrmarkt *m*

fungi ['fʌŋgaɪ] *npl of* **fungus**

fungus ['fʌŋgəs] *n* Pilz *m*

funnel ['fʌnl] *n* Trichter *m*; (*NAUT*) Schornstein *m*

funny ['fʌnɪ] *adj* komisch

fur [fəːʳ] *n* Pelz *m*; **~ coat** *n* Pelzmantel *m*

furious ['fjuərɪəs] *adj* wütend; (*attempt*) heftig

furlong ['fəːlɔŋ] *n* = 201.17 m

furnace ['fəːnɪs] *n* (Brenn)ofen *m*

furnish ['fəːnɪʃ] *vt* einrichten; (*supply*) versehen; **~ings** *npl* Einrichtung *f*

furniture ['fəːnɪtʃəʳ] *n* Möbel *pl*; **piece of ~** Möbelstück *nt*

furrow ['fʌrʌu] *n* Furche *f*

⚠ *For information on spelling reform see page 615*

furry ['fɜːrɪ] *adj* (*tongue*) pelzig; (*animal*) Pelz-
further ['fɜːðə*r*] *adj* weitere(r, s) ♦ *adv* weiter
♦ *vt* fördern; ~ **education** *n* Weiterbildung
f; Erwachsenenbildung *f*; **~more** *adv* ferner
furthest ['fɜːðɪst] *superl of* **far**
furtive ['fɜːtɪv] *adj* verstohlen
fury ['fjʊərɪ] *n* Wut *f*, Zorn *m*
fuse [fjuːz] (*US* **fuze**) *n* (*ELEC*) Sicherung *f*; (*of
bomb*) Zünder *m* ♦ *vt* verschmelzen ♦ *vi*
(*BRIT*: *ELEC*) durchbrennen; ~ **box** *n*
Sicherungskasten *m*
fuselage ['fjuːzəlɑːʒ] *n* Flugzeugrumpf *m*
fusion ['fjuːʒən] *n* Verschmelzung *f*
fuss [fʌs] *n* Theater *nt*; **~y** *adj* kleinlich
futile ['fjuːtaɪl] *adj* zwecklos, sinnlos; **futility**
[fjuːˈtɪlɪtɪ] *n* Zwecklosigkeit *f*
future ['fjuːtʃə*r*] *adj* zukünftig ♦ *n* Zukunft *f*;
in (the) ~ in Zukunft
fuze [fjuːz] (*US*) = **fuse**
fuzzy ['fʌzɪ] *adj* (*indistinct*) verschwommen;
(*hair*) kraus

G, g

G [dʒiː] *n* (*MUS*) G *nt*
G7 *n abbr* (= Group of Seven) G7 *f*
gabble ['gæbl] *vi* plappern
gable ['geɪbl] *n* Giebel *m*
gadget ['gædʒɪt] *n* Vorrichtung *f*
Gaelic ['geɪlɪk] *adj* gälisch ♦ *n* (*LING*) Gälisch
nt
gaffe [gæf] *n* Fauxpas *m*
gag [gæg] *n* Knebel *m*; (*THEAT*) Gag *m* ♦ *vt*
knebeln
gaiety ['geɪtɪ] *n* Fröhlichkeit *f*
gain [geɪn] *vt* (*obtain*) erhalten; (*win*)
gewinnen ♦ *vi* (*clock*) vorgehen ♦ *n* Gewinn
m; **to** ~ **in sth** an etw *dat* gewinnen; ~ **on**
vt fus einholen
gait [geɪt] *n* Gang *m*
gal. *abbr* = **gallon**
gala ['gɑːlə] *n* Fest *nt*
galaxy ['gæləksɪ] *n* Sternsystem *nt*
gale [geɪl] *n* Sturm *m*
gallant ['gælənt] *adj* tapfer; (*polite*) galant
gallbladder ['gɔːl-] *n* Gallenblase *f*

gallery ['gælərɪ] *n* (*also*: **art** ~) Galerie *f*
galley ['gælɪ] *n* (*ship's kitchen*) Kombüse *f*;
(*ship*) Galeere *f*
gallon ['gæln] *n* Gallone *f*
gallop ['gæləp] *n* Galopp *m* ♦ *vi* galoppieren
gallows ['gæləʊz] *n* Galgen *m*
gallstone ['gɔːlstəʊn] *n* Gallenstein *m*
galore [gəˈlɔːr] *adv* in Hülle und Fülle
galvanize ['gælvənaɪz] *vt* (*metal*)
galvanisieren; (*fig*) elektrisieren
gambit ['gæmbɪt] *n* (*fig*): **opening** ~
(einleitende(r)) Schachzug *m*
gamble ['gæmbl] *vi* (um Geld) spielen ♦ *vt*
(*risk*) aufs Spiel setzen ♦ *n* Risiko *nt*; ~ *r n*
Spieler(in) *m(f)*; **gambling** *n* Glücksspiel *nt*
game [geɪm] *n* Spiel *nt*; (*hunting*) Wild *nt*
♦ *adj*: ~ **(for)** bereit (zu); **~keeper** *n*
Wildhüter *m*; **~s console** *n* (*COMPUT*)
Gameboy *m* ®, Konsole *f*
gammon ['gæmən] *n* geräucherte(r)
Schinken *m*
gamut ['gæmət] *n* Tonskala *f*
gang [gæŋ] *n* (*of criminals, youths*) Bande *f*;
(*of workmen*) Kolonne *f* ♦ *vi*: **to** ~ **up on sb**
sich gegen jdn verschwören
gangrene ['gæŋgriːn] *n* Brand *m*
gangster ['gæŋstə*r*] *n* Gangster *m*
gangway ['gæŋweɪ] *n* (*NAUT*) Laufplanke *f*;
(*aisle*) Gang *m*
gaol [dʒeɪl] (*BRIT*) *n*, *vt* = **jail**
gap [gæp] *n* Lücke *f*
gape [geɪp] *vi* glotzen; **gaping** ['geɪpɪŋ] *adj*
(*wound*) klaffend; (*hole*) gähnend
garage ['gærɑːʒ] *n* Garage *f*; (*for repair*)
(Auto)reparaturwerkstatt *f*; (*for petrol*)
Tankstelle *f*
garbage ['gɑːbɪdʒ] *n* Abfall *m*; ~ **can** (*US*) *n*
Mülltonne *f*
garbled ['gɑːbld] *adj* (*story*) verdreht
garden ['gɑːdn] *n* Garten *m*; **~s** *npl* (*public
park*) Park *m*; (*private*) Gartenanlagen *pl*;
~er *n* Gärtner(in) *m(f)*; **~ing** *n* Gärtnern *nt*
gargle ['gɑːgl] *vi* gurgeln
gargoyle ['gɑːgɔɪl] *n* Wasserspeier *m*
garish ['gɛərɪʃ] *adj* grell
garland ['gɑːlənd] *n* Girlande *f*
garlic ['gɑːlɪk] *n* Knoblauch *m*

⚠ *Informationen zur Rechtschreibreform Seite 615*

garment ['gɑːmənt] n Kleidungsstück nt
garnish ['gɑːnɪʃ] vt (food) garnieren
garrison ['gærɪsn] n Garnison f
garter ['gɑːtə'] n Strumpfband nt; (US) Strumpfhalter m
gas [gæs] n Gas nt; (esp US: petrol) Benzin nt ♦ vt vergasen; ~ **cooker** (BRIT) n Gasherd m; ~ **cylinder** n Gasflasche f; ~ **fire** n Gasofen m
gash [gæʃ] n klaffende Wunde f ♦ vt tief verwunden
gasket ['gæskɪt] n Dichtungsring m
gas mask n Gasmaske f
gas meter n Gaszähler m
gasoline ['gæsəliːn] (US) n Benzin nt
gasp [gɑːsp] vi keuchen; (in surprise) tief Luft holen ♦ n Keuchen nt
gas: ~ **ring** n Gasring m; ~ **station** (US) n Tankstelle f; ~ **tap** n Gashahn m
gastric ['gæstrɪk] adj Magen-
gate [geɪt] n Tor nt; (barrier) Schranke f
gateau ['gætəu] (pl ~x) n Torte f
gatecrash ['geɪtkræʃ] (BRIT) vt (party) platzen in +acc
gateway ['geɪtweɪ] n Toreingang m
gather ['gæðə'] vt (people) versammeln; (things) sammeln; (understand) annehmen ♦ vi (assemble) sich versammeln; **to** ~ **speed** schneller werden; **to** ~ (**from**) schließen (aus); ~**ing** n Versammlung f
gauche [gəuʃ] adj linkisch
gaudy ['gɔːdɪ] adj schreiend
gauge [geɪdʒ] n (instrument) Meßgerät △ nt; (RAIL) Spurweite f; (dial) Anzeiger m; (measure) Maß nt ♦ vt (ab)messen; (fig) abschätzen
gaunt [gɔːnt] adj hager
gauze [gɔːz] n Gaze f
gave [geɪv] pt of give
gay [geɪ] adj (homosexual) schwul; (lively) lustig
gaze [geɪz] n Blick m ♦ vi starren; **to** ~ **at sth** etw dat anstarren
gazelle [gə'zel] n Gazelle f
gazumping [gə'zʌmpɪŋ] (BRIT) n Hausverkauf an Höherbietenden trotz Zusage an anderen

GB n abbr = Great Britain
GCE (BRIT) n abbr = General Certificate of Education
GCSE (BRIT) n abbr = General Certificate of Secondary Education
gear [gɪə'] n Getriebe nt; (equipment) Ausrüstung f; (AUT) Gang m ♦ vt (fig: adapt): **to be ~ed to** ausgerichtet sein auf +acc; **top** ~ höchste(r) Gang m; **high** ~ (US) höchste(r) Gang m; **low** ~ niedrige(r) Gang m; **in** ~ eingekuppelt; ~ **box** n Getriebe(gehäuse) nt; ~ **lever** n Schalthebel m; ~ **shift** (US) n Schalthebel m
geese [giːs] npl of goose
gel [dʒel] n Gel nt
gelatin(e) ['dʒelətiːn] n Gelatine f
gem [dʒem] n Edelstein m; (fig) Juwel nt
Gemini ['dʒemɪnaɪ] n Zwillinge pl
gender ['dʒendə'] n (GRAM) Geschlecht nt
gene [dʒiːn] n Gen nt
general ['dʒenərl] n General m ♦ adj allgemein; ~ **delivery** (US) n Ausgabe(schalter m) f postlagernder Sendungen; ~ **election** n allgemeine Wahlen pl; ~**ize** vi verallgemeinern; ~ **knowledge** n Allgemeinwissen nt; ~**ly** adv allgemein, im allgemeinen; ~ **practitioner** n praktische(r) Arzt m, praktische Ärztin f
generate ['dʒenəreɪt] vt erzeugen
generation [dʒenə'reɪʃən] n Generation f; (act) Erzeugung f
generator ['dʒenəreɪtə'] n Generator m
generosity [dʒenə'rɔsɪtɪ] n Großzügigkeit f
generous ['dʒenərəs] adj großzügig
genetic engineering [dʒɪ'netɪk] n Gentechnik f
genetic fingerprinting [-'fɪŋgəprɪntɪŋ] n genetische Fingerabdrücke pl
genetics [dʒɪ'netɪks] n Genetik f
Geneva [dʒɪ'niːvə] n Genf nt
genial ['dʒiːnɪəl] adj freundlich, jovial
genitals ['dʒenɪtlz] npl Genitalien pl
genius ['dʒiːnɪəs] n Genie nt
genocide ['dʒenəusaɪd] n Völkermord m
gent [dʒent] n abbr = gentleman
genteel [dʒen'tiːl] adj (polite) wohlanständig; (affected) affektiert

⚠ *For information on spelling reform see page 615*

gentle ['dʒɛntl] *adj* sanft, zart
gentleman ['dʒɛntlmən] (*irreg*) *n* Herr *m*; (*polite*) Gentleman *m*
gentleness ['dʒɛntlnɪs] *n* Zartheit *f*, Milde *f*
gently ['dʒɛntlɪ] *adv* zart, sanft
gentry ['dʒɛntrɪ] *n* Landadel *m*
gents [dʒɛnts] *n*: **G~** (*lavatory*) Herren *pl*
genuine ['dʒɛnjuɪn] *adj* echt
geographic(al) [dʒɪəˈgræfɪk(l)] *adj* geographisch △
geography [dʒɪˈɔgrəfɪ] *n* Geographie △ *f*
geological [dʒɪəˈlɔdʒɪkl] *adj* geologisch
geology [dʒɪˈɔlədʒɪ] *n* Geologie *f*
geometric(al) [dʒɪəˈmɛtrɪk(l)] *adj* geometrisch
geometry [dʒɪˈɔmətrɪ] *n* Geometrie *f*
geranium [dʒɪˈreɪnɪəm] *n* Geranie *f*
geriatric [dʒɛrɪˈætrɪk] *adj* Alten- ♦ *n* Greis(in) *m(f)*
germ [dʒɜːm] *n* Keim *m*; (*MED*) Bazillus *m*
German ['dʒɜːmən] *adj* deutsch ♦ *n* Deutsche(r) *f(m)*; (*LING*) Deutsch *nt*; **~ measles** *n* Röteln *pl*; **~y** *n* Deutschland *nt*
germination [dʒɜːmɪˈneɪʃən] *n* Keimen *nt*
gesticulate [dʒɛsˈtɪkjuleɪt] *vi* gestikulieren
gesture ['dʒɛstjəʳ] *n* Geste *f*

KEYWORD

get [gɛt] (*pt, pp* **got**, *pp* **gotten** (*US*)) *vi* **1** (*become, be*) werden; **to get old/tired** alt/ müde werden; **to get married** heiraten
2 (*go*) (an)kommen, gehen
3 (*begin*): **to get to know sb** jdn kennenlernen △; **let's get going** *or* **started!** fangen wir an!
4 (*modal aux vb*): **you've got to do it** du mußt es tun
♦ *vt* **1**: **to get sth done** (*do*) etw machen; (*have done*) etw machen lassen; **to get sth going** *or* **to go** etw in Gang bringen *or* bekommen; **to get sb to do sth** jdn dazu bringen, etw zu tun
2 (*obtain: money, permission, results*) erhalten; (*find: job, flat*) finden; (*fetch: person, object*) holen; **to get sth for sb** jdm etw besorgen; **get me Mr Jones, please** (*TEL*) verbinden Sie mich bitte mit Mr Jones

3 (*receive: present, letter*) bekommen, kriegen; (*acquire: reputation etc*) erwerben
4 (*catch*) bekommen, kriegen; (*hit: target etc*) treffen, erwischen; **get him!** (*to dog*) faß!
5 (*take, move*) bringen; **to get sth to sb** jdm etw bringen
6 (*understand*) verstehen; (*hear*) mitbekommen; **I've got it!** ich hab's!
7 (*have, possess*): **to have got sth** etw haben
get about *vi* herumkommen; (*news*) sich verbreiten
get along *vi* (*people*) (gut) zurechtkommen; (*depart*) sich *acc* auf den Weg machen
get at *vt* (*facts*) herausbekommen; **to get at sb** (*nag*) an jdm herumnörgeln
get away *vi* (*leave*) sich *acc* davonmachen; (*escape*): **to get away from sth** von etw *dat* entkommen; **to get away with sth** mit etw davon kommen
get back *vi* (*return*) zurückkommen ♦ *vt* zurückbekommen
get by *vi* (*pass*) vorbeikommen; (*manage*) zurechtkommen
get down *vi* (her)untergehen ♦ *vt* (*depress*) fertigmachen △; **to get down to** in Angriff nehmen; (*find time to do*) kommen zu
get in *vi* (*train*) ankommen; (*arrive home*) heimkommen
get into *vt* (*enter*) hinein-/hereinkommen in +*acc*; (*: car, train etc*) einsteigen in +*acc*; (*clothes*) anziehen
get off *vi* (*from train etc*) aussteigen; (*from horse*) absteigen ♦ *vt* aussteigen aus; absteigen von
get on *vi* (*progress*) vorankommen; (*be friends*) auskommen; (*age*) alt werden; (*onto train etc*) einsteigen; (*onto horse*) aufsteigen ♦ *vt* einsteigen in +*acc*; auf etw *acc* aufsteigen
get out *vi* (*of house*) herauskommen; (*of vehicle*) aussteigen ♦ *vt* (*take out*) herausholen
get out of *vt* (*duty etc*) herumkommen

um

get over *vt* (*illness*) sich *acc* erholen von; (*surprise*) verkraften; (*news*) fassen; (*loss*) sich abfinden mit

get round *vt* herumkommen; (*fig: person*) herumkriegen

get through to *vt* (*TEL*) durchkommen zu

get together *vi* zusammenkommen

get up *vi* aufstehen ♦ *vt* hinaufbringen; (*go up*) hinaufgehen; (*organize*) auf die Beine stellen

get up to *vt* (*reach*) erreichen; (*prank etc*) anstellen

getaway ['gɛtəweɪ] *n* Flucht *f*

get-up ['gɛtʌp] (*inf*) *n* Aufzug *m*

geyser ['giːzəʳ] *n* Geiser *m*; (*heater*) Durchlauferhitzer *m*

ghastly ['gɑːstlɪ] *adj* gräßlich △

gherkin ['gəːkɪn] *n* Gewürzgurke *f*

ghetto ['gɛtəu] *n* G(h)etto *nt*; **~ blaster** *n* (große(r)) Radiorekorder *m*

ghost [gəust] *n* Gespenst *nt*

giant ['dʒaɪənt] *n* Riese *m* ♦ *adj* riesig, Riesen-

gibberish ['dʒɪbərɪʃ] *n* dumme(s) Geschwätz *nt*

gibe [dʒaɪb] *n* spöttische Bemerkung *f*

giblets ['dʒɪblɪts] *npl* Geflügelinnereien *pl*

giddiness ['gɪdɪnɪs] *n* Schwindelgefühl *nt*

giddy ['gɪdɪ] *adj* schwindlig

gift [gɪft] *n* Geschenk *nt*; (*ability*) Begabung *f*; **~ed** *adj* begabt; **~ shop** *n* Geschenkeladen *m*; **~ token**, **~ voucher** *n* Geschenkgutschein *m*

gigantic [dʒaɪˈgæntɪk] *adj* riesenhaft

giggle ['gɪgl] *vi* kichern ♦ *n* Gekicher *nt*

gild [gɪld] *vt* vergolden

gill [dʒɪl] *n* (*1/4 pint*) Viertelpinte *f*

gills [gɪlz] *npl* (*of fish*) Kiemen *pl*

gilt [gɪlt] *n* Vergoldung *f* ♦ *adj* vergoldet; **~-edged** *adj* mündelsicher

gimmick ['gɪmɪk] *n* Gag *m*

gin [dʒɪn] *n* Gin *m*

ginger ['dʒɪndʒəʳ] *n* Ingwer *m*; **~ ale** *n* Ingwerbier *nt*; **~ beer** *n* Ingwerbier *nt*; **~bread** *n* Pfefferkuchen *m*; **~-haired** *adj* rothaarig

gingerly ['dʒɪndʒəlɪ] *adv* behutsam

gipsy ['dʒɪpsɪ] *n* Zigeuner(in) *m(f)*

giraffe [dʒɪˈrɑːf] *n* Giraffe *f*

girder ['gəːdəʳ] *n* Eisenträger *m*

girdle ['gəːdl] *n* Hüftgürtel *m*

girl [gəːl] *n* Mädchen *nt*; **an English ~** eine (junge) Engländerin; **~friend** *n* Freundin *f*; **~ish** *adj* mädchenhaft

giro ['dʒaɪrəu] *n* (*bank ~*) Giro *nt*; (*post office ~*) Postscheckverkehr *m*

girth [gəːθ] *n* (*measure*) Umfang *m*; (*strap*) Sattelgurt *m*

gist [dʒɪst] *n* Wesentliche(s) *nt*

give [gɪv] (*pt* **gave**, *pp* **given**) *vt* geben ♦ *vi* (*break*) nachgeben; **~ away** *vt* verschenken; (*betray*) verraten; **~ back** *vt* zurückgeben; **~ in** *vi* nachgeben ♦ *vt* (*hand in*) abgeben; **~ off** *vt* abgeben; **~ out** *vt* verteilen; (*announce*) bekanntgeben △; **~ up** *vt*, *vi* aufgeben; **to ~ o.s. up** sich stellen; (*after siege*) sich ergeben; **~ way** *vi* (*BRIT: traffic*) Vorfahrt lassen; (*to feelings*): **to ~ way to** nachgeben +*dat*

glacier ['glæsɪəʳ] *n* Gletscher *m*

glad [glæd] *adj* froh; **~ly** ['glædlɪ] *adv* gern(e)

glamorous ['glæmərəs] *adj* reizvoll

glamour ['glæməʳ] *n* Glanz *m*

glance [glɑːns] *n* Blick *m* ♦ *vi*: **to ~ (at)** (hin)blicken (auf +*acc*); **~ off** *vt fus* (*fly off*) abprallen von; **glancing** ['glɑːnsɪŋ] *adj* (*blow*) Streif-

gland [glænd] *n* Drüse *f*

glare [glɛəʳ] *n* (*light*) grelle(s) Licht *nt*; (*stare*) wilde(r) Blick *m* ♦ *vi* grell scheinen; (*angrily*): **to ~ at** böse ansehen; **glaring** ['glɛərɪŋ] *adj* (*injustice*) schreiend; (*mistake*) kraß △

glass [glɑːs] *n* Glas *nt*; (*mirror: also:* **looking ~**) Spiegel *m*; **~es** *npl* (*spectacles*) Brille *f*; **~house** *n* Gewächshaus *nt*; **~ware** *n* Glaswaren *pl*; **~y** *adj* glasig

glaze [gleɪz] *vt* verglasen; (*finish with a ~*) glasieren ♦ *n* Glasur *f*; **~d** *adj* (*eye*) glasig; (*pot*) glasiert; **glazier** ['gleɪzɪəʳ] *n* Glaser *m*

gleam [gliːm] *n* Schimmer *m* ♦ *vi* schimmern

△ *For information on spelling reform see page 615*

glean [gliːn] *vt (fig)* ausfindig machen
glen [glɛn] *n* Bergtal *nt*
glib [glɪb] *adj* oberflächlich
glide [glaɪd] *vi* gleiten; **~r** *n (AVIAT)* Segelflugzeug *nt*; **gliding** ['glaɪdɪŋ] *n* Segelfliegen *nt*
glimmer ['glɪməʳ] *n* Schimmer *m*
glimpse [glɪmps] *n* flüchtige(r) Blick *m* ♦ *vt* flüchtig erblicken
glint [glɪnt] *n* Glitzern *nt* ♦ *vi* glitzern
glisten ['glɪsn] *vi* glänzen
glitter ['glɪtəʳ] *vi* funkeln ♦ *n* Funkeln *nt*
gloat [gləut] *vi*: **to ~ over** sich weiden an +*dat*
global ['gləubl] *adj*: **~ warming** globale(r) Temperaturanstieg *m*
globe [gləub] *n* Erdball *m*; *(sphere)* Globus *m*
gloom [gluːm] *n (darkness)* Dunkel *nt*; *(depression)* düstere Stimmung *f*; **~y** *adj* düster
glorify ['glɔːrɪfaɪ] *vt* verherrlichen
glorious ['glɔːrɪəs] *adj* glorreich
glory ['glɔːrɪ] *n* Ruhm *m*
gloss [glɔs] *n (shine)* Glanz *m*; **~ over** *vt fus* übertünchen
glossary ['glɔsərɪ] *n* Glossar *nt*
glossy ['glɔsɪ] *adj (surface)* glänzend
glove [glʌv] *n* Handschuh *m*; **~ compartment** *n (AUT)* Handschuhfach *nt*
glow [gləu] *vi* glühen ♦ *n* Glühen *nt*
glower ['glauəʳ] *vi*: **to ~ at** finster anblicken
glucose ['gluːkəus] *n* Traubenzucker *m*
glue [gluː] *n* Klebstoff *m* ♦ *vt* kleben
glum [glʌm] *adj* bedrückt
glut [glʌt] *n* Überfluß ⚠ *m*
glutton ['glʌtn] *n* Vielfraß *m*; **a ~ for work** ein Arbeitstier *nt*
glycerin(e) ['glɪsəriːn] *n* Glyzerin *nt*
gnarled [nɑːld] *adj* knorrig
gnat [næt] *n* Stechmücke *f*
gnaw [nɔː] *vt* nagen an +*dat*
gnome [nəum] *n* Gnom *m*
go [gəu] *(pt* went, *pp* gone, *pl* **~es**) *vi* gehen; *(travel)* reisen, fahren; *(depart: train)* (ab)fahren; *(be sold)* verkauft werden; *(work)* gehen, funktionieren; *(fit, suit)* passen; *(become)* werden; *(break etc)*

nachgeben ♦ *n (energy)* Schwung *m*; *(attempt)* Versuch *m*; **he's ~ing to do it** er wird es tun; **to ~ for a walk** spazieren gehen; **to ~ dancing** tanzen gehen; **how did it ~?** wie war's?; **to ~ with** *(be suitable)* passen zu; **to have a ~ at sth** etw versuchen; **to be on the ~** auf Trab sein; **whose ~ is it?** wer ist dran?; **~ about** *vi (rumour)* umgehen ♦ *vt fus*: **how do I ~ about this?** wie packe ich das an?; **~ after** *vt fus (pursue: person)* nachgehen +*dat*; **~ ahead** *vi (proceed)* weitergehen; **~ along** *vi* dahingehen, dahinfahren ♦ *vt* entlanggehen, entlangfahren; **to ~ along with** *(support)* zustimmen +*dat*; **~ away** *vi (depart)* weggehen; **~ back** *vi (return)* zurückgehen; **~ back on** *vt fus (promise)* nicht halten; **~ by** *vi (years, time)* vergehen ♦ *vt fus* sich richten nach; **~ down** *vi (sun)* untergehen ♦ *vt fus* hinuntergehen, hinunterfahren; **~ for** *vt fus (fetch)* holen (gehen); *(like)* mögen; *(attack)* sich stürzen auf +*acc*; **~ in** *vi* hineingehen; **~ in for** *vt fus (competition)* teilnehmen an; **~ into** *vt fus (enter)* hineingehen in +*acc*; *(study)* sich befassen mit; **~ off** *vi (depart)* weggehen; *(lights)* ausgehen; *(milk etc)* sauer werden; *(explode)* losgehen ♦ *vt fus (dislike)* nicht mehr mögen; **~ on** *vi (continue)* weitergehen; *(inf: complain)* meckern; *(lights)* angehen; **to ~ on with sth** mit etw weitermachen; **~ out** *vi (fire, light)* ausgehen; *(of house)* hinausgehen; **~ over** *vi (ship)* kentern ♦ *vt fus (examine, check)* durchgehen; **~ past** *vi*: **to ~ past sth** an etw +*dat* vorbeigehen; **~ round** *vi (visit)*: **to ~ round (to sb's)** (bei jdm) vorbeigehen; **~ through** *vt fus (town etc)* durchgehen, durchfahren; **~ up** *vi (price)* steigen; **~ with** *vt fus (suit)* zu etw passen; **~ without** *vt fus* sich behelfen ohne; *(food)* entbehren
goad [gəud] *vt* anstacheln
go-ahead ['gəuəhɛd] *adj* zielstrebig; *(progressive)* fortschrittlich ♦ *n* grüne(s) Licht *nt*
goal [gəul] *n* Ziel *nt*; *(SPORT)* Tor *nt*;

~keeper n Torwart m; **~ post** n Torpfosten m

goat [gəut] n Ziege f

gobble ['gɔbl] vt (also: **~ down, ~ up**) hinunterschlingen

go-between ['gəubɪtwiːn] n Mittelsmann m

god [gɔd] n Gott m; **G~** n Gott m; **~child** n Patenkind nt; **~daughter** n Patentochter f; **~dess** n Göttin f; **~father** n Pate m; **~forsaken** adj gottverlassen; **~mother** n Patin f; **~send** n Geschenk nt des Himmels; **~son** n Patensohn m

goggles ['gɔglz] npl Schutzbrille f

going ['gəuɪŋ] n (HORSE-RACING) Bahn f ♦ adj (rate) gängig; (concern) gutgehend ⚠; **it's hard ~** es ist schwierig

gold [gəuld] n Gold nt ♦ adj golden; **~en** adj golden, Gold-; **~fish** n Goldfisch m; **~ mine** n Goldgrube f; **~-plated** adj vergoldet; **~smith** n Goldschmied(in) m(f)

golf [gɔlf] n Golf nt; **~ ball** n Golfball m; (on typewriter) Kugelkopf m; **~ club** n (society) Golfklub m; (stick) Golfschläger m; **~ course** n Golfplatz m; **~er** n Golfspieler(in) m(f)

gondola ['gɔndələ] n Gondel f

gone [gɔn] pp of **go**

gong [gɔŋ] n Gong m

good [gud] n (benefit) Wohl nt; (moral excellence) Güte f ♦ adj gut; **~s** npl (merchandise etc) Waren pl, Güter pl; **a ~ deal (of)** ziemlich viel; **a ~ many** ziemlich viele; **~ morning!** guten Morgen!; **~ afternoon!** guten Tag!; **~ evening!** guten Abend!; **~ night!** gute Nacht!; **would you be ~ enough to ...?** könnten Sie bitte ...?

goodbye [gud'baɪ] excl auf Wiedersehen!

good: G~ Friday n Karfreitag m; **~-looking** adj gutaussehend ⚠; **~-natured** adj gutmütig; (joke) harmlos; **~ness** n Güte f; (virtue) Tugend f; **~s train** (BRIT) n Güterzug m; **~will** n (favour) Wohlwollen nt; (COMM) Firmenansehen nt

goose [guːs] n (pl **geese**) Gans f

gooseberry ['guzbərɪ] n Stachelbeere f

gooseflesh ['guːsfleʃ] n Gänsehaut f

goose pimples npl Gänsehaut f

gore [gɔːʳ] vt aufspießen ♦ n Blut nt

gorge [gɔːdʒ] n Schlucht f ♦ vt: **to ~ o.s.** (sich voll)fressen ⚠

gorgeous ['gɔːdʒəs] adj prächtig

gorilla [gə'rɪlə] n Gorilla m

gorse [gɔːs] n Stechginster m

gory ['gɔːrɪ] adj blutig

go-slow ['gəu'sləu] (BRIT) n Bummelstreik m

gospel ['gɔspl] n Evangelium nt

gossip ['gɔsɪp] n Klatsch m; (person) Klatschbase f ♦ vi klatschen

got [gɔt] pt, pp of **get**

gotten ['gɔtn] (US) pp of **get**

gout [gaut] n Gicht f

govern ['gʌvən] vt regieren; verwalten

governess ['gʌvənɪs] n Gouvernante f

government ['gʌvnmənt] n Regierung f

governor ['gʌvənəʳ] n Gouverneur m

gown [gaun] n Gewand nt; (UNIV) Robe f

G.P. n abbr = **general practitioner**

grab [græb] vt packen

grace [greɪs] n Anmut f; (blessing) Gnade f; (prayer) Tischgebet nt ♦ vt (adorn) zieren; (honour) auszeichnen; **5 days' ~** 5 Tage Aufschub; **~ful** adj anmutig

gracious ['greɪʃəs] adj gnädig; (kind) freundlich

grade [greɪd] n Grad m; (slope) Gefälle nt ♦ vt (classify) einstufen; **~ crossing** (US) n Bahnübergang m; **~ school** (US) n Grundschule f

gradient ['greɪdɪənt] n Steigung f; Gefälle nt

gradual ['grædjuəl] adj allmählich; **~ly** adv allmählich

graduate [n 'grædjuɪt, vb 'grædjueɪt] n: **to be a ~** das Staatsexamen haben ♦ vi das Staatsexamen machen; **graduation** [grædju'eɪʃən] n Abschlußfeier ⚠ f

graffiti [grə'fiːtɪ] npl Graffiti pl

graft [grɑːft] n (hard work) Schufterei f; (MED) Verpflanzung f ♦ vt pfropfen; (fig) aufpfropfen; (MED) verpflanzen

grain [greɪn] n Korn nt; (in wood) Maserung f

gram [græm] n Gramm nt

grammar ['græməʳ] n Grammatik f; **~ school** (BRIT) n Gymnasium nt;

⚠ *For information on spelling reform see page 615*

grammatical [grə'mætɪkl] *adj* grammat(ikal)isch

gramme [græm] *n* = **gram**

granary ['grænərɪ] *n* Kornspeicher *m*

grand [grænd] *adj* großartig; **~child** (*pl* **~children**) *n* Enkelkind *nt*, Enkel(in) *m(f)*; **~dad** *n* Oma *m*; **~daughter** *n* Enkelin *f*; **~eur** ['grændʒər] *n* Erhabenheit *f*; **~father** *n* Großvater *m*; **~iose** ['grændɪəus] *adj* (*imposing*) großartig; (*pompous*) schwülstig; **~ma** *n* Oma *m*; **~mother** *n* Großmutter *f*; **~pa** *n* = **granddad**; **~parents** *npl* Großeltern *pl*; **~ piano** *n* Flügel *m*; **~son** *n* Enkel *m*; **~stand** *n* Haupttribüne *f*

granite ['grænɪt] *n* Granit *m*

granny ['grænɪ] *n* Oma *f*

grant [grɑːnt] *vt* gewähren ♦ *n* Unterstützung *f*; (*UNIV*) Stipendium *nt*; **to take sth for ~ed** etw als selbstverständlich (an)nehmen

granulated sugar ['grænjuleɪtɪd-] *n* Zuckerraffinade *f*

granule ['grænjuːl] *n* Körnchen *nt*

grape [greɪp] *n* (Wein)traube *f*

grapefruit ['greɪpfruːt] *n* Pampelmuse *f*, Grapefruit *f*

graph [grɑːf] *n* Schaubild *nt*; **~ic** ['græfɪk] *adj* (*descriptive*) anschaulich; (*drawing*) graphisch; **~ics** *npl* Grafik *f*

grapple ['græpl] *vi*: **to ~ with** kämpfen mit

grasp [grɑːsp] *vt* ergreifen; (*understand*) begreifen ♦ *n* Griff *m*; (*of subject*) Beherrschung *f*; **~ing** *adj* habgierig

grass [grɑːs] *n* Gras *nt*; **~hopper** *n* Heuschrecke *f*; **~land** *n* Weideland *nt*; **~roots** *adj* an der Basis; **~ snake** *n* Ringelnatter *f*

grate [greɪt] *n* Kamin *m* ♦ *vi* (*sound*) knirschen ♦ *vt* (*cheese etc*) reiben; **to ~ on the nerves** auf die Nerven gehen

grateful ['greɪtful] *adj* dankbar

grater ['greɪtər] *n* Reibe *f*

gratify ['grætɪfaɪ] *vt* befriedigen; **~ing** *adj* erfreulich

grating ['greɪtɪŋ] *n* (*iron bars*) Gitter *nt* ♦ *adj* (*noise*) knirschend

gratitude ['grætɪtjuːd] *n* Dankbarkeit *f*

gratuity [grə'tjuːɪtɪ] *n* Gratifikation *f*

grave [greɪv] *n* Grab *nt* ♦ *adj* (*serious*) ernst

gravel ['grævl] *n* Kies *m*

gravestone ['greɪvstəun] *n* Grabstein *m*

graveyard ['greɪvjɑːd] *n* Friedhof *m*

gravity ['grævɪtɪ] *n* Schwerkraft *f*; (*seriousness*) Schwere *f*

gravy ['greɪvɪ] *n* (Braten)soße *f*

gray [greɪ] *adj* = **grey**

graze [greɪz] *vi* grasen ♦ *vt* (*touch*) streifen; (*MED*) abschürfen ♦ *n* Abschürfung *f*

grease [griːs] *n* (*fat*) Fett *nt*; (*lubricant*) Schmiere *f* ♦ *vt* (ab)schmieren; **~proof** (*BRIT*) *adj* (*paper*) Butterbrot-; **greasy** ['griːsɪ] *adj* fettig

great [greɪt] *adj* groß; (*inf: good*) prima; **G~ Britain** *n* Großbritannien *nt*; **~-grandfather** *n* Urgroßvater *m*; **~-grandmother** *n* Urgroßmutter *f*; **~ly** *adv* sehr

Greece [griːs] *n* Griechenland *nt*

greed [griːd] *n* (*also:* **~iness**) Gier *f*; (*meanness*) Geiz *m*; **~(iness) for** Gier nach; **~y** *adj* gierig

Greek [griːk] *adj* griechisch ♦ *n* Grieche *m*, Griechin *f*; (*LING*) Griechisch *nt*

green [griːn] *adj* grün ♦ *n* (*village ~*) Dorfwiese *f*; **~ belt** *n* Grüngürtel *m*; **~ card** *n* (*AUT*) grüne Versicherungskarte *f*; **~ery** *n* Grün *nt*; grüne(s) Laub *nt*; **~gage** *n* Reineclaude *f*; **~grocer** (*BRIT*) *n* Obst- und Gemüsehändler *m*; **~house** *n* Gewächshaus *nt*; **~house effect** *n* Treibhauseffekt *m*; **~house gas** *n* Treibhausgas *nt*

Greenland ['griːnlənd] *n* Grönland *nt*

greet [griːt] *vt* grüßen; **~ing** *n* Gruß *m*; **~ing(s) card** *n* Glückwunschkarte *f*

gregarious [grə'gɛərɪəs] *adj* gesellig

grenade [grə'neɪd] *n* Granate *f*

grew [gruː] *pt of* **grow**

grey [greɪ] *adj* grau; **~-haired** *adj* grauhaarig; **~hound** *n* Windhund *m*

grid [grɪd] *n* Gitter *nt*; (*ELEC*) Leitungsnetz *nt*; (*on map*) Gitternetz *nt*

gridlock ['grɪdlɒk] *n* (*AUT: traffic jam*) totale(r) Stau *m*; **~ed** *adj*: **to be ~ed** (*roads*)

total verstopft sein; (*talks etc*) festgefahren
sein

grief [gri:f] *n* Gram *m*, Kummer *m*

grievance ['gri:vəns] *n* Beschwerde *f*

grieve [gri:v] *vi* sich grämen ♦ *vt* betrüben

grievous ['gri:vəs] *adj*: **~ bodily harm** (*JUR*)
schwere Körperverletzung *f*

grill [grɪl] *n* Grill *m* ♦ *vt* (*BRIT*) grillen;
(*question*) in die Mangel nehmen

grille [grɪl] *n* (*AUT*) (Kühler)gitter *nt*

grim [grɪm] *adj* grimmig; (*situation*) düster

grimace [grɪ'meɪs] *n* Grimasse *f* ♦ *vi*
Grimassen schneiden

grime [graɪm] *n* Schmutz *m*; **grimy** ['graɪmɪ]
adj schmutzig

grin [grɪn] *n* Grinsen *nt* ♦ *vi* grinsen

grind [graɪnd] (*pt, pp* **ground**) *vt* mahlen;
(*US: meat*) durch den Fleischwolf drehen;
(*sharpen*) schleifen; (*teeth*) knirschen mit ♦ *n*
(*bore*) Plackerei *f*

grip [grɪp] *n* Griff *m*; (*suitcase*) Handkoffer *m*
♦ *vt* packen; **~ping** *adj* (*exciting*) spannend

grisly ['grɪzlɪ] *adj* gräßlich ⚠

gristle ['grɪsl] *n* Knorpel *m*

grit [grɪt] *n* Splitt *m*; (*courage*) Mut *m* ♦ *vt*
(*teeth*) zusammenbeißen; (*road*) (mit Splitt
be)streuen

groan [grəun] *n* Stöhnen *nt* ♦ *vi* stöhnen

grocer ['grəusər] *n* Lebensmittelhändler *m*;
~ies *npl* Lebensmittel *pl*; **~'s (shop)** *n*
Lebensmittelgeschäft *nt*

groggy ['grɔgɪ] *adj* benommen

groin [grɔɪn] *n* Leistengegend *f*

groom [gru:m] *n* (*also:* **bridegroom**)
Bräutigam *m*; (*for horses*) Pferdeknecht *m*
♦ *vt* (*horse*) striegeln; (**well-**)**~ed** *adj* gepflegt

groove [gru:v] *n* Rille *f*, Furche *f*

grope [grəup] *vi* tasten; **~ for** *vt fus* suchen
nach

gross [grəus] *adj* (*coarse*) dick, plump; (*bad*)
grob, schwer; (*COMM*) brutto; **~ly** *adv*
höchst

grotesque [grə'tesk] *adj* grotesk

grotto ['grɔtəu] *n* Grotte *f*

ground [graund] *pt, pp of* **grind** ♦ *n* Boden
m; (*land*) Grundbesitz *m*; (*reason*) Grund *m*;
(*US: also:* **~ wire**) Endleitung *f* ♦ *vi* (*run*

ashore) stranden, auflaufen; **~s** *npl* (*dregs*)
Bodensatz *m*; (*around house*)
(Garten)anlagen *pl*; **on the ~** am Boden;
to the ~ zu Boden; **to gain/lose ~** Boden
gewinnen/verlieren; **~ cloth** (*US*) *n* =
groundsheet; **~ing** *n* (*instruction*)
Anfangsunterricht *m*; **~less** *adj* grundlos;
~sheet (*BRIT*) *n* Zeltboden *m*; **~ staff** *n*
Bodenpersonal *nt*; **~work** *n* Grundlage
f

group [gru:p] *n* Gruppe *f* ♦ *vt* (*also:* **~
together**) gruppieren ♦ *vi* sich gruppieren

grouse [graus] *n inv* (*bird*) schottische(s)
Moorhuhn *nt*

grove [grəuv] *n* Gehölz *nt*, Hain *m*

grovel ['grɔvl] *vi* (*fig*) kriechen

grow [grəu] (*pt* **grew**, *pp* **grown**) *vi*
wachsen; (*become*) werden ♦ *vt* (*raise*)
anbauen; **~ up** *vi* aufwachsen; **~er** *n*
Züchter *m*; **~ing** *adj* zunehmend

growl [graul] *vi* knurren

grown [grəun] *pp of* **grow**; **~-up** *n*
Erwachsene(r) *mf*

growth [grəuθ] *n* Wachstum *nt*; (*increase*)
Zunahme *f*; (*of beard etc*) Wuchs *m*

grub [grʌb] *n* Made *f*, Larve *f*; (*inf: food*)
Futter *nt*; **~by** ['grʌbɪ] *adj* schmutzig

grudge [grʌdʒ] *n* Groll *m* ♦ *vt*: **to ~ sb sth**
jdm etw mißgönnen ⚠; **to bear sb a ~**
einen Groll gegen jdn hegen

gruelling ['gruəlɪŋ] *adj* (*climb, race*)
mörderisch

gruesome ['gru:səm] *adj* grauenhaft

gruff [grʌf] *adj* barsch

grumble ['grʌmbl] *vi* murren

grumpy ['grʌmpɪ] *adj* verdrießlich

grunt [grʌnt] *vi* grunzen ♦ *n* Grunzen *nt*

G-string ['dʒi:strɪŋ] *n* Minislip *m*

guarantee [gærən'ti:] *n* Garantie *f* ♦ *vt*
garantieren

guard [gɑ:d] *n* (*sentry*) Wache *f*; (*BRIT: RAIL*)
Zugbegleiter *m* ♦ *vt* bewachen; **~ed** *adj*
vorsichtig; **~ian** *n* Vormund *m*; (*keeper*)
Hüter *m*; **~'s van** (*BRIT*) *n* (*RAIL*)
Dienstwagen *m*

guerrilla [gə'rɪlə] *n* Guerilla(kämpfer) *m*; **~
warfare** *n* Guerillakrieg *m*

⚠ *For information on spelling reform see page 615*

guess [ges] *vt, vi* (er)raten, schätzen ♦ *n* Vermutung *f*; **~work** *n* Raterei *f*

guest [gest] *n* Gast *m*; **~ house** *n* Pension *f*; **~ room** *n* Gastzimmer *nt*

guffaw [gʌ'fɔ:] *vi* schallend lachen

guidance ['gaidəns] *n* (*control*) Leitung *f*; (*advice*) Beratung *f*

guide [gaid] *n* Führer *m*; (*also:* **girl ~**) Pfadfinderin *f* ♦ *vt* führen; **~book** *n* Reiseführer *m*; **~ dog** *n* Blindenhund *m*; **~lines** *npl* Richtlinien *pl*

guild [gild] *n* (*HIST*) Gilde *f*

guillotine ['giləti:n] *n* Guillotine *f*

guilt [gilt] *n* Schuld *f*; **~y** *adj* schuldig

guinea pig ['gini-] *n* Meerschweinchen *nt*; (*fig*) Versuchskaninchen *nt*

guise [gaiz] *n*: **in the ~ of** in der Form +*gen*

guitar [gi'tɑ:ʳ] *n* Gitarre *f*

gulf [gʌlf] *n* Golf *m*; (*fig*) Abgrund *m*

gull [gʌl] *n* Möwe *f*

gullet ['gʌlit] *n* Schlund *m*

gullible ['gʌlibl] *adj* leichtgläubig

gully ['gʌli] *n* (Wasser)rinne *f*

gulp [gʌlp] *vt* (*also:* **~ down**) hinunterschlucken ♦ *vi* (*gasp*) schlucken

gum [gʌm] *n* (*around teeth*) Zahnfleisch *nt*; (*glue*) Klebstoff *m*; (*also:* **chewing ~**) Kaugummi *m* ♦ *vt* gummieren; **~boots** (*BRIT*) *npl* Gummistiefel *pl*

gun [gʌn] *n* Schußwaffe ⚠ *f*; **~boat** *n* Kanonenboot *nt*; **~fire** *n* Geschützfeuer *nt*; **~man** (*irreg*) *n* bewaffnete(r) Verbrecher *m*; **~point** *n*: **at ~point** mit Waffengewalt; **~powder** *n* Schießpulver *nt*; **~shot** *n* Schuß ⚠ *m*

gurgle ['gə:gl] *vi* gluckern

gush [gʌʃ] *vi* (*rush out*) hervorströmen; (*fig*) schwärmen

gust [gʌst] *n* Windstoß *m*, Bö *f*

gusto ['gʌstəu] *n* Genuß ⚠ *m*, Lust *f*

gut [gʌt] *n* (*ANAT*) Gedärme *pl*; (*string*) Darm *m*; **~s** *npl* (*fig*) Schneid *m*

gutter ['gʌtəʳ] *n* Dachrinne *f*; (*in street*) Gosse *f*

guttural ['gʌtərl] *adj* guttural, Kehl-

guy [gai] *n* (*also:* **~rope**) Halteseil *nt*; (*man*) Typ *m*, Kerl *m*

GUY FAWKES' NIGHT

ⓘ **Guy Fawkes' Night**, *auch Bonfire Night genannt, erinnert an den Gunpowder Plot, einen Attentatsversuch auf James I und sein Parlament am 5. November 1605. Einer der Verschwörer, Guy Fawkes, wurde auf frischer Tat ertappt, als er das Parlamentsgebäude in die Luft sprengen wollte. Vor der Guy Fawkes' Night basteln Kinder in Großbritannien eine Puppe des Guy Fawkes, mit der sie Geld für Feuerwerkskörper von Passanten erbetteln, und die dann am 5. November auf einem Lagerfeuer mit Feuerwerk verbrannt wird.*

---

guzzle ['gʌzl] *vt, vi* (*drink*) saufen; (*eat*) fressen

gym [dʒim] *n* (*also:* **~nasium**) Turnhalle *f*; (*also:* **~nastics**) Turnen *nt*; **~nast** ['dʒimnæst] *n* Turner(in) *m(f)*; **~nastics** [dʒim'næstiks] *n* Turnen *nt*, Gymnastik *f*; **~ shoes** *npl* Turnschuhe *pl*

gynaecologist [gainɪ'kɒlədʒist] (*US* **gynecologist**) *n* Frauenarzt(-ärztin) *m(f)*

gypsy ['dʒipsi] *n* = **gipsy**

gyrate [dʒai'reit] *vi* kreisen

H, h

haberdashery [hæbə'dæʃəri] (*BRIT*) *n* Kurzwaren *pl*

habit ['hæbit] *n* (An)gewohnheit *f*; (*monk's*) Habit *nt or m*

habitable ['hæbitəbl] *adj* bewohnbar

habitat ['hæbitæt] *n* Lebensraum *m*

habitual [hə'bitjuəl] *adj* gewohnheitsmäßig; **~ly** *adv* gewöhnlich

hack [hæk] *vt* hacken ♦ *n* Hieb *m*; (*writer*) Schreiberling *m*

hacker ['hækəʳ] *n* (*COMPUT*) Hacker *m*

hackneyed ['hæknid] *adj* abgedroschen

had [hæd] *pt, pp of* **have**

haddock ['hædək] (*pl* **~** *or* **~s**) *n* Schellfisch *m*

hadn't ['hædnt] = **had not**

---

haemorrhage ['hemərɪdʒ] (*US* **hemorrhage**) *n* Blutung *f*

haemorrhoids ['hemərɔɪdz] (*US* **hemorrhoids**) *npl* Hämorrhoiden ⚠ *pl*

haggard ['hægəd] *adj* abgekämpft

haggle ['hægl] *vi* feilschen

Hague [heɪg] *n*: **The ~** Den Haag *nt*

hail [heɪl] *n* Hagel *m* ♦ *vt* umjubeln ♦ *vi* hageln

hailstone *n* Hagelkorn *nt*

hair [heəʳ] *n* Haar *nt*, Haare *pl*; (*one ~*) Haar *nt*; **~brush** *n* Haarbürste *f*; **~cut** *n* Haarschnitt *m*; **to get a ~cut** sich *dat* die Haare schneiden lassen; **~do** *n* Frisur *f*; **~dresser** *n* Friseur *m*, Friseuse *f*; **~dresser's** *n* Friseursalon *m*; **~ dryer** *n* Trockenhaube *f*; (*hand-held*) Fön ⚠ *m* ®; **~ gel** *n* Haargel *nt*; **~grip** *n* Klemme *f*; **~net** *n* Haarnetz *nt*; **~pin** *n* Haarnadel *f*; **~pin bend** (*US* **~pin curve**) *n* Haarnadelkurve *f*; **~-raising** *adj* haarsträubend; **~ removing cream** *n* Enthaarungscreme *nt*; **~ spray** *n* Haarspray *nt*; **~style** *n* Frisur *f*; **~y** *adj* haarig

hake [heɪk] *n* Seehecht *m*

half [hɑːf] (*pl* **halves**) *n* Hälfte *f* ♦ *adj* halb ♦ *adv* halb, zur Hälfte; **an hour** eine halbe Stunde; **two and a ~** zweieinhalb; **to cut sth in ~** etw halbieren; **~ a dozen** ein halbes Dutzend, sechs; **~ board** *n* Halbpension *f*; **~-caste** *n* Mischling *m*; **~ fare** *n* halbe(r) Fahrpreis *m*; **~-hearted** *adj* lustlos; **~-hour** *n* halbe Stunde *f*; **~-price** *n*: **(at) ~-price** zum halben Preis; **~ term** (*BRIT*) *n* (*SCH*) Ferien *pl* in der Mitte des Trimesters; **~-time** *n* Halbzeit *f*; **~way** *adv* halbwegs, auf halbem Wege

halibut ['hælɪbət] *n inv* Heilbutt *m*

hall [hɔːl] *n* Saal *m*; (*entrance ~*) Hausflur *m*; (*building*) Halle *f*; **~ of residence** (*BRIT*) Studentenwohnheim *nt*

hallmark ['hɔːlmɑːk] *n* Stempel *m*

hallo [hə'ləʊ] *excl* = **hello**

Hallowe'en ['hæləʊ'iːn] *n* Tag *m* vor Allerheiligen

hallucination [həluːsɪ'neɪʃən] *n* Halluzination *f*

hallway ['hɔːlweɪ] *n* Korridor *m*

halo ['heɪləʊ] *n* Heiligenschein *m*

halt [hɔːlt] *n* Halt *m* ♦ *vt*, *vi* anhalten

halve [hɑːv] *vt* halbieren

halves [hɑːvz] *pl of* **half**

ham [hæm] *n* Schinken *m*

hamburger ['hæmbɜːgəʳ] *n* Hamburger *m*

hamlet ['hæmlɪt] *n* Weiler *m*

hammer ['hæməʳ] *n* Hammer *m* ♦ *vt*, *vi* hämmern

hammock ['hæmək] *n* Hängematte *f*

hamper ['hæmpəʳ] *vt* (be)hindern ♦ *n* Picknickkorb *m*

hamster ['hæmstəʳ] *n* Hamster *m*

hand [hænd] *n* Hand *f*; (*of clock*) (Uhr)zeiger *m*; (*worker*) Arbeiter *m* ♦ *vt* (*pass*) geben; **to give sb a ~** jdm helfen; **at ~** nahe; **to ~** zur Hand; **in ~** (*under control*) unter Kontrolle; (*being done*) im Gange; (*extra*) übrig; **on ~** zur Verfügung; **on the one ~ ..., on the other ~ ...** einerseits ..., andererseits ...; **~ in** *vt* abgeben; (*forms*) einreichen; **~ out** *vt* austeilen; **~ over** *vt* (*deliver*) übergeben; (*surrender*) abgeben; (: *prisoner*) ausliefern; **~bag** *n* Handtasche *f*; **~book** *n* Handbuch *nt*; **~brake** *n* Handbremse *f*; **~cuffs** *npl* Handschellen *pl*; **~ful** *n* Handvoll ⚠ *f*; (*inf*: *person*) Plage *f*

handicap ['hændɪkæp] *n* Handikap *nt* ♦ *vt* benachteiligen; **mentally/physically ~ped** geistig/körperlich behindert

handicraft ['hændɪkrɑːft] *n* Kunsthandwerk *nt*

handiwork ['hændɪwəːk] *n* Arbeit *f*; (*fig*) Werk *nt*

handkerchief ['hæŋkətʃɪf] *n* Taschentuch *nt*

handle ['hændl] *n* (*of door etc*) Klinke *f*; (*of cup etc*) Henkel *m*; (*for winding*) Kurbel *f* ♦ *vt* (*touch*) anfassen; (*deal with: things*) sich befassen mit; (: *people*) umgehen mit; **~bar(s)** *n(pl)* Lenkstange *f*

hand: **~ luggage** *n* Handgepäck *nt*; **~made** *adj* handgefertigt; **~out** *n* (*distribution*) Verteilung *f*; (*charity*) Geldzuwendung *f*; (*leaflet*) Flugblatt *nt*; **~rail** *n* Geländer *nt*; (*on ship*) Reling *f*; **~set** *n* (*TEL*) Hörer *m*; **please replace the ~set** bitte legen Sie auf; **~shake** *n* Händedruck *f*

handsome ['hænsəm] *adj* gutaussehend △

handwriting ['hændraɪtɪŋ] *n* Handschrift *f*

handy ['hændɪ] *adj* praktisch; (*shops*) leicht erreichbar; **~man** ['hændɪmæn] (*irreg*) *n* Bastler *m*

hang [hæŋ] (*pt, pp* **hung**) *vt* aufhängen; (*pt, pp* **hanged**) (*criminal*) hängen ♦ *vi* hängen ♦ *n*: **to get the ~ of sth** (*inf*) den richtigen Dreh für etw herauskriegen; **~ about, ~ around** *vi* sich herumtreiben; **~ on** *vi* (*wait*) warten; **~ up** *vi* (*TEL*) auflegen

hangar ['hæŋəʳ] *n* Hangar *m*

hanger ['hæŋəʳ] *n* Kleiderbügel *m*

hanger-on [hæŋərˈɔn] *n* Anhänger(in) *m(f)*

hang ['hæŋ-]: **~-gliding** *n* Drachenfliegen *nt*; **~over** *n* Kater *m*; **~-up** *n* Komplex *m*

hanker ['hæŋkəʳ] *vi*: **to ~ for** *or* **after** sich sehnen nach

hankie ['hæŋkɪ] *n abbr* = **handkerchief**

hanky ['hæŋkɪ] *n abbr* = **handkerchief**

haphazard [hæpˈhæzəd] *adj* zufällig

happen ['hæpən] *vi* sich ereignen, passieren; **as it ~s I'm going there today** zufällig(erweise) gehe ich heute (dort)hin; **~ing** *n* Ereignis *nt*

happily ['hæpɪlɪ] *adv* glücklich; (*fortunately*) glücklicherweise

happiness ['hæpɪnɪs] *n* Glück *nt*

happy ['hæpɪ] *adj* glücklich; **~ birthday!** alles Gute zum Geburtstag!; **~-go-lucky**

adj sorglos; **~ hour** *n* Happy Hour *f*

harass ['hærəs] *vt* plagen; **~ment** *n* Belästigung *f*

harbour ['hɑːbəʳ] (*US* **harbor**) *n* Hafen *m* ♦ *vt* (*hope etc*) hegen; (*criminal etc*) Unterschlupf gewähren

hard [hɑːd] *adj* (*firm*) hart; (*difficult*) schwer; (*harsh*) hart(herzig) ♦ *adv* (*work*) hart; (*try*) sehr; (*push, hit*) fest; **no ~ feelings!** ich nehme es dir nicht übel; **~ of hearing** schwerhörig; **to be ~ done by** übel dran sein; **~back** *n* kartonierte Ausgabe *f*; **~ cash** *n* Bargeld *nt*; **~ disk** *n* (*COMPUT*) Festplatte *f*; **~en** *vt* erhärten; (*fig*) verhärten ♦ *vi* hart werden; (*fig*) sich verhärten; **~-headed** *adj* nüchtern; **~ labour** *n* Zwangsarbeit *f*

hardly ['hɑːdlɪ] *adv* kaum

hard: **~ship** *n* Not *f*; **~ shoulder** (*BRIT*) *n* (*AUT*) Seitenstreifen *m*; **~ up** *adj* knapp bei Kasse; **~ware** *n* Eisenwaren *pl*; (*COMPUT*) Hardware *f*; **~ware shop** *n* Eisenwarenhandlung *f*; **~-wearing** *adj* strapazierfähig; **~-working** *adj* fleißig

hardy ['hɑːdɪ] *adj* widerstandsfähig

hare [hɛəʳ] *n* Hase *m*; **~-brained** *adj* schwachsinnig

harm [hɑːm] *n* Schaden *m* ♦ *vt* schaden +*dat*; **out of ~'s way** in Sicherheit; **~ful** *adj* schädlich; **~less** *adj* harmlos

harmonica [hɑːˈmɔnɪkə] *n* Mundharmonika *f*

harmonious [hɑːˈməunɪəs] *adj* harmonisch

harmonize ['hɑːmənaɪz] *vt* abstimmen ♦ *vi* harmonieren

harmony ['hɑːmənɪ] *n* Harmonie *f*

harness ['hɑːnɪs] *n* Geschirr *nt* ♦ *vt* (*horse*) anschirren; (*fig*) nutzbar machen

harp [hɑːp] *n* Harfe *f* ♦ *vi*: **to ~ on about sth** auf etw *dat* herumreiten

harpoon [hɑːˈpuːn] *n* Harpune *f*

harrowing ['hærəuɪŋ] *adj* nervenaufreibend

harsh [hɑːʃ] *adj* (*rough*) rauh △; (*severe*) streng; **~ness** *n* Härte *f*

harvest ['hɑːvɪst] *n* Ernte *f* ♦ *vt, vi* ernten

has [hæz] *vb see* **have**

hash [hæʃ] *vt* kleinhacken △ ♦ *n* (*mess*)

Kuddelmuddel m

hashish ['hæʃiʃ] n Haschisch nt

hasn't ['hæznt] = has not

hassle ['hæsl] (inf) n Theater nt

haste [heist] n Eile f; **~n** ['heisn] vt beschleunigen ♦ vi eilen; **hasty** adj hastig; (rash) vorschnell

hat [hæt] n Hut m

hatch [hætʃ] n (NAUT: also: **~way**) Luke f; (in house) Durchreiche f ♦ vi (young) ausschlüpfen ♦ vt (brood) ausbrüten; (plot) aushecken; **~back** ['hætʃbæk] n (AUT) (Auto nt mit) Heckklappe f

hatchet ['hætʃit] n Beil nt

hate [heit] vt hassen ♦ n Haß △ m; **~ful** adj verhaßt △

hatred ['heitrid] n Haß △ m

haughty ['hɔːti] adj hochnäsig, überheblich

haul [hɔːl] vt ziehen ♦ n (catch) Fang m; **~age** n Spedition f; **~ier** (US **hauler**) n Spediteur m

haunch [hɔːntʃ] n Lende f

haunt [hɔːnt] vt (ghost) spuken in +dat; (memory) verfolgen; (pub) häufig besuchen ♦ n Lieblingsplatz m; **the castle is ~ed in dem Schloß spukt es**

─────────────

KEYWORD

─────────────

have [hæv] (pt, pp **had**) aux vb 1 haben; (esp with vbs of motion) sein; **to have arrived/slept** angekommen sein/geschlafen haben; **to have been** gewesen sein; **having eaten or when he had eaten, he left** nachdem er gegessen hatte, ging er

2 (in tag questions): **you've done it, haven't you?** du hast es doch gemacht, oder nicht?

3 (in short answers and questions): **you've made a mistake – so I have/no I haven't** du hast einen Fehler gemacht – ja, stimmt/nein; **we haven't paid – yes we have!** wir haben nicht bezahlt – doch; **I've been there before, have you?** ich war schon einmal da, du auch?

♦ modal aux vb (be obliged): **to have (got) to do sth** etw tun müssen; **you haven't to tell her** du darfst es ihr nicht erzählen

♦ vt 1 (possess) haben; **he has (got) blue eyes** er hat blaue Augen; **I have (got) an idea** ich habe eine Idee

2 (referring to meals etc): **to have breakfast/a cigarette** frühstücken/eine Zigarette rauchen

3 (receive, obtain etc) haben; **may I have your address?** kann ich Ihre Adresse haben?; **to have a baby** ein Kind bekommen

4 (maintain, allow): **he will have it that he is right** er besteht darauf, daß er recht hat; **I won't have it** das lasse ich mir nicht bieten

5: **to have sth done** etw machen lassen; **to have sb do sth** jdn etw machen lassen; **he soon had them all laughing** er brachte sie alle zum Lachen

6 (experience, suffer): **she had her bag stolen** man hat ihr die Tasche gestohlen; **he had his arm broken** er hat sich den Arm gebrochen

7 (+noun: take, hold etc): **to have a walk/rest** spazierengehen/sich ausruhen; **to have a meeting/party** eine Besprechung/Party haben

have out vt: **to have it out with sb** (settle problem) etw mit jdm bereden

─────────────

haven ['heivn] n Zufluchtsort m

haven't ['hævnt] = have not

havoc ['hævək] n Verwüstung f

hawk [hɔːk] n Habicht m

hay [hei] n Heu nt; **~ fever** n Heuschnupfen m; **~stack** n Heuschober m

haywire ['heiwaiə] (inf) adj durcheinander

hazard ['hæzəd] n Risiko nt ♦ vt aufs Spiel setzen; **~ous** adj gefährlich; **~ (warning) lights** npl (AUT) Warnblinklicht nt

haze [heiz] n Dunst m

hazelnut ['heizlnʌt] n Haselnuß △ f

hazy ['heizi] adj (misty) dunstig; (vague) verschwommen

he [hiː] pron er

head [hed] n Kopf m; (leader) Leiter m ♦ vt (an)führen, leiten; (ball) köpfen; **~s (or tails)** Kopf (oder Zahl); **~ first** mit dem

△ For information on spelling reform see page 615

Kopf nach unten; ~ **over heels** kopfüber; ~ **for** *vt* *fus* zugehen auf +*acc*; ~**ache** *n* Kopfschmerzen *pl*; ~**dress** *n* Kopfschmuck *m*; ~**ing** *n* Überschrift *f*; ~**lamp** (*BRIT*) *n* Scheinwerfer *m*; ~**land** *n* Landspitze *f*; ~**light** *n* Scheinwerfer *m*; ~**line** *n* Schlagzeile *f*; ~**long** *adv* kopfüber; ~**master** *n* (*of primary school*) Rektor *m*; (*of secondary school*) Direktor *m*; ~**mistress** *n* Rektorin *f*; Direktorin *f*; ~ **office** *n* Zentrale *f*; ~**-on** *adj* Frontal-, ~**phones** *npl* Kopfhörer *pl*; ~**quarters** *npl* Zentrale *f*; (*MIL*) Hauptquartier *nt*; ~**rest** *n* Kopfstütze *f*; ~**room** *n* (*of bridges etc*) lichte Höhe *f*; ~**scarf** *n* Kopftuch *nt*; ~**strong** *adj* eigenwillig; ~**teacher** (*BRIT*) *n* Schulleiter(in) *m(f)*; (*of secondary school also*) Direktor(in) *m*; ~ **waiter** *n* Oberkellner *m*; ~**way** *n* Fortschritte *pl*; ~**wind** *n* Gegenwind *m*; ~**y** *adj* berauschend

heal [hi:l] *vt* heilen ♦ *vi* verheilen

health [helθ] *n* Gesundheit *f*; ~ **food** *n* Reformkost *f*; **H~ Service** (*BRIT*) *n*: **the H~ Service** das Gesundheitswesen; ~**y** *adj* gesund

heap [hi:p] *n* Haufen *m* ♦ *vt* häufen

hear [hiəʳ] (*pt, pp* **heard**) *vt* hören; (*listen to*) anhören ♦ *vi* hören; ~**d** [hɜ:d] *pt, pp of* **hear**; ~**ing** *n* Gehör *nt*; (*JUR*) Verhandlung *f*; ~**ing aid** *n* Hörapparat *m*; ~**say** *n* Hörensagen *nt*

hearse [hɜ:s] *n* Leichenwagen *m*

heart [hɑ:t] *n* Herz *nt*; ~**s** *npl* (*CARDS*) Herz *nt*; **by** ~ auswendig; ~ **attack** *n* Herzanfall *m*; ~**beat** *n* Herzschlag *m*; ~**breaking** *adj* herzzerbrechend; ~**broken** *adj* untröstlich; ~**burn** *n* Sodbrennen *nt*; ~ **failure** *n* Herzschlag *m*; ~**felt** *adj* aufrichtig

hearth [hɑ:θ] *n* Herd *m*

heartily ['hɑ:tɪlɪ] *adv* herzlich; (*eat*) herzhaft

heartless ['hɑ:tlɪs] *adj* herzlos

hearty ['hɑ:tɪ] *adj* kräftig; (*friendly*) freundlich

heat [hi:t] *n* Hitze *f*; (*of food, water etc*) Wärme *f*; (*SPORT: also: qualifying* ~) Ausscheidungsrunde *f* ♦ *vt* (*house*) heizen; (*substance*) heiß machen, erhitzen; ~ **up** *vi*

warm werden ♦ *vt* aufwärmen; ~**ed** *adj* erhitzt; (*fig*) hitzig; ~**er** *n* (Heiz)ofen *m*

heath [hi:θ] (*BRIT*) *n* Heide *f*

heathen ['hi:ðn] *n* Heide *m*/Heidin *f* ♦ *adj* heidnisch, Heiden-

heather ['heðəʳ] *n* Heidekraut *nt*

heat: ~ing *n* Heizung *f*; ~**-seeking** *adj* wärmesuchend; ~**stroke** *n* Hitzschlag *m*; ~ **wave** *n* Hitzewelle *f*

heave [hi:v] *vt* hochheben; (*sigh*) ausstoßen ♦ *vi* wogen; (*breast*) sich heben ♦ *n* Heben *nt*

heaven ['hevn] *n* Himmel *m*; ~**ly** *adj* himmlisch

heavily ['hevɪlɪ] *adv* schwer

heavy ['hevɪ] *adj* schwer; ~ **goods vehicle** *n* Lastkraftwagen *m*; ~**weight** *n* (*SPORT*) Schwergewicht *nt*

Hebrew ['hi:bru:] *adj* hebräisch ♦ *n* (*LING*) Hebräisch *nt*

Hebrides ['hebrɪdɪːz] *npl* Hebriden *pl*

heckle ['hekl] *vt* unterbrechen

hectic ['hektɪk] *adj* hektisch

he'd [hi:d] = **he had; he would**

hedge [hedʒ] *n* Hecke *f* ♦ *vt* einzäunen ♦ *vi* (*fig*) ausweichen; **to ~ one's bets** sich absichern

hedgehog ['hedʒhɔg] *n* Igel *m*

heed [hi:d] *vt* (*also: take ~ of*) beachten ♦ *n* Beachtung *f*; ~**less** *adj* achtlos

heel [hi:l] *n* Ferse *f*; (*of shoe*) Absatz *m* ♦ *vt* mit Absätzen versehen

hefty ['heftɪ] *adj* (*person*) stämmig; (*portion*) reichlich

heifer ['hefəʳ] *n* Färse *f*

height [haɪt] *n* (*of person*) Größe *f*; (*of object*) Höhe *f*; ~**en** *vt* erhöhen

heir [ɛəʳ] *n* Erbe *m*; ~**ess** ['ɛəres] *n* Erbin *f*; ~**loom** *n* Erbstück *nt*

held [held] *pt, pp of* **hold**

helicopter ['helɪkɔptəʳ] *n* Hubschrauber *m*

heliport ['helɪpɔːt] *n* Hubschrauberlandeplatz *m*

hell [hel] *n* Hölle *f* ♦ *excl* verdammt!

he'll [hi:l] = **he will; he shall**

hellish ['helɪʃ] *adj* höllisch, verteufelt

hello [hə'ləu] *excl* hallo

⚠ *Informationen zur Rechtschreibreform Seite 615*

helm [hɛlm] n Ruder nt, Steuer nt

helmet ['hɛlmɪt] n Helm m

help [hɛlp] n Hilfe f ♦ vt helfen +dat; **I can't ~ it** ich kann nichts dafür; **~ yourself** bedienen Sie sich; **~er** n Helfer m; **~ful** adj hilfreich; **~ing** n Portion f; **~less** adj hilflos

hem [hɛm] n Saum m ♦ vt säumen; **~ in** vt einengen

hemorrhage ['hɛmərɪdʒ] (US) n = **haemorrhage**

hemorrhoids ['hɛmərɔɪdz] (US) npl = **haemorrhoids**

hen [hɛn] n Henne f

hence [hɛns] adv von jetzt an; (therefore) daher; **~forth** adv von nun an; (from then on) von da an

henchman ['hɛntʃmən] (irreg) n Gefolgsmann m

her [hɜː] pron (acc) sie; (dat) ihr ♦ adj ihr; see also **me**; **my**

herald ['hɛrəld] n (Vor)bote m ♦ vt verkünden

heraldry ['hɛrəldrɪ] n Wappenkunde f

herb [hɜːb] n Kraut nt

herd [hɜːd] n Herde f

here [hɪə] adv hier; (to this place) hierher; **~after** [hɪər'ɑːftə] adv hernach, künftig ♦ n Jenseits nt; **~by** [hɪə'baɪ] adv hiermit

hereditary [hɪ'rɛdɪtrɪ] adj erblich

heredity [hɪ'rɛdɪtɪ] n Vererbung f

heritage ['hɛrɪtɪdʒ] n Erbe nt

hermit ['hɜːmɪt] n Einsiedler m

hernia ['hɜːnɪə] n Bruch m

hero ['hɪərəu] (pl **~es**) n Held m; **~ic** [hɪ'rəuɪk] adj heroisch

heroin ['hɛrəuɪn] n Heroin nt

heroine ['hɛrəuɪn] n Heldin f

heroism ['hɛrəuɪzəm] n Heldentum nt

heron ['hɛrən] n Reiher m

herring ['hɛrɪŋ] n Hering m

hers [hɜːz] pron ihre(r, s); see also **mine²**

herself [hɜː'sɛlf] pron sich (selbst); (emphatic) selbst; see also **oneself**

he's [hiːz] = he is; he has

hesitant ['hɛzɪtənt] adj zögernd

hesitate ['hɛzɪteɪt] vi zögern; **hesitation** [hɛzɪ'teɪʃən] n Zögern nt

heterosexual ['hɛtərəu'sɛksjuəl] adj heterosexuell ♦ n Heterosexuelle(r) mf

hew [hjuː] (pt **hewed**, pp **hewn**) vt hauen, hacken

hexagonal [hɛk'sægənl] adj sechseckig

heyday ['heɪdeɪ] n Blüte f, Höhepunkt m

HGV n abbr = **heavy goods vehicle**

hi [haɪ] excl he, hallo

hibernate ['haɪbəneɪt] vi Winterschlaf m halten; **hibernation** [haɪbə'neɪʃən] n Winterschlaf m

hiccough ['hɪkʌp] vi den Schluckauf haben; **~s** npl Schluckauf m

hiccup ['hɪkʌp] = **hiccough**

hid [hɪd] pt of **hide**; **~den** ['hɪdn] pp of **hide**

hide [haɪd] (pt **hid**, pp **hidden**) n (skin) Haut f, Fell nt ♦ vt verstecken ♦ vi sich verstecken; **~-and-seek** n Versteckspiel nt; **~away** n Versteck nt

hideous ['hɪdɪəs] adj abscheulich

hiding ['haɪdɪŋ] n (beating) Tracht f Prügel; **to be in ~** (concealed) sich versteckt halten; **~ place** n Versteck nt

hi-fi ['haɪfaɪ] n Hi-Fi nt ♦ adj Hi-Fi-

high [haɪ] adj hoch; (wind) stark ♦ adv hoch; **it is 20m ~** es ist 20 Meter hoch; **~brow** adj (betont) intellektuell; **~chair** n Hochstuhl m; **~er education** n Hochschulbildung f; **~-handed** adj eigenmächtig; **~-heeled** adj hochhackig; **~ jump** n (SPORT) Hochsprung m; **H~lands** npl: **the H~lands** das schottische Hochland; **~light** n (fig) Höhepunkt m ♦ vt hervorheben; **~ly** adv höchst; **~ly strung** adj überempfindlich; **~ness** n Höhe f; **Her H~ness** Ihre Hoheit f; **~-pitched** adj hoch; **~-rise block** n Hochhaus nt; **~ school** (US) n Oberschule f; **~ season** (BRIT) n Hochsaison f; **~ street** (BRIT) n Hauptstraße f

highway ['haɪweɪ] n Landstraße f; **H~ Code** (BRIT) n Straßenverkehrsordnung f

hijack ['haɪdʒæk] vt entführen; **~er** n Entführer(in) m(f)

hike [haɪk] vi wandern ♦ n Wanderung f; **~r** n Wanderer m; **hiking** n Wandern nt

hilarious [hɪ'lɛərɪəs] adj lustig

⚠ For information on spelling reform see page 615

hill [hɪl] n Berg m; **~side** n (Berg)hang m; **~ walking** n Bergwandern nt; **~y** adj hügelig

hilt [hɪlt] n Heft nt; **(up) to the ~** ganz und gar

him [hɪm] pron (acc) ihn; (dat) ihm; see also **me**; **~self** pron sich (selbst); (emphatic) selbst; see also **oneself**

hind [haɪnd] adj hinter, Hinter-

hinder ['hɪndə'] vt (stop) hindern; (delay) behindern; **hindrance** n (delay) Behinderung f; (obstacle) Hindernis nt

hindsight ['haɪndsaɪt] n: **with ~** im nachhinein △

Hindu ['hɪnduː] n Hindu m

hinge [hɪndʒ] n Scharnier nt; (on door) Türangel f ♦ vi (fig): **to ~ on** abhängen von

hint [hɪnt] n Tip △ m; (trace) Anflug m ♦ vt: **to ~ that** andeuten, daß △ ♦ vi: **to ~ at** andeuten

hip [hɪp] n Hüfte f

hippie ['hɪpɪ] n Hippie m

hippo ['hɪpəu] (inf) n Nilpferd nt

hippopotami [hɪpə'pɒtəmaɪ] npl of **hippopotamus**

hippopotamus [hɪpə'pɒtəməs] (pl **~es** or **hippopotami**) n Nilpferd nt

hire ['haɪə'] vt (worker) anstellen; (BRIT: car) mieten ♦ n Miete f; **for ~** (taxi) frei; **~(d) car** (BRIT) n Mietwagen m, Leihwagen m; **~ purchase** (BRIT) n Teilzahlungskauf m

his [hɪz] adj sein ♦ pron seine(r, s); see also **my**; **mine²**

hiss [hɪs] vi zischen ♦ n Zischen nt

historian [hɪ'stɔːrɪən] n Historiker m

historic [hɪ'stɒrɪk] adj historisch; **~al** adj historisch, geschichtlich

history ['hɪstərɪ] n Geschichte f

hit [hɪt] (pt, pp **hit**) vt schlagen; (injure) treffen ♦ n (blow) Schlag m; (success) Erfolg m; (MUS) Hit m; **to ~ it off with sb** prima mit jdm auskommen; **~-and-run driver** n jemand, der Fahrerflucht begeht

hitch [hɪtʃ] vt festbinden; (also: **~ up**) hochziehen ♦ n (difficulty) Haken m; **to ~ a lift** trampen; **~hike** vi trampen; **~hiker** n Tramper m; **~hiking** n Trampen nt

hi-tech ['haɪ'tek] adj Hi-tech- ♦ n

Spitzentechnologie f

hitherto [hɪðə'tuː] adv bislang

hit man (inf) (irreg) n Killer m

HIV n abbr: **HIV-negative/-positive** HIV-negativ/-positiv

hive [haɪv] n Bienenkorb m

HMS abbr = **His/Her Majesty's Ship**

hoard [hɔːd] n Schatz m ♦ vt horten, hamstern

hoarding ['hɔːdɪŋ] n Bretterzaun m; (BRIT: for posters) Reklamewand f

hoarse [hɔːs] adj heiser, rauh △

hoax [həuks] n Streich m

hob [hɒb] n Kochmulde f

hobble ['hɒbl] vi humpeln

hobby ['hɒbɪ] n Hobby nt

hobby-horse ['hɒbɪhɔːs] n (fig) Steckenpferd nt

hobo ['həubəu] (US) n Tippelbruder m

hockey ['hɒkɪ] n Hockey nt

hoe [həu] n Hacke f ♦ vt hacken

hog [hɒg] n Schlachtschwein nt ♦ vt mit Beschlag belegen; **to go the whole ~** aufs Ganze gehen

hoist [hɔɪst] n Winde f ♦ vt hochziehen

hold [həuld] (pt, pp **held**) vt halten; (contain) enthalten; (be able to contain) fassen; (breath) anhalten; (meeting) abhalten ♦ vi (withstand pressure) aushalten ♦ n (grasp) Halt m; (NAUT) Schiffsraum m; **~ the line!** (TEL) bleiben Sie am Apparat!; **to ~ one's own** sich behaupten; **~ back** vt zurückhalten; **~ down** vt niederhalten; (job) behalten; **~ off** vt (enemy) abwehren; **~ on** vi sich festhalten; (resist) durchhalten; (wait) warten; **~ on to** vt fus festhalten an +dat; (keep) behalten; **~ out** vt hinhalten ♦ vi aushalten; **~ up** vt (delay) aufhalten; (rob) überfallen; **~all** (BRIT) n Reisetasche f; **~er** n Behälter m; **~ing** n (share) (Aktien)anteil m; **~up** n (BRIT: in traffic) Stockung f; (robbery) Überfall m; (delay) Verzögerung f

hole [həul] n Loch nt; **~ in the wall** (inf) n (cash dispenser) Geldautomat m

holiday ['hɒlɪdeɪ] n (day) Feiertag m; freie(r) Tag m; (vacation) Urlaub m; (SCH) Ferien pl;

~ camp n Ferienlager nt; **~-maker** (BRIT) n Urlauber(in) m(f); **~ resort** n Ferienort m

Holland ['hɒlənd] n Holland nt

hollow ['hɒləʊ] adj hohl; (fig) leer ♦ n Vertiefung f; **~ out** vt aushöhlen

holly ['hɒlɪ] n Stechpalme f

holocaust ['hɒləkɔːst] n Inferno nt

holster ['həʊlstə*] n Pistolenhalfter m

holy ['həʊlɪ] adj heilig; **H~ Ghost** or **Spirit** n: **the H~ Ghost** or **Spirit** der Heilige Geist

homage ['hɒmɪdʒ] n Huldigung f; **to pay ~ to** huldigen +dat

home [həʊm] n Zuhause nt; (institution) Heim nt, Anstalt f ♦ adj einheimisch; (POL) inner ♦ adv heim, nach Hause; **at ~** zu Hause; **~ address** n Heimatadresse f; **~coming** n Heimkehr f; **~land** n Heimat(land nt) f; **~less** adj obdachlos; **~ly** adj häuslich; (US: ugly) unscheinbar; **~made** adj selbstgemacht ⚠; **~ match** adj Heimspiel nt; **H~ Office** (BRIT) n Innenministerium nt; **~ rule** n Selbstverwaltung f; **H~ Secretary** (BRIT) n Innenminister(in) m(f); **~sick** adj: **to be ~sick** Heimweh haben; **~ town** n Heimatstadt f; **~ward** adj (journey) Heim-; **~work** n Hausaufgaben pl

homicide ['hɒmɪsaɪd] (US) n Totschlag m

homoeopathic [həʊmɪə'pæθɪk] (US **homeopathic**) adj homöopathisch; **homoeopathy** [həʊmɪ'ɒpəθɪ] (US **homeopathy**) n Homöopathie f

homogeneous [hɒməʊ'dʒiːnɪəs] adj homogen

homosexual [hɒməʊ'sɛksjʊəl] adj homosexuell ♦ n Homosexuelle(r) mf

honest ['ɒnɪst] adj ehrlich; **~ly** adv ehrlich; **~y** n Ehrlichkeit f

honey ['hʌnɪ] n Honig m; **~comb** n Honigwabe f; **~moon** n Flitterwochen pl, Hochzeitsreise f; **~suckle** n Geißblatt nt

honk [hɒŋk] vi hupen

honor etc ['ɒnə*] (US) vt, n = **honour** etc

honorary ['ɒnərərɪ] adj Ehren-

honour ['ɒnə*] (US **honor**) vt ehren; (cheque) einlösen ♦ n Ehre f; **~able** adj ehrenwert; (intention) ehrenhaft; **~s degree** n (UNIV)

akademischer Grad mit Prüfung im Spezialfach

hood [hʊd] n Kapuze f; (BRIT: AUT) Verdeck nt; (US: AUT) Kühlerhaube f

hoof [huːf] (pl **hooves**) n Huf m

hook [hʊk] n Haken m ♦ vt einhaken

hooligan ['huːlɪgən] n Rowdy m

hoop [huːp] n Reifen m

hooray [huː'reɪ] excl = **hurrah**

hoot [huːt] vi (AUT) hupen; **~er** n (NAUT) Dampfpfeife f; (BRIT: AUT) (Auto)hupe f

Hoover ['huːvə*] ® (BRIT) n Staubsauger m ♦ vt: **to h~** staubsaugen

hooves [huːvz] pl of **hoof**

hop [hɒp] vi hüpfen, hopsen ♦ n (jump) Hopser m

hope [həʊp] vt, vi hoffen ♦ n Hoffnung f; **I ~ so/not** hoffentlich/hoffentlich nicht; **~ful** adj hoffnungsvoll; (promising) vielversprechend ⚠; **~fully** adv hoffentlich; **~less** adj hoffnungslos

hops [hɒps] npl Hopfen m

horizon [hə'raɪzn] n Horizont m; **~tal** [hɒrɪ'zɒntl] adj horizontal

hormone ['hɔːməʊn] n Hormon nt

horn [hɔːn] n Horn nt; (AUT) Hupe f

hornet ['hɔːnɪt] n Hornisse f

horny ['hɔːnɪ] adj schwielig; (US: inf) scharf

horoscope ['hɒrəskəʊp] n Horoskop nt

horrendous [hə'rendəs] adj (crime) abscheulich; (error) schrecklich

horrible ['hɒrɪbl] adj fürchterlich

horrid ['hɒrɪd] adj scheußlich

horrify ['hɒrɪfaɪ] vt entsetzen

horror ['hɒrə*] n Schrecken m; **~ film** n Horrorfilm m

hors d'oeuvre [ɔː'dɜːvrə] n Vorspeise f

horse [hɔːs] n Pferd nt; **~back** n: **on ~back** beritten; **~ chestnut** n Roßkastanie ⚠ f; **~man/woman** (irreg) n Reiter(in) m(f); **~power** n Pferdestärke f; **~-racing** n Pferderennen nt; **~radish** n Meerrettich m; **~shoe** n Hufeisen nt

horticulture ['hɔːtɪkʌltʃə*] n Gartenbau m

hose [həʊz] n (also: **~pipe**) Schlauch m

hosiery ['həʊzɪərɪ] n Strumpfwaren pl

hospitable ['hɒspɪtəbl] adj gastfreundlich

⚠ For information on spelling reform see page 615

hospital ['hɔspɪtl] n Krankenhaus nt
hospitality [hɔspɪ'tælɪtɪ] n Gastfreundschaft f
host [həust] n Gastgeber m; (innkeeper) (Gast)wirt m; (large number) Heerschar f; (ECCL) Hostie f
hostage ['hɔstɪdʒ] n Geisel f
hostel ['hɔstl] n Herberge f; (also: youth ~) Jugendherberge f
hostess ['həustɪs] n Gastgeberin f
hostile ['hɔstaɪl] adj feindlich; **hostility** [hɔ'stɪlɪtɪ] n Feindschaft f; **hostilities** npl (fighting) Feindseligkeiten pl
hot [hɔt] adj heiß; (food, water) warm; (spiced) scharf; **I'm ~** mir ist heiß; **~bed** n (fig) Nährboden m; **~ dog** n heiße(s) Würstchen nt
hotel [həu'tɛl] n Hotel nt; **~ier** n Hotelier m
hot: ~house n Treibhaus nt; **~ line** n (POL) heiße(r) Draht m; **~ly** adv (argue) hitzig; **~plate** n Kochplatte f; **~pot** ['hɔtpɔt] (BRIT) n Fleischeintopf m; **~-water bottle** n Wärmflasche f
hound [haund] n Jagdhund m ♦ vt hetzen
hour ['auə'] n Stunde f; (time of day) (Tages)zeit f; **~ly** adj, adv stündlich
house [n haus, vb hauz] n Haus nt ♦ vt unterbringen; **on the ~** auf Kosten des Hauses; **~ arrest** n (POL, MIL) Hausarrest m; **~boat** n Hausboot nt; **~breaking** n Einbruch m; **~coat** n Morgenmantel m; **~hold** n Haushalt m; **~keeper** n Haushälterin f; **~keeping** n Haushaltung f; **~-warming party** n Einweihungsparty f; **~wife** (irreg) n Hausfrau f; **~work** n Hausarbeit f
housing ['hauzɪŋ] n (act) Unterbringung f; (houses) Wohnungen pl; (POL) Wohnungsbau m; (covering) Gehäuse nt; **~ estate** (US **~ development**) n (Wohn)siedlung f
hovel ['hɔvl] n elende Hütte f
hover ['hɔvə'] vi (bird) schweben; (person) herumstehen; **~craft** n Luftkissenfahrzeug nt
how [hau] adv wie; **~ are you?** wie geht es Ihnen?; **~ much milk?** wieviel Milch?; **~**

many people? wie viele Leute?
however [hau'ɛvə'] adv (but) (je)doch, aber; **~ you phrase it** wie Sie es auch ausdrücken
howl [haul] n Heulen nt ♦ vi heulen
H.P. abbr = **hire purchase**
h.p. abbr = **horsepower**
H.Q. abbr = **headquarters**
hub [hʌb] n Radnabe f
hubbub ['hʌbʌb] n Tumult m
hubcap ['hʌbkæp] n Radkappe f
huddle ['hʌdl] vi: **to ~ together** sich zusammendrängen
hue [hju:] n Färbung f; **~ and cry** n Zetergeschrei nt
huff [hʌf] n: **to go into a ~** einschnappen
hug [hʌg] vt umarmen ♦ n Umarmung f
huge [hju:dʒ] adj groß, riesig
hulk [hʌlk] n (ship) abgetakelte(s) Schiff nt; (person) Koloß ⚠ m
hull [hʌl] n Schiffsrumpf m
hullo [hə'ləu] excl = **hello**
hum [hʌm] vt, vi summen
human ['hju:mən] adj menschlich ♦ n (also: **~ being**) Mensch m
humane [hju:'meɪn] adj human
humanitarian [hju:mænɪ'tɛərɪən] adj humanitär
humanity [hju:'mænɪtɪ] n Menschheit f; (kindliness) Menschlichkeit f
humble ['hʌmbl] adj demütig; (modest) bescheiden ♦ vt demütigen
humbug ['hʌmbʌg] n Humbug m; (BRIT: sweet) Pfefferminzbonbon nt
humdrum ['hʌmdrʌm] adj stumpfsinnig
humid ['hju:mɪd] adj feucht; **~ity** [hju:'mɪdɪtɪ] n Feuchtigkeit f
humiliate [hju:'mɪlɪeɪt] vt demütigen; **humiliation** [hju:mɪlɪ'eɪʃən] n Demütigung f
humility [hju:'mɪlɪtɪ] n Demut f
humor ['hju:mə'] (US) n, vt = **humour**
humorous ['hju:mərəs] adj humorvoll
humour ['hju:mə'] (US **humor**) n (fun) Humor m; (mood) Stimmung f ♦ vt bei Stimmung halten
hump [hʌmp] n Buckel m

⚠ *Informationen zur Rechtschreibreform Seite 615*

hunch [hʌntʃ] n Buckel m; (premonition) (Vor)ahnung f; **~back** n Bucklige(r) mf; **~ed** adj gekrümmt

hundred ['hʌndrəd] num hundert; **~weight** n Zentner m (BRIT = 50.8kg; US = 45.3kg)

hung [hʌŋ] pt, pp of **hang**

Hungarian [hʌŋ'gɛərɪən] adj ungarisch ♦ n Ungar(in) m(f); (LING) Ungarisch nt

Hungary ['hʌŋgərɪ] n Ungarn nt

hunger ['hʌŋgər] n Hunger m ♦ vi hungern

hungry ['hʌŋgrɪ] adj hungrig; **to be ~** Hunger haben

hunk [hʌŋk] n (of bread) Stück nt

hunt [hʌnt] vt, vi jagen ♦ n Jagd f; **to ~ for** suchen; **~er** n Jäger m; **~ing** n Jagd f

hurdle ['hɜːdl] n (also fig) Hürde f

hurl [hɜːl] vt schleudern

hurrah [hu'rɑː] n Hurra nt

hurray [hu'reɪ] n Hurra nt

hurricane ['hʌrɪkən] n Orkan m

hurried ['hʌrɪd] adj eilig; (hasty) übereilt; **~ly** adv übereilt, hastig

hurry ['hʌrɪ] n Eile f ♦ vi sich beeilen ♦ vt (an)treiben; (job) übereilen; **to be in a ~** es eilig haben; **~ up** vi sich beeilen ♦ vt (person) zur Eile antreiben; (work) vorantreiben

hurt [hɜːt] (pt, pp **hurt**) vt weh tun +dat; (injure, fig) verletzen ♦ vi weh tun; **~ful** adj schädlich; (remark) verletzend

hurtle ['hɜːtl] vi sausen

husband ['hʌzbənd] n (Ehe)mann m

hush [hʌʃ] n Stille f ♦ vt zur Ruhe bringen ♦ excl pst, still

husky ['hʌskɪ] adj (voice) rauh △ ♦ n Eskimohund m

hustle ['hʌsl] vt (push) stoßen; (hurry) antreiben ♦ n: **~ and bustle** Geschäftigkeit f

hut [hʌt] n Hütte f

hutch [hʌtʃ] n (Kaninchen)stall m

hyacinth ['haɪəsɪnθ] n Hyazinthe f

hydrant ['haɪdrənt] n (also: **fire ~**) Hydrant m

hydraulic [haɪ'drɔːlɪk] adj hydraulisch

hydroelectric ['haɪdrəu'lektrɪk] adj (energy) durch Wasserkraft erzeugt; **~ power**

station n Wasserkraftwerk nt

hydrofoil ['haɪdrəfɔɪl] n Tragflügelboot nt

hydrogen ['haɪdrədʒən] n Wasserstoff m

hyena [haɪ'iːnə] n Hyäne f

hygiene ['haɪdʒiːn] n Hygiene f; **hygienic** [haɪ'dʒiːnɪk] adj hygienisch

hymn [hɪm] n Kirchenlied nt

hype [haɪp] (inf) n Publicity f

hypermarket ['haɪpəmɑːkɪt] (BRIT) n Hypermarkt m

hyphen ['haɪfn] n Bindestrich m

hypnosis [hɪp'nəusɪz] n Hypnose f

hypnotize ['hɪpnətaɪz] vt hypnotisieren

hypocrisy [hɪ'pɔkrɪsɪ] n Heuchelei f

hypocrite ['hɪpəkrɪt] n Heuchler m; **hypocritical** [hɪpə'krɪtɪkl] adj scheinheilig, heuchlerisch

hypothermia [haɪpə'θəːmɪə] n Unterkühlung f

hypotheses [haɪ'pɔθɪsiːz] npl of **hypothesis**

hypothesis [haɪ'pɔθɪsɪs] (pl **hypotheses**) n Hypothese f

hypothetic(al) [haɪpəu'θetɪk(l)] adj hypothetisch

hysterical [hɪ'sterɪkl] adj hysterisch

hysterics [hɪ'sterɪks] npl hysterische(r) Anfall m

I, i

I [aɪ] pron ich

ice [aɪs] n Eis nt ♦ vt (COOK) mit Zuckerguß △ überziehen ♦ vi (also: **~ up**) vereisen; **~ axe** n Eispickel m; **~berg** n Eisberg m; **~box** n (US) Kühlschrank m; **~ cream** n Eis nt; **~ cube** n Eiswürfel m; **~d** adj (cake) mit Zuckerguß △ überzogen, glasiert; (tea, coffee) Eis-; **~ hockey** n Eishockey nt

Iceland ['aɪslənd] n Island nt

ice: ~ lolly (BRIT) n Eis nt am Stiel; **~ rink** n (Kunst)eisbahn f; **~ skating** n Schlittschuhlaufen nt

icicle ['aɪsɪkl] n Eiszapfen m

icing ['aɪsɪŋ] n (on cake) Zuckerguß △ m; (on window) Vereisung f; **~ sugar** (BRIT) n Puderzucker m

△ For information on spelling reform see page 615

icon ['aɪkɔn] *n* Ikone *f*

icy ['aɪsɪ] *adj* (*slippery*) vereist; (*cold*) eisig

I'd [aɪd] = I would; I had

idea [aɪ'dɪə] *n* Idee *f*

ideal [aɪ'dɪəl] *n* Ideal *nt* ♦ *adj* ideal

identical [aɪ'dɛntɪkl] *adj* identisch; (*twins*) eineiig

identification [aɪdɛntɪfɪ'keɪʃən] *n* Identifizierung *f*; **means of ~** Ausweispapiere *pl*

identify [aɪ'dɛntɪfaɪ] *vt* identifizieren; (*regard as the same*) gleichsetzen

Identikit [aɪ'dɛntɪkɪt] ® *n*: **~ picture** Phantombild *nt*

identity [aɪ'dɛntɪtɪ] *n* Identität *f*; **~ card** *n* Personalausweis *m*

ideology [aɪdɪ'ɔlədʒɪ] *n* Ideologie *f*

idiom ['ɪdɪəm] *n* (*expression*) Redewendung *f*; (*dialect*) Idiom *nt*; **~atic** [ɪdɪə'mætɪk] *adj* idiomatisch

idiosyncrasy [ɪdɪəu'sɪŋkrəsɪ] *n* Eigenart *f*

idiot ['ɪdɪət] *n* Idiot(in) *m(f)*; **~ic** [ɪdɪ'ɔtɪk] *adj* idiotisch

idle ['aɪdl] *adj* (*doing nothing*) untätig; (*lazy*) faul; (*useless*) nutzlos; (*machine*) still(stehend); (*threat, talk*) leer ♦ *vi* (*machine*) leerlaufen △ ♦ *vt*: **to ~ away the time** die Zeit vertrödeln; **~ness** *n* Müßiggang *m*; Faulheit *f*

idol ['aɪdl] *n* Idol *nt*; **~ize** *vt* vergöttern

i.e. *abbr* (= id est) d.h.

KEYWORD

if [ɪf] *conj* **1** wenn; (*in case also*) falls; **if I were you** wenn ich Sie wäre
2 (*although*): **(even) if** (selbst *or* auch) wenn
3 (*whether*) ob
4: if so/not wenn ja/nicht; **if only ...** wenn ... doch nur ...; **if only I could** wenn ich doch nur könnte; *see also* **as**

---

ignite [ɪg'naɪt] *vt* (an)zünden ♦ *vi* sich entzünden; **ignition** [ɪg'nɪʃən] *n* Zündung *f*; **to switch on/off the ignition** den Motor anlassen/abstellen; **ignition key** *n* (*AUT*) Zündschlüssel *m*

ignorance ['ɪgnərəns] *n* Unwissenheit *f*

ignorant ['ɪgnərənt] *adj* unwissend; **to be ~ of** nicht wissen

ignore [ɪg'nɔː] *vt* ignorieren

I'll [aɪl] = I will; I shall

ill [ɪl] *adj* krank ♦ *n* Übel *nt* ♦ *adv* schlecht; **~-advised** *adj* unklug; **~-at-ease** *adj* unbehaglich

illegal [ɪ'liːgl] *adj* illegal

illegible [ɪ'ledʒɪbl] *adj* unleserlich

illegitimate [ɪlɪ'dʒɪtɪmət] *adj* unehelich

ill-fated [ɪl'feɪtɪd] *adj* unselig

ill feeling *n* Verstimmung *f*

illicit [ɪ'lɪsɪt] *adj* verboten

illiterate [ɪ'lɪtərət] *adj* ungebildet

ill-mannered [ɪl'mænəd] *adj* ungehobelt

illness ['ɪlnɪs] *n* Krankheit *f*

illogical [ɪ'lɔdʒɪkl] *adj* unlogisch

ill-treat [ɪl'triːt] *vt* mißhandeln △

illuminate [ɪ'luːmɪneɪt] *vt* beleuchten; **illumination** [ɪluːmɪ'neɪʃən] *n* Beleuchtung *f*

illusion [ɪ'luːʒən] *n* Illusion *f*; **to be under the ~ that ...** sich *dat* einbilden, daß ...

illustrate ['ɪləstreɪt] *vt* (*book*) illustrieren; (*explain*) veranschaulichen; **illustration** [ɪlə'streɪʃən] *n* Illustration *f*; (*explanation*) Veranschaulichung *f*

illustrious [ɪ'lʌstrɪəs] *adj* berühmt

I'm [aɪm] = I am

image ['ɪmɪdʒ] *n* Bild *nt*; (*public ~*) Image *nt*; **~ry** *n* Symbolik *f*

imaginary [ɪ'mædʒɪnərɪ] *adj* eingebildet; (*world*) Phantasie- △

imagination [ɪmædʒɪ'neɪʃən] *n* Einbildung *f*; (*creative*) Phantasie △ *f*

imaginative [ɪ'mædʒɪnətɪv] *adj* phantasiereich △, einfallsreich

imagine [ɪ'mædʒɪn] *vt* sich vorstellen; (*wrongly*) sich einbilden

imbalance [ɪm'bæləns] *n* Unausgeglichenheit *f*

imbecile ['ɪmbəsiːl] *n* Schwachsinnige(r) *mf*

imitate ['ɪmɪteɪt] *vt* imitieren; **imitation** [ɪmɪ'teɪʃən] *n* Imitation *f*

immaculate [ɪ'mækjulət] *adj* makellos; (*dress*) tadellos; (*ECCL*) unbefleckt

---

△ *Informationen zur Rechtschreibreform Seite 615*

immaterial [ɪmə'tɪərɪəl] *adj* unwesentlich; **it is ~ whether ...** es ist unwichtig, ob ...

immature [ɪmə'tjʊəʳ] *adj* unreif

immediate [ɪ'miːdɪət] *adj* (*instant*) sofortig; (*near*) unmittelbar; (*relatives*) nächste(r, s); (*needs*) dringlich; **~ly** *adv* sofort; **~ly next to** direkt neben

immense [ɪ'mens] *adj* unermeßlich △

immerse [ɪ'məːs] *vt* eintauchen; **to be ~d in** (*fig*) vertieft sein in +*acc*

immersion heater [ɪ'məːʃən-] (*BRIT*) *n* Boiler *m*

immigrant ['ɪmɪɡrənt] *n* Einwanderer *m*

immigrate ['ɪmɪɡreɪt] *vi* einwandern; **immigration** [ɪmɪ'ɡreɪʃən] *n* Einwanderung *f*

imminent ['ɪmɪnənt] *adj* bevorstehend

immobile [ɪ'məubaɪl] *adj* unbeweglich; **immobilize** [ɪ'məubɪlaɪz] *vt* lähmen

immoral [ɪ'mɔrl] *adj* unmoralisch; **~ity** [ɪmɔ'rælɪtɪ] *n* Unsittlichkeit *f*

immortal [ɪ'mɔːtl] *adj* unsterblich

immune [ɪ'mjuːn] *adj* (*secure*) sicher; (*MED*) immun; **~ from** sicher vor +*dat*; **immunity** *n* (*MED, JUR*) Immunität *f*; (*fig*) Freiheit *f*; **immunize** ['ɪmjunaɪz] *vt* immunisieren

impact ['ɪmpækt] *n* Aufprall *m*; (*fig*) Wirkung *f*

impair [ɪm'peəʳ] *vt* beeinträchtigen

impart [ɪm'pɑːt] *vt* mitteilen; (*knowledge*) vermitteln; (*exude*) abgeben

impartial [ɪm'pɑːʃl] *adj* unparteiisch

impassable [ɪm'pɑːsəbl] *adj* unpassierbar

impassive [ɪm'pæsɪv] *adj* gelassen

impatience [ɪm'peɪʃəns] *n* Ungeduld *f*; **impatient** *adj* ungeduldig; **impatiently** *adv* ungeduldig

impeccable [ɪm'pekəbl] *adj* tadellos

impede [ɪm'piːd] *vt* (be)hindern; **impediment** [ɪm'pedɪmənt] *n* Hindernis *nt*; **speech impediment** Sprachfehler *m*

impending [ɪm'pendɪŋ] *adj* bevorstehend

impenetrable [ɪm'penɪtrəbl] *adj* (*also fig*) undurchdringlich

imperative [ɪm'perətɪv] *adj* (*necessary*) unbedingt erforderlich

imperceptible [ɪmpə'septɪbl] *adj* nicht wahrnehmbar

imperfect [ɪm'pəːfɪkt] *adj* (*faulty*) fehlerhaft; **~ion** [ɪmpə'fekʃən] *n* Unvollkommenheit *f*; (*fault*) Fehler *m*

imperial [ɪm'pɪərɪəl] *adj* kaiserlich

impersonal [ɪm'pəːsənl] *adj* unpersönlich

impersonate [ɪm'pəːsəneɪt] *vt* sich ausgeben als; (*for fun*) imitieren

impertinent [ɪm'pəːtɪnənt] *adj* unverschämt, frech

impervious [ɪm'pəːvɪəs] *adj* (*fig*): **~ (to)** unempfänglich (für)

impetuous [ɪm'petjuəs] *adj* ungestüm

impetus ['ɪmpɪtəs] *n* Triebkraft *f*; (*fig*) Auftrieb *m*

impinge [ɪm'pɪndʒ]: **~ on** *vt* beeinträchtigen

implacable [ɪm'plækəbl] *adj* unerbittlich

implement [*n* 'ɪmplɪmənt, *vb* 'ɪmplɪment] *n* Werkzeug *nt* ♦ *vt* ausführen

implicate ['ɪmplɪkeɪt] *vt* verwickeln; **implication** [ɪmplɪ'keɪʃən] *n* (*effect*) Auswirkung *f*; (*in crime*) Verwicklung *f*

implicit [ɪm'plɪsɪt] *adj* (*suggested*) unausgesprochen; (*utter*) vorbehaltlos

implore [ɪm'plɔːʳ] *vt* anflehen

imply [ɪm'plaɪ] *vt* (*hint*) andeuten; (*be evidence for*) schließen lassen auf +*acc*

impolite [ɪmpə'laɪt] *adj* unhöflich

import [*vb* ɪm'pɔːt, *n* 'ɪmpɔːt] *vt* einführen ♦ *n* Einfuhr *f*; (*meaning*) Bedeutung *f*

importance [ɪm'pɔːtns] *n* Bedeutung *f*

important [ɪm'pɔːtənt] *adj* wichtig; **it's not ~** es ist unwichtig

importer [ɪm'pɔːtəʳ] *n* Importeur *m*

impose [ɪm'pəuz] *vt, vi*: **to ~ (on)** auferlegen (+*dat*); (*penalty, sanctions*) verhängen (gegen); **to ~ (o.s.) on sb** sich jdm aufdrängen

imposing [ɪm'pəuzɪŋ] *adj* eindrucksvoll

imposition [ɪmpə'zɪʃən] *n* (*of burden, fine*) Auferlegung *f*; **to be an ~** (*on person*) eine Zumutung sein

impossible [ɪm'pɔsɪbl] *adj* unmöglich

impostor [ɪm'pɔstəʳ] *n* Hochstapler *m*

impotent ['ɪmpətnt] *adj* machtlos; (*sexually*) impotent

impound [ɪm'paund] *vt* beschlagnahmen

impoverished [ɪmˈpɔvərɪʃt] *adj* verarmt
impracticable [ɪmˈpræktɪkəbl] *adj* undurchführbar
impractical [ɪmˈpræktɪkl] *adj* unpraktisch
imprecise [ɪmprɪˈsaɪs] *adj* ungenau
impregnable [ɪmˈpregnəbl] *adj* (*castle*) uneinnehmbar
impregnate [ˈɪmpregneɪt] *vt* (*saturate*) sättigen; (*fertilize*) befruchten
impress [ɪmˈpres] *vt* (*influence*) beeindrucken; (*imprint*) (auf)drücken; **to ~ sth on sb** jdm etw einschärfen; **~ed** *adj* beeindruckt; **~ion** *n* Eindruck *m*; (*on wax, footprint*) Abdruck *m*; (*of book*) Auflage *f*; (*take-off*) Nachahmung *f*; **I was under the ~ion** ich hatte den Eindruck; **~ionable** *adj* leicht zu beeindrucken; **~ive** *adj* eindrucksvoll
imprint [ˈɪmprɪnt] *n* Abdruck *m*
imprison [ɪmˈprɪzn] *vt* ins Gefängnis schicken; **~ment** *n* Inhaftierung *f*
improbable [ɪmˈprɔbəbl] *adj* unwahrscheinlich
impromptu [ɪmˈprɔmptjuː] *adj, adv* aus dem Stegreif, improvisiert
improper [ɪmˈprɔpə*] *adj* (*indecent*) unanständig; (*unsuitable*) unpassend
improve [ɪmˈpruːv] *vt* verbessern ♦ *vi* besser werden; **~ment** *n* (Ver)besserung *f*
improvise [ˈɪmprəvaɪz] *vt, vi* improvisieren
imprudent [ɪmˈpruːdnt] *adj* unklug
impudent [ˈɪmpjudnt] *adj* unverschämt
impulse [ˈɪmpʌls] *n* Impuls *m*; **to act on ~** spontan handeln; **impulsive** [ɪmˈpʌlsɪv] *adj* impulsiv
impure [ɪmˈpjuə*] *adj* (*dirty*) verunreinigt; (*bad*) unsauber; **impurity** [ɪmˈpjuərɪti] *n* Unreinheit *f*; (*TECH*) Verunreinigung *f*

KEYWORD

in [ɪn] *prep* **1** (*indicating place, position*) in +*dat*; (*with motion*) in +*acc*; **in here/there** hier/dort; **in London** in London; **in the United States** in den Vereinigten Staaten
2 (*indicating time: during*) in +*dat*; **in summer** im Sommer; **in 1988** (im Jahre) 1988; **in the afternoon** nachmittags, am Nachmittag

3 (*indicating time: in the space of*) innerhalb von; **I'll see you in 2 weeks** *or* **in 2 weeks' time** ich sehe Sie in zwei Wochen
4 (*indicating manner, circumstances, state etc*) in +*dat*; **in the sun/rain** in der Sonne/im Regen; **in English/French** auf Englisch/Französisch; **in a loud/soft voice** mit lauter/leiser Stimme
5 (*with ratios, numbers*): **1 in 10** jeder zehnte; **20 pence in the pound** 20 Pence pro Pfund; **they lined up in twos** sie stellten sich in Zweierreihe auf
6 (*referring to people, works*): **the disease is common in children** bei Kindern ist die Krankheit häufig; **in Dickens** bei Dickens; **we have a loyal friend in him** er ist uns ein treuer Freund
7 (*indicating profession etc*): **to be in teaching/the army** Lehrer(in)/beim Militär sein; **to be in publishing** im Verlagswesen arbeiten
8 (*with present participle*): **in saying this, I ...** wenn ich das sage, ... ich; **in accepting this view, he ...** weil er diese Meinung akzeptierte, ... er
♦ *adv*: **to be in** (*person: at home, work*) dasein △; (*train, ship, plane*) angekommen sein; (*in fashion*) in sein; **to ask sb in** jdn hereinbitten; **to run/limp etc in** hereingerannt/gehumpelt *etc* kommen
♦ *n*: **the ins and outs** (*of proposal, situation etc*) die Feinheiten

in. *abbr* = **inch**
inability [ɪnəˈbɪlɪti] *n* Unfähigkeit *f*
inaccessible [ɪnəkˈsesɪbl] *adj* unzugänglich
inaccurate [ɪnˈækjurət] *adj* ungenau; (*wrong*) unrichtig
inactivity [ɪnækˈtɪvɪti] *n* Untätigkeit *f*
inadequate [ɪnˈædɪkwət] *adj* unzulänglich
inadvertently [ɪnədˈvəːtntli] *adv* unabsichtlich
inadvisable [ɪnədˈvaɪzəbl] *adj* nicht ratsam
inane [ɪˈneɪn] *adj* dumm, albern
inanimate [ɪnˈænɪmət] *adj* leblos
inappropriate [ɪnəˈprəuprɪət] *adj* (*clothing*) ungeeignet; (*remark*) unangebracht

inarticulate [ɪnɑːˈtɪkjulət] *adj* unklar

inasmuch as [ɪnəzˈmʌtʃ-] *adv* da; *(in so far as)* soweit

inaudible [ɪnˈɔːdɪbl] *adj* unhörbar

inaugurate [ɪˈnɔːgjureɪt] *vt (open)* einweihen; *(admit to office)* (feierlich) einführen

inauguration [ɪnɔːgjuˈreɪʃən] *n* Eröffnung *f*; *(feierliche)* Amtseinführung *f*

inborn [ɪnˈbɔːn] *adj* angeboren

inbred [ɪnˈbred] *adj* angeboren

Inc. *abbr* = **incorporated**

incalculable [ɪnˈkælkjuləbl] *adj (consequences)* unabsehbar

incapable [ɪnˈkeɪpəbl] *adj*: ~ **(of doing sth)** unfähig(, etw zu tun)

incapacitate [ɪnkəˈpæsɪteɪt] *vt* untauglich machen

incapacity [ɪnkəˈpæsɪtɪ] *n* Unfähigkeit *f*

incarcerate [ɪnˈkɑːsəreɪt] *vt* einkerkern

incarnation [ɪnkɑːˈneɪʃən] *n (ECCL)* Menschwerdung *f*; *(fig)* Inbegriff *m*

incendiary [ɪnˈsendɪərɪ] *adj* Brand-

incense [*n* ˈɪnsens, *vb* ɪnˈsens] *n* Weihrauch *m ♦ vt* erzürnen

incentive [ɪnˈsentɪv] *n* Anreiz *m*

incessant [ɪnˈsesnt] *adj* unaufhörlich; **~ly** *adv* unaufhörlich

incest [ˈɪnsest] *n* Inzest *m*

inch [ɪntʃ] *n* Zoll *m ♦ vi*: **to ~ forward** sich Stückchen für Stückchen vorwärts bewegen; **to be within an ~ of** kurz davor sein; **he didn't give an ~** er gab keinen Zentimeter nach

incidence [ˈɪnsɪdns] *n* Auftreten *nt*; *(of crime)* Quote *f*

incident [ˈɪnsɪdnt] *n* Vorfall *m*; *(disturbance)* Zwischenfall *m*

incidental [ɪnsɪˈdentl] *adj (music)* Begleit-; *(unimportant)* nebensächlich; *(remark)* beiläufig; **~ly** *adv* übrigens

incinerator [ɪnˈsɪnəreɪtə˞] *n* Verbrennungsofen *m*

incision [ɪnˈsɪʒən] *n* Einschnitt *m*

incisive [ɪnˈsaɪsɪv] *adj (style)* treffend; *(person)* scharfsinnig

incite [ɪnˈsaɪt] *vt* anstacheln

inclination [ɪnklɪˈneɪʃən] *n* Neigung *f*

incline [*n* ˈɪnklaɪn, *vb* ɪnˈklaɪn] *n* Abhang *m ♦ vt* neigen; *(fig)* veranlassen *♦ vi* sich neigen; **to be ~d to do sth** dazu neigen, etw zu tun

include [ɪnˈkluːd] *vt* einschließen; *(on list, in group)* aufnehmen; **including** *prep*: **including X** X inbegriffen; **inclusion** [ɪnˈkluːʒən] *n* Aufnahme *f*; **inclusive** [ɪnˈkluːsɪv] *adj* einschließlich; *(COMM)* inklusive; **inclusive of** einschließlich *+gen*

incoherent [ɪnkəʊˈhɪərənt] *adj* zusammenhanglos

income [ˈɪnkʌm] *n* Einkommen *nt*; *(from business)* Einkünfte *pl*; **~ tax** *n* Lohnsteuer *f*; *(of self-employed)* Einkommensteuer *f*

incoming [ˈɪnkʌmɪŋ] *adj*: **~ flight** eintreffende Maschine *f*

incomparable [ɪnˈkɒmpərəbl] *adj* unvergleichlich

incompatible [ɪnkəmˈpætɪbl] *adj* unvereinbar; *(people)* unverträglich

incompetence [ɪnˈkɒmpɪtns] *n* Unfähigkeit *f*; **incompetent** *adj* unfähig

incomplete [ɪnkəmˈpliːt] *adj* unvollständig

incomprehensible [ɪnkɒmprɪˈhensɪbl] *adj* unverständlich

inconceivable [ɪnkənˈsiːvəbl] *adj* unvorstellbar

incongruous [ɪnˈkɒŋgruəs] *adj* seltsam; *(remark)* unangebracht

inconsiderate [ɪnkənˈsɪdərət] *adj* rücksichtslos

inconsistency [ɪnkənˈsɪstənsɪ] *n* Widersprüchlichkeit *f*; *(state)* Unbeständigkeit *f*

inconsistent [ɪnkənˈsɪstnt] *adj (action, speech)* widersprüchlich; *(person, work)* unbeständig; **~ with** nicht übereinstimmend mit

inconspicuous [ɪnkənˈspɪkjuəs] *adj* unauffällig

incontinent [ɪnˈkɒntɪnənt] *adj (MED)* nicht fähig, Stuhl und Harn zurückzuhalten

inconvenience [ɪnkənˈviːnjəns] *n* Unbequemlichkeit *f*; *(trouble to others)* Unannehmlichkeiten *pl*

⚠ *For information on spelling reform see page 615*

inconvenient [ɪnkən'viːnjənt] *adj* ungelegen; (*journey*) unbequem

incorporate [ɪn'kɔːpəreɪt] *vt* (*include*) aufnehmen; (*contain*) enthalten; **~d** *adj*: **~d company** (*US*) eingetragene Aktiengesellschaft *f*

incorrect [ɪnkə'rekt] *adj* unrichtig

incorrigible [ɪn'kɒrɪdʒɪbl] *adj* unverbesserlich

incorruptible [ɪnkə'rʌptɪbl] *adj* unzerstörbar; (*person*) unbestechlich

increase [*n* 'ɪnkriːs, *vb* ɪn'kriːs] *n* Zunahme *f*; (*pay* ~) Gehaltserhöhung *f*; (*in size*) Vergrößerung *f* ♦ *vt* erhöhen; (*wealth, rage*) vermehren; (*business*) erweitern ♦ *vi* zunehmen; (*prices*) steigen; (*in size*) größer werden; (*in number*) sich vermehren; **increasing** *adj* steigend; **increasingly** [ɪn'kriːsɪŋlɪ] *adv* zunehmend

incredible [ɪn'kredɪbl] *adj* unglaublich

incredulous [ɪn'kredjuləs] *adj* ungläubig

increment ['ɪnkrɪmənt] *n* Zulage *f*

incriminate [ɪn'krɪmɪneɪt] *vt* belasten

incubation [ɪnkju'beɪʃən] *n* Ausbrüten *nt*

incubator ['ɪnkjubeɪtə'] *n* Brutkasten *m*

incumbent [ɪn'kʌmbənt] *adj*: **it is ~ on him to ...** es obliegt ihm, ...

incur [ɪn'kɜː'] *vt* sich zuziehen; (*debts*) machen

incurable [ɪn'kjuərəbl] *adj* unheilbar

indebted [ɪn'detɪd] *adj* (*obliged*): **~ (to sb)** (jdm) verpflichtet

indecent [ɪn'diːsnt] *adj* unanständig; **~ assault** (*BRIT*) *n* Notzucht *f*; **~ exposure** *n* Exhibitionismus *m*

indecisive [ɪndɪ'saɪsɪv] *adj* (*battle*) nicht entscheidend; (*person*) unentschlossen

indeed [ɪn'diːd] *adv* tatsächlich, in der Tat; **yes ~!** allerdings!

indefinite [ɪn'defɪnɪt] *adj* unbestimmt; **~ly** *adv* auf unbestimmte Zeit; (*wait*) unbegrenzt lange

indelible [ɪn'delɪbl] *adj* unauslöschlich

indemnity [ɪn'demnɪtɪ] *n* (*insurance*) Versicherung *f*; (*compensation*) Entschädigung *f*

independence [ɪndɪ'pendns] *n*

Unabhängigkeit *f*; **independent** *adj* unabhängig

INDEPENDENCE DAY

i **Independence Day** (*der 4. Juli*) ist in den USA ein gesetzlicher Feiertag zum Gedenken an die Unabhängigkeitserklärung am 4. Juli 1776, mit der die 13 amerikanischen Kolonien ihre Freiheit und Unabhängigkeit von Großbritannien erklärten.

---

indestructible [ɪndɪs'trʌktəbl] *adj* unzerstörbar

indeterminate [ɪndɪ'tɜːmɪnɪt] *adj* unbestimmt

index ['ɪndeks] (*pl* **~es** *or* **indices**) *n* Index *m*; **~ card** *n* Karteikarte *f*; **~ finger** *n* Zeigefinger *m*; **~-linked** (*US* **~ed**) *adj* (*salaries*) der Inflationsrate *dat* angeglichen; (*pensions*) dynamisch

India ['ɪndɪə] *n* Indien *nt*; **~n** *adj* indisch ♦ *n* Inder(in) *m(f)*; **American ~n** Indianer(in) *m(f)*; **~n Ocean** *n*: **the ~n Ocean** der Indische Ozean

indicate ['ɪndɪkeɪt] *vt* anzeigen; (*hint*) andeuten; **indication** [ɪndɪ'keɪʃən] *n* Anzeichen *nt*; (*information*) Angabe *f*; **indicative** [ɪn'dɪkətɪv] *adj*: **indicative of** bezeichnend für; **indicator** *n* (An)zeichen *nt*; (*AUT*) Richtungsanzeiger *m*

indict [ɪn'daɪt] *vt* anklagen; **~ment** *n* Anklage *f*

indifference [ɪn'dɪfrəns] *n* Gleichgültigkeit *f*; Unwichtigkeit *f*; **indifferent** *adj* gleichgültig; (*mediocre*) mäßig

indigenous [ɪn'dɪdʒɪnəs] *adj* einheimisch

indigestion [ɪndɪ'dʒestʃən] *n* Verdauungsstörung *f*

indignant [ɪn'dɪgnənt] *adj*: **to be ~ about sth** über etw *acc* empört sein

indignation [ɪndɪg'neɪʃən] *n* Entrüstung *f*

indignity [ɪn'dɪgnɪtɪ] *n* Demütigung *f*

indirect [ɪndɪ'rekt] *adj* indirekt

indiscreet [ɪndɪs'kriːt] *adj* (*insensitive*) taktlos; (*telling secrets*) indiskret; **indiscretion** [ɪndɪs'kreʃən] *n* Taktlosigkeit *f*;

Indiskretion f

indiscriminate [ɪndɪsˈkrɪmɪnət] *adj* wahllos; kritiklos

indispensable [ɪndɪsˈpɛnsəbl] *adj* unentbehrlich

indisposed [ɪndɪsˈpəʊzd] *adj* unpäßlich ⚠

indisputable [ɪndɪsˈpjuːtəbl] *adj* unbestreitbar; (*evidence*) unanfechtbar

indistinct [ɪndɪsˈtɪŋkt] *adj* undeutlich

individual [ɪndɪˈvɪdjʊəl] *n* Individuum *nt* ♦ *adj* individuell; (*case*) Einzel-; (*of, for one person*) eigen, individuell; (*characteristic*) eigentümlich; **~ly** *adv* einzeln, individuell

indivisible [ɪndɪˈvɪzɪbl] *adj* unteilbar

indoctrinate [ɪnˈdɒktrɪneɪt] *vt* indoktrinieren

Indonesia [ɪndəˈniːzɪə] *n* Indonesien *nt*

indoor [ˈɪndɔːʳ] *adj* Haus-; Zimmer-; Innen-; (*SPORT*) Hallen-; **~s** [ɪnˈdɔːz] *adv* drinnen, im Haus

induce [ɪnˈdjuːs] *vt* dazu bewegen; (*reaction*) herbeiführen

induction course [ɪnˈdʌkʃən-] (*BRIT*) *n* Einführungskurs *m*

indulge [ɪnˈdʌldʒ] *vt* (*give way*) nachgeben +*dat*; (*gratify*) frönen +*dat* ♦ *vi*: **to ~ (in)** frönen (+*dat*); **~nce** *n* Nachsicht *f*; (*enjoyment*) Genuß ⚠ *m*; **~nt** *adj* nachsichtig; (*pej*) nachgiebig

industrial [ɪnˈdʌstrɪəl] *adj* Industrie-, industriell; (*dispute, injury*) Arbeits-; **~ action** *n* Arbeitskampfmaßnahmen *pl*; **~ estate** (*BRIT*) *n* Industriegebiet *nt*; **~ist** *n* Industrielle(r) *mf*; **~ize** *vt* industrialisieren; **~ park** (*US*) *n* Industriegebiet *nt*

industrious [ɪnˈdʌstrɪəs] *adj* fleißig

industry [ˈɪndəstrɪ] *n* Industrie *f*; (*diligence*) Fleiß *m*

inebriated [ɪˈniːbrɪeɪtɪd] *adj* betrunken

inedible [ɪnˈɛdɪbl] *adj* ungenießbar

ineffective [ɪnɪˈfɛktɪv] *adj* unwirksam; (*person*) untauglich

ineffectual [ɪnɪˈfɛktʃʊəl] *adj* = **ineffective**

inefficiency [ɪnɪˈfɪʃənsɪ] *n* Ineffizienz *f*

inefficient [ɪnɪˈfɪʃənt] *adj* ineffizient; (*ineffective*) unwirksam

inept [ɪˈnɛpt] *adj* (*remark*) unpassend;

(*person*) ungeeignet

inequality [ɪnɪˈkwɒlɪtɪ] *n* Ungleichheit *f*

inert [ɪˈnɜːt] *adj* träge; (*CHEM*) inaktiv; (*motionless*) unbeweglich

inescapable [ɪnɪˈskeɪpəbl] *adj* unvermeidbar

inevitable [ɪnˈɛvɪtəbl] *adj* unvermeidlich; **inevitably** *adv* zwangsläufig

inexcusable [ɪnɪksˈkjuːzəbl] *adj* unverzeihlich

inexhaustible [ɪnɪɡˈzɔːstɪbl] *adj* unerschöpflich

inexpensive [ɪnɪksˈpɛnsɪv] *adj* preiswert

inexperience [ɪnɪksˈpɪərɪəns] *n* Unerfahrenheit *f*; **~d** *adj* unerfahren

inexplicable [ɪnɪksˈplɪkəbl] *adj* unerklärlich

inextricably [ɪnɪksˈtrɪkəblɪ] *adv* untrennbar

infallible [ɪnˈfælɪbl] *adj* unfehlbar

infamous [ˈɪnfəməs] *adj* (*deed*) schändlich; (*person*) niederträchtig

infancy [ˈɪnfənsɪ] *n* frühe Kindheit *f*; (*fig*) Anfangsstadium *nt*

infant [ˈɪnfənt] *n* kleine(s) Kind *nt*, Säugling *m*; **~ile** *adj* kindisch, infantil; **~ school** (*BRIT*) *n* Vorschule *f*

infatuated [ɪnˈfætjʊeɪtɪd] *adj* vernarrt; **to become ~ with** sich vernarren in +*acc*; **infatuation** [ɪnfætjʊˈeɪʃən] *n*: **infatuation (with)** Vernarrtheit *f* (in +*acc*)

infect [ɪnˈfɛkt] *vt* anstecken (*also fig*); **~ed with** (*illness*) infiziert mit; **~ion** [ɪnˈfɛkʃən] *n* Infektion *f*; **~ious** [ɪnˈfɛkʃəs] *adj* ansteckend

infer [ɪnˈfɜːʳ] *vt* schließen

inferior [ɪnˈfɪərɪəʳ] *adj* (*rank*) untergeordnet; (*quality*) minderwertig ♦ *n* Untergebene(r) *m*; **~ity** [ɪnfɪərɪˈɔrɪtɪ] *n* Minderwertigkeit *f*; (*in rank*) untergeordnete Stellung *f*; **~ity complex** *n* Minderwertigkeitskomplex *m*

infernal [ɪnˈfɜːnl] *adj* höllisch

infertile [ɪnˈfɜːtaɪl] *adj* unfruchtbar; **infertility** [ɪnfɜːˈtɪlɪtɪ] *n* Unfruchtbarkeit *f*

infested [ɪnˈfɛstɪd] *adj*: **to be ~ with** wimmeln von

infidelity [ɪnfɪˈdɛlɪtɪ] *n* Untreue *f*

infighting [ˈɪnfaɪtɪŋ] *n* Nahkampf *m*

infiltrate [ˈɪnfɪltreɪt] *vt* infiltrieren; (*spies*) einschleusen ♦ *vi* (*MIL, liquid*) einsickern;

⚠ *For information on spelling reform see page 615*

(POL): **to ~ (into)** unterwandern (+*acc*)

infinite ['ɪnfɪnɪt] *adj* unendlich

infinitive [ɪn'fɪnɪtɪv] *n* Infinitiv *m*

infinity [ɪn'fɪnɪtɪ] *n* Unendlichkeit *f*

infirm [ɪn'fɜːm] *adj* gebrechlich; **~ary** *n* Krankenhaus *nt*

inflamed [ɪn'fleɪmd] *adj* entzündet

inflammable [ɪn'flæməbl] *(BRIT) adj* feuergefährlich

inflammation [ɪnflə'meɪʃən] *n* Entzündung *f*

inflatable [ɪn'fleɪtəbl] *adj* aufblasbar

inflate [ɪn'fleɪt] *vt* aufblasen; *(tyre)* aufpumpen; *(prices)* hochtreiben; **inflation** [ɪn'fleɪʃən] *n* Inflation *f*; **inflationary** [ɪn'fleɪʃənərɪ] *adj (increase)* inflationistisch; *(situation)* inflationär

inflexible [ɪn'fleksɪbl] *adj (person)* nicht flexibel; *(opinion)* starr; *(thing)* unbiegsam

inflict [ɪn'flɪkt] *vt*: **to ~ sth on sb** jdm etw zufügen; *(wound)* jdm etw beibringen

influence ['ɪnfluəns] *n* Einfluß △ *m* ♦ *vt* beeinflussen

influential [ɪnflu'enʃl] *adj* einflußreich △

influenza [ɪnflu'enzə] *n* Grippe *f*

influx ['ɪnflʌks] *n (of people)* Zustrom *m*; *(of ideas)* Eindringen *nt*

infomercial ['ɪnfəuməːʃl] *n* Werbeinformationssendung *f*

inform [ɪn'fɔːm] *vt* informieren ♦ *vi*: **to ~ on sb** jdn denunzieren; **to keep sb ~ed** jdn auf dem laufenden halten

informal [ɪn'fɔːml] *adj* zwanglos; **~ity** [ɪnfɔː'mælɪtɪ] *n* Ungezwungenheit *f*

informant [ɪn'fɔːmənt] *n* Informant(in) *m(f)*

information [ɪnfə'meɪʃən] *n* Auskunft *f*, Information *f*; **a piece of ~** eine Auskunft, eine Information; **~ desk** *n* Auskunftsschalter *m*; **~ office** *n* Informationsbüro *nt*

informative [ɪn'fɔːmətɪv] *adj* informativ; *(person)* mitteilsam

informer [ɪn'fɔːmər] *n* Denunziant(in) *m(f)*

infra-red [ɪnfrə'red] *adj* infrarot

infrequent [ɪn'friːkwənt] *adj* selten

infringe [ɪn'frɪndʒ] *vt (law)* verstoßen gegen; **~ upon** *vt* verletzen; **~ment** *n*

Verstoß *m*, Verletzung *f*

infuriating [ɪn'fjuərɪeɪtɪŋ] *adj* ärgerlich

ingenuity [ɪndʒɪ'njuːɪtɪ] *n* Genialität *f*

ingenuous [ɪn'dʒenjuəs] *adj* aufrichtig; *(naive)* naiv

ingot ['ɪŋgət] *n* Barren *m*

ingrained [ɪn'greɪnd] *adj* tiefsitzend

ingratiate [ɪn'greɪʃɪeɪt] *vt*: **to ~ o.s. with sb** sich bei jdm einschmeicheln

ingratitude [ɪn'grætɪtjuːd] *n* Undankbarkeit *f*

ingredient [ɪn'griːdɪənt] *n* Bestandteil *m*; *(COOK)* Zutat *f*

inhabit [ɪn'hæbɪt] *vt* bewohnen; **~ant** *n* Bewohner(in) *m(f)*; *(of island, town)* Einwohner(in) *m(f)*

inhale [ɪn'heɪl] *vt* einatmen; *(MED, cigarettes)* inhalieren

inherent [ɪn'hɪərənt] *adj*: **~ (in)** innewohnend (+*dat*)

inherit [ɪn'herɪt] *vt* erben; **~ance** *n* Erbe *nt*, Erbschaft *f*

inhibit [ɪn'hɪbɪt] *vt* hemmen; **to ~ sb from doing sth** jdn daran hindern, etw zu tun; **~ion** [ɪnhɪ'bɪʃən] *n* Hemmung *f*

inhospitable [ɪnhɔs'pɪtəbl] *adj (person)* ungastlich; *(country)* unwirtlich

inhuman [ɪn'hjuːmən] *adj* unmenschlich

initial [ɪ'nɪʃl] *adj* anfänglich, Anfangs- ♦ *n* Initiale *f* ♦ *vt* abzeichnen; *(POL)* paraphieren; **~ly** *adv* anfangs

initiate [ɪ'nɪʃɪeɪt] *vt* einführen; *(negotiations)* einleiten; **to ~ proceedings against sb** *(JUR)* gerichtliche Schritte gegen jdn einleiten; **initiation** [ɪnɪʃɪ'eɪʃən] *n* Einführung *f*; Einleitung *f*

initiative [ɪ'nɪʃətɪv] *n* Initiative *f*

inject [ɪn'dʒekt] *vt* einspritzen; *(fig)* einflößen; **~ion** [ɪn'dʒekʃən] *n* Spritze *f*

injunction [ɪn'dʒʌŋkʃən] *n* Verfügung *f*

injure ['ɪndʒər] *vt* verletzen; **~d** *adj (person, arm)* verletzt; **injury** ['ɪndʒərɪ] *n* Verletzung *f*; **to play injury time** *(SPORT)* nachspielen

injustice [ɪn'dʒʌstɪs] *n* Ungerechtigkeit *f*

ink [ɪŋk] *n* Tinte *f*

inkling ['ɪŋklɪŋ] *n* (dunkle) Ahnung *f*

inlaid ['ɪnleɪd] *adj* eingelegt, Einlege-

inland [*adj* 'ınlənd, *adv* ın'lænd] *adj* Binnen-; (*domestic*) Inlands-♦ *adv* landeinwärts; ~ **revenue** (*BRIT*) *n* Fiskus *m*

in-laws ['ınlɔ:z] *npl* (*parents-in-law*) Schwiegereltern *pl*; (*others*) angeheiratete Verwandte *pl*

inlet ['ınlet] *n* Einlaß △ *m*; (*bay*) kleine Bucht *f*

inmate ['ınmeıt] *n* Insasse *m*

inn [ın] *n* Gasthaus *nt*, Wirtshaus *nt*

innate [ı'neıt] *adj* angeboren

inner ['ınə'] *adj* inner, Innen-; (*fig*) verborgen; ~ **city** *n* Innenstadt *f*; ~ **tube** *n* (*of tyre*) Schlauch *m*

innings ['ınıŋz] *n* (*CRICKET*) Innenrunde *f*

innocence ['ınəsns] *n* Unschuld *f*; (*ignorance*) Unkenntnis *f*

innocent ['ınəsnt] *adj* unschuldig

innocuous [ı'nɔkjuəs] *adj* harmlos

innovation [ınəu'veıʃən] *n* Neuerung *f*

innuendo [ınju'endəu] *n* (*versteckte*) Anspielung *f*

innumerable [ı'nju:mrəbl] *adj* unzählig

inoculation [ınɔkju'leıʃən] *n* Impfung *f*

inopportune [ın'ɔpətju:n] *adj* (*remark*) unangebracht; (*visit*) ungelegen

inordinately [ı'nɔ:dınətlı] *adv* unmäßig

inpatient ['ınpeıʃənt] *n* stationäre(r) Patient *m*/stationäre Patientin *f*

input ['ınput] *n* (*COMPUT*) Eingabe *f*; (*power* ~) Energiezufuhr *f*; (*of energy, work*) Aufwand *m*

inquest ['ınkwest] *n* gerichtliche Untersuchung *f*

inquire [ın'kwaıə'] *vi* sich erkundigen ♦ *vt* (*price*) sich erkundigen nach; ~ **into** *vt* untersuchen; **inquiry** [ın'kwaıərı] *n* (*question*) Erkundigung *f*; (*investigation*) Untersuchung *f*; **inquiries** Auskunft *f*; **inquiry office** (*BRIT*) *n* Auskunft(sbüro *nt*) *f*

inquisitive [ın'kwızıtıv] *adj* neugierig

ins. *abbr* = **inches**

insane [ın'seın] *adj* wahnsinnig; (*MED*) geisteskrank; **insanity** [ın'sænıtı] *n* Wahnsinn *m*

insatiable [ın'seıʃəbl] *adj* unersättlich

inscribe [ın'skraıb] *vt* eingravieren;

inscription [ın'skrıpʃən] *n* (*on stone*) Inschrift *f*; (*in book*) Widmung *f*

inscrutable [ın'skru:təbl] *adj* unergründlich

insect ['ınsekt] *n* Insekt *nt*; ~**icide** *n* Insektenvertilgungsmittel *nt*; ~ **repellent** *n* Insektenbekämpfungsmittel *nt*

insecure [ınsı'kjuə'] *adj* (*person*) unsicher; (*thing*) nicht fest *or* sicher; **insecurity** [ınsı'kjuərıtı] *n* Unsicherheit *f*

insemination [ınsemı'neıʃən] *n*: **artificial** ~ künstliche Befruchtung *f*

insensible [ın'sensıbl] *adj* (*unconscious*) bewußtlos △

insensitive [ın'sensıtıv] *adj* (*to pain*) unempfindlich; (*unfeeling*) gefühllos

inseparable [ın'seprəbl] *adj* (*people*) unzertrennlich; (*word*) untrennbar

insert [*vb* ın'sɜ:t, *n* 'ınsɜ:t] *vt* einfügen; (*coin*) einwerfen; (*stick into*) hineinstecken; (*advertisement*) aufgeben ♦ *n* (*in book*) Einlage *f*; (*in magazine*) Beilage *f*; ~**ion** [ın'sɜ:ʃən] *n* Einfügung *f*; (*PRESS*) Inserat *nt*

in-service ['ın'sɜ:vıs] *adj* (*training*) berufsbegleitend

inshore [ˈınˈʃɔ:ˈ] *adj* Küsten- ♦ *adv* an der Küste

inside ['ın'saıd] *n* Innenseite *f*, Innere(s) *nt* ♦ *adj* innere(r, s), Innen- ♦ *adv* (*place*) innen; (*direction*) nach innen, hinein ♦ *prep* (*place*) in +*dat*; (*direction*) in +*acc* ... hinein; (*time*) innerhalb +*gen*; ~**s** *npl* (*inf*) Eingeweide *nt*; ~ **10 minutes** unter 10 Minuten; ~ **information** *n* interne Informationen *pl*; ~ **lane** *n* (*AUT: in Britain*) linke Spur; ~ **out** *adv* linksherum; (*know*) in- und auswendig

insider dealing, insider trading [ın'saıdəˈ-] *n* (*STOCK EXCHANGE*) Insiderhandel *m*

insidious [ın'sıdıəs] *adj* heimtückisch

insight ['ınsaıt] *n* Einsicht *f*; ~ **into** Einblick *m* in +*acc*

insignificant [ınsıg'nıfıknt] *adj* unbedeutend

insincere [ınsın'sıə'] *adj* unaufrichtig

insinuate [ın'sınjueıt] *vt* (*hint*) andeuten

insipid [ın'sıpıd] *adj* fad(e)

△ *For information on spelling reform see page 615*

insist [ɪn'sɪst] *vi*: **to ~ (on)** bestehen (auf +*acc*); **~ence** *n* Bestehen *nt*; **~ent** *adj* hartnäckig; (*urgent*) dringend

insole ['ɪnsəʊl] *n* Einlegesohle *f*

insolence ['ɪnsələns] *n* Frechheit *f*

insolent ['ɪnsələnt] *adj* frech

insoluble [ɪn'sɒljʊbl] *adj* unlösbar; (*CHEM*) unlöslich

insolvent [ɪn'sɒlvənt] *adj* zahlungsunfähig

insomnia [ɪn'sɒmnɪə] *n* Schlaflosigkeit *f*

inspect [ɪn'spekt] *vt* prüfen; (*officially*) inspizieren; **~ion** [ɪn'spekʃən] *n* Inspektion *f*; **~or** *n* (*official*) Inspektor *m*; (*police*) Polizeikommissar *m*; (*BRIT: on buses, trains*) Kontrolleur *m*

inspiration [ɪnspə'reɪʃən] *n* Inspiration *f*

inspire [ɪn'spaɪə'] *vt* (*person*) inspirieren; **to ~ sth in sb** (*respect*) jdm etw einflößen; (*hope*) etw in jdm wecken

instability [ɪnstə'bɪlɪtɪ] *n* Unbeständigkeit *f*, Labilität *f*

install [ɪn'stɔːl] *vt* (*put in*) installieren; (*telephone*) anschließen; (*establish*) einsetzen; **~ation** [ɪnstə'leɪʃən] *n* (*of person*) (Amts)einsetzung *f*; (*of machinery*) Installierung *f*; (*machines etc*) Anlage *f*

instalment [ɪn'stɔːlmənt] (*US* **installment**) *n* Rate *f*; (*of story*) Fortsetzung *f*; **to pay in ~s** auf Raten zahlen

instance ['ɪnstəns] *n* Fall *m*; (*example*) Beispiel *nt*; **for ~** zum Beispiel; **in the first ~** zunächst

instant ['ɪnstənt] *n* Augenblick *m* ♦ *adj* augenblicklich, sofortig; **~aneous** [ɪnstən'teɪnɪəs] *adj* unmittelbar; **~ coffee** *n* Pulverkaffee *m*; **~ly** *adv* sofort

instead [ɪn'sted] *adv* statt dessen; **~ of** *prep* anstatt +*gen*

instep ['ɪnstep] *n* Spann *m*; (*of shoe*) Blatt *nt*

instil [ɪn'stɪl] *vt* (*fig*): **to ~ sth in sb** jdm etw beibringen

instinct ['ɪnstɪŋkt] *n* Instinkt *m*; **~ive** [ɪn'stɪŋktɪv] *adj* instinktiv

institute ['ɪnstɪtjuːt] *n* Institut *nt* ♦ *vt* einführen; (*search*) einleiten

institution [ɪnstɪ'tjuːʃən] *n* Institution *f*; (*home*) Anstalt *f*

instruct [ɪn'strʌkt] *vt* anweisen; (*officially*) instruieren; **~ion** [ɪn'strʌkʃən] *n* Unterricht *m*; **~ions** *npl* (*orders*) Anweisungen *pl*; (*for use*) Gebrauchsanweisung *f*; **~or** *n* Lehrer *m*

instrument ['ɪnstrumənt] *n* Instrument *nt*; **~al** [ɪnstru'mentl] *adj* (*MUS*) Instrumental-; (*helpful*): **~al (in)** behilflich (bei); **~ panel** *n* Armaturenbrett *nt*

insubordinate [ɪnsə'bɔːdənɪt] *adj* aufsässig, widersetzlich

insufferable [ɪn'sʌfrəbl] *adj* unerträglich

insufficient [ɪnsə'fɪʃənt] *adj* ungenügend

insular ['ɪnsjulə'] *adj* (*fig*) engstirnig

insulate ['ɪnsjuleɪt] *vt* (*ELEC*) isolieren; (*fig*): **to ~ (from)** abschirmen (vor +*dat*); **insulating tape** *n* Isolierband *nt*; **insulation** [ɪnsju'leɪʃən] *n* Isolierung *f*

insulin ['ɪnsjulɪn] *n* Insulin *nt*

insult [*n* 'ɪnsʌlt, *vb* ɪn'sʌlt] *n* Beleidigung *f* ♦ *vt* beleidigen

insurance [ɪn'ʃuərəns] *n* Versicherung *f*; **fire/life ~** Feuer-/Lebensversicherung; **~ agent** *n* Versicherungsvertreter *m*; **~ policy** *n* Versicherungspolice *f*

insure [ɪn'ʃuə'] *vt* versichern

intact [ɪn'tækt] *adj* unversehrt

intake ['ɪnteɪk] *n* (*place*) Einlaßöffnung *f*; (*act*) Aufnahme *f*; (*BRIT: SCH*): **an ~ of 200 a year** ein Neuzugang von 200 im Jahr

intangible [ɪn'tændʒɪbl] *adj* nicht greifbar

integral ['ɪntɪgrəl] *adj* (*essential*) wesentlich; (*complete*) vollständig; (*MATH*) Integral-

integrate ['ɪntɪgreɪt] *vt* integrieren ♦ *vi* sich integrieren

integrity [ɪn'tegrɪtɪ] *n* (*honesty*) Redlichkeit *f*, Integrität *f*

intellect ['ɪntəlekt] *n* Intellekt *m*; **~ual** [ɪntə'lektjuəl] *adj* geistig, intellektuell ♦ *n* Intellektuelle(r) *mf*

intelligence [ɪn'telɪdʒəns] *n* (*understanding*) Intelligenz *f*; (*news*) Information *f*; (*MIL*) Geheimdienst *m*; **~ service** *n* Nachrichtendienst *m*, Geheimdienst *m*

intelligent [ɪn'telɪdʒənt] *adj* intelligent; **~ly** *adv* klug; (*write, speak*) verständlich

intelligentsia [ɪnteli'dʒentsɪə] *n* Intelligenz *f*

intelligible [ɪnˈtelɪdʒɪbl] *adj* verständlich

intend [ɪnˈtend] *vt* beabsichtigen; **that was ~ed for you** das war für dich gedacht

intense [ɪnˈtens] *adj* stark, intensiv; (*person*) ernsthaft; **~ly** *adv* äußerst; (*study*) intensiv

intensify [ɪnˈtensɪfaɪ] *vt* verstärken, intensivieren

intensity [ɪnˈtensɪtɪ] *n* Intensität *f*

intensive [ɪnˈtensɪv] *adj* intensiv; **~ care unit** *n* Intensivstation *f*

intent [ɪnˈtent] *n* Absicht *f* ♦ *adj*: **to be ~ on doing sth** fest entschlossen sein, etw zu tun; **to all ~s and purposes** praktisch

intention [ɪnˈtenʃən] *n* Absicht *f*; **~al** *adj* absichtlich

intently [ɪnˈtentlɪ] *adv* konzentriert

interact [ɪntərˈækt] *vi* aufeinander einwirken; **~ion** [ɪntərˈækʃən] *n* Wechselwirkung *f*; **~ive** *adj* (*COMPUT*) interaktiv

intercept [ɪntəˈsept] *vt* abfangen

interchange [*n* ˈɪntətʃeɪndʒ, *vb* ɪntəˈtʃeɪndʒ] *n* (*exchange*) Austausch *m*; (*on roads*) Verkehrskreuz *nt* ♦ *vt* austauschen; **~able** [ɪntəˈtʃeɪndʒəbl] *adj* austauschbar

intercom [ˈɪntəkɔm] *n* (Gegen)sprechanlage *f*

intercourse [ˈɪntəkɔːs] *n* (*exchange*) Beziehungen *pl*; (*sexual*) Geschlechtsverkehr *m*

interest [ˈɪntrɪst] *n* Interesse *nt*; (*FIN*) Zinsen *pl*; (*COMM: share*) Anteil *m*; (*group*) Interessengruppe *f* ♦ *vt* interessieren; **~ed** *adj* (*having claims*) beteiligt; (*attentive*) interessiert; **to be ~ed in** sich interessieren für; **~ing** *adj* interessant; **~ rate** *n* Zinssatz *m*

interface [ˈɪntəfeɪs] *n* (*COMPUT*) Schnittstelle *f*, Interface *nt*

interfere [ɪntəˈfɪə] *vi*: **to ~ (with)** (*meddle*) sich einmischen (in *+acc*); (*disrupt*) stören *+acc*; **~nce** [ɪntəˈfɪərəns] *n* Einmischung *f*; (*TV*) Störung *f*

interim [ˈɪntərɪm] *n*: **in the ~** inzwischen

interior [ɪnˈtɪərɪə] *n* Innere(s) *nt* ♦ *adj* innere(r, s), Innen-; **~ designer** *n* Innenarchitekt(in) *m(f)*

interjection [ɪntəˈdʒekʃən] *n* Ausruf *m*

interlock [ɪntəˈlɔk] *vi* ineinandergreifen ⚠

interlude [ˈɪntəluːd] *n* Pause *f*

intermediary [ɪntəˈmiːdɪərɪ] *n* Vermittler *m*

intermediate [ɪntəˈmiːdɪət] *adj* Zwischen-, Mittel-

interminable [ɪnˈtəːmɪnəbl] *adj* endlos

intermission [ɪntəˈmɪʃən] *n* Pause *f*

intermittent [ɪntəˈmɪtnt] *adj* periodisch, stoßweise

intern [*vb* ɪnˈtəːn, *n* ˈɪntəːn] *vt* internieren ♦ *n* (*US*) Assistenzarzt *m*/-ärztin *f*

internal [ɪnˈtəːnl] *adj* (*inside*) innere(r, s); (*domestic*) Inlands-; **~ly** *adv* innen; (*MED*) innerlich; **"not to be taken ~ly"** "nur zur äußerlichen Anwendung"; **I~ Revenue Service** (*US*) *n* Finanzamt *nt*

international [ɪntəˈnæʃənl] *adj* international ♦ *n* (*SPORT*) Nationalspieler(in) *m(f)*; (*: match*) internationale(s) Spiel *nt*

Internet [ˈɪntənet] *n*: **the ~** das Internet

interplay [ˈɪntəpleɪ] *n* Wechselspiel *nt*

interpret [ɪnˈtəːprɪt] *vt* (*explain*) auslegen, interpretieren; (*translate*) dolmetschen; **~er** *n* Dolmetscher(in) *m(f)*

interrelated [ɪntərɪˈleɪtɪd] *adj* untereinander zusammenhängend

interrogate [ɪnˈterəgeɪt] *vt* verhören; **interrogation** [ɪnterəˈgeɪʃən] *n* Verhör *nt*

interrupt [ɪntəˈrʌpt] *vt* unterbrechen; **~ion** [ɪntəˈrʌpʃən] *n* Unterbrechung *f*

intersect [ɪntəˈsekt] *vt* (durch)schneiden ♦ *vi* sich schneiden; **~ion** [ɪntəˈsekʃən] *n* (*of roads*) Kreuzung *f*; (*of lines*) Schnittpunkt *m*

intersperse [ɪntəˈspəːs] *vt*: **to ~ sth with sth** etw mit etw durchsetzen

intertwine [ɪntəˈtwaɪn] *vt* verflechten ♦ *vi* sich verflechten

interval [ˈɪntəvl] *n* Abstand *m*; (*BRIT: SCH, THEAT, SPORT*) Pause *f*; **at ~s** in Abständen

intervene [ɪntəˈviːn] *vi* dazwischenliegen; (*act*): **to ~ (in)** einschreiten (gegen); **intervention** [ɪntəˈvenʃən] *n* Eingreifen *nt*, Intervention *f*

interview [ˈɪntəvjuː] *n* (*PRESS etc*) Interview *nt*; (*for job*) Vorstellungsgespräch *nt* ♦ *vt* interviewen; **~er** *n* Interviewer *m*

intestine [ɪnˈtestɪn] *n*: **large/small ~** Dick-

/Dünndarm *m*

intimacy ['ıntıməsı] *n* Intimität *f*

intimate [*adj* 'ıntımət, *vb* 'ıntımeıt] *adj* (*inmost*) innerste(r, s); (*knowledge*) eingehend; (*familiar*) vertraut; (*friends*) eng ♦ *vt* andeuten

intimidate [ın'tımıdeıt] *vt* einschüchtern

into ['ıntu] *prep* (*motion*) in +*acc* ... hinein; **5 ~ 25** 25 durch 5

intolerable [ın'tɔlərəbl] *adj* unerträglich

intolerant [ın'tɔlərnt] *adj*: **~ of** unduldsam gegen(über)

intoxicate [ın'tɔksıkeıt] *vt* berauschen; **~d** *adj* betrunken; **intoxication** [ıntɔksı'keıʃən] *n* Rausch *m*

intractable [ın'træktəbl] *adj* schwer zu handhaben; (*problem*) schwer lösbar

intransitive [ın'trænsıtıv] *adj* intransitiv

intravenous [ıntrə'viːnəs] *adj* intravenös

in-tray ['ıntreı] *n* Eingangskorb *m*

intrepid [ın'trepıd] *adj* unerschrocken

intricate ['ıntrıkət] *adj* kompliziert

intrigue [ın'triːg] *n* Intrige *f* ♦ *vt* faszinieren ♦ *vi* intrigieren

intrinsic [ın'trınsık] *adj* innere(r, s); (*difference*) wesentlich

introduce [ıntrə'djuːs] *vt* (*person*) vorstellen; (*sth new*) einführen; (*subject*) anschneiden; **to ~ sb to sb** jdm jdn vorstellen; **to ~ sb to sth** jdn in etw *acc* einführen; **introduction** [ıntrə'dʌkʃən] *n* Einführung *f*; (*to book*) Einleitung *f*; **introductory** [ıntrə'dʌktərı] *adj* Einführungs-, Vor-

introspective [ıntrəu'spektıv] *adj* nach innen gekehrt

introvert ['ıntrəuvəːt] *n* Introvertierte(r) *mf* ♦ *adj* introvertiert

intrude [ın'truːd] *vi*: **to ~ (on sb/sth)** (jdn/ etw) stören; **~r** *n* Eindringling *m*

intrusion [ın'truːʒən] *n* Störung *f*

intrusive [ın'truːsıv] *adj* aufdringlich

intuition [ıntjuː'ıʃən] *n* Intuition *f*

inundate ['ınʌndeıt] *vt* (*also fig*) überschwemmen

invade [ın'veıd] *vt* einfallen in +*acc*; **~r** *n* Eindringling *m*

invalid¹ ['ınvəlıd] *n* (*disabled*) Invalide *m*

♦ *adj* (*ill*) krank; (*disabled*) invalide

invalid² [ın'vælıd] *adj* (*not valid*) ungültig

invaluable [ın'væljuəbl] *adj* unschätzbar

invariable [ın'veərıəbl] *adj* unveränderlich; **invariably** *adv* ausnahmslos

invent [ın'vent] *vt* erfinden; **~ion** [ın'venʃən] *n* Erfindung *f*; **~ive** *adj* erfinderisch; **~or** *n* Erfinder *m*

inventory ['ınvəntrı] *n* Inventar *nt*

inverse [ın'vəːs] *n* Umkehrung *f* ♦ *adj* umgekehrt

invert [ın'vəːt] *vt* umdrehen; **~ed commas** (*BRIT*) *npl* Anführungszeichen *pl*

invest [ın'vest] *vt* investieren

investigate [ın'vestıgeıt] *vt* untersuchen; **investigation** [ınvestı'geıʃən] *n* Untersuchung *f*; **investigator** [ın'vestıgeıtə'] *n* Untersuchungsbeamte(r) *m*

investiture [ın'vestıtʃə'] *n* Amtseinsetzung *f*

investment [ın'vestmənt] *n* Investition *f*

investor [ın'vestə'] *n* (Geld)anleger *m*

invigilate [ın'vıdʒıleıt] *vi* (*in exam*) Aufsicht führen ♦ *vt* Aufsicht führen bei; **invigilator** *n* Aufsicht *f*

invigorating [ın'vıgəreıtıŋ] *adj* stärkend

invincible [ın'vınsıbl] *adj* unbesiegbar

invisible [ın'vızıbl] *adj* unsichtbar

invitation [ınvı'teıʃən] *n* Einladung *f*

invite [ın'vaıt] *vt* einladen

invoice ['ınvɔıs] *n* Rechnung *f* ♦ *vt* (*goods*): **to ~ sb for sth** jdm etw *acc* in Rechnung stellen

invoke [ın'vəuk] *vt* anrufen

involuntary [ın'vɔləntrı] *adj* unabsichtlich

involve [ın'vɔlv] *vt* (*entangle*) verwickeln; (*entail*) mit sich bringen; **~d** *adj* verwickelt; **~ment** *n* Verwicklung *f*

inward ['ınwəd] *adj* innere(r, s); (*curve*) Innen- ♦ *adv* nach innen; **~ly** *adv* im Innern; **~s** *adv* nach innen

I/O *abbr* (*COMPUT*) (= *input/output*) I/O

iodine ['aıəudiːn] *n* Jod *nt*

ioniser ['aıənaızə'] *n* Ionisator *m*

iota [aı'əutə] *n* (*fig*) bißchen ⚠ *nt*

IOU *n abbr* (= *I owe you*) Schuldschein *m*

IQ *n abbr* (= *intelligence quotient*) IQ *m*

IRA *n abbr* (= *Irish Republican Army*) IRA *f*

⚠ *Informationen zur Rechtschreibreform Seite 615*

Iran [ɪˈrɑːn] n Iran m; **~ian** [ɪˈreɪnɪən] adj iranisch ♦ n Iraner(in) m(f); (LING) Iranisch nt

Iraq [ɪˈrɑːk] n Irak m; **~i** adj irakisch ♦ n Iraker(in) m(f)

irate [aɪˈreɪt] adj zornig

Ireland [ˈaɪələnd] n Irland nt

iris [ˈaɪrɪs] (pl **~es**) n Iris f

Irish [ˈaɪrɪʃ] adj irisch ♦ npl: **the ~** die Iren pl, die Irländer pl; **~man** (irreg) n Ire m, Irländer m; **~ Sea** n: **the ~ Sea** die Irische See f; **~woman** (irreg) n Irin f, Irländerin f

iron [ˈaɪən] n Eisen nt; (for ironing) Bügeleisen nt ♦ adj eisern ♦ vt bügeln; **~ out** vt (also fig) ausbügeln; **Iron Curtain** n Eiserne(r) Vorhang m

ironic(al) [aɪˈrɒnɪk(l)] adj ironisch; (coincidence etc) witzig

iron: ~ing n Bügeln nt; (laundry) Bügelwäsche f; **~ing board** n Bügelbrett nt; **~monger's (shop)** n Eisen- und Haushaltswarenhandlung f

irony [ˈaɪrənɪ] n Ironie f

irrational [ɪˈræʃənl] adj irrational

irreconcilable [ɪrekənˈsaɪləbl] adj unvereinbar

irrefutable [ɪrɪˈfjuːtəbl] adj unwiderlegbar

irregular [ɪˈregjuləʳ] adj unregelmäßig; (shape) ungleich(mäßig); (fig) unüblich; (: behaviour) ungehörig

irrelevant [ɪˈreləvənt] adj belanglos, irrelevant

irreparable [ɪˈrepərəbl] adj nicht wiedergutzumachen △

irreplaceable [ɪrɪˈpleɪsəbl] adj unersetzlich

irresistible [ɪrɪˈzɪstɪbl] adj unwiderstehlich

irrespective [ɪrɪˈspektɪv]: **~ of** prep ungeachtet +gen

irresponsible [ɪrɪˈspɒnsɪbl] adj verantwortungslos

irreverent [ɪˈrevərənt] adj respektlos

irrevocable [ɪˈrevəkəbl] adj unwiderrufbar

irrigate [ˈɪrɪgeɪt] vt bewässern

irritable [ˈɪrɪtəbl] adj reizbar

irritate [ˈɪrɪteɪt] vt irritieren, reizen (also MED); **irritating** adj ärgerlich, irritierend; **he is irritating** er kann einem auf die Nerven

gehen; **irritation** [ɪrɪˈteɪʃən] n (anger) Ärger m; (MED) Reizung f

IRS n abbr = **Internal Revenue Service**

is [ɪz] vb see **be**

Islam [ˈɪzlɑːm] n Islam m; **~ic** [ɪzˈlæmɪk] adj islamisch

island [ˈaɪlənd] n Insel f; **~er** n Inselbewohner(in) m(f)

isle [aɪl] n (kleine) Insel f

isn't [ˈɪznt] = **is not**

isolate [ˈaɪsəleɪt] vt isolieren; **~d** adj isoliert; (case) Einzel-; **isolation** [aɪsəˈleɪʃən] n Isolierung f

Israel [ˈɪzreɪl] n Israel nt; **~i** [ɪzˈreɪlɪ] adj israelisch ♦ n Israeli mf

issue [ˈɪʃjuː] n (matter) Frage f; (outcome) Ausgang m; (of newspaper, shares) Ausgabe f; (offspring) Nachkommenschaft f ♦ vt ausgeben; (warrant) erlassen; (documents) ausstellen; (orders) erteilen; (books) herausgeben; (verdict) aussprechen; **to be at ~** zur Debatte stehen; **to take ~ with sb over sth** jdm in etw dat widersprechen

---

KEYWORD

it [ɪt] pron **1** (specific: subject) er/sie/es; (: direct object) ihn/sie/es; (: indirect object) ihm/ihr/ihm; **about/from/in/of it** darüber/daraus/darin/davon

2 (impers) es; **it's raining** es regnet; **it's Friday tomorrow** morgen ist Freitag; **who is it? – it's me** wer ist da? – ich (bin's)

Italian [ɪˈtæljən] adj italienisch ♦ n Italiener(in) m(f); (LING) Italienisch nt

italic [ɪˈtælɪk] adj kursiv; **~s** npl Kursivschrift f

Italy [ˈɪtəlɪ] n Italien nt

itch [ɪtʃ] n Juckreiz m; (fig) Lust f ♦ vi jucken; **to be ~ing to do sth** darauf brennen, etw zu tun; **~y** adj juckend

it'd [ˈɪtd] = **it would**; **it had**

item [ˈaɪtəm] n Gegenstand m; (on list) Posten m; (in programme) Nummer f; (in agenda) (Programm)punkt m; (in newspaper) (Zeitungs)notiz f; **~ize** vt verzeichnen

itinerant [ɪˈtɪnərənt] adj (person) umherreisend

△ For information on spelling reform see page 615

itinerary [aɪ'tɪnərərɪ] *n* Reiseroute *f*

it'll ['ɪtl] = **it will; it shall**

its [ɪts] *adj (masculine, neuter)* sein; *(feminine)* ihr

it's [ɪts] = **it is; it has**

itself [ɪt'self] *pron* sich (selbst); *(emphatic)* selbst

ITV *(BRIT) n abbr* = **Independent Television**

I.U.D. *n abbr* (= *intra-uterine device*) Pessar *nt*

I've [aɪv] = **I have**

ivory ['aɪvərɪ] *n* Elfenbein *nt*

ivy ['aɪvɪ] *n* Efeu *nt*

J, j

jab [dʒæb] *vt* (hinein)stechen ♦ *n* Stich *m*, Stoß *m*; *(inf)* Spritze *f*

jack [dʒæk] *n (AUT)* (Wagen)heber *m*; *(CARDS)* Bube *m*; **~ up** *vt* aufbocken

jackal ['dʒækl] *n (ZOOL)* Schakal *m*

jackdaw ['dʒækdɔ:] *n* Dohle *f*

jacket ['dʒækɪt] *n* Jacke *f*; *(of book)* Schutzumschlag *m*; *(TECH)* Ummantelung *f*; **~ potatoes** *npl* in der Schale gebackene Kartoffeln *pl*

jackknife ['dʒæknaɪf] *vi (truck)* sich zusammenschieben

jack plug *n (ELEC)* Buchsenstecker *m*

jackpot ['dʒækpɒt] *n* Haupttreffer *m*

jaded ['dʒeɪdɪd] *adj* ermattet

jagged ['dʒægɪd] *adj* zackig

jail [dʒeɪl] *n* Gefängnis *nt* ♦ *vt* einsperren; **~er** *n* Gefängniswärter *m*

jam [dʒæm] *n* Marmelade *f*; *(also:* **traffic ~**) (Verkehrs)stau *m*; *(inf: trouble)* Klemme *f* ♦ *vt (wedge)* einklemmen; *(cram)* hineinzwängen; *(obstruct)* blockieren ♦ *vi* sich verklemmen; **to ~ sth into sth** etw in etw *acc* hineinstopfen

Jamaica [dʒə'meɪkə] *n* Jamaika *nt*

jam jar *n* Marmeladenglas *nt*

jammed [dʒæmd] *adj*: **it's ~** es klemmt

jam-packed [dʒæm'pækt] *adj* überfüllt, proppenvoll

jangle ['dʒæŋgl] *vt, vi* klimpern

janitor ['dʒænɪtər] *n* Hausmeister *m*

January ['dʒænjuərɪ] *n* Januar *m*

Japan [dʒə'pæn] *n* Japan *nt*; **~ese** [dʒæpə'ni:z] *adj* japanisch ♦ *n inv* Japaner(in) *m(f)*; *(LING)* Japanisch *nt*

jar [dʒɑ:r] *n* Glas *nt* ♦ *vi* kreischen; *(colours etc)* nicht harmonieren

jargon ['dʒɑ:gən] *n* Fachsprache *f*, Jargon *m*

jaundice ['dʒɔ:ndɪs] *n* Gelbsucht *f*; **~d** *adj* *(fig)* mißgünstig ⚠

jaunt [dʒɔ:nt] *n* Spritztour *f*

javelin ['dʒævlɪn] *n* Speer *m*

jaw [dʒɔ:] *n* Kiefer *m*

jay [dʒeɪ] *n (ZOOL)* Eichelhäher *m*

jaywalker ['dʒeɪwɔ:kər] *n* unvorsichtige(r) Fußgänger *m*

jazz [dʒæz] *n* Jazz *m*; **~ up** *vt (MUS)* verjazzen; *(enliven)* aufpolieren

jealous ['dʒeləs] *adj (envious)* mißgünstig ⚠; *(husband)* eifersüchtig; **~y** *n* Mißgunst ⚠ *f*, Eifersucht *f*

jeans [dʒi:nz] *npl* Jeans *pl*

Jeep [dʒi:p] ® *n* Jeep *m* ®

jeer [dʒɪər] *vi*: **to ~ (at sb)** (über jdn) höhnisch lachen, (jdn) verspotten

Jehovah's Witness [dʒɪ'həuvəz-] *n* Zeuge *m*/Zeugin *f* Jehovas

jelly ['dʒelɪ] *n* Gelee *nt*; *(dessert)* Grütze *f*; **~fish** *n* Qualle *f*

jeopardize ['dʒepədaɪz] *vt* gefährden

jeopardy ['dʒepədɪ] *n*: **to be in ~** in Gefahr sein

jerk [dʒɔ:k] *n* Ruck *m*; *(inf: idiot)* Trottel *m* ♦ *vt* ruckartig bewegen ♦ *vi* sich ruckartig bewegen

jerky ['dʒɔ:kɪ] *adj (movement)* ruckartig; *(ride)* rüttelnd

jersey ['dʒɔ:zɪ] *n* Pullover *m*

jest [dʒest] *n* Scherz *m* ♦ *vi* spaßen; **in ~** im Spaß

Jesus ['dʒi:zəs] *n* Jesus *m*

jet [dʒet] *n (stream: of water etc)* Strahl *m*; *(spout)* Düse *f*; *(AVIAT)* Düsenflugzeug *nt*; **~-black** *adj* rabenschwarz; **~ engine** *n* Düsenmotor *m*; **~ lag** *n* Jet-lag *m*

jettison ['dʒetɪsn] *vt* über Bord werfen

jetty ['dʒetɪ] *n* Landesteg *m*, Mole *f*

Jew [dʒu:] *n* Jude *m*

jewel ['dʒuːəl] n (also fig) Juwel nt; **~ler** (US **jeweler**) n Juwelier m; **~ler's (shop)** n Juwelier m; **~lery** (US **jewelry**) n Schmuck m

Jewess ['dʒuːɪs] n Jüdin f

Jewish ['dʒuːɪʃ] adj jüdisch

jibe [dʒaɪb] n spöttische Bemerkung f

jiffy ['dʒɪfɪ] (inf) n: **in a ~** sofort

jigsaw ['dʒɪgsɔː] n (also: **~ puzzle**) Puzzle(spiel) nt

jilt [dʒɪlt] vt den Laufpaß ⚠ geben +dat

jingle ['dʒɪŋgl] n (advertisement) Werbesong m ♦ vi klimpern; (bells) bimmeln ♦ vt klimpern mit; bimmeln lassen

jinx [dʒɪŋks] n: **there's a ~ on it** es ist verhext

jitters ['dʒɪtəz] (inf) npl: **to get the ~** einen Bammel kriegen

job [dʒɔb] n (piece of work) Arbeit f; (position) Stellung f; (duty) Aufgabe f; (difficulty) Mühe f; **it's a good ~ he ...** es ist ein Glück, daß er ...; **just the ~** genau das Richtige; **J~centre** (BRIT) n Arbeitsamt nt; **~less** adj arbeitslos

jockey ['dʒɔkɪ] n Jockei m ♦ vi: **to ~ for position** sich in eine gute Position drängeln

jocular ['dʒɔkjulər] adj scherzhaft

jog [dʒɔg] vt (an)stoßen ♦ vi (run) joggen; **to ~ along** vor sich acc hinwursteln; (work) seinen Gang gehen; **~ging** n Jogging nt

join [dʒɔɪn] vt (club) beitreten +dat; (person) sich anschließen +dat; (fasten): **to ~ (sth to sth)** (etw mit etw) verbinden ♦ vi (unite) sich vereinigen ♦ n Verbindungsstelle f, Naht f; **~ in** vt, vi: **to ~ in (sth)** (bei etw) mitmachen; **~ up** vi (MIL) zur Armee gehen

joiner ['dʒɔɪnər] n Schreiner m; **~y** n Schreinerei f

joint [dʒɔɪnt] n (TECH) Fuge f; (of bones) Gelenk nt; (of meat) Braten m; (inf: place) Lokal nt ♦ adj gemeinsam; **~ account** n (with bank etc) gemeinsame(s) Konto nt; **~ly** adv gemeinsam

joke [dʒəuk] n Witz m ♦ vi Witze machen; **to play a ~ on sb** jdm einen Streich spielen;

~r n Witzbold m; (CARDS) Joker m

jolly ['dʒɔlɪ] adj lustig ♦ adv (inf) ganz schön

jolt [dʒəult] n (shock) Schock m; (jerk) Stoß m ♦ vt (push) stoßen; (shake) durchschütteln; (fig) aufrütteln ♦ vi holpern

Jordan ['dʒɔːdən] n Jordanien nt

jostle ['dʒɔsl] vt anrempeln

jot [dʒɔt] n: **not one ~** kein Jota nt; **~ down** vt notieren; **~ter** (BRIT) n Notizblock m

journal ['dʒəːnl] n (diary) Tagebuch nt; (magazine) Zeitschrift f; **~ism** n Journalismus m; **~ist** n Journalist(in) m(f)

journey ['dʒəːnɪ] n Reise f

jovial ['dʒəuvɪəl] adj jovial

joy [dʒɔɪ] n Freude f; **~ful** adj freudig; **~ous** adj freudig; **~ ride** n Schwarzfahrt f; **~rider** n Autodieb, der den Wagen nur für eine Spritztour stiehlt; **~stick** n Steuerknüppel m; (COMPUT) Joystick m

J.P. n abbr = **Justice of the Peace**

Jr abbr = **junior**

jubilant ['dʒuːbɪlnt] adj triumphierend

jubilee ['dʒuːbɪliː] n Jubiläum nt

judge [dʒʌdʒ] n Richter m; (fig) Kenner m ♦ vt (JUR: person) die Verhandlung führen über +acc; (case) verhandeln; (assess) beurteilen; (estimate) einschätzen; **~ment** n (JUR) Urteil nt; (ECCL) Gericht nt; (ability) Urteilsvermögen nt

judicial [dʒuːˈdɪʃl] adj gerichtlich, Justiz-

judiciary [dʒuːˈdɪʃɪərɪ] n Gerichtsbehörden pl; (judges) Richterstand m

judicious [dʒuːˈdɪʃəs] adj weise

judo ['dʒuːdəu] n Judo nt

jug [dʒʌg] n Krug m

juggernaut ['dʒʌgənɔːt] (BRIT) n (huge truck) Schwertransporter m

juggle ['dʒʌgl] vt, vi jonglieren; **~r** n Jongleur m

Jugoslav etc ['juːgəuˈslɑːv] = **Yugoslav** etc

juice [dʒuːs] n Saft m; **juicy** ['dʒuːsɪ] adj (also fig) saftig

jukebox ['dʒuːkbɔks] n Musikautomat m

July [dʒuːˈlaɪ] n Juli m

jumble ['dʒʌmbl] n Durcheinander nt ♦ vt (also: **~ up**) durcheinanderwerfen ⚠; (facts)

⚠ *For information on spelling reform see page 615*

durcheinanderbringen △; ~ **sale** (*BRIT*) *n*
Basar *m*, Flohmarkt *m*

JUMBLE SALE

ⓘ **Jumble sale** *ist ein*
Wohltätigkeitsbasar, meist in einer Aula
oder einem Gemeindehaus abgehalten, bei
dem alle möglichen Gebrauchtwaren (vor
allem Kleidung, Spielzeug, Bücher,
Geschirr und Möbel) verkauft werden. Der
Erlös fließt entweder einer
Wohltätigkeitsorganisation zu oder wird für
örtliche Zwecke verwendet, z.B. die
Pfadfinder, die Grundschule, Reparatur der
Kirche usw.

jumbo (jet) [ˈdʒʌmbəʊ-] *n* Jumbo(-Jet) *m*
jump [dʒʌmp] *vi* springen; (*nervously*)
zusammenzucken ♦ *vt* überspringen ♦ *n*
Sprung *m*; **to ~ the queue** (*BRIT*) sich
vordrängeln
jumper [ˈdʒʌmpəʳ] *n* (*BRIT*: *pullover*) Pullover
m; (*US*: *dress*) Trägerkleid *nt*
jump leads (*BRIT*) (*US* **jumper cables**) *npl*
Überbrückungskabel *nt*
jumpy [ˈdʒʌmpɪ] *adj* nervös
Jun. *abbr* = **junior**
junction [ˈdʒʌŋkʃən] *n* (*BRIT*: *of roads*)
(Straßen)kreuzung *f*; (*RAIL*) Knotenpunkt *m*
juncture [ˈdʒʌŋktʃəʳ] *n*: **at this ~** in diesem
Augenblick
June [dʒuːn] *n* Juni *m*
jungle [ˈdʒʌŋgl] *n* Dschungel *m*
junior [ˈdʒuːnɪəʳ] *adj* (*younger*) jünger; (*after*
name) junior; (*SPORT*) Junioren-; (*lower*
position) untergeordnet; (*for young people*)
Junioren- ♦ *n* Jüngere(r) *mf*; ~ **school**
(*BRIT*) *n* Grundschule *f*
junk [dʒʌŋk] *n* (*rubbish*) Plunder *m*; (*ship*)
Dschunke *f*; ~ **bond** (*COMM*) niedrig
eingestuftes Wertpapier mit hohen
Ertragschancen bei erhöhtem Risiko; ~
food *n* Junk food *nt*; ~ **mail** *n* Reklame,
die unangefordert in den Briefkasten
gesteckt wird; ~ **shop** *n* Ramschladen *m*
Junr *abbr* = **junior**
jurisdiction [dʒuərɪsˈdɪkʃən] *n*

Gerichtsbarkeit *f*; (*range of authority*)
Zuständigkeit(sbereich *m*) *f*
juror [ˈdʒuərəʳ] *n* Geschworene(r) *mf*; (*in*
competition) Preisrichter *m*
jury [ˈdʒuərɪ] *n* (*court*) Geschworene *pl*;
(*panel*) Jury *f*
just [dʒʌst] *adj* gerecht ♦ *adv* (*recently, now*)
gerade, eben; (*barely*) gerade noch;
(*exactly*) genau, gerade; (*only*) nur, bloß; (*a*
small distance) gleich; (*absolutely*) einfach; ~
as I arrived gerade als ich ankam; ~ **as**
nice genauso nett; ~ **as well** um so besser;
~ **now** soeben, gerade; ~ **try** versuch es
mal; **she's ~ left** sie ist gerade *or* (so)eben
gegangen; **he's ~ done it** er hat es gerade
or (so)eben getan; ~ **before** gerade *or* kurz
bevor; ~ **enough** gerade genug; **he ~**
missed er hat fast *or* beinahe getroffen
justice [ˈdʒʌstɪs] *n* (*fairness*) Gerechtigkeit *f*;
J~ of the Peace *n* Friedensrichter *m*
justifiable [dʒʌstɪˈfaɪəbl] *adj* berechtigt
justification [dʒʌstɪfɪˈkeɪʃən] *n*
Rechtfertigung *f*
justify [ˈdʒʌstɪfaɪ] *vt* rechtfertigen; (*text*)
justieren
justly [ˈdʒʌstlɪ] *adv* (*say*) mit Recht;
(*condemn*) gerecht
jut [dʒʌt] *vi* (*also:* ~ **out**) herausragen,
vorstehen
juvenile [ˈdʒuːvənaɪl] *adj* (*young*) jugendlich;
(*for the young*) Jugend- ♦ *n* Jugendliche(r)
mf
juxtapose [ˈdʒʌkstəpəʊz] *vt*
nebeneinanderstellen △

K, k

K [keɪ] *abbr* (= *one thousand*) Tsd.; (= *kilobyte*)
K
kangaroo [kæŋgəˈruː] *n* Känguruh △ *nt*
karate [kəˈrɑːtɪ] *n* Karate *nt*
kebab [kəˈbæb] *n* Kebab *m*
keel [kiːl] *n* Kiel *m*; **on an even ~** (*fig*) im
Lot
keen [kiːn] *adj* begeistert; (*wind, blade,*
intelligence) scharf; (*sight, hearing*) gut; **to**

be ~ to do or on doing sth etw unbedingt tun wollen; **to be ~ on sth/sb** scharf auf etw/jdn sein

keep [ki:p] (pt, pp **kept**) vt (retain) behalten; (have) haben; (animals, one's word) halten; (support) versorgen; (maintain in state) halten; (preserve) aufbewahren; (restrain) abhalten ♦ vi (continue in direction) sich halten; (food) sich halten; (remain: quiet etc) bleiben ♦ n Unterhalt m; (tower) Burgfried m; (inf): **for ~s** für immer; **to ~ sth to o.s.** etw für sich behalten; **it ~s happening** es passiert immer wieder; **~ back** vt fernhalten ⚠; (information) verschweigen; **~ on** vi: **on doing sth** etw immer weiter tun; **~ out** vt nicht hereinlassen; **"~ out"** „Eintritt verboten!"; **~ up** vi Schritt halten ♦ vt aufrechterhalten; (continue) weitermachen; **to ~ up with** Schritt halten mit; **~er** n Wärter(in) m(f); (goalkeeper) Torhüter(in) m(f); **~-fit** n Keep-fit nt; **~ing** n (care) Obhut f; **in ~ing with** in Übereinstimmung mit; **~sake** n Andenken nt

keg [keg] n Faß ⚠ nt

kennel ['kɛnl] n Hundehütte f; **~s** npl: **to put a dog in ~s** (for boarding) einen Hund in Pflege geben

Kenya ['kɛnjə] n Kenia nt; **~n** adj kenianisch ♦ n Kenianer(in) m(f)

kept [kɛpt] pt, pp of **keep**

kerb [kə:b] (BRIT) n Bordstein m

kernel ['kə:nl] n Kern m

kerosene ['kɛrəsi:n] n Kerosin nt

kettle ['kɛtl] n Kessel m; **~drum** n Pauke f

key [ki:] n Schlüssel m; (of piano, typewriter) Taste f; (MUS) Tonart f ♦ vt (also: **~ in**) eingeben; **~board** n Tastatur f; **~ed up** adj (person) überdreht; **~hole** n Schlüsselloch nt; **~hole surgery** n minimal invasive Chirurgie f, Schlüssellochchirurgie f; **~note** n Grundton m; **~ ring** n Schlüsselring m

khaki ['kɑ:ki] n K(h)aki nt ♦ adj k(h)aki(farben)

kick [kik] vt einen Fußtritt geben +dat, treten ♦ vi treten; (baby) strampeln; (horse)

ausschlagen ♦ n (Fuß)tritt m; (thrill) Spaß m; **he does it for ~s** er macht das aus Jux; **~ off** vi (SPORT) anstoßen; **~-off** n (SPORT) Anstoß m

kid [kid] n (inf: child) Kind nt; (goat) Zicklein nt; (leather) Glacéleder nt ♦ vi (inf) Witze machen

kidnap ['kidnæp] vt entführen; **~per** n Entführer m; **~ping** n Entführung f

kidney ['kidni] n Niere f

kill [kil] vt töten, umbringen ♦ vi töten ♦ n (hunting) (Jagd)beute f; **~er** n Mörder(in) m(f); **~ing** n Mord m; **~joy** n Spaßverderber(in) m(f)

kiln [kiln] n Brennofen m

kilo ['ki:ləu] n Kilo nt; **~byte** n (COMPUT) Kilobyte nt; **~gram(me)** n Kilogramm nt; **~metre** ['kiləmi:tə'] (US **kilometer**) n Kilometer m; **~watt** n Kilowatt nt

kilt [kilt] n Schottenrock m

kind [kaind] adj freundlich ♦ n Art f; **a ~ of** eine Art von; **(two) of a ~** (zwei) von der gleichen Art; **in ~** auf dieselbe Art; (in goods) in Naturalien

kindergarten ['kindəgɑ:tn] n Kindergarten m

kind-hearted [kaind'hɑ:tid] adj gutherzig

kindle ['kindl] vt (set on fire) anzünden; (rouse) reizen, (er)wecken

kindly ['kaindli] adj freundlich ♦ adv liebenswürdig(erweise); **would you ~ ...?** wären Sie so freundlich und ...?

kindness ['kaindnis] n Freundlichkeit f

kindred ['kindrid] adj: **~ spirit** Gleichgesinnte(r) mf

king [kiŋ] n König m; **~dom** n Königreich nt

kingfisher ['kiŋfiʃə'] n Eisvogel m

king-size(d) ['kiŋsaiz(d)] adj (cigarette) Kingsize

kinky ['kiŋki] (inf) adj (person, ideas) verrückt; (sexual) abartig

kiosk ['ki:ɔsk] (BRIT) n (TEL) Telefonhäuschen nt

kipper ['kipə'] n Räucherhering m

kiss [kis] n Kuß ⚠ m ♦ vt küssen ♦ vi: **they ~ed** sie küßten sich; **~ of life** (BRIT) n: **the ~ of life** Mund-zu-Mund-Beatmung f

⚠ *For information on spelling reform see page 615*

kit [kɪt] n Ausrüstung f; (tools) Werkzeug nt
kitchen ['kɪtʃɪn] n Küche f; ~ **sink** n
Spülbecken nt
kite [kaɪt] n Drachen m
kitten ['kɪtn] n Kätzchen nt
kitty ['kɪtɪ] n (money) Kasse f
km abbr (= kilometre) km
knack [næk] n Dreh m, Trick m
knapsack ['næpsæk] n Rucksack m; (MIL)
Tornister m
knead [niːd] vt kneten
knee [niː] n Knie nt; ~**cap** n Kniescheibe f
kneel [niːl] (pt, pp **knelt**) vi (also: ~ **down**)
knien
knelt [nɛlt] pt, pp of **kneel**
knew [njuː] pt of **know**
knickers ['nɪkəz] (BRIT) npl Schlüpfer m
knife [naɪf] (pl **knives**) n Messer nt ♦ vt
erstechen
knight [naɪt] n Ritter m; (chess) Springer m;
~**hood** n (title): **to get a ~hood** zum Ritter
geschlagen werden
knit [nɪt] vt stricken ♦ vi stricken; (bones)
zusammenwachsen; ~**ting** n (occupation)
Stricken nt; (work) Strickzeug nt; ~**ting**
needle n Stricknadel f; ~**wear** n
Strickwaren pl
knives [naɪvz] pl of **knife**
knob [nɔb] n Knauf m; (on instrument) Knopf
m; (BRIT: of butter etc) kleine(s) Stück nt
knock [nɔk] vt schlagen; (criticize)
heruntermachen ♦ vi: **to ~ at** or **on the**
door an die Tür klopfen ♦ n Schlag m; (on
door) Klopfen nt; ~ **down** vt umwerfen;
(with car) anfahren; ~ **off** vt (do quickly)
hinhauen; (inf: steal) klauen ♦ vi (finish)
Feierabend machen; ~ **out** vt ausschlagen;
(BOXING) k.o. schlagen; ~ **over** vt (person,
object) umwerfen; (with car) anfahren; ~**er**
n (on door) Türklopfer m; ~**out** n K.o.-
Schlag m; (fig) Sensation f
knot [nɔt] n Knoten m ♦ vt (ver)knoten
knotty ['nɔtɪ] adj (fig) kompliziert
know [nəʊ] (pt **knew**, pp **known**) vt, vi
wissen; (be able to) können; (be acquainted
with) kennen; (recognize) erkennen; **to ~**
how to do sth wissen, wie man etw

macht, etw tun können; **to ~ about** or **of**
sth/sb etw/jdn kennen; ~**all** n Alleswisser
m; ~**how** n Kenntnis f, Know-how nt;
~**ing** adj (look, smile) wissend; ~**ingly** adv
wissend; (intentionally) wissentlich
knowledge ['nɔlɪdʒ] n Wissen nt, Kenntnis
f; ~**able** adj informiert
known [nəʊn] pp of **know**
knuckle ['nʌkl] n Fingerknöchel m
K.O. n abbr = **knockout**
Koran [kɔˈrɑːn] n Koran m
Korea [kəˈrɪə] n Korea nt
kosher ['kəʊʃər] adj koscher

L, l

L [ɛl] abbr (BRIT: AUT: = learner) am Auto
angebrachtes Kennzeichen für Fahrschüler;
= **lake**; (= large) gr.; (= left) l.
l. abbr = **litre**
lab [læb] (inf) n Labor nt
label ['leɪbl] n Etikett nt ♦ vt etikettieren
labor etc ['leɪbər] (US) = **labour** etc
laboratory [ləˈbɔrətərɪ] n Laboratorium nt
laborious [ləˈbɔːrɪəs] adj mühsam
labour ['leɪbər] (US **labor**) n Arbeit f;
(workmen) Arbeitskräfte pl; (MED) Wehen pl
♦ vi: **to ~ (at)** sich abmühen (mit) ♦ vt
breittreten (inf); **in ~** (MED) in den Wehen;
L~ (BRIT: also: **the L~ party**) die Labour
Party; ~**ed** adj (movement) gequält; (style)
schwerfällig; ~**er** n Arbeiter m; **farm ~er**
(Land)arbeiter m
lace [leɪs] n (fabric) Spitze f; (of shoe)
Schnürsenkel m; (braid) Litze f ♦ vt (also: ~
up) (zu)schnüren
lack [læk] n Mangel m ♦ vt nicht haben; **sb**
~**s sth** jdm fehlt etw nom; **to be ~ing**
fehlen; **sb is ~ing in sth** es fehlt jdm an
etw dat; **for** or **through ~ of** aus Mangel an
+dat
lacquer ['lækər] n Lack m
lad [læd] n Junge m
ladder ['lædər] n Leiter f; (BRIT: in tights)
Laufmasche f ♦ vt (BRIT: tights) Laufmaschen
bekommen in +dat

⚠ *Informationen zur Rechtschreibreform Seite 615*

laden ['leɪdn] adj beladen, voll

ladle ['leɪdl] n Schöpfkelle f

lady ['leɪdɪ] n Dame f; (title) Lady f; **young ~** junge Dame; **the ladies' (room)** die Damentoilette; **~bird** (US **~bug**) n Marienkäfer m; **~like** adj damenhaft, vornehm; **~ship** n: **your L~ship** Ihre Ladyschaft

lag [læg] vi (also: **~ behind**) zurückbleiben
♦ vt (pipes) verkleiden

lager ['lɑːgəʳ] n helle(s) Bier nt

lagging ['lægɪŋ] n Isolierung f

lagoon [ləˈguːn] n Lagune f

laid [leɪd] pt, pp of **lay**; **~ back** (inf) adj cool

lain [leɪn] pp of **lie**

lair [leəʳ] n Lager nt

lake [leɪk] n See m

lamb [læm] n Lamm nt; (meat) Lammfleisch nt; **~ chop** n Lammkotelett nt; **~swool** n Lammwolle f

lame [leɪm] adj lahm; (excuse) faul

lament [ləˈment] n Klage f ♦ vt beklagen

laminated ['læmɪneɪtɪd] adj beschichtet

lamp [læmp] n Lampe f; (in street) Straßenlaterne f; **~post** n Laternenpfahl m; **~shade** n Lampenschirm m

lance [lɑːns] n Lanze f; **~ corporal** (BRIT) n Obergefreite(r) m

land [lænd] n Land nt ♦ vi (from ship) an Land gehen; (AVIAT, end up) landen ♦ vt (obtain) kriegen; (passengers) absetzen; (goods) abladen; (troops, space probe) landen; **~fill site** ['lændfɪl-] n Mülldeponie f; **~ing** n Landung f; (on stairs) (Treppen)absatz m; **~ing gear** n Fahrgestell nt; **~ing stage** (BRIT) n Landesteg m; **~ing strip** n Landebahn f; **~lady** n (Haus)wirtin f; **~locked** adj landumschlossen, Binnen-; **~lord** n (of house) Hauswirt m, Besitzer m; (of pub) Gastwirt m; (of area) Grundbesitzer m; **~mark** n Wahrzeichen nt; (fig) Meilenstein m; **~owner** n Grundbesitzer m; **~scape** n Landschaft f; **~scape gardener** n Landschaftsgärtner(in) m(f); **~slide** n (GEOG) Erdrutsch m; (POL) überwältigende(r) Sieg m

lane [leɪn] n (in town) Gasse f; (in country) Weg m; (of motorway) Fahrbahn f, Spur f; (SPORT) Bahn f; **"get in ~"** „bitte einordnen"

language ['læŋgwɪdʒ] n Sprache f; **bad ~** unanständige Ausdrücke pl; **~ laboratory** n Sprachlabor n

languish ['læŋgwɪʃ] vi schmachten

lank [læŋk] adj dürr

lanky ['læŋkɪ] adj schlaksig

lantern ['læntən] n Laterne f

lap [læp] n Schoß m; (SPORT) Runde f ♦ vt (also: **~ up**) auflecken ♦ vi (water) plätschern

lapel [ləˈpel] n Revers nt or m

Lapland ['læplænd] n Lappland nt

lapse [læps] n (moral) Fehltritt m ♦ vi (decline) nachlassen; (expire) ablaufen; (claims) erlöschen; **to ~ into bad habits** sich schlechte Gewohnheiten angewöhnen

laptop (computer) ['læptɔp-] n Laptop(-Computer) m

lard [lɑːd] n Schweineschmalz nt

larder ['lɑːdəʳ] n Speisekammer f

large [lɑːdʒ] adj groß; **at ~** auf freiem Fuß; **~ly** adv zum größten Teil; **~-scale** adj groß angelegt, Groß-

lark [lɑːk] n (bird) Lerche f; (joke) Jux m; **~ about** (inf) vi herumalbern

laryngitis [lærɪnˈdʒaɪtɪs] n Kehlkopfentzündung f

laser ['leɪzəʳ] n Laser m; **~ printer** n Laserdrucker m

lash [læʃ] n Peitschenhieb m; (eye~) Wimper f ♦ vt (rain) schlagen gegen; (whip) peitschen; (bind) festbinden; **~ out** vi (with fists) um sich schlagen

lass [læs] n Mädchen nt

lasso [læˈsuː] n Lasso nt

last [lɑːst] adj letzte(r, s) ♦ adv zuletzt; (~ time) das letztemal ⚠ ♦ vi (continue) dauern; (remain good) sich halten; (money) ausreichen; **at ~** endlich; **~ night** gestern abend; **~ week** letzte Woche; **~ but one** vorletzte(r, s); **~-ditch** adj (attempt) in letzter Minute; **~ing** adj dauerhaft; (shame etc) andauernd; **~ly** adv schließlich;

⚠ *For information on spelling reform see page 615*

~**-minute** *adj* in letzter Minute

latch [lætʃ] *n* Riegel *m*

late [leɪt] *adj* spät; *(dead)* verstorben ♦ *adv* spät; *(after proper time)* zu spät; **to be** ~ zu spät kommen; **of** ~ in letzter Zeit; **in** ~ **May** Ende Mai; ~**comer** *n* Nachzügler(in) *m(f)*; ~**ly** *adv* in letzter Zeit; ~**r** [ˈleɪtə] *adj (date)* später; *(version)* neuer ♦ *adv* später

lateral [ˈlætərəl] *adj* seitlich

latest [ˈleɪtɪst] *adj (fashion)* neueste(r, s) ♦ *n (news)* Neu(e)ste(s) *nt*; **at the** ~ spätestens

lathe [leɪð] *n* Drehbank *f*

lather [ˈlɑːðə] *n* (Seifen)schaum *m* ♦ *vt* einschäumen ♦ *vi* schäumen

Latin [ˈlætɪn] *n* Latein *nt* ♦ *adj* lateinisch; *(Roman)* römisch; ~ **America** *n* Lateinamerika *nt*; ~ **American** *adj* lateinamerikanisch

latitude [ˈlætɪtjuːd] *n (GEOG)* Breite *f*; *(freedom)* Spielraum *m*

latter [ˈlætə] *adj (second of two)* letztere; *(coming at end)* letzte(r, s), später ♦ *n*: **the** ~ der/die/das letztere, die letzteren; ~**ly** *adv* in letzter Zeit

lattice [ˈlætɪs] *n* Gitter *nt*

laudable [ˈlɔːdəbl] *adj* löblich

laugh [lɑːf] *n* Lachen *nt* ♦ *vi* lachen; ~ **at** *vt* lachen über +*acc*; ~ **off** *vt* lachend abtun; ~**able** *adj* lachhaft; ~**ing stock** *n* Zielscheibe *f* des Spottes; ~**ter** *n* Gelächter *nt*

launch [lɔːntʃ] *n (of ship)* Stapellauf *m*; *(of rocket)* Abschuß ⚠ *m*; *(boat)* Barkasse *f*; *(of product)* Einführung *f* ♦ *vt (set afloat)* vom Stapel lassen; *(rocket)* (ab)schießen; *(product)* auf den Markt bringen; ~**(ing) pad** *n* Abschußrampe ⚠ *f*

launder [ˈlɔːndə] *vt* waschen

Launderette [lɔːnˈdret] ® *BRIT)* *n* Waschsalon *m*

Laundromat [ˈlɔːndrəmæt] ® *US)* *n* Waschsalon *m*

laundry [ˈlɔːndrɪ] *n (place)* Wäscherei *f*; *(clothes)* Wäsche *f*; **to do the** ~ waschen

laureate [ˈlɔːrɪət] *adj see* **poet**

laurel [ˈlɔrl] *n* Lorbeer *m*

lava [ˈlɑːvə] *n* Lava *f*

lavatory [ˈlævətərɪ] *n* Toilette *f*

lavender [ˈlævəndə] *n* Lavendel *m*

lavish [ˈlævɪʃ] *adj (extravagant)* verschwenderisch; *(generous)* großzügig ♦ *vt (money)*: **to** ~ **sth on sth** etw auf etw *acc* verschwenden; *(attention, gifts)*: **to** ~ **sth on sb** jdn mit etw überschütten

law [lɔː] *n* Gesetz *nt*; *(system)* Recht *nt*; *(as studies)* Jura *no art*; ~**-abiding** *adj* gesetzestreu; ~ **and order** *n* Recht *nt* und Ordnung *f*; ~ **court** *n* Gerichtshof *m*; ~**ful** *adj* gesetzlich; ~**less** *adj* gesetzlos

lawn [lɔːn] *n* Rasen *m*; ~**mower** *n* Rasenmäher *m*; ~ **tennis** *n* Rasentennis *nt*

law: ~ **school** *n* Rechtsakademie *f*; ~**suit** *n* Prozeß ⚠ *m*; ~**yer** *n* Rechtsanwalt *m*, Rechtsanwältin *f*

lax [læks] *adj (behaviour)* nachlässig; *(standards)* lax

laxative [ˈlæksətɪv] *n* Abführmittel *nt*

lay [leɪ] *(pt, pp* **laid***)* *pt of* **lie** ♦ *adj* Laien- ♦ *vt (place)* legen; *(table)* decken; *(egg)* legen; *(trap)* stellen; *(money)* wetten; ~ **aside** *vt* zurücklegen; ~ **by** *vt (set aside)* beiseite legen; ~ **down** *vt* hinlegen; *(rules)* vorschreiben; *(arms)* strecken; **to** ~ **down the law** Vorschriften machen; ~ **off** *vt (workers)* (vorübergehend) entlassen; ~ **on** *vt (water, gas)* anschließen; *(concert etc)* veranstalten; ~ **out** *vt (her)auslegen; *(money)* ausgeben; *(corpse)* aufbahren; ~ **up** *vt (subj: illness)* ans Bett fesseln; ~**about** *n* Faulenzer *m*; ~**-by** *n (BRIT)* Parkbucht *f*; *(bigger)* Rastplatz *m*

layer [ˈleɪə] *n* Schicht *f*

layman [ˈleɪmən] *(irreg)* *n* Laie *m*

layout [ˈleɪaut] *n* Anlage *f*; *(ART)* Layout *nt*

laze [leɪz] *vi* faulenzen

laziness [ˈleɪzɪnɪs] *n* Faulheit *f*

lazy [ˈleɪzɪ] *adj* faul; *(slow-moving)* träge

lb. *abbr* = **pound** *(weight)*

lead¹ [led] *n (chemical)* Blei *nt*; *(of pencil)* (Bleistift)mine *f* ♦ *adj* bleiern, Blei-

lead² [liːd] *(pt, pp* **led***)* *n (front position)* Führung *f*; *(distance, time ahead)* Vorsprung *f*; *(example)* Vorbild *nt*; *(clue)* Tip ⚠ *m*; *(of police)* Spur *f*; *(THEAT)* Hauptrolle *f*; *(dog's)*

⚠ *Informationen zur Rechtschreibreform Seite 615*

Leine *f* ♦ *vt* (*guide*) führen; (*group etc*) leiten ♦ *vi* (*be first*) führen; **in the ~** (*SPORT, fig*) in Führung; **~ astray** *vt* irreführen; **~ away** *vt* wegführen; (*prisoner*) abführen; **~ back** *vi* zurückführen; **~ on** *vt* anführen; **~ on to** *vt* (*induce*) dazu bringen; **~ to** *vt* (*street*) (hin)führen nach; (*result in*) führen zu; **~ up to** *vt* (*drive*) führen zu; (*speaker etc*) hinführen auf +*acc*

leaded petrol ['lɛdɪd-] *n* verbleites Benzin *nt*

leaden ['lɛdn] *adj* (*sky, sea*) bleiern; (*heavy: footsteps*) bleischwer

leader ['liːdəʳ] *n* Führer *m*, Leiter *m*; (*of party*) Vorsitzende(r) *m*; (*PRESS*) Leitartikel *m*; **~ship** *n* (*office*) Leitung *f*; (*quality*) Führerschaft *f*

lead-free ['lɛdfriː] *adj* (*petrol*) bleifrei

leading ['liːdɪŋ] *adj* führend; **~ lady** *n* (*THEAT*) Hauptdarstellerin *f*; **~ light** *n* (*person*) führende(r) Geist *m*

lead singer [liːd-] *n* Leadsänger(in) *m(f)*

leaf [liːf] (*pl* **leaves**) *n* Blatt *nt* ♦ *vi*: **to ~ through** durchblättern; **to turn over a new ~** einen neuen Anfang machen

leaflet ['liːflɪt] *n* (*advertisement*) Prospekt *m*; (*pamphlet*) Flugblatt *nt*; (*for information*) Merkblatt *nt*

league [liːg] *n* (*union*) Bund *m*; (*SPORT*) Liga *f*; **to be in ~ with** unter einer Decke stecken mit

leak [liːk] *n* undichte Stelle *f*; (*in ship*) Leck *nt* ♦ *vt* (*liquid etc*) durchlassen ♦ *vi* (*pipe etc*) undicht sein; (*liquid etc*) auslaufen; **the information was ~ed to the enemy** die Information wurde dem Feind zugespielt; **~ out** *vi* (*liquid etc*) auslaufen; (*information*) durchsickern; **~y** ['liːkɪ] *adj* undicht

lean [liːn] (*pt, pp* **leaned** *or* **leant**) *adj* mager ♦ *vi* sich neigen ♦ *vt* (*an*)lehnen; **to ~ against sth** an etw *dat* angelehnt sein; sich an etw *acc* anlehnen; **~ back** *vi* sich zurücklehnen; **~ forward** *vi* sich vorbeugen; **to ~ on** *vt fus* sich stützen auf +*acc*; **~ out** *vi* sich hinauslehnen; **~ over** *vi* sich hinüberbeugen; **~ing** *n* Neigung *f* ♦ *adj* schief; **~t** [lɛnt] *pt, pp of* **lean**; **~-to** *n*

Anbau *m*

leap [liːp] (*pt, pp* **leaped** *or* **leapt**) *n* Sprung *m* ♦ *vi* springen; **~frog** *n* Bockspringen *nt*; **~t** [lɛpt] *pt, pp of* **leap**; **~ year** *n* Schaltjahr *nt*

learn [lɜːn] (*pt, pp* **learned** *or* **learnt**) *vt, vi* lernen; (*find out*) erfahren; **to ~ how to do sth** etw (er)lernen; **~ed** ['lɜːnɪd] *adj* gelehrt; **~er** *n* Anfänger(in) *m(f)*; (*AUT: BRIT: also:* **~er driver**) Fahrschüler(in) *m(f)*; **~ing** *n* Gelehrsamkeit *f*; **~t** [lɜːnt] *pt, pp of* **learn**

lease [liːs] *n* (*of property*) Mietvertrag *m* ♦ *vt* pachten

leash [liːʃ] *n* Leine *f*

least [liːst] *adj* geringste(r, s) ♦ *adv* am wenigsten ♦ *n* Mindeste(s) *nt*; **the ~ possible effort** möglichst geringer Aufwand; **at ~** zumindest; **not in the ~!** durchaus nicht!

leather ['lɛðəʳ] *n* Leder *nt*

leave [liːv] (*pt, pp* **left**) *vt* verlassen; (*~ behind*) zurücklassen; (*forget*) vergessen; (*allow to remain*) lassen; (*after death*) hinterlassen; (*entrust*): **to ~ sth to sb** jdm etw überlassen ♦ *vi* weggehen, abfahren; (*for journey*) abreisen; (*bus, train*) abfahren ♦ *n* Erlaubnis *f*; (*MIL*) Urlaub *m*; **to be left** (*remain*) übrigbleiben; **there's some milk left over** es ist noch etwas Milch übrig; **on ~** auf Urlaub; **~ behind** *vt* (*person, object*) dalassen; (*forget*) liegenlassen ⚠, stehenlassen ⚠; **~ out** *vt* auslassen; **~ of absence** *n* Urlaub *m*

leaves [liːvz] *pl of* **leaf**

Lebanon ['lɛbənən] *n* Libanon *m*

lecherous ['lɛtʃərəs] *adj* lüstern

lecture ['lɛktʃəʳ] *n* Vortrag *m*; (*UNIV*) Vorlesung *f* ♦ *vi* einen Vortrag halten; (*UNIV*) lesen ♦ *vt* (*scold*) abkanzeln; **to give a ~ on sth** einen Vortrag über etwas halten; **~r** ['lɛktʃərəʳ] *n* Vortragende(r) *mf*; (*BRIT: UNIV*) Dozent(in) *m(f)*

led [lɛd] *pt, pp of* **lead²**

ledge [lɛdʒ] *n* Leiste *f*; (*window ~*) Sims *m* or *nt*; (*of mountain*) (Fels)vorsprung *m*

ledger ['lɛdʒəʳ] *n* Hauptbuch *nt*

leech [liːtʃ] *n* Blutegel *m*

⚠ *For information on spelling reform see page 615*

leek [liːk] n Lauch m

leer [lɪəʳ] vi: **to ~ (at sb)** (nach jdm) schielen

leeway ['liːweɪ] n (fig): **to have some ~** etwas Spielraum haben

left [left] pt, pp of **leave** ♦ adj linke(r, s) ♦ n (side) linke Seite f ♦ adv links; **on the ~** links; **to the ~** nach links; **the L~** (POL) die Linke f; **~-hand** adj: **~-hand drive** mit Linkssteuerung f; **~-handed** adj linkshändig; **~-hand side** n linke Seite f; **~-luggage locker** n Gepäckschließfach nt; **~-luggage (office)** (BRIT) n Gepäckaufbewahrung f; **~-overs** npl Reste pl; **~-wing** adj linke(r, s)

leg [leg] n Bein nt; (of meat) Keule f; (stage) Etappe f; **1st/2nd ~** (SPORT) 1./2. Etappe

legacy ['legəsɪ] n Erbe nt, Erbschaft f

legal ['liːgl] adj gesetzlich; (allowed) legal; **~ holiday** (US) n gesetzliche(r) Feiertag m; **~ize** vt legalisieren; **~ly** adv gesetzlich; legal; **~ tender** n gesetzliche(s) Zahlungsmittel nt

legend ['ledʒənd] n Legende f; **~ary** adj legendär

leggings ['legɪŋz] npl Leggings pl

legible ['ledʒəbl] adj leserlich

legislation [ledʒɪs'leɪʃən] n Gesetzgebung f; **legislative** ['ledʒɪslətɪv] adj gesetzgebend; **legislature** ['ledʒɪslətʃəʳ] n Legislative f

legitimate [lɪ'dʒɪtɪmət] adj rechtmäßig, legitim; (child) ehelich

legroom ['legruːm] n Platz m für die Beine

leisure ['leʒəʳ] n Freizeit f; **to be at ~** Zeit haben; **~ centre** n Freizeitzentrum nt; **~ly** adj gemächlich

lemon ['lemən] n Zitrone f; (colour) Zitronengelb nt; **~ade** [lemə'neɪd] n Limonade f; **~ tea** n Zitronentee m

lend [lend] (pt, pp **lent**) vt leihen; **to ~ sb sth** jdm etw leihen; **~ing library** n Leihbibliothek f

length [leŋθ] n Länge f; (of road, pipe etc) Strecke f; (of material) Stück nt; **at ~** (lengthily) ausführlich; (at last) schließlich; **~en** vt verlängern ♦ vi länger werden; **~ways** adv längs; **~y** adj sehr lang, langatmig

lenient ['liːnɪənt] adj nachsichtig

lens [lenz] n Linse f; (PHOT) Objektiv nt

Lent [lent] n Fastenzeit f

lent [lent] pt, pp of **lend**

lentil ['lentɪl] n Linse f

Leo ['liːəu] n Löwe m

leotard ['liːətɑːd] n Trikot nt, Gymnastikanzug m

leper ['lepəʳ] n Leprakranke(r) f(m)

leprosy ['leprəsɪ] n Lepra f

lesbian ['lezbɪən] adj lesbisch ♦ n Lesbierin f

less [les] adj, adv weniger ♦ n weniger ♦ pron weniger; **~ than half** weniger als die Hälfte; **~ than ever** weniger denn je; **~ and ~** immer weniger; **the ~ he works** je **~ he works** weniger er arbeitet; **~en** ['lesn] vi abnehmen ♦ vt verringern, verkleinern; **~er** ['lesəʳ] adj kleiner, geringer; **to a ~er extent** in geringerem Maße

lesson ['lesn] n (SCH) Stunde f; (unit of study) Lektion f; (fig) Lehre f; (ECCL) Lesung f; **a maths ~** eine Mathestunde

lest [lest] conj: **~ it happen** damit es nicht passiert

let [let] (pt, pp **let**) vt lassen; (BRIT: lease) vermieten; **to ~ sb do sth** jdn etw tun lassen; **to ~ sb know sth** jdn etw wissen lassen; **~'s go!** gehen wir!; **~ him come** soll er doch kommen; **~ down** vt hinunterlassen; (disappoint) enttäuschen; **~ go** vi loslassen ♦ vt (things) loslassen; (person) gehen lassen; **~ in** vt hereinlassen; (water) durchlassen; **~ off** vt (gun) abfeuern; (steam) ablassen; (forgive) laufen lassen; **~ on** vi durchblicken lassen; (pretend) vorgeben; **~ out** vt herauslassen; (scream) fahren lassen; **~ up** vi nachlassen; (stop) aufhören

lethal ['liːθl] adj tödlich

lethargic [le'θɑːdʒɪk] adj lethargisch

letter ['letəʳ] n (of alphabet) Buchstabe m; (written) Brief m; (of credit) Akkreditiv m; **~ bomb** n Briefbombe f; **~box** (BRIT) n Briefkasten m; **~ing** n Beschriftung f; **~ of credit** n Akkreditiv m

lettuce ['letɪs] n (Kopf)salat m

let-up ['letʌp] (inf) n Nachlassen nt

leukaemia [luː'kiːmɪə] (US **leukemia**) n Leukämie f

level ['levl] *adj* (*ground*) eben; (*at same height*) auf gleicher Höhe; (*equal*) gleich gut; (*head*) kühl ♦ *adv* auf gleicher Höhe ♦ *n* (*instrument*) Wasserwaage *f*; (*altitude*) Höhe *f*; (*flat place*) ebene Fläche *f*; (*position on scale*) Niveau *nt*; (*amount, degree*) Grad *m* ♦ *vt* (*ground*) einebnen; **to draw ~ with** gleichziehen mit; **to be ~ with** auf einer Höhe sein mit; **A ~s** (*BRIT*) ≈ Abitur *nt*; **O ~s** (*BRIT*) ≈ mittlere Reife *f*; **on the ~** (*fig: honest*) ehrlich; **to ~ sth at sb** (*blow*) etw versetzen; (*remark*) etw gegen jdn richten; **~ off** *or* **out** *vi* flach *or* eben werden; (*fig*) sich ausgleichen; (*plane*) horizontal fliegen ♦ *vt* (*ground*) planieren; (*differences*) ausgleichen; **~ crossing** (*BRIT*) *n* Bahnübergang *m*; **~-headed** *adj* vernünftig

lever ['li:və'] *n* Hebel *m*; (*fig*) Druckmittel *nt* ♦ *vt* (hoch)stemmen; **~age** *n* Hebelkraft *f*; (*fig*) Einfluß △ *m*

levy ['levɪ] *n* (*of taxes*) Erhebung *f*; (*tax*) Abgaben *pl*; (*MIL*) Aushebung *f* ♦ *vt* erheben; (*MIL*) ausheben

lewd [lu:d] *adj* unzüchtig, unanständig

liability [laɪə'bɪlətɪ] *n* (*burden*) Belastung *f*; (*duty*) Pflicht *f*; (*debt*) Verpflichtung *f*; (*responsibility*) Haftung *f*; (*proneness*) Anfälligkeit *f*

liable ['laɪəbl] *adj* (*responsible*) haftbar; (*prone*) anfällig; **to be ~ for sth** etw *dat* unterliegen; **it's ~ to happen** es kann leicht vorkommen

liaise [li:'eɪz] *vi*: **to ~ (with sb)** (mit jdm) zusammenarbeiten; **liaison** *n* Verbindung *f*

liar ['laɪə'] *n* Lügner *m*

libel ['laɪbl] *n* Verleumdung *f* ♦ *vt* verleumden

liberal ['lɪbərl] *adj* (*generous*) großzügig; (*open-minded*) aufgeschlossen; (*POL*) liberal

liberate ['lɪbəreɪt] *vt* befreien; **liberation** [lɪbə'reɪʃən] *n* Befreiung *f*

liberty ['lɪbətɪ] *n* Freiheit *f*; (*permission*) Erlaubnis *f*; **to be at ~ to do sth** etw tun dürfen; **to take the ~ of doing sth** sich *dat* erlauben, etw zu tun

Libra ['li:brə] *n* Waage *f*

librarian [laɪ'brɛərɪən] *n* Bibliothekar(in) *m(f)*

library ['laɪbrərɪ] *n* Bibliothek *f*; (*lending ~*) Bücherei *f*

Libya ['lɪbɪə] *n* Libyen *nt*; **~n** *adj* libysch ♦ *n* Libyer(in) *m(f)*

lice [laɪs] *npl of* **louse**

licence ['laɪsns] (*US* **license**) *n* (*permit*) Erlaubnis *f*; (*also*: **driving ~,** (*US*) **driver's license**) Führerschein *m*

license ['laɪsns] *n* (*US*) = **licence** ♦ *vt* genehmigen, konzessionieren; **~d** *adj* (*for alcohol*) konzessioniert (*für den Alkoholausschank*); **~ plate** (*US*) *n* (*AUT*) Nummernschild *nt*

lichen ['laɪkən] *n* Flechte *f*

lick [lɪk] *vt* lecken ♦ *n* Lecken *nt*; **a ~ of paint** ein bißchen Farbe

licorice ['lɪkərɪs] (*US*) *n* = **liquorice**

lid [lɪd] *n* Deckel *m*; (*eye~*) Lid *nt*

lie [laɪ] (*pt* **lay**, *pp* **lain**) *vi* (*rest, be situated*) liegen; (*put o.s. in position*) sich legen; (*pt, pp* **lied**: *tell ~s*) lügen ♦ *n* Lüge *f*; **to ~ low** (*fig*) untertauchen; **~ about** *vi* (*things*) herumliegen; (*people*) faulenzen; **~-down** (*BRIT*) *n*: **to have a ~-down** ein Nickerchen machen; **~-in** (*BRIT*) *n*: **to have a ~-in** sich ausschlafen

lieu [lu:] *n*: **in ~ of** anstatt *+gen*

lieutenant [lɛf'tɛnənt, (*US*) lu:'tɛnənt] *n* Leutnant *m*

life [laɪf] (*pl* **lives**) *n* Leben *nt*; **~ assurance** (*BRIT*) *n* = **life insurance**; **~belt** (*BRIT*) *n* Rettungsring *m*; **~boat** *n* Rettungsboot *nt*; **~guard** *n* Rettungsschwimmer *m*; **~ insurance** *n* Lebensversicherung *f*; **~ jacket** *n* Schwimmweste *f*; **~less** *adj* (*dead*) leblos; (*dull*) langweilig; **~like** *adj* lebenswahr, naturgetreu; **~line** *n* Rettungsleine *f*; (*fig*) Rettungsanker *m*; **~long** *adj* lebenslang; **~ preserver** (*US*) *n* = **lifebelt**; **~-saver** *n* Lebensretter(in) *m(f)*; **~-saving** *adj* lebensrettend, Rettungs-; **~ sentence** *n* lebenslängliche Freiheitsstrafe *f*; **~ span** *n* Lebensspanne *f*; **~style** *n* Lebensstil *m*; **~ support system** *n* (*MED*) Lebenserhaltungssystem *nt*; **~time** *n*: **in his ~time** während er lebte; **once in a**

⚠ For information on spelling reform see page 615

~**time** einmal im Leben

lift [lɪft] *vt* hochheben ♦ *vi* sich heben ♦ *n* (*BRIT: elevator*) Aufzug *m*, Lift *m*; **to give sb a** ~ jdn mitnehmen; ~-**off** *n* Abheben *nt* (vom Boden)

ligament ['lɪgəmənt] *n* Band *nt*

light [laɪt] (*pt, pp* **lighted** *or* **lit**) *n* Licht *nt*; (*for cigarette etc*): **have you got a** ~? haben Sie Feuer? ♦ *vt* beleuchten; (*lamp*) anmachen; (*fire, cigarette*) anzünden ♦ *adj* (*bright*) hell; (*not heavy, easy*) leicht; (*punishment*) milde; (*touch*) leicht; ~**s** *npl* (*AUT*) Beleuchtung *f*; ~ **up** *vi* (*lamp*) angehen; (*face*) aufleuchten ♦ *vt* (*illuminate*) beleuchten; (*lights*) anmachen; ~ **bulb** *n* Glühbirne *f*; ~**en** *vi* (*brighten*) hell werden; (*lightning*) blitzen ♦ *vt* (*give light to*) erhellen; (*hair*) aufhellen; (*gloom*) aufheitern; (*make less heavy*) leichter machen; (*fig*) erleichtern; ~**er** *n* Feuerzeug *nt*; ~-**headed** *adj* (*thoughtless*) leichtsinnig; (*giddy*) schwindlig; ~-**hearted** *adj* leichtherzig, fröhlich; ~**house** *n* Leuchtturm *m*; ~**ing** *n* Beleuchtung *f*; ~**ly** *adv* leicht; (*irresponsibly*) leichtfertig; **to get off** ~**ly** mit einem blauen Auge davonkommen; ~**ness** *f* (*of weight*) Leichtigkeit *f*; (*of colour*) Helle *f*

lightning ['laɪtnɪŋ] *n* Blitz *m*; ~ **conductor** (*US* ~ **rod**) *n* Blitzableiter *m*

light: ~ **pen** *n* Lichtstift *m*; ~**weight** *adj* (*suit*) leicht; ~**weight** *n* (*BOXING*) Leichtgewichtler *m*; ~ **year** *n* Lichtjahr *nt*

like [laɪk] *vt* mögen, gern haben ♦ *prep* wie ♦ *adj* (*similar*) ähnlich; (*equal*) gleich ♦ *n*: **the** ~ dergleichen; **I would** *or* **I'd** ~ ich möchte gern; **would you** ~ **a coffee?** möchten Sie einen Kaffee?; **to be** *or* **look** ~ **sb/sth** jdm/etw ähneln; **that's just** ~ **him** das ist typisch für ihn; **do it** ~ **this** mach es so; **it is nothing** ~ ... es ist nicht zu vergleichen mit ...; **what does it look** ~? wie sieht es aus?; **what does it sound** ~? wie hört es sich an?; **what does it taste** ~? wie schmeckt es?; **his** ~**s and dislikes** was er mag und was er nicht mag; ~**able** *adj* sympathisch

likelihood ['laɪklɪhud] *n* Wahrscheinlichkeit *f*

likely ['laɪklɪ] *adj* wahrscheinlich; **he's** ~ **to leave** er geht möglicherweise; **not** ~! wohl kaum!

likeness ['laɪknɪs] *n* Ähnlichkeit *f*; (*portrait*) Bild *nt*

likewise ['laɪkwaɪz] *adv* ebenso

liking ['laɪkɪŋ] *n* Zuneigung *f*; (*taste*) Vorliebe *f*

lilac ['laɪlək] *n* Flieder *m* ♦ *adj* (*colour*) fliederfarben

lily ['lɪlɪ] *n* Lilie *f*; ~ **of the valley** *n* Maiglöckchen *nt*

limb [lɪm] *n* Glied *nt*

limber up ['lɪmbə'-] *vi* sich auflockern; (*fig*) sich vorbereiten

limbo ['lɪmbəu] *n*: **to be in** ~ (*fig*) in der Schwebe sein

lime [laɪm] *n* (*tree*) Linde *f*; (*fruit*) Limone *f*; (*substance*) Kalk *m*

limelight ['laɪmlaɪt] *n*: **to be in the** ~ (*fig*) im Rampenlicht stehen

limestone ['laɪmstəun] *n* Kalkstein *m*

limit ['lɪmɪt] *n* Grenze *f*; (*inf*) Höhe *f* ♦ *vt* begrenzen, einschränken; ~**ation** [lɪmɪ'teɪʃən] *n* Einschränkung *f*; ~**ed** *adj* beschränkt; **to be** ~**ed to** sich beschränken auf +*acc*; ~**ed** (**liability**) **company** (*BRIT*) *n* Gesellschaft *f* mit beschränkter Haftung

limousine ['lɪməzi:n] *n* Limousine *f*

limp [lɪmp] *n* Hinken *nt* ♦ *vi* hinken ♦ *adj* schlaff

limpet ['lɪmpɪt] *n* (*fig*) Klette *f*

line [laɪn] *n* Linie *f*; (*rope*) Leine *f*; (*on face*) Falte *f*; (*row*) Reihe *f*; (*of hills*) Kette *f*; (*US: queue*) Schlange *f*; (*company*) Linie *f*, Gesellschaft *f*; (*RAIL*) Strecke *f*; (*TEL*) Leitung *f*; (*written*) Zeile *f*; (*direction*) Richtung *f*; (*fig: business*) Branche *f*; (*range of items*) Kollektion *f* ♦ *vt* (*coat*) füttern; (*border*) säumen; ~**s** *npl* (*RAIL*) Gleise *pl*; **in** ~ **with** in Übereinstimmung mit; ~ **up** *vi* sich aufstellen ♦ *vt* aufstellen; (*prepare*) sorgen für; (*support*) mobilisieren; (*surprise*) planen; ~**ar** ['lɪnɪə'] *adj* gerade; (*measure*) Längen-; ~**d** *adj* (*face*) faltig; (*paper*) liniert

linen ['lɪnɪn] *n* Leinen *nt*; (*sheets etc*) Wäsche

⚠ *Informationen zur Rechtschreibreform Seite 615*

f

liner ['laɪnəʳ] n Überseedampfer m

linesman ['laɪnzmən] (irreg) n (SPORT) Linienrichter m

line-up ['laɪnʌp] n Aufstellung f

linger ['lɪŋgəʳ] vi (remain long) verweilen; (taste) (zurück)bleiben; (delay) zögern, verharren

lingerie ['lænʒəriː] n Damenunterwäsche f

lingering ['lɪŋgərɪŋ] adj (doubt) zurückbleibend; (disease) langwierig; (taste) nachhaltend; (look) lang

lingo ['lɪŋgəu] (pl ~es) (inf) n Sprache f

linguist ['lɪŋgwɪst] n Sprachkundige(r) mf; (UNIV) Sprachwissenschaftler(in) m(f); ~ic [lɪŋ'gwɪstɪk] adj sprachlich; sprachwissenschaftlich; ~ics n Sprachwissenschaft f, Linguistik f

lining ['laɪnɪŋ] n Futter nt

link [lɪŋk] n Glied nt; (connection) Verbindung f ♦ vt verbinden; ~s npl (GOLF) Golfplatz m; ~ up vt verbinden ♦ vi zusammenkommen; (companies) sich zusammenschließen; ~-up n (TEL) Verbindung f; (of spaceships) Kopplung f

lino ['laɪnəu] n = linoleum

linoleum [lɪ'nəuliəm] n Linoleum nt

linseed oil ['lɪnsiːd-] n Leinöl nt

lion ['laɪən] n Löwe m; ~ess n Löwin f

lip [lɪp] n Lippe f; (of jug) Schnabel m; to pay ~ service (to) ein Lippenbekenntnis ablegen (zu)

liposuction ['lɪpəusʌkʃən] n Fettabsaugen nt

lip: ~read (irreg) vi von den Lippen ablesen; ~ salve n Lippenbalsam m; ~stick n Lippenstift m

liqueur [lɪ'kjuəʳ] n Likör m

liquid ['lɪkwɪd] n Flüssigkeit f ♦ adj flüssig

liquidate ['lɪkwɪdeɪt] vt liquidieren

liquidize ['lɪkwɪdaɪz] vt (COOK) (im Mixer) pürieren; ~r n ['lɪkwɪdaɪzəʳ] n Mixgerät nt

liquor ['lɪkəʳ] n Alkohol m

liquorice ['lɪkərɪs] (BRIT) n Lakritze f

liquor store (US) n Spirituosengeschäft nt

Lisbon ['lɪzbən] n Lissabon nt

lisp [lɪsp] n Lispeln nt ♦ vt, vi lispeln

list [lɪst] n Liste f, Verzeichnis nt; (of ship) Schlagseite f ♦ vt (write down) eine Liste machen von; (verbally) aufzählen ♦ vi (ship) Schlagseite haben

listen ['lɪsn] vi hören; ~ to vt zuhören +dat; ~er n (Zu)hörer(in) m(f)

listless ['lɪstlɪs] adj lustlos

lit [lɪt] pt, pp of light

liter ['liːtəʳ] (US) n = litre

literacy ['lɪtərəsɪ] n Fähigkeit f zu lesen und zu schreiben

literal ['lɪtərəl] adj buchstäblich; (translation) wortwörtlich; ~ly adv wörtlich; buchstäblich

literary ['lɪtərərɪ] adj literarisch

literate ['lɪtərət] adj des Lesens und Schreibens kundig

literature ['lɪtrɪtʃəʳ] n Literatur f

litigation [lɪtɪ'geɪʃən] n Prozeß ⚠ m

litre ['liːtəʳ] (US liter) n Liter m

litter ['lɪtəʳ] n (rubbish) Abfall m; (of animals) Wurf m ♦ vt in Unordnung bringen; to be ~ed with übersät sein mit; ~ bin (BRIT) n Abfalleimer m

little ['lɪtl] adj klein ♦ adv, n wenig; a ~ ein bißchen; ~ by ~ nach und nach

live¹ [laɪv] adj lebendig; (MIL) scharf; (ELEC) geladen; (broadcast) live

live² [lɪv] vi leben; (dwell) wohnen ♦ vt (life) führen; ~ down vt: I'll never ~ it down das wird man mir nie vergessen; ~ on vi weiterleben ♦ vt fus: to ~ on sth von etw leben; ~ together vi zusammenleben; (share a flat) zusammenwohnen; ~ up to vt (standards) gerecht werden +dat; (principles) anstreben; (hopes) entsprechen +dat

livelihood ['laɪvlɪhud] n Lebensunterhalt m

lively ['laɪvlɪ] adj lebhaft, lebendig

liven up ['laɪvn-] vt beleben

liver ['lɪvəʳ] n (ANAT) Leber f

lives [laɪvz] pl of life

livestock ['laɪvstɔk] n Vieh nt

livid ['lɪvɪd] adj bläulich; (furious) fuchsteufelswild

living ['lɪvɪŋ] n (Lebens)unterhalt m ♦ adj lebendig; (language etc) lebend; to earn or

⚠ For information on spelling reform see page 615

make a ~ sich *dat* seinen Lebensunterhalt verdienen; **~ conditions** *npl* Wohnverhältnisse *pl*; **~ room** *n* Wohnzimmer *nt*; **~ standards** *npl* Lebensstandard *m*; **~ wage** *n* ausreichender Lohn *m*

lizard ['lɪzəd] *n* Eidechse *f*

load [ləʊd] *n* (*burden*) Last *f*; (*amount*) Ladung *f* ♦ *vt* (*also*: **~ up**) (be)laden; (*COMPUT*) laden; (*camera*) Film einlegen in +*acc*; (*gun*) laden; **a ~ of, ~s of** (*fig*) jede Menge; **~ed** *adj* beladen; (*dice*) präpariert; (*question*) Fang-; (*inf*: *rich*) steinreich; **~ing bay** *n* Ladeplatz *m*

loaf [ləʊf] (*pl* **loaves**) *n* Brot *nt* ♦ *vi* (*also*: **~ about, ~ around**) herumlungern, faulenzen

loan [ləʊn] *n* Leihgabe *f*; (*FIN*) Darlehen *nt* ♦ *vt* leihen; **on ~** geliehen

loath [ləʊθ] *adj*: **to be ~ to do sth** etw ungern tun

loathe [ləʊð] *vt* verabscheuen

loaves [ləʊvz] *pl of* **loaf**

lobby ['lɒbɪ] *n* Vorhalle *f*; (*POL*) Lobby *f* ♦ *vt* politisch beeinflussen (wollen)

lobster ['lɒbstə'] *n* Hummer *m*

local ['ləʊkl] *adj* ortsansässig, Orts- ♦ *n* (*pub*) Stammwirtschaft *f*; **the ~s** *npl* (*people*) die Ortsansässigen *pl*; **~ anaesthetic** *n* (*MED*) örtliche Betäubung *f*; **~ authority** *n* städtische Behörden *pl*; **~ call** *n* (*TEL*) Ortsgespräch *nt*; **~ government** *n* Gemeinde-/Kreisverwaltung *f*; **~ity** [ləʊ'kælɪtɪ] *n* Ort *m*; **~ly** *adv* örtlich, am Ort

locate [ləʊ'keɪt] *vt* ausfindig machen; (*establish*) errichten; **location** [ləʊ'keɪʃən] *n* Platz *m*, Lage *f*; **on location** (*CINE*) auf Außenaufnahme

loch [lɒx] (*SCOTTISH*) *n* See *m*

lock [lɒk] *n* Schloß ⚠ *nt*; (*NAUT*) Schleuse *f*; (*of hair*) Locke *f* ♦ *vt* (*fasten*) (ver)schließen ♦ *vi* (*door etc*) sich schließen (lassen); (*wheels*) blockieren; **~ up** *vt* (*criminal, mental patient*) einsperren; (*house*) abschließen

locker ['lɒkə'] *n* Spind *m*

locket ['lɒkɪt] *n* Medaillon *nt*

lock ['lɒk-]: **~out** *n* Aussperrung *f*; **~smith** *n*

Schlosser(in) *m(f)*; **~up** *n* (*jail*) Gefängnis *nt*; (*garage*) Garage *f*

locum ['ləʊkəm] *n* (*MED*) Vertreter(in) *m(f)*

lodge [lɒdʒ] *n* (*gatehouse*) Pförtnerhaus *nt*; (*freemasons'*) Loge *f* ♦ *vi* (*get stuck*) stecken(bleiben) ⚠; (*in Untermiete*): **to ~ (with)** wohnen (bei) ♦ *vt* (*protest*) einreichen; **~r** *n* (Unter)mieter *m*; **lodgings** *n* (Miet)wohnung *f*

loft [lɒft] *n* (Dach)boden *m*

lofty ['lɒftɪ] *adj* hoch(ragend); (*proud*) hochmütig

log [lɒg] *n* Klotz *m*; (*book*) = **logbook**

logbook ['lɒgbʊk] *n* Bordbuch *nt*; (*for lorry*) Fahrtenschreiber *m*; (*AUT*) Kraftfahrzeugbrief *m*

loggerheads ['lɒgəhedz] *npl*: **to be at ~** sich in den Haaren liegen

logic ['lɒdʒɪk] *n* Logik *f*; **~al** *adj* logisch

logistics [lɒ'dʒɪstɪks] *npl* Logistik *f*

logo ['ləʊgəʊ] *n* Firmenzeichen *nt*

loin [lɔɪn] *n* Lende *f*

loiter ['lɔɪtə'] *vi* herumstehen

loll [lɒl] *vi* (*also*: **~ about**) sich rekeln

lollipop ['lɒlɪpɒp] *n* (Dauer)lutscher *m*; **~ man/lady** (*irreg*) (*BRIT*) *n* ≈ Schülerlotse *m*

LOLLIPOP MAN/LADY

ⓘ **Lollipop man/lady** heißen in Großbritannien die Männer bzw. Frauen, die mit Hilfe eines runden Stoppschildes den Verkehr anhalten, damit Schulkinder die Straße gefahrlos überqueren können. Der Name bezieht sich auf die Form des Schildes, die an einen Lutscher erinnert.

---

lolly ['lɒlɪ] (*inf*) *n* (*sweet*) Lutscher *m*

London ['lʌndən] *n* London *nt*; **~er** *n* Londoner(in) *m(f)*

lone [ləʊn] *adj* einsam

loneliness ['ləʊnlɪnɪs] *n* Einsamkeit *f*

lonely ['ləʊnlɪ] *adj* einsam

loner ['ləʊnə'] *n* Einzelgänger(in) *m(f)*

long [lɒŋ] *adj* lang; (*distance*) weit ♦ *adv* lange ♦ *vi*: **to ~ for** sich sehnen nach; **before ~** bald; **as ~ as** solange; **in the ~**

⚠ *Informationen zur Rechtschreibreform Seite 615*

run auf die Dauer; **don't be ~!** beeil dich!; **how ~ is the street?** wie lang ist die Straße?; **how ~ is the lesson?** wie lange dauert die Stunde?; **6 metres ~** 6 Meter lang; **6 months ~** 6 Monate lang; **all night ~** die ganze Nacht; **he no ~er comes** er kommt nicht mehr; **~ ago** vor langer Zeit; **~ before** lange vorher; **at ~ last** endlich; **~-distance** adj Fern-

longevity [lɔnˈdʒevɪtɪ] n Langlebigkeit f

long: **~-haired** adj langhaarig; **~hand** n Langschrift f; **~ing** n Sehnsucht f ♦ adj sehnsüchtig

longitude [ˈlɔŋgɪtjuːd] n Längengrad m

long: **~ jump** n Weitsprung m; **~-life** adj (batteries etc) mit langer Lebensdauer; **~-lost** adj längst verloren geglaubt; **~-playing record** n Langspielplatte f; **~-range** adj Langstrecken-, Fern-; **~-sighted** adj weitsichtig; **~-standing** adj alt, seit langer Zeit bestehend; **~-suffering** adj schwer geprüft; **~-term** adj langfristig; **~ wave** n Langwelle f; **~-winded** adj langatmig

loo [luː] (BRIT: inf) n Klo nt

look [luk] vi schauen; (seem) aussehen; (building etc): **to ~ on to the sea** aufs Meer gehen ♦ n Blick m; **~s** npl (appearance) Aussehen nt; **~ after** vt (care for) sorgen für; (watch) aufpassen auf +acc; **~ at** vt ansehen; (consider) sich überlegen; **~ back** vi sich umsehen; (fig) zurückblicken; **~ down on** vt (fig) herabsehen auf +acc; **~ for** vt (seek) suchen; **~ forward to** vt sich freuen auf +acc; (in letters): **we ~ forward to hearing from you** wir hoffen, bald von Ihnen zu hören; **~ into** vt untersuchen; **~ on** vi zusehen; **~ out** vi hinaussehen; (take care) aufpassen; **~ out for** vt Ausschau halten nach; (be careful) achtgeben ⚠ auf +acc; **~ round** vi sich umsehen; **~ to** vt (take care of) achtgeben ⚠ auf +acc; (rely on) sich verlassen auf +acc; **~ up** vi aufblicken; (improve) sich bessern ♦ vt (word) nachschlagen; (person) besuchen; **~ up to** vt aufsehen zu; **~out** n (watch) Ausschau f; (person) Wachposten m;

(place) Ausguck m; (prospect) Aussichten pl; **to be on the ~out for sth** nach etw Ausschau halten

loom [luːm] n Webstuhl m ♦ vi sich abzeichnen

loony [ˈluːnɪ] (inf) n Verrückte(r) mf

loop [luːp] n Schlaufe f; **~hole** n (fig) Hintertürchen nt

loose [luːs] adj lose, locker; (free) frei; (inexact) unpräzise ♦ vt lösen, losbinden; **~ change** n Kleingeld nt; **~ chippings** npl (on road) Rollsplit m; **~ end** n: **to be at a ~ end** (BRIT) or **at ~ ends** (US) nicht wissen, was man tun soll; **~ly** adv locker, lose; **~n** vt lockern, losmachen

loot [luːt] n Beute f ♦ vt plündern

lop off [lɔp-] vt abhacken

lopsided [ˈlɔpˈsaɪdɪd] adj schief

lord [lɔːd] n (ruler) Herr m; (BRIT: title) Lord m; **the L~** (God) der Herr; **the (House of) L~s** das Oberhaus; **~ship** n: **Your L~ship** Eure Lordschaft

lorry [ˈlɔrɪ] (BRIT) n Lastwagen m; **~ driver** (BRIT) n Lastwagenfahrer(in) m(f)

lose [luːz] (pt, pp **lost**) vt verlieren; (chance) verpassen ♦ vi verlieren; **to ~ (time)** (clock) nachgehen; **~r** n Verlierer m

loss [lɔs] n Verlust m; **at a ~** (COMM) mit Verlust; (unable) außerstande ⚠

lost [lɔst] pt, pp of **lose** ♦ adj verloren; **~ property** (US **~ and found**) n Fundsachen pl

lot [lɔt] n (quantity) Menge f; (fate, at auction) Los nt; (inf: people, things) Haufen m; **the ~** alles; (people) alle; **a ~ of** (with sg) viel; (with pl) viele; **~s of** massenhaft, viel(e); **I read a ~** ich lese viel; **to draw ~s for sth** etw verlosen

lotion [ˈləuʃən] n Lotion f

lottery [ˈlɔtərɪ] n Lotterie f

loud [laud] adj laut; (showy) schreiend ♦ adv laut; **~ly** adv laut; **~speaker** n Lautsprecher m

lounge [laundʒ] n (in hotel) Gesellschaftsraum m; (in house) Wohnzimmer nt ♦ vi sich herumlümmeln

louse [laus] (pl **lice**) n Laus f

lousy [ˈlauzɪ] adj (fig) miserabel

⚠ For information on spelling reform see page 615

lout [laut] *n* Lümmel *m*

louvre ['luːvəʳ] (*US* **louver**) *adj* (*door, window*) Jalousie-

lovable ['lʌvəbl] *adj* liebenswert

love [lʌv] *n* Liebe *f*; (*person*) Liebling *m*; (*SPORT*) null ♦ *vt* (*person*) lieben; (*activity*) gerne mögen; **to be in ~ with sb** in jdn verliebt sein; **to make ~** sich lieben; **for the ~ of** aus Liebe zu; **"15 ~"** (*TENNIS*) „15 null"; **to ~ to do sth** etw (sehr) gerne tun; **~ affair** *n* (Liebes)verhältnis *nt*; **~ letter** *n* Liebesbrief *m*; **~ life** *n* Liebesleben *nt*

lovely ['lʌvlɪ] *adj* schön

lover ['lʌvəʳ] *n* Liebhaber(in) *m(f)*

loving ['lʌvɪŋ] *adj* liebend, liebevoll

low [ləu] *adj* niedrig; (*rank*) niedere(r, s); (*level, note, neckline*) tief; (*intelligence, density*) gering; (*vulgar*) ordinär; (*not loud*) leise; (*depressed*) gedrückt ♦ *adv* (*not high*) niedrig; (*not loudly*) leise ♦ *n* (~ *point*) Tiefstand *m*; (*MET*) Tief *nt*; **to feel ~** sich mies fühlen; **to turn (down) ~** leiser stellen; **~ alcohol** *adj* alkoholarm; **~-calorie** *adj* kalorienarm; **~-cut** *adj* (*dress*) tiefausgeschnitten ⚠; **~er** *vt* herunterlassen; (*eyes, gun*) senken; (*reduce*) herabsetzen, senken ♦ *vr*: **to ~er o.s. to** (*fig*) sich herablassen zu; **~er sixth** (*BRIT*) *n* (*SCOL*) ≈ zwölfte Klasse; **~-fat** *adj* fettarm, Mager-; **~lands** *npl* (*GEOG*) Flachland *nt*; **~ly** *adj* bescheiden; **~-lying** *adj* tiefgelegen

loyal ['lɔɪəl] *adj* treu; **~ty** *n* Treue *f*

lozenge ['lɒzɪndʒ] *n* Pastille *f*

L.P. *n abbr* = **long-playing record**

L-plates ['ɛlpleɪts] (*BRIT*) *npl* L-Schild *nt*

L-PLATES

ⓘ Als **L-Plates** werden in Großbritannien die weißen Schilder mit einem roten „L" bezeichnet, die vorne und hinten an jedem von einem Fahrschüler geführten Fahrzeug befestigt werden müssen. Fahrschüler müssen einen vorläufigen Führerschein beantragen und dürfen damit unter der Aufsicht eines erfahrenen Autofahrers auf allen Straßen außer Autobahnen fahren.

Ltd *abbr* (= *limited company*) GmbH

lubricant ['luːbrɪkənt] *n* Schmiermittel *nt*

lubricate ['luːbrɪkeɪt] *vt* schmieren

lucid ['luːsɪd] *adj* klar; (*sane*) bei klarem Verstand; (*moment*) licht

luck [lʌk] *n* Glück *nt*; **bad** *or* **hard** *or* **tough ~!** (so ein) Pech!; **good ~!** viel Glück!; **~ily** *adv* glücklicherweise, zum Glück; **~y** *adj* Glücks-; **to be ~y** Glück haben

lucrative ['luːkrətɪv] *adj* einträglich

ludicrous ['luːdɪkrəs] *adj* grotesk

lug [lʌg] *vt* schleppen

luggage ['lʌgɪdʒ] *n* Gepäck *nt*; **~ rack** *n* Gepäcknetz *nt*

lukewarm ['luːkwɔːm] *adj* lauwarm; (*indifferent*) lau

lull [lʌl] *n* Flaute *f* ♦ *vt* einlullen; (*calm*) beruhigen

lullaby ['lʌləbaɪ] *n* Schlaflied *nt*

lumbago [lʌm'beɪgəu] *n* Hexenschuß ⚠ *m*

lumber ['lʌmbəʳ] *n* Plunder *m*; (*wood*) Holz *nt*; **~jack** *n* Holzfäller *m*

luminous ['luːmɪnəs] *adj* Leucht-

lump [lʌmp] *n* Klumpen *m*; (*MED*) Schwellung *f*; (*in breast*) Knoten *m*; (*of sugar*) Stück *nt* ♦ *vt* (*also:* **~ together**) zusammentun; (*judge together*) in einen Topf werfen; **~ sum** *n* Pauschalsumme *f*; **~y** *adj* klumpig

lunacy ['luːnəsɪ] *n* Irrsinn *m*

lunar ['luːnəʳ] *adj* Mond-

lunatic ['luːnətɪk] *n* Wahnsinnige(r) *mf* ♦ *adj* wahnsinnig, irr

lunch. [lʌntʃ] *n* Mittagessen *nt*; **~eon** ['lʌntʃən] *n* Mittagessen *nt*; **~eon meat** *n* Frühstücksfleisch *nt*; **~eon voucher** (*BRIT*) *n* Essensmarke *f*; **~time** *n* Mittagszeit *f*

lung [lʌŋ] *n* Lunge *f*

lunge [lʌndʒ] *vi* (*also:* **~ forward**) (los)stürzen; **to ~ at** sich stürzen auf +*acc*

lurch [ləːtʃ] *vi* taumeln; (*NAUT*) schlingern ♦ *n* Ruck *m*; (*NAUT*) Schlingern *nt*; **to leave sb in the ~** jdn im Stich lassen

lure [luəʳ] *n* Köder *m*; (*fig*) Lockung *f* ♦ *vt* (ver)locken

lurid ['luərɪd] *adj* (*shocking*) grausig,

⚠ *Informationen zur Rechtschreibreform Seite 615*

widerlich; (*colour*) grell

lurk [lə:k] *vi* lauern

luscious ['lʌʃəs] *adj* köstlich

lush [lʌʃ] *adj* satt; (*vegetation*) üppig

lust [lʌst] *n* Wollust *f*; (*greed*) Gier *f* ♦ *vi*: **to ~ after** gieren nach

lustre ['lʌstər] (*US* **luster**) *n* Glanz *m*

Luxembourg ['lʌksəmbə:g] *n* Luxemburg *nt*

luxuriant [lʌg'zjuəriənt] *adj* üppig

luxurious [lʌg'zjuəriəs] *adj* luxuriös, Luxus-

luxury ['lʌkʃəri] *n* Luxus *m* ♦ *cpd* Luxus-

lying ['laiŋ] *n* Lügen *nt* ♦ *adj* verlogen

lynx [liŋks] *n* Luchs *m*

lyric ['lirik] *n* Lyrik *f* ♦ *adj* lyrisch; **~s** *pl* (*words for song*) (Lied)text *m*; **~al** *adj* lyrisch, gefühlvoll

M, m

m *abbr* = **metre**; **mile**; **million**

M.A. *n abbr* = **Master of Arts**

mac [mæk] (*BRIT: inf*) *n* Regenmantel *m*

macaroni [mækə'rəuni] *n* Makkaroni *pl*

machine [mə'ʃi:n] *n* Maschine *f* ♦ *vt* (*dress etc*) mit der Maschine nähen; **~ gun** *n* Maschinengewehr *nt*; **~ language** *n* (*COMPUT*) Maschinensprache *f*; **~ry** *n* Maschinerie *f*

macho ['mætʃəu] *adj* macho

mackerel ['mækrl] *n* Makrele *f*

mackintosh ['mækintɔʃ] (*BRIT*) *n* Regenmantel *m*

mad [mæd] *adj* verrückt; (*dog*) tollwütig; (*angry*) wütend; **~ about** (*fond of*) verrückt nach, versessen auf +*acc*

madam ['mædəm] *n* gnädige Frau *f*

madden ['mædn] *vt* verrückt machen; (*make angry*) ärgern

made [meid] *pt, pp of* **make**

made-to-measure ['meidtə'mɛʒə] (*BRIT*) *adj* Maß-

mad [mæd-]: **~ly** *adv* wahnsinnig; **~man** (*irreg*) *n* Verrückte(r) *m*, Irre(r) *m*; **~ness** *n* Wahnsinn *m*

magazine [mægə'zi:n] *n* Zeitschrift *f*; (*in gun*) Magazin *nt*

maggot ['mægət] *n* Made *f*

magic ['mædʒik] *n* Zauberei *f*, Magie *f*; (*fig*) Zauber *m* ♦ *adj* magisch, Zauber-; **~al** *adj* magisch; **~ian** [mə'dʒiʃən] *n* Zauberer *m*

magistrate ['mædʒistreit] *n* (Friedens)richter *m*

magnanimous [mæg'næniməs] *adj* großmütig

magnet ['mægnit] *n* Magnet *m*; **~ic** [mæg'netik] *adj* magnetisch; **~ic tape** *n* Magnetband *nt*; **~ism** *n* Magnetismus *m*; (*fig*) Ausstrahlungskraft *f*

magnificent [mæg'nifisnt] *adj* großartig

magnify ['mægnifai] *vt* vergrößern; **~ing glass** *n* Lupe *f*

magnitude ['mægnitju:d] *n* (*size*) Größe *f*; (*importance*) Ausmaß *nt*

magpie ['mægpai] *n* Elster *f*

mahogany [mə'hɔgəni] *n* Mahagoni *nt* ♦ *cpd* Mahagoni-

maid [meid] *n* Dienstmädchen *nt*; **old ~** alte Jungfer *f*

maiden ['meidn] *n* Maid *f* ♦ *adj* (*flight, speech*) Jungfern-; **~ name** *n* Mädchenname *m*

mail [meil] *n* Post *f* ♦ *vt* aufgeben; **~ box** (*US*) *n* Briefkasten *m*; **~ing list** *n* Anschreibeliste *f*; **~ order** *n* Bestellung *f* durch die Post; **~ order firm** *n* Versandhaus *nt*

maim [meim] *vt* verstümmeln

main [mein] *adj* hauptsächlich, Haupt- ♦ *n* (*pipe*) Hauptleitung *f*; **the ~s** *npl* (*ELEC*) das Stromnetz; **in the ~** im großen und ganzen; **~frame** *n* (*COMPUT*) Großrechner *m*; **~land** *n* Festland *nt*; **~ly** *adv* hauptsächlich; **~ road** *n* Hauptstraße *f*; **~stay** *n* (*fig*) Hauptstütze *f*; **~stream** *n* Hauptrichtung *f*

maintain [mein'tein] *vt* (*machine, roads*) instand halten; (*support*) unterhalten; (*keep up*) aufrechterhalten; (*claim*) behaupten; (*innocence*) beteuern

maintenance ['meintənəns] *n* (*TECH*) Wartung *f*; (*of family*) Unterhalt *m*

maize [meiz] *n* Mais *m*

⚠ *For information on spelling reform see page 615*

majestic [məˈdʒestɪk] *adj* majestätisch

majesty [ˈmædʒɪstɪ] *n* Majestät *f*

major [ˈmeɪdʒəʳ] *n* Major *m* ♦ *adj* (*MUS*) Dur; (*more important*) Haupt-; (*bigger*) größer

Majorca [məˈjɔːkə] *n* Mallorca *nt*

majority [məˈdʒɒrɪtɪ] *n* Mehrheit *f*; (*JUR*) Volljährigkeit *f*

make [meɪk] (*pt, pp* **made**) *vt* machen; (*appoint*) ernennen (zu); (*cause to do sth*) veranlassen; (*reach*) erreichen; (*in time*) schaffen; (*earn*) verdienen ♦ *n* Marke *f*; **to ~ sth happen** etw geschehen lassen; **to ~ it** es schaffen; **what time do you ~ it?** wie spät hast du es?; **to ~ do with** auskommen mit; **~ for** *vi* gehen/fahren nach; **~ out** *vt* (*write out*) ausstellen; (*understand*) verstehen; **~ up** *vt* machen; (*face*) schminken; (*quarrel*) beilegen; (*story etc*) erfinden ♦ *vi* sich versöhnen; **~ up for** *vt* wiedergutmachen △; (*COMM*) vergüten; **~-believe** *n* Phantasie △ *f*; **~r** *n* (*COMM*) Hersteller *m*; **~shift** *adj* behelfsmäßig, Not-; **~-up** *n* Schminke *f*, Make-up *nt*; **~-up remover** *n* Make-up-Entferner *m*; **making** *n*: **in the making** im Entstehen; **to have the makings of** das Zeug haben zu

malaria [məˈleərɪə] *n* Malaria *f*

Malaysia [məˈleɪzɪə] *n* Malaysia *nt*

male [meɪl] *n* Mann *m*; (*animal*) Männchen *nt* ♦ *adj* männlich

malevolent [məˈlevələnt] *adj* übelwollend △

malfunction [mælˈfʌŋkʃən] *n* (*MED*) Funktionsstörung *f*; (*of machine*) Defekt *m*

malice [ˈmælɪs] *n* Bosheit *f*; **malicious** [məˈlɪʃəs] *adj* böswillig, gehässig

malign [məˈlaɪn] *vt* verleumden ♦ *adj* böse

malignant [məˈlɪgnənt] *adj* bösartig

mall [mɔːl] *n* (*also:* **shopping ~**) Einkaufszentrum *nt*

malleable [ˈmælɪəbl] *adj* formbar

mallet [ˈmælɪt] *n* Holzhammer *m*

malnutrition [mælnjuːˈtrɪʃən] *n* Unterernährung *f*

malpractice [mælˈpræktɪs] *n* Amtsvergehen *nt*

malt [mɔːlt] *n* Malz *nt*

Malta [ˈmɔːltə] *n* Malta *nt*; **Maltese** [mɔːlˈtiːz] *adj inv* maltesisch ♦ *n inv* Malteser(in) *m(f)*

maltreat [mælˈtriːt] *vt* mißhandeln △

mammal [ˈmæml] *n* Säugetier *nt*

mammoth [ˈmæməθ] *n* Mammut *nt* ♦ *adj* Mammut-

man [mæn] (*pl* **men**) *n* Mann *m*; (*human race*) der Mensch, die Menschen *pl* ♦ *vt* bemannen; **an old ~** ein alter Mann, ein Greis *m*; **~ and wife** Mann und Frau

manage [ˈmænɪdʒ] *vi* zurechtkommen ♦ *vt* (*control*) führen, leiten; (*cope with*) fertigwerden △ mit; **~able** *adj* (*person, animal*) fügsam; (*object*) handlich; **~ment** *n* (*control*) Führung *f*, Leitung *f*; (*directors*) Management *nt*; **~r** *n* Geschäftsführer *m*; **~ress** [mænɪdʒəˈres] *n* Geschäftsführerin *f*; **~rial** [mænɪˈdʒɪərɪəl] *adj* (*post*) leitend; (*problem etc*) Management-; **managing** [ˈmænɪdʒɪŋ] *adj*: **managing director** Betriebsleiter *m*

mandarin [ˈmændərɪn] *n* (*fruit*) Mandarine *f*

mandatory [ˈmændətərɪ] *adj* obligatorisch

mane [meɪn] *n* Mähne *f*

maneuver [məˈnuːvəʳ] (*US*) = **manoeuvre**

manfully [ˈmænfəlɪ] *adv* mannhaft

mangle [ˈmæŋgl] *vt* verstümmeln ♦ *n* Mangel *f*

mango [ˈmæŋgəʊ] (*pl* **~es**) *n* Mango(pflaume) *f*

mangy [ˈmeɪndʒɪ] *adj* (*dog*) räudig

man [mæn-]: **~handle** *vt* grob behandeln; **~hole** *n* (*in street*) Schacht *m*; **~hood** *n* Mannesalter *nt*; **~-hour** *n* Arbeitsstunde *f*; **~hunt** *n* Fahndung *f*

mania [ˈmeɪnɪə] *n* Manie *f*; **~c** [ˈmeɪnɪæk] *n* Wahnsinnige(r) *mf*

manic [ˈmænɪk] *adj* (*behaviour, activity*) hektisch

manicure [ˈmænɪkjʊəʳ] *n* Maniküre *f*; **~ set** *n* Necessaire △ *nt*

manifest [ˈmænɪfest] *vt* offenbaren ♦ *adj* offenkundig; **~ation** [mænɪfesˈteɪʃən] *n* (*sign*) Anzeichen *nt*

manifesto [mænɪˈfestəʊ] *n* Manifest *nt*

manipulate [məˈnɪpjʊleɪt] *vt* handhaben;

△ *Informationen zur Rechtschreibreform Seite 615*

(fig) manipulieren

man [mæn'-]: **~kind** n Menschheit f; **~ly** ['mænlɪ] adj männlich; mannhaft; **~-made** adj *(fibre)* künstlich

manner ['mænə*] n Art f, Weise f; **~s** npl *(behaviour)* Manieren pl; **in a ~ of speaking** sozusagen; **~ism** n *(of person)* Angewohnheit f; *(of style)* Manieriertheit f

manoeuvre [mə'nu:və*] *(US* **maneuver**) vt, vi manövrieren ♦ n *(MIL)* Feldzug m; *(general)* Manöver nt, Schachzug m

manor ['mænə*] n Landgut nt

manpower ['mænpauə*] n Arbeitskräfte pl

mansion ['mænʃən] n Villa f

manslaughter ['mænslɔ:tə*] n Totschlag m

mantelpiece ['mæntlpi:s] n Kaminsims m

manual ['mænjuəl] adj manuell, Hand- ♦ n Handbuch nt

manufacture [mænju'fæktʃə*] vt herstellen ♦ n Herstellung f; **~r** n Hersteller m

manure [mə'njuə*] n Dünger m

manuscript ['mænjuskrɪpt] n Manuskript nt

Manx [mæŋks] adj der Insel Man

many ['menɪ] adj, pron viele; **a great ~** sehr viele; **~ a time** ein …

map [mæp] n *(Land)karte f; *(of town)* Stadtplan m ♦ vt eine Karte machen von; **~ out** vt *(fig)* ausarbeiten

maple ['meɪpl] n Ahorn m

mar [mɑ:*] vt verderben

marathon ['mærəθən] n *(SPORT)* Marathonlauf m; *(fig)* Marathon m

marble ['mɑ:bl] n Marmor m; *(for game)* Murmel f

March [mɑ:tʃ] n März m

march [mɑ:tʃ] vi marschieren ♦ n Marsch m

mare [meə*] n Stute f

margarine [mɑ:dʒə'ri:n] n Margarine f

margin ['mɑ:dʒɪn] n Rand m; *(extra amount)* Spielraum m; *(COMM)* Spanne f; **~al** adj *(note)* Rand-; *(difference etc)* geringfügig; **~al (seat)** n *(POL)* Wahlkreis, der nur mit knapper Mehrheit gehalten wird

marigold ['mærɪgəuld] n Ringelblume f

marijuana [mærɪ'wɑ:nə] n Marihuana nt

marina [mə'ri:nə] n Yachthafen m

marinate ['mærɪneɪt] vt marinieren

marine [mə'ri:n] adj Meeres-, See- ♦ n *(MIL)* Marineinfanterist m

marital ['mærɪtl] adj ehelich, Ehe-; **~ status** n Familienstand m

maritime ['mærɪtaɪm] adj See-

mark [mɑ:k] n *(coin)* Mark f; *(spot)* Fleck m; *(scar)* Kratzer m; *(sign)* Zeichen nt; *(target)* Ziel nt; *(SCH)* Note f ♦ vt *(make ~ on)* Flecken/Kratzer machen auf +acc; *(indicate)* markieren; *(exam)* korrigieren; **to ~ time** *(also fig)* auf der Stelle treten; **~ out** vt bestimmen; *(area)* abstecken; **~ed** adj deutlich; **~er** n *(in book)* (Lese)zeichen nt; *(on road)* Schild nt

market ['mɑ:kɪt] n Markt m; *(stock ~)* Börse f ♦ vt *(COMM: new product)* auf den Markt bringen; *(sell)* vertreiben; **~ garden** *(BRIT)* n Handelsgärtnerei f; **~ing** n Marketing nt; **~ research** n Marktforschung f; **~ value** n Marktwert m

marksman ['mɑ:ksmən] *(irreg)* n Scharfschütze m

marmalade ['mɑ:məleɪd] n Orangenmarmelade f

maroon [mə'ru:n] vt aussetzen ♦ adj *(colour)* kastanienbraun

marquee [mɑ:'ki:] n große(s) Zelt nt

marriage ['mærɪdʒ] n Ehe f; *(wedding)* Heirat f; **~ bureau** n Heiratsinstitut nt; **~ certificate** n Heiratsurkunde f

married ['mærɪd] adj *(person)* verheiratet; *(couple, life)* Ehe-

marrow ['mærəu] n *(Knochen)mark nt; *(BOT)* Kürbis m

marry ['mærɪ] vt *(join)* trauen; *(take as husband, wife)* heiraten ♦ vi *(also:* **get married)** heiraten

marsh [mɑ:ʃ] n Sumpf m

marshal ['mɑ:ʃl] n *(US)* Bezirkspolizeichef m ♦ vt (an)ordnen, arrangieren

marshy ['mɑ:ʃɪ] adj sumpfig

martial law ['mɑ:ʃl-] n Kriegsrecht nt

martyr ['mɑ:tə*] n *(also fig)* Märtyrer(in) m(f) ♦ vt zum Märtyrer machen; **~dom** n Martyrium nt

marvel ['mɑ:vl] n Wunder nt ♦ vi: **to ~ (at)** sich wundern (über +acc); **~lous** *(US*

⚠ *For information on spelling reform see page 615*

marvelous) adj wunderbar

Marxist ['mɑːksɪst] n Marxist(in) m(f)

marzipan ['mɑːzɪpæn] n Marzipan nt

mascara [mæs'kɑːrə] n Wimperntusche f

mascot ['mæskət] n Maskottchen nt

masculine ['mæskjulɪn] adj männlich

mash [mæʃ] n Brei m; **~ed potatoes** npl Kartoffelbrei m or -püree nt

mask [mɑːsk] n (also fig) Maske f ♦ vt maskieren, verdecken

mason ['meɪsn] n (stone~) Steinmetz m; (free~) Freimaurer m; **~ry** n Mauerwerk nt

masquerade [mæskə'reɪd] n Maskerade f ♦ vi: **to ~ as** sich ausgeben als

mass [mæs] n Masse f; (greater part) Mehrheit f; (REL) Messe f ♦ vi sich sammeln; **the ~es** npl (people) die Masse(n) f(pl)

massacre ['mæsəkər] n Blutbad nt ♦ vt niedermetzeln, massakrieren

massage ['mæsɑːʒ] n Massage f ♦ vt massieren

massive ['mæsɪv] adj gewaltig, massiv

mass media npl Massenmedien pl

mass production n Massenproduktion f

mast [mɑːst] n Mast m

master ['mɑːstər] n Herr m; (NAUT) Kapitän m; (teacher) Lehrer m; (artist) Meister m ♦ vt meistern; (language etc) beherrschen; **~ly** adj meisterhaft; **~mind** n Kapazität f ♦ vt geschickt lenken; **M~ of Arts** n Magister m der philosophischen Fakultät; **M~ of Science** n Magister m der naturwissenschaftlichen Fakultät; **~piece** n Meisterwerk nt; **~ plan** n kluge(r) Plan m; **~y** n Können n

masturbate ['mæstəbeɪt] vi masturbieren, onanieren

mat [mæt] n Matte f; (for table) Untersetzer m ♦ adj = **matt**

match [mætʃ] n Streichholz nt; (sth corresponding) Pendant nt; (SPORT) Wettkampf m; (ball games) Spiel nt ♦ vt (be like, suit) passen zu; (equal) gleichkommen +dat ♦ vi zusammenpassen; **it's a good ~ (for)** es paßt gut (zu); **~box** n Streichholzschachtel f; **~ing** adj passend

mate [meɪt] n (companion) Kamerad m;

(spouse) Lebensgefährte m; (of animal) Weibchen nt/Männchen nt; (NAUT) Schiffsoffizier m ♦ vi (animals) sich paaren ♦ vt (animals) paaren

material [mə'tɪərɪəl] n Material nt; (for book, cloth) Stoff m ♦ adj (important) wesentlich; (damage) Sach-; (comforts etc) materiell; **~s** npl (for building etc) Materialien pl; **~istic** [mətɪərɪə'lɪstɪk] adj materialistisch; **~ize** vi sich verwirklichen, zustande ⚠ kommen

maternal [mə'tɜːnl] adj mütterlich, Mutter-

maternity [mə'tɜːnɪtɪ] adj (dress) Umstands-; (benefit) Wochen-; **~ hospital** n Entbindungsheim nt

math [mæθ] n (US) n = **maths**

mathematical [mæθə'mætɪkl] adj mathematisch; **mathematics** n Mathematik f; **maths** (US **math**) n Mathe f

matinée ['mætɪneɪ] n Matinee f

matrices ['meɪtrɪsiːz] npl of **matrix**

matriculation [mətrɪkju'leɪʃən] n Immatrikulation f

matrimonial [mætrɪ'məunɪəl] adj ehelich, Ehe-

matrimony ['mætrɪmənɪ] n Ehestand m

matrix ['meɪtrɪks] (pl **matrices**) n Matrize f; (GEOL etc) Matrix f

matron ['meɪtrən] n (MED) Oberin f; (SCH) Hausmutter f

matt [mæt] adj (paint) matt

matted ['mætɪd] adj verfilzt

matter ['mætər] n (substance) Materie f; (affair) Angelegenheit f ♦ vi darauf ankommen; **no ~ how/what** egal wie/was; **what is the ~?** was ist los?; **as a ~ of course** selbstverständlich; **as a ~ of fact** eigentlich; **it doesn't ~** es macht nichts; **~-of-fact** adj sachlich, nüchtern

mattress ['mætrɪs] n Matratze f

mature [mə'tjuər] adj reif ♦ vi reif werden; **maturity** [mə'tjuərɪtɪ] n Reife f

maul [mɔːl] vt übel zurichten

maxima ['mæksɪmə] npl of **maximum**

maximum ['mæksɪməm] (pl **maxima**) adj Höchst-, Maximal- ♦ n Maximum nt

May [meɪ] n Mai m

may [meɪ] (conditional **might**) vi (be possible)

⚠ *Informationen zur Rechtschreibreform Seite 615*

können; (*have permission*) dürfen; **he ~ come** er kommt vielleicht; **~be** ['meɪbi:] *adv* vielleicht

May Day *n* der 1. Mai

mayhem ['meɪhem] *n* Chaos *nt*; (*US*) Körperverletzung *f*

mayonnaise [meɪə'neɪz] *n* Mayonnaise *f*

mayor [mɛəʳ] *n* Bürgermeister *m*; **~ess** *n* Bürgermeisterin *f*; (*wife*) (die) Frau *f* Bürgermeister

maypole ['meɪpəʊl] *n* Maibaum *m*

maze [meɪz] *n* Irrgarten *m*; (*fig*) Wirrwarr *nt*

M.D. *abbr* = **Doctor of Medicine**

KEYWORD
---

me [mi:] *pron* **1** (*direct*) mich; **it's me** ich bin's

2 (*indirect*) mir; **give them to me** gib sie mir

3 (*after prep*: +*acc*) mich; (: +*dat*) mir; **with/without me** mit mir/ohne mich

---

meadow ['mɛdəʊ] *n* Wiese *f*

meagre ['mi:gəʳ] (*US* **meager**) *adj* dürftig, spärlich

meal [mi:l] *n* Essen *nt*, Mahlzeit *f*; (*grain*) Schrotmehl *nt*; **to have a ~** essen (gehen); **~time** *n* Essenszeit *f*

mean [mi:n] (*pt, pp* **meant**) *adj* (*stingy*) geizig; (*spiteful*) gemein; (*average*) durchschnittlich, Durchschnitts- ♦ *vt* (*signify*) bedeuten; (*intend*) vorhaben, beabsichtigen ♦ *n* (*average*) Durchschnitt *m*; **~s** *npl* (*wherewithal*) Mittel *pl*; (*wealth*) Vermögen *nt*; **do you ~ me?** meinst du mich?; **do you ~ it?** meinst du das ernst?; **what do you ~?** was willst du damit sagen?; **to be ~t for sb/sth** für jdn/etw bestimmt sein; **by ~s of** durch; **by all ~s** selbstverständlich; **by no ~s** keineswegs

meander [mɪ'ændəʳ] *vi* sich schlängeln

meaning ['mi:nɪŋ] *n* Bedeutung *f*; (*of life*) Sinn *m*; **~ful** *adj* bedeutungsvoll; (*life*) sinnvoll; **~less** *adj* sinnlos

meanness ['mi:nnɪs] *n* (*stinginess*) Geiz *m*; (*spitefulness*) Gemeinheit *f*

meant [mɛnt] *pt, pp of* **mean**

meantime ['mi:ntaɪm] *adv* inzwischen

meanwhile ['mi:nwaɪl] *adv* inzwischen

measles ['mi:zlz] *n* Masern *pl*

measly ['mi:zlɪ] (*inf*) *adj* poplig

measure ['mɛʒəʳ] *vt, vi* messen ♦ *n* Maß *nt*; (*step*) Maßnahme *f*; **~ments** *npl* Maße *pl*

meat [mi:t] *n* Fleisch *nt*; **cold ~** Aufschnitt *m*; **~ ball** *n* Fleischkloß *m*; **~ pie** *n* Fleischpastete *f*; **~y** *adj* fleischig; (*fig*) gehaltvoll

Mecca ['mɛkə] *n* Mekka *nt* (*also fig*)

mechanic [mɪ'kænɪk] *n* Mechaniker *m*; **~al** *adj* mechanisch; **~s** *n* Mechanik *f* ♦ *npl* Technik *f*

mechanism ['mɛkənɪzəm] *n* Mechanismus *m*

mechanize ['mɛkənaɪz] *vt* mechanisieren

medal ['mɛdl] *n* Medaille *f*; (*decoration*) Orden *m*; **~list** (*US* **medalist**) *n* Medaillengewinner(in) *m(f)*

meddle ['mɛdl] *vi*: **to ~ (in)** sich einmischen (in +*acc*); **to ~ with sth** sich an etw *dat* zu schaffen machen

media ['mi:dɪə] *npl* Medien *pl*

mediaeval [mɛdɪ'i:vl] *adj* = **medieval**

median ['mi:dɪən] (*US*) *n* (*also*: **~ strip**) Mittelstreifen *m*

mediate ['mi:dɪeɪt] *vi* vermitteln; **mediator** *n* Vermittler *m*

Medicaid ['mɛdɪkeɪd] (®) *US*) *n* *medizinisches Versorgungsprogramm für Sozialschwache*

medical ['mɛdɪkl] *adj* medizinisch; Medizin-; ärztlich ♦ *n* (ärztliche) Untersuchung *f*

Medicare ['mɛdɪkɛəʳ] (*US*) *n* *staatliche Krankenversicherung besonders für Ältere*

medicated ['mɛdɪkeɪtɪd] *adj* medizinisch

medication [mɛdɪ'keɪʃən] *n* (*drugs etc*) Medikamente *pl*

medicinal [mɛ'dɪsɪnl] *adj* medizinisch, Heil-

medicine ['mɛdsɪn] *n* Medizin *f*; (*drugs*) Arznei *f*

medieval [mɛdɪ'i:vl] *adj* mittelalterlich

mediocre [mi:dɪ'əʊkəʳ] *adj* mittelmäßig

meditate ['mɛdɪteɪt] *vi* meditieren; **to ~ (on sth)** (über etw *acc*) nachdenken; **meditation** [mɛdɪ'teɪʃən] *n* Nachsinnen *nt*;

⚠ *For information on spelling reform see page 615*

Meditation *f*

Mediterranean [mɛdɪtə'reɪnɪən] *adj*
Mittelmeer-; (*person*) südländisch; **the ~
(Sea)** das Mittelmeer

medium ['miːdɪəm] *adj* mittlere(r, s),
Mittel-, mittel- ♦ *n* Mitte *f*; (*means*) Mittel
nt; (*person*) Medium *nt*; **happy ~**
goldener Mittelweg; **~-sized** *adj* mittelgroß; **~
wave** *n* Mittelwelle *f*

medley ['mɛdlɪ] *n* Gemisch *nt*

meek [miːk] *adj* sanft(mütig); (*pej*)
duckmäuserisch

meet [miːt] (*pt, pp* **met**) *vt* (*encounter*)
treffen, begegnen +*dat*; (*by arrangement*)
sich treffen mit; (*difficulties*) stoßen auf +*acc*;
(*get to know*) kennenlernen △; (*fetch*)
abholen; (*join*) zusammentreffen mit;
(*satisfy*) entsprechen +*dat* ♦ *vi* sich treffen;
(*become acquainted*) sich kennenlernen △;
~ with *vt* (*problems*) stoßen auf +*acc*; (*US:
people*) zusammentreffen mit; **~ing** *n*
Treffen *nt*; (*business meeting*) Besprechung *f*;
(*of committee*) Sitzung *f*; (*assembly*)
Versammlung *f*

mega- ['mɛgə-] (*inf*) *prefix* Mega-; **~byte** *n*
(*COMPUT*) Megabyte *nt*; **~phone** *n*
Megaphon △ *nt*

melancholy ['mɛlənkəlɪ] *adj* (*person*)
melancholisch; (*sight, event*) traurig

mellow ['mɛləu] *adj* mild, weich; (*fruit*) reif;
(*fig*) gesetzt ♦ *vi* reif werden

melodious [mɪ'ləudɪəs] *adj* wohlklingend

melody ['mɛlədɪ] *n* Melodie *f*

melon ['mɛlən] *n* Melone *f*

melt [mɛlt] *vi* schmelzen; (*anger*) verfliegen
♦ *vt* schmelzen; **~ away** *vi*
dahinschmelzen; **~ down** *vt*
einschmelzen; **~down** *n* (*in nuclear reactor*)
Kernschmelze *f*; **~ing point** *n*
Schmelzpunkt *m*; **~ing pot** *n* (*fig*)
Schmelztiegel *m*

member ['mɛmbər] *n* Mitglied *nt*; (*of tribe,
species*) Angehörige(r) *f(m)*; (*ANAT*) Glied *nt*;
M~ of Parliament (*BRIT*) *n*
Parlamentsmitglied *nt*; **M~ of the
European Parliament** (*BRIT*) *n* Mitglied *nt*
des Europäischen Parlaments; **~ship** *n*

Mitgliedschaft *f*; **to seek ~ship of** einen
Antrag auf Mitgliedschaft stellen; **~ship
card** *n* Mitgliedskarte *f*

memento [mə'mɛntəu] *n* Andenken *nt*

memo ['mɛməu] *n* Mitteilung *f*

memoirs ['mɛmwɑːz] *npl* Memoiren *pl*

memorable ['mɛmərəbl] *adj* denkwürdig

memoranda [mɛmə'rændə] *npl of*
memorandum

memorandum [mɛmə'rændəm] (*pl*
memoranda) *n* Mitteilung *f*

memorial [mɪ'mɔːrɪəl] *n* Denkmal *nt* ♦ *adj*
Gedenk-

memorize ['mɛməraɪz] *vt* sich einprägen

memory ['mɛmərɪ] *n* Gedächtnis *nt*; (*of
computer*) Speicher *m*; (*sth recalled*)
Erinnerung *f*

men [mɛn] *pl of* **man** ♦ *n* (*human race*) die
Menschen *pl*

menace ['mɛnɪs] *n* Drohung *f*; Gefahr *f* ♦ *vt*
bedrohen; **menacing** *adj* drohend

menagerie [mɪ'nædʒərɪ] *n* Tierschau *f*

mend [mɛnd] *vt* reparieren, flicken ♦ *vi*
(ver)heilen ♦ *n* ausgebesserte Stelle *f*; **on
the ~** auf dem Wege der Besserung; **~ing**
n (*articles*) Flickarbeit *f*

menial ['miːnɪəl] *adj* niedrig

meningitis [mɛnɪn'dʒaɪtɪs] *n*
Hirnhautentzündung *f*, Meningitis *f*

menopause ['mɛnəupɔːz] *n* Wechseljahre
pl, Menopause *f*

menstruation [mɛnstru'eɪʃən] *n*
Menstruation *f*

mental ['mɛntl] *adj* geistig, Geistes-;
(*arithmetic*) Kopf-; (*hospital*) Nerven-;
(*cruelty*) seelisch; (*inf: abnormal*) verrückt;
~ity [mɛn'tælɪtɪ] *n* Mentalität *f*

menthol ['mɛnθɔl] *n* Menthol *nt*

mention ['mɛnʃən] *n* Erwähnung *f* ♦ *vt*
erwähnen; **don't ~ it!** bitte (sehr), gern
geschehen

mentor ['mɛntɔːr] *n* Mentor *m*

menu ['mɛnjuː] *n* Speisekarte *f*

MEP *n abbr* = **Member of the European
Parliament**

mercenary ['məːsɪnərɪ] *adj* (*person*)
geldgierig ♦ *n* Söldner *m*

△ *Informationen zur Rechtschreibreform Seite 615*

merchandise ['mɜːtʃəndaɪz] n (Handels)ware f

merchant ['mɜːtʃənt] n Kaufmann m; ~ **bank** (BRIT) n Handelsbank f; ~ **navy** (US ~ **marine**) n Handelsmarine f

merciful ['mɜːsɪful] adj gnädig

merciless ['mɜːsɪlɪs] adj erbarmungslos

mercury ['mɜːkjurɪ] n Quecksilber nt

mercy ['mɜːsɪ] n Erbarmen nt; Gnade f; **at the ~ of** ausgeliefert +dat

mere [mɪəʳ] adj bloß; ~**ly** adv bloß

merge [mɜːdʒ] vt verbinden; (COMM) fusionieren ♦ vi verschmelzen; (roads) zusammenlaufen; (COMM) fusionieren; ~**r** n (COMM) Fusion f

meringue [mə'ræŋ] n Baiser nt

merit ['mɛrɪt] n Verdienst nt; (advantage) Vorzug m ♦ vt verdienen

mermaid ['mɜːmeɪd] n Wassernixe f

merry ['mɛrɪ] adj fröhlich; ~**-go-round** n Karussell nt

mesh [mɛʃ] n Masche f

mesmerize ['mɛzməraɪz] vt hypnotisieren; (fig) faszinieren

mess [mɛs] n Unordnung f; (dirt) Schmutz m; (trouble) Schwierigkeiten pl; (MIL) Messe f; ~ **about** or **around** vi (play the fool) herumalbern; (do nothing in particular) herumgammeln; ~ **about** or **around with** vt fus (tinker with) herummurksen an +dat; ~ **up** vt verpfuschen; (make untidy) in Unordnung bringen

message ['mɛsɪdʒ] n Mitteilung f; **to get the ~** kapieren

messenger ['mɛsɪndʒəʳ] n Bote m

Messrs ['mɛsəz] abbr (on letters) die Herren

messy ['mɛsɪ] adj schmutzig; (untidy) unordentlich

met [mɛt] pt, pp of **meet**

metabolism [mɛ'tæbəlɪzəm] n Stoffwechsel m

metal ['mɛtl] n Metall nt; ~**lic** adj metallisch; (made of metal) aus Metall

metaphor ['mɛtəfɔːʳ] n Metapher f

meteorology [miːtɪə'rɒlədʒɪ] n Meteorologie f

meter ['miːtəʳ] n Zähler m; (US) = **metre**

method ['mɛθəd] n Methode f; ~**ical** [mɪ'θɒdɪkl] adj methodisch; **M~ist** ['mɛθədɪst] adj methodistisch ♦ n Methodist(in) m(f); ~**ology** [mɛθə'dɒlədʒɪ] n Methodik f

meths [mɛθs] (BRIT) n(pl) = **methylated spirit(s)**

methylated spirit(s) ['mɛθɪleɪtɪd-] (BRIT) n (Brenn)spiritus m

meticulous [mɪ'tɪkjuləs] adj (über)genau

metre ['miːtəʳ] (US **meter**) n Meter m or nt

metric ['mɛtrɪk] adj (also: ~**al**) metrisch

metropolitan [mɛtrə'pɒlɪtn] adj der Großstadt; **M~ Police** (BRIT) n: **the M~ Police** die Londoner Polizei

mettle ['mɛtl] n Mut m

mew [mjuː] vi (cat) miauen

mews [mjuːz] n: ~ **cottage** ehemaliges Kutscherhäuschen

Mexican ['mɛksɪkən] adj mexikanisch ♦ n Mexikaner(in) m(f)

Mexico ['mɛksɪkəu] n Mexiko nt

miaow [miː'au] vi miauen

mice [maɪs] pl of **mouse**

micro ['maɪkrəu] n (also: ~**computer**) Mikrocomputer m; ~**chip** n Mikrochip m; ~**cosm** ['maɪkrəukɔzəm] n Mikrokosmos m; ~**phone** n Mikrophon ⚠ nt; ~**scope** n Mikroskop nt; ~**wave** n (also: ~**wave oven**) Mikrowelle(nherd nt) f

mid [mɪd] adj: **in ~ afternoon** am Nachmittag; **in ~ air** in der Luft; **in ~ May** Mitte Mai

midday [mɪd'deɪ] n Mittag m

middle ['mɪdl] n Mitte f; (waist) Taille f ♦ adj mittlere(r, s), Mittel-; **in the ~ of** mitten in +dat; ~**-aged** adj mittleren Alters; **M~ Ages** npl: **the M~ Ages** das Mittelalter; ~**-class** adj Mittelstands-; **M~ East** n: **the M~ East** der Nahe Osten; ~**man** (irreg) n (COMM) Zwischenhändler m; ~ **name** n zweiter Vorname m; ~ **weight** n (BOXING) Mittelgewicht nt

middling ['mɪdlɪŋ] adj mittelmäßig

midge [mɪdʒ] n Mücke f

midget ['mɪdʒɪt] n Liliputaner(in) m(f)

midnight ['mɪdnaɪt] n Mitternacht f

⚠ *For information on spelling reform see page 615*

midriff ['mɪdrɪf] *n* Taille *f*

midst [mɪdst] *n*: **in the ~ of** (*persons*) mitten unter +*dat*; (*things*) mitten in +*dat*

mid [mɪd'-]: **~summer** *n* Hochsommer *m*; **~way** *adv* auf halbem Wege ♦ *adj* Mittel-; **~week** *adv* in der Mitte der Woche

midwife ['mɪdwaɪf] (*irreg*) *n* Hebamme *f*; **~ry** *n* Geburtshilfe *f*

midwinter [mɪd'wɪntəʳ] *n* tiefste(r) Winter *m*

might [maɪt] *vi see* **may** ♦ *n* Macht *f*, Kraft *f*; **I ~ come** ich komme vielleicht; **~y** *adj, adv* mächtig

migraine ['miːɡreɪn] *n* Migräne *f*

migrant ['maɪɡrənt] *adj* Wander-; (*bird*) Zug-

migrate [maɪ'ɡreɪt] *vi* (ab)wandern; (*birds*) (fort)ziehen; **migration** [maɪ'ɡreɪʃən] *n* Wanderung *f*, Zug *m*

mike [maɪk] *n* = **microphone**

Milan [mɪ'læn] *n* Mailand *nt*

mild [maɪld] *adj* mild; (*medicine, interest*) leicht; (*person*) sanft ♦ *n* (*beer*) leichtes dunkles Bier

mildew ['mɪldjuː] *n* (*on plants*) Mehltau *m*; (*on food*) Schimmel *m*

mildly ['maɪldlɪ] *adv* leicht; **to put it ~** gelinde gesagt

mile [maɪl] *n* Meile *f*; **~age** *n* Meilenzahl *f*; **~ometer** *n* = **milometer**; **~stone** *n* (*also fig*) Meilenstein *m*

militant ['mɪlɪtnt] *adj* militant ♦ *n* Militante(r) *mf*

military ['mɪlɪtərɪ] *adj* militärisch, Militär-, Wehr-

militate ['mɪlɪteɪt] *vi*: **to ~ against** entgegenwirken +*dat*

militia [mɪ'lɪʃə] *n* Miliz *f*

milk [mɪlk] *n* Milch *f* ♦ *vt* (*also fig*) melken; **~ chocolate** *n* Milchschokolade *f*; **~man** (*irreg*) *n* Milchmann *m*; **~ shake** *n* Milchmixgetränk *nt*; **~y** *adj* milchig; **M~y Way** *n* Milchstraße *f*

mill [mɪl] *n* Mühle *f*; (*factory*) Fabrik *f* ♦ *vt* mahlen ♦ *vi* umherlaufen

millennia [mɪ'lenɪə] *npl of* **millennium**

millennium [mɪ'lenɪəm] (*pl* **~s** *or* **millennia**) *n* Jahrtausend *nt*

miller ['mɪləʳ] *n* Müller *m*

milligram(me) ['mɪlɪɡræm] *n* Milligramm *nt*

millimetre ['mɪlɪmiːtəʳ] (*US* **millimeter**) *n* Millimeter *m*

million ['mɪljən] *n* Million *f*; **a ~ times** tausendmal; **~aire** [mɪljə'neəʳ] *n* Millionär(in) *m(f)*

millstone ['mɪlstəʊn] *n* Mühlstein *m*

milometer [maɪ'lɒmɪtəʳ] *n* ≈ Kilometerzähler *m*

mime [maɪm] *n* Pantomime *f* ♦ *vt, vi* mimen

mimic ['mɪmɪk] *n* Mimiker *m* ♦ *vt, vi* nachahmen; **~ry** *n* Nachahmung *f*; (*BIOL*) Mimikry *f*

min. *abbr* = **minutes**; **minimum**

mince [mɪns] *vt* (zer)hacken ♦ *n* (*meat*) Hackfleisch *nt*; **~meat** *n* süße Pastetenfüllung *f*; **~ pie** *n* gefüllte (süße) Pastete *f*; **~r** *n* Fleischwolf *m*

mind [maɪnd] *n* Verstand *m*, Geist *m*; (*opinion*) Meinung *f* ♦ *vt* aufpassen auf +*acc*; (*object to*) etwas haben gegen; **on my ~** auf dem Herzen; **to my ~** meiner Meinung nach; **to be out of one's ~** wahnsinnig sein; **to bear** *or* **keep in ~** bedenken; **to change one's ~** es sich *dat* anders überlegen; **to make up one's ~** sich entschließen; **I don't ~** das macht mir nichts aus; **~ you, ...** allerdings ...; **never ~!** macht nichts!; **"~ the step"** „Vorsicht Stufe"; **~ your own business** kümmern Sie sich um Ihre eigenen Angelegenheiten; **~er** *n* Aufpasser(in) *m(f)*; **~ful** *adj*: **~ful of** achtsam auf +*acc*; **~less** *adj* sinnlos

mine¹ [maɪn] *n* (*coal-*) Bergwerk *nt*; (*MIL*) Mine *f* ♦ *vt* abbauen; (*MIL*) verminen

mine² [maɪn] *pron* meine(r, s); **that book is ~** das Buch gehört mir; **a friend of ~** ein Freund von mir

minefield ['maɪnfiːld] *n* Minenfeld *nt*

miner ['maɪnəʳ] *n* Bergarbeiter *m*

mineral ['mɪnərəl] *adj* mineralisch, Mineral- ♦ *n* Mineral *nt*; **~s** *npl* (*BRIT: soft drinks*) alkoholfreie Getränke *pl*; **~ water** *n* Mineralwasser *nt*

minesweeper ['maɪnswiːpəʳ] *n* Minensuchboot *nt*

⚠ *Informationen zur Rechtschreibreform Seite 615*

mingle ['mɪŋgl] *vi*: **to ~ (with)** sich mischen (unter +*acc*)

miniature ['mɪnətʃəʳ] *adj* Miniatur- ♦ *n* Miniatur *f*

minibus ['mɪnɪbʌs] *n* Kleinbus *m*

minimal ['mɪnɪml] *adj* minimal

minimize ['mɪnɪmaɪz] *vt* auf das Mindestmaß beschränken

minimum ['mɪnɪməm] (*pl* **minima**) *n* Minimum *nt* ♦ *adj* Mindest-

mining ['maɪnɪŋ] *n* Bergbau *m* ♦ *adj* Bergbau-, Berg-

miniskirt ['mɪnɪskə:t] *n* Minirock *m*

minister ['mɪnɪstəʳ] *n* (*BRIT: POL*) Minister *m*; (*ECCL*) Pfarrer *m* ♦ *vi*: **to ~ to sb/sb's needs** sich um jdn kümmern; **~ial** [mɪnɪs'tɪərɪəl] *adj* ministeriell, Minister-

ministry ['mɪnɪstrɪ] *n* (*BRIT: POL*) Ministerium *nt*; (*ECCL: office*) geistliche(s) Amt *nt*

mink [mɪŋk] *n* Nerz *m*

minnow ['mɪnəu] *n* Elritze *f*

minor ['maɪnəʳ] *adj* kleiner; (*operation*) leicht; (*problem, poet*) unbedeutend; (*MUS*) Moll ♦ *n* (*BRIT: under 18*) Minderjährige(r) *mf*

minority [mɪ'nɔrɪtɪ, maɪ'nɔrɪtɪ] *n* Minderheit *f*

mint [mɪnt] *n* Minze *f*; (*sweet*) Pfefferminzbonbon *nt* ♦ *vt* (*coins*) prägen; **the (Royal** (*BRIT*) **or US** (*US*)) **M~** die Münzanstalt; **in ~ condition** in tadellosem Zustand

minus ['maɪnəs] *n* Minuszeichen *nt*; (*amount*) Minusbetrag *m* ♦ *prep* minus, weniger

minuscule ['mɪnəskju:l] *adj* winzig

minute¹ [maɪ'nju:t] *adj* winzig; (*detailed*) minuziös

minute² ['mɪnɪt] *n* Minute *f*; (*moment*) Augenblick *m*; **~s** *npl* (*of meeting etc*) Protokoll *nt*

miracle ['mɪrəkl] *n* Wunder *nt*

miraculous [mɪ'rækjuləs] *adj* wunderbar

mirage ['mɪrɑ:ʒ] *n* Fata Morgana *f*

mire [maɪəʳ] *n* Morast *m*

mirror ['mɪrəʳ] *n* Spiegel *m* ♦ *vt* (wider)spiegeln

mirth [mə:θ] *n* Heiterkeit *f*

misadventure [mɪsəd'ventʃəʳ] *n* Mißgeschick ⚠ *nt*, Unfall *m*

misanthropist [mɪ'zænθrəpɪst] *n* Menschenfeind *m*

misapprehension ['mɪsæprɪ'henʃən] *n* Mißverständnis ⚠ *nt*

misbehave [mɪsbɪ'heɪv] *vi* sich schlecht benehmen

miscalculate [mɪs'kælkjuleɪt] *vt* falsch berechnen

miscarriage ['mɪskærɪdʒ] *n* (*MED*) Fehlgeburt *f*; **~ of justice** Fehlurteil *nt*

miscellaneous [mɪsɪ'leɪnɪəs] *adj* verschieden

mischief ['mɪstʃɪf] *n* Unfug *m*; **mischievous** ['mɪstʃɪvəs] *adj* (*person*) durchtrieben; (*glance*) verschmitzt; (*rumour*) bösartig

misconception ['mɪskən'sepʃən] *n* fälschliche Annahme *f*

misconduct [mɪs'kɔndʌkt] *n* Vergehen *nt*; **professional ~** Berufsvergehen *nt*

misconstrue [mɪskən'stru:] *vt* mißverstehen ⚠

misdemeanour [mɪsdɪ'mi:nəʳ] (*US* **misdemeanor**) *n* Vergehen *nt*

miser ['maɪzəʳ] *n* Geizhals *m*

miserable ['mɪzərəbl] *adj* (*unhappy*) unglücklich; (*headache, weather*) fürchterlich; (*poor*) elend; (*contemptible*) erbärmlich

miserly ['maɪzəlɪ] *adj* geizig

misery ['mɪzərɪ] *n* Elend *nt*, Qual *f*

misfire [mɪs'faɪəʳ] *vi* (*gun*) versagen; (*engine*) fehlzünden; (*plan*) fehlgehen

misfit ['mɪsfɪt] *n* Außenseiter *m*

misfortune [mɪs'fɔ:tʃən] *n* Unglück *nt*

misgiving(s) [mɪs'gɪvɪŋ(z)] *n(pl)* Bedenken *pl*

misguided [mɪs'gaɪdɪd] *adj* fehlgeleitet; (*opinions*) irrig

mishandle [mɪs'hændl] *vt* falsch handhaben

mishap ['mɪshæp] *n* Mißgeschick ⚠ *nt*

misinform [mɪsɪn'fɔ:m] *vt* falsch unterrichten

misinterpret [mɪsɪn'tə:prɪt] *vt* falsch

⚠ *For information on spelling reform see page 615*

auffassen

misjudge [mɪs'dʒʌdʒ] *vt* falsch beurteilen

mislay [mɪs'leɪ] (*irreg: like* **lay**) *vt* verlegen

mislead [mɪs'liːd] (*irreg: like* **lead²**) *vt* (*deceive*) irreführen; **~ing** *adj* irreführend

mismanage [mɪs'mænɪdʒ] *vt* schlecht verwalten

misnomer [mɪs'nəʊmə'] *n* falsche Bezeichnung *f*

misplace [mɪs'pleɪs] *vt* verlegen

misprint ['mɪsprɪnt] *n* Druckfehler *m*

Miss [mɪs] *n* Fräulein *nt*

miss [mɪs] *vt* (*fail to hit, catch*) verfehlen; (*not notice*) verpassen; (*be too late*) versäumen, verpassen; (*omit*) auslassen; (*regret the absence of*) vermissen ♦ *vi* fehlen ♦ *n* (*shot*) Fehlschuß △ *m*; (*failure*) Fehlschlag *m*; **I ~ you** du fehlst mir; **~ out** *vt* auslassen

misshapen [mɪs'ʃeɪpən] *adj* mißgestaltet △

missile ['mɪsaɪl] *n* Rakete *f*

missing ['mɪsɪŋ] *adj* (*person*) vermißt △; (*thing*) fehlend; **to be ~** fehlen

mission ['mɪʃən] *n* (*work*) Auftrag *m*; (*people*) Delegation *f*; (*REL*) Mission *f*; **~ary** *n* Missionar(in) *m(f)*; **~ statement** *n* Kurzdarstellung *f* der Firmenphilosophie

misspell ['mɪs'spel] (*irreg: like* **spell**) *vt* falsch schreiben

misspent ['mɪs'spent] *adj* (*youth*) vergeudet

mist [mɪst] *n* Dunst *m*, Nebel *m* ♦ *vi* (*also:* **~ over, ~ up**) sich trüben; (*BRIT: windows*) sich beschlagen

mistake [mɪs'teɪk] (*irreg: like* **take**) *n* Fehler *m* ♦ *vt* (*misunderstand*) mißverstehen △; (*mix up*): **to ~ (sth for sth)** (etw mit etw) verwechseln; **to make a ~** einen Fehler machen; **by ~** aus Versehen; **to ~ A for B** A mit B verwechseln; **~n** *pp* of **mistake** ♦ *adj* (*idea*) falsch; **to be ~n** sich irren

mister ['mɪstə'] *n* (*inf*) Herr *m*; *see* **Mr**

mistletoe ['mɪsltəʊ] *n* Mistel *f*

mistook [mɪs'tʊk] *pt* of **mistake**

mistress ['mɪstrɪs] *n* (*teacher*) Lehrerin *f*; (*in house*) Herrin *f*; (*lover*) Geliebte *f*; *see* **Mrs**

mistrust [mɪs'trʌst] *vt* mißtrauen △ +*dat*

misty ['mɪstɪ] *adj* neblig

misunderstand [mɪsʌndə'stænd] (*irreg: like* understand) *vt, vi* mißverstehen △, falsch verstehen; **~ing** *n* Mißverständnis △ *nt*; (*disagreement*) Meinungsverschiedenheit *f*

misuse [*n* mɪs'juːs, *vb* mɪs'juːz] *n* falsche(r) Gebrauch *m* ♦ *vt* falsch gebrauchen

mitigate ['mɪtɪgeɪt] *vt* mildern

mitt(en) ['mɪt(n)] *n* Fausthandschuh *m*

mix [mɪks] *vt* (*blend*) (ver)mischen ♦ *vi* (*liquids*) sich (ver)mischen lassen; (*people: get on*) sich vertragen; (*: associate*) Kontakt haben ♦ *n* (*mixture*) Mischung *f*; **~ up** *vt* zusammenmischen; (*confuse*) verwechseln; **~ed** *adj* gemischt; **~ed-up** *adj* durcheinander; **~er** *n* (*for food*) Mixer *m*; **~ture** *n* Mischung *f*; **~-up** *n* Durcheinander *nt*

mm *abbr* (= *millimetre(s)*) mm

moan [məʊn] *n* Stöhnen *nt*; (*complaint*) Klage *f* ♦ *vi* stöhnen; (*complain*) maulen

moat [məʊt] *n* (Burg)graben *m*

mob [mɒb] *n* Mob *m*; (*the masses*) Pöbel *m* ♦ *vt* herfallen über +*acc*

mobile ['məʊbaɪl] *adj* beweglich; (*library etc*) fahrbar ♦ *n* (*decoration*) Mobile *nt*; **~ home** *n* Wohnwagen *m*; **~ phone** *n* (*TEL*) Mobiltelefon *nt*; **mobility** [məʊ'bɪlɪtɪ] *n* Beweglichkeit *f*; **mobilize** ['məʊbɪlaɪz] *vt* mobilisieren

mock [mɒk] *vt* verspotten; (*defy*) trotzen +*dat* ♦ *adj* Schein-; **~ery** *n* Spott *m*; (*person*) Gespött *nt*

mod [mɒd] *adj see* **convenience**

mode [məʊd] *n* (Art *f* und) Weise *f*

model ['mɒdl] *n* Modell *nt*; (*example*) Vorbild *nt*; (*in fashion*) Mannequin *n* ♦ *adj* (*railway*) Modell-; (*perfect*) Muster-; vorbildlich ♦ *vt* (*make*) bilden; (*clothes*) vorführen ♦ *vi* als Mannequin arbeiten

modem ['məʊdem] *n* (*COMPUT*) Modem *nt*

moderate [*adj, n* 'mɒdərət, *vb* 'mɒdəreɪt] *adj* gemäßigt ♦ *n* (*POL*) Gemäßigte(r) *mf* ♦ *vi* sich mäßigen ♦ *vt* mäßigen; **moderation** [mɒdə'reɪʃən] *n* Mäßigung *f*; **in moderation** mit Maßen

modern ['mɒdən] *adj* modern; (*history, languages*) neuere(r, s); **~ize** *vt* modernisieren

modest ['mɒdɪst] adj bescheiden; **~y** n Bescheidenheit f

modicum ['mɒdɪkəm] n bißchen △ nt

modification [mɒdɪfɪ'keɪʃən] n (Ab)änderung f

modify ['mɒdɪfaɪ] vt abändern

module ['mɒdjuːl] n (component) (Bau)element nt; (SPACE) (Raum)kapsel f

mogul ['məʊɡl] n (fig) Mogul m

mohair ['məʊhɛəʳ] n Mohair m

moist [mɔɪst] adj feucht; **~en** ['mɔɪsn] vt befeuchten; **~ure** ['mɔɪstʃəʳ] n Feuchtigkeit f; **~urizer** ['mɔɪstʃəraɪzəʳ] n Feuchtigkeitscreme f

molar ['məʊləʳ] n Backenzahn m

molasses [mə'læsɪz] n Melasse f

mold [məʊld] (US) = **mould**

mole [məʊl] n (spot) Leberfleck m; (animal) Maulwurf m; (pier) Mole f

molest [mə'lest] vt belästigen

mollycoddle ['mɒlɪkɒdl] vt verhätscheln

molt [məʊlt] (US) vi = **moult**

molten ['məʊltən] adj geschmolzen

mom [mɒm] (US) n = **mum**

moment ['məʊmənt] n Moment m, Augenblick m; (importance) Tragweite f; **at the ~** im Augenblick; **~ary** adj kurz; **~ous** [məʊ'mentəs] adj folgenschwer

momentum [məʊ'mentəm] n Schwung m; **to gather ~** in Fahrt kommen

mommy ['mɒmɪ] (US) n = **mummy**

Monaco ['mɒnəkəʊ] n Monaco nt

monarch ['mɒnək] n Herrscher(in) m(f); **~y** n Monarchie f

monastery ['mɒnəstərɪ] n Kloster nt

monastic [mə'næstɪk] adj klösterlich, Kloster-

Monday ['mʌndɪ] n Montag m

monetary ['mʌnɪtərɪ] adj Geld-; (of currency) Währungs-

money ['mʌnɪ] n Geld nt; **to make ~** Geld verdienen; **~ belt** n Geldgürtel m; **~lender** n Geldverleiher m; **~ order** n Postanweisung f; **~-spinner** (inf) n Verkaufsschlager m

mongol ['mɒŋɡəl] n (MED) mongoloide(s) Kind nt ♦ adj mongolisch; (MED) mongoloid

mongrel ['mʌŋɡrəl] n Promenadenmischung f

monitor ['mɒnɪtəʳ] n (SCH) Klassenordner m; (television ~) Monitor m ♦ vt (broadcasts) abhören; (control) überwachen

monk [mʌŋk] n Mönch m

monkey ['mʌŋkɪ] n Affe m; **~ nut** (BRIT) n Erdnuß △ f; **~ wrench** n (TECH) Engländer m, Franzose m

monochrome ['mɒnəkrəʊm] adj schwarzweiß

monopolize [mə'nɒpəlaɪz] vt beherrschen

monopoly [mə'nɒpəlɪ] n Monopol nt

monosyllable ['mɒnəsɪləbl] n einsilbige(s) Wort nt

monotone ['mɒnətəʊn] n gleichbleibende(r) Ton(fall) m; **to speak in a ~** monoton sprechen; **monotonous** [mə'nɒtənəs] adj eintönig; **monotony** [mə'nɒtənɪ] n Eintönigkeit f, Monotonie f

monsoon [mɒn'suːn] n Monsun m

monster ['mɒnstəʳ] n Ungeheuer nt; (person) Scheusal nt

monstrosity [mɒn'strɒsɪtɪ] n Ungeheuerlichkeit f; (thing) Monstrosität f

monstrous ['mɒnstrəs] adj (shocking) gräßlich △, ungeheuerlich; (huge) riesig

month [mʌnθ] n Monat m; **~ly** adj monatlich, Monats- ♦ adv einmal im Monat ♦ n (magazine) Monatsschrift f

monument ['mɒnjumənt] n Denkmal nt; **~al** [mɒnju'mentl] adj (huge) gewaltig; (ignorance) ungeheuer

moo [muː] vi muhen

mood [muːd] n Stimmung f, Laune f; **to be in a good/bad ~** gute/schlechte Laune haben; **~y** adj launisch

moon [muːn] n Mond m; **~light** n Mondlicht nt; **~lighting** n Schwarzarbeit f; **~lit** adj mondhell

moor [muəʳ] n Heide f, Hochmoor nt ♦ vt (ship) festmachen, verankern ♦ vi anlegen; **~ings** npl Liegeplatz m; **~land** ['muələnd] n Heidemoor nt

moose [muːs] n Elch m

mop [mɒp] n Mop △ m ♦ vt (auf)wischen; **~ up** vt aufwischen

△ For information on spelling reform see page 615

mope [məup] *vi* Trübsal blasen

moped ['məupɛd] *n* Moped *nt*

moral ['mɔrl] *adj* moralisch; (*values*) sittlich; (*virtuous*) tugendhaft ♦ *n* Moral *f*; **~s** *npl* (*ethics*) Moral *f*

morale [mɔ'rɑ:l] *n* Moral *f*

morality [mə'ræliti] *n* Sittlichkeit *f*

morass [mə'ræs] *n* Sumpf *m*

morbid ['mɔ:bɪd] *adj* krankhaft; (*jokes*) makaber

KEYWORD

more [mɔ:ʳ] *adj* (*greater in number etc*) mehr; (*additional*) noch mehr; **do you want (some) more tea?** möchten Sie noch etwas Tee?; **I have no** *or* **I don't have any more money** ich habe kein Geld mehr
♦ *pron* (*greater amount*) mehr; (*further or additional amount*) noch mehr; **is there any more?** gibt es noch mehr?; (*left over*) ist noch etwas da?; **there's no more** es ist nichts mehr da
♦ *adv* mehr; **more dangerous/easily** *etc* (**than**) gefährlicher/einfacher *etc* (als); **more and more** immer mehr; **more and more excited** immer aufgeregter; **more or less** mehr oder weniger; **more than ever** mehr denn je; **more beautiful than ever** schöner denn je

---

moreover [mɔ:'rəuvəʳ] *adv* überdies

morgue [mɔ:g] *n* Leichenschauhaus *nt*

Mormon ['mɔ:mən] *n* Mormone *m*, Mormonin *f*

morning ['mɔ:nɪŋ] *n* Morgen *m*; **in the ~** am Morgen; **7 o'clock in the ~** 7 Uhr morgens; **~ sickness** *n* (Schwangerschafts)übelkeit *f*

Morocco [mə'rɔkəu] *n* Marokko *nt*

moron ['mɔ:rɔn] *n* Schwachsinnige(r) *mf*

morose [mə'rəus] *adj* mürrisch

morphine ['mɔ:fi:n] *n* Morphium *nt*

Morse [mɔ:s] *n* (*also:* **~ code**) Morsealphabet *nt*

morsel ['mɔ:sl] *n* Bissen *m*

mortal ['mɔ:tl] *adj* sterblich; (*deadly*) tödlich; (*very great*) Todes- ♦ *n* (*human being*)

Sterbliche(r) *mf*; **~ity** [mɔ:'tælɪtɪ] *n* Sterblichkeit *f*; (*death rate*) Sterblichkeitsziffer *f*

mortar ['mɔ:təʳ] *n* (*for building*) Mörtel *m*; (*MIL*) Granatwerfer *m*

mortgage ['mɔ:gɪdʒ] *n* Hypothek *f* ♦ *vt* hypothekarisch belasten; **~ company** (*US*) *n* ≈ Bausparkasse *f*

mortify ['mɔ:tɪfaɪ] *vt* beschämen

mortuary ['mɔ:tjuərɪ] *n* Leichenhalle *f*

mosaic [məu'zeɪɪk] *n* Mosaik *nt*

Moscow ['mɔskəu] *n* Moskau *nt*

Moslem ['mɔzləm] = **Muslim**

mosque [mɔsk] *n* Moschee *f*

mosquito [mɔs'ki:təu] (*pl* **~es**) *n* Moskito *m*

moss [mɔs] *n* Moos *nt*

most [məust] *adj* meiste(r, s) ♦ *adv* am meisten; (*very*) höchst ♦ *n* das meiste, der größte Teil; (*people*) die meisten; **~ men** die meisten Männer; **at the (very) ~** allerhöchstens; **to make the ~ of** das Beste machen aus; **a ~ interesting book** ein höchst interessantes Buch; **~ly** *adv* größtenteils

MOT (*BRIT*) *n abbr* (= *Ministry of Transport*): **the ~ (test)** ≈ der TÜV

motel [məu'tɛl] *n* Motel *nt*

moth [mɔθ] *n* Nachtfalter *m*; (*wool-eating*) Motte *f*; **~ball** *n* Mottenkugel *f*

mother ['mʌðəʳ] *n* Mutter *f* ♦ *vt* bemuttern; **~hood** *n* Mutterschaft *f*; **~-in-law** *n* Schwiegermutter *f*; **~ly** *adj* mütterlich; **~-of-pearl** *n* Perlmutt *nt*; **M~'s Day** (*BRIT*) *n* Muttertag *m*; **~-to-be** *n* werdende Mutter *f*; **~ tongue** *n* Muttersprache *f*

motif [məu'ti:f] *n* Motiv *nt*

motion ['məuʃən] *n* Bewegung *f*; (*in meeting*) Antrag *m* ♦ *vt*, *vi*: **to ~ (to) sb** jdm winken, jdm zu verstehen geben; **~less** *adj* regungslos; **~ picture** *n* Film *m*

motivated ['məutɪveɪtɪd] *adj* motiviert

motivation [məutɪ'veɪʃən] *n* Motivierung *f*

motive ['məutɪv] *n* Motiv *nt*, Beweggrund *m* ♦ *adj* treibend

motley ['mɔtlɪ] *adj* bunt

motor ['məutəʳ] *n* Motor *m*; (*BRIT: inf: vehicle*) Auto *nt* ♦ *adj* Motor-; **~bike** *n* Motorrad *nt*;

~**boat** n Motorboot nt; ~**car** (BRIT) n Auto nt; ~**cycle** n Motorrad nt; ~**cyclist** n Motorradfahrer(in) m(f); ~**ing** (BRIT) n Autofahren nt ♦ adj Auto-; ~**ist** n Autofahrer(in) m(f); ~ **mechanic** n Kraftfahrzeugmechaniker(in) m(f); Kfz-Mechaniker(in) m(f); ~ **racing** (BRIT) n Autorennen nt; ~ **vehicle** n Kraftfahrzeug nt; ~**way** (BRIT) n Autobahn f

mottled ['mɔtld] adj gesprenkelt

mould [məʊld] (US **mold**) n Form f; (mildew) Schimmel m ♦ vt (also fig) formen; ~**y** adj schimmelig

moult [məʊlt] (US **molt**) vi sich mausern

mound [maʊnd] n (Erd)hügel m

mount [maʊnt] n (liter: hill) Berg m; (horse) Pferd nt; (for jewel etc) Fassung f ♦ vt (horse) steigen auf +acc; (put in setting) fassen; (exhibition) veranstalten; (attack) unternehmen ♦ vi (also: ~ up) sich häufen; (on horse) aufsitzen

mountain ['maʊntɪn] n Berg m ♦ cpd Berg-; ~ **bike** n Mountain-Bike nt; ~**eer** n Bergsteiger(in) m(f); ~**eering** [maʊntɪ'nɪərɪŋ] n Bergsteigen nt; ~**ous** adj bergig; ~ **rescue team** n Bergwacht f; ~**side** n Berg(ab)hang m

mourn [mɔːn] vt betrauen, beklagen ♦ vi: to ~ **(for sb)** (um jdn) trauern; ~**er** n Trauernde(r) mf; ~**ful** adj traurig; ~**ing** n (grief) Trauer f ♦ cpd (dress) Trauer-; in ~**ing** (period etc) in Trauer; (dress) in Trauerkleidung f

mouse [maʊs] (pl **mice**) n Maus f; ~**trap** n Mausefalle f

mousse [muːs] n (COOK) Creme f; (cosmetic) Schaumfestiger m

moustache [məs'tɑːʃ] n Schnurrbart m

mousy ['maʊsɪ] adj (colour) mausgrau; (person) schüchtern

mouth [maʊθ] n Mund m; (opening) Öffnung f; (of river) Mündung f; ~**ful** n Mundvoll m; ~ **organ** n Mundharmonika f; ~**piece** n Mundstück nt; (fig) Sprachrohr nt; ~**wash** n Mundwasser nt; ~**watering** adj lecker, appetitlich

movable ['muːvəbl] adj beweglich

move [muːv] n (movement) Bewegung f; (in game) Zug m; (step) Schritt m; (of house) Umzug m ♦ vt bewegen; (people) transportieren; (in job) versetzen; (emotionally) bewegen ♦ vi sich bewegen; (vehicle, ship) fahren; (~ house) umziehen; to **get a ~ on** sich beeilen; to ~ **sb to do sth** jdn veranlassen, etw zu tun; ~ **about** or **around** vi sich hin- und herbewegen; (travel) unterwegs sein; ~ **along** vi weitergehen; (cars) weiterfahren; ~ **away** vi weggehen; ~ **back** vi zurückgehen; (to the rear) zurückweichen; ~ **forward** vi vorwärtsgehen △, sich vorwärtsbewegen △ ♦ vt vorschieben; (time) vorverlegen; ~ **in** vi (to house) einziehen; (troops) einrücken; ~ **on** vi weitergehen ♦ vt weitergehen lassen; ~ **out** vi (of house) ausziehen; (troops) abziehen; ~ **over** vi zur Seite rücken; ~ **up** vi aufsteigen; (in job) befördert werden ♦ vt nach oben bewegen; (in job) befördern; ~**ment** ['muːvmənt] n Bewegung f

movie ['muːvɪ] n Film m; to go to the ~**s** ins Kino gehen; ~ **camera** n Filmkamera f

moving ['muːvɪŋ] adj beweglich; (touching) ergreifend

mow [məʊ] (pt **mowed**, pp **mowed** or **mown**) vt mähen; ~ **down** vt (fig) niedermähen; ~**er** n (lawnmower) Rasenmäher m; ~**n** pp of **mow**

MP n abbr = Member of Parliament

m.p.h. abbr = miles per hour

Mr ['mɪstəʳ] (US **Mr.**) n Herr m

Mrs ['mɪsɪz] (US **Mrs.**) n Frau f

Ms [mɪz] (US **Ms.**) n (= Miss or Mrs) Frau f

M.Sc. n abbr = Master of Science

much [mʌtʃ] adj viel ♦ adv sehr; viel ♦ n viel, eine Menge; **how ~ is it?** wieviel kostet das?; **too ~** zuviel; **it's not ~** es ist nicht viel; **as ~ as** sosehr, soviel; **however ~ he tries** sosehr er es auch versucht

muck [mʌk] n Mist m; (fig) Schmutz m; ~ **about** or **around** (inf) vi: to ~ **about** or **around (with sth)** (an etw dat) herumalbern; ~ **up** vt (inf: ruin) vermasseln; (dirty) dreckig machen; ~**y** adj (dirty)

△ For information on spelling reform see page 615

dreckig

mud [mʌd] n Schlamm m

muddle ['mʌdl] n Durcheinander nt ♦ vt (also: ~ **up**) durcheinanderbringen △; ~ **through** vi sich durchwursteln

mud [mʌd-]: ~**dy** adj schlammig; ~**guard** n Schutzblech nt; ~**-slinging** (inf) n Verleumdung f

muesli ['mjuːzlɪ] n Müsli nt

muffin ['mʌfɪn] n süße(s) Teilchen nt

muffle ['mʌfl] vt (sound) dämpfen; (wrap up) einhüllen; ~**d** adj gedämpft; ~**r** (US) n (AUT) Schalldämpfer m

mug [mʌg] n (cup) Becher m; (inf: face) Visage f; (: fool) Trottel m ♦ vt überfallen und ausrauben; ~**ger** n Straßenräuber m; ~**ging** n Überfall m

muggy ['mʌgɪ] adj (weather) schwül

mule [mjuːl] n Maulesel m

mull [mʌl]: ~ **over** vt nachdenken über +acc

multicoloured ['mʌltɪkʌləd] (US **multicolored**) adj mehrfarbig

multi-level ['mʌltɪlevl] (US) adj = **multistorey**

multiple ['mʌltɪpl] n Vielfache(s) nt ♦ adj mehrfach; (many) mehrere; ~ **sclerosis** n multiple Sklerose f

multiplex cinema ['mʌltɪpleks-] n Kinocenter nt

multiplication [mʌltɪplɪ'keɪʃən] n Multiplikation f; (increase) Vervielfachung f

multiply ['mʌltɪplaɪ] vt: **to** ~ **(by)** multiplizieren (mit) ♦ vi (BIOL) sich vermehren

multistorey ['mʌltɪ'stɔːrɪ] (BRIT) adj (building, car park) mehrstöckig

multitude ['mʌltɪtjuːd] n Menge f

mum [mʌm] n (BRIT: inf) Mutti f ♦ adj: **to keep** ~ **(about)** den Mund halten (über +acc)

mumble ['mʌmbl] vt, vi murmeln ♦ n Gemurmel nt

mummy ['mʌmɪ] n (dead body) Mumie f; (BRIT: inf) Mami f

mumps [mʌmps] n Mumps m

munch [mʌntʃ] vt, vi mampfen

mundane [mʌn'deɪn] adj banal

municipal [mjuː'nɪsɪpl] adj städtisch, Stadt-

mural ['mjuərl] n Wandgemälde nt

murder ['mɜːdəʳ] n Mord m ♦ vt ermorden; ~**er** n Mörder m; ~**ous** adj Mord-; (fig) mörderisch

murky ['mɜːkɪ] adj finster

murmur ['mɜːməʳ] n Murmeln nt; (of water, wind) Rauschen nt ♦ vt, vi murmeln

muscle ['mʌsl] n Muskel m; ~ **in** vi mitmischen; **muscular** ['mʌskjuləʳ] adj Muskel-; (strong) muskulös

museum [mjuː'zɪəm] n Museum nt

mushroom ['mʌʃrum] n Champignon m; Pilz m ♦ vi (fig) emporschießen

music ['mjuːzɪk] n Musik f; (printed) Noten pl; ~**al** adj (sound) melodisch; (person) musikalisch ♦ n (show) Musical nt; ~**al instrument** n Musikinstrument nt; ~ **centre** n Stereoanlage f; ~ **hall** (BRIT) n Varieté △ nt; ~**ian** [mjuː'zɪʃən] n Musiker(in) m(f)

Muslim ['mʌzlɪm] adj moslemisch ♦ n Moslem m

muslin ['mʌzlɪn] n Musselin m

mussel ['mʌsl] n Miesmuschel f

must [mʌst] vb aux müssen; (in negation) dürfen ♦ n Muß △ nt; **the film is a** ~ den Film muß man einfach gesehen haben

mustard ['mʌstəd] n Senf m

muster ['mʌstəʳ] vt (MIL) antreten lassen; (courage) zusammennehmen

mustn't ['mʌsnt] = **must not**

musty ['mʌstɪ] adj muffig

mute [mjuːt] adj stumm ♦ n (person) Stumme(r) mf; (MUS) Dämpfer m; ~**d** adj gedämpft

mutilate ['mjuːtɪleɪt] vt verstümmeln

mutiny ['mjuːtɪnɪ] n Meuterei f ♦ vi meutern

mutter ['mʌtəʳ] vt, vi murmeln

mutton ['mʌtn] n Hammelfleisch nt

mutual ['mjuːtʃuəl] adj gegenseitig; beiderseitig; ~**ly** adv gegenseitig; für beide Seiten

muzzle ['mʌzl] n (of animal) Schnauze f; (for animal) Maulkorb m; (of gun) Mündung f ♦ vt einen Maulkorb anlegen +dat

my [maɪ] adj mein; **this is** ~ **car** das ist mein

△ *Informationen zur Rechtschreibreform Seite 615*

Auto; **I've washed ~ hair** ich habe mir die Haare gewaschen

myself [maɪˈself] *pron* mich *acc*; mir *dat*; (*emphatic*) selbst; *see also* **oneself**

mysterious [mɪsˈtɪərɪəs] *adj* geheimnisvoll

mystery [ˈmɪstərɪ] *n* (*secret*) Geheimnis *nt*; (*sth difficult*) Rätsel *nt*

mystify [ˈmɪstɪfaɪ] *vt* ein Rätsel sein +*dat*; verblüffen

mystique [mɪsˈtiːk] *n* geheimnisvolle Natur *f*

myth [mɪθ] *n* Mythos *m*; (*fig*) Erfindung *f*; **~ology** [mɪˈθɒlədʒɪ] *n* Mythologie *f*

N, n

n/a *abbr* (= *not applicable*) nicht zutreffend

nab [næb] (*inf*) *vt* schnappen

naff [næf] (*BRIT: inf*) *adj* blöd

nag [næg] *n* (*horse*) Gaul *m*; (*person*) Nörgler(in) *m(f)* ♦ *vt, vi*: **to ~ (at) sb** an jdm herumnörgeln; **~ging** *adj* (*doubt*) nagend ♦ *n* Nörgelei *f*

nail [neɪl] *n* Nagel *m* ♦ *vt* nageln; **to ~ sb down to doing sth** jdn darauf festnageln, etw zu tun; **~brush** *n* Nagelbürste *f*; **~file** *n* Nagelfeile *f*; **~ polish** *n* Nagellack *m*; **~ polish remover** *n* Nagellackentferner *m*; **~ scissors** *npl* Nagelschere *f*; **~ varnish** (*BRIT*) *n* = **nail polish**

naïve [naɪˈiːv] *adj* naiv

naked [ˈneɪkɪd] *adj* nackt

name [neɪm] *n* Name *m*; (*reputation*) Ruf *m* ♦ *vt* nennen; (*sth new*) benennen; (*appoint*) ernennen; **by ~** mit Namen; **I know him only by ~** ich kenne ihn nur dem Namen nach; **what's your ~?** wie heißen Sie?; **in the ~ of** im Namen +*gen*; (*for the sake of*) um +*gen* ...willen; **~less** *adj* namenlos; **~ly** *adv* nämlich; **~sake** *n* Namensvetter *m*

nanny [ˈnænɪ] *n* Kindermädchen *nt*

nap [næp] *n* (*sleep*) Nickerchen *nt*; (*on cloth*) Strich *m* ♦ *vi*: **to be caught ~ping** (*fig*) überrumpelt werden

nape [neɪp] *n* Nacken *m*

napkin [ˈnæpkɪn] *n* (*at table*) Serviette *f*;

(*BRIT: for baby*) Windel *f*

nappy [ˈnæpɪ] (*BRIT*) *n* (*for baby*) Windel *f*; **~ rash** *n* wunde Stellen *pl*

narcotic [nɑːˈkɒtɪk] *adj* betäubend ♦ *n* Betäubungsmittel *nt*

narrative [ˈnærətɪv] *n* Erzählung *f* ♦ *adj* erzählend

narrator [nəˈreɪtər] *n* Erzähler(in) *m(f)*

narrow [ˈnærəu] *adj* eng, schmal; (*limited*) beschränkt ♦ *vi* sich verengen; **to have a ~ escape** mit knapper Not davonkommen; **to ~ sth down to sth** etw auf etw *acc* einschränken; **~ly** *adv* (*miss*) knapp; (*escape*) mit knapper Not; **~-minded** *adj* engstirnig

nasty [ˈnɑːstɪ] *adj* ekelhaft, fies; (*business, wound*) schlimm

nation [ˈneɪʃən] *n* Nation *f*, Volk *nt*; **~al** [ˈnæʃənl] *adj* national, National-, Landes- ♦ *n* Staatsangehörige(r) *mf*; **~al anthem** (*BRIT*) *n* Nationalhymne *f*; **~al dress** *n* Tracht *f*; **N~al Health Service** (*BRIT*) *n* Staatliche(r) Gesundheitsdienst *m*; **N~al Insurance** (*BRIT*) *n* Sozialversicherung *f*; **~alism** [ˈnæʃnəlɪzəm] *n* Nationalismus *m*; **~alist** [ˈnæʃnəlɪst] *n* Nationalist(in) *m(f)* ♦ *adj* nationalistisch; **~ality** [næʃəˈnælɪtɪ] *n* Staatsangehörigkeit *f*; **~alize** [ˈnæʃnəlaɪz] *vt* verstaatlichen; **~ally** [ˈnæʃnəlɪ] *adv* national, auf Staatsebene; **~al park** (*BRIT*) *n* Nationalpark *m*; **~wide** [ˈneɪʃənwaɪd] *adj, adv* allgemein, landesweit

---

NATIONAL TRUST

Der **National Trust** *ist ein 1895 gegründeter Natur- und Denkmalschutzverband in Großbritannien, der Gebäude und Gelände von besonderem historischen oder ästhetischen Interesse erhält und der Öffentlichkeit zugänglich macht. Viele Gebäude im Besitz des National Trust sind (z.T. gegen ein Eintrittsgeld) zu besichtigen.*

---

native [ˈneɪtɪv] *n* (*born in*) Einheimische(r) *mf*; (*original inhabitant*) Eingeborene(r) *mf* ♦ *adj* einheimisch; Eingeborenen-;

⚠ *For information on spelling reform see page 615*

(*belonging by birth*) heimatlich, Heimat-; (*inborn*) angeboren, natürlich; **a ~ of Germany** ein gebürtiger Deutscher; **a ~ speaker of French** ein französischer Muttersprachler; **N~ American** *n* Indianer(in) *m(f)*, Ureinwohner(in) *m(f)* Amerikas; **~ language** *n* Muttersprache *f*

Nativity [nəˈtɪvɪtɪ] *n*: **the ~** Christi Geburt *no art*

NATO [ˈneɪtəʊ] *n abbr* (= *North Atlantic Treaty Organization*) NATO *f*

natural [ˈnætʃrəl] *adj* natürlich; Natur-; (*inborn*) (an)geboren, **~ gas** *n* Erdgas *nt*; **~ist** *n* Naturkundler(in) *m(f)*; **~ly** *adv* natürlich

nature [ˈneɪtʃər] *n* Natur *f*; **by ~** von Natur (aus)

naught [nɔːt] *n* = **nought**

naughty [ˈnɔːtɪ] *adj* (*child*) unartig, ungezogen; (*action*) ungehörig

nausea [ˈnɔːsɪə] *n* (*sickness*) Übelkeit *f*; (*disgust*) Ekel *m*; **~te** [ˈnɔːsɪeɪt] *vt* anekeln

nautical [ˈnɔːtɪkl] *adj* nautisch; See-; (*expression*) seemännisch

naval [ˈneɪvl] *adj* Marine-, Flotten-; **~ officer** *n* Marineoffizier *m*

nave [neɪv] *n* Kirchen(haupt)schiff *nt*

navel [ˈneɪvl] *n* Nabel *m*

navigate [ˈnævɪgeɪt] *vi* navigieren; **navigation** [nævɪˈgeɪʃən] *n* Navigation *f*; **navigator** [ˈnævɪgeɪtər] *n* Steuermann *m*; (*AVIAT*) Navigator *m*; (*AUT*) Beifahrer(in) *m(f)*

navvy [ˈnævɪ] (*BRIT*) *n* Straßenarbeiter *m*

navy [ˈneɪvɪ] *n* (Kriegs)marine *f* **♦** *adj* (*also:* **~ blue**) marineblau

Nazi [ˈnɑːtsɪ] *n* Nazi *m*

NB *abbr* (= *nota bene*) NB

near [nɪər] *adj* nah **♦** *adv* in der Nähe **♦** *prep* (*also:* **~ to**: *space*) in der Nähe +*gen*; (*also:* : *time*) um +*acc* ... herum **♦** *vt* sich nähern +*dat*; **a ~ miss** knapp daneben; **~by** *adj* nahe (gelegen) **♦** *adv* in der Nähe; **~ly** *adv* fast; **I ~ly fell** ich wäre fast gefallen; **~side** *n* (*AUT*) Beifahrerseite *f* **♦** *adj* auf der Beifahrerseite; **~-sighted** *adj* kurzsichtig

neat [niːt] *adj* (*tidy*) ordentlich; (*solution*) sauber; (*pure*) pur; **~ly** *adv* (*tidily*)

ordentlich

necessarily [ˈnesɪsrɪlɪ] *adv* unbedingt

necessary [ˈnesɪsrɪ] *adj* notwendig, nötig; **he did all that was ~** er erledigte alles, was nötig war; **it is ~ to/that ...** man muß ...

necessitate [nɪˈsesɪteɪt] *vt* erforderlich machen

necessity [nɪˈsesɪtɪ] *n* (*need*) Not *f*; (*compulsion*) Notwendigkeit *f*; (*poverty*) Not *f*; **necessities** *npl* (*things needed*) das Notwendigste

neck [nek] *n* Hals *m* **♦** *vi* (*inf*) knutschen; **~ and ~** Kopf an Kopf; **~lace** [ˈneklɪs] *n* Halskette *f*; **~line** [ˈneklaɪn] *n* Ausschnitt *m*; **~tie** [ˈnektaɪ] (*US*) *n* Krawatte *f*

née [neɪ] *adj* geborene

need [niːd] *n* Bedürfnis *nt*; (*lack*) Mangel *m*; (*necessity*) Notwendigkeit *f*; (*poverty*) Not *f* **♦** *vt* brauchen; **I ~ to do it** ich muß es tun; **you don't ~ to go** du brauchst nicht zu gehen

needle [ˈniːdl] *n* Nadel *f* **♦** *vt* (*fig: inf*) ärgern

needless [ˈniːdlɪs] *adj* unnötig; **~ to say** natürlich

needlework [ˈniːdlwɜːk] *n* Handarbeit *f*

needn't [ˈniːdnt] = **need not**

needy [ˈniːdɪ] *adj* bedürftig

negative [ˈnegətɪv] *n* (*PHOT*) Negativ *nt* **♦** *adj* negativ; (*answer*) abschlägig; **~ equity** *n* Differenz zwischen gefallenem Wert und hypothekarischer Belastung eines Wohnungseigentums

neglect [nɪˈglekt] *vt* vernachlässigen **♦** *n* Vernachlässigung *f*; **~ed** *adj* vernachlässigt

negligee [ˈneglɪʒeɪ] *n* Negligé △ *nt*

negligence [ˈneglɪdʒəns] *n* Nachlässigkeit *f*

negligible [ˈneglɪdʒɪbl] *adj* unbedeutend, geringfügig

negotiable [nɪˈgəʊʃɪəbl] *adj* (*cheque*) übertragbar, einlösbar

negotiate [nɪˈgəʊʃɪeɪt] *vi* verhandeln **♦** *vt* (*treaty*) abschließen; (*difficulty*) überwinden; (*corner*) nehmen; **negotiation** [nɪgəʊʃɪˈeɪʃən] *n* Verhandlung *f*; **negotiator** *n* Unterhändler *m*

Negro [ˈniːgrəʊ] *n* Neger *m*

neigh [neɪ] *vi* wiehern

neighbour ['neɪbər] (*US* **neighbor**) *n* Nachbar(in) *m(f)*; **~hood** *n* Nachbarschaft *f*; Umgebung *f*; **~ing** *adj* benachbart, angrenzend; **~ly** *adj* (*person, attitude*) nachbarlich

neither ['naɪðər] *adj, pron* keine(r, s) (von beiden) ♦ *conj*: **he can't do it, and ~ can I** er kann es nicht und ich auch nicht ♦ *adv*: **~ good nor bad** weder gut noch schlecht; **~ story is true** keine der beiden Geschichten stimmt

neon ['ni:ɔn] *n* Neon *nt*; **~ light** *n* Neonlampe *f*

nephew ['nevju:] *n* Neffe *m*

nerve [nɜ:v] *n* Nerv *m*; (*courage*) Mut *m*; (*impudence*) Frechheit *f*; **to have a fit of ~s** in Panik geraten; **~-racking** *adj* nervenaufreibend

nervous ['nɜ:vəs] *adj* (*of the nerves*) Nerven-; (*timid*) nervös, ängstlich; **~ breakdown** *n* Nervenzusammenbruch *m*; **~ness** *n* Nervosität *f*

nest [nest] *n* Nest *nt* ♦ *vi* nisten; **~ egg** *n* (*fig*) Notgroschen *m*

nestle ['nesl] *vi* sich kuscheln

net [net] *n* Netz *nt* ♦ *adj* netto, Netto- ♦ *vt* netto einnehmen; **~ball** *n* Netzball *m*

Netherlands ['neðələndz] *npl*: **the ~** die Niederlande *pl*

nett [net] *adj* = **net**

netting ['netɪŋ] *n* Netz(werk) *nt*

nettle ['netl] *n* Nessel *f*

network ['netwɜ:k] *n* Netz *nt*

neurotic [njuə'rɔtɪk] *adj* neurotisch

neuter ['nju:tər] *adj* (*BIOL*) geschlechtslos; (*GRAM*) sächlich ♦ *vt* kastrieren

neutral ['nju:trəl] *adj* neutral ♦ *n* (*AUT*) Leerlauf *m*; **~ity** [nju:'trælɪtɪ] *n* Neutralität *f*; **~ize** *vt* (*fig*) ausgleichen

never ['nevər] *adv* nie(mals); **I ~ went** ich bin gar nicht gegangen; **in ~ my life** nie im Leben; **~-ending** *adj* endlos; **~theless** [nevəðə'les] *adv* trotzdem, dennoch

new [nju:] *adj* neu; **N~ Age** *adj* New-Age-; **~born** *adj* neugeboren; **~comer** ['nju:kʌmər] *n* Neuankömmling *m*; **~-fangled** (*pej*) *adj* neumodisch; **~-found**

adj neuentdeckt △; **~ly** *adv* frisch, neu; **~ly-weds** *npl* Frischvermählte △ *pl*; **~ moon** *n* Neumond *m*

news [nju:z] *n* Nachricht *f*; (*RAD, TV*) Nachrichten *pl*; **a piece of ~** eine Nachricht; **~ agency** *n* Nachrichtenagentur *f*; **~agent** (*BRIT*) *n* Zeitungshändler *m*; **~caster** *n* Nachrichtensprecher(in) *m(f)*; **~ flash** *n* Kurzmeldung *f*; **~letter** *n* Rundschreiben *nt*; **~paper** *n* Zeitung *f*; **~print** *n* Zeitungspapier *nt*; **~reader** *n* = **newscaster**; **~reel** *n* Wochenschau *f*; **~ stand** *n* Zeitungsstand *m*

newt [nju:t] *n* Wassermolch *m*

New Year *n* Neujahr *nt*; **~'s Day** *n* Neujahrstag *m*; **~'s Eve** *n* Silvester(abend *m*) *nt*

New Zealand [-'zi:lənd] *n* Neuseeland *nt*; **~er** *n* Neuseeländer(in) *m(f)*

next [nekst] *adj* nächste(r, s) ♦ *adv* (*after*) dann, darauf; (*~ time*) das nächste Mal; **the ~ day** am nächsten *or* folgenden Tag; **~ time** das nächste Mal; **~ year** nächstes Jahr; **~ door** *adv* nebenan ♦ *adj* (*neighbour, flat*) von nebenan; **~ of kin** nächste(r) Verwandte(r) *mf*; **~ to** *prep* neben; **~ to nothing** so gut wie nichts

NHS *n abbr* = **National Health Service**

nib [nɪb] *n* Spitze *f*

nibble ['nɪbl] *vt* knabbern an +*dat*

nice [naɪs] *adj* (*person*) nett; (*thing*) schön; (*subtle*) fein; **~-looking** *adj* gutaussehend △; **~ly** *adv* gut, nett; **~ties** ['naɪsɪtɪz] *npl* Feinheiten *pl*

nick [nɪk] *n* Einkerbung *f* ♦ *vt* (*inf: steal*) klauen; **in the ~ of time** gerade rechtzeitig

nickel ['nɪkl] *n* Nickel *nt*; (*US*) Nickel *m* (*5 cents*)

nickname ['nɪkneɪm] *n* Spitzname *m* ♦ *vt* taufen

nicotine patch ['nɪkəti:n-] *n* Nikotinpflaster *nt*

niece [ni:s] *n* Nichte *f*

Nigeria [naɪ'dʒɪərɪə] *n* Nigeria *nt*

niggling ['nɪglɪŋ] *adj* pedantisch; (*doubt, worry*) quälend

△ *For information on spelling reform see page 615*

night [naɪt] *n* Nacht *f*; (*evening*) Abend *m*;
the ~ before last vorletzte Nacht; **at** *or* **by**
~ (*before midnight*) abends; (*after midnight*)
nachts; **~cap** *n* (*drink*) Schlummertrunk *m*;
~club *n* Nachtlokal *nt*; **~dress** *n*
Nachthemd *nt*; **~fall** *n* Einbruch *m* der
Nacht; **~ gown** *n* = **nightdress**; **~ie** (*inf*) *n*
Nachthemd *nt*

nightingale ['naɪtɪŋgeɪl] *n* Nachtigall *f*

night: ~life ['naɪtlaɪf] *n* Nachtleben *nt*; **~ly**
['naɪtlɪ] *adj, adv* jeden Abend; jede Nacht;
~mare ['naɪtmeəʳ] *n* Alptraum ⚠ *m*; **~**
porter *n* Nachtportier *m*; **~ school** *n*
Abendschule *f*; **~ shift** *n* Nachtschicht *f*;
~time *n* Nacht *f*

nil [nɪl] *n* Null *f*

Nile [naɪl] *n*: **the ~** der Nil

nimble ['nɪmbl] *adj* beweglich

nine [naɪn] *num* neun; **~teen** *num*
neunzehn; **~ty** *num* neunzig

ninth [naɪnθ] *adj* neunte(r, s)

nip [nɪp] *vt* kneifen ♦ *n* Kneifen *nt*

nipple ['nɪpl] *n* Brustwarze *f*

nippy ['nɪpɪ] (*inf*) *adj* (*person*) flink; (*BRIT: car*)
flott; (: *cold*) frisch

nitrogen ['naɪtrədʒən] *n* Stickstoff *m*

---KEYWORD---

no [nəʊ] (*pl* **noes**) *adv* (*opposite of yes*) nein;
to answer no (*to question*) mit Nein
antworten; (*to request*) nein sagen; **no**
thank you nein, danke
♦ *adj* (*not any*) kein(e); **I have no money/**
time ich habe kein Geld/keine Zeit; **"no**
smoking" „Rauchen verboten"
♦ *n* Nein *nt*; (*no vote*) Neinstimme *f*

---

nobility [nəʊ'bɪlɪtɪ] *n* Adel *m*

noble ['nəʊbl] *adj* (*rank*) adlig; (*splendid*)
nobel, edel

nobody ['nəʊbədɪ] *pron* niemand, keiner

nocturnal [nɔk'tə:nl] *adj* (*tour, visit*)
nächtlich; (*animal*) Nacht-

nod [nɔd] *vi* nicken ♦ *vt* nicken mit ♦ *n*
Nicken *nt*; **~ off** *vi* einnicken

noise [nɔɪz] *n* (*sound*) Geräusch *nt*;
(*unpleasant, loud*) Lärm *m*; **noisy** ['nɔɪzɪ] *adj*

laut; (*crowd*) lärmend

nominal ['nɔmɪnl] *adj* nominell

nominate ['nɔmɪneɪt] *vt* (*suggest*)
vorschlagen; (*in election*) aufstellen;
(*appoint*) ernennen; **nomination**
[nɔmɪ'neɪʃən] *n* (*election*) Nominierung *f*;
(*appointment*) Ernennung *f*; **nominee**
[nɔmɪ'ni:] *n* Kandidat(in) *m(f)*

non... [nɔn] *prefix* Nicht-, un-; **~alcoholic**
adj alkoholfrei

nonchalant ['nɔnʃələnt] *adj* lässig

non-committal [nɔnkə'mɪtl] *adj* (*reserved*)
zurückhaltend; (*uncommitted*) unverbindlich

nondescript ['nɔndɪskrɪpt] *adj* mittelmäßig

none [nʌn] *adj, pron* kein(e, er, es) ♦ *adv*:
he's ~ the worse for it es hat ihm nicht
geschadet; **~ of you** keiner von euch; **I've**
~ left ich habe keinen mehr

nonentity [nɔ'nentɪtɪ] *n* Null *f* (*inf*)

nonetheless ['nʌnðə'les] *adv*
nichtsdestoweniger

non-existent [nɔnɪg'zɪstənt] *adj* nicht
vorhanden

non-fiction [nɔn'fɪkʃən] *n* Sachbücher *pl*

nonplussed [nɔn'plʌst] *adj* verdutzt

nonsense ['nɔnsəns] *n* Unsinn *m*

non: ~-smoker *n* Nichtraucher(in) *m(f)*; **~-**
smoking *adj* Nichtraucher-; **~-stick** *adj*
(*pan, surface*) Teflon- ®; **~-stop** *adj*
Nonstop- ⚠

noodles ['nu:dlz] *npl* Nudeln *pl*

nook [nuk] *n* Winkel *m*; **~s and crannies**
Ecken und Winkel

noon [nu:n] *n* (12 Uhr) Mittag *m*

no one ['nəʊwʌn] *pron* = **nobody**

noose [nu:s] *n* Schlinge *f*

nor [nɔ:ʳ] *conj* = **neither** ♦ *adv see* **neither**

norm [nɔ:m] *n* (*convention*) Norm *f*; (*rule,
requirement*) Vorschrift *f*

normal ['nɔ:məl] *adj* normal; **~ly** *adv*
normal; (*usually*) normalerweise

Normandy ['nɔ:məndɪ] *n* Normandie *f*

north [nɔ:θ] *n* Norden *m* ♦ *adj* nördlich,
Nord- ♦ *adv* nördlich, nach *or* im Norden;
N~ Africa *n* Nordafrika *nt*; **N~ America** *n*
Nordamerika *nt*; **~-east** *n* Nordosten *m*;
~erly ['nɔ:ðəlɪ] *adj* nördlich; **~ern** ['nɔ:ðən]

adj nördlich, Nord-; **N~ern Ireland** *n* Nordirland *nt*; **N~ Pole** *n* Nordpol *m*; **N~ Sea** *n* Nordsee *f*; **~ward(s)** ['nɔːθwəd(z)] *adv* nach Norden; **~-west** *n* Nordwesten *m*

Norway ['nɔːweɪ] *n* Norwegen *nt*

Norwegian [nɔːˈwiːdʒən] *adj* norwegisch ♦ *n* Norweger(in) *m(f)*; (*LING*) Norwegisch *nt*

nose [nəʊz] *n* Nase *f* ♦ *vi*: **to ~ about** herumschnüffeln; **~bleed** *n* Nasenbluten *nt*; **~ dive** *n* Sturzflug *m*; **~y** *adj* = **nosy**

nostalgia [nɔsˈtældʒɪə] *n* Nostalgie *f*; **nostalgic** *adj* nostalgisch

nostril ['nɔstrɪl] *n* Nasenloch *nt*

nosy ['nəʊzɪ] (*inf*) *adj* neugierig

not [nɔt] *adv* nicht; **he is ~ or isn't here** er ist nicht hier; **it's too late, isn't it?** es ist zu spät, oder *or* nicht wahr?; **~ yet/now** noch nicht/nicht jetzt; *see also* **all**; **only**

notably ['nəʊtəblɪ] *adv* (*especially*) besonders; (*noticeably*) bemerkenswert

notary ['nəʊtərɪ] *n* Notar(in) *m(f)*

notch [nɔtʃ] *n* Kerbe *f*, Einschnitt *m*

note [nəʊt] *n* (*MUS*) Note *f*, Ton *m*; (*short letter*) Nachricht *f*; (*POL*) Note *f*; (*comment, attention*) Notiz *f*; (*of lecture etc*) Aufzeichnung *f*; (*bank~*) Schein *m*; (*fame*) Ruf *m* ♦ *vt* (*observe*) bemerken; (*also*: **~ down**) notieren; **~book** *n* Notizbuch *nt*; **~d** *adj* bekannt; **~pad** *n* Notizblock *m*; **~paper** *n* Briefpapier *nt*

nothing ['nʌθɪŋ] *n* nichts; **~ new/much** nichts Neues/nicht viel; **for ~** umsonst

notice ['nəʊtɪs] *n* (*announcement*) Bekanntmachung *f*; (*warning*) Ankündigung *f*; (*dismissal*) Kündigung *f* ♦ *vt* bemerken; **to take ~ of** beachten; **at short ~** kurzfristig; **until further ~** bis auf weiteres; **to hand in one's ~** kündigen; **~able** *adj* merklich; **~ board** *n* Anschlagtafel *f*

notify ['nəʊtɪfaɪ] *vt* benachrichtigen

notion ['nəʊʃən] *n* Idee *f*

notorious [nəʊˈtɔːrɪəs] *adj* berüchtigt

notwithstanding [nɔtwɪθˈstændɪŋ] *adv* trotzdem; **~ this** ungeachtet dessen

nought [nɔːt] *n* Null *f*

noun [naʊn] *n* Substantiv *nt*

nourish ['nʌrɪʃ] *vt* nähren; **~ing** *adj* nahrhaft; **~ment** *n* Nahrung *f*

novel ['nɔvl] *n* Roman *m* ♦ *adj* neu(artig); **~ist** *n* Schriftsteller(in) *m(f)*; **~ty** *n* Neuheit *f*

November [nəʊˈvɛmbər] *n* November *m*

novice ['nɔvɪs] *n* Neuling *m*

now [naʊ] *adv* jetzt; **right ~** jetzt, gerade; **by ~** inzwischen; **just ~** gerade; **~ and then, ~ and again** ab und zu, manchmal; **from ~ on** von jetzt an; **~adays** *adv* heutzutage

nowhere ['nəʊwɛər] *adv* nirgends

nozzle ['nɔzl] *n* Düse *f*

nuclear ['njuːklɪər] *adj* (*energy etc*) Atom-, Kern-

nuclei ['njuːklɪaɪ] *npl of* **nucleus**

nucleus ['njuːklɪəs] *n* Kern *m*

nude [njuːd] *adj* nackt ♦ *n* (*ART*) Akt *m*; **in the ~** nackt

nudge [nʌdʒ] *vt* leicht anstoßen

nudist ['njuːdɪst] *n* Nudist(in) *m(f)*

nudity ['njuːdɪtɪ] *n* Nacktheit *f*

nuisance ['njuːsns] *n* Ärgernis *nt*; **what a ~!** wie ärgerlich!

nuke [njuːk] (*inf*) *n* Kernkraftwerk *nt* ♦ *vt* atomar vernichten

null [nʌl] *adj*: **~ and void** null und nichtig

numb [nʌm] *adj* taub, gefühllos ♦ *vt* betäuben

number ['nʌmbər] *n* Nummer *f*; (*numeral also*) Zahl *f*; (*quantity*) (An)zahl *f* ♦ *vt* numerieren △; (*amount to*) sein; **to be ~ed among** gezählt werden zu; **a ~ of** (*several*) einige; **they were ten in ~** sie waren zehn an der Zahl; **~ plate** *n* (*AUT*) Nummernschild *nt*

numeral ['njuːmərəl] *n* Ziffer *f*

numerate ['njuːmərɪt] *adj* rechenkundig

numerical [njuːˈmɛrɪkl] *adj* (*order*) zahlenmäßig

numerous ['njuːmərəs] *adj* zahlreich

nun [nʌn] *n* Nonne *f*

nurse [nɜːs] *n* Krankenschwester *f*; (*for children*) Kindermädchen *nt* ♦ *vt* (*patient*) pflegen; (*doubt etc*) hegen

nursery ['nɜːsərɪ] *n* (*for children*)

⚠ *For information on spelling reform see page 615*

Kinderzimmer nt; (for plants) Gärtnerei f; (for trees) Baumschule f; ~ **rhyme** n Kinderreim m; ~ **school** n Kindergarten m; ~ **slope** (BRIT) n (SKI) Idiotenhügel m (inf), Anfängerhügel m

nursing ['nɜːsɪŋ] n (profession) Krankenpflege f; ~ **home** n Privatklinik f

nurture ['nɜːtʃər] vt aufziehen

nut [nʌt] n Nuß △ f; (TECH) Schraubenmutter f; (inf) Verrückte(r) mf; **he's ~s** er ist verrückt; ~**crackers** ['nʌtkrækəz] npl Nußknacker △ m

nutmeg ['nʌtmeɡ] n Muskat(nuß △ f) m

nutrient ['njuːtrɪənt] n Nährstoff m

nutrition [njuːˈtrɪʃən] n Nahrung f; **nutritious** [njuːˈtrɪʃəs] adj nahrhaft

nutshell ['nʌtʃel] n Nußschale △ f; **in a ~** (fig) kurz gesagt

nutter ['nʌtər] (BRIT: inf) n Spinner(in) m(f)

nylon ['naɪlɒn] n Nylon nt ♦ adj Nylon-

O, o

oak [əʊk] n Eiche f ♦ adj Eichen(holz)-

O.A.P. abbr = **old-age pensioner**

oar [ɔːr] n Ruder nt

oases [əʊˈeɪsiːz] npl of **oasis**

oasis [əʊˈeɪsɪs] n Oase f

oath [əʊθ] n (statement) Eid m, Schwur m; (swearword) Fluch m

oatmeal ['əʊtmiːl] n Haferschrot m

oats [əʊts] npl Hafer m

obedience [əˈbiːdɪəns] n Gehorsam m

obedient [əˈbiːdɪənt] adj gehorsam

obesity [əʊˈbiːsɪtɪ] n Fettleibigkeit f

obey [əˈbeɪ] vt, vi: **to ~ (sb)** (jdm) gehorchen

obituary [əˈbɪtjuərɪ] n Nachruf m

object [n 'ɒbdʒɪkt, vb əbˈdʒekt] n (thing) Gegenstand m, Objekt nt; (purpose) Ziel nt ♦ vi dagegen sein; **expense is no ~** Ausgaben spielen keine Rolle; **I ~!** ich protestiere!; **to ~ to sth** Einwände gegen etw haben; (morally) Anstoß an etw acc nehmen; **to ~ that** einwenden, daß; ~**ion** [əbˈdʒekʃən] n (reason against) Einwand m,

Einspruch m; (dislike) Abneigung f; **I have no ~ion to ...** ich habe nichts gegen ... einzuwenden; ~**ionable** [əbˈdʒekʃənəbl] adj nicht einwandfrei; (language) anstößig

objective [əbˈdʒektɪv] n Ziel nt ♦ adj objektiv

obligation [ɒblɪˈɡeɪʃən] n Verpflichtung f; **without ~** unverbindlich; **obligatory** [əˈblɪɡətərɪ] adj obligatorisch

oblige [əˈblaɪdʒ] vt (compel) zwingen; (do a favour) einen Gefallen tun +dat; **to be ~d to sb for sth** jdm für etw verbunden sein

obliging [əˈblaɪdʒɪŋ] adj entgegenkommend

oblique [əˈbliːk] adj schräg, schief ♦ n Schrägstrich m

obliterate [əˈblɪtəreɪt] vt auslöschen

oblivion [əˈblɪvɪən] n Vergessenheit f

oblivious [əˈblɪvɪəs] adj nicht bewußt △

oblong ['ɒblɒŋ] n Rechteck nt ♦ adj länglich

obnoxious [əbˈnɒkʃəs] adj widerlich

oboe ['əʊbəʊ] n Oboe f

obscene [əbˈsiːn] adj obszön; **obscenity** [əbˈsenɪtɪ] n Obszönität f; **obscenities** npl (oaths) Zoten pl

obscure [əbˈskjuər] adj unklar; (indistinct) undeutlich; (unknown) unbekannt, obskur; (dark) düster ♦ vt verdunkeln; (view) verbergen; (confuse) verwirren; **obscurity** [əbˈskjuərɪtɪ] n Unklarheit f; (darkness) Dunkelheit f

observance [əbˈzɜːvəns] n Befolgung f

observant [əbˈzɜːvənt] adj aufmerksam

observation [ɒbzəˈveɪʃən] n (noticing) Beobachtung f; (surveillance) Überwachung f; (remark) Bemerkung f

observatory [əbˈzɜːvətrɪ] n Sternwarte f, Observatorium nt

observe [əbˈzɜːv] vt (notice) bemerken; (watch) beobachten; (customs) einhalten; ~**r** n Beobachter(in) m(f)

obsess [əbˈses] vt verfolgen, quälen; ~**ion** [əbˈseʃən] n Besessenheit f, Wahn m; ~**ive** adj krankhaft

obsolete ['ɒbsəliːt] adj überholt, veraltet

obstacle ['ɒbstəkl] n Hindernis nt; ~ **race** n Hindernisrennen nt

obstetrics [ɒbˈstetrɪks] n Geburtshilfe f

△ Informationen zur Rechtschreibreform Seite 615

obstinate ['ɔbstɪnɪt] *adj* hartnäckig, stur
obstruct [əb'strʌkt] *vt* versperren; *(pipe)* verstopfen; *(hinder)* hemmen; **~ion** [əb'strʌkʃən] *n* Versperrung *f*; Verstopfung *f*; *(obstacle)* Hindernis *nt*
obtain [əb'teɪn] *vt* erhalten, bekommen; *(result)* erzielen
obtrusive [əb'truːsɪv] *adj* aufdringlich
obvious ['ɔbvɪəs] *adj* offenbar, offensichtlich; **~ly** *adv* offensichtlich
occasion [ə'keɪʒən] *n* Gelegenheit *f*; *(special event)* Ereignis *nt*; *(reason)* Anlaß Δ *m ♦ vt* veranlassen; **~al** *adj* gelegentlich; **~ally** *adv* gelegentlich
occupant ['ɔkjupənt] *n* Inhaber(in) *m(f)*; *(of house)* Bewohner(in) *m(f)*
occupation [ɔkju'peɪʃən] *n* *(employment)* Tätigkeit *f*, Beruf *m*; *(pastime)* Beschäftigung *f*; *(of country)* Besetzung *f*, Okkupation *f*; **~al hazard** *n* Berufsrisiko *nt*
occupier ['ɔkjupaɪə'] *n* Bewohner(in) *m(f)*
occupy ['ɔkjupaɪ] *vt* *(take possession of)* besetzen; *(seat)* belegen; *(live in)* bewohnen; *(position, office)* bekleiden; *(position in sb's life)* einnehmen; *(time)* beanspruchen; **to ~ o.s. with sth** sich mit etw beschäftigen; **to ~ o.s. by doing sth** sich damit beschäftigen, etw zu tun
occur [ə'kəː'] *vi* vorkommen; **to ~ to sb** jdm einfallen; **~rence** *n* *(event)* Ereignis *nt*; *(appearing)* Auftreten *nt*
ocean ['əuʃən] *n* Ozean *m*, Meer *nt*; **~-going** *adj* Hochsee-
o'clock [ə'klɔk] *adv*: **it is 5 ~** es ist 5 Uhr
OCR *n abbr* = **optical character reader**
octagonal [ɔk'tægənl] *adj* achteckig
October [ɔk'təubə'] *n* Oktober *m*
octopus ['ɔktəpəs] *n* Krake *f*; *(small)* Tintenfisch *m*
odd [ɔd] *adj* *(strange)* sonderbar; *(not even)* ungerade; *(sock etc)* einzeln; *(surplus)* übrig; **60-~** so um die 60; **at ~ times** ab und zu; **to be the ~ one out** *(person)* das fünfte Rad am Wagen sein; *(thing)* nicht dazugehören; **~ity** *n* *(strangeness)* Merkwürdigkeit *f*; *(queer person)* seltsame(r) Kauz *m*; *(thing)* Kuriosität *f*; **~-job man**

(irreg) *n* Mädchen *nt* für alles; **~ jobs** *npl* gelegentlich anfallende Arbeiten; **~ly** *adv* seltsam; **~ments** *npl* Reste *pl*; **~s** *npl* Chancen *pl*; *(betting)* Gewinnchancen *pl*; **it makes no ~s** es spielt keine Rolle; **at ~s** uneinig; **~s and ends** *npl* Krimskrams *m*
odometer [ɔ'dɔmɪtə'] *(esp US)* *n* Tacho(meter) *m*
odour ['əudə'] *(US* **odor**) *n* Geruch *m*

KEYWORD

of [ɔv, əv] *prep* **1** von +*dat*; *use of gen* **the history of Germany** die Geschichte Deutschlands; **a friend of ours** ein Freund von uns; **a boy of 10** ein 10-jähriger Junge; **that was kind of you** das war sehr freundlich von Ihnen
2 *(expressing quantity, amount, dates etc)*: **a kilo of flour** ein Kilo Mehl; **how much of this do you need?** wieviel brauchen Sie (davon)?; **there were 3 of them** *(people)* sie waren zu dritt; *(objects)* es gab 3 (davon); **a cup of tea/vase of flowers** eine Tasse Tee/Vase mit Blumen; **the 5th of July** der 5 Juli
3 *(from, out of)* aus; **a bridge made of wood** eine Holzbrücke, eine Brücke aus Holz

off [ɔf] *adj, adv* *(absent)* weg, fort; *(switch)* aus(geschaltet), ab(geschaltet); *(BRIT: food: bad)* schlecht; *(cancelled)* abgesagt ♦ *prep* von +*dat*; **to be ~** *(to leave)* gehen; **to be ~ sick** krank sein; **a day ~** ein freier Tag; **to have an ~ day** einen schlechten Tag haben; **he had his coat ~** er hatte seinen Mantel aus; **10% ~** *(COMM)* 10% Rabatt; **5 km ~ (the road)** 5 km (von der Straße) entfernt; **~ the coast** vor der Küste; **I'm ~ meat** *(no longer eat it)* ich esse kein Fleisch mehr; *(no longer like it)* ich mag kein Fleisch mehr; **on the ~ chance** auf gut Glück
offal ['ɔfl] *n* Innereien *pl*
off-colour ['ɔf'kʌlə'] *adj* nicht wohl
offence [ə'fens] *(US* **offense**) *n* *(crime)* Vergehen *nt*, Straftat *f*; *(insult)* Beleidigung *f*; **to take ~ at** gekränkt sein wegen

Δ *For information on spelling reform see page 615*

offend [əˈfɛnd] vt beleidigen; ~er n Gesetzesübertreter m

offense [əˈfɛns] (US) n = offence

offensive [əˈfɛnsɪv] adj (unpleasant) übel, abstoßend; (weapon) Kampf-; (remark) verletzend ♦ n Angriff m

offer [ˈɔfər] n Angebot f ♦ vt anbieten; (opinion) äußern; (resistance) leisten; **on ~** zum Verkauf angeboten; **~ing** n Gabe f

offhand [ɔfˈhænd] adj lässig ♦ adv ohne weiteres

office [ˈɔfɪs] n Büro nt; (position) Amt nt; **doctor's ~** (US) Praxis f; **to take ~** sein Amt antreten; (POL) die Regierung übernehmen; **~ automation** n Büroautomatisierung f; **~ block** (US **~ building**) n Büro(hoch)haus nt; **~ hours** npl Dienstzeit f; (US: MED) Sprechstunde f

officer [ˈɔfɪsər] n (MIL) Offizier m; (public ~) Beamte(r) m

official [əˈfɪʃl] adj offiziell, amtlich ♦ n Beamte(r) m; **~dom** n Beamtentum nt

officiate [əˈfɪʃɪeɪt] vi amtieren

officious [əˈfɪʃəs] adj aufdringlich

offing [ˈɔfɪŋ] n: **in the ~** in (Aus)sicht

OFF-LICENCE

Off-licence ist ein Geschäft (oder eine Theke in einer Gaststätte), wo man alkoholische Getränke kaufen kann, die aber anderswo konsumiert werden müssen. In solchen Geschäften, die oft von landesweiten Ketten betrieben werden, kann man auch andere Getränke, Süßigkeiten, Zigaretten und Knabbereien kaufen.

---

off: **~-licence** (BRIT) n (shop) Wein- und Spirituosenhandlung f; **~-line** adj (COMPUT) Off-line- ♦ adv (COMPUT) off line; **~-peak** adj (charges) verbilligt; **~-putting** (BRIT) adj (person, remark etc) abstoßend; **~-road vehicle** n Geländefahrzeug nt; **~-season** adj außer Saison; **~set** (irreg: like **set**) vt ausgleichen ♦ n (also: **~set printing**) Offset(druck) m; **~shoot** n (fig: of organization) Zweig m; (: of discussion etc) Randergebnis nt; **~shore** adv in einiger

Entfernung von der Küste ♦ adj küstennah, Küsten-; **~side** adj (SPORT) im Abseits ♦ adv abseits ♦ n (AUT) Fahrerseite f; **~spring** n Nachkommenschaft f; (one) Sprößling △ m; **~stage** adv hinter den Kulissen; **~-the-cuff** adj unvorbereitet, aus dem Stegreif; **~-the-peg** (US **~-the-rack**) adv von der Stange; **~-white** adj naturweiß

Oftel [ˈɔftɛl] n Überwachungsgremium zum Verbraucherschutz nach Privatisierung der Telekommunikationsindustrie

often [ˈɔfn] adv oft

Ofwat [ˈɔfwɔt] n Überwachungsgremium zum Verbraucherschutz nach Privatisierung der Wasserindustrie

ogle [ˈəʊgl] vt liebäugeln mit

oil [ɔɪl] n Öl nt ♦ vt ölen; **~can** n Ölkännchen nt; **~field** n Ölfeld nt; **~ filter** n (AUT) Ölfilter m; **~-fired** adj Öl-; **~ painting** n Ölgemälde nt; **~ rig** n Ölplattform f; **~skins** npl Ölzeug nt; **~ slick** n Ölteppich m; **~ tanker** n (Öl)tanker m; **~ well** n Ölquelle f; **~y** adj ölig; (dirty) ölbeschmiert

ointment [ˈɔɪntmənt] n Salbe f

O.K. [ˈəʊˈkeɪ] excl in Ordnung, O.K. ♦ adj in Ordnung ♦ vt genehmigen

okay [ˈəʊˈkeɪ] = **O.K.**

old [əʊld] adj alt; **how ~ are you?** wie alt bist du?; **he's 10 years ~** er ist 10 Jahre alt; **~er brother** ältere(r) Bruder m; **~ age** n Alter nt; **~-age pensioner** (BRIT) n Rentner(in) m(f); **~-fashioned** adj altmodisch

olive [ˈɔlɪv] n (fruit) Olive f; (colour) Olive nt ♦ adj Oliven-; (coloured) olivenfarbig; **~ oil** n Olivenöl nt

Olympic [əʊˈlɪmpɪk] adj olympisch; **the ~ Games, the ~s** die Olympischen Spiele

omelet(te) [ˈɔmlɪt] n Omelett nt

omen [ˈəʊmən] n Omen nt

ominous [ˈɔmɪnəs] adj bedrohlich

omission [əʊˈmɪʃən] n Auslassung f; (neglect) Versäumnis nt

omit [əʊˈmɪt] vt auslassen; (fail to do) versäumen

on [ɔn] *prep* 1 (*indicating position*) auf +*dat*; (*with vb of motion*) auf +*acc*; (*on vertical surface, part of body*) an +*dat/acc*; **it's on the table** es ist auf dem Tisch; **she put the book on the table** sie legte das Buch auf den Tisch; **on the left** links
2 (*indicating means, method, condition etc*): **on foot** (*go, be*) zu Fuß; **on the train/plane** (*go*) mit dem Zug/Flugzeug; (*be*) im Zug/Flugzeug; **on the telephone/television** am Telefon/im Fernsehen; **to be on drugs** Drogen nehmen; **to be on holiday/business** im Urlaub/auf Geschäftsreise sein
3 (*referring to time*): **on Friday** (am) Freitag; **on Fridays** freitags; **on June 20th** am 20. Juni; **a week on Friday** Freitag in einer Woche; **on arrival he ...** als er ankam, ... er ...
4 (*about, concerning*) über +*acc*
♦ *adv* 1 (*referring to dress*) an; **she put her boots/hat on** sie zog ihre Stiefel an/setzte ihren Hut auf
2 (*further, continuously*) weiter; **to walk on** weitergehen
♦ *adj* 1 (*functioning, in operation: machine, TV, light*) an; (: *tap*) aufgedreht; (: *brakes*) angezogen; **is the meeting still on?** findet die Versammlung noch statt?; **there's a good film on** es läuft ein guter Film
2: **that's not on!** (*inf: of behaviour*) das liegt nicht drin!

once [wʌns] *adv* einmal ♦ *conj* wenn ... einmal; ~ **he had left/it was done** nachdem er gegangen war/es fertig war; **at** ~ sofort; (*at the same time*) gleichzeitig; ~ **a week** einmal in der Woche; ~ **more** noch einmal; ~ **and for all** ein für alle Mal; ~ **upon a time** es war einmal

oncoming ['ɔnkʌmɪŋ] *adj* (*traffic*) Gegen-, entgegenkommend

one [wʌn] *num* eins; (*with noun, referring back to noun*) ein/eine/ein; **it is one (o'clock)** es ist eins, es ist ein Uhr; **one hundred and fifty** einhundertfünfzig
♦ *adj* 1 (*sole*) einzige(r, s); **the one book which** das einzige Buch, welches
2 (*same*) derselbe/dieselbe/dasselbe; **they came in the one car** sie kamen alle in dem einen Auto
3 (*indef*): **one day I discovered ...** eines Tages bemerkte ich ...
♦ *pron* 1 eine(r, s); **do you have a red one?** haben Sie einen roten/eine rote/ein rotes?; **this one** diese(r, s); **that one** der/die/das; **which one?** welche(r, s)?; **one by one** einzeln
2: **one another** einander; **do you two ever see one another?** seht ihr beide euch manchmal?
3 (*impers*) man; **one never knows** man kann nie wissen; **to cut one's finger** sich in den Finger schneiden

one: ~-**armed bandit** *n* einarmiger Bandit *m*; ~-**day excursion** (*US*) *n* (*day return*) Tagesrückfahrkarte *f*; ~-**man** *adj* Einmann-; ~-**man band** *n* Einmannkapelle *f*; (*fig*) Einmannbetrieb *m*; ~-**off** (*BRIT: inf*) *n* Einzelfall *m*

oneself [wʌnˈsɛlf] *pron* (*reflexive: after prep*) sich; (~ *personally*) sich selbst *or* selber; (*emphatic*) (sich) selbst; **to hurt** ~ sich verletzen

one: ~-**sided** *adj* (*argument*) einseitig; ~-**to-**~ *adj* (*relationship*) eins-zu-eins; ~-**upmanship** *n* die Kunst, anderen um eine Nasenlänge voraus zu sein; ~-**way** *adj* (*street*) Einbahn-

ongoing ['ɔngəʊɪŋ] *adj* momentan; (*progressing*) sich entwickelnd

onion ['ʌnjən] *n* Zwiebel *f*

on-line ['ɔnlaɪn] *adj* (*COMPUT*) On-line-

onlooker ['ɔnlʊkəʳ] *n* Zuschauer(in) *m(f)*

only ['əʊnlɪ] *adv* nur, bloß ♦ *adj* einzige(r, s) ♦ *conj* nur, bloß; **an** ~ **child** ein Einzelkind; **not** ~ ... **but also ...** nicht nur ... sondern auch ...

onset ['ɔnsɛt] *n* (*start*) Beginn *m*

⚠ *For information on spelling reform see page 615*

onshore ['ɔnʃɔːʳ] adj (wind) See-
onslaught ['ɔnslɔːt] n Angriff m
onto ['ɔntu] prep = **on to**
onus ['əunəs] n Last f, Pflicht f
onward(s) ['ɔnwəd(z)] adv (place) voran,
vorwärts; **from that day ~** von dem Tag
an; **from today ~** ab heute
ooze [uːz] vi sickern
opaque [əu'peɪk] adj undurchsichtig
OPEC ['əupek] n abbr (= Organization of
Petroleum-Exporting Countries) OPEC f
open ['əupn] adj offen; (public) öffentlich;
(mind) aufgeschlossen ♦ vt öffnen,
aufmachen; (trial, motorway, account)
eröffnen ♦ vi (begin) anfangen; (shop)
aufmachen; (door, flower) aufgehen; (play)
Premiere haben; **in the ~ (air)** im Freien; **~
on to** vt fus sich öffnen auf +acc; **~ up** vt
(route) erschließen; (shop, prospects)
eröffnen ♦ vi öffnen; **~ing** n (hole) Öffnung
f; (beginning) Anfang m; (good chance)
Gelegenheit f; **~ing hours** npl
Öffnungszeiten pl; **~ learning centre** n
Weiterbildungseinrichtung auf
Teilzeitbasis; **~ly** adv offen; (publicly)
öffentlich; **~-minded** adj aufgeschlossen;
~-necked adj offen; **~-plan** adj (office)
Großraum-; (flat etc) offen angelegt

┌─────────────────────────────────┐
│ **OPEN UNIVERSITY**   │
└─────────────────────────────────┘

🛈 **Open University** ist eine 1969 in
Großbritannien gegründete
Fernuniversität für Spätstudierende. Der
Unterricht findet durch Fernseh- und
Radiosendungen statt, schriftliche Arbeiten
werden mit der Post verschickt, und der
Besuch von Sommerkursen ist Pflicht. Die
Studenten müssen eine bestimmte Anzahl
von Unterrichtseinheiten in einem
bestimmten Zeitraum absolvieren und für
die Verleihung eines akademischen Grades
eine Mindestzahl von Scheinen machen.

opera ['ɔpərə] n Oper f; **~ house** n
Opernhaus nt
operate ['ɔpəreɪt] vt (machine) bedienen;
(brakes, light) betätigen ♦ vi (machine)

laufen, in Betrieb sein; (person) arbeiten;
(MED): **to ~ on** operieren
operatic [ɔpə'rætɪk] adj Opern-
operating ['ɔpəreɪtɪŋ] adj: **~ table/theatre**
Operationstisch m/-saal m
operation [ɔpə'reɪʃən] n (working) Betrieb m;
(MED) Operation f; (undertaking)
Unternehmen nt; (MIL) Einsatz m; **to be in
~** (JUR) in Kraft sein; (machine) in Betrieb
sein; **to have an ~** (MED) operiert werden;
~al adj einsatzbereit
operative ['ɔpərətɪv] adj wirksam
operator ['ɔpəreɪtəʳ] n (of machine) Arbeiter
m; (TEL) Telefonist(in) m(f)
opinion [ə'pɪnjən] n Meinung f; **in my ~**
meiner Meinung nach; **~ated** adj
starrsinnig; **~ poll** n Meinungsumfrage f
opponent [ə'pəunənt] n Gegner m
opportunity [ɔpə'tjuːnɪtɪ] n Gelegenheit f,
Möglichkeit f; **to take the ~ of doing sth**
die Gelegenheit ergreifen, etw zu tun
oppose [ə'pəuz] vt entgegentreten +dat;
(argument, idea) ablehnen; (plan)
bekämpfen; **to be ~d to sth** gegen etw
sein; **as ~d to** im Gegensatz zu; **opposing**
adj gegnerisch; (points of view)
entgegengesetzt
opposite ['ɔpəzɪt] adj (house)
gegenüberliegend; (direction)
entgegengesetzt ♦ adv gegenüber ♦ prep
gegenüber ♦ n Gegenteil nt
opposition [ɔpə'zɪʃən] n (resistance)
Widerstand m; (POL) Opposition f; (contrast)
Gegensatz m
oppress [ə'pres] vt unterdrücken; (heat etc)
bedrücken; **~ion** [ə'preʃən] n
Unterdrückung f; **~ive** adj (authority, law)
repressiv; (burden, thought) bedrückend;
(heat) drückend
opt [ɔpt] vi: **to ~ for** sich entscheiden für; **to
~ to do sth** sich entscheiden, etw zu tun;
to ~ out of sich drücken vor +dat
optical ['ɔptɪkl] adj optisch; **~ character
reader** n optische(s) Lesegerät nt
optician [ɔp'tɪʃən] n Optiker m
optimist ['ɔptɪmɪst] n Optimist m; **~ic**
[ɔptɪ'mɪstɪk] adj optimistisch

⚠ Informationen zur Rechtschreibreform Seite 615

optimum ['ɔptɪməm] *adj* optimal

option ['ɔpʃən] *n* Wahl *f*; (COMM) Option *f*; **to keep one's ~s open** sich alle Möglichkeiten offenhalten; **~al** *adj* freiwillig; (*subject*) wahlfrei; **~al extras** *npl* Extras auf Wunsch

or [ɔː] *conj* oder; **he could not read ~ write** er konnte weder lesen noch schreiben; **~ else** sonst

oral ['ɔːrəl] *adj* mündlich ♦ *n* (*exam*) mündliche Prüfung *f*

orange ['ɔrɪndʒ] *n* (*fruit*) Apfelsine *f*, Orange *f*; (*colour*) Orange *nt* ♦ *adj* orange

orator ['ɔrətər] *n* Redner(in) *m(f)*

orbit ['ɔːbɪt] *n* Umlaufbahn *f*

orbital (motorway) ['ɔːbɪtəl-] *n* Ringautobahn *f*

orchard ['ɔːtʃəd] *n* Obstgarten *m*

orchestra ['ɔːkɪstrə] *n* Orchester *nt*; (US: *seating*) Parkett *nt*; **~l** [ɔːˈkestrəl] *adj* Orchester-, orchestral

orchid ['ɔːkɪd] *n* Orchidee *f*

ordain [ɔːˈdeɪn] *vt* (ECCL) weihen

ordeal [ɔːˈdiːl] *n* Qual *f*

order ['ɔːdər] *n* (*sequence*) Reihenfolge *f*; (*good arrangement*) Ordnung *f*; (*command*) Befehl *m*; (JUR) Anordnung *f*; (*peace*) Ordnung *f*; (*condition*) Zustand *m*; (*rank*) Klasse *f*; (COMM) Bestellung *f*; (ECCL, *honour*) Orden *m* ♦ *vt* (*also*: **put in ~**) ordnen; (*command*) befehlen; (COMM) bestellen; **in ~** in der Reihenfolge; **in (working) ~** in gutem Zustand; **in ~ to do sth** um etw zu tun; **on ~** (COMM) auf Bestellung; **to ~ sb to do sth** jdm befehlen, etw zu tun; **to ~ sth** (*command*) etw acc befehlen; **~ form** *n* Bestellschein *m*; **~ly** *n* (MIL) Sanitäter *m*; (MED) Pfleger *m* ♦ *adj* (*tidy*) ordentlich; (*well-behaved*) ruhig

ordinary ['ɔːdnrɪ] *adj* gewöhnlich ♦ *n*: **out of the ~** außergewöhnlich

Ordnance Survey ['ɔːdnəns] (BRIT) *n* amtliche(r) Kartographiedienst *m*

ore [ɔː] *n* Erz *nt*

organ ['ɔːgən] *n* (MUS) Orgel *f*; (BIOL, *fig*) Organ *nt*

organic [ɔːˈgænɪk] *adj* (*food, farming etc*) biodynamisch

organization [ɔːgənaɪˈzeɪʃən] *n* Organisation *f*; (*make-up*) Struktur *f*

organize ['ɔːgənaɪz] *vt* organisieren; **~r** *n* Organisator *m*, Veranstalter *m*

orgasm ['ɔːgæzəm] *n* Orgasmus *m*

orgy ['ɔːdʒɪ] *n* Orgie *f*

Orient ['ɔːrɪənt] *n* Orient *m*; **o~al** [ɔːrɪˈentl] *adj* orientalisch

origin ['ɔrɪdʒɪn] *n* Ursprung *m*; (*of the world*) Anfang *m*, Entstehung *f*; **~al** [əˈrɪdʒɪnl] *adj* (*first*) ursprünglich; (*painting*) original; (*idea*) originell ♦ *n* Original *nt*; **~ally** *adv* ursprünglich; originell; **~ate** [əˈrɪdʒɪneɪt] *vi* entstehen ♦ *vt* ins Leben rufen; **to ~ate from** stammen aus

Orkney ['ɔːknɪ] *npl* (*also*: **the ~ Islands**) die Orkneyinseln *pl*

ornament ['ɔːnəmənt] *n* Schmuck *m*; (*on mantelpiece*) Nippesfigur *f*; **~al** [ɔːnəˈmentl] *adj* Zier-

ornate [ɔːˈneɪt] *adj* reich verziert

orphan ['ɔːfn] *n* Waise *f*, Waisenkind *nt* ♦ *vt*: **to be ~ed** Waise werden; **~age** *n* Waisenhaus *nt*

orthodox ['ɔːθədɔks] *adj* orthodox; **~y** *n* Orthodoxie *f*; (*fig*) Konventionalität *f*

orthopaedic [ɔːθəˈpiːdɪk] (US **orthopedic**) *adj* orthopädisch

ostentatious [ɔstenˈteɪʃəs] *adj* großtuerisch, protzig

ostracize ['ɔstrəsaɪz] *vt* ausstoßen

ostrich ['ɔstrɪtʃ] *n* Strauß *m*

other ['ʌðər] *adj* andere(r, s) ♦ *pron* andere(r, s) ♦ *adv*: **~ than** anders als; **the ~ (one)** der/die/das andere; **the ~ day** neulich; **~s** (~ *people*) andere; **~wise** *adv* (*in a different way*) anders; (*or else*) sonst

otter ['ɔtər] *n* Otter *m*

ouch [autʃ] *excl* aua

ought [ɔːt] *vb aux* sollen; **I ~ to do it** ich sollte es tun; **this ~ to have been corrected** das hätte korrigiert werden sollen

ounce [auns] *n* Unze *f*

our ['auər] *adj* unser; *see also* **my**; **~s** *pron* unsere(r, s); *see also* **mine²**; **~selves** *pron*

⚠ *For information on spelling reform see page 615*

uns (selbst); (*emphatic*) (wir) selbst; *see also*
oneself

oust [aust] *vt* verdrängen

out [aut] *adv* hinaus/heraus; (*not indoors*)
draußen; (*not alight*) aus; (*unconscious*)
bewußtlos ⚠; (*results*) bekanntgegeben; **to
eat/go ~** auswärts essen/ausgehen; **~
there** da draußen; **he is ~** (*absent*) er ist
nicht da; **he was ~ in his calculations**
seine Berechnungen waren nicht richtig; **~
loud** laut; **~ of** aus; (*away from*) außerhalb
+*gen*; **to be ~ of milk** *etc* keine Milch *etc*
mehr haben; **~ of order** außer Betrieb; **~-
and-~** *adj* (*liar, thief etc*) ausgemacht;
~back *n* Hinterland *nt*; **~board (motor)** *n*
Außenbordmotor *m*; **~break** *n* Ausbruch
m; **~burst** *n* Ausbruch *m*; **~cast** *n*
Ausgestoßene(r) *mf*; **~come** *n* Ergebnis *nt*;
~crop *n* (*of rock*) Felsnase *f*; **~cry** *n* Protest
m; **~dated** *adj* überholt; **~do** (*irreg: like
do*) *vt* übertrumpfen; **~door** *adj* Außen-;
(*SPORT*) im Freien; **~doors** *adv* im Freien

outer ['autər] *adj* äußere(r, s); **~ space** *n*
Weltraum *m*

outfit ['autfit] *n* Kleidung *f*

out: ~going *adj* (*character*) aufgeschlossen;
~goings (*BRIT*) *npl* Ausgaben *pl*; **~grow**
(*irreg: like* **grow**) *vt* (*clothes*) herauswachsen
aus; (*habit*) ablegen; **~house** *n*
Nebengebäude *nt*

outing ['autɪŋ] *n* Ausflug *m*

outlandish [aut'lændɪʃ] *adj* eigenartig

out: ~law *n* Geächtete(r) *f(m)* ♦ *vt* ächten;
(*thing*) verbieten; **~lay** *n* Auslage *f*; **~let** *n*
Auslaß ⚠ *m*, Abfluß ⚠ *m*; (*also:* **retail
~let**) Absatzmarkt *m*; (*US: ELEC*) Steckdose *f*;
(*for emotions*) Ventil *nt*

outline ['autlaɪn] *n* Umriß ⚠ *m*

out: ~live *vt* überleben; **~look** *n* (*also fig*)
Aussicht *f*; (*attitude*) Einstellung *f*; **~lying**
adj entlegen; (*district*) Außen-; **~moded** *adj*
veraltet; **~number** *vt* zahlenmäßig
überlegen sein +*dat*; **~-of-date** *adj*
(*passport*) abgelaufen; (*clothes etc*)
altmodisch; (*ideas etc*) überholt; **~-of-the-
way** *adj* abgelegen; **~patient** *n*
ambulante(r) Patient *m*/ambulante

Patientin *f*; **~post** *n* (*MIL, fig*) Vorposten *m*;
~put *n* Leistung *f*, Produktion *f*; (*COMPUT*)
Ausgabe *f*

outrage ['autreɪdʒ] *n* (*cruel deed*)
Ausschreitung *f*; (*indecency*) Skandal *m* ♦ *vt*
(*morals*) verstoßen gegen; (*person*)
empören; **~ous** [aut'reɪdʒəs] *adj* unerhört

outreach worker [aut'riːtʃ-] *n*
Streetworker(in) *m(f)*

outright [*adv* aut'raɪt, *adj* 'autraɪt] *adv* (*at
once*) sofort; (*openly*) ohne Umschweife
♦ *adj* (*denial*) völlig; (*sale*) Total-; (*winner*)
unbestritten

outset ['autset] *n* Beginn *m*

outside [aut'saɪd] *n* Außenseite *f* ♦ *adj*
äußere(r, s), Außen-; (*chance*) gering ♦ *adv*
außen ♦ *prep* außerhalb +*gen*; **at the ~** (*fig*)
maximal; (*time*) spätestens; **to go ~** nach
draußen gehen; **~ lane** (*AUT*) äußere
Spur *f*; **~ line** *n* (*TEL*) Amtsanschluß ⚠ *m*;
~r *n* Außenseiter(in) *m(f)*

out: ~size *adj* übergroß; **~skirts** *npl*
Stadtrand *m*; **~spoken** *adj* freimütig;
~standing *adj* hervorragend; (*debts etc*)
ausstehend; **~stay** *vt*: **to ~stay one's
welcome** länger bleiben als erwünscht;
~stretched *adj* ausgestreckt; **~strip** *vt*
übertreffen; **~ tray** *n* Ausgangskorb *m*

outward ['autwəd] *adj* äußere(r, s); (*journey*)
Hin-; (*freight*) ausgehend ♦ *adv* nach außen;
~ly *adv* äußerlich

outweigh [aut'weɪ] *vt* (*fig*) überwiegen

outwit [aut'wɪt] *vt* überlisten

oval ['əuvl] *adj* oval ♦ *n* Oval *nt*

OVAL OFFICE

ⓘ **Oval Office**, *ein großer ovaler Raum im
Weißen Haus, ist das private Büro des
amerikanischen Präsidenten. Im weiteren
Sinne bezieht sich dieser Begriff oft auf die
Präsidentschaft selbst.*

---

ovary ['əuvəri] *n* Eierstock *m*

ovation [əu'veɪʃən] *n* Beifallssturm *m*

oven ['ʌvn] *n* Backofen *m*; **~proof** *adj*
feuerfest

over ['əuvər] *adv* (*across*) hinüber/herüber;

(*finished*) vorbei; (*left*) übrig; (*again*) wieder, noch einmal ♦ *prep* über ♦ *prefix* (*excessively*) übermäßig; ~ **here** hier(hin); ~ **there** dort(hin); **all** ~ (*everywhere*) überall; (*finished*) vorbei; ~ **and** ~ immer wieder; ~ **and above** darüber hinaus; **to ask sb** ~ jdn einladen; **to bend** ~ sich bücken

overall [*adj, n* 'əʊvərɔːl, *adv* əʊvər'ɔːl] *adj* (*situation*) allgemein; (*length*) Gesamt- ♦ *n* (*BRIT*) Kittel *m* ♦ *adv* insgesamt; ~**s** *npl* (*for man*) Overall *m*

over: ~**awe** *vt* (*frighten*) einschüchtern; (*make impression*) überwältigen; ~**balance** *vi* Übergewicht bekommen; ~**bearing** *adj* aufdringlich; ~**board** *adv* über Bord; ~**book** *vi* überbuchen

overcast ['əʊvəkɑːst] *adj* bedeckt

overcharge [əʊvə'tʃɑːdʒ] *vt*: **to ~ sb** von jdm zuviel ⚠ verlangen

overcoat ['əʊvəkəʊt] *n* Mantel *m*

overcome [əʊvə'kʌm] (*irreg: like* **come**) *vt* überwinden

over: ~**crowded** *adj* überfüllt; ~**crowding** *n* Überfüllung *f*; ~**do** (*irreg: like* **do**) *vt* (*cook too much*) verkochen; (*exaggerate*) übertreiben; ~**done** *adj* übertrieben; (*COOK*) verbraten, verkocht; ~**dose** *n* Überdosis *f*; ~**draft** *n* (*Konto*)überziehung *f*; ~**drawn** *adj* (*account*) überzogen; ~**due** *adj* überfällig; ~**estimate** *vt* überschätzen; ~**excited** *adj* überreizt; (*children*) aufgeregt

overflow [əʊvə'fləʊ] *vi* überfließen ♦ *n* (*excess*) Überschuß ⚠ *m*; (*also:* ~ **pipe**) Überlaufrohr *nt*

overgrown [əʊvə'grəʊn] *adj* (*garden*) verwildert

overhaul [*vb* əʊvə'hɔːl, *n* 'əʊvəhɔːl] *vt* (*car*) überholen; (*plans*) überprüfen ♦ *n* Überholung *f*

overhead [*adv* əʊvə'hed, *adj, n* 'əʊvəhed] *adv* oben ♦ *adj* Hoch-; (*wire*) oberirdisch; (*lighting*) Decken- ♦ *n* (*US*) = **overheads**; ~**s** *npl* (*costs*) allgemeine Unkosten *pl*; ~ **projector** *n* Overheadprojektor *m*

over: ~**hear** (*irreg: like* **hear**) *vt* (mit an)hören; ~**heat** *vi* (*engine*) heiß laufen;

~**joyed** *adj* überglücklich; ~**kill** *n* (*fig*) Rundumschlag *m*

overland ['əʊvəlænd] *adj* Überland- ♦ *adv* (*travel*) über Land

overlap [*vb* əʊvə'læp, *n* 'əʊvəlæp] *vi* sich überschneiden; (*objects*) sich teilweise decken ♦ *n* Überschneidung *f*

over: ~**leaf** *adv* umseitig; ~**load** *vt* überladen; ~**look** *vt* (*view from above*) überblicken; (*not notice*) übersehen; (*pardon*) hinwegsehen über +*acc*

overnight [*adv* əʊvə'naɪt, *adj* 'əʊvənaɪt] *adv* über Nacht ♦ *adj* (*journey*) Nacht-; ~ **stay** Übernachtung *f*; **to stay** ~ übernachten

overpass ['əʊvəpɑːs] *n* Überführung *f*

overpower [əʊvə'paʊə] *vt* überwältigen

over: ~**rate** *vt* überschätzen; ~**ride** (*irreg: like* **ride**) *vt* (*order, decision*) aufheben; (*objection*) übergehen; ~**riding** *adj* vorherrschend; ~**rule** *vt* verwerfen; ~**run** (*irreg: like* **run**) *vt* (*country*) einfallen in; (*time limit*) überziehen

overseas [əʊvə'siːz] *adv* nach/in Übersee ♦ *adj* überseeisch, Übersee-

overseer ['əʊvəsɪə] *n* Aufseher *m*

overshadow [əʊvə'ʃædəʊ] *vt* überschatten

overshoot [əʊvə'ʃuːt] (*irreg: like* **shoot**) *vt* (*runway*) hinausschießen über +*acc*

oversight ['əʊvəsaɪt] *n* (*mistake*) Versehen *nt*

over: ~**sleep** (*irreg: like* **sleep**) *vi* verschlafen; ~**spill** *n* (*Bevölkerungs*)-überschuß ⚠ *m*; ~**state** *vt* übertreiben; ~**step** *vt*: **to ~step the mark** zu weit gehen

overt [əʊ'vɜːt] *adj* offen(kundig)

overtake [əʊvə'teɪk] (*irreg: like* **take**) *vt, vi* überholen

over: ~**throw** (*irreg: like* **throw**) *vt* (*POL*) stürzen; ~**time** *n* Überstunden *pl*; ~**tone** *n* (*fig*) Note *f*

overture ['əʊvətʃʊə] *n* Ouvertüre *f*

over: ~**turn** *vt, vi* umkippen; ~**weight** *adj* zu dick; ~**whelm** *vt* überwältigen; ~**work** *n* Überarbeitung *f* ♦ *vt* überlasten *vi* sich überarbeiten; ~**wrought** *adj* überreizt

owe [əʊ] *vt* schulden; **to ~ sth to sb** (*money*) jdm etw schulden; (*favour etc*) jdm etw verdanken; **owing to** *prep* wegen +*gen*

⚠ *For information on spelling reform see page 615*

owl [aul] *n* Eule *f*

own [əun] *vt* besitzen ♦ *adj* eigen; **a room of my ~** mein eigenes Zimmer; **to get one's ~ back** sich rächen; **on one's ~** allein; **~ up** *vi*: **to ~ up (to sth)** (etw) zugeben; **~er** *n* Besitzer(in) *m(f)*; **~ership** *n* Besitz *m*

ox [ɔks] *n (pl ~en) n* Ochse *m*

oxtail ['ɔksteɪl] *n*: **~ soup** Ochsenschwanzsuppe *f*

oxygen ['ɔksɪdʒən] *n* Sauerstoff *m*; **~ mask** *n* Sauerstoffmaske *f*; **~ tent** *n* Sauerstoffzelt *nt*

oyster ['ɔɪstə*r*] *n* Auster *f*

oz. *abbr* = **ounce(s)**

ozone ['əuzəun] *n* Ozon *nt*; **~-friendly** *adj (aerosol)* ohne Treibgas; *(fridge)* FCKW-frei; **~ hole** *n* Ozonloch *nt*; **~ layer** *n* Ozonschicht *f*

P, p

p *abbr* = **penny; pence**

pa [pɑ:] *(inf) n* Papa *m*

P.A. *n abbr* = **personal assistant; public address system**

p.a. *abbr* = **per annum**

pace [peɪs] *n* Schritt *m*; *(speed)* Tempo *nt* ♦ *vi* schreiten; **to keep ~ with** Schritt halten mit; **~maker** *n* Schrittmacher *m*

pacific [pə'sɪfɪk] *adj* pazifisch ♦ *n*: **the P~ (Ocean)** der Pazifik

pacifist ['pæsɪfɪst] *n* Pazifist *m*

pacify ['pæsɪfaɪ] *vt* befrieden; *(calm)* beruhigen

pack [pæk] *n (of goods)* Packung *f*; *(of hounds)* Meute *f*; *(of cards)* Spiel *nt*; *(gang)* Bande *f* ♦ *vt (case)* packen; *(clothes)* einpacken ♦ *vi* packen; **to ~ sb off to ...** jdn nach ... schicken; **~ it in!** laß es gut sein!

package ['pækɪdʒ] *n* Paket *nt*; **~ tour** *n* Pauschalreise *f*

packed [pækt] *adj* abgepackt; **~ lunch** *n* Lunchpaket *nt*

packet ['pækɪt] *n* Päckchen *nt*

packing ['pækɪŋ] *n (action)* Packen *nt*;

(material) Verpackung *f*; **~ case** *n* (Pack)kiste *f*

pact [pækt] *n* Pakt *m*, Vertrag *m*

pad [pæd] *n (of paper)* (Schreib)block *m*; *(stuffing)* Polster *nt* ♦ *vt* polstern; **~ding** *n* Polsterung *f*

paddle ['pædl] *n* Paddel *nt*; *(US: SPORT)* Schläger *m* ♦ *vt (boat)* paddeln ♦ *vi (in sea)* planschen; **~ steamer** *n* Raddampfer *m*

paddling pool ['pædlɪŋ-] *(BRIT) n* Planschbecken *nt*

paddock ['pædək] *n* Koppel *f*

paddy field ['pædɪ-] *n* Reisfeld *nt*

padlock ['pædlɔk] *n* Vorhängeschloß ⚠ *nt* ♦ *vt* verschließen

paediatrics [pi:dɪ'ætrɪks] *(US* **pediatrics***) n* Kinderheilkunde *f*

pagan ['peɪgən] *adj* heidnisch ♦ *n* Heide *m*, Heidin *f*

page [peɪdʒ] *n* Seite *f*; *(person)* Page *m* ♦ *vt (in hotel)* ausrufen lassen

pageant ['pædʒənt] *n* Festzug *m*; **~ry** *n* Gepränge *nt*

pager ['peɪdʒə*r*] *n (TEL)* Funkrufempfänger *m*, Piepser *m (inf)*

paging device ['peɪdʒɪŋ-] *n (TEL)* = **pager**

paid [peɪd] *pt, pp* of **pay** ♦ *adj* bezahlt; **to put ~ to** *(BRIT)* zunichte machen

pail [peɪl] *n* Eimer *m*

pain [peɪn] *n* Schmerz *m*; **to be in ~** Schmerzen haben; **on ~ of death** bei Todesstrafe; **to take ~s to do sth** sich *dat* Mühe geben, etw zu tun; **~ed** *adj (expression)* gequält; **~ful** *adj (physically)* schmerzhaft; *(embarrassing)* peinlich; *(difficult)* mühsam; **~fully** *adv (fig: very)* schrecklich; **~killer** *n* Schmerzmittel *nt*; **~less** *adj* schmerzlos; **~staking** ['peɪnzteɪkɪŋ] *adj* gewissenhaft

paint [peɪnt] *n* Farbe *f* ♦ *vt* anstreichen; *(picture)* malen; **to ~ the door blue** die Tür blau streichen; **~brush** *n* Pinsel *m*; **~er** *n* Maler *m*; **~ing** *n* Malerei *f*; *(picture)* Gemälde *nt*; **~work** *n* Anstrich *m*; *(of car)* Lack *m*

pair [peə*r*] *n* Paar *nt*; **~ of scissors** Schere *f*; **~ of trousers** Hose *f*

pajamas [pə'dʒɑːməz] (US) npl Schlafanzug m

Pakistan [pɑːkɪ'stɑːn] n Pakistan nt; **~i** adj pakistanisch ♦ n Pakistani mf

pal [pæl] (inf) n Kumpel m

palace ['pæləs] n Palast m, Schloß △ nt

palatable ['pælɪtəbl] adj schmackhaft

palate ['pælɪt] n Gaumen m

palatial [pə'leɪʃəl] adj palastartig

pale [peɪl] adj blaß △, bleich ♦ n: **to be beyond the ~** die Grenzen überschreiten

Palestine ['pælɪstaɪn] n Palästina nt; **Palestinian** [pælɪs'tɪnɪən] adj palästinensisch ♦ n Palästinenser(in) m(f)

palette ['pælɪt] n Palette f

paling ['peɪlɪŋ] n (stake) Zaunpfahl m; (fence) Lattenzaun m

pall [pɔːl] vi jeden Reiz verlieren, verblassen

pallet ['pælɪt] n (for goods) Palette f

pallid ['pælɪd] adj blaß △, bleich

pallor ['pælə'] n Blässe f

palm [pɑːm] n (of hand) Handfläche f; (also: **~ tree**) Palme f ♦ vt: **to ~ sth off on sb** jdm etw andrehen; **P~ Sunday** n Palmsonntag m

palpable ['pælpəbl] adj (also fig) greifbar

palpitation [pælpɪ'teɪʃən] n Herzklopfen nt

paltry ['pɔːltrɪ] adj armselig

pamper ['pæmpə'] vt verhätscheln

pamphlet ['pæmflət] n Broschüre f

pan [pæn] n Pfanne f ♦ vi (CINE) schwenken

panache [pə'næʃ] n Schwung m

pancake ['pænkeɪk] n Pfannkuchen m

pancreas ['pæŋkrɪəs] n Bauchspeicheldrüse f

panda ['pændə] n Panda m; **~ car** (BRIT) n (Funk)streifenwagen m

pandemonium [pændɪ'məʊnɪəm] n Hölle f; (noise) Höllenlärm m

pander ['pændə'] vi: **to ~** sich richten nach

pane [peɪn] n (Fenster)scheibe f

panel ['pænl] n (of wood) Tafel f; (TV) Diskussionsrunde f; **~ling** (US **paneling**) n Täfelung f

pang [pæŋ] n: **~s of hunger** quälende(r) Hunger m; **~s of conscience** Gewissensbisse pl

panic ['pænɪk] n Panik f ♦ vi in Panik geraten; **don't ~** (nur) keine Panik; **~ky** adj (person) überängstlich; **~-stricken** adj von panischem Schrecken erfaßt; (look) panisch

pansy ['pænzɪ] n Stiefmütterchen nt; (inf) Schwule(r) m

pant [pænt] vi keuchen; (dog) hecheln

panther ['pænθə'] n Panther △ m

panties ['pæntɪz] npl (Damen)slip m

pantihose ['pæntɪhəʊz] (US) n Strumpfhose f

pantomime ['pæntəmaɪm] (BRIT) n Märchenkomödie f um Weihnachten

---
PANTOMIME

ⓘ Pantomime oder umgangssprachlich **panto** ist in Großbritannien ein zur Weihnachtszeit aufgeführtes Märchenspiel mit possenhaften Elementen, Musik, Standardrollen (ein als Frau verkleideter Mann, ein Junge, ein Bösewicht) und aktuellen Witzen. Publikumsbeteiligung wird gern gesehen (z.B. warnen die Kinder den Helden mit dem Ruf "He's behind you" vor einer drohenden Gefahr), und viele der Witze sprechen vor allem Erwachsene an, so daß pantomimes Unterhaltung für die ganze Familie bieten.

---

pantry ['pæntrɪ] n Vorratskammer f

pants [pænts] npl (BRIT: woman's) Schlüpfer m; (: man's) Unterhose f; (US: trousers) Hose f

papal ['peɪpəl] adj päpstlich

paper ['peɪpə'] n Papier nt; (news~) Zeitung f; (essay) Referat nt ♦ adj Papier-, aus Papier ♦ vt (wall) tapezieren; **~s** npl (identity ~s) Ausweis(papiere pl) m; **~back** n Taschenbuch nt; **~ bag** n Tüte f; **~ clip** n Büroklammer f; **~ hankie** n Tempotaschentuch nt ®; **~weight** n Briefbeschwerer m; **~work** n Schreibarbeit f

par [pɑː'] n (COMM) Nennwert m; (GOLF) Par nt; **on a ~ with** ebenbürtig +dat

△ For information on spelling reform see page 615

parable ['pærəbl] n (REL) Gleichnis nt
parachute ['pærəʃuːt] n Fallschirm m ♦ vi (mit dem Fallschirm) abspringen
parade [pə'reɪd] n Parade f ♦ vt aufmarschieren lassen; (fig) zur Schau stellen ♦ vi paradieren, vorbeimarschieren
paradise ['pærədaɪs] n Paradies nt
paradox ['pærədɔks] n Paradox nt; **~ically** [pærə'dɔksɪklɪ] adv paradoxerweise
paraffin ['pærəfɪn] (BRIT) n Paraffin nt
paragraph ['pærəgrɑːf] n Absatz m
parallel ['pærəlel] adj parallel ♦ n Parallele f
paralyse ['pærəlaɪz] (US **paralyze**) vt (MED) lähmen, paralysieren; (fig: organization, production etc) lahmlegen; **~d** adj gelähmt; **paralysis** [pə'rælɪsɪs] n Lähmung f
paralyze ['pærəlaɪz] (US) = **paralyse**
parameter [pə'ræmɪtər] n Parameter m; **~s** npl (framework, limits) Rahmen m
paramount ['pærəmaunt] adj höchste(r, s), oberste(r, s)
paranoid ['pærənɔɪd] adj (person) an Verfolgungswahn leidend, paranoid; (feeling) krankhaft
parapet ['pærəpɪt] n Brüstung f
paraphernalia [pærəfə'neɪlɪə] n Zubehör nt, Utensilien pl
paraphrase ['pærəfreɪz] vt umschreiben
paraplegic [pærə'pliːdʒɪk] n Querschnittsgelähmte(r) f(m)
parasite ['pærəsaɪt] n (also fig) Schmarotzer m, Parasit m
parasol ['pærəsɔl] n Sonnenschirm m
paratrooper ['pærətruːpər] n Fallschirmjäger m
parcel ['pɑːsl] n Paket nt ♦ vt (also: **~ up**) einpacken
parch [pɑːtʃ] vt (aus)dörren; **~ed** adj ausgetrocknet; (person) am Verdursten
parchment ['pɑːtʃmənt] n Pergament nt
pardon ['pɑːdn] n Verzeihung f ♦ vt (JUR) begnadigen; **~ me!, I beg your ~!** verzeihen Sie bitte!; **~ me?** (US) wie bitte?; **(I beg your) ~?** wie bitte?
parent ['pɛərənt] n Elternteil m; **~s** npl (mother and father) Eltern pl; **~al** [pə'rentl] adj elterlich, Eltern-

parentheses [pə'renθɪsiːz] npl of **parenthesis**
parenthesis [pə'renθɪsɪs] n Klammer f; (sentence) Parenthese f
Paris ['pærɪs] n Paris nt
parish ['pærɪʃ] n Gemeinde f
park [pɑːk] n Park m ♦ vt, vi parken
parking ['pɑːkɪŋ] n Parken nt; **"no ~"** „Parken verboten"; **~ lot** (US) n Parkplatz m; **~ meter** n Parkuhr f; **~ ticket** n Strafzettel m
parlance ['pɑːləns] n Sprachgebrauch m
parliament ['pɑːləmənt] n Parlament nt; **~ary** [pɑːlə'mentərɪ] adj parlamentarisch, Parlaments-
parlour ['pɑːlər] (US **parlor**) n Salon m
parochial [pə'rəukɪəl] adj (narrow-minded) eng(stirnig)
parole [pə'rəul] n: **on ~** (prisoner) auf Bewährung
parrot ['pærət] n Papagei m
parry ['pærɪ] vt parieren, abwehren
parsley ['pɑːslɪ] n Petersilie m
parsnip ['pɑːsnɪp] n Pastinake f
parson ['pɑːsn] n Pfarrer m
part [pɑːt] n (piece) Teil m; (THEAT) Rolle f; (of machine) Teil m ♦ adv = **partly** ♦ vt trennen; (hair) scheiteln ♦ vi (people) sich trennen; **to take ~ in** teilnehmen an +dat; **to take sth in good ~** etw nicht übelnehmen; **to take sb's ~** sich auf jds Seite acc stellen; **for my ~** ich für meinen Teil; **for the most ~** meistens, größtenteils; **in ~ exchange** (BRIT) in Zahlung; **~ with** vt fus hergeben; (renounce) aufgeben; **~ial** ['pɑːʃl] adj (incomplete) teilweise; (biased) parteiisch; **to be ~ial to** eine (besondere) Vorliebe haben für
participant [pɑː'tɪsɪpənt] n Teilnehmer(in) m(f)
participate [pɑː'tɪsɪpeɪt] vi: **to ~ (in)** teilnehmen (an +dat); **participation** [pɑːtɪsɪ'peɪʃən] n Teilnahme f; (sharing) Beteiligung f
participle ['pɑːtɪsɪpl] n Partizip nt
particle ['pɑːtɪkl] n Teilchen nt
particular [pə'tɪkjulər] adj bestimmt; (exact)

genau; *(fussy)* eigen; **in ~** besonders; **~ly** *adv* besonders

particulars *npl (details)* Einzelheiten *pl; (of person)* Personalien *pl*

parting ['pɑːtɪŋ] *n (separation)* Abschied *m; (BRIT: of hair)* Scheitel *m ♦ adj* Abschieds-

partition [pɑː'tɪʃən] *n (wall)* Trennwand *f; (division)* Teilung *f ♦ vt* aufteilen

partly ['pɑːtlɪ] *adv* zum Teil, teilweise

partner ['pɑːtnəʳ] *n* Partner *m ♦ vt* der Partner sein von; **~ship** *n* Partnerschaft *f; (COMM)* Teilhaberschaft *f*

partridge ['pɑːtrɪdʒ] *n* Rebhuhn *nt*

part-time ['pɑːt'taɪm] *adj* Teilzeit- ♦ *adv* stundenweise

party ['pɑːtɪ] *n (POL, JUR)* Partei *f; (group)* Gesellschaft *f; (celebration)* Party *f ♦ adj (dress)* Party-; *(politics)* Partei-; **~ line** *n (TEL)* Gemeinschaftsanschluß △ *m*

pass [pɑːs] *vt (on foot)* vorbeigehen an +*dat; (driving)* vorbeifahren an +*dat; (surpass)* übersteigen; *(hand on)* weitergeben; *(approve)* genehmigen; *(time)* verbringen; *(exam)* bestehen ♦ *vi (go by)* vorbeigehen; vorbeifahren; *(years)* vergehen; *(be successful)* bestehen ♦ *n (in mountains, SPORT)* Paß △ *m; (permission)* Passierschein *m; (in exam):* **to get a ~** bestehen; **to ~ sth through sth** etw durch etw führen; **to make a ~ at sb** *(inf)* bei jdm Annäherungsversuche machen; **~ away** *vi (euph)* verscheiden; **~ by** *vi* vorbeigehen; vorbeifahren; *(years)* vergehen; **~ on** *vt* weitergeben; **~ out** *vi (faint)* ohnmächtig werden; **~ up** *vt* vorbeigehen lassen; **~able** *adj (road)* passierbar; *(fairly good)* passabel

passage ['pæsɪdʒ] *n (corridor)* Gang *m; (in book)* (Text)stelle *f; (voyage)* Überfahrt *f;* **~way** *n* Durchgang *m*

passbook ['pɑːsbʊk] *n* Sparbuch *nt*

passenger ['pæsɪndʒəʳ] *n* Passagier *m; (on bus)* Fahrgast *m*

passer-by [pɑːsə'baɪ] *n* Passant(in) *m(f)*

passing ['pɑːsɪŋ] *adj (car)* vorbeifahrend; *(thought, affair)* momentan ♦ *n:* **in ~** beiläufig; **~ place** *n (AUT)* Ausweichstelle *f*

passion ['pæʃən] *n* Leidenschaft *f;* **~ate** *adj* leidenschaftlich

passive ['pæsɪv] *adj* passiv; *(LING)* passivisch; **~ smoking** *n* Passivrauchen *nt*

Passover ['pɑːsəʊvəʳ] *n* Passahfest *nt*

passport ['pɑːspɔːt] *n* (Reise)paß △ *m;* **~ control** *n* Paßkontrolle △ *f;* **~ office** *n* Paßamt △ *nt*

password ['pɑːswɜːd] *n* Parole *f,* Kennwort *nt,* Losung *f*

past [pɑːst] *prep (motion)* an +*dat* ... vorbei; *(position)* hinter +*dat; (later than)* nach ♦ *adj (years)* vergangen; *(president etc)* ehemalig ♦ *n* Vergangenheit *f;* **he's ~ forty** er ist über vierzig; **for the ~ few/3 days** in den letzten paar/3 Tagen; **to run ~** vorbeilaufen; **ten/quarter ~ eight** zehn/viertel nach acht

pasta ['pæstə] *n* Teigwaren *pl*

paste [peɪst] *n (fish ~ etc)* Paste *f; (glue)* Kleister *m ♦ vt* kleben

pasteurized ['pæstʃəraɪzd] *adj* pasteurisiert

pastime ['pɑːstaɪm] *n* Zeitvertreib *m*

pastor ['pɑːstəʳ] *n* Pfarrer *m*

pastry ['peɪstrɪ] *n* Blätterteig *m;* **pastries** *npl (tarts etc)* Stückchen *pl*

pasture ['pɑːstʃəʳ] *n* Weide *f*

pasty [*n* 'pæstɪ, *adj* 'peɪstɪ] *n* (Fleisch)pastete *f ♦ adj* bläßlich △, käsig

pat [pæt] *n* leichte(r) Schlag *m,* Klaps *m ♦ vt* tätscheln

patch [pætʃ] *n* Fleck *m ♦ vt* flicken; **(to go through) a bad ~** eine Pechsträhne (haben); **~ up** *vt* flicken; *(quarrel)* beilegen; **~ed** *adj* geflickt; **~y** *adj (irregular)* ungleichmäßig

pâté ['pæteɪ] *n* Pastete *f*

patent ['peɪtnt] *n* Patent *nt ♦ vt* patentieren lassen; *(by authorities)* patentieren ♦ *adj* offenkundig; **~ leather** *n* Lackleder *nt*

paternal [pə'tɜːnl] *adj* väterlich

paternity [pə'tɜːnɪtɪ] *n* Vaterschaft *f*

path [pɑːθ] *n* Pfad *m;* Weg *m*

pathetic [pə'θetɪk] *adj (very bad)* kläglich

pathological [pæθə'lɒdʒɪkl] *adj* pathologisch

pathology [pə'θɒlədʒɪ] *n* Pathologie *f*

△ *For information on spelling reform see page 615*

pathos ['peɪθɔs] *n* Rührseligkeit *f*
pathway ['pɑːθweɪ] *n* Weg *m*
patience ['peɪʃns] *n* Geduld *f*; (*BRIT: CARDS*) Patience *f*
patient ['peɪʃnt] *n* Patient(in) *m(f)*, Kranke(r) *mf* ♦ *adj* geduldig
patio ['pætɪəʊ] *n* Terrasse *f*
patriotic [pætrɪ'ɔtɪk] *adj* patriotisch
patrol [pə'trəʊl] *n* Patrouille *f*; (*police*) Streife *f* ♦ *vt* patrouillieren in +*dat* ♦ *vi* (*police*) die Runde machen; (*MIL*) patrouillieren; ~ **car** *n* Streifenwagen *m*; ~**man** (*US*) (*irreg*) *n* (Streifen)polizist *m*
patron ['peɪtrən] *n* (*in shop*) (Stamm)kunde *m*; (*in hotel*) (Stamm)gast *m*; (*supporter*) Förderer *m*; ~ **of the arts** Mäzen *m*; ~**age** ['pætrənɪdʒ] *n* Schirmherrschaft *f*; ~**ize** ['pætrənaɪz] *vt* (*support*) unterstützen; (*shop*) besuchen; (*treat condescendingly*) von oben herab behandeln; ~ **saint** *n* Schutzpatron(in) *m(f)*
patter ['pætə'] *n* (*sound: of feet*) Trappeln *nt*; (: *of rain*) Prasseln *nt*; (*sales talk*) Gerede *nt* ♦ *vi* (*feet*) trappeln; (*rain*) prasseln
pattern ['pætən] *n* Muster *nt*; (*SEWING*) Schnittmuster *nt*; (*KNITTING*) Strickanleitung *f*
pauper ['pɔːpə'] *n* Arme(r) *mf*
pause [pɔːz] *n* Pause *f* ♦ *vi* innehalten
pave [peɪv] *vt* pflastern; **to ~ the way for** den Weg bahnen für
pavement ['peɪvmənt] (*BRIT*) *n* Bürgersteig *m*
pavilion [pə'vɪlɪən] *n* Pavillon *m*; (*SPORT*) Klubhaus *nt*
paving ['peɪvɪŋ] *n* Straßenpflaster *nt*; ~ **stone** *n* Pflasterstein *m*
paw [pɔː] *n* Pfote *f*; (*of big cats*) Tatze *f*, Pranke *f* ♦ *vt* (*scrape*) scharren; (*handle*) betatschen
pawn [pɔːn] *n* Pfand *nt*; (*chess*) Bauer *m* ♦ *vt* verpfänden; ~**broker** *n* Pfandleiher *m*; ~**shop** *n* Pfandhaus *nt*
pay [peɪ] (*pt, pp* **paid**) *n* Bezahlung *f*, Lohn *m* ♦ *vt* bezahlen ♦ *vi* zahlen; (*be profitable*) sich bezahlt machen; **to ~ attention (to)** achtgeben (auf +*acc*); **to ~ sb a visit** jdn

besuchen; ~ **back** *vt* zurückzahlen; ~ **for** *vt fus* bezahlen; ~ **in** *vt* einzahlen; ~ **off** *vt* abzahlen ♦ *vi* (*scheme, decision*) sich bezahlt machen; ~ **up** *vi* bezahlen; ~**able** *adj* zahlbar, fällig; ~**ee** *n* Zahlungsempfänger *m*; ~ **envelope** (*US*) *n* Lohntüte *f*; ~**ment** *n* Bezahlung *f*; **advance ~ment** Vorauszahlung *f*; **monthly ~ment** monatliche Rate *f*; ~ **packet** (*BRIT*) *n* Lohntüte *f*; ~**phone** *n* Münzfernsprecher *m*; ~**roll** *n* Lohnliste *f*; ~ **slip** *n* Lohn-/Gehaltsstreifen *m*; ~ **television** *n* Abonnenten-Fernsehen *nt*
PC *n abbr* = **personal computer**
p.c. *abbr* = **per cent**
pea [piː] *n* Erbse *f*
peace [piːs] *n* Friede(n) *m*; ~**able** *adj* friedlich; ~**ful** *adj* friedlich, ruhig; ~**keeping** *adj* Friedens-
peach [piːtʃ] *n* Pfirsich *m*
peacock ['piːkɔk] *n* Pfau *m*
peak [piːk] *n* Spitze *f*; (*of mountain*) Gipfel *m*; (*fig*) Höhepunkt *m*; ~ **hours** *npl* (*traffic*) Hauptverkehrszeit *f*; (*telephone, electricity*) Hauptbelastungszeit *f*; ~ **period** *n* Stoßzeit *f*, Hauptzeit *f*
peal [piːl] *n* (Glocken)läuten *nt*; ~**s of laughter** schallende(s) Gelächter *nt*
peanut ['piːnʌt] *n* Erdnuß △ *f*; ~ **butter** *n* Erdnußbutter △ *f*
pear [pεə'] *n* Birne *f*
pearl [pəːl] *n* Perle *f*
peasant ['peznt] *n* Bauer *m*
peat [piːt] *n* Torf *m*
pebble ['pebl] *n* Kiesel *m*
peck [pek] *vt, vi* picken ♦ *n* (*with beak*) Schnabelhieb *m*; (*kiss*) flüchtige(r) Kuß △ *m*; ~**ing order** *n* Hackordnung *f*; ~**ish** (*BRIT: inf*) *adj* ein bißchen △ hungrig
peculiar [pɪ'kjuːlɪə'] *adj* (*odd*) seltsam; ~ **to** charakteristisch für; ~**ity** [pɪkjuːlɪ'ærɪtɪ] *n* (*singular quality*) Besonderheit *f*; (*strangeness*) Eigenartigkeit *f*
pedal ['pedl] *n* Pedal *nt* ♦ *vt, vi* (*cycle*) fahren, radfahren
pedantic [pɪ'dæntɪk] *adj* pedantisch
peddler ['pedlə'] *n* Hausierer(in) *m(f)*; (*of*

drugs) Drogenhändler(in) *m(f)*
pedestal ['pedəstl] *n* Sockel *m*
pedestrian [pi'destriən] *n* Fußgänger *m*
♦ *adj* Fußgänger-; *(humdrum)* langweilig; ~
crossing *(BRIT)* *n* Fußgängerüberweg *m*;
~**ized** *n* in eine Fußgängerzone
umgewandelt; ~ **precinct** *(BRIT),* ~ **zone**
(US) *n* Fußgängerzone *f*
pediatrics [pi:dɪˈætrɪks] *(US)* *n* =
paediatrics
pedigree ['pedɪgriː] *n* Stammbaum *m* ♦ *cpd*
(animal) reinrassig, Zucht-
pee [piː] *(inf)* *vi* pissen, pinkeln
peek [piːk] *vi* gucken
peel [piːl] *n* Schale *f* ♦ *vt* schälen ♦ *vi (paint*
etc) abblättern; *(skin)* sich schälen
peep [piːp] *n (BRIT: look)* kurze(r) Blick *m*;
(sound) Piepsen *nt* ♦ *vi (BRIT: look)* gucken;
~ **out** *vi* herausgucken; ~**hole** *n* Guckloch
nt
peer [pɪər] *vi* starren; *(peep)* gucken ♦ *n*
(nobleman) Peer *m*; *(equal)* Ebenbürtige(r)
m; ~**age** *n* Peerswürde *f*
peeved [piːvd] *adj (person)* sauer
peg [peg] *n (stake)* Pflock *m*; *(BRIT: also:*
clothes ~*)* Wäscheklammer *f*
Pekinese [piːkɪˈniːz] *n (dog)* Pekinese *m*
pelican ['pelɪkən] *n* Pelikan *m*; ~ **crossing**
(BRIT) *n (AUT)* Ampelüberweg *m*
pellet ['pelɪt] *n* Kügelchen *nt*
pelmet ['pelmɪt] *n* Blende *f*
pelt [pelt] *vt* bewerfen ♦ *vi (rain)* schütten
♦ *n* Pelz *m*, Fell *nt*
pelvis ['pelvɪs] *n* Becken *nt*
pen [pen] *n (fountain* ~*)* Federhalter *m*; *(ball-*
point ~*)* Kuli *m*; *(for sheep)* Pferch *m*
penal ['piːnl] *adj* Straf-; ~**ize** *vt (punish)*
bestrafen; *(disadvantage)* benachteiligen
penalty ['penltɪ] *n* Strafe *f*; *(FOOTBALL)*
Elfmeter *m*; ~ **(kick)** *n* Elfmeter *m*
penance ['penəns] *n* Buße *f*
pence [pens] *(BRIT) npl of* **penny**
pencil ['pensl] *n* Bleistift *m*; ~ **case** *n*
Federmäppchen *nt*; ~ **sharpener** *n*
Bleistiftspitzer *m*
pendant ['pendnt] *n* Anhänger *m*
pending ['pendɪŋ] *prep* bis (zu) ♦ *adj*

unentschieden, noch offen
pendulum ['pendjuləm] *n* Pendel *nt*
penetrate ['penɪtreɪt] *vt* durchdringen;
(enter into) eindringen in +*acc*;
penetration [penɪˈtreɪʃən] *n* Durchdringen
nt; Eindringen *nt*
penfriend ['penfrend] *(BRIT)* *n*
Brieffreund(in) *m(f)*
penguin ['peŋgwɪn] *n* Pinguin *m*
penicillin [penɪˈsɪlɪn] *n* Penizillin *nt*
peninsula [pəˈnɪnsjulə] *n* Halbinsel *f*
penis ['piːnɪs] *n* Penis *m*
penitentiary [penɪˈtenʃərɪ] *(US)* *n* Zuchthaus
nt
penknife ['pennaɪf] *n* Federmesser *nt*
pen name *n* Pseudonym *nt*
penniless ['penɪlɪs] *adj* mittellos
penny ['penɪ] *(pl* **pennies** *or (BRIT)* **pence**) *n*
Penny *m*; *(US)* Centstück *nt*
penpal ['penpæl] *n* Brieffreund(in) *m(f)*
pension ['penʃən] *n* Rente *f*; ~**er** *(BRIT)* *n*
Rentner(in) *m(f)*; ~ **fund** *n* Rentenfonds *m*;
~ **plan** *n* Rentenversicherung *f*
pensive ['pensɪv] *adj* nachdenklich

PENTAGON

🛈 **Pentagon** *heißt das fünfeckige Gebäude*
in Arlington, Virginia, in dem das
amerikanische Verteidigungsministerium
untergebracht ist. Im weiteren Sinne bezieht
sich dieses Wort auf die amerikanische
Militärführung.

---

pentathlon [pen'tæθlən] *n* Fünfkampf *m*
Pentecost ['pentɪkɒst] *n* Pfingsten *pl or nt*
penthouse ['penthaus] *n*
Dachterrassenwohnung *f*
pent-up ['pentʌp] *adj (feelings)* angestaut
penultimate [peˈnʌltɪmət] *adj* vorletzte(r, s)
people ['piːpl] *n (nation)* Volk *nt* ♦ *npl*
(persons) Leute *pl*; *(inhabitants)* Bevölkerung
f ♦ *vt* besiedeln; **several ~ came** mehrere
Leute kamen; ~ **say that ...** man sagt,
daß ...
pepper ['pepər] *n* Pfeffer *m*; *(vegetable)*
Paprika *m* ♦ *vt (pelt)* bombardieren; ~ **mill**
n Pfeffermühle *f*; ~**mint** *n (plant)*

⚠ *For information on spelling reform see page 615*

Pfefferminze f; (*sweet*) Pfefferminz nt
pep talk [pep] (*inf*) n Anstachelung f
per [pəːʳ] *prep* pro; ~ **day/person** pro Tag/
Person; ~ **annum** *adv* pro Jahr; ~ **capita**
adj (*income*) Pro-Kopf- ♦ *adv* pro Kopf
perceive [pə'siːv] *vt* (*realize*) wahrnehmen;
(*understand*) verstehen
per cent n Prozent nt; **percentage**
[pə'sentɪdʒ] n Prozentsatz m
perception [pə'sepʃən] n Wahrnehmung f;
(*insight*) Einsicht f
perceptive [pə'septɪv] *adj* (*person*)
aufmerksam; (*analysis*) tiefgehend △
perch [pəːtʃ] n Stange f; (*fish*) Flußbarsch △
m ♦ *vi* sitzen, hocken
percolator ['pəːkəleɪtəʳ] n Kaffeemaschine f
percussion [pə'kʌʃən] n (*MUS*) Schlagzeug
nt
perennial [pə'renɪəl] *adj* wiederkehrend;
(*everlasting*) unvergänglich
perfect [*adj*, n 'pəːfɪkt, *vb* pə'fekt] *adj*
vollkommen; (*crime, solution*) perfekt ♦ n
(*GRAM*) Perfekt nt ♦ *vt* vervollkommnen;
~**ion** n Vollkommenheit f; ~**ly** *adv*
vollkommen, perfekt; (*quite*) ganz, einfach
perforate ['pəːfəreɪt] *vt* durchlöchern;
perforation [pəːfə'reɪʃən] n Perforieren nt;
(*line of holes*) Perforation f
perform [pə'fɔːm] *vt* (*carry out*) durch- or
ausführen; (*task*) verrichten; (*THEAT*) spielen,
geben ♦ *vi* (*THEAT*) auftreten; ~**ance** n
Durchführung f; (*efficiency*) Leistung f;
(*show*) Vorstellung f; ~**er** n Künstler(in) m(f)
perfume ['pəːfjuːm] n Duft m; (*lady's*)
Parfüm nt
perhaps [pə'hæps] *adv* vielleicht
peril ['perɪl] n Gefahr f
perimeter [pə'rɪmɪtəʳ] n Peripherie f; (*of
circle etc*) Umfang m
period ['pɪərɪəd] n Periode f; (*GRAM*) Punkt
m; (*MED*) Periode f ♦ *adj* (*costume*)
historisch; ~**ic** [pɪərɪ'ɔdɪk] *adj* periodisch;
~**ical** [pɪərɪ'ɔdɪkl] n Zeitschrift f; ~**ically**
[pɪərɪ'ɔdɪklɪ] *adv* periodisch
peripheral [pə'rɪfərəl] *adj* Rand-, peripher
♦ n (*COMPUT*) Peripheriegerät nt
perish ['perɪʃ] *vi* umkommen; (*fruit*)

verderben; ~**able** *adj* leicht verderblich
perjury ['pəːdʒərɪ] n Meineid m
perk [pəːk] (*inf*) n (*fringe benefit*)
Vergünstigung f; ~ **up** *vi* munter werden;
~**y** *adj* keck
perm [pəːm] n Dauerwelle f
permanent ['pəːmənənt] *adj* dauernd,
ständig
permeate ['pəːmɪeɪt] *vt, vi* durchdringen
permissible [pə'mɪsɪbl] *adj* zulässig
permission [pə'mɪʃən] n Erlaubnis f
permissive [pə'mɪsɪv] *adj* nachgiebig; **the
~ society** die permissive Gesellschaft
permit [n 'pəːmɪt, vb pə'mɪt] n Zulassung f
♦ *vt* erlauben, zulassen
perpendicular [pəːpən'dɪkjuləʳ] *adj*
senkrecht
perpetrate ['pəːpɪtreɪt] *vt* begehen
perpetual [pə'petjuəl] *adj* dauernd, ständig
perpetuate [pə'petjueɪt] *vt* verewigen,
bewahren
perplex [pə'pleks] *vt* verblüffen
persecute ['pəːsɪkjuːt] *vt* verfolgen;
persecution [pəːsɪ'kjuːʃən] n Verfolgung f
perseverance [pəːsɪ'vɪərns] n Ausdauer f
persevere [pəːsɪ'vɪəʳ] *vi* durchhalten
Persian ['pəːʃən] *adj* persisch ♦ n Perser(in)
m(f); **the (~) Gulf** der Persische Golf
persist [pə'sɪst] *vi* (*in belief etc*) bleiben;
(*rain, smell*) andauern; (*continue*) nicht
aufhören; **to ~ in** bleiben bei; ~**ence** n
Beharrlichkeit f; ~**ent** *adj* beharrlich;
(*unending*) unend
person ['pəːsn] n Person f; **in ~** persönlich;
~**able** *adj* gutaussehend △; ~**al** *adj*
persönlich; (*private*) privat; (*of body*)
körperlich, Körper-; ~**al assistant** n
Assistent(in) m(f); ~**al column** n private
Kleinanzeigen pl; ~**al computer** n
Personalcomputer m; ~**ality** [pəːsə'nælɪtɪ] n
Persönlichkeit f; ~**ally** *adv* persönlich; ~**al
organizer** n Terminplaner m, Zeitplaner
m; (*electronic*) elektronisches Notizbuch nt;
~**al stereo** n Walkman m ®; ~**ify**
[pəː'sɔnɪfaɪ] *vt* verkörpern
personnel [pəːsə'nel] n Personal nt
perspective [pə'spektɪv] n Perspektive f

Perspex ['pə:speks] ® n Acrylglas nt

perspiration [pə:spɪ'reɪʃən] n Transpiration f

perspire [pə'spaɪəʳ] vi transpirieren

persuade [pə'sweɪd] vt überreden; (convince) überzeugen

persuasion [pə'sweɪʒən] n Überredung f; Überzeugung f

persuasive [pə'sweɪsɪv] adj überzeugend

pert [pə:t] adj keck

pertaining [pə:'teɪnɪŋ]: ~ **to** prep betreffend +acc

pertinent ['pə:tɪnənt] adj relevant

perturb [pə'tə:b] vt beunruhigen

pervade [pə'veɪd] vt erfüllen

perverse [pə'və:s] adj pervers; (obstinate) eigensinnig

pervert [n 'pə:və:t, vb pə'və:t] n perverse(r) Mensch m ♦ vt verdrehen; (morally) verderben

pessimist ['pesɪmɪst] n Pessimist m; **~ic** adj pessimistisch

pest [pest] n (insect) Schädling m; (fig: person) Nervensäge f; (: thing) Plage f; **~er** ['pestəʳ] vt plagen; **~icide** ['pestɪsaɪd] n Insektenvertilgungsmittel nt

pet [pet] n (animal) Haustier nt ♦ vt liebkosen, streicheln

petal ['petl] n Blütenblatt nt

peter out ['pi:tə-] vi allmählich zu Ende gehen

petite [pə'ti:t] adj zierlich

petition [pə'tɪʃən] n Bittschrift f

petrified ['petrɪfaɪd] adj versteinert; (person) starr (vor Schreck)

petrify ['petrɪfaɪ] vt versteinern; (person) erstarren lassen

petrol ['petrəl] (BRIT) n Benzin nt, Kraftstoff m; **two-/four-star ~** ≈ Normal-/ Superbenzin nt; **~ can** n Benzinkanister m

petroleum [pə'trəʊlɪəm] n Petroleum nt

petrol: ~ pump (BRIT) n (in car) Benzinpumpe f; (at garage) Zapfsäule f; **~ station** (BRIT) n Tankstelle f; **~ tank** (BRIT) n Benzintank m

petticoat ['petɪkəʊt] n Unterrock m

petty ['petɪ] adj (unimportant) unbedeutend;

(mean) kleinlich; **~ cash** n Portokasse f; **~ officer** n Maat m

pew [pju:] n Kirchenbank f

pewter ['pju:təʳ] n Zinn nt

phantom ['fæntəm] n Phantom nt

pharmacist ['fɑ:məsɪst] n Pharmazeut m; (druggist) Apotheker m

pharmacy ['fɑ:məsɪ] n Pharmazie f; (shop) Apotheke f

phase [feɪz] n Phase f ♦ vt: **to ~ sth in** etw allmählich einführen; **to ~ sth out** etw auslaufen lassen

Ph.D. n abbr = Doctor of Philosophy

pheasant ['feznt] n Fasan m

phenomena [fə'nɒmɪnə] npl of **phenomenon**

phenomenon [fə'nɒmɪnən] n Phänomen nt

philanthropist [fɪ'lænθrəpɪst] n Philanthrop m, Menschenfreund m

Philippines ['fɪlɪpi:nz] npl: **the ~** die Philippinen pl

philosopher [fɪ'lɒsəfəʳ] n Philosoph m; **philosophical** [fɪlə'sɒfɪkl] adj philosophisch; **philosophy** [fɪ'lɒsəfɪ] n Philosophie f

phlegm [flem] n (MED) Schleim m

phobia ['fəʊbjə] n (irrational fear: of insects, flying, water etc) Phobie f

phone [fəʊn] n Telefon nt ♦ vt, vi telefonieren, anrufen; **to be on the ~** telefonieren; **~ back** vt, vi zurückrufen; **~ up** vt, vi anrufen; **~ bill** n Telefonrechnung f; **~ book** n Telefonbuch nt; **~ booth** n Telefonzelle f; **~ box** n Telefonzelle f; **~ call** n Telefonanruf m; **~card** n (TEL) Telefonkarte f; **~-in** n (RAD, TV) Phone-in nt; **~ number** n Telefonnummer f

phonetics [fə'netɪks] n Phonetik f

phoney ['fəʊnɪ] (inf) adj unecht ♦ n (person) Schwindler m; (thing) Fälschung f; (banknote) Blüte f

phony ['fəʊnɪ] adj, n = **phoney**

photo ['fəʊtəʊ] n Foto nt; **~copier** ['fəʊtəʊkɒpɪəʳ] n Kopiergerät nt; **~copy** ['fəʊtəʊkɒpɪ] n Fotokopie f ♦ vt fotokopieren; **~genic** [fəʊtəʊ'dʒenɪk] adj fotogen; **~graph** n Fotografie f, Aufnahme f ♦ vt

⚠ For information on spelling reform see page 615

fotografieren; **~grapher** [ˈfəʊtəgræf] n
Fotograf m; **~graphic** [fəʊtəˈgræfɪk] adj
fotografisch; **~graphy** [fəˈtɒgrəfɪ] n
Fotografie f

phrase [freɪz] n Satz m; (expression)
Ausdruck m ♦ vt ausdrücken, formulieren; ~
book n Sprachführer m

physical [ˈfɪzɪkl] adj physikalisch; (bodily)
körperlich, physisch; ~ **education** n
Turnen nt; **~ly** adv physikalisch

physician [fɪˈzɪʃən] n Arzt m

physicist [ˈfɪzɪsɪst] n Physiker(in) m(f)

physics [ˈfɪzɪks] n Physik f

physiotherapist [fɪzɪəʊˈθerəpɪst] n
Physiotherapeut(in) m(f)

physiotherapy [fɪzɪəʊˈθerəpɪ] n
Heilgymnastik f, Physiotherapie f

physique [fɪˈziːk] n Körperbau m

pianist [ˈpiːənɪst] n Pianist(in) m(f)

piano [pɪˈænəʊ] n Klavier nt

pick [pɪk] n (tool) Pickel m; (choice) Auswahl f
♦ vt (fruit) pflücken; (choose) aussuchen;
take your ~ such dir etwas aus; **to ~ sb's**
pocket jdn bestehlen; **~ on** vt fus (person)
herumhacken auf +dat; **~ out** vt
auswählen; **~ up** vi (improve) sich erholen
♦ vt (lift up) aufheben; (learn) (schnell)
mitbekommen; (collect) abholen; (girl) (sich
dat) anlachen; (AUT: passenger) mitnehmen;
(speed) gewinnen an +dat; **to ~ o.s. up**
aufstehen

picket [ˈpɪkɪt] n (striker) Streikposten m ♦ vt
(factory) (Streik)posten aufstellen vor +dat
♦ vi (Streik)posten stehen

pickle [ˈpɪkl] n (salty mixture) Pökel m; (inf)
Klemme f ♦ vt (in Essig) einlegen; einpökeln

pickpocket [ˈpɪkpɒkɪt] n Taschendieb m

pick-up [ˈpɪkʌp] n (BRIT: on record player)
Tonabnehmer m; (small truck) Lieferwagen
m

picnic [ˈpɪknɪk] n Picknick nt ♦ vi picknicken;
~ **area** n Rastplatz m

pictorial [pɪkˈtɔːrɪəl] adj in Bildern

picture [ˈpɪktʃə] n Bild nt ♦ vt (visualize) sich
dat vorstellen; **the ~s** npl (BRIT) das Kino; ~
book n Bilderbuch nt

picturesque [pɪktʃəˈresk] adj malerisch

pie [paɪ] n (meat) Pastete f; (fruit) Torte f

piece [piːs] n Stück nt ♦ vt: **to ~ together**
zusammenstückeln; (fig) sich dat
zusammenreimen; **to take to ~s** in
Einzelteile zerlegen; **~meal** adv stückweise,
Stück für Stück; **~work** n Akkordarbeit f

pie chart n Kreisdiagramm nt

pier [pɪə] n Pier m, Mole f

pierce [pɪəs] vt durchstechen, durchbohren
(also look); **~d** adj durchgestochen;
piercing [ˈpɪəsɪŋ] adj (cry) durchdringend

pig [pɪg] n Schwein nt

pigeon [ˈpɪdʒən] n Taube f; **~hole** n
(compartment) Ablegefach nt

piggy bank [ˈpɪgɪ-] n Sparschwein nt

pig: ~headed [ˈpɪgˈhedɪd] adj dickköpfig;
~let [ˈpɪglɪt] n Ferkel nt; **~skin** [ˈpɪgskɪn] n
Schweinsleder nt; **~sty** [ˈpɪgstaɪ] n
Schweinestall m; **~tail** [ˈpɪgteɪl] n Zopf m

pike [paɪk] n Pike f; (fish) Hecht m

pilchard [ˈpɪltʃəd] n Sardine f

pile [paɪl] n Haufen m; (of books, wood)
Stapel m; (in ground) Pfahl m; (on carpet)
Flausch m ♦ vt (also: ~ up) anhäufen ♦ vi
(also: ~ up) sich anhäufen

piles [paɪlz] npl Hämorrhoiden ⚠ pl

pile-up [ˈpaɪlʌp] n (AUT)
Massenzusammenstoß m

pilfering [ˈpɪlfərɪŋ] n Diebstahl m

pilgrim [ˈpɪlgrɪm] n Pilger(in) m(f); **~age** n
Wallfahrt f

pill [pɪl] n Tablette f, Pille f; **the ~** die
(Antibaby)pille

pillage [ˈpɪlɪdʒ] vt plündern

pillar [ˈpɪlə] n Pfeiler m, Säule f (also fig); ~
box (BRIT) n Briefkasten m

pillion [ˈpɪljən] n Soziussitz m

pillow [ˈpɪləʊ] n Kissen nt; **~case** n
Kissenbezug m

pilot [ˈpaɪlət] n Pilot m; (NAUT) Lotse m ♦ adj
(scheme etc) Versuchs- ♦ vt führen; (ship)
lotsen; ~ **light** n Zündflamme f

pimp [pɪmp] n Zuhälter m

pimple [ˈpɪmpl] n Pickel m

PIN n abbr (= personal identification number)
PIN f

pin [pɪn] n Nadel f; (for sewing) Stecknadel f;

(TECH) Stift m, Bolzen m ♦ vt stecken; (keep in one position) pressen, drücken; **to ~ sth to sth** etw an etw acc heften; **to ~ sth on sb** (fig) jdm etw anhängen; **~s and needles** Kribbeln nt; **~ down** vt (fig: person): **to ~ sb down (to sth)** jdn (auf etw acc) festnageln

pinafore ['pɪnəfɔː'] n Schürze f; **~ dress** n Kleiderrock m

pinball ['pɪnbɔːl] n Flipper m

pincers ['pɪnsəz] npl Kneif- or Beißzange f; (MED) Pinzette f

pinch [pɪntʃ] n Zwicken nt, Kneifen nt; (of salt) Prise f ♦ vt zwicken, kneifen; (inf: steal) klauen ♦ vi (shoe) drücken; **at a ~** notfalls, zur Not

pincushion ['pɪnkʊʃən] n Nadelkissen nt

pine [paɪn] n (also: **~ tree**) Kiefer f ♦ vi: **to ~ for** sich sehnen nach; **~ away** vi sich zu Tode sehnen

pineapple ['paɪnæpl] n Ananas f

ping [pɪŋ] n Klingeln nt; **~-pong** ® n Pingpong nt

pink [pɪŋk] adj rosa inv ♦ n Rosa nt; (BOT) Nelke f

pinnacle ['pɪnəkl] n Spitze f

PIN number n PIN-Nummer f

pinpoint ['pɪnpɔɪnt] vt festlegen

pinstripe ['pɪnstraɪp] n Nadelstreifen m

pint [paɪnt] n Pint nt; (BRIT: inf: of beer) große(s) Bier nt

pioneer [paɪə'nɪə'] n Pionier m; (fig also) Bahnbrecher m

pious ['paɪəs] adj fromm

pip [pɪp] n Kern m; **the ~s** npl (BRIT: RAD) das Zeitzeichen

pipe [paɪp] n (smoking) Pfeife f; (tube) Rohr nt; (in house) (Rohr)leitung f ♦ vt (durch Rohre) leiten; (MUS) blasen; **~s** npl (also: **bagpipes**) Dudelsack m; **~ down** vi (be quiet) die Luft anhalten; **~ cleaner** n Pfeifenreiniger m; **~ dream** n Luftschloß △ nt; **~line** n (for oil) Pipeline f; **~r** n Pfeifer m; (bagpipes) Dudelsackbläser m

piping ['paɪpɪŋ] adv: **~ hot** siedend heiß

pique ['piːk] n gekränkte(r) Stolz m

pirate ['paɪərət] n Pirat m, Seeräuber m; **~d**

adj: **~d version** Raubkopie f; **~ radio** (BRIT) n Piratensender m

Pisces ['paɪsiːz] n Fische pl

piss [pɪs] (inf) vi pissen; **~ed** (inf) adj (drunk) voll

pistol ['pɪstl] n Pistole f

piston ['pɪstən] n Kolben m

pit [pɪt] n Grube f; (THEAT) Parterre nt; (orchestra ~) Orchestergraben m ♦ vt (mark with scars) zerfressen; (compare): **to ~ sb against sb** jdn vergleichen mit; **the ~s** npl (MOTOR RACING) die Boxen

pitch [pɪtʃ] n Wurf m; (of trader) Stand m; (SPORT) (Spiel)feld nt; (MUS) Tonlage f; (substance) Pech m ♦ vt werfen; (set up) aufschlagen ♦ vi (NAUT) rollen; **to ~ a tent** ein Zelt aufbauen; **~-black** adj pechschwarz; **~ed battle** n offene Schlacht f

piteous ['pɪtɪəs] adj kläglich, erbärmlich

pitfall ['pɪtfɔːl] n (fig) Falle f

pith [pɪθ] n Mark nt

pithy ['pɪθɪ] adj prägnant

pitiful ['pɪtɪful] adj (deserving pity) bedauernswert; (contemptible) jämmerlich

pitiless ['pɪtɪlɪs] adj erbarmungslos

pittance ['pɪtns] n Hungerlohn m

pity ['pɪtɪ] n (sympathy) Mitleid nt ♦ vt Mitleid haben mit; **what a ~!** wie schade!

pivot ['pɪvət] n Drehpunkt m ♦ vi: **to ~ (on)** sich drehen (um)

pizza ['piːtsə] n Pizza f

placard ['plækɑːd] n Plakat nt, Anschlag m

placate [plə'keɪt] vt beschwichtigen

place [pleɪs] n Platz m; (spot) Stelle f; (town etc) Ort m ♦ vt setzen, stellen, legen; (order) aufgeben; (SPORT) plazieren △; (identify) unterbringen; **to take ~** stattfinden; **out of ~** nicht am rechten Platz; (fig: remark) unangebracht; **in the first ~** erstens; **to change ~s with sb** mit jdm den Platz tauschen; **to be ~d third** (in race, exam) auf dem dritten Platz liegen

placid ['plæsɪd] adj gelassen, ruhig

plagiarism ['pleɪdʒɪərɪzəm] n Plagiat nt

plague [pleɪg] n Pest f; (fig) Plage f ♦ vt plagen

△ For information on spelling reform see page 615

plaice [pleɪs] n Scholle f
plaid [plæd] n Plaid nt
plain [pleɪn] adj (clear) klar, deutlich; (simple) einfach, schlicht; (not beautiful) alltäglich ♦ n Ebene f; **in ~ clothes** (police) in Zivil(kleidung); **~ chocolate** n Bitterschokolade f
plaintiff ['pleɪntɪf] n Kläger m
plaintive ['pleɪntɪv] adj wehleidig
plait [plæt] n Zopf m ♦ vt flechten
plan [plæn] n Plan m ♦ vt, vi planen; **according to ~** planmäßig; **to ~ to do sth** vorhaben, etw zu tun
plane [pleɪn] n Ebene f; (AVIAT) Flugzeug nt; (tool) Hobel m; (tree) Platane f
planet ['plænɪt] n Planet m
plank [plæŋk] n Brett nt
planning ['plænɪŋ] n Planung f; **family ~** Familienplanung f; **~ permission** n Baugenehmigung f
plant [plɑːnt] n Pflanze f; (TECH) (Maschinen)anlage f; (factory) Fabrik f, Werk nt ♦ vt pflanzen; (set firmly) stellen; **~ation** [plænˈteɪʃən] n Plantage f
plaque [plæk] n Gedenktafel f; (on teeth) (Zahn)belag m
plaster ['plɑːstər] n Gips m; (in house) Verputz m; (BRIT: also: **sticking ~**) Pflaster nt; (for fracture: ~ of Paris) Gipsverband m ♦ vt gipsen; (hole) zugipsen; (ceiling) verputzen; (fig: with pictures etc) bekleben, verkleben; **~ed** (inf) adj besoffen; **~er** n Gipser m
plastic ['plæstɪk] n Plastik nt or f ♦ adj (made of ~) Plastik-; (ART) plastisch, bildend; **~ bag** n Plastiktüte f
plasticine ['plæstɪsiːn] ® n Plastilin nt
plastic surgery n plastische Chirurgie f
plate [pleɪt] n Teller m; (gold/silver ~) vergoldete(s)/versilberte(s) Tafelgeschirr nt; (in book) (Bild)tafel f
plateau ['plætəu] (pl **~s** or **~x**) n (GEOG) Plateau nt, Hochebene f
plateaux ['plætəuz] npl of **plateau**
plate glass n Tafelglas nt
platform ['plætfɔːm] n (at meeting) Plattform f, Podium nt; (RAIL) Bahnsteig m; (POL) Parteiprogramm nt; **~ ticket** n Bahnsteigkarte f
platinum ['plætɪnəm] n Platin nt
platoon [pləˈtuːn] n (MIL) Zug m
platter ['plætər] n Platte f
plausible ['plɔːzɪbl] adj (theory, excuse, statement) plausibel; (person) überzeugend
play [pleɪ] n (also TECH) Spiel nt; (THEAT) (Theater)stück nt ♦ vt spielen; (another team) spielen gegen ♦ vi spielen; **to ~ safe** auf Nummer sicher gehen; **~ down** vt herunterspielen; **~ up** vi (cause trouble) frech werden; (bad leg etc) weh tun ♦ vt (person) plagen; **to ~ up to sb** jdm flattieren; **~-acting** n Schauspielerei f; **~er** n Spieler(in) m(f); **~ful** adj spielerisch; **~ground** n Spielplatz m; **~group** n Kindergarten m; **~ing card** n Spielkarte f; **~ing field** n Sportplatz m; **~mate** n Spielkamerad m; **~-off** n (SPORT) Entscheidungsspiel nt; **~pen** n Laufstall m; **~school** n = **playgroup**; **~thing** n Spielzeug nt; **~time** n (kleine) Pause f; **~wright** ['pleɪraɪt] n Theaterschriftsteller m
plc abbr (= public limited company) AG
plea [pliː] n Bitte f; (general appeal) Appell m; (JUR) Plädoyer nt; **~ bargaining** n (LAW) Aushandeln der Strafe zwischen Staatsanwaltschaft und Verteidigung
plead [pliːd] vt (poverty) zur Entschuldigung anführen; (JUR: sb's case) vertreten ♦ vi (beg) dringend bitten; (JUR) plädieren; **to ~ with sb** jdn dringend bitten
pleasant ['plɛznt] adj angenehm; **~ries** npl (polite remarks) Nettigkeiten pl
please [pliːz] vt, vi (be agreeable to) gefallen +dat; **~! bitte!; ~ yourself!** wie du willst!; **~d** adj zufrieden; (glad): **~d (about sth)** erfreut (über etw acc); **~d to meet you** angenehm; **pleasing** ['pliːzɪŋ] adj erfreulich
pleasure ['plɛʒər] n Freude f ♦ cpd Vergnügungs-; **"it's a ~"** „gern geschehen"
pleat [pliːt] n Falte f
plectrum ['plɛktrəm] n Plektron nt
pledge [plɛdʒ] n Pfand nt; (promise) Versprechen nt ♦ vt verpfänden; (promise)

geloben, versprechen

plentiful ['plentiful] *adj* reichlich

plenty ['plenti] *n* Fülle *f*, Überfluß △ *m*; **~ of** eine Menge, viel

pleurisy ['pluərisi] *n* Rippenfellentzündung *f*

pliable ['plaiəbl] *adj* biegsam; *(person)* beeinflußbar

pliers ['plaiəz] *npl* (Kneif)zange *f*

plight [plait] *n* Notlage *f*

plimsolls ['plimsəlz] *(BRIT)* *npl* Turnschuhe *pl*

plinth [plinθ] *n* Sockel *m*

P.L.O. *n abbr* (= *Palestine Liberation Organization*) PLO *f*

plod [plɔd] *vi* (*work*) sich abplagen; (*walk*) trotten

plonk [plɔŋk] *n* (*BRIT: inf: wine*) billige(r) Wein *m* ♦ *vt:* **to ~ sth down** etw hinknallen

plot [plɔt] *n* Komplott *nt*; (*story*) Handlung *f*; (*of land*) Grundstück *nt* ♦ *vt* markieren; (*curve*) zeichnen; (*movements*) nachzeichnen ♦ *vi* (*plan secretly*) sich verschwören

plough [plau] *(US* **plow**) *n* Pflug *m* ♦ *vt* pflügen; **~ back** *vt* (*COMM*) wieder in das Geschäft stecken; **~ through** *vt fus* (*water*) durchpflügen; (*book*) sich kämpfen durch

plow [plau] *(US)* = **plough**

ploy [plɔi] *n* Masche *f*

pluck [plʌk] *vt* (*fruit*) pflücken; (*guitar*) zupfen; (*goose etc*) rupfen ♦ *n* Mut *m*; **to ~ up courage** all seinen Mut zusammennehmen

plug [plʌg] *n* Stöpsel *m*; (*ELEC*) Stecker *m*; (*inf: publicity*) Schleichwerbung *f*; (*AUT*) Zündkerze *f* ♦ *vt* (zu)stopfen; (*inf: advertise*) Reklame machen für; **~ in** *vt* (*ELEC*) anschließen

plum [plʌm] *n* Pflaume *f*, Zwetsch(g)e *f*

plumage ['plu:midʒ] *n* Gefieder *nt*

plumber ['plʌmə*r*] *n* Klempner *m*, Installateur *m*; **plumbing** ['plʌmiŋ] *n* (*craft*) Installieren *nt*; (*fittings*) Leitungen *pl*

plummet ['plʌmit] *vi* (ab)stürzen

plump [plʌmp] *adj* rundlich, füllig ♦ *vt* plumpsen lassen; **to ~ for** (*inf: choose*) sich entscheiden für

plunder ['plʌndə*r*] *n* Plünderung *f*; (*loot*) Beute *f* ♦ *vt* plündern

plunge [plʌndʒ] *n* Sturz *m* ♦ *vt* stoßen ♦ *vi* (sich) stürzen; **to take the ~** den Sprung wagen; **plunging** ['plʌndʒiŋ] *adj* (*neckline*) offenherzig

plural ['pluərl] *n* Plural *m*, Mehrzahl *f*

plus [plʌs] *n* (*also:* **~ sign**) Plus(zeichen) *nt* ♦ *prep* plus, und; **ten/twenty ~** mehr als zehn/zwanzig

plush [plʌʃ] *adj* (*also:* **~y:** *inf*) feudal

ply [plai] *vt* (*trade*) (be)treiben; (*with questions*) zusetzen +*dat*; (*ship, taxi*) befahren ♦ *vi* (*ship, taxi*) verkehren ♦ *n:* **three-~** (*wool*) Dreifach-; **to ~ sb with drink** jdn zum Trinken animieren; **~wood** *n* Sperrholz *nt*

P.M. *n abbr* = **prime minister**

p.m. *adv abbr* (= *post meridiem*) nachmittags

pneumatic drill *n* Preßlufthammer △ *m*

pneumonia [nju:'məuniə] *n* Lungenentzündung *f*

poach [pəutʃ] *vt* (*COOK*) pochieren; (*game*) stehlen ♦ *vi* (*steal*) wildern; **~ed** *adj* (*egg*) verloren; **~er** *n* Wilddieb *m*

P.O. Box *n abbr* = **Post Office Box**

pocket ['pɔkit] *n* Tasche *f*; (*of resistance*) (Widerstands)nest *nt* ♦ *vt* einstecken; **to be out of ~** (*BRIT*) draufzahlen; **~book** *n* Taschenbuch *nt*; **~ calculator** *n* Taschenrechner *m*; **~ knife** *n* Taschenmesser *nt*; **~ money** *n* Taschengeld *nt*

pod [pɔd] *n* Hülse *f*; (*of peas also*) Schote *f*

podgy ['pɔdʒi] *adj* pummelig

podiatrist [pɔ'di:ətrist] *(US)* *n* Fußpfleger(in) *m(f)*

poem ['pəuim] *n* Gedicht *nt*

poet ['pəuit] *n* Dichter *m*, Poet *m*; **~ic** [pəu'etik] *adj* poetisch, dichterisch; **~ laureate** *n* Hofdichter *m*; **~ry** *n* Poesie *f*; (*poems*) Gedichte *pl*

poignant ['pɔinjənt] *adj* (*touching*) ergreifend

point [pɔint] *n* (*also in discussion, scoring*) Punkt *m*; (*spot*) Punkt *m*, Stelle *f*; (*sharpened tip*) Spitze *f*; (*moment*) (Zeit)punkt *m*;

△ *For information on spelling reform see page 615*

(purpose) Zweck m; *(idea)* Argument nt; *(decimal)* Dezimalstelle f; *(personal characteristic)* Seite f ♦ vt zeigen mit; *(gun)* richten ♦ vi zeigen; ~s npl *(RAIL)* Weichen pl; **to be on the ~ of doing sth** drauf und dran sein, etw zu tun; **to make a ~ of** Wert darauf legen; **to get the ~** verstehen, worum es geht; **to come to the ~** zur Sache kommen; **there's no ~ (in doing sth)** es hat keinen Sinn(, etw zu tun); **~ out** vt hinweisen auf +acc; **~ to** vt fus zeigen auf +acc; **~-blank** adv *(at close range)* aus nächster Entfernung; *(bluntly)* unverblümt; **~ed** adj *(also fig)* spitz, scharf; **~edly** adv *(fig)* spitz; **~er** n Zeigestock m; *(on dial)* Zeiger m; **~less** adj sinnlos; **~ of view** n Stand- or Gesichtspunkt m

poise [pɔɪz] n Haltung f; *(fig)* Gelassenheit f

poison [ˈpɔɪzn] n *(also fig)* Gift nt ♦ vt vergiften; **~ing** n Vergiftung f; **~ous** adj giftig, Gift-

poke [pəʊk] vt stoßen; *(put)* stecken; *(fire)* schüren; *(hole)* bohren; **~ about** vi herumstochern; *(nose around)* herumwühlen

poker [ˈpəʊkəʳ] n Schürhaken m; *(CARDS)* Poker nt

poky [ˈpəʊkɪ] adj eng

Poland [ˈpəʊlənd] n Polen nt

polar [ˈpəʊləʳ] adj Polar-, polar; **~ bear** n Eisbär m

Pole [pəʊl] n Pole m, Polin f

pole [pəʊl] n Stange f, Pfosten m; *(flag~, telegraph ~)* Stange f, Mast m; *(ELEC, GEOG)* Pol m; *(SPORT: vaulting ~)* Stab m; *(ski ~)* Stock m; **~ bean** n *(US)* *(runner bean)* Stangenbohne f; **~ vault** n Stabhochsprung m

police [pəˈliːs] n Polizei f ♦ vt kontrollieren; **~ car** n Polizeiwagen m; **~man** *(irreg)* n Polizist m; **~ state** n Polizeistaat m; **~ station** n (Polizei)revier nt, Wache f; **~woman** *(irreg)* n Polizistin f

policy [ˈpɒlɪsɪ] n Politik f; *(insurance)* (Versicherungs)police f

polio [ˈpəʊlɪəʊ] n *(spinale)* Kinderlähmung f, Polio f

Polish [ˈpəʊlɪʃ] adj polnisch ♦ n *(LING)* Polnisch nt

polish [ˈpɒlɪʃ] n Politur f; *(for floor)* Wachs nt; *(for shoes)* Creme f; *(for nails)* Lack m; *(shine)* Glanz m; *(of furniture)* Politur f; *(fig)* Schliff m ♦ vt polieren; *(shoes)* putzen; *(fig)* den letzten Schliff geben +dat; **~ off** vt *(inf: food)* wegputzen; (: drink) hinunterschütten; **~ed** adj glänzend; *(manners)* verfeinert

polite [pəˈlaɪt] adj höflich; **~ly** adv höflich; **~ness** n Höflichkeit f

political [pəˈlɪtɪkl] adj politisch; **~ly** adv politisch; **~ly correct** politisch korrekt

politician [pɒlɪˈtɪʃən] n Politiker m

politics npl Politik f

polka dot [ˈpɒlkə-] n Tupfen m

poll [pəʊl] n Abstimmung f; *(in election)* Wahl f; *(votes cast)* Wahlbeteiligung f; *(opinion ~)* Umfrage f ♦ vt *(votes)* erhalten

pollen [ˈpɒlən] n *(BOT)* Blütenstaub m, Pollen m

polling [ˈpəʊlɪŋ-]: **~ booth** *(BRIT)* n Wahlkabine f; **~ day** *(BRIT)* n Wahltag m; **~ station** *(BRIT)* n Wahllokal nt

pollute [pəˈluːt] vt verschmutzen, verunreinigen; **~d** adj verschmutzt; **pollution** [pəˈluːʃən] n Verschmutzung f

polo [ˈpəʊləʊ] n Polo nt; **~ neck** n *(also: ~- necked sweater)* Rollkragen m; Rollkragenpullover m; **~ shirt** n Polohemd nt

polystyrene [pɒlɪˈstaɪriːn] n Styropor nt

polytechnic [pɒlɪˈteknɪk] n technische Hochschule f

polythene [ˈpɒlɪθiːn] n Plastik nt; **~ bag** n Plastiktüte f

pomegranate [ˈpɒmɪɡrænɪt] n Granatapfel m

pompom [ˈpɒmpɒm] n Troddel f, Pompon m

pompous [ˈpɒmpəs] adj aufgeblasen; *(language)* geschwollen

pond [pɒnd] n Teich m, Weiher m

ponder [ˈpɒndəʳ] vt nachdenken über +acc; **~ous** adj schwerfällig

pong [pɒŋ] *(BRIT: inf)* n Mief m

pontiff ['pɒntɪf] n Pontifex m

pontoon [pɒn'tuːn] n Ponton m; (CARDS) 17-und-4 nt

pony ['pəʊnɪ] n Pony nt; **~tail** n Pferdeschwanz m; **~ trekking** (BRIT) n Ponyreiten nt

poodle ['puːdl] n Pudel m

pool [puːl] n (swimming ~) Schwimmbad nt; (: private) Swimmingpool m; (of liquid, blood) Lache f; (fund) (gemeinsame) Kasse f; (billiards) Poolspiel nt ♦ vt (money etc) zusammenlegen; **typing ~** Schreibzentrale f; **(football) ~s** Toto nt

poor [pʊəʳ] adj arm; (not good) schlecht ♦ npl: **the ~** die Armen pl; **~ in** (resources) arm an +dat; **~ly** adv schlecht; (dressed) ärmlich ♦ adj schlecht

pop [pɒp] n Knall m; (music) Popmusik f; (drink) Limo(nade) f; (US: inf) Pa m ♦ vt (put) stecken; (balloon) platzen lassen ♦ vi knallen; **~ in** vi kurz vorbeigehen or vorbeikommen; **~ out** vi (person) kurz rausgehen; (thing) herausspringen; **~ up** vi auftauchen; **~corn** n Puffmais m

pope [pəʊp] n Papst m

poplar ['pɒpləʳ] n Pappel f

poppy ['pɒpɪ] n Mohn m

Popsicle ['pɒpsɪkl] (® US) n (ice lolly) Eis nt am Stiel

populace ['pɒpjʊləs] n Volk nt

popular ['pɒpjʊləʳ] adj beliebt, populär; (of the people) volkstümlich; (widespread) allgemein; **~ity** [pɒpjʊ'lærɪtɪ] n Beliebtheit f, Popularität f; **~ly** adv allgemein, überall

population [pɒpjʊ'leɪʃən] n Bevölkerung f; (of town) Einwohner pl

populous ['pɒpjʊləs] adj dicht besiedelt

porcelain ['pɔːslɪn] n Porzellan nt

porch [pɔːtʃ] n Vorbau m, Veranda f

porcupine ['pɔːkjupaɪn] n Stachelschwein nt

pore [pɔːʳ] n Pore f ♦ vi: **to ~ over** brüten über +dat

pork [pɔːk] n Schweinefleisch nt

porn [pɔːn] n Porno m; **~ographic** [pɔːnə'græfɪk] adj pornographisch △; **~ography** [pɔː'nɔgrəfɪ] n Pornographie △ f

porous ['pɔːrəs] adj porös; (skin) porig

porpoise ['pɔːpəs] n Tümmler m

porridge ['pɒrɪdʒ] n Haferbrei m

port [pɔːt] n Hafen m; (town) Hafenstadt f; (NAUT: left side) Backbord nt; (wine) Portwein m; **~ of call** Anlaufhafen m

portable ['pɔːtəbl] adj tragbar

porter ['pɔːtəʳ] n Pförtner(in) m(f); (for luggage) (Gepäck)träger m

portfolio [pɔːt'fəʊlɪəʊ] n (case) Mappe f; (POL) Geschäftsbereich m; (FIN) Portefeuille nt; (of artist) Kollektion f

porthole ['pɔːthəʊl] n Bullauge nt

portion ['pɔːʃən] n Teil m, Stück nt; (of food) Portion f

portrait ['pɔːtreɪt] n Porträt nt

portray [pɔː'treɪ] vt darstellen; **~al** n Darstellung f

Portugal ['pɔːtjugl] n Portugal nt

Portuguese [pɔːtju'giːz] adj portugiesisch ♦ n inv Portugiese m, Portugiesin f; (LING) Portugiesisch nt

pose [pəʊz] n Stellung f, Pose f; (affectation) Pose f ♦ vi posieren ♦ vt stellen

posh [pɒʃ] (inf) adj (piek)fein

position [pə'zɪʃən] n Stellung f; (place) Lage f; (job) Stelle f; (attitude) Standpunkt m ♦ vt aufstellen

positive ['pɒzɪtɪv] adj positiv; (convinced) sicher; (definite) eindeutig

posse ['pɒsɪ] (US) n Aufgebot nt

possess [pə'zes] vt besitzen; **~ion** [pə'zeʃən] n Besitz m; **~ive** adj besitzergreifend, eigensüchtig

possibility [pɒsɪ'bɪlɪtɪ] n Möglichkeit f

possible ['pɒsɪbl] adj möglich; **as big as ~** so groß wie möglich, möglichst groß; **possibly** adv möglicherweise, vielleicht; **I cannot possibly come** ich kann unmöglich kommen

post [pəʊst] n (BRIT: letters, delivery) Post f; (pole) Pfosten m, Pfahl m; (place of duty) Posten m; (job) Stelle f ♦ vt (notice) anschlagen; (BRIT: letters) aufgeben; (: appoint) versetzen; (soldiers) aufstellen; **~age** n Postgebühr f, Porto nt; **~al** adj Post-; **~al order** n Postanweisung f; **~box** (BRIT) n Briefkasten m; **~card** n Postkarte f;

△ For information on spelling reform see page 615

~code (*BRIT*) n Postleitzahl f

postdate ['pəust'deɪt] vt (*cheque*) nachdatieren

poster ['pəustə*r*] n Plakat nt, Poster nt

poste restante [pəust'restã:nt] n Aufbewahrungsstelle f für postlagernde Sendungen

posterior [pɒs'tɪərɪə*r*] (*inf*) n Hintern m

posterity [pɒs'terɪtɪ] n Nachwelt f

postgraduate ['pəust'grædjuət] n Weiterstudierende(r) mf

posthumous ['pɒstjuməs] adj post(h)um

postman ['pəustmən] (*irreg*) n Briefträger m

postmark ['pəustmɑ:k] n Poststempel m

post-mortem [pəust'mɔ:təm] n Autopsie f

post office n Postamt nt, Post f; (*organization*) Post f; **Post Office Box** n Postfach nt

postpone [pəus'pəun] vt verschieben

postscript ['pəustskrɪpt] n Postskript nt; (*to affair*) Nachspiel nt

posture ['pɒstʃə*r*] n Haltung f ♦ vi posieren

postwar [pəust'wɔ:*r*] adj Nachkriegs-

postwoman ['pəustwumən] (*irreg*) n Briefträgerin f

posy ['pəuzɪ] n Blumenstrauß m

pot [pɒt] n Topf m; (*tea~*) Kanne f; (*inf: marijuana*) Hasch m ♦ vt (*plant*) eintopfen; **to go to ~** (*inf: work*) auf den Hund kommen

potato [pə'teɪtəu] (*pl* **~es**) n Kartoffel f; **~ peeler** n Kartoffelschäler m

potent ['pəutnt] adj stark; (*argument*) zwingend

potential [pə'tenʃl] adj potentiell △ ♦ n Potential △ nt; **~ly** adv potentiell △

pothole ['pɒthəul] n (*in road*) Schlagloch nt; (*BRIT: underground*) Höhle f; **potholing** (*BRIT*) n: **to go potholing** Höhlen erforschen

potion ['pəuʃən] n Trank m

potluck [pɒt'lʌk] n: **to take ~ with sth** etw auf gut Glück nehmen

pot plant n Topfpflanze f

potter ['pɒtə*r*] n Töpfer m ♦ vi herumhantieren; **~y** n Töpferwaren pl; (*place*) Töpferei f

potty ['pɒtɪ] adj (*inf: mad*) verrückt ♦ n Töpfchen nt

pouch [pautʃ] n Beutel m

pouf(fe) [pu:f] n Sitzkissen nt

poultry ['pəultrɪ] n Geflügel nt

pounce [pauns] vi sich stürzen ♦ n Sprung m, Satz m; **to ~ on** sich stürzen auf +acc

pound [paund] n (*FIN, weight*) Pfund nt; (*for cars, animals*) Auslösestelle f ♦ vt (*zer*)stampfen ♦ vi klopfen, hämmern; **~ sterling** n Pfund Sterling nt

pour [pɔ:*r*] vt gießen, schütten ♦ vi gießen; (*crowds etc*) strömen; **~ away** vt abgießen; **~ in** vi (*people*) hereinströmen; **~ off** vt abgießen; **~ out** vi (*people*) herausströmen ♦ vt (*drink*) einschenken; **~ing** adj: **~ing rain** strömende(r) Regen m

pout [paut] vi schmollen

poverty ['pɒvətɪ] n Armut f; **~-stricken** adj verarmt, sehr arm

powder ['paudə*r*] n Pulver nt; (*cosmetic*) Puder m ♦ vt pulverisieren; **to ~ one's nose** sich dat die Nase pudern; **~ compact** n Puderdose f; **~ed milk** n Milchpulver nt; **~ room** n Damentoilette f; **~y** adj pulverig

power ['pauə*r*] n (*also POL*) Macht f; (*ability*) Fähigkeit f; (*strength*) Stärke f; (*MATH*) Potenz f; (*ELEC*) Strom m ♦ vt betreiben, antreiben; **to be in ~** (*POL etc*) an der Macht sein; **~ cut** n Stromausfall m; **~ed** adj: **~ed by** betrieben mit; **~ failure** (*US*) n Stromausfall m; **~ful** adj (*person*) mächtig; (*engine, government*) stark; **~less** adj machtlos; **~ point** (*BRIT*) n elektrische(r) Anschluß △ m; **~ station** n Elektrizitätswerk nt; **~ struggle** n Machtkampf m

p.p. abbr (= *per procurationem*): **p.p. J. Smith** i.A. J. Smith

PR n abbr = **public relations**

practicable ['præktɪkəbl] adj durchführbar

practical ['præktɪkl] adj praktisch; **~ity** [præktɪ'kælɪtɪ] n (*of person*) praktische Veranlagung f; (*of situation etc*) Durchführbarkeit f; **~ joke** n Streich m; **~ly** adv praktisch

practice ['præktɪs] n Übung f; (*reality, also of*

doctor, lawyer) Praxis f; (custom) Brauch m; (in business) Usus m ♦ vt, vi (US) = **practise**; **in ~** (in reality) in der Praxis; **out of ~** außer Übung; **practicing** (US) adj = **practising**

practise ['præktɪs] (US **practice**) vt üben; (profession) ausüben ♦ vi (sich) üben; (doctor, lawyer) praktizieren; **practising** (US **practicing**) adj praktizierend; (Christian etc) aktiv

practitioner [præk'tɪʃənər] n praktische(r) Arzt m, praktische Ärztin f

pragmatic [præg'mætɪk] adj pragmatisch

prairie ['prɛərɪ] n Prärie f, Steppe f

praise [preɪz] n Lob nt ♦ vt loben; **~worthy** adj lobenswert

pram [præm] (BRIT) n Kinderwagen m

prance [prɑːns] vi (horse) tänzeln; (person) stolzieren

prank [præŋk] n Streich m

prawn [prɔːn] n Garnele f, Krabbe f; **~ cocktail** n Krabbencocktail m

pray [preɪ] vi beten; **~er** [prɛər] n Gebet nt

preach [priːtʃ] vi predigen; **~er** n Prediger m

preamble [prɪ'æmbl] n Einleitung f

precarious [prɪ'kɛərɪəs] adj prekär, unsicher

precaution [prɪ'kɔːʃən] n (Vorsichts)maßnahme f

precede [prɪ'siːd] vi vorausgehen ♦ vt vorausgehen +dat; **~nce** ['presɪdəns] n Vorrang m; **~nt** ['presɪdənt] n Präzedenzfall m; **preceding** [prɪ'siːdɪŋ] adj vorhergehend

precinct ['priːsɪŋkt] n (US: district) Bezirk m; **~s** npl (round building) Gelände nt; (area, environs) Umgebung f; **pedestrian ~** Fußgängerzone f; **shopping ~** Geschäftsviertel nt

precious ['preʃəs] adj kostbar, wertvoll; (affected) preziös, geziert

precipice ['presɪpɪs] n Abgrund m

precipitate [adj prɪ'sɪpɪtɪt, vb prɪ'sɪpɪteɪt] adj überstürzt, übereilt ♦ vt hinunterstürzen; (events) heraufbeschwören

precise [prɪ'saɪs] adj genau, präzis; **~ly** adv genau, präzis

precision [prɪ'sɪʒən] n Präzision f

preclude [prɪ'kluːd] vt ausschließen

precocious [prɪ'kəʊʃəs] adj frühreif

preconceived [priːkən'siːvd] adj (idea) vorgefaßt ⚠

precondition ['priːkən'dɪʃən] n Vorbedingung f, Voraussetzung f

precursor [priː'kɜːsər] n Vorläufer m

predator ['predətər] n Raubtier nt

predecessor ['priːdɪsesər] n Vorgänger m

predicament [prɪ'dɪkəmənt] n mißliche ⚠ Lage f

predict [prɪ'dɪkt] vt voraussagen; **~able** adj vorhersagbar; **~ion** [prɪ'dɪkʃən] n Voraussage f

predominantly [prɪ'dɒmɪnəntlɪ] adv überwiegend, hauptsächlich

predominate [prɪ'dɒmɪneɪt] vi vorherrschen; (fig) vorherrschen, überwiegen

pre-eminent [priː'emɪnənt] adj hervorragend, herausragend

pre-empt [priː'emt] vt (action, decision) vorwegnehmen

preen [priːn] vt putzen; **to ~ o.s.** (person) sich brüsten

prefab ['priːfæb] n Fertighaus nt

preface ['prefəs] n Vorwort nt

prefect ['priːfekt] n Präfekt m; (SCH) Aufsichtsschüler(in) m(f)

prefer [prɪ'fɜːr] vt vorziehen, lieber mögen; **to ~ to do sth** etw lieber tun; **~ably** ['prefrəblɪ] adv vorzugsweise, am liebsten; **~ence** ['prefrəns] n Präferenz f, Vorzug m; **~ential** [prefə'renʃəl] adj bevorzugt, Vorzugs-

prefix ['priːfɪks] n Vorsilbe f, Präfix nt

pregnancy ['pregnənsɪ] n Schwangerschaft f

pregnant ['pregnənt] adj schwanger

prehistoric ['priːhɪs'tɒrɪk] adj prähistorisch, vorgeschichtlich

prejudice ['predʒʊdɪs] n (bias) Voreingenommenheit f; (opinion) Vorurteil nt; (harm) Schaden m ♦ vt beeinträchtigen; **~d** adj (person) voreingenommen

preliminary [prɪ'lɪmɪnərɪ] adj einleitend, Vor-

⚠ *For information on spelling reform see page 615*

prelude ['prelju:d] n Vorspiel nt; (fig) Auftakt m

premarital ['pri:'mærɪtl] adj vorehelich

premature ['premətʃuə'] adj vorzeitig, verfrüht; (birth) Früh-

premeditated [pri:'medɪteɪtɪd] adj geplant; (murder) vorsätzlich

premenstrual syndrome [pri:'menstrʊəl-] n prämenstruelles Syndrom nt

premier ['premɪə'] adj erste(r, s) ♦ n Premier m

première ['premɪeə'] n Premiere f; Uraufführung f

Premier League [-li:g] n ≈ 1. Bundesliga (höchste Spielklasse im Fußball)

premise ['premɪs] n Voraussetzung f, Prämisse f; ~s npl (shop) Räumlichkeiten pl; (grounds) Gelände nt; on the ~s im Hause

premium ['pri:mɪəm] n Prämie f; to be at a ~ über pari stehen; ~ bond (BRIT) n Prämienanleihe f

premonition [premə'nɪʃən] n Vorahnung f

preoccupation [pri:ɔkju'peɪʃən] n Sorge f

preoccupied [pri:'ɔkjupaɪd] adj (look) geistesabwesend

prep [prep] n (SCH) Hausaufgabe f

prepaid [pri:'peɪd] adj vorausbezahlt; (letter) frankiert

preparation [prepə'reɪʃən] n Vorbereitung f

preparatory [prɪ'pærətərɪ] adj Vor(bereitungs)-; ~ school n (BRIT) private Vorbereitungsschule für die Public School; (US) private Vorbereitungsschule für die Hochschule

prepare [prɪ'peə'] vt vorbereiten ♦ vi sich vorbereiten; to ~ for/prepare sth for sich/etw vorbereiten auf +acc; to be ~d to ... bereit sein zu ...

preponderance [prɪ'pɔndərns] n Übergewicht nt

preposition [prepə'zɪʃən] n Präposition f, Verhältniswort nt

preposterous [prɪ'pɔstərəs] adj absurd

prep school n = preparatory school

prerequisite [pri:'rekwɪzɪt] n (unerläßliche ⚠) Voraussetzung f

prerogative [prɪ'rɔgətɪv] n Vorrecht nt

Presbyterian [prezbɪ'tɪərɪən] adj presbyterianisch ♦ n Presbyterier(in) m(f)

preschool ['pri:'sku:l] adj Vorschul-

prescribe [prɪ'skraɪb] vt vorschreiben; (MED) verschreiben

prescription [prɪ'skrɪpʃən] n (MED) Rezept nt

presence ['prezns] n Gegenwart f; ~ of mind Geistesgegenwart f

present [adj, n 'preznt, vb pri'zent] adj (here) anwesend; (current) gegenwärtig ♦ n Gegenwart f; (gift) Geschenk nt ♦ vt vorlegen; (introduce) vorstellen; (show) zeigen; (give): to ~ sb with sth jdm etw überreichen; at ~ im Augenblick; to give sb a ~ jdm ein Geschenk machen; ~able [prɪ'zentəbl] adj präsentabel; ~ation [prezn'teɪʃən] n Überreichung f; ~-day adj heutig; ~er [prɪ'zentə'] n (RAD, TV) Moderator(in) m(f); ~ly adv bald; (at present) im Augenblick

preservation [prezə'veɪʃən] n Erhaltung f

preservative [prɪ'zə:vətɪv] n Konservierungsmittel nt

preserve [prɪ'zə:v] vt erhalten; (food) einmachen ♦ n (jam) Eingemachte(s) nt; (reserve) Schutzgebiet nt

preside [prɪ'zaɪd] vi den Vorsitz haben

president ['prezɪdənt] n Präsident m; ~ial [prezɪ'denʃl] adj Präsidenten-; (election) Präsidentschafts-; (system) Präsidial-

press [pres] n Presse f; (printing house) Druckerei f ♦ vt drücken; (iron) bügeln; (urge) (be)drängen ♦ vi (push) drücken; to be ~ed for time unter Zeitdruck stehen; to ~ for sth drängen auf etw acc; ~ on vi vorwärtsdrängen ⚠; ~ agency n Presseagentur f; ~ conference n Pressekonferenz f; ~ed adj (clothes) gebügelt; ~ing adj dringend; ~ stud (BRIT) n Druckknopf m; ~-up (BRIT) n Liegestütz m

pressure ['preʃə'] n Druck m; ~ cooker n Schnellkochtopf m; ~ gauge n Druckmesser m

pressurized ['preʃəraɪzd] adj Druck-

prestige [pres'ti:ʒ] n Prestige nt;

prestigious [prɛsˈtɪdʒəs] adj Prestige-
presumably [prɪˈzjuːməblɪ] adv vermutlich
presume [prɪˈzjuːm] vt, vi annehmen; **to ~ to do sth** sich erlauben, etw zu tun;
presumption [prɪˈzʌmpʃən] n Annahme f;
presumptuous [prɪˈzʌmpʃəs] adj anmaßend
pretence [prɪˈtɛns] (US **pretense**) n Vorgabe f, Vortäuschung f; (false claim) Vorwand m
pretend [prɪˈtɛnd] vt vorgeben, so tun als ob ... ♦ vi so tun; **to ~ to sth** Anspruch erheben auf etw acc
pretense [prɪˈtɛns] (US) n = **pretence**
pretension [prɪˈtɛnʃən] n Anspruch m; (impudent claim) Anmaßung f
pretentious [prɪˈtɛnʃəs] adj angeberisch
pretext [ˈpriːtɛkst] n Vorwand m
pretty [ˈprɪtɪ] adj hübsch ♦ adv (inf) ganz schön
prevail [prɪˈveɪl] vi siegen; (custom) vorherrschen; **to ~ against** or **over** siegen über +acc; **to ~ (up)on sb to do sth** jdn dazu bewegen, etw zu tun; **~ing** adj vorherrschend
prevalent [ˈprɛvələnt] adj vorherrschend
prevent [prɪˈvɛnt] vt (stop) verhindern, verhüten; **to ~ sb from doing sth** jdn (daran) hindern, etw zu tun; **~ative** n Vorbeugungsmittel nt; **~ion** [prɪˈvɛnʃən] n Verhütung f; **~ive** adj vorbeugend, Schutz-
preview [ˈpriːvjuː] n private Voraufführung f; (trailer) Vorschau f
previous [ˈpriːvɪəs] adj früher, vorherig; **~ly** adv früher
prewar [ˈpriːˈwɔːᵗ] adj Vorkriegs-
prey [preɪ] n Beute f; **~ on** vt fus Jagd machen auf +acc; **it was ~ing on his mind** es quälte sein Gewissen
price [praɪs] n Preis m; (value) Wert m ♦ vt (label) auszeichnen; **~less** adj (also fig) unbezahlbar; **~ list** n Preisliste f
prick [prɪk] n Stich m ♦ vt, vi stechen; **to ~ up one's ears** die Ohren spitzen
prickle [ˈprɪkl] n Stachel m, Dorn m
prickly [ˈprɪklɪ] adj stachelig; (fig: person) reizbar; **~ heat** n Hitzebläschen pl

pride [praɪd] n Stolz m; (arrogance) Hochmut m ♦ vt: **to ~ o.s. on sth** auf etw acc stolz sein
priest [priːst] n Priester m; **~hood** n Priesteramt nt
prim [prɪm] adj prüde
primarily [ˈpraɪmərɪlɪ] adv vorwiegend
primary [ˈpraɪmərɪ] adj (main) Haupt-; (SCH) Grund-; **~ school** (BRIT) n Grundschule f
prime [praɪm] adj erste(r, s); (excellent) erstklassig ♦ vt vorbereiten; (gun) laden; **in the ~ of life** in der Blüte der Jahre; **~ minister** n Premierminister m, Ministerpräsident m; **~r** [ˈpraɪməᵗ] n Fibel f
primeval [praɪˈmiːvl] adj vorzeitlich; (forests) Ur-
primitive [ˈprɪmɪtɪv] adj primitiv
primrose [ˈprɪmrəʊz] n (gelbe) Primel f
primus (stove) [ˈpraɪməs-] (® BRIT) n Primuskocher m
prince [prɪns] n Prinz m; (ruler) Fürst m; **~ss** [prɪnˈsɛs] n Prinzessin f; Fürstin f
principal [ˈprɪnsɪpl] adj Haupt- ♦ n (SCH) (Schul)direktor m, Rektor m; (money) (Grund)kapital nt
principle [ˈprɪnsɪpl] n Grundsatz m, Prinzip nt; **in ~** im Prinzip; **on ~** aus Prinzip, prinzipiell
print [prɪnt] n Druck m; (made by feet, fingers) Abdruck m; (PHOT) Abzug m ♦ vt drucken; (name) in Druckbuchstaben schreiben; (PHOT) abziehen; **out of ~** vergriffen; **~ed matter** n Drucksache f; **~er** n Drucker m; **~ing** n Drucken nt; (of photos) Abziehen nt; **~out** n (COMPUT) Ausdruck m
prior [ˈpraɪəᵗ] adj früher ♦ n Prior m; **~ to** vor etw dat; **~ to going abroad, she had ...** bevor sie ins Ausland ging, hatte sie ...
priority [praɪˈɒrɪtɪ] n Vorrang m, Priorität f
prise [praɪz] vt: **to ~ open** aufbrechen
prison [ˈprɪzn] n Gefängnis nt ♦ adj Gefängnis-; (system etc) Strafvollzugs-; **~er** n Gefangene(r) mf
pristine [ˈprɪstiːn] adj makellos
privacy [ˈprɪvəsɪ] n Ungestörtheit f, Ruhe f; Privatleben nt

⚠ For information on spelling reform see page 615

private ['praɪvɪt] *adj* privat, Privat-; *(secret)* vertraulich, geheim ♦ *n* einfache(r) Soldat *m*; "**~**" *(on envelope)* "persönlich"; *(on door)* „Privat"; **in ~** privat, unter vier Augen; **~ enterprise** *n* Privatunternehmen *nt*; **~ eye** *n* Privatdetektiv *m*; **~ property** *n* Privatbesitz *m*; **~ school** *n* Privatschule *f*; **privatize** *vt* privatisieren

privet ['prɪvɪt] *n* Liguster *m*

privilege ['prɪvɪlɪdʒ] *n* Privileg *nt*; **~d** *adj* bevorzugt, privilegiert

privy ['prɪvɪ] *adj* geheim, privat; **P~ Council** *n* Geheime(r) Staatsrat *m*

prize [praɪz] *n* Preis *m* ♦ *adj (example)* erstklassig; *(idiot)* Voll- ♦ *vt* (hoch)schätzen ⚠; **~-giving** *n* Preisverteilung *f*; **~winner** *n* Preisträger(in) *m(f)*

pro [prəʊ] *n (professional)* Profi *m*; **the ~s and cons** das Für und Wider

probability [prɒbə'bɪlɪtɪ] *n* Wahrscheinlichkeit *f*

probable ['prɒbəbl] *adj* wahrscheinlich; **probably** *adv* wahrscheinlich

probation [prə'beɪʃən] *n* Probe(zeit) *f*; *(JUR)* Bewährung *f*; **on ~** auf Probe; auf Bewährung

probe [prəʊb] *n* Sonde *f*; *(enquiry)* Untersuchung *f* ♦ *vt, vi* erforschen

problem ['prɒbləm] *n* Problem *nt*; **~atic** [prɒblə'mætɪk] *adj* problematisch

procedure [prə'siːdʒər] *n* Verfahren *nt*

proceed [prə'siːd] *vi (advance)* vorrücken; *(start)* anfangen; *(carry on)* fortfahren; *(set about)* vorgehen; **~ings** *npl* Verfahren *nt*

proceeds ['prəʊsiːdz] *npl* Erlös *m*

process ['prəʊses] *n* Prozeß ⚠ *m*; *(method)* Verfahren *nt* ♦ *vt* bearbeiten; *(food)* verarbeiten; *(film)* entwickeln; **~ing** *n (PHOT)* Entwickeln *nt*

procession [prə'seʃən] *n* Prozession *f*, Umzug *m*; **funeral ~** Trauerprozession *f*

pro-choice [prəʊ'tʃɔɪs] *adj (movement)* Pro-Abtreibungs-; **~ campaigner** Abtreibungsbefürworter(in) *m(f)*

proclaim [prə'kleɪm] *vt* verkünden

procrastinate [prəʊ'kræstɪneɪt] *vi* zaudern

procure [prə'kjʊər] *vt* beschaffen

prod [prɒd] *vt* stoßen ♦ *n* Stoß *m*

prodigal ['prɒdɪgl] *adj*: **~ (with** or **of)** verschwenderisch (mit)

prodigy ['prɒdɪdʒɪ] *n* Wunder *nt*

produce [*n* 'prɒdjuːs, *vb* prə'djuːs] *n (AGR)* (Boden)produkte *pl*, (Natur)erzeugnis *nt* ♦ *vt* herstellen, produzieren; *(cause)* hervorrufen; *(farmer)* erzeugen; *(yield)* liefern, bringen; *(play)* inszenieren; **~r** *n* Hersteller *m*, Produzent *m* *(also CINE)*; Erzeuger *m*

product ['prɒdʌkt] *n* Produkt *nt*, Erzeugnis *nt*; **~ion** [prə'dʌkʃən] *n* Produktion *f*, Herstellung *f*; *(thing)* Erzeugnis *nt*, Produkt *nt*; *(THEAT)* Inszenierung *f*; **~ion line** *n* Fließband *nt*; **~ive** [prə'dʌktɪv] *adj* produktiv; *(fertile)* ertragreich, fruchtbar; **~ivity** [prɒdʌk'tɪvɪtɪ] *n* Produktivität *f*

profane [prə'feɪn] *adj* weltlich, profan; *(language etc)* gotteslästerlich

profess [prə'fes] *vt* bekennen; *(show)* zeigen; *(claim to be)* vorgeben

profession [prə'feʃən] *n* Beruf *m*; *(declaration)* Bekenntnis *nt*; **~al** *n* Fachmann *m*; *(SPORT)* Berufsspieler(in) *m(f)* ♦ *adj* Berufs-; *(expert)* fachlich; *(player)* professionell; **~ally** *adv* beruflich, fachmännisch

professor [prə'fesər] *n* Professor *m*

proficiency [prə'fɪʃənsɪ] *n* Können *nt*

proficient [prə'fɪʃənt] *adj* fähig

profile ['prəʊfaɪl] *n* Profil *nt*; *(fig: report)* Kurzbiographie ⚠ *f*

profit ['prɒfɪt] *n* Gewinn *m* ♦ *vi*: **to ~ (by** or **from)** profitieren (von); **~ability** [prɒfɪtə'bɪlɪtɪ] *n* Rentabilität *f*; **~able** *adj* einträglich, rentabel; **~eering** [prɒfɪ'tɪərɪŋ] *n* Profitmacherei *f*

profound [prə'faʊnd] *adj* tief

profuse [prə'fjuːs] *adj* überreich; **~ly** [prə'fjuːslɪ] *adv* überschwenglich ⚠; *(sweat)* reichlich; **profusion** [prə'fjuːʒən] *n*: **profusion (of)** Überfülle *f* (von), Überfluß ⚠ *m* (an *+dat*)

program ['prəʊgræm] *n (COMPUT)* Programm *nt* ♦ *vt (machine)* programmieren; **~me** *(US* **program)** *n*

Programm nt ♦ vt planen; (computer)
programmieren; **~mer** (US **programer**) n
Programmierer(in) m(f)

progress [n 'prəʊgrɛs, vb prə'grɛs] n
Fortschritt m ♦ vi fortschreiten,
weitergehen; **in ~** im Gang; **~ion**
[prə'grɛʃən] n Folge f; **~ive** [prə'grɛsɪv] adj
fortschrittlich, progressiv

prohibit [prə'hɪbɪt] vt verbieten; **to ~ sb
from doing sth** jdm untersagen, etw zu
tun; **~ion** [prəʊɪ'bɪʃən] n Verbot nt; (US)
Alkoholverbot nt, Prohibition f; **~ive** adj
unerschwinglich

project [n 'prɔdʒɛkt, vb prə'dʒɛkt] n Projekt
nt ♦ vt vorausplanen; (film etc) projizieren;
(personality, voice) zum Tragen bringen ♦ vi
(stick out) hervorragen, (her)vorstehen

projectile [prə'dʒɛktaɪl] n Geschoß Δ nt

projection [prə'dʒɛkʃən] n Projektion f; (sth
prominent) Vorsprung m

proletariat [prəʊlɪ'tɛərɪət] n Proletariat nt

pro-life [prəʊ'laɪf] adj (movement) Anti-
Abtreibungs-; **~ campaigner**
Abtreibungsgegner(in) m(f)

prolific [prə'lɪfɪk] adj fruchtbar; (author etc)
produktiv

prologue ['prəʊlɒg] n Prolog m; (event)
Vorspiel nt

prolong [prə'lɒŋ] vt verlängern

prom [prɒm] n abbr = **promenade**;
promenade concert

*Prom (promenade concert) ist in
Großbritannien ein Konzert, bei dem ein
Teil der Zuhörer steht (ursprünglich
spazierengehg). Die seit 1895 alljährlich
stattfindenden Proms (seit 1941 immer in
der Londoner Royal Albert Hall) zählen zu
den bedeutendsten Musikereignissen in
England. Der letzte Abend der Proms steht
ganz im Zeichen des Patriotismus und
gipfelt im Singen des Lieds "Land of Hope
and Glory". In den USA und Kanada steht
das Wort für promenade, ein Ball an einer
High School oder einem College.*

promenade [prɔmə'nɑːd] n Promenade f; **~
concert** n Promenadenkonzert nt

prominence ['prɔmɪnəns] n (große)
Bedeutung f

prominent ['prɔmɪnənt] adj bedeutend;
(politician) prominent; (easily seen)
herausragend, auffallend

promiscuous [prə'mɪskjʊəs] adj lose

promise ['prɔmɪs] n Versprechen nt; (hope:
~ of sth) Aussicht f auf etw acc ♦ vt, vi
versprechen; **promising** adj
vielversprechend Δ

promontory ['prɔmɔntrɪ] n Vorsprung m

promote [prə'məʊt] vt befördern; (help on)
fördern, unterstützen; **~r** n (in
entertainment, sport) Veranstalter m; (for
charity etc) Organisator m; **promotion**
[prə'məʊʃən] n (in rank) Beförderung f;
(furtherance) Förderung f; (COMM):
promotion (of) Werbung f
(für)

prompt [prɔmpt] adj prompt, schnell ♦ adv
(punctually) genau ♦ n (COMPUT) Meldung f
♦ vt veranlassen; (THEAT) soufflieren +dat; **to
~ sb to do sth** jdn dazu veranlassen, etw
zu tun; **~ly** adv sofort

prone [prəʊn] adj hingestreckt; **to be ~ to
sth** zu etw neigen

prong [prɔŋ] n Zinke f

pronoun ['prəʊnaʊn] n Fürwort nt

pronounce [prə'naʊns] vt aussprechen;
(JUR) verkünden ♦ vi: **to ~ (on)** sich äußern
(zu)

pronunciation [prənʌnsɪ'eɪʃən] n
Aussprache f

proof [pruːf] n Beweis m; (PRINT)
Korrekturfahne f; (of alcohol) Alkoholgehalt
m ♦ adj sicher

prop [prɒp] n (also fig) Stütze f; (THEAT)
Requisit nt ♦ vt (also: ~ up) (ab)stützen

propaganda [prɔpə'gændə] n Propaganda f

propel [prə'pɛl] vt (an)treiben; **~ler** n
Propeller m; **~ling pencil** (BRIT) n
Drehbleistift m

propensity [prə'pɛnsɪtɪ] n Tendenz f

proper ['prɔpə*] adj richtig; (seemly)
schicklich; **~ly** adv richtig; **~ noun** n

Δ *For information on spelling reform see page 615*

Eigenname m

property ['prɔpətɪ] n Eigentum nt; (quality) Eigenschaft f; (land) Grundbesitz m; ~ **owner** n Grundbesitzer m

prophecy ['prɔfɪsɪ] n Prophezeiung f

prophesy ['prɔfɪsaɪ] vt prophezeien

prophet ['prɔfɪt] n Prophet m

proportion [prə'pɔ:ʃən] n Verhältnis nt; (share) Teil m ♦ vt: **to ~ (to)** abstimmen (auf +acc); ~**al** adj proportional; ~**ate** adj verhältnismäßig

proposal [prə'pəuzl] n Vorschlag m; (of marriage) Heiratsantrag m

propose [prə'pəuz] vt vorschlagen; (toast) ausbringen ♦ vi (offer marriage) einen Heiratsantrag machen; **to ~ to do sth** beabsichtigen, etw zu tun

proposition [prɔpə'zɪʃən] n Angebot nt; (statement) Satz m

proprietor [prə'praɪətəʳ] n Besitzer m, Eigentümer m

propriety [prə'praɪɪtɪ] n Anstand m

pro rata [prəu'rɑ:tə] adv anteilmäßig

prose [prəuz] n Prosa f

prosecute ['prɔsɪkju:t] vt (strafrechtlich) verfolgen; **prosecution** [prɔsɪ'kju:ʃən] n (JUR) strafrechtliche Verfolgung f; (party) Anklage f; **prosecutor** n Vertreter m der Anklage; **Public Prosecutor** Staatsanwalt m

prospect [n 'prɔspekt, vb prə'spekt] n Aussicht f ♦ vt auf Bodenschätze hin untersuchen ♦ vi: **to ~ (for)** suchen (nach); ~**ing** ['prɔspektɪŋ] n (for minerals) Suche f; ~**ive** [prə'spektɪv] adj (son-in-law etc) zukünftig; (customer, candidate) voraussichtlich

prospectus [prə'spektəs] n (Werbe)prospekt m

prosper ['prɔspəʳ] vi blühen, gedeihen; (person) erfolgreich sein; ~**ity** [prɔ'spɛrɪtɪ] n Wohlstand m; ~**ous** adj wohlhabend, reich

prostitute ['prɔstɪtju:t] n Prostituierte f

prostrate ['prɔstreɪt] adj ausgestreckt (liegend)

protagonist [prə'tægənɪst] n Hauptperson f, Held m

protect [prə'tekt] vt (be)schützen; ~**ed species** n geschützte Art; ~**ion** [prə'tekʃən] n Schutz m; ~**ive** adj Schutz-, (be)schützend

protégé ['prəuteʒeɪ] n Schützling m

protein ['prəuti:n] n Protein nt, Eiweiß nt

protest [n 'prəutest, vb prə'test] n Protest m ♦ vi protestieren ♦ vt (affirm) beteuern

Protestant ['prɔtɪstənt] adj protestantisch ♦ n Protestant(in) m(f)

protester [prə'testəʳ] n (demonstrator) Demonstrant(in) m(f)

protracted [prə'træktɪd] adj sich hinziehend

protrude [prə'tru:d] vi (her)vorstehen

proud [praud] adj: ~ **(of)** stolz (auf +acc)

prove [pru:v] vt beweisen ♦ vi: **to ~ (to be) correct** sich als richtig erweisen; **to ~ o.s.** sich bewähren

proverb ['prɔvə:b] n Sprichwort nt; ~**ial** [prə'və:bɪəl] adj sprichwörtlich

provide [prə'vaɪd] vt versehen; (supply) besorgen; **to ~ sb with sth** jdn mit etw versorgen; ~ **for** vt fus sorgen für; (emergency) Vorkehrungen treffen für; ~**d (that)** conj vorausgesetzt(, daß) ⚠

providing [prə'vaɪdɪŋ] conj vorausgesetzt (, daß) ⚠

province ['prɔvɪns] n Provinz f; (division of work) Bereich m; **provincial** [prə'vɪnʃəl] adj provinziell, Provinz-

provision [prə'vɪʒən] n Vorkehrung f; (condition) Bestimmung f; ~**s** npl (food) Vorräte pl, Proviant m; ~**al** adj provisorisch

proviso [prə'vaɪzəu] n Bedingung f

provocative [prə'vɔkətɪv] adj provozierend

provoke [prə'vəuk] vt provozieren; (cause) hervorrufen

prowess ['prauɪs] n überragende(s) Können nt

prowl [praul] vi herumstreichen; (animal) schleichen ♦ n: **on the ~** umherstreifend; ~**er** n Herumtreiber(in) m(f)

proximity [prɔk'sɪmɪtɪ] n Nähe f

proxy ['prɔksɪ] n (Stell)vertreter m; (authority, document) Vollmacht f; **by ~** durch einen Stellvertreter

prudent ['pru:dnt] adj klug, umsichtig

⚠ Informationen zur Rechtschreibreform Seite 615

prudish ['pruːdɪʃ] *adj* prüde
prune [pruːn] *n* Backpflaume *f* ♦ *vt* ausputzen; *(fig)* zurechtstutzen
pry [praɪ] *vi*: **to ~ (into)** seine Nase stecken (in +*acc*)
PS *n abbr* (= *postscript*) PS
pseudonym ['sjuːdənɪm] *n* Pseudonym *nt*, Deckname *m*
psychiatric [saɪkɪˈætrɪk] *adj* psychiatrisch
psychiatrist [saɪˈkaɪətrɪst] *n* Psychiater *m*
psychic ['saɪkɪk] *adj* (*also*: **~al**) übersinnlich; *(person)* paranormal begabt
psychoanalyse [saɪkəʊˈænəlaɪz] (*US* **psychoanalyze**) *vt* psychoanalytisch behandeln; **psychoanalyst** [saɪkəʊˈænəlɪst] *n* Psychoanalytiker(in) *m(f)*
psychological [saɪkəˈlɒdʒɪkl] *adj* psychologisch; **psychologist** [saɪˈkɒlədʒɪst] *n* Psychologe *m*, Psychologin *f*; **psychology** [saɪˈkɒlədʒɪ] *n* Psychologie *f*
PTO *abbr* = **please turn over**
pub [pʌb] *n abbr* (= *public house*) Kneipe *f*

┌─────────────────────────────────┐
| **PUB** |
| |
| ℹ **Pub** ist ein Gasthaus mit einer Lizenz |
| zum Ausschank von alkoholischen |
| Getränken. Ein Pub besteht meist aus |
| verschiedenen gemütlichen (**lounge, snug**) |
| oder einfacheren Räumen (**public bar**), in |
| denen auch Spiele wie Darts, Domino |
| und Poolbillard zur Verfügung stehen. In |
| Pubs werden vor allem Mittags oft auch |
| Mahlzeiten angeboten. Pubs sind |
| normalerweise von 11 bis 23 Uhr geöffnet, |
| aber manchmal nachmittags geschlossen. |
└─────────────────────────────────┘

pubic ['pjuːbɪk] *adj* Scham-
public ['pʌblɪk] *adj* öffentlich ♦ *n* (*also*: **general ~**) Öffentlichkeit *f*; **in ~** in der Öffentlichkeit; **~ address system** *n* Lautsprecheranlage *f*
publican ['pʌblɪkən] *n* Wirt *m*
publication [pʌblɪˈkeɪʃən] *n* Veröffentlichung *f*
public: **~ company** *n* Aktiengesellschaft *f*; **~ convenience** (*BRIT*) *n* öffentliche Toiletten *pl*; **~ holiday** *n* gesetzliche(r)

Feiertag *m*; **~ house** (*BRIT*) *n* Lokal *nt*, Kneipe *f*
publicity [pʌbˈlɪsɪtɪ] *n* Publicity *f*, Werbung *f*
publicize ['pʌblɪsaɪz] *vt* bekanntmachen ⚠; *(advertise)* Publicity machen für
publicly ['pʌbɪklɪ] *adv* öffentlich
public: **~ opinion** *n* öffentliche Meinung *f*; **~ relations** *npl* Public Relations *pl*; **~ school** *n* (*BRIT*) Privatschule *f*; (*US*) staatliche Schule *f*; **~-spirited** *adj* mit Gemeinschaftssinn; **~ transport** *n* öffentliche Verkehrsmittel *pl*
publish ['pʌblɪʃ] *vt* veröffentlichen; *(event)* bekanntgeben ⚠; **~er** *n* Verleger *m*; **~ing** *n* (*business*) Verlagswesen *nt*
pub lunch *n* in Pubs servierter Imbiß
pucker ['pʌkəʳ] *vt* (*face*) verziehen; *(lips)* kräuseln
pudding ['pʊdɪŋ] *n* (*BRIT: course*) Nachtisch *m*; Pudding *m*; **black ~** ≈ Blutwurst *f*
puddle ['pʌdl] *n* Pfütze *f*
puff [pʌf] *n* (*of wind etc*) Stoß *m*; *(cosmetic)* Puderquaste *f* ♦ *vt* blasen, pusten; *(pipe)* paffen ♦ *vi* keuchen, schnaufen; *(smoke)* paffen; **to ~ out smoke** Rauch ausstoßen; **~ pastry** (*US* **~ paste**) *n* Blätterteig *m*; **~y** *adj* aufgedunsen
pull [pʊl] *n* Ruck *m*; *(influence)* Beziehung *f* ♦ *vt* ziehen; *(trigger)* abdrücken ♦ *vi* ziehen; **to ~ sb's leg** jdn auf den Arm nehmen; **to ~ to pieces** in Stücke reißen; *(fig)* verreißen; **to ~ one's punches** sich zurückhalten; **to ~ one's weight** sich in die Riemen legen; **to ~ o.s. together** sich zusammenreißen; **~ apart** *vt* (*break*) zerreißen; *(dismantle)* auseinandernehmen ⚠; *(separate)* trennen; **~ down** *vt* (*house*) abreißen; **~ in** *vi* hineinfahren; *(stop)* anhalten; (*RAIL*) einfahren; **~ off** *vt* (*deal etc*) abschließen; **~ out** *vi* (*car*) herausfahren; *(fig: partner)* aussteigen ♦ *vt* herausziehen; **~ over** *vi* (*AUT*) an die Seite fahren; **~ through** *vi* durchkommen; **~ up** *vi* anhalten ♦ *vt* (*uproot*) herausreißen; *(stop)* anhalten
pulley ['pʊlɪ] *n* Rolle *f*, Flaschenzug *m*
pullover ['pʊləʊvəʳ] *n* Pullover *m*

⚠ *For information on spelling reform see page 615*

pulp [pʌlp] n Brei m; (of fruit) Fruchtfleisch nt
pulpit ['pulpɪt] n Kanzel f
pulsate [pʌl'seɪt] vi pulsieren
pulse [pʌls] n Puls m; ~s npl (BOT) Hülsenfrüchte pl
pummel ['pʌml] vt mit den Fäusten bearbeiten
pump [pʌmp] n Pumpe f; (shoe) leichter (Tanz)schuh m ♦ vt pumpen; ~ **up** vt (tyre) aufpumpen
pumpkin ['pʌmpkɪn] n Kürbis m
pun [pʌn] n Wortspiel nt
punch [pʌntʃ] n (tool) Locher m; (blow) (Faust)schlag m; (drink) Punsch m, Bowle f ♦ vt lochen; (strike) schlagen, boxen; ~ **line** n Pointe f; ~**-up** (BRIT: inf) n Keilerei f
punctual ['pʌŋktjuəl] adj pünktlich
punctuate ['pʌŋktjueɪt] vt mit Satzzeichen versehen; (fig) unterbrechen; **punctuation** [pʌŋktju'eɪʃən] n Zeichensetzung f, Interpunktion f
puncture ['pʌŋktʃər] n Loch nt; (AUT) Reifenpanne f ♦ vt durchbohren
pundit ['pʌndɪt] n Gelehrte(r) m
pungent ['pʌndʒənt] adj scharf
punish ['pʌnɪʃ] vt bestrafen; (in boxing etc) übel zurichten; ~**ment** n Strafe f; (action) Bestrafung f
punk [pʌŋk] n (also: ~ **rocker**) Punker(in) m(f); (also: ~ **rock**) Punk m; (US: inf: hoodlum) Ganove m
punt [pʌnt] n Stechkahn m
punter ['pʌntər] (BRIT) n (better) Wetter m
puny ['pju:nɪ] adj kümmerlich
pup [pʌp] n = **puppy**
pupil ['pju:pl] n Schüler(in) m(f); (in eye) Pupille f
puppet ['pʌpɪt] n Puppe f; Marionette f
puppy ['pʌpɪ] n junge(r) Hund m
purchase ['pə:tʃɪs] n Kauf m; (grip) Halt m ♦ vt kaufen, erwerben; ~**r** n Käufer(in) m(f)
pure [pjuər] adj (also fig) rein; ~**ly** ['pjuəlɪ] adv rein
purgatory ['pə:gətərɪ] n Fegefeuer nt
purge [pə:dʒ] n (also POL) Säuberung f ♦ vt reinigen; (body) entschlacken
purify ['pjuərɪfaɪ] vt reinigen

purity ['pjuərɪtɪ] n Reinheit f
purple ['pə:pl] adj violett; (face) dunkelrot
purport [pə:'pɔ:t] vi vorgeben
purpose ['pə:pəs] n Zweck m, Ziel nt; (of person) Absicht f; **on** ~ absichtlich; ~**ful** adj zielbewußt △, entschlossen
purr [pə:r] n Schnurren nt ♦ vi schnurren
purse [pə:s] n Portemonnaie △ nt, Geldbeutel m ♦ vt (lips) zusammenpressen, schürzen
purser ['pə:sər] n Zahlmeister m
pursue [pə'sju:] vt verfolgen; (study) nachgehen +dat; ~**r** n Verfolger m; **pursuit** [pə'sju:t] n Verfolgung f; (occupation) Beschäftigung f
pus [pʌs] n Eiter m
push [puʃ] n Stoß m, Schub m; (MIL) Vorstoß m ♦ vt stoßen, schieben; (button) drücken; (idea) durchsetzen ♦ vi stoßen, schieben; ~ **aside** vt beiseite schieben; ~ **off** (inf) vi abschieben; ~ **on** vi weitermachen; ~ **through** vt durchdrücken; (policy) durchsetzen; ~ **up** vt (total) erhöhen; (prices) hochtreiben; ~**chair** (BRIT) n (Kinder)sportwagen m; ~**er** n (drug dealer) Pusher m; ~**over** (inf) n Kinderspiel nt; ~**-up** (US) n (press-up) Liegestütz m; ~**y** (inf) adj aufdringlich
puss [pus] n Mieze(katze) f; ~**y(cat)** n Mieze(katze) f
put [put] (pt, pp **put**) vt setzen, stellen, legen; (express) ausdrücken, sagen; (write) schreiben; ~ **about** vi (turn back) wenden ♦ vt (spread) verbreiten; ~ **across** vt (explain) erklären; ~ **away** vt weglegen; (store) beiseite legen; ~ **back** vt zurückstellen or -legen; ~ **by** vt zurücklegen, sparen; ~ **down** vt hinstellen or -legen; (rebellion) niederschlagen; (animal) einschläfern; (in writing) niederschreiben; ~ **forward** vt (idea) vorbringen; (clock) vorstellen; ~ **in** vt (application, complaint) einreichen; ~ **off** vt verschieben; (discourage): **to** ~ **sb off sth** jdn von etw abbringen; ~ **on** vt (clothes etc) anziehen; (light etc) anschalten, anmachen; (play etc) aufführen; (brake)

anziehen; **~ out** vt (hand etc)
(her)ausstrecken; (news, rumour) verbreiten;
(light etc) ausschalten, ausmachen; **~
through** vt (TEL: person) verbinden; (: call)
durchstellen; **~ up** vt (tent) aufstellen;
(building) errichten; (price) erhöhen; (person)
unterbringen; **~ up with** vt fus sich
abfinden mit

putrid ['pju:trɪd] adj faul
putt [pʌt] vt (golf) putten ♦ n (golf) Putten nt;
~ing green n kleine(r) Golfplatz m nur
zum Putten
putty ['pʌtɪ] n Kitt m; (fig) Wachs nt
put-up ['putʌp] adj: **~-~ job** abgekartete(s)
Spiel nt
puzzle ['pʌzl] n Rätsel nt; (toy) Geduldspiel
nt ♦ vt verwirren ♦ vi sich den Kopf
zerbrechen; **~d** adj verdutzt, verblüfft;
puzzling adj rätselhaft, verwirrend
pyjamas [pə'dʒɑːməz] (BRIT) npl Schlafanzug
m, Pyjama m
pylon ['paɪlən] n Mast m
pyramid ['pɪrəmɪd] n Pyramide f

Q, q

quack [kwæk] n Quaken nt; (doctor)
Quacksalber m ♦ vi quaken
quad [kwɒd] n abbr = **quadrangle**;
quadruplet
quadrangle ['kwɒdræŋgl] n (court) Hof m;
(MATH) Viereck nt
quadruple [kwɒ'dru:pl] vi sich vervierfachen
♦ vt vervierfachen
quadruplets [kwɒ'dru:plɪts] npl Vierlinge pl
quagmire ['kwægmaɪə] n Morast m
quail [kweɪl] n (bird) Wachtel f ♦ vi (vor
Angst) zittern
quaint [kweɪnt] adj kurios; malerisch
quake [kweɪk] vi beben, zittern ♦ n abbr =
earthquake
qualification [kwɒlɪfɪ'keɪʃən] n Qualifikation
f; (sth which limits) Einschränkung f
qualified ['kwɒlɪfaɪd] adj (competent)
qualifiziert; (limited) bedingt
qualify ['kwɒlɪfaɪ] vt (prepare) befähigen;

(limit) einschränken ♦ vi sich qualifizieren;
to ~ as a doctor / lawyer sein
medizinisches/juristisches Staatsexamen
machen
quality ['kwɒlɪtɪ] n Qualität f; (characteristic)
Eigenschaft f

quality time n intensiv genutzte Zeit
qualm [kwɑːm] n Bedenken nt
quandary ['kwɒndrɪ] n: **to be in a ~** in
Verlegenheit sein
quantity ['kwɒntɪtɪ] n Menge f; **~ surveyor**
n Baukostenkalkulator m
quarantine ['kwɒrntiːn] n Quarantäne f
quarrel ['kwɒrl] n Streit m ♦ vi sich streiten;
~some adj streitsüchtig
quarry ['kwɒrɪ] n Steinbruch m; (animal)
Wild nt; (fig) Opfer nt
quarter ['kwɔːtə] n Viertel nt; (of year)
Quartal nt ♦ vt (divide) vierteln; (MIL)
einquartieren; **~s** npl (esp MIL) Quartier nt;
~ of an hour Viertelstunde f; **~ final** n
Viertelfinale nt; **~ly** adj vierteljährlich
quartet(te) [kwɔː'tet] n Quartett nt
quartz [kwɔːts] n Quarz m
quash [kwɒʃ] vt (verdict) aufheben
quaver ['kweɪvə] vi (tremble) zittern
quay [kiː] n Kai m
queasy ['kwiːzɪ] adj übel
queen [kwiːn] n Königin f; **~ mother** n
Königinmutter f
queer [kwɪə] adj seltsam ♦ n (inf:
homosexual) Schwule(r) m
quell [kwel] vt unterdrücken
quench [kwentʃ] vt (thirst) löschen
querulous ['kwerʊləs] adj nörglerisch
query ['kwɪərɪ] n (question) (An)frage f;

⚠ *For information on spelling reform see page 615*

(*question mark*) Fragezeichen *nt* ♦ *vt* in Zweifel ziehen, in Frage stellen

quest [kwest] *n* Suche *f*

question ['kwestʃən] *n* Frage *f* ♦ *vt* (*ask*) (be)fragen; (*suspect*) verhören; (*doubt*) in Frage stellen, bezweifeln; **beyond ~** ohne Frage; **out of the ~** ausgeschlossen; **~able** *adj* zweifelhaft; **~ mark** *n* Fragezeichen *nt*

questionnaire [kwestʃə'neəʳ] *n* Fragebogen *m*

queue [kju:] (*BRIT*) *n* Schlange *f* ♦ *vi* (*also: ~ up*) Schlange stehen

quibble ['kwɪbl] *vi* kleinlich sein

quick [kwɪk] *adj* schnell ♦ *n* (*of nail*) Nagelhaut *f*; **be ~!** mach schnell!; **cut to the ~** (*fig*) tief getroffen; **~en** *vt* (*hasten*) beschleunigen ♦ *vi* sich beschleunigen; **~ly** *adv* schnell; **~sand** *n* Treibsand *m*; **~-witted** *adj* schlagfertig

quid [kwɪd] (*BRIT: inf*) *n* Pfund *nt*

quiet ['kwaɪət] *adj* (*without noise*) leise; (*peaceful, calm*) still, ruhig ♦ *n* Stille *f*, Ruhe *f* ♦ *vt, vi* (*US*) = **quieten**; **keep ~!** sei still!; **~en** *vi* (*also: ~en down*) ruhig werden ♦ *vt* beruhigen; **~ly** *adv* leise, ruhig; **~ness** *n* Ruhe *f*, Stille *f*

quilt [kwɪlt] *n* (*continental ~*) Steppdecke *f*

quin [kwɪn] *n abbr* = **quintuplet**

quintuplets [kwɪn'tju:plɪts] *npl* Fünflinge *pl*

quip [kwɪp] *n* witzige Bemerkung *f*

quirk [kwɜːk] *n* (*oddity*) Eigenart *f*

quit [kwɪt] (*pt, pp* **quit** *or* **quitted**) *vt* verlassen ♦ *vi* aufhören

quite [kwaɪt] *adv* (*completely*) ganz, völlig; (*fairly*) ziemlich; **~ a few of them** ziemlich viele von ihnen; **~ (so)!** richtig!

quits [kwɪts] *adj* quitt; **let's call it ~** lassen wir's gut sein

quiver ['kwɪvəʳ] *vi* zittern ♦ *n* (*for arrows*) Köcher *m*

quiz [kwɪz] *n* (*competition*) Quiz *nt* ♦ *vt* prüfen; **~zical** *adj* fragend

quota ['kwəʊtə] *n* Anteil *m*; (*COMM*) Quote *f*

quotation [kwəʊ'teɪʃən] *n* Zitat *nt*; (*price*) Kostenvoranschlag *m*; **~ marks** *npl* Anführungszeichen *pl*

quote [kwəʊt] *n* = **quotation** ♦ *vi* (*from book*)

zitieren ♦ *vt* zitieren; (*price*) angeben

R, r

rabbi ['ræbaɪ] *n* Rabbiner *m*; (*title*) Rabbi *m*

rabbit ['ræbɪt] *n* Kaninchen *nt*; **~ hole** *n* Kaninchenbau *m*; **~ hutch** *n* Kaninchenstall *m*

rabble ['ræbl] *n* Pöbel *m*

rabies ['reɪbiːz] *n* Tollwut *f*

RAC (*BRIT*) *n abbr* = **Royal Automobile Club**

raccoon [rə'ku:n] *n* Waschbär *m*

race [reɪs] *n* (*species*) Rasse *f*; (*competition*) Rennen *nt*; (*on foot*) Rennen *nt*, Wettlauf *m*; (*rush*) Hetze *f* ♦ *vt* um die Wette laufen mit; (*horses*) laufen lassen ♦ *vi* (*run*) rennen; (*in contest*) am Rennen teilnehmen; **~ car** (*US*) *n* = **racing car**; **~ car driver** (*US*) *n* = **racing driver**; **~course** *n* (*for horses*) Rennbahn *f*; **~horse** *n* Rennpferd *nt*; **~r** *n* (*person*) Rennfahrer(in) *m(f)*; (*car*) Rennwagen *m*; **~track** *n* (*for cars etc*) Rennstrecke *f*

racial ['reɪʃl] *adj* Rassen-

racing ['reɪsɪŋ] *n* Rennen *nt*; **~ car** (*BRIT*) *n* Rennwagen *m*; **~ driver** (*BRIT*) *n* Rennfahrer *m*

racism ['reɪsɪzəm] *n* Rassismus *m*; **racist** ['reɪsɪst] *n* Rassist *m* ♦ *adj* rassistisch

rack [ræk] *n* Ständer *m*, Gestell *nt* ♦ *vt* plagen; **to go to ~ and ruin** verfallen; **to ~ one's brains** sich *dat* den Kopf zerbrechen

racket ['rækɪt] *n* (*din*) Krach *m*; (*scheme*) (Schwindel)geschäft *nt*; (*TENNIS*) (Tennis)schläger *m*

racquet ['rækɪt] *n* (Tennis)schläger *m*

racy ['reɪsɪ] *adj* gewagt; (*style*) spritzig

radar ['reɪdɑːʳ] *n* Radar *nt or m*

radial ['reɪdɪəl] *adj* (*also: US:* **~-ply**) radial

radiant ['reɪdɪənt] *adj* strahlend; (*giving out rays*) Strahlungs-

radiate ['reɪdɪeɪt] *vi* ausstrahlen; (*roads, lines*) strahlenförmig wegführen ♦ *vt* ausstrahlen; **radiation** [reɪdɪ'eɪʃən] *n* (Aus)strahlung *f*

radiator ['reɪdɪeɪtəʳ] *n* (*for heating*) Heizkörper *m*; (*AUT*) Kühler *m*

radical ['rædɪkl] *adj* radikal

radii ['reɪdiaɪ] *npl of* **radius**

radio ['reɪdɪəʊ] *n* Rundfunk *m*, Radio *nt*; (*set*) Radio *nt*, Radioapparat *m*; **on the ~** im Radio; **~active** ['reɪdɪəʊ'æktɪv] *adj* radioaktiv; **~ cassette** *n* Radiorecorder *m*; **~-controlled** *adj* ferngesteuert; **~logy** [reɪdɪ'ɒlədʒɪ] *n* Strahlenkunde *f*; **~ station** *n* Rundfunkstation *f*; **~therapy** ['reɪdɪəʊ'θerəpɪ] *n* Röntgentherapie *f*

radish ['rædɪʃ] *n* (*big*) Rettich *m*; (*small*) Radieschen *nt*

radius ['reɪdɪəs] (*pl* **radii**) *n* Radius *m*; (*area*) Umkreis *m*

RAF *n abbr* = **Royal Air Force**

raffle ['ræfl] *n* Verlosung *f*, Tombola *f* ♦ *vt* verlosen

raft [rɑːft] *n* Floß *nt*

rafter ['rɑːftə*] *n* Dachsparren *m*

rag [ræg] *n* (*cloth*) Lumpen *m*, Lappen *m*; (*inf: newspaper*) Käseblatt *nt*; (*UNIV: for charity*) studentische Sammelaktion *f* ♦ *vt* (*BRIT*) auf den Arm nehmen; **~s** *npl* (*cloth*) Lumpen *pl*; **~ doll** *n* Flickenpuppe *f*

rage [reɪdʒ] *n* Wut *f*; (*fashion*) große Mode *f* ♦ *vi* wüten, toben

ragged ['rægɪd] *adj* (*edge*) gezackt; (*clothes*) zerlumpt

raid [reɪd] *n* Überfall *m*; (*MIL*) Angriff *m*; (*by police*) Razzia *f* ♦ *vt* überfallen

rail [reɪl] *n* (*also* RAIL) Schiene *f*; (*on stair*) Geländer *nt*; (*of ship*) Reling *f*; **~s** (*RAIL*) Geleise *pl*; **by ~** per Bahn; **~ing(s)** *n(pl)* Geländer *nt*; **~road** (*US*) *n* Eisenbahn *f*; **~way** (*BRIT*) *n* Eisenbahn *f*; **~way line** (*BRIT*) *n* (Eisen)bahnlinie *f*; (*track*) Gleis *nt*; **~wayman** (*irreg: BRIT*) *n* Eisenbahner *m*; **~way station** (*BRIT*) *n* Bahnhof *m*

rain [reɪn] *n* Regen *m* ♦ *vt, vi* regnen; **in the ~** im Regen; **it's ~ing** es regnet; **~bow** *n* Regenbogen *m*; **~coat** *n* Regenmantel *m*; **~drop** *n* Regentropfen *m*; **~fall** *n* Niederschlag *m*; **~forest** *n* Regenwald *m*; **~y** *adj* (*region, season*) Regen-; (*day*) regnerisch, verregnet

raise [reɪz] *n* (*esp US: increase*) (Gehalts)erhöhung *f* ♦ *vt* (*lift*) (hoch)heben;

(*increase*) erhöhen; (*question*) aufwerfen; (*doubts*) äußern; (*funds*) beschaffen; (*family*) großziehen; (*livestock*) züchten; **to ~ one's voice** die Stimme erheben

raisin ['reɪzn] *n* Rosine *f*

rake [reɪk] *n* Rechen *m*, Harke *f*; (*person*) Wüstling *m* ♦ *vt* rechen, harken; (*search*) (durch)suchen

rally ['rælɪ] *n* (*POL etc*) Kundgebung *f*; (*AUT*) Rallye *f* ♦ *vt* (*MIL*) sammeln ♦ *vi* Kräfte sammeln; **~ round** *vt fus* (sich) scharen um; (*help*) zu Hilfe kommen +*dat* ♦ *vi* zu Hilfe kommen

RAM [ræm] *n abbr* (= *random access memory*) RAM *m*

ram [ræm] *n* Widder *m* ♦ *vt* (*hit*) rammen; (*stuff*) (hinein)stopfen

ramble ['ræmbl] *n* Wanderung *f* ♦ *vi* (*talk*) schwafeln; **~r** *n* Wanderer *m*; **rambling** *adj* (*speech*) weitschweifig; (*town*) ausgedehnt

ramp [ræmp] *n* Rampe *f*; **on/off ~** (*US: AUT*) Ein-/Ausfahrt *f*

rampage [ræm'peɪdʒ] *n*: **to be on the ~** randalieren ♦ *vi* randalieren

rampant ['ræmpənt] *adj* wild wuchernd

rampart ['ræmpɑːt] *n* (Schutz)wall *m*

ram raid *n* Raubüberfall, bei dem eine Geschäftsfront mit einem Fahrzeug gerammt wird

ramshackle ['ræmʃækl] *adj* baufällig

ran [ræn] *pt of* **run**

ranch [rɑːntʃ] *n* Ranch *f*

rancid ['rænsɪd] *adj* ranzig

rancour ['ræŋkə*] (*US* **rancor**) *n* Verbitterung *f*, Groll *m*

random ['rændəm] *adj* ziellos, wahllos ♦ *n*: **at ~** aufs Geratewohl; **~ access** *n* (*COMPUT*) wahlfreie(r) Zugriff *m*

randy ['rændɪ] (*BRIT: inf*) *adj* geil, scharf

rang [ræŋ] *pt of* **ring**

range [reɪndʒ] *n* Reihe *f*; (*of mountains*) Kette *f*; (*COMM*) Sortiment *nt*; (*reach*) (Reich)weite *f*; (*of gun*) Schußweite ⚠ *f*; (*for shooting practice*) Schießplatz *m*; (*stove*) (großer) Herd *m* ♦ *vt* (*set in row*) anordnen, aufstellen; (*roam*) durchstreifen ♦ *vi*: **to ~ over** (*wander*) umherstreifen in +*dat*;

⚠ *For information on spelling reform see page 615*

(*extend*) sich erstrecken auf +*acc*; **a ~ of** (*selection*) eine (große) Auswahl an +*dat*; **prices ranging from £5 to £10** Preise, die sich zwischen £5 und £10 bewegen; **~r** ['reɪndʒəʳ] n Förster m

rank [ræŋk] n (*row*) Reihe f; (*BRIT: also: taxi ~*) (Taxi)stand m; (*MIL*) Rang m; (*social position*) Stand m ♦ vi (*have ~*): **to ~ among** gehören zu ♦ adj (*strong-smelling*) stinkend; (*extreme*) kraß △; **the ~ and file** (*fig*) die breite Masse

rankle ['ræŋkl] vi nagen

ransack ['rænsæk] vt (*plunder*) plündern; (*search*) durchwühlen

ransom ['rænsəm] n Lösegeld nt; **to hold sb to ~** jdn gegen Lösegeld festhalten

rant [rænt] vi hochtrabend reden

rap [ræp] n Schlag m; (*music*) Rap m ♦ vt klopfen

rape [reɪp] n Vergewaltigung f; (*BOT*) Raps m ♦ vt vergewaltigen; **~(seed) oil** n Rapsöl nt

rapid ['ræpɪd] adj rasch, schnell; **~ity** [rə'pɪdɪtɪ] n Schnelligkeit f; **~s** npl Stromschnellen pl

rapist ['reɪpɪst] n Vergewaltiger m

rapport [ræ'pɔːʳ] n gute(s) Verhältnis nt

rapture ['ræptʃəʳ] n Entzücken nt; **rapturous** ['ræptʃərəs] adj (*applause*) stürmisch; (*expression*) verzückt

rare [rɛəʳ] adj selten, rar; (*underdone*) nicht durchgebraten; **~ly** ['rɛəlɪ] adv selten

raring ['rɛərɪŋ] adj: **to be ~ to go** (*inf*) es kaum erwarten können, bis es losgeht

rarity ['rɛərɪtɪ] n Seltenheit f

rascal ['rɑːskl] n Schuft m

rash [ræʃ] adj übereilt; (*reckless*) unbesonnen ♦ n (*Haut*)ausschlag m

rasher ['ræʃəʳ] n Speckscheibe f

raspberry ['rɑːzbərɪ] n Himbeere f

rasping ['rɑːspɪŋ] adj (*noise*) kratzend; (*voice*) krächzend

rat [ræt] n (*animal*) Ratte f; (*person*) Halunke m

rate [reɪt] n (*proportion*) Rate f; (*price*) Tarif m; (*speed*) Tempo nt ♦ vt (ein)schätzen; **~s** npl (*BRIT: tax*) Grundsteuer f; **to ~ as** für etw halten; **~able value** (*BRIT*) n

Einheitswert m (*als Bemessungsgrundlage*); **~payer** (*BRIT*) n Steuerzahler(in) m(f)

rather ['rɑːðəʳ] adv (*in preference*) lieber, eher; (*to some extent*) ziemlich; **I would** or **I'd ~ go** ich würde lieber gehen; **it's ~ expensive** (*quite*) es ist ziemlich teuer; (*too*) es ist etwas zu teuer; **there's ~ a lot** es ist ziemlich viel

ratify ['rætɪfaɪ] vt (*POL*) ratifizieren

rating ['reɪtɪŋ] n Klasse f

ratio ['reɪʃɪəu] n Verhältnis nt; **in the ~ of 100 to 1** im Verhältnis 100 zu 1

ration ['ræʃən] n (*usu pl*) Ration f ♦ vt rationieren

rational ['ræʃənl] adj rational

rationale [ræʃə'nɑːl] n Grundprinzip nt

rationalize ['ræʃnəlaɪz] vt rationalisieren

rat race n Konkurrenzkampf m

rattle ['rætl] n (*sound*) Rasseln nt; (*toy*) Rassel f ♦ vi ratteln, klappern ♦ vt rasseln mit; **~snake** n Klapperschlange f

raucous ['rɔːkəs] adj heiser, rauh △

rave [reɪv] vi (*talk wildly*) phantasieren △; (*rage*) toben ♦ n (*BRIT: inf: party*) Rave m, Fete f

raven ['reɪvən] n Rabe m

ravenous ['rævənəs] adj heißhungrig

ravine [rə'viːn] n Schlucht f

raving ['reɪvɪŋ] adj: **~ lunatic** völlig Wahnsinnige(r) mf

ravishing ['rævɪʃɪŋ] adj atemberaubend

raw [rɔː] adj (*tender*) wund(gerieben); (*inexperienced*) unerfahren; **to get a ~ deal** (*inf*) schlecht wegkommen; **~ material** n Rohmaterial nt

ray [reɪ] n (*of light*) Strahl m; **~ of hope** Hoffnungsschimmer m

raze [reɪz] vt (*also: ~ to the ground*) dem Erdboden gleichmachen

razor ['reɪzəʳ] n Rasierapparat m; **~ blade** n Rasierklinge f

Rd abbr = **road**

RE (*BRIT: SCH*) abbr (= *religious education*) Religionsunterricht m

re [riː] prep (*COMM*) betreffs +*gen*

reach [riːtʃ] n Reichweite f; (*of river*) Strecke f ♦ vt (*arrive at*) erreichen; (*give*) reichen ♦ vi

△ *Informationen zur Rechtschreibreform Seite 615*

(*stretch*) sich erstrecken; **within ~** (*shops etc*) in erreichbarer Weite or Entfernung; **out of ~** außer Reichweite; **to ~ for** (*try to get*) langen nach; **~ out** *vi* die Hand ausstrecken; **to ~ out for sth** nach etw greifen

react [riːˈækt] *vi* reagieren; **~ion** [riːˈækʃən] *n* Reaktion *f*; **~or** [riːˈæktər] *n* Reaktor *m*

read¹ [rɛd] *pt, pp of* **read**

read² [riːd] (*pt, pp* read) *vt, vi* lesen; (*aloud*) vorlesen; **~ out** *vt* vorlesen; **~able** *adj* leserlich; (*worth reading*) lesenswert; **~er** *n* (*person*) Leser(in) *m(f)*; **~ership** *n* Leserschaft *f*

readily [ˈrɛdɪlɪ] *adv* (*willingly*) bereitwillig; (*easily*) prompt

readiness [ˈrɛdɪnɪs] *n* (*willingness*) Bereitwilligkeit *f*; (*being ready*) Bereitschaft *f*; **in ~** (*prepared*) bereit

reading [ˈriːdɪŋ] *n* Lesen *nt*

readjust [riːəˈdʒʌst] *vt* neu einstellen ♦ *vi* (*person*): **to ~ to** sich wieder anpassen an +*acc*

ready [ˈrɛdɪ] *adj* (*prepared, willing*) bereit ♦ *adv*: **~-cooked** vorgekocht ♦ *n*: **at the ~** bereit; **~-made** *adj* gebrauchsfertig, Fertig-; (*clothes*) Konfektions-; **~ money** *n* Bargeld *nt*; **~ reckoner** *n* Rechentabelle *f*; **~-to-wear** *adj* Konfektions-

real [rɪəl] *adj* wirklich; (*actual*) eigentlich; (*not fake*) echt; **in ~ terms** effektiv; **~ estate** *n* Grundbesitz *m*; **~istic** [rɪəˈlɪstɪk] *adj* realistisch

reality [riːˈælɪtɪ] *n* Wirklichkeit *f*, Realität *f*; **in ~** in Wirklichkeit

realization [rɪəlaɪˈzeɪʃən] *n* (*understanding*) Erkenntnis *f*; (*fulfilment*) Verwirklichung *f*

realize [ˈrɪəlaɪz] *vt* (*understand*) begreifen; (*make real*) verwirklichen; **I didn't ~ ...** ich wußte nicht, ...

really [ˈrɪəlɪ] *adv* wirklich; **~?** (*indicating interest*) tatsächlich?; (*expressing surprise*) wirklich?

realm [rɛlm] *n* Reich *nt*

realtor [ˈrɪəltɔːr] (*US*) *n* Grundstücksmakler(in) *m(f)*

reap [riːp] *vt* ernten

reappear [riːəˈpɪər] *vi* wieder erscheinen

rear [rɪər] *adj* hintere(r, s), Rück- ♦ *n* Rückseite *f*; (*last part*) Schluß △ *m* ♦ *vt* (*bring up*) aufziehen ♦ *vi* (*horse*) sich aufbäumen; **~guard** *n* Nachhut *f*

rearmament [riːˈɑːməmənt] *n* Wiederaufrüstung *f*

rearrange [riːəˈreɪndʒ] *vt* umordnen

rear-view mirror [ˈrɪəvjuː-] *n* Rückspiegel *m*

reason [ˈriːzn] *n* (*cause*) Grund *m*; (*ability to think*) Verstand *m*; (*sensible thoughts*) Vernunft *f* ♦ *vi* (*think*) denken; (*use arguments*) argumentieren; **it stands to ~ that** es ist logisch, daß; **to ~ with sb** mit jdm diskutieren; **~able** *adj* vernünftig; **~ably** *adv* vernünftig; (*fairly*) ziemlich; **~ed** *adj* (*argument*) durchdacht; **~ing** *n* Urteilen *nt*; (*argumentation*) Beweisführung *f*

reassurance [riːəˈʃuərəns] *n* Beruhigung *f*; (*confirmation*) Bestätigung *f*; **reassure** [riːəˈʃuər] *vt* beruhigen; **to reassure sb of sth** jdm etw versichern

rebate [ˈriːbeɪt] *n* Rückzahlung *f*

rebel [*n* ˈrɛbl, *vb* rɪˈbɛl] *n* Rebell *m* ♦ *vi* rebellieren; **~lion** [rɪˈbɛljən] *n* Rebellion *f*, Aufstand *m*; **~lious** [rɪˈbɛljəs] *adj* rebellisch

rebirth [riːˈbɜːθ] *n* Wiedergeburt *f*

rebound [*vb* rɪˈbaund, *n* ˈriːbaund] *vi* zurückprallen ♦ *n* Rückprall *m*

rebuff [rɪˈbʌf] *n* Abfuhr *f* ♦ *vt* abblitzen lassen

rebuild [riːˈbɪld] (*irreg*) *vt* wiederaufbauen △; (*fig*) wiederherstellen △

rebuke [rɪˈbjuːk] *n* Tadel *m* ♦ *vt* tadeln, rügen

rebut [rɪˈbʌt] *vt* widerlegen

recall [*vb* rɪˈkɔːl, *n* ˈriːkɔːl] *vt* (*call back*) zurückrufen; (*remember*) sich erinnern an +*acc* ♦ *n* Rückruf *m*

recap [ˈriːkæp] *vt, vi* wiederholen

rec'd *abbr* (= *received*) Eing.

recede [rɪˈsiːd] *vi* zurückweichen; **receding** *adj*: **receding hairline** Stirnglatze *f*

receipt [rɪˈsiːt] *n* (*document*) Quittung *f*; (*receiving*) Empfang *m*; **~s** *npl* (*ECON*) Einnahmen *pl*

△ *For information on spelling reform see page 615*

receive [rɪ'siːv] *vt* erhalten; (*visitors etc*) empfangen; **~r** *n* (*TEL*) Hörer *m*

recent ['riːsnt] *adj* vor kurzem (geschehen), neulich; (*modern*) neu; **~ly** *adv* kürzlich, neulich

receptacle [rɪ'septɪkl] *n* Behälter *m*

reception [rɪ'sepʃən] *n* Empfang *m*; **~ desk** *n* Empfang *m*; (*in hotel*) Rezeption *f*; **~ist** *n* (*in hotel*) Empfangschef *m*, Empfangsdame *f*; (*MED*) Sprechstundenhilfe *f*

receptive [rɪ'septɪv] *adj* aufnahmebereit

recess [rɪ'ses] *n* (*break*) Ferien *pl*; (*hollow*) Nische *f*

recession [rɪ'seʃən] *n* Rezession *f*

recharge [riː'tʃɑːdʒ] *vt* (*battery*) aufladen

recipe ['resɪpɪ] *n* Rezept *nt*

recipient [rɪ'sɪpɪənt] *n* Empfänger *m*

reciprocal [rɪ'sɪprəkl] *adj* gegenseitig; (*mutual*) wechselseitig

recital [rɪ'saɪtl] *n* Vortrag *m*

recite [rɪ'saɪt] *vt* vortragen, aufsagen

reckless ['rekləs] *adj* leichtsinnig; (*driving*) fahrlässig

reckon ['rekən] *vt* (*count*) rechnen, berechnen, errechnen; (*estimate*) schätzen; (*think*): **I ~ that ...** ich nehme an, daß ...; **~ on** *vt fus* rechnen mit; **~ing** *n* (*calculation*) Rechnen *nt*

reclaim [rɪ'kleɪm] *vt* (*expenses*) zurückverlangen; (*land*): **to ~ (from sth)** (etw *dat*) gewinnen; **reclamation** [reklə'meɪʃən] *n* (*of land*) Gewinnung *f*

recline [rɪ'klaɪn] *vi* sich zurücklehnen; **reclining** *adj* Liege-

recluse [rɪ'kluːs] *n* Einsiedler *m*

recognition [rekəg'nɪʃən] *n* (*recognizing*) Erkennen *nt*; (*acknowledgement*) Anerkennung *f*; **transformed beyond ~** völlig verändert

recognizable ['rekəgnaɪzəbl] *adj* erkennbar

recognize ['rekəgnaɪz] *vt* erkennen; (*POL, approve*) anerkennen; **to ~ as** anerkennen als; **to ~ by** erkennen an +*dat*

recoil [rɪ'kɔɪl] *vi* (*in horror*) zurückschrecken; (*rebound*) zurückprallen; (*person*): **to ~ from doing sth** davor zurückschrecken, etw zu tun

recollect [rekə'lekt] *vt* sich erinnern an +*acc*; **~ion** [rekə'lekʃən] *n* Erinnerung *f*

recommend [rekə'mend] *vt* empfehlen; **~ation** [rekəmen'deɪʃən] *n* Empfehlung *f*

recompense ['rekəmpens] *n* (*compensation*) Entschädigung *f*; (*reward*) Belohnung *f* ♦ *vt* entschädigen; belohnen

reconcile ['rekənsaɪl] *vt* (*facts*) vereinbaren; (*people*) versöhnen; **to ~ o.s. to sth** sich mit etw abfinden; **reconciliation** [rekənsɪlɪ'eɪʃən] *n* Versöhnung *f*

recondition [riːkən'dɪʃən] *vt* (*machine*) generalüberholen

reconnoitre [rekə'nɔɪtəʳ] (*US* **reconnoiter**) *vt* erkunden ♦ *vi* aufklären

reconsider [riːkən'sɪdəʳ] *vt* von neuem erwägen, noch einmal überdenken ♦ *vi* es noch einmal überdenken

reconstruct [riːkən'strʌkt] *vt* wiederaufbauen △; (*crime*) rekonstruieren

record [*n* 'rekɔːd, *vb* rɪ'kɔːd] *n* Aufzeichnung *f*; (*MUS*) Schallplatte *f*; (*best performance*) Rekord *m* ♦ *vt* aufzeichnen; (*music etc*) aufnehmen; **off the ~** (*as adj*) inoffiziell, vertraulich; (*as adv*) im Vertrauen; **in ~ time** in Rekordzeit; **~ card** *n* (*in file*) Karteikarte *f*; **~ed delivery** (*BRIT*) *n* (*POST*) Einschreiben *nt*; **~er** *n* (*TECH*) Registriergerät *nt*; (*MUS*) Blockflöte *f*; **~ holder** *n* (*SPORT*) Rekordinhaber *m*; **~ing** *n* (*MUS*) Aufnahme *f*; **~ player** *n* Plattenspieler *m*

recount [rɪ'kaunt] *vt* (*tell*) berichten

re-count ['riːkaunt] *n* Nachzählung *f*

recoup [rɪ'kuːp] *vt*: **to ~ one's losses** seinen Verlust wiedergutmachen △

recourse [rɪ'kɔːs] *n*: **to have ~ to** Zuflucht nehmen zu *or* bei

recover [rɪ'kʌvəʳ] *vt* (*get back*) zurückerhalten ♦ *vi* sich erholen

re-cover [riː'kʌvəʳ] *vt* (*quilt etc*) neu überziehen

recovery [rɪ'kʌvərɪ] *n* Wiedererlangung *f*; (*of health*) Erholung *f*

recreate [riːkrɪ'eɪt] *vt* wiederherstellen △

recreation [rekrɪ'eɪʃən] *n* Erholung *f*; **~al** *adj* Erholungs-; **~al drug** *n* Freizeitdroge *f*

recrimination [rɪkrɪmɪ'neɪʃən] *n*

Gegenbeschuldigung f

recruit [rɪ'kru:t] n Rekrut m ♦ vt rekrutieren; **~ment** n Rekrutierung f

rectangle ['rektæŋgl] n Rechteck nt; **rectangular** [rek'tæŋgjuləʳ] adj rechteckig, rechtwinklig

rectify ['rektɪfaɪ] vt berichtigen

rector ['rektəʳ] n (REL) Pfarrer m; (SCH) Direktor(in) m(f); **~y** ['rektərɪ] n Pfarrhaus nt

recuperate [rɪ'kju:pəreɪt] vi sich erholen

recur [rɪ'kə:ʳ] vi sich wiederholen; **~rence** n Wiederholung f; **~rent** adj wiederkehrend

recycle [ri:'saɪkl] vt wiederverwerten △, wiederaufbereiten △; **recycling** n Recycling nt

red [red] n Rot nt; (POL) Rote(r) m ♦ adj rot; **in the ~** in den roten Zahlen; **~ carpet treatment** n Sonderbehandlung f, große(r) Bahnhof m; **R~ Cross** n Rote(s) Kreuz nt; **~currant** n rote Johannisbeere f; **~den** vi sich röten; (blush) erröten ♦ vt röten; **~dish** adj rötlich

redecorate [ri:'dekəreɪt] vt neu tapezieren, neu streichen

redeem [rɪ'di:m] vt (COMM) einlösen; (save) retten; **~ing** adj: **~ing feature** versöhnende(s) Moment nt

redeploy [ri:dɪ'plɔɪ] vt (resources) umverteilen

red: ~-haired [red'heəd] adj rothaarig; **~-handed** [red'hændɪd] adv: **to be caught ~-handed** auf frischer Tat ertappt werden; **~head** ['redhed] n Rothaarige(r) mf; **~ herring** n Ablenkungsmanöver nt; **~-hot** [red'hɒt] adj rotglühend △

redirect [ri:daɪ'rekt] vt umleiten

red light n: **to go through a ~** (AUT) bei Rot über die Ampel fahren; **red-light district** n Strichviertel nt

redo [ri:'du:] (irreg: like do) vt nochmals machen

redolent ['redələnt] adj: **~ of** (fig) erinnernd an +acc

redouble [ri:'dʌbl] vt: **to ~ one's efforts** seine Anstrengungen verdoppeln

redress [rɪ'dres] vt wiedergutmachen △

red: R~ Sea n: **the R~ Sea** das Rote Meer;

~skin ['redskɪn] n Rothaut f; **~ tape** n Bürokratismus m

reduce [rɪ'dju:s] vt (speed, temperature) vermindern; (photo) verkleinern; **"~ speed now"** (AUT) ≈ "langsam"; **to ~ the price (to)** den Preis herabsetzen (auf +acc); **at a ~d price** zum ermäßigten Preis

reduction [rɪ'dʌkʃən] n Verminderung f; Verkleinerung f; Herabsetzung f; (amount of money) Nachlaß △ m

redundancy [rɪ'dʌndənsɪ] n Überflüssigkeit f; (of workers) Entlassung f

redundant [rɪ'dʌndnt] adj überflüssig; (workers) ohne Arbeitsplatz; **to be made ~** arbeitslos werden

reed [ri:d] n Schilf nt; (MUS) Rohrblatt nt

reef [ri:f] n Riff nt

reek [ri:k] vi: **to ~ (of)** stinken (nach)

reel [ri:l] n Spule f, Rolle f ♦ vt (also: ~ in) wickeln; vi (stagger) taumeln

ref [ref] (inf) n abbr (= referee) Schiri m

refectory [rɪ'fektərɪ] n (UNIV) Mensa f; (SCH) Speisesaal m; (ECCL) Refektorium nt

refer [rɪ'fə:ʳ] vt: **to ~ sb to sb/sth** jdn an jdn/etw verweisen ♦ vi: **to ~ to** (to book) nachschlagen in +dat; (mention) sich beziehen auf +acc

referee [refə'ri:] n Schiedsrichter m; (BRIT: for job) Referenz f ♦ vt schiedsrichtern

reference ['refrəns] n (for job) Referenz f; (in book) Verweis m; (number, code) Aktenzeichen nt; (allusion): **~ (to)** Anspielung (auf +acc); **with ~ to** in bezug auf +acc; **~ book** n Nachschlagewerk nt; **~ number** n Aktenzeichen nt

referenda [refə'rendə] npl of **referendum**

referendum [refə'rendəm] (pl **-da**) n Volksabstimmung f

refill [vb ri:'fɪl, n 'ri:fɪl] vt nachfüllen ♦ n (for pen) Ersatzmine f

refine [rɪ'faɪn] vt (purify) raffinieren; **~d** adj kultiviert; **~ment** n Kultiviertheit f; **~ry** n Raffinerie f

reflect [rɪ'flekt] vt (light) reflektieren; (fig) (wider)spiegeln ♦ vi (meditate): **to ~ (on)** nachdenken (über +acc); **it ~s badly/well on him** das stellt ihn in ein schlechtes/

△ *For information on spelling reform see page 615*

gutes Licht; **~ion** [rɪˈflekʃən] n Reflexion f; (*image*) Spiegelbild nt; (*thought*) Überlegung f; **on ~ion** wenn man sich *dat* das recht überlegt

reflex [ˈriːfleks] adj Reflex- ♦ n Reflex m; **~ive** [rɪˈfleksɪv] adj reflexiv

reform [rɪˈfɔːm] n Reform f ♦ vt (*person*) bessern; **~atory** (*US*) n Besserungsanstalt f

refrain [rɪˈfreɪn] vi: **to ~ from** unterlassen ♦ n Refrain m

refresh [rɪˈfreʃ] vt erfrischen; **~er course** (*BRIT*) n Wiederholungskurs m; **~ing** adj erfrischend; **~ments** npl Erfrischungen pl

refrigeration [rɪfrɪdʒəˈreɪʃən] n Kühlung f

refrigerator [rɪˈfrɪdʒəreɪtər] n Kühlschrank m

refuel [riːˈfjuəl] vt, vi auftanken

refuge [ˈrefjuːdʒ] n Zuflucht f; **to take ~ in** sich flüchten in +*acc*; **~e** [refjuːˈdʒiː] n Flüchtling m

refund [n ˈriːfʌnd, vb rɪˈfʌnd] n Rückvergütung f ♦ vt zurückerstatten

refurbish [riːˈfɜːbɪʃ] vt aufpolieren

refusal [rɪˈfjuːzəl] n (Ver)weigerung f; **first ~** Vorkaufsrecht nt

refuse¹ [rɪˈfjuːz] vt abschlagen ♦ vi sich weigern

refuse² [ˈrefjuːs] n Abfall m, Müll m; **~ collection** n Müllabfuhr f

refute [rɪˈfjuːt] vt widerlegen

regain [rɪˈgeɪn] vt wiedergewinnen; (*consciousness*) wiedererlangen

regal [ˈriːgl] adj königlich

regalia [rɪˈgeɪlɪə] npl Insignien pl

regard [rɪˈgɑːd] n Achtung f ♦ vt ansehen; **to give one's ~s to sb** jdn grüßen lassen; **"with kindest ~s"** „mit freundlichen Grüßen"; **~ing** or **as ~s** or **with ~ to** bezüglich +*gen*, in bezug △ auf +*acc*; **~less** adj: **~less of** ohne Rücksicht auf +*acc* ♦ adv trotzdem

regenerate [rɪˈdʒenəreɪt] vt erneuern

régime [reɪˈʒiːm] n Regime nt

regiment [n ˈredʒɪmənt, vb ˈredʒɪment] n Regiment nt ♦ vt (*fig*) reglementieren; **~al** [redʒɪˈmentl] adj Regiments-

region [ˈriːdʒən] n Region f; **in the ~ of** (*fig*) so um; **~al** adj örtlich, regional

register [ˈredʒɪstər] n Register nt ♦ vt (*list*) registrieren; (*emotion*) zeigen; (*write down*) eintragen ♦ vi (*at hotel*) sich eintragen; (*with police*) sich melden; (*make impression*) wirken, ankommen; **~ed** (*BRIT*) adj (*letter*) Einschreibe-, eingeschrieben; **~ed trademark** n eingetragene(s) Warenzeichen nt

registrar [ˈredʒɪstrɑːr] n Standesbeamte(r) m

registration [redʒɪsˈtreɪʃən] n (*act*) Registrierung f; (*AUT: also:* **~ number**) polizeiliche(s) Kennzeichen nt

registry [ˈredʒɪstrɪ] n Sekretariat nt; **~ office** (*BRIT*) n Standesamt nt; **to get married in a ~ office** standesamtlich heiraten

regret [rɪˈgret] n Bedauern nt ♦ vt bedauern; **~fully** adv mit Bedauern, ungern; **~table** adj bedauerlich

regroup [riːˈgruːp] vt umgruppieren ♦ vi sich umgruppieren

regular [ˈregjulər] adj regelmäßig; (*usual*) üblich; (*inf*) regelrecht ♦ n (*client etc*) Stammkunde m; **~ity** [regjuˈlærɪtɪ] n Regelmäßigkeit f; **~ly** adv regelmäßig

regulate [ˈregjuleɪt] vt regeln, regulieren; **regulation** [regjuˈleɪʃən] n (*rule*) Vorschrift f; (*control*) Regulierung f

rehabilitation [ˈriːəbɪlɪˈteɪʃən] n (*of criminal*) Resozialisierung f

rehearsal [rɪˈhɜːsəl] n Probe f

rehearse [rɪˈhɜːs] vt proben

reign [reɪn] n Herrschaft f ♦ vi herrschen

reimburse [riːɪmˈbɜːs] vt: **to ~ sb for sth** jdn für etw entschädigen, jdm etw zurückzahlen

rein [reɪn] n Zügel m

reincarnation [riːɪnkɑːˈneɪʃən] n Wiedergeburt f

reindeer [ˈreɪndɪər] n Ren nt

reinforce [riːɪnˈfɔːs] vt verstärken; **~d concrete** n Stahlbeton m; **~ment** n Verstärkung f; **~ments** npl (*MIL*) Verstärkungstruppen pl

reinstate [riːɪnˈsteɪt] vt wiedereinsetzen △

reissue [riːˈɪʃuː] vt neu herausgeben

reiterate [riːˈɪtəreɪt] vt wiederholen

reject [n ˈriːdʒekt, vb rɪˈdʒekt] n (*COMM*)

Ausschuß(artikel) △ *m* ♦ *vt* ablehnen; **~ion** [rɪ'dʒekʃən] *n* Zurückweisung *f*

rejoice [rɪ'dʒɔɪs] *vi*: **to ~ at** or **over** sich freuen über +*acc*

rekindle [riː'kɪndl] *vt* wieder anfachen

relapse [rɪ'læps] *n* Rückfall *m*

relate [rɪ'leɪt] *vt* (*tell*) erzählen; (*connect*) verbinden ♦ *vi*: **to ~ to** zusammenhängen mit; (*form relationship*) eine Beziehung aufbauen zu; **~d** *adj*: **~d (to)** verwandt (mit); **relating** *prep*: **relating to** bezüglich +*gen*; **relation** [rɪ'leɪʃən] *n* Verwandte(r) *mf*; (*connection*) Beziehung *f*; **relationship** *n* Verhältnis *nt*, Beziehung *f*

relative ['relətɪv] *n* Verwandte(r) *mf* ♦ *adj* relativ; **~ly** *adv* verhältnismäßig

relax [rɪ'læks] *vi* (*slacken*) sich lockern; (*muscles, person*) sich entspannen ♦ *vt* (*ease*) lockern, entspannen; **~ation** [riːlæk'seɪʃən] *n* Entspannung *f*; **~ed** *adj* entspannt, locker; **~ing** *adj* entspannend

relay [*n* 'riːleɪ, *vb* rɪ'leɪ] *n* (*SPORT*) Staffel *f* ♦ *vt* (*message*) weiterleiten; (*RAD, TV*) übertragen

release [rɪ'liːs] *n* (*freedom*) Entlassung *f*; (*TECH*) Auslöser *m* ♦ *vt* befreien; (*prisoner*) entlassen; (*report, news*) verlautbaren, bekanntgeben △

relegate ['relɪgeɪt] *vt* (*SPORT*): **to be ~d** absteigen

relent [rɪ'lent] *vi* nachgeben; **~less** *adj* unnachgiebig

relevant ['relɪvənt] *adj* wichtig, relevant; **~ to** relevant für

reliability [rɪlaɪə'bɪlɪtɪ] *n* Zuverlässigkeit *f*

reliable [rɪ'laɪəbl] *adj* zuverlässig; **reliably** *adv* zuverlässig; **to be reliably informed that ...** aus zuverlässiger Quelle wissen, daß ...

reliance [rɪ'laɪəns] *n*: **~ (on)** Abhängigkeit *f* (von)

relic ['relɪk] *n* (*from past*) Überbleibsel *nt*; (*REL*) Reliquie *f*

relief [rɪ'liːf] *n* Erleichterung *f*; (*help*) Hilfe *f*; (*person*) Ablösung *f*

relieve [rɪ'liːv] *vt* (*ease*) erleichtern; (*help*) entlasten; (*person*) ablösen; **to ~ sb of sth** jdm etw abnehmen; **to ~ o.s.** (*euph*) sich

erleichtern (*euph*); **~d** *adj* erleichtert

religion [rɪ'lɪdʒən] *n* Religion *f*; **religious** [rɪ'lɪdʒəs] *adj* religiös

relinquish [rɪ'lɪŋkwɪʃ] *vt* aufgeben

relish ['relɪʃ] *n* Würze *f* ♦ *vt* genießen; **to ~ doing** gern tun

relocate [riːləʊ'keɪt] *vt* verlegen ♦ *vi* umziehen

reluctance [rɪ'lʌktəns] *n* Widerstreben *nt*, Abneigung *f*

reluctant [rɪ'lʌktənt] *adj* widerwillig; **~ly** *adv* ungern

rely [rɪ'laɪ] *vt fus*: **to ~ on** sich verlassen auf +*acc*

remain [rɪ'meɪn] *vi* (*be left*) übrigbleiben △; (*stay*) bleiben; **~der** *n* Rest *m*; **~ing** *adj* übrig(geblieben) △; **~s** *npl* Überreste *pl*

remake ['riːmeɪk] *n* (*CINE*) Neuverfilmung *f*

remand [rɪ'mɑːnd] *n*: **on ~** in Untersuchungshaft ♦ *vt*: **to ~ in custody** in Untersuchungshaft schicken; **~ home** (*BRIT*) *n* Untersuchungsgefängnis *nt* für Jugendliche

remark [rɪ'mɑːk] *n* Bemerkung *f* ♦ *vt* bemerken; **~able** *adj* bemerkenswert; **remarkably** *adv* außergewöhnlich

remarry [riː'mærɪ] *vi* sich wieder verheiraten

remedial [rɪ'miːdɪəl] *adj* Heil-; (*teaching*) Hilfsschul-

remedy ['remədɪ] *n* Mittel *nt* ♦ *vt* (*pain*) abhelfen +*dat*; (*trouble*) in Ordnung bringen

remember [rɪ'membə*] *vt* sich erinnern an +*acc*; **remembrance** [rɪ'membrəns] *n* Erinnerung *f*; (*official*) Gedenken *nt*; **R~ Day** *n* ≈ Volkstrauertag *m*

REMEMBRANCE DAY

i Remembrance Day oder Remembrance Sunday *ist der britische Gedenktag für die Gefallenen der beiden Weltkriege und anderer Konflikte. Er fällt auf einen Sonntag vor oder nach dem 11. November (am 11. November 1918 endete der erste Weltkrieg) und wird mit einer Schweigeminute, Kranzniederlegungen an Kriegerdenkmälern und dem Tragen von Anstecknadeln in Form einer Mohnblume*

△ *For information on spelling reform see page 615*

begangen.

remind [rɪˈmaɪnd] vt: **to ~ sb to do sth** jdn daran erinnern, etw zu tun; **to ~ sb of sth** jdn an etw acc erinnern; **she ~s me of her mother** sie erinnert mich an ihre Mutter; **~er** n Mahnung f

reminisce [remɪˈnɪs] vi in Erinnerungen schwelgen; **~nt** [remɪˈnɪsnt] adj: **to be ~nt of sth** an etw acc erinnern

remiss [rɪˈmɪs] adj nachlässig

remission [rɪˈmɪʃən] n Nachlaß △ m; (of debt, sentence) Erlaß △ m

remit [rɪˈmɪt] vt (money): **to ~ (to)** überweisen (an +acc); **~tance** n Geldanweisung f

remnant [ˈremnənt] n Rest m; **~s** npl (COMM) Einzelstücke pl

remorse [rɪˈmɔːs] n Gewissensbisse pl; **~ful** adj reumütig; **~less** adj unbarmherzig

remote [rɪˈməʊt] adj abgelegen; (slight) gering; **~ control** n Fernsteuerung f; **~ly** adv entfernt

remould [ˈriːməʊld] (BRIT) n runderneuerte(r) Reifen m

removable [rɪˈmuːvəbl] adj entfernbar

removal [rɪˈmuːvəl] n Beseitigung f; (of furniture) Umzug m; (from office) Entlassung f; **~ van** (BRIT) n Möbelwagen m

remove [rɪˈmuːv] vt beseitigen, entfernen; **~rs** npl Möbelspedition f

remuneration [rɪmjuːnəˈreɪʃən] n Vergütung f, Honorar nt

render [ˈrendər] vt machen; (translate) übersetzen; **~ing** n (MUS) Wiedergabe f

rendezvous [ˈrɒndɪvuː] n (meeting) Rendezvous nt; (place) Treffpunkt m ♦ vi sich treffen

renew [rɪˈnjuː] vt erneuern; (contract, licence) verlängern; (replace) ersetzen; **~able** adj regenerierbar; **~al** n Erneuerung f; Verlängerung f

renounce [rɪˈnaʊns] vt (give up) verzichten auf +acc; (disown) verstoßen

renovate [ˈrenəveɪt] vt renovieren; (building) restaurieren

renown [rɪˈnaʊn] n Ruf m; **~ed** adj namhaft

rent [rent] n Miete f; (for land) Pacht f ♦ vt (hold as tenant) mieten; pachten; (let) vermieten; verpachten; (car etc) mieten; (firm) vermieten; **~al** n Miete f

renunciation [rɪnʌnsɪˈeɪʃən] n: **~ (of)** Verzicht m (auf +acc)

reorganize [riːˈɔːɡənaɪz] vt umgestalten, reorganisieren

rep [rep] n abbr (COMM) = **representative**; (THEAT) **repertory**

repair [rɪˈpeər] n Reparatur f ♦ vt reparieren; (damage) wiedergutmachen △; **in good/ bad ~** in gutem/schlechtem Zustand; **~ kit** n Werkzeugkasten m

repartee [repɑːˈtiː] n Witzeleien pl

repatriate [riːˈpætrɪeɪt] vt in die Heimat zurückschicken

repay [riːˈpeɪ] (irreg) vt zurückzahlen; (reward) vergelten; **~ment** n Rückzahlung f; (fig) Vergeltung f

repeal [rɪˈpiːl] vt aufheben

repeat [rɪˈpiːt] n (RAD, TV) Wiederholung(ssendung) f ♦ vt wiederholen; **~edly** adv wiederholt

repel [rɪˈpel] vt (drive back) zurückschlagen; (disgust) abstoßen; **~lent** adj abstoßend ♦ n: **insect ~lent** Insektenmittel nt

repent [rɪˈpent] vt, vi: **to ~ (of)** bereuen; **~ance** n Reue f

repercussion [riːpəˈkʌʃən] n Auswirkung f; **to have ~s** ein Nachspiel haben

repertory [ˈrepətəri] n Repertoire nt

repetition [repɪˈtɪʃən] n Wiederholung f

repetitive [rɪˈpetɪtɪv] adj sich wiederholend

replace [rɪˈpleɪs] vt ersetzen; (put back) zurückstellen; **~ment** n Ersatz m

replay [ˈriːpleɪ] n (of match) Wiederholungsspiel nt; (of tape, film) Wiederholung f

replenish [rɪˈplenɪʃ] vt ergänzen

replica [ˈreplɪkə] n Kopie f

reply [rɪˈplaɪ] n Antwort f ♦ vi antworten; **~ coupon** n Antwortschein m

report [rɪˈpɔːt] n Bericht m; (BRIT: SCH) Zeugnis nt ♦ vt (tell) berichten; (give information against) melden; (to police) anzeigen ♦ vi (make ~) Bericht erstatten;

(*present o.s.*): **to ~ (to sb)** sich (bei jdm) melden; **~ card** (US, SCOTTISH) n Zeugnis nt; **~edly** adv wie verlautet; **~er** n Reporter m

reprehensible [reprɪˈhensɪbl] adj tadelnswert

represent [reprɪˈzent] vt darstellen; (*speak for*) vertreten; **~ation** [reprɪzenˈteɪʃən] n Darstellung f; (*being represented*) Vertretung f; **~ations** npl (*protest*) Vorhaltungen pl; **~ative** n (*person*) Vertreter m; (US: POL) Abgeordnete(r) mf ♦ adj repräsentativ

repress [rɪˈpres] vt unterdrücken; **~ion** [rɪˈpreʃən] n Unterdrückung f

reprieve [rɪˈpriːv] n (JUR) Begnadigung f; (*fig*) Gnadenfrist f ♦ vt (JUR) begnadigen

reprimand [ˈreprɪmɑːnd] n Verweis m ♦ vt einen Verweis erteilen +dat

reprint [n ˈriːprɪnt, vb riːˈprɪnt] n Neudruck m ♦ vt wieder abdrucken

reprisal [rɪˈpraɪzl] n Vergeltung f

reproach [rɪˈprəʊtʃ] n Vorwurf m ♦ vt Vorwürfe machen +dat; **to ~ sb with sth** jdm etw vorwerfen; **~ful** adj vorwurfsvoll

reproduce [riːprəˈdjuːs] vt reproduzieren ♦ vi (*have offspring*) sich vermehren; **reproduction** [riːprəˈdʌkʃən] n (ART, PHOT) Reproduktion f; (*breeding*) Fortpflanzung f; **reproductive** [riːprəˈdʌktɪv] adj reproduktiv; (*breeding*) Fortpflanzungs-

reprove [rɪˈpruːv] vt tadeln

reptile [ˈreptaɪl] n Reptil nt

republic [rɪˈpʌblɪk] n Republik f

repudiate [rɪˈpjuːdɪeɪt] vt zurückweisen

repugnant [rɪˈpʌgnənt] adj widerlich

repulse [rɪˈpʌls] vt (*drive back*) zurückschlagen; (*reject*) abweisen

repulsive [rɪˈpʌlsɪv] adj abstoßend

reputable [ˈrepjutəbl] adj angesehen

reputation [repjuˈteɪʃən] n Ruf m

reputed [rɪˈpjuːtɪd] adj angeblich; **~ly** [rɪˈpjuːtɪdlɪ] adv angeblich

request [rɪˈkwest] n Bitte f ♦ vt (*thing*) erbitten; **to ~ sth of** or **from sb** jdn um etw bitten; (*formally*) jdn um etw ersuchen; **~ stop** (BRIT) n Bedarfshaltestelle f

require [rɪˈkwaɪə*] vt (*need*) brauchen;

(*demand*) erfordern; **~ment** n (*condition*) Anforderung f; (*need*) Bedarf m

requisite [ˈrekwɪzɪt] adj erforderlich

requisition [rekwɪˈzɪʃən] n Anforderung f ♦ vt beschlagnahmen

rescue [ˈreskjuː] n Rettung f ♦ vt retten; **~ party** n Rettungsmannschaft f; **~r** n Retter m

research [rɪˈsəːtʃ] n Forschung f ♦ vi forschen ♦ vt erforschen; **~er** n Forscher m

resemblance [rɪˈzembləns] n Ähnlichkeit f

resemble [rɪˈzembl] vt ähneln +dat

resent [rɪˈzent] vt übelnehmen △; **~ful** adj nachtragend, empfindlich; **~ment** n Verstimmung f, Unwille m

reservation [rezəˈveɪʃən] n (*booking*) Reservierung f; (THEAT) Vorbestellung f; (*doubt*) Vorbehalt m; (*land*) Reservat nt

reserve [rɪˈzəːv] n (*store*) Vorrat m, Reserve f; (*manner*) Zurückhaltung f; (*game ~*) Naturschutzgebiet nt; (SPORT) Ersatzspieler(in) m(f) ♦ vt reservieren; (*judgement*) sich dat vorbehalten; **~s** npl (MIL) Reserve f; **in ~** in Reserve; **~d** adj reserviert

reshuffle [riːˈʃʌfl] n (POL): **cabinet ~** Kabinettsumbildung f ♦ vt (POL) umbilden

reside [rɪˈzaɪd] vi wohnen, ansässig sein

residence [ˈrezɪdəns] n (*house*) Wohnsitz m; (*living*) Aufenthalt m; **~ permit** (BRIT) n Aufenthaltserlaubnis f

resident [ˈrezɪdənt] n (*in house*) Bewohner m; (*in area*) Einwohner m ♦ adj wohnhaft, ansässig; **~ial** [rezɪˈdenʃəl] adj Wohn-

residue [ˈrezɪdjuː] n Rest m; (CHEM) Rückstand m; (*fig*) Bodensatz m

resign [rɪˈzaɪn] vt (*office*) aufgeben, zurücktreten von ♦ vi (*from office*) zurücktreten; (*employee*) kündigen; **to be ~ed to sth, to ~ o.s. to sth** sich mit etw abfinden; **~ation** [rezɪgˈneɪʃən] n (*from job*) Kündigung f; (POL) Rücktritt m; (*submission*) Resignation f; **~ed** adj resigniert

resilience [rɪˈzɪlɪəns] n Spannkraft f; (*of person*) Unverwüstlichkeit f; **resilient** [rɪˈzɪlɪənt] adj unverwüstlich

resin [ˈrezɪn] n Harz nt

△ *For information on spelling reform see page 615*

resist [rɪ'zɪst] vt widerstehen +dat; **~ance** n Widerstand m

resit [vb riː'sɪt, n 'riːsɪt] vt (exam) wiederholen ♦ n Wiederholung(sprüfung) f

resolute ['rezəluːt] adj entschlossen, resolut; **resolution** [rezə'luːʃən] n (firmness) Entschlossenheit f; (intention) Vorsatz m; (decision) Beschluß △ m

resolve [rɪ'zɒlv] n Entschlossenheit f ♦ vt (decide) beschließen ♦ vi sich lösen; **~d** adj (fest) entschlossen

resonant ['rezənənt] adj voll

resort [rɪ'zɔːt] n (holiday place) Erholungsort m; (help) Zuflucht f ♦ vi: **to ~ to** Zuflucht nehmen zu; **as a last ~** als letzter Ausweg

resound [rɪ'zaund] vi: **to ~ (with)** widerhallen (von); **~ing** adj nachhallend; (success) groß

resource [rɪ'sɔːs] n Findigkeit f; **~s** npl (financial) Geldmittel pl; (natural) Bodenschätze pl; **~ful** adj findig

respect [rɪs'pekt] n Respekt m ♦ vt achten, respektieren; **~s** npl (regards) Grüße pl; **with ~ to** in bezug auf +acc, hinsichtlich +gen; **in this ~** in dieser Hinsicht; **~able** adj anständig; (not bad) leidlich; **~ful** adj höflich

respective [rɪs'pektɪv] adj jeweilig; **~ly** adv beziehungsweise

respiration [respɪ'reɪʃən] n Atmung f

respite ['respaɪt] n Ruhepause f

resplendent [rɪs'plendənt] adj strahlend

respond [rɪs'pɒnd] vi antworten; (react): **to ~ (to)** reagieren (auf +acc); **response** [rɪs'pɒns] n Antwort f; Reaktion f; (to advert) Resonanz f

responsibility [rɪspɒnsɪ'bɪlɪtɪ] n Verantwortung f

responsible [rɪs'pɒnsɪbl] adj verantwortlich; (reliable) verantwortungsvoll

responsive [rɪs'pɒnsɪv] adj empfänglich

rest [rest] n Ruhe f; (break) Pause f; (remainder) Rest m ♦ vi sich ausruhen; (be supported) (auf)liegen ♦ vt (lean): **to ~ sth on/against sth** etw gegen etw acc lehnen; **the ~ of them** die übrigen; **it ~s with him to ...** es liegt bei ihm, zu ...

restaurant ['restərɒŋ] n Restaurant nt; **~ car** (BRIT) n Speisewagen m

restful ['restful] adj erholsam, ruhig

rest home n Erholungsheim nt

restive ['restɪv] adj unruhig

restless ['restlɪs] adj unruhig

restoration [restə'reɪʃən] n Rückgabe f; (of building etc) Rückerstattung f

restore [rɪs'tɔː] vt (order) wiederherstellen △; (customs) wieder einführen; (person to position) wiedereinsetzen △; (give back) zurückgeben; (renovate) restaurieren

restrain [rɪs'treɪn] vt zurückhalten; (curiosity etc) beherrschen; (person): **to ~ sb from doing sth** jdn davon abhalten, etw zu tun; **~ed** adj (style etc) gedämpft, verhalten; **~t** n (self-control) Zurückhaltung f

restrict [rɪs'trɪkt] vt einschränken; **~ion** [rɪs'trɪkʃən] n Einschränkung f; **~ive** adj einschränkend

rest room (US) n Toilette f

restructure [riː'strʌktʃəʳ] vt umstrukturieren

result [rɪ'zʌlt] n Resultat nt, Folge f; (of exam, game) Ergebnis nt ♦ vi: **to ~ in sth** etw zur Folge haben; **as a ~ of** als Folge +gen

resume [rɪ'zjuːm] vt fortsetzen; (occupy again) wieder einnehmen ♦ vi (work etc) wieder beginnen

résumé ['reɪzjuːmeɪ] n Zusammenfassung f

resumption [rɪ'zʌmpʃən] n Wiederaufnahme f

resurgence [rɪ'səːdʒəns] n Wiedererwachen nt

resurrection [rezə'rekʃən] n Auferstehung f

resuscitate [rɪ'sʌsɪteɪt] vt wiederbeleben △; **resuscitation** [rɪsʌsɪ'teɪʃən] n Wiederbelebung f

retail ['riːteɪl] n Einzelhandel m ♦ adj Einzelhandels- ♦ vt im kleinen verkaufen ♦ vi im Einzelhandel kosten; **~er** n Einzelhändler m, Kleinhändler m; **~ price** n Ladenpreis m

retain [rɪ'teɪn] vt (keep) (zurück)behalten; **~er** n (fee) (Honorar)vorschuß m

retaliate [rɪ'tælɪeɪt] vi zum Vergeltungsschlag ausholen; **retaliation**

[rɪtælʳeɪʃən] n Vergeltung f

retarded [rɪˈtɑːdɪd] adj zurückgeblieben

retch [retʃ] vi würgen

retentive [rɪˈtentɪv] adj (memory) gut

reticent [ˈretɪsnt] adj schweigsam

retina [ˈretɪnə] n Netzhaut f

retire [rɪˈtaɪəʳ] vi (from work) in den Ruhestand treten; (withdraw) sich zurückziehen; (go to bed) schlafen gehen; ~**d** adj (person) pensioniert, im Ruhestand; ~**ment** n Ruhestand m

retiring [rɪˈtaɪərɪŋ] adj zurückhaltend

retort [rɪˈtɔːt] n (reply) Erwiderung f ♦ vi (scharf) erwidern

retrace [rɪˈtreɪs] vt zurückverfolgen; **to ~ one's steps** denselben Weg zurückgehen

retract [rɪˈtrækt] vt (statement) zurücknehmen; (claws) einziehen ♦ vi einen Rückzieher machen; ~**able** adj (aerial) ausziehbar

retrain [riːˈtreɪn] vt umschulen

retread [ˈriːtred] n (tyre) Reifen m mit erneuerter Lauffläche

retreat [rɪˈtriːt] n Rückzug m; (place) Zufluchtsort m ♦ vi sich zurückziehen

retribution [retrɪˈbjuːʃən] n Strafe f

retrieval [rɪˈtriːvəl] n Wiedergewinnung f

retrieve [rɪˈtriːv] vt wiederbekommen; (rescue) retten; ~**r** n Apportierhund m

retrograde [ˈretrəɡreɪd] adj (step) Rück-; (policy) rückschrittlich

retrospect [ˈretrəspekt] n: **in ~** im Rückblick, rückblickend; ~**ive** [retrəˈspektɪv] adj (action) rückwirkend; (look) rückblickend

return [rɪˈtɜːn] n Rückkehr f; (profits) Ertrag m; (BRIT: rail ticket etc) Rückfahrkarte f; (: plane ticket) Rückflugkarte f ♦ adj (journey, match) Rück- ♦ vi zurückkehren, zurückkommen ♦ vt zurückgeben, zurücksenden; (pay back) zurückzahlen; (elect) wählen; (verdict) aussprechen; ~**s** npl (COMM) Gewinn m; (receipts) Einkünfte pl; **in ~** dafür; **by ~ of post** postwendend; **many happy ~s (of the day)!** herzlichen Glückwunsch zum Geburtstag!

reunion [riːˈjuːnɪən] n Wiedervereinigung f; (SCH etc) Treffen nt

reunite [riːjuːˈnaɪt] vt wiedervereinigen △

reuse [riːˈjuːz] vt wiederverwenden △, wiederverwerten △

rev [rev] n abbr (AUT) (= revolution) Drehzahl f

revamp [riːˈvæmp] vt aufpolieren

reveal [rɪˈviːl] vt enthüllen; ~**ing** adj aufschlußreich △

revel [ˈrevl] vi: **to ~ in sth/in doing sth** seine Freude an etw dat haben/daran haben, etw zu tun

revelation [revəˈleɪʃən] n Offenbarung f

revelry [ˈrevlrɪ] n Rummel m

revenge [rɪˈvendʒ] n Rache f; **to take ~ on** sich rächen an +dat

revenue [ˈrevənjuː] n Einnahmen pl

reverberate [rɪˈvɜːbəreɪt] vi widerhallen

revere [rɪˈvɪəʳ] vt (ver)ehren; ~**nce** [ˈrevərəns] n Ehrfurcht f

Reverend [ˈrevərənd] adj: **the ~ Robert Martin** ≈ Pfarrer Robert Martin

reversal [rɪˈvɜːsl] n Umkehrung f

reverse [rɪˈvɜːs] n Rückseite f; (AUT: gear) Rückwärtsgang m ♦ adj (order, direction) entgegengesetzt ♦ vt umkehren ♦ vi (BRIT: AUT) rückwärts fahren; ~**-charge call** (BRIT) n R-Gespräch nt; **reversing lights** npl (AUT) Rückfahrscheinwerfer pl

revert [rɪˈvɜːt] vi: **to ~ to** zurückkehren zu; (to bad state) zurückfallen in +acc

review [rɪˈvjuː] n (of book) Rezension f; (magazine) Zeitschrift f ♦ vt Rückschau halten auf +acc; (MIL) mustern; (book) rezensieren; (reexamine) von neuem untersuchen; ~**er** n (critic) Rezensent m

revise [rɪˈvaɪz] vt (book) überarbeiten; (reconsider) ändern, revidieren; **revision** [rɪˈvɪʒən] n Prüfung f; (COMM) Revision f; (SCH) Wiederholung f

revitalize [riːˈvaɪtəlaɪz] vt neu beleben

revival [rɪˈvaɪvəl] n Wiederbelebung f; (REL) Erweckung f; (THEAT) Wiederaufnahme f

revive [rɪˈvaɪv] vt wiederbeleben △; (fig) wieder auffrischen ♦ vi wiedererwachen △; (fig) wieder aufleben

revoke [rɪˈvəʊk] vt aufheben

revolt [rɪˈvəʊlt] n Aufstand m, Revolte f ♦ vi sich auflehnen ♦ vt entsetzen; ~**ing** adj

△ For information on spelling reform see page 615

widerlich

revolution [rɛvə'lu:ʃən] n (*turn*) Umdrehung f; (*POL*) Revolution f; **~ary** adj revolutionär ♦ n Revolutionär m; **~ize** vt revolutionieren

revolve [rɪ'vɔlv] vi kreisen; (*on own axis*) sich drehen

revolver [rɪ'vɔlvəʳ] n Revolver m

revolving door [rɪ'vɔlvɪŋ-] n Drehtür f

revulsion [rɪ'vʌlʃən] n Ekel m

reward [rɪ'wɔ:d] n Belohnung f ♦ vt belohnen; **~ing** adj lohnend

rewind [ri:'waɪnd] (*irreg: like* **wind**) vt (*tape etc*) zurückspulen

rewire [ri:'waɪəʳ] vt (*house*) neu verkabeln

reword [ri:'wɜːd] vt anders formulieren

rewrite [ri:'raɪt] (*irreg: like* **write**) vt umarbeiten, neu schreiben

rheumatism ['ru:mətɪzəm] n Rheumatismus m, Rheuma nt

Rhine [raɪn] n: **the ~** der Rhein

rhinoceros [raɪ'nɔsərəs] n Nashorn nt

Rhone [rəun] n: **the ~** die Rhone

rhubarb ['ru:bɑːb] n Rhabarber m

rhyme [raɪm] n Reim m

rhythm ['rɪðm] n Rhythmus m

rib [rɪb] n Rippe f ♦ vt (*mock*) hänseln, aufziehen

ribbon ['rɪbən] n Band nt; **in ~s** (*torn*) in Fetzen

rice [raɪs] n Reis m; **~ pudding** n Milchreis m

rich [rɪtʃ] adj reich; (*food*) reichhaltig ♦ npl: **the ~** die Reichen pl; **~es** npl Reichtum m; **~ly** adv reich; (*deserve*) völlig

rickets ['rɪkɪts] n Rachitis f

rickety ['rɪkɪtɪ] adj wack(e)lig

rickshaw ['rɪkʃɔː] n Rikscha f

ricochet ['rɪkəʃeɪ] n Abprallen nt; (*shot*) Querschläger m ♦ vi abprallen

rid [rɪd] (*pt, pp* **rid**) vt befreien; **to get ~ of** loswerden

riddle ['rɪdl] n Rätsel nt ♦ vt: **to be ~d with** völlig durchlöchert sein von

ride [raɪd] (*pt* **rode**, *pp* **ridden**) n (*in vehicle*) Fahrt f; (*on horse*) Ritt m ♦ vt (*horse*) reiten; (*bicycle*) fahren ♦ vi fahren, reiten; **to take sb for a ~** mit jdm eine Fahrt *etc* machen;

(*fig*) jdn aufs Glatteis führen; **~r** n Reiter m

ridge [rɪdʒ] n Kamm m; (*of roof*) First m

ridicule ['rɪdɪkjuːl] n Spott m ♦ vt lächerlich machen

ridiculous [rɪ'dɪkjuləs] adj lächerlich

riding ['raɪdɪŋ] n Reiten nt; **~ school** n Reitschule f

rife [raɪf] adj weit verbreitet; **to be ~** grassieren; **to be ~ with** voll sein von

riffraff ['rɪfræf] n Pöbel m

rifle ['raɪfl] n Gewehr nt ♦ vt berauben; **~ range** n Schießstand m

rift [rɪft] n Spalte f; (*fig*) Bruch m

rig [rɪg] n (*oil ~*) Bohrinsel f ♦ vt (*election etc*) manipulieren; **~ out** (*BRIT*) vt ausstatten; **~ up** vt zusammenbasteln; **~ging** n Takelage f

right [raɪt] adj (*correct, just*) richtig, recht; (*~ side*) rechte(r, s) ♦ n Recht nt; (*not left, POL*) Rechte f ♦ adv (*on the ~*) rechts; (*to the ~*) nach rechts; (*look, work*) richtig, recht; (*directly*) gerade; (*exactly*) genau ♦ vt in Ordnung bringen, korrigieren ♦ excl gut; **on the ~** rechts; **to be in the ~** im Recht sein; **by ~s** von Rechts wegen; **to be ~** recht haben; **~ away** sofort; **~ now** in diesem Augenblick, eben; **~ in the middle** genau in der Mitte; **~ angle** n rechte(r) Winkel m; **~eous** ['raɪtʃəs] adj rechtschaffen; **~ful** adj rechtmäßig; **~-hand** adj; **~-hand drive** mit Rechtssteuerung; **~-handed** adj rechtshändig; **~-hand man** (*irreg*) n rechte Hand f; **~-hand side** n rechte Seite f; **~ly** adv mit Recht; **~ of way** n Vorfahrt f; **~-wing** adj rechtsorientiert

rigid ['rɪdʒɪd] adj (*stiff*) starr, steif; (*strict*) streng; **~ity** [rɪ'dʒɪdɪtɪ] n Starrheit f; Strenge f

rigmarole ['rɪgmərəul] n Gewäsch nt

rigor ['rɪgəʳ] (*US*) n = **rigour**

rigorous ['rɪgərəs] adj streng

rigour ['rɪgəʳ] (*US* **rigor**) n Strenge f, Härte f

rile [raɪl] vt ärgern

rim [rɪm] n (*edge*) Rand m; (*of wheel*) Felge f

rind [raɪnd] n Rinde f

ring [rɪŋ] (*pt* **rang**, *pp* **rung**) n Ring m; (*of* people) Kreis m; (arena) Manege f; (of telephone) Klingeln nt ♦ vt, vi (bell) läuten; (BRIT) anrufen; ~ **back** (BRIT) vt, vi zurückrufen; ~ **off** (BRIT) vi aufhängen; ~ **up** (BRIT) vt anrufen; ~ **binder** n Ringbuch nt; **~ing** n Klingeln nt; (of large bell) Läuten nt; (in ears) Klingen nt; **~ing tone** n (TEL) Rufzeichen nt

ringleader ['rɪŋliːdər] n Anführer m, Rädelsführer m

ringlets ['rɪŋlɪts] npl Ringellocken pl

ring road (BRIT) n Umgehungsstraße f

rink [rɪŋk] n (ice ~) Eisbahn f

rinse [rɪns] n Spülen nt ♦ vt spülen

riot ['raɪət] n Aufruhr m ♦ vi randalieren; **to run ~** (people) randalieren; (vegetation) wuchern; **~er** n Aufrührer m; **~ous** adj aufrührerisch; (noisy) lärmend

rip [rɪp] n Schlitz m, Riß △ m ♦ vt, vi (zer)reißen; **~cord** n Reißleine f

ripe [raɪp] adj reif; **~n** vi reifen ♦ vt reifen lassen

rip-off ['rɪpɔf] (inf) n: **it's a ~-~!** das ist Wucher!

ripple ['rɪpl] n kleine Welle f ♦ vt kräuseln ♦ vi sich kräuseln

rise [raɪz] (pt rose, pp risen) n (slope) Steigung f; (esp in wages: BRIT) Erhöhung f; (growth) Aufstieg m ♦ vi aufgehen; (sun) aufgehen; (mountain) sich erheben; (ground) ansteigen; (prices) steigen; (in revolt) sich erheben; **to give ~ to** Anlaß geben zu; **to ~ to the occasion** sich der Lage gewachsen zeigen; **~n** [rɪzn] pp of **rise**; **~r** ['raɪzər] n: **to be an early ~r** ein(e) Frühaufsteher(in) m(f) sein; **rising** ['raɪzɪŋ] adj (tide, prices) steigend; (sun, moon) aufgehend ♦ n (uprising) Aufstand m

risk [rɪsk] n Gefahr f, Risiko nt ♦ vt (venture) wagen; (chance loss of) riskieren, aufs Spiel setzen; **to take** or **run the ~ of doing** das Risiko eingehen, zu tun; **at ~** in Gefahr; **at one's own ~** auf eigene Gefahr; **~y** adj riskant

risqué ['riːskeɪ] adj gewagt

rissole ['rɪsəul] n Fleischklößchen nt

rite [raɪt] n Ritus m; **last ~s** Letzte Ölung f

ritual ['rɪtjuəl] n Ritual nt ♦ adj ritual, Ritual-; (fig) rituell

rival ['raɪvl] n Rivale m, Konkurrent m ♦ adj rivalisierend ♦ vt rivalisieren mit; (COMM) konkurrieren mit; **~ry** n Rivalität f; Konkurrenz f

river ['rɪvər] n Fluß △ m, Strom m ♦ cpd (port, traffic) Fluß- △; **up/down ~** flußaufwärts/-abwärts; **~bank** n Flußufer △ nt; **~bed** n Flußbett △ nt

rivet ['rɪvɪt] n Niete f ♦ vt (fasten) (ver)nieten

Riviera [rɪvɪ'eərə] n: **the ~** die Riviera

road [rəud] n Straße f ♦ cpd Straßen-; **major/minor ~** Haupt-/Nebenstraße f; **~ accident** n Verkehrsunfall m; **~block** n Straßensperre f; **~hog** n Verkehrsrowdy m; **~ map** n Straßenkarte f; **~ rage** n Aggressivität f im Straßenverkehr; **~ safety** n Verkehrssicherheit f; **~side** n Straßenrand m ♦ adj an der Landstraße (gelegen); **~ sign** n Straßenschild nt; **~ user** n Verkehrsteilnehmer m; **~way** n Fahrbahn f; **~ works** npl Straßenbauarbeiten pl; **~worthy** adj verkehrssicher

roam [rəum] vi (umher)streifen ♦ vt durchstreifen

roar [rɔːr] n Brüllen nt, Gebrüll nt ♦ vi brüllen; **to ~ with laughter** vor Lachen brüllen; **to do a ~ing trade** ein Riesengeschäft machen

roast [rəust] n Braten m ♦ vt braten, schmoren; **~ beef** n Roastbeef nt

rob [rɒb] vt bestehlen, berauben; (bank) ausrauben; **to ~ sb of sth** jdm etw rauben; **~ber** n Räuber m; **~bery** n Raub m

robe [rəub] n (dress) Gewand nt; (US) Hauskleid nt; (judge's) Robe f

robin ['rɒbɪn] n Rotkehlchen nt

robot ['rəubɔt] n Roboter m

robust [rəu'bʌst] adj (person) robust; (appetite, economy) gesund

rock [rɒk] n Felsen m; (BRIT: sweet) Zuckerstange f ♦ vt, vi wiegen, schaukeln; **on the ~s** (drink) mit Eis(würfeln); (marriage) gescheitert; (ship) aufgelaufen; **~ and roll** n Rock and Roll m; **~-bottom** n (fig) Tiefpunkt m; **~ery** n Steingarten m

△ *For information on spelling reform see page 615*

rocket [ˈrɒkɪt] *n* Rakete *f*
rocking chair [ˈrɒkɪŋ-] *n* Schaukelstuhl *m*
rocking horse *n* Schaukelpferd *nt*
rocky [ˈrɒkɪ] *adj* felsig
rod [rɒd] *n* (*bar*) Stange *f*; (*stick*) Rute *f*
rode [rəud] *pt of* **ride**
rodent [ˈrəudnt] *n* Nagetier *nt*
roe [rəu] *n* (*also:* **~ deer**) Reh *nt*; (*of fish: also:* **hard ~**) Rogen *m*; **soft ~** Milch *f*
rogue [rəug] *n* Schurke *m*
role [rəul] *n* Rolle *f*; **~ play** *n* Rollenspiel *nt*
roll [rəul] *n* Rolle *f*; (*bread*) Brötchen *nt*; (*list*) (Namens)liste *f*; (*of drum*) Wirbel *m* ♦ *vt* (*turn*) rollen, (herum)wälzen; (*grass etc*) walzen ♦ *vi* (*swing*) schlingern; (*sound*) rollen, grollen; **~ about** *or* **around** *vi* herumkugeln; (*ship*) schlingern; (*dog etc*) sich wälzen; **~ by** *vi* (*time*) verfließen; **~ over** *vi* sich (herum)drehen; **~ up** *vi* (*arrive*) kommen, auftauchen ♦ *vt* (*carpet*) aufrollen; **~ call** *n* Namensaufruf *m*; **~er** *n* Rolle *f*, Walze *f*; (*road roller*) Straßenwalze *f*; **~blade** *n* Rollerblade *m*; **~er coaster** *n* Achterbahn *f*; **~er skates** *npl* Rollschuhe *pl*; **~-skating** *n* Rollschuhlaufen *nt*
rolling [ˈrəulɪŋ] *adj* (*landscape*) wellig; **~ pin** *n* Nudel- *or* Wellholz *nt*; **~ stock** *n* Wagenmaterial *nt*
ROM [rɒm] *n abbr* (= *read only memory*) ROM *m*
Roman [ˈrəumən] *adj* römisch ♦ *n* Römer(in) *m(f)*; **~ Catholic** *adj* römisch-katholisch ♦ *n* Katholik(in) *m(f)*
romance [rəˈmæns] *n* Romanze *f*; (*story*) (Liebes)roman *m*
Romania [rəuˈmeɪnɪə] *n* = **Rumania**; **~n** *n* = **Rumanian**
Roman numeral *n* römische Ziffer
romantic [rəˈmæntɪk] *adj* romantisch; **~ism** [rəˈmæntɪsɪzəm] *n* Romantik *f*
Rome [rəum] *n* Rom *nt*
romp [rɒmp] *n* Tollen *f* ♦ *vi* (*also:* **~ about**) herumtollen
rompers [ˈrɒmpəz] *npl* Spielanzug *m*
roof [ruːf] (*pl* **~s**) *n* Dach *nt*; (*of mouth*) Gaumen *m* ♦ *vt* überdachen, überdecken; **~ing** *n* Deckmaterial *nt*; **~ rack** *n* (*AUT*)

Dachgepäckträger *m*
rook [ruk] *n* (*bird*) Saatkrähe *f*; (*chess*) Turm *m*
room [ruːm] *n* Zimmer *nt*, Raum *m*; (*space*) Platz *m*; (*fig*) Spielraum *m*; **~s** *npl* (*accommodation*) Wohnung *f*; **"~s to let** (*BRIT*) *or* **for rent** (*US*)" „Zimmer zu vermieten"; **single/double ~** Einzel-/ Doppelzimmer *nt*; **~ing house** (*US*) *n* Mietshaus *nt* (*mit möblierten Wohnungen*); **~mate** *n* Mitbewohner(in) *m(f)*; **~ service** *n* Zimmerbedienung *f*; **~y** *adj* geräumig
roost [ruːst] *n* Hühnerstange *f* ♦ *vi* auf der Stange hocken
rooster [ˈruːstə*] *n* Hahn *m*
root [ruːt] *n* (*also fig*) Wurzel *f* ♦ *vi* wurzeln; **~ about** *vi* (*fig*) herumwühlen; **~ for** *vt fus* Stimmung machen für; **~ out** *vt* ausjäten; (*fig*) ausrotten
rope [rəup] *n* Seil *nt* ♦ *vt* (*tie*) festschnüren; **to know the ~s** sich auskennen; **to ~ sb in** jdn gewinnen; **~ off** *vt* absperren; **~ ladder** *n* Strickleiter *f*
rosary [ˈrəuzərɪ] *n* Rosenkranz *m*
rose [rəuz] *pt of* **rise** ♦ *n* Rose *f* ♦ *adj* Rosen-, rosenrot
rosé [ˈrəuzeɪ] *n* Rosé *m*
rosebud [ˈrəuzbʌd] *n* Rosenknospe *f*
rosebush [ˈrəuzbuʃ] *n* Rosenstock *m*
rosemary [ˈrəuzmərɪ] *n* Rosmarin *m*
rosette [rəuˈzɛt] *n* Rosette *f*
roster [ˈrɒstə*] *n* Dienstplan *m*
rostrum [ˈrɒstrəm] *n* Rednerbühne *f*
rosy [ˈrəuzɪ] *adj* rosig
rot [rɒt] *n* Fäulnis *f*; (*nonsense*) Quatsch *m* ♦ *vi* verfaulen ♦ *vt* verfaulen lassen
rota [ˈrəutə] *n* Dienstliste *f*
rotary [ˈrəutərɪ] *adj* rotierend
rotate [rəuˈteɪt] *vt* rotieren lassen; (*take turns*) turnusmäßig wechseln ♦ *vi* rotieren; **rotating** *adj* rotierend; **rotation** [rəuˈteɪʃən] *n* Umdrehung *f*
rote [rəut] *n*: **by ~** auswendig
rotten [ˈrɒtn] *adj* faul; (*fig*) schlecht, gemein; **to feel ~** (*ill*) sich elend fühlen
rotund [rəuˈtʌnd] *adj* rundlich
rouble [ˈruːbl] (*US* **ruble**) *n* Rubel *m*

⚠ *Informationen zur Rechtschreibreform Seite 615*

rough [rʌf] adj (not smooth) rauh △; (path)
uneben; (violent) roh, grob; (crossing)
stürmisch; (without comforts) hart,
unbequem; (unfinished, makeshift) grob;
(approximate) ungefähr ♦ n (BRIT: person)
Rowdy m, Rohling m; (GOLF): **in the ~** im
Rauh ♦ vt: **to ~ it** primitiv leben; **to sleep ~**
im Freien schlafen; **~age** n Ballaststoffe pl;
~-and-ready adj provisorisch; (work)
zusammengehauen; **~ copy** n Entwurf m;
~ draft n Entwurf m; **~ly** adv grob; (about)
ungefähr; **~ness** n Rauheit f; (of manner)
Ungeschliffenheit f

roulette [ru:'let] n Roulett(e) nt

Roumania [ru:'meɪnɪə] n = **Rumania**

round [raund] adj rund; (figures)
aufgerundet ♦ adv (in a circle) rundherum
♦ prep um ... herum ♦ n Runde f; (of
ammunition) Magazin nt ♦ vt (corner) biegen
um; **all ~** überall; **the long way ~** der
Umweg; **all the year ~** das ganze Jahr
über; **it's just ~ the corner** (fig) es ist
gerade um die Ecke; **~ the clock** rund um
die Uhr; **to go ~ to sb's (house)** jdn
besuchen; **to go ~ the back** hintenherum
gehen; **enough to go ~** genug für alle; **to
go the ~s** (story) die Runde machen; **a ~ of
applause** ein Beifall m; **a ~ of drinks** eine
Runde Drinks; **a ~ of sandwiches** ein
Sandwich nt or m, ein belegtes Brot; **~ off**
vt abrunden; **~ up** vt (end) abschließen;
(figures) aufrunden; (criminals)
hochnehmen; **~about** n (BRIT: traffic)
Kreisverkehr m; (: merry-go-round) Karussell
nt ♦ adj auf Umwegen; **~ers** npl (game) ≈
Schlagball m; **~ly** adv (fig) gründlich; **~-
shouldered** adj mit abfallenden Schultern;
~ trip n Rundreise f; **~up** n
Zusammentreiben nt, Sammeln nt

rouse [rauz] vt (waken) (auf)wecken; (stir up)
erregen; **rousing** adj (welcome) stürmisch;
(speech) zündend

route [ru:t] n Weg m, Route f; **~ map** (BRIT)
n (for journey) Streckenkarte f

routine [ru:'ti:n] n Routine f ♦ adj Routine-

row¹ [rau] n (noise) Lärm m; (dispute) Streit
m ♦ vi sich streiten

row² [rəu] n (line) Reihe f ♦ vt, vi (boat)
rudern; **in a ~** (fig) hintereinander; **~boat**
['rəubaut] (US) n Ruderboot nt

rowdy ['raudɪ] adj rüpelhaft ♦ n (person)
Rowdy m

rowing ['rəuɪŋ] n Rudern nt; (SPORT)
Rudersport m; **~ boat** (BRIT) n Ruderboot nt

royal ['rɔɪəl] adj königlich, Königs-; **R~ Air
Force** n Königliche Luftwaffe f; **~ty** ['rɔɪəltɪ]
n (family) königliche Familie f; (for novel etc)
Tantieme f

rpm abbr (= revs per minute) U/min

R.S.V.P. abbr (= répondez s'il vous plaît)
u.A.w.g.

Rt. Hon. (BRIT) abbr (= Right Honourable)
Abgeordnete(r) mf

rub [rʌb] n (with cloth) Polieren nt; (on
person) Reiben nt ♦ vt reiben; **to ~ sb up**
(BRIT) or **to ~ sb** (US) **the wrong way** jdn
aufreizen; **~ off** vi (also fig): **to ~ off (on)**
abfärben (auf +acc); **~ out** vt herausreiben;
(with eraser) ausradieren

rubber ['rʌbər] n Gummi m; (BRIT)
Radiergummi m; **~ band** n Gummiband
nt; **~ plant** n Gummibaum m

rubbish ['rʌbɪʃ] n (waste) Abfall m;
(nonsense) Blödsinn m, Quatsch m; **~ bin**
(BRIT) n Mülleimer m; **~ dump** n
Müllabladeplatz m

rubble ['rʌbl] n (Stein)schutt m

ruby ['ru:bɪ] n Rubin m ♦ adj rubinrot

rucksack ['rʌksæk] n Rucksack m

rudder ['rʌdər] n Steuerruder nt

ruddy ['rʌdɪ] adj (colour) rötlich; (inf: bloody)
verdammt

rude [ru:d] adj unverschämt; (shock) hart;
(awakening) unsanft; (unrefined, rough) grob;
~ness n Unverschämtheit f; Grobheit f

rudiment ['ru:dɪmənt] n Grundlage f

rueful ['ru:ful] adj reuevoll

ruffian ['rʌfɪən] n Rohling m

ruffle ['rʌfl] vt kräuseln

rug [rʌg] n Brücke f; (in bedroom)
Bettvorleger m; (BRIT: for knees) (Reise)decke
f

rugby ['rʌgbɪ] n (also: ~ **football**) Rugby nt

rugged ['rʌgɪd] adj (coastline) zerklüftet;

△ For information on spelling reform see page 615

(*features*) markig

rugger ['rʌgəʳ] (*BRIT: inf*) *n* = **rugby**

ruin ['ru:ɪn] *n* Ruine *f*; (*downfall*) Ruin *m* ♦ *vt* ruinieren; **~s** *npl* (*fig*) Trümmer *pl*; **~ous** *adj* ruinierend

rule [ru:l] *n* Regel *f*; (*government*) Regierung *f*; (*for measuring*) Lineal *nt* ♦ *vt* (*govern*) herrschen über +*acc*, regieren; (*decide*) anordnen, entscheiden; (*make lines on*) linieren ♦ *vi* herrschen, regieren; entscheiden; **as a ~** in der Regel; **~ out** ausschließen; **~d** *adj* (*paper*) liniert; **~r** *n* Lineal *nt*; Herrscher *m*; **ruling** ['ru:lɪŋ] *adj* (*party*) Regierungs-; (*class*) herrschend ♦ *n* (*JUR*) Entscheid *m*

rum [rʌm] *n* Rum *m*

Rumania [ru:'meɪnɪə] *n* Rumänien *nt*; **~n** *adj* rumänisch ♦ *n* Rumäne *m*, Rumänin *f*; (*LING*) Rumänisch *nt*

rumble ['rʌmbl] *n* Rumpeln *nt*; (*of thunder*) Grollen *nt* ♦ *vi* rumpeln; grollen

rummage ['rʌmɪdʒ] *vi* durchstöbern

rumour ['ru:məʳ] (*US* **rumor**) *n* Gerücht *nt* ♦ *vt*: **it is ~ed that** man sagt *or* man munkelt, daß

rump [rʌmp] *n* Hinterteil *nt*; **~ steak** *n* Rumpsteak *nt*

rumpus ['rʌmpəs] *n* Spektakel *m*

run [rʌn] (*pt* **ran**, *pp* **run**) *n* Lauf *m*; (*in car*) (Spazier)fahrt *f*; (*series*) Serie *f*, Reihe *f*; (*ski ~*) (Ski)abfahrt *f*; (*in stocking*) Laufmasche *f* ♦ *vt* (*cause to ~*) laufen lassen; (*car, train, bus*) fahren; (*race, distance*) laufen, rennen; (*manage*) leiten; (*COMPUT*) laufen lassen; (*pass: hand, eye*) gleiten lassen ♦ *vi* laufen; (*move quickly*) laufen, rennen; (*bus, train*) fahren; (*flow*) fließen, laufen; (*colours*) (ab)färben; **there was a ~ on** (*meat, tickets*) es gab einen Ansturm auf +*acc*; **on the ~** auf der Flucht; **in the long ~** auf die Dauer; **I'll ~ you to the station** ich fahre dich zum Bahnhof; **to ~ a risk** ein Risiko eingehen; **~ about** *or* **around** *vi* (*children*) umherspringen; **~ across** *vt fus* (*find*) stoßen auf +*acc*; **~ away** *vi* weglaufen; **~ down** *vi* (*clock*) ablaufen ♦ *vt* (*production, factory*) allmählich auflösen; (*with car*)

überfahren; (*talk against*) heruntermachen; **to be ~ down** erschöpft *or* abgespannt sein; **~ in** (*BRIT*) *vt* (*car*) einfahren; **~ into** *vt fus* (*meet: person*) zufällig treffen; (*trouble*) bekommen; (*collide with*) rennen gegen; fahren gegen; **~ off** *vi* fortlaufen; **~ out** *vi* (*person*) hinausrennen; (*liquid*) auslaufen; (*lease*) ablaufen; (*money*) ausgehen; **he ran out of money / petrol** ihm ging das Geld / Benzin aus; **~ over** *vt* (*in accident*) überfahren; **~ through** *vt* (*instructions*) durchgehen; **~ up** *vt* (*debt, bill*) machen; **~ up against** *vt fus* (*difficulties*) stoßen auf +*acc*; **~away** *adj* (*horse*) ausgebrochen; (*person*) flüchtig

rung [rʌŋ] *pp of* **ring** ♦ *n* Sprosse *f*

runner ['rʌnəʳ] *n* Läufer(in) *m(f)*; (*for sleigh*) Kufe *f*; **~ bean** (*BRIT*) *n* Stangenbohne *f*; **~-up** *n* Zweite(r) *mf*

running ['rʌnɪŋ] *n* (*of business*) Leitung *f*; (*of machine*) Betrieb *m* ♦ *adj* laufend, fließend; (*commentary*) laufend; **to be in / out of the ~ for sth** im / aus dem Rennen für etw sein; **3 days ~** 3 Tage lang *or* hintereinander; **~ costs** *npl* (*of car, machine*) Unterhaltungskosten *pl*

runny ['rʌnɪ] *adj* dünn; (*nose*) laufend

run-of-the-mill ['rʌnəvðə'mɪl] *adj* gewöhnlich, alltäglich

runt [rʌnt] *n* (*animal*) Kümmerer *m*

run-up ['rʌnʌp] *n*: **the ~-~ to** (*election etc*) die Endphase vor +*dat*

runway ['rʌnweɪ] *n* Startbahn *f*

rupture ['rʌptʃəʳ] *n* (*MED*) Bruch *m*

rural ['ruərl] *adj* ländlich, Land-

ruse [ru:z] *n* Kniff *m*, List *f*

rush [rʌʃ] *n* Eile *f*, Hetze *f*; (*FIN*) starke Nachfrage *f* ♦ *vt* (*carry along*) auf dem schnellsten Wege schaffen *or* transportieren; (*attack*) losstürmen auf +*acc* ♦ *vi* (*hurry*) eilen, stürzen; **don't ~ me** dräng mich nicht; **~ hour** *n* Hauptverkehrszeit *f*

rusk [rʌsk] *n* Zwieback *m*

Russia ['rʌʃə] *n* Rußland ⚠ *nt*; **~n** *adj* russisch ♦ *n* Russe *m*, Russin *f*; (*LING*) Russisch *nt*

⚠ *Informationen zur Rechtschreibreform Seite 615*

rust [rʌst] n Rost m ♦ vi rosten
rustic ['rʌstɪk] adj bäuerlich, ländlich
rustle ['rʌsl] vi rauschen, rascheln ♦ vt rascheln lassen
rustproof ['rʌstpruːf] adj rostfrei
rusty ['rʌstɪ] adj rostig
rut [rʌt] n (in track) Radspur f; **to be in a ~** im Trott stecken
ruthless ['ruːθlɪs] adj rücksichtslos
rye [raɪ] n Roggen m; **~ bread** n Roggenbrot nt

S, s

sabbath ['sæbəθ] n Sabbat m
sabotage ['sæbətɑːʒ] n Sabotage f ♦ vt sabotieren
saccharin ['sækərɪn] n Saccharin nt
sachet ['sæʃeɪ] n (of shampoo etc) Briefchen nt, Kissen nt
sack [sæk] n Sack m ♦ vt (inf) hinauswerfen; (pillage) plündern; **to get the ~** rausfliegen; **~ing** n (material) Sackleinen nt; (inf) Rausschmiß ⚠ m
sacrament ['sækrəmənt] n Sakrament nt
sacred ['seɪkrɪd] adj heilig
sacrifice ['sækrɪfaɪs] n Opfer nt ♦ vt (also fig) opfern
sacrilege ['sækrɪlɪdʒ] n Schändung f
sad [sæd] adj traurig; **~den** vt traurig machen, betrüben
saddle ['sædl] n Sattel m ♦ vt (burden): **to ~ sb with sth** jdm etw aufhalsen; **~bag** n Satteltasche f
sadistic [sə'dɪstɪk] adj sadistisch
sadly ['sædlɪ] adv traurig; (unfortunately) leider
sadness ['sædnɪs] n Traurigkeit f
s.a.e. abbr (= stamped addressed envelope) adressierte(r) Rückumschlag m
safe [seɪf] adj (careful) vorsichtig ♦ n Safe m; **~ and sound** gesund und wohl; **(just) to be on the ~ side** um ganz sicher zu gehen; **~ from** (attack) sicher vor +dat; **~conduct** n freie(s) Geleit nt; **~deposit** n (vault) Tresorraum m; (box) Banksafe m;

~guard n Sicherung f ♦ vt sichern, schützen; **~keeping** n sichere Verwahrung f; **~ly** adv sicher; (arrive) wohlbehalten; **~ sex** n geschützter Sex m
safety ['seɪftɪ] n Sicherheit f; **~ belt** n Sicherheitsgurt m; **~ pin** n Sicherheitsnadel f; **~ valve** n Sicherheitsventil nt
sag [sæg] vi (durch)sacken
sage [seɪdʒ] n (herb) Salbei m; (person) Weise(r) mf
Sagittarius [sædʒɪ'tɛərɪəs] n Schütze m
Sahara [sə'hɑːrə] n: **the ~ (Desert)** die (Wüste) Sahara
said [sed] pt, pp of **say**
sail [seɪl] n Segel nt; (trip) Fahrt f ♦ vt segeln ♦ vi segeln; (begin voyage: person) abfahren; (: ship) auslaufen; (fig: cloud etc) dahinsegeln; **to go for a ~** segeln gehen; **they ~ed into Copenhagen** sie liefen in Kopenhagen ein; **~ through** vt fus, vi (fig) (es) spielend schaffen; **~boat** (US) n Segelboot nt; **~ing** n Segeln nt; **~ing ship** n Segelschiff nt; **~or** n Matrose m, Seemann m
saint [seɪnt] n Heilige(r) mf; **~ly** adj heilig, fromm
sake [seɪk] n: **for the ~ of** um +gen willen
salad ['sæləd] n Salat m; **~ bowl** n Salatschüssel f; **~ cream** (BRIT) n gewürzte Mayonnaise f; **~ dressing** n Salatsoße f
salary ['sælərɪ] n Gehalt nt
sale [seɪl] n Verkauf m; (reduced prices) Schlußverkauf ⚠ m; **"for ~"** „zu verkaufen"; **on ~** zu verkaufen; **~room** n Verkaufsraum m; **~s assistant** n Verkäufer(in) m(f); **~s clerk** (US) n Verkäufer(in) m(f); **~sman** (irreg) n Verkäufer m; (representative) Vertreter m; **~s rep** n (COMM) Vertreter(in) m(f); **~swoman** (irreg) n Verkäuferin f
salient ['seɪlɪənt] adj bemerkenswert
saliva [sə'laɪvə] n Speichel m
sallow ['sæləʊ] adj fahl; (face) bleich
salmon ['sæmən] n Lachs m
salon ['sælɒn] n Salon m
saloon [sə'luːn] n (BRIT: AUT) Limousine f; (ship's lounge) Salon m; **~ car** (BRIT) n

Limousine *f*

salt [sɔːlt] *n* Salz *nt* ♦ *vt* (*cure*) einsalzen; (*flavour*) salzen; **~cellar** *n* Salzfaß △ *nt*; **~water** *adj* Salzwasser-; **~y** *adj* salzig

salute [sə'luːt] *n* (*MIL*) Gruß *m*; (*with guns*) Salutschüsse *pl* ♦ *vt* (*MIL*) salutieren

salvage ['sælvɪdʒ] *n* (*from ship*) Bergung *f*; (*property*) Rettung *f* ♦ *vt* bergen; retten

salvation [sæl'veɪʃən] *n* Rettung *f*; **S~ Army** *n* Heilsarmee *f*

same [seɪm] *adj*, *pron* (*similar*) gleiche(r, s); (*identical*) derselbe/dieselbe/dasselbe; **the ~ book as** das gleiche Buch wie; **at the ~ time** zur gleichen Zeit, gleichzeitig; (*however*) zugleich, andererseits; **all** *or* **just the ~** trotzdem; **the ~ to you!** gleichfalls!; **to do the ~ (as sb)** das gleiche tun (wie jd)

sample ['sɑːmpl] *n* Probe *f* ♦ *vt* probieren

sanctify ['sæŋktɪfaɪ] *vt* weihen

sanctimonious [sæŋktɪ'məʊnɪəs] *adj* scheinheilig

sanction ['sæŋkʃən] *n* Sanktion *f*

sanctity ['sæŋktɪtɪ] *n* Heiligkeit *f*; (*fig*) Unverletzlichkeit *f*

sanctuary ['sæŋktjʊərɪ] *n* (*for fugitive*) Asyl *nt*; (*refuge*) Zufluchtsort *m*; (*for animals*) Schutzgebiet *nt*

sand [sænd] *n* Sand *m* ♦ *vt* (*furniture*) schmirgeln

sandal ['sændl] *n* Sandale *f*

sand: ~box (*US*) *n* = **sandpit**; **~castle** *n* Sandburg *f*; **~ dune** *n* (Sand)düne *f*; **~paper** *n* Sandpapier *nt*; **~pit** *n* Sandkasten *m*; **~stone** *n* Sandstein *m*

sandwich ['sændwɪtʃ] *n* Sandwich *m or nt* ♦ *vt* (*also*: **~ in**) einklemmen; **cheese-/ham ~** Käse-/Schinkenbrot; **~ed between** eingeklemmt zwischen; **~ board** *n* Reklametafel *f*; **~ course** (*BRIT*) *n* in Theorie und Praxis abwechselnde(r) Ausbildungsgang *m*

sandy ['sændɪ] *adj* sandig; (*hair*) rotblond

sane [seɪn] *adj* geistig gesund *or* normal; (*sensible*) vernünftig, gescheit

sang [sæŋ] *pt of* **sing**

sanitary ['sænɪtərɪ] *adj* hygienisch; **~ towel** *n* (Monats)binde *f*

sanitation [sænɪ'teɪʃən] *n* sanitäre Einrichtungen *pl*; **~ department** (*US*) *n* Stadtreinigung *f*

sanity ['sænɪtɪ] *n* geistige Gesundheit *f*; (*sense*) Vernunft *f*

sank [sæŋk] *pt of* **sink**

Santa Claus [sæntə'klɔːz] *n* Nikolaus *m*, Weihnachtsmann *m*

sap [sæp] *n* (*of plants*) Saft *m* ♦ *vt* (*strength*) schwächen

sapling ['sæplɪŋ] *n* junge(r) Baum *m*

sapphire ['sæfaɪə*] *n* Saphir *m*

sarcasm ['sɑːkæzm] *n* Sarkasmus *m*

sarcastic [sɑː'kæstɪk] *adj* sarkastisch

sardine [sɑː'diːn] *n* Sardine *f*

Sardinia [sɑː'dɪnɪə] *n* Sardinien *nt*

sardonic [sɑː'dɔnɪk] *adj* zynisch

sash [sæʃ] *n* Schärpe *f*

sat [sæt] *pt, pp of* **sit**

Satan ['seɪtn] *n* Satan *m*

satchel ['sætʃl] *n* (*for school*) Schulmappe *f*

satellite ['sætəlaɪt] *n* Satellit *m*; **~ dish** *n* (*TECH*) Parabolantenne *f*, Satellitenantenne *f*; **~ television** *n* Satellitenfernsehen *nt*

satisfaction [sætɪs'fækʃən] *n* Befriedigung *f*, Genugtuung *f*; **satisfactory** [sætɪs'fæktərɪ] *adj* zufriedenstellend △, befriedigend; **satisfied** *adj* befriedigt

satisfy ['sætɪsfaɪ] *vt* befriedigen, zufriedenstellen △; (*convince*) überzeugen; (*conditions*) erfüllen; **~ing** *adj* befriedigend; (*meal*) sättigend

saturate ['sætʃəreɪt] *vt* (durch)tränken

Saturday ['sætədɪ] *n* Samstag *m*, Sonnabend *m*

sauce [sɔːs] *n* Soße *f*, Sauce *f*; **~pan** *n* Kasserolle *f*

saucer ['sɔːsə*] *n* Untertasse *f*

saucy ['sɔːsɪ] *adj* frech, keck

Saudi: ~ Arabia *n* Saudi-Arabien *nt*; **~ (Arabian)** *adj* saudiarabisch ♦ *n* Saudiaraber(in) *m(f)*

sauna ['sɔːnə] *n* Sauna *f*

saunter ['sɔːntə*] *vi* schlendern

sausage ['sɔsɪdʒ] *n* Wurst *f*; **~ roll** *n* Wurst *f* im Schlafrock, Wurstpastete *f*

△ *Informationen zur Rechtschreibreform Seite 615*

sauté ['sɔute] *adj* Röst-

savage ['sævɪdʒ] *adj* wild ♦ *n* Wilde(r) *mf* ♦ *vt* (*animals*) zerfleischen

save [seɪv] *vt* retten; (*money, electricity etc*) sparen; (*strength etc*) aufsparen; (*COMPUT*) speichern ♦ *vi* (*also:* ~ **up**) sparen ♦ *n* (*SPORT*) (Ball)abwehr *f* ♦ *prep, conj* außer, ausgenommen

saving ['seɪvɪŋ] *adj:* **the ~ grace of** das Versöhnende an +*dat* ♦ *n* Sparen *nt*, Ersparnis *f*; **~s** *npl* (*money*) Ersparnisse *pl*; **~s account** *n* Sparkonto *nt*; **~s bank** *n* Sparkasse *f*

saviour ['seɪvjəʳ] (*US* **savior**) *n* (*REL*) Erlöser *m*

savour ['seɪvəʳ] (*US* **savor**) *vt* (*taste*) schmecken; (*fig*) genießen; **~y** *adj* pikant, würzig

saw [sɔː] (*pt* **sawed**, *pp* **sawed** *or* **sawn**) *pt of* **see** ♦ *n* (*tool*) Säge *f* ♦ *vt, vi* sägen; **~dust** *n* Sägemehl *nt*; **~mill** *n* Sägewerk *nt*; **~n** *pp of* **saw**; **~n-off shotgun** *n* Gewehr *nt* mit abgesägtem Lauf

sax [sæks] (*inf*) *n* Saxophon ⚠ *nt*

saxophone ['sæksəfəun] *n* Saxophon ⚠ *nt*

say [seɪ] (*pt, pp* **said**) *n:* **to have a/no ~ in sth** Mitspracherecht/kein Mitspracherecht bei etw haben ♦ *vt, vi* sagen; **let him have his ~** laß ihn doch reden; **to ~ yes/no** ja/ nein sagen; **that goes without ~ing** das versteht sich von selbst; **that is to ~** das heißt; **~ing** *n* Sprichwort *nt*

scab [skæb] *n* Schorf *m*; (*pej*) Streikbrecher *m*

scaffold ['skæfəld] *n* (*for execution*) Schafott *nt*; **~ing** *n* (*Bau*)gerüst *nt*

scald [skɔːld] *n* Verbrühung *f* ♦ *vt* (*burn*) verbrühen

scale [skeɪl] *n* (*of fish*) Schuppe *f*; (*MUS*) Tonleiter *f*; (*on map, size*) Maßstab *m*; (*gradation*) Skala *f* ♦ *vt* (*climb*) erklimmen; **~s** *npl* (*balance*) Waage *f*; **on a large ~** (*fig*) im großen, in großem Umfang; **~ of charges** Gebührenordnung *f*; **~ down** *vt* verkleinern; **~ model** *n* maßstabgetreue(s) Modell *nt*

scallop ['skɔləp] *n* Kammuschel ⚠ *f*

scalp [skælp] *n* Kopfhaut *f*

scamper ['skæmpəʳ] *vi:* **to ~ away** *or* **off** sich davonmachen

scampi ['skæmpɪ] *npl* Scampi *pl*

scan [skæn] *vt* (*examine*) genau prüfen; (*quickly*) überfliegen; (*horizon*) absuchen

scandal ['skændl] *n* Skandal *m*; (*piece of gossip*) Skandalgeschichte *f*

Scandinavia [skændɪ'neɪvɪə] *n* Skandinavien *nt*; **~n** *adj* skandinavisch ♦ *n* Skandinavier(in) *m(f)*

scant [skænt] *adj* knapp; **~ily** *adv* knapp, dürftig; **~y** *adj* knapp, unzureichend

scapegoat ['skeɪpgəut] *n* Sündenbock *m*

scar [skɑː] *n* Narbe *f* ♦ *vt* durch Narben entstellen

scarce [skɛəs] *adj* selten, rar; (*goods*) knapp; **~ly** *adv* kaum; **scarcity** *n* Mangel *m*

scare [skɛəʳ] *n* Schrecken *m* ♦ *vt* erschrecken; **bomb ~** Bombendrohung *f*; **to ~ sb stiff** jdn zu Tode erschrecken; **to be ~d** Angst haben; **~ away** *vt* (*animal*) verscheuchen; **~ off** *vt* = **scare away**; **~crow** *n* Vogelscheuche *f*

scarf [skɑːf] (*pl* **scarves**) *n* Schal *m*; (*head~*) Kopftuch *nt*

scarlet ['skɑːlɪt] *adj* scharlachrot ♦ *n* Scharlachrot *nt*; **~ fever** *n* Scharlach *m*

scarves [skɑːvz] *npl of* **scarf**

scary ['skɛərɪ] (*inf*) *adj* schaurig

scathing ['skeɪðɪŋ] *adj* scharf, vernichtend

scatter ['skætəʳ] *vt* (*sprinkle*) (ver)streuen; (*disperse*) zerstreuen ♦ *vi* sich zerstreuen; **~brained** *adj* flatterhaft, schusselig

scavenger ['skævəndʒəʳ] *n* (*animal*) Aasfresser *m*

scenario [sɪ'nɑːrɪəu] *n* (*THEAT, CINE*) Szenarium *nt*; (*fig*) Szenario *nt*

scene [siːn] *n* (*of happening*) Ort *m*; (*of play, incident*) Szene *f*; (*view*) Anblick *m*; (*argument*) Szene *f*, Auftritt *m*; **~ry** ['siːnərɪ] *n* (*THEAT*) Bühnenbild *nt*; (*landscape*) Landschaft *f*

scenic ['siːnɪk] *adj* landschaftlich

scent [sent] *n* Parfüm *nt*; (*smell*) Duft *m* ♦ *vt* parfümieren

sceptical ['skeptɪkl] (*US* **skeptical**) *adj*

⚠ *For information on spelling reform see page 615*

skeptisch

schedule ['ʃedjuːl, (*US*) 'skedjuːl] *n* (*list*) Liste *f*; (*plan*) Programm *nt*; (*of work*) Zeitplan *m* ♦ *vt* planen; **on ~** pünktlich; **to be ahead of/behind ~** dem Zeitplan voraus/im Rückstand sein; **~d flight** *n* (*not charter*) Linienflug *m*

scheme [skiːm] *n* Schema *nt*; (*dishonest*) Intrige *f*; (*plan of action*) Plan *m* ♦ *vi* intrigieren ♦ *vt* planen; **scheming** ['skiːmɪŋ] *adj* intrigierend

scholar ['skɒləʳ] *n* Gelehrte(r) *m*; (*holding ~ship*) Stipendiat *m*; **~ly** *adj* gelehrt; **~ship** *n* Gelehrsamkeit *f*; (*grant*) Stipendium *nt*

school [skuːl] *n* Schule *f*; (*UNIV*) Fakultät *f* ♦ *vt* schulen; **~ age** *n* schulpflichtige(s) Alter *nt*; **~book** *n* Schulbuch *nt*; **~boy** *n* Schüler *m*; **~children** *npl* Schüler *pl*, Schulkinder *pl*; **~days** *npl* (alte) Schulzeit *f*; **~girl** *n* Schülerin *f*; **~ing** *n* Schulung *f*, Ausbildung *f*; **~master** *n* Lehrer *m*; **~mistress** *n* Lehrerin *f*; **~teacher** *n* Lehrer(in) *m(f)*

sciatica [saɪ'ætɪkə] *n* Ischias *m* or *nt*

science ['saɪəns] *n* Wissenschaft *f*; (*natural ~*) Naturwissenschaft *f*; **~ fiction** *n* Science-fiction *f*; **scientific** [saɪən'tɪfɪk] *adj* wissenschaftlich; (*natural sciences*) naturwissenschaftlich; **scientist** ['saɪəntɪst] *n* Wissenschaftler(in) *m(f)*

scintillating ['sɪntɪleɪtɪŋ] *adj* sprühend

scissors ['sɪzəz] *npl* Schere *f*; **a pair of ~** eine Schere

scoff [skɒf] *vt* (*BRIT*: *inf*: *eat*) fressen ♦ *vi* (*mock*): **to ~ (at)** spotten (über +*acc*)

scold [skəʊld] *vt* schimpfen

scone [skɒn] *n* weiche(s) Teegebäck *nt*

scoop [skuːp] *n* Schaufel *f*; (*news*) sensationelle Erstmeldung *f*; **~ out** *vt* herausschaufeln; **~ up** *vt* aufschaufeln; (*liquid*) aufschöpfen

scooter ['skuːtəʳ] *n* Motorroller *m*; (*child's*) Roller *m*

scope [skəʊp] *n* Ausmaß *nt*; (*opportunity*) (Spiel)raum *m*

scorch [skɔːtʃ] *n* Brandstelle *f* ♦ *vt* versengen; **~ing** *adj* brennend

score [skɔːʳ] *n* (*in game*) Punktzahl *f*; (*final ~*) (Spiel)ergebnis *nt*; (*MUS*) Partitur *f*; (*line*) Kratzer *m*; (*twenty*) zwanzig, zwanzig Stück ♦ *vt* (*goal*) schießen; (*points*) machen; (*mark*) einritzen ♦ *vi* (*keep record*) Punkte zählen; **on that ~** in dieser Hinsicht; **what's the ~?** wie steht's?; **to ~ 6 out of 10** 6 von 10 Punkten erzielen; **~ out** *vt* ausstreichen; **~board** *n* Anschreibetafel *f*; **~r** *n* Torschütze *m*; (*recorder*) (Auf)schreiber *m*

scorn [skɔːn] *n* Verachtung *f* ♦ *vt* verhöhnen; **~ful** *adj* verächtlich

Scorpio ['skɔːpɪəʊ] *n* Skorpion *m*

Scot [skɒt] *n* Schotte *m*, Schottin *f*

Scotch [skɒtʃ] *n* Scotch *m*

scotch [skɒtʃ] *vt* (*end*) unterbinden

scot-free ['skɒt'friː] *adv*: **to get off ~-~** (*unpunished*) ungeschoren davonkommen

Scotland ['skɒtlənd] *n* Schottland *nt*

Scots [skɒts] *adj* schottisch; **~man/woman** (*irreg*) *n* Schotte *m*/Schottin *f*

Scottish ['skɒtɪʃ] *adj* schottisch

scoundrel ['skaʊndrl] *n* Schuft *m*

scour ['skaʊəʳ] *vt* (*search*) absuchen; (*clean*) schrubben

scourge [skɜːdʒ] *n* (*whip*) Geißel *f*; (*plague*) Qual *f*

scout [skaʊt]·*n* (*MIL*) Späher *m*; (*also*: **boy ~**) Pfadfinder *m*; **~ around** *vi*: **to ~ around (for)** sich umsehen (nach)

scowl [skaʊl] *n* finstere(r) Blick *m* ♦ *vi* finster blicken

scrabble ['skræbl] *vi* (*also*: **~ around**: *search*) (herum)tasten; (*claw*): **to ~ (at)** kratzen (an +*dat*) ♦ *n*: **S~** ® Scrabble *nt* ®

scraggy ['skrægɪ] *adj* dürr, hager

scram [skræm] (*inf*) *vi* abhauen

scramble ['skræmbl] *n* (*climb*) Kletterei *f*; (*struggle*) Kampf *m* ♦ *vi* klettern; (*fight*) sich schlagen; **to ~ out/through** krabbeln aus/ durch; **to ~ for sth** sich um etw raufen; **~d eggs** *npl* Rührei *nt*

scrap [skræp] *n* (*bit*) Stückchen *nt*; (*fight*) Keilerei *f*; (*also*: **~ iron**) Schrott *m* ♦ *vt* verwerfen ♦ *vi* (*fight*) streiten, sich prügeln;

⚠ *Informationen zur Rechtschreibreform Seite 615*

~s npl (leftovers) Reste pl; (waste) Abfall m; **~book** n Einklebealbum nt; **~ dealer** n Schrotthändler(in) m(f)

scrape [skreɪp] n Kratzen nt; (trouble) Klemme f ♦ vt kratzen; (car) zerkratzen; (clean) abkratzen ♦ vi (make harsh noise) kratzen; **to ~ through** gerade noch durchkommen; **~r** n Kratzer m

scrap: **~ heap** n Schrotthaufen m; **on the ~ heap** (fig) beim alten Eisen; **~ iron** n Schrott m; **~ merchant** (BRIT) n Altwarenhändler(in) m(f); **~ paper** n Schmierpapier nt

scrappy ['skræpɪ] adj zusammengestoppelt

scratch [skrætʃ] n (wound) Kratzer m, Schramme f ♦ adj: **~ team** zusammengewürfelte Mannschaft ♦ vt kratzen; (car) zerkratzen ♦ vi (sich) kratzen; **to start from ~** ganz von vorne anfangen; **to be up to ~** den Anforderungen entsprechen

scrawl [skrɔːl] n Gekritzel nt ♦ vt, vi kritzeln

scrawny ['skrɔːnɪ] adj (person, neck) dürr

scream [skriːm] n Schrei m ♦ vi schreien

scree [skriː] n Geröll(halde f) nt

screech [skriːtʃ] n Schrei m ♦ vi kreischen

screen [skriːn] n (protective) Schutzschirm m; (CINE) Leinwand f; (TV) Bildschirm m ♦ vt (shelter) (be)schirmen; (film) zeigen, vorführen; **~ing** n (MED) Untersuchung f; **~play** n Drehbuch nt

screw [skruː] n Schraube f ♦ vt (fasten) schrauben; (vulgar) bumsen; **~ up** vt (paper etc) zerknüllen; (inf: ruin) vermasseln (inf); **~driver** n Schraubenzieher m

scribble ['skrɪbl] n Gekritzel nt ♦ vt kritzeln

script [skrɪpt] n (handwriting) Handschrift f; (for film) Drehbuch nt; (THEAT) Manuskript nt, Text m

Scripture ['skrɪptʃər] n Heilige Schrift f

scroll [skrəʊl] n Schriftrolle f

scrounge [skraʊndʒ] (inf) vt: **to ~ sth off** or **from sb** etw bei jdm abstauben ♦ n: **on the ~** beim Schnorren

scrub [skrʌb] n (clean) Schrubben nt; (in countryside) Gestrüpp nt ♦ vt (clean) schrubben

scruff [skrʌf] n: **by the ~ of the neck** am Genick

scruffy ['skrʌfɪ] adj unordentlich, vergammelt

scrum(mage) ['skrʌm(ɪdʒ)] n Getümmel nt

scruple ['skruːpl] n Skrupel m, Bedenken pl

scrupulous ['skruːpjʊləs] adj peinlich genau, gewissenhaft

scrutinize ['skruːtɪnaɪz] vt genau prüfen; **scrutiny** ['skruːtɪnɪ] n genaue Untersuchung f

scuff [skʌf] vt (shoes) abstoßen

scuffle ['skʌfl] n Handgemenge nt

sculptor ['skʌlptər] n Bildhauer(in) m(f)

sculpture ['skʌlptʃər] n (ART) Bildhauerei f; (statue) Skulptur f

scum [skʌm] n (also fig) Abschaum m

scurry ['skʌrɪ] vi huschen

scuttle ['skʌtl] n (also: coal ~) Kohleneimer m ♦ vt (ship) versenken ♦ vi (scamper): **to ~ away** or **off** sich davonmachen

scythe [saɪð] n Sense f

SDP (BRIT) n abbr = **Social Democratic Party**

sea [siː] n Meer nt, See f; (fig) Meer nt ♦ adj Meeres-, See-; **by ~** (travel) auf dem Seeweg; **on the ~** (boat) auf dem Meer; (town) am Meer; **out to ~** aufs Meer hinaus; **out at ~** aufs Meer; **~board** n Küste f; **~food** n Meeresfrüchte pl; **~ front** n Strandpromenade f; **~going** adj seetüchtig, Hochsee-; **~gull** n Möwe f

seal [siːl] n (animal) Robbe f, Seehund m; (stamp, impression) Siegel nt ♦ vt versiegeln; **~ off** vt (place) abriegeln

sea level n Meeresspiegel m

sea lion n Seelöwe m

seam [siːm] n Saum m; (edges joining) Naht f; (of coal) Flöz m

seaman ['siːmən] (irreg) n Seemann m

seaplane ['siːpleɪn] n Wasserflugzeug nt

seaport ['siːpɔːt] n Seehafen m

search [sɜːtʃ] n (for person, thing) Suche f; (of drawer, pockets, house) Durchsuchung f ♦ vi suchen ♦ vt durchsuchen; **in ~ of** auf der Suche nach; **to ~ for** suchen nach; **~ through** vt durchsuchen; **~ing** adj (look)

forschend; **~light** n Scheinwerfer m; **~
party** n Suchmannschaft f; **~ warrant** n
Durchsuchungsbefehl m

sea: ~shore ['si:ʃɔːr] n Meeresküste f; **~sick**
['si:sɪk] adj seekrank; **~side** ['si:saɪd] n Küste
f; **~side resort** n Badeort m

season ['si:zn] n Jahreszeit f; (*Christmas etc*)
Zeit f, Saison f ♦ vt (*flavour*) würzen; **~al** adj
Saison-; **~ed** adj (*fig*) erfahren; **~ing** n
Gewürz nt, Würze f; **~ ticket** n (*RAIL*)
Zeitkarte f; (*THEAT*) Abonnement nt

seat [si:t] n Sitz m, Platz m; (*in Parliament*)
Sitz m; (*part of body*) Gesäß nt; (*of trousers*)
Hosenboden m ♦ vt (*place*) setzen; (*have
space for*) Sitzplätze bieten für; **to be ~ed**
sitzen; **~ belt** n Sicherheitsgurt m

sea: ~ water n Meerwasser nt; **~weed**
['si:wi:d] n (See)tang m; **~worthy** ['si:wə:ðɪ]
adj seetüchtig

sec. abbr (= *second(s)*) Sek.

secluded [sɪ'klu:dɪd] adj abgelegen

seclusion [sɪ'klu:ʒən] n Zurückgezogenheit
f

second ['sekənd] adj zweite(r,s) ♦ adv (*in ~
position*) an zweiter Stelle ♦ n Sekunde f;
(*person*) Zweite(r) mf; (*COMM: imperfect*)
zweite Wahl f; (*SPORT*) Sekundant m; (*AUT:
also: ~ gear*) zweite(r) Gang m; (*BRIT: UNIV:
degree*) mittlere Note bei Abschluß-
prüfungen ♦ vt (*support*) unterstützen; **~ary**
adj zweitrangig; **~ary school** n höhere
Schule f, Mittelschule f; **~-class** adj
zweiter Klasse; **~ hand** adj aus zweiter
Hand; (*car etc*) gebraucht; **~ hand** n (*on
clock*) Sekundenzeiger m; **~ly** adv zweitens

secondment [sɪ'kɔndmənt] (*BRIT*) n
Abordnung f

second-rate ['sekənd'reɪt] adj mittelmäßig

second thoughts npl: **to have ~** es sich
dat anders überlegen; **on ~** (*BRIT*) or
second thought (*US*) oder lieber (nicht)

secrecy ['si:krəsɪ] n Geheimhaltung f

secret ['si:krɪt] n Geheimnis nt ♦ adj
geheim, Geheim-; **in ~** adv

secretarial [sekrɪ'teərɪəl] adj Sekretärinnen-

secretary ['sekrətərɪ] n Sekretär(in) m(f); **S~
of State** (*BRIT*) n (*POL*): **S~ of State (for)**

Minister(in) m(f) (für)

secretion [sɪ'kri:ʃən] n Absonderung f

secretive ['si:krətɪv] adj geheimtuerisch

secretly ['si:krɪtlɪ] adv geheim

sectarian [sek'teərɪən] adj (*riots etc*)
Konfessions-, zwischen den Konfessionen

section ['sekʃən] n Teil m; (*department*)
Abteilung f; (*of document*) Abschnitt m

sector ['sektər] n Sektor m

secular ['sekjulər] adj weltlich, profan

secure [sɪ'kjuər] adj (*safe*) sicher; (*firmly
fixed*) fest ♦ vt (*make firm*) befestigen,
sichern; (*obtain*) sichern; **security**
[sɪ'kjuərɪtɪ] n Sicherheit f; (*pledge*) Pfand nt;
(*document*) Wertpapier nt; (*national security*)
Staatssicherheit f; **security guard** n
Sicherheitsbeamte(r) m, Wächter m, Wache
f

sedan [sə'dæn] (*US*) n (*AUT*) Limousine f

sedate [sɪ'deɪt] adj gesetzt ♦ vt (*MED*) ein
Beruhigungsmittel geben +dat; **sedation**
[sɪ'deɪʃən] n (*MED*) Einfluß ⚠ m von
Beruhigungsmitteln; **sedative** ['sedɪtɪv] n
Beruhigungsmittel nt ♦ adj beruhigend,
einschläfernd

sediment ['sedɪmənt] n (Boden)satz m

seduce [sɪ'dju:s] vt verführen; **seductive**
[sɪ'dʌktɪv] adj verführerisch

see [si:] (*pt* saw, *pp* seen) vt sehen;
(*understand*) (ein)sehen, erkennen; (*visit*)
besuchen ♦ vi (*be aware*) sehen; (*find out*)
nachsehen ♦ n (*ECCL: R.C.*) Bistum nt;
(: *Protestant*) Kirchenkreis m; **to ~ sb to the
door** jdn hinausbegleiten; **to ~ that** (*ensure*)
dafür sorgen, daß; **~ you soon!** bis bald!; **~
about** vt fus sich kümmern um; **~ off** vt:
to ~ sb off jdn zum Zug etc begleiten; **~
through** vt: **to ~ sth through** etw
durchfechten; **~ through sb/sth** jdn/
etw durchschauen; **~ to** vt fus: **to ~ to it**
dafür sorgen

seed [si:d] n Samen m ♦ vt (*TENNIS*)
plazieren ⚠; **to go to ~** (*plant*) schießen;
(*fig*) herunterkommen; **~ling** n Setzling m

seedy adj (*café*) übel; (*person*)
zweifelhaft

seeing ['si:ɪŋ] conj: **~ (that)** da

seek [siːk] (*pt, pp* **sought**) *vt* suchen
seem [siːm] *vi* scheinen; **it ~s that ...** es scheint, daß ...; **~ingly** *adv* anscheinend
seen [siːn] *pp of* **see**
seep [siːp] *vi* sickern
seesaw ['siːsɔː] *n* Wippe *f*
seethe [siːð] *vi:* **to ~ with anger** vor Wut kochen
see-through ['siːθruː] *adj* (*dress etc*) durchsichtig
segment ['segmənt] *n* Teil *m*; (*of circle*) Ausschnitt *m*
segregate ['segrɪgeɪt] *vt* trennen
seize [siːz] *vt* (*grasp*) (er)greifen, packen; (*power*) ergreifen; (*take legally*) beschlagnahmen; **~ (up)on** *vt fus* sich stürzen auf +*acc*; **~ up** *vi* (*TECH*) sich festfressen; **seizure** ['siːʒəʳ] *n* (*illness*) Anfall *m*
seldom ['seldəm] *adv* selten
select [sɪ'lekt] *adj* ausgewählt ♦ *vt* auswählen; **~ion** [sɪ'lekʃən] *n* Auswahl *f*; **~ive** *adj* (*person*) wählerisch
self [self] (*pl* **selves**) *pron* selbst ♦ *n* Selbst *nt*, Ich *nt*; **the ~** das Ich; **~-assured** *adj* selbstbewußt △; **~-catering** (*BRIT*) *adj* für Selbstversorger; **~-centred** (*US* **self-centered**) *adj* egozentrisch; **~-coloured** (*US* **self-colored**) *adj* (*of one colour*) einfarbig, uni; **~-confidence** *n* Selbstvertrauen *nt*, Selbstbewußtsein △ *nt*; **~-conscious** *adj* gehemmt, befangen; **~-contained** *adj* (*complete*) (in sich) geschlossen; (*person*) verschlossen; (*BRIT: flat*) separat; **~-control** *n* Selbstbeherrschung *f*; **~-defence** (*US* **self-defense**) *n* Selbstverteidigung *f*; (*JUR*) Notwehr *f*; **~-discipline** *n* Selbstdisziplin *f*; **~-employed** *adj* frei(schaffend); **~-evident** *adj* offensichtlich; **~-governing** *adj* selbstverwaltet △; **~-indulgent** *adj* zügellos; **~-interest** *n* Eigennutz *m*
selfish ['selfɪʃ] *adj* egoistisch, selbstsüchtig; **~ness** *n* Egoismus *m*, Selbstsucht *f*
self: **~lessly** *adv* selbstlos; **~-made** *adj:* **~-made man** Selfmademan *m*; **~-pity** *n* Selbstmitleid *nt*; **~-portrait** *n* Selbstbildnis

nt; **~-possessed** *adj* selbstbeherrscht; **~-preservation** *n* Selbsterhaltung *f*; **~-reliant** *adj* unabhängig; **~-respect** *n* Selbstachtung *f*; **~-righteous** *adj* selbstgerecht; **~-sacrifice** *n* Selbstaufopferung *f*; **~-satisfied** *adj* selbstzufrieden; **~-service** *adj* Selbstbedienungs-; **~-sufficient** *adj* selbstgenügsam; **~-taught** *adj* selbsterlernt; **~-taught person** Autodidakt *m*
sell [sel] (*pt, pp* **sold**) *vt* verkaufen ♦ *vi* verkaufen; (*goods*) sich verkaufen; **to ~ at** *or* **for £10** für £10 verkaufen; **~ off** *vt* verkaufen; **~ out** *vi* alles verkaufen; **~-by date** *n* Verfalldatum *nt*; **~er** *n* Verkäufer *m*; **~ing price** *n* Verkaufspreis *m*
Sellotape ['seləuteɪp] (® *BRIT*) *n* Tesafilm *nt* ®
sellout ['selaut] *n* (*of tickets*): **it was a ~** es war ausverkauft
selves [selvz] *npl of* **self**
semaphore ['seməfɔːʳ] *n* Winkzeichen *pl*
semblance ['semblns] *n* Anschein *m*
semen ['siːmən] *n* Sperma *nt*
semester [sɪ'mestəʳ] (*US*) *n* Semester *nt*
semi ['semɪ] *n* = **semidetached house;** **~circle** *n* Halbkreis *m*; **~colon** *n* Semikolon *nt*; **~conductor** *n* Halbleiter *m*; **~detached house** (*BRIT*) *n* halbe(s) Doppelhaus *nt*; **~final** *n* Halbfinale *nt*
seminary ['semɪnərɪ] *n* (*REL*) Priesterseminar *nt*
semiskilled [semɪ'skɪld] *adj* angelernt
semi-skimmed [semɪ'skɪmd] *adj* (*milk*) teilentrahmt, Halbfett-
senate ['senɪt] *n* Senat *m*; **senator** *n* Senator *m*
send [send] (*pt, pp* **sent**) *vt* senden, schicken; (*inf: inspire*) hinreißen; **~ away** *vt* wegschicken; **~ away for** *vt fus* anfordern; **~ back** *vt* zurückschicken; **~ for** *vt fus* holen lassen; **~ off** *vt* (*goods*) abschicken; (*BRIT: SPORT: player*) vom Feld schicken; **~ out** *vt* (*invitation*) aussenden; **~ up** *vt* hinaufsenden; (*BRIT: parody*) verulken; **~er** *n* Absender *m*; **~-off** *n:* **to**

△ *For information on spelling reform see page 615*

give sb a good ~-off jdn (ganz) groß verabschieden

senior ['siːnɪə'] *adj* (*older*) älter; (*higher rank*) Ober- ♦ *n* (*older person*) Ältere(r) *mf*; (*higher ranking*) Rangälteste(r) *mf*; **~ citizen** *n* ältere(r) Mitbürger(in) *m(f)*; **~ity** [siːnɪ'ɒrɪtɪ] *n* (*of age*) höhere(s) Alter *nt*; (*in rank*) höhere(r) Dienstgrad *m*

sensation [sen'seɪʃən] *n* Gefühl *nt*; (*excitement*) Sensation *f*, Aufsehen *nt*; **~al** *adj* (*wonderful*) wunderbar; (*result*) sensationell; (*headlines etc*) reißerisch

sense [sens] *n* Sinn *m*; (*understanding*) Verstand *m*, Vernunft *f*; (*feeling*) Gefühl *nt* ♦ *vt* fühlen, spüren; **~ of humour** Humor *m*; **to make ~** Sinn ergeben; **~less** *adj* sinnlos; (*unconscious*) besinnungslos

sensibility [sensɪ'bɪlɪtɪ] *n* Empfindsamkeit *f*; (*feeling hurt*) Empfindlichkeit *f*; **sensibilities** *npl* (*feelings*) Zartgefühl *nt*

sensible ['sensɪbl] *adj* vernünftig

sensitive ['sensɪtɪv] *adj*: **~ (to)** empfindlich (gegen); **sensitivity** [sensɪ'tɪvɪtɪ] *n* Empfindlichkeit *f*; (*artistic*) Feingefühl *nt*; (*tact*) Feinfühligkeit *f*

sensual ['sensjʊəl] *adj* sinnlich

sensuous ['sensjʊəs] *adj* sinnlich

sent [sent] *pt, pp of* **send**

sentence ['sentns] *n* (*LING*) Satz *m*; (*JUR*) Strafe *f*; Urteil *nt* ♦ *vt*: **to ~ sb to death/to 5 years** jdn zum Tode/zu 5 Jahren verurteilen

sentiment ['sentɪmənt] *n* Gefühl *nt*; (*thought*) Gedanke *m*; **~al** [sentɪ'mentl] *adj* sentimental; (*of feelings rather than reason*) gefühlsmäßig

sentry ['sentrɪ] *n* (Schild)wache *f*

separate [*adj* 'seprɪt, *vb* 'sepəreɪt] *adj* getrennt, separat ♦ *vt* trennen ♦ *vi* sich trennen; **~ly** *adv* getrennt; **~s** *npl* (*clothes*) Röcke, Pullover *etc*; **separation** [sepə'reɪʃən] *n* Trennung *f*

September [sep'tembə'] *n* September *m*

septic ['septɪk] *adj* vereitert, septisch; **~ tank** *n* Klärbehälter *m*

sequel ['siːkwl] *n* Folge *f*

sequence ['siːkwəns] *n* (Reihen)folge *f*

sequin ['siːkwɪn] *n* Paillette *f*

Serbia ['səːbɪə] *n* Serbien *nt*

serene [sɪ'riːn] *adj* heiter

sergeant ['saːdʒənt] *n* Feldwebel *m*; (*POLICE*) (Polizei)wachtmeister *m*

serial ['sɪərɪəl] *n* Fortsetzungsroman *m*; (*TV*) Fernsehserie *f* ♦ *adj* (*number*) (fort)laufend; **~ize** *vt* in Fortsetzungen veröffentlichen; in Fortsetzungen senden

series ['sɪəriːz] *n inv* Serie *f*, Reihe *f*

serious ['sɪərɪəs] *adj* ernst; (*injury*) schwer; **~ly** *adv* ernst(haft); (*hurt*) schwer; **~ness** *n* Ernst *m*, Ernsthaftigkeit *f*

sermon ['səːmən] *n* Predigt *f*

serrated [sɪ'reɪtɪd] *adj* gezackt

servant ['səːvənt] *n* Diener(in) *m(f)*

serve [səːv] *vt* dienen +*dat*; (*guest, customer*) bedienen; (*food*) servieren ♦ *vi* dienen, nützen; (*at table*) servieren; (*TENNIS*) geben, aufschlagen; **it ~s him right** das geschieht ihm recht; **that'll ~ as a table** das geht als Tisch; **to ~ a summons (on sb)** (jdn) vor Gericht laden; **~ out** *or* **up** *vt* (*food*) auftragen, servieren

service ['səːvɪs] *n* (*help*) Dienst *m*; (*trains etc*) Verbindung *f*; (*hotel*) Service *m*, Bedienung *f*; (*set of dishes*) Service *nt*; (*REL*) Gottesdienst *m*; (*car*) Inspektion *f*; (*for TVs etc*) Kundendienst *m*; (*TENNIS*) Aufschlag *m* ♦ *vt* (*AUT, TECH*) warten, überholen; **the S~s** *npl* (*armed forces*) die Streitkräfte *pl*; **to be of ~ to sb** jdm einen großen Dienst erweisen; **~ included/not included** Bedienung inbegriffen/nicht inbegriffen; **~able** *adj* brauchbar; **~ area** *n* (*on motorway*) Raststätte *f*; **~ charge** (*BRIT*) *n* Bedienung *f*; **~man** (*irreg*) *n* (*soldier etc*) Soldat *m*; **~ station** *n* (Groß)tankstelle *f*

serviette [səːvɪ'et] *n* Serviette *f*

servile ['səːvaɪl] *adj* unterwürfig

session ['seʃən] *n* Sitzung *f*; (*POL*) Sitzungsperiode *f*; **to be in ~** tagen

set [set] (*pt, pp* **set**) *n* (*collection of things*) Satz *m*, Set *nt*; (*RAD, TV*) Apparat *m*; (*TENNIS*) Satz *m*; (*group of people*) Kreis *m*; (*CINE*) Szene *f*; (*THEAT*) Bühnenbild *n* ♦ *adj* festgelegt; (*ready*) bereit ♦ *vt* (*place*) setzen, stellen, legen; (*arrange*) (an)ordnen; (*table*)

⚠ *Informationen zur Rechtschreibreform Seite 615*

decken; (*time, price*) festsetzen; (*alarm, watch, task*) stellen; (*jewels*) (ein)fassen; (*exam*) ausarbeiten ♦ *vi* (*sun*) untergehen; (*become hard*) fest werden; (*bone*) zusammenwachsen; **to be ~ on doing sth** etw unbedingt tun wollen; **to ~ to music** vertonen; **to ~ on fire** anstecken; **to ~ free** freilassen; **to ~ sth going** etw in Gang bringen; **to ~ sail** losfahren; **~ about** *vt fus* (*task*) anpacken; **~ aside** *vt* beiseite legen; **~ back** *vt*: **to ~ back (by)** zurückwerfen (um); **~ off** *vi* aufbrechen ♦ *vt* (*explode*) sprengen; (*alarm*) losgehen lassen; (*show up well*) hervorheben; **~ out** *vi*: **to ~ out to do sth** vorhaben, etw zu tun ♦ *vt* (*arrange*) anlegen, arrangieren; (*state*) darlegen; **~ up** *vt* (*organization*) aufziehen; (*record*) aufstellen; (*monument*) erstellen; **~back** *n* Rückschlag *m*; **~ meal** *n* Menü *nt*; **~ menu** *n* Tageskarte *f*

settee [sɛˈtiː] *n* Sofa *nt*

setting [ˈsɛtɪŋ] *n* Hintergrund *m*

settle [ˈsɛtl] *vt* beruhigen; (*pay*) begleichen, bezahlen; (*agree*) regeln ♦ *vi* sich einleben; (*come to rest*) sich niederlassen; (*sink*) sich setzen; (*calm down*) sich beruhigen; **to ~ for sth** sich mit etw zufriedengeben; **to ~ on sth** sich für etw entscheiden; **to ~ up with sb** mit jdm abrechnen; **~ down** *vi* (*feel at home*) sich einleben; (*calm down*) sich beruhigen; **~ in** *vi* sich eingewöhnen; **~ment** *n* Regelung *f*; (*payment*) Begleichung *f*; (*colony*) Siedlung *f*; **~r** *n* Siedler *m*

setup [ˈsɛtʌp] *n* (*situation*) Lage *f*

seven [ˈsɛvn] *num* sieben; **~teen** *num* siebzehn; **~th** *adj* siebte(r, s) ♦ *n* Siebtel *nt*; **~ty** *num* siebzig

sever [ˈsɛvəʳ] *vt* abtrennen

several [ˈsɛvrəl] *adj* mehrere, verschiedene ♦ *pron* mehrere; **~ of us** einige von uns

severance [ˈsɛvərəns] *n*: **~ pay** Abfindung *f*

severe [sɪˈvɪəʳ] *adj* (*strict*) streng; (*serious*) schwer; (*climate*) rauh △; **severity** [sɪˈvɛrɪtɪ] *n* Strenge *f*; Schwere *f*; Rauheit *f*

sew [səu] (*pt* **sewed**, *pp* **sewn**) *vt*, *vi* nähen; **~ up** *vt* zunähen

sewage [ˈsuːɪdʒ] *n* Abwässer *pl*

sewer [ˈsuːəʳ] *n* (Abwasser)kanal *m*

sewing [ˈsəuɪŋ] *n* Näharbeit *f*; **~ machine** *n* Nähmaschine *f*

sewn [səun] *pp of* **sew**

sex [sɛks] *n* Sex *m*; (*gender*) Geschlecht *nt*; **to have ~ with sb** mit jdm Geschlechtsverkehr haben; **~ism** *n* Sexismus *m*; **~ist** *adj* sexistisch ♦ *n* Sexist(in) *m(f)*; **~ual** [ˈsɛksjuəl] *adj* sexuell, geschlechtlich, Geschlechts-; **~uality** [sɛksjuˈælɪtɪ] *n* Sexualität *f*; **~y** *adj* sexy

shabby [ˈʃæbɪ] *adj* (*also fig*) schäbig

shack [ʃæk] *n* Hütte *f*

shackles [ˈʃæklz] *npl* (*also fig*) Fesseln *pl*, Ketten *pl*

shade [ʃeɪd] *n* Schatten *m*; (*for lamp*) Lampenschirm *m*; (*colour*) Farbton *m* ♦ *vt* abschirmen; **in the ~** im Schatten; **a ~ smaller** ein bißchen kleiner

shadow [ˈʃædəu] *n* Schatten *m* ♦ *vt* (*follow*) beschatten ♦ *adj*: **~ cabinet** (*BRIT: POL*) Schattenkabinett *nt*; **~y** *adj* schattig

shady [ˈʃeɪdɪ] *adj* schattig; (*fig*) zwielichtig

shaft [ʃɑːft] *n* (*of spear etc*) Schaft *m*; (*in mine*) Schacht *m*; (*TECH*) Welle *f*; (*of light*) Strahl *m*

shaggy [ˈʃægɪ] *adj* struppig

shake [ʃeɪk] (*pt* **shook**, *pp* **shaken**) *vt* schütteln, rütteln; (*shock*) erschüttern ♦ *vi* (*move*) schwanken; (*tremble*) zittern, beben ♦ *n* (*jerk*) Ruck *nt*, Rütteln *nt*; **to ~ hands with** die Hand geben +*dat*; **to ~ one's head** den Kopf schütteln; **~ off** *vt* abschütteln; **~ up** *vt* aufschütteln; (*fig*) aufrütteln; **~n** [ˈʃeɪkn] *pp of* **shake**; **shaky** [ˈʃeɪkɪ] *adj* zittrig; (*weak*) unsicher

shall [ʃæl] *vb aux*: **I ~ go** ich werde gehen; **~ I open the door?** soll ich die Tür öffnen?; **I'll buy some cake, ~ I?** soll ich Kuchen kaufen?, ich kaufe Kuchen, oder?

shallow [ˈʃæləu] *adj* seicht

sham [ʃæm] *n* Schein *m* ♦ *adj* unecht, falsch

shambles [ˈʃæmblz] *n* Durcheinander *nt*

shame [ʃeɪm] *n* Scham *f*; (*disgrace, pity*) Schande *f* ♦ *vt* beschämen; **it is a ~ that** es ist schade, daß; **it is a ~ to do ...** es ist

⚠ *For information on spelling reform see page 615*

eine Schande, ... zu tun; **what a ~!** wie schade!; **~faced** adj beschämt; **~ful** adj schändlich; **~less** adj schamlos

shampoo [ʃæm'puː] n Shampoo(n) nt ♦ vt (hair) waschen; **~ and set** n Waschen nt und Legen

shamrock ['ʃæmrɔk] n Kleeblatt nt

shandy ['ʃændɪ] n Bier nt mit Limonade

shan't [ʃɑːnt] = **shall not**

shantytown ['ʃæntɪtaʊn] n Bidonville f

shape [ʃeɪp] n Form f ♦ vt formen, gestalten ♦ vi (also: **~ up**) sich entwickeln; **to take ~** Gestalt annehmen; **-~d** suffix: **heart-~d** herzförmig; **~less** adj formlos; **~ly** adj wohlproportioniert

share [ʃeəʳ] n (An)teil m; (FIN) Aktie f ♦ vt teilen; **to ~ out (among/between)** verteilen (unter/zwischen); **~holder** n Aktionär(in) m(f)

shark [ʃɑːk] n Hai(fisch) m; (swindler) Gauner m

sharp [ʃɑːp] adj scharf; (pin) spitz; (person) clever; (MUS) erhöht ♦ n Kreuz nt ♦ adv zu hoch; **nine o'clock ~** Punkt neun; **~en** vt schärfen; (pencil) spitzen; **~ener** n (also: **pencil ~ener**) Anspitzer m; **~-eyed** adj scharfsichtig; **~ly** adv (turn, stop) plötzlich; (stand out, contrast) deutlich; (criticize, retort) scharf

shatter ['ʃætəʳ] vt zerschmettern; (fig) zerstören ♦ vi zerspringen

shave [ʃeɪv] n Rasur f ♦ vt rasieren ♦ vi sich rasieren; **to have a ~** sich rasieren (lassen); **~r** n (also: **electric ~r**) Rasierapparat m

shaving ['ʃeɪvɪŋ] n (action) Rasieren nt; **~s** npl (of wood etc) Späne pl; **~ brush** n Rasierpinsel m; **~ cream** n Rasierkrem f; **~ foam** n Rasierschaum n

shawl [ʃɔːl] n Schal m, Umhang m

she [ʃiː] pron sie ♦ adj weiblich; **~-bear** Bärenweibchen nt

sheaf [ʃiːf] n (pl **sheaves**) n Garbe f

shear [ʃɪəʳ] n (pt **sheared**, pp **sheared** or **shorn**) vt scheren; **~ off** vi abbrechen; **~s** npl Heckenschere f

sheath [ʃiːθ] n Scheide f; (condom) Kondom m or nt

sheaves [ʃiːvz] npl of **sheaf**

shed [ʃed] (pt, pp **shed**) n Schuppen m; (for animals) Stall m ♦ vt (leaves etc) verlieren; (tears) vergießen

she'd [ʃiːd] = **she had**; **she would**

sheen [ʃiːn] n Glanz m

sheep [ʃiːp] n inv Schaf nt; **~dog** n Schäferhund m; **~ish** adj verlegen; **~skin** n Schaffell nt

sheer [ʃɪəʳ] adj bloß, rein; (steep) steil; (transparent) (hauch)dünn ♦ adv (directly) direkt

sheet [ʃiːt] n Bettuch △ nt, Bettlaken nt; (of paper) Blatt nt; (of metal etc) Platte f; (of ice) Fläche f

sheik(h) [ʃeɪk] n Scheich m

shelf [ʃelf] (pl **shelves**) n Bord nt, Regal nt

shell [ʃel] n Schale f; (sea~) Muschel f; (explosive) Granate f ♦ vt (peas) schälen; (fire on) beschießen

she'll [ʃiːl] = **she will**; **she shall**

shellfish ['ʃelfɪʃ] n Schalentier nt; (as food) Meeresfrüchte pl

shell suit n Ballonseidenanzug m

shelter ['ʃeltəʳ] n Schutz m; (air-raid ~) Bunker m ♦ vt schützen, bedecken; (refugees) aufnehmen ♦ vi sich unterstellen; **~ed** adj (life) behütet; (spot) geschützt; **~ housing** n (for old people) Altenwohnungen pl; (for handicapped people) Behindertenwohnungen pl

shelve [ʃelv] vt aufschieben ♦ vi abfallen

shelves [ʃelvz] npl of **shelf**

shepherd ['ʃepəd] n Schäfer m ♦ vt treiben, führen; **~'s pie** n Auflauf aus Hackfleisch und Kartoffelbrei

sheriff ['ʃerɪf] n Sheriff m; (SCOTTISH) Friedensrichter m

sherry ['ʃerɪ] n Sherry m

she's [ʃiːz] = **she is**; **she has**

Shetland ['ʃetlənd] n (also: **the ~s, the ~ Isles**) die Shetlandinseln pl

shield [ʃiːld] n Schild m; (fig) Schirm m ♦ vt (be)schirmen; (TECH) abschirmen

shift [ʃɪft] n Verschiebung f; (work) Schicht f ♦ vt (ver)rücken, verschieben; (arm) wegnehmen ♦ vi sich verschieben; **~less**

adj (*person*) träge; **~ work** *n* Schichtarbeit
f; **~y** *adj* verschlagen

shilly-shally [ˈʃɪlɪʃælɪ] *vi* zögern

shin [ʃɪn] *n* Schienbein *nt*

shine [ʃaɪn] (*pt, pp* **shone**) *n* Glanz *m*,
Schein *m* ♦ *vt* polieren ♦ *vi* scheinen; (*fig*)
glänzen; **to ~ a torch on sb** jdn (mit einer
Lampe) anleuchten

shingle [ˈʃɪŋgl] *n* Strandkies *m*; **~s** *npl* (MED)
Gürtelrose *f*

shiny [ˈʃaɪnɪ] *adj* glänzend

ship [ʃɪp] *n* Schiff *nt* ♦ *vt* verschiffen;
~building *n* Schiffbau *m*; **~ment** *n*
Schiffsladung *f*; **~per** *n* Verschiffer *m*;
~ping *n* (*act*) Verschiffung *f*; (*ships*)
Schiffahrt △ *f*; **~wreck** *n* Schiffbruch *m*;
(*destroyed ship*) Wrack *n* ♦ *vt*: **to be
~wrecked** Schiffbruch erleiden; **~yard** *n*
Werft *f*

shire [ˈʃaɪə*] (BRIT) *n* Grafschaft *f*

shirk [ʃɜːk] *vt* ausweichen +*dat*

shirt [ʃɜːt] *n* (Ober)hemd *nt*; **in ~ sleeves** in
Hemdsärmeln

shit [ʃɪt] (*infl*) *excl* Scheiße (!)

shiver [ˈʃɪvə*] *n* Schauer *m* ♦ *vi* frösteln,
zittern

shoal [ʃəʊl] *n* (Fisch)schwarm *m*

shock [ʃɔk] *n* Erschütterung *f*; (*mental*)
Schock *m*; (*ELEC*) Schlag *m* ♦ *vt* erschüttern;
(*offend*) schockieren; **~ absorber** *n*
Stoßdämpfer *m*; **~ed** *adj* geschockt,
schockiert, erschüttert; **~ing** *adj* unerhört

shod [ʃɔd] *pt, pp of* **shoe**

shoddy [ˈʃɔdɪ] *adj* schäbig

shoe [ʃuː] (*pt, pp* **shod**) *n* Schuh *m*; (*of
horse*) Hufeisen *nt* ♦ *vt* (*horse*) beschlagen;
~brush *n* Schuhbürste *f*; **~horn** *n*
Schuhlöffel *m*; **~lace** *n* Schnürsenkel *m*; **~
polish** *n* Schuhcreme *f*; **~ shop** *n*
Schuhgeschäft *nt*; **~string** *n* (*fig*): **on a
~string** mit sehr wenig Geld

shone [ʃɔn] *pt, pp of* **shine**

shoo [ʃuː] *excl* sch; (*to dog etc*) pfui

shook [ʃʊk] *pt of* **shake**

shoot [ʃuːt] (*pt, pp* **shot**) *n* (*branch*)
Schößling △ *m* ♦ *vt* (*gun*) abfeuern; (*goal,
arrow*) schießen; (*person*) anschießen; (*kill*)

erschießen; (*film*) drehen ♦ *vi* (*move quickly*)
schießen; **to ~ (at)** schießen (auf +*acc*); **~
down** *vt* abschießen; **~ in** *vi*
hineinschießen; **~ out** *vi* hinausschießen; **~
up** *vi* (*fig*) aus dem Boden schießen;
~ing *n* Schießerei *f*; **~ing star** *n*
Sternschnuppe *f*

shop [ʃɔp] *n* (*esp* BRIT) Geschäft *nt*, Laden *m*;
(*work~*) Werkstatt *f* ♦ *vi* (*also:* **go ~ping**)
einkaufen gehen; **~ assistant** (BRIT) *n*
Verkäufer(in) *m(f)*; **~ floor** (BRIT) *n*
Werkstatt *f*; **~keeper** *n* Geschäftsinhaber
m; **~lifting** *n* Ladendiebstahl *m*; **~per** *n*
Käufer(in) *m(f)*; **~ping** *n* Einkaufen *nt*,
Einkauf *m*; **~ping bag** *n* Einkaufstasche *f*;
~ping centre (US **shopping center**) *n*
Einkaufszentrum *nt*; **~-soiled** *adj*
angeschmutzt; **~ steward** (BRIT) *n*
(INDUSTRY) Betriebsrat *m*; **~ window** *n*
Schaufenster *nt*

shore [ʃɔː*] *n* Ufer *nt*; (*of sea*) Strand *m* ♦ *vt*:
to ~ up abstützen

shorn [ʃɔːn] *pp of* **shear**

short [ʃɔːt] *adj* kurz; (*person*) klein; (*curt*) kurz
angebunden; (*measure*) zu knapp ♦ *n* (*also:*
~ film) Kurzfilm *m* ♦ *adv* (*suddenly*) plötzlich
♦ *vi* (ELEC) einen Kurzschluß △ haben; **~s**
npl (*clothes*) Shorts *pl*; **to be ~ of sth** nicht
genug von etw haben; **in ~** kurz gesagt; **~
of doing sth** ohne so weit zu gehen, etw
zu tun; **everything ~ of ...** alles außer ...; **it
is ~ for** das ist die Kurzform von; **to cut ~**
abkürzen; **to fall ~ of sth** etw nicht
erreichen; **to stop ~** plötzlich anhalten; **to
stop ~ of** haltmachen vor; **~age** *n*
Knappheit *f*, Mangel *m*; **~bread** *n*
Mürbegebäck *nt*; **~-change** *vt*: **to ~-
change sb** jdm zuwenig △ herausgeben;
~-circuit *n* Kurzschluß △ *m* ♦ *vi* einen
Kurzschluß △ haben ♦ *vt* kurzschließen;
~coming *n* Mangel *m*; **~(crust) pastry**
(BRIT) *n* Mürbeteig *m*; **~ cut** *n* Abkürzung *f*;
~en *vt* (ab)kürzen; (*clothes*) kürzer machen;
~fall *n* Defizit *nt*; **~hand** (BRIT) *n*
Stenographie △ *f*; **~hand typist** (BRIT) *n*
Stenotypistin *f*; **~ list** (BRIT) *n* (*for job*)
engere Wahl *f*; **~-lived** *adj* kurzlebig; **~ly**

△ *For information on spelling reform see page 615*

adv bald; **~ notice** *n*: **at ~ notice** kurzfristig; **~-sighted** (*BRIT*) *adj* (*also fig*) kurzsichtig; **~-staffed** *adj*: **to be ~-staffed** zu wenig Personal haben; **~-stay** *n* (*car park*) Kurzparken *nt*; **~ story** *n* Kurzgeschichte *f*; **~-tempered** *adj* leicht aufbrausend; **~-term** *adj* (*effect*) kurzfristig; **~ wave** *n* (*RAD*) Kurzwelle *f*

shot [ʃɔt] *pt, pp of* **shoot** ♦ *n* (*from gun*) Schuß △ *m*; (*person*) Schütze *m*; (*try*) Versuch *m*; (*injection*) Spritze *f*; (*PHOT*) Aufnahme *f*; **like a ~** wie der Blitz; **~gun** *n* Schrotflinte *f*

should [ʃʊd] *vb aux*: **I ~ go now** ich sollte jetzt gehen; **he ~ be there now** er sollte eigentlich schon da sein; **I ~ go if I were you** ich würde gehen, wenn ich du wäre; **I ~ like to** ich möchte gerne

shoulder ['ʃəʊldə*] *n* Schulter *f*; (*BRIT*: *of road*): **hard ~** Seitenstreifen *m* ♦ *vt* (*rifle*) schultern; (*fig*) auf sich nehmen; **~ bag** *n* Umhängetasche *f*; **~ blade** *n* Schulterblatt *nt*; **~ strap** *n* (*of dress etc*) Träger *m*

shouldn't ['ʃʊdnt] = **should not**

shout [ʃaʊt] *n* Schrei *m*; (*call*) Ruf *m* ♦ *vt* rufen ♦ *vi* schreien; **~ down** *vt* niederbrüllen; **~ing** *n* Geschrei *nt*

shove [ʃʌv] *n* Schubs *m*, Stoß *m* ♦ *vt* schieben, stoßen, schubsen; (*inf*: *put*): **to ~ sth in(to) sth** etw in etw *acc* hineinschieben; **~ off** *vi* (*NAUT*) abstoßen; (*fig*: *inf*) abhauen

shovel ['ʃʌvl] *n* Schaufel *f* ♦ *vt* schaufeln

show [ʃəʊ] (*pt* **showed**, *pp* **shown**) *n* (*display*) Schau *f*; (*exhibition*) Ausstellung *f*; (*CINE, THEAT*) Vorstellung *f*, Show *f* ♦ *vt* zeigen; (*kindness*) erweisen ♦ *vi* zu sehen sein; **to be on ~** (*exhibits etc*) ausgestellt sein; **to ~ sb in** jdn hereinführen; **to ~ sb out** jdn hinausbegleiten; **~ off** *vi* (*pej*) angeben ♦ *vt* (*display*) ausstellen; **~ up** *vi* (*stand out*) sich abheben; (*arrive*) erscheinen ♦ *vt* aufzeigen; (*unmask*) bloßstellen; **~ business** *n* Showbusineß △ *nt*; **~down** *n* Kraftprobe *f*

shower ['ʃaʊə*] *n* Schauer *m*; (*of stones*) (Stein)hagel *m*; (*~ bath*) Dusche *f* ♦ *vi*

duschen ♦ *vt*: **to ~ sb with sth** jdn mit etw überschütten; **~proof** *adj* wasserabstoßend △

showing ['ʃəʊɪŋ] *n* Vorführung *f*

show jumping *n* Turnierreiten *nt*

shown [ʃəʊn] *pp of* **show**

show: **~-off** ['ʃəʊɔf] *n* Angeber(in) *m(f)*; **~piece** ['ʃəʊpiːs] *n* Paradestück *nt*; **~room** ['ʃəʊruːm] *n* Ausstellungsraum *m*

shrank [ʃræŋk] *pt of* **shrink**

shred [ʃred] *n* Fetzen *m* ♦ *vt* zerfetzen; (*COOK*) raspeln; **~der** *n* (*COOK*) Gemüseschneider *m*; (*for documents*) Reißwolf *m*

shrewd [ʃruːd] *adj* clever

shriek [ʃriːk] *n* Schrei *m* ♦ *vt, vi* kreischen, schreien

shrill [ʃrɪl] *adj* schrill

shrimp [ʃrɪmp] *n* Krabbe *f*, Garnele *f*

shrine [ʃraɪn] *n* Schrein *m*; (*fig*) Gedenkstätte *f*

shrink [ʃrɪŋk] (*pt* **shrank**, *pp* **shrunk**) *vi* schrumpfen, eingehen ♦ *vt* einschrumpfen lassen; **to ~ from doing sth** davor zurückschrecken, etw zu tun; **~age** *n* Schrumpfung *f*; **~-wrap** *vt* einschweißen

shrivel ['ʃrɪvl] *vt, vi* (*also*: **~ up**) schrumpfen, schrumpeln

shroud [ʃraʊd] *n* Leichentuch *nt* ♦ *vt*: **~ed in mystery** mit einem Geheimnis umgeben

Shrove Tuesday ['ʃrəʊv-] *n* Fastnachtsdienstag *m*

shrub [ʃrʌb] *n* Busch *m*, Strauch *m*; **~bery** *n* Gebüsch *nt*

shrug [ʃrʌg] *n* Achselzucken *nt* ♦ *vt, vi*: **to ~ (one's shoulders)** die Achseln zucken; **~ off** *vt* auf die leichte Schulter nehmen

shrunk [ʃrʌŋk] *pp of* **shrink**

shudder ['ʃʌdə*] *n* Schauder *m* ♦ *vi* schaudern

shuffle ['ʃʌfl] *vt* (*cards*) mischen; **to ~ (one's feet)** schlurfen

shun [ʃʌn] *vt* scheuen, (ver)meiden

shunt [ʃʌnt] *vt* rangieren

shut [ʃʌt] (*pt, pp* **shut**) *vt* schließen, zumachen ♦ *vi* sich schließen (lassen); **~ down** *vt, vi* schließen; **~ off** *vt* (*supply*) abdrehen; ~ **up** vi (keep quiet) den Mund halten ♦ vt (close) zuschließen; **~ter** n Fensterladen m; (PHOT) Verschluß △ m

shuttle ['ʃʌtl] n (plane, train etc) Pendelflugzeug nt/-zug m etc; (space ~) Raumtransporter m; (also: ~ **service**) Pendelverkehr m; **~cock** ['ʃʌtlkɔk] n Federball m; ~ **diplomacy** n Pendeldiplomatie f

shy [ʃaɪ] adj schüchtern; **~ness** n Schüchternheit f

Siamese [saɪə'miːz] adj: ~ **cat** Siamkatze f

Siberia [saɪ'bɪərɪə] n Sibirien nt

sibling ['sɪblɪŋ] n Geschwister nt

Sicily ['sɪsɪlɪ] n Sizilien nt

sick [sɪk] adj krank; (joke) makaber; **I feel** ~ mir ist schlecht; **I was** ~ ich habe gebrochen; **to be** ~ **of sb/sth** jdn/etw satt haben; ~ **bay** n (Schiffs)lazarett nt; **~en** vt (disgust) krankmachen ♦ vi krank werden; **~ening** adj (annoying) zum Weinen

sickle ['sɪkl] n Sichel f

sick: ~ **leave** n: **to be on** ~ **leave** krank geschrieben sein; **~ly** adj kränklich, blaß △; (causing nausea) widerlich; **~ness** n Krankheit f; (vomiting) Übelkeit f, Erbrechen nt; ~ **note** n Arbeitsunfähigkeitsbescheinigung f; ~ **pay** n Krankengeld nt

side [saɪd] n Seite f ♦ adj (door, entrance) Seiten-, Neben- ♦ vi: **to** ~ **with sb** jds Partei ergreifen; **by the** ~ **of** neben; ~ **by** ~ nebeneinander; **on all** ~**s** von allen Seiten; **to take** ~**s (with)** Partei nehmen (für); **from all** ~**s** von allen Seiten; **~board** n Sideboard nt; **~boards** (BRIT) npl Koteletten pl; **~burns** npl Koteletten pl; **~car** n Beiwagen m; ~ **drum** n (MUS) kleine Trommel; ~ **effect** n Nebenwirkung f; **~light** n (AUT) Parkleuchte f; **~line** n (SPORT) Seitenlinie f; (fig: hobby) Nebenbeschäftigung f; **~long** adj Seiten-; ~ **order** n Beilage f; **~saddle** adv im Damensattel; ~ **show** n Nebenausstellung f; **~step** vt (fig) ausweichen; ~ **street** n Seitenstraße f; **~track** vt (fig) ablenken; **~walk** (US) n Bürgersteig m; **~ways** adv

seitwärts

siding ['saɪdɪŋ] n Nebengleis nt

sidle ['saɪdl] vi: **to** ~ **up (to)** sich heranmachen (an +acc)

siege [siːdʒ] n Belagerung f

sieve [sɪv] n Sieb nt ♦ vt sieben

sift [sɪft] vt sieben; (fig) sichten

sigh [saɪ] n Seufzer m ♦ vi seufzen

sight [saɪt] n (power of seeing) Sehvermögen nt; (look) Blick m; (fact of seeing) Anblick m; (of gun) Visier nt ♦ vt sichten; **in** ~ in Sicht; **out of** ~ außer Sicht; **~seeing** n Besuch m von Sehenswürdigkeiten; **to go ~seeing** Sehenswürdigkeiten besichtigen

sign [saɪn] n Zeichen nt; (notice, road ~ etc) Schild nt ♦ vt unterschreiben; **to** ~ **sth over to sb** jdm etw überschreiben; ~ **on** vi (as unemployed) sich (arbeitslos) melden ♦ vt (employee) anstellen; ~ **up** vi (MIL) sich verpflichten ♦ vt verpflichten

signal ['sɪgnl] n Signal nt ♦ vt ein Zeichen geben +dat; **~man** n (irreg) (RAIL) Stellwerkswärter m

signature ['sɪgnətʃəʳ] n Unterschrift f; ~ **tune** n Erkennungsmelodie f

signet ring ['sɪgnət-] n Siegelring m

significance [sɪg'nɪfɪkəns] n Bedeutung f

significant [sɪg'nɪfɪkənt] adj (meaning sth) bedeutsam; (important) bedeutend

signify ['sɪgnɪfaɪ] vt bedeuten; (show) andeuten, zu verstehen geben

sign language n Zeichensprache f, Fingersprache f

signpost ['saɪnpəʊst] n Wegweiser m

silence ['saɪləns] n Stille f; (of person) Schweigen nt ♦ vt zum Schweigen bringen; **~r** n (on gun) Schalldämpfer m; (BRIT: AUT) Auspufftopf m

silent ['saɪlənt] adj still; (person) schweigsam; **to remain** ~ schweigen; ~ **partner** n (COMM) stille(r) Teilhaber m

silicon chip ['sɪlɪkən-] n Siliciumchip nt

silk [sɪlk] n Seide f ♦ adj seiden, Seiden-; **~y** adj seidig

silly ['sɪlɪ] adj dumm, albern

silt [sɪlt] n Schlamm m, Schlick m

silver ['sɪlvəʳ] n Silber nt ♦ adj silbern,

Silber-; ~ **paper** (*BRIT*) *n* Silberpapier *nt*;
~-**plated** *adj* versilbert; ~**smith** *n*
Silberschmied *m*; ~**ware** *n* Silber *nt*; ~**y** *adj*
silbern

similar ['sɪmɪlər] *adj*: ~ **(to)** ähnlich (+*dat*);
~**ity** [sɪmɪ'lærɪtɪ] *n* Ähnlichkeit *f*; ~**ly** *adv* in
ähnlicher Weise

simmer ['sɪmər] *vi* sieden ♦ *vt* sieden lassen

simple ['sɪmpl] *adj* einfach; ~**(-minded)** *adj*
einfältig

simplicity [sɪm'plɪsɪtɪ] *n* Einfachheit *f*; (*of
person*) Einfältigkeit *f*

simplify ['sɪmplɪfaɪ] *vt* vereinfachen

simply ['sɪmplɪ] *adv* einfach

simulate ['sɪmjuleɪt] *vt* simulieren

simultaneous [sɪməl'teɪnɪəs] *adj*
gleichzeitig

sin [sɪn] *n* Sünde *f* ♦ *vi* sündigen

since [sɪns] *adv* seither ♦ *prep* seit, seitdem
♦ *conj* (*time*) seit; (*because*) da, weil; ~ **then**
seitdem

sincere [sɪn'sɪər] *adj* aufrichtig; ~**ly** *adv*:
yours ~ly mit freundlichen Grüßen;
sincerity [sɪn'serɪtɪ] *n* Aufrichtigkeit *f*

sinew ['sɪnjuː] *n* Sehne *f*

sinful ['sɪnful] *adj* sündig, sündhaft

sing [sɪŋ] (*pt* **sang**, *pp* **sung**) *vt, vi* singen

Singapore [sɪŋgə'pɔːr] *n* Singapur *nt*

singe [sɪndʒ] *vt* versengen

singer ['sɪŋər] *n* Sänger(in) *m(f)*

singing ['sɪŋɪŋ] *n* Singen *nt*, Gesang *m*

single ['sɪŋgl] *adj* (*one only*) einzig; (*bed,
room*) Einzel-, einzeln; (*unmarried*) ledig;
(*BRIT: ticket*) einfach; (*having one part only*)
einzeln ♦ *n* (*BRIT: also:* ~ **ticket**) einfache
Fahrkarte *f*; **in** ~ **file** hintereinander; ~ **out**
vt aussuchen, auswählen; ~ **bed** *n*
Einzelbett *nt*; ~-**breasted** *adj* einreihig; ~-
handed *adj* allein; ~-**minded** *adj*
zielstrebig; ~ **parent** *n* Alleinerziehende(r)
f(m); ~ **room** *n* Einzelzimmer *nt*; ~**s** *n*
(*TENNIS*) Einzel *nt*; ~-**track road** *n*
einspurige Straße (mit Ausweichestellen);
singly *adv* einzeln, allein

singular ['sɪŋgjulər] *adj* (*odd*) merkwürdig,
seltsam ♦ *n* (*GRAM*) Einzahl *f*, Singular *m*

sinister ['sɪnɪstər] *adj* (*evil*) böse; (*ghostly*)

unheimlich

sink [sɪŋk] (*pt* **sank**, *pp* **sunk**) *n* Spülbecken
nt ♦ *vt* (*ship*) versenken ♦ *vi* sinken; **to** ~ **sth
into** (*teeth, claws*) etw schlagen in +*acc*; ~
in *vi* (*news etc*) eingehen

sinner ['sɪnər] *n* Sünder(in) *m(f)*

sinus ['saɪnəs] *n* (*ANAT*) Sinus *m*

sip [sɪp] *n* Schlückchen *nt* ♦ *vt* nippen an
+*dat*

siphon ['saɪfən] *n* Siphon(flasche *f*) *m*; ~ **off**
vt absaugen; (*fig*) abschöpfen

sir [sər] *n* (*respect*) Herr *m*; (*knight*) Sir *m*; **S~
John Smith** Sir John Smith; **yes** ~ ja(wohl,
mein Herr)

siren ['saɪərn] *n* Sirene *f*

sirloin ['sɜːlɔɪn] *n* Lendenstück *nt*

sissy ['sɪsɪ] (*inf*) *n* Waschlappen *m*

sister ['sɪstər] *n* Schwester *f*; (*BRIT: nurse*)
Oberschwester *f*; (*nun*) Ordensschwester *f*;
~-**in-law** *n* Schwägerin *f*

sit [sɪt] (*pt, pp* **sat**) *vi* sitzen; (*hold session*)
tagen ♦ *vt* (*exam*) machen; ~ **down** *vi*
sich hinsetzen; ~ **in on** *vt fus* dabeisein ⚠
bei; ~ **up** *vi* (*after lying*) sich aufsetzen;
(*straight*) sich gerade setzen; (*at night*)
aufbleiben

sitcom ['sɪtkɔm] *n abbr* (= *situation comedy*)
Situationskomödie *f*

site [saɪt] *n* Platz *m*; (*also:* **building** ~)
Baustelle *f* ♦ *vt* legen

sitting ['sɪtɪŋ] *n* (*meeting*) Sitzung *f*; ~ **room**
n Wohnzimmer *nt*

situated ['sɪtjueɪtɪd] *adj*: **to be** ~ liegen

situation [sɪtju'eɪʃən] *n* Situation *f*, Lage *f*;
(*place*) Lage *f*; (*employment*) Stelle *f*; **"~s
vacant"** (*BRIT*) „Stellenangebote" *pl*

six [sɪks] *num* sechs; ~**teen** *num* sechzehn;
~**th** *adj* sechste(r, s) ♦ *n* Sechstel *nt*; ~**ty**
num sechzig

size [saɪz] *n* Größe *f*; (*of project*) Umfang *m*;
~ **up** *vt* (*assess*) abschätzen, einschätzen;
~**able** *adj* ziemlich groß, ansehnlich

sizzle ['sɪzl] *vi* zischen; (*COOK*) brutzeln

skate [skeɪt] *n* Schlittschuh *m*; (*fish: pl inv*)
Rochen *m* ♦ *vi* Schlittschuh laufen; ~**board**
n Skateboard *nt*; ~**boarding** *n*
Skateboardfahren *nt*; ~**r** *n*

Schlittschuhläufer(in) m(f); **skating**
['skeɪtɪŋ] n Eislauf m; **to go skating** Eislaufen
gehen; **skating rink** n Eisbahn f

skeleton ['skelɪtn] n Skelett nt; (fig) Gerüst
nt; ~ **key** n Dietrich m; ~ **staff** n
Notbesetzung f

skeptical ['skeptɪkl] (US) adj = **sceptical**

sketch [sketʃ] n Skizze f; (THEAT) Sketch m
♦ vt skizzieren; ~**book** n Skizzenbuch nt;
~**y** adj skizzenhaft

skewer ['skjuːəʳ] n Fleischspieß m

ski [skiː] n Ski m, Schi m ♦ vi Ski or Schi
laufen; ~ **boot** n Skistiefel m

skid [skɪd] n (AUT) Schleudern nt ♦ vi
rutschen; (AUT) schleudern

ski: ~**er** ['skiːəʳ] n Skiläufer(in) m(f); ~**ing**
['skiːɪŋ] n: **to go** ~**ing** Skilaufen gehen; ~-
jump n Sprungschanze f ♦ vi Ski springen

skilful ['skɪlful] adj geschickt

ski-lift n Skilift m

skill [skɪl] n Können nt; (worker) Fach-, gelernt

skim [skɪm] vt (liquid) abschöpfen; (glide
over) gleiten über +acc ♦ vi: ~ **through**
(book) überfliegen; ~**med milk** n
Magermilch f

skimp [skɪmp] vt (do carelessly) oberflächlich
tun; ~**y** adj (dress) knapp

skin [skɪn] n Haut f; (peel) Schale f ♦ vt
abhäuten; schälen; ~ **cancer** n Hautkrebs
m; ~-**deep** adj oberflächlich; ~ **diving** n
Schwimmtauchen nt; ~**head** n Skinhead
m; ~**ny** adj dünn; ~**tight** adj (dress etc)
hauteng

skip [skɪp] n Sprung m ♦ vi hüpfen; (with
rope) Seil springen ♦ vt (pass over)
übergehen

ski: ~ **pants** npl Skihosen pl; ~ **pass** n
Skipaß △ nt; ~ **pole** n Skistock m

skipper ['skɪpəʳ] n Kapitän m ♦ vt führen

skipping rope ['skɪpɪŋ-] (BRIT) n Hüpfseil nt

skirmish ['skɜːmɪʃ] n Scharmützel nt

skirt [skɜːt] n Rock m ♦ vt herumgehen um;
(fig) umgehen; ~**ing board** (BRIT) n
Fußleiste f

ski suit n Skianzug m

skit [skɪt] n Parodie f

ski tow n Schlepplift m

skittle ['skɪtl] n Kegel m; ~**s** n (game) Kegeln
nt

skive [skaɪv] (BRIT: inf) vi schwänzen

skulk [skʌlk] vi sich herumdrücken

skull [skʌl] n Schädel m

skunk [skʌŋk] n Stinktier nt

sky [skaɪ] n Himmel m; ~**light** n Oberlicht
nt; ~**scraper** n Wolkenkratzer m

slab [slæb] n (of stone) Platte f

slack [slæk] adj (loose) locker; (business) flau;
(careless) nachlässig, lasch ♦ vi nachlässig
sein ♦ n: **to take up the** ~ straffziehen; ~**s**
npl (trousers) Hose(n pl) f; ~**en** vi (also: ~**en
off**) locker werden; (: slow down) stocken,
nachlassen ♦ vt (: loosen) lockern

slag [slæg] (BRIT) vt: ~ **off** (criticize)
(he)runtermachen

slag heap [slæg-] n Halde f

slain [sleɪn] pp of **slay**

slam [slæm] n Knall m ♦ vt (door)
zuschlagen; (throw down) knallen ♦ vi
zuschlagen

slander ['slɑːndəʳ] n Verleumdung f ♦ vt
verleumden

slang [slæŋ] n Slang m; (jargon) Jargon m

slant [slɑːnt] n Schräge f; (fig) Tendenz f
♦ vt schräg legen ♦ vi schräg liegen; ~**ed**
adj schräg; ~**ing** adj schräg

slap [slæp] n Klaps m ♦ vt einen Klaps geben
+dat ♦ adv (directly) geradewegs; ~**dash** adj
salopp; ~**stick** n (comedy) Klamauk m; ~-
up (BRIT) adj (meal) erstklassig, prima

slash [slæʃ] n Schnittwunde f ♦ vt
(auf)schlitzen

slat [slæt] n Leiste f

slate [sleɪt] n (stone) Schiefer m; (roofing)
Dachziegel m ♦ vt (criticize) verreißen

slaughter ['slɔːtəʳ] n (of animals) Schlachten
nt; (of people) Gemetzel nt ♦ vt schlachten;
(people) niedermetzeln; ~**house** n
Schlachthof m

Slav [slɑːv] adj slawisch

slave [sleɪv] n Sklave m, Sklavin f ♦ vi
schuften, sich schinden; ~**ry** n Sklaverei f

slay [sleɪ] (pt **slew**, pp **slain**) vt ermorden

sleazy ['sliːzɪ] adj (place) schmierig

△ *For information on spelling reform see page 615*

sledge [slɛdʒ] *n* Schlitten *m*

sledgehammer ['slɛdʒhæməʳ] *n* Schmiedehammer *m*

sledging *n* Schlittenfahren *nt*

sleek [sliːk] *adj* glatt; (*shape*) rassig

sleep [sliːp] (*pt, pp* **slept**) *n* Schlaf *m* ♦ *vi* schlafen; **to go to ~** einschlafen; **~ in** *vi* ausschlafen; (*oversleep*) verschlafen; **~er** *n* (*person*) Schläfer *m*; (*BRIT: RAIL*) Schlafwagen *m*; (*: beam*) Schwelle *f*; **~ing bag** *n* Schlafsack *m*; **~ing car** *n* Schlafwagen *m*; **~ing partner** *n* = **silent partner**; **~ing pill** *n* Schlaftablette *f*; **~less** *adj* (*night*) schlaflos; **~walker** *n* Schlafwandler(in) *m(f)*; **~y** *adj* schläfrig

sleet [sliːt] *n* Schneeregen *m*

sleeve [sliːv] *n* Ärmel *m*; (*of record*) Umschlag *m*; **~less** *adj* ärmellos

sleigh [sleɪ] *n* Pferdeschlitten *m*

sleight [slaɪt] *n*: **~ of hand** Fingerfertigkeit *f*

slender ['slɛndəʳ] *adj* schlank; (*fig*) gering

slept [slɛpt] *pt, pp of* **sleep**

slew [sluː] *vi* (*veer*) (herum)schwenken ♦ *pt of* **slay**

slice [slaɪs] *n* Scheibe *f* ♦ *vt* in Scheiben schneiden

slick [slɪk] *adj* (*clever*) raffiniert, aalglatt ♦ *n* Ölteppich *m*

slid [slɪd] *pt, pp of* **slide**

slide [slaɪd] (*pt, pp* **slid**) *n* Rutschbahn *f*; (*PHOT*) Dia(positiv) *nt*; (*BRIT: for hair*) (Haar)spange *f* ♦ *vt* schieben ♦ *vi* (*slip*) gleiten, rutschen; **sliding** ['slaɪdɪŋ] *adj* (*door*) Schiebe-; **sliding scale** *n* gleitende Skala *f*

slight [slaɪt] *adj* zierlich; (*trivial*) geringfügig; (*small*) gering ♦ *n* Kränkung *f* ♦ *vt* (*offend*) kränken; **not in the ~est** nicht im geringsten; **~ly** *adv* etwas, ein bißchen △

slim [slɪm] *adj* schlank; (*book*) dünn; (*chance*) gering ♦ *vi* eine Schlankheitskur machen

slime [slaɪm] *n* Schleim *m*

slimming ['slɪmɪŋ] *n* Schlankheitskur *f*

slimy ['slaɪmɪ] *adj* glitschig; (*dirty*) schlammig; (*person*) schmierig

sling [slɪŋ] (*pt, pp* **slung**) *n* Schlinge *f*; (*weapon*) Schleuder *f* ♦ *vt* schleudern

slip [slɪp] *n* (*mistake*) Flüchtigkeitsfehler *m*; (*petticoat*) Unterrock *m*; (*of paper*) Zettel *m* ♦ *vt* (*put*) stecken, schieben ♦ *vi* (*lose balance*) ausrutschen; (*move*) gleiten, rutschen; (*decline*) nachlassen; (*move smoothly*): **to ~ in/out** (*person*) hinein-/hinausschlüpfen; **to give sb the ~** jdm entwischen; **~ of the tongue** Versprecher *m*; **it ~ped my mind** das ist mir entfallen; **to ~ sth on/off** etw über-/abstreifen; **~ away** *vi* sich wegstehlen; **~ in** *vt* hineingleiten lassen ♦ *vi* (*errors*) sich einschleichen; **~ped disc** *n* Bandscheibenschaden *m*

slipper ['slɪpəʳ] *n* Hausschuh *m*

slippery ['slɪpərɪ] *adj* glatt

slip: **~ road** (*BRIT*) *n* Auffahrt *f*/Ausfahrt *f*; **~shod** *adj* schlampig; **~-up** *n* Panne *f*; **~way** *n* Auslaufbahn *f*

slit [slɪt] (*pt, pp* **slit**) *n* Schlitz *m* ♦ *vt* aufschlitzen

slither ['slɪðəʳ] *vi* schlittern; (*snake*) sich schlängeln

sliver ['slɪvəʳ] *n* (*of glass, wood*) Splitter *m*; (*of cheese*) Scheibchen *nt*

slob [slɔb] (*inf*) *n* Klotz *m*

slog [slɔg] *vi* (*work hard*) schuften ♦ *n*: **it was a ~** es war eine Plackerei

slogan ['sləʊgən] *n* Schlagwort *nt*; (*COMM*) Werbespruch *m*

slop [slɔp] *vi* (*also:* **~ over**) überschwappen ♦ *vt* verschütten

slope [sləʊp] *n* Neigung *f*; (*of mountains*) (Ab)hang *m* ♦ *vi*: **to ~ down** sich senken; **to ~ up** ansteigen; **sloping** ['sləʊpɪŋ] *adj* schräg

sloppy ['slɔpɪ] *adj* schlampig

slot [slɔt] *n* Schlitz *m* ♦ *vt*: **to ~ sth in** etw einlegen

sloth [sləʊθ] *n* (*laziness*) Faulheit *f*

slot machine *n* (*BRIT*) Automat *m*; (*for gambling*) Spielautomat *m*

slouch [slaʊtʃ] *vi*: **to ~ about** (*laze*) herumhängen (*inf*)

slovenly ['slʌvənlɪ] *adj* schlampig; (*speech*) salopp

slow [sləʊ] *adj* langsam ♦ *adv* langsam; **to**

be ~ (clock) nachgehen; (stupid) begriffsstutzig sein; **"~"** (road sign) „Langsam"; **in ~ motion** in Zeitlupe; **~ down** vi langsamer werden ♦ vt verlangsamen; **~ up** vi sich verlangsamen, sich verzögern ♦ vt aufhalten, langsamer machen; **~ly** adv langsam

sludge [slʌdʒ] n Schlamm m

slug [slʌg] n Nacktschnecke f; (inf. bullet) Kugel f

sluggish ['slʌgɪʃ] adj träge; (COMM) schleppend

sluice [slu:s] n Schleuse f

slum [slʌm] n (house) Elendsquartier nt

slump [slʌmp] n Rückgang m ♦ vi fallen, stürzen

slung [slʌŋ] pt, pp of **sling**

slur [slɜ:ʳ] n Undeutlichkeit f; (insult) Verleumdung f; **~red** [slɜ:d] adj (pronunciation) undeutlich

slush [slʌʃ] n (snow) Schneematsch m; **~ fund** n Schmiergeldfonds m

slut [slʌt] n Schlampe f

sly [slaɪ] adj schlau

smack [smæk] n Klaps m ♦ vt einen Klaps geben +dat ♦ vi: **to ~ of** riechen nach; **to ~ one's lips** schmatzen, sich dat die Lippen lecken

small [smɔ:l] adj klein; **in the ~ hours** in den frühen Morgenstunden; **~ ads** (BRIT) npl Kleinanzeigen pl; **~ change** n Kleingeld nt; **~holder** (BRIT) n Kleinbauer m; **~pox** n Pocken pl; **~ talk** n Geplauder nt

smart [smɑ:t] adj (fashionable) elegant, schick; (neat) adrett; (clever) clever; (quick) scharf ♦ vi brennen, schmerzen; **~ card** n Chipkarte f; **~en up** vi sich in Schale werfen ♦ vt herausputzen

smash [smæʃ] n Zusammenstoß m; (TENNIS) Schmetterball m ♦ vt (break) zerschmettern; (destroy) vernichten ♦ vi (break) zersplittern, zerspringen; **~ing** (inf) adj toll

smattering ['smætərɪŋ] n oberflächliche Kenntnis f

smear [smɪəʳ] n Fleck m ♦ vt beschmieren

smell [smel] (pt, pp **smelt** or **smelled**) n Geruch m; (sense) Geruchssinn m ♦ vt

riechen ♦ vi: **to ~ (of)** riechen (nach); (fragrantly) duften (nach); **~y** adj übelriechend ⚠

smile [smaɪl] n Lächeln nt ♦ vi lächeln

smiling ['smaɪlɪŋ] adj lächelnd

smirk [smɜ:k] n blöde(s) Grinsen nt

smock [smɔk] n Kittel m

smoke [sməuk] n Rauch m ♦ vt rauchen; (food) räuchern ♦ vi rauchen; **~d** adj (bacon) geräuchert; (glass) Rauch-; **~r** n Raucher(in) m(f); (RAIL) Raucherabteil nt; **~ screen** n Rauchwand f

smoking ['sməukɪŋ] n: **"no ~"** „Rauchen verboten"; **~ compartment** (BRIT), **~ car** (US) n Raucherabteil nt

smoky ['sməukɪ] adj rauchig; (room) verraucht; (taste) geräuchert

smolder ['sməuldəʳ] (US) vi = **smoulder**

smooth [smu:ð] adj glatt ♦ vt (also: **~ out**) glätten, glattstreichen ⚠

smother ['smʌðəʳ] vt ersticken

smoulder ['sməuldəʳ] (US **smolder**) vi schwelen

smudge [smʌdʒ] n Schmutzfleck m ♦ vt beschmieren

smug [smʌg] adj selbstgefällig

smuggle ['smʌgl] vt schmuggeln; **~r** n Schmuggler m

smuggling ['smʌglɪŋ] n Schmuggel m

smutty ['smʌtɪ] adj schmutzig

snack [snæk] n Imbiß ⚠ m; **~ bar** n Imbißstube ⚠ f

snag [snæg] n Haken m

snail [sneɪl] n Schnecke f

snake [sneɪk] n Schlange f

snap [snæp] n Schnappen nt; (photograph) Schnappschuß ⚠ m ♦ adj (decision) schnell ♦ vt (break) zerbrechen; (PHOT) knipsen ♦ vi (break) brechen; (speak) anfauchen; **to ~ shut** zuschnappen; **~ at** vt fus schnappen nach; **~ off** vt (break) abbrechen; **~ up** vt aufschnappen; **~shot** n Schnappschuß ⚠ m

snare [snɛəʳ] n Schlinge f ♦ vt mit einer Schlinge fangen

snarl [snɑ:l] n Zähnefletschen nt ♦ vi (dog) knurren

⚠ For information on spelling reform see page 615

snatch [snætʃ] n (*small amount*) Bruchteil m
♦ vt schnappen, packen

sneak [sni:k] vi schleichen ♦ n (*inf*) Petze(r)
mf; **~ers** ['sni:kəz] (US) npl Freizeitschuhe
pl; **~y** ['sni:kɪ] adj raffiniert

sneer [snɪə'] n Hohnlächeln nt ♦ vi spötteln

sneeze [sni:z] n Niesen nt ♦ vi niesen

sniff [snɪf] n Schnüffeln nt ♦ vi schnieben;
(*smell*) schnüffeln ♦ vt schnuppern

snigger ['snɪgə'] n Kichern nt ♦ vi hämisch
kichern

snip [snɪp] n Schnippel m, Schnipsel m ♦ vt
schnippeln

sniper ['snaɪpə'] n Heckenschütze m

snippet ['snɪpɪt] n Schnipsel m; (*of
conversation*) Fetzen m

snivelling ['snɪvlɪŋ] adj weinerlich

snob [snɔb] n Snob m

snooker ['snu:kə'] n Snooker nt

snoop [snu:p] vi: **to ~ about**
herumschnüffeln

snooze [snu:z] n Nickerchen nt ♦ vi ein
Nickerchen machen, dösen

snore [snɔː'] vi schnarchen ♦ n Schnarchen
nt

snorkel ['snɔːkl] n Schnorchel m

snort [snɔːt] n Schnauben nt ♦ vi schnauben

snout [snaut] n Schnauze f

snow [snəu] n Schnee m ♦ vi schneien;
~ball n Schneeball m ♦ vi eskalieren;
~bound adj eingeschneit; **~drift** n
Schneewehe f; **~drop** n Schneeglöckchen
nt; **~fall** n Schneefall m; **~flake** n
Schneeflocke f; **~man** (*irreg*) n
Schneemann m; **~plough** (US **snowplow**)
n Schneepflug m; **~ shoe** n Schneeschuh
m; **~storm** n Schneesturm m

snub [snʌb] vt schroff abfertigen ♦ n Verweis
m; **~-nosed** adj stupsnasig

snuff [snʌf] n Schnupftabak m

snug [snʌg] adj gemütlich, behaglich

snuggle ['snʌgl] vi: **to ~ up to sb** sich an
jdn kuscheln

KEYWORD
---

so [səu] adv 1 (*thus*) so; (*likewise*) auch; **so
saying he walked away** indem er das

sagte, ging er; **if so** wenn ja; **I didn't do it
- you did so!** ich hab das nicht gemacht –
hast du wohl!; **so do I, so am I** *etc* ich
auch; **so it is!** tatsächlich!; **I hope/think so**
hoffentlich/ich glaube schon; **so far** bis
jetzt

2 (*in comparisons etc: to such a degree*) so;
so quickly/big (that) so schnell/groß, daß;
I'm so glad to see you ich freue mich so,
dich zu sehen

3: **so many** so viele; **so much work** so viel
Arbeit; **I love you so much** ich liebe dich
so sehr

4 (*phrases*): **10 or so** etwa 10; **so long!**
(*inf: goodbye*) tschüs!

♦ conj 1 (*expressing purpose*): **so as to** um
... zu; **so (that)** damit

2 (*expressing result*) also; **so I was right
after all** ich hatte also doch recht; **so you
see ...** wie du siehst ...

soak [səuk] vt durchnässen; (*leave in liquid*)
einweichen ♦ vi (ein)weichen; **~ in** vi
einsickern; **~ up** vt aufsaugen; **~ed** adj
völlig durchnäßt; **~ing** adj klitschnaß ⚠,
patschnaß ⚠

so-and-so ['səuənsəu] n (*somebody*) .
Soundso m

soap [səup] n Seife f; **~flakes** npl
Seifenflocken pl; **~ opera** n Familienserie f
(*im Fernsehen, Radio*); **~ powder** n
Waschpulver nt; **~y** adj seifig, Seifen-

soar [sɔː'] vi aufsteigen; (*prices*) in die Höhe
schnellen

sob [sɔb] n Schluchzen nt ♦ vi schluchzen

sober ['səubə'] adj (*also fig*) nüchtern; **~ up**
vi nüchtern werden

so-called ['səu'kɔːld] adj sogenannt

soccer ['sɔkə'] n Fußball m

sociable ['səuʃəbl] adj gesellig

social ['səuʃl] adj sozial; (*friendly, living with
others*) gesellig ♦ n gesellige(r) Abend m; **~
club** n Verein m (*für Freizeitgestaltung*);
~ism n Sozialismus m; **~ist** n Sozialist(in)
m(f) ♦ adj sozialistisch; **~ize** vi: **to ~ize
(with)** gesellschaftlich verkehren (mit); **~ly**
adv gesellschaftlich, privat; **~ security** n

⚠ *Informationen zur Rechtschreibreform Seite 615*

Sozialversicherung f; ~ **work** n Sozialarbeit
f; ~ **worker** n Sozialarbeiter(in) m(f)
society [sə'saɪətɪ] n Gesellschaft f;
(fashionable world) die große Welt
sociology [saʊsɪ'ɒlədʒɪ] n Soziologie f
sock [sɒk] n Socke f
socket ['sɒkɪt] n (ELEC) Steckdose f; (of eye)
Augenhöhle f
sod [sɒd] n Rasenstück nt; (inf!) Saukerl m (!)
soda ['səʊdə] n Soda f; (also: ~ **water**)
Soda(wasser) nt; (US: also: ~ **pop**)
Limonade f
sodden ['sɒdn] adj durchweicht
sodium ['səʊdɪəm] n Natrium nt
sofa ['səʊfə] n Sofa nt
soft [sɒft] adj weich; (not loud) leise; (weak)
nachgiebig; ~ **drink** n alkoholfreie(s)
Getränk nt; ~**en** ['sɒfn] vt weich machen;
(blow) abschwächen, mildern ♦ vi weich
werden; ~**ly** adv sanft; leise; ~**ness** n
Weichheit f; (fig) Sanftheit f
software ['sɒftweə'] n (COMPUT) Software f
soggy ['sɒgɪ] adj (ground) sumpfig; (bread)
aufgeweicht
soil [sɔɪl] n Erde f ♦ vt beschmutzen
solace ['sɒlɪs] n Trost m
solar ['səʊlə'] adj Sonnen-; ~ **cell** n
Solarzelle f; ~ **energy** n Sonnenenergie f;
~ **panel** n Sonnenkollektor m; ~ **power** n
Sonnenenergie f
sold [səʊld] pt, pp of **sell**; ~ **out** (COMM)
ausverkauft
solder ['səʊldə'] vt löten
soldier ['səʊldʒə'] n Soldat m
sole [səʊl] n Sohle f; (fish) Seezunge f ♦ adj
alleinig, Allein-; ~**ly** adv ausschließlich
solemn ['sɒləm] adj feierlich
sole trader n (COMM) Einzelunternehmen
nt
solicit [sə'lɪsɪt] vt (request) bitten um ♦ vi
(prostitute) Kunden anwerben
solicitor [sə'lɪsɪtə'] n Rechtsanwalt m/-
anwältin f
solid ['sɒlɪd] adj (hard) fest; (of same material,
not hollow) massiv; (without break) voll,
ganz; (reliable, sensible) solide ♦ n Festkörper
m; ~**arity** [sɒlɪ'dærɪtɪ] n Solidarität f; ~**ify**

[sə'lɪdɪfaɪ] vi fest werden
solitary ['sɒlɪtərɪ] adj einsam, einzeln; ~
confinement n Einzelhaft f
solitude ['sɒlɪtju:d] n Einsamkeit f
solo ['səʊləʊ] n Solo nt; ~**ist** ['səʊləʊɪst] n
Solist(in) m(f)
soluble ['sɒljʊbl] adj (substance) löslich;
(problem) (auf)lösbar
solution [sə'lu:ʃən] n (also fig) Lösung f; (of
mystery) Erklärung f
solve [sɒlv] vt (auf)lösen
solvent ['sɒlvənt] adj (FIN) zahlungsfähig ♦ n
(CHEM) Lösungsmittel nt
sombre ['sɒmbə'] (US **somber**) adj düster

| KEYWORD |

some [sʌm] adj **1** (a certain amount or
number of) einige; (a few) ein paar; (with
singular nouns) etwas; **some tea/biscuits**
etwas Tee/ein paar Plätzchen; **I've got
some money, but not much** ich habe ein
bißchen Geld, aber nicht viel
2 (certain: in contrasts) manche(r, s); **some
people say that ...** manche Leute sagen,
daß ...
3 (unspecified) irgendein(e); **some woman
was asking for you** da hat eine Frau nach
Ihnen gefragt; **some day** eines Tages;
some day next week irgendwann nächste
Woche
♦ pron **1** (a certain number) einige; **have
you got some?** haben Sie welche?
2 (a certain amount) etwas; **I've read some
of the book** ich habe das Buch teilweise
gelesen
♦ adv: **some 10 people** etwa 10 Leute

somebody ['sʌmbədɪ] pron = **someone**
somehow ['sʌmhaʊ] adv (in some way, for
some reason) irgendwie
someone ['sʌmwʌn] pron jemand; (direct
obj) jemand(en); (indirect obj) jemandem
someplace ['sʌmpleɪs] (US) adv =
somewhere
somersault ['sʌməsɔ:lt] n Salto m ♦ vi
einen Salto machen
something ['sʌmθɪŋ] pron etwas

⚠ For information on spelling reform see page 615

sometime ['sʌmtaɪm] *adv* (irgend)einmal

sometimes ['sʌmtaɪmz] *adv* manchmal

somewhat ['sʌmwɒt] *adv* etwas

somewhere ['sʌmweəʳ] *adv* irgendwo; (*to a place*) irgendwohin; **~ else** irgendwo anders

son [sʌn] *n* Sohn *m*

sonar ['səʊnɑːʳ] *n* Echolot *nt*

song [sɒŋ] *n* Lied *nt*

sonic boom ['sɒnɪk-] *n* Überschallknall *m*

son-in-law ['sʌnɪnlɔː] *n* Schwiegersohn *m*

soon [suːn] *adv* bald; **~ afterwards** kurz danach; **~er** *adv* (*time*) früher; (*for preference*) lieber; **~er or later** früher oder später

soot [sʊt] *n* Ruß *m*

soothe [suːð] *vt* (*person*) beruhigen; (*pain*) lindern

sophisticated [sə'fɪstɪkeɪtɪd] *adj* (*person*) kultiviert; (*machinery*) hochentwickelt ⚠

sophomore ['sɒfəmɔːʳ] (*US*) *n* College-Student *m* im 2. Jahr

soporific [sɒpə'rɪfɪk] *adj* einschläfernd

sopping ['sɒpɪŋ] *adj* patschnaß ⚠

soppy ['sɒpɪ] (*inf*) *adj* schmalzig

soprano [sə'prɑːnəʊ] *n* Sopran *m*

sorcerer ['sɔːsərəʳ] *n* Hexenmeister *m*

sordid ['sɔːdɪd] *adj* erbärmlich

sore [sɔːʳ] *adj* schmerzend; (*point*) wund ♦ *n* Wunde *f*; **~ly** *adv* (*tempted*) stark, sehr

sorrow ['sɒrəʊ] *n* Kummer *m*, Leid *nt*; **~ful** *adj* sorgenvoll

sorry ['sɒrɪ] *adj* traurig, erbärmlich; **~!** Entschuldigung!; **to feel ~ for sb** jdn bemitleiden; **I feel ~ for him** er tut mir leid; **~?** (*pardon*) wie bitte?

sort [sɔːt] *n* Art *f*, Sorte *f* ♦ *vt* (*also:* **~ out**: *papers*) sortieren; (: *problems*) sichten, in Ordnung bringen; **~ing office** *n* Sortierstelle *f*

SOS *n* SOS *nt*

so-so ['səʊsəʊ] *adv* so(-so) la-la

sought [sɔːt] *pt, pp of* **seek**

soul [səʊl] *n* Seele *f*; (*music*) Soul *m*; **~-destroying** *adj* trostlos; **~ful** *adj* seelenvoll

sound [saʊnd] *adj* (*healthy*) gesund; (*safe*) sicher; (*sensible*) vernünftig; (*theory*)
stichhaltig; (*thorough*) tüchtig, gehörig ♦ *adv*: **to be ~ asleep** fest schlafen ♦ *n* (*noise*) Geräusch *nt*, Laut *m*; (*GEOG*) Sund *m* ♦ *vt* erschallen lassen; (*alarm*) (Alarm) schlagen ♦ *vi* (*make a ~*) schallen, tönen; (*seem*) klingen; **to ~ like** sich anhören wie; **~ out** *vt* erforschen; (*person*) auf den Zahn fühlen +*dat*; **~ barrier** *n* Schallmauer *f*; **~ bite** *n* (*RAD, TV*) prägnante(s) Zitat *nt*; **~ effects** *npl* Toneffekte *pl*; **~ly** *adv* (*sleep*) fest; (*beat*) tüchtig; **~proof** *adj* (*room*) schalldicht; **~ track** *n* Tonstreifen *m*; (*music*) Filmmusik *f*

soup [suːp] *n* Suppe *f*; **~ plate** *n* Suppenteller *m*; **~spoon** *n* Suppenlöffel *m*

sour ['saʊəʳ] *adj* (*also fig*) sauer; **it's ~ grapes** (*fig*) die Trauben hängen zu hoch

source [sɔːs] *n* (*also fig*) Quelle *f*

south [saʊθ] *n* Süden *m* ♦ *adj* Süd-, südlich ♦ *adv* nach Süden, südwärts; **S~ Africa** *n* Südafrika *nt*; **S~ African** *adj* südafrikanisch ♦ *n* Südafrikaner(in) *m(f)*; **S~ America** *n* Südamerika *nt*; **S~ American** *adj* südamerikanisch ♦ *n* Südamerikaner(in) *m(f)*; **~-east** *n* Südosten *m*; **~erly** ['sʌðəlɪ] *adj* südlich; **~ern** ['sʌðən] *adj* südlich, Süd-; **S~ Pole** *n* Südpol *m*; **S~ Wales** *n* Südwales *nt*; **~ward(s)** *adv* südwärts, nach Süden; **~-west** *n* Südwesten *m*

souvenir [suːvə'nɪəʳ] *n* Souvenir *nt*

sovereign ['sɒvrɪn] *n* (*ruler*) Herrscher(in) *m(f)* ♦ *adj* (*independent*) souverän

soviet ['səʊvɪət] *adj* sowjetisch; **the S~ Union** die Sowjetunion

sow¹ [saʊ] *n* Sau *f*

sow² [səʊ] (*pt* **sowed**, *pp* **sown**) *vt* (*also fig*) säen

soya ['sɔɪə] (*US* **soy**) *n*: **~ bean** Sojabohne *f*; **~ sauce** Sojasauce *f*

spa [spɑː] *n* (*place*) Kurort *m*

space [speɪs] *n* Platz *m*, Raum *m*; (*universe*) Weltraum *m*, All *nt*; (*length of time*) Abstand *m* ♦ *vt* (*also:* **~ out**) verteilen; **~craft** *n* Raumschiff *nt*; **~man** (*irreg*) *n* Raumfahrer *m*; **~ ship** *n* Raumschiff *nt*

spacing ['speɪsɪŋ] *n* Abstand *m*; (*also:* **~ out**) Verteilung *f*

⚠ *Informationen zur Rechtschreibreform Seite 615*

spacious ['speɪʃəs] adj geräumig, weit
spade [speɪd] n Spaten m; **~s** npl (CARDS) Pik nt
Spain [speɪn] n Spanien nt
span [spæn] n Spanne f; (of bridge etc) Spannweite f ♦ vt überspannen
Spaniard ['spænjəd] n Spanier(in) m(f)
spaniel ['spænjəl] n Spaniel m
Spanish ['spænɪʃ] adj spanisch ♦ n (LING) Spanisch nt; **the ~** npl (people) die Spanier pl
spank [spæŋk] vt verhauen, versohlen
spanner ['spænəʳ] (BRIT) n Schraubenschlüssel m
spar [spɑːʳ] n (NAUT) Sparren m ♦ vi (BOXING) einen Sparring machen
spare [spɛəʳ] adj Ersatz- ♦ n = **spare part** ♦ vt (lives, feelings) verschonen; (trouble) ersparen; **to ~** (surplus) übrig; **~ part** n Ersatzteil nt; **~ time** n Freizeit f; **~ wheel** n (AUT) Reservereifen m
sparing ['spɛərɪŋ] adj: **to be ~ with** geizen mit; **~ly** adv sparsam; (eat, spend etc) in Maßen
spark [spɑːk] n Funken m; **~(ing) plug** n Zündkerze f
sparkle ['spɑːkl] n Funkeln nt; (gaiety) Schwung m ♦ vi funkeln; **sparkling** adj funkelnd; (wine) Schaum-; (mineral water) mit Kohlensäure; (conversation) spritzig, geistreich
sparrow ['spærəu] n Spatz m
sparse [spɑːs] adj spärlich
spasm ['spæzəm] n (MED) Krampf m; (fig) Anfall m; **~odic** [spæz'mɔdɪk] adj (fig) sprunghaft
spastic ['spæstɪk] (old) n Spastiker(in) m(f) ♦ adj spastisch
spat [spæt] pt, pp of spit
spate [speɪt] n (fig) Flut f, Schwall m; **in ~** (river) angeschwollen
spatter ['spætəʳ] vt bespritzen, verspritzen
spatula ['spætjulə] n Spatel m
spawn [spɔːn] vi laichen ♦ n Laich m
speak [spiːk] (pt spoke, pp spoken) vt sprechen, reden; (truth) sagen; (language) sprechen ♦ vi: **to ~ (to)** sprechen (mit or zu); **to ~ to sb** of or about sth mit jdm über etw acc sprechen; **~ up!** sprich lauter!; **~er** n Sprecher(in) m(f), Redner(in) m(f); (loudspeaker) Lautsprecher m; (POL): **the S~er** der Vorsitzende des Parlaments (BRIT) or des Kongresses (US)
spear [spɪəʳ] n Speer m ♦ vt aufspießen; **~head** vt (attack etc) anführen
spec [spɛk] (inf) n: **on ~** auf gut Glück
special ['spɛʃl] adj besondere(r, s); **~ist** n (TECH) Fachmann m; (MED) Facharzt m/Fachärztin f; **~ity** [spɛʃɪ'ælɪtɪ] n Spezialität f; (study) Spezialgebiet nt; **~ize** vi: **to ~ize (in)** sich spezialisieren (auf +acc); **~ly** adv besonders; (explicitly) extra; **~ needs** adj: **~ needs children** behinderte Kinder pl; **~ty** (esp US) n = **speciality**
species ['spiːʃiːz] n Art f
specific [spə'sɪfɪk] adj spezifisch; **~ally** adv spezifisch
specification [spɛsɪfɪ'keɪʃən] n Angabe f; (stipulation) Bedingung f; **~s** npl (TECH) technische Daten pl
specify ['spɛsɪfaɪ] vt genau angeben
specimen ['spɛsɪmən] n Probe f
speck [spɛk] n Fleckchen nt
speckled ['spɛkld] adj gesprenkelt
specs [spɛks] (inf) npl Brille f
spectacle ['spɛktəkl] n Schauspiel nt; **~s** npl (glasses) Brille f
spectacular [spɛk'tækjuləʳ] adj sensationell; (success etc) spektakulär
spectator [spɛk'teɪtəʳ] n Zuschauer(in) m(f)
spectre ['spɛktəʳ] (US **specter**) n Geist m, Gespenst nt
speculate ['spɛkjuleɪt] vi spekulieren
speech [spiːtʃ] n Sprache f; (address) Rede f; (way one speaks) Sprechweise f; **~less** adj sprachlos
speed [spiːd] n Geschwindigkeit f; (gear) Gang m ♦ vi (JUR) (zu) schnell fahren; **at full** or **top ~** mit Höchstgeschwindigkeit; **~ up** vt beschleunigen ♦ vi schneller werden; schneller fahren; **~boat** n Schnellboot nt; **~ily** adv schleunigst; **~ing** n Geschwindigkeitsüberschreitung f; **~ limit** n Geschwindigkeitsbegrenzung f; **~ometer**

[spɪ'dɒmɪtə] n Tachometer m; **~way** n (bike racing) Motorradrennstrecke f; **~y** adj schnell

spell [spɛl] (pt, pp **spelt** (BRIT) or **spelled**) n (magic) Bann m; (period of time) Zeitlang △ f ♦ vt buchstabieren; (imply) bedeuten; **to cast a ~ on sb** jdn verzaubern; **~bound** adj (wie) gebannt; **~ing** n Rechtschreibung f

spelt [spɛlt] (BRIT) pt, pp of **spell**

spend [spɛnd] (pt, pp **spent**) vt (money) ausgeben; (time) verbringen; **~thrift** n Verschwender(in) m(f)

spent [spɛnt] pt, pp of **spend**

sperm [spəːm] n (BIOL) Samenflüssigkeit f

spew [spjuː] vt (er)brechen

sphere [sfɪə] n (globe) Kugel f; (fig) Sphäre f, Gebiet nt; **spherical** ['sfɛrɪkl] adj kugelförmig

spice [spaɪs] n Gewürz nt ♦ vt würzen

spick-and-span ['spɪkən'spæn] adj blitzblank

spicy ['spaɪsɪ] adj (food) stark gewürzt; (fig) pikant

spider ['spaɪdə] n Spinne f

spike [spaɪk] n Dorn m, Spitze f

spill [spɪl] (pt, pp **spilt** or **spilled**) vt verschütten ♦ vi sich ergießen; **~ over** vi überlaufen; (fig) sich ausbreiten

spilt [spɪlt] pt, pp of **spill**

spin [spɪn] (pt, pp **spun**) n (trip in car) Spazierfahrt f; (AVIAT) (Ab)trudeln nt; (on ball) Drall m ♦ vt (thread) spinnen; (like top) (herum)wirbeln ♦ vi sich drehen; **~ out** vt in die Länge ziehen

spinach ['spɪnɪtʃ] n Spinat m

spinal ['spaɪnl] adj Rückgrat-; **~ cord** n Rückenmark nt

spindly ['spɪndlɪ] adj spindeldürr

spin doctor n PR-Fachmann m, PR-Frau f

spin-dryer [spɪn'draɪə] (BRIT) n Wäscheschleuder f

spine [spaɪn] n Rückgrat nt; (thorn) Stachel m; **~less** adj (also fig) rückgratlos

spinning ['spɪnɪŋ] n Spinnen nt; **~ top** n Kreisel m; **~ wheel** n Spinnrad nt

spin-off ['spɪnɒf] n Nebenprodukt nt

spinster ['spɪnstə] n unverheiratete Frau f; (pej) alte Jungfer f

spiral ['spaɪərl] n Spirale f ♦ adj spiralförmig; (movement etc) in Spiralen ♦ vi sich (hoch)winden; **~ staircase** n Wendeltreppe f

spire [spaɪə] n Turm m

spirit ['spɪrɪt] n Geist m; (humour, mood) Stimmung f; (courage) Mut m; (verve) Elan m; (alcohol) Alkohol m; **~s** npl (drink) Spirituosen pl; **in good ~s** gut aufgelegt; **~ed** adj beherzt; **~ level** n Wasserwaage f

spiritual ['spɪrɪtjuəl] adj geistig, seelisch; (REL) geistlich ♦ n Spiritual nt

spit [spɪt] (pt, pp **spat**) n (for roasting) (Brat)spieß m; (saliva) Spucke f ♦ vi spucken; (rain) sprühen; (make a sound) zischen; (cat) fauchen

spite [spaɪt] n Gehässigkeit f ♦ vt kränken; **in ~ of** trotz; **~ful** adj gehässig

spittle ['spɪtl] n Speichel m, Spucke f

splash [splæʃ] n Spritzer m, (of colour) (Farb)fleck m ♦ vt bespritzen ♦ vi spritzen

spleen [spliːn] n (ANAT) Milz f

splendid ['splɛndɪd] adj glänzend

splendour ['splɛndə] (US **splendor**) n Pracht f

splint [splɪnt] n Schiene f

splinter ['splɪntə] n Splitter m ♦ vi (zer)splittern

split [splɪt] (pt, pp **split**) n Spalte f; (fig) Spaltung f; (division) Trennung f ♦ vt spalten vi ♦ vi (divide) reißen; **~ up** vi sich trennen

splutter ['splʌtə] vi stottern

spoil [spɔɪl] (pt, pp **spoilt** or **spoiled**) vt (ruin) verderben; (child) verwöhnen; **~s** npl Beute f; **~sport** n Spielverderber m; **~t** pt, pp of **spoil**

spoke [spəuk] pt of **speak** ♦ n Speiche f; **~n** pp of **speak**

spokesman ['spəuksmən] (irreg) n Sprecher m; **spokeswoman** ['spəukswumən] (irreg) n Sprecherin f

sponge [spʌndʒ] n Schwamm m ♦ vt abwaschen ♦ vi: **to ~ on** auf Kosten leben +gen; **~ bag** (BRIT) n Kulturbeutel m; **~**

cake n Rührkuchen m

sponsor ['spɒnsə'] n Sponsor m ♦ vt fördern; **~ship** n Finanzierung f; (public) Schirmherrschaft f

spontaneous [spɒn'teɪnɪəs] adj spontan

spooky ['spu:kɪ] (inf) adj gespenstisch

spool [spu:l] n Spule f, Rolle f

spoon [spu:n] n Löffel m; **~-feed** (irreg) vt mit dem Löffel füttern; (fig) hochpäppeln; **~ful** n Löffel(voll) m

sport [spɔ:t] n Sport m; (person) feine(r) Kerl m; **~ing** adj (fair) sportlich, fair; **to give sb a ~ing chance** jdm eine faire Chance geben; **~ jacket** (US) n = **sports jacket**; **~s car** n Sportwagen m; **~s jacket** n Sportjackett nt; **~sman** (irreg) n Sportler m; **~smanship** n Sportlichkeit f; **~swear** n Sportkleidung f; **~swoman** (irreg) n Sportlerin f; **~y** adj sportlich

spot [spɒt] n Punkt m; (dirty) Fleck(en) m; (place) Stelle f; (MED) Pickel m ♦ vt erspähen; (mistake) bemerken; **on the ~** an Ort und Stelle; (at once) auf der Stelle; **~ check** n Stichprobe f; **~less** adj fleckenlos; **~light** n Scheinwerferlicht nt; (lamp) Scheinwerfer m; **~ted** adj gefleckt; **~ty** adj (face) pickelig

spouse [spaʊs] n Gatte m/Gattin f

spout [spaʊt] n (of pot) Tülle f; (jet) Wasserstrahl m ♦ vi speien

sprain [spreɪn] n Verrenkung f ♦ vt verrenken

sprang [spræŋ] pt of **spring**

sprawl [sprɔ:l] vi sich strecken

spray [spreɪ] n Spray nt; (off sea) Gischt f; (of flowers) Zweig m ♦ vt besprühen, sprayen

spread [spred] (pt, pp **spread**) n (extent) Verbreitung f; (inf: meal) Schmaus m; (for bread) Aufstrich m ♦ vt ausbreiten; (scatter) verbreiten; (butter) streichen ♦ vi sich ausbreiten; **~-eagled** ['spredi:gld] adj: **to be ~-eagled** alle viere von sich strecken; **~ out** vi (move apart) sich verteilen; **~sheet** n Tabellenkalkulation f

spree [spri:] n (shopping) Einkaufsbummel m; **to go on a ~** einen draufmachen

sprightly ['spraɪtlɪ] adj munter, lebhaft

spring [sprɪŋ] (pt **sprang**, pp **sprung**) n (leap) Sprung m; (TECH) Feder f; (season) Frühling m; (water) Quelle f ♦ vi (leap) springen; **~ up** vi (problem) auftauchen; **~board** n Sprungbrett nt; **~-clean** n (also: **~-cleaning**) Frühjahrsputz m; **~time** n Frühling m; **~y** adj federnd, elastisch

sprinkle ['sprɪŋkl] vt (salt) streuen; (liquid) sprenkeln; **to ~ water on, to ~ with water** mit Wasser besprengen; **~r** ['sprɪŋklə'] n (for lawn) Sprenger m; (for fire fighting) Sprinkler m

sprint [sprɪnt] n (race) Sprint m ♦ vi (run fast) rennen; (SPORT) sprinten; **~er** n Sprinter(in) m(f)

sprout [spraʊt] vi sprießen

sprouts [spraʊts] npl (also: **Brussels ~**) Rosenkohl m

spruce [spru:s] n Fichte f ♦ adj schmuck, adrett

sprung [sprʌŋ] pp of **spring**

spry [spraɪ] adj flink, rege

spun [spʌn] pt, pp of **spin**

spur [spə:'] n Sporn m; (fig) Ansporn m ♦ vt (also: **~ on**: fig) anspornen; **on the ~ of the moment** spontan

spurious ['spjʊərɪəs] adj falsch

spurn [spə:n] vt verschmähen

spurt [spə:t] n (jet) Strahl m; (acceleration) Spurt m ♦ vi (liquid) schießen

spy [spaɪ] n Spion(in) m(f) ♦ vi spionieren ♦ vt erspähen; **~ing** n Spionage f

sq. abbr = **square**

squabble ['skwɒbl] n Zank m ♦ vi sich zanken

squad [skwɒd] n (MIL) Abteilung f; (POLICE) Kommando nt

squadron ['skwɒdrn] n (cavalry) Schwadron f; (NAUT) Geschwader nt; (air force) Staffel f

squalid ['skwɒlɪd] adj verkommen

squall [skwɔ:l] n Bö f, Windstoß m

squalor ['skwɒlə'] n Verwahrlosung f

squander ['skwɒndə'] vt verschwenden

square [skweə'] n Quadrat nt; (open space) Platz m; (instrument) Winkel m; (inf: person) Spießer m ♦ adj viereckig; (inf: ideas, tastes) spießig ♦ vt (arrange) ausmachen; (MATH)

⚠ For information on spelling reform see page 615

ins Quadrat erheben ♦ *vi* (*agree*)
übereinstimmen; **all ~** quitt; **a ~ meal** eine
ordentliche Mahlzeit; **2 metres ~** 2 Meter
im Quadrat; **1 ~ metre** 1 Quadratmeter;
~ly *adv* fest, gerade

squash [skwɔʃ] *n* (*BRIT: drink*) Saft *m*; (*game*)
Squash *nt* ♦ *vt* zerquetschen

squat [skwɔt] *adj* untersetzt ♦ *vi* hocken;
~ter *n* Hausbesetzer *m*

squawk [skwɔːk] *vi* kreischen

squeak [skwiːk] *vi* quiek(s)en; (*spring, door
etc*) quietschen

squeal [skwiːl] *vi* schrill schreien

squeamish [ˈskwiːmɪʃ] *adj* empfindlich

squeeze [skwiːz] *vt* pressen, drücken;
(*orange*) auspressen; **~ out** *vt*
ausquetschen

squelch [skwɛltʃ] *vi* platschen

squib [skwɪb] *n* Knallfrosch *m*

squid [skwɪd] *n* Tintenfisch *m*

squiggle [ˈskwɪgl] *n* Schnörkel *m*

squint [skwɪnt] *vi* schielen ♦ *n*: **to have a ~**
schielen; **to ~ at sb/sth** nach jdm/etw
schielen

squirm [skwəːm] *vi* sich winden

squirrel [ˈskwɪrəl] *n* Eichhörnchen *nt*

squirt [skwəːt] *vt, vi* spritzen

Sr *abbr* (= *senior*) sen.

St *abbr* (= *saint*) hl., St.; (= *street*) Str.

stab [stæb] *n* (*blow*) Stich *m*; (*inf: try*)
Versuch *m* ♦ *vt* erstechen

stabilize [ˈsteɪbəlaɪz] *vt* stabilisieren ♦ *vi* sich
stabilisieren

stable [ˈsteɪbl] *adj* stabil ♦ *n* Stall *m*

stack [stæk] *n* Stapel *m* ♦ *vt* stapeln

stadium [ˈsteɪdɪəm] *n* Stadion *nt*

staff [stɑːf] *n* (*stick, MIL*) Stab *m*; (*personnel*)
Personal *nt*; (*BRIT: SCH*) Lehrkräfte *pl* ♦ *vt*
besetzen

stag [stæg] *n* Hirsch *m*

stage [steɪdʒ] *n* Bühne *f*; (*of journey*) Etappe
f; (*degree*) Stufe *f*; (*point*) Stadium *nt* ♦ *vt*
(*put on*) aufführen; (*simulate*) inszenieren;
(*demonstration*) veranstalten; **in ~s**
etappenweise; **~coach** *n* Postkutsche *f*; **~
door** *n* Bühneneingang *m*; **~ manager** *n*
Intendant *m*

stagger [ˈstægər] *vi* wanken, taumeln ♦ *vt*
(*amaze*) verblüffen; (*hours*) staffeln; **~ing**
adj unglaublich

stagnant [ˈstægnənt] *adj* stagnierend;
(*water*) stehend; **stagnate** [stægˈneɪt] *vi*
stagnieren

stag party *n* Männerabend *m* (vom
Bräutigam vor der Hochzeit gegeben)

staid [steɪd] *adj* gesetzt

stain [steɪn] *n* Fleck *m* ♦ *vt* beflecken; **~ed
glass window** buntes Glasfenster *nt*; **~less**
adj (*steel*) rostfrei; **~ remover** *n*
Fleckentferner *m*

stair [steər] *n* (*Treppen*)stufe *f*; **~s** *npl* (*flight
of steps*) Treppe *f*; **~case** *n* Treppenhaus
nt, Treppe *f*; **~way** *n* Treppenaufgang *m*

stake [steɪk] *n* (*post*) Pfahl *m*; (*money*)
Einsatz *m* ♦ *vt* (*bet: money*) setzen; **to be at
~** auf dem Spiel stehen

stale [steɪl] *adj* alt; (*bread*) altbacken

stalemate [ˈsteɪlmeɪt] *n* (*CHESS*) Patt *nt*; (*fig*)
Stillstand *m*

stalk [stɔːk] *n* Stengel △ *m*, Stiel *m* ♦ *vt*
(*game*) jagen; **~ off** *vi* abstolzieren

stall [stɔːl] *n* (*in stable*) Stand *m*, Box *f*; (*in
market*) (Verkaufs)stand *m* ♦ *vt* (*AUT*)
abwürgen ♦ *vi* (*AUT*) stehenbleiben △; (*fig*)
Ausflüchte machen; **~s** *npl* (*BRIT: THEAT*)
Parkett *nt*

stallion [ˈstæljən] *n* Zuchthengst *m*

stalwart [ˈstɔːlwət] *n* treue(r) Anhänger *m*

stamina [ˈstæmɪnə] *n* Durchhaltevermögen
nt, Zähigkeit *f*

stammer [ˈstæmər] *n* Stottern *nt* ♦ *vt, vi*
stottern, stammeln

stamp [stæmp] *n* Briefmarke *f*; (*for document*)
Stempel *m* ♦ *vi* stampfen ♦ *vt* (*mark*)
stempeln; (*mail*) frankieren; (*foot*) stampfen
mit; **~ album** *n* Briefmarkenalbum *nt*; **~
collecting** *n* Briefmarkensammeln *nt*

stampede [stæmˈpiːd] *n* panische Flucht *f*

stance [stæns] *n* Haltung *f*

stand [stænd] (*pt, pp stood*) *n* (*for objects*)
Gestell *nt*; (*seats*) Tribüne *f* ♦ *vi* stehen;
(*rise*) aufstehen; (*decision*) feststehen ♦ *vt*
setzen, stellen; (*endure*) aushalten; (*person*)
ausstehen; (*nonsense*) dulden; **to make a ~**

Widerstand leisten; **to ~ for parliament** (*BRIT*) für das Parlament kandidieren; **~ by** *vi* (*be ready*) bereitstehen ♦ *vt fus* (*opinion*) treu bleiben +*dat*; **~ down** *vi* (*withdraw*) zurücktreten; **~ for** *vt fus* (*signify*) stehen für; (*permit, tolerate*) hinnehmen; **~ in for** *vt fus* (*be prominent*) hervorstehen; **~ up** *vi* (*rise*) aufstehen; **~ up for** *vt fus* sich einsetzen für; **~ up to** *vt fus*: **to ~ up to sth** einer Sache *dat* gewachsen sein; **to ~ up to sb** sich jdm gegenüber behaupten

standard ['stændəd] *n* (*measure*) Norm *f*; (*flag*) Fahne *f* ♦ *adj* (*size etc*) Normal-; **~s** *npl* (*morals*) Maßstäbe *pl*; **~ize** *vt* vereinheitlichen; **~ lamp** (*BRIT*) *n* Stehlampe *f*; **~ of living** *n* Lebensstandard *m*

stand: **~-by** *n* Reserve *f*; **to be on ~-by** in Bereitschaft sein; **~-by ticket** *n* (*AVIAT*) Standby-Ticket *nt*; **~-in** ['stændɪn] *n* Ersatz *m*

standing ['stændɪŋ] *adj* (*erect*) stehend; (*permanent*) ständig; (*invitation*) offen ♦ *n* (*duration*) Dauer *f*; (*reputation*) Ansehen *nt*; **of many years' ~** langjährig; **~ order** (*BRIT*) *n* (*at bank*) Dauerauftrag *m*; **~ room** *n* Stehplatz *m*

stand: **~-offish** [stænd'ɔfɪʃ] *adj* zurückhaltend, sehr reserviert; **~point** ['stændpɔɪnt] *n* Standpunkt *m*; **~still** ['stændstɪl] *n*: **to be at a ~still** stillstehen; **to come to a ~still** zum Stillstand kommen

stank [stæŋk] *pt of* **stink**

staple ['steɪpl] *n* (*in paper*) Heftklammer *f*; (*article*) Haupterzeugnis *nt* ♦ *adj* Grund-, Haupt- ♦ *vt* (*fest*)klammern; **~r** *n* Heftmaschine *f*

star [stɑːr] *n* Stern *m*; (*person*) Star *m* ♦ *vi* die Hauptrolle spielen ♦ *vt*: **~ring ...** in der Hauptrolle/den Hauptrollen ...

starboard ['stɑːbɔːd] *n* Steuerbord *nt*

starch [stɑːtʃ] *n* Stärke *f*

stardom ['stɑːdəm] *n* Berühmtheit *f*

stare [stɛər] *n* starre(r) Blick *m* ♦ *vi*: **to ~ at** starren auf +*acc*, anstarren

starfish ['stɑːfɪʃ] *n* Seestern *m*

stark [stɑːk] *adj* öde ♦ *adv*: **~ naked** splitternackt

starling ['stɑːlɪŋ] *n* Star *m*

starry ['stɑːrɪ] *adj* Sternen-; **~-eyed** *adj* (*innocent*) blauäugig

start [stɑːt] *n* Anfang *m*; (*SPORT*) Start *m*; (*lead*) Vorsprung *m* ♦ *vt* in Gang setzen; (*car*) anlassen ♦ *vi* anfangen; (*car*) anspringen; (*on journey*) aufbrechen; (*SPORT*) starten; (*with fright*) zusammenfahren; **to ~ doing** *or* **to do sth** anfangen, etw zu tun; **~ off** *vi* anfangen; (*begin moving*) losgehen; losfahren; **~ up** *vi* anfangen ♦ *vt* beginnen; (*car*) anlassen; (*engine*) starten; **~er** *n* (*AUT*) Anlasser *m*; (*for race*) Starter *m*; (*BRIT: COOK*) Vorspeise *f*; **~ing point** *n* Ausgangspunkt *m*

startle ['stɑːtl] *vt* erschrecken; **startling** *adj* erschreckend

starvation [stɑːˈveɪʃən] *n* Verhungern *nt*

starve [stɑːv] *vi* verhungern ♦ *vt* verhungern lassen; **I'm starving** ich sterbe vor Hunger

state [steɪt] *n* (*condition*) Zustand *m*; (*POL*) Staat *m* ♦ *vt* erklären; (*facts*) angeben; **the S~s** (*USA*) die Staaten; **to be in a ~** durchdrehen; **~ly** *adj* würdevoll; **~ly home** *n* herrschaftliches Anwesen *nt*, Schloß ⚠ *nt*; **~ment** *n* Aussage *f*; (*POL*) Erklärung *f*; **~sman** (*irreg*) *n* Staatsmann *m*

static ['stætɪk] *n* (*also:* **~ electricity**) Reibungselektrizität *f*

station ['steɪʃən] *n* (*RAIL etc*) Bahnhof *m*; (*police etc*) Wache *f*; (*in society*) Stand *m* ♦ *vt* stationieren

stationary ['steɪʃnərɪ] *adj* stillstehend; (*car*) parkend

stationer's *n* (*shop*) Schreibwarengeschäft *nt*; **~y** *n* Schreibwaren *pl*

station master *n* Bahnhofsvorsteher *m*

station wagon *n* Kombiwagen *m*

statistics [stəˈtɪstɪks] *n* Statistik *f*

statue ['stætjuː] *n* Statue *f*

stature ['stætʃər] *n* Größe *f*

status ['steɪtəs] *n* Status *m*

statute ['stætjuːt] *n* Gesetz *nt*; **statutory** ['stætjutrɪ] *adj* gesetzlich

staunch [stɔːntʃ] *adj* standhaft

⚠ *For information on spelling reform see page 615*

stay [steɪ] n Aufenthalt m ♦ vi bleiben; (*reside*) wohnen; **to ~ put** an Ort und Stelle bleiben; **to ~ the night** übernachten; **~ behind** vi zurückbleiben; **~ in** vi (*at home*) zu Hause bleiben; **~ on** vi (*continue*) länger bleiben; **~ out** vi (*of house*) wegbleiben; **~ up** vi (*at night*) aufbleiben; **~ing power** n Durchhaltevermögen nt

stead [stɛd] n: **in sb's ~** an jds Stelle dat; **to stand sb in good ~** jdm zugute kommen

steadfast ['stɛdfɑ:st] adj standhaft, treu

steadily ['stɛdɪlɪ] adv stetig, regelmäßig

steady ['stɛdɪ] adj (*firm*) fest, stabil; (*regular*) gleichmäßig; (*reliable*) beständig; (*hand*) ruhig; (*job, boyfriend*) fest ♦ vt festigen; **to ~ o.s. on/against sth** sich stützen auf/gegen etw acc

steak [steɪk] n Steak nt; (*fish*) Filet nt

steal [sti:l] (pt **stole**, pp **stolen**) vt stehlen ♦ vi stehlen; (*go quietly*) sich stehlen

stealth [stɛlθ] n Heimlichkeit f; **~y** adj verstohlen, heimlich

steam [sti:m] n Dampf m ♦ vt (COOK) im Dampfbad erhitzen ♦ vi dampfen; **~ engine** n Dampfmaschine f; **~er** n Dampfer m; **~roller** n Dampfwalze f; **~ship** n = **steamer**; **~y** adj dampfig

steel [sti:l] n Stahl m ♦ adj Stahl-; (*fig*) stählern; **~works** n Stahlwerke pl

steep [sti:p] adj steil; (*price*) gepfeffert ♦ vt einweichen

steeple ['sti:pl] n Kirchturm m; **~chase** n Hindernisrennen nt

steer [stɪəʳ] vt, vi steuern; (*car etc*) lenken; **~ing** n (AUT) Steuerung f; **~ing wheel** n Steuer- od Lenkrad nt

stem [stem] n Stiel m ♦ vt aufhalten; **~ from** vt fus abstammen von

stench [stentʃ] n Gestank m

stencil ['stensl] n Schablone f ♦ vt (auf)drucken

stenographer [stɛˈnɔgrəfəʳ] (US) n Stenograph(in) ⚠ m(f)

step [step] n Schritt m; (*stair*) Stufe f ♦ vi treten, schreiten; **~s** npl (BRIT) = **stepladder**; **to take ~s** Schritte

unternehmen; **in/out of ~ (with)** im/nicht im Gleichklang (mit); **~ down** vi (*fig*) abtreten; **~ off** vt fus aussteigen aus; **~ up** vt steigern

stepbrother ['stɛpbrʌðəʳ] n Stiefbruder m

stepdaughter ['stɛpdɔ:təʳ] n Stieftochter f

stepfather ['stɛpfɑ:ðəʳ] n Stiefvater m

stepladder ['stɛplædəʳ] n Trittleiter f

stepmother ['stɛpmʌðəʳ] n Stiefmutter f

stepping stone ['stɛpɪŋ-] n Stein m; (*fig*) Sprungbrett n

stepsister ['stɛpsɪstəʳ] n Stiefschwester f

stepson ['stɛpsʌn] n Stiefsohn m

stereo ['stɛrɪəu] n Stereoanlage f ♦ adj (also: **~phonic**) stereophonisch ⚠

stereotype ['stɪərətaɪp] n (*fig*) Klischee nt ♦ vt stereotypieren; (*fig*) stereotyp machen

sterile ['stɛraɪl] adj steril; (*person*) unfruchtbar; **sterilize** vt sterilisieren

sterling ['stɜ:lɪŋ] adj (FIN) Sterling-; (*character*) gediegen ♦ n (ECON) das Pfund Sterling; **a pound ~** ein Pfund Sterling

stern [stɜ:n] adj streng ♦ n Heck nt, Achterschiff nt

stew [stju:] n Eintopf m ♦ vt, vi schmoren

steward ['stju:əd] n Steward m; **~ess** n Stewardess ⚠ f

stick [stɪk] (pt, pp **stuck**) n Stock m; (*of chalk etc*) Stück nt ♦ vt (*stab*) stechen; (*fix*) stecken; (*put*) stellen; (*gum*) (an)kleben; (*inf: tolerate*) vertragen ♦ vi (*stop*) steckenbleiben ⚠; (*get stuck*) klemmen; (*hold fast*) kleben, haften; **~ out** vi (*project*) hervorstehen; **~ up** vi (*project*) in die Höhe stehen; **~ up for** vt fus (*defend*) eintreten für; **~er** n Aufkleber m; **~ing plaster** n Heftpflaster nt

stickler ['stɪkləʳ] n: **~ (for)** Pedant m (in +acc)

stick-up ['stɪkʌp] (inf) n (Raub)überfall m

sticky ['stɪkɪ] adj klebrig; (*atmosphere*) stickig

stiff [stɪf] adj steif; (*difficult*) hart; (*paste*) dick; (*drink*) stark; **to have a ~ neck** einen steifen Hals haben; **~en** vt versteifen, (ver)stärken ♦ vi sich versteifen

stifle ['staɪfl] vt unterdrücken; **stifling** adj drückend

stigma ['stɪgmə] (pl BOT, MED, REL **~ta;** fig

⚠ *Informationen zur Rechtschreibreform Seite 615*

~s) n Stigma nt
stigmata [stɪgˈmɑːtə] npl of **stigma**
stile [staɪl] n Steige f
stiletto [stɪˈletəu] (BRIT) n (also: ~ **heel**) Pfennigabsatz m
still [stɪl] adj still ♦ adv (immer) noch; (anyhow) immerhin; **~born** adj totgeboren △; ~ **life** n Stilleben △ nt
stilt [stɪlt] n Stelze f
stilted ['stɪltɪd] adj gestelzt
stimulate ['stɪmjuleɪt] vt anregen, stimulieren
stimuli ['stɪmjulaɪ] npl of **stimulus**
stimulus ['stɪmjuləs] (pl -li) n Anregung f, Reiz m
sting [stɪŋ] (pt, pp **stung**) n Stich m; (organ) Stachel m ♦ vi stechen; (on skin) brennen ♦ vt stechen
stingy ['stɪndʒɪ] adj geizig, knauserig
stink [stɪŋk] (pt **stank**, pp **stunk**) n Gestank m ♦ vi stinken; **~ing** adj (fig) widerlich
stint [stɪnt] n (period) Betätigung f; **to do one's ~** seine Arbeit tun; (share) seinen Teil beitragen
stipulate ['stɪpjuleɪt] vt festsetzen
stir [stəːʳ] n Bewegung f; (COOK) Rühren nt; (sensation) Aufsehen nt ♦ vt (um)rühren ♦ vi sich rühren; **~ up** vt (mob) aufhetzen; (mixture) umrühren; (dust) aufwirbeln
stirrup ['stɪrəp] n Steigbügel m
stitch [stɪtʃ] n (with needle) Stich m; (MED) Faden m; (of knitting) Masche f; (pain) Stich m ♦ vt nähen
stoat [stəut] n Wiesel nt
stock [stɔk] n Vorrat m; (COMM) (Waren)lager nt; (live~) Vieh nt; (COOK) Brühe f; (FIN) Grundkapital nt ♦ adj stets vorrätig; (standard) Normal- ♦ vt (in shop) führen; **~s** npl (FIN) Aktien pl; **in/out of ~** vorrätig/nicht vorrätig; **to take ~ of** Inventur machen von; (fig) Bilanz ziehen aus; **~s and shares** Effekten pl; ~ **up** vi: **to ~ up (with)** Reserven anlegen (von); **~broker** ['stɔkbrəukəʳ] n Börsenmakler m; ~ **cube** n Brühwürfel m; ~ **exchange** n Börse f
stocking ['stɔkɪŋ] n Strumpf m

stock: ~ **market** n Börse f; ~ **phrase** n Standardsatz m; **~pile** n Vorrat m ♦ vt aufstapeln; **~taking** (BRIT) n (COMM) Inventur f, Bestandsaufnahme f
stocky ['stɔkɪ] adj untersetzt
stodgy ['stɔdʒɪ] adj pampig
stoke [stəuk] vt schüren
stole [stəul] pt of **steal** ♦ n Stola f
stolen ['stəuln] pp of **steal**
stomach ['stʌmək] n Bauch m, Magen m ♦ vt vertragen; **~-ache** n Magen- or Bauchschmerzen pl
stone [stəun] n Stein m; (BRIT: weight) Gewichtseinheit = 6.35 kg ♦ vt (olive) entkernen; (kill) steinigen; **~-cold** adj eiskalt; **~-deaf** adj stocktaub; **~work** n Mauerwerk nt; **stony** ['stəunɪ] adj steinig
stood [stud] pt, pp of **stand**
stool [stuːl] n Hocker m
stoop [stuːp] vi sich bücken
stop [stɔp] n Halt m; (bus ~) Haltestelle f; (punctuation) Punkt m ♦ vt anhalten; (bring to an end) aufhören (mit), sein lassen ♦ vi aufhören; (clock) stehenbleiben △; bleiben; **to ~ doing sth** aufhören, etw zu tun; **to ~ dead** innehalten; ~ **off** vi kurz haltmachen △; ~ **up** vt (hole) zustopfen, verstopfen; **~gap** n Notlösung f; **~lights** npl (AUT) Bremslichter pl; **~over** n (on journey) Zwischenaufenthalt m; **~page** ['stɔpɪdʒ] n (An)halten nt; (traffic) Verkehrsstockung f; (strike) Arbeitseinstellung f; **~per** ['stɔpəʳ] n Propfen m, Stöpsel m; ~ **press** n letzte Meldung f; **~watch** ['stɔpwɔtʃ] n Stoppuhr f
storage ['stɔːrɪdʒ] n Lagerung f; ~ **heater** n (Nachtstrom)speicherofen m
store [stɔːʳ] n Vorrat m; (place) Lager nt, Warenhaus nt; (BRIT: large shop) Kaufhaus nt; (US) Laden m ♦ vt lagern; **~s** npl (supplies) Vorräte pl; ~ **up** vt sich eindecken mit; **~room** n Lagerraum m, Vorratsraum m
storey ['stɔːrɪ] (US **story**) n Stock m
stork [stɔːk] n Storch m
storm [stɔːm] n (also fig) Sturm m ♦ vt, vi stürmen; **~y** adj stürmisch

△ *For information on spelling reform see page 615*

story ['stɔːrɪ] n Geschichte f; (lie) Märchen nt; (US) = **storey**; **~book** n Geschichtenbuch nt; **~teller** n Geschichtenerzähler m

stout [staut] adj (bold) tapfer; (fat) beleibt ♦ n Starkbier nt; (also: **sweet ~**) ≈ Malzbier nt

stove [stəuv] n (Koch)herd m; (for heating) Ofen m

stow [stəu] vt verstauen; **~away** n blinde(r) Passagier m

straddle ['strædl] vt (horse, fence) rittlings sitzen auf +dat; (fig) überbrücken

straggle ['strægl] vi (people) nachhinken; **~r** n Nachzügler m; **straggly** adj (hair) zottig

straight [streɪt] adj gerade; (honest) offen, ehrlich; (drink) pur ♦ adv (direct) direkt, geradewegs; **to put** or **get sth ~** etw in Ordnung bringen; **~ away** sofort; **~ off** sofort; **~en** vt (also: **~en out**) gerade machen; (fig) klarstellen; **~-faced** adv ohne die Miene zu verziehen ♦ adj: **to be ~-faced** keine Miene verziehen; **~forward** adj einfach, unkompliziert

strain [streɪn] n Belastung f; (streak, trace) Zug m; (of music) Fetzen m ♦ vt überanstrengen; (stretch) anspannen; (muscle) zerren; (filter) (durch)seihen ♦ vi sich anstrengen; **~ed** adj (laugh) gezwungen; (relations) gespannt; **~er** n Sieb nt

strait [streɪt] n Straße f, Meerenge f; **~jacket** n Zwangsjacke f; **~-laced** adj engherzig, streng

strand [strænd] n (of hair) Strähne f; (also fig) Faden m

stranded ['strændɪd] adj (also fig) gestrandet

strange [streɪndʒ] adj fremd; (unusual) seltsam; **~r** n Fremde(r) mf

strangle ['stræŋgl] vt erwürgen; **~hold** n (fig) Umklammerung f

strap [stræp] n Riemen m; (on clothes) Träger m ♦ vt (fasten) festschnallen

strapping ['stræpɪŋ] adj stramm

strata ['strɑːtə] npl of **stratum**

strategic [strə'tiːdʒɪk] adj strategisch

strategy ['strætɪdʒɪ] n (fig) Strategie f

stratum ['strɑːtəm] (pl **-ta**) n Schicht f

straw [strɔː] n Stroh nt; (single stalk, drinking ~) Strohhalm m; **that's the last ~!** das ist der Gipfel!

strawberry ['strɔːbərɪ] n Erdbeere f

stray [streɪ] adj (animal) verirrt ♦ vi herumstreunen

streak [striːk] n Streifen m; (in character) Einschlag m; (in hair) Strähne f ♦ vt streifen ♦ vi zucken; (move quickly) flitzen; **~ of bad luck** Pechsträhne f; **~y** adj gestreift; (bacon) durchwachsen

stream [striːm] n (brook) Bach m; (fig) Strom m ♦ vt (SCH) in (Leistungs)gruppen einteilen ♦ vi strömen; **to ~ in/out** (people) hinein-/hinausströmen

streamer ['striːmə'] n (flag) Wimpel m; (of paper) Luftschlange f

streamlined ['striːmlaɪnd] adj stromlinienförmig; (effective) rationell

street [striːt] n Straße f ♦ adj Straßen-; **~car** (US) n Straßenbahn f; **~ lamp** n Straßenlaterne f; **~ plan** n Stadtplan m; **~wise** (inf) adj: **to be ~wise** wissen, wo es lang geht

strength [streŋθ] n (also fig) Stärke f; Kraft f; **~en** vt (ver)stärken

strenuous ['strenjuəs] adj anstrengend

stress [stres] n Druck m; (mental) Streß ⚠ m; (GRAM) Betonung f ♦ vt betonen

stretch [stretʃ] n Strecke f ♦ vt ausdehnen, strecken ♦ vi sich erstrecken; (person) sich strecken; **~ out** vi sich ausstrecken ♦ vt ausstrecken

stretcher ['stretʃə'] n Tragbahre f

stretchy ['stretʃɪ] adj elastisch, dehnbar

strewn [struːn] adj: **~ with** übersät mit

stricken ['strɪkən] adj (person) ergriffen; (city, country) heimgesucht; **~ with** (disease) leidend unter +dat

strict [strɪkt] adj (exact) genau; (severe) streng; **~ly** adv streng, genau

stridden ['strɪdn] pp of **stride**

stride [straɪd] (pt **strode**, pp **stridden**) n lange(r) Schritt m ♦ vi schreiten

strident ['straɪdnt] adj schneidend, durchdringend

strife [straɪf] n Streit m

strike [straɪk] (pt, pp **struck**) n Streik m; (attack) Schlag m ♦ vt (hit) schlagen; (collide) stoßen gegen; (come to mind) einfallen +dat; (stand out) auffallen +dat; (find) finden ♦ vi (stop work) streiken; (attack) zuschlagen; (clock) schlagen; **on ~** (workers) im Streik; **to ~ a match** ein Streichholz anzünden; **~ down** vt (lay low) niederschlagen; **~ out** vt (cross out) ausstreichen; **~ up** vt (music) anstimmen; (friendship) schließen; **~r** n Streikende(r) mf; **striking** ['straɪkɪŋ] adj auffallend

string [strɪŋ] (pt, pp **strung**) n Schnur f; (row) Reihe f; (MUS) Saite f ♦ vt: **to ~ together** aneinanderreihen △ ♦ vi: **to ~ out** (sich) verteilen; **the ~s** npl (MUS) die Streichinstrumente pl; **to pull ~s** (fig) Fäden ziehen; **~ bean** n grüne Bohne f; **~(ed) instrument** n (MUS) Saiteninstrument nt

stringent ['strɪndʒənt] adj streng

strip [strɪp] n Streifen m ♦ vt (uncover) abstreifen, abziehen; (clothes) ausziehen; (TECH) auseinandernehmen △ ♦ vi (undress) sich ausziehen; **~ cartoon** n Bildserie f

stripe [straɪp] n Streifen m; **~d** adj gestreift

strip lighting n Neonlicht nt

stripper ['strɪpə'] n Striptaenzerin f

strip-search ['strɪpsɜːtʃ] n Leibesvisitation f (bei der man sich ausziehen muß) ♦ vt: **to be ~~ed** sich ausziehen müssen und durchsucht werden

stripy ['straɪpɪ] adj gestreift

strive [straɪv] (pt **strove**, pp **striven**) vi: **to ~ (for)** streben (nach)

strode [strəud] pt of **stride**

stroke [strəuk] n Schlag m; (SWIMMING, ROWING) Stoß m; (MED) Schlaganfall m; (caress) Streicheln nt ♦ vt streicheln; **at a ~** mit einem Schlag

stroll [strəul] n Spaziergang m ♦ vi schlendern; **~er** (US) n (pushchair) Sportwagen m

strong [strɒŋ] adj stark; (firm) fest; **they are 50 ~** sie sind 50 Mann stark; **~box** n Kassette f; **~hold** n Hochburg f; **~ly** adv stark; **~room** n Tresor m

strove [strəuv] pt of **strive**

struck [strʌk] pt, pp of **strike**

structure ['strʌktʃə'] n Struktur f, Aufbau m; (building) Bau m

struggle ['strʌgl] n Kampf m ♦ vi (fight) kämpfen

strum [strʌm] vt (guitar) klimpern auf +dat

strung [strʌŋ] pt, pp of **string**

strut [strʌt] n Strebe f, Stütze f ♦ vi stolzieren

stub [stʌb] n Stummel m; (of cigarette) Kippe f ♦ vt: **to ~ one's toe** sich dat den Zeh anstoßen; **~ out** vt ausdrücken

stubble ['stʌbl] n Stoppel f

stubborn ['stʌbən] adj hartnäckig

stuck [stʌk] pt, pp of **stick** ♦ adj (jammed) klemmend; **~-up** adj hochnäsig

stud [stʌd] n (button) Kragenknopf m; (place) Gestüt nt ♦ vt (fig): **~ded with** übersät mit

student ['stjuːdənt] n Student(in) m(f); (US) Student(in) m(f), Schüler(in) m(f) ♦ adj Studenten-; **~ driver** (US) n Fahrschüler(in) m(f)

studio ['stjuːdɪəu] n Studio nt; (for artist) Atelier nt; **~ apartment** (US) n Appartement nt; **~ flat** n Appartement nt

studious ['stjuːdɪəs] adj lernbegierig

study ['stʌdɪ] n (investigation) Studium nt, Untersuchung f; (room) Arbeitszimmer nt; (essay etc) Studie f ♦ vt studieren; (face) erforschen; (evidence) prüfen ♦ vi studieren

stuff [stʌf] n Stoff m; (inf) Zeug nt ♦ vt stopfen, füllen; (animal) ausstopfen; **~ing** n Füllung f; **~y** adj (room) schwül; (person) spießig

stumble ['stʌmbl] vi stolpern; **to ~ across** (fig) zufällig stoßen auf +acc

stumbling block ['stʌmblɪŋ-] n Hindernis nt

stump [stʌmp] n Stumpf m

stun [stʌn] vt betäuben; (shock) niederschmettern

stung [stʌŋ] pt, pp of **sting**

stunk [stʌŋk] pp of **stink**

stunned adj benommen, fassungslos

stunning ['stʌnɪŋ] adj betäubend; (news)

△ *For information on spelling reform see page 615*

überwältigend, umwerfend
stunt [stʌnt] *n* Kunststück *nt*, Trick *m*
stunted ['stʌntɪd] *adj* verkümmert
stuntman ['stʌntmæn] (*irreg*) *n* Stuntman *m*
stupefy ['stju:pɪfaɪ] *vt* betäuben; (*by news*) bestürzen
stupendous [stju:'pɛndəs] *adj* erstaunlich, enorm
stupid ['stju:pɪd] *adj* dumm; **~ity** [stju:'pɪdɪtɪ] *n* Dummheit *f*
stupor ['stju:pər] *n* Betäubung *f*
sturdy ['stɜ:dɪ] *adj* kräftig, robust
stutter ['stʌtər] *n* Stottern *nt* ♦ *vi* stottern
sty [staɪ] *n* Schweinestall *m*
stye [staɪ] *n* Gerstenkorn *nt*
style ['staɪlɪʃ, staɪl] *n* Stil *m*; (*fashion*) Mode *f*; **stylish** ['staɪlɪʃ] *adj* modisch; **stylist** *n* (*hair stylist*) Friseur *m*, Friseuse *f*
stylus ['staɪləs] *n* (Grammophon)nadel △ *f*
suave [swɑ:v] *adj* zuvorkommend
sub... [sʌb] *prefix* Unter...; **~conscious** *adj* unterbewußt △ ♦ *n*: **the ~conscious** das Unterbewußte △; **~contract** *vt* (vertraglich) untervermitteln; **~divide** *vt* unterteilen; **~dued** *adj* (*lighting*) gedämpft; (*person*) still
subject [*n, adj* 'sʌbdʒɪkt, *vb* səb'dʒɛkt] *n* (*of kingdom*) Untertan *m*; (*citizen*) Staatsangehörige(r) *mf*; (*topic*) Thema *nt*; (*SCH*) Fach *nt*; (*GRAM*) Subjekt *nt* ♦ *adj*: **to be ~ to** unterworfen sein +*dat*; (*exposed*) ausgesetzt sein +*dat* ♦ *vt* (*subdue*) unterwerfen; (*expose*) aussetzen; **~ive** [səb'dʒɛktɪv] *adj* subjektiv; **~ matter** *n* Thema *nt*
sublet [sʌb'lɛt] (*irreg: like* **let**) *vt* untervermieten
sublime [sə'blaɪm] *adj* erhaben
submachine gun ['sʌbmə'ʃi:n-] *n* Maschinenpistole *f*
submarine [sʌbmə'ri:n] *n* Unterseeboot *nt*, U-Boot *nt*
submerge [səb'mə:dʒ] *vt* untertauchen; (*flood*) überschwemmen ♦ *vi* untertauchen
submission [səb'mɪʃən] *n* (*obedience*) Gehorsam *m*; (*claim*) Behauptung *f*; (*of plan*) Unterbreitung *f*; **submissive**

[sə'mɪsɪv] *adj* demütig, unterwürfig (*pej*)
submit [səb'mɪt] *vt* behaupten; (*plan*) unterbreiten ♦ *vi* sich ergeben
subnormal [sʌb'nɔ:ml] *adj* minderbegabt
subordinate [sə'bɔ:dɪnət] *adj* untergeordnet ♦ *n* Untergebene(r) *mf*
subpoena [səb'pi:nə] *n* Vorladung *f* ♦ *vt* vorladen
subscribe [səb'skraɪb] *vi*: **to ~ to** (*view etc*) unterstützen; (*newspaper*) abonnieren; **~r** *n* (*to periodical*) Abonnent *m*; (*TEL*) Telefonteilnehmer *m*
subscription [səb'skrɪpʃən] *n* Abonnement *nt*; (*money subscribed*) (Mitglieds)beitrag *m*
subsequent ['sʌbsɪkwənt] *adj* folgend, später; **~ly** *adv* später
subside [səb'saɪd] *vi* sich senken; **subsidence** [səb'saɪdns] *n* Senkung *f*
subsidiarity [səbsɪdɪ'ærɪtɪ] *n* (*POL*) Subsidiarität *f*
subsidiary [səb'sɪdɪərɪ] *adj* Neben- ♦ *n* Tochtergesellschaft *f*
subsidize ['sʌbsɪdaɪz] *vt* subventionieren
subsidy ['sʌbsɪdɪ] *n* Subvention *f*
subsistence [səb'sɪstəns] *n* Unterhalt *m*
substance ['sʌbstəns] *n* Substanz *f*
substantial [səb'stænʃl] *adj* (*strong*) fest, kräftig; (*important*) wesentlich; **~ly** *adv* erheblich
substantiate [səb'stænʃɪeɪt] *vt* begründen, belegen
substitute ['sʌbstɪtju:t] *n* Ersatz *m* ♦ *vt* ersetzen; **substitution** [sʌbstɪ'tju:ʃən] *n* Ersetzung *f*
subterfuge ['sʌbtəfju:dʒ] *n* Vorwand *m*; (*trick*) Trick *m*
subterranean [sʌbtə'reɪnɪən] *adj* unterirdisch
subtitle ['sʌbtaɪtl] *n* Untertitel *m*; **~d** *adj* untertitelt, mit Untertiteln versehen
subtle ['sʌtl] *adj* fein; **~ty** *n* Feinheit *f*
subtotal [sʌb'təutl] *n* Zwischensumme *f*
subtract [səb'trækt] *vt* abziehen; **~ion** [səb'trækʃən] *n* Abziehen *nt*, Subtraktion *f*
suburb ['sʌbə:b] *n* Vorort *m*; **the ~s** die Außenbezirke *pl*; **~an** [sə'bə:bən] *adj* Vorort(s)-, Stadtrand-; **~ia** [sə'bə:bɪə] *n*

Vorstadt *f*

subversive [səb'vɜːsɪv] *adj* subversiv

subway ['sʌbweɪ] *n* (*US*) U-Bahn *f*; (*BRIT*) Unterführung *f*

succeed [sək'siːd] *vi* (*person*) erfolgreich sein, Erfolg haben; (*plan etc also*) gelingen ♦ *vt* (nach)folgen +*dat*; **he ~ed in doing it** es gelang ihm, es zu tun; **~ing** *adj* (nach)folgend

success [sək'ses] *n* Erfolg *m*; **~ful** *adj* erfolgreich; **to be ~ful (in doing sth)** Erfolg haben (bei etw); **~fully** *adv* erfolgreich

succession [sək'sefən] *n* (Aufeinander)folge *f*; (*to throne*) Nachfolge *f*

successive [sək'sesɪv] *adj* aufeinanderfolgend ⚠

successor [sək'sesər] *n* Nachfolger(in) *m(f)*

succinct [sək'sɪŋkt] *adj* knapp

succulent ['sʌkjulənt] *adj* saftig

succumb [sə'kʌm] *vi*: **to ~ (to)** erliegen (+*dat*); (*yield*) nachgeben (+*dat*)

such [sʌtʃ] *adj* solche(r, s); **~ a book** so ein Buch; **~ books** solche Bücher; **~ courage** so ein Mut; **~ a long trip** so eine lange Reise; **~ a lot of** so viel(e); **~ as** wie; **a noise ~ as to** ein derartiger Lärm, daß; **as ~** an sich; **~-and-~ a time** die und die Zeit

suck [sʌk] *vt* saugen; (*lollipop etc*) lutschen

sucker ['sʌkər] (*inf*) *n* Idiot *m*

suction ['sʌkfən] *n* Saugkraft *f*

sudden ['sʌdn] *adj* plötzlich; **all of a ~** auf einmal; **~ly** *adv* plötzlich

suds [sʌdz] *npl* Seifenlauge *f*; (*lather*) Seifenschaum *m*

sue [suː] *vt* verklagen

suede [sweɪd] *n* Wildleder *nt*

suet ['suɪt] *n* Nierenfett *nt*

Suez ['suːɪz] *n*: **the ~ Canal** der Suezkanal

suffer ['sʌfər] *vt* (er)leiden ♦ *vi* leiden; **~er** *n* Leidende(r) *mf*; **~ing** *n* Leiden *nt*

suffice [sə'faɪs] *vi* genügen

sufficient [sə'fɪʃənt] *adj* ausreichend; **~ly** *adv* ausreichend

suffix ['sʌfɪks] *n* Nachsilbe *f*

suffocate ['sʌfəkeɪt] *vt*, *vi* ersticken

suffrage ['sʌfrɪdʒ] *n* Wahlrecht *nt*

sugar ['fugər] *n* Zucker *m* ♦ *vt* zuckern; **~**

beet *n* Zuckerrübe *f*; **~ cane** *n* Zuckerrohr *nt*; **~y** *adj* süß

suggest [sə'dʒest] *vt* vorschlagen; (*show*) schließen lassen auf +*acc*; **~ion** [sə'dʒestfən] *n* Vorschlag *m*; **~ive** *adj* anregend; (*indecent*) zweideutig

suicide ['suɪsaɪd] *n* Selbstmord *m*; **to commit ~** Selbstmord begehen

suit [suːt] *n* Anzug *m*; (*CARDS*) Farbe *f* ♦ *vt* passen +*dat*; (*clothes*) stehen +*dat*; **well ~ed** (*well matched*) gut zusammenpassend; **~able** *adj* geeignet, passend; **~ably** *adv* passend, angemessen

suitcase ['suːtkeɪs] *n* (Hand)koffer *m*

suite [swiːt] *n* (*of rooms*) Zimmerflucht *f*; (*of furniture*) Einrichtung *f*; (*MUS*) Suite *f*

suitor ['suːtər] *n* (*JUR*) Kläger(in) *m(f)*

sulfur ['sʌlfər] (*US*) *n* = **sulphur**

sulk [sʌlk] *vi* schmollen; **~y** *adj* schmollend

sullen ['sʌlən] *adj* mürrisch

sulphur ['sʌlfər] (*US* **sulfur**) *n* Schwefel *m*

sultana [sʌl'tɑːnə] *n* (*fruit*) Sultanine *f*

sultry ['sʌltrɪ] *adj* schwül

sum [sʌm] *n* Summe *f*; (*money*) Betrag *m*; Summe *f*; (*arithmetic*) Rechenaufgabe *f*; **~ up** *vt*, *vi* zusammenfassen

summarize ['sʌmər022] *vt* kurz zusammenfassen

summary ['sʌmərɪ] *n* Zusammenfassung *f* ♦ *adj* (*justice*) kurzerhand erteilt

summer ['sʌmər] *n* Sommer *m* ♦ *adj* Sommer-; **~house** *n* (*in garden*) Gartenhaus *nt*; **~time** *n* Sommerzeit *f*

summit ['sʌmɪt] *n* Gipfel *m*; **~ (conference)** *n* Gipfelkonferenz *f*

summon ['sʌmən] *vt* herbeirufen; (*JUR*) vorladen; (*gather up*) aufbringen; **~s** (*JUR*) *n* Vorladung *f* ♦ *vt* vorladen

sump [sʌmp] (*BRIT*) *n* (*AUT*) Ölwanne *f*

sumptuous ['sʌmptjuəs] *adj* prächtig

sun [sʌn] *n* Sonne *f*; **~bathe** *vi* sich sonnen; **~block** *n* Sonnenschutzcreme *f*; **~burn** *n* Sonnenbrand *m*; **~burnt** *adj* sonnenverbrannt, sonnengebräunt; **to be ~burnt** (*painfully*) einen Sonnenbrand haben

Sunday ['sʌndɪ] *n* Sonntag *m*; **~ school** *n*

⚠ *For information on spelling reform see page 615*

Sonntagsschule f

sundial ['sʌndaɪəl] n Sonnenuhr f

sundown ['sʌndaun] n Sonnenuntergang m

sundries ['sʌndrɪz] npl (*miscellaneous items*) Verschiedene(s) nt

sundry ['sʌndrɪ] adj verschieden; **all and ~** alle

sunflower ['sʌnflauə'] n Sonnenblume f

sung [sʌŋ] pp of **sing**

sunglasses ['sʌnglɑːsɪz] npl Sonnenbrille f

sunk [sʌŋk] pp of **sink**

sun: ~light ['sʌnlaɪt] n Sonnenlicht nt; **~lit** ['sʌnlɪt] adj sonnenbeschienen; **~ny** ['sʌnɪ] adj sonnig; **~rise** n Sonnenaufgang m; **~roof** n (AUT) Schiebedach nt; **~screen** ['sʌnskriːn] n Sonnenschutzcreme f; **~set** ['sʌnset] n Sonnenuntergang m; **~shade** ['sʌnʃeɪd] n Sonnenschirm m; **~shine** ['sʌnʃaɪn] n Sonnenschein m; **~stroke** ['sʌnstrəuk] n Hitzschlag m; **~tan** ['sʌntæn] n (Sonnen)bräune f; **~tan oil** n Sonnenöl nt

super ['suːpə'] (inf) adj prima, klasse

superannuation [suːpərænjuˈeɪʃən] n Pension f

superb [suːˈpəːb] adj ausgezeichnet, hervorragend

supercilious [suːpəˈsɪlɪəs] adj herablassend

superficial [suːpəˈfɪʃəl] adj oberflächlich

superfluous [suˈpəːfluəs] adj überflüssig

superhuman [suːpəˈhjuːmən] adj (effort) übermenschlich

superimpose ['suːpərɪmˈpəuz] vt übereinanderlegen △

superintendent [suːpərɪnˈtendənt] n Polizeichef m

superior [suˈpɪərɪə'] adj überlegen; (better) besser ♦ n Vorgesetzte(r) mf; **~ity** [supɪərɪˈɒrɪtɪ] n Überlegenheit f

superlative [suˈpəːlətɪv] adj überragend

super: ~man ['suːpəmæn] (irreg) n Übermensch m; **~market** ['suːpəmɑːkɪt] n Supermarkt m; **~natural** [suːpəˈnætʃərəl] adj übernatürlich; **~power** ['suːpəpauə'] n Weltmacht f

supersede [suːpəˈsiːd] vt ersetzen

supersonic ['suːpəˈsɒnɪk] adj Überschall-

superstition [suːpəˈstɪʃən] n Aberglaube m;

superstitious [suːpəˈstɪʃəs] adj abergläubisch

supervise ['suːpəvaɪz] vt beaufsichtigen, kontrollieren; **supervision** [suːpəˈvɪʒən] n Aufsicht f; **supervisor** ['suːpəvaɪzə'] n Aufsichtsperson f; **supervisory** ['suːpəvaɪzərɪ] adj Aufsichts-

supper ['sʌpə'] n Abendessen nt

supplant [səˈplɑːnt] vt (person, thing) ersetzen

supple ['sʌpl] adj geschmeidig

supplement [n 'sʌplɪmənt, vb sʌplɪˈment] n Ergänzung f; (in book) Nachtrag m ♦ vt ergänzen; **~ary** [sʌplɪˈmentərɪ] adj ergänzend; **~ary benefit** (BRIT: old) n ≈ Sozialhilfe f

supplier [səˈplaɪə'] n Lieferant m

supplies [səˈplaɪz] npl (food) Vorräte pl; (MIL) Nachschub m

supply [səˈplaɪ] vt liefern ♦ n Vorrat m; (supplying) Lieferung f; see also **supplies**; **~ teacher** (BRIT) n Aushilfslehrer(in) m(f)

support [səˈpɔːt] n Unterstützung f; (TECH) Stütze f ♦ vt (hold up) stützen, tragen; (provide for) ernähren; (be in favour of) unterstützen; **~er** n Anhänger(in) m(f)

suppose [səˈpəuz] vt, vi annehmen; **to be ~d to do sth** etw tun sollen; **~dly** [səˈpəuzɪdlɪ] adv angeblich; **supposing** conj angenommen; **supposition** [sʌpəˈzɪʃən] n Voraussetzung f

suppress [səˈpres] vt unterdrücken

supremacy [suˈpreməsɪ] n Vorherrschaft f, Oberhoheit f

supreme [suˈpriːm] adj oberste(r, s), höchste(r, s)

surcharge ['səːtʃɑːdʒ] n Zuschlag m

sure [ʃuə'] adj sicher, gewiß △; **~!** (of course) klar!; **to make ~ of sth/that** sich einer Sache gen vergewissern/vergewissern, daß; **~ enough** (with past) tatsächlich; (with future) ganz bestimmt; **~-footed** adj sicher (auf den Füßen); **~ly** adv (certainly) sicherlich, gewiß △; **~ly it's wrong** das ist doch wohl falsch

surety ['ʃuərətɪ] n Sicherheit f

surf [səːf] n Brandung f

surface ['sɜːfɪs] *n* Oberfläche *f* ♦ *vt* (*roadway*) teeren ♦ *vi* auftauchen; ~ **mail** *n* gewöhnliche Post *f*

surfboard ['sɜːfbɔːd] *n* Wellenreiterbrett *nt*

surfeit ['sɜːfɪt] *n* Übermaß *nt*

surfing ['sɜːfɪŋ] *n* Wellenreiten *nt*

surge [sɜːdʒ] *n* Woge *f* ♦ *vi* wogen

surgeon ['sɜːdʒən] *n* Chirurg(in) *m(f)*

surgery ['sɜːdʒərɪ] *n* (*BRIT: place*) Praxis *f*; (*: time*) Sprechstunde *f*; (*treatment*) Operation *f*; **to undergo** ~ operiert werden; ~ **hours** (*BRIT*) *npl* Sprechstunden *pl*

surgical ['sɜːdʒɪkl] *adj* chirurgisch; ~ **spirit** (*BRIT*) *n* Wundbenzin *nt*

surly ['sɜːlɪ] *adj* verdrießlich, grob

surmount [sɜːmaunt] *vt* überwinden

surname ['sɜːneɪm] *n* Zuname *m*

surpass [sɜːpɑːs] *vt* übertreffen

surplus ['sɜːpləs] *n* Überschuß △ *m* ♦ *adj* überschüssig, Über(schuß)- △

surprise [sə'praɪz] *n* Überraschung *f* ♦ *vt* überraschen; ~**d** *adj* überrascht; **surprising** *adj* überraschend; **surprisingly** *adv* überraschend(erweise)

surrender [sə'rendər] *n* Kapitulation *f* ♦ *vi* sich ergeben

surreptitious [sʌrəp'tɪʃəs] *adj* heimlich; (*look also*) verstohlen

surrogate ['sʌrəgɪt] *n* Ersatz *m*; ~ **mother** *n* Leihmutter *f*

surround [sə'raund] *vt* umgeben; ~**ing** *adj* (*countryside*) umliegend; ~**ings** *npl* Umgebung *f*; (*environment*) Umwelt *f*

surveillance [sɜː'veɪləns] *n* Überwachung *f*

survey [*n* 'sɜːveɪ, *vb* sɜː'veɪ] *n* Übersicht *f* ♦ *vt* überblicken; (*land*) vermessen; ~**or** [sə'veɪər] *n* Land(ver)messer(in) *m(f)*

survival [sə'vaɪvl] *n* Überleben *nt*

survive [sə'vaɪv] *vt*, *vi* überleben; **survivor** [sə'vaɪvər] *n* Überlebende(r) *mf*

susceptible [sə'septəbl] *adj*: ~ (**to**) empfindlich (gegen); (*charms etc*) empfänglich (für)

suspect [*n* 'sʌspekt, *vb* səs'pekt] *n* Verdächtige(r) *mf* ♦ *adj* verdächtig ♦ *vt* verdächtigen; (*think*) vermuten

suspend [səs'pend] *vt* verschieben; (*from work*) suspendieren; (*hang up*) aufhängen; (*SPORT*) sperren; ~**ed sentence** *n* (*JUR*) zur Bewährung ausgesetzte Strafe; ~**er belt** *n* Strumpf(halter)gürtel *m*; ~**ers** *npl* (*BRIT*) Strumpfhalter *m*; (*US*) Hosenträger *m*

suspense [səs'pens] *n* Spannung *f*

suspension [səs'penʃən] *n* (*from work*) Suspendierung *f*; (*SPORT*) Sperrung *f*; (*AUT*) Federung *f*; ~ **bridge** *n* Hängebrücke *f*

suspicion [səs'pɪʃən] *n* Mißtrauen △ *nt*; Verdacht *m*; **suspicious** [səs'pɪʃəs] *adj* mißtrauisch △; (*causing suspicion*) verdächtig

sustain [səs'teɪn] *vt* (*maintain*) aufrechterhalten; (*confirm*) bestätigen; (*injury*) davontragen; ~**able** *adj* (*development, growth etc*) aufrechtzuerhalten; ~**ed** *adj* (*effort*) anhaltend

sustenance ['sʌstɪnəns] *n* Nahrung *f*

swab [swɒb] *n* (*MED*) Tupfer *m*

swagger ['swægər] *vi* stolzieren

swallow ['swɒləʊ] *n* (*bird*) Schwalbe *f*; (*of food etc*) Schluck *m* ♦ *vt* (ver)schlucken; ~ **up** *vt* verschlingen

swam [swæm] *pt of* **swim**

swamp [swɒmp] *n* Sumpf *m* ♦ *vt* überschwemmen

swan [swɒn] *n* Schwan *m*

swap [swɒp] *n* Tausch *m* ♦ *vt*: **to** ~ **sth (for sth)** etw (gegen etw) tauschen *or* eintauschen

swarm [swɔːm] *n* Schwarm *m* ♦ *vi*: **to** ~ *or* **be** ~**ing with** wimmeln von

swarthy ['swɔːðɪ] *adj* dunkel, braun

swastika ['swɒstɪkə] *n* Hakenkreuz *nt*

swat [swɒt] *vt* totschlagen

sway [sweɪ] *vi* schwanken; (*branches*) schaukeln, sich wiegen ♦ *vt* schwenken; (*influence*) beeinflussen

swear [sweər] (*pt* **swore**, *pp* **sworn**) *vi* (*promise*) schwören; (*curse*) fluchen; **to** ~ **to sth** schwören auf etw *acc*; ~**word** *n* Fluch *m*

sweat [swet] *n* Schweiß *m* ♦ *vi* schwitzen

sweater ['swetər] *n* Pullover *m*

△ *For information on spelling reform see page 615*

sweatshirt ['swetʃɔ:t] n Sweatshirt nt

sweaty ['swetɪ] adj verschwitzt

Swede [swi:d] n Schwede m, Schwedin f

swede [swi:d] (BRIT) n Steckrübe f

Sweden ['swi:dn] n Schweden nt

Swedish ['swi:dɪʃ] adj schwedisch ♦ n (LING) Schwedisch nt

sweep [swi:p] (pt, pp swept) n (chimney ~) Schornsteinfeger m ♦ vt fegen, kehren; ~ **away** vt wegfegen; ~ **past** vi vorbeisausen; ~ **up** vt zusammenkehren; ~ing adj (gesture) schwungvoll; (statement) verallgemeinernd

sweet [swi:t] n (course) Nachtisch m; (candy) Bonbon nt ♦ adj süß; ~**corn** n Zuckermais m; ~en vt süßen; (fig) versüßen; ~**heart** n Liebste(r) mf; ~**ness** n Süße f; ~ **pea** n Gartenwicke f

swell [swel] (pt swelled, pp swollen or swelled) n Seegang m ♦ adj (inf) todschick ♦ vt (numbers) vermehren ♦ vi (also: ~ up) (an)schwellen; ~ing n Schwellung f

sweltering ['sweltərɪŋ] adj drückend

swept [swept] pt, pp of sweep

swerve [swɜ:v] vt, vi ausscheren

swift [swɪft] n Mauersegler m ♦ adj geschwind, schnell, rasch; ~**ly** adv geschwind, schnell, rasch

swig [swɪg] n Zug m

swill [swɪl] n (for pigs) Schweinefutter nt ♦ vt spülen

swim [swɪm] (pt swam, pp swum) n: **to go for a ~** schwimmen gehen ♦ vi schwimmen ♦ vt (cross) (durch)schwimmen; ~**mer** n Schwimmer(in) m(f); ~**ming** n Schwimmen nt; ~**ming cap** n Badehaube f, Badekappe f; ~**ming costume** (BRIT) n Badeanzug m; ~**ming pool** n Schwimmbecken nt; (private) Swimmingpool m; ~**ming trunks** npl Badehose f; ~**suit** n Badeanzug m

swindle ['swɪndl] n Schwindel m, Betrug m ♦ vt betrügen

swine [swaɪn] n (also fig) Schwein nt

swing [swɪŋ] (pt, pp swung) n (child's) Schaukel f; (movement) Schwung m ♦ vt schwingen ♦ vi schwingen, schaukeln; (turn quickly) schwenken; **in full ~** in vollem Gange; ~ **bridge** n Drehbrücke f; ~ **door** (BRIT) n Schwingtür f

swingeing ['swɪndʒɪŋ] (BRIT) adj hart; (taxation, cuts) extrem

swinging door ['swɪŋɪŋ-] (US) n Schwingtür f

swipe [swaɪp] n Hieb m ♦ vt (inf: hit) hart schlagen; (: steal) klauen

swirl [swɜ:l] vi wirbeln

swish [swɪʃ] adj (inf: smart) schick ♦ vi zischen; (grass, skirts) rascheln

Swiss [swɪs] adj Schweizer, schweizerisch ♦ n Schweizer(in) m(f); **the ~** npl (people) die Schweizer pl

switch [swɪtʃ] n (ELEC) Schalter m; (change) Wechsel m ♦ vt (ELEC) schalten; (change) wechseln ♦ vi wechseln; ~ **off** vt ab- or ausschalten; ~ **on** vt an- or einschalten; ~**board** n Zentrale f; (board) Schaltbrett nt

Switzerland ['swɪtsələnd] n die Schweiz

swivel ['swɪvl] vt (also: ~ round) drehen ♦ vi (also: ~ round) sich drehen

swollen ['swəʊlən] pp of swell

swoon [swu:n] vi (old) in Ohnmacht fallen

swoop [swu:p] n Sturzflug m; (esp by police) Razzia f ♦ vi (also: ~ down) stürzen

swop [swɔp] = swap

sword [sɔ:d] n Schwert nt; ~**fish** n Schwertfisch m

swore [swɔ:ʳ] pt of swear

sworn [swɔ:n] pp of swear

swot [swɔt] vt, vi pauken

swum [swʌm] pp of swim

swung [swʌŋ] pt, pp of swing

sycamore ['sɪkəmɔ:ʳ] n (US) Platane f; (BRIT) Bergahorn m

syllable ['sɪləbl] n Silbe f

syllabus ['sɪləbəs] n Lehrplan m

symbol ['sɪmbl] n Symbol nt; ~**ic(al)** [sɪm'bɒlɪk(l)] adj symbolisch

symmetry ['sɪmɪtrɪ] n Symmetrie f

sympathetic [sɪmpə'θetɪk] adj mitfühlend

sympathize ['sɪmpəθaɪz] vi mitfühlen; ~**r** n (POL) Sympathisant(in) m(f)

sympathy ['sɪmpəθɪ] n Mitleid nt, Mitgefühl nt; (condolence) Beileid nt; **with our**

deepest ~ mit tiefempfundenem Beileid
symphony ['sɪmfənɪ] *n* Sinfonie *f*
symptom ['sɪmptəm] *n* Symptom *nt*; **~atic**
[sɪmptə'mætɪk] *adj* (*fig*): **~atic of**
bezeichnend für
synagogue ['sɪnəgɒg] *n* Synagoge *f*
synchronize ['sɪŋkrənaɪz] *vt*
synchronisieren
syndicate ['sɪndɪkɪt] *n* Konsortium *nt*
synonym ['sɪnənɪm] *n* Synonym *nt*
synonymous [sɪ'nɒnɪməs] *adj*
gleichbedeutend
synopsis [sɪ'nɒpsɪs] *n* Zusammenfassung *f*
synthetic [sɪn'θetɪk] *adj* synthetisch; **~s** *npl*
(*man-made fabrics*) Synthetik *f*
syphon ['saɪfən] = **siphon**
Syria ['sɪrɪə] *n* Syrien *nt*
syringe [sɪ'rɪndʒ] *n* Spritze *f*
syrup ['sɪrəp] *n* Sirup *m*; (*of sugar*) Melasse
f
system ['sɪstəm] *n* System *nt*; **~atic**
[sɪstə'mætɪk] *adj* systematisch; **~ disk** *n*
(*COMPUT*) Systemdiskette *f*; **~s analyst** *n*
Systemanalytiker(in) *m(f)*

T, t

ta [tɑː] (*BRIT: inf*) *excl* danke!
tab [tæb] *n* Aufhänger *m*; (*name ~*) Schild *nt*;
to keep ~s on (*fig*) genau im Auge
behalten
tabby ['tæbɪ] *n* (*also: ~ cat*) getigerte Katze
f
table ['teɪbl] *n* Tisch *m*; (*list*) Tabelle *f* ♦ *vt*
(*PARL: propose*) vorlegen, einbringen; **to lay**
or **set the ~** den Tisch decken; **~cloth** *n*
Tischtuch *nt*; **~ d'hôte** [tɑːbl'dəʊt] *n*
Tagesmenü *nt*; **~ lamp** *n* Tischlampe *f*;
~mat *n* Untersatz *m*; **~ of contents** *n*
Inhaltsverzeichnis *nt*; **~spoon** *n* Eßlöffel △
m; **~spoonful** *n* Eßlöffel(voll) △ *m*
tablet ['tæblɪt] *n* (*MED*) Tablette *f*
table tennis *n* Tischtennis *nt*
table wine *n* Tafelwein *m*
tabloid ['tæblɔɪd] *n* Zeitung *f* in kleinem
Format; (*pej*) Boulevardzeitung *f*

TABLOID PRESS

ⓘ *Der Ausdruck* **tabloid press** *bezieht
sich auf kleinformatige Zeitungen (ca 30
x 40cm); sie sind in Großbritannien fast
ausschließlich Massenblätter. Im Gegensatz
zur* **quality press** *verwenden diese
Massenblätter viele Fotos und einen
knappen, oft reißerischen Stil. Sie kommen
den Lesern entgegen, die mehr Wert auf
Unterhaltung legen.*

---

tabulate ['tæbjuleɪt] *vt* tabellarisch ordnen
tacit ['tæsɪt] *adj* stillschweigend
taciturn ['tæsɪtɜːn] *adj* wortkarg
tack [tæk] *n* (*small nail*) Stift *m*; (*US: thumb~*)
Reißzwecke *f*; (*stitch*) Heftstich *m*; (*NAUT*)
Lavieren *nt*; (*course*) Kurs *m* ♦ *vt* (*nail*)
nageln; (*stitch*) heften ♦ *vi* aufkreuzen
tackle ['tækl] *n* (*for lifting*) Flaschenzug *m*;
(*NAUT*) Takelage *f*; (*SPORT*) Tackling *nt* ♦ *vt*
(*deal with*) anpacken, in Angriff nehmen;
(*person*) festhalten; (*player*) angehen
tacky ['tækɪ] *adj* klebrig
tact [tækt] *n* Takt *m*; **~ful** *adj* taktvoll
tactical ['tæktɪkl] *adj* taktisch
tactics ['tæktɪks] *npl* Taktik *f*
tactless ['tæktlɪs] *adj* taktlos
tadpole ['tædpəʊl] *n* Kaulquappe *f*
taffy ['tæfɪ] (*US*) *n* Sahnebonbon *nt*
tag [tæg] *n* (*label*) Schild *nt*, Anhänger *m*;
(*maker's name*) Etikett *nt*; **~ along** *vi*
mitkommen
tail [teɪl] *n* Schwanz *m*; (*of list*) Schluß △ *m*
♦ *vt* folgen +*dat*; **~ away** *or* **off** *vi*
abfallen, schwinden; **~back** (*BRIT*) *n* (*AUT*)
(Rück)stau *m*; **~ coat** *n* Frack *m*; **~ end** *n*
Schluß △ *m*, Ende *nt*; **~gate** *n* (*AUT*)
Heckklappe *f*
tailor ['teɪləᵊ] *n* Schneider *m*; **~ing** *n*
Schneidern *nt*; **~-made** *adj*
maßgeschneidert; (*fig*): **~-made for sb** jdm
wie auf den Leib geschnitten
tailwind ['teɪlwɪnd] *n* Rückenwind *m*
tainted ['teɪntɪd] *adj* verdorben
take [teɪk] (*pt* **took**, *pp* **taken**) *vt* nehmen;
(*trip, exam, PHOT*) machen; (*capture: person*)

△ *For information on spelling reform see page 615*

fassen; (: *town; also* COMM, FIN) einnehmen; (*carry to a place*) bringen; (*get for o.s.*) sich *dat* nehmen; (*gain, obtain*) bekommen; (*put up with*) hinnehmen; (*respond to*) aufnehmen; (*interpret*) auffassen; (*assume*) annehmen; (*contain*) Platz haben für; (GRAM) stehen mit; **to ~ sth from sb** jdm etw wegnehmen; **to ~ sth from sth** (MATH: *subtract*) etw von etw abziehen; (*extract, quotation*) etw einer Sache *dat* entnehmen; **~ after** *vt fus* ähnlich sein +*dat*; **~ apart** *vt* auseinandernehmen △; **~ away** *vt* (*remove*) wegnehmen; (*carry off*) wegbringen; **~ back** *vt* (*return*) zurückbringen; (*retract*) zurücknehmen; **~ down** *vt* (*pull down*) abreißen; (*write down*) aufschreiben; **~ in** *vt* (*deceive*) hereinlegen; (*understand*) begreifen; (*include*) einschließen; **~ off** *vi* (*plane*) starten ♦ *vt* (*remove*) wegnehmen; (*clothing*) ausziehen; (*imitate*) nachmachen; **~ on** *vt* (*undertake*) übernehmen; (*engage*) einstellen; (*opponent*) antreten gegen; **~ out** *vt* (*girl, dog*) ausführen; (*extract*) herausnehmen; (*insurance*) abschließen; (*licence*) sich geben lassen; (*book*) ausleihen; (*remove*) entfernen; **to ~ sth out of sth** (*drawer, pocket etc*) etw aus etw herausnehmen; **~ over** *vt* übernehmen ♦ *vi*: **to ~ over from sb** jdn ablösen; **~ to** *vt fus* (*like*) mögen; (*adopt as practice*) sich *dat* angewöhnen; **~ up** *vt* (*raise*) aufnehmen; (*dress etc*) kürzer machen; (*occupy*) in Anspruch nehmen; (*engage in*) sich befassen mit; **~away** *adj* zum Mitnehmen; **~-home pay** *n* Nettolohn *m*; **~n** *pp of* **take**; **~off** *n* (AVIAT) Start *m*; (*imitation*) Nachahmung *f*; **~out** (US) *adj* = **takeaway**; **~over** *n* (COMM) Übernahme *f*; **takings** ['teɪkɪŋz] *npl* (COMM) Einnahmen *pl*

talc [tælk] *n* (*also:* **~um powder**) Talkumpuder *m*

tale [teɪl] *n* Geschichte *f*, Erzählung *f*; **to tell ~s** (*fig: lie*) Geschichten erfinden

talent ['tælnt] *n* Talent *nt*; **~ed** *adj* begabt

talk [tɔːk] *n* (*conversation*) Gespräch *nt*; (*rumour*) Gerede *nt*; (*speech*) Vortrag *m* ♦ *vi*

sprechen, reden; **~s** *npl* (POL etc) Gespräche *pl*; **to ~ about** sprechen von +*dat* or über +*acc*; **to ~ sb into doing sth** jdn überreden, etw zu tun; **to ~ sb out of doing sth** jdm ausreden, etw zu tun; **to ~ shop** fachsimpeln; **~ over** *vt* besprechen; **~ative** *adj* gesprächig

tall [tɔːl] *adj* groß; (*building*) hoch; **to be 1 m 80 ~** 1,80 m groß sein; **~boy** (BRIT) *n* Kommode *f*; **~ story** *n* übertriebene Geschichte *f*

tally ['tælɪ] *n* Abrechnung *f* ♦ *vi* übereinstimmen

talon ['tælən] *n* Kralle *f*

tame [teɪm] *adj* zahm; (*fig*) fade

tamper ['tæmpəʳ] *vi*: **to ~ with** herumpfuschen an +*dat*

tampon ['tæmpɔn] *n* Tampon *m*

tan [tæn] *n* (Sonnen)bräune *f*; (*colour*) Gelbbraun *nt* ♦ *adj* (*colour*) (gelb)braun ♦ *vt* bräunen ♦ *vi* braun werden

tang [tæŋ] *n* Schärfe *f*

tangent ['tændʒənt] *n* Tangente *f*; **to go off at a ~** (*fig*) vom Thema abkommen

tangerine [tændʒəˈriːn] *n* Mandarine *f*

tangible ['tændʒəbl] *adj* greifbar

tangle ['tæŋgl] *n* Durcheinander *nt*; (*trouble*) Schwierigkeiten *pl*; **to get in(to) a ~** sich verheddern

tank [tæŋk] *n* (*container*) Tank *m*, Behälter *m*; (MIL) Panzer *m*; **~er** ['tæŋkəʳ] *n* (*ship*) Tanker *m*; (*vehicle*) Tankwagen *m*

tanned [tænd] *adj* gebräunt

tantalizing ['tæntəlaɪzɪŋ] *adj* verlockend; (*annoying*) quälend

tantamount ['tæntəmaunt] *adj*: **~ to** gleichbedeutend mit

tantrum ['tæntrəm] *n* Wutanfall *m*

tap [tæp] *n* Hahn *m*; (*gentle blow*) Klopfen *nt* ♦ *vt* (*strike*) klopfen; (*supply*) anzapfen; (*telephone*) abhören; **on ~** (*fig: resources*) zur Hand; **~-dancing** *n* Steppen *nt*

tape [teɪp] *n* Band *nt*; (*magnetic*) (Ton)band *nt*; (*adhesive*) Klebstreifen *m* ♦ *vt* (*record*) aufnehmen; **~ deck** *n* Tapedeck *nt*; **~ measure** *n* Maßband *nt*

taper ['teɪpəʳ] *vi* spitz zulaufen

tape recorder n Tonbandgerät nt

tapestry ['tæpɪstrɪ] n Wandteppich m

tar [tɑː] n Teer m

target ['tɑːgɪt] n Ziel nt; (board) Zielscheibe f

tariff ['tærɪf] n (duty paid) Zoll m; (list) Tarif m

tarmac ['tɑːmæk] n (AVIAT) Rollfeld nt

tarnish ['tɑːnɪʃ] vt matt machen; (fig) beflecken

tarpaulin [tɑː'pɔːlɪn] n Plane f

tarragon ['tærəgən] n Estragon m

tart [tɑːt] n (Obst)torte f; (inf) Nutte f ♦ adj scharf; ~ **up** (inf) vt aufmachen; (person) auftakeln

tartan ['tɑːtn] n Schottenkaro nt ♦ adj mit Schottenkaro

tartar ['tɑːtər] n Zahnstein m

tartar(e) sauce ['tɑːtə-] n Remouladensoße f

task [tɑːsk] n Aufgabe f; **to take sb to ~** sich dat jdn vornehmen; ~ **force** n Sondertrupp m

tassel ['tæsl] n Quaste f

taste [teɪst] n Geschmack m; (sense) Geschmackssinn m; (small quantity) Kostprobe f; (liking) Vorliebe f ♦ vt schmecken; (try) probieren ♦ vi schmecken; **can I have a ~ of this wine?** kann ich diesen Wein probieren?; **to have a ~ for sth** etw mögen; **in good/bad ~** geschmackvoll/geschmacklos; **you can ~ the garlic (in it)** man kann den Knoblauch herausschmecken; **to ~ of sth** nach einer Sache schmecken; ~**ful** adj geschmackvoll; ~**less** adj (insipid) fade; (in bad taste) geschmacklos; **tasty** ['teɪstɪ] adj schmackhaft

tattered ['tætəd] adj = **in tatters**

tatters ['tætəz] npl: **in ~** in Fetzen

tattoo [tə'tuː] n (MIL) Zapfenstreich m; (on skin) Tätowierung f ♦ vt tätowieren

tatty ['tætɪ] (BRIT: inf) adj schäbig

taught [tɔːt] pt, pp of **teach**

taunt [tɔːnt] n höhnische Bemerkung f ♦ vt verhöhnen

Taurus ['tɔːrəs] n Stier m

taut [tɔːt] adj straff

tawdry ['tɔːdrɪ] adj (bunt und) billig

tax [tæks] n Steuer f ♦ vt besteuern; (strain) strapazieren; (strength) angreifen; ~**able** adj (income) steuerpflichtig; ~**ation** [tæk'seɪʃən] n Besteuerung f; ~ **avoidance** n Steuerumgehung f; ~ **disc** (BRIT) n (AUT) Kraftfahrzeugsteuerplakette f; ~ **evasion** n Steuerhinterziehung f; ~**-free** adj steuerfrei

taxi ['tæksɪ] n Taxi nt ♦ vi (plane) rollen; ~ **driver** n Taxifahrer m; ~ **rank** (BRIT) n Taxistand m; ~ **stand** n Taxistand m

tax: ~**payer** n Steuerzahler m; ~ **relief** n Steuerermäßigung f; ~ **return** n Steuererklärung f

TB n abbr (= tuberculosis) Tb f, Tbc f .

tea [tiː] n Tee m; (meal) (frühes) Abendessen nt; **high ~** (BRIT) Abendessen nt; ~ **bag** n Teebeutel m; ~ **break** (BRIT) n Teepause f

teach [tiːtʃ] (pt, pp **taught**) vt lehren, unterrichten; (show): **to ~ sb sth** jdm etw beibringen ♦ vi lehren, unterrichten; ~**er** n Lehrer(in) m(f); ~**er's pet** n Lehrers Liebling m; ~**ing** n (teacher's work) Unterricht m; (doctrine) Lehre f

tea: ~ **cloth** n Geschirrtuch nt; ~ **cosy** n Teewärmer m; ~**cup** n Teetasse f; ~ **leaves** npl Teeblätter pl

team [tiːm] n (workers) Team nt; (SPORT) Mannschaft f; (animals) Gespann nt; ~**work** n Gemeinschaftsarbeit f, Teamarbeit f

teapot ['tiːpɔt] n Teekanne f

tear¹ [teə^r] (pt **tore**, pp **torn**) n Riß ⚠ m ♦ vt zerreißen; (muscle) zerren ♦ vi (zer)reißen; (rush) rasen; ~ **along** vi (rush) entlangrasen; ~ **up** vt (sheet of paper etc) zerreißen

tear² [tɪə^r] n Träne f; ~**ful** adj ['tɪəful] weinend; (voice) weinerlich; ~ **gas** ['tɪəgæs] n Tränengas nt

tearoom ['tiːruːm] n Teestube f

tease [tiːz] n Hänsler m ♦ vt necken

tea set n Teeservice nt

teaspoon ['tiːspuːn] n Teelöffel m

teat [tiːt] n (of bottle) Sauger m

teat [tiːt] n Brustwarze f; (of animal) Zitze f; (of bottle) Sauger m

tea time n (in the afternoon) Teestunde f; (mealtime) Abendessen nt

tea towel n Geschirrtuch nt

⚠ *For information on spelling reform see page 615*

technical ['tɛknɪkl] *adj* technisch; (*knowledge, terms*) Fach-; **~ity** [tɛknɪ'kælɪtɪ] *n* technische Einzelheit *f*; (*JUR*) Formsache *f*; **~ly** *adv* technisch; (*speak*) spezialisiert; (*fig*) genau genommen

technician [tɛk'nɪʃən] *n* Techniker *m*

technique [tɛk'niːk] *n* Technik *f*

techno ['tɛknəʊ] *n* Techno *m*

technological [tɛknə'lɒdʒɪkl] *adj* technologisch

technology [tɛk'nɒlədʒɪ] *n* Technologie *f*

teddy (bear) ['tɛdɪ-] *n* Teddybär *m*

tedious ['tiːdɪəs] *adj* langweilig, ermüdend

tee [tiː] *n* (*GOLF*: *object*) Tee *nt*

teem [tiːm] *vi* (*swarm*): **to ~ (with)** wimmeln (von); **it is ~ing (with rain)** es gießt in Strömen

teenage ['tiːneɪdʒ] *adj* (*fashions etc*) Teenager-, jugendlich; **~r** *n* Teenager *m*, Jugendliche(r) *mf*

teens [tiːnz] *npl* Teenageralter *nt*

tee-shirt ['tiːʃəːt] *n* T-Shirt *nt*

teeter ['tiːtəʳ] *vi* schwanken

teeth [tiːθ] *npl of* **tooth**

teethe [tiːð] *vi* zahnen; **teething ring** *n* Beißring *m*; **teething troubles** *npl* (*fig*) Kinderkrankheiten *pl*

teetotal ['tiː'təʊtl] *adj* abstinent

tele: **~communications** *npl* Fernmeldewesen *nt*; **~conferencing** *n* Telefon- *or* Videokonferenz; **~gram** *n* Telegramm *nt*; **~graph** *n* Telegraf *m*; **~graph pole** *n* Telegrafenmast *m*

telephone ['tɛlɪfəʊn] *n* Telefon *nt*, Fernsprecher *m ♦ vt* anrufen; (*message*) telefonisch mitteilen; **to be on the ~** (*talking*) telefonieren; (*possessing phone*) Telefon haben; **~ booth** *n* Telefonzelle *f*; **~ box** (*BRIT*) *n* Telefonzelle *f*; **~ call** *n* Telefongespräch *nt*, Anruf *m*; **~ directory** *n* Telefonbuch *nt*; **~ number** *n* Telefonnummer *f*; **telephonist** [tə'lɛfənɪst] (*BRIT*) *n* Telefonist(in) *m(f)*

telephoto lens ['tɛlɪ'fəʊtəʊ-] *n* Teleobjektiv *nt*

telescope ['tɛlɪskəʊp] *n* Teleskop *nt*, Fernrohr *nt ♦ vt* ineinanderschieben ⚠

televise ['tɛlɪvaɪz] *vt* durch das Fernsehen übertragen

television ['tɛlɪvɪʒən] *n* Fernsehen *nt*; **on ~** im Fernsehen; **~ (set)** *n* Fernsehapparat *m*, Fernseher *m*

telex ['tɛlɛks] *n* Telex *nt ♦ vt* per Telex schicken

tell [tɛl] (*pt, pp* **told**) *vt* (*story*) erzählen; (*secret*) ausplaudern; (*say, make known*) sagen; (*distinguish*) erkennen; (*be sure*) wissen *♦ vi* (*talk*) sprechen; (*be sure*) wissen; (*divulge*) es verraten; (*have effect*) sich auswirken; **to ~ sb to do sth** jdm sagen, daß er etw tun soll; **to ~ sb sth** *or* **sth to sb** jdm etw sagen; **to ~ sb by sth** jdn an etw *dat* erkennen; **to ~ sth from** etw unterscheiden von; **to ~ of sth** von etw sprechen; **~ off** *vt*: **to ~ sb off** jdn ausschimpfen

teller ['tɛləʳ] *n* Kassenbeamte(r) *mf*

telling ['tɛlɪŋ] *adj* verräterisch; (*blow*) hart

telltale ['tɛlteɪl] *adj* verräterisch

telly ['tɛlɪ] (*BRIT*: *inf*) *n abbr* (= **television**) TV *nt*

temp [tɛmp] *n abbr* (= **temporary**) Aushilfssekretärin *f*

temper ['tɛmpəʳ] *n* (*disposition*) Temperament *nt*; (*anger*) Zorn *m ♦ vt* (*tone down*) mildern; (*metal*) härten; **to be in a (bad) ~** wütend sein; **to lose one's ~** die Beherrschung verlieren

temperament ['tɛmprəmənt] *n* Temperament *nt*; **~al** [tɛmprə'mɛntl] *adj* (*moody*) launisch

temperate ['tɛmprət] *adj* gemäßigt

temperature ['tɛmprətʃəʳ] *n* Temperatur *f*; (*MED*: *high ~*) Fieber *nt*; **to have** *or* **run a ~** Fieber haben

template ['tɛmplɪt] *n* Schablone *f*

temple ['tɛmpl] *n* Tempel *m*; (*ANAT*) Schläfe *f*

temporal ['tɛmpərl] *adj* (*of time*) zeitlich; (*worldly*) irdisch, weltlich

temporarily ['tɛmpərərɪlɪ] *adv* zeitweilig, vorübergehend

temporary ['tɛmpərərɪ] *adj* vorläufig; (*road, building*) provisorisch

tempt [tɛmpt] *vt* (*persuade*) verleiten;

(*attract*) reizen, (ver)locken; **to ~ sb into doing sth** jdn dazu verleiten, etw zu tun; **~ation** [tempˈteɪʃən] n Versuchung f; **~ing** adj (*person*) verführerisch; (*object, situation*) verlockend

ten [ten] num zehn

tenable [ˈtenəbl] adj haltbar

tenacious [təˈneɪʃəs] adj zäh, hartnäckig

tenacity [təˈnæsɪtɪ] n Zähigkeit f, Hartnäckigkeit f

tenancy [ˈtenənsɪ] n Mietverhältnis nt

tenant [ˈtenənt] n Mieter m; (*of larger property*) Pächter m

tend [tend] vt (*look after*) sich kümmern um ♦ vi: **to ~ to do sth** etw gewöhnlich tun

tendency [ˈtendənsɪ] n Tendenz f; (*of person*) Tendenz f, Neigung f

tender [ˈtendəʳ] adj zart; (*loving*) zärtlich ♦ n (COMM: *offer*) Kostenanschlag m ♦ vt (an)bieten; (*resignation*) einreichen; **~ness** n Zartheit f; (*being loving*) Zärtlichkeit f

tendon [ˈtendən] n Sehne f

tenement [ˈtenəmənt] n Mietshaus nt

tennis [ˈtenɪs] n Tennis nt; **~ ball** n Tennisball m; **~ court** n Tennisplatz m; **~ player** n Tennisspieler(in) m(f); **~ racket** n Tennisschläger m; **~ shoes** npl Tennisschuhe pl

tenor [ˈtenəʳ] n Tenor m

tenpin bowling [ˈtenpɪn-] n Bowling nt

tense [tens] adj angespannt ♦ n Zeitform f

tension [ˈtenʃən] n Spannung f

tent [tent] n Zelt nt

tentacle [ˈtentəkl] n Fühler m; (*of sea animals*) Fangarm m

tentative [ˈtentətɪv] adj (*movement*) unsicher; (*offer*) Probe-; (*arrangement*) vorläufig; (*suggestion*) unverbindlich; **~ly** adv versuchsweise; (*try, move*) vorsichtig

tenterhooks [ˈtentəhʊks] npl: **to be on ~** auf die Folter gespannt sein

tenth [tenθ] adj zehnte(r, s)

tent peg n Hering m

tent pole n Zeltstange f

tenuous [ˈtenjʊəs] adj schwach

tenure [ˈtenjʊəʳ] n (*of land*) Besitz m; (*of office*) Amtszeit f

tepid [ˈtepɪd] adj lauwarm

term [tɜːm] n (*period of time*) Zeit(raum m) f; (*limit*) Frist f; (SCH) Quartal nt; (UNIV) Trimester nt; (*expression*) Ausdruck m ♦ vt (be)nennen; **~s** npl (*conditions*) Bedingungen pl; **in the short/long ~** auf kurze/lange Sicht; **to be on good ~s with sb** gut mit jdm auskommen; **to come to ~s with** (*person*) sich einigen mit; (*problem*) sich abfinden mit

terminal [ˈtɜːmɪnl] n (BRIT: *also*: **coach ~**) Endstation f; (AVIAT) Terminal m; (COMPUT) Terminal nt or m ♦ adj Schluß- △; (MED) unheilbar; **~ly** adj (MED): **~ly ill** unheilbar krank

terminate [ˈtɜːmɪneɪt] vt beenden ♦ vi enden, aufhören

termini [ˈtɜːmɪnaɪ] npl of **terminus**

terminus [ˈtɜːmɪnəs] (pl **termini**) n Endstation f

terrace [ˈterəs] n (BRIT: *row of houses*) Häuserreihe f; (*in garden etc*) Terrasse f; **the ~s** npl (BRIT: SPORT) die Ränge; **~d** adj (*garden*) terrassenförmig angelegt; (*house*) Reihen-

terrain [teˈreɪn] n Gelände nt

terrible [ˈterɪbl] adj schrecklich, entsetzlich, fürchterlich; **terribly** adv fürchterlich

terrier [ˈterɪəʳ] n Terrier m

terrific [təˈrɪfɪk] adj unwahrscheinlich; **~!** klasse!

terrified adj: **to be ~ of sth** vor etw schreckliche Angst haben

terrify [ˈterɪfaɪ] vt erschrecken

territorial [terɪˈtɔːrɪəl] adj Gebiets-, territorial

territory [ˈterɪtərɪ] n Gebiet nt

terror [ˈterəʳ] n Schrecken m

terrorism [ˈterərɪzəm] n Terrorismus m; **~ist** n Terrorist(in) m(f); **~ize** vt terrorisieren

terse [tɜːs] adj knapp, kurz, bündig

test [test] n Probe f; (*examination*) Prüfung f; (PSYCH, TECH) Test m ♦ vt prüfen; (PSYCH) testen

testicle [ˈtestɪkl] n (ANAT) Hoden m

testify [ˈtestɪfaɪ] vi aussagen; **to ~ to sth** etw bezeugen

testimony [ˈtestɪmənɪ] n (JUR)

△ *For information on spelling reform see page 615*

Zeugenaussage *f*; *(fig)* Zeugnis *nt*
test match *n (SPORT)* Länderkampf *m*
test tube *n* Reagenzglas *nt*
tetanus ['tetənəs] *n* Wundstarrkrampf *m*, Tetanus *m*
tether ['tɛðər] *vt* anbinden ♦ *n*: **at the end of one's ~** völlig am Ende
text [tɛkst] *n* Text *m*; *(of document)* Wortlaut *m*; **~book** *n* Lehrbuch *nt*
textiles ['tɛkstaɪlz] *npl* Textilien *pl*
texture ['tɛkstʃər] *n* Beschaffenheit *f*
Thai [taɪ] *adj* thailändisch ♦ *n* Thailänder(in) *m(f)*; **~land** *n* Thailand *nt*
Thames [tɛmz] *n*: **the ~** die Themse
than [ðæn, ðən] *prep (in comparisons)* als
thank [θæŋk] *vt* danken *+dat*; **you've him to ~ for your success** Sie haben Ihren Erfolg ihm zu verdanken; **~ you (very much)** danke (vielmals), danke schön; **~ful** *adj* dankbar; **~less** *adj* undankbar; **~s** *npl* Dank *m* ♦ *excl* danke!; **~s to** dank *+gen*; **T~sgiving (Day)** *(US)* *n* Thanksgiving Day *m*

THANKSGIVING (DAY)

i Thanksgiving (Day) *ist ein Feiertag in den USA, der auf den vierten Donnerstag im November fällt. Er soll daran erinnern, wie die Pilgerväter die gute Ernte im Jahre 1621 feierten. In Kanada gibt es einen ähnlichen Erntedanktag (der aber nichts mit den Pilgervätern zu tun hat) am zweiten Montag im Oktober.*

KEYWORD

that [ðæt, ðət] *adj (demonstrative: pl those)* der/die/das; jene(r, s); **that one** das da ♦ *pron* **1** *(demonstrative: pl those)* der/die/das; **who's/what's that?** wer ist da/was ist das?; **is that you?** bist du das?; **that's what he said** genau das hat er gesagt; **what happened after that?** was passierte danach?; **that is** das heißt
2 *(relative: subj)* der/die/das, die; *(: direct obj)* den/die/das, die; *(: indirect obj)* dem/der/dem, denen; **all (that) I have** alles, was

ich habe
3 *(relative: of time)*: **the day (that)** an dem Tag, als; **the winter (that) he came** in dem Winter, in dem er kam
♦ *conj* daß ⚠; **he thought that I was ill** er dachte, daß ich krank sei, er dachte, ich sei krank
♦ *adv (demonstrative)* so; **I can't work that much** ich kann nicht soviel arbeiten

thatched [θætʃt] *adj* strohgedeckt; *(cottage)* mit Strohdach
thaw [θɔ:] *n* Tauwetter *nt* ♦ *vi* tauen; *(frozen foods, fig: people)* auftauen ♦ *vt* (auf)tauen lassen

KEYWORD

the [ði:, ðə] *def art* **1** der/die/das; **to play the piano/violin** Klavier/Geige spielen; **I'm going to the butcher's/the cinema** ich gehe zum Fleischer/ins Kino; **Elizabeth the First** Elisabeth die Erste
2 *(+adj to form noun)* das, die; **the rich and the poor** die Reichen und die Armen
3 *(in comparisons)*: **the more he works the more he earns** je mehr er arbeitet, desto mehr verdient er

theatre ['θɪətər] *(US* **theater)** *n* Theater *nt*; *(for lectures etc)* Saal *m*; *(MED)* Operationssaal *m*; **~goer** *n* Theaterbesucher(in) *m(f)*; **theatrical** [θɪˈætrɪkl] *adj* Theater-; *(career)* Schauspieler-; *(showy)* theatralisch
theft [θɛft] *n* Diebstahl *m*
their [ðɛər] *adj* ihr; *see also* **my**; **~s** *pron* ihre(r, s); *see also* **mine²**
them [ðɛm, ðəm] *pron (acc)* sie; *(dat)* ihnen; *see also* **me**
theme [θi:m] *n* Thema *nt*; *(MUS)* Motiv *nt*; **~ park** *n* (thematisch gestalteter) Freizeitpark *m*; **~ song** *n* Titelmusik *f*
themselves [ðəmˈsɛlvz] *pl pron (reflexive)* sich (selbst); *(emphatic)* selbst; *see also* **oneself**
then [ðɛn] *adv (at that time)* damals; *(next)* dann ♦ *conj* also, folglich; *(furthermore)*

⚠ *Informationen zur Rechtschreibreform Seite 615*

ferner ♦ adj damalig; **from ~ on** von da an; **by ~** bis dahin; **the ~ president** der damalige Präsident

theology [θɪˈɔlədʒɪ] n Theologie f

theoretical [θɪəˈrɛtɪkl] adj theoretisch; **~ly** adv theoretisch

theory [ˈθɪərɪ] n Theorie f

therapist [ˈθɛrəpɪst] n Therapeut(in) m(f)

therapy [ˈθɛrəpɪ] n Therapie f

KEYWORD

there [ðɛəʳ] adv **1: there is, there are** es or da ist/sind; (there exists/exist also) es gibt; **there are 3 of them** (people, things) es gibt 3 davon; **there has been an accident** da war ein Unfall

2 (place) da, dort; (direction) dahin, dorthin; **put it in/on there** leg es dahinein/dorthinauf

3: there, there (esp to child) na, na

---

there: ~abouts [ˈðɛərəˈbauts] adv (place) dort in der Nähe, dort irgendwo; (amount): **20 or ~abouts** ungefähr 20; **~after** [ðɛərˈɑːftəʳ] adv danach; **~by** [ˈðɛəbaɪ] adv dadurch, damit

therefore [ˈðɛəfɔːʳ] adv deshalb, daher

there's [ˈðɛəz] = **there is; there has**

thermometer [θəˈmɔmɪtəʳ] n Thermometer nt

Thermos [ˈθəːməs] ® n Thermosflasche f

thesaurus [θɪˈsɔːrəs] n Synonymwörterbuch nt

these [ðiːz] pron, adj (pl) diese

theses [ˈθiːsiːz] npl of **thesis**

thesis [ˈθiːsɪs] (pl **theses**) n (for discussion) These f; (UNIV) Dissertation f, Doktorarbeit f

they [ðeɪ] pl pron sie; (people in general) man; **~ say that ...** (it is said that) es wird gesagt, daß ...; **~'d = they had; they would; ~'ll they shall = they will; ~'re = they are; ~'ve = they have**

thick [θɪk] adj dick; (forest) dicht; (liquid) dickflüssig; (slow, stupid) dumm, schwer von Begriff ♦ n: **in the ~ of** mitten in +dat; **it's 20 cm ~** es ist 20 cm dick or stark; **~en** vi (fog) dichter werden ♦ vt (sauce etc)

verdicken; **~ness** n Dicke f; Dichte f; Dickflüssigkeit f; **~set** adj untersetzt; **~-skinned** adj dickhäutig

thief [θiːf] (pl **thieves**) n Dieb(in) m(f)

thieves [θiːvz] npl of **thief**

thieving [ˈθiːvɪŋ] n Stehlen nt ♦ adj diebisch

thigh [θaɪ] n Oberschenkel m

thimble [ˈθɪmbl] n Fingerhut m

thin [θɪn] adj dünn; (person) dünn, mager; (excuse) schwach ♦ vt: **to ~ (down)** (sauce, paint) verdünnen

thing [θɪŋ] n Ding nt; (affair) Sache f; **my ~s** meine Sachen pl; **the best ~ would be to** ... das Beste wäre, ...; **how are ~s?** wie geht's?

think [θɪŋk] (pt, pp **thought**) vt, vi denken; **what did you ~ of them?** was halten Sie von ihnen?; **to ~ about sth/sb** nachdenken über etw/jdn; **I'll ~ about it** ich überlege es mir; **to ~ of doing sth** vorhaben or beabsichtigen, etw zu tun; **I ~ so/not** ich glaube (schon)/glaube nicht; **to ~ well of sb** viel von jdm halten; **~ over** vt überdenken; **~ up** vt sich dat ausdenken; **~ tank** n Expertengruppe f

thinly [ˈθɪnlɪ] adv dünn; (disguised) kaum

third [θəːd] adj dritte(r, s) ♦ n (person) Dritte(r) mf; (part) Drittel nt; **~ly** adv drittens; **~ party insurance** (BRIT) n Haftpflichtversicherung f; **~-rate** adj minderwertig; **T~ World** n: **the T~ World** die Dritte Welt f

thirst [θəːst] n (also fig) Durst m; **~y** adj (person) durstig; (work) durstig machend; **to be ~y** Durst haben

thirteen [θəːˈtiːn] num dreizehn

thirty [ˈθəːtɪ] num dreißig

KEYWORD

this [ðɪs] adj (demonstrative: pl **these**) diese(r, s); **this evening** heute abend; **this one** diese(r, s) (da)

♦ pron (demonstrative: pl **these**) dies, das; **who/what is this?** wer/was ist das?; **this is where I live** hier wohne ich; **this is what he said** das hat er gesagt; **this is Mr Brown** dies ist Mr Brown; (on telephone)

⚠ For information on spelling reform see page 615

hier ist Mr Brown
♦ *adv* (*demonstrative*): **this high/long** *etc* so
groß/lang *etc*

---

thistle ['θɪsl] *n* Distel *f*

thorn [θɔːn] *n* Dorn *m*; **~y** *adj* dornig;
(*problem*) schwierig

thorough ['θʌrə] *adj* gründlich; **~bred** *n*
Vollblut *nt* ♦ *adj* reinrassig, Vollblut-; **~fare**
n Straße *f*; **"no ~fare"** „Durchfahrt
verboten"; **~ly** *adv* gründlich; (*extremely*)
äußerst

those [ðəuz] *pl pron* die (da), jene ♦ *adj* die,
jene

though [ðəu] *conj* obwohl ♦ *adv* trotzdem

thought [θɔːt] *pt, pp of* **think** ♦ *n* (*idea*)
Gedanke *m*; (*thinking*) Denken *nt*,
Denkvermögen *nt*; **~ful** *adj* (*thinking*)
gedankenvoll, nachdenklich; (*kind*)
rücksichtsvoll, aufmerksam; **~less** *adj*
gedankenlos, unbesonnen; (*unkind*)
rücksichtslos

thousand ['θauzənd] *num* tausend; **two ~**
zweitausend; **~s of** Tausende (von); **~th** *adj*
tausendste(r, s)

thrash [θræʃ] *vt* verdreschen; (*fig*)
(vernichtend) schlagen; **~ about** *vi* um
sich schlagen; **~ out** *vt* ausdiskutieren

thread [θrɛd] *n* Faden *m*, Garn *nt*; (*TECH*)
Gewinde *nt*; (*in story*) Faden *m* ♦ *vt* (*needle*)
einfädeln; **~bare** *adj* fadenscheinig

threat [θrɛt] *n* Drohung *f*; (*danger*) Gefahr *f*;
~en *vt* bedrohen ♦ *vi* drohen; **to ~en sb
with sth** jdm etw androhen

three [θriː] *num* drei; **~-dimensional** *adj*
dreidimensional; **~-piece suite** *n*
dreiteilige Polstergarnitur *f*; **~-wheeler** *n*
Dreiradwagen *m*

thresh [θrɛʃ] *vt, vi* dreschen

threshold ['θrɛʃhəuld] *n* Schwelle *f*

threw [θruː] *pt of* **throw**

thrift [θrɪft] *n* Sparsamkeit *f*; **~y** *adj* sparsam

thrill [θrɪl] *n* Reiz *m*, Erregung *f* ♦ *vt*
begeistern, packen; **to be ~ed with** (*gift
etc*) sich unheimlich freuen über +*acc*; **~er**
n Krimi *m*; **~ing** *adj* spannend; (*news*)
aufregend

thrive [θraɪv] (*pt* **thrived**, *pp* **thrived**) *vi*: **to
~ (on)** gedeihen (bei); **thriving** ['θraɪvɪŋ]
adj blühend

throat [θrəut] *n* Hals *m*, Kehle *f*; **to have a
sore ~** Halsschmerzen haben

throb [θrɔb] *vi* klopfen, pochen

throes [θrəuz] *npl*: **in the ~ of** mitten in
+*dat*

throne [θrəun] *n* Thron *m*; **on the ~** auf
dem Thron

throng ['θrɔŋ] *n* (Menschen)schar *f* ♦ *vt* sich
drängen in +*dat*

throttle ['θrɔtl] *n* Gashebel *m* ♦ *vt* erdrosseln

through [θruː] *prep* durch; (*time*) während
+*gen*; (*because of*) aus, durch ♦ *adv* durch
♦ *adj* (*ticket, train*) durchgehend; (*finished*)
fertig; **to be ~ (to)** jdn verbinden (mit);
to be ~ (*TEL*) eine Verbindung haben;
(*have finished*) fertig sein; **no ~ way** (*BRIT*)
Sackgasse *f*; **~out** [θruː'aut] *prep* (*place*)
überall in +*dat*; (*time*) während +*gen* ♦ *adv*
überall; die ganze Zeit

throw [θrəu] (*pt* **threw**, *pp* **thrown**) *n* Wurf
m ♦ *vt* werfen; **to ~ a party** eine Party
geben; **~ away** *vt* wegwerfen; (*waste*)
verschenken; (*money*) verschwenden; **~ off**
vt abwerfen; (*pursuer*) abschütteln; **~ out** *vt*
hinauswerfen; (*rubbish*) wegwerfen; (*plan*)
verwerfen; **~ up** *vt, vi* (*vomit*) speien;
~away *adj* Wegwerf-; **~-in** *n* Einwurf *m*;
~n *pp of* **throw**

thru [θruː] (*US*) = **through**

thrush [θrʌʃ] *n* Drossel *f*

thrust [θrʌst] (*pt, pp* **thrust**) *vt, vi* (*push*)
stoßen

thud [θʌd] *n* dumpfe(r) (Auf)schlag *m*

thug [θʌg] *n* Schlägertyp *m*

thumb [θʌm] *n* Daumen *m* ♦ *vt* (*book*)
durchblättern; **to ~ a lift** per Anhalter
fahren (wollen); **~tack** (*US*) *n* Reißzwecke *f*

thump [θʌmp] *n* (*blow*) Schlag *m*; (*noise*)
Bums *m* ♦ *vi* hämmern, pochen ♦ *vt*
schlagen auf +*acc*

thunder ['θʌndəʳ] *n* Donner *m* ♦ *vi* donnern;
(*train etc*): **to ~ past** vorbeidonnern ♦ *vt*
brüllen; **~bolt** *n* Blitz *nt*; **~clap** *n*
Donnerschlag *m*; **~storm** *n* Gewitter *nt*,

⚠ *Informationen zur Rechtschreibreform Seite 615*

Unwetter nt; **~y** adj gewitterschwül

Thursday ['θɜːzdɪ] n Donnerstag m

thus [ðʌs] adv (in this way) so; (therefore) somit, also, folglich

thwart [θwɔːt] vt vereiteln, durchkreuzen; (person) hindern

thyme [taɪm] n Thymian m

thyroid ['θaɪrɔɪd] n Schilddrüse f

tiara [tɪ'ɑːrə] n Diadem nt

tic [tɪk] n Tick m

tick [tɪk] n (sound) Ticken nt; (mark) Häkchen nt ♦ vi ticken ♦ vt abhaken; **in a ~** (BRIT: inf) sofort; **~ off** vt abhaken; (person) ausschimpfen; **~ over** vi (engine) im Leerlauf laufen; (fig) auf Sparflamme laufen

ticket ['tɪkɪt] n (for travel) Fahrkarte f; (for entrance) (Eintritts)karte f; (price ~) Preisschild nt; (luggage ~) (Gepäck)schein m; (raffle ~) Los nt; (parking ~) Strafzettel m; (in car park) Parkschein m; **~ collector** n Fahrkartenkontrolleur m; **~ inspector** n Fahrkartenkontrolleur m; **~ office** n (THEAT etc) Kasse f; (RAIL etc) Fahrkartenschalter m

tickle ['tɪkl] n Kitzeln nt ♦ vt kitzeln; (amuse) amüsieren; **ticklish** ['tɪklɪʃ] adj (also fig) kitzlig

tidal ['taɪdl] adj Flut-, Tide-; **~ wave** n Flutwelle f

tidbit ['tɪdbɪt] (US) n Leckerbissen m

tiddlywinks ['tɪdlɪwɪŋks] n Floh(hüpf)spiel nt

tide [taɪd] n Gezeiten pl; **high/low ~** Flut f/ Ebbe f

tidy ['taɪdɪ] adj ordentlich ♦ vt aufräumen, in Ordnung bringen

tie [taɪ] n (BRIT: neck) Krawatte f, Schlips m; (sth connecting) Band nt; (SPORT) Unentschieden nt ♦ vt (fasten, restrict) binden ♦ vi (SPORT) unentschieden spielen; (in competition) punktgleich sein; **to ~ in a bow** zur Schleife binden; **to ~ a knot in sth** einen Knoten in etw acc machen; **~ down** vt festbinden; **to ~ sb down to** jdn binden an +acc; **~ up** vt (dog) anbinden; (parcel) verschnüren; (boat) festmachen; (person) fesseln; **to be ~d up** (busy) beschäftigt sein

tier [tɪə²] n Rang m; (of cake) Etage f

tiff [tɪf] n Krach m

tiger ['taɪgə²] n Tiger m

tight [taɪt] adj (close) eng, knapp; (schedule) gedrängt; (firm) fest; (control) streng; (stretched) stramm, (an)gespannt; (inf: drunk) blau, stramm ♦ adv (squeeze) fest; **~en** vt anziehen, anspannen; (restrictions) verschärfen ♦ vi sich spannen; **~-fisted** adj knauserig; **~ly** adv eng; fest; (stretched) straff; **~-rope** n Seil nt; **~s** npl (esp BRIT) Strumpfhose f

tile [taɪl] n (on roof) Dachziegel m; (on wall or floor) Fliese f; **~d** adj (roof) gedeckt, Ziegel-; (floor, wall) mit Fliesen belegt

till [tɪl] n Kasse f ♦ vt bestellen ♦ prep, conj = **until**

tiller ['tɪlə²] n Ruderpinne f

tilt [tɪlt] vt kippen, neigen ♦ vi sich neigen

timber ['tɪmbə²] n (wood) Holz nt

time [taɪm] n Zeit f; (occasion) Mal nt; (rhythm) Takt m ♦ vt zur rechten Zeit tun, zeitlich einrichten; (SPORT) stoppen; **in 2 weeks' ~** in 2 Wochen; **a long ~** lange; **for the ~ being** vorläufig; **4 at a ~** zu jeweils 4; **from ~ to ~** gelegentlich; **to have a good ~** sich amüsieren; **in ~** (soon enough) rechtzeitig; (after some ~) mit der Zeit; (MUS) im Takt; **in no ~** im Handumdrehen; **any ~** jederzeit; **on ~** pünktlich, rechtzeitig; **five ~s 5** fünfmal 5; **what ~ is it?** wieviel Uhr ist es?, wie spät ist es?; **at ~s** manchmal; **~ bomb** n Zeitbombe f; **~less** adj (beauty) zeitlos; **~ limit** n Frist f; **~ly** adj rechtzeitig; günstig; **~ off** n freie Zeit f; **~r** n (timer switch: in kitchen) Schaltuhr f; **~ scale** n Zeitspanne f; **~-share** adj Time-sharing-; **~ switch** (BRIT) n Zeitschalter m; **~table** n Fahrplan m; (SCH) Stundenplan m; **~ zone** n Zeitzone f

timid ['tɪmɪd] adj ängstlich, schüchtern

timing ['taɪmɪŋ] n Wahl f des richtigen Zeitpunkts, Timing nt

timpani ['tɪmpənɪ] npl Kesselpauken pl

tin [tɪn] n (metal) Blech nt; (BRIT: can) Büchse f, Dose f; **~foil** n Stanniolpapier nt

tinge [tɪndʒ] n (colour) Färbung f; (fig)

⚠ For information on spelling reform see page 615

Anflug *m* ♦ *vt* färben; **~d with** mit einer Spur von

tingle ['tɪŋgl] *n* Prickeln *nt* ♦ *vi* prickeln

tinker ['tɪŋkəʳ] *n* Kesselflicker *m*; **~ with** *vt fus* herumpfuschen an +*dat*

tinkle ['tɪŋkl] *vi* klingeln

tinned [tɪnd] (*BRIT*) *adj* (*food*) Dosen-, Büchsen-

tin opener [-əupnəʳ] (*BRIT*) *n* Dosen- or Büchsenöffner *m*

tinsel ['tɪnsl] *n* Rauschgold *nt*

tint [tɪnt] *n* Farbton *m*; (*slight colour*) Anflug *m*; (*hair*) Tönung *f*; **~ed** *adj* getönt

tiny ['taɪnɪ] *adj* winzig

tip [tɪp] *n* (*pointed end*) Spitze *f*; (*money*) Trinkgeld *nt*; (*hint*) Wink *m*, Tip ⚠ *m* ♦ *vt* (*slant*) kippen; (*hat*) antippen; (~ *over*) umkippen; (*waiter*) ein Trinkgeld geben +*dat*; **~-off** *n* Hinweis *m*, Tip ⚠ *m*; **~ped** (*BRIT*) *adj* (*cigarette*) Filter-

tipsy ['tɪpsɪ] *adj* beschwipst

tiptoe ['tɪptəu] *n*: **on ~** auf Zehenspitzen

tiptop [tɪp'tɒp] *adj*: **in ~ condition** tipptopp, erstklassig

tire ['taɪəʳ] *n* (*US*) = **tyre** ♦ *vt*, *vi* ermüden, müde machen/werden; **~d** *adj* müde; **to be ~d of sth** etw satt haben; **~less** *adj* unermüdlich; **~some** *adj* lästig

tiring ['taɪərɪŋ] *adj* ermüdend

tissue ['tɪʃuː] *n* Gewebe *nt*; (*paper handkerchief*) Papiertaschentuch *nt*; **~ paper** *n* Seidenpapier *nt*

tit [tɪt] *n* (*bird*) Meise *f*; **~ for tat** wie du mir, so ich dir

titbit ['tɪtbɪt] (*US* **tidbit**) *n* Leckerbissen *m*

titillate ['tɪtɪleɪt] *vt* kitzeln

title ['taɪtl] *n* Titel *m*; **~ deed** *n* Eigentumsurkunde *f*; **~ role** *n* Hauptrolle *f*

titter ['tɪtəʳ] *vi* kichern

titular ['tɪtjʊləʳ] *adj* (*in name only*) nominell

TM *abbr* (= *trademark*) Wz

KEYWORD

to [tuː, tə] *prep* **1** (*direction*) zu, nach; **I go to France/school** ich gehe nach Frankreich/zur Schule; **to the left** nach links

2 (*as far as*) bis

3 (*with expressions of time*) vor; **a quarter to 5** Viertel vor 5

4 (*for, of*) für; **secretary to the director** Sekretärin des Direcktors

5 (*expressing indirect object*): **to give sth to sb** jdm etw geben; **to talk to sb** mit jdm sprechen; **I sold it to a friend** ich habe es einem Freund verkauft

6 (*in relation to*) zu; **30 miles to the gallon** 30 Meilen pro Gallone

7 (*purpose, result*) zu; **to my surprise** zu meiner Überraschung

♦ *with vb* **1** (*infin*): **to go/eat** gehen/essen; **to want to do sth** etw tun wollen; **to try/start to do sth** versuchen/anfangen, etw zu tun; **he has a lot to lose** er hat viel zu verlieren

2 (*with vb omitted*): **I don't want to** ich will (es) nicht

3 (*purpose, result*) um; **I did it to help you** ich tat es, um dir zu helfen

4 (*after adj etc*): **ready to use** gebrauchsfertig; **too old/young to ...** zu alt/jung, um ... zu ...

♦ *adv*: **push/pull the door to** die Tür zuschieben/zuziehen

---

toad [təud] *n* Kröte *f*; **~stool** *n* Giftpilz *m*

toast [təust] *n* (*bread*) Toast *m*; (*drinking*) Trinkspruch *m* ♦ *vt* trinken auf +*acc*; (*bread*) toasten; (*warm*) wärmen; **~er** *n* Toaster *m*

tobacco [tə'bækəu] *n* Tabak *m*; **~nist** [tə'bækənɪst] *n* Tabakhändler *m*; **~nist's (shop)** *n* Tabakladen *m*

toboggan [tə'bɒgən] *n* (Rodel)schlitten *m*; **~ing** *n* Rodeln *nt*

today [tə'deɪ] *adv* heute; (*at the present time*) heutzutage

toddler ['tɒdləʳ] *n* Kleinkind *nt*

toddy ['tɒdɪ] *n* (Whisky)grog *m*

to-do [tə'duː] *n* Theater *nt*

toe [təu] *n* Zehe *f*; (*of sock, shoe*) Spitze *f* ♦ *vt*: **to ~ the line** (*fig*) sich einfügen; **~nail** *n* Zehennagel *m*

toffee ['tɒfɪ] *n* Sahnebonbon *nt*; **~ apple** (*BRIT*) *n* kandierte(r) Apfel *m*

together [tə'geðəʳ] *adv* zusammen; (*at the*

same time) gleichzeitig; **~ with** zusammen mit; gleichzeitig mit

toil [tɔɪl] *n* harte Arbeit *f*, Plackerei *f* ♦ *vi* sich abmühen, sich plagen

toilet ['tɔɪlət] *n* Toilette *f* ♦ *cpd* Toiletten-; **~ bag** *n* Waschbeutel *m*; **~ paper** *n* Toilettenpapier *nt*; **~ries** ['tɔɪlətrɪz] *npl* Toilettenartikel *pl*; **~ roll** *n* Rolle *f* Toilettenpapier; **~ water** *n* Toilettenwasser *nt*

token ['təʊkən] *n* Zeichen *nt*; *(gift ~)* Gutschein *m*; **book/record ~** *(BRIT)* Bücher-/Plattengutschein *m*

Tokyo ['təʊkjəʊ] *n* Tokio *nt*

told [təʊld] *pt, pp of* **tell**

tolerable ['tɔlərəbl] *adj (bearable)* erträglich; *(fairly good)* leidlich

tolerant ['tɔlərnt] *adj:* **be ~ (of)** vertragen +*acc*

tolerate ['tɔləreɪt] *vt* dulden; *(noise)* ertragen

toll [təʊl] *n* Gebühr *f* ♦ *vi (bell)* läuten

tomato [tə'mɑːtəʊ] *(pl ~es) n* Tomate *f*

tomb [tuːm] *n* Grab(mal) *nt*

tomboy ['tɔmbɔɪ] *n* Wildfang *m*

tombstone ['tuːmstəʊn] *n* Grabstein *m*

tomcat ['tɔmkæt] *n* Kater *m*

tomorrow [tə'mɔrəʊ] *n* Morgen *nt* ♦ *adv* morgen; **the day after ~** übermorgen; ~ **morning** morgen früh; **a week ~** morgen in einer Woche

ton [tʌn] *n* Tonne *f (BRIT = 1016kg; US = 907kg);* **~s of** *(inf)* eine Unmenge von

tone [təʊn] *n* Ton *m;* ~ **down** *vt (criticism, demands)* mäßigen; *(colours)* abtönen; ~ **up** *vt* in Form bringen; **~-deaf** *adj* ohne musikalisches Gehör

tongs [tɔŋz] *npl* Zange *f;* *(curling ~)* Lockenstab *m*

tongue [tʌŋ] *n* Zunge *f;* *(language)* Sprache *f;* **with ~ in cheek** scherzhaft; **~-tied** *adj* stumm, sprachlos; ~ **twister** *n* Zungenbrecher *m*

tonic ['tɔnɪk] *n (drink)* Tonic *nt;* *(MED)* Stärkungsmittel *nt*

tonight [tə'naɪt] *adv* heute abend △

tonsil ['tɔnsl] *n* Mandel *f;* **~litis** [tɔnsɪ'laɪtɪs] *n* Mandelentzündung *f*

too [tuː] *adv* zu; *(also)* auch; ~ **bad!** Pech!; ~ **many** zu viele

took [tʊk] *pt of* **take**

tool [tuːl] *n (also fig)* Werkzeug *nt;* **~box** *n* Werkzeugkasten *m*

toot [tuːt] *n* Hupen *nt* ♦ *vi* tuten; *(AUT)* hupen

tooth [tuːθ] *(pl teeth) n* Zahn *m;* **~ache** *n* Zahnschmerzen *pl*, Zahnweh *nt;* **~brush** *n* Zahnbürste *f;* **~paste** *n* Zahnpasta *f;* **~pick** *n* Zahnstocher *m*

top [tɔp] *n* Spitze *f;* *(of mountain)* Gipfel *m;* *(of tree)* Wipfel *m;* *(toy)* Kreisel *m;* *(~ gear)* vierte(r)/fünfte(r) Gang *m* ♦ *adj* oberste(r, s) ♦ *vt (list)* an erster Stelle stehen auf +*dat;* **on ~ of** oben auf +*dat;* **from ~ to bottom** von oben bis unten; ~ **off** *(US)* vt auffüllen; ~ **up** *vt* auffüllen; ~ **floor** *n* oberste(s) Stockwerk *nt;* ~ **hat** *n* Zylinder *m;* **~- heavy** *adj* kopflastig

topic ['tɔpɪk] *n* Thema *nt*, Gesprächsgegenstand *m;* **~al** *adj* aktuell

top: **~less** ['tɔplɪs] *adj (bather etc)* oben ohne; **~-level** *adj* auf höchster Ebene; **~most** ['tɔpməʊst] *adj* oberste(r, s)

topple ['tɔpl] *vt, vi* stürzen, kippen

top-secret ['tɔp'siːkrɪt] *adj* streng geheim

topsy-turvy ['tɔpsɪ'tɜːvɪ] *adv* durcheinander ♦ *adj* auf den Kopf gestellt

torch [tɔːtʃ] *n (BRIT: ELEC)* Taschenlampe *f;* *(with flame)* Fackel *f*

tore [tɔːr] *pt of* **tear¹**

torment [*n* 'tɔːment, *vb* tɔː'ment] *n* Qual *f* ♦ *vt (distress)* quälen

torn [tɔːn] *pp of* **tear¹** ♦ *adj* hin- und hergerissen

torrent ['tɔrnt] *n* Sturzbach *m;* **~ial** [tɔ'renʃl] *adj* wolkenbruchartig

torrid ['tɔrɪd] *adj* heiß

tortoise ['tɔːtəs] *n* Schildkröte *f;* **~shell** ['tɔːtəʃel] *n* Schildpatt *m*

torture ['tɔːtʃər] *n* Folter *f* ♦ *vt* foltern

Tory ['tɔːrɪ] *(BRIT) n (POL)* Tory *m* ♦ *adj* Tory-, konservativ

toss [tɔs] *vt* schleudern; **to ~ a coin** *or* **to ~ up for sth** etw mit einer Münze entscheiden; **to ~ and turn** *(in bed)* sich hin

△ *For information on spelling reform see page 615*

und her werfen

tot [tɔt] n (small quantity) bißchen ⚠ nt; (small child) Knirps m

total ['təutl] n Gesamtheit f; (money) Endsumme f ♦ adj Gesamt-, total ♦ vt (add up) zusammenzählen; (amount to) sich belaufen auf

totalitarian [təutælɪ'tɛərɪən] adj totalitär

totally ['təutəlɪ] adv total

totter ['tɔtər] vi wanken, schwanken

touch [tʌtʃ] n Berührung f; (sense of feeling) Tastsinn m ♦ vt (feel) berühren; (come against) leicht anstoßen; (emotionally) rühren; **a ~ of** (fig) eine Spur von; **to get in ~ with sb** sich mit jdm in Verbindung setzen; **to lose ~** (friends) Kontakt verlieren; **~ on** vt fus (topic) berühren, erwähnen; **~ up** vt (paint) auffrischen; **~-and-go** adj riskant, knapp; **~down** n Landen nt, Niedergehen nt; **~ed** adj (moved) gerührt; **~ing** adj rührend; **~line** n Seitenlinie f; **~-sensitive screen** n (COMPUT) berührungsempfindlicher Bildschirm m; **~y** adj empfindlich, reizbar

tough [tʌf] adj zäh; (difficult) schwierig ♦ n Schläger(typ) m; **~en** vt zäh machen; (make strong) abhärten

toupee ['tu:peɪ] n Toupet nt

tour ['tuər] n Tour f ♦ vi umherreisen; (THEAT) auf Tour sein; auf Tour gehen; **~ guide** n Reiseleiter(in) m(f)

tourism ['tuərɪzm] n Fremdenverkehr m, Tourismus m

tourist ['tuərɪst] n Tourist(in) m(f) ♦ cpd (class) Touristen-; **~ office** n Verkehrsamt nt

tournament ['tuənəmənt] n Turnier nt

tousled ['tauzld] adj zerzaust

tout [taut] vi: **to ~ for** auf Kundenfang gehen für ♦ n: **ticket ~** Kundenschlepper(in) m(f)

tow [təu] vt (ab)schleppen; **on** (BRIT) or **in** (US) **~** (AUT) im Schlepp

toward(s) [tə'wɔ:d(z)] prep (with time) gegen; (in direction of) nach

towel ['tauəl] n Handtuch nt; **~ling** n (fabric) Frottee nt or m; **~ rack** (US) n

Handtuchstange f; **~ rail** n Handtuchstange f

tower ['tauər] n Turm m; **~ block** (BRIT) n Hochhaus nt; **~ing** adj hochragend

town [taun] n Stadt f; **to go to ~** (fig) sich ins Zeug legen; **~ centre** n Stadtzentrum nt; **~ clerk** n Stadtdirektor m; **~ council** n Stadtrat m; **~ hall** n Rathaus nt; **~ plan** n Stadtplan m; **~ planning** n Stadtplanung f

towrope ['təurəup] n Abschlepptau nt

tow truck (US) n Abschleppwagen m

toxic ['tɔksɪk] adj giftig, Gift-

toy [tɔɪ] n Spielzeug nt; **~ with** vt fus spielen mit; **~shop** n Spielwarengeschäft nt

trace [treɪs] n Spur f ♦ vt (follow a course) nachspüren +dat; (find out) aufspüren; (copy) durchpausen; **tracing paper** n Pauspapier n

track [træk] n (mark) Spur f; (path) Weg m; (race~) Rennbahn f; (RAIL) Gleis nt ♦ vt verfolgen; **to keep ~ of sb** jdn im Auge behalten; **~ down** vt aufspüren; **~suit** n Trainingsanzug m

tract [trækt] n (of land) Gebiet nt

traction ['trækʃən] n (power) Zugkraft f; (AUT: grip) Bodenhaftung f; (MED): **in ~** im Streckverband

tractor ['træktər] n Traktor m

trade [treɪd] n (commerce) Handel m; (business) Geschäft nt, Gewerbe nt; (people) Geschäftsleute pl; (skilled manual work) Handwerk nt ♦ vi: **to ~ (in)** handeln (mit) ♦ vt tauschen; **~ in** vt in Zahlung geben; **~ fair** n Messe nt; **~-in price** n Preis, zu dem etw in Zahlung genommen wird; **~mark** n Warenzeichen nt; **~ name** n Handelsbezeichnung f; **~r** n Händler m; **~sman** (irreg) n (shopkeeper) Geschäftsmann m; (workman) Handwerker m; (delivery man) Lieferant m; **~ union** n Gewerkschaft f; **~ unionist** n Gewerkschaftler(in) m(f)

trading ['treɪdɪŋ] n Handel m; **~ estate** (BRIT) n Industriegelände nt

tradition [trə'dɪʃən] n Tradition f; **~al** adj traditionell, herkömmlich

⚠ *Informationen zur Rechtschreibreform Seite 615*

traffic ['træfɪk] n Verkehr m; (esp in drugs): ~ **(in)** Handel m (mit) ♦ vi: **to ~ in** (esp drugs) handeln mit; ~ **calming** n Verkehrsberuhigung f; ~ **circle** (US) n Kreisverkehr m; ~ **jam** n Verkehrsstauung f; ~ **lights** npl Verkehrsampel f; ~ **warden** n ≈ Verkehrspolizist m (ohne amtliche Befugnisse), Politesse f (ohne amtliche Befugnisse)

tragedy ['trædʒədɪ] n Tragödie f

tragic ['trædʒɪk] adj tragisch

trail [treɪl] n (track) Spur f; (of smoke) Rauchfahne f; (of dust) Staubwolke f; (road) Pfad m, Weg m ♦ vt (animal) verfolgen; (person) folgen +dat; (drag) schleppen ♦ vi (hang loosely) schleifen; (plants) sich ranken; (be behind) hinterherhinken; (SPORT) weit zurückliegen; (walk) zuckeln; ~ **behind** vi zurückbleiben; **~er** n Anhänger m; (US: caravan) Wohnwagen m; (for film) Vorschau f; **~er truck** (US) n Sattelschlepper m

train [treɪn] n Zug m; (of dress) Schleppe f; (series) Folge f ♦ vt (teach: person) ausbilden; (: animal) abrichten; (: mind) schulen; (SPORT) trainieren; (aim) richten ♦ vi (exercise) trainieren; (study) ausgebildet werden; ~ **of thought** Gedankengang m; **to ~ sth on** (aim) etw richten auf +acc; **~ed** adj (eye) geschult; (person, voice) ausgebildet; **~ee** n Lehrling m; Praktikant(in) m(f); **~er** n (SPORT) Trainer m; Ausbilder m; **~ers** npl Turnschuhe pl; **~ing** n (for occupation) Ausbildung f; (SPORT) Training nt; **in ~ing** im Training; **~ing college** n Pädagogische Hochschule f, Lehrerseminar nt; **~ing shoes** npl Turnschuhe pl

traipse [treɪps] vi latschen

trait [treɪt] n Zug m, Merkmal nt

traitor ['treɪtəʳ] n Verräter m

trajectory [trə'dʒɛktərɪ] n Flugbahn f

tram [træm] (BRIT) n (also: ~**car**) Straßenbahn f

tramp [træmp] n Landstreicher m ♦ vi (trudge) stampfen, stapfen

trample ['træmpl] vt (nieder)trampeln ♦ vi (herum)trampeln; **to ~ (underfoot)** herumtrampeln auf +dat

trampoline ['træmpəliːn] n Trampolin m

tranquil ['træŋkwɪl] adj ruhig, friedlich; **~lity** [træŋ'kwɪlɪtɪ] (US **tranquility**) n Ruhe f; **~lizer** (US **tranquilizer**) n Beruhigungsmittel nt

transact [træn'zækt] vt abwickeln; **~ion** [træn'zækʃən] n Abwicklung f; (piece of business) Geschäft nt, Transaktion f

transcend [træn'sɛnd] vt übersteigen

transcription [træn'skrɪpʃən] n Transkription f; (product) Abschrift f

transfer [n 'trænsfəʳ, vb træns'fɜːʳ] n (transferring) Übertragung f; (of business) Umzug m; (being ~red) Versetzung f; (design) Abziehbild nt; (SPORT) Transfer m ♦ vt (business) verlegen; (person) versetzen; (prisoner) überführen; (drawing) übertragen; (money) überweisen; **to ~ the charges** (BRIT: TEL) ein R-Gespräch führen; ~ **desk** n (AVIAT) Transitschalter m

transform [træns'fɔːm] vt umwandeln; **~ation** [trænsfə'meɪʃən] n Umwandlung f, Verwandlung f

transfusion [træns'fjuːʒən] n Blutübertragung f, Transfusion f

transient ['trænzɪənt] adj kurz(lebig)

transistor [træn'zɪstəʳ] n (ELEC) Transistor m; (RAD) Transistorradio nt

transit ['trænzɪt] n: **in ~** unterwegs

transition [træn'zɪʃən] n Übergang m; **~al** adj Übergangs-

transit lounge n Warteraum m

translate [trænz'leɪt] vt, vi übersetzen; **translation** [trænz'leɪʃən] n Übersetzung f; **translator** [trænz'leɪtəʳ] n Übersetzer(in) m(f)

transmission [trænz'mɪʃən] n (of information) Übermittlung f; (ELEC, MED, TV) Übertragung f; (AUT) Getriebe nt

transmit [trænz'mɪt] vt (message) übermitteln; (ELEC, MED, TV) übertragen; **~ter** n Sender m

transparency [træns'pɛərnsɪ] n Durchsichtigkeit f; (BRIT: PHOT) Dia(positiv) nt

transparent [træns'pærnt] adj durchsichtig;

⚠ *For information on spelling reform see page 615*

(fig) offenkundig

transpire [træns'paɪəʳ] *vi (turn out)* sich herausstellen; *(happen)* passieren

transplant [*vb* træns'plɑːnt, *n* 'trænsplɑːnt] *vt* umpflanzen; *(MED, also fig: person)* verpflanzen ♦ *n (MED)* Transplantation *f*; *(organ)* Transplantat *nt*

transport [*n* 'trænspɔːt, *vb* træns'pɔːt] *n* Transport *m*, Beförderung *f* ♦ *vt* befördern; transportieren; **means of ~** Transportmittel *nt*; **~ation** ['trænspɔː'teɪʃən] *n* Transport *m*, Beförderung *f*; *(means)* Beförderungsmittel *nt*; *(cost)* Transportkosten *pl*; **~ café** *(BRIT)* *n* Fernfahrerlokal *nt*

trap [træp] *n* Falle *f*; *(carriage)* zweirädrige(r) Einspänner *m*; *(inf: mouth)* Klappe *f* ♦ *vt* fangen; *(person)* in eine Falle locken; **~door** *n* Falltür *f*

trappings ['træpɪŋz] *npl* Aufmachung *f*

trash [træʃ] *n (rubbish)* Plunder *m*; *(nonsense)* Mist *m*; *(US n)* Mülleimer *m*; **~y** *(inf)* *adj* minderwertig, wertlos; *(novel)* Schund-

traumatic [trɔː'mætɪk] *adj* traumatisch

travel ['trævl] *n* Reisen *nt* ♦ *vi* reisen ♦ *vt (distance)* zurücklegen; *(country)* bereisen; **~s** *npl (journeys)* Reisen *pl*; **~ agency** *n* Reisebüro *nt*; **~ agent** *n* Reisebürokaufmann(-frau) *m(f)*; **~ler** *(US* **traveler)** *n* Reisende(r) *mf*; *(salesman)* Handlungsreisende(r) *m*; **~ler's cheque** *(US* **traveler's check)** *n* Reisescheck *m*; **~ling** *(US* **traveling)** *n* Reisen *nt*; **~sick** *adj* reisekrank; **~ sickness** *n* Reisekrankheit *f*

trawler ['trɔːləʳ] *n (NAUT, FISHING)* Fischdampfer *m*, Trawler *m*

tray [treɪ] *n (tea ~)* Tablett *nt*; *(for mail)* Ablage *f*

treacherous ['tretʃərəs] *adj* verräterisch; *(road)* tückisch

treachery ['tretʃərɪ] *n* Verrat *m*

treacle ['triːkl] *n* Sirup *m*, Melasse *f*

tread [tred] *(pt* **trod**, *pp* **trodden)** *n* Schritt *m*, Tritt *m*; *(of stair)* Stufe *f*; *(on tyre)* Profil *nt* ♦ *vi* treten; **~ on** *vt fus* treten auf +*acc*

treason ['triːzn] *n* Verrat *m*

treasure ['treʒəʳ] *n* Schatz *m* ♦ *vt* schätzen

treasurer ['treʒərəʳ] *n* Kassenverwalter *m*, Schatzmeister *m*

treasury ['treʒərɪ] *n (POL)* Finanzministerium *nt*

treat [triːt] *n* besondere Freude *f* ♦ *vt (deal with)* behandeln; **to ~ sb to sth** jdm etw spendieren

treatise ['triːtɪz] *n* Abhandlung *f*

treatment ['triːtmənt] *n* Behandlung *f*

treaty ['triːtɪ] *n* Vertrag *m*

treble ['trebl] *adj* dreifach ♦ *vt* verdreifachen; **~ clef** *n* Violinschlüssel *m*

tree [triː] *n* Baum *m*; **~ trunk** *n* Baumstamm *m*

trek [trek] *n* Treck *m*, Zug *m*; *(inf)* anstrengende(r) Weg *m* ♦ *vi* trecken

trellis ['trelɪs] *n* Gitter *nt*; *(for gardening)* Spalier *nt*

tremble ['trembl] *vi* zittern; *(ground)* beben

tremendous [trɪ'mendəs] *adj* gewaltig, kolossal; *(inf: good)* prima

tremor ['treməʳ] *n* Zittern *nt*; *(of earth)* Beben *nt*

trench [trentʃ] *n* Graben *m*; *(MIL)* Schützengraben *m*

trend [trend] *n* Tendenz *f*; **~y** *(inf)* *adj* modisch

trepidation [trepɪ'deɪʃən] *n* Beklommenheit *f*

trespass ['trespəs] *vi*: **to ~ on** widerrechtlich betreten; **"no ~ing"** „Betreten verboten"

trestle ['tresl] *n* Bock *m*; **~ table** *n* Klapptisch *m*

trial ['traɪəl] *n (JUR)* Prozeß △ *m*; *(test)* Versuch *m*, Probe *f*; *(hardship)* Prüfung *f*; **by ~ and error** durch Ausprobieren; **~ period** *n* Probezeit *f*

triangle ['traɪæŋgl] *n* Dreieck *nt*; *(MUS)* Triangel *f*; **triangular** [traɪ'æŋgjuləʳ] *adj* dreieckig

tribal ['traɪbl] *adj* Stammes-

tribe [traɪb] *n* Stamm *m*; **~sman** *(irreg)* *n* Stammesangehörige(r) *m*

tribulation [trɪbju'leɪʃən] *n* Not *f*, Mühsal *f*

tribunal [traɪ'bjuːnl] *n* Gericht *nt*; *(inquiry)* Untersuchungsausschuß △ *m*

△ *Informationen zur Rechtschreibreform Seite 615*

tributary ['trɪbjutərɪ] n Nebenfluß △ m

tribute ['trɪbjuːt] n (admiration) Zeichen nt der Hochachtung; **to pay ~ to sb/sth** jdm/einer Sache Tribut zollen

trick [trɪk] n Trick m; (CARDS) Stich m ♦ vt überlisten, beschwindeln; **to play a ~ on sb** jdm einen Streich spielen; **that should do the ~** das müßte eigentlich klappen; **~ery** n Tricks pl

trickle ['trɪkl] n Tröpfeln nt; (small river) Rinnsal nt ♦ vi tröpfeln; (seep) sickern

tricky ['trɪkɪ] adj (problem) schwierig; (situation) kitzlig

tricycle ['traɪsɪkl] n Dreirad nt

trifle ['traɪfl] n Kleinigkeit f; (COOK) Trifle m ♦ adv: **a ~ ...** ein bißchen △ ...; **trifling** adj geringfügig

trigger ['trɪɡə'] n Drücker m; **~ off** vt auslösen

trim [trɪm] adj gepflegt; (figure) schlank ♦ n (gute) Verfassung f; (embellishment, on car) Verzierung f ♦ vt (clip) schneiden; (trees) stutzen; (decorate) besetzen; (sails) trimmen; **~mings** npl (decorations) Verzierung f, Verzierungen pl; (extras) Zubehör nt

Trinity ['trɪnɪtɪ] n: **the ~** die Dreieinigkeit f

trinket ['trɪŋkɪt] n kleine(s) Schmuckstück nt

trip [trɪp] n (kurze) Reise f; (outing) Ausflug m; (stumble) Stolpern nt ♦ vi (stumble) stolpern; **on a ~** auf Reisen; **~ up** vi stolpern; (fig) stolpern, einen Fehler machen ♦ vt zu Fall bringen; (fig) hereinlegen

tripe [traɪp] n (food) Kutteln pl; (rubbish) Mist m

triple ['trɪpl] adj dreifach

triplets ['trɪplɪts] npl Drillinge pl

triplicate ['trɪplɪkət] n: **in ~** in dreifacher Ausfertigung

tripod ['traɪpɔd] n (PHOT) Stativ nt

trite [traɪt] adj banal

triumph ['traɪʌmf] n Triumph m ♦ vi: **to ~ (over)** triumphieren (über +acc); **~ant** [traɪˈʌmfənt] adj triumphierend

trivia ['trɪvɪə] npl Trivialitäten pl

trivial ['trɪvɪəl] adj gering(fügig), trivial

trod [trɔd] pt of **tread**; **~den** pp of **tread**

trolley ['trɔlɪ] n Handwagen m; (in shop) Einkaufswagen m; (for luggage) Kofferkuli m; (table) Teewagen m; **~ bus** n Oberleitungsbus m, Obus m

trombone [trɔm'bəun] n Posaune f

troop [truːp] n Schar f; (MIL) Trupp m; **~s** npl (MIL) Truppen pl; **~ in/out** vi hinein-/hinausströmen; **~ing the colour** n (ceremony) Fahnenparade f

trophy ['trəufɪ] n Trophäe f

tropic ['trɔpɪk] n Wendekreis m; **~al** adj tropisch

trot [trɔt] n Trott m ♦ vi trotten; **on the ~** (BRIT: fig: inf) in einer Tour

trouble ['trʌbl] n (problems) Ärger m; (worry) Sorge f; (in country, industry) Unruhen pl; (effort) Mühe f; (MED): **stomach ~** Magenbeschwerden pl ♦ vt (disturb) stören; **~s** npl (POL etc) Unruhen pl; **to ~ to do sth** sich bemühen, etw zu tun; **to be in ~** Probleme or Ärger haben; **to go to the ~ of doing sth** sich die Mühe machen, etw zu tun; **what's the ~?** was ist los?; (to sick person) wo fehlt's?; **~d** adj (person) beunruhigt; (country) geplagt; **~-free** adj sorglos; **~maker** n Unruhestifter m; **~shooter** n Vermittler m; **~some** adj lästig, unangenehm; (child) schwierig

trough [trɔf] n Trog m; (channel) Rinne f, Kanal m; (MET) Tief nt

trousers ['trauzəz] npl Hose f

trout [traut] n Forelle f

trowel ['trauəl] n Kelle f

truant ['truənt] n: **to play ~** (BRIT) (die Schule) schwänzen

truce [truːs] n Waffenstillstand m

truck [trʌk] n Lastwagen m; (RAIL) offene(r) Güterwagen m; **~ driver** n Lastwagenfahrer m; **~ farm** (US) n Gemüsegärtnerei f

trudge [trʌdʒ] vi sich (mühselig) dahinschleppen

true [truː] adj (exact) wahr; (genuine) echt; (friend) treu

truffle ['trʌfl] n Trüffel f or m

truly ['truːlɪ] adv wirklich; **yours ~** Ihr sehr

△ For information on spelling reform see page 615

ergebener

trump [trʌmp] n (CARDS) Trumpf m

trumpet ['trʌmpɪt] n Trompete f

truncheon ['trʌntʃən] n Gummiknüppel m

trundle ['trʌndl] vt schieben ♦ vi: **to ~ along** entlangrollen

trunk [trʌŋk] n (of tree) (Baum)stamm m; (ANAT) Rumpf m; (box) Truhe f, Überseekoffer m; (of elephant) Rüssel m; (US: AUT) Kofferraum m; **~s** npl (also: **swimming ~s**) Badehose f

truss [trʌs] vt (also: **~ up**) fesseln

trust [trʌst] n (confidence) Vertrauen nt; (for land etc) Treuhandvermögen nt ♦ vt (rely on) vertrauen +dat, sich verlassen auf +acc; (hope) hoffen; (entrust): **to ~ sth to sb** jdm etw anvertrauen; **~ed** adj treu; **~ee** [trʌs'tiː] n Vermögensverwalter m; **~ful** adj vertrauensvoll; **~ing** adj vertrauensvoll; **~worthy** adj vertrauenswürdig; (account) glaubwürdig

truth [truːθ] n Wahrheit f; **~ful** adj ehrlich

try [traɪ] n Versuch m ♦ vt (attempt) versuchen; (test) (aus)probieren; (JUR: person) unter Anklage stellen; (: case) verhandeln; (courage, patience) auf die Probe stellen ♦ vi (make effort) versuchen, sich bemühen; **to have a ~** es versuchen; **to ~ to do sth** versuchen, etw zu tun; **~ on** vt (dress) anprobieren; (hat) aufprobieren; **~ out** vt ausprobieren; **~ing** adj schwierig

T-shirt ['tiːʃəːt] n T-shirt nt

T-square ['tiːskwɛəʳ] n Reißschiene f

tub [tʌb] n Wanne f, Kübel m; (for margarine etc) Becher m

tubby ['tʌbɪ] adj rundlich

tube [tjuːb] n Röhre f, Rohr nt; (for toothpaste etc) Tube f; (underground) U-Bahn f; (AUT) Schlauch m

tuberculosis [tjubəːkjuˈləusɪs] n Tuberkulose f

tube station n (in London) U-Bahnstation f; **tubing** ['tjuːbɪŋ] n Schlauch m; **tubular** ['tjuːbjuləʳ] adj röhrenförmig

TUC (BRIT) n abbr = **Trades Union Congress**

tuck [tʌk] n (fold) Falte f, Einschlag m ♦ vt (put) stecken; (gather) fälteln, einschlagen; **~ away** vt wegstecken; **~ in** vt hineinstecken; (blanket etc) feststecken; (person) zudecken ♦ vi (eat) hineinhauen, zulangen; **~ up** vt (child) warm zudecken; **~ shop** n Süßwarenladen m

Tuesday ['tjuːzdɪ] n Dienstag m

tuft [tʌft] n Büschel m

tug [tʌg] n (jerk) Zerren nt, Ruck m; (NAUT) Schleppdampfer m ♦ vt, vi zerren, ziehen; (boat) schleppen; **~ of war** n Tauziehen nt

tuition [tjuːˈɪʃən] n (BRIT) Unterricht m; (: private ~) Privatunterricht m; (US: school fees) Schulgeld nt

tulip ['tjuːlɪp] n Tulpe f

tumble ['tʌmbl] n (fall) Sturz m ♦ vi fallen, stürzen; **~ to** vt fus kapieren; **~down** adj baufällig; **~ dryer** (BRIT) n Trockner m; **~r** ['tʌmbləʳ] n (glass) Trinkglas nt

tummy ['tʌmɪ] (inf) n Bauch m; **~ upset** n Magenverstimmung f

tumour ['tjuːməʳ] (US **tumor**) n Geschwulst f, Tumor m

tumultuous [tjuːˈmʌltjuəs] adj (welcome, applause etc) stürmisch

tuna ['tjuːnə] n Thunfisch ⚠ m

tune [tjuːn] n Melodie f ♦ vt (MUS) stimmen; (AUT) richtig einstellen; **to sing in ~/out of ~** richtig/falsch singen; **to be out of ~ with** nicht harmonieren mit; **~ in** vi einschalten; **~ up** vi (MUS) stimmen; **~ful** adj melodisch; **~r** n (RAD) Tuner m; (person) (Instrumenten)stimmer m; **piano ~r** Klavierstimmer(in) m(f)

tunic ['tjuːnɪk] n Waffenrock m; (loose garment) lange Bluse f

tuning ['tjuːnɪŋ] n (RAD, AUT) Einstellen nt; (MUS) Stimmen nt; **~ fork** n Stimmgabel f

Tunisia [tjuːˈnɪzɪə] n Tunesien nt

tunnel ['tʌnl] n Tunnel m, Unterführung f ♦ vi einen Tunnel anlegen

turbulent ['təːbjulənt] adj stürmisch

tureen [təˈriːn] n Terrine f

turf [təːf] n Rasen m; (piece) Sode f ♦ vt mit Grassoden belegen; **~ out** (inf) vt rauswerfen

⚠ *Informationen zur Rechtschreibreform Seite 615*

turgid ['tɜːdʒɪd] *adj* geschwollen
Turk [tɜːk] *n* Türke *m*, Türkin *f*
Turkey ['tɜːkɪ] *n* Türkei *f*
turkey ['tɜːkɪ] *n* Puter *m*, Truthahn *m*
Turkish ['tɜːkɪʃ] *adj* türkisch ♦ *n* (*LING*)
Türkisch *nt*
turmoil ['tɜːmɔɪl] *n* Aufruhr *m*, Tumult *m*
turn [tɜːn] *n* (*rotation*) (Um)drehung *f*;
(*performance*) (Programm)nummer *f*; (*MED*)
Schock *m* ♦ *vt* (*rotate*) drehen; (*change
position of*) umdrehen, wenden; (*page*)
umblättern; (*transform*): **to ~ sth into sth**
etw in etw *acc* verwandeln; (*direct*)
zuwenden ♦ *vi* (*rotate*) sich drehen; (*change
direction: in car*) abbiegen; (*: wind*) drehen;
(*~ round*) umdrehen, wenden; (*become*)
werden; (*leaves*) sich verfärben; (*milk*) sauer
werden; (*weather*) umschlagen; **to do sb a
good ~** jdm etwas Gutes tun; **it's your ~**
du bist dran *or* an der Reihe; **in ~, by ~s**
abwechselnd; **to take ~s** sich abwechseln;
it gave me quite a ~ das hat mich schön
erschreckt; **"no left ~"** (*AUT*)
„Linksabbiegen verboten"; **~ away** *vi* sich
abwenden; **~ back** *vi* umdrehen; (*person*)
zurückschicken; (*clock*) zurückstellen ♦ *vi*
umkehren; **~ down** *vt* (*refuse*) ablehnen;
(*fold down*) umschlagen; **~ in** *vi* (*go to bed*)
ins Bett gehen ♦ *vt* (*fold inwards*) einwärts
biegen; **~ off** *vi* abbiegen ♦ *vt* ausschalten;
(*tap*) zudrehen; (*machine, electricity*)
abstellen; **~ on** *vt* (*light*) anschalten,
einschalten; (*tap*) aufdrehen; (*machine*)
anstellen; **~ out** *vi* (*prove to be*) sich
erweisen; (*people*) sich entwickeln ♦ *vt*
(*light*) ausschalten; (*gas*) abstellen; (*produce*)
produzieren; **how did the cake ~ out?** wie
ist der Kuchen geworden?; **~ over** *vi*
(*person*) sich umdrehen ♦ *vt* (*object*)
umdrehen, wenden; (*page*) umblättern; **~
round** *vi* (*person, vehicle*) sich
herumdrehen; (*rotate*) sich drehen; **~ up** *vi*
auftauchen ♦ *vt* (*collar*) hochklappen,
hochstellen; (*nose*) rümpfen; (*increase: radio*)
lauter stellen; (*: heat*) höher drehen; **~ing** *n*
(*in road*) Abzweigung *f*; **~ing point** *n*
Wendepunkt *m*

turnip ['tɜːnɪp] *n* Steckrübe *f*
turnout ['tɜːnaʊt] *n* (*Besucher*)zahl *f*
turnover ['tɜːnəʊvəʳ] *n* Umsatz *m*; (*of staff*)
Wechsel *m*
turnpike ['tɜːnpaɪk] (*US*) *n*
gebührenpflichtige Straße *f*
turn: ~stile ['tɜːnstaɪl] *n* Drehkreuz *nt*;
~table ['tɜːnteɪbl] *n* (*of record player*)
Plattenteller *m*; (*RAIL*) Drehscheibe *f*; **~-up**
['tɜːnʌp] (*BRIT*) *n* (*on trousers*) Aufschlag *m*
turpentine ['tɜːpəntaɪn] *n* Terpentin *nt*
turquoise ['tɜːkwɔɪz] *n* (*gem*) Türkis *m*;
(*colour*) Türkis *nt* ♦ *adj* türkisfarben
turret ['tʌrɪt] *n* Turm *m*
turtle ['tɜːtl] *n* Schildkröte *f*; **~ neck
(sweater)** *n* Pullover *m* mit
Schildkrötkragen
tusk [tʌsk] *n* Stoßzahn *m*
tussle ['tʌsl] *n* Balgerei *f*
tutor ['tjuːtəʳ] *n* (*teacher*) Privatlehrer *m*;
(*college instructor*) Tutor *m*; **~ial** [tjuːˈtɔːrɪəl]
n (*UNIV*) Kolloquium *nt*, Seminarübung *f*
tuxedo [tʌkˈsiːdəʊ] (*US*) *n* Smoking *m*
TV [tiːˈviː] *n abbr* (= *television*) TV *nt*
twang [twæŋ] *n* scharfe(r) Ton *m*; (*of voice*)
Näseln *nt*
tweezers ['twiːzəz] *npl* Pinzette *f*
twelfth [twelfθ] *adj* zwölfte(r, s)
twelve [twelv] *num* zwölf; **at ~ o'clock**
(*midday*) um 12 Uhr; (*midnight*) um Null
Uhr
twentieth ['twentɪɪθ] *adj* zwanzigste(r, s)
twenty ['twentɪ] *num* zwanzig
twice [twaɪs] *adv* zweimal; **~ as much**
doppelt soviel
twiddle ['twɪdl] *vt, vi*: **to ~ (with) sth** an
etw *dat* herumdrehen; **to ~ one's thumbs**
(*fig*) Däumchen drehen
twig [twɪg] *n* dünne(r) Zweig *m* ♦ *vt* (*inf*)
kapieren, merken
twilight ['twaɪlaɪt] *n* Zwielicht *nt*
twin [twɪn] *n* Zwilling *m* ♦ *adj* Zwillings-;
(*very similar*) Doppel- ♦ *vt* (*towns*) zu
Partnerstädten machen; **~-bedded room**
n Zimmer *nt* mit zwei Einzelbetten; **~ beds**
npl zwei (gleiche) Einzelbetten *pl*
twine [twaɪn] *n* Bindfaden *m* ♦ *vi* (*plants*)

⚠ *For information on spelling reform see page 615*

sich ranken

twinge [twɪndʒ] *n* stechende(r) Schmerz *m*, Stechen *nt*

twinkle ['twɪŋkl] *n* Funkeln *nt*, Blitzen *nt* ♦ *vi* funkeln

twinned *adj*: **to be ~ with** die Partnerstadt von ... sein

twirl [twəːl] *n* Wirbel *m* ♦ *vt, vi* (herum)wirbeln

twist [twɪst] *n* (~*ing*) Drehung *f*; (*bend*) Kurve *f* ♦ *vt* (*turn*) drehen; (*make crooked*) verbiegen; (*distort*) verdrehen ♦ *vi* (*wind*) sich drehen; (*curve*) sich winden

twit [twɪt] (*inf*) *n* Idiot *m*

twitch [twɪtʃ] *n* Zucken *nt* ♦ *vi* zucken

two [tuː] *num* zwei; **to put ~ and ~ together** seine Schlüsse ziehen; **~-door** *adj* zweitürig; **~-faced** *adj* falsch; **~-fold** *adj, adv* zweifach, doppelt; **to increase ~fold** verdoppeln; **~-piece** *adj* zweiteilig; **~-piece (suit)** *n* Zweiteiler *m*; **~-piece (swimsuit)** *n* zweiteilige(r) Badeanzug *m*; **~-seater** *n* (*plane, car*) Zweisitzer *m*; **~some** *n* Paar *nt*; **~-way** *adj* (*traffic*) Gegen-

tycoon [taɪˈkuːn] *n*: **(business) ~** (Industrie)magnat *m*

type [taɪp] *n* Typ *m*, Art *f*; (*PRINT*) Type *f* ♦ *vt, vi* maschineschreiben ⚠, tippen; **~-cast** *adj* (*THEAT, TV*) auf eine Rolle festgelegt; **~face** *n* Schrift *f*; **~script** *n* maschinegeschriebene(r) Text *m*; **~writer** *n* Schreibmaschine *f*; **~written** *adj* maschinegeschrieben

typhoid ['taɪfɔɪd] *n* Typhus *m*

typical ['tɪpɪkl] *adj*: **~ (of)** typisch (für)

typify ['tɪpɪfaɪ] *vt* typisch sein für

typing ['taɪpɪŋ] *n* Maschineschreiben *nt*

typist ['taɪpɪst] *n* Maschineschreiber(in) *m(f)*, Tippse *f* (*inf*)

tyrant ['taɪərnt] *n* Tyrann *m*

tyre ['taɪəʳ] (*US* **tire**) *n* Reifen *m*; **~ pressure** *n* Reifendruck *m*

U, u

U-bend ['juːbend] *n* (*in pipe*) U-Bogen *m*

udder ['ʌdəʳ] *n* Euter *nt*

UFO ['juːfəu] *n abbr* (= *unidentified flying object*) UFO *nt*

ugh [əːh] *excl* hu

ugliness ['ʌglɪnɪs] *n* Häßlichkeit ⚠ *f*

ugly ['ʌglɪ] *adj* häßlich ⚠; (*bad*) böse, schlimm

UHT *abbr* (= *ultra heat treated*): **UHT milk** H-Milch *f*

UK *n abbr* = **United Kingdom**

ulcer ['ʌlsəʳ] *n* Geschwür *nt*

Ulster ['ʌlstəʳ] *n* Ulster *nt*

ulterior [ʌlˈtɪərɪəʳ] *adj*: **~ motive** Hintergedanke *m*

ultimate ['ʌltɪmət] *adj* äußerste(r, s), allerletzte(r, s); **~ly** *adv* schließlich, letzten Endes

ultrasound ['ʌltrəsaund] *n* (*MED*) Ultraschall *m*

umbilical cord [ʌmˈbɪlɪkl-] *n* Nabelschnur *f*

umbrella [ʌmˈbrelə] *n* Schirm *m*

umpire ['ʌmpaɪəʳ] *n* Schiedsrichter *m* ♦ *vt, vi* schiedsrichtern

umpteenth [ʌmpˈtiːnθ] (*inf*) *adj* zig; **for the ~ time** zum X-ten Mal

UN *n abbr* = **United Nations**

unable [ʌnˈeɪbl] *adj*: **to be ~ to do sth** etw nicht tun können

unacceptable [ʌnəkˈseptəbl] *adj* unannehmbar, nicht akzeptabel

unaccompanied [ʌnəˈkʌmpənɪd] *adj* ohne Begleitung

unaccountably [ʌnəˈkauntəblɪ] *adv* unerklärlich

unaccustomed [ʌnəˈkʌstəmd] *adj* nicht gewöhnt; (*unusual*) ungewohnt; **~ to** nicht gewöhnt an +*acc*

unanimous [juːˈnænɪməs] *adj* einmütig; (*vote*) einstimmig; **~ly** *adv* einmütig; einstimmig

unarmed [ʌnˈɑːmd] *adj* unbewaffnet

unashamed [ʌnəˈʃeɪmd] adj schamlos

unassuming [ʌnəˈsjuːmɪŋ] adj bescheiden

unattached [ʌnəˈtætʃt] adj ungebunden

unattended [ʌnəˈtendɪd] adj (person) unbeaufsichtigt; (thing) unbewacht

unauthorized [ʌnˈɔːθəraɪzd] adj unbefugt

unavoidable [ʌnəˈvɔɪdəbl] adj unvermeidlich

unaware [ʌnəˈweəʳ] adj: **to be ~ of sth** sich dat einer Sache gen nicht bewußt Δ sein; **~s** adv unversehens

unbalanced [ʌnˈbælənst] adj unausgeglichen; (mentally) gestört

unbearable [ʌnˈbeərəbl] adj unerträglich

unbeatable [ʌnˈbiːtəbl] adj unschlagbar

unbeknown(st) [ʌnbɪˈnəʊn(st)] adv: **~ to me** ohne mein Wissen

unbelievable [ʌnbɪˈliːvəbl] adj unglaublich

unbend [ʌnˈbend] (irreg: like bend) vt geradebiegen ♦ vi aus sich herausgehen

unbias(s)ed [ʌnˈbaɪəst] adj unparteiisch

unborn [ʌnˈbɔːn] adj ungeboren

unbreakable [ʌnˈbreɪkəbl] adj unzerbrechlich

unbridled [ʌnˈbraɪdld] adj ungezügelt

unbroken [ʌnˈbrəʊkən] adj (period) ununterbrochen; (spirit) ungebrochen; (record) unübertroffen

unburden [ʌnˈbɜːdn] vt: **to ~ o.s.** (jdm) sein Herz ausschütten

unbutton [ʌnˈbʌtn] vt aufknöpfen

uncalled-for [ʌnˈkɔːldfɔːʳ] adj unnötig

uncanny [ʌnˈkænɪ] adj unheimlich

unceasing [ʌnˈsiːsɪŋ] adj unaufhörlich

unceremonious [ʌnserɪˈməʊnɪəs] adj (abrupt, rude) brüsk; (exit, departure) überstürzt

uncertain [ʌnˈsɜːtn] adj unsicher; (doubtful) ungewiß Δ; (unreliable) unbeständig; (vague) undeutlich, vag(e); **~ty** n Ungewißheit Δ f

unchanged [ʌnˈtʃeɪndʒd] adj unverändert

unchecked [ʌnˈtʃekt] adj ungeprüft; (not stopped: advance) ungehindert

uncivilized [ʌnˈsɪvɪlaɪzd] adj unzivilisiert

uncle [ˈʌŋkl] n Onkel m

uncomfortable [ʌnˈkʌmfətəbl] adj unbequem, ungemütlich

uncommon [ʌnˈkɒmən] adj ungewöhnlich; (outstanding) außergewöhnlich

uncompromising [ʌnˈkɒmprəmaɪzɪŋ] adj kompromißlos Δ, unnachgiebig

unconcerned [ʌnkənˈsɜːnd] adj unbekümmert; (indifferent) gleichgültig

unconditional [ʌnkənˈdɪʃənl] adj bedingungslos

unconscious [ʌnˈkɒnʃəs] adj (MED) bewußtlos Δ; (not meant) unbeabsichtigt ♦ n: **the ~** das Unbewußte Δ; **~ly** adv unbewußt Δ

uncontrollable [ʌnkənˈtrəʊləbl] adj unkontrollierbar, unbändig

unconventional [ʌnkənˈvenʃənl] adj unkonventionell

uncouth [ʌnˈkuːθ] adj grob

uncover [ʌnˈkʌvəʳ] vt aufdecken

undecided [ʌndɪˈsaɪdɪd] adj unschlüssig

undeniable [ʌndɪˈnaɪəbl] adj unleugbar

under [ˈʌndəʳ] prep unter ♦ adv darunter; **~ there** da drunter; **~ repair** in Reparatur

underage [ʌndərˈeɪdʒ] adj minderjährig

undercarriage [ˈʌndəkærɪdʒ] (BRIT) n (AVIAT) Fahrgestell nt

undercharge [ʌndəˈtʃɑːdʒ] vt: **to ~ sb** jdm zu wenig berechnen

undercoat [ˈʌndəkəʊt] n (paint) Grundierung f

undercover [ʌndəˈkʌvəʳ] adj Geheim-

undercurrent [ˈʌndəkʌrnt] n Unterströmung f

undercut [ʌndəˈkʌt] (irreg: like cut) vt unterbieten

underdeveloped [ˈʌndədɪˈveləpt] adj Entwicklungs-, unterentwickelt

underdog [ˈʌndədɒg] n Unterlegene(r) mf

underdone [ʌndəˈdʌn] adj (COOK) nicht gar, nicht durchgebraten

underestimate [ʌndərˈestɪmeɪt] vt unterschätzen

underexposed [ˈʌndərɪksˈpəʊzd] adj unterbelichtet

underfoot [ʌndəˈfʊt] adv am Boden

undergo [ʌndəˈgəʊ] (irreg: like go) vt (experience) durchmachen; (test, operation)

Δ For information on spelling reform see page 615

sich unterziehen +*dat*

undergraduate [ʌndə'grædjuɪt] *n* Student(in) *m(f)*

underground ['ʌndəgraund] *n* U-Bahn *f* ♦ *adj* Untergrund-

undergrowth ['ʌndəgrəuθ] *n* Gestrüpp *nt*, Unterholz *nt*

underhand(ed) [ʌndə'hænd(ɪd)] *adj* hinterhältig

underlie [ʌndə'laɪ] (*irreg: like* lie) *vt* zugrundeliegen +*dat*

underline [ʌndə'laɪn] *vt* unterstreichen; (*emphasize*) betonen

underling ['ʌndəlɪŋ] *n* Handlanger *m*

undermine [ʌndə'maɪn] *vt* untergraben

underneath [ʌndə'niːθ] *adv* darunter ♦ *prep* unter

underpaid [ʌndə'peɪd] *adj* unterbezahlt

underpants ['ʌndəpænts] *npl* Unterhose *f*

underpass ['ʌndəpɑːs] (*BRIT*) *n* Unterführung *f*

underprivileged [ʌndə'prɪvɪlɪdʒd] *adj* benachteiligt, unterprivilegiert

underrate [ʌndə'reɪt] *vt* unterschätzen

undershirt ['ʌndəʃəːt] (*US*) *n* Unterhemd *nt*

undershorts ['ʌndəʃɔːts] (*US*) *npl* Unterhose *f*

underside ['ʌndəsaɪd] *n* Unterseite *f*

underskirt ['ʌndəskəːt] (*BRIT*) *n* Unterrock *m*

understand [ʌndə'stænd] (*irreg: like* stand) *vt*, *vi* verstehen; **I ~ that ...** ich habe gehört, daß ...; **am I to ~ that ...?** soll das (etwa) heißen, daß ...?; **what do you ~ by that?** was verstehen Sie darunter?; **it is understood that ...** es wurde vereinbart, daß ...; **to make o.s. understood** sich verständlich machen; **is that understood?** ist das klar?; **~able** *adj* verständlich; **~ing** *n* Verständnis *nt* ♦ *adj* verständnisvoll

understatement ['ʌndəsteɪtmənt] *n* (*quality*) Untertreibung *f*; **that's an ~!** das ist untertrieben!

understood [ʌndə'stud] *pt*, *pp of* **understand** ♦ *adj* klar; (*implied*) angenommen

understudy ['ʌndəstʌdɪ] *n* Ersatz(schau)spieler(in) *m(f)*

undertake [ʌndə'teɪk] (*irreg: like* take) *vt* unternehmen ♦ *vi*: **to ~ to do sth** sich verpflichten, etw zu tun

undertaker ['ʌndəteɪkəʳ] *n* Leichenbestatter *m*

undertaking ['ʌndəteɪkɪŋ] *n* (*enterprise*) Unternehmen *nt*; (*promise*) Verpflichtung *f*

undertone ['ʌndətəun] *n*: **in an ~** mit gedämpfter Stimme

underwater ['ʌndə'wɔːtəʳ] *adv* unter Wasser ♦ *adj* Unterwasser-

underwear ['ʌndəweəʳ] *n* Unterwäsche *f*

underworld ['ʌndəwəːld] *n* (*of crime*) Unterwelt *f*

underwriter ['ʌndəraɪtəʳ] *n* Assekurant *m*

undesirable [ʌndɪ'zaɪərəbl] *adj* unerwünscht

undies ['ʌndɪz] (*inf*) *npl* (Damen)unterwäsche *f*

undisputed ['ʌndɪs'pjuːtɪd] *adj* unbestritten

undo [ʌn'duː] (*irreg: like* do) *vt* (*unfasten*) öffnen, aufmachen; (*work*) zunichte machen; **~ing** *n* Verderben *nt*

undoubted [ʌn'dautɪd] *adj* unbezweifelt; **~ly** *adv* zweifellos, ohne Zweifel

undress [ʌn'drɛs] *vt* ausziehen ♦ *vi* sich ausziehen

undue [ʌn'djuː] *adj* übermäßig

undulating ['ʌndjuleɪtɪŋ] *adj* wellenförmig; (*country*) wellig

unduly [ʌn'djuːlɪ] *adv* übermäßig

unearth [ʌn'əːθ] *vt* (*dig up*) ausgraben; (*discover*) ans Licht bringen

unearthly [ʌn'əːθlɪ] *adj* (*hour*) nachtschlafen

uneasy [ʌn'iːzɪ] *adj* (*worried*) unruhig; (*feeling*) ungut

uneconomic(al) ['ʌniːkə'nɔmɪk(l)] *adj* unwirtschaftlich

uneducated [ʌn'edjukeɪtɪd] *adj* ungebildet

unemployed [ʌnɪm'plɔɪd] *adj* arbeitslos ♦ *npl*: **the ~** die Arbeitslosen *pl*

unemployment [ʌnɪm'plɔɪmənt] *n* Arbeitslosigkeit *f*

unending [ʌn'endɪŋ] *adj* endlos

unerring [ʌn'əːrɪŋ] *adj* unfehlbar

uneven [ʌn'iːvn] *adj* (*surface*) uneben; (*quality*) ungleichmäßig

⚠ *Informationen zur Rechtschreibreform Seite 615*

unexpected [ʌnɪks'pektɪd] *adj* unerwartet;
~**ly** *adv* unerwartet

unfailing [ʌn'feɪlɪŋ] *adj* nie versagend

unfair [ʌn'feəʳ] *adj* ungerecht, unfair

unfaithful [ʌn'feɪθful] *adj* untreu

unfamiliar [ʌnfə'mɪlɪəʳ] *adj* ungewohnt;
(*person, subject*) unbekannt; **to be ~ with**
nicht kennen +*acc*, nicht vertraut sein mit

unfashionable [ʌn'fæʃnəbl] *adj* unmodern;
(*area etc*) nicht in Mode

unfasten [ʌn'fɑːsn] *vt* öffnen, aufmachen

unfavourable [ʌn'feɪvrəbl] (*US*
unfavorable) *adj* ungünstig

unfeeling [ʌn'fiːlɪŋ] *adj* gefühllos, kalt

unfinished [ʌn'fɪnɪʃt] *adj* unvollendet

unfit [ʌn'fɪt] *adj* ungeeignet; (*in bad health*)
nicht fit; **~ for sth** *or* für etw ungeeignet

unfold [ʌn'fəuld] *vt* entfalten; (*paper*)
auseinanderfalten △ ♦ *vi* (*develop*) sich
entfalten

unforeseen ['ʌnfɔː'siːn] *adj*
unvorhergesehen

unforgettable [ʌnfə'getəbl] *adj*
unvergeßlich △

unforgivable [ʌnfə'gɪvəbl] *adj* unverzeihlich

unfortunate [ʌn'fɔːtʃənət] *adj* unglücklich,
bedauerlich; ~**ly** *adv* leider

unfounded [ʌn'faundɪd] *adj* unbegründet

unfriendly [ʌn'frendlɪ] *adj* unfreundlich

ungainly [ʌn'geɪnlɪ] *adj* linkisch

ungodly [ʌn'gɔdlɪ] *adj* (*hour*)
nachtschlafend; (*row*) heillos

ungrateful [ʌn'greɪtful] *adj* undankbar

unhappiness [ʌn'hæpɪnɪs] *n* Unglück *nt*,
Unglückseligkeit *f*

unhappy [ʌn'hæpɪ] *adj* unglücklich; **~ with**
(*arrangements etc*) unzufrieden mit

unharmed [ʌn'hɑːmd] *adj* wohlbehalten,
unversehrt

UNHCR *n abbr* (= *United Nations High
Commission for Refugees*)
*Flüchtlingshochkommissariat der Vereinten
Nationen*

unhealthy [ʌn'helθɪ] *adj* ungesund

unheard-of [ʌn'hɜːdɔv] *adj* unerhört

unhurt [ʌn'hɜːt] *adj* unverletzt

unidentified [ʌnaɪ'dentɪfaɪd] *adj* unbekannt,
nicht identifiziert

uniform ['juːnɪfɔːm] *n* Uniform *f* ♦ *adj*
einheitlich; ~**ity** [juːnɪ'fɔːmɪtɪ] *n*
Einheitlichkeit *f*

unify ['juːnɪfaɪ] *vt* vereinigen

unilateral [juːnɪ'lætərəl] *adj* einseitig

uninhabited [ʌnɪn'hæbɪtɪd] *adj* unbewohnt

unintentional [ʌnɪn'tenʃənəl] *adj*
unabsichtlich

union ['juːnjən] *n* (*uniting*) Vereinigung *f*;
(*alliance*) Bund *m*, Union *f*; (*trade ~*)
Gewerkschaft *f*; **U~ Jack** *n* Union Jack *m*

unique [juː'niːk] *adj* einzig(artig)

UNISON ['juːnɪsn] *n Gewerkschaft der
Angestellten im Öffentlichen Dienst*

unison ['juːnɪsn] *n* Einstimmigkeit *f*; **in ~**
einstimmig

unit ['juːnɪt] *n* Einheit *f*; **kitchen ~**
Küchenelement *nt*

unite [juː'naɪt] *vt* vereinigen ♦ *vi* sich
vereinigen; ~**d** *adj* vereinigt; (*together*)
vereint; **U~d Kingdom** *n* Vereinigte(s)
Königreich *nt*; **U~d Nations
(Organization)** *n* Vereinte Nationen *pl*;
U~d States (of America) *n* Vereinigte
Staaten *pl* (von Amerika)

unit trust (*BRIT*) *n* Treuhandgesellschaft *f*

unity ['juːnɪtɪ] *n* Einheit *f*; (*agreement*)
Einigkeit *f*

universal [juːnɪ'vɜːsl] *adj* allgemein

universe ['juːnɪvɜːs] *n* (Welt)all *nt*

university [juːnɪ'vɜːsɪtɪ] *n* Universität *f*

unjust [ʌn'dʒʌst] *adj* ungerecht

unkempt [ʌn'kempt] *adj* ungepflegt

unkind [ʌn'kaɪnd] *adj* unfreundlich

unknown [ʌn'nəun] *adj*: **~ (to sb)** (jdm)
unbekannt

unlawful [ʌn'lɔːful] *adj* illegal

unleaded ['ʌn'ledɪd] *adj* bleifrei, unverbleit;
I use ~ ich fahre bleifrei

unleash [ʌn'liːʃ] *vt* entfesseln

unless [ʌn'les] *conj* wenn nicht, es sei denn;
~ he comes es sei denn, er kommt; **~
otherwise stated** sofern nicht anders
angegeben

unlike [ʌn'laɪk] *adj* unähnlich ♦ *prep* im
Gegensatz zu

△ *For information on spelling reform see page 615*

unlikely [ʌn'laɪklɪ] *adj* (*not likely*) unwahrscheinlich; (*unexpected: combination etc*) merkwürdig

unlimited [ʌn'lɪmɪtɪd] *adj* unbegrenzt

unlisted ['ʌn'lɪstɪd] (*US*) *adj* nicht im Telefonbuch stehend

unload [ʌn'ləud] *vt* entladen

unlock [ʌn'lɒk] *vt* aufschließen

unlucky [ʌn'lʌkɪ] *adj* unglücklich; (*person*) unglückselig; **to be ~** Pech haben

unmarried [ʌn'mærɪd] *adj* unverheiratet, ledig

unmask [ʌn'mɑːsk] *vt* entlarven

unmistakable [ʌnmɪs'teɪkəbl] *adj* unverkennbar

unmitigated [ʌn'mɪtɪgeɪtɪd] *adj* ungemildert, ganz

unnatural [ʌn'nætʃrəl] *adj* unnatürlich

unnecessary [ʌn'nesəsərɪ] *adj* unnötig

unnoticed [ʌn'nəutɪst] *adj*: **to go ~** unbemerkt bleiben

UNO ['juːnəu] *n abbr* = **United Nations Organization**

unobtainable [ʌnəb'teɪnəbl] *adj*: **this number is ~** kein Anschluß △ unter dieser Nummer

unobtrusive [ʌnəb'truːsɪv] *adj* unauffällig

unofficial [ʌnə'fɪʃl] *adj* inoffiziell

unpack [ʌn'pæk] *vt, vi* auspacken

unparalleled [ʌn'pærəleld] *adj* beispiellos

unpleasant [ʌn'pleznt] *adj* unangenehm

unplug [ʌn'plʌg] *vt* den Stecker herausziehen von

unpopular [ʌn'pɒpjulər] *adj* (*person*) unbeliebt; (*decision etc*) unpopulär

unprecedented [ʌn'presɪdentɪd] *adj* beispiellos

unpredictable [ʌnprɪ'dɪktəbl] *adj* unvorhersehbar; (*weather, person*) unberechenbar

unprofessional [ʌnprə'feʃənl] *adj* unprofessionell

UNPROFOR *n abbr* (= *United Nations Protection Force*) UNPROFOR *f*

unqualified [ʌn'kwɒlɪfaɪd] *adj* (*success*) uneingeschränkt, voll; (*person*) unqualifiziert

unquestionably [ʌn'kwestʃənəblɪ] *adv* fraglos

unravel [ʌn'rævl] *vt* (*disentangle*) ausfasern, entwirren; (*solve*) lösen

unreal [ʌn'rɪəl] *adj* unwirklich

unrealistic ['ʌnrɪə'lɪstɪk] *adj* unrealistisch

unreasonable [ʌn'riːznəbl] *adj* unvernünftig; (*demand*) übertrieben

unrelated [ʌnrɪ'leɪtɪd] *adj* ohne Beziehung; (*family*) nicht verwandt

unrelenting [ʌnrɪ'lentɪŋ] *adj* unerbittlich

unreliable [ʌnrɪ'laɪəbl] *adj* unzuverlässig

unremitting [ʌnrɪ'mɪtɪŋ] *adj* (*efforts, attempts*) unermüdlich

unreservedly [ʌnrɪ'zɜːvɪdlɪ] *adv* offen; (*believe, trust*) uneingeschränkt; (*cry*) rückhaltlos

unrest [ʌn'rest] *n* (*discontent*) Unruhe *f*; (*fighting*) Unruhen *pl*

unroll [ʌn'rəul] *vt* aufrollen

unruly [ʌn'ruːlɪ] *adj* (*child*) undiszipliniert; schwer lenkbar

unsafe [ʌn'seɪf] *adj* nicht sicher

unsaid [ʌn'sed] *adj*: **to leave sth ~** etw ungesagt lassen

unsatisfactory ['ʌnsætɪs'fæktərɪ] *adj* unbefriedigend; unzulänglich

unsavoury [ʌn'seɪvərɪ] (*US* **unsavory**) *adj* (*fig*) widerwärtig

unscathed [ʌn'skeɪðd] *adj* unversehrt

unscrew [ʌn'skruː] *vt* aufschrauben

unscrupulous [ʌn'skruːpjuləs] *adj* skrupellos

unsettled [ʌn'setld] *adj* (*person*) rastlos; (*weather*) wechselhaft

unshaven [ʌn'ʃeɪvn] *adj* unrasiert

unsightly [ʌn'saɪtlɪ] *adj* unansehnlich

unskilled [ʌn'skɪld] *adj* ungelernt

unspeakable [ʌn'spiːkəbl] *adj* (*joy*) unsagbar; (*crime*) scheußlich

unstable [ʌn'steɪbl] *adj* instabil; (*mentally*) labil

unsteady [ʌn'stedɪ] *adj* unsicher

unstuck [ʌn'stʌk] *adj*: **to come ~** sich lösen; (*fig*) ins Wasser fallen

unsuccessful [ʌnsək'sesful] *adj* erfolglos

unsuitable [ʌn'suːtəbl] *adj* unpassend

unsure [ʌn'ʃuər] *adj* unsicher; **to be ~ of**

o.s. unsicher sein
unsuspecting [ʌnsəsˈpektɪŋ] *adj*
nichtsahnend △
unsympathetic [ˈʌnsɪmpəˈθetɪk] *adj*
gefühllos; (*response*) abweisend; (*unlikeable*)
unsympathisch
untapped [ʌnˈtæpt] *adj* (*resources*)
ungenützt
unthinkable [ʌnˈθɪŋkəbl] *adj* unvorstellbar
untidy [ʌnˈtaɪdɪ] *adj* unordentlich
untie [ʌnˈtaɪ] *vt* aufschnüren
until [ənˈtɪl] *prep, conj* bis; ~ **he comes** bis er
kommt; ~ **then** bis dann; ~ **now** bis jetzt
untimely [ʌnˈtaɪmlɪ] *adj* (*death*) vorzeitig
untold [ʌnˈtəʊld] *adj* unermeßlich △
untoward [ʌntəˈwɔːd] *adj* widrig
untranslatable [ʌntrænzˈleɪtəbl] *adj*
unübersetzbar
unused [ʌnˈjuːzd] *adj* unbenutzt
unusual [ʌnˈjuːʒuəl] *adj* ungewöhnlich
unveil [ʌnˈveɪl] *vt* enthüllen
unwanted [ʌnˈwɒntɪd] *adj* unerwünscht
unwavering [ʌnˈweɪvərɪŋ] *adj* standhaft,
unerschütterlich
unwelcome [ʌnˈwelkəm] *adj* (*at a bad time*)
unwillkommen; (*unpleasant*) unerfreulich
unwell [ʌnˈwel] *adj*: **to feel** *or* **be** ~ sich
nicht wohl fühlen
unwieldy [ʌnˈwiːldɪ] *adj* sperrig
unwilling [ʌnˈwɪlɪŋ] *adj*: **to be** ~ **to do sth**
nicht bereit sein, etw zu tun; ~**ly** *adv*
widerwillig
unwind [ʌnˈwaɪnd] (*irreg: like* **wind²**) *vt*
abwickeln ♦ *vi* (*relax*) sich entspannen
unwise [ʌnˈwaɪz] *adj* unklug
unwitting [ʌnˈwɪtɪŋ] *adj* unwissentlich
unworkable [ʌnˈwəːkəbl] *adj* (*plan*)
undurchführbar
unworthy [ʌnˈwəːðɪ] *adj* (*person*): ~ **(of sth)**
(einer Sache *gen*) nicht wert
unwrap [ʌnˈræp] *vt* auspacken
unwritten [ʌnˈrɪtn] *adj* ungeschrieben

───── KEYWORD ─────

up [ʌp] *prep*: **to be up sth** oben auf etw *dat*
sein; **to go up sth** (auf) etw *acc* hinauf
gehen; **go up that road** gehen Sie die
Straße hinauf
♦ *adv* **1** (*upwards, higher*) oben; **put it up a
bit higher** stell es etwas weiter nach oben;
up there da oben, dort oben; **up above**
hoch oben
2: **to be up** (*out of bed*) auf sein; (*prices,
level*) gestiegen sein; (*building, tent*) stehen
3: **up to** (*as far as*) bis; **up to now** bis jetzt
4: **to be up to** (*depending on*): **it's up to
you** das hängt von dir ab; (*equal to*): **he's
not up to it** (*job, task etc*) er ist dem nicht
gewachsen; (*inf: be doing: showing
disapproval, suspicion*): **what is he up to?**
was führt er im Schilde?; **it's not up to me
to decide** die Entscheidung liegt nicht bei
mir; **his work is not up to the required
standard** seine Arbeit entspricht nicht dem
geforderten Niveau
♦ *n*: **ups and downs** (*in life, career*) Höhen
und Tiefen *pl*

up-and-coming [ʌpəndˈkʌmɪŋ] *adj*
aufstrebend
upbringing [ˈʌpbrɪŋɪŋ] *n* Erziehung *f*
update [ʌpˈdeɪt] *vt* auf den neuesten Stand
bringen
upgrade [ʌpˈgreɪd] *vt* höher einstufen
upheaval [ʌpˈhiːvl] *n* Umbruch *m*
uphill [ˈʌpˈhɪl] *adj* ansteigend; (*fig*) mühsam
♦ *adv*: **to go** ~ bergauf gehen/fahren
uphold [ʌpˈhəʊld] (*irreg: like* **hold**) *vt*
unterstützen
upholstery [ʌpˈhəʊlstərɪ] *n* Polster *nt*;
Polsterung *f*
upkeep [ˈʌpkiːp] *n* Instandhaltung *f*
upon [əˈpɒn] *prep* auf
upper [ˈʌpəʳ] *n* (*on shoe*) Oberleder *nt* ♦ *adj*
obere(r, s), höhere(r, s); **to have the** ~
hand die Oberhand haben; ~**-class** *adj*
vornehm; ~**most** *adj* oberste(r, s),
höchste(r, s); **what was** ~**most in my mind**
was mich in erster Linie beschäftigte; ~
sixth (*BRIT: SCOL*) ≈ Abschlußklasse △ *f*
upright [ˈʌpraɪt] *adj* aufrecht
uprising [ˈʌpraɪzɪŋ] *n* Aufstand *m*
uproar [ˈʌprɔːʳ] *n* Aufruhr *m*
uproot [ʌpˈruːt] *vt* ausreißen

upset [*n* 'ʌpset, *vb, adj* ʌp'set] (*irreg: like* **set**) *n* Aufregung *f* ♦ *vt* (*overturn*) umwerfen; (*disturb*) aufregen, bestürzen; (*plans*) durcheinanderbringen △ ♦ *adj* (*person*) aufgeregt; (*stomach*) verdorben

upshot ['ʌpʃɒt] *n* (End)ergebnis *nt*

upside-down ['ʌpsaɪd-] *adv* verkehrt herum

upstairs [ʌp'stɛəz] *adv* oben; (*go*) nach oben ♦ *adj* (*room*) obere(r, s), Ober- ♦ *n* obere(s) Stockwerk *nt*

upstart ['ʌpstɑːt] *n* Emporkömmling *m*

upstream [ʌp'striːm] *adv* stromaufwärts

uptake ['ʌpteɪk] *n*: **to be quick on the ~** schnell begreifen; **to be slow on the ~** schwer von Begriff sein

uptight [ʌp'taɪt] (*inf*) *adj* (*nervous*) nervös; (*inhibited*) verklemmt

up-to-date ['ʌptə'deɪt] *adj* (*clothes*) modisch, modern; (*information*) neueste(r, s)

upturn ['ʌptɜːn] *n* Aufschwung *m*

upward ['ʌpwəd] *adj* nach oben gerichtet; **~(s)** *adv* aufwärts

uranium [juə'reɪnɪəm] *n* Uran *nt*

urban ['ɜːbən] *adj* städtisch, Stadt-; **~ clearway** *n* Stadtautobahn *f*

urchin ['ɜːtʃɪn] *n* (*boy*) Schlingel *m*; (*sea ~*) Seeigel *m*

urge [ɜːdʒ] *n* Drang *m* ♦ *vt*: **to ~ sb to do sth** jdn (dazu) drängen, etw zu tun

urgency ['ɜːdʒənsɪ] *n* Dringlichkeit *f*

urgent ['ɜːdʒənt] *adj* dringend

urinal ['juərɪnl] *n* (*public*) Pissoir *nt*

urinate ['juərɪneɪt] *vi* urinieren

urine ['juərɪn] *n* Urin *m*, Harn *m*

urn [ɜːn] *n* Urne *f*; (*tea ~*) Teemaschine *f*

US *n abbr* = **United States**

us [ʌs] *pron* uns; *see also* **me**

USA *n abbr* = **United States of America**

usage ['juːzɪdʒ] *n* Gebrauch *m*; (*esp LING*) Sprachgebrauch *m*

use [*n* juːs, *vb* juːz] *n* (*employment*) Gebrauch *m*; (*point*) Zweck *m* ♦ *vt* gebrauchen; **in ~** in Gebrauch; **out of ~** außer Gebrauch; **to be of ~** nützlich sein; **it's no ~** es hat keinen Zweck; **what's the ~?** was soll's?;

~d to (*accustomed to*) gewöhnt an +*acc*; **she ~d to live here** (*formerly*) sie hat früher mal hier gewohnt; **~ up** *vt* aufbrauchen, verbrauchen; **~d** *adj* (*car*) Gebraucht-; **~ful** *adj* nützlich; **~fulness** *n* Nützlichkeit *f*; **~less** *adj* nutzlos, unnütz; **~r** *n* Benutzer *m*; **~r-friendly** *adj* (*computer*) benutzerfreundlich

usher ['ʌʃə'] *n* Platzanweiser *m*; **~ette** [ʌʃə'rɛt] *n* Platzanweiserin *f*

usual ['juːʒuəl] *adj* gewöhnlich, üblich; **as ~** wie üblich; **~ly** *adv* gewöhnlich

usurp [juː'zɜːp] *vt* an sich reißen

utensil [juː'tensl] *n* Gerät *nt*; **kitchen ~s** Küchengeräte *pl*

uterus ['juːtərəs] *n* Gebärmutter *f*

utilitarian [juːtɪlɪ'tɛərɪən] *adj* Nützlichkeits-

utility [juː'tɪlɪtɪ] *n* (*usefulness*) Nützlichkeit *f*; (*also*: **public ~**) öffentliche(r) Versorgungsbetrieb *m*; **~ room** *n* Hauswirtschaftsraum *m*

utilize ['juːtɪlaɪz] *vt* benützen

utmost ['ʌtməust] *adj* äußerste(r, s) ♦ *n*: **to do one's ~** sein möglichstes tun

utter ['ʌtə'] *adj* äußerste(r, s), höchste(r, s), völlig ♦ *vt* äußern, aussprechen; **~ance** *n* Äußerung *f*; **~ly** *adv* äußerst, absolut, völlig

U-turn ['juː'tɜːn] *n* (*AUT*) Kehrtwendung *f*

V, v

v. *abbr* = **verse; versus; volt;** (= *vide*) siehe

vacancy ['veɪkənsɪ] *n* (*BRIT: job*) offene Stelle *f*; (*room*) freie(s) Zimmer *nt*; **"no vacancies"** „belegt"

vacant ['veɪkənt] *adj* leer; (*unoccupied*) frei; (*house*) leerstehend △, unbewohnt; (*stupid*) (gedanken)leer; **~ lot** (*US*) *n* unbebaute(s) Grundstück *nt*

vacate [və'keɪt] *vt* (*seat*) frei machen; (*room*) räumen

vacation [və'keɪʃən] *n* Ferien *pl*, Urlaub *m*; **~ist** (*US*) *n* Ferienreisende(r) *f(m)*

vaccinate ['væksɪneɪt] *vt* impfen

vaccine ['væksiːn] *n* Impfstoff *m*

vacuum ['vækjum] *n* Vakuum *nt*; **~ bottle**

△ *Informationen zur Rechtschreibreform Seite 615*

(*US*) *n* Thermosflasche *f*; ~ **cleaner** *n* Staubsauger *m*; ~ **flask** (*BRIT*) *n* Thermosflasche *f*; **~-packed** *adj* vakuumversiegelt

vagina [və'dʒaɪnə] *n* Scheide *f*

vague [veɪg] *adj* vag(e); (*absent-minded*) geistesabwesend; **~ly** *adv* unbestimmt, vag(e)

vain [veɪn] *adj* eitel; (*attempt*) vergeblich; **in ~** vergebens, umsonst

valentine ['væləntaɪn] *n* (*also:* ~ **card**) Valentinsgruß *m*; **V~'s Day** *n* Valentinstag *m*

valet ['vælɪt] *n* Kammerdiener *m*

valiant ['væliənt] *adj* tapfer

valid ['vælɪd] *adj* gültig; (*argument*) stichhaltig; (*objection*) berechtigt; **~ity** [və'lɪdɪtɪ] *n* Gültigkeit *f*

valley ['vælɪ] *n* Tal *nt*

valour ['vælər] (*US* **valor**) *n* Tapferkeit *f*

valuable ['væljuəbl] *adj* wertvoll; (*time*) kostbar; **~s** *npl* Wertsachen *pl*

valuation [vælju'eɪʃən] *n* (*FIN*) Schätzung *f*; Beurteilung *f*

value ['vælju:] *n* Wert *m*; (*usefulness*) Nutzen *m* ♦ *vt* (*prize*) (hoch)schätzen ⚠, werthalten; (*estimate*) schätzen; ~ **added tax** (*BRIT*) *n* Mehrwertsteuer *f*; **~d** *adj* (hoch)geschätzt ⚠

valve [vælv] *n* Ventil *nt*; (*BIOL*) Klappe *f*; (*RAD*) Röhre *f*

van [væn] *n* Lieferwagen *m*; (*BRIT: RAIL*) Waggon *m* ⚠ *nt*

vandal ['vændl] *n* Rowdy *m*; **~ism** ['vændəlɪzəm] *n* mutwillige Beschädigung *f*; **~ize** ['vændəlaɪz] *vt* mutwillig beschädigen

vanguard ['vænga:d] *n* (*fig*) Spitze *f*

vanilla [və'nɪlə] *n* Vanille *f*; ~ **ice cream** *n* Vanilleeis *m*

vanish ['vænɪʃ] *vi* verschwinden

vanity ['vænɪtɪ] *n* Eitelkeit *f*; ~ **case** *n* Schminkkoffer *m*

vantage ['vɑ:ntɪdʒ] *n*: ~ **point** gute(r) Aussichtspunkt *m*

vapour ['veɪpər] (*US* **vapor**) *n* (*mist*) Dunst *m*; (*gas*) Dampf *m*

variable ['veərɪəbl] *adj* wechselhaft,

veränderlich; (*speed, height*) regulierbar

variance ['veərɪəns] *n*: **to be at ~ (with)** nicht übereinstimmen (mit)

variation [veərɪ'eɪʃən] *n* Variation *f*; (*in prices etc*) Schwankung *f*

varicose ['værɪkəus] *adj*: ~ **veins** Krampfadern *pl*

varied ['veərɪd] *adj* unterschiedlich; (*life*) abwechslungsreich

variety [və'raɪətɪ] *n* (*difference*) Abwechslung *f*; (*varied collection*) Vielfalt *f*; (*COMM*) Auswahl *f*; (*sort*) Sorte *f*, Art *f*; ~ **show** *n* Varieté ⚠ *nt*

various ['veərɪəs] *adj* verschieden; (*several*) mehrere

varnish ['vɑ:nɪʃ] *n* Lack *m*; (*on pottery*) Glasur *f* ♦ *vt* lackieren

vary ['veərɪ] *vt* (*alter*) verändern; (*give variety to*) abwechslungsreicher gestalten ♦ *vi* sich (ver)ändern; (*prices*) schwanken; (*weather*) unterschiedlich sein

vase [vɑ:z] *n* Vase *f*

Vaseline ['væsɪli:n] ® *n* Vaseline *f*

vast [vɑ:st] *adj* weit, groß, riesig

VAT [væt] *n abbr* (= *value added tax*) MwSt *f*

vat [væt] *n* große(s) Faß ⚠ *nt*

vault [vɔ:lt] *n* (*of roof*) Gewölbe *nt*; (*tomb*) Gruft *f*; (*in bank*) Tresorraum *m*; (*leap*) Sprung *m* ♦ *vt* (*also:* ~ **over**) überspringen

vaunted ['vɔ:ntɪd] *adj*: **much-~** vielgerühmt

VCR *n abbr* = **video cassette recorder**

VD *n abbr* = **venereal disease**

VDU *n abbr* = **visual display unit**

veal [vi:l] *n* Kalbfleisch *nt*

veer [vɪər] *vi* sich drehen; (*of car*) ausscheren

vegan ['vi:gən] *n* Vegan *m*, radikale(r) Vegetarier(in) *m(f)*

vegeburger ['vedʒɪbə:gər] *n* vegetarische Frikadelle *f*

vegetable ['vedʒtəbl] *n* Gemüse *nt* ♦ *adj* Gemüse-; **~s** *npl* (*CULIN*) Gemüse *nt*

vegetarian [vedʒɪ'teərɪən] *n* Vegetarier(in) *m(f)* ♦ *adj* vegetarisch

vegetate ['vedʒɪteɪt] *vi* (dahin)vegetieren

veggieburger ['vedʒɪbə:gər] *n* = **vegeburger**

vehement ['vi:mənt] *adj* heftig

⚠ *For information on spelling reform see page 615*

vehicle [ˈviːɪkl] n Fahrzeug nt; (fig) Mittel nt

veil [veɪl] n (also fig) Schleier m ♦ vt verschleiern

vein [veɪn] n Ader f; (mood) Stimmung f

velocity [vɪˈlɒsɪtɪ] n Geschwindigkeit f

velvet [ˈvelvɪt] n Samt m ♦ adj Samt-

vendetta [venˈdetə] n Fehde f; (in family) Blutrache f

vending machine [ˈvendɪŋ-] n Automat m

vendor [ˈvendəʳ] n Verkäufer m

veneer [vəˈnɪəʳ] n Furnier(holz) nt; (fig) äußere(r) Anstrich m

venereal disease [vɪˈnɪərɪəl-] n Geschlechtskrankheit f

Venetian blind [vɪˈniːʃən-] n Jalousie f

vengeance [ˈvendʒəns] n Rache f; **with a ~** gewaltig

venison [ˈvenɪsn] n Reh(fleisch) nt

venom [ˈvenəm] n Gift nt

vent [vent] n Öffnung f; (in coat) Schlitz m; (fig) Ventil nt ♦ vt (emotion) abreagieren

ventilate [ˈventɪleɪt] vt belüften; **ventilator** [ˈventɪleɪtəʳ] n Ventilator m

ventriloquist [venˈtrɪləkwɪst] n Bauchredner m

venture [ˈventʃəʳ] n Unternehmung f, Projekt nt ♦ vt wagen; (life) aufs Spiel setzen ♦ vi sich wagen

venue [ˈvenjuː] n Schauplatz m

verb [vɜːb] n Zeitwort nt, Verb nt; **~al** adj (spoken) mündlich; (translation) wörtlich; **~ally** adv mündlich

verbatim [vɜːˈbeɪtɪm] adv Wort für Wort ♦ adj wortwörtlich

verbose [vɜːˈbəʊs] adj wortreich

verdict [ˈvɜːdɪkt] n Urteil nt

verge [vɜːdʒ] n (BRIT) Rand m ♦ vi: **to ~ on** grenzen an +acc; **"soft ~s"** (BRIT: AUT) „Seitenstreifen nicht befahrbar"; **on the ~ of doing sth** im Begriff, etw zu tun

verify [ˈverɪfaɪ] vt (über)prüfen; (confirm) bestätigen; (theory) beweisen

veritable [ˈverɪtəbl] adj wirklich, echt

vermin [ˈvɜːmɪn] npl Ungeziefer nt

vermouth [ˈvɜːməθ] n Wermut m

versatile [ˈvɜːsətaɪl] adj vielseitig

verse [vɜːs] n (poetry) Poesie f; (stanza)

Strophe f; (of Bible) Vers m; **in ~** in Versform

version [ˈvɜːʃən] n Version f; (of car) Modell nt

versus [ˈvɜːsəs] prep gegen

vertebrate [ˈvɜːtɪbrɪt] adj Wirbel-

vertical [ˈvɜːtɪkl] adj senkrecht

vertigo [ˈvɜːtɪɡəʊ] n Schwindel m

very [ˈverɪ] adv sehr ♦ adj (extreme) äußerste(r, s); **the ~ book which** genau das Buch, welches; **the ~ last** der/die/das allerletzte; **at the ~ least** allerwenigstens; **~ much** sehr

vessel [ˈvesl] n (ship) Schiff nt; (container) Gefäß nt

vest [vest] n (BRIT) Unterhemd nt; (US: waistcoat) Weste f

vested interests [ˈvestɪd-] npl finanzielle Beteiligung f; (people) finanziell Beteiligte pl; (fig) persönliche(s) Interesse nt

vestige [ˈvestɪdʒ] n Spur f

vestry [ˈvestrɪ] n Sakristei f

vet [vet] n abbr (= veterinary surgeon) Tierarzt(-ärztin) m(f)

veteran [ˈvetərn] n Veteran(in) m(f)

veterinarian [vetrɪˈnɛərɪən] (US) n Tierarzt m/-ärztin f

veterinary [ˈvetrɪnərɪ] adj Veterinär-; **~ surgeon** (BRIT) n Tierarzt m/-ärztin f

veto [ˈviːtəʊ] (pl **~es**) n Veto nt ♦ vt sein Veto einlegen gegen

vex [veks] vt ärgern; **~ed** adj verärgert; **~ed question** umstrittene Frage f

VHF abbr (= very high frequency) UKW f

via [ˈvaɪə] prep über +acc

viable [ˈvaɪəbl] adj (plan) durchführbar; (company) rentabel

vibrant [ˈvaɪbrnt] adj (lively) lebhaft; (bright) leuchtend; (full of emotion: voice) bebend

vibrate [vaɪˈbreɪt] vi zittern, beben; (machine, string) vibrieren; **vibration** [vaɪˈbreɪʃən] n Schwingung f; (of machine) Vibrieren nt

vicar [ˈvɪkəʳ] n Pfarrer m; **~age** n Pfarrhaus nt

vice [vaɪs] n (evil) Laster nt; (TECH) Schraubstock m

vice-chairman [vaɪs'tʃɛəmən] n stellvertretende(r) Vorsitzende(r) m

vice-president [vaɪs'prezɪdənt] n Vizepräsident m

vice squad n ≈ Sittenpolizei f

vice versa [vaɪsɪ'vɜːsə] adv umgekehrt

vicinity [vɪ'sɪnɪtɪ] n Umgebung f; (closeness) Nähe f

vicious ['vɪʃəs] adj gemein, böse; ~ **circle** n Teufelskreis m

victim ['vɪktɪm] n Opfer nt

victor ['vɪktə*] n Sieger m

Victorian [vɪk'tɔːrɪən] adj viktorianisch; (fig) (sitten)streng

victorious [vɪk'tɔːrɪəs] adj siegreich

victory ['vɪktərɪ] n Sieg m

video ['vɪdɪəʊ] adj Fernseh-, Bild- ♦ n (~ film) Video nt; (also: ~ **cassette**) Videokassette f; (also: ~ **cassette recorder**) Videorekorder m; ~ **tape** n Videoband nt; ~ **wall** n Videowand m

vie [vaɪ] vi wetteifern

Vienna [vɪ'enə] n Wien nt

Vietnam ['vjet'næm] n Vietnam nt; **~ese** [vjetnə'miːz] adj vietnamesisch ♦ n inv (person) Vietnamese m, Vietnamesin f

view [vjuː] n (sight) Sicht f, Blick m; (scene) Aussicht f; (opinion) Ansicht f; (intention) Absicht f ♦ vt (situation) betrachten; (house) besichtigen; **to have sth in ~** etw beabsichtigen; **on ~** ausgestellt; **in ~ of** wegen +gen, angesichts +gen; **~er** n (PHOT: small projector) Gucki m; (TV) Fernsehzuschauer(in) m(f); **~finder** n Sucher m; **~point** n Standpunkt m

vigil ['vɪdʒɪl] n (Nacht)wache f; **~ant** adj wachsam

vigorous ['vɪgərəs] adj kräftig; (protest) energisch, heftig

vile [vaɪl] adj (mean) gemein; (foul) abscheulich

villa ['vɪlə] n Villa f

village ['vɪlɪdʒ] n Dorf nt; **~r** n Dorfbewohner(in) m(f)

villain ['vɪlən] n Schurke m

vindicate ['vɪndɪkeɪt] vt rechtfertigen

vindictive [vɪn'dɪktɪv] adj nachtragend, rachsüchtig

vine [vaɪn] n Rebstock m, Rebe f

vinegar ['vɪnɪgə*] n Essig m

vineyard ['vɪnjɑːd] n Weinberg m

vintage ['vɪntɪdʒ] n (of wine) Jahrgang m; ~ **car** n Oldtimer m (zwischen 1919 und 1930 gebaut); ~ **wine** n edle(r) Wein m

viola [vɪ'əʊlə] n Bratsche f

violate ['vaɪəleɪt] vt (law) übertreten; (rights, rule, neutrality) verletzen; (sanctity, woman) schänden; **violation** [vaɪə'leɪʃən] n Übertretung f; Verletzung f

violence ['vaɪələns] n (force) Heftigkeit f; (brutality) Gewalttätigkeit f

violent ['vaɪələnt] adj (strong) heftig; (brutal) gewalttätig, brutal; (contrast) kraß ⚠; (death) gewaltsam

violet ['vaɪələt] n Veilchen nt ♦ adj veilchenblau, violett

violin [vaɪə'lɪn] n Geige f, Violine f; **~ist** n Geiger(in) m(f)

VIP n abbr (= very important person) VIP m

virgin ['vɜːdʒɪn] n Jungfrau f ♦ adj jungfräulich, unberührt; **~ity** [və:'dʒɪnɪtɪ] n Unschuld f

Virgo ['vɜːgəʊ] n Jungfrau f

virile ['vɪraɪl] adj männlich; **virility** [vɪ'rɪlɪtɪ] n Männlichkeit f

virtually ['vɜːtjʊəlɪ] adv praktisch, fast

virtual reality ['vɜːtjʊəl-] n (COMPUT) virtuelle Realität f

virtue ['vɜːtjuː] n (moral goodness) Tugend f; (good quality) Vorteil m, Vorzug m; **by ~ of** aufgrund +gen

virtuous ['vɜːtjʊəs] adj tugendhaft

virulent ['vɪrʊlənt] adj (poisonous) bösartig; (bitter) scharf, geharnischt

virus ['vaɪərəs] n (also COMPUT) Virus m

visa ['viːzə] n Visum nt

vis-à-vis [viːzə'viː] prep gegenüber

viscous ['vɪskəs] adj zähflüssig

visibility [vɪzɪ'bɪlɪtɪ] n (MET) Sicht(weite) f

visible ['vɪzəbl] adj sichtbar; **visibly** adv sichtlich

vision ['vɪʒən] n (ability) Sehvermögen nt; (foresight) Weitblick m; (in dream, image) Vision f

⚠ For information on spelling reform see page 615

visit ['vɪzɪt] *n* Besuch *m* ♦ *vt* besuchen; *(town, country)* fahren nach; **~ing hours** *npl (in hospital etc)* Besuchszeiten *pl;* **~or** *n (in house)* Besucher(in) *m(f);* (*in hotel)* Gast *m;* **~or centre** *n* Touristeninformation *f*

visor ['vaɪzə^r] *n* Visier *nt;* (*on cap)* Schirm *m;* (AUT) Blende *f*

vista ['vɪstə] *n* Aussicht *f*

visual ['vɪzjuəl] *adj* Seh-, visuell; **~ aid** *n* Anschauungsmaterial *nt;* **~ display unit** *n* Bildschirm(gerät *nt*) *m;* **~ize** *vt* sich +*dat* vorstellen; **~ly-impaired** *adj* sehbehindert

vital ['vaɪtl] *adj (important)* unerläßlich △; *(necessary for life)* Lebens-, lebenswichtig; *(lively)* vital; **~ity** [vaɪˈtælɪtɪ] *n* Vitalität *f;* **~ly** *adv:* **~ly important** äußerst wichtig; **~ statistics** *npl* (*fig)* Maße *pl*

vitamin ['vɪtəmɪn] *n* Vitamin *nt*

vivacious [vɪˈveɪʃəs] *adj* lebhaft

vivid ['vɪvɪd] *adj (graphic)* lebendig; *(memory)* lebhaft; *(bright)* leuchtend; **~ly** *adv* lebendig; lebhaft; leuchtend

V-neck ['viːnek] *n* V-Ausschnitt *m*

vocabulary [vəʊˈkæbjulərɪ] *n* Wortschatz *m,* Vokabular *nt*

vocal ['vəʊkl] *adj* Vokal-, Gesang-; *(fig)* lautstark; **~ cords** *npl* Stimmbänder *pl*

vocation [vəʊˈkeɪʃən] *n (calling)* Berufung *f;* **~al** *adj* Berufs-

vociferous [vəˈsɪfərəs] *adj* lautstark

vodka ['vɒdkə] *n* Wodka *m*

vogue [vəʊg] *n* Mode *f*

voice [vɔɪs] *n* Stimme *f;* (*fig)* Mitspracherecht *nt* ♦ *vt* äußern

void [vɔɪd] *n* Leere *f* ♦ *adj (invalid)* nichtig, ungültig; *(empty):* **~ of** ohne, bar +*gen; see* **null**

volatile ['vɒlətaɪl] *adj (gas)* flüchtig; *(person)* impulsiv; *(situation)* brisant

volcano [vɒlˈkeɪnəʊ] *n* Vulkan *m*

volition [vəˈlɪʃən] *n* Wille *m;* **of one's own ~** aus freiem Willen

volley ['vɒlɪ] *n (of guns)* Salve *f;* (*of stones)* Hagel *m;* (*tennis)* Flugball *m;* **~ball** *n* Volleyball *m*

volt [vəʊlt] *n* Volt *nt;* **~age** *n* (Volt)spannung *f*

volume ['vɒljuːm] *n (book)* Band *m;* (*size)* Umfang *m;* (*space)* Rauminhalt *m;* (*of sound)* Lautstärke *f*

voluntarily ['vɒləntrɪlɪ] *adv* freiwillig

voluntary ['vɒləntərɪ] *adj* freiwillig

volunteer [vɒlənˈtɪə^r] *n* Freiwillige(r) *mf* ♦ *vi* sich freiwillig melden; **to ~ to do sth** sich anbieten, etw zu tun

vomit ['vɒmɪt] *n* Erbrochene(s) *nt* ♦ *vt* spucken ♦ *vi* sich übergeben

vote [vəʊt] *n* Stimme *f;* (*ballot)* Abstimmung *f;* (*result)* Abstimmungsergebnis *nt;* (*franchise)* Wahlrecht *nt* ♦ *vt, vi* wählen; **~ of thanks** *n* Dankesworte *pl;* **~r** *n* Wähler(in) *m(f);* **voting** ['vəʊtɪŋ] *n* Wahl *f*

voucher ['vautʃə^r] *n* Gutschein *m*

vouch for [vautʃ-] *vt* bürgen für

vow [vau] *n* Versprechen *nt;* (REL) Gelübde *nt* ♦ *vt* geloben

vowel ['vauəl] *n* Vokal *m*

voyage ['vɔɪdʒ] *n* Reise *f*

vulgar ['vʌlgə^r] *adj (rude)* vulgär; **~ity** [vʌlˈgærɪtɪ] *n* Vulgarität *f*

vulnerable ['vʌlnərəbl] *adj (easily injured)* verwundbar; *(sensitive)* verletzlich

vulture ['vʌltʃə^r] *n* Geier *m*

W, w

wad [wɒd] *n (bundle)* Bündel *nt;* (*of paper)* Stoß *m;* (*of money)* Packen *m*

waddle ['wɒdl] *vi* watscheln

wade [weɪd] *vi:* **to ~ through** waten durch

wafer ['weɪfə^r] *n* Waffel *f;* (REL) Hostie *f;* (COMPUT) Wafer *f*

waffle ['wɒfl] *n* Waffel *f;* (*inf: empty talk)* Geschwafel *nt* ♦ *vi* schwafeln

waft [wɒft] *vt, vi* wehen

wag [wæg] *vt (tail)* wedeln mit ♦ *vi* wedeln

wage [weɪdʒ] *n (also:* **~s**) (Arbeits)lohn *m* ♦ *vt:* **to ~ war** Krieg führen; **~ earner** *n* Lohnempfänger(in) *m(f);* **~ packet** *n* Lohntüte *f*

wager ['weɪdʒə^r] *n* Wette *f* ♦ *vt, vi* wetten

waggle ['wægl] *vi* wackeln

wag(g)on ['wægən] *n (horse-drawn)*

Fuhrwerk nt; (US: AUT) Wagen m; (BRIT: RAIL) Waggon △ m

wail [weɪl] n Wehgeschrei nt ♦ vi wehklagen, jammern

waist [weɪst] n Taille f; **~coat** (BRIT) n Weste f; **~line** n Taille f

wait [weɪt] n Wartezeit f ♦ vi warten; **to lie in ~ for sb** jdm auflauern; **I can't ~ to see him** ich kann's kaum erwarten, ihn zu sehen; **"no ~ing"** (BRIT: AUT) „Halteverbot"; **~ behind** vi zurückbleiben; **~ for** vt fus warten auf +acc; **~ on** vt fus bedienen; **~er** n Kellner m; **~ing list** n Warteliste f; **~ing room** n (MED) Wartezimmer nt; (RAIL) Wartesaal m; **~ress** n Kellnerin f

waive [weɪv] vt verzichten auf +acc

wake [weɪk] (pt **woke, waked**, pp **woken**) vt wecken ♦ vi (also: ~ **up**) aufwachen ♦ n (NAUT) Kielwasser nt; (for dead) Totenwache f; **to ~ up to** (fig) sich bewußt werden +gen

waken ['weɪkn] vt aufwecken

Wales [weɪlz] n Wales nt

walk [wɔːk] n Spaziergang m; (gait) Gang m; (route) Weg m ♦ vi gehen; (stroll) spazierengehen △; (longer) wandern; **~s of life** Sphären pl; **a 10-minute ~** 10 Minuten zu Fuß; **to ~ out on sb** (inf) jdn sitzenlassen △; **~er** n Spaziergänger m; (hiker) Wanderer m; **~ie-talkie** ['wɔːkɪ'tɔːkɪ] n tragbare(s) Sprechfunkgerät nt; **~ing** n Gehen nt; (hiking) Wandern nt ♦ adj Wander-; **~ing shoes** npl Wanderschuhe pl; **~ing stick** n Spazierstock m; **W~man** ['wɔːkmən] ® n Walkman m ®; **~out** n Streik m; **~over** (inf) n leichte(r) Sieg m; **~way** n Fußweg m

wall [wɔːl] n (inside) Wand f; (outside) Mauer f; **~ed** adj von Mauern umgeben

wallet ['wɔlɪt] n Brieftasche f

wallflower ['wɔːlflauə'] n Goldlack m; **to be a ~** (fig) ein Mauerblümchen sein

wallop ['wɔləp] (inf) vt schlagen, verprügeln

wallow ['wɔləu] vi sich wälzen

wallpaper ['wɔːlpeɪpə'] n Tapete f

walnut ['wɔːlnʌt] n Walnuß △ f

walrus ['wɔːlrəs] n Walroß △ nt

waltz [wɔːlts] n Walzer m ♦ vi Walzer tanzen

wan [wɔn] adj bleich

wand [wɔnd] n (also: **magic ~**) Zauberstab m

wander ['wɔndə'] vi (roam) (herum)wandern; (fig) abschweifen

wane [weɪn] vi abnehmen; (fig) schwinden

wangle ['wæŋgl] (BRIT: inf) vt: **to ~ sth** etw richtig hindrehen

want [wɔnt] n (lack) Mangel m ♦ vt (need) brauchen; (desire) wollen; (lack) nicht haben; **~s** npl (needs) Bedürfnisse pl; **for ~ of** aus Mangel an +dat; mangels +gen; **to ~ to do sth** etw tun wollen; **to ~ sb to do sth** wollen, daß jd etw tut; **~ed** adj (criminal etc) gesucht; **"cook ~ed"** (in adverts) „Koch/Köchin gesucht"; **~ing** adj: **to be found ~ing** sich als unzulänglich erweisen

wanton ['wɔntn] adj mutwillig, zügellos

war [wɔː] n Krieg m; **to make ~** Krieg führen

ward [wɔːd] n (in hospital) Station f; (of city) Bezirk m; (child) Mündel nt; **~ off** vt abwenden, abwehren

warden ['wɔːdn] n (guard) Wächter m, Aufseher m; (BRIT: in youth hostel) Herbergsvater m; (UNIV) Heimleiter m; (BRIT: also: **traffic ~**) ≈ Verkehrspolizist m, ≈ Politesse f

warder ['wɔːdə'] (BRIT) n Gefängniswärter m

wardrobe ['wɔːdrəub] n Kleiderschrank m; (clothes) Garderobe f

warehouse ['wɛəhaus] n Lagerhaus nt

wares [wɛəz] npl Ware f

warfare ['wɔːfɛə'] n Krieg m; Kriegsführung f

warhead ['wɔːhɛd] n Sprengkopf m

warily ['wɛərɪlɪ] adv vorsichtig

warlike ['wɔːlaɪk] adj kriegerisch

warm [wɔːm] adj warm; (welcome) herzlich ♦ vt, vi wärmen; **I'm ~** mir ist warm; **it's ~** es ist warm; **~ up** vt aufwärmen ♦ vi warm werden; **~-hearted** adj warmherzig; **~ly** adv warm; herzlich; **~th** n Wärme f; Herzlichkeit f

warn [wɔːn] vt: **to ~ (of** or **against)** warnen (vor +dat); **~ing** n Warnung f; **without ~ing** unerwartet; **~ing light** n Warnlicht nt;

~ing triangle n (AUT) Warndreieck nt

warp [wɔːp] vt verziehen; **~ed** adj wellig; (fig) pervers

warrant ['wɔrnt] n (for arrest) Haftbefehl m

warranty ['wɔrəntɪ] n Garantie f

warren ['wɔrən] n Labyrinth nt

Warsaw ['wɔːsɔː] n Warschau nt

warship ['wɔːʃɪp] n Kriegsschiff nt

wart [wɔːt] n Warze f

wartime ['wɔːtaɪm] n Krieg m

wary ['wɛərɪ] adj mißtrauisch △

was [wɔz] pt of **be**

wash [wɔʃ] n Wäsche f ♦ vt waschen; (dishes) abwaschen ♦ vi sich waschen; (do ~ing) waschen; **to have a ~** sich waschen; **~ away** vt abwaschen, wegspülen; **~ off** vt abwaschen; **~ up** vi (BRIT) spülen; (US) sich waschen; **~able** adj waschbar; **~basin** n Waschbecken nt; **~ bowl** (US) n Waschbecken nt; **~ cloth** (US) n (face cloth) Waschlappen m; **~er** n (TECH) Dichtungsring m; (machine) Waschmaschine f; **~ing** n Wäsche f; **~ing machine** n Waschmaschine f; **~ing powder** (BRIT) n Waschpulver nt; **~ing-up** n Abwasch m; **~ing-up liquid** n Spülmittel nt; **~-out** (inf) n (event) Reinfall m; (person) Niete f; **~room** n Waschraum m

wasn't ['wɔznt] = **was not**

wasp [wɔsp] n Wespe f

wastage ['weɪstɪdʒ] n Verlust m; **natural ~** Verschleiß m

waste [weɪst] n (wasting) Verschwendung f; (what is wasted) Abfall m ♦ adj (useless) überschüssig, Abfall- ♦ vt (object) verschwenden; (time, life) vergeuden ♦ vi: **to ~ away** verfallen, verkümmern; **~s** npl (land) Einöde f; **~ disposal unit** (BRIT) n Müllschlucker m; **~ful** adj verschwenderisch; (process) aufwendig △; **~ ground** (BRIT) n unbebaute(s) Grundstück nt; **~land** n Ödland nt; **~paper basket** n Papierkorb m; **~ pipe** n Abflußrohr △ nt

watch [wɔtʃ] n Wache f; (for time) Uhr f ♦ vt ansehen; (observe) beobachten; (be careful of) aufpassen auf +acc; (guard) bewachen

♦ vi zusehen; **to be on the ~ (for sth)** (auf etw acc) aufpassen; **to ~ TV** fernsehen; **to ~ sb doing sth** jdm bei etw zuschauen; **~ out** vi Ausschau halten; (be careful) aufpassen; **~ out!** paß auf!; **~dog** n Wachhund m; (fig) Wächter m; **~ful** adj wachsam; **~maker** n Uhrmacher m; **~man** (irreg) n (also: **night ~man**) (Nacht)wächter m; **~ strap** n Uhrarmband nt

water ['wɔːtə*] n Wasser nt ♦ vt (be)gießen; (river) bewässern; (horses) tränken ♦ vi (eye) tränen; **~s** npl (of sea, river etc) Gewässer nt; **~ down** vt verwässern; **~ closet** (BRIT) n (Wasser)klosett nt; **~colour** (US **watercolor**) n (painting) Aquarell nt; (paint) Wasserfarbe f; **~cress** n (Brunnen)kresse f; **~fall** n Wasserfall m; (fig) Wächter m; **~ heater** n Heißwassergerät nt; **~ing can** n Gießkanne f; **~ level** n Wasserstand m; **~lily** n Seerose f; **~line** n Wasserlinie f; **~logged** adj (ground) voll Wasser; **~ main** n Haupt(wasser)leitung f; **~mark** n Wasserzeichen nt; (on wall) Wasserstandsmarke f; **~melon** n Wassermelone f; **~ polo** n Wasserball(spiel) nt; **~proof** adj wasserdicht; **~shed** n Wasserscheide f; **~-skiing** n Wasserskilaufen nt; **~ tank** n Wassertank m; **~tight** adj wasserdicht; **~way** n Wasserweg m; **~works** npl Wasserwerk nt; **~y** adj wäss(e)rig

watt [wɔt] n Watt nt

wave [weɪv] n Welle f; (with hand) Winken nt ♦ vt (move to and fro) schwenken; (hand, flag) winken mit ♦ vi (person) winken; (flag) wehen; **~length** n (also fig) Wellenlänge f

waver ['weɪvə*] vi schwanken

wavy ['weɪvɪ] adj wellig

wax [wæks] n Wachs nt; (sealing ~) Siegellack m; (in ear) Ohrenschmalz nt ♦ vt (floor) (ein)wachsen ♦ vi (moon) zunehmen; **~works** npl Wachsfigurenkabinett nt

way [weɪ] n Weg m; (method) Art und Weise f; (direction) Richtung f; (habit) Gewohnheit f; (distance) Entfernung f; (condition) Zustand m; **which ~? - this ~** welche Richtung? - hier entlang; **on the ~** (en route) unterwegs; **to be in the ~** im Weg sein; **to go out of one's ~ to do sth** sich besonders anstrengen, um etw zu tun; **to lose one's ~** sich verirren; **"give ~"** (*BRIT: AUT*) „Vorfahrt achten!"; **in a ~** in gewisser Weise; **by the ~** übrigens; **in some ~** in gewisser Hinsicht; **"~ in"** (*BRIT*) „Eingang"; **"~ out"** (*BRIT*) „Ausgang"

waylay [weɪˈleɪ] (*irreg: like* lay) *vt* auflauern +*dat*

wayward [ˈweɪwəd] *adj* eigensinnig

W.C. (*BRIT*) *n* WC *nt*

we [wiː] *pl pron* wir

weak [wiːk] *adj* schwach; **~en** *vt* schwächen ♦ *vi* schwächer werden; **~ling** *n* Schwächling *m*; **~ness** *n* Schwäche *f*

wealth [welθ] *n* Reichtum *m*; (*abundance*) Fülle *f*; **~y** *adj* reich

wean [wiːn] *vt* entwöhnen

weapon [ˈwepən] *n* Waffe *f*

wear [weər] (*pt* wore, *pp* worn) *n* (*clothing*): **sports/baby ~** Sport-/Babykleidung *f*; (*use*) Verschleiß *m* ♦ *vt* (*have on*) tragen; (*smile etc*) haben; (*use*) abnutzen ♦ *vi* (*last*) halten; (*become old*) (sich) verschleißen; **evening ~** Abendkleidung *f*; **~ and tear** Verschleiß *m*; **~ away** *vt* verbrauchen ♦ *vi* schwinden; **~ down** *vt* (*people*) zermürben; **~ off** *vi* sich verlieren; **~ out** *vt* verschleißen; (*person*) erschöpfen

weary [ˈwɪərɪ] *adj* müde ♦ *vt* ermüden ♦ *vi* überdrüssig werden

weasel [ˈwiːzl] *n* Wiesel *nt*

weather [ˈweðər] *n* Wetter *nt* ♦ *vt* verwittern lassen; (*resist*) überstehen; **under the ~** (*fig:* ill) angeschlagen (*inf*); **~-beaten** *adj* verwittert; **~cock** *n* Wetterhahn *m*; **~ forecast** *n* Wettervorhersage *f*; **~ vane** *n* Wetterfahne *f*

weave [wiːv] (*pt* wove, *pp* woven) *vt* weben; **~r** *n* Weber(in) *m(f)*; **weaving** *n* (*craft*) Webkunst *f*

web [web] *n* Netz *nt*; (*membrane*) Schwimmhaut *f*

wed [wed] (*pt, pp* wedded) *vt* heiraten ♦ *n*: **the newly-~s** ♦ *npl* die Frischvermählten △ *pl*

we'd [wiːd] = **we had; we would**

wedding [ˈwedɪŋ] *n* Hochzeit *f*; **silver/golden ~ anniversary** Silberhochzeit *f*/Goldene Hochzeit *f*; **~ day** *n* Hochzeitstag *m*; **~ dress** *n* Hochzeitskleid *nt*; **~ present** *n* Hochzeitsgeschenk *nt*; **~ ring** *n* Trauring *m*, Ehering *m*

wedge [wedʒ] *n* Keil *m*; (*of cheese etc*) Stück *nt* ♦ *vt* (*fasten*) festklemmen; (*pack tightly*) einkeilen

Wednesday [ˈwednzdɪ] *n* Mittwoch *m*

wee [wiː] (*SCOTTISH*) *adj* klein, winzig

weed [wiːd] *n* Unkraut *nt* ♦ *vt* jäten; **~-killer** *n* Unkrautvertilgungsmittel *nt*

weedy [ˈwiːdɪ] *adj* (*person*) schmächtig

week [wiːk] *n* Woche *f*; **a ~ today/on Friday** heute/Freitag in einer Woche; **~day** *n* Wochentag *m*; **~end** *n* Wochenende *nt*; **~ly** *adj* wöchentlich; (*wages, magazine*) Wochen- ♦ *adv* wöchentlich

weep [wiːp] (*pt, pp* wept) *vi* weinen; **~ing willow** *n* Trauerweide *f*

weigh [weɪ] *vt, vi* wiegen; **to ~ anchor** den Anker lichten; **~ down** *vt* niederdrücken; **~ up** *vt* abschätzen

weight [weɪt] *n* Gewicht *nt*; **to lose/put on ~** abnehmen/zunehmen; **~ing** *n* (*allowance*) Zulage *f*; **~lifter** *n* Gewichtheber *m*; **~lifting** *n* Gewichtheben *nt*; **~y** *adj* (*heavy*) gewichtig; (*important*) schwerwiegend

weir [wɪər] *n* (Stau)wehr *nt*

weird [wɪəd] *adj* seltsam

welcome [ˈwelkəm] *n* Willkommen *nt*, Empfang *m* ♦ *vt* begrüßen; **thank you - you're ~!** danke - nichts zu danken

welder [ˈweldər] *n* (*person*) Schweißer(in) *m(f)*

welding [ˈweldɪŋ] *n* Schweißen *nt*

welfare [ˈwelfeər] *n* Wohl *nt*; (*social*) Fürsorge *f*; **~ state** *n* Wohlfahrtsstaat *m*; **~ work** *n* Fürsorge *f*

well [wel] *n* Brunnen *m*; (*oil ~*) Quelle *f* ♦ *adj* (*in good health*) gesund ♦ *adv* gut ♦ *excl* nun!, na schön!; **I'm ~** es geht mir gut; **get ~ soon!** gute Besserung!; **as ~** auch; **as ~ as** sowohl als auch; **~ done!** gut

△ *For information on spelling reform see page 615*

gemacht!; **to do ~** (*person*) gut
zurechtkommen; (*business*) gut gehen; **~
up** *vi* emporsteigen; (*fig*) aufsteigen

we'll [wi:l] = **we will; we shall**

well: **~-behaved** ['welbı'heıvd] *adj*
wohlerzogen; **~-being** ['wel'bi:ıŋ] *n* Wohl
nt; **~-built** ['wel'bılt] *adj* kräftig gebaut; **~-
deserved** ['weldı'zə:vd] *adj* wohlverdient;
~-dressed ['wel'drest] *adj* gut gekleidet;
~-heeled ['wel'hi:ld] (*inf*) *adj* (*wealthy*) gut
gepolstert

wellingtons ['welıŋtənz] *npl* (*also:*
wellington boots) Gummistiefel *pl*

well: **~-known** ['wel'nəun] *adj* bekannt; **~-
mannered** ['wel'mænəd] *adj* wohlerzogen;
~-meaning ['wel'mi:nıŋ] *adj* (*person*)
wohlmeinend; (*action*) gutgemeint ⚠; **~-
off** ['wel'ɔf] *adj* gut situiert; **~-read**
['wel'red] *adj* (sehr) belesen; **~-to-do**
['weltə'du:] *adj* wohlhabend; **~-wisher**
['welwıʃə'] *n* Gönner *m*

Welsh [welʃ] *adj* walisisch ♦ *n* (*LING*)
Walisisch *nt*; **the ~** *npl* (*people*) die Waliser
pl; **~man, ~woman** (*irreg*) *n* Waliser(in)
m(f)

went [went] *pt of* **go**

wept [wept] *pt, pp of* **weep**

were [wə:'] *pt pl of* **be**

we're [wıə'] = **we are**

weren't [wə:nt] = **were not**

west [west] *n* Westen *m* ♦ *adj* West-,
westlich ♦ *adv* westwärts, nach Westen; **the
W~** der Westen; **W~ Country** (*BRIT*) *n*:
the W~ Country der Südwesten Englands;
~erly *adj* westlich; **~ern** *adj* westlich,
West- ♦ *n* (*CINE*) Western *m*; **W~ Indian**
adj westindisch ♦ *n* Westindier(in) *m(f)*; **W~
Indies** *npl* Westindische Inseln *pl*;
~ward(s) *adv* westwärts

wet [wet] *adj* naß ⚠; **to get ~** naß werden;
"~ paint" „frisch gestrichen"; **~ blanket** *n*
(*fig*) Triefel *m*; **~ suit** *n* Taucheranzug *m*

we've [wi:v] = **we have**

whack [wæk] *n* Schlag *m* ♦ *vt* schlagen

whale [weıl] *n* Wal *m*

wharf [wɔ:f] *n* Kai *m*

wharves [wɔ:vz] *npl of* **wharf**

---

what [wɔt] *adj* **1** (*in questions*) welche(r, s),
was für ein(e); **what size is it?** welche
Größe ist das?

2 (*in exclamations*) was für ein(e); **what a
mess!** was für ein Durcheinander!

♦ *pron* (*interrogative/relative*) was; **what are
you doing?** was machst du gerade?; **what
are you talking about?** wovon reden Sie?;
what is it called? wie heißt das?; **what
about ...?** wie wär's mit ...?; **I saw what
you did** ich habe gesehen, was du
gemacht hast

♦ *excl* (*disbelieving*) wie, was; **what, no
coffee!** wie, kein Kaffee?; **I've crashed the
car - what!** ich hatte einen Autounfall -
was!

---

whatever [wɔt'evə'] *adj*: **~ book** welches
Buch auch immer ♦ *pron*: **do ~ is
necessary** tu, was (immer auch) nötig ist;
~ happens egal, was passiert; **nothing ~**
überhaupt *or* absolut gar nichts; **do ~ you
want** tu, was (immer) du (auch) möchtest;
no reason ~ *or* **whatsoever** überhaupt *or*
absolut kein Grund

whatsoever [wɔtsəu'evə'] *adj see* **whatever**

wheat [wi:t] *n* Weizen *m*

wheedle ['wi:dl] *vt*: **to ~ sb into doing sth**
jdn dazu überreden, etw zu tun; **to ~ sth
out of sb** jdm etw abluchsen

wheel [wi:l] *n* Rad *nt*; (*steering ~*) Lenkrad
nt; (*disc*) Scheibe *f* ♦ *vt* schieben; **~barrow**
n Schubkarren *m*; **~chair** *n* Rollstuhl *m*; **~
clamp** *n* (*AUT*) Parkkralle *f*

wheeze [wi:z] *vi* keuchen

when [wen] *adv* wann

♦ *conj* **1** (*at, during, after the time that*)
wenn; (*in past*) als; **she was reading when
I came in** sie las, als ich hereinkam; **be
careful when you cross the road** seien Sie
vorsichtig, wenn Sie über die Straße gehen
2 (*on, at which*) als; **on the day when I met
him** an dem Tag, an dem ich ihn traf

⚠ *Informationen zur Rechtschreibreform Seite 615*

3 (*whereas*) wo ... doch

whenever [wɛn'ɛvər] *adv* wann (auch) immer; (*every time that*) jedesmal wenn ♦ *conj* (*any time*) wenn

where [wɛər] *adv* (*place*) wo; (*direction*) wohin; **this is ~ ...** hier ...; **~abouts** ['wɛərəbauts] *adv* wo ♦ *n* Aufenthaltsort *m*; **nobody knows his ~abouts** niemand weiß, wo er ist; **~as** [wɛər'æz] *conj* während, wo ... doch; **~by** *pron* woran, wodurch, womit, wovon; **~upon** *conj* worauf, wonach; (*at beginning of sentence*) daraufhin; **~ver** [wɛər'ɛvər] *adv* wo (immer)

wherewithal ['wɛəwɪðɔːl] *n* nötige (Geld)mittel *pl*

whet [wɛt] *vt* (*appetite*) anregen

whether ['wɛðər] *conj* ob; **I don't know ~ to accept or not** ich weiß nicht, ob ich es annehmen soll oder nicht; **~ you go or not** ob du gehst oder nicht; **it's doubtful/ unclear ~ ...** est ist zweifelhaft/nicht klar, ob ...

KEYWORD

which [wɪtʃ] *adj* **1** (*interrogative: direct, indirect*) welche(r, s); **which one?** welche(r, s)?

2: in which case in diesem Fall; **by which time** zu dieser Zeit

♦ *pron* **1** (*interrogative*) welche(r, s); (*of people also*) wer; (*of people*) der/die/das; (*referring to people*) was; **the apple which you ate/which is on the table** der Apfel, den du gegessen hast/der auf dem Tisch liegt; **he said he saw her, which is true** er sagte, er habe sie gesehen, was auch stimmt

whichever [wɪtʃ'ɛvər] *adj* welche(r, s) auch immer; (*no matter which*) ganz gleich welche(r, s); **~ book you take** welches Buch du auch nimmst; **~ car you prefer** egal, welches Auto du vorziehst

whiff [wɪf] *n* Hauch *m*

while [waɪl] *n* Weile *f* ♦ *conj* während; **for a**

~ eine Zeitlang; **~ away** *vt* (*time*) sich *dat* vertreiben

whim [wɪm] *n* Laune *f*

whimper ['wɪmpər] *n* Wimmern *nt* ♦ *vi* wimmern

whimsical ['wɪmzɪkəl] *adj* launisch

whine [waɪn] *n* Gewinsel *nt*, Gejammer *nt* ♦ *vi* heulen, winseln

whip [wɪp] *n* Peitsche *f*; (*POL*) Fraktionsführer *m* ♦ *vt* (*beat*) peitschen; (*snatch*) reißen; **~ped cream** *n* Schlagsahne *f*

whip-round ['wɪpraund] (*BRIT: inf*) *n* Geldsammlung *f*

whirl [wɜːl] *n* Wirbel *m* ♦ *vt, vi* (herum)wirbeln; **~pool** *n* Wirbel *m*; **~wind** *n* Wirbelwind *m*

whirr [wɜːr] *vi* schwirren, surren

whisk [wɪsk] *n* Schneebesen *m* ♦ *vt* (*cream etc*) schlagen; **to ~ sb away** *or* **off** mit jdm davon sausen

whisker ['wɪskər] *n*: **~s** (*of animal*) Barthaare *pl*; (*of man*) Backenbart *m*

whisky ['wɪski] (*US, IRISH* **whiskey**) *n* Whisky *m*

whisper ['wɪspər] *n* Flüstern *nt* ♦ *vt, vi* flüstern

whistle ['wɪsl] *n* Pfiff *m*; (*instrument*) Pfeife *f* ♦ *vt, vi* pfeifen

white [waɪt] *n* Weiß *nt*; (*of egg*) Eiweiß *nt* ♦ *adj* weiß; **~ coffee** (*BRIT*) *n* Kaffee *m* mit Milch; **~-collar worker** *n* Angestellte(r) *m*; **~ elephant** *n* (*fig*) Fehlinvestition *f*; **~ lie** *n* Notlüge *f*; **~ paper** *n* (*POL*) Weißbuch *nt*; **~wash** *n* (*paint*) Tünche *f*; (*fig*) Ehrenrettung *f* ♦ *vt* weißen, tünchen; (*fig*) reinwaschen △

whiting ['waɪtɪŋ] *n* Weißfisch *m*

Whitsun ['wɪtsn] *n* Pfingsten *nt*

whittle ['wɪtl] *vt*: **to ~ away** *or* **down** stutzen, verringern

whizz [wɪz] *vi*: **to ~ past** *or* **by** vorbeizischen, vorbeischwirren; **~ kid** (*inf*) *n* Kanone *f*

KEYWORD

who [huː] *pron* **1** (*interrogative*) wer; (*acc*) wen; (*dat*) wem; **who is it?, who's there?**

△ *For information on spelling reform see page 615*

wer ist da?

2 (*relative*) der/die/das; **the woman/man who spoke to me** die Frau/der Mann, die/der mit mir sprach

---

whodu(n)nit [huːˈdʌnɪt] (*inf*) *n* Krimi *m*
whoever [huːˈɛvəʳ] *pron* wer/wen/wem auch immer; (*no matter who*) ganz gleich wer/wen/wem

whole [həʊl] *adj* ganz ♦ *n* Ganze(s) *nt*; **the ~ of the town** die ganze Stadt; **on the ~** im großen und ganzen; **as a ~** im großen und ganzen; **~food(s)** [ˈhəʊlfuːd(z)] *n(pl)* Vollwertkost *f*; **~hearted** [həʊlˈhɑːtɪd] *adj* rückhaltlos; **~heartedly** *adv* von ganzem Herzen; **~meal** *adj* (*bread, flour*) Vollkorn-; **~sale** *n* Großhandel *m* ♦ *adj* (*trade*) Großhandels-; (*destruction*) Massen-; **~saler** *n* Großhändler *m*; **~some** *adj* bekömmlich, gesund; **~wheat** *adj* = **wholemeal**
wholly [ˈhəʊlɪ] *adv* ganz, völlig

KEYWORD

whom [huːm] *pron* **1** (*interrogative: acc*) wen; (: *dat*) wem; **whom did you see?** wen haben Sie gesehen?; **to whom did you give it?** wem haben Sie es gegeben?
2 (*relative: acc*) den/die/das; (: *dat*) dem/der/dem; **the man whom I saw/to whom I spoke** der Mann, den ich sah/mit dem ich sprach

---

whooping cough [ˈhuːpɪŋ-] *n* Keuchhusten *m*
whore [hɔːʳ] *n* Hure *f*
whose [huːz] *adj* (*possessive: interrogative*) wessen; (: *relative*) dessen; (*after f and pl*) deren ♦ *pron* wessen; **~ book is this?, ~ is this book?** wessen Buch ist dies?; **~ is this?** wem gehört das?

KEYWORD

why [waɪ] *adv* warum, weshalb
♦ *conj* warum, weshalb; **that's not why I'm here** ich bin nicht deswegen hier; **that's the reason why** deshalb
♦ *excl* (*expressing surprise, shock*) na so was;

(*explaining*) also dann; **why, it's you!** na so was, du bist es!

---

wick [wɪk] *n* Docht *m*
wicked [ˈwɪkɪd] *adj* böse
wicker [ˈwɪkəʳ] *n* (*also:* **~work**) Korbgeflecht *nt*
wicket [ˈwɪkɪt] *n* Tor *nt*, Dreistab *m*
wide [waɪd] *adj* breit; (*plain*) weit; (*in firing*) daneben ♦ *adv:* **to open ~** weit öffnen; **to shoot ~** daneben schießen; **~-angle lens** *n* Weitwinkelobjektiv *nt*; **~-awake** *adj* hellwach; **~ly** *adv* weit; (*known*) allgemein; **~n** *vt* erweitern; **~ open** weit geöffnet; **~spread** *adj* weitverbreitet △
widow [ˈwɪdəʊ] *n* Witwe *f*; **~ed** *adj* verwitwet; **~er** *n* Witwer *m*
width [wɪdθ] *n* Breite *f*, Weite *f*
wield [wiːld] *vt* schwingen, handhaben
wife [waɪf] (*pl* **wives**) *n* (Ehe)frau *f*, Gattin *f*
wig [wɪg] *n* Perücke *f*
wiggle [ˈwɪgl] *n* Wackeln *nt* ♦ *vt* wackeln mit ♦ *vi* wackeln
wild [waɪld] *adj* wild; (*violent*) heftig; (*plan, idea*) verrückt; (*angry*) in Wildnis *f*, Wüste *f*; **~-goose chase** *n* (*fig*) fruchtlose(s) Unternehmen *nt*; **~life** *n* Tierwelt *f*; **~ly** *adv* wild, ungestüm; (*exaggerated*) irrsinnig; **~s** *npl:* **the ~s** die Wildnis *f*
wilful [ˈwɪlful] (*US* **willful**) *adj* (*intended*) vorsätzlich; (*obstinate*) eigensinnig

---

KEYWORD

will [wɪl] *aux vb* **1** (*forms future tense*) werden; **I will finish it tomorrow** ich mache es morgen zu Ende
2 (*in conjectures, predictions*): **he will** *or* **he'll be there by now** er dürfte jetzt da sein; **that will be the postman** das wird der Postbote sein
3 (*in commands, requests, offers*): **will you be quiet!** sei endlich still!; **will you help me?** hilfst du mir?; **will you have a cup of tea?** trinken Sie eine Tasse Tee?; **I won't put up with it!** das lasse ich mir nicht gefallen!
♦ *vt* wollen

△ *Informationen zur Rechtschreibreform Seite 615*

♦ *n* Wille *m*; (*JUR*) Testament *nt*

willing ['wɪlɪŋ] *adj* gewillt, bereit; **~ly** *adv* bereitwillig, gern; **~ness** *n* (Bereit)willigkeit *f*

willow ['wɪləu] *n* Weide *f*

willpower ['wɪl'pauə'] *n* Willenskraft *f*

willy-nilly ['wɪlɪ'nɪlɪ] *adv* einfach so

wilt [wɪlt] *vi* (ver)welken

wily ['waɪlɪ] *adj* gerissen

win [wɪn] (*pt, pp* **won**) *n* Sieg *m* ♦ *vt, vi* gewinnen; **to ~ sb over** *or* **round** jdn gewinnen, jdn dazu bringen

wince [wɪns] *vi* zusammenzucken

winch [wɪntʃ] *n* Winde *f*

wind¹ [wɪnd] *n* Wind *m*; (*MED*) Blähungen *pl*

wind² [waɪnd] (*pt, pp* **wound**) *vt* (*rope*) winden; (*bandage*) wickeln ♦ *vi* (*turn*) sich winden; **~ up** *vt* (*clock*) aufziehen; (*debate*) (ab)schließen

windfall ['wɪndfɔːl] *n* unverhoffte(r) Glücksfall *m*

winding ['waɪndɪŋ] *adj* (*road*) gewunden

wind instrument ['wɪnd-] *n* Blasinstrument *nt*

windmill ['wɪndmɪl] *n* Windmühle *f*

window ['wɪndəu] *n* Fenster *nt*; **~ box** *n* Blumenkasten *m*; **~ cleaner** *n* Fensterputzer *m*; **~ envelope** *n* Fensterbriefumschlag *m*; **~ ledge** *n* Fenstersims *m*; **~ pane** *n* Fensterscheibe *f*; **~-shopping** *n* Schaufensterbummel *m*; **to go ~-shopping** einen Schaufensterbummel machen; **~sill** *n* Fensterbank *f*

wind: **~pipe** *n* Luftröhre *f*; **~ power** *n* Windenergie *f*; **~screen** (*BRIT*) *n* Windschutzscheibe *f*; **~screen washer** *n* Scheibenwaschanlage *f*; **~screen wiper** *n* Scheibenwischer *m*; **~shield** (*US*) *n* = **windscreen**; **~swept** *adj* vom Wind gepeitscht; (*person*) zerzaust; **~y** *adj* windig

wine [waɪn] *n* Wein *m*; **~ bar** *n* Weinlokal *nt*; **~ cellar** *n* Weinkeller *m*; **~glass** *n* Weinglas *nt*; **~ list** *n* Weinkarte *f*; **~ merchant** *n* Weinhändler *m*; **~ tasting** *n* Weinprobe *f*; **~ waiter** *n* Weinkellner *m*

wing [wɪŋ] *n* Flügel *m*; (*MIL*) Gruppe *f*; **~s** *npl* (*THEAT*) Seitenkulisse *f*; **~er** *n* (*SPORT*) Flügelstürmer *m*

wink [wɪŋk] *n* Zwinkern *nt* ♦ *vi* zwinkern, blinzeln

winner ['wɪnə'] *n* Gewinner *m*; (*SPORT*) Sieger *m*

winning ['wɪnɪŋ] *adj* (*team*) siegreich, Sieger-; (*goal*) entscheidend; **~ post** *n* Ziel *nt*; **~s** *npl* Gewinn *m*

winter ['wɪntə'] *n* Winter *m* ♦ *adj* (*clothes*) Winter- ♦ *vi* überwintern; **~ sports** *npl* Wintersport *m*; **wintry** ['wɪntrɪ] *adj* Winter-, winterlich

wipe [waɪp] *n*: **to give sth a ~** etw (ab)wischen ♦ *vt* wischen; **~ off** *vt* abwischen; **~ out** *vt* (*debt*) löschen; (*destroy*) auslöschen; **~ up** *vt* aufwischen

wire ['waɪə'] *n* Draht *m*; (*telegram*) Telegramm *nt* ♦ *vt* telegrafieren; **to ~ sb** jdm telegrafieren; **~less** ['waɪəlɪs] (*BRIT*) *n* Radio(apparat *m*) *nt*

wiring ['waɪərɪŋ] *n* elektrische Leitungen *pl*

wiry ['waɪərɪ] *adj* drahtig

wisdom ['wɪzdəm] *n* Weisheit *f*; (*of decision*) Klugheit *f*; **~ tooth** *n* Weisheitszahn *m*

wise [waɪz] *adj* klug, weise ♦ *suffix*: **timewise** zeitlich gesehen

wisecrack ['waɪzkræk] *n* Witzelei *f*

wish [wɪʃ] *n* Wunsch *m* ♦ *vt* wünschen; **best ~es** (*on birthday etc*) alles Gute; **with best ~es** (*in letter*) herzliche Grüße; **to ~ sb goodbye** jdn verabschieden; **he ~ed me well** er wünschte mir Glück; **to ~ to do sth** etw tun wollen; **~ for** *vt fus* sich *dat* wünschen; **~ful thinking** *n* Wunschdenken *nt*

wishy-washy ['wɪʃɪ'wɔʃɪ] (*inf*) *adj* (*ideas, argument*) verschwommen

wisp [wɪsp] *n* (*Haar*)strähne *f*; (*of smoke*) Wölkchen *nt*

wistful ['wɪstful] *adj* sehnsüchtig

wit [wɪt] *n* (*also*: **~s**) Verstand *m no pl*; (*amusing ideas*) Witz *m*; (*person*) Witzbold *m*

witch [wɪtʃ] *n* Hexe *f*; **~craft** *n* Hexerei *f*

KEYWORD

with [wɪð, wɪθ] *prep* **1** (*accompanying, in the*

⚠ *For information on spelling reform see page 615*

company of) mit; **we stayed with friends**
wir übernachteten bei Freunden; **I'll be
with you in a minute** einen Augenblick,
ich bin sofort da; **I'm not with you** (*I don't
understand*) das verstehe ich nicht; **to be
with it** (*inf: up-to-date*) auf dem laufenden
sein; (: *alert*) (voll) da sein (*inf*)
2 (*descriptive, indicating manner etc*) mit; **the
man with the grey hat** der Mann mit dem
grauen Hut; **red with anger** rot vor Wut

withdraw [wɪθ'drɔː] (*irreg: like* **draw**) *vt*
zurückziehen; (*money*) abheben; (*remark*)
zurücknehmen ♦ *vi* sich zurückziehen; **~al**
n Zurückziehung *f*; Abheben *nt*;
Zurücknahme *f*; **~n** *adj* (*person*)
verschlossen
wither ['wɪðəʳ] *vi* (ver)welken
withhold [wɪθ'həuld] (*irreg: like* **hold**) *vt*: **to
~ sth (from sb)** (jdm) etw vorenthalten
within [wɪð'ɪn] *prep* innerhalb +*gen* ♦ *adv*
innen; **~ sight of** in Sichtweite von; **~ the
week** innerhalb dieser Woche; **~ a mile of**
weniger als eine Meile von
without [wɪð'aut] *prep* ohne; **~ speaking/
sleeping** *etc* ohne zu sprechen/schlafen *etc*
withstand [wɪθ'stænd] (*irreg: like* **stand**) *vt*
widerstehen +*dat*
witness ['wɪtnɪs] *n* Zeuge *m*, Zeugin *f* ♦ *vt*
(*see*) sehen, miterleben; (*document*)
beglaubigen; **~ box** *n* Zeugenstand *m*; **~
stand** (*US*) *n* Zeugenstand *m*
witticism ['wɪtɪsɪzəm] *n* witzige Bemerkung
f
witty ['wɪtɪ] *adj* witzig, geistreich
wives [waɪvz] *pl of* **wife**
wk *abbr* = **week**
wobble ['wɒbl] *vi* wackeln
woe [wəu] *n* Kummer *m*
woke [wəuk] *pt of* **wake**
woken ['wəukn] *pp of* **wake**
wolf [wulf] (*pl* **wolves**) *n* Wolf *m*
woman ['wumən] (*pl* **women**) *n* Frau *f*; **~
doctor** *n* Ärztin *f*; **~ly** *adj* weiblich
womb [wuːm] *n* Gebärmutter *f*
women ['wɪmɪn] *npl of* **woman**; **~'s lib** (*inf*)
n Frauenrechtsbewegung *f*

won [wʌn] *pt, pp of* **win**
wonder ['wʌndəʳ] *n* (*marvel*) Wunder *nt*;
(*surprise*) Staunen *nt*, Verwunderung *f* ♦ *vi*
sich wundern ♦ *vt*: **I ~ whether ...** ich frage
mich, ob ...; **it's no ~ that** es ist kein
Wunder, daß; **to ~ at** sich wundern über
+*acc*; **to ~ about** sich Gedanken machen
über +*acc*; **~ful** *adj* wunderbar, herrlich
won't [wəunt] = **will not**
woo [wuː] *vt* (*audience etc*) umwerben
wood [wud] *n* Holz *nt*; (*forest*) Wald *m*; **~
carving** *n* Holzschnitzerei *f*; **~ed** *adj*
bewaldet; **~en** *adj* (*also fig*) hölzern;
~pecker *n* Specht *m*; **~wind** *n*
Blasinstrumente *pl*; **~work** *n* Holzwerk *nt*;
(*craft*) Holzarbeiten *pl*; **~worm** *n* Holzwurm
m
wool [wul] *n* Wolle *f*; **to pull the ~ over
sb's eyes** (*fig*) jdm Sand in die Augen
streuen; **~len** (*US* **woolen**) *adj* Woll-; **~lens**
npl Wollsachen *pl*; **~ly** (*US* **wooly**) *adj*
wollig, (*fig*) schwammig
word [wɜːd] *n* Wort *nt*; (*news*) Bescheid *m*
♦ *vt* formulieren; **in other ~s** anders
gesagt; **to break/keep one's ~** sein Wort
brechen/halten; **~ing** *n* Wortlaut *m*; **~
processing** *n* Textverarbeitung *f*; **~
processor** *n* Textverarbeitung *f*
wore [wɔːʳ] *pt of* **wear**
work [wɜːk] *n* Arbeit *f*; (*ART, LITER*) Werk *nt*
♦ *vi* arbeiten; (*machine*) funktionieren;
(*medicine*) wirken; (*succeed*) klappen; **~s** *n sg*
(*BRIT: factory*) Fabrik *f*, Werk *nt* ♦ *npl* (*of
watch*) Werk *nt*; **to be out of ~** arbeitslos
sein; **in ~ing order** in betriebsfähigem
Zustand; **~ loose** *vi* sich lockern; **~ on** *vi*
weiterarbeiten ♦ *vt fus* arbeiten an +*dat*;
(*influence*) bearbeiten; **~ out** *vi* (*sum*)
aufgehen; (*plan*) klappen ♦ *vt* (*problem*)
lösen; (*plan*) ausarbeiten; **it ~s out at £100**
das gibt *or* macht £100; **~ up** *vt*: **to get
~ed up** sich aufregen; **~able** *adj* (*soil*)
bearbeitbar; (*plan*) ausführbar; **~aholic**
[wɜːkə'hɒlɪk] *n* Arbeitssüchtige(r) *f(m)*; **~er** *n*
Arbeiter(in) *m(f)*; **~ experience** *n*
Praktikum *nt*; **~force** *n* Arbeiterschaft *f*;
~ing class *n* Arbeiterklasse *f*; **~ing-class**

adj Arbeiter-; **~man** (*irreg*) *n* Arbeiter *m*; **~manship** *n* Arbeit *f*, Ausführung *f*; **~sheet** *n* Arbeitsblatt *nt*; **~shop** *n* Werkstatt *f*; **~ station** *n* Arbeitsplatz *m*; **~-to-rule** (*BRIT*) *n* Dienst *m* nach Vorschrift

world [wɜːld] *n* Welt *f*; **to think the ~ of sb** große Stücke auf jdn halten; **~ly** *adj* weltlich, irdisch; **~-wide** *adj* weltweit

World-Wide Web *n* World Wide Web *nt*

worm [wɜːm] *n* Wurm *m*

worn [wɔːn] *pp of* **wear ♦** *adj* (*clothes*) abgetragen; **~-out** *adj* (*object*) abgenutzt; (*person*) völlig erschöpft

worried ['wʌrɪd] *adj* besorgt, beunruhigt

worry ['wʌrɪ] *n* Sorge *f* ♦ *vt* beunruhigen ♦ *vi* (*feel uneasy*) sich sorgen, sich *dat* Gedanken machen; **~ing** *adj* beunruhigend

worse [wɜːs] *adj* schlechter, schlimmer ♦ *adv* schlimmer, ärger ♦ *n* Schlimmere(s) *nt*, Schlechtere(s) *nt*; **a change for the ~** eine Verschlechterung; **~n** *vt* verschlimmern ♦ *vi* sich verschlechtern; **~ off** *adj* (*fig*) schlechter dran

worship ['wɜːʃɪp] *n* Verehrung *f* ♦ *vt* anbeten; **Your W~** (*BRIT*: *to mayor*) Herr/Frau Bürgermeister; (: *to judge*) Euer Ehren

worst [wɜːst] *adj* schlimmste(r, s), schlechteste(r, s) ♦ *adv* am schlimmsten, am ärgsten ♦ *n* Schlimmste(s) *nt*, Ärgste(s) *nt*; **at ~** schlimmstenfalls

worth [wɜːθ] *n* Wert *m* ♦ *adj* wert; **it's ~ it** es lohnt sich; **to be ~ one's while (to do sth)** die Mühe wert sein, (etw zu tun); **~less** *adj* wertlos; (*person*) nichtsnutzig; **~while** *adj* lohnend, der Mühe wert; **~y** *adj* wert, würdig

---

KEYWORD

would [wʊd] *aux vb* **1** (*conditional tense*): **if you asked him he would do it** wenn du ihn fragtest, würde er es tun; **if you had asked him he would have done it** wenn du ihn gefragt hättest, hätte er es getan

2 (*in offers, invitations, requests*): **would you like a biscuit?** möchten Sie ein Plätzchen?; **would you ask him to come in?** würden Sie ihn bitte hineinbitten?

3 (*in indirect speech*): **I said I would do it** ich sagte, ich würde es tun

4 (*emphatic*): **it WOULD have to snow today!** es mußte △ ja ausgerechnet heute schneien!

5 (*insistence*): **she wouldn't behave** sie wollte sich partout nicht anständig benehmen

6 (*conjecture*): **it would have been midnight** es mag ungefähr Mitternacht gewesen sein; **it would seem so** es sieht wohl so aus

7 (*indicating habit*): **he would go there on Mondays** er ging jeden Montag dorthin

---

would-be ['wʊdbiː] (*pej*) *adj* Möchtegern-

wouldn't ['wʊdnt] = **would not**

wound¹ [wuːnd] *n* (*also fig*) Wunde *f* ♦ *vt* verwunden, verletzen (*also fig*)

wound² [waʊnd] *pt, pp of* **wind²**

wove [wəʊv] *pt of* **weave**; **~n** *pp of* **weave**

wrangle ['ræŋgl] *n* Streit *m* ♦ *vi* sich zanken

wrap [ræp] *vt* einwickeln; **~ up** *vt* einwickeln; (*deal*) abschließen; **~per** *n* Umschlag *m*, Schutzhülle *f*; **~ping paper** *n* Einwickelpapier *nt*

wrath [rɔθ] *n* Zorn *m*

wreak [riːk] *vt* (*havoc*) anrichten; (*vengeance*) üben

wreath [riːθ] *n* Kranz *m*

wreck [rek] *n* (*ship*) Wrack *nt*; (*sth ruined*) Ruine *f* ♦ *vt* zerstören; **~age** *n* Trümmer *pl*

wren [ren] *n* Zaunkönig *m*

wrench [rentʃ] *n* (*spanner*) Schraubenschlüssel *m*; (*twist*) Ruck *m* ♦ *vt* reißen, zerren; **to ~ sth from sb** jdm etw entreißen *or* entwinden

wrestle ['resl] *vi*: **to ~ (with sb)** (mit jdm) ringen; **~r** *n* Ringer(in) *m(f)*; **wrestling** *n* Ringen *nt*

wretched ['retʃɪd] *adj* (*inf*) verflixt

wriggle ['rɪgl] *n* Schlängeln *nt* ♦ *vi* sich winden

wring [rɪŋ] (*pt, pp* **wrung**) *vt* wringen

wrinkle ['rɪŋkl] *n* Falte *f*, Runzel *f* ♦ *vt* runzeln ♦ *vi* sich runzeln; (*material*) knittern; **~d** *adj* faltig, schrumpelig

△ *For information on spelling reform see page 615*

wrist [rɪst] *n* Handgelenk *nt*; **~watch** *n* Armbanduhr *f*

writ [rɪt] *n* gerichtliche(r) Befehl *m*

write [raɪt] (*pt* **wrote**, *pp* **written**) *vt, vi* schreiben; **~ down** *vt* aufschreiben; **~ off** *vt* (*dismiss*) abschreiben; **~ out** *vt* (*copy*) abschreiben; (*cheque*) ausstellen; **~ up** *vt* schreiben; **~-off** *n*: **it is a ~-off** das kann man abschreiben; **~r** *n* Schriftsteller *m*

writhe [raɪð] *vi* sich winden

writing ['raɪtɪŋ] *n* (*act*) Schreiben *nt*; (*hand~*) (Hand)schrift *f*; **in ~** schriftlich; **~ paper** *n* Schreibpapier *nt*

written ['rɪtn] *pp of* **write**

wrong [rɒŋ] *adj* (*incorrect*) falsch; (*morally*) unrecht ♦ *n* Unrecht *nt* ♦ *vt* Unrecht tun +*dat*; **he was ~ in doing that** es war nicht recht von ihm, das zu tun; **you are ~ about that, you've got it ~** da hast du unrecht; **to be in the ~** im Unrecht sein; **what's ~ with your leg?** was ist mit deinem Bein los?; **to go ~** (*plan*) schiefgehen; (*person*) einen Fehler machen; **~ful** *adj* unrechtmäßig; **~ly** *adv* falsch; (*accuse*) zu Unrecht

wrong number *n* (*TEL*): **you've got the ~** Sie sind falsch verbunden

wrote [rəʊt] *pt of* **write**

wrought [rɔːt] *adj*: **~ iron** Schmiedeeisen *nt*

wrung [rʌŋ] *pt, pp of* **wring**

wry [raɪ] *adj* ironisch

wt. *abbr* = **weight**

X, x

Xmas ['eksməs] *n abbr* = **Christmas**

X-ray ['eksreɪ] *n* Röntgenaufnahme *f* ♦ *vt* röntgen; **~-~s** *npl* Röntgenstrahlen *pl*

xylophone ['zaɪləfəʊn] *n* Xylophon ⚠ *nt*

Y, y

yacht [jɒt] *n* Jacht *f*; **~ing** *n* (Sport)segeln *nt*; **~sman** (*irreg*) *n* Sportsegler *m*

Yank [jæŋk] (*inf*) *n* Ami *m*

yap [jæp] *vi* (*dog*) kläffen

yard [jɑːd] *n* Hof *m*; (*measure*) (englische) Elle *f*, Yard *nt* (*0,91 m*); **~stick** *n* (*fig*) Maßstab *m*

yarn [jɑːn] *n* (*thread*) Garn *nt*; (*story*) (Seemanns)garn *nt*

yawn [jɔːn] *n* Gähnen *nt* ♦ *vi* gähnen; **~ing** *adj* (*gap*) gähnend

yd. *abbr* = **yard(s)**

yeah [jeə] (*inf*) *adv* ja

year [jɪəʳ] *n* Jahr *nt*; **to be 8 ~s old** acht Jahre alt sein; **an eight-~-old child** ein achtjähriges Kind; **~ly** *adj, adv* jährlich

yearn [jɜːn] *vi*: **to ~ (for)** sich sehnen (nach); **~ing** *n* Verlangen *nt*, Sehnsucht *f*

yeast [jiːst] *n* Hefe *f*

yell [jel] *n* gellende(r) Schrei *m* ♦ *vi* laut schreien

yellow ['jeləʊ] *adj* gelb ♦ *n* Gelb *nt*

yelp [jelp] *n* Gekläff *nt* ♦ *vi* kläffen

yes [jes] *adv* ja ♦ *n* Ja *nt*, Jawort *nt*; **to say ~** ja sagen; **to answer ~** mit Ja antworten

yesterday ['jestədɪ] *adv* gestern ♦ *n* Gestern *nt*; **~ morning/evening** gestern morgen/abend; **all day ~** gestern den ganzen Tag; **the day before ~** vorgestern

yet [jet] *adv* noch; (*in question*) schon; (*up to now*) bis jetzt ♦ *conj* doch, dennoch; **it is not finished ~** es ist noch nicht fertig; **the best ~** das bisher beste; **as ~** bis jetzt; (*in past*) bis dahin

yew [juː] *n* Eibe *f*

yield [jiːld] *n* Ertrag *m* ♦ *vt* (*result, crop*) hervorbringen; (*interest, profit*) abwerfen; (*concede*) abtreten ♦ *vi* nachgeben; (*MIL*) sich ergeben; **"~"** (*US: AUT*) „Vorfahrt gewähren"

YMCA *n abbr* (= *Young Men's Christian Association*) CVJM *m*

yob [jɒb] (*BRIT: inf*) *n* Halbstarke(r) *f(m)*,

Rowdy m

yoga ['jəʊgə] n Joga m

yoghourt ['jəʊgət] n Joghurt △ m

yog(h)urt ['jəʊgət] n = **yoghourt**

yoke [jəʊk] n (also fig) Joch nt

yolk [jəʊk] n Eidotter m, Eigelb nt

KEYWORD
---

you [juː] pron 1 (subj, in comparisons: familiar form: sg) du; (: pl) ihr; (in letters also) Du, Ihr; (: polite form) Sie; **you Germans** ihr Deutschen; **she's younger than you** sie ist jünger als du/Sie

2 (direct object, after prep +acc: familiar form: sg) dich; (: pl) euch; (in letters also) Dich, Euch; (: polite form) Sie; **I know you** ich kenne dich/euch/Sie

3 (indirect object, after prep +dat: familiar form: sg) dir; (: pl) euch; (in letters also) Dir, Euch; (: polite form) Ihnen; **I gave it to you** ich gab es dir/euch/Ihnen

4 (impers: one: subj) man; (: direct object) einen; (: indirect object) einem; **fresh air does you good** frische Luft tut gut

---

you'd [juːd] = **you had; you would**

you'll [juːl] = **you will; you shall**

young [jʌŋ] adj jung ♦ npl: **the ~** die Jungen pl; **~ster** n Junge m, junge(r) Bursche m, junge(s) Mädchen nt

your [jɔːr] adj (familiar: sg) dein; (: pl) euer, eure pl; (: polite) Ihr; see also **my**

you're [jʊər] = **you are**

yours [jɔːz] pron (familiar: sg) deine(r, s); (: pl) eure(r, s); (: polite) Ihre(r, s); see also **mine²**

yourself [jɔːˈsɛlf] pron (emphatic) selbst; (familiar: sg: acc) dich (selbst); (: dat) dir (selbst); (: pl) euch (selbst); (: polite) sich (selbst); see also **oneself**; **yourselves** pl pron (reflexive: familiar) euch; (: polite) sich; (emphatic) selbst; see also **oneself**

youth [juːθ] n Jugend f; (young man) junge(r) Mann m; **~s** npl (young people)

Jugendliche pl; **~ club** n Jugendzentrum nt; **~ful** adj jugendlich; **~ hostel** n Jugendherberge f

you've [juːv] = **you have**

YTS (BRIT) n abbr (= Youth Training Scheme) staatliches Förderprogramm für arbeitslose Jugendliche

Yugoslav ['juːgəʊslɑːv] adj jugoslawisch ♦ n Jugoslawe m, Jugoslawin f; **~ia** ['juːgəʊˈslɑːvɪə] n Jugoslawien nt

yuppie ['jʌpɪ] (inf) n Yuppie m ♦ adj yuppiehaft, Yuppie-

YWCA n abbr (= Young Women's Christian Association) CVJF m

Z, z

zany ['zeɪnɪ] adj (ideas, sense of humour) verrückt

zap [zæp] vt (COMPUT) löschen

zeal [ziːl] n Eifer m; **~ous** adj eifrig

zebra ['ziːbrə] n Zebra nt; **~ crossing** (BRIT) n Zebrastreifen m

zero ['zɪərəʊ] n Null f; (on scale) Nullpunkt m

zest [zɛst] n Begeisterung f

zigzag ['zɪgzæg] n Zickzack m

Zimbabwe [zɪmˈbɑːbwɪ] n Zimbabwe nt

Zimmer frame ['zɪmə-] n Laufgestell nt

zip [zɪp] n Reißverschluß m ♦ vt (also: ~ up) den Reißverschluß zumachen +gen

zip code (US) n Postleitzahl f

zipper ['zɪpər] (US) n Reißverschluß m

zit [zɪt] (inf) n Pickel m

zodiac ['zəʊdɪæk] n Tierkreis m

zombie ['zɒmbɪ] n: **like a ~** (fig) wie im Tran

zone [zəʊn] n (also MIL) Zone f, Gebiet nt; (in town) Bezirk m

zoo [zuː] n Zoo m

zoology [zuːˈɒlədʒɪ] n Zoologie f

zoom [zuːm] vi: **to ~ past** vorbeisausen; **~ lens** n Zoomobjektiv nt

zucchini [zuːˈkiːnɪ] (US) npl Zucchini pl

△ For information on spelling reform see page 615

GERMAN IRREGULAR VERBS

*with 'sein'

infinitive	present indicative (2nd, 3rd sg)	imperfect	past participle
aufschrecken*	schrickst auf, schrickt auf	schrak or schreckte auf	aufgeschreckt
ausbedingen	bedingst aus, bedingt aus	bedang or bedingte aus	ausbedungen
backen	bäckst, bäckt	backte or buk	gebacken
befehlen	befiehlst, befiehlt	befahl	befohlen
beginnen	beginnst, beginnt	begann	begonnen
beißen	beißt, beißt	biß	gebissen
bergen	birgst, birgt	barg	geborgen
bersten*	birst, birst	barst	geborsten
bescheißen*	bescheißt, bescheißt	beschiß	beschissen
bewegen	bewegst, bewegt	bewog	bewogen
biegen	biegst, biegt	bog	gebogen
bieten	bietest, bietet	bot	geboten
binden	bindest, bindet	band	gebunden
bitten	bittest, bittet	bat	gebeten
blasen	bläst, bläst	blies	geblasen
bleiben*	bleibst, bleibt	blieb	geblieben
braten	brätst, brät	briet	gebraten
brechen*	brichst, bricht	brach	gebrochen
brennen	brennst, brennt	brannte	gebrannt
bringen	bringst, bringt	brachte	gebracht
denken	denkst, denkt	dachte	gedacht
dreschen	drisch(e)st, drischt	drosch	gedroschen
dringen*	dringst, dringt	drang	gedrungen
dürfen	darfst, darf	durfte	gedurft
empfehlen	empfiehlst, empfiehlt	empfahl	empfohlen
erbleichen*	erbleichst, erbleicht	erbleichte	erblichen
erlöschen*	erlischt, erlischt	erlosch	erloschen
erschrecken*	erschrickst, erschrickt	erschrak	erschrocken
essen	ißt, ißt	aß	gegessen
fahren*	fährst, fährt	fuhr	gefahren
fallen*	fällst, fällt	fiel	gefallen
fangen	fängst, fängt	fing	gefangen
fechten	fichtst, ficht	focht	gefochten

infinitive	present indicative (2nd, 3rd sg)	imperfect	past participle
finden	findest, findet	fand	gefunden
flechten	flichtst, flicht	flocht	geflochten
fliegen*	fliegst, fliegt	flog	geflogen
fliehen*	fliehst, flieht	floh	geflohen
fließen*	fließt, fließt	floß	geflossen
fressen	frißt, frißt	fraß	gefressen
frieren	frierst, friert	fror	gefroren
gären*	gärst, gärt	gor	gegoren
gebären	gebierst, gebiert	gebar	geboren
geben	gibst, gibt	gab	gegeben
gedeihen*	gedeihst, gedeiht	gedieh	gediehen
gehen*	gehst, geht	ging	gegangen
gelingen*	——, gelingt	gelang	gelungen
gelten	giltst, gilt	galt	gegolten
genesen*	gene(se)st, genest	genas	genesen
genießen	genießt, genießt	genoß	genossen
geraten*	gerätst, gerät	geriet	geraten
geschehen*	——, geschieht	geschah	geschehen
gewinnen	gewinnst, gewinnt	gewann	gewonnen
gießen	gießt, gießt	goß	gegossen
gleichen	gleichst, gleicht	glich	geglichen
gleiten*	gleitest, gleitet	glitt	geglitten
glimmen	glimmst, glimmt	glomm	geglommen
graben	gräbst, gräbt	grub	gegraben
greifen	greifst, greift	griff	gegriffen
haben	hast, hat	hatte	gehabt
halten	hältst, hält	hielt	gehalten
hängen	hängst, hängt	hing	gehangen
hauen	haust, haut	haute	gehauen
heben	hebst, hebt	hob	gehoben
heißen	heißt, heißt	hieß	geheißen
helfen	hilfst, hilft	half	geholfen
kennen	kennst, kennt	kannte	gekannt
klimmen*	klimmst, klimmt	klomm	geklommen
klingen	klingst, klingt	klang	geklungen
kneifen	kneifst, kneift	kniff	gekniffen
kommen*	kommst, kommt	kam	gekommen
können	kannst, kann	konnte	gekonnt
kriechen*	kriechst, kriecht	kroch	gekrochen
laden	lädst, lädt	lud	geladen
lassen	läßt, läßt	ließ	gelassen
laufen*	läufst, läuft	lief	gelaufen
leiden	leidest, leidet	litt	gelitten
leihen	leihst, leiht	lieh	geliehen
lesen	liest, liest	las	gelesen

infinitive	present indicative (2nd, 3rd sg)	imperfect	past participle
liegen*	liegst, liegt	lag	gelegen
lügen	lügst, lügt	log	gelogen
mahlen	mahlst, mahlt	mahlte	gemahlen
meiden	meidest, meidet	mied	gemieden
melken	melkst, melkt	melkte	gemolken
messen	mißt, mißt	maß	gemessen
mißlingen*	——, mißlingt	mißlang	mißlungen
mögen	magst, mag	mochte	gemocht
müssen	mußt, muß	mußte	gemußt
nehmen	nimmst, nimmt	nahm	genommen
nennen	nennst, nennt	nannte	genannt
pfeifen	pfeifst, pfeift	pfiff	gepfiffen
preisen	preist, preist	pries	gepriesen
quellen*	quillst, quillt	quoll	gequollen
raten	rätst, rät	riet	geraten
reiben	reibst, reibt	rieb	gerieben
reißen*	reißt, reißt	riß	gerissen
reiten*	reitest, reitet	ritt	geritten
rennen*	rennst, rennt	rannte	gerannt
riechen	riechst, riecht	roch	gerochen
ringen	ringst, ringt	rang	gerungen
rinnen*	rinnst, rinnt	rann	geronnen
rufen	rufst, ruft	rief	gerufen
salzen	salzt, salzt	salzte	gesalzen
saufen	säufst, säuft	soff	gesoffen
saugen	saugst, saugt	sog	gesogen
schaffen	schaffst, schafft	schuf	geschaffen
scheiden	scheidest, scheidet	schied	geschieden
scheinen	scheinst, scheint	schien	geschienen
schelten	schiltst, schilt	schalt	gescholten
scheren	scherst, schert	schor	geschoren
schieben	schiebst, schiebt	schob	geschoben
schießen	schießt, schießt	schoß	geschossen
schinden	schindest, schindet	schindete	geschunden
schlafen	schläfst, schläft	schlief	geschlafen
schlagen	schlägst, schlägt	schlug	geschlagen
schleichen*	schleichst, schleicht	schlich	geschlichen
schleifen	schleifst, schleift	schliff	geschliffen
schließen	schließt, schließt	schloß	geschlossen
schlingen	schlingst, schlingt	schlang	geschlungen
schmeißen	schmeißt, schmeißt	schmiß	geschmissen
schmelzen*	schmilzt, schmilzt	schmolz	geschmolzen

infinitive	present indicative (2nd, 3rd sg)	imperfect	past participle
schneiden	schneidest, schneidet	schnitt	geschnitten
schreiben	schreibst, schreibt	schrieb	geschrieben
schreien	schreist, schreit	schrie	geschrie(e)n
schreiten	schreitest, schreitet	schritt	geschritten
schweigen	schweigst, schweigt	schwieg	geschwiegen
schwellen*	schwillst, schwillt	schwoll	geschwollen
schwimmen*	schwimmst, schwimmt	schwamm	geschwommen
schwinden*	schwindest, schwindet	schwand	geschwunden
schwingen	schwingst, schwingt	schwang	geschwungen
schwören	schwörst, schwört	schwor	geschworen
sehen	siehst, sieht	sah	gesehen
sein*	bist, ist	war	gewesen
senden	sendest, sendet	sandte	gesandt
singen	singst, singt	sang	gesungen
sinken*	sinkst, sinkt	sank	gesunken
sinnen	sinnst, sinnt	sann	gesonnen
sitzen*	sitzt, sitzt	saß	gesessen
sollen	sollst, soll	sollte	gesollt
speien	speist, speit	spie	gespie(e)n
spinnen	spinnst, spinnt	spann	gesponnen
sprechen	sprichst, spricht	sprach	gesprochen
sprießen*	sprießt, sprießt	sproß	gesprossen
springen*	springst, springt	sprang	gesprungen
stechen	stichst, sticht	stach	gestochen
stecken	steckst, steckt	steckte or stak	gesteckt
stehen	stehst, steht	stand	gestanden
stehlen	stiehlst, stiehlt	stahl	gestohlen
steigen*	steigst, steigt	stieg	gestiegen
sterben*	stirbst, stirbt	starb	gestorben
stinken	stinkst, stinkt	stank	gestunken
stoßen	stößt, stößt	stieß	gestoßen
streichen	streichst, streicht	strich	gestrichen
streiten*	streitest, streitet	stritt	gestritten
tragen	trägst, trägt	trug	getragen
treffen	triffst, trifft	traf	getroffen
treiben*	treibst, treibt	trieb	getrieben
treten*	trittst, tritt	trat	getreten
trinken	trinkst, trinkt	trank	getrunken
trügen	trügst, trügt	trog	getrogen

infinitive	present indicative (2nd, 3rd sg)	imperfect	past participle
tun	tust, tut	tat	getan
verderben	verdirbst, verdirbt	verdarb	verdorben
verdrießen	verdrießt, verdrießt	verdroß	verdrossen
vergessen	vergißt, vergißt	vergaß	vergessen
verlieren	verlierst, verliert	verlor	verloren
verschleißen	verschleißt, verschleißt	verschliß	verschlissen
wachsen*	wächst, wächst	wuchs	gewachsen
weben	webst, webt	webte *or* wob	gewoben
wägen	wägst, wägt	wog	gewogen
waschen	wäschst, wäscht	wusch	gewaschen
weichen*	weichst, weicht	wich	gewichen
weisen	weist, weist	wies	gewiesen
wenden	wendest, wendet	wandte	gewandt
werben	wirbst, wirbt	warb	geworben
werden*	wirst, wird	wurde	geworden
werfen	wirfst, wirft	warf	geworfen
wiegen	wiegst, wiegt	wog	gewogen
winden	windest, windet	wand	gewunden
wissen	weißt, weiß	wußte	gewußt
wollen	willst, will	wollte	gewollt
wringen	wringst, wringt	wrang	gewrungen
zeihen	zeihst, zeiht	zieh	geziehen
ziehen*	ziehst, zieht	zog	gezogen
zwingen	zwingst, zwingt	zwang	gezwungen

GERMAN SPELLING CHANGES

In July 1996, all German–speaking countries signed a declaration concerning the reform of German spelling, with the result that the new spelling rules can now be taught in all schools. To ensure that you have the most up–to–date information at your fingertips, the following list contains the old and new spellings of all German headwords and translations in this dictionary which are affected by the reform.

ALT/OLD	NEU/NEW	ALT/OLD	NEU/NEW
abend	Abend	**auseinanderbrechen**	auseinander brechen
Abfluß	Abfluss	**auseinanderbringen**	auseinander bringen
Abflußrohr	Abflussrohr	**auseinanderfallen**	auseinander fallen
Abschluß	Abschluss	**auseinanderfalten**	auseinander falten
Abschlußexamen	Abschlussexamen	**auseinandergehen**	auseinander gehen
Abschlußfeier	Abschlussfeier	**auseinanderhalten**	auseinander halten
Abschlußklasse	Abschlussklasse	**auseinandernehmen**	auseinander nehmen
Abschlußprüfung	Abschlussprüfung	**auseinandersetzen**	auseinander setzen
Abschuß	Abschuss	**Ausfluß**	Ausfluss
Abschußrampe	Abschussrampe	**Ausguß**	Ausguss
Abszeß	Abszess	**Auslaß**	Auslass
achtgeben	Acht geben	**Ausschluß**	Ausschluss
Adreßbuch	Adressbuch	**Ausschuß**	Ausschuss
Alleinerziehende(r)	Alleinerziehende(r)	**Ausschuß(artikel)**	Ausschuss(artikel)
	or allein Erziehende(r)	**aussein**	aus sein
alleinstehend	allein stehend	**außerstande**	außer Stande
allgemeingültig	allgemein gültig	**Autobiographie**	Autobiographie
allzuoft	allzu oft		or Autobiografie
allzuviel	allzu viel	**Baß**	Bass
Alptraum	Alptraum	**Baßstimme**	Bassstimme
	or Albtraum		or Bass–Stimme
Amboß	Amboss	**Ballettänzer(in)**	Balletttänzer(in)
Amtsanschluß	Amtsanschluss		or Ballett–Tänzer(in)
(Amts)mißbrauch	(Amts)missbrauch	**beeinflußbar**	beeinflussbar
andersdenkend	anders denkend	**beiseitelegen**	beiseite legen
aneinandergeraten	aneinander geraten	**bekanntgeben**	bekannt geben
aneinanderreihen	aneinander reihen	**bekanntmachen**	bekannt machen
Anlaß	Anlass	**Beschluß**	Beschluss
anläßlich	anlässlich	**Beschuß**	Beschuss
Anschluß	Anschluss	**bessergehen**	besser gehen
Anschlußflug	Anschlussflug	**Bettuch**	Betttuch
As	Ass		or Bett–Tuch
aufeinanderfolgen	aufeinander folgen	**(Bevölkerungs)überschuß**	
aufeinanderfolgend	aufeinander folgend		(Bevölkerungs)überschuss
aufeinanderlegen	aufeinander legen	**bewußt**	bewusst
aufeinanderprallen	aufeinander prallen	**bewußtlos**	bewusstlos
aufschlußreich	aufschlussreich	**Bewußtlosigkeit**	Bewusstlosigkeit
aufsehenerregend	Aufsehen erregend	**Bewußtsein**	Bewusstsein
aufsein	auf sein	**bezug**	Bezug
aufwendig	aufwendig	**Bibliographie**	Bibliographie
	or aufwändig		or Bibliografie

ALT/OLD	NEU/NEW	ALT/OLD	NEU/NEW
Biographie	Biographie	Einlaß	Einlass
	or Biografie	ekelerregend	Ekel erregend
Biß	Biss	Elsaß	Elsass
biß	biss	Engpaß	Engpass
bißchen	bisschen	Entschluß	Entschluss
blaß	blass	entschlußfreudig	entschlussfreudig
bläßlich	blässlich	Entschlußkraft	Entschlusskraft
bleibenlassen	bleiben lassen	epochemachend	Epoche machend
Bluterguß	Bluterguss	Erdgeschoß	Erdgeschoss
Boß	Boss	Erdnuß	Erdnuss
braungebrannt	braun gebrannt	Erdnußbutter	Erdnussbutter
breitmachen	breit machen	erfolgversprechend	Erfolg versprechend
Brenn(n)essel	Brennnessel	Erguß	Erguss
	or Brenn-Nessel	Erlaß	Erlass
Büroschluß	Büroschluss	ernstgemeint	ernst gemeint
Butterfaß	Butterfass	erstemal	erste Mal
Cashewnuß	Cashewnuss	erstenmal	ersten Mal
Chicorée	Chicorée	eßbar	essbar
	or Schikoree	Eßbesteck	Essbesteck
Choreograph(in)	Choreograph(in)	Eßecke	Essecke
	or Choreograf(in)	Eßgeschirr	Essgeschirr
Computertomographie	Computertomographie	Eßkastanie	Esskastanie
	or Computertomografie	Eßlöffel	Esslöffel
dabeisein	dabei sein	Eßlöffel(voll)	Esslöffel (voll)
dafürkönnen	dafür können	(Eß)stäbchen	(Ess)stäbchen
dahinterkommen	dahinter kommen		or (Ess-)Stäbchen
darauffolgend	darauf folgend	Eßtisch	Esstisch
dasein	da sein	Eßwaren	Esswaren
daß	dass	Eßzimmer	Esszimmer
Dekolleté	Dekolleté	Expreß	Express
	or Dekolletee	Expreßgut	Expressgut
Delphin	Delphin	Expreßzug	Expresszug
	or Delfin	Facette	Facette
dessenungeachtet	dessen ungeachtet		or Fassette
dichtbevölkert	dicht bevölkert	Fährenanschluß	Fährenanschluss
diensthabend	Dienst habend	Fairneß	Fairness
Differentialrechnung	Differentialrechnung	fallenlassen	fallen lassen
	or Differenzialrechnung	Faß	Fass
Diktaphon	Diktaphon	faßbar	fassbar
	or Diktafon	Fehlschuß	Fehlschuss
dreiviertel	drei Viertel	fernhalten	fern halten
durcheinanderbringen	durcheinander bringen	fertigbringen	fertig bringen
durcheinanderreden	durcheinander reden	fertigmachen	fertig machen
durcheinanderwerfen	durcheinander werfen	fertigstellen	fertig stellen
durchnumerieren	durchnummerieren	fertigwerden	fertig werden
ehrfurchtgebietend	Ehrfurcht gebietend	festangestellt	fest angestellt
Einfluß	Einfluss	Fitneß	Fitness
Einflußbereich	Einflussbereich	fleischfressend	Fleisch fressend
einflußreich	einflussreich	floß	floss
einigemal	einige Mal	Fluß	Fluss
einiggehen	einig gehen	Fluß-	Fluss-

ALT/OLD	NEU/NEW	ALT/OLD	NEU/NEW
flußabwärts	flussabwärts	(Grammophon)nadel	(Grammophon)nadel
Flußbarsch	Flussbarsch		or (Grammofon)nadel
Flußbett	Flussbett	gräßlich	grässlich
Flußdiagramm	Flussdiagramm	Greuel	Gräuel
flüssigmachen	flüssig machen	Greueltat	Gräueltat
Flußufer	Flussufer	greulich	gräulich
Fön ®	Fön	Grundriß	Grundriss
	or Föhn ®	Guß	Guss
fönen	föhnen	Gußeisen	Gusseisen
Fönfrisur	Föhnfrisur	gutaussehend	gut aussehend
Friedensschluß	Friedensschluss	gutgehen	gut gehen
Frischvermählte	frisch Vermählte	gutgehend	gut gehend
Frischvermählten	frisch Vermählten	gutgemeint	gut gemeint
frißt	frisst	guttun	gut tun
fritieren	frittieren	haftenbleiben	haften bleiben
Gebiß	Gebiss	halboffen	halb offen
Gebührenerlaß	Gebührenerlass	haltmachen	Halt machen
gefangen(gehalten)	gefangen (gehalten)	Hämorrhoiden	Hämorrhoiden
gefangenhalten	gefangen halten		or Hämorriden
gefangennehmen	gefangen nehmen	Handvoll	Hand voll
gefaßt	gefasst	hängenbleiben	hängen bleiben
geheimhalten	geheim halten	hängenlassen	hängen lassen
gehenlassen	gehen lassen	hartgekocht	hart gekocht
Gemeinschaftsanschluß		Haselnuß	Haselnuss
	Gemeinschaftsanschluss	Haß	Hass
Gemse	Gämse	häßlich	hässlich
gemußt	gemusst	Häßlichkeit	Hässlichkeit
genaugenommen	genau genommen	haushalten	haushalten
Genuß	Genuss		or Haus halten
genüßlich	genüsslich	heiligsprechen	heilig sprechen
Genußmittel	Genussmittel	Hexenschuß	Hexenschuss
Geograph	Geograph	hierbehalten	hier behalten
	or Geograf	hierbleiben	hier bleiben
Geographie	Geographie	hierlassen	hier lassen
	or Geografie	hierzulande	hierzulande
geographisch	geographisch		or hier zu Lande
	or geografisch	hochachten	hoch achten
geringachten	gering achten	hochbegabt	hoch begabt
Geschäftsschluß	Geschäftsschluss	hochdotiert	hoch dotiert
Geschoß	Geschoss	hochentwickelt	hoch entwickelt
gewinnbringend	Gewinn bringend	(hoch)geschätzt	(hoch) geschätzt
gewiß	gewiss	(hoch)schätzen	(hoch) schätzen
Gewißheit	Gewissheit	(Honorar)vorschuß	(Honorar)vorschuss
gewußt	gewusst	Imbiß	Imbiss
glattrasiert	glatt rasiert	Imbißraum	Imbissraum
glattstreichen	glatt streichen	Imbißstube	Imbissstube
gleichbleibend	gleich bleibend		or Imbiss-Stube
gleichgesinnt	gleich gesinnt	immerwährend	immer während
Glimmstengel	Glimmstängel	imstande	imstande
Grammophon	Grammophon		or im Stande
	or Grammofon	ineinandergreifen	ineinander greifen

ALT/OLD	NEU/NEW	ALT/OLD	NEU/NEW
ineinanderschieben	ineinander schieben	Ladenschluß	Ladenschluss
Intercity-Expreßzug	Intercity-Expresszug	Laufpaß	Laufpass
ißt	isst	leerlaufen	leer laufen
Jahresabschluß	Jahresabschluss	leerstehend	leer stehend
jedesmal	jedes Mal	leichtfallen	leicht fallen
Joghurt	Joghurt	leichtmachen	leicht machen
	or Jogurt	Lenkradschloß	Lenkradschloss
kahlgeschoren	kahl geschoren	letztemal	letzte Mal
kaltbleiben	kalt bleiben	liebgewinnen	lieb gewinnen
Kammuschel	Kammuschel	liebhaben	lieb haben
	or Kamm-Muschel	liegenbleiben	liegen bleiben
Känguruh	Känguru	liegenlassen	liegen lassen
Karamel	Karamell	Litfaßsäule	Litfasssäule
Karamelbonbon	Karamellbonbon		*or* Litfass-Säule
Katarrh	Katarrh	Luftschloß	Luftschloss
	or Katarr	maschineschreiben	Maschine schreiben
Kellergeschoß	Kellergeschoss	maßhalten	Maß halten
kennenlernen	kennen lernen	Megaphon	Megaphon
keß	kess		*or* Megafon
klarsehen	klar sehen	Meldeschluß	Meldeschluss
klarwerden	klar werden	meßbar	messbar
klassenbewußt	klassenbewusst	Meßbecher	Messbecher
Klassenbewußtsein	Klassenbewusstsein	Meßgerät	Messgerät
klatschnaß	klatschnass	Mikrophon	Mikrophon
kleinhacken	klein hacken		*or* Mikrofon
kleinschneiden	klein schneiden	mißachten	missachten
klitschnaß	klitschnass	Mißachtung	Missachtung
knapphalten	knapp halten	Mißbehagen	Missbehagen
Kokosnuß	Kokosnuss	Mißbildung	Missbildung
Koloß	Koloss	mißbilligen	missbilligen
Kombinationsschloß	Kombinationsschloss	Mißbilligung	Missbilligung
Kommuniqué	Kommuniqué	Mißbrauch	Missbrauch
	or Kommunikee	mißbrauchen	missbrauchen
Kompaß	Kompass	Mißerfolg	Misserfolg
Kompromiß	Kompromiss	Mißfallen	Missfallen
kompromißbereit	kompromissbereit	mißfallen	missfallen
kompromißlos	kompromisslos	Mißgeschick	Missgeschick
Kompromißlösung	Kompromisslösung	mißgestaltet	missgestaltet
Kongreß	Kongress	mißglücken	missglücken
Kongreßzentrum	Kongresszentrum	mißgönnen	missgönnen
Kontrabaß	Kontrabass	Mißgriff	Missgriff
kraß	krass	Mißgunst	Missgunst
Kreppapier	Krepppapier	mißgünstig	missgünstig
	or Krepp-Papier	mißhandeln	misshandeln
kriegführend	Krieg führend	Mißhandlung	Misshandlung
krummnehmen	krumm nehmen	Mißklang	Missklang
Kurzbiographie	Kurzbiographie	Mißkredit	Misskredit
	or Kurzbiografie	mißlich	misslich
kurzhalten	kurz halten	mißlingen	misslingen
Kurzschluß	Kurzschluss	mißlungen	misslungen
Kuß	Kuss	Mißmut	Missmut

ALT/OLD	NEU/NEW	ALT/OLD	NEU/NEW
mißmutig	missmutig	**Nußschale**	Nussschale
mißraten	missraten		or Nuss–Schale
Mißstand	Missstand	**obenerwähnt**	oben erwähnt
	or Miss–Stand	**obengenannt**	oben genannt
Mißtrauen	Misstrauen	**Obergeschoß**	Obergeschoss
mißtrauen	misstrauen	**offenbleiben**	offen bleiben
Mißtrauensantrag	Misstrauensantrag	**offenhalten**	offen halten
Mißtrauensvotum	Misstrauensvotum	**offenlassen**	offen lassen
mißtrauisch	misstrauisch	**offenstehen**	offen stehen
Mißverhältnis	Missverhältnis	**Ölmeßstab**	Ölmessstab
Mißverständnis	Missverständnis		or Ölmess–Stab
mißverstehen	missverstehen	**Orthographie**	Orthographie
Mißwirtschaft	Misswirtschaft		or Orthografie
mittag	Mittag	**orthographisch**	orthographisch
Mop	Mopp		or orthografisch
Muß	Muss	**paarmal**	paar Mal
mußte	musste	**Panther**	Panther
nachhinein	Nachhinein		or Panter
Nachlaß	Nachlass	**Paragraph**	Paragraph
nahegehen	nahe gehen		or Paragraf
nahekommen	nahe kommen	**Paranuß**	Paranuss
nahelegen	nahe legen	**Parlamentsbeschluß**	Parlamentsbeschluss
naheliegen	nahe liegen	**Paß**	Pass
naheliegend	nahe liegend	**Paßamt**	Passamt
näherkommen	näher kommen	**Paßbild**	Passbild
näherrücken	näher rücken	**Paßkontrolle**	Passkontrolle
nahestehen	nahe stehen	**Paßstelle**	Passstelle
nahestehend	nahe stehend		or Pass–Stelle
nahetreten	nahe treten	**Paßstraße**	Passstraße
naß	nass		or Pass–Straße
naßkalt	nasskalt	**patschnaß**	patschnass
Naßrasur	Nassrasur	**pflichtbewußt**	pflichtbewusst
Nebenanschluß	Nebenanschluss	**Phantasie**	Phantasie
nebeneinanderlegen	nebeneinander legen		or Fantasie
nebeneinanderstellen	nebeneinander stellen	**Phantasie–**	Phantasie–
Nebenfluß	Nebenfluss		or Fantasie–
Necessaire	Necessaire	**phantasielos**	phantasielos
	or Nessessär		or fantasielos
Negligé	Negligé	**phantasiereich**	phantasiereich
	or Negligee		or fantasiereich
Netzanschluß	Netzanschluss	**phantasieren**	phantasieren
neuentdeckt	neu entdeckt		or fantasieren
nichtsahnend	nichts ahnend	**phantasievoll**	phantasievoll
nichtssagend	nichts sagend		or fantasievoll
Nonstop–	Nonstop–	**phantastisch**	phantastisch
	or Non–Stop–		or fantastisch
notleidend	Not leidend	**platschnaß**	platschnass
numerieren	nummerieren	**plazieren**	platzieren
Nuß	Nuss	**Pornographie**	Pornographie
Nußbaum	Nussbaum		or Pornografie
Nußknacker	Nussknacker	**pornographisch**	pornographisch

ALT/OLD	NEU/NEW	ALT/OLD	NEU/NEW
	or pornografisch	(Schluß)folgerung	(Schluss)folgerung
Portemonnaie	Portemonnaie	Schlußlicht	Schlusslicht
	or Portmonee	Schlußrunde	Schlussrunde
Potential	Potential	Schlußrundenteilnehmer	
	or Potenzial		Schlussrundenteilnehmer
potentiell	potentiell	Schlußstrich	Schlussstrich
	or potenziell		*or* Schluss-Strich
preisbewußt	preisbewusst	Schlußverkauf	Schlussverkauf
Preßluft	Pressluft	Schmiß	Schmiss
Preßluftbohrer	Pressluftbohrer	Schnappschloß	Schnappschloss
Preßlufthammer	Presslufthammer	Schnappschuß	Schnappschuss
Prozeß	Prozess	Schnellimbiß	Schnellimbiss
Prüfungsausschuß	Prüfungsausschuss	schneuzen	schnäuzen
radfahren	Rad fahren	schoß	schoss
(Raketen)abschuß	(Raketen)abschuss	Schößling	Schössling
Rassenhaß	Rassenhass	Schritt(t)empo	Schritttempo
rauh	rau		*or* Schritt-Tempo
Rauhreif	Raureif	Schuß	Schuss
Raumschiffahrt	Raumschifffahrt	Schußbereich	Schussbereich
	or Raumschiff-Fahrt	Schußlinie	Schusslinie
Rausschmiß	Rausschmiss	Schußverletzung	Schussverletzung
Rechnungsabschluß	Rechnungsabschluss	Schußwaffe	Schusswaffe
reinwaschen	rein waschen	Schußweite	Schussweite
Reisepaß	Reisepass	schwererziehbar	schwer erziehbar
Reißverschluß	Reißverschluss	schwerfallen	schwer fallen
richtigstellen	richtig stellen	schwermachen	schwer machen
Riß	Riss	schwernehmen	schwer nehmen
Rolladen	Rollladen	schwertun	schwer tun
	or Roll-Laden	schwerverdaulich	schwer verdaulich
Roß	Ross	schwerverletzt	schwer verletzt
Roßkastanie	Rosskastanie	Seismograph	Seismograph
rotglühend	rot glühend		*or* Seismograf
Rückschluß	Rückschluss	selbständig	selbständig
Rußland	Russland		*or* selbstständig
Safe(r) Sex	Safe(r) Sex	Selbständigkeit	Selbständigkeit
	or Safe(r)-sex		*or* Selbstständigkeit
Salzfaß	Salzfass	selbstbewußt	selbstbewusst
sauberhalten	sauber halten	Selbstbewußtsein	Selbstbewusstsein
Saxophon	Saxophon	selbstgemacht	selbst gemacht
	or Saxofon	selbstverständlich	selbst verständlich
Schattenriß	Schattenriss	selbstverwaltet	selbst verwaltet
schiefgehen	schief gehen	seßhaft	sesshaft
Schiffahrt	Schifffahrt	Showbineß	Showbusiness
	or Schiff-Fahrt	Sicherheitsschloß	Sicherheitsschloss
Schlangenbiß	Schlangenbiss	sitzenbleiben	sitzen bleiben
schlechtgehen	schlecht gehen	sitzenlassen	sitzen lassen
schlechtmachen	schlecht machen	Skipaß	Skipass
Schlegel	Schlägel	sogenannt	so genannt
Schloß	Schloss	Sommerschlußverkauf	Sommerschlussverkauf
Schluß	Schluss	sonstjemand	sonst jemand
Schluß-	Schluss-	sonstwo	sonst wo

ALT/OLD	NEU/NEW	ALT/OLD	NEU/NEW
sonstwoher	sonst woher	Überschuß	Überschuss
sonstwohin	sonst wohin	überschwenglich	überschwänglich
Spannbettuch	Spannbetttuch	übrigbleiben	übrig bleiben
	or Spann-Tuch	übriggeblieben	übrig geblieben
spazierenfahren	spazieren fahren	übriglassen	übrig lassen
spazierengehen	spazieren gehen	Umriß	Umriss
Sprößling	Sprössling	unbewußt	unbewusst
steckenbleiben	stecken bleiben	Unbewußte	Unbewusste
steckenlassen	stecken lassen	unerläßlich	unerlässlich
stehenbleiben	stehen bleiben	unermeßlich	unermesslich
stehenlassen	stehen lassen	unfaßbar	unfassbar
Stengel	Stängel	ungewiß	ungewiss
Stenographie	Stenographie	Ungewißheit	Ungewissheit
	or Stenografie	unmißverständlich	unmissverständlich
stenographieren	stenographieren	unpäßlich	unpässlich
	or stenografieren	unselbständig	unselbständig
Stenograph(in)	Stenograph(in)		or unselbstständig
	or Stenograf(in)	unterbewußt	unterbewusst
stereophonisch	stereophonisch	Unterbewußte	Unterbewusste
	or stereofonisch	Unterbewußtsein	Unterbewusstsein
Stewardeß	Stewardess	Untergeschoß	Untergeschoss
Stilleben	Stillleben	Untersuchungsausschuß	
	or Still-Leben		Untersuchungsausschuss
stillegen	stilllegen	unvergeßlich	unvergesslich
Streifschuß	Streifschuss	Varieté	Varieté
strenggenommen	streng genommen		or Varietee
Streß	Stress	verantwortungsbewußt	
telegraphieren	telegraphieren		verantwortungsbewusst
	or telegrafieren	Verdruß	Verdruss
Thunfisch	Thunfisch	vergeßlich	vergesslich
	or Tunfisch	Vergeßlichkeit	Vergesslichkeit
tiefausgeschnitten	tief ausgeschnitten	Vergißmeinnicht	Vergissmeinnicht
tiefgehend	tief gehend	vergißt	vergisst
tiefgekühlt	tief gekühlt	verhaßt	verhasst
tiefgreifend	tief greifend	Verlaß	Verlass
tiefschürfend	tief schürfend	verläßlich	verlässlich
Tip	Tipp	verlorengehen	verloren gehen
topographisch	topographisch	vermißt	vermisst
	or topografisch	Verschluß	Verschluss
totenblaß	totenblass	vertrauenerweckend	Vertrauen erweckend
totgeboren	tot geboren	vielsagend	viel sagend
Trugschluß	Trugschluss	vielversprechend	viel versprechend
tschüs	tschüs	(voll)fressen	(voll) fressen
	or tschüss	vollgepfropft	voll gepfropft
übelgelaunt	übel gelaunt	vollpfropfen	voll pfropfen
übelnehmen	übel nehmen	vollstopfen	voll stopfen
übelriechend	übel riechend	volltanken	voll tanken
übelwollend	übel wollend	vorgefaßt	vorgefasst
Überdruß	Überdruss	Vorhängeschloß	Vorhängeschloss
übereinanderlegen	übereinander legen	vorhinein	Vorhinein
Überfluß	Überfluss	vorliebnehmen	vorlieb nehmen

ALT/OLD	NEU/NEW	ALT/OLD	NEU/NEW
Vorschuß	Vorschuss	Xylophon	Xylophon
vorwärtsbewegen	vorwärts bewegen		or Xylofon
vorwärtsdrängen	vorwärts drängen	Zahlenschloß	Zahlenschloss
vorwärtsgehen	vorwärts gehen	zeitlang	Zeit lang
vorwärtskommen	vorwärts kommen	zielbewußt	zielbewusst
Waggon	Waggon	Zuckerguß	Zuckerguss
	or Wagon	zufriedengeben	zufrieden geben
Walnuß	Walnuss	zufriedenstellen	zufrieden stellen
Walroß	Walross	zufriedenstellend	zufrieden stellend
wasserabstoßend	Wasser abstoßend	zugrunde	zugrunde
wäßrig	wässrig		or zu Grunde
Weißrußland	Weißrussland	zugunsten	zugunsten
weitblickend	weitblickend		or zu Gunsten
	or weit blickend	zuleide	zuleide
weitreichend	weitreichend		or zu Leide
	or weit reichend	zumute	zumute
weitverbreitet	weitverbreitet		or zu Mute
	or weit verbreitet	Zündschloß	Zündschloss
wiederaufbauen	wieder aufbauen	Zungenkuß	Zungenkuss
wiederaufbereiten	wieder aufbereiten	zunutze	zunutze
wiederaufnehmen	wieder aufnehmen		or zu Nutze
wiederbeleben	wieder beleben	Zusammenschluß	Zusammenschluss
wiedereinsetzen	wieder einsetzen	zuschulden	zuschulden
wiedererkennen	wieder erkennen		or zu Schulden
wiedererwachen	wieder erwachen	Zuschuß	Zuschuss
wiedergutmachen	wieder gutmachen	zustande	zustande
wiedergutzumachen	wieder gutzumachen		or zu Stande
wiederherstellen	wieder herstellen	zustande bringen	zustande bringen
wiedersehen	wieder sehen		or zu Stande bringen
wiedervereinigen	wieder vereinigen	zustande kommen	zustande kommen
wiederverwenden	wieder verwenden		or zu Stande kommen
wiederverwerten	wieder verwerten	zutage	zutage
wieviel	wie viel		or zu Tage
Wißbegier(de)	Wissbegier(de)	zuviel	zu viel
wißbegierig	wissbegierig	zuwege	zuwege
wohltun	wohl tun		or zu Wege
wußte	wusste	zuwenig	zu wenig